CW00404194

BUSINESS TURBOPROPS INTERNATIONAL 2009

Compiled by Mark Checkley

in collaboration with Sean Meagher, Barry Collman and Barrie Towey

Published by: Air-Britain (Historians) Limited

Sales Department: 41 Penshurst Road, Leigh, Tonbridge, Kent TN11 8HL, UK

Sales e-mail: sales@air-britain.co.uk

Membership: 1 Rose Cottages, 179 Penn Road, Hazlemere, Bucks HP15 7NE, UK
(email: barry.collman@air-britain.co.uk)

Web-site: http://www.air-britain.co.uk

ISBN: 978-0-85130-402-1

Cover photographs:

Front cover:

Rockwell 690B N81783 c/n 11521 on a pre-delivery flight during 1979 resplendent in factory paint design #6A comprising Matterhorn White with stripes of Velvet Brown, Light Sienna and Condor Gold. (Rockwell via Barry Collman)

Back cover:

Top: EMB.121A Xingu 084/YH c/n 121084 at Olbia - Costa Smeralda, Italy on 22nd August 2006. (Juha Ritaranta / http://www.abpic.co.uk/photo/1102474)

Centre: Pilatus PC-12/47E HB-FVD c/n 1072 at Rotterdam - Zestienhoven, Netherlands on 25th June 2009. (Henk Wadman / http://www.abpic.co.uk/photo/1180429)

Bottom: Beech B200 PT-MMB c/n BB-971 at Sao Paulo - Congonhas, Brazil on 19th September 2005. (Mark J Davies)

Printed by Bell & Bain Ltd, Glasgow G46 7UQ

Air-Britain supports the fight against terrorism and the efforts of the Police and other Authorities in protecting airports and airfields from criminal activity.
If you see anything suspicious do not hesitate to call the
Anti-Terrorist Hotline 0800 789321
or alert a Police Officer.

INTRODUCTION

Nearly nine years have passed since the last edition of Business Turboprops International, during which time many of the first generation turboprops have soldiered on only to be replaced by a new generation of frugal singles as the economics of operating an older twin have been eroded by high fuel and maintenance costs. Many of the piston types included in previous editions of this book have now been omitted to make way for the additional space required by subsequent fates as many of the first generation turboprops come to the end of their working lives. The Cessna 208 Caravan family which featured in the second edition remains with our sister publication Turboprop Airliners & Military Transports of the World, a new edition of which is expected to be published shortly.

As in previous editions, additional construction numbers covering future production of each type are included for those types currently in production, enabling readers to update their own copy of the book with details of new aircraft as they appear in Air-Britain News.

This edition has been some four years in the making with significant updates to the production listings resulting in a master index which now contains over 49,000 individual registrations and serials. Many examples of new information have come to light during this research period and I would like to convey my sincere thanks to the Air-Britain specialists who have given so much of their time in providing information, much of which has never been previously published. Particular mention must go to Barry Collman for providing Turbo Commander information, Colin Smith for Piper, Rod Brickell for Beech, Allan Wright of BN Historians for the Islander/Trislander and Marcus Herzig for the PC-6. Invaluable additional research has been provided from the extensive records of Graham Slack and my research mentor Barrie Towey.

In keeping with previous editions, current registrations are highlighted in the master index with grateful thanks to the programming skills of Sean Meagher who has taken the raw data and turned it into a polished final product. The market for new aircraft has been growing steadily in recent years with a near 17% hike in deliveries between 2007 and 2008. Smaller single-engined models such as the Pilatus PC-12 continue to sell well although at the larger end of the market there is a lack of confidence in the short term, demonstrated by recent retrenchment at some manufacturers. New utility single-engined types are slowly establishing a reputation and bringing turbine performance into territory previously held by piston twins with the PAC750XL and Quest Kodiak notable examples. At the high end of the market Piaggio are still working through their order backlog and Hawker Beechcraft have recently won large military orders for the Super King Air 350. Sadly the very basement of the used market comprises many venerable old twins which can now be purchased so cheaply they are disposable commodities to be exported to Central and South America not always with the best of intentions in mind.

The lack of verified data sources from Central and parts of South America remains an obstacle to completing many aircraft histories, with large swathes of the registers from some countries proving to be a continual thorn in the side. Reports from this part of the world are always most gratefully received. Whilst every effort has been made to check and re-check the production lists, it is inevitable that the occasional error will slip through. Corrections are welcome and can be addressed to;

August 2009

Mark Checkley
57 Foxyards Road,
TIPTON, West Midlands,
DY4 8AU, England
e-mail : mark.checkley@air-britain.co.uk

ACKNOWLEDGEMENTS

Business Turboprops International has been produced with the valued assistance of the following companies, individuals and publications;
Paul R Compton/Nordic Research AB, Air-Britain News, Aviation Letter, Robert Branbergen, Ian Burnett, Paul Simpson, The Graham Slack Collection, Ton van Soest, Pete Webber, Colin Clarke, Stephen Hay, Robert Hobbelman, Kevin Latham, Steve Mitchell, Tony Orr, Kevin Palmer, Justin Palmer, Dave Richardson, Mark Sheen, Andy Vass, Enhanced Aero, BLR Aerospace, Raisbeck Engineering, Dodson Aviation, White Industries, Pilatus Flugzeugwerke AG, Hawker Beechcraft Corp, Turbine Aircraft Marketing, Marcelo Alemany, Alexis Antonakis, Tony Arbon, Archive Flugzeugerkennung Bern, Tony Beales, Dave Buckingham, Nigel Burch, Richard Bye, Mike Cain, Aidan Curley, Howard Curtis, Steve Darke, Alud Davies, Andy Durrant, Jamie Eagles, Ian Evans, Mark Gale, Steve Garner, Peter Gerhard, Ian Gibson, Malcolm Greenbaum, Kieran Gildea, Jerry Gunner, Dave Haines, Arno Landewers, Clive Lynch, Chris Jacewicz, Terry Judge, Derek King, Carl Knight, Phillip Linley, Matt Lusted, Michael Magnusson, George Maidens, Simon Neville, Mike Ody, Izabella Osawa, Steve Parslow, Roger Peperell, Christian Pscheidt, Dave Rock, Luis Rossi, Doug Rough, Oliver Schmid, Martin Sidwells, Terry Smith, Steven Sowter, Iain Thomson, Jeff DeVore, Kevin Widdowson, Luc Wittemans, Phil Yeadon plus the proof-reading team of Don Schofield and Lisa Checkley. Finally a special thank you to Laurence Jones & Mark Davies who created FreeBird Aviation Database (http://www.freebirddb.com), my involvement in which served as the catalyst that created my interest in this genre of aircraft.

EXPLANATORY NOTES

The following abbreviations have been used in the text:

b/u	broken up	canx	cancelled	cvtd	converted
dam	damaged	dbf	destroyed by fire	dbr	damaged beyond repair
exp	expired	inst	instuctional	pres	preserved
std	stored	wfu	withdrawn from use	w/o	written off

* An asterisk following the last registration indicates that at the time of compilation these marks were reserved or assigned to the aircraft in question.
( ) Brackets around a registration indicate that these marks were reserved but not taken up.
" " Inverted commas indicate false or illegally-carried marks and registrations assigned/painted in error.

NOTES : When an aircraft has been exported to another country and the new marks are not known at the time of compilation, the country prefix only is shown. A significant number of aircraft have been sold in Mexico, Venezuela, Colombia and Panama although in many cases the aircraft have been sold on to another country without adopting marks in the country they were officially exported to.

CONTENTS

AERITALIA-PARTENAVIA P.68T

c/n	Identities
6001	I-PAIT [wfu; CofA exp 29Oct81]

Production complete

AERITALIA-PARTENAVIA AP.68TP-100

c/n	Identities
6002	I-RAIO [w/o 05Oct82 Mare Al Largo Di Gaeta, Italy]
6003	I-RAIP [w/o 30Jul82 Ogliaro, Italy]

Production complete

AERITALIA-PARTENAVIA AP.68TP-300 SPARTACUS

c/n	Identities					
8001	I-RAIP	I-SPRV	HB-LQW	N313LC	N75CY	
8002	I-RAIK	I-SPRS	N802AT	YV-2510P	YV1832	
8003	I-SPRT	[wfu; CofA exp 05Jan85]				
8004	I-SPRU	[wfu; CofA exp 11Dec90]				
8005	YV-696P	YV2199				
8006	I-RAIZ	LN-LMX				
8007	9Y-THI	N3116C	[w/o 09Jan96 in Pacific Ocean nr El Segundo, CA, USA; canx 19Nov96]			
8008	I-SPRX	5A-DSD	9H-AFO			
8009	I-MAAA	N809AM	YV-2373P	YV2299		
8010	CP-1997					
8011	I-RAIZ	I-AITT	I-VULE	N98AG	[cvtd to Vulcanair AP.68TP-300 Spartacus]	

Production complete

AERITALIA-PARTENAVIA AP.68TP-600 VIATOR

c/n	Identities				
9001	I-RAIL	I-BAML	N901TP		
9002	I-AITN	N902TP	5R-MKC	D-IVIS	T7-BMM
9003	I-RAIS	9L-LBC	N903TP		
9004	N7028M	C9-ATQ	ZS-MGI	N904TP	
9005	I-RAIL	I-TLRN			
9006	I-AITE				
9007	[to Tajena Aerospace and built as c/n 1A-002]				

Production complete

AERO COMMANDER/ROCKWELL 680T/680V TURBO COMMANDER

680T/V = Built as a 680T, later modified to 680V - gross weight increased from 8950lbs to 9400lbs

$ = has been modified from original TPE331-43 to TPE331-1-151K series engines
+ = has been modified with the installation of Commander-Aero winglets

c/n	Series/Mod	Identities
1473-1	680T/V	N6381U N686N (N48AD) N686N [b/u; canx 17Jul92]
1532-2	680T/V	(N36A) (ZS-EUI) N1186Z G-AWXL HB-GEK N399T [w/o 31Jan75 Olathe-Johnson County, KS, USA; canx 20Aug75]
1534-3	680T	N1156Z N499N N441LM N602PA [wfu c1984 Bethany, OK, USA; b/u; canx 30Oct84]
1536-4	680T/V	N6359U (N696SA) N6359U [w/o 22Jan70 White Horse Springs, Aspen, CO, USA; canx 18Jun70]
1538-5	680T/V $+	N6382U (D-IKAO) N1444C N925HB N1444C N100BP N722LJ YV-1151CP YV1035
1540-6	680T/680V-TU	N6300 G-AWXK F-WSTM F-BSTM [cvtd to use Astafan II turbojet engines (ff 08Apr71 as a jet); pres Mas Pelegry Aviation Museum, Perpignan, France; canx 18Nov91]
1542-7	680T/V $	N1168Z N45Q N45QC [wfu & b/u for spares c1984]
1544-8	680T/V	(N1171Z) N357X N146E C-GSVQ [wfu cFeb85 (TT 4418); pres inst airframe Northern Lights College, Dawson Creek, BC, Canada]
1546-9	680T/V	N75D N300HH N800HH N800HA (C-GVCF) N9031X (N800HA) C-GJCA N2549E C-FAXN [pres British Columbia Institute of Technology, Burnaby, BC, Canada; canx 03Apr09]
1548-10	680T/V	N1185Z N7610U CF-HAP N7610U [abandoned Chetumal, Quintana Roo, Mexico]
1550-11	680T/V	(N6387U) CF-SVJ N4470H [wfu & b/u; canx 07Aug84]
1552-12	680T	N592DC N5920C [wfu before Mar69; canx 02Jun69; fuselage used to construct Model 690 c/n 11000]
1554-13	680T	(N6509V) (N5415) N5419 N541W [w/o 03Oct70 off Pompano Beach, FL, USA; registration revoked 24Nov71]
1556-14	680T	(N1187Z) N543S [b/u; registration revoked 31Oct75]
1557-15	680T	N1171Z [wfu, parts to White Industries, Bates City, MO, USA; location "S-24"]
1558-16	680T/V	N1188Z N818 (N99517) N818EC N818L [dbr late 1980's at Matagorda Island, TX, USA; b/u]
1560-17	680T/V	N1163Z N419S C-GMNC N419S C-GMNC N419S N687L
1562-18	680T/V	(N1183Z) N6539V N962BL C-GFAF [wfu Pacific Vocational Institute, Burnaby, BC, Canada; canx 13Feb85]
1563-19	680T/V $	(N1195Z) N272E N22LY N200CT N400G HK-2539G FAC542 (Colombian AF) [impounded in Colombia & tfd to military; still current as N400G]
1564-20	680T	N1199Z I-ARBO EC-DSA [dbr 04Dec85 Palma de Mallorca, Spain; b/u c1991]
1565-21	680T/V	N245E OB-T-924 N2655 N9006N N18EL N444GP N444GB [w/o 05Aug90 Keflavik, Iceland; canx 31Aug90]
1566-22	680T/V	N1192Z N292Z
1567-23	680T	N76D N76BT [wfu c1989 OK Aircraft Parts, Hayward, CA, USA; b/u; canx 13Jun02]
1568-24	680T/V $	N6519V CF-AAP N2637M (C-GLRI) N666MN
1570-25	680T/V +	N370K (N222JK) N370K
1571-26	680T/V	N6540V [wfu cJan91; pres inst airframe Portland, OR, USA]
1572-27	680T/V	N6506V N900RJ N681AC N900RJ
1573-28	680T	N1179Z PI-C797 RP-C797 PK-OBB N54553 N80SS HS-TFB [w/o 22Jul84 12km N of Don Muang Apt, Bangkok, Thailand]
1575-29	680T/V	N1195Z (CF-VAA) N1195Z [w/o 09Dec72 Augusta Regional/Bush Field, GA, USA; canx 26Jun73]
1576-30	680T/V	N1187Z N917RG [w/o cAug76 nr Mazatlan, Sinaloa, Mexico; canx 14Jul77]
1577-31	680T/V	N1178Z N725SF N17690 C-GIXF N17690 [w/o 03Dec85 Concord-Buchanan Field, CA, USA; canx 31Jul87]
1579-32	680T/V	N6536V N808GU [seized in Mexico c1991 - status?]
1580-33	680T	(N6503V) N78D [w/o 05Dec71 nr New Orleans-Lakefront, LA, USA; canx 22Jan72]
1581-34	680T	N6514V [dbr 02Mar80 Atlanta-DeKalb/Peachtree, GA, USA; b/u c1985]
1583-35	680T	N6523V [wfu 31Oct68 & b/u; canx 26Jun70]
1584-36	680T	(N1181Z) N512JC N512JD
1585-37	680T/V	(N1282) N1154Z [b/u c1983; canx 02Dec83]
1587-38	680T/V	(N1284) N6543V N944WH N55B N251B C-GJNH [dbr 09Jul81 Red Deer-Industrial, AB, Canada; b/u cFeb83; canx 23Feb83]
1588-39	680T/V	N6507V N932 N932E [w/o 11Jul84 Castle Rock, WA, USA; canx 03Aug87]
1589-40	680T/V	N360X N91D N699GN N698GN [wfu cApr96 Hayward-Air Terminal, CA, USA]
1593-41	680T/V	N6541V N688NA N111WE TG-PYD [canx as exported; no further details]
1597-42	680T $	(N6520V) N676MB N6969B N688SH [b/u c1999; canx 01Feb99]
1601-43	680T/V $	(N6532V) N5418 N541X N577VM N577RH (N22WG) C-GFAB [wfu cFeb87 (TT7475); pres inst airframe New Brunswick Community College, Fredericton, NB, Canada; canx 09Apr87]
1605-44	680T/V	N6537V N601G [w/o 08Aug76 nr Alapaha, GA, USA; canx 11Nov76]
1609-45	680V	N5413 N541F C-GPRO N541F [w/o 03Nov90 Fort Lauderdale-Executive, FL, USA; canx 12Dec90]
1610-46	680T/V	(N78D) N79D N79BT N79BJ [wfu cApr79; pres inst airframe Atlanta Area Technical School, GA, USA; canx 16Jan04]
1612-47	680T	(N4598E) N688DC [b/u cDec84 Oklahoma City-Wiley Post, OK, USA; canx 13Jun06]
1614-48	680T/V	N4556E [impounded Santo Domingo-Herrera, Dominican Republic]
1616-49	680T/V $	N4576E N677PV N311MH N311PD N348BP N171AT
1618-50	680T/V $	N4693E N100CT [w/o 03Sep84 in sea off Bridgeport, CT, USA, parts to White Industries, Bates City, MO, USA; b/u; canx 21Aug87]
1620-51	680T/V	(N4594E) OE-FCB D-IBOE N801RA N132AT ZP-TYE N680PD N680MH N11HM
1622-52	680T/V	(N5418) (N5420) N4527E [wfu cNov87, parts to White Industries, Bates City, MO, USA; location "Ramp North"]
1624-53	680T/V	(N4558E) N1010M N32DF [b/u date & location unkn]
1626-54	680T/V	N4875E N200E N212CW N212CM [b/u c1983 Hillsboro, OR, USA]

AERO COMMANDER/ROCKWELL 680T/680V

c/n	Series/Mod	Identities
1628-55	680T/V $	(N79D) N2755H [w/o 07Jul80 Jackson-Allen C Thompson, MS, USA]
1630-56	680V	N4682E [wfu cJan89; pres inst airframe Cincinnati Technical College, OH, USA]
1632-57	680T/V	(N196KC) N4901E N73AC HK-2285X HK-2285 HK-2285P [w/o 13Sep94 between Mariquita, Tolima & Armenia, Quindio, Colombia; canx 22Nov00]
1675-58	680T/V	N4517E N1540Y N12KW N12KV [b/u date & location unkn]
1676-59	680T/V	N4345R N580M N66FV [pres at tech school, Harlingen-Rio Grande Valley International, TX, USA]
1677-60	680V	(N4633E) N86D N8QD N2UL N677KA
1679-61	680V	N4710E N330LC N888DD [wfu; b/u by Island Aircraft Parts, St Simons Island, GA, USA; canx 15Dec95]
1680-62	680V	N710JK N3CC N3CG [wfu Smyrna, TN, USA; canx 23Oct07]
1681-63	680V $	(N4700E) AE104 (Argentinian Army) AE129 (Argentinian Army) AE128 (Argentinian Army) LV-OFX [wfu Buenos Aires-Aeroparque, Argentina]
1683-64	680V	N4549E YV-O-MOP-8 YV-O-MAR-2 [w/o 17Aug78 in Venezuela]
1684-65	680T/V $	N81D N1BA N1UT N10TG EC-HDE D-IABC
1685-66	680T/V $	(N4859E) N949ET N11MC N10QZ YV-2435P YV-744CP YV-2740P
1687-67	680V $+	(N4930E) N5411 N54117 N110PC N2TF (N42TE) N42TF N680FS N688TM
1688-68	680V	N4938E N4F N4FB
1689-69	680V +	(N4860E) YV-T-ZTA YV-T-OTZ YV-T-ZTZ YV-TAKP YV-03CP YV-834P YV-714CP (YV1551) YV-714CP [w/o 03Feb06 nr Sevilla, Magdalena, Colombia]
1691-70	680V	(N4859E) N4585E N47HM [pres inst airframe Cochise Community College, Douglas, AZ, USA]
1692-71	680V	N4638E N375A [b/u date & location unkn]
1693-72	680T/V	(N4648E) CF-FEO C-FFEO [dbf 15Feb93 Mount Hope, ON, Canada; canx 22Feb93]
1694-73	680T/V	(N4664E) (N344) N334 N334JG N334TP N999WT I-MLWT [CofA exp 08Nov89; canx c1995 - status?]
1697-74	680T/V	(N4669E) N85D N99AF N1963R N400LR N400LP [wfu, parts to White Industries, Bates City, MO, USA; canx 01Apr99; location R-22]
1698-75	680T/V +	(N4599E) CF-VNX N420J N20BM
1699-76	680T/V	(N85D) N375A N4638E CF-IIG C-FIIG N7029P N29DE [std Las Vegas-North Air Terminal, NV, USA]
1701-77	680V	N4648E N163D (N58B) N11CK N163D [b/u c1992; canx 31Mar92]
1702-78	680V	(N4664E) N89D N89DA [w/o 15Nov82 Damphries, Jamaica; canx 02Nov83]
1703-79	680V	N4557E N299F N299FL N161X N161XX PT- [canx 07Jul92 as exported to Brazil]
1704-80	680V	(N36A) N830 N830WM N2KS C-GKFV N2173Z [wfu c1988 Kelowna, BC, Canada; canx 09Sep97]
1705-81	680V	N87D N87BT [wfu cJul82; pres inst airframe Aviation High School, Long Island City, NY, USA]
1707-82	680T/V $	N7000H N616MC N616E [wfu c1988; b/u ; canx 07Sep00]
1708-83	680V	N4603E N500HY (C-GFAC) N200TB [inst airframe East Coast Aero Technical School, Bedford-Hanscom Field, MA, USA]
1709-84	680V	(N36A) 9J-RGD G-AYTX ZS-HSA N33511 N335H N300KC N300KQ TI- [b/u date & location unkn]
1710-85	680V $	N4947E N897AW N801MF N111ST N111SK
1711-86	680V	(N36A) N535SM EC-DXG [wfu c1990; pres cMay00 as inst airframe Globalia Training Centre, Lluchmayor, Mallorca, Spain]
1713-87	680V $	(N344) (N4704E) (N677PV) (N36A) N1123V N88WZ [b/u c1991; canx 23Dec91]
1714-88	680V $+	(N344) (N4928E) XB-CED N50655
1718-89	680V	(N4566E) (N4992E) (D-IDIG) D-IATI N3DG C-GJQM N3253U YV-340CP YV-344P (YV1217) YV2224
1719-90	680V	(N36A) YV-O-CVG-2 YV-1405P
1720-91	680V	(N288W) N228W OO-SKF N8042N [b/u c1984 Bethany, OK, USA]
1721-92	680V	[built as Rockwell Commander 680W c/n 1721-1]
1722-93	680V	[built as Rockwell Commander 680W c/n 1722-2]
1723-94	680V	[built as Rockwell Commander 680W c/n 1723-3]
1519-95	680T/V	N1161Z N175DB FAC551 (Colombian AF) [wfu Bogota-El Dorado, Distrito Capital, Colombia]

Production complete

AERO COMMANDER/ROCKWELL 680W TURBO II COMMANDER

$ = has been modified from original TPE331-43 to TPE331-1-151K series engines
+ = has been modified with the installation of Commander-Aero winglets

c/n	Series/Mod	Identities
1721-1	680W $	(N36A) (N677PV) N4928E N299DE N299ED N954HF N954HE N39AS
1722-2	680W	N93D N93RA [w/o 23Mar80 off Bimini Island, Bahamas]
1723-3	680W $	N4622E
1751-4	680W $	N5052E VH-KRX N5052E N951HF N951HE [wfu cMay86; pres inst airframe Memphis Area Vocational-Technical School, TN, USA]
1752-5	680W	N5051E N505RT [wfu Sorocaba, Sao Paulo State, Brazil]
1760-6	680W	N5049E N177DC N5ER [wfu & canx 20Aug91 as inst airframe, Embry-Riddle University, Daytona Beach, FL, USA; registered but never marked N5ER; b/u cMar03]
1761-7	680W $	N5057E N242A N16TE C-GNYD N3833P [wfu cAug93; parts at Red Deer-Industrial, AB, Canada]
1762-8	680W $+	N91D N2755B YV1044
1763-9	680W $	N4704E N4561 ZS-RSM N97011 N200DT
1772-10	680W $	N4730E N615 N611 N611MF 83-24126 (US Army) N514NA [inst airframe University of the District of Columbia, Washington, DC, USA]
1773-11	680W	N4852E N11CT
1774-12	680W $+	(N4860E) N5416 N54163 (N680SJ) N54163
1775-13	680W	(N4930E) N5417 N122NM N9RN YV-820CP
1776-14	680W	N4988E N13TV N121AB N680W EC-EAG [wfu c1990 Palma de Mallorca-Son Bonet, Spain]
1777-15	680W	N4992E YV-2175P N24099 N107DC [wfu, parts to Dodson International Parts, Rantoul, KS, USA]
1778-16	680W	N5022E C-GPNV N680X [dbr 24Aug92 Miami International, FL, USA by Hurricane Andrew; canx 18Mar93]
1787-17	680W	N5058E [w/o 20Nov82 Atlanta-Hartsfield International, GA, USA]
1788-18	680W	N5021E N5E N5EQ N5EV XA-DII N5EV XA-DII XB-DTD [wfu cMar99, parts to Orange Coast College-Aviation Technology, Costa Mesa, CA, USA; b/u cMar09]
1789-19	680W	N192MH N1928H (N260RC) N1928H
1790-20	680W $	N5061E (N68TC) N410TH N7UP
1791-21	680W	N5062E N77JL N345TT
1792-22	680W	N5064E N5064C N43W N43WL N680JD
1793-23	680W	N5069E N22RT N22ET [wfu & b/u cMay93 by Tri-City Air Parts, Norman, OK, USA]
1802-24	680W	N5078E N17JG (N102US) HP-898 N17JG [wfu cMar83; inst airframe Tulsa County Area Vocational Technical School, Tulsa-R.Lloyd Jones, OK, USA]
1803-25	680W	N5079E N4100B [wfu cAug93, parts to White Industries, Bates City, MO, USA; b/u]
1804-26	680W +	N5081E YV-O-INOS-3 YV-2280P
1805-27	680W	N5082E N713SP [w/o 04Oct79 nr Alexandria, LA, USA]
1811-28	680W	N5017E N505JC N94HC N94HD [w/o 11Nov78 nr Lucerne, CA, USA; canx 31Jan85]
1812-29	680W	N5029E N500QE N500NR N680KM [dbr 18Sep87 Reno-Tahoe Intl, NV, USA, parts to White Industries, Bates City, MO, USA; location "Ramp North"]
1813-30	680W	(N5031E) YV-T-VTY YV-533P YV-536P
1814-31	680W +	(N5036E) N6733 N6733H N77MF N71AF YV-2436P
1818-32	680W	(N6517V) N5418 N1NR N15ES N3RA C-GKMV N3RA N5RE [wfu cJun00; pres inst airframe at Pennsylvania College of Technology, Williamsport Regional Apt, PA, USA]
1819-33	680W	(N6520V) D-IMON [w/o 27Dec78 Lake Walchensee, nr Niedernach, Bavaria, West Germany; canx cJan79]
1820-34	680W	(N6525V) N340BK N319FB N319PB N3SK (N219D) HK-3975X HP-1433 HK-4289X
1821-35	680W	N6532V TG-DAM N424PP [wfu c2003,parts to Aviation Warehouse, El Mirage, CA, USA]
1828-36	680W	N9003N CF-KEX N94490 N9003N [b/u date & location unkn; canx 21Nov91]
1829-37	680W	N9004N [wfu cAug88; b/u by Arkansas Airframe, Clinton, AR, USA; canx 20Sep91; some parts to Dawson Aircraft, Clinton, AR, USA]
1833-38	680W	(N9008N) PP-FNK PT-FNK PT-KYY N8061Q [noted 30Nov07 still marked as PT-KYY]
1834-39	680W $	N9009N N847CE N300CT N200CT N200QT [b/u c1993 possibly in Mexico; canx 13Aug93]
1835-40	680W	N9010N CF-ANG N81LC CP- [canx 05Nov82 as exported to Bolivia]
1842-41	680W	N9017N N333TE C-GKFG N39480 (N456A) N345CA [wfu cAug93, parts to White Industries, Bates City, MO, USA; location R-24]
1843-42	680W $	(N9018W) N9018N N300CF N308CF N20ME N20MB N8416B (YV-723P) N940U
1844-43	680W	N9019N [w/o 28Dec71 Elkhart, IN, USA in hangar bomb blast; canx 22Nov72]
1848-44	680W	(N9023N) EP-FSS
1849-45	680W	(N9024N) EP-FIA
1850-46	680W	(N9025N) EP-FIB

Production complete

AERO COMMANDER/ROCKWELL 681/681B TURBO COMMANDER

$ = has been modified from original TPE331-43 to TPE331-1-151K series engines
+ = has been modified with the installation of Commander-Aero winglets

c/n	Series/Mod	Identities
6001	681	N9051N (N355HC) N102DE N66CP N22RT
6002	681	N9052N N6E
6003	681	N9053N N90DA N9053N CF-FDB N500JP (N711MV) N500JP [w/o 27Jan81 nr Winnemucca, NV, USA; canx 08Feb83]
6004	681	N9054N N740ES (N110PG) VH-NYG [w/o 14Feb91 Tamworth, NSW, Australia; canx 11Feb93]
6005	681 +	N9055N N180VW N35WA YV-2383P YV1775
6006	681 $	N9056N N2725B N113CT
6007	681 $+	N9057N LV-JOJ N68VH
6008	681	N9058N YV-06CP N9058N [wfu cJun91; pres inst airframe Broward Community College, Hollywood-North Perry, FL, USA; canx 19May04]
6009	681	N9059N 5-59 (Iranian AF) 5-4081 (Iranian Army) [pres Aerospace Exhibition Centre, Tehran-Mehrabad, Iran]
6010	681	N9065N XB-PAO N3867N
6011	681	N9060N [w/o 25Nov70 Altus Municipal, OK, USA; canx 18Jan71]
6012	681	N9061N EP-AGU [forward fuselage pres in museum at Tehran, Iran]
6013	681	(N9062N) N84D N60BC N70RF [dbr 30Jun95 Nassau, Bahamas]
6014	681	N9063N N123GT N666PC N88RK LV-VHP N681SM YV [canx 09Jun02 as exported to Venezuela]
6015	681	N9066N CP-894 [w/o 18Jun71 between Puerto Suarez & Santa Cruz, Bolivia]
6016	681	(N9067N) N126JW N1100M N444JB (N344AC) VH-NYH [pres Darwin Aviation Heritage Museum, NT, Australia; canx 08Apr94]
6017	681	[built as Rockwell Commander 685 c/n 12000]
6018	681 $	N9068N PT-DQX N9068N N29PR
6019	681 $	N9069N C-GFAE N3203P
6020	681 $	(N9670N) N9070N (N371DG) N371DR N9DF N114MR C-FATR [wfu cMay97, parts to Global Aircraft Industries, Edmonton-Villeneuve, AB, Canada; (TT 10132); canx 16May01]
6021	681	N9071N N10RN PT-OQQ
6022	681	N9073N N53CC N58CC N58PP N250AC C-GBIT TG-WIZ
6023	681	N9012N XB-CUF XA-CAG XB-DJN
6024	681 $	N9020N N22WK YV-2501P
6025	681 $	N9023N N10HC N10HG CP-2042
6026	681 $	N9024N VH-NYF [wfu & canx 05Aug97]
6027	681 $+	N9025N N711TT N211TT N3754C N3738J N681AS N548GQ N681SP
6028	681 $	N9028N C-GFAD N9028N N100GL
6029	681 +	N9074N YV-2404P
6030	681	N9035N D-IGAD 9Q-CGL [dbr 08Apr90 Lubudi, Zaire, parts to Dodson International Parts, Rantoul, KS, USA; b/u]
6031	681	[built as Rockwell Commander 690 c/n 11001]
6032	681	N9079N OH-ACE N32TC N75GM TG-GMI TG-AMI [wfu Toluca, Mexico State, Mexico; CofA exp 04Mar92; canx]
6033	681	N9086N SE-FGE [w/o 23Jul73 Mestersvig, Greenland; canx 31Jan74]
6034	681	N9087N VH-NYD [wfu Darwin, NT, Australia; canx 10Mar92; b/u cAug04]
6035	681	N9088N HK-1977X HK-1977W HK-1977 HK-1977P HK-1977 [canx 27Sep99 - status?]
6036	681 +	N9089N PI-C1977 RP-C1977 N681DC TG- [canx 17Aug05 as exported to Guatemala]
6037	681	N9090N N10TN [pres cMay86 ICAO Apprentice Training School, Kurmitola, Bangladesh; canx 11Jun86]
6038	681 $	N9091N N46JC N78CH
6039	681	N9092N N420MA VH-JWO [wfu & b/u cJun99; canx 06May99]
6040	681 $+	N9097N XB-AUR
6041	681 $	N9101N (N73SJ) N25BE
6042	681	N9102N N5NR N5NP [w/o 08Mar78 Greenup, KY, USA; registration revoked 09Jan81]
6043	681	(N9105N) N5410 N3NR N20NT N30RS N240AC HK-2376X HK-2376P HK-2376W HK-2376 HK-2376W HK-2376P HK-2376
6044	681 $+	N5411 N4NR N4NB N8RA C-GKFR N4798M C-GLMC N529JC YV-2697P (YV1254) YV-2697P [dbf 06Mar06 El Zumbador, nr Trujillo, Honduras]
6045	681B	N9107N F-BXPU N9107N 9Q-CBU
6046	681B	N9108N HK-2986X HK-3236X HK-3236P [impounded Medellin, Antioquia, Colombia; canx 06Mar00]
6047	681B $+	N9109N N121SP VH-NYE (VH-UJN) VH-NBT
6048	681 $	N9110N ZS-JMF N9110N (N660JC) N911JM N676DM N337FG
6049	681B	N9111N N578KA N587KA HC-BPY N681HV
6050	681B $	N9067N N97AB N9067N N56MC N56MQ N772CB [w/o 28Mar85 Calhan, CO, USA; canx 19Aug87]
6051	681B $	N9117N N14M N681FV N162RB N200M N12MU N19MU
6052	681B $+	(N9118N) XB-WID N48213 N130TT N10269 (N269CA) N105SS YV-2475P YV2178
6053	681B	N9121N N3701F HK-2217X HK-2217 HK-2217W HK-2217P [w/o 13Mar86 nr Medellin, Antioquia, Colombia in mid-air collision with PA-34 HK-2453W; canx 08Apr88]
6054	681B $+	N9124N N21HC C-FCMJ
6055	681B $	N9127N CF-PNB C-FPNB N18KK
6056	681B $+	N9129N [w/o 30Nov96 nr Mansfield-Lahm Municipal, OH, USA; canx 03Jun98]
6057	681B	N9130N HL5223 [w/o 13Sep74 in South Korea; canx 04Oct74]
6058	681B $+	N9137N N4MF N4ME N47CK [wfu, parts to White Industries, Bates City, MO, USA; location "Ramp No 14"]
6059	681B $	N9138N N333RK N30BG (N681NR) N30BG
6060	681B	N9142N F-BTFG EI-BAH F-BXPV N2643B 9Q-CGE N2643B (EC-) N2643B [wfu engineless & derelict Seville-San Pablo, Spain]

c/n	Series/Mod	Identities
6061	681B $+	(N9143N) XB-YET N22EE N520CS YV1066
6062	681B	(N9144N) 5-280 (Iranian AF) 5-8901 (Iranian Defence Force)
6063	681B	N9146N (N111RA) N9146N N111RA N111RG XB-HUL XA-SHP XB-SHP
6064	681B	(N9149N) LV-PSE LQ-LDB LV-LDB [wfu Buenos Aires-Don Torcuato, Argentina]
6065	681B	(N9151N) (N9154N) EP-AKA [pres Tehran Civil Aviation Technical School, Tehran, Iran]
6066	681B	(N9153N) (N5412) N2NR N9NB RP-C775 [pres Camp Aquino Army Museum, Tarlac, Luzon, Philippines]
6067	681B	(N9161N) EP-AKB [pres Aerospace Exhibition Centre, Tehran-Mehrabad, Iran]
6068	681B	(N9162N) 5-281 (Iranian AF) 5-8902 (Iranian Defence Force)
6069	681B +	(N9163N) PT-IEC
6070	681B	(N9164N) PT-IED
6071	681B	(N9165N) PT-IEE [w/o 16Dec00 nr Sao Paulo-Congonhas, Sao Paulo State, Brazil]
6072	681B	(N9166N) 5-282 (Iranian AF) 5-8903 (Iranian Defence Force) [pres Aerospace Exhibition Centre, Tehran-Mehrabad, Iran]

Production complete

AERO COMMANDER/ROCKWELL 690 TURBO COMMANDER

$ = has been modified from original TPE331-5 to TPE331-10 series engines
+ = has been modified with the installation of Commander-Aero winglets

c/n	Series/Mod	Identities
11000	690	N9001N [w/o 05May69 Rosedale, OK, USA; canx 07Jun73]
11001	690	N9100N N700CB CP-1016 N700CB N41T
11002	690	N9202N [w/o 26Jun70 Bethany, OK, USA; canx 02Jul70]
11003	690	N9203N (N512JC) HP- "HK-3147X" N9203N N72TT C-FNAS N72TT N302WB [w/o 16Sep03 nr Soto la Marina, Tamaulipas, Mexico; canx 30Dec05]
11004	690 +	N9204N SE-FGF N37546 N57175
11005	690	(N9205N) TG-JAC 633 (Guatemalan AF) TG-JAC TG-BAD HK-2055X HK-2055W HK-2055 [canx 25Feb00 - status?]
11006	690	N9206N N1JW N15JW N150W (N33AR) N515AR (N515AP) N690SP HZ-SS1 ZK-MOH
11007	690	N9207N ZS-NHG N9207N N711TT N171TT EC-EIL [dbr 29May91 Palma de Mallorca, Spain; b/u]
11008	690	N9201N OB-M-1031 [w/o 14Feb79 Cerro Valle Punta, nr Yauyos, Peru; canx 16Jan80]
11009	690 +	N9209N CF-DLE N9209N N25BD
11010	690 +	N9210N N28AD N23AD XA-RYF N690RA
11011	690	N9211N PT-OQH [dbr 28May95 Lages, Santa Catarina, Brazil; canx 12Mar97]
11012	690 +	(N9212N) N921HB N885RA YV [canx 20Jul09 as exported to Venezuela]
11013	690	D-INIX [w/o 21Jun72 between Reykjavik, Iceland and Narsarsuaq, South Greenland]
11014	690	N9214N HK-1982X HK-1982W HK-1982P HK-1982 HK-1982W [canx 07Apr00 - status?]
11015	690	N9215N N412FS (N412FB) N662DM [w/o 21Jun87 nr Bridgeport-Bryant Field, CA, USA; canx 19Jul94]
11016	690	N9216N N333UP N333UR N428SJ C-GKDZ [fleet no.54]
11017	690	N9217N N101RW N101RQ N690WC
11018	690	N9218N N173LP N173AL N690BW (N690PG) N63PG XA-PUY
11019	690	N9219N LV-LEY [canx c1996; b/u Buenos Aires-Base Area Moron, Argentina]
11020	690 +	N9220N N340BK N340BP N14CV C-GZON [fleet no.55]
11021	690	XC-RAM [wfu Mexico City-Benito Juarez International, Mexico]
11022	690 +	N9222N N14BH N98MR TI-MEL N184RL LV-BCJ
11023	690	N9223N [wfu c1996 Hayward-Air Terminal, CA, USA]
11024	690	N1NR [w/o 14Aug72 Wellsburg, WV, USA]
11025	690 +	(N919MD) N9225N N100LS C-FZRQ [fleet no.51]
11026	690	N9226N VH-NYC
11027	690	N568H [w/o 21Oct76 Los Angeles, CA, USA in mid-air collision with Beech 35C-33 N21TH; canx 25Nov76]
11028	690	N9228N (N12BU) N2DB [stolen c1981 never recovered; canx 22Sep06]
11029	690	N569H (N888KN) N569H [pres inst airframe Clayton College & State University, Jonesboro, GA, USA; canx 28Jul89]
11030	690	(TG-JAC) N5028E D-ICKS VH-WLS VH-WLO N399GM YV [canx 06May05 as exported to Venezuela]
11031	690 +	XA-COS N17244 N93WW (N83SS) N1SS N84DT N690GK
11032	690	N8LB N8LD N349AC C-GFPP [fleet no.52]
11033	690	N9233N N100DG HK-2281X HK-2281 HK-2281P HK-2281 [canx 16Jun97 - status?]
11034	690	(N414EA) N9234N N400JJ EC-EFS N690TR
11035	690 +	N9235N N882GS N15VZ C-GJFO [fleet no.53]
11036	690	PP-FRC PT-FRC PT-LDA
11037	690	PP-FRD PT-FRD PT-LDL
11038	690	OO-GPL N9238N (N77PR) N33WG [reportedly b/u]
11039	690	N9239N CR-AOI C9-AOI 9Q-CIH N690NH C-GICX N690NH VH-NYB [pres at Hi-Way Inn (intersection of Carpentaria and Stuart Highways), NT, Australia; canx 08Apr94]
11040	690	N9240N N701CB N690CM N690DC C-FAKP [fleet no.56]
11041	690	N9241N (N5PT) N924PC (N54MH) N924PC
11042	690	(XC-FEL) XC-FUJ XA-KUU [wfu, parts to Eagle Creek Aviation, Eagle Creek Apt, IN, USA; b/u; fuselage to Indianapolis International, IN, USA; canx 03Aug94; b/u c2008]
11043	690 +	(N9143N) N2VA N2VQ N71VT N71VE

AERO COMMANDER/ROCKWELL 690

c/n	Series/Mod	Identities
11044	690	N9144N N471SC VH-BSS [w/o 14Jan94 in sea nr Sydney, NSW, Australia; canx 01Feb94]
11045	690	EP-AGV 1406 (Iranian Police)
11046	690 +	N2155B
11047	690	EP-AGW
11048	690	(N5NR) N1NR N182 [w/o 15Jan80 nr Goldsboro, MD, USA; canx 06Dec82]
11049	690	501 (Iranian Navy) 5-8997 (Iranian AF) 1403 (Iranian Police)
11050	690	XC-FUV XA-IIW [wfu Mexico City-Benito Juarez International, Mexico; canx 07Jul94 reportedly on sale to USA]
11051	690	N9151N N500R N567R
11052	690	(N9132N) N1230D N780BP (ZP-) N780BP
11053	690	CP-1016 [w/o 09Aug93 Pacajes, nr La Paz, Bolivia]
11054	690	CP-1017 [w/o 13Feb74 nr Lima-Jorge Chavez Apt, Peru]
11055	690 +	(N9162N) HB-GFH N83TC N100MB CP-2182 ARC601 (Colombian Navy) [w/o 05Nov98 Bogota-El Dorado, Distrito Capital, Colombia]
11056	690	N9156N HK-1844X HK-1844W HK-1844P [wfu cJan00 Caracas-Oscar Machado Zuloaga International, Venezuela; canx 07Feb00]
11057	690	N9126N N37T N37TB N376TC C-GWEW [fleet no.130]
11058	690	N9148N N11VS N690JC CX-BOE N2069B N690PJ EC-HNH N691CL
11059	690	N9131N HK-3465X HK-3465 HK-3465P [canx 11Apr00 - status?]
11060	690	(XA-GAC) XA-DER
11061	690 +	N28G YV-853CP N853CP YV-854CP YV2252
11062	690	N9147N VH-BLH VH-NEY VH-UJG [wfu cOct07 Melbourne-Essendon, VIC, Australia]
11063	690	(N2VA) N9150N [w/o 25Aug84 nr Little America, WY, USA]
11064	690	N9154N N830 N83G [wfu cAug93, parts to White Industries, Bates City, MO, USA; location "Ramp North"]
11065	690	(N9165N) XB-KUE XB-CZX XB-FYD
11066	690 +	N9166N N36WR N68TD [wfu cAug08, parts to Alliance Air Parts, Oklahoma City, OK, USA]
11067	690	(N9196N) CP-1076 FAB-028 (Bolivian AF)
11068	690	N9168N C-GGOO [dbf 16Oct00 Red Deer-Industrial, AB, Canada; canx 07Nov00]
11069	690	N123CF N321MG (5Y-) N321MG [wfu c1998 Malindi, Kenya]
11070	690	[built as Rockwell Commander 690A c/n 11100]
11071	690	N9175N
11072	690	(N9149N) OH-ACH N70WA RP-C1956 N690JM [dbr 14Oct01 Temecula-French Valley, CA, USA; canx 08Nov03]
11073	690 +	N9140N N999WW N680AD HP- [canx 03Jun03 as exported to Panama]
11074	690	(N9192N) XA-DIF XB-AEL XB-GJL
11075	690	(N9187N) EP-AKI 1405 (Iranian Police)
11076	690	(N9227N) 501 (Iranian Navy) 5-2501 (Iranian Navy) [pres Aerospace Exhibition Centre, Tehran-Mehrabad, Iran]
11077	690	(N9229N) 4-901 (Iranian Army)
11078	690	(N9231N) 4-902 (Iranian Army)
11079	690	(N9232N) 4-903 (Iranian Army)

Production complete

AERO COMMANDER/ROCKWELL 690A TURBO COMMANDER

$ = has been modified from original TPE331-5 to TPE331-10 series engines
+ = has been modified with the installation of Commander-Aero winglets

c/n	Series/Mod	Identities
11100	690A	N9200N HK-2415X HK-2415 [w/o 07Sep91 nr San Andres, San Andre y Providencia, Colombia; canx 06Mar00]
11101	690A	N57101 VH-AAG [std cOct07 Melbourne-Essendon, VIC, Australia]
11102	690A	N57102 CF-ALI C-FALI N690FP C-GADI N157TA N677JM N697JM HK-4330X HK-4330W
11103	690A	N690AC N690MF N690CE 5Y-BTL
11104	690A +	(N3KS) N2KS N17RM N690CB N320M TR-LXY N3279Y N96BW N690DA N690AZ C-GAAL [fleet no.131]
11105	690A +	N57105 N45ST N57105 N666K N112CE N712CE (N321GM) ZS-MXE A2-AIH ZS-LRM
11106	690A +	N57106 C-FCZZ [fleet no.133]
11107	690A $+	(N57097) N14GG (N14FS) N115CW XB-FXS N813PR N69010 CP-2467
11108	690A	N57108 HB-GFP N46866 [wfu cAug93, parts to White Industries, Bates City, MO, USA; location "Ramp Mid"; canx 29Dec94]
11109	690A	N57109 N690TB N920AU N690TB [w/o 11Aug02 nr Bishop, CA, USA; canx 05Apr04]
11110	690A	N57110 N711LV (N444UP) N444MS ZP-PVO ZP-TVO N6607H HK-3597X HK-3597 [canx 29May02 - status?]
11111	690A +	N57111 N801EB (XB-) N801EB
11112	690A	N299F [w/o 27May78 nr Calumet, OK, USA; canx 21Jan81]
11113	690A +	N57113
11114	690A +	N57114 YV-834CP YV2247
11115	690A	(N57115) N200M N200MB XB-XUC XC-NAY
11116	690A	(N57116) N40MP [w/o 12Nov74 over Bryce Canyon, UT, USA in mid-air collision with USAF F-111A 67-0055; canx 09Jun75]
11117	690A	N333CA [w/o 22Aug73 Alex, OK, USA]
11118	690A	(N57118) (SE-GER) SE-FLN N91384
11119	690A +	(N57118) N57119 N471SC N471SQ (F-BPQQ) EI-BBL N65169 XA-RTQ N690AH
11120	690A +	N57096 [w/o 28Jul06 23 mls WSW of Anchorage, AK, USA; canx 07Feb08]
11121	690A	(N57121) D-IGAF S5-CAI LN-ACE SE-LZU
11122	690A	(N57122) (ZS-GCC) N57122 ZS-GKR N9229Y [w/o 20Dec84 Pea Ridge, nr Rogers Municipal/Carters Field, AR, USA; canx 08Sep86]
11123	690A $+	N57123 N53CC N32BW N122PG N112EF
11124	690A	N57124 (N690MC) N83MC (N83RV) N83MC [w/o 20Jan84 Liberty, MO, USA; canx 13Sep91]
11125	690A $	N57125 (N100AK) OO-WAT P4-PHC N690AE N690EM
11126	690A	N57037 (N345SP) N132JH
11127	690A	N57127 N100CL N199WP N17HF
11128	690A	(N57098) XA-DOG XC-GIG XC-TAB N9015P HK-2282X HK-2282 HK-2282P HK-2282W HK-2282P HK-2282 HK-2282P
11129	690A $+	N57129 N37BW (N500AL) N37BW
11130	690A	(N57130) N570H N294BC N111VS EC-EFH [wfu c1995; pres Madrid-Barajas, Spain]
11131	690A +	N57099 N8535 YV1348
11132	690A	N57054 CR-LAA D2-LAA D2-EAA
11133	690A	N57133 [dbr 07Jan87 Miles City-Frank Wiley Field, MT, USA; canx 28Dec92]
11134	690A	N7RB N45VT (N690DW) C-GHWF [fleet no.132]
11135	690A	N57135 N16GG N160G N744JD [canx 27May05 as exported to Venezuela; reportedly shot down 01Jun05 Yucatan State, Mexico]
11136	690A +	N333CA N318TK
11137	690A $+	N57137 N876MC N331RC
11138	690A $+	(N57138) N77EC N111FF N921AC N690EC N690RK
11139	690A +	N57059 I-FSAB N61WA N7EV TI-AXU
11140	690A	N57053 N847 [w/o 23Apr77 Lake Michigan, nr Chicago-Meigs Field, IL, USA; canx 14Dec77]
11141	690A	(N57141) (9K-ANP) 9K-ACP (N92TC) HB-GFQ N62366 N3869F
11142	690A	(N57142) D-IOET [dbr 01Dec81 Luton, UK; canx cAug82]
11143	690A	N57143 EP-AHL
11144	690A +	N57144 XA-RAO XB-FQC XA-CLE XB-NBI
11145	690A +	N57145 N295BC N86345 LV-PGE LV-VGS N86345 N102JK XB-ISC
11146	690A +	(N57146) N200M N368T (N368L) N721BU F-OHAU N8912B F-OHJE N690SG
11147	690A	(N57147) EP-AHN [w/o 09Jul79 in Iran]
11148	690A	N57148 N2SN N2KN N2KC N13TV [wfu & b/u; canx 12Jun95]
11149	690A	N57149 N5KW N57RS
11150	690A	(N57150) N690WC N47150 N333HC
11151	690A	N57151 CR-LNX 9Q-CCB "CR-LHL" ZS-JWS 3D-BYZ 6O-SBQ [wore illegal marks CR-LHL; wfu Mombasa-Moi, later moved to Nairobi-Wilson, Kenya]
11152	690A $	(N57152) HB-GFO SE-GSB N9101F N42MM VH-NYA VH-NMT VH-CLT
11153	690A	N57074 N53RF N46663 N690CL
11154	690A	N57154 N102JK N31DV
11155	690A +	N57155 N55CM (N55CD) XA-RAS N222MT N536 CC-CRE N155TA N690AR
11156	690A	N57077 N400N (N490N) N400N [w/o 30Nov90 nr Ryderwood, WA, USA; canx 10Apr91]
11157	690A	N57086 L-701 (Lebanese Ministry of National Defence) [dbr cJun82 Beirut International, Lebanon by Israeli bomb attack]
11158	690A +	N57158 VH-ATF
11159	690A $+	(N57091) N28BP N100TT N555GG N655GG N2ES N690HM N690DD
11160	690A +	N57092 N446JB YV [canx 09Jul09 as exported to Venezuela]
11161	690A $+	N57093 HB-GFR SE-GSL OH-ALK SE-GSL OH-ALK N28958 N690KC XA-RZS N291RB YV2428

AERO COMMANDER/ROCKWELL 690A

c/n	Series/Mod	Identities
11162	690A +	N124H HC-BMI N124HQ XB-FYK N124HQ N777TE TG- [canx 29Aug05 as exported to Guatemala]
11163	690A	(N57163) OE-FIX D-IFIX N9769S N111FL [w/o 29Mar92 nr Taos, NM, USA]
11164	690A +	N57152 N700SR (N690RW) N700SR [w/o 03Jan04 nr Cortez-Municipal, CO, USA; canx 23Aug04]
11165	690A +	N57091 G-BEJN N803RA N690LP HK-3466X HK-3466 HK-3466P [dbf 16Mar09 nr La Encantada, Guatemala]
11166	690A +	N57166 N777T (N7787) N77HS N78BA C-GRRO
11167	690A +	(N57167) (N3NR) N5NR N5NZ N48T N48TL N541AM I-BERF N36BA N85AB C-FIIL [fleet no.57]
11168	690A $+	N57168 N261WR N361WR N1CN N5JP N510CH XA-LEY N62MA TI-AXM N690AZ N690CF
11169	690A	XC-GIM XB-FLF N38WA
11170	690A	XA-FEG XC-CAU XA-JUY [wfu c1996 OK Parts, Hollister, CA, USA; b/u; canx 23Apr96]
11171	690A +	N57171 CS-APV N690EM N690JJ YV303T YV2538
11172	690A	(N57172) N9164N TF-ERR C-GERR TF-ERR (D-IIGI) N60B N60BM [canx 17May00 as exported to United Kingdom; reinstated 10Jan07 as N60BM; no G- registration ever issued]
11173	690A $+	(N57143) N501MC N501MQ N950M VH-YJP
11174	690A +	N57174 C-GAJB N2292Z N6B N66GW
11175	690A +	(N57175) N276H XA-SPW N722EJ TG-ATP
11176	690A +	LV-PTC LV-LMU N690WD
11177	690A +	N57177 N77WN N16TG N16TB N15CD YV [canx 24Jul09 as exported to Venezuela]
11178	690A $+	N57147 N4SB N124SB XA-POW N124SB N57EC N57EG
11179	690A	N57179 N375AA
11180	690A	(N57180) YV-T-ZTA YV-900P YV-907CP YV2229
11181	690A	G-3201 (Iranian Police) 6-3201 (Iranian Police) 1401 (Iranian Police)
11182	690A	EP-AHM
11183	690A	5-2505 (Iranian Navy)
11184	690A	(N57180) (N57167) N110GM N1176W [dbr 09Aug89 Greeley-Weld County, CO, USA, parts to Hayward-Air Terminal, CA, USA; canx 06Dec89]
11185	690A +	N57181 N45Q N45QA (N147DA) N53JJ EC-FRR (N815MA) N690JB XA-TQD
11186	690A	N57186 [w/o 17Nov76 nr Independence, KS, USA; canx 07Feb77]
11187	690A $+	N57187 N440CA HC-BPX N449LC
11188	690A	(XB-RAB) XA-FIZ XB-BED
11189	690A +	N57189 N300CH N737E
11190	690A +	N57190 N8KG YV-2488P YV2418
11191	690A	N57191 N917WP N616SD N440CC YV [fate unkn; possibly sold in Venezuela cOct94]
11192	690A +	N57192 C-GDCL [fleet no.134]
11193	690A +	CP-1106
11194	690A	N57194 N101UC N953HF N690WS
11195	690A $	(N57195) F-BXJC N690DD N55JS [w/o 15Oct06 nr Antlers, OK, USA, parts to Aircraft Salvage of Dallas, Lancaster Municipal, TX, USA]
11196	690A $+	(N57196) N9149N N55PP N52PB N52PY
11197	690A	N9197N LV-PTI LV-LTA [w/o 26Oct75 nr Loma Verde, Buenos Aires Province, Argentina]
11198	690A	(N57198) N605KC (N40AC) (N783CB) N600CB N600VW N700MP N707MP YV-O-GPA-1 YV0145
11199	690A	XB-AEA [w/o 30Jan80 nr Newcastle, OK, USA]
11200	690A +	(N57134) N921ST
11201	690A $+	N12Q N50ST (CC-CBS) N24CC
11202	690A	XB-AEB XC-ROX N100EJ N600PB N690AT
11203	690A	N57169 [w/o 24Jun87 Hilliard, FL, USA; canx 04Apr90]
11204	690A	(N57209) D-IGAA SE-GSR OH-UTI
11205	690A $+	N57136 N76CP N9007 N690HB
11206	690A +	(N57162) N121JW N1213W N75RR N74GB
11207	690A +	(N57196) YV-E-DPK YV-TAPP YV-733P YV1459
11208	690A	D-IMBB OO-TCA "N90492" N90420 N74RR N76EC
11209	690A +	N57208 G-BCXS N570WA N570GB (N500SR) N500TS N107JJ HP-1607 [w/o 20Dec07 at "LAP-2" airstrip nr La Pendejada, Cordoba, Colombia; aircraft forced down and destroyed by Colombian AF]
11210	690A	N57210 (N86SS) N1SS N188 N1SS N70MD *N690KM
11211	690A	D-IBAG N414MG ZS-SLI
11212	690A	N9165N C-GIAA N690BT EC-EIH [dbr 18Dec94 Seville, Spain & b/u]
11213	690A	N57123 (N747MC) N925MC [w/o 31Jan84 Chihuahua, Chihuahua State, Mexico; canx 18Jul86]
11214	690A $	N57214 XB-EIH
11215	690A +	N57215 LN-LMF N215BA N32GA
11216	690A	(N9193N) N57216 HK-1770G (YV1566) HK-1770G
11217	690A	N9227N HK-1771G
11218	690A $+	N9229N XA-BOG N690VM N321DB N690TP N75U
11219	690A	N57212 N50MP N242TC [w/o 27Sep93 5 mls SW of Lansing-Capital City Apt, MI, USA; canx 17Dec02]
11220	690A +	(N57220) YV-TAYT YV-45CP YV-236P N4717V (N690TB) N4717V
11221	690A	N57221 5N-AKS HB-GFY N132RD HK-3514X HK-3514 HK-3514P [canx 03Apr03 - status?]
11222	690A	(N57222) AN-ASD N8059Y OB-M-1212 ZP-PRY OB-M-1212 OB-1212 [stolen 07May92 Uchiza, Peru; never recovered; canx 21Dec01]
11223	690A	N57223 N847CE [w/o 12Sep75 Nemacolin, PA, USA; canx 07Nov75]

AERO COMMANDER/ROCKWELL 690A

c/n	Series/Mod	Identities
11224	690A	(N57220) (LV-PTK) N81413 N200JN N200JQ [status?]
11225	690A	(N57225) N123G XB-EXC XA-EOC XB-HSE
11226	690A $+	N57227 N717AP N690DB N674NM
11227	690A +	N57218 N131JN N50DX
11228	690A +	LV-PTJ LV-LRF N690HV YV-2812P YV2256
11229	690A	N57220 LV-PTZ LV-LTO N30854
11230	690A	N57116 (LV-PTX) LV-PTY LV-LTY [wfu; canx 28Jun01]
11231	690A +	N9169N N115BH N115AB
11232	690A	N11NP N618 N618B [wfu cFeb92, parts to White Industries, Bates City, MO, USA; location "Ramp Mid"; canx 31Jan94]
11233	690A $+	N9192N HR-AAJ N9192N N67TC [dbr 31Jan05 Courcheval, France, parts to Eagle Creek Aviation, Eagle Creek Apt, IN, USA; canx 26May05]
11234	690A +	(N57216) N200M N200ML (N200GE) N630RH N680RH N550NP N698CE N693VM
11235	690A $+	N57235 HC-BPF N75PD N46BA N1KG N122AV [export cert to Mexico issued 29Jul08; still current on US register]
11236	690A	N9231N LV-PTT LV-LRH [possibly seized in Mexico c1993]
11237	690A +	N57237 C-GHMD N57237 N977DG
11238	690A	(N57216) N9193N LV-PUA LV-LTB
11239	690A $+	(N57271) N57217 YV-2317P YV1841
11240	690A/690A-TU	(N9232N) F-BXAS F-WXAS F-BXAS [cvtd to use Astafan IV-F turbojet engines (ff 24Jan76 as a jet); wfu Pau-Pont-Long-Uzein, France & later b/u; canx 06Jun97]
11241	690A	(N9237N) LV-PUB LV-LTC
11242	690A	N57229 N38GP N72VT N72VF (N690EC) N72VF [w/o 12Dec97 Yakima, WA, USA]
11243	690A	N57230 HB-GFS G-NISR N677WA (N911RX) N677WA
11244	690A	N57263 YV-TOCO YV-02P YV-109CP YV1758
11245	690A	N57231 (LV-PUF) N57115 N71NB N236SC YV-69CP YV1177
11246	690A	N57232 (LV-PUG) LV-PUW LV-LZL
11247	690A	N57233 [w/o 01Oct79 Columbus-Ohio State University Apt, OH, USA; canx 20Mar81]
11248	690A	(N57236) (N122K) N57032 (LV-PUE) N57268 ZS-JRB
11249	690A $+	N57030 ZS-JRZ N5776P N161JB N723AC
11250	690A +	YV-TARW YV-69CP N4560E N44WV 11250 (Philippine AF)
11251	690A $+	(N57035) N200U N690RC N251ES
11252	690A $+	N57042 EC-CRB N690ML XA-SEQ N35WA (N690AR) N690PT
11253	690A +	N57043 YV-TSJM YV-31CP YV-2593P YV1959
11254	690A +	N57056 N8FC N691AC N163ME XA-RMZ N24GT
11255	690A	N57063 N14GH HK-3314X HK-3314 HK-3314W [canx 06Mar00 - status?]
11256	690A	EP-KCD [possibly tfd to Iranian Police]
11257	690A	XC-BAP XB-HGG N121FM YV2490
11258	690A	(N57117) LV-PUH LV-LTX [wfu, parts to Atlanta Air Salvage, Griffin-Spalding County, GA, USA]
11259	690A	N57090 OY-BEO SE-IYX OY-BEO SE-KYY N70RR VP-BRR N425RR ZS-PXR
11260	690A	N57097 N6B N324BT I-TASE (N891WA) I-TASE [wfu engineless Bergamo-Orio al Serio, Italy; canx]
11261	690A	(N57098) LV-PUI LV-LTU [wfu, parts to Atlanta Air Salvage, Griffin-Spalding County, GA, USA]
11262	690A $	N57104 N690DS
11263	690A +	N57112
11264	690A	(N57115) YV-01P YV1787
11265	690A	(N57118) (LV-PUP) N81540 UN77 (United Nations) J-11265 (Turkish Police) TC-RZL N81540 I-MAGJ
11266	690A	(N57121) (LV-PUQ) LV-PUV LV-MBR [w/o 14Sep80 Rio de la Plata, nr Buenos Aires, Argentina; canx 16Jan07]
11267	690A	(N81391) N57035 XA-GEM [w/o 21Nov85 nr Chetumal, Quintana Roo, Mexico]
11268	690A	(N57130) (LV-PUR) LV-PUX LV-LZM [b/u Buenos Aires-Moron, Argentina; canx 11Jun91]
11269	690A	N57146 N156G N690DM N4PZ
11270	690A	N57292
11271	690A $+	N57138 XC-PPM N1100M N161WC N690JT N5007 N690RC N690RE [dbr 15Jul02 Crescent Lake State Apt, OR, USA, parts to Byerly Aviation, Peoria-Regional, IL, USA; canx 18Aug06]
11272	690A +	N57141 N888R N256RR N888PB N90AT
11273	690A	N57142 N222JP I-TASA (N892WA) (N678WA) N892WA (N678WA) N892WA
11274	690A	N57195 YV-316P YV-386CP N4432W ZP-THN PT-OFG [w/o 07Jun97 Garuva, Santa Catarina, Brazil; canx 04Jul97]
11275	690A	N57170 N952HF N952HE N254PW [w/o 09Oct85 nr Cadillac-Wexford County, MI, USA]
11276	690A	(N57170) N57172 N118CR YV [canx 21Apr09 as exported to Venezuela]
11277	690A +	N57175 (LV-PUF) XC-MLM XB-EBD XB-GQU N690AS (N612DM) N690AS
11278	690A	N57176 YV-246CP (YV2143) YV-246CP [w/o 13Jan07 Finca La Carolina, nr Pueblo Bello, Cesar, Colombia]
11279	690A $+	(N57179) N57180 C-GEOS
11280	690A $+	(N81394) XC-VER XC-CDA (N53AR) N699SB
11281	690A	N57183 YV-O-MC-5 YV-O-MTC-5 [wfu Caracas-Oscar Machado Zuloaga International, Venezuela]
11282	690A $+	N57193 N429K N20EB
11283	690A $	N57228 VH-PCV
11284	690A +	N57273 ZS-JRA
11285	690A +	N57275 (YV-971P) YV-80CP YV-818P YV-81CP YV2184
11286	690A	N57280 (LV-PUF) N321MT 7Q-YSC 3D-ADM ZS-NXK N286AF
11287	690A $+	N57286 N777HE N690SD
11288	690A	N57287 YV-757P YV-192CP YV1846
11289	690A	N57236 N24BT (N27JT) N95JM
11290	690A +	N57294 N122LA XB-EJW N100JJ N290PF N95LF
11291	690A	(N81397) N28AD [w/o 17May93 River Sepahua, nr Sepahua, Peru]

AERO COMMANDER/ROCKWELL 690A

c/n	Series/Mod	Identities
11292	690A	(N81389) HB-GEH PJ-CEB
11293	690A	G-3202 (Iranian Police) 6-3202 (Iranian Police) 1402 (Iranian Police)
11294	690A	N9187N 5-4035 (Iranian Army)
11295	690A	N81427 5-4036 (Iranian Army)
11296	690A	N57098 N161X N161G HK-2414X HK-2414 HK-2414P 3932 (Mexican AF)
11297	690A $+	N81398 N755N N514GP N208CL
11298	690A $+	(N9237N) (D-IGAB) N80LP (N80FE) N690HF
11299	690A +	N81399 N813NH LV-WIH N856MA N855MA N121JW (N121DK) N121JW
11300	690A	N9181N N471SC N80TB N490KC
11301	690A	(N81400) OH-ACN
11302	690A	N81406 N10PP N690LJ XA-PIR N302BA HR-CEM
11303	690A	N81409 N848CE
11304	690A $+	N81410 N932 (N441LM) EC-EAQ N304HC (N29AA) N823SB
11305	690A	N81392 C-GIAB N660RB [w/o 17May88 Little Rock-Adams Field, AR, USA; canx 21Mar91]
11306	690A	N81416 (N25JM) N81416 [w/o 13Feb83 Winter Haven-Gilbert Apt, FL, USA; canx 21Nov83]
11307	690A $+	(N31418) N81418 N16WL N900DS N48AZ (N46AZ) N690TD C-FMFP
11308	690A $+	N81419 N99WC VH-YJG
11309	690A +	N2NR N2NQ N690EH
11310	690A $+	N57121 LV-PUF LV-LTW N331JA N690RC
11311	690A +	N57118 N690BM
11312	690A	N9232N N700CD N1QL N111QL (N55SR) N111QL [w/o 18Sep83 Nacogdoches-A.L.Mangham Jnr Regional, TX, USA; canx 11Jan93]
11313	690A +	N81389 N245CT N245CF (N179KC) (N112BG) N245CF
11314	690A	N57252 N8AD N14AD (HP-) HK-3656X HK-3656 HK-3656P [impounded El Libertador AFB, Palo Negro, Aragua, Venezuela; canx 19Aug05]
11315	690A +	(N57172) (N81432) N319FB N34SC N34RT N561TC
11316	690A $+	(N81430) (N77EC) N76EC N77EC N90TT N666K N690DE (N690PB) N362SH
11317	690A $+	(N57163) (N57196) N615 N615DP
11318	690A +	(N57170) (N57198) YV-902P YV-402CP N4581U YV-902P YV-980P "HK-3245" HK-3245G
11319	690A +	N81434 N727CC N727CQ N106TC N22HP C-GPDX N690AJ N690GZ
11320	690A	N81436 N25ES (N25RE) (N24RE) XA-PAC N220HC N98PJ
11321	690A	N81430 VH-DLK ZK-PVB
11322	690A +	N81437 N18SS N4601L N69TM [w/o 12Feb95 nr Cashion, OK, USA; canx 25May95]
11323	690A	N81438 YV-711P YV-29CP YV-2437P YV-O-MAR-10
11324	690A	N81441 N111LA [wfu & b/u; canx 07Jul92]
11325	690A $+	N81442 (YV-1020P) YV-07CP YV2037
11326	690A	N81444 N10VG N707BP [w/o 30Jul93 nr Norfolk-Karl Stefan Memorial Apt, NE, USA in mid-air collision with PA-28 N33056; canx 07Mar94]
11327	690A $+	N81448
11328	690A	N81449 D-IHVB EC-DXA [wfu c1997 - location?]
11329	690A +	N81460 YV-86CP (N81460) (N72AB) YV-950CP YV1796
11330	690A +	(N57280) (N57267) N100WC N666LW N567H N112EM
11331	690A	(N81463) N43EC N20AS XC-CIR XB-ECX XC-JCT
11332	690A $+	N81464 N72AB XA-TFQ N32PR (N216PL) N32PR
11333	690A	N57196 5-4037 (Iranian Army)
11334	690A	N81467 5-4038 (Iranian Army)
11335	690A	N81470 [wfu cFeb92, parts to White Industries, Bates City, MO, USA; location "Ramp Mid"; canx 31Jan94]
11336	690A +	N81473 N321M N16GL N3WU N96LF
11337	690A +	N81476 N1547A N690SM
11338	690A +	(N81477) C-GIAC N46906 N222ME
11339	690A $+	N81483 ZS-JRL N32WS
11340	690A	N81491 HS-TFA 11340 (Thai Army) 81491 (Thai AF) [wfu c1988; pres Foundation for the Preservation and Development of Thai Aircraft Museum, Bangkok-Don Muang International, Thailand]
11341	690A $+	N81493 N20BP N690PC
11342	690A $	N81497 N924MC XA-RPD N76WA
11343	690A +	(N81499) D-IMCA F-GBGL N706US N706KC [dbr 26Aug93 Bishop, CA, USA; b/u cJan95]
11344	690A	N81500 ZS-JRE N81500 N900FT EC-676 EC-FFE [w/o 29Nov95 Mysiadlo, nr Warsaw, Poland; canx 29Nov95]

Production complete

AERO COMMANDER/ROCKWELL 690B TURBO COMMANDER

$ = has been modified from original TPE331-5 to TPE331-10 series engines
+ = has been modified with the installation of Commander-Aero winglets

c/n	Series/Mod	Identities
11350	690B +	N81516 HK-2051X HK-2051C HK-2051 HK-2051W N690RD (PR-MSM) N690RD PR-MSM
11351	690B	N81521 [w/o 07Jan81 Burns, OR, USA; canx 19Feb81]
11352	690B +	(N81523) N690HC N7AR N46JC N721TB
11353	690B	N81525 N4TX C-GHQG N690JT N31WD
11354	690B $+	(N81526) YV-99CP HK-2490X HK-2490 HK-2490P HK-2490 HK-2490W HP-1415 HK-4323X HK-4323 [w/o cJul05 & buried Villa de Carmen, Managua, Nicaragua]
11355	690B +	N81527 N303G (N517DW) N89CU
11356	690B +	N81528 N690PC N653PC N711PB
11357	690B $+	N81529 N690RT OO-MRT OY-BHO CS-ARX N690MH N690GH N690GF
11358	690B +	N81531 (N12RS) N402ST N210ED N810GF YV-663CP YV2096
11359	690B +	N81533 XB-OCI N690NA YV189T (YV1019) YV2182
11360	690B	(N81535) (N1100M) N100WC XB-DMT
11361	690B	(N81536) (N300M) N100AM N690BH
11362	690B	N81537 D-ICMS N81537 N711TT [dbr 08Oct87 Albuquerque-Coronado, NM, USA, parts to White Industries, Bates City, MO, USA; location R-26]
11363	690B +	N81541 N690JB N690GS YV [canx 29Jan09 as exported to Venezuela]
11364	690B	(N81543) HR-ABN N9049X HK-2291X HK-2291 [stolen 01Jun79 in Colombia; never recovered; canx 02Aug95]
11365	690B +	(N81544) LV-PVA LV-LZS HK-3561X HK-3561 HK-3561P HK-3561
11366	690B +	N81546 N777KD N777RD YV-775CP YV2094
11367	690B	N81547 D-IAWW N888TB OY-BEJ LN-FAH SE-LZX
11368	690B	N81548 N22VF N77PA N77PE HP-77PE
11369	690B +	N81550 N45ST N369GM N1VQ
11370	690B	(N81553) N1100M N200TT N200TE XA-NTC
11371	690B +	N81556 ZS-JRD N15AJ XB-EGT XA-RMG XB-GDS
11372	690B	N81557 N23LS [reportedly w/o cAug82; registration revoked 24Sep82]
11373	690B +	N81558 N911AC N279DD
11374	690B	N81562 5N-ALA G-BGXM OO-MRU N602CA N7872L N81562 N300CP [w/o 31Dec92 nr Herlong, CA, USA; canx 11Apr96]
11375	690B	N81563 N412AC N882AC XB-KWX
11376	690B	N81567 YV-177CP N81567 PT-LHV
11377	690B +	(N81568) YV-116CP YV1632
11378	690B	(N81569) N222BE (N222BF) N25PF YV-143CP YV2122
11379	690B +	(N81575) N690CC
11380	690B	(N81579) YV-33CP N3980U ZK-PIP VH-FOZ VH-SVQ [w/o 02Oct94 in sea between Williamtown & Lord Howe Island, NSW, Australia; canx 02Oct94]
11381	690B +	N81593 (CP-1335) C-GIAD N81593 N46HA N690BG
11382	690B $	N81599 HR-ADI N81599 N690JP (N58DC) XA-REB XC-JBP XC-AA85 XC-TAG XB-TWL
11383	690B $+	N81601 (YV-O-DAC-2) YV-149CP N45AZ
11384	690B $+	N81602 N690LL 7Q-YLL N2950L N295NM N690KC N690AX
11385	690B $+	N81603 (N300CH) VH-EXT N690TC
11386	690B	(N81604) N568H HK-
11387	690B +	N81609 N690CB N44NC
11388	690B +	N81610 N818 N221SV N532 N690ES YV2406
11389	690B	(N8LB) N81615 N8LB N8LX N90CH (N90QH) N700PC N700PQ
11390	690B $+	(N81619) YV-77CP YV-991P YV-63CP YV-649P YV1085
11391	690B +	N81621 D-IHVF N73MA (PT-) 708 (Peruvian AF)
11392	690B +	(N81622) LV-PVH LV-MAG N460K YV2576
11393	690B +	N81623 N699GN N690FD
11394	690B	(N81625) LV-PVL LV-MAU N531GK ZP-TIW
11395	690B +	N81626 N816PC CP-2266
11396	690B	N81628 [dbr 22Sep90 North Castle, NY, USA, parts to White Industries, Bates City, MO, USA; location R-23; canx 16Oct91]
11397	690B	(N81631) LV-PVM LV-MAV [w/o 12Sep84 5km East of Chapelco, Neuquen, Argentina; canx 27Sep95]
11398	690B	(N81632) LV-PVN LV-MAW
11399	690B $+	N81633 N690WM N1ER N302WC N727JA
11400	690B +	N81634 (HK-) XA-RFG XA-THE N25CE (N3TJ) (N23TJ) N25CE
11401	690B $+	(N81636) N33DW N211NK N62DW N28SE N78NA
11402	690B +	N81638 YV-181CP N81638 N345CM N444H
11403	690B +	N81639 YV-145CP N29773 (N690BG) N11HY N127AA
11404	690B $+	N81640 N100MF N205BN N205BL N815CC
11405	690B +	N81641 CP-1335 HP-235 N5387V YV-454CP YV2160
11406	690B	N81642 XC-SPI XB-FKC XB-SAH [wfu Toluca, Mexico State, Mexico]
11407	690B	N81643 N799V [w/o 02Nov91 Milton, KS, USA; canx 21Nov91]
11408	690B	(N81465) N81645 N200HT YV-420CP N68HL N58WB (N690SA) N79BE
11409	690B $+	N81646 OO-ROB (PH-ISM) OO-ROB
11410	690B +	(N81467) N81647 XC-SPP XB-DZP XA-AFI XB-DZP N366FG YV [canx 24Jun09 as exported to Venezuela]
11411	690B $+	N81648 N95GR N690GG
11412	690B	N81653 LV-PXN LV-MBY
11413	690B +	N1NR N90CR N528BE N690DT N502DT YV2341 [dam 07Apr07 Los Roques, Venezuela]
11414	690B +	N81654 VH-PCD 9M-AZM VH-PCD N93ME
11415	690B +	D-IATS N2888A OY-BSG N57AC N700SS N730SS N690LN
11416	690B	N81658 N108SA
11417	690B	N81662 XC-JAL

AERO COMMANDER/ROCKWELL 690B

c/n	Series/Mod	Identities
11418	690B	N81664 N555MT N773CA N555MT
11419	690B	N81668 LV-PYH LV-BNA
11420	690B $+	N81671 N813AW N60DB
11421	690B +	N81672 ZS-JRH
11422	690B $+	N81673 N500MM N77UA N310GA ZS-PFD V5-MFN [may have become D2-EBX]
11423	690B $+	N81674 N690MG XA- [canx 23Jan08 as exported to Mexico]
11424	690B +	N81677 N38LR N28LR N38LM CP-2299 N38LM
11425	690B +	N81680 N690CP ZP-GAR ZP-TWV N996AB
11426	690B $	N81682 N9KG (N690DM) N9KG
11427	690B	N81683 XA-LIY N46802 N55WJ
11428	690B +	(N81684) N112SA N1BC N91CS N91CT N91CU YV [canx 15Apr09 as exported to Venezuela]
11429	690B +	(N81687) D-IBMA N771BA (D-ILAT) (N690EE) N771BA
11430	690B	(N81689) YV-O-DAC-2 YV-O-MTC-12 YV-O-MTC-2YV-O-MIF-2YV0112
11431	690B $	N81692 N72RF C-GPCA N690HS YV [canx 21May09 as exported to Venezuela]
11432	690B +	N81694 ZS-JRC V5-MGF
11433	690B $+	N81695 N237SC EC-EBG N703MA (N690BW) N690XY
11434	690B	(N81697) N113SA N700R [dbf 25Dec85 Pekin-Municipal, IL, USA; canx 09Jan86]
11435	690B +	N81698 N333UP N338UP N878MS N200M N600WS
11436	690B	(N81699) D-IFAB F-GBBE D-IFAB N690FR N751BR
11437	690B +	(N81701) N114SA G-BMIC N9171S HL5261 N167R
11438	690B	N81703
11439	690B +	N81706 D-IADH N364WA
11440	690B	(N81707) N115SA N47CF N20ME
11441	690B +	N81708 N333GC ZS-KOG N6900K [dbr 01Oct00 Sao Tome & Principe International; acquired by OK Aviation for spares]
11442	690B	(N81701) (N81702) LV-PYT LV-MDN
11443	690B +	(N81709) N116SA N1110M N104RG (N104JM) YV-102CP YV-1050P YV2056
11444	690B +	(N81710) D-IFAC F-GBBF D-IFAC F-GCQK N13625 N777JN I-PAIR N35WA N690GM N1KC N690TG N318WA [w/o 03Dec08 nr Rio Grande, PR]
11445	690B	N81717 [w/o 17Jan84 Greenville, SC, USA; canx 03Dec85]
11446	690B	(N81721) N117SA N137BW C-FMCX
11447	690B	(N81723) XC-STA [canx cSep87; no recent sightings; fate unkn]
11448	690B +	N81726 N246MC (D-IHDM) HK-2492X HK-2492 HK-2492P XC-COL N246MC (N104RG) YV2048
11449	690B +	(N81728) N118SA D-ICSM N28TC
11450	690B	N81729 LV-PZL LV-BNB N81729 XC-HHS
11451	690B +	N81733 LV-PAD LV-MSR N71MA N690CP
11452	690B +	(N81734) N119SA N210EC N115SB (CS-) N115SB CS-ASG N5016H
11453	690B $	N81736 HK-2218X HK-2218W
11454	690B	N81737 YV-182CP N81737 XA-ABH
11455	690B +	N81748 N690JL N13PF N206BN XA-JPV
11456	690B	(N81750) D-IGLB N267R N267RD
11457	690B $+	N81752 N93RM N900JP N900R N691CP N615SB
11458	690B $	N81754 ZS-KEF N81754 ZS-KEF N98AJ
11459	690B $+	N81756 N333KD N40WG (N80LG) N40WG
11460	690B	N81762 N40DR N42DK XB-GCU
11461	690B	(N81763) YV-188CP
11462	690B +	N81764 N225MM
11463	690B $	(N81765) N93SA N101RG VH-TSS CP-259_ [canx 01Jul09 as exported to Bolivia]
11464	690B	N81766 YV-227CP YV1271
11465	690B +	N81767 EI-BFL N81767 G-IANS HB-GHE F-GFPT CS-ASA PT-MPN
11466	690B +	(N81769) (YV-104CP) YV-204CP YV-2631P YV1082
11467	690B $	N81771 N771WW N774WW N690PG N690HT N690XT
11468	690B +	(N81772) N94SA N94JP XA-KAB N2AC YV-797CP YV-2588P YV2222
11469	690B $+	(N81773) D-IAFB F-GCMJ N13622
11470	690B $+	N81774 N86MP N744CH
11471	690B $	N122SA XC-ROX N122SA N60CR N68QR N70ES N177EM N3TJ (N622HC) YV319T
11472	690B +	(N81775) TG-MEE N699CP YV-2694P YV223T
11473	690B	(N81776) 5H-TAA [dbr, parts to Dodson International Parts, Rantoul, KS, USA cFeb95]
11474	690B	(N81783) 5H-ASP 5H-MTY 5Y-BMY
11475	690B $+	(N81765) (N81785) N690CA VH-SFV ZK-WLH VH-NPT VH-PJC N690CA N690LS
11476	690B +	(N81795) ZK-PVA N690SC N330ES
11477	690B	N124SA (N333EC) (N25SM) N690SB C-FHNL N690CB [dbr 27May03 Chapleau, ON, Canada; registered N690CB 18Feb04 presumably for spares use; canx 12Apr07]
11478	690B	N81797 N36JF
11479	690B	(N81798) D-IAFC N51MF N690JC [w/o 25Jun92 nr Konawa, OK, USA; canx 28Aug92]
11480	690B $+	N81799 N690JK
11481	690B	N126SA XC-VES XB-LGR
11482	690B	(N81805) YV-212CP N4224U N745T HS-TFG G-CECN N95590
11483	690B	(N81806) YV-218CP YV1998
11484	690B	N81877 (N106SA) G-LACY G-BLPT (N720US) N2141B (N690SC) N2141B
11485	690B	N81809 N46NH N173DB
11486	690B	N127SA N954HF N34EF N94AC (N39CG) N94AC
11487	690B $+	N81811 N810K N810KM C-GCIA N26952 N690PR N690LH N690BB N690TH
11488	690B +	(N81812) (D-IAFE) (D-ICKH) D-IMWT OY-SUU N70AC YV-243CP YV2176
11489	690B	(N81818) N478DC N7701L HK-2551X HK-2551W HK-2551P
11490	690B $+	(N81819) YV-220CP YV-209CP YV-2096P YV-918CP YV1456
11491	690B	N81820 ZS-JRF (N690RC) ZS-JRF [w/o 05Dec84 in Atlantic between Windhoek, Namibia and Abidjan, Ivory Coast; canx 16Aug93]

AERO COMMANDER/ROCKWELL 690B

c/n	Series/Mod	Identities
11492	690B $+	N81822 N42MS N691SM C-FACC N691SM
11493	690B $+	(N128SA) N951HF N34FF YV-1444P N988AS N1HR N690RP
11494	690B	N81826 (N78AW) YV-2302P ETE-1332 (Mexican AF)
11495	690B	(N81827) N76EC N130TT
11496	690B	(N81830) D-IKOA N2646W [wfu cOct93, parts to White Industries, Bates City, MO, USA; location R-25]
11497	690B +	N81831 C-FNWD [wfu Abbotsford, BC, Canada for spares use; fleet no.135]
11498	690B	N131SA D-IKOC [w/o 21Feb81 nr Auxerre, France; canx cMar81]
11499	690B +	N81832 N499WC YV2009
11500	690B	N81833 YV-O-FDU-1 YVO115
11501	690B $	N81835 N22CC (N22QC) N25CL N12DE
11502	690B +	(N81842) YV-229CP YV-229P
11503	690B +	N81843 XC-ALI XB-DKQ XB-GJQ N690EL N15WD N86BP XB-IGG N222EA XB-IRY XB-JNA N503B [dbr cOct05 Acapulco, Guerrero, Mexico, parts to Alliance Air Parts, Oklahoma City, OK, USA & registered N503B]
11504	690B	(N81845) N106SA XC-TAB
11505	690B $+	N81846 D-IKOB EC-DFY D-IAAN N28WR CP-2262 N28WR N36SW
11506	690B	(N81849) D-IKAH I-TELM "HB-CPA" [CofA exp 02May87; canx c1993; wfu on fire dump Lugano-Agno, Switzerland (painted red with false registration HB-CPA, then 9HB-CPA)]
11507	690B	N81850 EI-BGL [w/o 13Nov84 nr Jevington, East Sussex, UK]
11508	690B $+	N81861 N307CL N690BK
11509	690B $+	(N81863) N690TL C-GBOT N3160G N78TT
11510	690B +	(N690TL) N81865 N690MS N1NG N1JG N61TS [canx 29Jun09 as exported to Venezuela]
11511	690B $+	N81795 (D-IKOC) N87WZ
11512	690B	N81872 YV-252CP (N3754C) G-TYME N400DS
11513	690B $+	N81873 N818HT I-ACCT N74WA N690BA (N690KG) PR-MPD
11514	690B $+	N81876 C-GRVJ N14BU N20MA
11515	690B	N81879 N515WC YV-2422P YV1932
11516	690B +	(N81871) XC-SAH
11517	690B +	(N9237N) N690EX G-SWAN N9054F N101RW N517HP YV306T
11518	690B	(N51798) N57198 HK-3354X HK-3354W N25RZ
11519	690B +	N57267 XB-BNB N57267 N425DT CP-2225 N425DT
11520	690B $+	N81785 N77VF N47EP (N471HP) N47EP
11521	690B +	N81783 N5ER N19HC XB-JYM (XA-SLL) N81746 N7KS
11522	690B $+	N81776 N30AB (N30AG) N50MS (N50MG) N691WM N691TP N84GU
11523	690B $+	N81775 C-GMDD N333PA N53LG [w/o 27Mar03 nr Homerville, GA, USA; canx 02Oct03]
11524	690B $+	N81773 N22CK YV [canx 16Jul09 as exported to Venezuela]
11525	690B	N500CR N690DS HK-3379X HK-3379 HK-3379P HK-3379W
11526	690B $+	N81769 N50PT XA-SCJ N64EZ N691PA N121ML
11527	690B +	N81765 (N11EX) N690AC
11528	690B	N81763 N690DM N690SH N15SF
11529	690B +	N81750 N690MT N690SE N500MT XB-ETM N226BP N690JH
11530	690B +	N81734 G-JRMM G-TVSA N489GA N559CG
11531	690B	(N81728) N4NR N4NH N101RF N244MP
11532	690B +	(N81723) YV-281CP YV-690P YV2001
11533	690B	N81721 N376RF N27MT [w/o 08Oct94 Springfield, MO, USA; canx 05May95]
11534	690B	(N81710) (YV-268CP) XB-BGH XA-SFD
11535	690B $	N81709 N999FG
11536	690B	N81707 N260WE
11537	690B $	N81702 N700PC N700PQ (N400JW) N911JW N611MT N434CC XB-KCY XB-PSA
11538	690B +	N81701 N777EL *PR-ORB
11539	690B +	N81699 N729CC YV246T
11540	690B +	N81697 N67CG
11541	690B +	N81689 G-NATS N81689 N321MC N821MC N9177N D-IHKH N690BD N270DP
11542	690B $+	N81687 (N690DT) N76DT N690CH
11543	690B +	(N81684) LV-PBS LV-MOO N480K
11544	690B $+	N81655 I-ACLR N690BE N690LL
11545	690B	(N81636) (N690TL) N25LS N32BW ZS-KUS
11546	690B $+	N81632 (D-IDGR) G-BHLI (EI-BJU) (YV-280CP) EI-BPC N690SC YV-416CP YV-998C YV-2737P YV1540 N555VE
11547	690B	N81631 YV-670CP YV-2772P YV-842C YV-532CP YV1994
11548	690B $+	N81625 N29KG XB-CDI
11549	690B	N81622 N444NC N444NR XA- [canx 19May06 as exported to Mexico]
11550	690B	(N81689) N690EA N31GH N9LV N690SS YV [canx 11May09 as exported to Venezuela]
11551	690B +	(N81604) N690AG N87TC N431JS XA-RPY (N692T) N358HF N253JM VH-LVG
11552	690B	(N81592) N690LB N888SL N37RR
11553	690B +	N81591 N27VE N27VG N586DV
11554	690B $+	(N81582) D-IDGR F-GCJX N1362W I-GEBA F-GIMP N84WA N107GL
11555	690B +	N81579 N150SP N692T
11556	690B	(N81569) XC-GAS
11557	690B $	(N81568) LV-PCZ LV-MYI N75WA V5-MAC
11558	690B	(N81553) LV-PDI LV-MYA
11559	690B +	(N81552) N40SM
11560	690B +	N81544 (N690RB) XC-HMO
11561	690B +	(N81543) D-IDAF F-GCJY N9196Q N690WP YV [canx 01Jun09 as exported to Venezuela]
11562	690B	N81538 HK-2996X HK-2996P FAB-023 (Bolivian AF) [dbr 30May92 La Paz-Alto International, Bolivia]
11563	690B	N81536 N140CA XB-KLY

AERO COMMANDER/ROCKWELL 690B/690C

c/n	Series/Mod	Identities
11564	690B	N81535 (YV-268CP) N101RW N101RZ (N666A) N726A N401SP CP-2224 *PT-FLA
11565	690B	(N81526) N81HK HP- [canx 24Sep85 as exported to Panama; may have been sold in Venezuela]
11566	690B $+	N81523 N30BM N186EC N186E
11567	690B	[void - airframe not built]
11568	690B	(YV-360CP) [void - airframe not built]
11569	690B	[void - airframe not built]
11570	690B	[void - airframe not built]
11571	690B	[void - airframe not built]
11572	690B	(YV-317CP) [void - airframe not built]
11573	690B	[void - airframe not built]
11574	690B	[void - airframe not built]
11575	690B	[void - airframe not built]
11576	690B	(YV-318CP) [void - airframe not built]
11577	690B	[void - airframe not built]
11578	690B	(YV-319CP) [void - airframe not built]
11579	690B	(N81394) [void - airframe not built]

Production complete

AERO COMMANDER/ROCKWELL 690C TURBO COMMANDER Jetprop 840

$ = has been modified from original TPE331-5 to TPE331-10 series engines
All aircraft built with winglets installed

c/n	Series/Mod	Identities
11600	690C	N81400 (N690CR) N840RC N47TT
11601	690C $	(N5852K) N840JP N840GB N840CM N63DL N63DU
11602	690C	(N5853K) N840R G-BHZC N2647C HK- [canx cJul95; no recent sightings; fate unkn]
11603	690C $	N5854K N5NR N5NK YV-170CP YV2099
11604	690C	N5855K HK- [canx cJul95; may have been seized in Mexico]
11605	690C	N5856K D-ILAN HB-GPB N125MM
11606	690C	N5858K N911BB N911BP N5833N PJ- XC-ALO ZP- XC-AA29 XC-LIM
11607	690C	(N5859K) N840SA N840EA N840VM
11608	690C	N5860K [w/o 12Dec81 nr Patterson-Harry P Williams Memorial Apt, LA, USA; canx 07Apr83]
11609	690C	N5861K HK-2478X HK-2478 HK-2478W HK-2478P XC-IFA
11610	690C $	(N5862) (N5862K) N840AA (N6EL) YV-849CP YV-609CP N840AA N840SE
11611	690C	N5863K N35DR HK-3424X HK-3424 [canx 08Jul05 - status?]
11612	690C	(N5864K) LV-PGD LV-OEI
11613	690C	N5865K D-IBOB SE-GSS LN-FWB SE-GSS
11614	690C	(N5866K) N840AC N3DS N74RR N74RF N74EF
11615	690C $	(N5867K) N82SA N990CH N990QH N811LC N811EC HC-BXT N840GH
11616	690C	N5868K N133DL D-IGEL N133DL [status? possibly sold in Colombia cOct88; still current on USCAR]
11617	690C	N5869K ZS-KOF N3263Y ZS-KOF N840LC N73EF
11618	690C	(N5870K) N118SA YV-39CP YV1315
11619	690C	N5871K VH-UVT N16TG (N18TG) N86ST N72TB
11620	690C	N5872K (G-NATZ) G-BXYZ HK-3680X HK-3680 [canx 11Apr00 - status?]
11621	690C	(N5873K) (YV-351CP) XA-JUY XC-GIR XB-DWX XC-KAG XA-RKO (N23TX) N920WJ HP-1888
11622	690C	(N5874K) N49BB N926SC
11623	690C	(N5875K) D-IBEI N11EX N45Q [w/o 12Oct90 nr Deadhorse, AK, USA; canx 26Apr94]
11624	690C	(N5876K) N119SA N840XL OY-BHG N840XL N840CF
11625	690C	N5877K N690HC ZP-ASH N690HC PT-WIC
11626	690C $	N5878K
11627	690C $	N5879K N24RE N41VY (N650) N24A N88BJ
11628	690C	(N5880K) LV-PHJ LV-OEV [w/o 26Aug81 Irigoyen, Entre Rios, Argentina; canx 19Apr82]
11629	690C/695	N5881K VH-NCM N940AC
11630	690C	(N5882K) D-INRO N106TT
11631	690C	N5883K XA-KOO XC-TXA XB-DSH XC-CEN
11632	690C	(N5884K) N67SA N711QP XA-PUM N711QP YV [canx cAug91 as exported to Venezuela]
11633	690C	N5885K HK-2495X HK-2495 HK-2495P [canx 26Jan00 - status?]
11634	690C	N5886K HC-BHU [hijacked 27Oct91 between Guayaquil and Lago Agrio, Ecuador - status?]
11635	690C	(N5887K) D-IMAG C-GPVE N331SC N489SC N431MS XA-UFZ
11636	690C	(N5888K) N68SA N17GG (N42GG) N37LP YV-83P N7649J N980AK
11637	690C	N5889K YV-394CP
11638	690C $	N5890K N840SF N3XY N840MG
11639	690C	(N9790S) (N5891K) N63RB HB-LOL D-IUTA
11640	690C $	N5892K VH-BSO YV-630CP YV-914CP YV-993CP N840VB N840KB
11641	690C $	(N5893K) XC-DUZ XB-GBR XA-SYV XB-SYV TG-SYV-PA N850GA N977JC
11642	690C	N5894K HK-2599X HK-2599P HK-2599W HK-2599P [canx 06Mar00 - status?]
11643	690C	N840JC
11644	690C	N5896K ZS-KRS [w/o 16Sep81 Parys-Arwa Field, Orange Free State, South Africa; canx 04Jan82]

AERO COMMANDER/ROCKWELL 690C

c/n	Series/Mod	Identities
11645	690C	(N5897K) YV-310CP [w/o 27Apr96 nr Caracas, Venezuela]
11646	690C	N5898K (LV-PIY) N65Y N165BC
11647	690C	(N78SA) N100NW HK-3460X HK-3460W HK-3460 HK-3460P [canx 23Feb00 - status?]
11648	690C	N5900K
11649	690C	(N5901K) N155WP (C-GZOA) N840PH N155WP (N82BA) HK-3448X HK-3448W HK-3448 XC-HHH
11650	690C	(N78SA) N5902K XA-JPA XB-DTW
11651	690C	N5903K (N840JP) HK-2601X HK-2601 HK-2601P HK-2601W HK-2601P [canx 02Apr03 - status?]
11652	690C	N5904K N1929J HK-3541X HK-3541 XC-HGJ XC-AA27 XC-PGB
11653	690C	N5905K N840CL HK-3290X HK-3290 HK-3290P [reportedly dbr 16Feb95; canx 06Oct99]
11654	690C	N5906K N840CR N1NR N1NT YV-87CP
11655	690C	(N5907K) YV-406CP N406CP
11656	690C $	(N5908K) (D-IBAP) XC-OAX
11657	690C	(N5909K) YV-O-KWH-3 YV0149
11658	690C $	N5910K N840CC N840FK N840JW
11659	690C	N5911K ZS-KYU N402AB XC-BAD N402AB
11660	690C	N5912K N550JB (N840WZ) HK-3221X HK-3221 HK-3221P HK-3221 HK-3221P ETE-1361 (Mexican AF) (N140WJ) N81JN (D-IUTA) N81JN [wfu Mexico City-Benito Juarez Intl, Mexico; canx 23Dec05]
11661	690C	(N5913K) N5915K N840TC N840DC XA-TOR
11662	690C	N5914K OY-SVG N5914K XC-LJQ
11663	690C $	N5913K N840NB N840BC
11664	690C	N5916K N110RS G-RNCO N7057A
11665	690C $	N5917K (N38SA) N40KW D-IWKW N48BA
11666	690C	(N5918K) (D-IMOW) (D-IHOW) YV-435CP "HK-3290" YV-626CP YV-773CP YV-717P YV1385
11667	690C	N5919K 11667 (Pakistan Army)
11668	690C	(N5920K) YV-417CP YV-2413P HK-3912X HK-3912 HK-3912P [canx 11Apr00 - status?]
11669	690C	N5921K N60DR N53MF OY-CRM N844MA HC-BUD
11670	690C	N5922K ZS-KZP N2937A [w/o 31Oct84 Wooster-Wayne County, OH, USA; canx 04Sep86]
11671	690C	(N5923K) YV-439CP YV-2346P
11672	690C $	(N5924K) D-IKOM OE-FIT VR-BLK VP-BLK N41462 N840PS
11673	690C	N5925K N777WY YV-779CP HK-4065X HK-4065W [canx 14Mar03 - status?]
11674	690C	N5926K [w/o 16Oct81 Freeport, Bahamas]
11675	690C	N39SA N319BF [status?]
11676	690C	N5928K N129TB
11677	690C	(N5929K) (D-IBAI) XC-HAA XB-GCV XB-GMT
11678	690C	N74SA YV-483CP XC-AA36 XC-HHY XC-JEH [w/o 02May04 Milpillas, 24km from Aguascalientes, Aguascalientes State, Mexico]
11679	690C $	(N5913K) N5931K N840VB (N5931K) ZS-SLL N840PN
11680	690C $	(N5932K) YV-415CP N7052J XA-JYM N680WA N777NV
11681	690C	N5933K ZS-KZO N110WE SE-IUV (LN-FAN) LN-FWA SE-IUV
11682	690C	N5934K N910EC N910FC
11683	690C $	N5935K N840AS N840BM N60VS N171DR N840G
11684	690C $	N5936K N51WF
11685	690C	N5937K N840BC YV-105CP FAC (Colombian AF) [stolen 16Nov88 in Venezuela; possibly seized]
11686	690C	N5938K (N38SA) N5938K [dbr 07Mar94 25 mls North of Hayden-Yampa Valley, CO, USA, parts to White Industries, Bates City, MO, USA; location R-09; canx 01Oct96]
11687	690C	N5939K N840DW N748GM XA-RWA N90WE N900LL
11688	690C $	(N5940K) XC-HAB N840TC
11689	690C $	N5941K (D-IBOS) N265JH N840TW
11690	690C	N5942K N81TR [w/o 22Dec92 nr Golden, CO, USA; canx 09Feb93]
11691	690C $	N5943K N600BM N800BM C-GIIT N800BM N32PH
11692	690C	(N5944K) N152X C-FNRM
11693	690C	N79SA N840MD
11694	690C	N5946K N101KJ YV [canx 30Oct90 as exported to Venezuela]
11695	690C	N5947K N818EK HK-3365X HK-3365 HK-3365P XB-JIO XC-AA56
11696	690C	N5948K N88PD N884D
11697	690C $	N5949K N690CA N97696 N840AA N840JK
11698	690C	N5950K YV-485CP N5950K YV-485CP YV-601P YV-1102CP YV1325
11699	690C	N5951K N822MS XB-DYZ XA-PEW TG-LEF N425MM
11700	690C	(N83SA) N5952K N840SM
11701	690C	N5953K N50WF N844SC
11702	690C	N5954K N64PS
11703	690C $	N5955K
11704	690C	(N5956K) [void - airframe not built]
11705	690C	(N5957K) [void - airframe not built]
11706	690C	(N5958K) [void - airframe not built]
11707	690C	(N5959K) (N89SA) [void - airframe not built]
11708	690C	(N5960K) [void - airframe not built]
11709	690C $	N5961K ZS-KZM N690BA N840LE N97WT
11710	690C	[void - airframe not built]
11711	690C	[void - airframe not built]
11712	690C	[void - airframe not built]
11713	690C	[void - airframe not built]
11714	690C	[void - airframe not built]
11715	690C	[void - airframe not built]
11716	690C	[void - airframe not built]
11717	690C	[void - airframe not built]
11718	690C	[void - airframe not built]

c/n	Series/Mod	Identities
11719	690C	N5956K TI-AQM N5956K PT-LRQ N5956K
11720	690C	N5957K [w/o 29Mar82 nr Hughes, AR, USA; canx 10Jul82]
11721	690C	N5958K N940BR N555GG N62CE XA-REC HK-3700X HK-3700 [canx 23Feb00 - status?]
11722	690C	N5959K HK-3447X HK-3447 HK-3447P [canx 11Ap/00 - status?]
11723	690C	N5960K YV-45CP FAC (Colombian AF) [hijacked 14Oct88; reportedly tfd to Colombian AF]
11724	690C	(N5961K) N5962K N37SB
11725	690C	N5963K YV-260CP YV-535CP N66RA YV-792CP YV1835
11726	690C $	N5964K YV-505CP YV-170P YV-505CP YV-2505P YV1892
11727	690C	N5965K N840V (N840EE) N840V
11728	690C	N5966K HK-3385X HK-3385 HK-3385P [seized 05Dec96 wearing false registration YV-1070; canx 16Jan02 - status?]
11729	690C $	N5967K N67FE
11730	690C	(N5968K) N28GA N835CC
11731	690C	(N5969K) N43GA N43ME XA-SOE N840DA N815BC C-FNAO
11732	690C $	(N5970K) N52GA (D-IBOY) C-GMPP N29DS N8VL V5-DAC
11733	690C	N56GA 11733 (Pakistan Army)
11734	690C $	N130GA N193SS N1931S N600BM N840NK [w/o 15Jan09 nr Wray, CO, USA]
11735	690C	N241GA N888KN YV-212P YV1851

Production complete

AERO COMMANDER/ROCKWELL 690D TURBO COMMANDER Jetprop 900

$ = has been modified from original TPE331-5 to TPE331-10 series engines
All aircraft built with winglets installed

c/n	Series/Mod	Identities
15001	690D $	N5779N N82BA N351SS XA-TCK N14072 N711DW N690TP
15002	690D $	N5833N N911BB N900MA N131KS N721MR N721ML C-FSPM
15003	690D	N5836N N900RH HP- [canx 16Sep91 as exported to Panama]
15004	690D	N5838N HP- [canx 05Sep91 as exported to Panama]
15005	690D	N5841N (N900CD) HI-423 N5841N ZP-TWZ
15006	690D	N5852N YV-492CP [stolen 25Dec88 Valencia, Carabobo, Venezuela; never recovered]
15007	690D/695A	N5855N HK-3473X HK-3473 HK-3473W HK-3473 N23EF N695LD N337DR [dbr 05May05 Las Vegas-North Air Terminal, NV, USA, parts to Dodson International Parts, Rantoul, KS, USA]
15008	690D	N5860N ZS-KZT N6BZ N900NE
15009	690D	N5862N N810P HP- XC-BDR XC-AA39 XC-JDB
15010	690D	N5863N N900BE HP- FAC5454 (Colombian AF)
15011	690D	N5865N N990JC [canx 03Apr89 as exported to Cayman Islands; Cayman authorities deny aircraft has ever been registered]
15012	690D	N5866N (D-ILAS) N83JH YV-903P
15013	690D $	N5867N N900AB (HS-TFC) N42SL N927SM
15014	690D $	N5869N N771FF
15015	690D	N5874N G-IBLL G-NTMN N27MW N544GA
15016	690D $	(N5876N) N382AC N900CP N27KG N950TJ N601WT
15017	690D $	N5880N YV-880CP YV1617
15018	690D $	(N5886N) N611
15019	690D	N5889N (N16GG) N5889N [reportedly dbr before Apr86; b/u; canx 09Sep86]
15020	690D/695A	N5894N (C-GWSR) N102VF N600CM C-GOVT
15021	690D	N5896N N900TN N908TN ZP- [canx 25Oct90 as exported to Paraguay]
15022	690D	N5905N D-ILAS YV-521CP YV1173
15023	690D	N5906N N88RC HC- [canx 29Jan90 as exported to Ecuador]
15024	690D/695A	N5911N N79SZ "HK-2784" EJC-103 (Colombian Army) EJC-111 (Colombian Army) EJC-021 (Colombian Army)
15025	690D $	(N5912N) N29GA
15026	690D/695A	N5914N N28BF N120EK N995HP VH-LMC
15027	690D	N5915N N700PC N900SR PT-WLD
15028	690D	N5916N XC-MLM
15029	690D	(N5919N) N36GA N200PR [w/o 07May86 Price, UT, USA; canx 10May00]
15030	690D	(N5920N) N98GA N900HC XA-EMO YV-822CP YV2249
15031	690D $	(N5922N) N37GA N913RM N615JB N471SC N471JS N901TE
15032	690D $	(N5924N) N112GA HP- HK-4063X HK-4063W N900HV YV-777CP YV1777
15033	690D	(N5925N) N49GA G-MFAL VR-BMZ VP-BMZ
15034	690D	(N5926N) N113GA N900DJ YV [canx 06Mar90 as exported to Venezuela]
15035	690D $	N51GA OE-FGS N900DS N909HH N84LG N29GD
15036	690D	N45GA OE-FCS [w/o 23Feb89 Lake Constance, Switzerland; canx cNov90]
15037	690D $	(N53GA) (C-GVSO) C-GSVO N62GA N911AE N90BA C-FAWG N900ET
15038	690D	(N57GA) N77PH N77PK PT-OQY
15039	690D	N61GA N144JB [reportedly w/o 02Oct96 in South America]
15040	690D	N65GA N4NT (N76NA) XA-CHM
15041	690D $	N68GA EI-CCR N82BA N77HS
15042	690D	N71GA C-FGWT
15043	690D	(N74GA) [void - airframe not built]
15044	690D	(N76GA) [void - airframe not built]
15045	690D	(N136GA) [void - airframe not built]

Production complete

AERO COMMANDER/ROCKWELL 695 TURBO COMMANDER Jetprop 980

All aircraft built with winglets installed

c/n	Series/Mod	Identities
95000	695	N81575 N980RC N13BJ N303E YV XC-AA67 XC-UJW
95001	695	(N980JP) N980AA (N980AN) N980AA [status? possibly exported to Colombia; still current on USCAR]
95002	695	N980R N8LB N8LN N980BH (N905BL) N980BH
95003	695	N9756S N501NB N9756S [status? possibly exported to Colombia; still current on USCAR]
95004	695	N9757S N555GG N100TK N100TT CP-2078 [unconfirmed but possibly FAB-030]
95005	695	N9758S ZS-KVB [w/o 20Jun84 Dingle Farm, nr Sishen, Cape Province, South Africa; canx 30Sep93]
95006	695	N9759S YV-366CP N4468F N171CP N171CT N980HB
95007	695	N9760S (N123RC) YV-581CP ARV-0211 (Venezuelan Navy)
95008	695	N9761S N515AM
95009	695	(N9762S) N333GC 3D-ABH ZS-KZW N214GA ZS-KZW YV-2566P YV224T
95010	695	(N9763S) D-IHEL N8534Z N980BC PJ-BRW HK-3412X HK-3412 HK-3412W YV0154
95011	695	N9764S N980EC
95012	695	(N9765S) N980SA YV-129P N980SA
95013	695	N9766S N200M N500TH N519HB N25TN
95014	695	N9767S (N321MD) N9767S [dbr 02Aug81 Peoria-Greater Peoria Regional, IL, USA]
95015	695	N9768S N655PC N695WR
95016	695	N9769S N245KK (N54GP) N600TC YV-83CP N70505 HK-3474X HK-3474
95017	695	N9770S YV-56CP YV2090
95018	695	N9771S (N121LA) N123LA XC-PFB
95019	695	N9772S (N980JC) PK-ODR [almost certainly became A-2022 with the Indonesian Army]
95020	695	(N9773S) N900LC N980H YV-119CP XC-HFX XC-AA38 [w/o 19Oct92 Pesqueria, Nuevo Leon, Mexico]
95021	695	(N9774S) ZP-PTU ZP-TTU [canx 20May86 as exported to USA; not actually imported - status?]
95022	695	N9775S N20HG HK-3484X HK-3484 HK-3484P
95023	695	(N9776S) D-IMKO N888SF N700PC
95024	695	(N9778S) N66FP N36JT
95025	695	N9779S N54UM "HK-3230P" N136AR
95026	695	(N9757S) N9780S N999FE N90BL N903L HC- [canx 09May89 as exported to Ecuador]
95027	695	(N83SA) (N9792S) N7101L
95028	695	N9781S (N980AC) N980CF YV-980CP
95029	695	(N9782S) N700MM N600MM [stolen 16Dec87 Vero Beach, FL, USA; never recovered]
95030	695	(N9783S) N980AB N980MD
95031	695	N9784S HP-1132P N980EA [status? possibly exported to Colombia]
95032	695	N9785S N265EX
95033	695	N87SA N8774P N126M
95034	695	N9786S N980WM N980GM YV1532
95035	695	N9787S N200JN ZP- [canx 31Oct88 as exported to Paraquay]
95036	695	(N9788S) (D-IBOS) D-IOEB (OE-) N5356M
95037	695	N9789S [w/o 12May82 Carlsbad-Cavern City Air Terminal, NM, USA]
95038	695	N91SA PT- [canx 01Jul88 as exported to Brazil]
95039	695	N9790S D-IHSI
95040	695	N980AD N980E HK- XC-HHI XB-AOC MT-219 (Mexican Navy)
95041	695	N9793S N400DK N400DW N3U N218MS
95042	695	N9794S XA-LEK XB-DTO XB-DXX
95043	695	N9795S N9NR (N9WZ) N74CD YV HK-3461X HK-3461 [w/o 23Aug90 Cerro de la Cruz, Queretaro, Mexico]
95044	695	N9796S (XA-LEI) XC-FUT N65664 JA8604 [w/o 24Mar03 nr Ogawa Village, nr Tokyo, Ibaraki Prefecture, Japan; canx 30Apr03]
95045	695	N9797S HK- "HK-268P82" XC-TXA XC-AA98 (XC-DAC) N981WJ
95046	695	N9798S XA-LEJ XB-DSA (N94MA) MT-221 (Mexican Navy) AMP-130 (Mexican Navy) XB-DIV
95047	695	N9799S N1981S (TG-) (N301MP) N1981S
95048	695	N9800S N980DT [stolen 11Dec88 Lebanon, MO, USA; never recovered; canx 02Apr98]
95049	695	(N9801S) CP-1640 FAB-019 (Bolivian AF) CP-1640 N3982C N980GR
95050	695	N9802S N707SC HK-3408X HK-3408W HK-3408 [canx 06Mar00 - status?]
95051	695	(N9803S) LV-PLS LV-OOE HK-3443X HK-3443 XC-HGG XB-ACO MT-224 (Mexican Navy) AMP-131 (Mexican Navy)
95052	695	N9804S HK-2738X HK-2738 HK-2738P HK-2738W XC-ENL XC-AA84 XC-ALB XB-KFD
95053	695	N9805S N73DC N73DQ ZP-TFV
95054	695	(N9806S) D-IBAR [w/o 30Jan85 Steinhausen, Switzerland; canx cFeb85]
95055	695	(N9807S) N29SA FAC5553 (Colombian AF)
95056	695	N9808S (N980JD) N980GC N980BM TI-MEL
95057	695	N9809S HK-3444X HK-3444 [canx 23Feb00 - status?]
95058	695	(N9810S) D-IMOL N125DC N243AR YV-893CP YV2175
95059	695	N9811S (N980CT) HK-3819X HK-3819 [canx 29Feb00 - status?]
95060	695	N9812S
95061	695	(N9813S) N30SA (N9818S) HK-2608X HK-2608 HK-2608P XC-HGL XC-AA15 XC-PPF N980WJ HK-4583X HK-4583
95062	695	N9814S N200BD N92MT HK-3406X HK-3406 [canx 11Apr00 - status?]
95063	695	(N9814S) (N9815S) N4712W ZS-KZN N4712W N331NF N980GM N980GZ
95064	695	(N9816S) [built as Rockwell Commander 690C c/n 11709]
95065	695	N9817S N20ER N980JS HK-3455X HK-3455 [possibly seized in Colombia; canx 18Apr00 - status?]

AERO COMMANDER/ROCKWELL 695/695A

c/n	Series/Mod	Identities
95066	695	N9818S HK-2682X HK-2682 HK-2682P XB-ORA EJC-115 (Colombian Army) EJC-022 (Colombian Army)
95067	695	(N9819S) YV-407CP [stolen 13Jan87 Caracas-Oscar Machado Zuloaga International, Venezuela; possibly since seized by Colombian AF]
95068	695	N9820S ZS-KZR N9820S HK-3409X HK-3409W XC-AA62
95069	695	N9821S N14CN N14CX VR-CBP HB-LQA N695EC D-IHUC PR-DBR
95070	695	(N9822S) N35SA JA8600 N38AA JA8600
95071	695	(N9823S) N810EC [status? possibly exported to South America c1987; still current on USCAR]
95072	695	(N9824S) D-IBAI N96MA HK-3492X HK-3492 XC-HHM XC-HGH
95073	695	N9825S N200TT [status? possibly exported to Colombia c1988]
95074	695	N9826S N980DW HK-3405X HK-3405 "C-FRMP" C-GREV N3212A YV-980CP N357ST (N980GK) (N123MZ) N357ST
95075	695	N9827S N716CC HK-3407X HK-3407 [canx 02Feb00 - status?]
95076	695	N9828S N76HH [status? possibly exported to Colombia cApr89]
95077	695	N9829S N221K [status? possibly sold in Colombia cDec88; still current on USCAR]
95078	695	N9830S JA8826 N980MH JA860A [canx 10May01 - status?]
95079	695	N9831S HK-3481X HK-3481
95080	695	(N9832S) (N37SA) N81405 N999ST "HK-3394X" PNP-218 (Peruvian Police)
95081	695	N9833S N888NT N808NT [status? possibly exported to Colombia cJul90; still current on USCAR]
95082	695	N9834S N810K HK-3453X HK-3453 MT-222 (Mexican Navy) AMP-133 (Mexican Navy)
95083	695	(N9835S) N980JP C-GTCI N70318 HK-3450X HK-3450W HK-3450 HK-3450P [canx 17Feb97 - status?]
95084	695	(N9836S) N980JC YV-787CP YV2020

Production complete

AERO COMMANDER/ROCKWELL 695A TURBO COMMANDER Jetprop 1000

All aircraft built with winglets installed

c/n	Series/Mod	Identities
96000	695A	N81502 [w/o 09Oct84 Checotah, OK, USA; canx 05Feb91]
96001	695A	N9900S N333UP HK-3364X HK-3364 XC-AA23 TP-216/XC-UTA (Mexican AF)
96002	695A	N9902S (N96002) TG-LEM [canx by Apr08 - status?]
96003	695A	N9906S OY-BPA ZS-LLL N17CG N9906S [N17CG canx 24Apr90 as exported to Panama; reinstated 02May06 as N9906S; no Panamanian marks ever issued]
96004	695A	(N9907S) XA-LUU XB-ECT
96005	695A	(N9910S) D-IHOP N815S N94PA
96006	695A	N9913S 018 (Panama Defence Force) HP-1108 N7031J "HK-3497X" 070 (Guatemalan AF) N7031J (N496MA) N444WD
96007	695A	(N9915S) N695PA N9456T N2267U (N6361U) N695AM
96008	695A	N9917S PJ-NAF
96009	695A	(N9924S) N8LB N8LV N695JC HK-3271X HK-3271 (HH-) N7031K [status? possibly exported to Colombia cAug89]
96010	695A	(N9926S) XC-CUL N104TT N104DT HK-3239X HK-3239P HK-3239W HK-3239P ETE-1363 (Mexican AF) 3963 (Mexican AF) [incorrectly quoted as c/n 95010 on official Mexican AF papers]
96011	695A	(N9928S) N99AK N8159G N2270T N5422P N695GJ
96012	695A	(N9931S) C-GJEI N695BA N95AB
96013	695A	(N9933S) N84H HK-3328X HK-3328 HK-3328W HK-3328P HK-3328W "HK-3377" XC-HHZ MT-218 (Mexican Navy)
96014	695A	N9934S N51DM
96015	695A	(N9935S) XC-HAC XB-DSF N325MM N333UP
96016	695A	(N9936S) (YV-477CP) YV-O-MTC-1YV-O-MIF-1YV0100
96017	695A	N9937S (YV-461CP) (N17QC) N17ZD HP- [reportedly exported to Panama and subsequently w/o]
96018	695A	(N9939S) (N9938S) YV-416CP HK-3367X HK-3367 YV-364C
96019	695A	(N9939S) N200DK [status? possibly exported to Colombia cMar86]
96020	695A	N9940S YV-441CP N9940S HP-1078P HK-3240X HK-3240 HK-3240W ETE-1349 (Mexican AF) N93NM [vandalised & dbr in Mexico; canx 23Dec05]
96021	695A	N9941S N132PR HK-3439X HK-3439
96022	695A	N9942S
96023	695A	N9943S ZS-KZV HB-GHK PR-MRN
96024	695A	(N9944S) YV-484CP N5450J XC-AA33 XC-LGC
96025	695A	N9945S [status?]
96026	695A	N9946S HK-3157X HK-3157 HK-3157P HK-3157W MT-217 (Mexican Navy) (N46BA) MT-217 (Mexican Navy) [wfu Veracruz-Las Bajadas, Veracruz, Mexico]
96027	695A	N9947S N727CC [stolen 16Feb88 Phoenix, AZ, USA; never recovered; canx 03Feb05]
96028	695A	N9948S [status?]
96029	695A	(N9949S) N282AC N79PH
96030	695A	(N9950S) N73H PJ- HK- FAC5198 (Colombian AF)
96031	695A	N9951S (YV-546CP) (N318FE) C-FDGD HP-1149P [reportedly canx - status?]
96032	695A	N9952S VH-GAB N695NC
96033	695A	(N9953S) G-IOOO HK-3366X HK-3366 HK-3366P
96034	695A	N9954S ZS-KZS G-BWMP N508AB C-GMMO N508AB (N24A) N700L

AERO COMMANDER/ROCKWELL 695A

c/n	Series/Mod	Identities
96035	695A	(N9955S) D-IBER N93MA HK- XC-HFZ [canx 06Mar00 - status?]
96036	695A	(N9956S) YV-461CP N4676U ZK-FRC N20GT N695GG
96037	695A	N9957S HK-3389X HK-3389 HK-3389P
96038	695A	N9958S N707TS N695HT
96039	695A	N9959S HK-3060X HK-3060 HK-3060P HK-3060 [canx 07Apr00 - status?]
96040	695A	N9960S N900JP HP- MT-214 (Mexican Navy) AMP-132 (Mexican Navy) N900JP
96041	695A	N9961S HK-2912X HK-2912 HK-2912P ETE-1318 (Mexican AF) 3918 (Mexican AF)
96042	695A	N9962S N303GM
96043	695A	N9963S XC-HFN
96044	695A	N9964S HK-2908X HK-2908 HK-2908P HK-2908 FAC5600 (Colombian AF) [wfu Bogota-El Dorado, Distrito Capital, Colombia]
96045	695A	N9965S HK-2909X HK-2909 HK-2909P [canx 06Mar00 - status?]
96046	695A	N9966S [status? possibly exported to South America cMar91; still current on USCAR]
96047	695A	N9967S N88NW N51228 HK-3390X HK-3390 [w/o 11Jun88 Cali, Valle Del Cauca, Colombia; canx 13Aug92]
96048	695A	N9968S [status? possibly exported to Colombia cJul89]
96049	695A	N9969S HK-2951X HK-2951P HK-2951 [canx 12May03 - status?]
96050	695A	N9970S ZS-KZX N900EC N45LG N695MM
96051	695A	N9971S ZS-KZY
96052	695A	N9972S ZS-KZZ
96053	695A	N9973S
96054	695A	N9974S N8LB N71MR
96055	695A	N9975S CP-2050 N695AB
96056	695A	(N9976S) N31GA (CP-2140) HK-3263X HK-3263 HK-3263P HK-3263 HK-3263P ETE-1358 (Mexican AF) 3958 (Mexican AF) XC-HFV XC-AA19 XC-LHD [reportedly dbr 19Oct92 Monterrey, Nuevo Leon, Mexico; noted cMar06 as XC-LHD, c/n plate checked]
96057	695A	(N9977S) N34GA
96058	695A	N9978S (YV-506CP) N711GT HP-11GT "HP-1078" N711GT N36AG
96059	695A	(N9979S) N39GA HK-3391X HK-3391 HK-3391W HK-3391P [canx 09Mar00 - status?]
96060	695A	N9980S HK-3194X HK-3194 HK-3194W FAH006 (Honduran AF)
96061	695A	N9981S N184BB HK-3218X HK-3218 3960 (Mexican AF)
96062	695A/B	(N9982S) N120GA N2VA N12VA [used as prototype Jetprop 1200, cvtd to model 695B]
96063	695A/B	VH-LTI N61508 N83WA
96064	695A	(N9984S) N48GA OY-BPF N6767M [stolen 22Jan87 in TX, USA; never recovered]
96065	695A	(N9985S) N46GA PJ- [canx cDec96 as exported to Netherlands Antilles]
96066	695A	(N9986S) N54GA
96067	695A	(N9987S) N59GA N200PT YV-53CP
96068	695A	(N9988S) N62GA N519CC [status? possibly exported to Colombia cJul89]
96069	695A/B	VH-LTJ N6151T HK-3961X [canx 30Aug99 - status?]
96070	695A	(N9990S) N67GA N7896G N695YP
96071	695A	(N9991S) N69GA (N695PR) N69GA
96072	695A	(N9992S) N72GA HK-3279X HK-3279 HK-3279W HK-3279 [canx 11Oct01 - status?]
96073	695A	(N9993S) N75GA N85DJ HK-3278X HK-3278 [w/o 21Mar90 Llanos del Yari, Caqueta, Colombia; canx 31Aug90]
96074	695A	N78GA N900EZ HK-3253X HK-3253 HK-3253P [canx 10Jun97 - status?]
96075	695A/B	VH-LTK N6151W XA- [canx cSep93 as exported to Mexico]
96076	695A	N79GA HK-3275X HK-3275 HK-3275P EJC-112 (Colombian Army)
96077	695A	N83GA HK-3192X HK-3192 HK-3192W T-8 (Jamaica Defence Force) N695DA N695FA
96078	695A/B	VH-LTN N6151X N85WA N85NM N695GH
96079	695A	N84GA N169CR ZP-TXF
96080	695A	N86GA (N777T) HK-3284X HK-3284 HK-3284W HK-3284G HK-3284W HK-3284 N999EF N960AC HK-4370X HK-4370
96081	695A	N87GA N600BM HP- [canx 21Oct88 as exported to Panama]
96082	695A	N89GA HP- [canx 30Jun88 as exported to Panama]
96083	695A	(N90GA) G-YABU N901AS HK-3376X HK-3376 HK-3376P HK-3376 HK-3376P EJC-114 (Colombian Army) [w/o 19Feb01 Puerto Lopez, nr Carimagua Apt, Meta, Colombia]
96084	695A	N93GA HK-3417X HK-3417 XC-HGW XC-AA16 XC-ZCL
96085	695A/B	VH-LTO N205AB N808NC
96086	695A	N94GA HK-3193X HK-3193 HK-3193P "XC-NCL" HK-3193 [dam 11Jun88 Ejido San Rafael de los Milagros, Coahuila, Mexico wearing false registration XC-NCL]
96087	695A	N95GA N722SG N695RC
96088	695A	N96GA HK-3291X HK-3291 HK-3291W HK-3291P HK-3291W
96089	695A	N97GA N20TX N7812 N45RF
96090	695A	(N115GA) [built as Gulfstream Commander 695B c/n 96201]
96091	695A	N119GA N17EE HK-3414X HK-3414 XB-ATC XC-HGX XC-AA20 XC-HUA
96092	695A	N127GA N211AD
96093	695A	N129GA C-FALI ZP- [canx 11Dec87 as exported to Paraguay]
96094	695A	N131GA N94EA
96095	695A	N132GA N73DC ZP-TWY
96096	695A	(N133GA) N44SF N44SD N695CT
96097	695A	N134GA N112CE [status? possibly exported to Colombia cMar86]
96098	695A	N135GA N12ZA N699GN N269M [w/o 21Jan98 nr Delray Beach, FL, USA; canx 10Sep98]
96099	695A	(N137GA) N147RP HK-3283X HK-3283 HK-3283W
96100	695A	(N14GA) N111VY HK-3324X HK-3324 HK-3324P [canx 11Oct01 - status?]

Production complete

AERO COMMANDER/ROCKWELL 695B TURBO COMMANDER

All aircraft built with winglets installed

c/n	Series/Mod	Identities				
96201	695B	N115GA				
96202	695B	(N221GA)	PK-ZNS	PK-ENS	N695P	N27VE
96203	695B	N223GA	N64JT	ZP-TXG		
96204	695B	(N224GA)	N4751W	N30059	N695MG	
96205	695B	(N226GA)	N5852K	N91575	N695EE	
96206	695B	(N227GA)	N9915S	N97315	N224EZ	
96207	695B	(N229GA)	N81432	N695KG		
96208	695B	(N230GA)	VH-LTM	VH-PJC	N695BE	VP-BCT
96209	695B	(N235GA)	[void - airframe not built]			
96210	695B	(N238GA)	[void - airframe not built]			

Production complete

AERO COMMANDER/ROCKWELL TURBO COMMANDER Jetprop 1200

Proposed 695B variant with TPE331-12 engines & four bladed props, production abandoned

c/n	Series/Mod	Identities
98001	1200	(N228GA)
98002	1200	(N232GA)
98003	1200	(N236GA)
98004	1200	(N240GA)

AEROSPATIALE/SOCATA/TBM INTERNATIONAL TBM.700

c/n	Series	Identities
01		F-WTBM
02		F-WKPG F-GKPG
03		F-WKDL
1		F-OHBM N300PW F-GLBE D-FTBM OE-ESM N755PG
2		F-GLBA N700JJ N100PB N702BM
3		F-GJTS HB-KEI F-HBGC OO-TBM
4		F-OHBA HS-PBA N701MR N700DE N750AB
5		N107BP N800GS N731TM N781TM
6		(N700XL) F-WNGU F-GLBB N700ZL N157JB
7		OE-EDB D-FGYY N138JM
8		F-OHBB JA8892 N56WF
9		N969RF N5HT
10		N19AP N69BS [dbr 04Aug98 nr Spearfish-Black Hills/Clyde Ice Field, SD, USA, parts to Dodson International Parts, Rantoul, KS, USA; canx 10May00]
11		F-GKJV N877PC N700BS
12		(N107RP) F-OHBD EC-FPF
13		(F-GKDJ) F-GJPY LX-JFB F-GJPY N700MV
14		(N33DF) N2DF N711GH N292RG N700MX
15		N700PU
16		N400ST N700CT N283BS
17		N717Y
18		F-GLBC [w/o 15Nov91 in France; canx 12Feb92]
19		N79Z D-FWGJ N635DS C-GBTS
20		F-OHBE N91BM (N700RF) N95BM N50ST
21		N700EF N708EF *N554CA
22		F-OHBF F-GLBM D-FFBU N994DF
23		N700XL F-WNGO F-GLBF D-FSOC F-GLBR N700AR [w/o 13May02 Moulins, France; canx 04Oct05]
24		F-GLBD PH-AJS D-FTAN D-FOOO
25		N303WB N700TJ N751JB N751J
26		N700SF
27		N700GB N700WD N700TJ
28		OE-EHG [dbr 07Dec95 Braunschweig, Germany, parts to Dodson International Parts, Rantoul, KS, USA]
29		N700PW N708PW
30		N715MC
31		N64TW N701PF N829BC
32		N356M F-GLBZ
33		33/65-XA (French AF) 33/330-ID (French AF) 33/43-XA (French AF)
34		N8EG
35		35/43-XB (French AF) 35/65-XB (French AF) 35/43-XB (French AF) 35/ABW (French Army)
36		[void - airframe not built]
37		[void - airframe not built]
38		F-OHBG JA8894
39		N339W [w/o 22Aug92 South Lake Tahoe-Lake Tahoe Apt, CA, USA; canx 21Oct92]
40		[void - airframe not built]
41		[void - airframe not built]
42		[void - airframe not built]
43		[void - airframe not built]
44		[void - airframe not built]
45		[void - airframe not built]
46		N844S N701ES N1967H
47		[void - airframe not built]
48		[void - airframe not built]
49		N567T N722SR
50		N700YB N84HS (N67LF) N84HS
51		[void - airframe not built]
52		F-OHBH (VH-FIS) VH-PTG F-OHEV N700PK N700RE
53		N700BF C-GTBM
54		[void - airframe not built]
55		[void - airframe not built]
56		[void - airframe not built]
57		N57SL
58		[void - airframe not built]
59		N700PP [w/o 01Mar03 nr Leesburg-Executive, VA, USA; canx 28Feb06]
60		(SE-KNX) F-OHBN N700HK (N95DW) N700HK
61		N661DW
62		N45PM N762JK [dbr 15Dec00 Harrisburg, IL, USA; b/u c2003 Dodson Aviation, Rantoul, KS, USA]
63		(F-GLJE) F-GLJS LX-JFA
64		[void - airframe not built]
65		[void - airframe not built]
66		[void - airframe not built]
67		N62LM
68		F-OHBI JA8896 [w/o 26Apr96 Kushiro, Hokkaido Prefecture, Japan; canx 08May96]
69		F-OHBL VH-ICO 9M-DSR
70		70/43-XC (French AF) 70/43-VX (French AF) 70/43-XC (French AF) 70/ABX (French Army)
71		N888RA (N838JW) N838RA
72		N700VM

TBM.700

c/n	Series	Identities			
73		OE-EDU [w/o 02Apr93 Wieden, Germany]			
74		(D-FASC) F-OHBK D-FBFS	N93BN		
75		F-OHBJ C-GXXD N79RA	N975TB		
76		N345RD [dbr 13Mar98 nr Truckee-Tahoe, CA, USA, parts to White Industries, Bates City, MO, USA; located "West Building 06"; canx 29Mar02]			
77		77/65-XD (French AF)	77/40-XD (French AF)		
78		78/65-XE (French AF)	78/44-XE (French AF)	78/65-XE (French AF)	
79		[void - airframe not built]			
80		80/65-XF (French AF)	80/41-XF (French AF)	80/40-XF (French AF)	
		80/ABY (French Army)			
81		[void - airframe not built]			
82		N300WC [w/o 26Mar01 nr Denver-Centennial/Arapahoe County, CO, USA; canx 25Jan02]			
83		N783DJ N883CA N883CR			
84		N228CX			
85		N300PW PH-TBD N702JP	N650DM		
86		N700LL (N110JM) N700LL			
87		N874RJ N700ZR			
88		N700KL N217DC			
89		N930SU D-FEIN N5BR			
90		N57HC N57HQ			
91		N700WT			
92		F-OHBP VH-KFT			
93		93/330-IC (French AF)	93/43-XL (French AF)		
94		94/65-XG (French AF)	94/44-XG (French AF)	94/70-XG (French AF)	
		94/ABZ (French Army)			
95		95/65-XH (French AF)			
96		N767CW N442DS			
97		N300AE			
98		N700SP N776RM			
99		99/ABO (French Army)			
100		100/ABP (French Army)			
101		N755DM			
102		F-GNHP N700GJ N88WF	(N700KN) N579NC		
103		103/65-XI (French AF)	103/41-XI (French AF)	103/40-XI (French AF)	
		103/65-XI (French AF)			
104		104/65-XJ (French AF)	104/41-XJ (French AF)	104/65-XJ (French AF)	
		104/70-XJ (French AF)			
105		105/65-XK (French AF)			
106		106/F-ZVMN (French AF)			
107		F-GLBG F-GLLL N701LT			
108		N555HP (N555HN) N715V			
109		N700CS			
110		110/65-XL (French AF)	110/41-XP (French AF)	110/40-XP (French AF)	
111		111/65-XM (French AF)			
112		F-GLBH N12WY N702H			
113		F-OHBU N700CC			
114		F-WNGN F-OHBS PK-CAL			
115		115/ABQ (French Army)			
116		F-GLBK N116VL N700ZZ			
117		117/65-XN (French AF)	117/44-XN (French AF)		
118		F-WNGF F-GLBI N700VX			
119		F-OHBQ PK-AHA			
120		F-OHBR PK-AHC			
121		F-OHBT PK-CAM			
122		F-GLBJ N461LM			
123		N700TB N700CF			
124		F-WWRO N701PP N701MK			
125		125/65-XO (French AF)			
126		F-WWRK F-GLBL N811SW	N701QD		
127		F-WWRL F-OHBV PH-HUB			
128		F-WWRP N91BM N128PC	N63TP		
129	B	F-WWRL F-GLBP LX-JFC	N703QD		
130		F-WWRM N700AP C-GSMO	N38KJ	D-FSJP	
131		131/65-XQ (French AF)			
132		F-WWRO N700AN			
133		F-WWRP N98NF			
134		F-WWRR N700DT			
135		N88U			
136		136/ABR (French Army)			
137	B	D-FIRE			
138		F-GLBN N198X [w/o 27Dec05 nr Lancaster-General Wm.J Fox Airfireld, CA, USA]			
139		139/ABS (French Army)			
140		(N709DM) N1421Z			
141		N500FF			
142		D-FNRE			
143	B	(N709DM) N724DM			
144		N144JT			
145		F-GTJM			
146		146/65-XR (French AF)			
147		147/65-XS (French AF)			
148	B	N700TB (D-FMOR) (N700EV)	N790TB		

TBM.700

c/n	Series	Identities
149		N800GS
150	B	N241TL N449CA (N225AS) N449CA
151	B	N70LT (N950WA) N70LT
152		N767HP
153		N4MD (N40DN) (N344MD) N40DN
154		N435DM
155	B	N345HB N321CW
156		156/ABT (French Army)
157	B	F-WWRN D-FALF
158	B	N700KM
159	B	159/ABU (French Army)
160	B	160/ABV (French Army)
161	B	F-OHBY I-AESR N18SR
162	B	D-FGYY
163		N700DN N700VJ
164	B	F-WWRR N164PG ZS-TBM N700VV
165	B	N700DY N702QD
166	B	F-OHBZ OH-TJJ F-OHBZ F-GZRB 9M-TBM VH-XTB F-HBGG
167	B	N788RB N788RR
168		N709MC
169	B	N4920Y
170		N58HP
171	B	F-WWRP D-FBOY N129AG
172		F-OIKA (D-FBOY) PH-TBM F-GLBT N700WS N70PH
173	B	N22WZ VH-JSO
174		F-GLBS N700QD [w/o 06Dec03 nr Reading-Regional, PA, USA]
175	B	D-FFBU N700WK
176		F-WWRO N700CB
177	B	F-WWRP N702GS
178	B	N277GM N888TF C-FPBL
179		N701AV (N69FR) N701AV
180	B	F-WWRK D-FWIR N700VP N444JV N606SF
181		N721SR
182		N702AV
183		N770DC
184	B	N527TS N552JF
185	B	N700AJ N700AU F-HBGB
186	B	D-FIVE
187	B	N769JS
188	B	N704QD
189		[void - airframe not built]
190	B	N705AV N700VD N700AP
191		N706AV C-GRBV
192		F-WWRJ N71EE N71FF (N12EN) N6842D
193	B	N700S
194	B	N19SG D-FERY
195	B	F-WWRM (N700EN) HB-KFR
196		F-WWRI N843BH
197		F-WWRK N707AV
198	B	N700ER
199	B	F-OIKC LX-JFD N762RS
200	B	N275CA
201		F-WWRK N30LT [w/o 06Dec03 Oxford-Kidlington, UK; canx 17Jun04]
202		N709AV N724RN
203	B	N700BN
204		N700HN
205	C	F-WWRL N778C VH-ICA
206		(D-FAJS) N944CA [w/o 03Feb07 New Bedford Regional, MA, USA]
207	B	N356F
208	B	F-OIKE LX-JFE
209	B	N701AR N700EL
210	B	(N708AV) N700KH
211		N700PW
212	B	F-OIKF LX-JFF
213	B	N559CA
214		N703AV N700WE
215		N700PV
216		N702AA
217	B	N700ND F-GLBU F-HIGH N700ND N623RT N217TM
218		(N700NE) F-GLBV F-HOPE N700NE HB-KOL
219		F-GMLV
220	B	F-WWRI F-GLBX VH-TBO N2WF
221		F-WWRJ N700CV
222	B	F-WWRK N700YN
223		N700BY C-GITC
224		N700XL N9LE N9UE
225	B	F-OIKG I-AESW N70LR *N900DG
226	B	N226GS N226PB
227		N700TL
228	B	N700KP
229		F-GLBY F-HELO (N778C) N123ZC

TBM.700

c/n	Series	Identities				
230	B	N242CA	N324JS			
231	B	N705QD	[w/o 25Apr03 nr Mobile-Downtown, AL, USA; canx 10Jul06]			
232		F-OIKH	EI-TBM	F-WWRO	EI-TBM	N868AT
233	B	(F-OIKI)	N700VA	[dbr 24Oct03 nr Dundee Apt, Scotland; fuselage stored Fairoaks, UK]		
234	B	N811SW	N811SV	N711PM		
235	B	N335MA				
236		N700CT				
237	B	F-OIKJ	N700VB			
238	B	N459CA	(N700EF)	C-GBCO		
239		N115KC				
240	C2	F-WWRO	N811SW			
241	C	N700GJ	(N702RM)	N700GJ		
242	B	N827VG	N700JJ			
243	C	F-WWRI	N217DH	N700KK		
244	C1	F-WWRI	(N700DY)	F-GLBQ	LX-JFG	N997JM
245	C2	F-WWRM	N6720Y	N700WH	ZS-TBM	N700JV
246	C	F-WWRJ	N700GN			
247	C	F-WWRN	N15SB			
248	C2	F-WWRM	N220MA			
249	C2	F-WWRK	N700PX			
250	C2	N700AD				
251	C2	F-WWRP	N700MK			
252	C2	N700AQ				
253	C2	F-WWRQ	N700BH	N700RK		
254	C2	N700AZ				
255	C2	N700GE				
256	C1	F-GZRA	N700TB	N702RW		
257	C	N700SL				
258	C	OH-KJJ	(D-FTBM)	OH-KJJ		
259	C	N459MA				
260	C2	N738C	N700XS	N701CN		
261	C	N181PC	G-MCMC			
262	C2	N700BK				
263	C2	N700BU	N263CW			
264	C2	N700MZ	N700JD			
265	C2	(N700EV)	N6720Y			
266	C2	N700CL				
267	C2	N700FT				
268	C	(N785MA)	N700PT			
269	C2	F-WWRI				
270	C	N700LF	(N700HS)	N700LF		
271	C2	(D-FAJS)	N700DQ			
272	C2	N272MA				
273	C	N703CA	(N943CA)	N703CA		
274	C2	N582C				
275	C	N702AR				
276	C	N700GT				
277	C2	N700SN	N924JP	N700QQ		
278	C2	N700HY	(N702SB)	N700HY		
279	C1	OE-ESK	N824RH	N396AW		
280	C	N785MA				
281	C	N700HL				
282	C	N988C				
283	C2	N700SY				
284	C2	N700EG				
285	C	N706CA	N90CP	N792CA		
286	C2	N386MA	N9EE			
287	C	N700EV				
288	C1	D-FKAI				
289	C	N700GQ	N220JM			
290	C	N700GV				
291	C2	F-WWRK	N700EJ			
292	C2	F-WWRL	N262J			
293	C2	N693MA				
294	C	N883CA	N777FX			
295	C2	N700DZ				
296	C	N700KV				
297	C	N700HM	PR-FIC			
298	C2	N700BQ				
299	C2	F-WWRP	F-OIKL	PH-CLZ		
300	C2	F-WWRO	N300AZ			
301	C2	N700CZ				
302	C1	D-FBFT	N700GY			
303	C	(N903MA)	N210CL			
304	C	N700EK	N8KF	N8KU		
305	C	N700DN	(N700KD)	N700DM		
306	C2	N557CA	(ZS-FEP)	N887TC		
307	C2	N700EZ				
308	C2	N903MA				
309	C2	N930CA	N101NX			
310	C	N716MA				

TBM.700/850

c/n	Series	Identities			
311	C2	N700TK			
312	C2	F-WWRJ	F-GZRC	N773TC	
313	C	N700HD			
314	C2	N702MB			
315	C2	OE-EMS	N700ZM		
316	C2	N820SM			
317	C2	N700ZA			
318	C2	F-WWRL	N12MA		
319	C2	N319TB			
320	C2	N700BD	N700GK		
321	C2	(N700ZB)	F-HBCF		
322	C2	N700ZP	N700KD		
323	C2	N223EA			
324	C2	N700QT	N700WB		
325	C2	N700SX			
326	C2	F-WWRM	N700ZB	N710M	
327	C2	N732C	N300CX		
328	C2	N700ZC	N627DB		
329	C2	N700EN	(N825KM)	N700EN	
330	C2	N611MA			
331	C2	N701MA	N701JF		
332	C2	N731CA			
333	C2	N484RJ	[w/o 15Jul08 nr Kennesaw-Cobb County/McCollum Field, GA, USA]		
334	C2	N334JR			
335	C2	N700ZE	N386CP	(N700QB)	C-GPQB
336	C2	N700ZF			
337	C2	N700QT			
338	C2	N787CA	N436CB	N439CB	N815RD
339	C2	N751CM			
340	C2	N930MA			
341	C2	N790CA			
342	C2	(N948C)	HB-KHC		
343	C2	N2UX	N71EE		
344	C2	(N794CA)	F-OIKD	VH-CZM	
345	C2	F-OIKM	I-TICO		
346	850	F-WWRE	N850TB		
347	850	N850L			
348	850	N850AZ	N850JR		
349	850	F-HBGA	HB-KOR		
350	850	N850MA	N850LL		
351	850	N351CK			
352	850	(N850WM)	N850XS		
353	850	N850WM			
354	850	N850DL			
355	850	N850HM	C-GMET		
356	850	(N850XX)	N257JM		
357	850	F-WWRD	N850TX	N850SB	
358	850	N850SL	N37SV	PH-FSB	
359	850	N850GS			
360	850	N874CA			
361	850	N850SC	N850TG	(N850TL)	PP-PIV
362	850	N850JD	N850JT		
363	850	N885CA			
364	850	N226RA	N226RC		
365	850	F-WWRN	N850JB		
366	850	N318EA	VH-SMZ		
367	850	N850CA	N850BG		
368	850	N854MA			
369	850	N850LA	N288CC		
370	850	N850DD			
371	850	N853MA	N371CW		
372	850	N850WZ	PH-UKK		
373	850	N851TB			
374	850	F-WWRR	N850LH		
375	850	N850JM			
376	850	N850CW			
377	850	N897CA			
378	850	N378FC			
379	850	N850AP			
380	850	N850U			
381	850	N850AB			
382	850	N507BC			
383	850	F-GSCF			
384	850	N850AZ			
385	850	F-WWRM	N74MA		
386	850	F-WWRP	N850AR	N864DM	
387	850	F-WWRR	D-FBFS		
388	850	F-WWRJ	N850TM	N220JM	N850PL
389	850	F-HBGD	VH-MRJ	*N850VT	
390	850	N850PW			
391	850	F-OIKN	LX-JFL		

TBM.850

c/n	Series	Identities			
392	850	N851MA			
393	850	N893CA			
394	850	N851WA			
395	850	N850RB	N788RB		
396	850	N85JE	N2711E		
397	850	F-OIKI	ZS-BCI		
398	850	N850KL			
399	850	N850AA			
400	850	N32WZ			
401	850	N850MD			
402	850	N855MA	N555HP		
403	850	N850LW	N850MK		
404	850	N950WA			
405	850	N924BB			
406	850	F-WWRR	N223JG		
407	850	F-WWRJ	N850KM		
408	850	F-WWRL	N892CA	N850MW	
409	850	N850EE	N63DL		
410	850	N367EA			
411	850	N850WE			
412	850	N849MA	[dbr 04Jun08 Iowa City-Municipal, ID, USA, parts to Dodson International Parts, Rantoul, KS, USA]		
413	850	N850KK	D-FGPE	N850KK	
414	850	N850AG			
415	850	N6868C			
416	850	N894EA	(N850SJ)	N894EA	
417	850	N850LD			
418	850	N654CW	PR-GAB		
419	850	F-GSLV			
420	850	N11T	N850BQ	*N850BL	
421	850	LZ-TBM			
422	850	F-OIKQ	LX-JFO		
423	850	N850DP	N51LG		
424	850	N842MA			
425	850	N302RJ			
426	850	(N850WC)	HB-KHP	N850WC	N850AC
427	850	N850BZ			
428	850	PH-TJA			
429	850	N988V	*PP-OPV		
430	850	F-WWRP	N850WT		
431	850	F-WWRR	D-FIBG		
432	850	F-WWRL	N850DB		
433	850	N850BT			
434	850	F-WWRJ	N847MA	N313BP	
435	850	F-WWRK	N850GX		
436	850	F-WWRO	N850JS	EI-LCM	
437	850	F-WWRP	N850LK		
438	850	F-WWRQ	N294PJ	N851SH	
439	850	N654CW			
440	850	G-PMHT			
441	850	N850GC	N37SV		
442	850	N851GC	F-OJGL		
443	850	N22MY			
444	850	N850AD			
445	850	(N440EA)	N888LF		
446	850	N850BD			
447	850	N440EA	N850SJ		
448	850	N824RH			
449	850	N850TG			
450	850	N850NW	N731TM		
451	850	N4884M			
452	850	(N492B)	LX-JFT		
453	850	EC-KQP			
454	850	N850MB	PR-HLT		
455	850	N492B			
456	850	M-USCA			
457	850	N850PC	PR-MLF		
458	850	N15NM			
459	850	N850MF			
460	850	F-HBGE			
461	850	N155PM	N850TD		
462	850	N528MD			
463	850	N463RD			
464	850	OE-EEE			
465	850	N436CB			
466	850	N8KF			
467	850	M-SHEP			
468	850	N850TX			
469	850	N285JE	N85JE		
470	850	N850TT			
471	850	N850FA			

TBM.850

c/n	Series	Identities
472	850	N375BZ
473	850	N850PB N850ED
474	850	N12ZM
475	850	G-KEMW
476	850	N850KP
477	850	N550CP (N386CP) N386CP
478	850	N850MY
479	850	N850GG
480	850	N85ZG
481	850	N850SC
482	850	N226RA
483	850	N23MY
484	850	N850DX *PR-KRC
485	850	N850PD
486	850	N535DM
487	850	N218TG
488	850	N850LR
489	850	N850MT
490	850	N850FC
491	850	N599G
492	850	N850JE PR-DPR
493	850	N850ZM N72SR
494	850	N857WC N219GR
495	850	N850SF
496	850	N850NW *N850DK
497	850	N851SB
498	850	N850SD
499	850	
500	850	N4MD
501	850	N850EA
502	850	N221MA
503	850	F-HBGH
504	850	N850CD
505	850	N850WW
506	850	N850PT
507	850	N850VM
508	850	N850BU
509	850	N859CA
510	850	N850ZZ
511	850	N850LE
512	850	N562CC
513	850	N850TV
514	850	(N850WC)
515	850	N898CA
516	850	N551MA
517	850	N850BN
518	850	N850MV
519	850	N756TW
520	850	N850RT
521	850	(N43EA)
522	850	N850WC
523	850	N850JD
524	850	N850RB
525	850	N676MA
526	850	N881CA
527	850	
528	850	
529	850	
530	850	
531	850	
532	850	
533	850	
534	850	
535	850	
536	850	
537	850	
538	850	
539	850	
540	850	
541	850	
542	850	
543	850	
544	850	
545	850	
546	850	
547	850	
548	850	
549	850	
550	850	
551	850	
552	850	

c/n	Series	Identities
553	850	
554	850	
555	850	
556	850	
557	850	
558	850	
559	850	
560	850	
561	850	
562	850	
563	850	
564	850	
565	850	
566	850	
567	850	
568	850	
569	850	
570	850	
571	850	
572	850	
573	850	
574	850	
575	850	
576	850	
577	850	
578	850	
579	850	
580	850	
581	850	
582	850	
583	850	
584	850	
585	850	
586	850	
587	850	
588	850	
589	850	
590	850	
591	850	
592	850	
593	850	
594	850	
595	850	
596	850	
597	850	
598	850	
599	850	
600	850	
601	850	
602	850	
603	850	
604	850	
605	850	
606	850	
607	850	
608	850	
609	850	
610	850	
611	850	
612	850	
613	850	
614	850	
615	850	
616	850	
617	850	
618	850	
619	850	
620	850	
621	850	
622	850	
623	850	
624	850	
625	850	
626	850	
627	850	
628	850	
629	850	
630	850	

BEECH 65-90/A90/B90/C90/C90-1/C90B/C90GT KING AIR

$ = Raisbeck dual aft body strakes fitted
# = Raisbeck nacelle wing lockers fitted
+ = Raisbeck dual aft body strakes and nacelle wing lockers fitted
^ - Blackhawk XP135A engine upgrade fitted

c/n	Series/Mod	Identities
LJ-1	65-90	N5690K N925X N924K N26CH N925X
LJ-2	65-90	N799K (N135NK) N155NK N5CJ N48TB N271W N812Q N812P
LJ-3	65-90	CF-UAC C-FUAC "N90VU" [pres inst airframe at Vincennes University Facility, Indianapolis-International, IN, USA; canx 15May92; wears false marks N90VU]
LJ-4	65-90	N790K HB-GCI PH-ILK F-BUFI TR-LBB F-GDRT [CofA exp cAug88; wfu for spares Aero Stock, Paris-Le Bourget, France]
LJ-5	65-90	N702K N357JR [possibly sold in Panama c2003]
LJ-6	65-90	N770K D-ILTE N5PC N5PQ N7CJ N7CQ C-GSFC N43DT [b/u c1995 White Industries, Bates City, MO, USA; canx 07Jun95]
LJ-7	65-90	(HB-GBK) D-ILMU N17776 N180K C-GJBK N46DT [wfu cMay95 Dalfort Aircraft Technical School, Atlanta, GA, USA]
LJ-8	65-90	N5652K N19R N4R N19R N4RY (N16CG) N4RY
LJ-9	65-90	N13309 N649MC N613BR
LJ-10	65-90	N10J N10JE
LJ-11	65-90	D-ILDB N17BC CF-WHV N2JJ N101GA [w/o 03Jan95 Hot Springs, AR, USA; canx 10Apr96]
LJ-12	65-90	N316M N420M N1LC N90MR N654C
LJ-13	65-90	N99W C-FBPT [wfu cMar95 Calgary-International, AB, Canada; canx 11Mar86]
LJ-14	65-90	HB-GCB I-ERRE EC-BNN D-ILTI N155S [wfu Stevenson Aviation & Aerospace Training, Winnipeg-International, MB, Canada; canx 08Nov01]
LJ-15	65-90	N733K N733KL N37GP
LJ-16	65-90	N51K N51KA PT-
LJ-17	65-90	N4900W N23UT (N110AS) N134CA N440TP [wfu cMay87 - status?]
LJ-18	65-90	N2400X [w/o 17Apr76 off Akutan Island, AK, USA]
LJ-19	65-90	CF-JCN N821U [canx 04May06 as exported to Mexico; impounded 16Jun06 Malambo, Atlantico, Colombia]
LJ-20	65-90	N808K N808S CF-MLC C-FMLC N249DA [wfu, parts to Dodson International Parts, Rantoul, KS, USA; canx 31Aug89]
LJ-21	65-90	N5Y N249PA [wfu, parts to Aviation Warehouse, El Mirage, CA, USA]
LJ-22	65-90	N212Q N412Q N710TK N9502Q N113TC [w/o 16Jul74 Knoxville-Downtown Island, TX, USA]
LJ-23	65-90	CF-CAS [w/o 01May79 Sherrington, QC, Canada; canx 04Feb80]
LJ-24	65-90	CF-CAU C-FCAU [dbr 29Aug85 Quebec City, QC, Canada; b/u & canx 05Apr89]
LJ-25	65-90	N895K [dbr 05Aug82 Billings-Logan International, MT, USA; b/u at Dodson International Parts, Rantoul, KS, USA; canx 15Jun93]
LJ-26	65-90	D-ILVW D-ILGK F-BVVM [b/u c1994 Toussus Le Noble, France; canx 13Apr94]
LJ-27	65-90	N403NW N403N N400PC N400PQ N330CB [wfu, parts to Dodson International Parts, Rantoul, KS, USA]
LJ-28	65-90	N142LM [wfu & b/u; canx cAug87]
LJ-29	65-90	D-ILMI F-BXSF [wfu, parts to Dodson International Parts, Rantoul, KS, USA; canx 24Mar93]
LJ-30	65-90	N538M N1290A
LJ-31	65-90	N34W N740R N7009 N4948W (N505M) N4948W [pres Steward Davies Technical School, North Hollywood, CA, USA]
LJ-32	65-90	HB-GCF PH-FSS F-BTOK F-GGAM [b/u c1986 in France; canx 15May98]
LJ-33	65-90	N5767K N420X N420G CF-RCL [w/o 28Aug76 Prince Albert, SK, Canada; canx 19Jan77]
LJ-34	65-90	N1920H N200SW N275DP [pres Washington-Smithsonian National Air & Space Museum, Steven F Udvar-Hazy Center, VA, USA]
LJ-35	65-90	N735K [pres South Seattle Community College, Seattle, WA, USA]
LJ-36	65-90	D-ILME N5724M N414GN N5PQ N3DS (N312DS) N3DF
LJ-37	65-90	N720K [wfu in scrapyard adjacent to Deland Municipal-Sidney H Taylor Field, FL, USA]
LJ-38	65-90	N1128M N1128B C-GGGL N141RR [stored Deland Municipal-Sidney H Taylor Field, FL, USA; still marked as C-GGGL]
LJ-39	65-90	N410WA N410W [wfu, parts to White Industries, Bates City, MO, USA; location F-10]
LJ-40	65-90	HB-GCH I-GNIS F-BTQP
LJ-41	65-90	N370V N123JB N9SA N10NW N777AG N877AG N877AQ [wfu, parts to Dodson International Parts, Rantoul, KS, USA]
LJ-42	65-90	N376D N367DF N711KA N81CC N816C [wfu, parts to White Industries, Bates City, MO, USA; location F-27; canx 18Oct88]
LJ-43	65-90	N721K [wfu, parts to Dodson International Parts, Rantoul, KS, USA; canx 10Oct96]
LJ-44	65-90	XB-YAZ N93227 N333CS [wfu, parts to White Industries, Bates City, MO, USA; location F-40; canx 14Jul04]
LJ-45	65-90$	HB-GBK N12AB [wfu; canx 17Apr92; pres as inst airframe FAA Technical Centre, Building 207 Atlantic City Apt, NJ, USA]
LJ-46	65-90	N190K N190N C-GZIZ N38GP [wfu in scrapyard adjacent to Deland Municipal-Sidney H Taylor Field, FL, USA]
LJ-47	65-90	N613M N6137 [pres Hinds Junior College, Raymond, MS, USA]
LJ-48	65-90	D-ILMA [w/o 13Aug69 nr Munster-Osnabruck, West Germany; canx 19Jan70]
LJ-49	65-90	N55GP N4990Y N2AK N777TG N401HT C-GNUX N32229
LJ-50	65-90	N75X N75XA S9-NAA [dbr c1988, parts to White Industries, Bates City, MO, USA; location F-35]
LJ-51	65-90	N747K [wfu, parts to White Industries, Bates City, MO, USA; location F-28; canx 10Feb92]

BEECH 90

c/n	Series/Mod	Identities
LJ-52	65-90	OY-BAL N90BL N134W
LJ-53	65-90	N810K N81PS N81PA N55JM N123PP N818MS N539DP YV [canx 03Sep08 as exported to Venezuela]
LJ-54	65-90	N880K N661JB N6619B N66MR N66MS N66WC F-GDMM [dbf cSep92 Dinard/Pleurtuit-St.Malo, France; canx 10Sep92]
LJ-55	65-90	N595MG (N122AS) N50KK N711BU HP- [canx 18Jun03 as exported to Panama]
LJ-56	65-90	N776K [wfu, parts to White Industries, Bates City, MO, USA; location F-14]
LJ-57	65-90	N234MM N2340M RP-C2340 [b/u; parts to Dodson International Parts, Rantoul, KS, USA; nose section displayed inside ADS Hangar, Manila Domestic, Philippines; CofA exp 31Aug94]
LJ-58	65-90	D-ILMY N11ER N11JP C-GXHD N58KA
LJ-59	65-90	N579B N5799 N1909R N190BT
LJ-60	65-90	N763K N1WJ
LJ-61	65-90	N764K N3078W N900BP [pres Columbus State Community College, Columbus-Bolton Field, OH, USA]
LJ-62	65-90	N512W N512WP N212WP [wfu; location unkn]
LJ-63	65-90	XB-ZAA XA-MUR XB-ZAA XB-GTP
LJ-64	65-90	N740E N740F N243Q N512Q N512G [w/o 03Jan83 nr Grand Cayman, Cayman Islands]
LJ-65	65-90	N991LL N981LL N981LE N46WA [w/o 13Jan94 off Marseille, France; canx 08Dec99]
LJ-66	65-90	D-IFLU N4PC N1SA N901SA
LJ-67	65-90	N780K N777NR N777NP (N21AM) N777NP
LJ-68	65-90	D-ILNE D-IKAO OY-BVA [pres Roskilde, Denmark as an engine test vehicle; canx 12Nov03]
LJ-69	65-90	N742K N742UT N120DP N190JL
LJ-70	65-90	N516W N516WB
LJ-71	65-90	N1100X N110EL
LJ-72	65-90	N901W YV-299P [w/o 31Jan79 in Venezuela]
LJ-73	65-90	N277F N399GT N6GT N90NY [wfu, parts to White Industries, Bates City, MO, USA; location F-30]
LJ-74	65-90	N3711H N3711M XC-GFM XC-FER XB-DKJ XA-RMH N32FH [pres Gateway Technical College, Kenosha, WI, USA; later moved to White Industries, Bates City, MO, USA]
LJ-75	65-90	N902W C-GJBE N75368
LJ-76	65-90	N866K N100AN N866K [b/u; canx 19Oct93]
LJ-77	65-90	N817M N52BW N56SC N56SQ N58AC
LJ-78	65-90	N730K N95UF [wfu in scrapyard adjacent to Deland Municipal-Sidney H Taylor Field, FL, USA; canx 30Apr08]
LJ-79	65-90	N41LZ N33JC N332K [w/o 03Sep79 Laredo, TX, USA; canx 01Oct82]
LJ-80	65-90	(G-ATGB) N774K N577NK ZS-NED D2-ALS
LJ-81	65-90	N950K N276VM
LJ-82	65-90	N724N [w/o 22Dec79 nr Leeville, LA, USA]
LJ-83	65-90	N827T (YV-980P) N827T [dbr 12Apr67 Alcova, WY, USA, parts to Quest Aviation, Lake City, FL, USA]
LJ-84	65-90	I-SNAT D-IKOR N619GS C-FUFW [wfu cMay02, pres College D'Enseignement General Et Professionnel, Longueuil, PQ, Canada]
LJ-85	65-90	N576D N576DU N5760U N223MD N900CF N900CK
LJ-86	65-90	N801K N90FH N60RJ N17WT
LJ-87	65-90	N98B
LJ-88	65-90	HB-GCW N10AT (N90233) N10AY [dbr 26Feb82 Atlanta-DeKalb/Peachtree, GA, USA]
LJ-89	65-90	N195D N195DR N195DP
LJ-90	65-90	N165NL N65NL N85NL [wfu, parts to Dodson International Parts, Rantoul, KS, USA; listed on Dodson inventory as N165NL]
LJ-91	65-90	N2085W N825K [pres Rock Valley College, Rockford, IL, USA]
LJ-92	65-90	XC-DEY XA-CAK XB-VUW XC-FUR N5245F
LJ-93	65-90	N48W N48A N9901 [pres Great Oaks Inst of Technology Joint Vocational School, Cincinnati, OH, USA]
LJ-94	65-90	N962M N96RE N300HC N300HG [wfu, parts to White Industries, Bates City, MO, USA; location F-21]
LJ-95	65-90	N795K [wfu cFeb96, pres Vaughn College of Aeronautics and Technology, La Guardia, NY, USA]
LJ-96	65-90	D-ILVV N3PC N2MF [w/o 19Mar78 Houston, TX, USA]
LJ-97	65-90	N709K (N504M) N709K [b/u; front fuselage to Meyers-Diver's, Tecumseh, MI, USA; rear fuselage at location B-13, White Industries, Bates City, MO, USA; canx 09Jul96]
LJ-98	65-90	N158GD N158G OY-ANP F-GBPB
LJ-99	65-90	HB-GCK N292A
LJ-100	65-90	N191DM N1NL N191DM [wfu, parts to White Industries, Bates City, MO, USA; location F-13; canx 18Mar93]
LJ-101	65-90	N630M N6308 N42B N333G [b/u c2005 Manaus-Eduardo Gomes, Amazonas, Brazil]
LJ-102	65-90	N787K
LJ-103	65-90	N3002S [reportedly b/u]
LJ-104	65-90	N712K N710K N1TP N37PP N814G (N314G) (N819C) N814G
LJ-105	65-90	PP-CIJ PP-ENF PT-LHM
LJ-106	65-90	N177G N44F N44FL N271MB N411RS
LJ-107	65-90	N1153S N1183S N157CA N7BF N7BQ N311SR [pres inst airframe at International Airline Training Academy, Tucson-International, AZ, USA]
LJ-108	65-90	N1154S C6-CAM
LJ-109	65-90	N528N N48N N48XP
LJ-110	65-90	N704K N677WP N677W N695V N29AA [b/u cDec92 Dallas, TX, USA; canx 08Dec92]

BEECH 90

c/n	Series/Mod	Identities
LJ-111	65-90	CF-WHV N808DP N808Y N88CV N33BB N36BB N33BB N27LR N50ES [reportedly b/u cJun96]
LJ-112	65-90	N529N [w/o 11Mar66 nr Green Castle, MO, USA]
LJ-113	65-90	N117K N117KL N16CS N105K
LJ-114	65-A90	N890K (VH-FBK) VH-CMT N114KA N114CW [b/u; canx 24Jul84]
LJ-115	65-A90	N899K N299K N396DP N3969P N30KS N7377 [wfu c2003, parts to White Industries, Bates City, MO, USA; location "Ramp SO A-12"]
LJ-116	65-A90	D-ILNI [w/o 22Sep67 nr Saluzzo, Italy; canx 07Feb68]
LJ-116A	65-A90	N885K N88SP [cvtd from Beech 65-88 c/n LP-29]
LJ-117	65-A90	N444SA N3000W N100TB N20RT N10430 N115PA
LJ-118	65-A90	CF-CGE C-FCGE
LJ-119	65-A90	D-ILMO N719W N7782 N25CA N34F [dbr 10Mar77 Kankakee, IL, USA, parts to White Industries, Bates City, MO, USA; location N/P-2; canx 17Feb81]
LJ-120	65-A90	N601T N601TA [wfu cOct89, pres Metro Tech College, Oklahoma City, OK, USA]
LJ-121	65-A90	D-ILNA HB-GCU F-GERH N666FG N948RM F-GVRM [w/o 24Dec04 Montpellier, France]
LJ-122	65-A90	N860K HR-IAH
LJ-123	65-A90$	N815K N812AC
LJ-124	65-A90	N253MZ N253ZM N2536Z N1965M N253ZM F-BINE N6238N YV [canx 22Dec03 as exported to Venezuela]
LJ-125	65-A90	N925X N333LT N913RM N120JM PT-OUL [w/o 02Mar99 Franca, Sao Paulo State, Brazil]
LJ-126	65-A90	N570M N57MM [wfu, parts to White Industries, Bates City, MO, USA; location F-43]
LJ-127	65-A90	N727X N72RD F-GCFH [wfu Marseille-Marignane, France; canx 09Aug96]
LJ-128	65-A90	D-IMTW F-BOSY
LJ-129	65-A90	N714K N714KL N333GG 86-1683 (US Army) N7202L N129LA
LJ-130	65-A90	N70TG N70TQ N70UA YV [canx 04Aug04 as exported to Venezuela]
LJ-131	65-A90	N700S N80DG
LJ-132	65-A90	N365G HB-GDW N365G N3650 N3650P N3500P N8500B ZP-TYF N290CC
LJ-133	65-A90	N1905L N90SA N90FA [wfu cJan96, pres Fox Valley Technical College, Appleton, WI, USA]
LJ-134	65-A90	N815CE N8156E N37LA N38LA C-GLRR [wfu, parts to Westcan Aircraft Sales & Salvage, Kamloops, BC, Canada; canx 08Feb02]
LJ-135	65-A90$	N571M N571L [wfu, parts to White Industries, Bates City, MO, USA; location F-41]
LJ-136	65-A90	HB-GDF F-BFRE 5N-ATU [wfu cMay94; b/u Gamston, UK]
LJ-137	65-A90	N18X N18KA N7117 N1ZA N24PL N24PR N80GP [dbr 14Nov97 Wheeling-Ohio County, WV, USA; canx 04Jun98]
LJ-138	65-A90	N4000 N65190 N100SC N100UF N100UE
LJ-139	65-A90	N1515T N100WB
LJ-140	65-A90	D-INAW N307LW N50GH N437CF
LJ-141	65-A90	N530N [w/o 01May93 Mount Ida, AR, USA; canx 06Oct93]
LJ-142	65-A90	N723K N101NK N181NK
LJ-143	65-A90	N5000 N5006 N751PC (N280KA) N751PC [wfu cAug04, parts to White Industries, Bates City, MO, USA; location "Ramp SO B-34"; canx 06Nov07]
LJ-144	65-A90	N1413B D-IBMA N111ER N14CE N101FC (N3DG) N331AM [wfu c2003, parts to White Industries, Bates City, MO, USA; location "Ramp SO B-31"; canx 29Apr09]
LJ-145	65-A90	N8999A N89991 N45PR
LJ-146	65-A90	N722K N49E N49EL N77DA YV [canx 21Mar05 as exported to Venezuela]
LJ-147	65-A90	N100UP N100UB N102RC N483JM N198BC YV [canx 24Feb04 as exported to Venezuela]
LJ-148	65-A90$	N200UP N100WL N671L N671LL
LJ-149	65-A90	F-BNMC [w/o 28Aug97 L'Isles sur la Sorgue, France]
LJ-150	65-A90	N1151S N4646S N123NA N100HC N900W SE-FNU D-ICPD F-GEDV [CofA exp 28Sep97; canx 05Oct05; wfu Cergy-Pontoise, France]
LJ-151	65-A90	N3926M N22HS N28AB YV [canx 23Sep03 as exported to Venezuela]
LJ-152	65-A90	N8180 PT-OVP
LJ-153	VC-6A	N901R 66-15361 (US Army) N901R [pres at White Sands Missile Range, Alamogordo, NM, USA; canx 13Feb73]
LJ-154	65-A90	N5104 N5111 N5111U [wfu; fuselage located at Titusville/Cocoa Beach-Space Centre Executive, FL, USA]
LJ-155	65-A90	N5105 N5112 N124J N7HL N7HU N40RM [wfu, parts to White Industries, Bates City, MO, USA; location N/P-2; canx 30Jun93]
LJ-156	65-A90	N2 N22 N3754V N8520L [wfu cNov98; b/u c2006 Philadelphia-International, PA, USA]
LJ-157	65-A90	N400V N176K N330PM N288HH N90GN
LJ-158	65-A90	D-IEHL N54GA (N900WM) N503M
LJ-159	65-A90	N288RG N108RJ N27465 N7078S N50525 86-0092 (US Army) N50525
LJ-160	65-A90	N1152S N111XL N111XE N66WB N42CG N616AS [dbr 19Apr97 Salt Lake City-South Valley, UT, USA, parts to Dodson International Parts, Rantoul, KS, USA; canx 24Apr98; listed in Dodson inventory as N42CG]
LJ-161	65-A90	N173A ZS-MAN ZS-IRJ ZS-EFC
LJ-162	65-A90	N235HM N13ST N198T N198KA
LJ-163	65-A90	N636SC N636SQ N2RR N20BL
LJ-164	65-A90	N531N N8GT N8GF N17SA [w/o 03Aug08 Pitt Meadows Regional, BC, Canada; canx 09Apr09]
LJ-165	65-A90	N592DC N592DQ N6HF N616F [w/o 14Jan01 Great Salt Lake, nr Lake Point, UT, USA; canx 14Jan02]
LJ-166	65-A90	N28J N777AT [wfu c2003, parts to White Industries, Bates City, MO, USA; location "Taxiway S01"; canx 29Apr09]
LJ-167	65-A90	N239CT N41SC C-FIYA N789TW N290RD YV [canx 28Jul05 as exported to Venezuela]

BEECH 90

c/n	Series/Mod	Identities
LJ-168	65-A90	N23W XB-BOF XB-FOT [w/o 15Feb78 in Mexico]
LJ-169	65-A90	N293WX N903K N983K
LJ-170	65-A90	N767K [b/u c1987; location unkn; canx 18Aug88]
LJ-171	65-A90	N755K N611VP [dbr 01Apr88 Narsarsuaq, Greenland; parts to Dodson International Parts, Rantoul, KS, USA]
LJ-172	65-A90	N2000E N2000F N2000E
LJ-173	65-A90$	N901TC N901UC N613M N623R XB-SFS N623R N629CD
LJ-174	65-A90	N6000 N9WW N660PC N83SF N93SF (N193SF) N93RY
LJ-175	65-A90	N706K N720X N800TB N50RM N501M [wfu, parts to White Industries, Bates City, MO, USA; location F-33]
LJ-176	65-A90	N820K N565RA N5656A XC-ICP [w/o 28Jan73 Veracruz, Veracruz State, Mexico]
LJ-177	65-A90	N572M N2AE N31NC N90SJ [wfu, parts to White Industries, Bates City, MO, USA; location F-08]
LJ-178	65-A90	D-ILNU [w/o 16Feb67 nr Bremen-Nieuenland, West Germany; canx 20Feb67]
LJ-178A	65-A90	N798K [cvtd from Beech 65-88 c/n LP-27]
LJ-179	65-A90	N49R N49D N711CF N511BF [w/o 17Oct03 Fentress, TX, USA]
LJ-180	65-A90	N643JA N610W OB-1457 N171TE [w/o 29Nov98 in sea 20 mls N of Haiti]
LJ-181	65-A90	N1823B N223KD PT-LBZ PR-PJC
LJ-182	65-A90	N1000C N1009C N92W N92WG
LJ-183	65-A90	N870K CF-PCB C-FPCB N151BU [wfu cSep96 Baylor University, Waco, TX, USA, parts to Global Aircraft Industries, Edmonton-Villeneuve, AB, Canada; TT 14784 hours; canx 28Oct99]
LJ-184	65-A90	N858K (N127RS) N566CA HP- [canx 17Jan07 as exported to Panama]
LJ-185	65-A90	N769K N769 N89JR [wfu, parts to White Industries, Bates City, MO, USA; location F-06; canx 26Jun89]
LJ-186	65-A90	N821U CF-JCN N881M N814SW [dbf 16Nov96 Orange County Apt, VA, USA; canx 24Apr98]
LJ-187	65-A90	N610K (N510L) N743K [wfu, parts to White Industries, Bates City, MO, USA; location "Mid Ramp"]
LJ-188	65-A90	N703K N703WC [w/o 18Oct68 Cleveland-Hopkins, OH, USA]
LJ-189	65-A90$	N889K N555CB N123KA PK-VKZ
LJ-190	65-A90	YV-T-GTX (YV-52CP) YV-O-MMH-2 YV-1391P N700US N216AJ N216LJ
LJ-191	65-A90	N737K PT-WAE
LJ-192	65-A90	N792K N15CT
LJ-193	65-A90	N600BW N600BF
LJ-194	65-A90	N1952 N1952L N55FW N55FY
LJ-195	65-A90	N740K N31CP N98DD ZP-TXP N98DD YV [canx 26Sep03 as exported to Venezuela]
LJ-196	65-A90	N3000R N300DD N348AC
LJ-197	65-A90	N725K N2510L PK-VKY
LJ-198	65-A90	N898K C-GBFF N898K [b/u; canx 01Dec92]
LJ-199	65-A90	N500X [w/o 26Nov69 off Galveston, TX, USA]
LJ-200	65-A90	N243D N50RP XA- [canx 07Jan05 as exported to Mexico]
LJ-201	65-A90	(D-ILNY) N866A [w/o 27Nov99 St.George Municipal, SC, USA; canx 09Aug05]
LJ-202	65-A90	N404G N464G N474DP N464G YV [canx 01Nov05 as exported to Venezuela]
LJ-203	65-A90	CF-CGH C-FCGH
LJ-204	65-A90	N165U N52EL
LJ-205	65-A90	N140CN N126C N416CS N7111H N707PR YV-1700P [w/o 13Jun98 in sea off Adicora, Venezuela]
LJ-206	65-A90	HB-GDG F-BTAK F-GHDO
LJ-207	65-A90	N23Y N77577 N7177 N383JC N962AT [pres inst airframe FlygTeknikCentrum Hasslo, Vasteras-Hasslo, Sweden; canx 13Mar03]
LJ-208	65-A90	N29S N29SA N296A [pres Sowela Regional Technical Institute, Lake Charles, LA, USA]
LJ-209	65-A90	D-ILNY N2PC N400CE N400QE N517LF N90BE N54WW
LJ-210	65-A90	N75A N3PC N1UC N11UC N43TT YV [canx 27Feb03 as exported to Venezuela]
LJ-211	65-A90	N867K N550Z N553Z N76CB N76CV N90JR (D-ILKC) N90JR [wfu, parts to Dodson International Parts, Rantoul, KS, USA; canx 10May96]
LJ-212	65-A90	CF-SIV N483G N483D [b/u; canx 08Sep92]
LJ-213	65-A90	N417CS N250U [pres Midland College, Midland, TX, USA]
LJ-214	65-A90	N24S N66PC N718VA N718VN N22WC N813AA N985AA N412MA N316AF
LJ-215	65-A90	D-IEVW HB-GEV N127HT N479SA
LJ-216	65-A90	N129GP [w/o 16Apr67 Endicott, NY, USA]
LJ-217	65-A90	N601R (F-GHRD) F-GJRD F-WJRD CN-TGL
LJ-218	65-A90	N49UC N46CB N360M N380M N801KM
LJ-219	65-A90	N581WC N52C N101XC [wfu, parts to White Industries, Bates City, MO, USA; location F-38]
LJ-220	65-A90	CF-CGI C-FCGI
LJ-221	65-A90	N38V PP-OTK PT-KGV
LJ-222	65-A90	N19M N7LH N10127 (N901AS) YV [canx 14Nov03 as exported to Venezuela]
LJ-223	65-A90	N1127M N1127D [w/o 19Nov96 Quincy-Municipal, IL, USA; collided with Be1900 N87GL]
LJ-224	65-A90	N464AL N464AB YV [canx 20May05 as exported to Venezuela]
LJ-225	65-A90	CF-VMH C-FVMH [wfu c1991; canx 25Jul91]
LJ-226	65-A90	N463AL N195DR N14TG N271WN
LJ-227	65-A90	N5401U VH-BIB N239K N25DC CC-CII CC-PIR CC-COT [wfu c1999 Punta Arenas, Chile; canx 27May99]
LJ-228	65-A90	N946K OB-1567
LJ-229	65-A90	N435A [dbr 27Jul07 Wallkill-Kobelt, NY, USA, parts to Dodson International Parts, Rantoul, KS, USA]
LJ-230	65-A90	N750K N93BA N77SS

BEECH 90

c/n	Series/Mod	Identities
LJ-231	65-A90	CF-CGJ C-FCGJ [wfu cApr91; canx 17Apr91]
LJ-232	65-A90	N602 N602E N602 N707EB CP-2287 [w/o 12Apr96 Robore, Bolivia]
LJ-233	65-A90	N456PH N100HT N700MB [b/u; canx 08Jul05]
LJ-234	65-A90	N723T N338GW N320F N800BP N212D N3XB
LJ-235	65-A90	N708K N75D N440D [wfu Vero Beach-Municipal, FL, USA; canx to Norway 27May99; possibly b/u]
LJ-236	65-A90	N363N [wfu, parts to White Industries, Bates City, MO, USA; location F-09]
LJ-237	65-A90	N232A N66GS
LJ-238	65-A90	N802K N7HD N190RF N6KZ
LJ-239	65-A90	N28S N28SE [w/o 30Jun85 nr Apalachicola-St.George Island Apt, FL, USA; canx 11Jul89]
LJ-240	65-A90	N36030 N360D YV [canx 21Nov02 as exported to Venezuela]
LJ-241	65-A90	N18S N27UU N22BB
LJ-242	65-A90	N925G N1975L N812PS N41VC [w/o 12Aug97 Alice-International, TX, USA; canx 09Dec98]
LJ-243	65-A90	N578DU N278DU (N509W) N278DU [w/o 10Jul78 nr Denver-Stapleton, CO, USA]
LJ-244	65-A90	N295X [w/o 01May72 Racine, WI, USA; canx 07Jul72]
LJ-245	65-A90	N3000C N68395 N5BW N42CC N42CQ (N221ML) N42CQ [wfu cAug88, pres Oklahoma State Department For Vocational Technologies, Stillwater, OK, USA]
LJ-246	65-A90	N878T [w/o 27Feb78 Big Piney, WY, USA]
LJ-247	65-A90	N9507Q N515PC PI-C990 RP-C990 [w/o 28Jul99 nr Mankayan, Ilocos Sur, Philippines; CofR exp 30Aug99]
LJ-248	65-A90	N333X N338X N562R N562P N202RW N562P HK- [canx 23Oct02 as exported to Colombia]
LJ-249	65-A90	N8000 N800S N800VT [wfu, parts to White Industries, Bates City, MO, USA; location F-19; canx 07Dec95]
LJ-250	65-A90	N6200D N900CA N6200B (N66FS) N6200B [wfu, parts to White Industries, Bates City, MO, USA; location "Mid Ramp"; canx 09Dec04]
LJ-251	65-A90	N516DM N518DM [dbr 31Jul99 Marine City, MI, USA, parts to Dodson International Parts, Rantoul, KS, USA; canx 01May00]
LJ-252	65-A90	N728K N33SB
LJ-253	65-A90	N791K [w/o 13Mar73 Portland, ME, USA]
LJ-254	65-A90	N804K N3D N977QA N781JT N911KA [dbr 22Jan98 Selmer-Robert Sibley, TN, USA, parts to Dodson International Parts, Rantoul, KS, USA; canx 30Mar00]
LJ-255	65-A90	N5113 N14TK [wfu, parts to White Industries, Bates City, MO, USA; location F-31]
LJ-256	65-A90	N5114 N111KA N530D N53TT C-FOLR N256TA [wfu cNov07, parts to Calgary-Springbank, AB, Canada]
LJ-257	65-A90	N55V N44US N711VP C-FXNB N299D
LJ-258	65-A90	N915BD N123V [pres inst airframe Milwaukee Area Technical College, WI, USA]
LJ-259	65-A90	N727K N3333X N3333D [w/o 10Oct96 Itaguazurenda, Bolivia]
LJ-260	65-A90	N920K N1851T N1853T N35HM N303NH N96AG
LJ-261	65-A90	N5115 N5115D N990SA [status? possibly b/u by Aviation Parts Exchange, TX, USA]
LJ-262	65-A90	N5116 N111ME F-GFJF [CofA exp cJan89; canx cAug96; wfu Dinard/Pleurtuit-St.Malo, France]
LJ-263	65-A90	N929K N426JX N526BT N526RR
LJ-264	65-A90	HB-GCV N86JR N86MG [status? possibly b/u by Aviation Parts Exchange, TX, USA]
LJ-265	65-A90	HB-GDI I-MEDI I-MUDI N10YP (N126AT) N10YP
LJ-266	65-A90	D-IGTW N11AB N77CA N55GM N55LH YV [canx 05Nov04 as exported to Venezuela]
LJ-267	65-A90	N868K N503LA N5963H N416LF N416MR
LJ-268	65-A90	N573M N573ML N57V [w/o 25Jan75 Washington-National, DC, USA; canx cJun90]
LJ-269	65-A90$	N788K N507W N41DZ
LJ-270	65-A90	CF-ACB N41758 XC-FUS TP-213/XC-UTG (Mexican AF) MT-213(Mexican Navy) XB-GMY N26540 BDF-06 (Belize AF) N26540 TG-ZUM
LJ-271	65-A90	LN-VIP [w/o 28Jun68 Bodo, Norway]
LJ-272	65-A90	N5Y
LJ-273	65-A90	N620HM N5JR N585S N430C N5JR [wfu, parts to Dodson International Parts, Rantoul, KS, USA; listed in Dodson inventory as N620HM]
LJ-274	65-A90	N904K N984K N30AA N469JK [wfu, parts to Quest Aviation, Lake City, FL, USA]
LJ-275	65-A90	N905K N985K N457SR N457CP [pres Texas State Technical College, Waco, TX, USA]
LJ-276	65-A90	N574M N90VP
LJ-277	65-A90	N876K N100GB N1002B N100K N140GL N228CF N623BB
LJ-278	65-A90	N741E N741L N18LP [wfu, parts to Dodson International Parts, Rantoul, KS, USA; canx 02Nov98]
LJ-279	65-A90	N211X [b/u cSep91 Aviation Parts Exchange, TX, USA; canx 28Mar90]
LJ-280	65-A90	N46G N6228Q [pres Cumberland County Board Of Vocational Education, Bridgeton, VA, USA]
LJ-281	65-A90	N5415U VH-DYN RP-C3318 XU-999 9L-LDA C-FFRZ N39TE C-FUPD N40TE
LJ-282	65-A90	N853K N623AW [dbr 24Aug04 Atlanta-DeKalb/Peachtree, GA, USA, parts to White Industries, Bates City, MO, USA c2005; location "Taxiway SO"; canx 22Sep05]
LJ-283	65-A90	N773S
LJ-284	65-A90	N148X N2EP [w/o 13Nov90 Crestview-Bob Sikes, FL, USA; canx 23May91]
LJ-285	65-A90	N6789 N6788 PH-IND N98HB
LJ-286	65-A90$	N925B N935K N37DA N43JT
LJ-287	65-A90	N823K N502W XA- [canx 06Jan04 as exported to Mexico]
LJ-288	65-A90	N270M
LJ-289	65-A90	N579B N90D CF-VLR N90BT N35P N5WG
LJ-290	65-A90	N2046D N50JP N50JJ [wfu, parts to MTW Aerospace, Montgomery, AL, USA; canx 10Aug09]
LJ-291	65-A90	N6069C [wfu, parts to White Industries, Bates City, MO, USA; location F-20]
LJ-292	65-A90	CF-VPM N114FC N100HM N100JF LV-ZTO N827FM LV-ZTO

BEECH 90

c/n	Series/Mod	Identities
LJ-293	65-A90	N793K XC-ONA
LJ-294	65-A90+	N930K
LJ-295	65-A90	N625W N9031Y N57FM N57EM
LJ-296	65-A90	N19J N19JX N30EH XB-FJF N30EH R701 (Guatemalan AF)
LJ-297	65-A90	N839K N140PA
LJ-298	65-A90	N788W N615AA
LJ-299	65-A90	N312RF N312VF (N312MH) N312VF
LJ-300	65-A90	N886T N222MB C-GMHJ N310KR N70VM
LJ-301	65-A90	N800Q N11FL A9C-?? [canx 30Jun06 as exported to Bahrain]
LJ-302	65-A90	N229C N229CH N999LL OB-1305 [w/o 11Oct91 Rio Diamante, Peru; canx 21Dec01]
LJ-303	65-A90	N848K N55MP N55MG [w/o 26Nov77 nr Charleston, SC, USA]
LJ-304	65-A90	N656A [wfu, parts to White Industries, Bates City, MO, USA; location F-29]
LJ-305	65-A90	N732NM (N962HB) (N722NM) N525JK
LJ-306	65-A90+	N129GP N720R N720RL OY-ASH N223K YV-70CP YV-722P YV-06CP YV-2683P N124SA
LJ-307	65-A90+	N338 N833 N966CY N66RE (N811LT) N66RE
LJ-308	65-A90	N7010N VT-DXU N970GA N577DC
LJ-309	65-A90	N329H CF-HWI C-FHWI [b/u; canx 10May04]
LJ-310	65-A90	N772K [wfu, parts to Dodson International Parts, Rantoul, KS, USA]
LJ-311	65-A90	N909K N10XL N114SV F-GIGP HB-GIN F-GNBA N712DB [dbr 22Aug06 Knock, Eire, parts to Westcan Aircraft Sales & Salvage, Kamloops, BC, Canada]
LJ-312	65-A90	N675SP N45TT [w/o 17Aug04 Pensacola-Regional, FL, USA; canx 23Aug07]
LJ-313	65-A90	CF-CGN C-FCGN
LJ-314	65-A90	N991LL N971LL N971EL N707CE [w/o 29May90 Tamanrasset, Algeria]
LJ-315	65-A90	N940K N110EC N940K XB-FJM N34HA [dam 22Sep03 nr Summerville-Dorchester County, SC, USA]
LJ-316	65-A90	N758K N30PC N30PQ YV-79CP XB-BZQ N758K
LJ-317	65-A90	N46A N46AX
LJ-318	B90	N725K N425K [pres inst airframe, Middle Georgia Technical College, GA, USA; canx 16Jan04]
LJ-319	B90	N845K N1999G
LJ-320	VC-6A	N2085W 66-7943 (USAF) [pres USAF Museum, Dayton-Wright/Patterson AFB USAF Museum, OH, USA]
LJ-321	B90	N877K N15MR N22RJ N22WE N269RR N223CH
LJ-322	B90	N8133 N45SC OB-1594
LJ-323	B90	N716K N90SM LV-VHR
LJ-324	B90	N719K N512PC N829DF D2-EQC
LJ-325	B90	N717K N10121 N900LD (N900FP) N900LD C-FJHP [w/o 23Aug98 St-Tite-Des-Caps, QC, Canada; canx 24Sep98]
LJ-326	B90	N770M N7702 OB-T-1297 OB-1297
LJ-327	B90	N827K (N507M) OY-JRO G-OJRO N902WW
LJ-328	B90	N7041N N777W N730K C-GQDD [wfu, parts to Dodson International Parts, Rantoul, KS, USA; listed in Dodson inventory as C-GOOD; canx 11May87]
LJ-329	B90	N303X N17CD HK-1805X HK-1805E HK-1805 [b/u; canx 09May00]
LJ-330	B90	N404X N66MS N19MK N711GD OB-1364 [dbr 04Jun92 Tingo Maria, Peru; CofA exp 28Apr98]
LJ-331	B90	N19Y N20Z N107VM N86BD N886BD F-GEXK [w/o 21Feb94 Propriano, Corsica; canx 21Feb94]
LJ-332	B90	N919K N7127 N440TC (N1301L) N442TC [dbr 23Feb93 Albert Lea-Municipal, MN, USA, parts to White Industries, Bates City, MO, USA; location F-16]
LJ-333	B90	N891K OB-1495 LV-WRM
LJ-334	B90	N744K N611ER N611EP N722TS N621TB
LJ-335	B90	N7644R
LJ-336	B90	CF-HBW C-FHBW [pres Danish Government Training School, Copenhagen-Kastrup; canx 19Apr91]
LJ-337	B90	N9551Q ZS-NOK N67262 N69J C-GHVR
LJ-338	B90	N7138N VR-UDV N280K C-FCBJ N280K ZS-LWZ 9J-YVZ
LJ-339	B90$	N766K N211SC N120LG N143KB (F-GKTY) F-WKTY LX-KTY
LJ-340	B90#	N925B N240K
LJ-341	B90	N91MK N91ML N91NC N33FM N83FM YV [canx 24Jul07 as exported to Venezuela]
LJ-342	B90	XB-GIW XA-CIC XB-PEZ XA-MIM N876L
LJ-343	B90	N880X (N57AJ) N57AG
LJ-344	B90	N873K [impounded cMar96 wearing false marks HK-3965P]
LJ-345	B90	N914K N5500S N550TS C-GWCY [w/o 12Oct81 Lynn Lake, MB, Canada; canx 06Dec88]
LJ-346	B90	PP-FNZ PT-FNZ PP-FHG PP-EOC PT-WTN
LJ-347	B90	D-IEVV N333JJ N76RJ N76AS N38RH N3290A N1TV N777SB F-GFHQ N2ZN
LJ-348	B90	N805K C-GTMA
LJ-349	B90	N939K
LJ-350	B90	N579DU (N5798) N579DU N7BF *N319D
LJ-351	B90	N2100E N105K C-GNIS N62BW N90LG [dbr 20Feb97 in Antigua, parts to Dodson International Parts, Rantoul, KS, USA]
LJ-352	B90	N345RC C-GBTV VR-BHT C-GBTI [dbr 06Jun91 Fort Frances, ON, Canada, parts to Atlanta Air Salvage, Griffin-Spalding County, GA, USA; canx 01Nov91]
LJ-353	B90	PT-FOA PT-OBW
LJ-354	B90	N558DB N1000W N400AM (N506M) N400AM [w/o 10Oct83 Burlington-Municipal, CO, USA]
LJ-355	B90	PT-DEU
LJ-356	B90	PI-C202 RP-C202 [b/u c1992 Manila, Philippines, parts to Dodson International Parts, Rantoul, KS, USA; CofA exp 05Jan90]

BEECH 90

c/n	Series/Mod	Identities
LJ-357	B90	N887K N887KU YV [canx 26Apr04 as exported to Venezuela; hijacked & stolen 24Apr04 still as N887KU]
LJ-358	B90	N603H N40CK N934LD N61HT N60HT YV [canx 20Apr09 as exported to Venezuela]
LJ-359	B90	N7077N D-ILTU [w/o 22Jan71 Altkonig Mountain, nr Frankfurt-am-Main, West Germany; canx 29Jan71]
LJ-360	B90	N1250 N1250B N125A
LJ-361	B90	N530M N587M
LJ-362	B90	N1290B N869D N869U N31SV N31SN
LJ-363	B90	N959B N95GR N81648 N43TC N303WJ F-GICE
LJ-364	B90	N713K N49LD N49FD N555TB N110SL [wfu, parts to Atlanta Air Salvage, Griffin-Spalding County, GA, USA; canx 08Aug98]
LJ-365	B90$	N833K N14V N14VK RP-C2208
LJ-366	B90	N920P N812M N812G N66CD N68CD
LJ-367	B90F	N726K N72WE N9711B N321DZ
LJ-368	B90	N1100D C-GDOM [w/o 16Oct88 Fort Simpson, NT, Canada; canx 03Jul91]
LJ-369	B90	N1899 N18991 (N621CF) N700U N70CU N20LA N129RW N672LS
LJ-370	B90$	N7529N N9820 YV-P-DPN YV-555CP YV-40CP YV-1947P YV-898CP YV1599 [also reported as YV1094 in INAC records]
LJ-371	B90	N718K
LJ-372	B90	N534H N600BN N600NW N800KA N301TS (N302TS) N301DK [w/o 22May99 in Pacific ocean off Mokuleia, HI, USA; canx 13Aug99]
LJ-373	B90	CF-PAW N23KA C-GWGT N136J N99KA N275LE
LJ-374	B90	N290WL CF-DCA N725F C-GLEB N54CF N32SV N54CF YV1568
LJ-375	B90	N920K N90BW N90RW N101BS N110BS N101BS
LJ-376	B90	N729K N919GT N3UA N300RV C-FMKD
LJ-377	B90	N8473N N777KU [w/o 17Feb04 nr Dodge City Regional, KS, USA]
LJ-378	B90	N727K N595AF N320E YV-2816P [dam 15Nov04 by Yak-40 YV-1100CP at Caracas-Gen.Franc de Miranda AB, Venezuela]
LJ-379	B90	N732K N73LC N9TW [wfu & canx 15Jun01]
LJ-380	B90	N738K N30XY N70Q N4270 C-GHLA N66AD
LJ-381	B90	N117VA N1VA N11VA N91DT N48A N49GN
LJ-382	B90	N922K N25DC EC-860 F-GLED F-WQCC EC-939 EC-GIJ
LJ-383	B90	N734K N19GR N17GR N49M N607AB N607AE N63GA N63GB N388MC YV [canx 15May04 as exported to Venezuela]
LJ-384	B90	N736K N563MC HP- [canx 22Jun06 as exported to Panama]
LJ-385	B90	N745K N33AS N130DM (N777WN) N130DM
LJ-386	B90	N743K N610K N899D
LJ-387	B90	N824K XB-CIO [w/o 07Mar97 Pesqueira, Nuevo Leon, Mexico]
LJ-388	B90	N654MT N94BA N93HA N93EJ XB-HCL
LJ-389	B90	N829K N75Z N410PD (N412PD) N429K N745JB C-GPPN [w/o 22Dec84 Sanikiluaq, NT, Canada; canx 12Dec88]
LJ-390	B90	N741K N567CS YV-94P N741K N701AT
LJ-391	B90	CF-FAR N22JJ N55MG
LJ-392	B90	N771HM N64406 N392CA N121HC N392TW [impounded 15Jun03 in Guatemala]
LJ-393	B90	N757K N300CT N800CT N221NC (F-GSJL) N221NC [dbr 25Jun99 Creede-Mineral County Memorial, CO, USA, parts to White Industries, Bates City, MO, USA; location "Taxiway SO"; canx 02Jul02]
LJ-394	B90	N803K N500TM C-GASR N394AL [dam 10Aug03 Louisa-County/Freeman Field, VA, USA]
LJ-395	B90	N604 N604B N81PA N81PG ZS-PFA
LJ-396	B90	N783K N70SM YV [canx 25Feb04 as exported to Venezuela]
LJ-397	B90	N8482N ZS-TBS ZS-INY ZS-BEN (ZS-OYN) ZS-OYS A6-SKY
LJ-398	B90	PT-DIQ
LJ-399	B90	N5511A N55UA N551E N551F N551AT XA- [canx 10Jun04 as exported to Mexico]
LJ-400	B90	N773K N73BF N3500R N500PP N3500R N500PP N501PP OB-1595 [w/o 02Apr93 Tingo Maria, Peru; canx 21Dec01]
LJ-401	B90	N419D N396DP N396DR N8NP N8NM N500NA N590SA
LJ-402	B90	N925B N925BA ZS-IBE 9Q-CKM
LJ-403	B90	N746K N241Q N2000X N603PA (N603RE) N603PA
LJ-404	B90	N233MW N238MW N825T N835BG N90MT N90NM (N900JA) N90NM
LJ-405	B90	N751K N474L N473L N68RT OB-1558 YV1342 [dbr 17Oct94 San Miguel, Peru; registered 13Oct05 as YV1342]
LJ-406	B90+	N749K N438 N226JW
LJ-407	B90	D-ILTP N98949 [w/o 05May82 Charlotte, TX, USA]
LJ-408	B90	D-ILTA N107GA N481SA ZS-MUM
LJ-409	B90	PP-EUE
LJ-410	B90	N838K XB-MAZ N961K N33CS N901WL
LJ-411	B90$	N807K N14V
LJ-412	B90	N753K N56K N20Z N8093W N41DZ [b/u; canx 17Dec98]
LJ-413	B90	N907K CP-872 FAB-001 (Bolivian AF) FAB-006 (Bolivian AF) [w/o 26Apr79 El Alto, Bolivia]
LJ-414	B90	N45V N11WC N1U N1UA C-GVCC N57MA
LJ-415	B90	N210X N87MM
LJ-416	B90	N869K N444SR [w/o 17Feb85 Los Alamitos, CA, USA]
LJ-417	B90	G-AWPM N29TC N44RG
LJ-418	B90	N725K N715K N49CM (N49CN) OY-BVS OK-XKN SE-LEN OY-BVS [wfu cJul08]
LJ-419	B90	N885W N88AT N63BW N11TE N11TN
LJ-420	B90	N759K N759KX N642DH
LJ-421	B90	N9426

BEECH 90

c/n	Series/Mod	Identities
LJ-422	B90	N360X N360XL N513SC C-GSFM
LJ-423	B90	HB-GDT 7T-VSH [w/o cJan76 in Algeria]
LJ-424	B90F	N638D
LJ-425	B90	N754K N109KH N110SM N41LH N93WB N767LD N90BU
LJ-426	B90	N761K (N713JF) N761K
LJ-427	B90	N784K [wfu, parts to Atlanta Air Salvage, Griffin-Spalding County, GA, USA; canx 15Mar89]
LJ-428	B90	N1590B N74GP N74GR LV-VHO
LJ-429	B90	N363DB N363CB N811AA N984AA
LJ-430	B90	N573DU (N573P) N551SS (N225CF) N41WC
LJ-431	B90	N925S 9Q-CVT ZS-OHB
LJ-432	B90	N778K N345CS N345LL N919AG
LJ-433	B90	HB-GDV [w/o 24Jan86 Klein-Ober, Austria; canx 05Mar86]
LJ-434	B90	HB-GDU OE-FDU N14GA C-GRCN F-GFIR
LJ-435	B90	D-ILVW (D-IHGH) D-IHCH N9838Z
LJ-436	B90	N309L N221CH [w/o 14May01 San Jon, NM, USA; canx 05Jul01]
LJ-437	B90	N177G N12JG N90DN
LJ-438	B90	N1153S N1PB N2296W N7PB N720HC N910E N900LS N988SL
LJ-439	B90	N480K [w/o 27Dec71 in Atlantic nr Bahamas]
LJ-440	B90	N785K N711HS N1HS N19HS N181LL [w/o 05Apr88 St.Paul, MN, USA; canx 09Apr91]
LJ-441	B90	CC-ECF 209 (Chilean Army) CC-PBZ CC-CVZ CC-PTZ CC-PBE CC-CVZ
LJ-442	B90	N36MK N365K N36PR N45MC N388MC N745LP N388MC [w/o 10Jan78 nr Yazoo City-Barrier Field, MS, USA]
LJ-443	B90	N796K N411FT
LJ-444	B90	N5111C N40BA
LJ-445	B90	N832K N700CS N70CS N230TW [w/o 05Jan94 nr Okeechobee, FL, USA]
LJ-446	B90	G-AWWK G-BHGT G-BLNA N7138C [wfu, parts to Dodson International Parts, Rantoul, KS, USA; canx cJul93]
LJ-447	B90	N926S C-GSUN N926S [wfu Dillingham Field, Oahu, HI, USA; canx 12Apr06]
LJ-448	B90	CF-YFD N211BT N722S N428DN OB-1362 [w/o 31Jul90 Huanuco, Peru; canx 30Apr93]
LJ-449	B90	LV-PIZ LV-JJW
LJ-450	B90	N977LX N979LX N6881S [wfu, parts to Dodson International Parts, Rantoul, KS, USA]
LJ-451	B90	N896K OB-1361 [dbr 18Feb91 Uchiza, Peru, parts to Dodson International Parts, Rantoul, KS, USA & b/u; canx 30Apr93]
LJ-452	B90	D-ILKA N452TT YV [canx 10May05 as exported to Venezuela]
LJ-453	B90	D-ILTO (F-GFPI) F-GIFB (D-IAMX) 5V-TTD
LJ-454	B90	N297LE N297PT N297W N12AM N12AQ N113SD N105RJ N105RG
LJ-455	B90	N806K N712J N712K N712KA N111US N211WT HI-605 N444WG PT-OYD N444WG HP- [canx 06Feb07 as exported to Panama]
LJ-456	B90	D-ILTY F-GIFC J5-GTF
LJ-457	B90	N855K N25BL N606MM N696MM N405BC N299MS [canx 03Sep08 - fate unkn]
LJ-458	B90$	N963M N9636 HK-853X HK-853P HK-853W 458 (Guatemalan AF)
LJ-459	B90$	N843K N2JR N9HW
LJ-460	B90	N814K N55LM N10KF F-ODMQ N460KA F-GHAU N113TT PT-WBQ
LJ-461	B90	N809K (N753SR) N453SR N90WL
LJ-462	B90	N821K N2GG [w/o 15Feb75 nr Joliet-Municipal, IL, USA; canx 04Mar76]
LJ-463	B90	N431U N43RE N43MB (N300A) N43MB
LJ-464	B90	N813K N36DD YV [canx 10Jun05 as exported to Venezuela]
LJ-465	B90	OB-M-932 OB-S-932 OB-T-932 OB-932 [w/o 26Jun96 Lima, Peru; canx 21Dec01]
LJ-466	B90	PT-CGK PP-IAG PT-ODA
LJ-467	B90	N944K
LJ-468	B90	N831K N1FC C-FNCN
LJ-469	B90	N836K XA-COQ N90GB HK- [canx 14Nov05 as exported to Colombia]
LJ-470	B90	N490K SE-GUU [w/o 15Oct85 Sindal Flyveplads, Denmark; canx 10Jan86]
LJ-471	B90	N861K [b/u Dodson International Parts, Rantoul, KS, USA]
LJ-472	B90	N104Z (N204FW) N148Z
LJ-473	B90	N9390C N90CB [status in question - may have been pres as inst airframe]
LJ-474	B90	N943K N14RA N474H [wfu, parts to White Industries, Bates City, MO, USA; location F-22; canx 12Sep89]
LJ-475	B90	N851K N500RK N32BA
LJ-476	B90	N882K N21CT N21AK N41AA N10TM [w/o 19Sep07 nr Chattanooga-Lovell Field, TN, USA; canx 12Jun09]
LJ-477	B90	N841K N7777 OB-1593 OB-1593-P [wfu; CofA exp 10Nov03; canx 20Feb04]
LJ-478	B90	N40WS N7TW
LJ-479	B90	N10A N11PA N11LA (N502M) N74MA [wfu c1998 Denver-Centennial/Arapahoe County, CO, USA; canx 24Oct02]
LJ-480	B90	N847K N270SF N270SE N31SV N92BA N2UV
LJ-481	B90#	G-AXFE G-KJET G-BVRS N670AT
LJ-482	B90	HB-GEE F-BRNO
LJ-483	B90	N210K N83TC
LJ-484	B90	9J-AAT A2-ZGT ZS-KLW N242DA [wfu, parts to White Industries, Bates City, MO, USA; still marked as ZS-KLW; canx 31May90]
LJ-485	B90	9J-AAU ZS-AAU Z-WNB ZS-AAU 9J-TAF ZS-PRT
LJ-486	B90	9J-AAV A2-JZT 9J-AAV
LJ-487	B90	N529M N529V [wfu, parts to White Industries, Bates City, MO, USA; location F-17]
LJ-488	B90	YV-P-HPN YV-O-KWH-1 YV-2229P YV-258CP
LJ-489	B90	N933K N75GP N750P HR-IAI N90RZ LV-ZXZ LV-BDU

BEECH 90

c/n	Series/Mod	Identities
LJ-490	B90	N814K N44WC N45BC N881M N881MX N881LT N81AT [wfu cJan08, parts to MTW Aerospace, Montgomery, AL, USA]
LJ-491	B90	N727K N900BR N88RB N88RP
LJ-492	B90	N852K N1653H N111WA N171VA LN-KAR N160H LN-HAC N492PA
LJ-493	B90	N826K F-BSRP N388AS LV-WMD N338AS [w/o 03Sep99 nr West Palm Beach International, FL, USA]
LJ-494	B90	N884K N4HC (N15LM) N4HC 9Q-CKZ [wfu Lubumbashi, Zaire; canx 29Oct96]
LJ-495	B90	N950K N803SM N395DA (N600AL) N71WH YV [canx 03Sep04 as exported to Venezuela]
LJ-496	B90	N878K (F-GFLQ) N579PS
LJ-497	B90	N9019Q ZS-IHZ [w/o 26Dec92 Cape Town-D.F.Malan International, Cape Province, South Africa; canx 16Aug93]
LJ-498	B90	N918K (XB-SIR) N100CH N100CQ N76GM [dbr 24Jan97 Longmont, CO, USA, parts to Dodson International Parts, Rantoul, KS, USA]
LJ-499	B90	8P-BAR N87720 YV-TASK YV-273P N44454 PT-OUO YV2327 [w/o 21Dec07 off Saona Island, Dominican Republic]
LJ-500	B90	N21CH N20WC C-GCFL
LJ-501	B90	N865M N865MA N43WA (N144SL) N43WA
LJ-502	C90^	N881K N88HM
LJ-503	C90	N193A "N423M" FAC5730 (Colombian AF) [canx 19Aug05 as exported to Venezuela; impounded cSep05 wearing false marks N423M & tfd to Colombian military]
LJ-504	C90	N908K VH-WWA N908K (N479SJ) N908K
LJ-505	C90	N886K N1PT [wfu, parts to Dodson International Parts, Rantoul, KS, USA; canx 31May90]
LJ-506	C90	N90KA N10AC N3TH N63TH N30HF N32CC
LJ-507	C90	N92090 N91074 N1PT N5PT N25ST [w/o 21Aug89 Gold Beach, OR, USA; canx 16Nov89]
LJ-508	C90	N938K N801MP N706DG N708DG
LJ-509	C90	D-ILHA [wfu 13Sep88; canx 07Mar89 (TT 13408); pres as inst airframe Hamburg-Fuhlsbuttel, Germany; moved 12Feb03 to Ahrenlohe, Germany]
LJ-510	C90$	D-ILHB F-GHBB XU-HBB
LJ-511	C90	N812NB N516SW N616PA N45BA N1UV YV144T YV1250 [also reported as YV1011 in INAC records]
LJ-512	C90	N659H N221MJ [w/o 04Nov75 Charleston-Kanawha, WV, USA; canx 14Jan76]
LJ-513	C90	N913K N886J D-IFTC N913K 4X-DZT
LJ-514	C90	N111JW N111HR N88CR [w/o 16Jan79 nr Houston-Andrau Airpark, TX, USA]
LJ-515	C90	N953K PT-OIU
LJ-516	C90	N555RH N711FC [w/o 20Dec73 Columbia Metropolitan, SC, USA]
LJ-517	C90$	N733K N33KA N733KA N738RH N738R
LJ-518	C90	HB-GEZ F-BTCA 518/F-ZBBF (French Customs) [w/o 17Jul94 Ajaccio, Corsica]
LJ-519	C90	XB-GAS XA-RUI N82307 N290PA
LJ-520	C90	N880M N1869 HP- [canx 08Apr03 as exported to Panama]
LJ-521	C90	N700Z N70QZ N901BK
LJ-522	C90	D-IHVB F-BXAP
LJ-523	C90	N9258Q ZS-INN N523CR ZS-INN V5-INN ZS-INN [w/o 23Dec01 nr Cradock, Eastern Cape Province, South Africa; canx 22Aug06]
LJ-524	C90	N77RC N77RQ N19CM N19UM
LJ-525	C90	N1857W N1857A ZK-UPA N70MT N90WJ
LJ-526	C90	N948K ZS-MLO N54EC
LJ-527	C90	N55SC N55SG EC-GOY
LJ-528	C90	N928K N92PL N5GA ZS-MNT (5R-M??) N883AV 5Y-NBB [wfu Nairobi-Wilson, Kenya]
LJ-529	C90#	N89BF N898F N55MP (N55MJ) N78AM N78SE (N74DE) LV-WJP N290DP
LJ-530	C90	N404VW N3KF [wfu cJun08, parts to MTW Aerospace, Montgomery, AL, USA]
LJ-531	C90	PT-IBE [CofA exp c1978; b/u]
LJ-532	C90	G-AZBM N900TB N57SC N575C
LJ-533	C90	N739K N75RS
LJ-534	C90	N7SP N79P N120JJ PT-OFC
LJ-535	C90	N794K PT-OXU
LJ-536	C90	N21WF N31WB XA- [canx 03Sep03 as exported to Mexico]
LJ-537	C90	N9030V VT-ECA N537EC N133LA N101SS
LJ-538	C90	N854K N8088V VH-LLS N65TA
LJ-539	C90	N936K [w/o 03Jan73 Blairstown, IA, USA]
LJ-540	C90	N9298Q N80WA N123SK
LJ-541	C90	N9314Q N4TS [w/o 24Oct83 Fort Wayne, IN, USA]
LJ-542	C90+	N9442Q N90KH
LJ-543	C90	G-AZGG N29791 PT-LTF
LJ-544	C90	D-ILHC (F-GHFC) F-GHFE [wfu Cergy-Pontoise, France]
LJ-545	C90	D-ILHD F-GHBD
LJ-546	C90$	N715DM N508T N45PL N45BE N90RG [dbr 06Aug92 Pontiac-Oakland, MI, USA; tfd to Dynamic Aviation Group for spares use]
LJ-547	C90	[completed as c/n LW-1]
LJ-548	C90	N937K N800PW XA-ACG
LJ-549	C90	N9449Q N600DJ N531CS
LJ-550	C90	N9450Q XB-FRW N9450Q
LJ-551	C90	N9376Q ZS-ITH ZS-XAC ZS-MCA
LJ-552	C90	N927K (N100JW) N928K N614ML N456VC P2-PNB P2-DCA VH-AMH VH-WNT N53EC
LJ-553	C90	XC-FOC
LJ-554	C90	N897K G-BJMN F-GESC N12AC N697MB N12AC N697MB N697MP YV2410
LJ-555	C90	N9498Q N100JD N108JD N977AA

BEECH 90

c/n	Series/Mod	Identities
LJ-556	C90	N9456Q YV-T-ADF YV-818P YV-465CP [hijacked Tocuyito, Venezuela 15Jul00; fate unkn]
LJ-557	C90	N9457Q N870D N870B N101CG N101GG C-GQPC N9066N [w/o 12Jul94 Ciudad Construction, Peru; registration was canx 08Jul94 as exported to Peru but no marks were ever allocated]
LJ-558	C90	PT-ICP
LJ-559	C90	[completed as c/n LW-2]
LJ-560	C90	F-BTDP [w/o 17Dec74 Marseille, France; canx 10Mar76]
LJ-561	C90	N962M N25BW N8AF N8AH N10120 N80CM N851MK N777NW N904DJ
LJ-562	C90	N137B (N333FJ) D-IIHA
LJ-563	C90	N139B
LJ-564	C90	N146B VH-CRG N246DA N777GF
LJ-565	C90	N711MD N711MP N45RL
LJ-566	C90	N77CT N79CT N67PC N67PL N515KJ
LJ-567	C90	PP-FBW PT-FBW PP-IAF PT-OCT
LJ-568	C90	N1790W N100KU N108KU
LJ-569	C90	N180B [wfu, parts to White Industries, Bates City, MO, USA; location F-23; canx 22Jan09]
LJ-570	C90	N100FB N100FF N240RL C-GMPA N240RL N240RE N73MH
LJ-571	C90	N1811W N666HB D-IEWT HB-GIB D-ILKB N183SA
LJ-572	C90	N4PS N46RF N35TV
LJ-573	C90	N25620 N210MA N707RW N90LB
LJ-574	C90	N25674 N78AM N318F (N1097S) N318F
LJ-575	C90	N90BW N90BR N92996 N12RF 9J-DCF
LJ-576	C90	N3GC
LJ-577	C90	N57KA EC-HMA
LJ-578	C90	N58KA N58GP N8BG N84JH N71KA
LJ-579	C90	D-INAF F-BVTB
LJ-580	C90	N9LD N9EN (F-GFYI) N580RA
LJ-581	C90$	N1090W (N109JB) (N581VP) N717X N717XP N717X
LJ-582	C90$	N66KA
LJ-583	C90	N216K N21WB N200TG (N202W) N820SL
LJ-584	C90	N33GB D-IHKR N18CD N243TC PT-LYW N73LK XA-TXK
LJ-585	C90	N14CP
LJ-586	C90$	N60KA PR-XKY
LJ-587	C90	N61KA TC-AUV
LJ-588	C90	N4333W N298S N711BL N711BN
LJ-589	C90	N59KA
LJ-590	C90	N24BL N243L 9J-GCF [w/o 16Aug90 Serenje, Zambia]
LJ-591	C90	N68KA D-IKCC HB-GIF F-GJFL N108TT YV-2466P [w/o 13Jun01 Fort Lauderdale-International, FL, USA]
LJ-592	C90$	N3CR N77DE N77BE N777WC N41CV N383DA N90EL
LJ-593	C90	N90KA OY-AZA [w/o 15Jan79 Copenhagen-Kastrup, Denmark; canx 27Jul82]
LJ-594	C90	N3094W N90ZH
LJ-595	C90$	N3095W N3KT N3UT N19LW N119LW N19UW (N595AS) N767MC
LJ-596	C90	N2896W N880H
LJ-597	TC-90	N1845W 6801 (JMSDF)
LJ-598	TC-90	N1846W 6802 (JMSDF) [wfu Tokushima AB, Tokushima Prefecture, Japan]
LJ-599	TC-90	N1847W 6803 (JMSDF) [wfu Hachinohe AB, Aomori Prefecture, Japan]
LJ-600	C90	N3PR N73MC
LJ-601	C90	N99CD HP-918 N99CD N611AY
LJ-602	C90	F-BUTV [dbf 28Jul92 Toussus Le Noble, France; canx 28Jul92]
LJ-603	C90	EC-CDI E.22-1 (Spanish AF) E.22-04/42-33 (Spanish AF) E.22-04/409-33 (Spanish AF)
LJ-604	C90	N1GC N1GV G-BKID [w/o 26Dec83 nr Copenhagen-Kastrup, Denmark; canx 13Aug84]
LJ-605	C90	EC-CDJ E.22-2 (Spanish AF) E.22-05/42-34 (Spanish AF) E.22-05/409-34 (Spanish AF)
LJ-606	C90	N64KA
LJ-607	C90	N678GP N48DA C-GKBB
LJ-608	C90	EC-CDK E.22-3 (Spanish AF) EC-CDK
LJ-609	C90	N963M (N963E) Z-TAB Z-WSG N38BA C-GRSL
LJ-610	C90	N62HB N624B N537JH (N16GM) N55GM N555AN F-GFJD N89TM (N169WD) N89TM
LJ-611	C90	N65KA
LJ-612	C90	N3112W N999ES
LJ-613	C90	N3053W ZS-LTF
LJ-614	C90	G-BBKN G-COTE G-OMET G-BNAT [w/o 25Jan88 East Midlands, UK; canx 03Oct88]
LJ-615	C90	N444PS (N38DG) N444PS
LJ-616	C90	N1970T N1MB N1MX SE-GXD I-LIPO C-GMVP
LJ-617	C90	CF-FAS C-FFAS N65GH N1310T
LJ-618	C90	N4318W N92AM N900DG N900DZ
LJ-619	C90	N166SM G-BKAK ST-AIR G-BKAK N7128J ZS-NDH "5Y-MEL" 5Y-MAL (ZS-NDH) N72154 [wfu, parts to Dodson International Parts, Rantoul, KS, USA]
LJ-620	C90	N74CC [w/o 18Jan00 Somerset, KY, USA]
LJ-621	C90	EC-CHA E.22-4 (Spanish AF) E.22-02/42-31 (Spanish AF) E.22-02/409-31 (Spanish AF)
LJ-622	C90	F-BUYS N104TT TC-AUT
LJ-623	C90	EC-CHB E.22-5 (Spanish AF) EC-CHB [w/o 01Oct80 Salamanca, Spain; parts used as a simulator]
LJ-624	C90	EC-CHC E.22-6 (Spanish AF) E.22-03/42-32 (Spanish AF) [w/o 18Feb04 Parla, Spain]
LJ-625	C90$	N4425W N50AB ZS-NWC
LJ-626	C90	N4488W N3CR N9CR N500MS N501MS
LJ-627	C90+	N4447W
LJ-628	C90+	F-BVEZ (D-IDSB) 3A-MIE F-GNUV N800RP (N800KD) N308RM
LJ-629	C90	YV-E-APM YV-39CP N4950C

BEECH 90

c/n	Series/Mod	Identities
LJ-630	C90	N1974H G-BMXO N840SW XA-SGQ N22BM N21SP
LJ-631	C90	G-BBVK N100VM N103FG C-FLTC
LJ-632	C90	N71FN N71EN
LJ-633	C90	N4463W [w/o 30Nov87 Beaufort, SC, USA]
LJ-634	C90	N634KA N19R N1801B
LJ-635	C90	N5GC N5WU [dbr 16Feb98 Charleston-Yeager, WV, USA, parts to Dodson International Parts, Rantoul, KS, USA; canx 01Sep98]
LJ-636	C90	N1899 N60JT N60JE G-BIFS N85GA N222BJ N66TL
LJ-637	C90	N7311R N95BD N95DD F-GCLD
LJ-638	C90	PT-KFV PP-EHE
LJ-639	C90	N3019W [w/o 25Jun99 Munson, FL, USA]
LJ-640	C90	N4484W N94AM N942M N750RC
LJ-641	C90	N7338R N27CG N7338R G-BMEF N7128H D-IKIW N9UZ
LJ-642	TC-90	N7312R 6804 (JMSDF)
LJ-643	C90	N2WC N2WX N80AM N36JF N159G (N36CW) N36BE N999HC N909HC N96AH
LJ-644	C90	N9026R N333NB N333MW (N888MW) N888DR N777SJ N66CN VH-LQH [w/o 27Nov01 Toowoomba, QLD, Australia; canx 18Jan02]
LJ-645	C90^	N9027R N90CT (N999MJ) N90CT
LJ-646	C90	N4146S [w/o 18Apr75 Grand Rapids, MN, USA]
LJ-647	C90	N9075S LX-DAK D-IDAK
LJ-648	C90	F-BXSL N118HC
LJ-649	C90	N7249R N77WD N33HC N38CA F-GIJD (OO-MLC) N102AJ YV [canx 07Jan08 as exported to Venezuela]
LJ-650	C90	N9077S N103FL N103BL
LJ-651	C90	N7256R YV-T-ASS YV-127P N3834P N7300N (N7300K) PT-LUF
LJ-652	C90	N4072S N43GT [w/o 01Oct89 Atlanta, GA, USA; canx 14Jun90]
LJ-653	C90	N9053S N400N N585TC N586TC
LJ-654	C90$	N917K N152WW
LJ-655	C90	N4095S VH-NQH VH-SAM
LJ-656	C90	N600PC N15GA N888MA
LJ-657	C90	N9030R C-GTWW
LJ-658	C90	F-BXAR N2270B [w/o cJan79 in California, USA]
LJ-659	C90$^	YV-T-AOV YV-02P YV-410CP YV-2034P YV-1037CP YV1595
LJ-660	C90	N9060S N906GP N70FG ZS-LXL [Illegally exported from South Africa 30Aug93; wfu Kinshasa, Democratic Republic of Congo]
LJ-661	C90	N4140S N26CS (N969BH) N88SD N90ME
LJ-662	C90$	RP-C3650 N136PA
LJ-663	C90	EC-COI E.22-7 (Spanish AF) EC-COI [dbr 19Oct89 Salamanca, Spain; parts to Ocana, Spain cMay96]
LJ-664	C90	EC-COJ E.22-8 (Spanish AF) EC-COJ [w/o 04Oct83 Salamanca, Spain]
LJ-665	C90	EC-COK E.22-9 (Spanish AF) EC-COK N665JK
LJ-666	C90	EC-COL E.22-10 (Spanish AF) EC-COL E.22-01/42-30 (Spanish AF) E.22-01/409-30 (Spanish AF)
LJ-667	C90	N9067S G-BMZD N888GN (F-GJDQ) F-GQJD
LJ-668	C90	N9069S N906RS F-GGMO F-OGOX N668WJ HK-4357X HK-4357P
LJ-669	C90$^	N9397S ST-AFO ZS-OHR
LJ-670	TC-90	N9399S 6805 (JMSDF)
LJ-671	C90	N9071S N4RT N4RS C-GDPC N771CP ZS-MNC N99LM ZS-MNC N89FF *PR-CGN
LJ-672	C90	(N672KA) F-BXOM HB-GIC N989GA N221TM (N11AB) N717JG
LJ-673	C90	N9073S N666JM N660JM N660GW
LJ-674	C90	N9074S N332DE
LJ-675	C90$	N1870S N1876S N456Q N458Q V5-CSB ZS-ODV N973GA
LJ-676	C90	N9114S N90MM N224BH N37KH N605DK N1DK N26RE
LJ-677	C90$	N12AW N555WF N555CK N990LS
LJ-678	C90+	N9091S N150VE
LJ-679	C90$	N90ML N90MU
LJ-680	C90#	N1580L N185G G-BKZW N7138E N928RD C-FNED
LJ-681	C90$	N1581L N90PW
LJ-682	C90$	N9082S HP-752 N3980D N682KA
LJ-683	C90	N1583L PT-MPC N269SC (F-GVEP) N269SC
LJ-684	C90	F-BXPY
LJ-685	C90	N1585L N110SF N110SE (N912SM) C-FATW C-FHLP
LJ-686	C90$	N100BX N100BT N400BX
LJ-687	C90$	N165CB N127P Z-WRD
LJ-688	C90	N14KA N195KC (N57CC) N195KQ N911FN
LJ-689	C90	N431BT HP-823 N114NB N156SC N5WF N689EB N100QT
LJ-690	C90	N2090L N80TB N690JP [dbr 09Oct01 nr Dallas-Love Field, TX, USA, parts to Dodson International Parts, Rantoul, KS, USA; canx 28Oct02]
LJ-691	C90$	N9061S N752HB JA8839 N62525
LJ-692	C90+	N4292S N438SP (N14WL) N925JW N822TJ N70FH N711KP
LJ-693	C90	YV-994P [w/o 04Feb82 Caracas, Venezuela]
LJ-694	C90$	N712K N901JA N246CK
LJ-695	C90$	N225S N93BB N695JJ
LJ-696	C90	N68DK N68DR N644SP (N144WA) (N525PC) N644SP
LJ-697	C90$	N2297L N80RE (N280RE) N384JB N90AW C-GSAX N90AW
LJ-698	C90$	TG-RBL N9872C
LJ-699	C90	N976JT N806WB
LJ-700	C90	N23700 N700FC N700CP
LJ-701	C90$	N300GC N90LJ N90MV

BEECH 90

c/n	Series/Mod	Identities
LJ-702	C90	N44HP
LJ-703	C90	N300CK (F-GKSR) N793MA TC-DBZ [w/o 24Jan00 Ankara, Turkey]
LJ-704	C90	N1565L N296AS
LJ-705	C90$	N2075L VT-EFF [w/o 30Sep01 Kanpur, Uttar Pradesh, India]
LJ-706	C90	N23856 VT-EFB
LJ-707	C90^	(N22WL) N22NL N122K (N32HF) N122K
LJ-708	C90	N90MK N26TC (N36JC) N312P N500KS N500KR
LJ-709	C90	N33TW N114CM [w/o 16Jun86 nr Jackson, WY, USA; canx 17Jan95]
LJ-710	C90	D-IAFH 3A-MON F-GJRK
LJ-711	C90	N23875 VT-EFE VT-UBA [wfu Bombay-Juhu, India; still marked as VT-EFE]
LJ-712	C90$	N900SC C-GUNG N70AB N85GW
LJ-713	C90+	N17510 N11TE N114J PR-TLL N954TG
LJ-714	C90	N17573
LJ-715	C90$	N9076S
LJ-716	C90	N25KW N25DL
LJ-717	C90	N200BX F-GFHC
LJ-718	C90	N90BP [w/o 07Aug93 Augusta Regional/Bush Field, GA, USA; canx 28Feb96]
LJ-719	C90	N23917 VT-EFG
LJ-720	C90+	N23929 VT-EFP N720RD
LJ-721	C90$	N23721 N777JJ N770TJ N757AL CS-DBT N111AA N596CU
LJ-722	C90	N23903 N90PR N1188A N35HP N38RP
LJ-723	C90	OY-ASI SE-IIB
LJ-724	C90	N5TW N5TA
LJ-725	C90	D-IHDE N939RK
LJ-726	C90$	N23947 ST-AGZ N387GA (N469PC) N434EM N405EM
LJ-727	C90	N360GK N833BK N888BK N75GC [w/o 31Jan04 Everglades National Park, FL, USA]
LJ-728	C90	N23728 (N111QP) N15JW N275Z N275X N275L N291CC
LJ-729	C90	N17647 N711VC N110LT [w/o 13Feb90 Burlington, NC, USA; canx 07Jul98]
LJ-730	C90	N23959 ZS-KAM 3D-ACO ZS-KAM N730WB VH-SQH
LJ-731	C90#	N23731 N37PW N37PT N731KA [dbr 26Jan04 Richmond-Ashland, VA, USA, parts to White Industries, Bates City, MO, USA; location "Ramp SO B-38"; canx 25Oct07]
LJ-732	C90	N214B N473LP N473BP N56DL YV [canx 17Aug09 as exported to Venezuela]
LJ-733	C90$	N18383 N977FC HK-4460X HK-4460W
LJ-734	C90	N37T F-GIBR N928JR (N700BN) N284PM
LJ-735	C90	F-GATR N190TT N819MH
LJ-736	C90$	N516SW N19HT N635AF
LJ-737	C90	N23796 [w/o 23Sep77 Pontiac, IL, USA; canx 21Dec81]
LJ-738	C90$	N23738 N738W N666PC N239C N20WP
LJ-739	C90+	YV-152CP EJC-116 (Colombian Army) EJC-010 (Colombian Army)
LJ-740	C90	N502SE (N390YH) N502SE
LJ-741	C90	I-AZIO HB-GGW F-GFLD "N33FL" (N90FL) N30FL
LJ-742	C90	YV-158CP
LJ-743	C90	N160AC N1602C N161AC N620WE
LJ-744	C90	N23744 N19HM N771PS N91TJ
LJ-745	C90+^	N92BD N92BE N384H N37CN
LJ-746	C90$	N65JL (N122RG) N322R
LJ-747	C90+^	N23756 ECT-014 EC-DDS G-MEDI G-OFBL N529JH N8MG
LJ-748	C90+	N23748 ZS-MRZ N974GA N915CD
LJ-749	C90	N93BD N93BA N552R N90EJ
LJ-750	C90$	N214D N10MD N70FE
LJ-751	C90	YV-167CP
LJ-752	C90	N4571M N100JB FAC570 (Colombian AF) FAC5570 (Colombian AF)
LJ-753	C90	N601SC N990DA
LJ-754	C90	N9078S N3030C N303QC N754TW
LJ-755	C90	N9085S 5N-AMZ
LJ-756	C90$	YV-172CP YV1245
LJ-757	C90$	N23675 N104LC
LJ-758	C90	N900SC N157CB
LJ-759	C90	N633D N11DW N133K N133E N895FK
LJ-760	C90	N319D N707CB (N90AJ) N700JP F-GHEM N362MC
LJ-761	C90	N9064S N25HB N410MC
LJ-762	C90+	N24176 N178RC N350WA
LJ-763	C90$	N78JD N9VC
LJ-764	C90$	N201KA N775DM
LJ-765	C90$	N24172 5N-WNL N191A [wfu cMay05, parts to MTW Aerospace, Montgomery, AL, USA]
LJ-766	C90$	N23804 YV-193CP YV-1930P N44VC N642TD
LJ-767	C90$	N9092S N85DR
LJ-768	C90$	OY-SBU LN-KCG OY-SBU
LJ-769	C90	N23669 N200EK N2KQ N911UM N24GJ
LJ-770	C90#	N4770M N88CG (YV-2301P) OH-BCX
LJ-771	C90$	N4774M TC-IHC
LJ-772	C90	N90JS N90RW F-GFBO N11692
LJ-773	C90+	N4773M N305AS N8TZ N728DS N711CC N711CQ
LJ-774	C90	N4742M (N713PA) N911ND N911FG
LJ-775	C90+	(D-ILMO) D-IBPL I-KWYX HB-GIW N386GA
LJ-776	C90	N4776M
LJ-777	C90	N9AN VH-KFG
LJ-778	TC-90	N23780 6806 (JMSDF)
LJ-779	C90	N216KA (N170RE) N117MF
LJ-780	C90	N4947M
LJ-781	C90	N4953M N495NM

BEECH 90

c/n	Series/Mod	Identities
LJ-782	C90	TG-VAS
LJ-783	C90$	N5083M (N11EA) (N3DF) N197SC N197CC
LJ-784	C90$	N4847M YV-254CP N62SK YV-2835P YV1349
LJ-785	C90	N666PC N666PD N999VB N998VB [dbr 28Dec96 Rhinelander, WI, USA, parts to White Industries, Bates City, MO, USA; location F-18; canx 06Dec97]
LJ-786	C90	YV-202CP YV-2620P N973AC YV-972CP YV1054
LJ-787	C90$	N40MB N31MT N81MT N170DB TC-NAZ N787TT
LJ-788	C90$	N2030W N107SC
LJ-789	C90	N2016L YV-223CP
LJ-790	C90	N4908M VT-EFZ VT-RAM
LJ-791	C90	N2035S F-GFDF N791RC PT-WDU
LJ-792	C90	N2019U [w/o 14Feb85 nr St.Marys Municipal Apt, PA, USA]
LJ-793	C90	LN-KCR [dbr 02Apr87 Skien, Norway, parts to Dodson International Parts, Rantoul, KS, USA; canx 13Sep04]
LJ-794	C90	N57JB PT-LSO
LJ-795	C90$	F-GBDY N551GA ZS-MBZ
LJ-796	C90$	N700GC N100V
LJ-797	C90	YV-216CP N310KR D-IMUC F-GIAT N61GA N797CF
LJ-798	C90	N2029N [w/o 30Dec78 Houston-Intercontinental, TX, USA; canx 21Jul82]
LJ-799	C90	OY-AZV N220TM ZP-TXE N799GK
LJ-800	C90	N2032N N60KW
LJ-801	C90	YV-217CP YV-181P N44917 N40JT N18BG TC-CSA N808SW
LJ-802	C90	N101LR [w/o 15Sep81 Quito, Ecuador; canx 28Nov82]
LJ-803	C90	G-BFVX G-OLAF N9TN N75GA N469B
LJ-804	C90$	N45EL HK-3276X HK-3276 N429DM N427DM
LJ-805	C90+	N2068W ZS-KGO G-BJSY VR-BKW VP-BKW N364UZ
LJ-806	C90	N2039B N1MB (N67AS) N105CG N611DD
LJ-807	C90	N2038Z N877W N877WL N802DG
LJ-808	C90	N2930A (N711WT) PT-LZH
LJ-809	C90	N777PR N922DT N549BR
LJ-810	C90	N359D N90CD ZS-MZG N811GA YV1973
LJ-811	C90$	N330V
LJ-812	C90	G-BFVY N627KP PT-OJI
LJ-813	C90	N2050A N517PC N2050A
LJ-814	C90+^	N20506 N96DC N96DQ
LJ-815	C90	N2057N N946AM
LJ-816	C90	N111RL N4C N40PS N416BK
LJ-817	C90$^	YV-104CP N3981Y PT-LPS
LJ-818	C90$	N97SF N77NB
LJ-819	C90	N2063A G-SHAM G-RACI
LJ-820	C90	N100KB
LJ-821	C90	N60KC C-GKCA N821CT N959MC
LJ-822	C90	F-GBLU (F-GNCY) F-GBLU
LJ-823	C90	N6023R N580C ST-ANH
LJ-824	C90$	G-RCCL N2687W N724TD N1MT
LJ-825	C90	N11LS N601DM
LJ-826	C90+^	N6026K (N20GT) (N69TX) N701XP
LJ-827	C90$	N2057C
LJ-828	C90	N6037C F-GFME I-BOMY (F-GPJC) F-GNMP
LJ-829	C90$	N6026R N7000Z HB-GIY D-IFCL N901AJ N829FC (N11FX) N98AR
LJ-830	C90	N6023Y N711WW (N911DR) N85BX N45PK N45PE N911CX
LJ-831	C90+	N6029M HK-3429X HK-3429W HK-3429
LJ-832	C90	N6032L N91LE N10CW N10QW N512RR
LJ-833	C90	N85TB (N45AW) N85TB
LJ-834	C90	N6034D N42CC N42QC PT-LVI
LJ-835	C90	D-IHCO N414AF PT-OVY
LJ-836	C90	N6646R
LJ-837	C90	N364D OK-DSH
LJ-838	C90	N445DW N445DR N445CR
LJ-839	C90	N6034Z ZS-MFA 9G-SAM N299K [w/o 29May03 in Mexico]
LJ-840	C90	N6040M [w/o 05Aug79 nr Indianapolis, IN, USA]
LJ-841	C90^	YV-249CP N249CP
LJ-842	C90	N6052F VH-FDT N23Q N90CE A2-MJM
LJ-843	C90	N6053H N605CW N843MC N843CP N404SC
LJ-844	C90	N20736 ZS-KHB N1346N N707CV PT-LQD
LJ-845	C90^	N60533 N28KC N28KP
LJ-846	C90	OY-MBA N29TB
LJ-847	C90	N90UB N317EC PT-OCY
LJ-848	C90	OY-MBB G-BKNC PH-DMJ N5397W N584NR N584PM (N317EC) TR-LCS Z-LCS
LJ-849	C90+	N6647P C-GCFZ
LJ-850	C90	N6681S
LJ-851	C90	N970V N4B N851KA
LJ-852	C90	YV-250CP N90LF
LJ-853	C90	N66853 N6LD N400RV
LJ-854	C90	N712D F-GERN [w/o 30Dec93 St.Broladre, France]
LJ-855	TC-90	N6062X 6807 (JMSDF)
LJ-856	C90$	N6652G N27RF N965J N904JS N904US
LJ-857	C90	N6064A RP-C290 [wfu cSep93; std Manila, Philippines; CofA exp 07Sep93]
LJ-858	C90	N50KW N50KJ N644S (F-GHFO) F-GHFS N270TC [w/o 18May01 Islip-Long Island MacArthur, NY, USA; canx 26Jul01]
LJ-859	C90+^	TG-POL HR-AHJ N9081R N48AZ

BEECH 90

c/n	Series/Mod	Identities
LJ-860	C90	F-GBPZ
LJ-861	C90$	N70Q N30XY N30BY N905GP N903GP N908GR
LJ-862	C90	N25CU N93DC N190CC F-GMJP N380SC N321FJ
LJ-863	C90	N6663Y N200SC N777EB
LJ-864	C90	N6663A N199TD N773PW
LJ-865	C90	YV-263CP YV1695
LJ-866	C90	N6664P N844C
LJ-867	C90	(D-IFOM) D-IIIS HB-GIH D-IEKG 3A-MKB LX-APB [wfu Singapore-Seletar; canx cSep07]
LJ-868	C90	SE-GXK N508GA F-GERL N139SC
LJ-869	C90$	N6662D N732WJ N811KC
LJ-870	C90	N19P N500MB PT-OPR
LJ-871	C90$	N348D N25AW (N25GW) (N28BE) N29EB N290AJ
LJ-872	C90	N6668U N555MS N248MC
LJ-873	C90	N6670C N318DS N44TF N44TG I-KWYR [w/o 10Feb89 Rome-Ciampino, Italy]
LJ-874	C90	G-BHAP G-SPTS N44486 D-IFUN SX-BGO OY-JAP
LJ-875	C90	N6672N N73PH
LJ-876	C90$	N66712 HP-1118 HP-1118P N876NA N153PM N227DC
LJ-877	C90	N66877 N300VA
LJ-878	C90$	N6673R N440KC N440KF
LJ-879	C90^	N6656D N725AR
LJ-880	C90	N60659 ZS-KLC 7Q-YMM [dbr 09Nov90 Blantyre-Chileka, Malawi, parts to Dodson International Parts, Rantoul, KS, USA]
LJ-881	C90	N66810 N32SJ N32CM
LJ-882	C90	N66828 N333JA N1818W N181GA PT-OOY
LJ-883	C90+	N7801L N410WC G-BSGA N12TA D-IAXX N380AA (N527JD) N984MA
LJ-884	C90	N6736L N88RB PT-OLQ
LJ-885	C90	N92P (N722WB) N1WB N123LL
LJ-886	C90$	N6685Y N15SL C-GCFM
LJ-887	C90$	N66864 N444DC N10XH G-LAMB D-IIWN D-IGLI N887CF N751KC
LJ-888	C90	N67511 (N111GF) N67511
LJ-889	C90$	YV-354CP YV-O-CBL-5 YV0136
LJ-890	C90	OY-AUV (PH-CAV) (PH-CCA) ZS-LOL N140SP N610W ZS-LOL VT-NEF [dbr cFeb98 in India, parts to Dodson International Parts, Rantoul, KS, USA]
LJ-891	C90$	N6754H
LJ-892	C90	N6690L N105AW N103LC N318LA HK-3277X HK-3277P [w/o 31Jul02 nr Puerto Leguizamo, Putumayo, Colombia]
LJ-893	C90	N16
LJ-894	C90$	F-GCGA
LJ-895	C90$	YV-355CP N4449Q
LJ-896	C90	N17
LJ-897	C90	N758D PT-LLV
LJ-898	C90	N67599 OH-BKI N41AJ YV-741CP N113AP LX-FRZ N898CM
LJ-899	C90$	N6732V N813JB
LJ-900	C90	D-ILGA OE-FHG N415MA PT-OJU
LJ-901	C90$	N23LF N93LP
LJ-902	C90	N18 N5 N21
LJ-903	C90$	N33GB N1UM N45SA
LJ-904	C90	N6743V N90HB N94HB
LJ-905	C90	CP-1600 EB-003 (Bolivian Army)
LJ-906	C90$	N5371 N957JF N925ES
LJ-907	C90	N6749C N175BC N302DK N900TJ N900BE N900WC
LJ-908	C90$	N6794W N234DP N334DP N234DP N101SG N101SZ N91HM N1078 N38TR
LJ-909	C90	N19
LJ-910	C90$	(YV-322CP) XA-KOM (D-IOTO) N217GA TC-FRT N211PC
LJ-911	C90$	N107K N84TP
LJ-912	C90	N20
LJ-913	C90	N6759J N715AT PT-LMI N715AT PT-LMI
LJ-914	C90	N36880 N6RU PT-OEH N914TT N402EM (N774EM) N402EM
LJ-915	C90$	N3688P
LJ-916	TC-90	N67233 6808 (JMSDF)
LJ-917	TC-90	N6724D 6809 (JMSDF)
LJ-918	C90$	N499M N21HA N918SA
LJ-919	C90$	N18MB ZS-LTZ VH-TAM
LJ-920	C90	C-GBYB N42KA PT-OPD
LJ-921	C90	N3690F
LJ-922	C90$	(F-GCPN) CN-TAX
LJ-923	C90^	XA-KUE XB-DJZ XA-REH N30GK N108JD
LJ-924	C90	N3695W
LJ-925	C90$	N3703L (N925G) N925GS N925BC N925MM N149CF
LJ-926	C90	(D-IBBI) D-IHNA [w/o 27May94 nr Mindelheim-Mattsies, Germany; canx cJun94]
LJ-927	C90$	N3701F YV-454CP N4492D PT-LMJ PT-OSO
LJ-928	C90	HI-366 HI-366CT N5095K N132AS
LJ-929	C90	N81DD C-GCFB
LJ-930	C90+	N3717J ZS-KMA
LJ-931	C90	HB-GHB N931KA I-FIRS HB-GIE D-IBMC
LJ-932	C90	N37132 N34CE (N90CE) N34CE
LJ-933	C90+	N3709S N3AT N760EB
LJ-934	C90$	F-GCTA N369GA N101WR
LJ-935	C90	N3709W N600FL N600FE
LJ-936	C90	N917BH N912BH N207R N207E N49FA PT-OSI

BEECH 90

c/n	Series/Mod	Identities
LJ-937	C90$	OY-BEK PT-OUX
LJ-938	C90^	N3817H
LJ-939	C90$	SE-IGS N26803 N94CD
LJ-940	C90	N82P PT-OPE
LJ-941	C90	N3804C F-GEOU
LJ-942	C90	D-IKES N321AV
LJ-943	C90+	N3805E
LJ-944	C90$^	G-BIEE G-PTER HB-GHT (N135JA) N944TT N9DA
LJ-945	C90	N979C N88GL
LJ-946	C90	CP-1600 N3236T PT-LLR
LJ-947	C90	N3804F [w/o 05Nov89 Gadsden-Municipal, AL, USA in mid-air collision with Cessna 172 N52244; canx 21Nov90]
LJ-948	C90	YV-381CP N4495U N205MS
LJ-949	C90$	N8300C N100HS N269JG
LJ-950	C90$	HK-2595X HK-2595W N108TT N401EM
LJ-951	C90	N511D PT-OZJ
LJ-952	C90	YV-178CP N4490L PT-OJA
LJ-953	C90	N38280
LJ-954	C90$	F-GDCC C9-ASK ZS-SGO
LJ-955	C90	N678SB N768SB F-GIZB
LJ-956	C90	N3850H N9933E N41PS ZS-MSD N225AT (N210JM) PT-WMT
LJ-957	C90	HK-2596X HK-2596G HK-2596
LJ-958	C90^	N908G N458P N500MT N505MT N11FT
LJ-959	C90$^	(D-IFIP) N38353 ZS-KZI
LJ-960	C90	N3861H PT-OCC
LJ-961	C90	(XA-LOP) XA-ISL N16KM
LJ-962	C90	N18299 N1213P TC-MCK N962TT
LJ-963	C90	N38589 PT-OLX
LJ-964	C90$	N38595 N595PC N595RC N501GS
LJ-965	C90	(YV-424CP) N1841G N62BB N205SP N205ST (N965TT) N205ST
LJ-966	C90	N181JH PT-LQS
LJ-967	C90	N3832X VT-EGR N967WJ
LJ-968	C90	N102EP VH-FDP VH-FOP N277SW
LJ-969	C90	HB-GHC I-SUSE 9Q-CHE N77HE
LJ-970	C90	N121P
LJ-971	C90$	OY-BEB N971CF N959CM N959GM
LJ-972	C90$	N18080 HB-GJH
LJ-973	C90	YV-436CP YV1607
LJ-974	C90	N555RA N55MN
LJ-975	C90	N1830H N94SC PT-OHH
LJ-976	TC-90	N3832G 6810 (JMSDF)
LJ-977	C90$	N1813P D-IFHI
LJ-978	C90+	N3835Z ZS-LBF N725KR OH-BEX
LJ-979	C90$	N12LA N777NG N777NQ N777VH D-IAAK 5B-CJL
LJ-980	TC-90	N3832K 6811 (JMSDF)
LJ-981	C90	N220F [w/o 27Nov85 East Greenwich, RI, USA]
LJ-982	C90	N1820P N102FL N102FK
LJ-983	C90	N61776 N491BT (N491BF) N391BT N971AM
LJ-984	C90+	N1823A LN-FOD OH-BAX
LJ-985	C90	EI-BLI N409ND PT-OLW
LJ-986	C90-1	N18300 HC-
LJ-987	C90	N1834H N100CH N180CH N90WC ZS-LZP N390L N722VB
LJ-988	C90$	N18267 ZS-LUU A2-DBH
LJ-989	C90	(YV-442CP) N62300
LJ-990	C90$	N1836H
LJ-991	C90	(YV-442CP) G-BIXM G-SALV G-BIXM N504AB N19LW
LJ-992	C90$	N13PA N992LJ HB-GJA N305TT
LJ-993	C90$	N1837F [canx 15Feb94 to Philippines, never registered there] N81NA
LJ-994	C90	HK-2873X HK-2873 HK-2873P HK-2873W HK-4387
LJ-995	C90	N1855H PT-OOT
LJ-996	C90-1	N150TH N34TM N600SB HB-GDA N502MS N679FS
LJ-997	C90$	N1853T N503CB
LJ-998	C90-1$	N1853X (N17AK) N17EN PT-OCI
LJ-999	C90$^	N18488 N333TP N333TL
LJ-1000	C90$	N18536 N90SG HI-469 HI-469SP N6623D PT-OOD N323MC N982FA N403EM
LJ-1001	C90	N18548 (N4GU) N4GC N88EL N91LW N979MC
LJ-1002	C90+	N713D N643PU D-ICLE N900VA C-GAWA
LJ-1003	C90	N90DL N747SF XA-SCG N31LA N972AM
LJ-1004	C90	N6111S N45US (N458S) PT-ORW [wfu; canx 15Jun99]
LJ-1005	C90	YV-464CP YV-2260P N6661J PT-OQS
LJ-1006	C90	N61188 N123NA N175AZ
LJ-1007	C90	N61254 N68PC N964GB
LJ-1008	C90	N1842A VT-EHY [w/o 29Oct08 Chandigarh, India]
LJ-1009	C90$	N61383 (N155RG) N61383
LJ-1010	C90$	N6135Z PT-LHJ
LJ-1011	C90-1	N6139U VH-FDW N278SW
LJ-1012	C90-1$	N61797 N617LM N278AB
LJ-1013	C90-1$	N2872B N6723Y
LJ-1014	C90-1	N6173C
LJ-1015	C90-1	N6280E [wfu, parts to Dodson International Parts, Rantoul, KS, USA]
LJ-1016	C90-1	N6199P N790A

BEECH 90

c/n	Series/Mod	Identities
LJ-1017	C90-1$	N6207F *N468M
LJ-1018	C90-1	N501LA PT-ONQ
LJ-1019	C90-1	N502LA N25AJ PT-OEP
LJ-1020	C90-1$	N62358 (N315B) N10HE N10HY N63LB N71SL VH-LJG VH-LYG
LJ-1021	C90-1+	N117D VH-FDZ P2-NTR
LJ-1022	C90-1+	N6280P PT-OAB N922AA N522SC
LJ-1023	C90-1^	N6262M N77AK N88AP PT-OKW N731RJ N32MA N332MS
LJ-1024	C90-1	N6424Q N618DB VH-FDM VH-FOM P2-NTJ [wfu Goroka, Papua New Guinea]
LJ-1025	C90-1	N6272C [w/o 10Mar82 nr Azores]
LJ-1026	C90-1$	N6364H PT-LPJ
LJ-1027	C90-1	N83P
LJ-1028	C90-1	N6420H G-BKFY N6420H VR-CCT VP-CCT N213CT G-BKFY LV-BLV
LJ-1029	C90-1$	N6567C N28TM N423TJ
LJ-1030	C90-1	N6504H N357HP N901JB
LJ-1031	C90-1	N1844K ZS-LFN N612MR SU-PAC N982BA N397CA N1GF
LJ-1032	C90-1$	N6563K
LJ-1033	C90-1	N6717T ZS-LFL
LJ-1034	C90-1$	(D-IFOC) D-IARF (N98RF) ZS-CPM ZS-CSC
LJ-1035	C90-1	N9933E G-BKIP G-NUIG F-GLJD N396CA
LJ-1036	C90-1^	N36803 N440M N44QM (N59WP) N11SN
LJ-1037	C90-1	N6382H N283DP PT-LYT
LJ-1038	UC-90	N1839D 9102 (JMSDF)
LJ-1039	C90-1	N6746S N404JP
LJ-1040	C90-1$	N545D N115MX N115KU N444KU C-FAGA
LJ-1041	C90-1$	N63459 OH-BKO N106AJ PT-OVN N541AA YV [canx 24Oct08 as exported to Venezuela]
LJ-1042	TC-90	N18460 6812 (JMSDF)
LJ-1043	TC-90	N1846B 6813 (JMSDF)
LJ-1044	TC-90	N1846D 6814 (JMSDF)
LJ-1045	C90-1$	N84P
LJ-1046	C90-1+^	N6445N N644PU N90PU N990KB
LJ-1047	TC-90	N1846F 6815 (JMSDF)
LJ-1048	C90-1$	N6473V PT-OOG N46CR N777HF N900MT
LJ-1049	C90-1	N7931D
LJ-1050	C90-1	N6492C
LJ-1051	C90-1+^	N44KA HP-976 HP-976P N111KA
LJ-1052	C90-1	N6356C
LJ-1053	C90-1$	N6691L ZS-LIN
LJ-1054	C90-1	N63908 N10AU N10AV N167BB
LJ-1055	C90-1	N303D N771PA
LJ-1056	C90-1$	N6574C N90GH PT-LQE [dam 13Jun09 Nanuque, Minas Gerais, Brazil]
LJ-1057	C90-1$	N424TV N47SW
LJ-1058	C90-1$	N6586K ZS-NXY [w/o 13Dec96 nr Cape Town, Western Cape Province, South Africa]
LJ-1059	C90-1	N6581B PT-OZR
LJ-1060	TC-90	N1875Z 6816 (JMSDF)
LJ-1061	TC-90	N1876Z 6817 (JMSDF)
LJ-1062	TC-90	N6886S 6818 (JMSDF)
LJ-1063	C90A	N66775 N79DS N76DS (N28MM) PT-LSE
LJ-1064	C90A	N6763K
LJ-1065	C90-1	N6727L F-GFLY N93BA N900LE N722KR
LJ-1066	C90A	N6727M N300FL N300FN F-HDCS
LJ-1067	C90A	N224P N200TR
LJ-1068	C90A$	D-ILBA N96MR N666PC N613RF
LJ-1069	C90A	N67516 N223CG G-BMKD
LJ-1070	C90A$	N67554 N210EC
LJ-1071	C90A$^	N67569 ZS-LOK N68AJ
LJ-1072	C90A	N6692D
LJ-1073	C90A$	G-BKUX N7049U HP-1152P N120TT
LJ-1074	C90A	N6583K N923CR
LJ-1075	C90A	N68474 N130MA N129RP N120RP
LJ-1076	C90A	N69275 (N692AC) N86JG PR-VOT
LJ-1077	C90A$^	N69297 N4CH N4B D-IGKN [canx 23Oct08 as exported to San Marino; still active as D-IGKN]
LJ-1078	C90A	N6555C N78SR PT-ONJ
LJ-1079	C90A$	N69301
LJ-1080	C90A	N6931W TC-LMK [dbr 21Mar00 nr Bursa, Turkey, parts to Dodson International Parts, Rantoul, KS, USA]
LJ-1081	C90A	N7200U N60CW PT-OYN
LJ-1082	C90A$^	N398D N666GW N686GW
LJ-1083	TC-90	N6923Z 6819 (JMSDF)
LJ-1084	TC-90	N69237 6820 (JMSDF)
LJ-1085	C90A$^	N72055 N720CT N360MP
LJ-1086	C90A$	N7200R N1818W N18182 N105TC
LJ-1087	C90A	N7252S N377P
LJ-1088	C90A$	N72073 N71WW N124MB N904RB
LJ-1089	C90A	N46KA D-IEXT HB-GHW N993RC N904DK
LJ-1090	C90A	N7210H D-ILGI
LJ-1091	C90A	N179D N179MD
LJ-1092	C90A	N7212D N91TR N88CW PT-OXY N11755 PT-WNW
LJ-1093	C90A#^	N7204V N720DK D-IDSR HB-GHN N70PJ HB-GHN F-GLLA N126WA
LJ-1094	C90A	N7215L PT-OFY

BEECH 90

c/n	Series/Mod	Identities								
LJ-1095	C90A^	N850BE	N850CE	N617KM	N617RM					
LJ-1096	C90A$	N7216H	(N400SR)	PT-OTG						
LJ-1097	C90A	N69261	JA8838	OY-JAJ	N114DB					
LJ-1098	C90$	N7218V	F-GFCO	N294TT	F-HJCM					
LJ-1099	C90A	N7219D	D-IHSA	N8109N	ZS-MKI	Z-MKI	ZS-MKI			
LJ-1100	C90A	N7219K	VT-EJZ							
LJ-1101	C90A$	N72206	N17FL	N17EL	D-IFMI					
LJ-1102	C90A$	N72223	RP-C2446	N682TA	N109DT					
LJ-1103	C90A	N72226	N55LC	N8GT	N8GU					
LJ-1104	C90A$^	N7223X	(N72AM)	N7223X						
LJ-1105	C90A	N72233	F-GLRA	[w/o 19Oct94 Samur, France; canx 06Oct95]						
LJ-1106	C90A	N6690C	N222WJ							
LJ-1107	C90A$^	N72260	N101BU	N155GB						
LJ-1108	C90A	N7227R	N438SP	N958JH						
LJ-1109	C90A+^	N95PC								
LJ-1110	TC-90	N7238J	6821 (JMSDF)							
LJ-1111	C90A$	N7228Y	D-IOPL	N597DM	N500DY	(N500PN)	C-FGXC	N140TT	C-GJVC	N204EA
		N96FA								
LJ-1112	C90A+	N7229Z	N737L	N66LM	N37XX	N135AA				
LJ-1113	C90A	N7230H	(N268PS)	(N69PS)	N7230H					
LJ-1114	C90A$	N7232U	N808W	N55WF						
LJ-1115	C90A	D-IBPE	OE-FHL							
LJ-1116	C90A$	N76RJ	N76RU	G-COWE	N25AE	VT-NEI				
LJ-1117	C90A$	N7234H	N3030C	N3030G						
LJ-1118	C90A	N7234Z	N937BC	ZS-LZR						
LJ-1119	C90A	N72369	N386CP	N261GB						
LJ-1120	C90A$	N7237K	D-IIKM							
LJ-1121	C90A	N7238B	N123ML	N123ME	N20LB	(N20LK)	N904JP	N311TJ		
LJ-1122	C90A$^	N7244J	N992C	N190EF						
LJ-1123	C90A$^	N7245Z	N917BH	N621TD						
LJ-1124	C90A$	N7246B	D-IALL	N90EP	OE-FRS	N999LK				
LJ-1125	C90A+	N7208L	OE-FAK	N124RC	N299KA	N299VM				
LJ-1126	C90A	N3070S	N311CK	N300CK	N497P	N319MB				
LJ-1127	C90A$	N7254B	PT-OXH	(N779JM)	N814CP					
LJ-1128	C90A$^	N7248G	PT-ODH							
LJ-1129	C90A+	N7248M	N717DW	N817F	N506F					
LJ-1130	C90A$	N72149	D-IMAG	N504EC	N90DJ	C-FGXB	N330RC	N518TS		
LJ-1131	C90A$	N72508	N811R							
LJ-1132	C90A	N7251H	XA-GSM	XB-FMJ	XC-AGS	XB-ECL				
LJ-1133	C90A$	N7257P	N300HH	N77WM						
LJ-1134	C90A	N223P	D-IEVO	N303CA						
LJ-1135	C90A	N2602M	VT-EMI							
LJ-1136	C90A$^	N2648M	N90RK	N359JT	(N901XP)	N902XP				
LJ-1137	C90A	N6690N	VT-EMJ							
LJ-1138	C90A$	N2706E	XA-ESM	XA-POK	N17KA	D-ITCH				
LJ-1139	C90A	N2785A	JA8840	N121RL	C-FGXG					
LJ-1140	C90A	N30573	JA8841	N8841	C-FGXU					
LJ-1141	C90A	N2736D	JA8844							
LJ-1142	C90A	N2860A	JA8845							
LJ-1143	C90A	N7239S	JA8846							
LJ-1144	C90A	N7239U	JA8847							
LJ-1145	C90A	N7239Y	JA8848							
LJ-1146	TC-90	N72400	6822 (JMSDF)							
LJ-1147	C90A$	N475JA	(N1147W)	N475JA						
LJ-1148	C90A	N7240D	JA8849	N120RL	N8887B					
LJ-1149	C90A	N7240E	JA8850							
LJ-1150	C90A	N7240K	JA8851							
LJ-1151	C90A	N7240L	JA8852	N126RL	C-FGXX					
LJ-1152	C90A+	N3090A	C-FGXA	N252RC						
LJ-1153	C90A	YV-333CP	N70491	VT-EQO						
LJ-1154	C90A$	N3076U	N67CL							
LJ-1155	C90A	N3077Y	N32MT							
LJ-1156	C90A$	N18264	N817DP	N342CF						
LJ-1157	C90A	N36805	N288MT	N85PH						
LJ-1158	C90A	N793PA	N38H	D-IHKM						
LJ-1159	C90A	N3078D	PT-ODE	N425SV	VT-AJV					
LJ-1160	C90A	N7242V	JA8856	N909GA	VT-ETI	N6031W	N919CL			
LJ-1161	C90A	N476JA	N4764A							
LJ-1162	C90A	N477JA	C-FGXH							
LJ-1163	C90A	N478JA	N777J	HI-776SP						
LJ-1164	C90A	N3079Z	ZS-MIL	N104AJ						
LJ-1165	C90A^	N3081K	N39FB	(N325A)	N39FB					
LJ-1166	C90A	N3100W	2201 (Mexican AF)		5201 (Mexican AF)					
LJ-1167	C90A	N31174	VT-EQN							
LJ-1168	C90A	N3082W	2203 (Mexican AF)		5203 (Mexican AF)					
LJ-1169	C90A^	N30844	N585R							
LJ-1170	C90A$^	N3085Y	G-OAKZ	G-SVSS	N4131S	N581B				
LJ-1171	C90A	N3086G	2205 (Mexican AF)		5205 (Mexican AF)					
LJ-1172	C90A	N30833	N904TH	N904TD	N32JP					
LJ-1173	C90A	PT-LPD								
LJ-1174	C90A	N31398	PT-OIZ							

c/n	Series/Mod	Identities						
LJ-1175	C90A	N3139T	2204 (Mexican AF)	5204 (Mexican AF)				
LJ-1176	C90A	N3108K	2202 (Mexican AF)	5202 (Mexican AF)				
LJ-1177	C90A	N479JA	(N357CA)	C-FGXZ				
LJ-1178	C90A	N480JA	N357CY	C-FGXJ				
LJ-1179	C90A	N481JA	N179RC	C-FGXE				
LJ-1180	C90A	N190CA	LV-PAJ	LV-ROC				
LJ-1181	C90A	N3083E	N90PE	RP-C1807	N904P			
LJ-1182	LC90	N3228V	9301 (JMSDF)					
LJ-1183	C90A	N482JA	N779JM					
LJ-1184	C90A	N483JA	N149CM					
LJ-1185	C90A$^	N44GP	N50VP					
LJ-1186	C90A	N31434	[w/o 30May90 Manaus, Amazonas, Brazil]					
LJ-1187	C90A^	N31447	(N15PT)	N524TS				
LJ-1188	C90A	N1537H	PT-LYK					
LJ-1189	C90A	N200SL	(N203SL)	C-FGXL				
LJ-1190	C90A$	N3190S						
LJ-1191	C90A	N1157R	YV-32P					
LJ-1192	C90A	N15023	(N30BM)	D-ISAG	N616SC	C-FGXQ		
LJ-1193	C90A$	N1528T	N28VM	PT-OJZ	D2-ETJ	ZS-OTK		
LJ-1194	C90A+	N15234	(N90DS)	N15234				
LJ-1195	C90A	N31187	N70PA	PT-OKQ				
LJ-1196	C90A	N484JA	N119SA					
LJ-1197	C90A	N485JA	N485JD	N779MJ	N255DF			
LJ-1198	C90A	N486JA	N486JD	N611CF	JA55HA			
LJ-1199	C90A	N487JA	N487JD	N717RD	XB-JNN			
LJ-1200	C90A	(N485JA)	N1546U	N68TW	C-FGXO			
LJ-1201	C90A$^	(N486JA)	N2789B	PT-LVK				
LJ-1202	C90A#	N5519C	(D-IMPW)	HB-GIZ	N417VN	N902DB		
LJ-1203	C90A	(N487JA)	N3084B	N505EB	N115MX	N115MZ	N485AT	
LJ-1204	C90A	N1552D	ZS-COP					
LJ-1205	C90A	N1552F	N169DR					
LJ-1206	C90A	N1552G						
LJ-1207	C90A	N31559	D-ISEM	N578P	N207RC	C-FGXS		
LJ-1208	C90A	(N485JA)	N621WP	N427RB	(N928P)	N44GP		
LJ-1209	C90A	N1571T	N3030C	N53TJ	(F-GUPM)	N53TJ		
LJ-1210	C90A	N1553D	N948AM					
LJ-1211	C90A	N1551H						
LJ-1212	C90A	N1551J	PT-WHP					
LJ-1213	C90A	N1559T	N20FD	[wfu c1999, parts to White Industries, Bates City, MO, USA; canx 07Jul99]				
LJ-1214	C90A	N1553G						
LJ-1215	C90A	N15615	N105FL	[w/o 09Apr92 St.Augustine, FL, USA; canx 22Jun92]				
LJ-1216	C90A	N1562Z	D-IHAH	D-IEAH				
LJ-1217	C90A#^	N1567G						
LJ-1218	C90A	N15628	N224CC					
LJ-1219	C90A	N5519V	N61HB	PT-MTD	N771AW	N155RG	N367EA	N523TH
LJ-1220	C90A	N5520X	PT-OMZ					
LJ-1221	C90A	N1563U	N416P	N94SR	N400GW	N407GW	N891AA	
LJ-1222	C90A	N15627	OK-VKE	OM-VKE	N322BR			
LJ-1223	C90A+^	N5522X	OY-JAB	N90MT	N8CA	N191TP		
LJ-1224	C90A$^	N1556Z	PT-OBF	N123AT	F-WQVX	F-GIDL		
LJ-1225	C90A	N1564M	PT-LLO					
LJ-1226	C90A	N2854B	XA-RQM	N369B	N2854B	F-GULM		
LJ-1227	C90A+	N1556G	N200SC	N200SY	N89KA	P2-DRS		
LJ-1228	C90A	N5590L	N90KA	N90BJ	N190JS	N681EV		
LJ-1229	C90A	N5547Y	N422RJ	N422TW	D-IAFF	N94MG		
LJ-1230	C90A	N1564P	(N999KH)	C-FGXT				
LJ-1231	C90A	N5595K	N101SG	N101SQ	N931AJ	N931WC	N358K	N567MD
LJ-1232	C90A	N1564Q	XA-RGL	N91KA				
LJ-1233	C90A	N5502D	N113TP	PT-ORZ				
LJ-1234	C90A#	N1564W	N611CR					
LJ-1235	C90A	N1569N	D-IABB	N92FC				
LJ-1236	C90A+	N5598L	D-IPEL	OE-FMG	N905DR	UN-K9001	UP-K9001	
LJ-1237	C90A	N5537W	N330DR	N338DR	PT-OTI			
LJ-1238	C90A	N1553N	N947AM					
LJ-1239	C90A+	N5639K						
LJ-1240	C90A+	N1565X	N691AS					
LJ-1241	C90A	N5641X						
LJ-1242	C90A	N15696	N88PD					
LJ-1243	C90A	N5582K	HS-TFH	HS-SLB	N243JB			
LJ-1244	C90A$^	N5644E	N247MD					
LJ-1245	C90A	N5654E	PT-WAH					
LJ-1246	C90A	XA-RFN	N308MD					
LJ-1247	C90A^	N5651J	D-IAAH					
LJ-1248	LC90	N56633	9302 (JMSDF)					
LJ-1249	LC90	N56638	9303 (JMSDF)					
LJ-1250	C90A	N2855B	F-GKGT	F-OGUY	F-GTRM	N938P		
LJ-1251	C90A	N5607X	N87HB					
LJ-1252	C90A+^	N55008	N92CD	N72TG				
LJ-1253	C90A	N309P	PT-WHA					
LJ-1254	C90A^	N55486	N31GM	N770VF	N779VF			

BEECH 90

c/n	Series/Mod	Identities
LJ-1255	C90A	N55495 N595TM
LJ-1256	C90A$	N90KA N904HB
LJ-1257	C90A	N2790B N8255A N155A
LJ-1258	C90A+	N56531 N80CK N40MH N111KC
LJ-1259	C90A	N712JC N702DK
LJ-1260	C90A	N5618Z PT-OSN
LJ-1261	C90A^	N56787 F-GJSD LX-LLM N72GL
LJ-1262	C90A	N15527 (N1347J) N200HV N700RF
LJ-1263	C90A	N5680S D-IDIW 9A-DAC N230JS N927JJ N927JT
LJ-1264	C90A	PT-OFF
LJ-1265	C90A	N8001V
LJ-1266	C90A	N421HV
LJ-1267	C90A$	HB-GIM A6-FAE D-IEBE N368RK
LJ-1268	C90A+^	N1CR N131CR N636 N131CL N525P N555AL *N455AL
LJ-1269	C90A	N8021P
LJ-1270	C90A	N5685K N324AB VT-SLK
LJ-1271	C90A	N80904 N242NS
LJ-1272	C90A	N8045T HP-1203 N770AJ PR-SIA
LJ-1273	C90A$	N1564M YV-2282P YV-1000CP YV1726
LJ-1274	C90A#^	N8099G N513JM
LJ-1275	C90A#^	N8108E TC-AEM (N275TT) N275LA
LJ-1276	C90A	N8065R TC-MSS
LJ-1277	C90A	N8012U N871KS
LJ-1278	C90A$	N8141K VT-RLK N851GA VT-JPK
LJ-1279	C90A	N8087V XA-RXE N717A N71VG N611KA PR-AVT
LJ-1280	C90A	XA-RXT XB-HQW
LJ-1281	LC90	N81538 9304 (JMSDF)
LJ-1282	LC90	(N191SP) N8154G 9305 (JMSDF)
LJ-1283	C90A^	N8108Z D-IHMW N700GM
LJ-1284	C90A^	OY-GEF N25GA OE-FHM
LJ-1285	C90A$	N191SP HP-1264 N900BT SP-NEB
LJ-1286	C90A$	N56534 N301ER N800PG
LJ-1287	C90A	N8049R LV-WLV N881JT N718MB
LJ-1288	C90B$	N90KA N90KB N27BM N736EA
LJ-1289	C90A	N563AC N1NP N522JP
LJ-1290	C90A	N81763 JA8882
LJ-1291	C90A	N8178W JA8883
LJ-1292	C90A	N81826 JA8884
LJ-1293	C90A$	N214P
LJ-1294	C90A	N82025 PT-OMO N19BK PT-WPN
LJ-1295	C90B	N8248H N1CR N91CR N91LY N191WB
LJ-1296	C90A	F-OGRZ (F-GJDK) F-GLRZ
LJ-1297	C90A	N8239Q N779DD
LJ-1298	C90A+^	N8264G ZS-NAG N170AJ N190SS
LJ-1299	C90A	N8253D F-GNMA
LJ-1300	C90B	C-GMBC/901 N920TT
LJ-1301	C90B	C-GMBD/902 N924TT *PR-WFM
LJ-1302	C90B	N5670D N322TC
LJ-1303	C90B	N80513 (F-GIAO) F-GMPM
LJ-1304	C90B	C-GMBG/903 N465JB
LJ-1305	C90B$	N488JD N488JR C-GPNB C-FSXG
LJ-1306	C90B$^	N8290T N422RJ N65CL
LJ-1307	C90B#	N8053U D-IBDH [w/o 09Dec07 Kiev-Zhulyany, Ukraine]
LJ-1308	C90B	PT-ORG
LJ-1309	C90B	C-GMBH/904 N709EA
LJ-1310	C90B	C-GMBW/905 N463JB
LJ-1311	C90B	N489JD N489JS PR-MZP
LJ-1312	C90B	N490JD N490JT N490J N640DF
LJ-1313	C90B+^	C-GMBX/906 N928TT
LJ-1314	C90B+	N8022Q N198PP
LJ-1315	C90B^	N8103E D-IHSW
LJ-1316	C90B	N8114P N49LL [dbr 13Jun05 Marble Canyon, AZ, USA, parts to Alliance Air Parts, Oklahoma City, OK, USA]
LJ-1317	C90B	C-GMBY/907 N929TT
LJ-1318	C90B$^	CC-CDL N131SA N17KK
LJ-1319	C90B	C-GMBZ/908 N719EA
LJ-1320	C90B#	N8119N N65GP (N65GE) N572BB
LJ-1321	C90B	N8232L D-IOMG F-GYGL LX-GNG F-GVPD [w/o 19Oct06 Besancon, France]
LJ-1322	C90B^	N8121C N500QT N530CH
LJ-1323	C90B$	N90KA D-IUDE
LJ-1324	C90B+	N82430 D-IKIM
LJ-1325	C90B	N8135M D-IHMV
LJ-1326	C90B$^	N8096U
LJ-1327	C90B	(D-IOMG) N8227P D-IHHE
LJ-1328	C90B	N8250K N90HB F-GNEE
LJ-1329	C90B+	N8061Q YV-839CP YV-1069CP YV1649
LJ-1330	C90B	N8064A N266F N555VW
LJ-1331	C90B+^	N8089J PT-WVI
LJ-1332	C90B	N8259Q PR-GBS
LJ-1333	C90B	N8156Z
LJ-1334	C90B	N8148N N5VK N5VN N22VK D-IIKY SX-BKY *F-HAYP

BEECH 90

c/n	Series/Mod	Identities				
LJ-1335	C90B	N82323	9306 (JMSDF)		6823 (JMSDF)	
LJ-1336	C90B	N82326	9307 (JMSDF)		6824 (JMSDF)	
LJ-1337	C90B	N82349	9308 (JMSDF)		6825 (JMSDF)	
LJ-1338	C90B	N82366	9309 (JMSDF)		6826 (JMSDF)	
LJ-1339	C90B	N82376	9310 (JMSDF)		6827 (JMSDF)	
LJ-1340	C90B$	LV-PGL	LV-WCW	N10799	D-IIWB	
LJ-1341	C90B	PT-OZL				
LJ-1342	C90B$	C-FTPE				
LJ-1343	C90B	N8208C	N971SC			
LJ-1344	C90B	N8220V	N903P			
LJ-1345	C90B$^	N415P	(N117HP)	VH-ZGQ	N43KM	[w/o 14Dec08 nr Rocksprings, TX, USA]
LJ-1346	C90B	LV-PGN	LV-WDP	PT-WFN		
LJ-1347	C90B$^	N8210C	N551CN			
LJ-1348	C90B$	N451A	UR-CRV			
LJ-1349	C90B	N491JV				
LJ-1350	C90B	N492JW	JA007C	VH-KQB		
LJ-1351	C90B	N493JX	N424EM			
LJ-1352	C90B	N494JY	N426EM			
LJ-1353	C90B	N8292Y	SU-ZAA	[w/o 15Jan08 Port Said, Egypt]		
LJ-1354	C90B	N8294Z	LV-PHP	LV-WJE		
LJ-1355	C90B$	N8105D	D-ISIX	N995PA	D-ISIX	
LJ-1356	C90B	N8287E				
LJ-1357	C90B	N1560T				
LJ-1358	C90B$	N80927	N94TK			
LJ-1359	C90B	N8280K	7T-WCF			
LJ-1360	C90B	N1560U	S5-CMO			
LJ-1361	C90B	N5521T	F-HHAM			
LJ-1362	C90B	N990CB				
LJ-1363	C90B	N1534T	PT-WGU			
LJ-1364	C90B$^	TG-CCA	TG-EME			
LJ-1365	C90B$	N1551C				
LJ-1366	C90B	N1544V				
LJ-1367	C90GTi	N15599	N111MD	N111MU	ZK-MKG	
LJ-1368	C90B	N1568X				
LJ-1369	C90B	(N15527)	N3222K	VT-RLL	N127ZW	
LJ-1370	C90B$	N1570C	D-IHAH			
LJ-1371	C90B$^	C-FSGZ	N696WW	VT-PPC	N34RF	
LJ-1372	C90B	N1562V	N151JL	(N121EB)	N454P	
LJ-1373	C90B	TG-RWC	TG-SAQ	HP-8000		
LJ-1374	C90B$	N15116	VT-VIL	N190CB	VH-EMJ	
LJ-1375	C90B$	N3194K	XA-TDW	N35HC	VH-ILB	
LJ-1376	C90B	N15542	VT-HYA			
LJ-1377	C90B	N3042K	PT-WCS			
LJ-1378	C90B	N3083K	N555HJ			
LJ-1379	C90B	N3112K	7T-WCG			
LJ-1380	C90B	N3128K	7T-WCH			
LJ-1381	C90B	LV-PHH	LV-WIU	N381SC	N92BK	N707FF
LJ-1382	C90B	N3120U	N96TH			
LJ-1383	C90B	N90WP	N118MF			
LJ-1384	C90B$	N3196K				
LJ-1385	C90B	N3198K	PT-WRA			
LJ-1386	C90B	N3165M	PT-WJF			
LJ-1387	C90B	N500ED	N500EQ			
LJ-1388	C90B	N83KK	N580AC	YV1146		
LJ-1389	C90B	N3204K	CC-CTW	N200U		
LJ-1390	C90B#^	N8203C	N3237K	N75PG		
LJ-1391	C90B$	HB-GJE	3A-MRL	F-GPLK		
LJ-1392	C90B+^	N3216K				
LJ-1393	C90B	N3217M	VT-TIS			
LJ-1394	C90B	N3217K	PT-WIT			
LJ-1395	C90B	LV-PHZ	LV-WMG			
LJ-1396	C90A	N3218K	PT-WIH			
LJ-1397	C90B	N3216U				
LJ-1398	C90B	N3238K	N996TT	N441CG	N12MU	
LJ-1399	C90B	N3212Y	TG-BAC	TG-BAQ	HR-ATP	
LJ-1400	C90B	N3239K	VT-UPZ			
LJ-1401	C90B	N3270K	YV-660CP	YV2350		
LJ-1402	C90B	N3234K	VT-NKF			
LJ-1403	C90B+^	N903SE	N275FA	N424MF	RP-C898	
LJ-1404	C90B	N3106P	VT-DEJ			
LJ-1405	C90B	N59MS				
LJ-1406	C90B	N207P				
LJ-1407	C90B$	HB-GJF	N789WA	C-GRCW		
LJ-1408	C90B	N749RH	N749RN	N587PB		
LJ-1409	C90B	(F-GKDG)	F-GKSP			
LJ-1410	C90B	N3245Y	N771SC	N771SG	N90CN	
LJ-1411	C90B+^	N3218P				
LJ-1412	C90B	N3106Y	TC-MAZ	N412KA	N14GG	N422PM
LJ-1413	C90B	(N90KA)	N3242L	N573P	N773SD	
LJ-1414	C90B	N3234X	LV-WFB	N523P	N344DP	
LJ-1415	C90B	N30CN				

BEECH 90

c/n	Series/Mod	Identities
LJ-1416	C90B	N3254E LV-WPB
LJ-1417	C90B	N3217X N387AS
LJ-1418	C90B	N3218X SU-UAA [w/o 10Jun00 Inshas, Egypt]
LJ-1419	C90B	N257CG N257CQ
LJ-1420	C90B#	N3220L (N844CH) N3220L
LJ-1421	C90B	N3252B N61GN
LJ-1422	C90B$	N3242V OY-IFH N2123Y N511KV
LJ-1423	C90B	N3253Q N4488L
LJ-1424	C90B	N3252J D-IHBP N665CF [dbr 29Apr99 in Germany; registered N665CF 08Sep05 for spares recovery]
LJ-1425	C90B	N3223H (N54TF) N3223H
LJ-1426	C90B	N724KW N724KH
LJ-1427	C90B	N3251E PT-WJD
LJ-1428	C90B	N3242Z N370U
LJ-1429	C90B	N3251Q N96JF
LJ-1430	C90B	N3251U OK-BKS N178JM F-HDGC [dam cJan06 Toulouse-Blagnac, France; tfd 09Feb06 to Agen-La Garenne, France for rebuild]
LJ-1431	C90B	N1031Y
LJ-1432	C90A$	N3263C
LJ-1433	C90B	N3254A N100RU (N248SB) N700SB
LJ-1434	C90B	N3264N N313DW
LJ-1435	C90B	N1095M N16KW
LJ-1436	C90B	N8236B N196HA N196LA N823FC N828FC
LJ-1437	C90B	N1067L N90PR
LJ-1438	C90B	N3268M N389AS
LJ-1439	C90B$	N1089L C-GNKX
LJ-1440	C90B	N1070F
LJ-1441	C90B	N3271S ZS-NUE N995TA F-GSDM D-IKMS PR-TCA
LJ-1442	C90B	N1072G PT-WNI PP-EPS
LJ-1443	C90B	N1083S
LJ-1444	C90B	N1084N N366NC
LJ-1445	C90B$	N209P N90CH
LJ-1446	C90B	N1086Z N222NF N446AS
LJ-1447	C90B$	N569GR (N9690B) N234ST N444LR
LJ-1448	C90B	N1068K
LJ-1449	C90B#^	N72PK N825SD
LJ-1450	C90B	N3265K D-IWID
LJ-1451	C90B+^	N3270V N688LL LV- [canx 08May09 as exported to Argentina]
LJ-1452	C90B#	N1097B N548JG N22FS
LJ-1453	C90B#	N1092G (N25HE) N25HB
LJ-1454	C90B	N1092H
LJ-1455	C90B	N1085V N1848S
LJ-1456	C90B	N1095W
LJ-1457	C90B	N1057L
LJ-1458	C90B#^	N488LL N992WS N901TS
LJ-1459	C90B	N70VP N994WS N902TS
LJ-1460	C90B+^	N1067K N99ML N99MN N313MK N800MK
LJ-1461	C90B	N1076K (N83LS) N1076K
LJ-1462	C90B	N1079D
LJ-1463	C90B	N1099K N771SC N771SQ N930MC
LJ-1464	C90B	N1083K CC-PBK N2040E VH-JET
LJ-1465	C90B^	N1102K C- [canx 13Aug09 as exported to Canada]
LJ-1466	C90B	N1108K LV-PML LV-WXC N466SC LV-WXC
LJ-1467	C90B	N1130J
LJ-1468	C90B	N1134G TI-AZI
LJ-1469	C90B	N97KE N97KA
LJ-1470	C90B	N1099Z JA881C N118MB N529JM
LJ-1471	C90B	N1099D PT-FCM
LJ-1472	C90B	N1099L N100JD (N21WY) N100JD
LJ-1473	C90B	N1090X PT-XHP
LJ-1474	C90B	N205P N478CR
LJ-1475	C90B	N1103G (N900KW) N1103G
LJ-1476	C90B	N1106M P4-SSI
LJ-1477	C90B	N1107W
LJ-1478	C90B$^	N1108M N200HV
LJ-1479	C90B	N1119U XA-YAS
LJ-1480	C90B	N902LT
LJ-1481	C90B^	N1101U N110PM
LJ-1482	C90B	N3035T
LJ-1483	C90B^	N1126J
LJ-1484	C90B	N1134D N24YC
LJ-1485	C90B	N886AT VT-JRD [dbr 26Apr06 Jamshedpur, India; canx 09May07]
LJ-1486	C90A	N1110K
LJ-1487	C90B	N970P N85LG
LJ-1488	C90B$^	N1135G N555XY
LJ-1489	C90B	N1069F LV-YBP
LJ-1490	C90B	N1127U N1TP N9174P N720AM (N520AM) N197SC
LJ-1491	C90B	N2316H PT-WTU
LJ-1492	C90B	N2029Z N97CV ZS-TKB
LJ-1493	C90B	N90KA N98WP
LJ-1494	C90B	N1135X PT-WKX

BEECH 90

c/n	Series/Mod	Identities				
LJ-1495	C90B	N919SA	N1135K	D-IDIX	N495TM	[dbr 12Nov99 Poznan, Poland; re-registered N495TM and b/u by Turbine Aircraft Marketing, San Angelo-Mathis Field, TX, USA]
LJ-1496	C90A	N101SG	N101SQ	VT-SFL		
LJ-1497	C90A	N2297C				
LJ-1498	C90A	N21868	PT-WOZ	PT-MVJ		
LJ-1499	C90B	N862CC	XB-MSF	N440KA		
LJ-1500	C90B	N98XK	N18XJ	(N290JS)	HP-1608	
LJ-1501	C90A	N401TS	N401TT	PT-XOU		
LJ-1502	C90B	N5VK	N5UL	N98KS		
LJ-1503	C90B#	N9MU	N128SB			
LJ-1504	C90B	N333BM				
LJ-1505	C90B+	N800JF	N28XJ	HC-BZD	N901PC	
LJ-1506	C90B	N988P	N54AM			
LJ-1507	C90B#	N2097W	N202FG			
LJ-1508	C90A	N2178F				
LJ-1509	C90B	N769GR				
LJ-1510	C90A	N2310K				
LJ-1511	C90A	N2311J	PT-WUG			
LJ-1512	C90B	N38XJ				
LJ-1513	C90A	N2313K	N600CF	N878K		
LJ-1514	C90B#	N1114Z				
LJ-1515	C90A	N2315L				
LJ-1516	C90B	N60VP				
LJ-1517	C90A+	N90KA	N90KS			
LJ-1518	C90B	N2290C	N982SB			
LJ-1519	C90A#	N800JF	N500VA	N520JA		
LJ-1520	C90A$	N55EP	N128JV	N355CL		
LJ-1521	C90A	N2291F	N91CT			
LJ-1522	C90A	N58XJ	N98BK			
LJ-1523	C90B^	N982SS				
LJ-1524	C90A	N78XJ	XA-TTR			
LJ-1525	C90A	N88XJ				
LJ-1526	C90B	N998P	(F-GPRG)	LX-PRG		
LJ-1527	C90A	N488XJ				
LJ-1528	C90B	N2273A	N20FD			
LJ-1529	C90B	N66CK	N78BA			
LJ-1530	C90A	N588XJ				
LJ-1531	C90B	N2709J	N150GW			
LJ-1532	C90B	N2354Y				
LJ-1533	C90B$	N3133L	N628VK	XB-RYA		
LJ-1534	C90A	N2325L	N121EB	N268P	N291DF	
LJ-1535	C90A	N3035P	LV-ZNS	N3035P	LV-ZNS	
LJ-1536	C90B	N3066W				
LJ-1537	C90B	N99ML	N299RP			
LJ-1538	C90A	N3138B	PT-WZC			
LJ-1539	C90A	(D-IUWM)	N2217Q	D-IGAH	LX-PBL	
LJ-1540	C90A	N2187J	N600FL	N396AS		
LJ-1541	C90A	N438CA				
LJ-1542	C90A	N2178A	N330DB			
LJ-1543	C90B	N3143T	CP-2526			
LJ-1544	C90B	N3068Z				
LJ-1545	C90B	N3145F	N786RM			
LJ-1546	C90A	N3071H	PR-RFB			
LJ-1547	C90A	N399WS				
LJ-1548	C90A	N2342N	LV-ZPS	N574P	N990TF	N90SD
LJ-1549	C90A	N3076U	XB-HMI			
LJ-1550	C90B	N477P	N261GB	N993CB		
LJ-1551	C90A	N3111K	XA-GSA	D-INAS		
LJ-1552	C90A	N3132D	LQ-ZRB			
LJ-1553	C90B	N394B	N147TA	N1962		
LJ-1554	C90B#	N3014R	N90RK			
LJ-1555	C90B	N3205W	PT-PAC	[dam 03Sep08 Rio de Janeiro-Congonhas, Rio de Janeiro State, Brazil]		
LJ-1556	C90B	N3156F	CC-CVT			
LJ-1557	C90A	(N557SA)	N540GA			
LJ-1558	C90B	N3258P	N543GA			
LJ-1559	C90B$	N547GA				
LJ-1560	C90B	N3160P	VT-RSL			
LJ-1561	C90B	N3171A	N100SM	N2MP		
LJ-1562	C90B	N3262R				
LJ-1563	C90B	N3263N				
LJ-1564	C90B	N3164R	PT-MJQ			
LJ-1565	C90B	N213NC	G-ERAD	ZS-LEE		
LJ-1566	C90B	N988XJ	D-INMA			
LJ-1567	C90B	N31279	JA01KA			
LJ-1568	C90A	N568SA				
LJ-1569	C90B	N505P	PT-XOV			
LJ-1570	C90B+^	N3252W	N214KF	N300AW		
LJ-1571	C90B#	N90KA	D-IDIX	D-IKIA	D-IDIX	
LJ-1572	C90B	N33LA	N931GG			
LJ-1573	C90B	N3203L	VT-JIL			
LJ-1574	C90B	N422P	N406RL	(N286WA)	(N432TL)	N406RL

BEECH 90

c/n	Series/Mod	Identities				
LJ-1575	C90B	N971P	N395AS			
LJ-1576	C90B	N3246S				
LJ-1577	C90B	N4477N	PT-WQW			
LJ-1578	C90B	N3178R	PP-ETR			
LJ-1579	C90B	N775D				
LJ-1580	C90B	N32238				
LJ-1581	C90B	N32211	N326PT	(N581RA)	N584SK	
LJ-1582	C90B	N46AE				
LJ-1583	C90B+^	N902PL	F-HADR	D-IAVI		
LJ-1584	C90B	N3184F	6828 (JMSDF)			
LJ-1585	C90B#	(N233SA)	N929FD			
LJ-1586	C90B	N3066U	YV-1066CP	N15GZ	VH-PFK	VH-PFJ
LJ-1587	C90B	N617MM				
LJ-1588	C90B	N588SA				
LJ-1589	C90B	N439PW	CC-PTS			
LJ-1590	C90B	N4060Z	PT-WXH	N13GZ		
LJ-1591	C90B#	N395P	N400TG	JA21EG	N399MB	N946TS
LJ-1592	C90B	N40490	6829 (JMSDF)			
LJ-1593	C90B	N44693	XB-AHK			
LJ-1594	C90B	N590GM	[w/o 27Sep07 nr Pagosa Springs, CO, USA]			
LJ-1595	C90B	N31950				
LJ-1596	C90B	N43046	6830 (JMSDF)			
LJ-1597	C90B	N3197L	LV-ZTP	N597P		
LJ-1598	C90B	N4298X				
LJ-1599	C90B#	N3151P	N4368Y			
LJ-1600	C90B	N812LP	N477PT			
LJ-1601	C90B#	N903TS	N801BS			
LJ-1602	C90B	N3202A	(N700KB)	N807RS		
LJ-1603	C90B#	N445D	N298D	PP-ASD		
LJ-1604	C90B#	N906TS	N925BS	N928US	VT-REL	
LJ-1605	C90B	N4005J	YV-1074CP	YV197T	N353Z	
LJ-1606	C90B#	N4206U	D-ITOP	LZ-ADK		
LJ-1607	C90B	N782P	N73PG			
LJ-1608	C90B	N4408U	PR-CCF			
LJ-1609	C90B+^	N609SA				
LJ-1610	C90B	N44406	OY-LSA	F-GULY		
LJ-1611	C90B	N688P	N74B	N530AG	N530AC	N322MR
LJ-1612	C90B#	N3212Y	N724DR			
LJ-1613	C90B	N5013J	N549GA			
LJ-1614	C90B	N614SA	C6-SPL			
LJ-1615	C90B	N3151P	N700KB	N156MG		
LJ-1616	C90B#	N342P	N24DS			
LJ-1617	C90B	N3217P	N363K	LV-ARU		
LJ-1618	C90B	N5024W	PP-COP			
LJ-1619	C90B	N756P	N90VF	N67CC	N67CQ	
LJ-1620	C90B	N3220E	N543HC			
LJ-1621	C90B	N3221M				
LJ-1622	C90B	N4172Q	D-IDCV			
LJ-1623	C90B	N5023T	XA-JAG			
LJ-1624	C90B	N4324K	XA-EGE			
LJ-1625	C90B	N5025R				
LJ-1626	C90B	N5026C	N369RC	N1875C		
LJ-1627	C90B	N5027V				
LJ-1628	C90B$	N3228M	PR-TIN			
LJ-1629	C90B	N465P	N224JV	(N229J)	N224JE	
LJ-1630	C90B#	N5037W				
LJ-1631	C90B	N4031K	N86LD			
LJ-1632	C90B+^	N608P	N928KG	N928K		
LJ-1633	C90B	N4473M	N266RD			
LJ-1634	C90B	N50344	6831 (JMSDF)			
LJ-1635	C90B	N5035M	N771PD			
LJ-1636	TC-90	N50785	6832 (JMSDF)			
LJ-1637	C90B	N290SA	N915MP	N915MR		
LJ-1638	TC-90	N50778	6833 (JMSDF)			
LJ-1639	C90B	N51139	PR-XIB			
LJ-1640	C90B	N40XJ				
LJ-1641	C90B	N5141G	N654P	N770VF		
LJ-1642	C90B	N4392K				
LJ-1643	C90B	N643EA				
LJ-1644	C90B	N4474Y	N90XP	PR-MLZ		
LJ-1645	C90B	N4115H	XA-TXE	N345BH	N7736M	
LJ-1646	C90B	N4446D	PP-BAF			
LJ-1647	C90B	N169P	YV-477CP	N169P	N778DB	
LJ-1648	C90B	N3178H	HP-1500			
LJ-1649	C90B	N4479W	N490W			
LJ-1650	C90B	N5150K	N831E			
LJ-1651	C90B	N70VR				
LJ-1652	C90B	N722JM	N772JB			
LJ-1653	C90B	N5153V	C-GPPA	N653TF	XA-MSC	
LJ-1654	C90B#	N545C				
LJ-1655	C90B+	N5154E	N387GC	(N125AR)	(N146RT)	N387GC

BEECH 90

c/n	Series/Mod	Identities					
LJ-1656	C90B	N656SA	N447DB				
LJ-1657	C90B+^	N777MN	N777YN				
LJ-1658	C90B	N4YF	PR-GPO				
LJ-1659	C90B	N4409U	YV-731CP	N4409U	YV-931CP	YV218T	
LJ-1660	C90B	N4470M	F-WTCR	F-GTCR			
LJ-1661	C90B	N5061X	N199CG				
LJ-1662	C90B	N4482A	N552E	N410PT	N313PT	N788KC	*N313PT
LJ-1663	C90B$	N5133W	N588SD	HP-1635	[dam 06Jun08 Contadora Island, Panama]		
LJ-1664	C90B	N5064L	N789KP				
LJ-1665	C90B	N4465F	(N904GM)	N289RP			
LJ-1666	C90B	N867P					
LJ-1667	C90B^	N5067L					
LJ-1668	C90B	N4468F	N9DC	N990DW			
LJ-1669	C90B	N4469Z	N126MM				
LJ-1670	C90B	N4470K	N70CM	(PR-RIP)	PR-WNF		
LJ-1671	C90B	N4471M					
LJ-1672	C90B	N5072R	PR-EDP				
LJ-1673	C90B	N3251H	N5431M				
LJ-1674	C90B+	N4484T	N821CS	PR-FAZ			
LJ-1675	C90B	N4415F					
LJ-1676	C90B	N5076G	N771JB	N771JC	PP-WCA		
LJ-1677	C90B	N6077X	(N444ES)	N6077X			
LJ-1678	C90B$	N786P	N53PB	N57WR	[w/o 01Feb08 nr Mount Airy-Surry County Apt, NC, USA; canx 13Jun09]		
LJ-1679	C90B	N4479M	PR-USA				
LJ-1680	C90B	N790W	N74B	N904TH			
LJ-1681	C90B#	N4481P	N954BL	N954BS			
LJ-1682	C90B	N6082A	N21LE	PP-UNI			
LJ-1683	C90B	N6183A	N683GW				
LJ-1684	C90B	N5084J	PR-JQM				
LJ-1685	C90B#^	N1685S					
LJ-1686	C90B+^	N272EA					
LJ-1687	C90B	N6187L	N437JB				
LJ-1688	C90B	N629JG					
LJ-1689	C90B	N557P					
LJ-1690	TC-90	N61669	6834 (JMSDF)				
LJ-1691	C90B	N991SA					
LJ-1692	C90B	N692W					
LJ-1693	C90B	N6193J	PR-RMA				
LJ-1694	C90B	N90KA	N694CT				
LJ-1695	C90B	N124LL					
LJ-1696	C90B	N61906	N93QR	VT-KPC			
LJ-1697	C90B	N50847	N461EP				
LJ-1698	C90B	N61698					
LJ-1699	C90B$^	N90KP	N456PP	M-ONTI			
LJ-1700	C90B	N923P	N550SW				
LJ-1701	C90B	N5134S	PR-FKY				
LJ-1702	C90B	N6190S					
LJ-1703	C90B	N90KU	(N713US)	N45PF	N707PC		
LJ-1704	C90B	N794P	N50PD				
LJ-1705	C90B	N5115H					
LJ-1706	C90B	N5066N	N648JG	PR-VIT			
LJ-1707	C90B	N495Y					
LJ-1708	C90B	N974C	N170S				
LJ-1709	C90B	N744P	N426HM				
LJ-1710	C90B	N785JP					
LJ-1711	C90B	N6111V					
LJ-1712	C90B	N785P	N999NH	PR-GSW			
LJ-1713	C90B+^	N546C	N713EA	N888GD			
LJ-1714	C90B	N6172Y	N422AS				
LJ-1715	C90B	N508CB	PR-CMI				
LJ-1716	C90B	N61716	D-IBBP				
LJ-1717	C90B	N32217	PR-RHH				
LJ-1718	C90B	N720AF	PH-KBB				
LJ-1719	C90B	N36719	N304TC				
LJ-1720	C90B	N22HD					
LJ-1721	C90B	N6196S	N145AF				
LJ-1722	C90B	N37222					
LJ-1723	C90B#	N546C					
LJ-1724	C90B	N79PE					
LJ-1725	C90B	N30025	PR-AGV				
LJ-1726	C90B	N901JS					
LJ-1727	C90GT	N713US	N690GT	PP-AMC			
LJ-1728	C90B	N6028Y	N58GG	XA-	[canx 02May08 as exported to Mexico]		
LJ-1729	C90B	N36929					
LJ-1730	C90B	N36720	LV-BDG	*PR-EQM			
LJ-1731	C90B	N3731V	N851CM	N35HD			
LJ-1732	C90B	N501P	N52BG				
LJ-1733	C90B$	N590PS	M-OTOR				
LJ-1734	C90B	N36634	N59GG	M-GLAS			
LJ-1735	C90B	N36735	ZS-FON				

BEECH 90

c/n	Series/Mod	Identities			
LJ-1736	C90B	N35436	N164WS		
LJ-1737	C90B+^	N36937	N619SH		
LJ-1738	C90B	N51148	XA-EAM	N106DD	
LJ-1739	C90B	N36839	PR-ARC		
LJ-1740	C90B	N36640	C-FMFQ		
LJ-1741	C90B	N36741	XA-RFH		
LJ-1742	C90B+	N36742	PR-MFG		
LJ-1743	C90B	N36883	PR-IRB		
LJ-1744	C90B	N60724	C-FMFR		
LJ-1745	C90B	N36745	C-FMFS		
LJ-1746	C90B	N30246	C-FMFU		
LJ-1747	C90B	N36667	C-FMFX		
LJ-1748	C90B	N36648	N405DD		
LJ-1749	C90B	N37149	C-FMFY		
LJ-1750	C90B	N36850	C-FMFZ		
LJ-1751	C90B	N36891	N12LE	VT-SSL	
LJ-1752	C90B	N6152U	VT-EBG		
LJ-1753	C90B	N37123	XA-	[canx 25Oct06 as exported to Mexico]	
LJ-1754	C90GT#	N24FH	N247CH		
LJ-1755	C90B	N896P	N97DA		
LJ-1756	C90GT#	N741JP	N331JP		
LJ-1757	C90GT$	N157EA	N106ML		
LJ-1758	C90GT	N390GT	XA-CPR		
LJ-1759	C90GT	N590GT			
LJ-1760	C90GT	N23HD	N23HF	D-IBSG	
LJ-1761	C90GT	N790GT			
LJ-1762	C90GT	N762GT	N599HL		
LJ-1763	C90GT	N61788	PR-BOM		
LJ-1764	C90GT	N904JG			
LJ-1765	C90GT	N64GT			
LJ-1766	C90GT	N753P	N74B		
LJ-1767	C90GT	N6197V			
LJ-1768	C90GT	N990GT			
LJ-1769	C90GTi	N36799	PR-CMM		
LJ-1770	C90GT	N770WA	PR-SDA		
LJ-1771	C90GT	N429K	PR-JAG		
LJ-1772	C90GT	N36688	PP-AMJ		
LJ-1773	C90GT+	N37093	XA-	[canx 27Mar09 as exported to Mexico]	
LJ-1774	C90GT	N730EB	N31JN		
LJ-1775	C90GT+	N508GT			
LJ-1776	C90GT	N774EA	N15UB	(N825U)	N575NM
LJ-1777	C90GT	N6178V	N386TH		
LJ-1778	C90GT	N71878			
LJ-1779	C90GT$	N541RK			
LJ-1780	C90GT	N6180P	N51CT	PR-CMB	
LJ-1781	C90GT	N781GT			
LJ-1782	C90GT	N782EA	N155RG		
LJ-1783	C90GT	N333TK	PR-UMU		
LJ-1784	C90GT	N37124	PR-PIB		
LJ-1785	C90GT#	N73415			
LJ-1786	C90GT+	N7086V			
LJ-1787	C90GT	N71957	YV2152		
LJ-1788	C90GT+	N36888	XA-	[canx 01Jul08 as exported to Mexico]	
LJ-1789	C90GT	N417SH			
LJ-1790	C90GT	N42MJ	N125AR	PR-SOF	
LJ-1791	C90GT	N7191N			
LJ-1792	C90GT+	N904PA			
LJ-1793	C90GT+	N825P			
LJ-1794	C90GT	N37324	PR-SGB		
LJ-1795	C90GT	N7295T	N90GP	N90GE	M-TSRI
LJ-1796	C90GT	N71296	PR-DIN		
LJ-1797	C90GT	N427SE			
LJ-1798	C90GT	N37198	(N295AW)	N513BT	
LJ-1799	C90GT	N70189	PR-PDG		
LJ-1800	C90GT	N37200			
LJ-1801	C90GT	N73991	HL5200		
LJ-1802	C90GT$	N7102V	ZS-TWP	ZS-TGM	
LJ-1803	C90GT	N71873	PR-BIO		
LJ-1804	C90GT$	N804GT			
LJ-1805	C90GT	N991GT			
LJ-1806	C90GT	N963P	N91PD		
LJ-1807	C90GT	N7007Y	PR-CEB		
LJ-1808	C90GT	N730EB	N730EZ		
LJ-1809	C90GT	N71909	9M-JPL		
LJ-1810	C90GT	N71650	VT-SKM		
LJ-1811	C90GT	N22CR			
LJ-1812	C90GT#	N73712	C-FPLZ		
LJ-1813	C90GT	N826P	N775SR	PT-GAR	
LJ-1814	C90GT	N70944	C-FJTN		
LJ-1815	C90GT	N3735M	XB-SSL		
LJ-1816	C90GT	N995GT			

c/n	Series/Mod	Identities			
LJ-1817	C90GT	N610SC			
LJ-1818	C90GT	N7218Y	N178EJ		
LJ-1819	C90GT	N70689	LV-BIC		
LJ-1820	C90GT#	N722PM			
LJ-1821	C90GT	N7221Y	PR-GFB		
LJ-1822	C90GT	N73220	TG-RWC		
LJ-1823	C90GT	N7193Q	(PR-LOV)	PT-MBF	
LJ-1824	C90GT	N884EA	N465KC		
LJ-1825	C90GT	N7125Y	(PR-DHA)	PR-DHD	
LJ-1826	C90GT	N3726Y	PR-CAR		
LJ-1827	C90GT	N7207M	PR-BTS		
LJ-1828	C90GT	N7328B	YV2419		
LJ-1829	C90GT+	N71839	XA-CGT		
LJ-1830	C90GT#	N7030B	N790RV		
LJ-1831	C90GT#	N831EB	N618HG	N402MD	
LJ-1832	C90GT	N7282X			
LJ-1833	C90GT	N37064	D-IMAG		
LJ-1834	C90GT	N3734Y	YV	[canx 04Feb09 as exported to Venezuela]	
LJ-1835	C90GT	N7185C	CC-CGS	N718BE	*N835BL
LJ-1836	C90GT	N793P			
LJ-1837	C90GT	N7277F			
LJ-1838	C90GT	N838GT			
LJ-1839	C90GT	N72709	OK-NHR		
LJ-1840	C90GT	N73920	XA-	[canx 07May08 as exported to Mexico]	
LJ-1841	C90GT	N841TB	PR-JME		
LJ-1842	C90GT	N842KA	XA-EAM		
LJ-1843	C90GT	N843KA	XA-	[canx 04Aug08 as exported to Mexico]	
LJ-1844	C90GT	N1844B	PR-JCA		
LJ-1845	C90GT	N845KA	D-IHRG		
LJ-1846	C90GT	N846KA	PR-XGT		
LJ-1847	C90GTi#	N31947	N26TP		
LJ-1848	C90GT	N771JB			
LJ-1849	C90GT	N809P	N407CF		
LJ-1850	C90GT	N527SE			
LJ-1851	C90GT	N851HB	6835 (JMSDF)		
LJ-1852	C90GT	N852HB	6836 (JMSDF)		
LJ-1853	C90GTi	N34003	PR-LMT		
LJ-1854	C90GTi	N890LG			
LJ-1855	C90GTi$	N88DW	N2NC		
LJ-1856	C90GTi#	N271AK			
LJ-1857	C90GTi	N826TM			
LJ-1858	C90GTi#	N623DT	PP-UMU		
LJ-1859	C90GTi	N158J			
LJ-1860	C90GTi	N46MJ			
LJ-1861	C90GTi	N31861	(PP-RCA)	PR-SRA	
LJ-1862	C90GTi	N80KA	PR-OTE		
LJ-1863	C90GTi	N559MC	N989GT		
LJ-1864	C90GTi	N996BL			
LJ-1865	C90GTi	N34975	(D-ITDK)	D-IDKE	
LJ-1866	C90GTi	N33226	I-INVG		
LJ-1867	C90GTi	N921RA			
LJ-1868	C90GTi	N788JM			
LJ-1869	C90GTi	N31869	D-ISTT		
LJ-1870	C90GTi$	N3270T	N65MV		
LJ-1871	C90GTi	N588KM			
LJ-1872	C90GTi	N31872	XA-	[canx 01Apr08 as exported to Mexico]	
LJ-1873	C90GTi	N3133L	HK-	[canx 04Aug08 as exported to Colombia]	
LJ-1874	C90GTi	N32974	VH-GTI		
LJ-1875	C90GTi	N32075	"ZS-DGC"	ZS-GDC	
LJ-1876	C90GTi	N825TL	*PR-LMT		
LJ-1877	C90GTi	N856P	N843RM		
LJ-1878	C90GTi	N463CP			
LJ-1879	C90GTi	N3289T	N890GT		
LJ-1880	C90GTi	N31780	LV-BPB		
LJ-1881	C90GTi#	N232BS	N232BG		
LJ-1882	C90GTi	N31882	PR-JJM		
LJ-1883	C90GTi	N484BW			
LJ-1884	C90GTi	N3184W			
LJ-1885	C90GTi	N90GP	PR-JAV		
LJ-1886	C90GTi	N3186W	PR-LYG		
LJ-1887	C90GTi	N32087	F-HTCR		
LJ-1888	C90GTi+	N989W	N908EF		
LJ-1889	C90GTi	N3289Z	OY-PCM		
LJ-1890	C90GTi#	N3400H	G-CFBX		
LJ-1891	C90GTi	N3191E	PR-AVG		
LJ-1892	C90GTi#	N998GT			
LJ-1893	C90GTi	N11T			
LJ-1894	C90GTi	N528GM			
LJ-1895	C90GTi	N3195B	CC-CNP		
LJ-1896	C90GTi	N3296J	PP-AGR		
LJ-1897	C90GTi	N3197A	N527PM		

BEECH 90

c/n	Series/Mod	Identities			
LJ-1898	C90GTi	N520JK			
LJ-1899	C90GTi$	N3500E	N81MV		
LJ-1900	C90GTi	N3400T	F-HARC		
LJ-1901	C90GTi	N3201W	N254P		
LJ-1902	C90GTi	N3202A	G-WLLM	M-WLLM	
LJ-1903	C90GTi	N904W	N47WY		
LJ-1904	C90GTi	N3204Y	(PR-MJB)	PR-FCI	
LJ-1905	C90GTi	N3305E	XA-	[canx 05Dec08 as exported to Mexico]	
LJ-1906	C90GTi	N3306X	(PP-CMA)	PR-ERM	
LJ-1907	C90GTi	N7HG			
LJ-1908	C90GTi+	N3208T	OE-FDY		
LJ-1909	C90GTi	N909EA			
LJ-1910	C90GTi	N903TT			
LJ-1911	C90GTi	N3501B			
LJ-1912	C90GTi	N3192M	PR-IPI		
LJ-1913	C90GTi	N3388C	PH-JAX		
LJ-1914	C90GTi	N32217	N38HL	*PR-LOL	
LJ-1915	C90GTi	N915WA	VH-PFK		
LJ-1916	C90GTi+	N412WC			
LJ-1917	C90GTi	N330PE			
LJ-1918	C90GTi#	N3298D			
LJ-1919	C90GTi	N335AP			
LJ-1920	C90GTi	N88DW			
LJ-1921	C90GTi	N921KA	(N113LY)	N324JP	
LJ-1922	C90GTi+	N922WA	C-GTSV		
LJ-1923	C90GTi	N929P	*N970P		
LJ-1924	C90GTi#	N3242Q	XA-ULE		
LJ-1925	C90GTi#	N3225V	XA-ULF		
LJ-1926	C90GTi	N926KA	PR-SJE		
LJ-1927	C90GTi	N227GA			
LJ-1928	C90GTi+	N3188W	D-ICMK		
LJ-1929	C90GTi	N6029H	N49FR		
LJ-1930	C90GTi	N6030K			
LJ-1931	C90GTi	N6211J			
LJ-1932	C90GTi	N6032F			
LJ-1933	C90GTi	N933KA			
LJ-1934	C90GTi	N6234M	N590HB		
LJ-1935	C90GTi	N60FR	N890HB	N190EU	D-ISBC
LJ-1936	C90GTi	N6436U	HB-GPL		
LJ-1937	C90GTi	N63937	*PR-LLL		
LJ-1938	C90GTi	N6338P	PR-JCF		
LJ-1939	C90GTi	N6439R	*PR-RPN		
LJ-1940	C90GTi	N63540	(PR-MDA)	PR-CMG	
LJ-1941	C90GTi	N62541	YV	[canx 11Aug09 as exported to Venezuela]	
LJ-1942	C90GTi	N6042K	HP-	[canx 27May09 as exported to Panama]	
LJ-1943	C90GTi	N6043Z			
LJ-1944	C90GTi	N890HB			
LJ-1945	C90GTi	N6005Y	B-7751		
LJ-1946	C90GTi+	N6446Q	N904GT		
LJ-1947	C90GTi	N64347	A2-	[canx 30Jul09 as exported to Botswana]	
LJ-1948	C90GTi	N6148Z			
LJ-1949	C90GTi	N6449B	*PP-MSE		
LJ-1950	C90GTi	N69GT			
LJ-1951	C90GTi	N6151A			
LJ-1952	C90GTi	N6352J			
LJ-1953	C90GTi	N6253B			
LJ-1954	C90GTi	N60FR			
LJ-1955	C90GTi	N6055W	*PP-AGM		
LJ-1956	C90GTi	N6356V			
LJ-1957	C90GTi	N64576			
LJ-1958	C90GTi	N61678			
LJ-1959	C90GTi				
LJ-1960	C90GTi	N6260Q			
LJ-1961	C90GTi	N6061L			
LJ-1962	C90GTi				
LJ-1963	C90GTi				
LJ-1964	C90GTi	N6204U			
LJ-1965	C90GTi				
LJ-1966	C90GTi	N6466G			
LJ-1967	C90GTi				
LJ-1968	C90GTi	N6168T			
LJ-1969	C90GTi				
LJ-1970	C90GTi				
LJ-1971	C90GTi				
LJ-1972	C90GTi	N64392			
LJ-1973	C90GTi				
LJ-1974	C90GTx				
LJ-1975	C90GTx				
LJ-1976	C90GTx				
LJ-1977	C90GTx				
LJ-1978	C90GTx				

BEECH 90

c/n	Series/Mod	Identities
LJ-1979	C90GTx	
LJ-1980	C90GTx	
LJ-1981	C90GTx	
LJ-1982	C90GTx	
LJ-1983	C90GTx	
LJ-1984	C90GTx	
LJ-1985	C90GTx	
LJ-1986	C90GTx	
LJ-1987	C90GTx	
LJ-1988	C90GTx	
LJ-1989	C90GTx	
LJ-1990	C90GTx	
LJ-1991	C90GTx	
LJ-1992	C90GTx	
LJ-1993	C90GTx	
LJ-1994	C90GTx	
LJ-1995	C90GTx	
LJ-1996	C90GTx	
LJ-1997	C90GTx	
LJ-1998	C90GTx	
LJ-1999	C90GTx	
LJ-2000	C90GTx	
LJ-2001	C90GTx	
LJ-2002	C90GTx	
LJ-2003	C90GTx	
LJ-2004	C90GTx	
LJ-2005	C90GTx	
LJ-2006	C90GTx	
LJ-2007	C90GTx	
LJ-2008	C90GTx	
LJ-2009	C90GTx	
LJ-2010	C90GTx	
LJ-2011	C90GTx	
LJ-2012	C90GTx	
LJ-2013	C90GTx	
LJ-2014	C90GTx	
LJ-2015	C90GTx	
LJ-2016	C90GTx	
LJ-2017	C90GTx	
LJ-2018	C90GTx	
LJ-2019	C90GTx	
LJ-2020	C90GTx	
LJ-2021	C90GTx	
LJ-2022	C90GTx	
LJ-2023	C90GTx	
LJ-2024	C90GTx	
LJ-2025	C90GTx	
LJ-2026	C90GTx	
LJ-2027	C90GTx	
LJ-2028	C90GTx	
LJ-2029	C90GTx	
LJ-2030	C90GTx	
LJ-2031	C90GTx	
LJ-2032	C90GTx	
LJ-2033	C90GTx	
LJ-2034	C90GTx	
LJ-2035	C90GTx	
LJ-2036	C90GTx	
LJ-2037	C90GTx	
LJ-2038	C90GTx	
LJ-2039	C90GTx	
LJ-2040	C90GTx	
LJ-2041	C90GTx	
LJ-2042	C90GTx	
LJ-2043	C90GTx	
LJ-2044	C90GTx	
LJ-2045	C90GTx	
LJ-2046	C90GTx	
LJ-2047	C90GTx	
LJ-2048	C90GTx	
LJ-2049	C90GTx	
LJ-2050	C90GTx	
LJ-2051	C90GTx	
LJ-2052	C90GTx	
LJ-2053	C90GTx	
LJ-2054	C90GTx	
LJ-2055	C90GTx	
LJ-2056	C90GTx	
LJ-2057	C90GTx	
LJ-2058	C90GTx	

BEECH E90 KING AIR

$ = Raisbeck dual aft body strakes fitted
# = Raisbeck nacelle wing lockers fitted
+ = Raisbeck dual aft body strakes and nacelle wing lockers fitted
^ - Blackhawk XP135A engine upgrade fitted

c/n	Series/Mod	Identities
LW-1	E90	N934K N64RA N64RJ N190RM N190RL
LW-2	E90	N9502Q N710TK N412SR N100MW
LW-3	E90	N9493Q N888BH F-GJAD
LW-4	E90	N111JW N112LS N44EC N77WF
LW-5	E90	N1575W N222TR N200CU N730K N999SE N999SF
LW-6	E90	N1631W (D-IMAS) HB-GFG N511J (N60DC) N722M N905TF
LW-7	E90	N107B N51SG N51DN
LW-8	E90	N132B N132HS
LW-9	E90	PT-IGD
LW-10	E90	N214B N711EK N14MW N977SB
LW-11	E90	N241B N11DT
LW-12	E90	N2KA RP-C289 N12GJ
LW-13	E90	N239B N21DJ N383AA
LW-14	E90	N226W N226B YV-72CP N4495N XA- [canx 22Jul05 as exported to Mexico]
LW-15	E90	PP-EFC [dbr 30May00 Goiania, Goias, Brazil; parts to Sorocaba, Sao Paulo State, Brazil]
LW-16	E90	N48V N48VL N80NC N43WS
LW-17	E90#	N932K N945M N305PC N305BC LV-WEY N259SC (N906BB) N259SC
LW-18	E90	N22EH N22ER
LW-19	E90	N1716W N102RB [w/o 18Mar93 Julcan, Peru; canx 11Mar08]
LW-20	E90	N37D N37DC N84LS N87CH
LW-21	E90$	N121B
LW-22	E90	CF-ASD N428TB N90BJ N90DA OB-1602 N90DA [w/o 28Mar97 Choque, Peru; canx 11Oct03]
LW-23	E90	N345V
LW-24	E90	N90CA N76LB N7134J N95RB N95LB
LW-25	E90	G-BABW N4406W N1100M YV N1100M [canx 23Oct06 as exported to Venezuela; reinstated 23Jul07]
LW-26	E90	N1769W 1769 (Royal Thai AF) 00-923 (Royal Thai AF)
LW-27	E90	N169B N1HR N999ES N379VM
LW-28	E90	G-BAAM N56MC N56ME (N44AB) (N56MF) N42MP YV-1765P N2XZ FAB-026 (Bolivian AF)
LW-29	E90	N1739W N90AF [w/o 26Sep93 Cuzco-Teniente Alejandro Velasco Astete International, Peru]
LW-30	E90	N159B N20WS (N24TF) N20WS
LW-31	E90	N1741W N17GD N90WT
LW-32	E90	N1HP N1HT N123PP N291MM
LW-33	E90	XC-FUY [w/o; date & location unkn]
LW-34	E90	N214K N690G
LW-35	E90	N147E N811JB N14NM
LW-36	E90	N1679E OB-1598 PNP-230 (Peruvian Police)
LW-37	E90	N1837W I-ELTR N1837W N777EC [dbf 07Jan79 in New York State, USA]
LW-38	E90	N5000T N4GN [w/o 10Mar80 Flushing, NY, USA]
LW-39	E90	HB-GFI N99447 N6UM OB-1466 HK-3907X HK-3907W
LW-40	E90$	N1PC N99TC N81PS N61PS N61NA N155CG N523CJ N891PC
LW-41	E90	N2AS N12KA [w/o 21Jul02 Bloomington-Central Illinois Regional, IL, USA; canx 20Oct05]
LW-42	E90	N52KA
LW-43	E90	D-INAC N600CX
LW-44	E90	N101PC N14CE N166A N666DC
LW-45	E90	N111JA N777SS N200RM
LW-46	E90	N56KA [dbr 27Dec92 nr Dixon-Municipal, IL, USA, parts to Dodson International Parts, Rantoul, KS, USA; canx 17Jan95]
LW-47	E90	(F-BUFY) F-ASFA 5R- [canx 02Jul09 as exported to Madagascar]
LW-48	E90	N5500F N3500F OK-DKH N70MV N22N
LW-49	E90	N100NS N700NS (N700AB) N3000W N103SB N20QD N777NG N777AJ N12LA
LW-50	E90	N10J N10JQ N88GC N150TW
LW-51	E90	N7LR N35CM N35CG N35CM N779AF
LW-52	E90	I-PIAB N72589 N741KA N74171 N181Z
LW-53	E90	YV-TADJ [w/o 10May73 nr Pratt, KS, USA]
LW-54	E90	N771HM N77JX
LW-55	E90^	N55KA XB-IEI N3929G
LW-56	E90	PT-FGA PP-FPP
LW-57	E90$	N414GC N414GQ N89BC N86TR N88TR N511WM
LW-58	E90$	N4PC N500MB N250HP N350AT N625PP
LW-59	E90+	G-BAVG N4718C G-OOAG G-FAVI VR-CGK (N303MF) D-IMWA N992MA N290KA
LW-60	E90$	N3090W N17CP N660L N999TB N90PH
LW-61	E90	N3061W N735TD N100JW N7001L N220B N321DH N56TJ N120GR N129C
LW-62	E90	N21XL N21XE N21XL N7CJ N96DA N16NM N14C N26E
LW-63	E90	N3063W N200CL N250MM VH-ICV N808GA N93A
LW-64	E90	N8PC N213DS N47LC [w/o 03Jul07 Carlsbad-McClellan Palomar, CA, USA; canx 21Jan09]
LW-65	E90	N3065W N987GM
LW-66	E90$	N3166W N554CF (N106TB) N554CF
LW-67	E90	N4400W N575HW N575HC [w/o 19May85 Pine Bluff-Grider Field, AR, USA; canx 26Mar91]
LW-68	E90	F-BUTS [wfu, parts to Dodson International Parts, Rantoul, KS, USA; canx 19Sep03]

BEECH E90

c/n	Series/Mod	Identities
LW-69	E90$	N27L N271 YV-1894P N4264D HK-2550X HK-2550 ZP-TWT N69AM N769AM N5462G
LW-70	E90	N4PT N133K N5911P LV-WZR
LW-71	E90$	N121EG
LW-72	E90	N25655 N310GF (N73JC) N101WL N102MC N81HP
LW-73	E90#	N743JA (N743EC) N111WA
LW-74	E90	N713X N71BX N717PP
LW-75	E90	N3075W XB-AEU N75LW
LW-76	E90	9Q-CZD ZS-LJF N176TW N76TW N176TW
LW-77	E90	N3177W [w/o 31May93 Bellavista, Peru]
LW-78	E90	N4378W N15WN
LW-79	E90	XB-PUF XA-RNF N12AK N60BA
LW-80	E90+	N2ZC N3ZC N20LH N522MJ
LW-81	E90	N10JP YV-T-AJP YV-416P [wfu, parts to Atlanta Air Salvage, Griffin-Spalding County, GA, USA]
LW-82	E90$^	YV-O-MH-01 YV-O-MAC-6 YV-O-SAS-3N820RD
LW-83	E90	G-BBKM N99855 G-BHUL [w/o 22Apr85 Goodwood, UK; canx 04Feb87]
LW-84	E90	N3026W N999MC N999MK TF-DCA N111JA
LW-85	E90$	N3125W N312MP N20RF N42PC
LW-86	E90	N3126W N410PD N410PB (N429K) (N505N) F-GFDJ
LW-87	E90	N309D N107TB N800BF ZS-OGT 9J-OGT V5-MED
LW-88	E90	N90CJ N1LC N1LQ N1TQ 9Q-CTQ F-GELL N29M
LW-89	E90	N3189W N550Z N22KW (N22KD) N22KF N77PA N98HF
LW-90	E90$	N3190W N319MP N319P N86AT N81PL N114AT HK- [canx 13Sep91 as exported to Colombia]
LW-91	E90	F-BUYZ N75DA F-GBRD [w/o 02Nov86 Barcelonnette, France]
LW-92	E90	N300PS N308PS [w/o 18Nov88 Locust Grove-Batesville Regional, AR, USA]
LW-93	E90$	N1PC N655F N352GR
LW-94	E90	N23DB N13DB N50RD N98ME YV-467CP
LW-95	E90	N3195W N350MH N351MH N270FS OY-CFO N567GJ
LW-96	E90	N35KA N214SC
LW-97	E90	TR-LRX F-ODID D-IDTB F-WZIG F-GESJ TL- [canx 14Jun07 as exported to Central African Republic]
LW-98	E90	N4398W N439EE N987GM [dbr 31May89 Tuba City, AZ, USA, parts to White Industries, Bates City, MO, USA; location F-34; canx 21Sep89]
LW-99	E90	N31JJ N31WP
LW-100	E90	N5AJ N5AX N31FM N31FN N28MS
LW-101	E90	D-IDAH F-BXPL N64795 N111XT N111PC N70SW N211CG
LW-102	E90	N4423W CS-TFA F-GABV [w/o 01May98 nr Alencon, France; canx 03Dec99]
LW-103	E90	N5RE N35BH C-FMGL D-IDEA N898WW
LW-104	E90$	N130S N130SB N133PL N123MH
LW-105	E90	N205CA N111FW N111FV
LW-106	E90	I-FASJ SE-IIU OB-1420 [w/o 08Mar94 Palmapampa, Peru; canx 28Feb95]
LW-107	E90	N4487W N44WL N990CF N27BM N96TB N44MV
LW-108	E90$	N28356 N51KA N1105X N37X N37HC
LW-109	E90	N388SC N989GM N39U
LW-110	E90	N8PC 9Q-CCG
LW-111	E90	N11GE C-GBTI
LW-112	E90	N3034W N67PS
LW-113	E90	XA-FEX XB-QIY [w/o 02Mar81 Monterrey, Nuevo Leon, Mexico]
LW-114	E90	N9024R N89L N700DH
LW-115	E90	N80WP N37MC N76SK N176JR
LW-116	E90	F-BVRS TF-ELT 9J-STA
LW-117	E90	N7387R N3LK N31EE N76PW N10XJ
LW-118	E90	N8118R
LW-119	E90	N111JW N100CU N102CU N152D N994RD (N800C) N152D
LW-120	E90+	N9GC N99AC (N870BB) N99AC
LW-121	E90$	N500TR N515BC
LW-122	E90	N8554R VH-DDG N114K [w/o 26Oct81 Mineral Wells, TX, USA; canx 18Dec82]
LW-123	E90#	N158D N5NM N5NV N121GW N500MS
LW-124	E90$	N8594R N859MB N859LP (N759LP) N859LB N883AC N31GA N90GK N90BF
LW-125	E90+	N122NC N122NN N543MB N504CB
LW-126	E90$	(G-BCKE) RP-C201 N103AP N115YS
LW-127	E90$	N948V N711RP N711RQ N71WB
LW-128	E90	N444KA N1CB N50EB
LW-129	E90$	N9051S N423JD LV-WFP
LW-130	E90	N7309R ZS-AMR N52457 N75KC N47AW [wfu cOct08, parts to MTW Aerospace, Montgomery, AL, USA]
LW-131	E90	N9031R N98PC N98PM
LW-132	E90	N9029R
LW-133	E90$^	N581M (N52CB) PT-LHZ
LW-134	E90	N44KA N663LS N55HC
LW-135	E90	N7275R N74VR LV-AYG
LW-136	E90	TR-LTT N328TB N84GA N30CW N750DC G-DEXY G-ORTH
LW-137	E90	N6843S [w/o 29Nov76 nr Tok, AK, USA]
LW-138	E90	N914D (N105WW) N90WW N90GD PT-WAG
LW-139	E90	N4139S N413AP C-FFOL N345KA N249WM
LW-140	E90$	8P-BAR N8069S N1UC
LW-141	E90	N9704S ZS-JFW N9296Z N77CA N167CA (N167JR) N382TW TI-SFC N382TW
LW-142	E90+	N4138S N7WS N7WU
LW-143	E90+	N9093S N30MR N30MD N300BA N300MT

BEECH E90

c/n	Series/Mod	Identities
LW-144	E90$	YV-T-APD YV-66CP YV-2503P N812KB
LW-145	E90	N9065S N122HC RP-C879 N737LC
LW-146	E90$	N4467M (YV-T-AOL) YV-T-HTZ YV-71P N4467M N711BP N141DA N41HH LV-BXF
LW-147	E90	N111JA N26SE N4RG C-FATX N553MA N28M
LW-148	E90	N90MB N500PR N300KD N300CH N80BT
LW-149	E90	N102PC N177KA N177MK
LW-150	E90	N23AE N100EC
LW-151	E90	(F-BXLF) TR-LVH ZS-OAE
LW-152	E90	N9052S N2000F N9046G N7400V
LW-153	E90	FAC498 (Chilean AF) CC-EAB CC-PTQ CC-DAG CC-DSN
LW-154	E90$	N222RL N211DG GN-7593 (Venezuelan National Guard)
LW-155	E90^	N9095S N903HC N505GA N505MW
LW-156	E90	N5PC N414GN
LW-157	E90	TR-LVJ N114K C-GXJQ N81AS N199TT
LW-158	E90	N42KA N940SR N75JP
LW-159	E90	N9059S
LW-160	E90	N9080S N251CM N251SR N53CE
LW-161	E90	F-BXON
LW-162	E90#	N2162L N200E N2006 N100SC N100SK N36GS N369CD [w/o 05Aug07 Ruidoso, NM, USA; canx 18Sep07]
LW-163	E90+	N9063S (N112CM) N34MF
LW-164	E90	N200RE
LW-165	E90$	N6833S N700DH N701X
LW-166	E90	D-IBUR N26902 N300SP [w/o 31Jan96 Humphreys Peak, Flagstaff, AZ, USA; canx 23Mar99]
LW-167	E90	N9097S N214RW N213RW N199PL
LW-168	E90$	N9068S N112AR N500CT N711HA N220PB (N616DD) N23EW
LW-169	E90+	N600SC N600KC N17SE ZS-IAN
LW-170	E90	N1570L (ZS-KEC) ZS-KCE N444GA N500TL N555TT XB-JCT [impounded Managua, Nicaragua]
LW-171	E90$	N6571S
LW-172	E90	YV-326P YV1167
LW-173	E90	N1573L N707TL
LW-174	E90	N1574L N21KE N45RM [w/o 01Jul92 Yurimaguas, Peru; aircraft had been canx 06Feb92 although never officially registered in Peru before accident]
LW-175	E90	F-BXSN F-HAAA
LW-176	E90+	YV-735P N190TC N103AL N500HJ N1MW N70EA N662JS
LW-177	E90	N2177L N944RS
LW-178	E90	HC-DAC
LW-179	E90	N2111L N211MH N676J
LW-180	E90	N2180L F-GIML [w/o 13Nov00 Reims, France]
LW-181	E90	N2181L [dbr 07Dec80 Michigan City, IN, USA, parts to Dodson International Parts, Rantoul, KS, USA]
LW-182	E90$	YV-O-BIV-2 YV-726CP [dbr 27Mar94 Caracas, Venezuela, parts to Dodson International Parts, Rantoul, KS, USA]
LW-183	E90	YV-940P HK-2491X HK-2491
LW-184	E90	F-BXPK N555LW N999GP N899GP N4MR N314MR
LW-185	E90$	N600AC
LW-186	E90+	N2186L
LW-187	E90	N2187L N900MH N816EP N66BP N816RL
LW-188	E90$	N2188L N16TE N68PM N428V
LW-189	E90	YV-O-INAV-3 YV-O-INV-3 YV-O-SATA-7 YV0107 YV2352
LW-190	E90$	RP-C415
LW-191	E90$	N2191L N300BJ N63EC N258JC *N63LW
LW-192	E90	N2192L
LW-193	E90	N9057S N46RP (N6410X) N46RP
LW-194	E90$	N2194L N70LS N194KA N117FH C-GSNM
LW-195	E90	N2195L AN-BME N195BV N195WF N195B [dbr 14Oct86 Beverly-Municipal, MA, USA, parts to Dodson International Parts, Rantoul, KS, USA]
LW-196	E90$	N2269L N3813C N3818C
LW-197	E90$	N222JD N228RA N533SS
LW-198	E90	N202CC (N7PB) G-WELL N46BM
LW-199	E90	F-GALZ [reportedly dbr 01Apr94 - status?]
LW-200	E90$	N4210S N913VS N918VS
LW-201	E90	YV-O-NCE-2 [w/o 13Nov95 Caracas-La Carlota, Venezuela]
LW-202	E90+^	N31KA N127 N934DC N65MS
LW-203	E90$	YV-O-SAS-3 N203RD
LW-204	E90+	N4204S N965LC N965LG
LW-205	E90+	N6666N N252CM ZS-NDR Z-DJF Z-AHL
LW-206	E90	N6406S N290MC
LW-207	E90	N4207S [w/o 31Jul77 nr Sitka, AK, USA]
LW-208	E90	YV-706P
LW-209	E90$	N700DC N32NS N282DB
LW-210	E90$^	N4284S N957MC N717TM N860MH
LW-211	E90	N4216S N88RG N4216S
LW-212	E90	N75CF [w/o 19Dec99 nr Beaufort-County Apt, SC, USA; canx 26Jun01]
LW-213	E90	N2274L
LW-214	E90$	N17603 N14SB
LW-215	E90^	(F-GAME) N99342 I-MCCC N56HT (N215AM) N90AL N56HT
LW-216	E90	N200SF N24DA D-IBPD N91SF N81SF N190DB N439WA

BEECH E90

c/n	Series/Mod	Identities
LW-217	E90	N16LH
LW-218	E90	N1824S N18243 HP-1246 N700WD N406SF
LW-219	E90$	N77A N77AG N83FE
LW-220	E90	N17619 C-GIIX N220Y I-RWWW [CofA exp 08Apr90; reportedly wfu & b/u]
LW-221	E90$	N400SF N429DM N429DW N48VZ LV-BRS
LW-222	E90$	N17620 N1762K VH-MTG ZS-NYE
LW-223	E90$	N77M N7UM N333LE
LW-224	E90	D-IATA ZS-NXI
LW-225	E90$	N700AC N700DC N101CG N181CG (N419HM) N181CG
LW-226	E90#	N22675 N976 N711TZ [dbr 19Mar03 nr McElroy Field, Kremmling, CO, USA, parts to Dodson International Parts, Rantoul, KS, USA; canx 31Jan05]
LW-227	E90	N77P N7ZP N901TM
LW-228	E90	N22844 N130S N132S N21EH N26EH N53BB N692M
LW-229	E90	EV-7702 (Venezuelan Army)
LW-230	E90	N464AL N70DW N333AS N345MB N126RD N48T N48TE N23W
LW-231	E90	YV-122CP YV-27P N4954S (N388CP) N304LG
LW-232	E90	N23250 N2325G N232CL N112SB N448CP
LW-233	E90	N908CM [w/o 25Aug80 nr Kotzebue, AK, USA]
LW-234	E90$	YV-118CP YV1465
LW-235	E90	D-IMAA N16GA C-FBCS N776DC
LW-236	E90+	N23600 N48V N948CC [w/o 14Mar02 nr Reno/Tahoe International, NV, USA; canx 03Aug06]
LW-237	E90	N23707 N714F (N113SB) N5NM N17NM
LW-238	E90	N23800 N707BC N707DC N25TG XB-DLS N4107W XA- [canx 24Mar08 as exported to Mexico]
LW-239	E90	N6EA N89FN N24SM G-SFSG N25EN
LW-240	E90	N80WP N500EA HP-5000H TI-AZO
LW-241	E90	N17844 N30KC
LW-242	E90+	G-GBSC N555GA N34WW N34BS C-GGRS (N95KA) N963KA
LW-243	E90	N18343
LW-244	E90	D-IMBI OY-ASU N611R
LW-245	E90$	N22453 N823PW N18DN N18DV F-GKJD (N7084B) N18DV N3LS
LW-246	E90	N23646 N711NV N711HV
LW-247	E90	F-GAPO TR-LYA [w/o 10Apr78 Libreville, Gabon]
LW-248	E90	N9FC N555FW
LW-249	E90$^	N30KC (N28CC) N68CC N521LB
LW-250	E90$	N18750 N5555L N600EF N321DM TI-BBN
LW-251	E90	TG-BET N7050J N483 N7ZU F-GJCR
LW-252	E90$	N202KA N505RG N1975G N969CL N30CV
LW-253	E90$	N18753 N709DB N43PC
LW-254	E90	N22654 N48W
LW-255	E90	N258D VH-LFH [w/o 25Jul90 Wondai, nr Kingaroy, QLD, Australia; canx 22Apr92]
LW-256	E90	N961DM N63BW N63BV
LW-257	E90+	N20695 N136K N711BL N711BX N355JS N77CE
LW-258	E90	N20316 N203PC
LW-259	E90	N23509 ZP-PMX N103HC N269JB LV-WHV
LW-260	E90	(YV-171CP) GN-7839 (Venezuelan National Guard)
LW-261	E90	N8SP N8SD CP-2183 N4283R ZP-TZW
LW-262	E90$	N77W N7ZW N790RB YV [canx 13Aug09 as exported to Venezuela]
LW-263	E90$	N78K N184JS N1840S XA- [canx 20Aug08 as exported to Mexico]
LW-264	E90	TR-0201 (Venezuelan Navy) ARV-0201 (Venezuelan Navy)
LW-265	E90	N362D
LW-266	E90^	N9081S N525KA N215HC N702XP
LW-267	E90$	N23726 N468SC N23726 N20S
LW-268	E90	N23681 TI-GEV YS-210P *N210YS
LW-269	E90	N23802 N288CB N288CR
LW-270	E90	YV-1500P
LW-271	E90	N23798 N123LN N727MT
LW-272	E90	N221KA N300HC (N301HC) N62BL [w/o 23Jun05 New Roads-False River Regional, LA, USA]
LW-273	E90	N800AC N555TB N10SA N273NA
LW-274	E90#^	N90EA (N2296Y) N90TT C-GTIO N274KA
LW-275	E90$	N4725M N47BH C-FYCB
LW-276	E90	D-IAHC N138GA N125L N7TD
LW-277	E90	N4977M RP-C292 [CofA exp 10Nov01; canx; fate unkn]
LW-278	E90	YV-195CP N4757C N700MA F-GHUV
LW-279	E90	N4763M N390MT N390PS
LW-280	E90	N4820M N41WE [dbr 11Jan05 nr Rawlins-Municipal, WY, USA, parts to Weld County Apt, CO, USA; canx 10Aug06]
LW-281	E90	N4821M N30A N502SC N31A
LW-282	E90	N50MB N900AC
LW-283	E90	N4915M I-MOFN SE-IKM N845MC N48TA
LW-284	E90	N4992M N200WB N300RK N200WB ZP-TJW ZP-TMA
LW-285	E90	N777KA
LW-286	E90	N18754 N155LS
LW-287	E90$	N23660 C-FNCB
LW-288	E90	N500GC N500DC HB-GGY N717US N700DD
LW-289	E90$	D-ILMP N85DH N222MC N222MQ N83WE
LW-290	E90	N20162 N50MT N51MT N79NS N60MH
LW-291	E90+	N2017Y N27GT N10GP N291AV 5U-ABV N824AC
LW-292	E90$	N2017N N179CA N7MA N92DV

BEECH E90

c/n	Series/Mod	Identities
LW-293	E90	N12AU N12AX
LW-294	E90	N20281 N9DF N677J
LW-295	E90	F-GBDZ [w/o 15Dec82 Paris, France]
LW-296	E90$^	YV-207CP N4424V N207CP F-GETJ *F-GZZB
LW-297	E90$	OY-AZG SE-IKD LX-LTX PH-AXS
LW-298	E90	N2029X N44GK (N118SB) N44GK
LW-299	E90$	N821AD N37CP N127BB N127EC N33FR
LW-300	E90	N2035C N911AZ (N912AZ) N911AZ
LW-301	E90$	N550P N618RD
LW-302	E90$	N2035N RP-C298 (N209DM) RP-C298 [assigned import as N209DM since 1989]
LW-303	E90+^	N20351 N79CT
LW-304	E90	G-BGNU G-SANB (N113SB) F-GMRN
LW-305	E90+	N500GC N625W N605W N942RM N111TC
LW-306	E90	N2043W N90SR N67V
LW-307	E90	N2041Y N25RT ZS-KYH N300EH N47WM [dbr 20Jan95 Kingston, ON, Canada, parts to Dodson International Parts, Rantoul, KS, USA]
LW-308	E90	N2044C N777EC N777EQ N717DC N62CS HR-ANW N2DD N132DD
LW-309	E90$	N2045N N20GM N25AP N630AM N160TT LN-ACY N375EM YV [canx 23Jul09 as exported to Venezuela]
LW-310	E90+	LV-PAY LV-MRN N10WG
LW-311	E90(WL)	N2048K N83RH N551MS N505RP N282TC
LW-312	E90	N20509 N505BG N510ME
LW-313	E90	(N54RC) N491KA N491KD N916PA [w/o 10Jun96 Woolwich-Wiscasset Apt, ME, USA; canx 25Mar97]
LW-314	E90	N20564 (N404RW) CP-2494
LW-315	E90	HB-GGU N666ZT (N770MT) N888ZT
LW-316	E90+	N70KC N70YC N46HM N38CR F-GJHM N57MS N77WZ OO-VHV
LW-317	E90	N2062A N703LW
LW-318	E90$	F-GBLV N702US ZK-RIL N702US N999HE N943CL N443CL
LW-319	E90^	N2065K N1205S
LW-320	E90	N2065D N366JM N366GW
LW-321	E90	N60253 EI-BHL TJ-MJP
LW-322	E90	N6050F N600FC YV-516CP
LW-323	E90	N323KA N323HA
LW-324	E90	N2043C N351GR
LW-325	E90$	N60575 RP-C291
LW-326	E90	D-IHCE N90XY TN-AFG
LW-327	E90	N6671M G-JGAL N788SW
LW-328	E90	N1AM N797PA N551M F-GPJD
LW-329	E90$	N122MM N122BW N320LH F-GJBG N652L
LW-330	E90	LV-PFJ LV-PDA LV-OBB
LW-331	E90$	N67262 RP-C319 N54PT
LW-332	E90#	N636JM N636GW C-FJWU
LW-333	E90	G-BHKS N90BE XB-JLA
LW-334	E90	N22TL
LW-335	E90	F-GCJN [w/o 18Aug81 location unkn; canx 22Oct86]
LW-336	E90	N6759P N675J N21NM
LW-337	E90	N290K
LW-338	E90	N3682E N50RV N199DW
LW-339	E90	SE-IES (D-ILAF) N290TC LV-VFC N339KA
LW-340	E90	N3700M
LW-341	E90+	N3722G RP-C1990 N341MH
LW-342	E90+^	N3741M N90XS
LW-343	E90	N3710Y PT-OUF
LW-344	E90#	N3818H N16TB (N16TE) N344W N810V N888RT N999SE
LW-345	E90	N336JM N38561 N86Q N911MM N811MM N336JM N173AS
LW-346	E90	N3821S N114WA
LW-347	E90	N3841V PT-LCE

Production complete

BEECH F90/F90-1 KING AIR

$ = Raisbeck dual aft body strakes fitted
# = Raisbeck nacelle wing lockers fitted
+ = Raisbeck dual aft body strakes and nacelle wing lockers fitted
^ - Blackhawk XP135A engine upgrade fitted

c/n	Series/Mod	Identities
LA-1	F90	N9079S [wfu c1987 Wichita-Beech Field, KS, USA]
LA-2	F90^	N290KA N58AU N58AB N49CH
LA-3	F90+	N9090S N1MA (N87AG) N1MA
LA-4	F90+	N66489 N64JB OY-BVD N24MK N1DE N1HE N502SP HB-GJQ N502SP HB-GJQ
LA-5	F90	N90FD N602EB N901PS
LA-6	F90	N6642B N51K N7PB C-GSSA N111AA
LA-7	F90	N66447 N717EP N50GH N67RP PT-LLP
LA-8	F90	YV-288CP [w/o 18May84 Caracas, Venezuela]
LA-9	F90$	N66549 N23WE N200FA N300TA
LA-10	F90$	N91P N90BN N325WP N325WR
LA-11	F90$	N6750C N18EA N18EH PT-LXI
LA-12	F90	N66912 N19R N19RK N200E N19RK
LA-13	F90$	C-GGJH N20AM D-ICBA N909K N18BL N132AS N911CF
LA-14	F90^	N214KA N210PP N205PC N205BC N581RJ
LA-15	F90+	(F-GBTK) HB-GGX N804RM (F-GHAF) F-GHGP N10GA ZS-NSC N237JS N124BK
LA-16	F90	N6725T YV-289CP YV-2289P YV-1013P HK-3852X HK-3852 [canx 15Jun94 - status?]
LA-17	F90	N6651H XB-HPC N19EG N117TJ
LA-18	F90#	N22JW N65SF N84JL
LA-19	F90	N6686A N90MT N90NS F-GETI
LA-20	F90+	N754D N117W N717W N13JV (N85JG) N90ET N810CM
LA-21	F90	N66LP N20UN
LA-22	F90	D-ICET N4269Y (N444EM) F-GHIV
LA-23	F90$	N6731A N32PM N14TT N27WH N16BM
LA-24	F90	N93KA
LA-25	F90+	N6667K N875DA N616BH N616CP N128JP
LA-26	F90+^	N6668C N96TT
LA-27	F90+	N6671Z N44SR N40BR N246CA
LA-28	F90	N6065L JA8822 N110RK N90GT N90LL PT-LPL
LA-29	F90	N6673V N667HE N88TW [stolen 17Feb97 Treasure Cay, Bahamas, dbr & b/u; canx 24Aug01]
LA-30	F90	N6690C N199BC (N483JM) N199BC
LA-31	F90$^	N6675W N960V
LA-32	F90	N969MC N123CH
LA-33	F90	N6726Z N90FL N49PH
LA-34	F90+	N6739H N43WS N57TM
LA-35	F90	YV-290CP YV1537
LA-36	F90^	N6736C N102WK
LA-37	F90	N30GT
LA-38	F90+	N160S N70637 N888EM D-IAGB N65MT
LA-39	F90+	YV-342CP N703JT N454GC
LA-40	F90	N6748P N66BS
LA-41	F90	N37BT N37JT N321JG N37UT N37JT N311DS [dbr 11Jan91 Nacogdoches, TX, USA, parts to White Industries, Bates City, MO, USA; location F-42]
LA-42	F90	N43PS N47PE N18CM N47PE N190FD D-ILIM N190FD
LA-43	F90$	N6749E XA-TAY
LA-44	F90$	N67242 ZS-KLT V5-KLT N244J XA-TMP
LA-45	F90	N6752C N68DK N748GM XA-LGT
LA-46	F90	N208PP N208PC N208RC ZP-TZF
LA-47	F90	D-IDIC N984GA ZS-MHM *ZS-CSI
LA-48	F90+	N3685C C-FOMH N30NH N910JS *N555LD
LA-49	F90	N3685P N200BM PT-OIF
LA-50	F90	F-GCLS HB-GHD
LA-51	F90$	N44KA N901WP N901NB ZS-NFO
LA-52	F90	N769D
LA-53	F90#	N3667U N366SP N514LM N5AH
LA-54	F90	(YV-371CP) HK-2484X HK-2484 N540WJ TG- [canx 11Mar08 as exported to Guatemala]
LA-55	F90+	N3679A N10K N311DB N701NC N300GC N311GC
LA-56	F90	N3684P N777AG N777AQ N68DK
LA-57	F90	N3685G N700SF HP-80P HP-805 N9PU [w/o 09Dec89 Lincoln, NM, USA]
LA-58	F90$	C-GBTL N67TM N59EK
LA-59	F90+	N7P G-FLTI N146FL *G-FLTI
LA-60	F90$	N3680A N233PT N44VP N41WL YV2343
LA-61	F90	N3694C N444RS N189JR
LA-62	F90	N714D D-ICBD F-GIFK (F-HAAG) F-GIFK
LA-63	F90	N3686V ZS-LTD
LA-64	F90	N3698H N322GK
LA-65	F90	N711SD N1MB C-GMIT C-GMTI N867MA
LA-66	F90	(YV-373CP) N3720W N90TP
LA-67	F90	N614ML N927K N614ML N614ME N416P
LA-68	F90+^	N99LM N77PV
LA-69	F90	N6727C ZS-KLZ
LA-70	F90$	N3687S N990BM N119FJ
LA-71	F90	N555WF N45WL N541MM (N576P) N600WA
LA-72	F90$	OY-AUL N90SE N90SK N770SD

BEECH F90

c/n	Series/Mod	Identities
LA-73	F90	N3694F N369BR N81GC
LA-74	F90	N81PS N79EC
LA-75	F90+	N3686B N600WM
LA-76	F90$^	D-IMMO N9716G N77CJ N78NW N781VC TI-AWM
LA-77	F90	N3704S N827DP N277SP
LA-78	F90$	N816EP N90MH PT-WET
LA-79	F90	(YV-372CP) XA-KUR XB-DQP N2164L
LA-80	F90$	G-BHUS G-KFIT N614RG N17AE [dbr 24Jan01 Nashville-International, TN, USA, parts to MTW Aerospace, Montgomery, AL, USA; canx 28Jun01]
LA-81	F90	G-BHUT G-STYR N42636 N1976M N432DA N444MF C-FCDF
LA-82	F90$	N33KA N131CD N531DS N501TD N501DU
LA-83	F90+	N3701B N771JB N186DD N323DB N994ST
LA-84	F90	HB-GGZ N122GA
LA-85	F90+	N3697P PT-ODN
LA-86	F90	N3717E VH-CRM N6659V (D-IILL) PT-OLM N249RC N242LF
LA-87	F90	N3699U (N522CC) N527CC N92UK N200SC N696RA
LA-88	F90	F-GCTB F-ODGU F-GVJV N6VJ
LA-89	F90$^	N3706F N888RE N871RC N24TL N77PA LV-ZPY
LA-90	F90$	N3735D N290DK N236JS
LA-91	F90$	N3709B N77PK N90GS N641PE N333WT
LA-92	F90	N3715T PT-ONO
LA-93	F90	LV-PJY N1187K PT-LJR [w/o 02Oct88 Sao Pedro da Aldeia, Rio de Janeiro State, Brazil]
LA-94	F90	N3735W PT-LSH
LA-95	F90	XB-CGP XA-SAW
LA-96	F90$	N3739C N37390 N932G D-IXIE N96NA D-IXIE N47TE D-IDVK
LA-97	F90+	YV-371CP N371CP N58EZ N114CW
LA-98	F90+	N77JT N103CB
LA-99	F90+	N3741U N711KW N803HC
LA-100	F90	G-BIED HB-GHP D-IWAL (OO-SAL) OO-IAL *D-IWAL
LA-101	F90+	N37990
LA-102	F90$	YV-399CP N44882 N429DM
LA-103	F90	N3802F PT-LTT
LA-104	F90$	N3824H N222ML TC-NML D-IEEE N90NA (N900BK) N90NA
LA-105	F90+	N21WF D-IAWK N188BF C-GVLH
LA-106	F90	D-ICIL OE-FML D-IBTU N19112 C-GQGA N173PL
LA-107	F90	N38051 N844TS N4237M N700BK N188JB PP-JCA
LA-108	F90	YV-400CP N627AC N411RJ
LA-109	F90	N3806U PT-LYZ
LA-110	F90+	N3824V N759FS
LA-111	F90$	G-BIEZ HB-GHO N632RR N10DH *N138RB
LA-112	F90	N3809C
LA-113	F90	N1822D N890GA N890CA C-GKSC
LA-114	F90	N77AK N379D N313BH D-IMWH [w/o 06Dec87 5km N of Dusseldorf-Rhine Ruhr, West Germany; canx cJan88]
LA-115	F90	F-GCTR
LA-116	F90	N3825E N197AS
LA-117	F90	N3721Z VH-WJT N7775 N120RC
LA-118	F90$	N38164 N50MW N943CL N715GW PT-OFD
LA-119	F90+^	N3826T N100PL N100PH N900HM N994RD (N800C) N800BK
LA-120	F90$	N80CK N879PC ZS-PGW
LA-121	F90$	N82DD N182CA
LA-122	F90	N3723N ZS-LBC
LA-123	F90+	N38246 N211EC N513KL
LA-124	F90	N13 N94U [w/o 24Nov00 Lynchburg-Regional, VA, USA]
LA-125	F90+	N3845S N65MM N145MR
LA-126	F90	N3848V PT-LYP
LA-127	F90	YV-410CP N410CP YV-410CP YV-02CP N812CP
LA-128	F90	N3867A PT-ONU
LA-129	F90	OY-BEL F-GKKK 3A-MON N605EA
LA-130	F90+	N81SD N402BL
LA-131	F90	N14 N46KA N42SC N42SY N210AJ
LA-132	F90	N38649 PT-LQC
LA-133	F90$	N1803P N31TL
LA-134	F90$	C-GDMN N2420M N993M N90BD
LA-135	F90+	N422Z
LA-136	F90$	RP-C410 [assigned import as N215DM since cOct89]
LA-137	F90	N18150 N200MW N488FT
LA-138	F90	N15
LA-139	F90+^	N1829H N22FR A2-AFI N333EB N94JD
LA-140	F90	YV-428CP N190GM N607DK
LA-141	F90	F-GDAK
LA-142	F90$	N1815T N50AW
LA-143	F90+	N624LF N69AD
LA-144	F90	N18121 (N300BF) PT-ONE
LA-145	F90	N18
LA-146	F90	N1824T N90LM N90TM N90TX N90RT
LA-147	F90	(D-IEDI) XA-LOO XA-ROE (N221DR) N722DR XA-TWB
LA-148	F90$	N1826P PT-LER
LA-149	F90	N9BX N577VM N577LM N707DR (N10DR) N44PA
LA-150	F90	N700RL N80M

BEECH F90

c/n	Series/Mod	Identities
LA-151	F90+	YV-445CP HK-3935X HK-3935W HK-4358X HK-4358
LA-152	F90$	N297D N5UT HP-1215 N152WE N89CA *N494AL
LA-153	F90	N3838S (VH-DHW) VH-NZA N4428V N200RA PT-ORY [w/o 03Feb93 nr Sao Paulo, Sao Paulo State, Brazil]
LA-154	F90+	C-GFFY N9491Y N90SB
LA-155	F90	N1837V D-IICL N155GA PT-OUJ
LA-156	F90$	N1827F PT-LTO
LA-157	F90	N69084
LA-158	F90$	N1839G ZS-LFF N123GM N122SC N580PA
LA-159	F90	N150BA N150BZ N90GT N76HC N222AG
LA-160	F90$	N92P N335R HP-1266 N982SA ZS-ALD
LA-161	F90	N18471
LA-162	F90	N1845L N90BL PT-OOX
LA-163	F90+	N1853D N483 N483K N90FP PT-OIV N163AJ PP-DPS N154AJ N85PJ
LA-164	F90	N1860C (F-GFDM) N990F
LA-165	F90	N18571 N686LD N300DM
LA-166	F90$	N6133H HB-GHM F-GFVN
LA-167	F90	N1857F
LA-168	F90	N6128P N32BG N43LA XA- [canx 17Jun04 as exported to Mexico]
LA-169	F90	N61228
LA-170	F90+	N6643D N605CC N314P C-FLTL
LA-171	F90$	N61429 PT-LMC N32HF N46JW N46JX
LA-172	F90$	N1842N N141JW N101ET (N808DS) N68AM [dbr 13Dec04 Monroe, GA, USA; canx 31Jan06]
LA-173	F90^	N6176A N25RT N56TW PT-OHZ
LA-174	F90$	(C-GBBY) N1846W N877W N90LL YV-606CP YV-702CP YV1693
LA-175	F90$	N6292H N415GN PT-OZP
LA-176	F90+	N6344H N766RB N517AB N90HK
LA-177	F90	N6262B N200CU N200CG PT-OHR N200CG N416DY N418DY N127DC N11WN
LA-178	F90+	N6253V N82HR N53G N178LA
LA-179	F90$	YV-486CP YV-886CP YV1601
LA-180	F90+	N6261C N999KK N357CC
LA-181	F90	HK-2888X HK-2888P HK-2888W TG-CFA 700 (Guatemalan AF)
LA-182	F90$	N761D N100CU N125TS N424CP
LA-183	F90	N6411E N25CU N82WC N90TD
LA-184	F90+	N62760 N55K OY-CCC C-FCLH
LA-185	F90	D-IBBO N45845 N61DH PT-LYM
LA-186	F90+	N350BA N928RS N600SF XB-JRF XB-JMC
LA-187	F90$	N6416P PT-OTA
LA-188	F90#	N6429M N41CK N41AK (N46BA) N41AK
LA-189	F90$	N18436 ZS-LFP N107AJ N555TZ
LA-190	F90$	N6335F
LA-191	F90#	TR-LAJ (F-GRLN) N822BA HK-4433X HK-4433W
LA-192	F90	N6331Q N17TS D-ITLL [canx 21Nov08 as exported - to where?]
LA-193	F90$	YV-490CP (YV-2253P) N193GM N604DK XA-AGG
LA-194	F90$	N6685P N27SE
LA-195	F90	N678DW HI-446 N70132 PT-LXY
LA-196	F90+	N117JM N7ZU HP-1252 N196JP N196WC CC-CTE
LA-197	F90	YV-494CP N4488N PT-LSP
LA-198	F90$	(G-BJXS) HK-3118X HK-3118W HK-3118 N198FM HK-4298X HK-4298 N198FM
LA-199	F90+	(N678DW) N196HA N211NA N5NW N118MJ
LA-200	F90$	N6685H PT-OFB
LA-201	F90+	N6530B N653LP N955RA
LA-202	F90+	N14KA D-IIBB N777AS N840SB PP-CMM
LA-203	F90+	N6530E N721DR PT-OOZ N72KA OY-CVC N42GA N399TW
LA-204	F90	N6569H XA-PEM N75MS [wfu cMar02, parts to Dodson International Parts, Rantoul, KS, USA]
LA-205	F90-1$	N6690R N205SM N94PG
LA-206	F90-1	N146D D-IIBS N131SP (N4UC) N131SP
LA-207	F90-1	N83VB HI-449 N2DF YV-622CP
LA-208	F90-1$	N6654V N901SA N999RC
LA-209	F90-1$	N6727U N444KK YV [canx 21Jan09 as exported to Venezuela]
LA-210	F90-1$	N917BH N917BA N715JT N415RB N415HS A2-SID
LA-211	F90-1$	N67146 N600BG (JA8865) PT-OHX N22SN N808TC
LA-212	F90-1$	N6726P A2-AHV [dbf 19Jan09 in Botswana]
LA-213	F90-1$	N77M PT-ODO
LA-214	F90-1	N77P N773
LA-215	F90-1$	N6730S PT-LUT
LA-216	F90-1$	N390D PT-LZT
LA-217	F90-1$	N6756L PT-OCE
LA-218	F90-1+	N6781W N137AL N137JP D-IWKA N218BA N299KP
LA-219	F90-1$	N6821W N71NH D-IREI N513RB N8YK N18CM
LA-220	F90-1	N6837C PT-OLP [w/o 18Aug92 Navegantes, Santa Catarina, Brazil]
LA-221	F90-1$	N6845L N499MC N300AA N71612 HK-3505X HK-3505 HK-3505W HK-3505P [canx 02Apr03 - status?]
LA-222	F90-1+	N69283 N711L
LA-223	F90-1$	N83KA PT-LIF
LA-224	F90-1	N3855K N29GB N991GC
LA-225	F90-1	N6930L N7MC N713DH N713DB PT-OFS
LA-226	F90-1+	N6690L N16WG
LA-227	F90-1#	N7206Z N330VP D-ISTB

BEECH F90

c/n	Series/Mod	Identities							
LA-228	F90-1	N7206N	N80WP	PP-CSE					
LA-229	F90-1	N7209Z	D-IRIS						
LA-230	F90-1	N7215C	N393CF	N393CE	N111EL	N111EN			
LA-231	F90-1+	N7220T	N27PA	VP-CLA	N427PA	C-GHUN	N129JS	N78FB	
LA-232	F90-1$	N7219G	D-IWPF	PT-ASN					
LA-233	F90-1	N72224	VT-ELZ	[w/o 02Feb98 nr Bhilai, Chhattisgarh, India]					
LA-234	F90-1	N7206E							
LA-235	F90-1$	N7225K	N901GS	N722PT	N77WW				
LA-236	F90-1+	N6790F	XA-RQD	N236ML	PT-OZE	N234CW	(N230RM)	N957JF	N18SF

Production complete

BEECH T-44A/B (H90) KING AIR

c/n	Series/Mod	Identities	
LL-1	T-44A	160839 (US Navy)	[w/o 25Mar96 Corpus Christi NAS, TX, USA]
LL-2	T-44A	160840 (US Navy)	
LL-3	T-44A	160841 (US Navy)	
LL-4	T-44A	160842 (US Navy)	
LL-5	T-44A	160843 (US Navy)	
LL-6	T-44A	160844 (US Navy)	
LL-7	T-44A	160845 (US Navy)	
LL-8	T-44A	160846 (US Navy)	
LL-9	T-44A	160847 (US Navy)	
LL-10	T-44A	160848 (US Navy)	
LL-11	T-44A	160849 (US Navy)	
LL-12	T-44A	160850 (US Navy)	
LL-13	T-44A	160851 (US Navy)	
LL-14	T-44A	160852 (US Navy)	
LL-15	T-44A	160853 (US Navy)	
LL-16	T-44A	160854 (US Navy)	
LL-17	T-44A	160855 (US Navy)	
LL-18	T-44A	160856 (US Navy)	
LL-19	T-44A	160967 (US Navy)	[w/o 08Jul82 Corpus Christi-Cabaniss Field, TX, USA in collision with T-44A 161067]
LL-20	T-44A	160968 (US Navy)	
LL-21	T-44A	160969 (US Navy)	
LL-22	T-44A	160970 (US Navy)	
LL-23	T-44A	160971 (US Navy)	
LL-24	T-44A	160972 (US Navy)	
LL-25	T-44A	160973 (US Navy)	
LL-26	T-44A	160974 (US Navy)	
LL-27	T-44A	160975 (US Navy)	[wfu, parts to Dodson International Parts, Rantoul, KS, USA]
LL-28	T-44A	160976 (US Navy)	[dbr 23Oct02 Corpus Christi NAS, TX, USA by hail during a thunderstorm]
LL-29	T-44A	160977 (US Navy)	
LL-30	T-44A	160978 (US Navy)	N8109J
LL-31	T-44A	160979 (US Navy)	
LL-32	T-44A	160980 (US Navy)	[dbr 08Mar84 nr Orange Grove, Naval Auxiliary Landing Field, TX, USA; parts located Corpus Christi NAS, TX, USA]
LL-33	T-44A	160981 (US Navy)	
LL-34	T-44A	160982 (US Navy)	
LL-35	T-44A	160983 (US Navy)	
LL-36	T-44A	160984 (US Navy)	
LL-37	T-44A	160985 (US Navy)	
LL-38	T-44A	160986 (US Navy)	
LL-39	T-44A	161057 (US Navy)	
LL-40	T-44A	161058 (US Navy)	
LL-41	T-44A	161059 (US Navy)	[w/o 21Feb80 location unkn]
LL-42	T-44A	161060 (US Navy)	
LL-43	T-44A	161061 (US Navy)	
LL-44	T-44A	161062 (US Navy)	
LL-45	T-44A	161063 (US Navy)	
LL-46	T-44A	161064 (US Navy)	
LL-47	T-44A	161065 (US Navy)	
LL-48	T-44A	161066 (US Navy)	
LL-49	T-44A	161067 (US Navy)	[w/o 08Jul82 Corpus Christi-Cabaniss Field, TX, USA in collision with T-44A 160967]
LL-50	T-44A	161068 (US Navy)	
LL-51	T-44A	161069 (US Navy)	
LL-52	T-44A	161070 (US Navy)	
LL-53	T-44A	161071 (US Navy)	
LL-54	T-44A	161072 (US Navy)	
LL-55	T-44A	161073 (US Navy)	
LL-56	T-44A	161074 (US Navy)	
LL-57	T-44A	161075 (US Navy)	
LL-58	T-44A	161076 (US Navy)	
LL-59	T-44A	161077 (US Navy)	
LL-60	T-44A	161078 (US Navy)	

c/n	Series/Mod	Identities
LL-61	T-44A	161079 (US Navy)
LL-62	T-44B	(164579) (US Navy)[order cancelled - aircraft not built]
LL-63	T-44B	(164580) (US Navy)[order cancelled - aircraft not built]
LL-64	T-44B	(164581) (US Navy)[order cancelled - aircraft not built]
LL-65	T-44B	(164582) (US Navy)[order cancelled - aircraft not built]
LL-66	T-44B	(164583) (US Navy)[order cancelled - aircraft not built]

Production complete

BEECH U-21 (A90-1) KING AIR

c/n	Series/Mod	Identities
LM-1	EU-21A	66-18000 (US Navy) N7000B
LM-2	U-21A	66-18001 (US Army) N7007G
LM-3	JU-21A	66-18002 (US Army)[w/o 14Apr77 location unkn]
LM-4	U-21A	66-18003 (US Army)[reportedly w/o; no further details]
LM-5	U-21A	66-18004 (US Navy) N7007Q N87E
LM-6	U-21A	66-18005 (US Army) N70088 [std Muskogee-Davis Field, OK, USA]
LM-7	U-21A	66-18006 (US Army) N7010L [std Muskogee-Davis Field, OK, USA]
LM-8	U-21A	66-18007 (US Army)[w/o 16Mar69 Loc Thuy mountains, Vietnam]
LM-9	JU-21A	66-18008 (US Army) N70135 N85Z
LM-10	JU-21A	66-18009 (US Army) N7014L
LM-11	U-21A	66-18010 (US Army) N611ND (N49K) N60C
LM-12	U-21A	66-18011 (US Army)[w/o 20Jan78 in Turkey]
LM-13	U-21A	66-18012 (US Army) N7018F
LM-14	EU-21A	66-18013 (US Army) N70224 N67X
LM-15	U-21A	66-18014 (US Army) N7026H N76Q
LM-16	U-21A	66-18015 (US Army) N823SB XA-TJD
LM-17	U-21A	66-18016 (US Army) N70264 N78K N990JM
LM-18	U-21A	66-18017 (US Army) N70292 [std Muskogee-Davis Field, OK, USA]
LM-19	U-21A	66-18018 (US Army) N7031F N72L
LM-20	U-21A	66-18019 (US Army)[pres cOct98 Savannah-Hunter AAF, GA, USA]
LM-21	U-21A	66-18020 (US Army) N7031L (N39U) N80R
LM-22	U-21A	66-18021 (US Army) N7034K CS-DCP N3634K N79Z
LM-23	U-21A	66-18022 (US Army)[w/o; date & location unkn]
LM-24	U-21A	66-18023 (US Army) N7035B N67K
LM-25	U-21A	66-18024 (US Army) N70356 [std Muskogee-Davis Field, OK, USA]
LM-26	U-21A	66-18025 (US Army) N7036L [std Muskogee-Davis Field, OK, USA]
LM-27	U-21A	66-18026 (US Army)[w/o 25May70; location unkn]
LM-28	EU-21A	66-18027 (US Army) N7038Y [std Muskogee-Davis Field, OK, USA]
LM-29	U-21A	66-18028 (US Army)[w/o; date & location unkn]
LM-30	U-21A	66-18029 (US Army) N7039T [std Muskogee-Davis Field, OK, USA]
LM-31	U-21A	66-18030 (US Army) N7040J N32P
LM-32	U-21A	66-18031 (US Army) N7040V N64C [std Muskogee-Davis Field, OK, USA]
LM-33	U-21A	66-18032 (US Army) N7041M N84G
LM-34	U-21A	66-18033 (US Army) N7042R N65JA N89N
LM-35	U-21A	66-18034 (US Army) N7043D [std Muskogee-Davis Field, OK, USA]
LM-36	U-21A	66-18035 (US Army)[b/u; no further details known]
LM-37	JU-21A	66-18036 (US Army) N7043G [w/o 12Jun06 Tampa-Peter O'Knight Field, FL, USA]
LM-38	U-21A	66-18037 (US Army) N7043N
LM-39	U-21A	66-18038 (US Army) N7043Y N541MC
LM-40	U-21A	66-18039 (US Army)[w/o 26Apr75 Stockdale, TX, USA]
LM-41	U-21A	66-18040 (US Army) N7047D [std Muskogee-Davis Field, OK, USA]
LM-42	U-21A	66-18041 (US Army)[w/o 14Dec71 nr Da Nang, South Vietnam]
LM-43	U-21A	66-18042 (US Army) N70503
LM-44	U-21A	66-18043 (US Army) N7051K
LM-45	U-21A	66-18044 (US Army) N7052X
LM-46	U-21A	66-18045 (US Army)[w/o; date & location unkn]
LM-47	U-21A	66-18046 (US Army) N7052Y
LM-48	U-21A	66-18047 (US Army) N7059H N37H
LM-49	U-21A	67-18048 (US Army) N7062W [std Muskogee-Davis Field, OK, USA]
LM-50	U-21A	67-18049 (US Army) N7063D
LM-51	U-21A	67-18050 (US Army) N7063W N70U
LM-52	U-21A	67-18051 (US Army) N7064Q [std Muskogee-Davis Field, OK, USA]
LM-53	U-21A	67-18052 (US Army) N70648
LM-54	U-21A	67-18053 (US Army) N7066X
LM-55	U-21A	67-18054 (US Army) N7067S
LM-56	U-21A	67-18055 (US Army) N7069F
LM-57	U-21A	67-18056 (US Army) N7070Z N75N
LM-58	U-21A	67-18057 (US Army) N7071H [std Muskogee-Davis Field, OK, USA]
LM-59	EU-21A	67-18058 (US Army) N7071N N67B
LM-60	U-21A	67-18059 (US Army) N7076X N87Q
LM-61	U-21A	67-18060 (US Army) N7201S N75Z
LM-62	U-21A	67-18061 (US Army)[w/o 20Jan87 Kansas City, KS, USA; collided with PA-31 N60SE]
LM-63	U-21A	67-18062 (US Army)[w/o 12Dec84 Ft.Bragg, NC, USA]
LM-64	JU-21A	67-18063 (US Army) N70766 TZ-ZBE
LM-65	U-21A	67-18064 (US Army)
LM-66	JU-21A	67-18065 (US Army)[w/o 04May71 in Vietnam]
LM-67	U-21A	67-18066 (US Army) N7078J

BEECH U-21 (A90-1)

c/n	Series/Mod	Identities
LM-68	U-21A	67-18067 (US Army) N117CP (N73Q) N66W
LM-69	U-21A	67-18068 (US Army) N7078L [std Muskogee-Davis Field, OK, USA]
LM-70	JU-21A	67-18069 (US Army) N7079S [std Muskogee-Davis Field, OK, USA]
LM-71	U-21A	67-18070 (US Army) [b/u cMay96 Fort Lauderdale, FL, USA]
LM-72	U-21A	67-18071 (US Army) N7081L N72J
LM-73	U-21A	67-18072 (US Army) N70841 N65L
LM-74	U-21A	67-18073 (US Army) N7087U N62V
LM-75	U-21A	67-18074 (US Army) N70876
LM-76	U-21A	67-18075 (US Army) N70879 [std Muskogee-Davis Field, OK, USA]
LM-77	U-21A	67-18076 (US Army) N7089Q N79W
LM-78	U-21A	67-18078 (US Army) N70890 N78D [std Muskogee-Davis Field, OK, USA]
LM-79	U-21A	67-18079 (US Army) N70904 N65U N80Y
LM-80	U-21A	67-18080 (US Army) N518NA [pres inst airframe Lake Area Technical Institute, Watertown, SD, USA]
LM-81	U-21A	67-18081 (US Army) [w/o 10Feb77 nr Mount Iliamna, AK, USA]
LM-82	U-21A	67-18082 (US Army) N28HF
LM-83	U-21A	67-18083 (US Army) N7092K N75G
LM-84	U-21A	67-18084 (US Army) N70926
LM-85	U-21A	67-18086 (US Army) 67-18086 (Korean AF) [reportedly wfu]
LM-86	U-21A	67-18088 (US Army) N70950
LM-87	U-21A	67-18090 (US Army) N7112M N65U [std Muskogee-Davis Field, OK, USA]
LM-88	U-21A	67-18091 (US Army) N7112T
LM-89	U-21A	67-18092 (US Army) N7113Z N41J
LM-90	U-21A	67-18094 (US Army) N7120P
LM-91	U-21A	67-18095 (US Army) [w/o 10Feb71; location unkn]
LM-92	U-21A	67-18096 (US Army) N7123C N61Q
LM-93	U-21A	67-18097 (US Army) N7126U
LM-94	U-21A	67-18098 (US Army) N7128H
LM-95	U-21A	67-18099 (US Army) N7132Z
LM-96	U-21A	67-18100 (US Army) N71347
LM-97	U-21A	67-18101 (US Army) N71351 [std Muskogee-Davis Field, OK, USA]
LM-98	U-21A	67-18102 (US Army) N7136M N903MD
LM-99	U-21A	67-18103 (US Army) N7137G [std Muskogee-Davis Field, OK, USA]
LM-100	RU-21D	67-18104 (US Army) N7201Z [std Muskogee-Davis Field, OK, USA]
LM-101	RU-21H	67-18105 (US Army) N7139Z [std Muskogee-Davis Field, OK, USA]
LM-102	U-21D	67-18106 (US Army) [w/o 30Mar81 location unkn]
LM-103	RU-21D	67-18107 (US Army) N7143Y N75V
LM-104	RU-21D	67-18108 (US Army) N7146X [std Muskogee-Davis Field, OK, USA]
LM-105	RU-21D	67-18109 (US Army) N7148A N38V
LM-106	RU-21D	67-18110 (US Army) N7154W N39Q
LM-107	RU-21H	67-18111 (US Army) N7155P
LM-108	RU-21A	67-18112 (US Army) [w/o 24Jul85 location unkn]
LM-109	RU-21A	67-18113 (US Army) [wfu, parts to JW Duff scrapyard Denver, CO, USA]
LM-110	RU-21A	67-18114 (US Army) [wfu, parts to JW Duff scrapyard Denver, CO, USA]
LM-111	RU-21A	67-18115 (US Army) [wfu, parts to JW Duff scrapyard Denver, CO, USA]
LM-112	U-21A	67-18116 (US Army) N7155S [std Muskogee-Davis Field, OK, USA]
LM-113	U-21A	67-18117 (US Army) N7156J N65V [std Muskogee-Davis Field, OK, USA]
LM-114	U-21A	67-18118 (US Army) [status?]
LM-115	RU-21H	67-18119 (US Army) N7157K [std Muskogee-Davis Field, OK, USA]
LM-116	RU-21A	67-18120 (US Army) N71581 [std Muskogee-Davis Field, OK, USA]
LM-117	RU-21A	67-18121 (US Army) [w/o 17Jan91 nr Yakima-Air Terminal, WA, USA]
LM-118	RU-21D	67-18122 (US Army) N71597
LM-119	U-21D	67-18123 (US Army) N7165J
LM-120	U-21D	67-18124 (US Army) N7165Y
LM-121	JRU-21D	67-18125 (US Army) [w/o 30Mar78 in Alabama, USA]
LM-122	U-21D	67-18126 (US Army) N7169U [std Muskogee-Davis Field, OK, USA]
LM-123	U-21D	67-18127 (US Army) N7169Z
LM-124	U-21D	67-18128 (US Army) N72014 N89F
LM-125	RU-21H	70-15891 (US Army) N7170A N95S [std Muskogee-Davis Field, OK, USA]
LM-126	U-21G	70-15892 (US Army) N7171A LX-RAD OO-SAD
LM-127	U-21H	70-15893 (US Army) N7173K N97T
LM-128	RU-21H	70-15894 (US Army) N7173Y N93J [std Muskogee-Davis Field, OK, USA]
LM-129	RU-21H	70-15895 (US Army) N7174J N99G [std Muskogee-Davis Field, OK, USA]
LM-130	U-21G	70-15896 (US Army) N71764 N87V [w/o 02Nov08 in Guyana]
LM-131	U-21G	70-15897 (US Army) N71797 [std Muskogee-Davis Field, OK, USA]
LM-132	RU-21H	70-15898 (US Army) N7181E N92B [std Muskogee-Davis Field, OK, USA]
LM-133	RU-21H	70-15899 (US Army) N7202D N94S [std Muskogee-Davis Field, OK, USA]
LM-134	U-21G	70-15900 (US Army) N7181H
LM-135	JU-21G	70-15901 (US Army) N7181J
LM-136	RU-21H	70-15902 (US Army) N7181Z N410SP
LM-137	U-21G	70-15903 (US Army) N7182H N97D
LM-138	U-21H	70-15904 (US Army) N7191W N418SP
LM-139	U-21G	70-15905 (US Army) N7193M [std Muskogee-Davis Field, OK, USA]
LM-140	U-21G	70-15906 (US Army) N7194P N906HF
LM-141	U-21G	70-15907 (US Army) N7198B
LM-142	U-21J	[built as U-21J c/n B-95]
LM-143	U-21J	[built as U-21J c/n B-96]
LM-144	U-21J	[built as U-21J c/n B-97]
LM-145	U-21J	[built as U-21J c/n B-98]
LM-146	U-21J	[built as U-21J c/n B-99]

Production complete

BEECH RU-21B (A90-2) KING AIR

c/n	Series/Mod	Identities
LS-1	RU-21B	67-18077 (US Army)
LS-2	RU-21B	67-18087 (US Army)
LS-3	RU-21B	67-18093 (US Army)[status?]

Production complete

BEECH RU-21C (A90-3) KING AIR

c/n	Series/Mod	Identities		
LT-1	RU-21C	67-18085 (US Army)	N5079K	[wfu, parts to JW Duff scrapyard Denver, CO, USA; canx 05Mar96]
LT-2	RU-21C	67-18089 (US Army)	N5079L	[wfu, parts to JW Duff scrapyard Denver, CO, USA; canx 05Mar96]

Production complete

BEECH U-21B (A90-4) KING AIR

c/n	Series/Mod	Identities			
LU-1	U-21A	70-15875 (US Army)	N7198S		
LU-2	RU-21H	70-15876 (US Army)	N7198Y		
LU-3	RU-21H	70-15877 (US Army)	N71982	N93V	[std Muskogee-Davis Field, OK, USA]
LU-4	U-21H	70-15878 (US Army)	N71984	N94N	[std Muskogee-Davis Field, OK, USA]
LU-5	RU-21H	70-15879 (US Army)	N7199B	N92S	[std Muskogee-Davis Field, OK, USA]
LU-6	RU-21H	70-15880 (US Army)	N7199D		
LU-7	U-21H	70-15881 (US Army)	N7199H		
LU-8	RU-21H	70-15882 (US Army)	N7199J	N96Y	[std Muskogee-Davis Field, OK, USA]
LU-9	U-21H	70-15883 (US Army)	N7199L		
LU-10	RU-21H	70-15884 (US Army)	N7199N	N90D	
LU-11	RU-21H	70-15885 (US Army)	N7199S		
LU-12	RU-21H	70-15886 (US Army)	N71992	N92J	[std Muskogee-Davis Field, OK, USA]
LU-13	RU-21H	70-15887 (US Army)	N71996	N96S	[std Muskogee-Davis Field, OK, USA]
LU-14	JU-21H	70-15888 (US Army)[std Fort Rucker-Cairns AAF, AL, USA]			
LU-15	RU-21H	70-15889 (US Army)	N71998	N91S	
LU-16	RU-21E	70-15890 (US Army)[dbf 19Oct75 Fort Bliss, TX, USA]			

Production complete

BEECH 100/A100 KING AIR

$ = Raisbeck dual aft body strakes fitted
# = Raisbeck nacelle wing lockers fitted
+ = Raisbeck dual aft body strakes and nacelle wing lockers fitted

c/n	Series/Mod	Identities
B-1	100	N3100K [wfu, parts to White Industries, Bates City, MO, USA; location F-52]
B-2	100$	N6100K N725K D-IGVW N21J N3RC N11JJ N211VP [std Deland Municipal-Sidney H Taylor Field, FL, USA]
B-3	100	N13303 N101UA N1284 N128L N128RC C-FIDN
B-4	100	N925B N925BD XB-WUI [status?]
B-5	100	N1020K N280RA N288RA
B-6	100$	N1008J N1008G N78FC N78FQ N85BC N85BH N208AJ N203AJ N169MM N122ZZ
B-7	100	N819K N101AF N101AP N271SC N271SG OE-FEM N800MD PT-OQP [w/o 07Feb93 Foz do Iguacu, Parana, Brazil]
B-8	100$	N100PA N705S N103RH N59T C-FDAM
B-9	100$	CF-QDI C-FQDI N55796 ZS-PBH 3C-PBH ZS-PBH
B-10	100	D-IMDB N500TB N220JB N400BE N204AJ [w/o 16Sep89 Houston, TX, USA; canx 11Mar92]
B-11	100	N100KA
B-12	100	N912K N100UT N912K N152X N999CR [dbr 18Mar81 Houston-William P Hobby, TX, USA, parts to White Industries, Bates City, MO, USA; location B-19; canx cApr82]
B-13	100	N100BW N696JB [w/o 28Mar90 nr Uvalde-Garner Field, TX, USA; canx 12Jun90]
B-14	100$	N921K N40TG N402G C-GJKS
B-15	100	N947K PI-C710 RP-C710 [dbr 28Nov96 San Jose, Philippines, parts to White Industries, Bates City, MO, USA; location F-03; CofR exp 22Aug97; Canx cMar99]
B-16	100$	N925K YV-801CP YV1486 [also reported as YV1091 in INAC records]
B-17	100	N951K
B-18	100$	N915BD N7007 C-GXVX N503AB (N901AT) N503AB
B-19	100	N50PC [w/o 01Dec74 Birmingham-Municipal, AL, USA; canx cNov91]
B-20	100	N570DU N570 OH-BKB N195MA N49GW N195MA (N28WL) N195MA [wfu cAug04, parts to White Industries, Bates City, MO, USA; location "Sec-1 R-1 03"]
B-21	100	N11AG N360C N411HA
B-22	100$	N577DU N577L N577D
B-23	100$	N98HF N98UC N711 N711AU N701RJ C-GNCV
B-24	100$	N204CS N2040S N382WC C-GNAA
B-25	100	N565RA N565RP N5649F N72LT N352NR N136JH
B-26	100	N942K N666DC N666DA (N20RT) N9300P N74TF N610JM N610KR N696JB
B-27	100	N871K 9M-CAA 9M-JPA N5377C 5B-CGM G-BOFN C-GWWA
B-28	100$	N212Q N218Q N22JR N27JE N27JJ C-FWYO
B-29	100	N2400E N8300E N830EM [wfu, parts to White Industries, Bates City, MO, USA]
B-30	100	N3600A N1653H N360BT N3606T
B-31	100	N2100T N688CC N688CQ N688CW N8JG N38HB N711GM
B-32	100	N122H N122U C-GSAM N122U
B-33	100$	N883K OY-GAP 9Q-CRF
B-34	100$	D-ILRA N7332 XB-NOE XB-ING N61MR XA-SWE HI-663SP N2225H YV [canx in error 05Mar08 as exported to Venezuela; reinstated 04Apr08; canx 20Jun08]
B-35	100$	N925B CF-BFP C-FBFP C-GPPK N711AV N77WM N178WM C-GTLS
B-36	100$	N256K N600CB C-GXRX
B-37	100	N846K N627L N524SC [wfu c1997 parts to White Industries, Bates City, MO, USA; location "Taxiway South"; canx 05Mar97]
B-38	100$	N931M C-FQOV [wfu Calgary-Springbank, AB, Canada]
B-39	100	HB-GEN OH-BKA [pres Mantta, Finland; canx 26Oct07]
B-40	100$	N923K C-FMXY
B-41	100	N500LR N111AT N500LR N500EH N502CW N93BC N1100A C-FAXE
B-42	100	LN-VIP CF-AFD C-FAFD
B-43	100	PT-DKV
B-44	100	N4100H N6666K N5546K N962R (N101PF) N440SM C-FCAZ
B-45	100$	N45V N704S C-GPCB
B-46	100+	N6789 N6780 N678RM N283PM N770RL
B-47	100$	XB-WOS XA-PAK XB-CIP C-GNAX C-FWYN
B-48	100+	N572DU N572 N5727
B-49	100	N945K N887PL N887PE [w/o 15Sep89 nr Mayfield-Graves County, KY, USA; canx 16Jul90]
B-50	100	N99BW N166TR N65TD [w/o 10Dec86 Windsor, nr Pittsfield-Municipal, MA, USA; canx 05Jan89]
B-51	100	N8100H N8100D N14VB N16SW C-FWPN [wfu, parts to Global Aircraft Industries, Edmonton-Villeneuve, AB, Canada; canx 02Feb06]
B-52	100+	N899K N610K N8NP C-FKIJ [wfu, parts to Westcan Aircraft Sales & Salvage, Kamloops, BC, Canada; canx 02Nov01]
B-53	100	N879K N850DB N153JW N153JA
B-54	100	N100SA N100LB N1776L N776L [wfu, parts to Dodson International Parts, Rantoul, KS, USA]
B-55	100	N8100R N101CJ N45GT LN-KCK LN-PAO OY-CCP N4167P N911RL
B-56	100	PT-DNP [w/o 25Nov01 Buriti Alegre, Goias, Brazil]
B-57	100$	N18X N18U N190CA ZS-OUS
B-58	100	CF-JLJ C-FJLJ N750FC (N100JJ) N750FC
B-59	100	D-IKOR N88879 N702JL C-FMWM
B-60	100	N926K N110BP N100BP N110BP N2FA N54JW [wfu c1990; b/u at Dodson International Parts, Rantoul, KS, USA; canx 31May90]
B-61	100	N418GA N418LA C-GSYN C-FTUA
B-62	100	D-IAVW (OY-ASO) LN-VIT OY-AUF SE-IIE LN-NLB C-GKBQ

BEECH 100

c/n	Series/Mod	Identities
B-63	100	N4600A N711MC F-GGFE N20880 C-FHKB [wfu Airdrie, AB, Canada]
B-64	100	N4200A
B-65	100	N856K N14V N856K (N3FA) N102RS N102LF
B-66	100	N42319 N4000D N106PA C-GBFD N265K HP-1411B HP-1411 N525ZS [w/o 28Oct08 nr Bauru, Sao Paulo State, Brazil; canx 10Feb09]
B-67	100$	N311UL N311UE N1WD N26KW C-FWPG
B-68	100	XA-DEA XB-REA [w/o 01Aug75 in Mexico]
B-69	100	N862K N1SC N2SC N207SB (N501KS) N207SB
B-70	100	N123ST N128ST N25JL N77PF
B-71	100$	N77711 N7771R N431R
B-72	100$	D-IMSH N5476R C-GTLF C-FRKB
B-73	100$	N155PT N155T N73KA (N73PD) YV-04CP YV1300
B-74	100	N931K N14PC N233MW N239MW N3500P N3500E N74JV
B-75	100	N925B N410WA N410WB N24MK (N104RA) C-FCSD N75LA
B-76	100$	N9138Q PK-BTW N300DA C-GWWQ
B-77	100	N9477Q PI-C1978 RP-C1978
B-78	100$	N9378Q PI-C282 RP-C282 N626SA
B-79	100	G-AYGY N104TB N265K CC-CIH CC-PIE CC-CLY
B-80	100$	G-AYLW N9021J N99KA N424SW YV2010
B-81	100	N945K N858B N707SS
B-82	100	AE100 (Argentine Army) LV-WDO
B-83	100$	N917K YV-T-ETM YV-04P YV-631CP YV2129 [w/o 01Mar09 nr Loma Rejo Tiezo, Venezuela; also reported as YV1092 in INAC records]
B-84	100$	N422X N422D N422P N42BP N303CB N401TJ C-FWOL TI-AYN C-FDJQ [canx 31Dec04 as exported to USA for scrapping; parts to White Industries, Bates City, MO, USA; location "Sec-1 R-1 06"]
B-85	100	N894K LN-PAJ C-GKBZ
B-86	100$	N916K N500Y N53MD C-FTYZ
B-87	100	N125DB (YV-04CP) N70JL
B-88	100$	N100PA N100GM N100ZM C-GJSU
B-89	100+	D-IHEI OE-FCW N4209L N169RA C-FWYF
B-90	A100	N875K N601T N601U F-GFDV N515AS YV-2423P N515AS
B-91	A100	N9050V F-GHHV 6V- [canx 01Jul09 as exported to Senegal]
B-92	A100	N6789 N6739 N700SP [w/o 26Apr75 Hilton Head Island-Hilton Head Apt, SC, USA; canx 22Mar76]
B-93	A100	N9369Q 7T-VCV
B-94	A100	N925B N925BB N3GT N3GW YV-101CP N8479Y N32KC N32KG N117SH N94CP N12AQ N945WS
B-95	U-21J	70-15908 (US Army)
B-96	U-21J	70-15909 (US Army) N96GJ N116RJ C-FCAK
B-97	U-21J	70-15910 (US Army) N997RC
B-98	U-21J	70-15911 (US Army) N998RC C-GHYT
B-99	U-21J	70-15912 (US Army) N100GJ N324EC
B-100	A100	N88BW N100S C-GJBV
B-101	A100	(XC-ONA) XC-FIS N6619B N98TR N696AB N921SA N13K
B-102	A100$	N1KA N1KQ N777ST N777SD (N777SZ) N799DD
B-103	A100	CF-DOR C-FDOR
B-104	A100+	N9412Q N72X C-GCFD C-GAIK
B-105	A100$	N9324Q ZS-INY ZS-TBS A2-ABS ZS-TBS 9Q-CEM
B-106	A100$	CF-DOS C-FDOS
B-107	A100	N9355Q N101SE LN-AAH C-GNAJ
B-108	A100$	N9366Q N110JJ C-GASW [w/o 14Jun99 Thunder Bay, ON, Canada; canx 14Apr00]
B-109	A100	N1GT N1GX N51V N51VK N78CA N78MK N870MA [wfu, parts to Atlanta Air Salvage, Griffin-Spalding County, GA, USA; canx 11Feb05]
B-110	A100	XC-FIW
B-111	A100	N941K [w/o 22Jun78 Muscle Shoals, AL, USA; canx cOct81]
B-112	A100	CF-DOU C-FDOU
B-113	A100	N9439Q N72BS [w/o 01Feb85 Cedarville, nr Millville Municipal, NJ, USA; canx cAug87]
B-114	A100	XC-FIX N1347Z [wfu and believed b/u]
B-115	A100	N875K N111JW N22T N22TE [wfu, parts to White Industries, Bates City, MO, USA; location F-26; canx 28Apr89]
B-116	A100$	N531M (N90208) N531DF N100GV N601LM
B-117	A100#	CF-DOV C-FDOV
B-118	A100	N1818W N31BH N100MX N18AH
B-119	A100	N9494Q N45D N45DZ (N45RJ) N82982 OH-BKC N7GA [w/o 04Aug94 Williamstown, nr Harriman-and-West Apt, MA, USA; canx 17Sep97]
B-120	A100	CF-DOY C-FDOY
B-121	A100	PP-FBT PP-EGK PT-LJN
B-122	A100$	5R-MHC F-BHLG OY-ATA SE-IRH LN-AAF N8181Z C-FXAJ
B-123	A100	N100SA N5BA N50M (N55FF) N741EB C-GJJF
B-124	A100	N100PA N100PL N100SJ C-GILM [w/o 07Dec97 Sioux Lookout, ON, Canada; canx 13May98]
B-125	A100	N898SR N898ST N91LP N91LR N89JM C-FWRM
B-126	A100$	N45V N1MT N23BW C-GASI
B-127	A100	N1128M N112J N1125M N1129M N128F C-GJVK N710AS
B-128	A100	N196B XB-NUV [w/o 13Oct76 San Luis Potosi, San Luis Potosi State, Mexico]
B-129	A100	N235B F-GEJV [wfu Le Havre-Octeville, France; canx 25Oct05]
B-130	A100$	N225AD N9065D N455PM N91U N9UG N83TM N467BW
B-131	A100	N90C N90CC N102FG C-FLRB
B-132	A100+	N1528L XC-FUC XA-MUS XB-SLG C-GXHP C-FAIO

BEECH 100

c/n	Series/Mod	Identities
B-133	A100	N189B N1200Z N22BJ [wfu c2006, parts to White Industries, Bates City, MO, USA; location "Sec-1 R-1 11"]
B-134	A100	N84B N129D [w/o 17Aug93 Vieques, PR]
B-135	A100	N4GT C-GVCE [w/o 21Nov84 Calgary, AB, Canada; canx 25Mar85]
B-136	A100	N925B (N45PL) N925BC N700AT YV1838
B-137	A100	F-BPPM TR-LAE N95GA PT-OVQ N629SC LV-BRL
B-138	A100	N500DB N7114E N711UG OY-ASF N711UG N611CC N600DK N700NC [dbr 05Jan06 Sault Ste Marie-Chippewa County International, MI, USA, parts to MTW Aerospace, Montgomery, AL, USA]
B-139	A100	N247B
B-140	A100	N875K N475K N102ME N44UF N44UE [dbr 18Jan90 in collision with Boeing 727 N8867E (c/n 20823) Atlanta-Hartsfield, GA, USA, parts to White Industries, Bates City, MO, USA; location F-44; canx 23Oct90]
B-141	A100	G-BABX [w/o 12Jan77 Sturgate, UK; canx 19Jan77]
B-142	A100	PP-FOY
B-143	A100	N96GM N96QM N151E C-GBOG N102GP N151U C-GNVB C-GZUZ
B-144	A100	N50AC N999TB N999G C- [canx 04Feb09 as exported to Canada]
B-145	A100	N1800W N380W C-FMAI [dbr 19Apr04 Chapais, QC, Canada, parts to MTW Aerospace, Montgomery, AL, USA; canx 22Jul04]
B-146	A100	N2PW N2PQ N208SB N410SP N410SB N200AJ N410SB N200AJ
B-147	A100	N1828W 7T-VRF
B-148	A100	N1788W N103DC N103DQ N67V C-GJLP
B-149	A100$	(N149KA) N53KA N883CA C-FLTS
B-150	A100	N54KA N54MG N51BL F-GGLV 6V- [canx 01Jul09 as exported to Senegal]
B-151	A100$	N532M N324B C-FPAJ
B-152	A100	N25652 N65LC N65LG N67LC (N67LG) C-GISH
B-153	A100+	N25616 N3U N53JK N120AS C-GYQK
B-154	A100	N25628 VH-CGL N700TB N70MN N919WM N46JK C-FONY
B-155	A100$	YV-O-SID-2 YV-979CP YV1507 [w/o 26Dec05 nr Paparo, Venezuela]
B-156	A100	N9MA N71WW N21RX C-GDPI
B-157	A100$	N123CS C-GUPP
B-158	A100	N62KA N62NC XA- [canx 09Oct03 as exported to Mexico]
B-159	A100	N91D N91DE N110KF C-GLPG
B-160	A100$	N925B N369DP N896DR (N806DR) N896SB OY-CCS N896SB
B-161	A100$	PP-EFL PT-LJM N62526 YV-2615P YV1257
B-162	A100	N3D N3DG N96AM N96AL N224LB C-FUPQ
B-163	A100	N22X SE-ING C-FASB
B-164	A100	N246B N1129M N112BM N164RA C-FGIN
B-165	A100$	N64KA N911CB N911CE C-GTLA N811CU C-FDJX
B-166	A100	N27C N27CE N221SS C-FAMU N79NB VP-LV? [canx 09Dec08 as exported to British Virgin Isles]
B-167	A100	N67KA N67HC N78L [dbr 08Nov86 Brooksville-Hernando County, FL, USA]
B-168	A100	N875K F-GFVM N715WA YV [canx 30Jun08 as exported to Venezuela]
B-169	A100#	N27LS (N27GS) N305TZ C-FAPP
B-170	A100	N63KA N76AS N900DH N900DN XB-JVV [w/o 04Nov07 Santa Elena, Guatemala; reportedly wearing false marks YV1568]
B-171	A100$	G-BAVE N888TB C-FJFH N720C
B-172	A100	N733K N733KY N2300Z N16FA N753DB C-GIZX
B-173	A100	N100LJ N371H N37TH N98CH (N980H) F-GECV C-GAST HP-1336A
B-174	A100	N1WV N1WJ N763K N671L N151A C-FTMA
B-175	A100$	N92D N92DL C-GJHW
B-176	A100	N3076W YV-O-CVG-4 N3076W (N110VU) C-FXDE
B-177	A100$	N626RM N30GC (N31AS) (N100BX) N30GC [w/o 06Nov07 Chino, CA, USA; canx 14Nov08]
B-178	A100	N3078W N764K C-FNIF [w/o 25Oct07 Chibougamau, QC, Canada; canx 30Nov07]
B-179	A100	N25747 N20EG N127Z
B-180	A100	CNA-NA (Royal Moroccan AF) [w/o cOct78 in Morocco]
B-181	A100	CNA-NB (Royal Moroccan AF)
B-182	A100	CNA-NC (Royal Moroccan AF)
B-183	A100	CNA-ND (Royal Moroccan AF)
B-184	A100	CF-GNL C-FGNL [pres College of the North Atlantic, Gander, NL as a ground trainer; canx 12Dec00]
B-185	A100	N567DC OY-ATS N567DC N81CC N337K F-GSAR N818AS N220KW
B-186	A100	CNA-NE (Royal Moroccan AF)
B-187	A100	CNA-NF (Royal Moroccan AF)
B-188	A100	N545GM 5X-UWS OO-TLS [dbr 08Jan94 Bacau, Romania, parts to Atlanta Air Salvage, Griffin-Spalding County, GA, USA; canx 04Mar94]
B-189	A100	N538M N22220 C-GYQT [w/o 21Feb95 Big Trout Lake, 3.4 mls NW of Big Trout Lake Airport, ON, Canada; canx 25Apr95]
B-190	A100	N117MC LN-AAG C-GNAR C-GFFN [w/o 07Jan07 Sandy Bay, SK, Canada]
B-191	A100	N4391W N777NR N4391W N214CK C-GJBQ
B-192	A100	N4392W (N458HW) (N169TM) N4392W [wfu cFeb03, parts to MTW Aerospace, Montgomery, AL, USA; canx 06Apr06]
B-193	A100+	EC-CHD E.23-1 (Spanish AF) EC-CHD F-GXAB C-FAIP
B-194	A100	C-GHOC
B-195	A100	EC-CHE E.23-2 (Spanish AF) EC-CHE
B-196	A100	N5ST N773SK F-GJJJ [wfu c2003, parts to White Industries, Bates City, MO, USA; location "Ramp SO B-17"]
B-197	A100	N74KA 5X-UWT JW-9027 (Tanzanian AF)
B-198	A100	N8157R (5H-MPD) 5H-MCW N58309 C-GWLR N712AS C-GAPK [w/o 30Dec05 La Ronge, SK, Canada; canx 03Aug06]

BEECH 100

c/n	Series/Mod	Identities
B-199	A100	G-BBVL N82TC G-BBVL N600AC N110TD F-GEXV
B-200	A100	N1042W PT-FOB PT-LZA
B-201	A100	G-BBVM C-GAVI
B-202	A100	N8570R (5H-MPE) 5H-TRA N5831A F-GEFV N2038Q N5831A N72TA N45MF N45MN N919JP
B-203	A100	N7373R N81MD [w/o 11Aug78 Lagos, Nigeria; canx cJan82]
B-204	A100#	N7374R N813Q (N75HW) N813Q N108JL C-FBGS
B-205	A100	[cvtd to Beech B100 c/n BE-1]
B-206	A100$	N7200R N72HB N711AE N86PA N86BM C-FEYP
B-207	A100$	N727LE C-FHGG
B-208	A100$	N4475W 9Y-TJA N208SR
B-209	A100	N25623 N4KT (N440CA) N100AN N14CF YV2424
B-210	A100	N9731S N1GV N75Z N75ZZ N75GR C-FEYT
B-211	A100	C-GNEX
B-212	A100$	N115D N115DT (N29N) N15L
B-213	A100$	N7243R N660CB F-GFEV SE-LDL LN-AWA
B-214	A100	HZ-AFC N46BE YV1239
B-215	A100	N4545S N665D N100QR OY-CCA N552GA C-GPBA
B-216	A100$	T-3 (Jamaican Defence Force) N28C
B-217	A100$	OO-SNA F-WNAK (F-GNAK) N730EJ LN-AWB [dbr c2007 Haugesund, Norway; b/u cApr08 Stockholm-Bromma, Sweden; canx 14Jul08]
B-218	A100	N4318S N80MD C-GJUL [w/o 29Nov88 Chapleau, ON, Canada; canx 21Mar89]
B-219	A100	CC-ESA 331 (Chilean AF)
B-220	A100	N600GC N700K F-GEFR [w/o 28Aug86 Lille, France; canx 16Oct86]
B-221	A100	HZ-AFE N100BE [dbr 21Dec97 Colorado Springs-Municipal, CO, USA, parts to Dodson International Parts, Rantoul, KS, USA; canx 05Nov98]
B-222	A100	N1523L PK-CAE (N304TC) N232AL [wfu Calgary-Springbank, AB, Canada]
B-223	A100+	N1524L PK-CAF (N306TC) N233AL N223LH
B-224	A100	N16SM C-FPLG
B-225	A100+	N3060C N306BC N666RH N696RH N723W N601PC [w/o 22Aug08 nr Canyonlands Field, UT, USA; canx 01May09]
B-226	A100	N9126S N91RK (N190WA) N91RK
B-227	A100$	N2227L N77711 N77715 N77711 N227BC C-FSNA [w/o 22Nov08 God's Lake Narrows, MB, Canada]
B-228	A100	N32868 ZS-XGB ZS-LVL N23868 F-GKEL
B-229	A100$	N4209S N2017M N15LR N100HC C-GMAG
B-230	A100	(N18RC) N1811L D-IKUL N1362N YV2458
B-231	A100	N600SC N3EP N38P YV-1148CP YV1104
B-232	A100	N9129S N400WH C-GKAJ
B-233	A100	N99HE N711RE
B-234	A100	(N5CE) N23404
B-235	A100	N23517 C-GJLJ
B-236	A100	N23605
B-237	A100	N43FC YV-1104CP YV1306
B-238	A100	N9100S N1TR
B-239	A100$	N750S F-GELR N154TC C-FSKA
B-240	A100	N390KA (N112CA) N87CA YV [originally allocated as Beech C100 c/n BF-1; canx 21Oct08 as exported to Venezuela]
B-241	A100	N777NR N777GF N777GS
B-242	A100	IGM-240 (Ecuador AF) [also reported as IGM-242]
B-243	A100+	N17CP (N117CM) N72EH PT-OFZ N63SJ C-FLRD
B-244	A100	N2025G N31JL N51VW N942DS N842DS
B-245	A100	(N2030B) N41BP OY-BHA N41BE [w/o 25Oct02 nr Eveleth, MN, USA; canx 05Apr04]
B-246	A100	(N4857M) LN-SAE N107GA N20FS N30SA N995SA [dbr 10Dec97 Charlotte, NC, USA, parts to Dodson International Parts, Rantoul, KS, USA; re-registered N995SA 08Apr05]
B-247	A100$	N116KA F-GJPA N153TC C-GFKS [w/o 11Jan06 Dryden, ON, Canada; canx 01May07]

Production complete

BEECH B100 KING AIR

$ = Raisbeck dual aft body strakes fitted
# = Raisbeck nacelle wing lockers fitted
+ = Raisbeck dual aft body strakes and nacelle wing lockers fitted

c/n	Series/Mod	Identities
BE-1	B100	N41KA [b/u c1983 Wichita-Beech Field, KS, USA]
BE-2	B100	N43KA N729MS
BE-3	B100	N9103S N150TJ
BE-4	B100	N9104S N786CB C6-BHV N786CB
BE-5	B100	N1555L YV-91CP N39130 N1KC N1MG N900TJ N90EM N577RW N220AA
BE-6	B100	N9116S HB-GEP N8514B N24EM
BE-7	B100	N1907L N22KW N22XW (N41PC) N681PC N57HT C-GVIK
BE-8	B100	N1808L N33GK N38GK N27WT N688DS N45LU
BE-9	B100	N361D YV-36CP (N360BA) N236CP
BE-10	B100	N1910L [w/o 26Nov83 Midland-Regional, TX, USA; canx 15Nov89]
BE-11	B100	N1911L N78DA
BE-12	B100	N400AC
BE-13	B100	N4213S (N113SF) N93SF
BE-14	B100	N4214S N86FD N68DA
BE-15	B100	YV-O-CPI-2 N6599A N300LE N300DG C-GDFJ
BE-16	B100	N331GB C-GDFZ C-FJDQ
BE-17	B100	N17508 N17WD N178NC (N178NQ) (N1981B) C-FASN
BE-18	B100	N4218S N95CM N95JJ N818PA N93AJ N700TF YV [canx 08Jul09 as exported to Venezuela]
BE-19	B100	YV-95CP
BE-20	B100	N17580 N525WE N443TC
BE-21	B100	N17821 N60TJ
BE-22	B100	N17822 N50BS N50SS N86TR *N213RJ
BE-23	B100#	N13KA N93D
BE-24	B100	YV-117CP N117EP N187J N234TK
BE-25	B100	N400GC N1250 N125U N125VH
BE-26	B100	N18426 N60575 N7PD N50NE N73JC N36WH C-GPRU
BE-27	B100	N777CR N87JE (N297SL) C-FIDC
BE-28	B100	N23756 (YV-126CP) YV-125CP YV-1276P YV-127CP YV2226
BE-29	B100	N18429 N888RK N333NB N7729B D-IERI D-IZAC D-IDPL
BE-30	B100	N18430 N10EC N110EC N111YF
BE-31	B100	N18487 N80DB C-FAFS
BE-32	B100	N18436 N56SC N568C N712MA N1PN N493DT
BE-33	B100	N23634 N953RC N532EB N900RD
BE-34	B100	N203KA N711PJ N949SW (N17TV) N949SW
BE-35	B100	N23735 N564BC N364BC N821CB
BE-36	B100	N18317 N200TV N3GS [wfu c1993 parts to Atlanta Air Salvage, Griffin-Spalding County, GA, USA; canx 01Apr93]
BE-37	B100	N111XP N49SS N68MU
BE-38	B100	N24169 [dbr 22Nov91 Romeo, MI, USA, parts to White Industries, Bates City, MO, USA; location F-32; canx 20Sep00]
BE-39	B100	YV-129CP N129CP C-FSIK
BE-40	B100	N24203
BE-41	B100	N17792
BE-42	B100+	N700SB N87NW
BE-43	B100	N4975M N32RL N32RT N70BA N544FD N487JH
BE-44	B100	N300MP C-FPBC
BE-45	B100	N4841M A40-SL N2411A N263DC PT-WPV
BE-46	B100	N18482 N502SM N45BT N146BT N988JR
BE-47	B100	N4996M N49E
BE-48	B100	N5009M N2830S
BE-49	B100	N5008M N98D N400RK C-GGKJ
BE-50	B100+	N18495 N102WB N188JB N955FC N136MB
BE-51	B100	N702Z N2016T (N10AT) N750TJ N1DA N100TW
BE-52	B100	N2052B N771S N771CW
BE-53	B100	N2037C N53TD
BE-54	B100	N2025S N241CW
BE-55	B100	N50KA N546BZ N813BL
BE-56	B100	N2066C C-GBWF N251DA N9933S N98TA
BE-57	B100	N9898 N57AK (N47AP) N75AP
BE-58	B100	N300MT N299MT N100P N564CA
BE-59	B100	N293D N777DC (N133GA) N777DQ (N47KS) C-FODC
BE-60	B100	N2060Y N100HW N650TJ (N331BB) N650JT (N650UT) N650JT
BE-61	B100	N2073X YV-309CP YV1159
BE-62	B100	N6044B N85LF N991DM N350TC
BE-63	B100	N6028P N83ED N444EW N921ER N924WS N924RM N27CS
BE-64	B100+	YV-248CP N4490M (N497SL) N4490M
BE-65	B100	N6045S
BE-66	B100	N6032E N37PC
BE-67	B100	N6035H N522CF 90-0060 (US Army) N4415L
BE-68	B100	N6052C N66820
BE-69	B100	N70KA N710KC N794WB N794CE
BE-70	B100	N700GC N117FS N808CC N808GC N5007X N808GC C-GAPT N926HS N120MG
BE-71	B100	N66480 N200MB [wfu c1992, parts to White Industries, Bates City, MO, USA; location F-04; canx 08Mar93]
BE-72	B100	N2830B XA-OCI YV-321CP N2425J N20FL ZS-MZS C-FAFE

BEECH B100

c/n	Series/Mod	Identities
BE-73	B100	N6645B N76AE N76BF N300MV N256DJ N730BR N54CK C-GBTS [dbr 27Feb99 Muskoka, ON, Canada, parts to White Industries, Bates City, MO, USA; location "Ramp North"; canx 13Apr99]
BE-74	B100	N6730S N486DC N488A N56FL N88FA
BE-75	B100	N6645P N814GT N48AF ZS-MSG [w/o 23Dec94 Vrede, Free State Province, South Africa]
BE-76	B100	(YV-322CP) N812WJ N301TS
BE-77	B100	N444RK N444RL N55US N580S
BE-78	B100	N3LL N3UL N500ML [w/o 13Nov97 Madison, MS, USA; canx 27May98]
BE-79	B100$	N6685H N500JE N500KD
BE-80	B100	N53JC N53JQ (N53WT) N53JQ N13PR N13DR N93WT
BE-81	B100$	N6736S N73WL N987B (N3737G) N10655
BE-82	B100	N66804 (N200JL) N66804
BE-83	B100	N6733H N412FS N412FC N123BL
BE-84	B100	N6695L N812M N412M N300TN N700BA
BE-85	B100	N6723T N222LP
BE-86	B100	N85KA (N624PA) N264PA
BE-87	B100	N67259 (ZP-PSP) N980KA N19DA [wfu, parts to Alliance Air Parts, Oklahoma City, OK, USA]
BE-88	B100	N130AT [w/o 04May93 Clarksburg-Benedum Field, WV, USA; canx 07Aug95]
BE-89	B100#	N6737C N737MG C-GKNP N499SW
BE-90	B100	N67460 N770D
BE-91	B100	N6740D N717D N847D
BE-92	B100	N6756P
BE-93	B100	(XC-DIR) XC-IMC N142JC N1QL
BE-94	B100	N3663B
BE-95	B100	N3668P [wfu, parts to White Industries, Bates City, MO, USA]
BE-96	B100	N3669U N55MP N55TJ N802RD N802GC
BE-97	B100	N3675B N42CC N43RJ N97WD
BE-98	B100	N753D N948HB
BE-99	B100	N3699P N25EG N524BA C-GBVX
BE-100	B100	N3688F N10AG
BE-101	B100	N3695A N311CM
BE-102	B100	N81P (N91L) N57TJ C-GNSC
BE-103	B100	N3699T N2TX
BE-104	B100	N67KA N67BS N321TH
BE-105	B100	N3735H N27MH N700TJ N287GS N28PH N87XX C-FHSC
BE-106	B100	N6666K N568K (N59SS) N568K
BE-107	B100	N3699B C-GPJL
BE-108	B100$	N38005 N108EB
BE-109	B100	N3811F N105VY
BE-110	B100+	N3806N N48MB N48VB N48AF N300R N500N N702R N702JL N702TD
BE-111	B100	N38052 N360SC N361SC N622RP (N622AM) N400TJ N118NL
BE-112	B100+	N3818C N990PT N990BT N990SV N727RS
BE-113	B100	N3810Q N1883M N1888M N88TL
BE-114	B100+	N125D YV [canx 16Jan08 as exported to Venezuela]
BE-115	B100$	N124CM N124CN N126HU N104LS C-FXRJ C-FIME
BE-116	B100#	N3852V N116AC N116DG
BE-117	B100	N32RL [w/o 30Sep87 Gold Beach-Municipal, OR, USA; canx cJan88]
BE-118	B100	N3866B N4700K N101SN
BE-119	B100	N1807H N188LL
BE-120	B100	N1814P C-GBWB N2QE N110CE
BE-121	B100	N3836H VT-EGQ VT-AVB C-FAFZ N770AB
BE-122	B100	XA-LOZ XA-RMR N74RR N54US
BE-123	B100+	N1838H N55FR N827RM
BE-124	B100	N150YR N150YA
BE-125	B100	N1854S N314EB N350TJ
BE-126	B100	N1861D (N4GC) (N3LL) D-IALT N123WH (N512DS) N248JH
BE-127	B100	N6129C N62GC N25CJ N2000M N666AC N686AC
BE-128	B100	N137D YV1191
BE-129	B100	N6187U LV-VCU N2074M C-GSWF
BE-130	B100	N6241P C-GTCL N339JG
BE-131	B100	N6354H C-GSWG
BE-132	B100+	N150YR
BE-133	B100	N6338C N531CM N531CB
BE-134	B100	N6378E N888RK N363EA C-FOGP
BE-135	B100	N106SP N106SB N135AR N997ME
BE-136	B100	N18348 N221TC N223DG
BE-137	B100	N65187 N444RK

Production complete

BEECH 200/B200/1300 SUPER KING AIR

$ = Raisbeck dual aft body strakes fitted
# = Raisbeck nacelle wing lockers fitted
+ = Raisbeck dual aft body strakes and nacelle wing lockers fitted
^4 - Blackhawk XP42 engine upgrade fitted
^5 - Blackhawk XP52 engine upgrade fitted
^6 - Blackhawk XPR61 engine upgrade fitted
GTO = Enhanced Aero GTO package fitted
(WL) = BLR winglets fitted

c/n	Series/Mod	Identities
BB-1	200	N38B [wfu c1976; b/u cMar80 Wichita-Beech Field, KS, USA; canx 13Mar95]
BB-2	200	N51KA N200KA N200KP C-GARO [wfu Montreal-St.Hubert, QC, Canada; canx 10Apr97]
BB-3	RU-21J	72-21058 (US Army) N24SP
BB-4	RU-21J	72-21059 (US Army) N200LN N397SA N410RE
BB-5	RU-21J	72-21060 (US Army) N200KE N399SA YV-O-SATA-6 YV0106
BB-6	200	N925B N92BA N201TT N201LB (N301TT) N300TR XB-IVQ EJC-124 (Colombian Army) [impounded 13Aug05 Barranquilla, Atlantico, Colombia & tfd to Colombian military]
BB-7	200$	CF-BCN C-FBCN
BB-8	200	CF-BCO C-FBCO N210AJ N923WS XB-TFS XB-IMT N343CL N343CP YV [canx 31Oct08 as exported to Venezuela]
BB-9	200	N42319 N319SF N5PC N200EZ
BB-10	200	N7210R N660M (N980DB) N660M C-FALQ
BB-11	200	N200MM FAB-001 (Bolivian AF) FAB-002 (Bolivian AF)
BB-12	200$	N4473W VH-THS VH-NSS (N5CA) C-GYSK VH-NSS VH-NIH N193GA [wfu, parts to Quest Aviation, Lake City, FL, USA; still marked as VH-NIH]
BB-13	200	N200PB N595A N83MA F-GIJB
BB-14	200	N418CS C-GWWN
BB-15	200	N8415B (N841BA) N999TC N3500P ZS-MNF V5-MNF ZS-MNF N385GA [dbr 03Nov95 Cuando, Angola, parts to Dodson International Parts, Rantoul, KS, USA; canx 26Feb97]
BB-16	200	N1PC N830CE N700CP N711CR
BB-17	200	N9BK N233MW (N17TJ) N900CP N900CV YV [canx 06Aug03 as exported to Venezuela]
BB-18	200$	N90C N90CL N941JD N211JB N346CM N846CM
BB-19	200	N40FC N221B ZS-MGR [w/o 21Oct95 Marunga, Eastern Cape Province, South Africa]
BB-20	200$	N9023R OB-1509
BB-21	200	F-BVET [b/u; canx 22Oct03]
BB-22	200$	N7300R N73MW [w/o 28Nov05 Kaduna, Nigeria]
BB-23	200#	N814KA N153ML
BB-24	200$	N80MC N183MC C-FCGB
BB-25	200	N1555N N601CF PR- [canx 04Mar05 as exported to Brazil]
BB-26	200	N4299S N200MM N200MN N815CE N815CL N57FM ZS-LYA N57FM ZS-LYA "N100ND" N10825
BB-27	200$	N9379S XA-FUB XA-MAW N62MR N25BL N120DP C-GFOL
BB-28	200	N1952 N41JR F-GKPL 6V-AGS
BB-29	200$	N570M (N57VS) N570VS C-GTJW N500KB C-GKBN LN-ASG C-GKBN [wfu Airdrie, AB, Canada]
BB-30	200$	N200CA N3030C N3090C N211JB N244JB G-HAMA G-ONAL
BB-31	200	N719HC N61RR N7RW N600KW YV [canx 15Dec04 as exported to Venezuela]
BB-32	200$	(N100S) N100SF N160SF
BB-33	200	N8798R ZS-AAA (N8798R) N90806 HP- [canx 03Feb04 as exported to Panama]
BB-34	200$	N204CS N204CA N74BL N72LT N72GC N87BP N878RA
BB-35	200$	YV-T-MTI YV-732P YV-734CP N200YY N35KD N213UV
BB-36	200	N946V N90LP N816RB N44UF
BB-37	200	N217CS N217GS C-GHOL N245K XA-IOE XA-PAU N460CR ZS-NXH
BB-38	200	F-BVRP [w/o 03Apr83 Guangzhou, China; canx 24Aug94]
BB-39	200+	N925B N100NS N55BP N888VG N37SM N63JR N39YV [w/o 10May89 Azusa, CA, USA; canx 17Jan95]
BB-40	200	N926S N35TT N4TJ
BB-41	200	N200ZC
BB-42	200	N200KA N3GT N3GY N66TJ
BB-43	200#	N4201S N500CT N500GT N500UR N520MC
BB-44	200	F-BVRD (N3232U) N3235U F-GHAL D2-ECL [w/o 28May97 Luanda, Angola]
BB-45	200$	N10TM N70TM C-GARM N200TK C-GBQM N200TK N911WC N46JK PT-OZK
BB-46	200	N760NB N760NP
BB-47	200	RP-C200 VH-SKC [w/o 04Sep00 65km ENE of Burketown, QLD, Australia; canx 10Jul01]
BB-48	200	N2809B XA-GAY XB-ACM XB-EDZ XA-PEU XC-AA38 N750HL
BB-49	200$	N222KA XA- [canx 11Apr07 as exported to Mexico]
BB-50	200	N12KA N2AS N1JP N200EJ N500FE N888TR N60SM
BB-51	200	N4202S N702Z (N702ZA) N601PA N104TM ZS-LST (F-GGBT) (5Y-BIQ) 5Y-BIR ZS-LST 5Y-BIR
BB-52	200	YV-T-AOU YV-36CP N36CP (N36JP) N85CC F-GFTA N400AJ ZS-NWK
BB-53	200	N6ES N280RA
BB-54	200	0697/5-T-31 (Argentinian Navy) 0697/1-G-31 (Argentinian Navy) 0697/6-G-41 (Argentinian Navy)
BB-55	200	N9755S G-BCUZ G-OAKM N200BC C-FDEB
BB-56	200$	N55BH N55BN N44US
BB-57	200$	N32TP C-FCGZ N121DA C-FAFT
BB-58	200$	N60PC N60PD
BB-59	200$	N571M N56GR N500WR N504WR N500KS

BEECH 200

c/n	Series/Mod	Identities
BB-60	200	N51JH N510H N320LB (N36AD) N202AD XA-PEX XA-CAH XA-SBG N530JA HK-4108X HK-4108
BB-61	200	C-GSEP N58280 [b/u; canx 28Dec94]
BB-62	200GTO	N246K N300GN N500GN
BB-63	200$	N916MP (N33GG) N83CK N248JM N10DM HK-3705X HK-3705 [canx 11Apr00 - status?]
BB-64	200	N96GM N96QM N174PW N608DK N56CD
BB-65	200$	N99DE N890E N90ML (N901BR) N440ST XB-JZO [c/n checked 17Jan07; current on USCAR as N440ST]
BB-66	200	N1287F N440A (N219DM) RP-C223 RP-223 [assigned import as N219DM since 1989; appears on FAA record card dated 18Sep89]
BB-67	200	N200PB N400DB N78DV YV [canx 03Nov04 as exported to Venezuela]
BB-68	200#	N90WP N349D N844N C-GMWR
BB-69	200$	N45V N45VV N1US N5UB N204JS N812DP
BB-70	200	N6351S N6666K N6666Q N87JR N747KF [stolen 05Apr91 in Peru; canx 09Mar96]
BB-71	200	0698/5-T-32 (Argentinian Navy) 0698/4-G-42 (Argentinian Navy) 0698/4-F-42 (Argentinian Navy)
BB-72	200	N9728S ZS-JKB 3D-ABY ZS-JKB C9-MMB ZS-JKB V5-JKB ZS-JKB 5Y-JKB [w/o 06Nov98 Nairobi Game Park, Kenya]
BB-73	200#	VH-SGT
BB-74	200	N9730S VH-IBC [pres Powerhouse Museum, Sydney, NSW, Australia; canx 21Mar88]
BB-75	200	D-IDMA N42091 D-IHEB F-GIMF N70LA HK-3902X HK-3936X HK-3936W
BB-76	200	N8416B N334LS (N384LS) 025/N86DA (Royal Saudi AF) N500DR C-GPCD [wfu; canx 26Apr06; location?]
BB-77	200$	N2077L (F-BXLE) N300CP C-GWUY 145201 (Canadian Armed Forces) C-GWUY
BB-78	200	N733DY N783DY N694AB N694FC YV [canx 14Jan04 as exported to Venezuela]
BB-79	200	N1FV N63CB N155WC N155RJ N155QS XA- [canx 07Mar08 as exported to Mexico]
BB-80	200	N925B N73LC N78LC (N104AG) N200AL N444TW F-GGMS F-ORCE
BB-81	200$	N1PC N396DP N398DP N402CE N69TD N697D N18DN N200FM [dbr 09Nov08 Puerto San Francisquito, Sonora, Mexico; canx 26Jan09]
BB-82	200	8R-GFB N788AA LZ-RGP LZ-FEO LZ-YUK
BB-83	200	RP-C711 N283KA
BB-84	200	C-GFSB
BB-85	200	N1KA N123A N95WC ZS-NTL V5-CIC ZS-NTL [wfu Lanseria, Gauteng Province, South Africa; still marked as V5-CIC]
BB-86	200$	YV-312P N44640 N677BC 5Y-BKM N677BC TZ-ZBC N677BC
BB-87	200+	F-BXOL N87GA D-ITEC N87GA TI-TCT
BB-88	200$	N79 N4 N35
BB-89	200#	N1282 N16BF N200WZ
BB-90	200	N1283 [w/o 11Sep88 nr Jackson, WY, USA; canx 06Feb89]
BB-91	200	N24MK N9CJ N884PG
BB-92	200	N227US C-FJRT 145201 (Canadian Armed Forces) C-FJRT N192SA "N326BA" N192SA N8117N 3250 (Venezuelan AF) [canx 17Dec04 as exported to Venezuela; impounded Belize wearing false marks N326BA; re-registered in USA 10Jan05; canx 10Jun05 to Venezuela but not registered; reinstated 20Mar06; canx to Venezuela 23Apr08]
BB-93	200	OE-FMC D-IBAF [w/o 27Jul77 Bourgas, Bulgaria; canx cOct77]
BB-94	200	N572M (N10FL) (N12FL) N12L N12LB N51SD N467JM N28AH N17HM
BB-95	200	N9741S ZS-JPD A2-AHZ
BB-96	200	N256TM [w/o 18Apr77 nr Ruddock, LA, USA; canx 12Mar79]
BB-97	200	N4297S N7EG N65RT
BB-98	200	N100HC [dbr 12Aug85 Quinlan, TX, USA, parts to White Industries, Bates City, MO, USA; location B-48; canx cOct87]
BB-99	200$	(N774T) N274T C-FSKQ 5Y-SEL C-FSKQ
BB-100	200	N75KA XC-DIJ
BB-101	200	N31XL N76SG N535JR ZS-MYA D2-EXW
BB-102	200$	C-GPNB F-GGDJ N997MA N200AF
BB-103	200$	N201CH
BB-104	200$	N40RA
BB-105	200#	N4205S N120VE N71TZ C-FKJI
BB-106	200	N4206S N43CC N43CQ TR-LWZ N43CQ N545RC N888DE F-GFLO N383AS N52SF
BB-107	200	N145MC N581MW N585FL N191FL N115TT YV [canx 17Jun04 as exported to Venezuela]
BB-108	200+	(TR-LWC) RP-C1979 N108BM G-OMNH G-SAXN
BB-109	200	N1PC N908R N244JP N308RH
BB-110	200	N11PA TC-FBZ OE-FIM N110BM N202DB
BB-111	200	N4211S (N65WL) N633EB N22071 A2-FMB
BB-112	200	N456L [w/o 27Mar80 nr Parker, CO, USA]
BB-113	200$	PK-TRA [dbr during maintenance; canx c2002; b/u by Wessex Aero, UK]
BB-114	200	N2114L N25KW XA-PMX N300PW
BB-115	200$^6	N2115L N80XY N80X N80XC N330BR N335TM N700KW
BB-116	200$	PK-TRB [b/u c1993]
BB-117	200$	N117TP N999WP N200TM N200TN N1DE N21DE (N410SH) N21DE
BB-118	200	C-GCSL [dbf 10Jan93 Quebec-Jean Lesage International, QC, Canada; canx 22Feb93]
BB-119	200	N204CS OY-AUJ LN-PAG [dbr 13Mar87 Stord-Soerstokken, Norway; canx 17Jul92]
BB-120	200	N6773S C-GHOP
BB-121	200$	N403MP N14V N14VT N16GM F-GHOA TR-LDX ZS-OCI
BB-122	200	TC-TAA N122TJ N122RF XA- [canx 01Dec06 as exported to Mexico]
BB-123	200+	N9123S N711AR N911LR N123YV N120DA PH-ATM D-IBIC PH-ATM
BB-124	200	N111LS N44HT N344T F-GFFB N124AJ N109TM C-GCET

BEECH 200

c/n	Series/Mod	Identities
BB-125	200$	FAG001 (Guatemalan AF) TG-UGA N90PB
BB-126	200+	N600DC N777WJ N388CC N208AJ N777XS N777XZ ZS-PBB N777XZ D2-FFL
BB-127	200	N2127L N200JL [w/o 03Nov08 nr Santa Rosalia, Baja California Sur, Mexico; canx 05Jan09]
BB-128	200	F-BXSI N110TA HP-1591
BB-129	200$	N143CP N148CP [w/o 09Jun85 Hamptonburgh, NY, USA]
BB-130	200	N200SB N333NB N323MB N682DR
BB-131	200	TC-TAB N131SJ
BB-132	200	N1528L (HS-TFF) HS-FFI HS-DCB
BB-133	200	N2133L SE-GSU G-BJZG G-OAKL N113RL N717HT YV [canx 13Jan06 as exported to Venezuela; stolen 15Feb06 Valencia-Arturo Michelena International, Venezuela still wearing N717HT]
BB-134	200	D-IAAK N200EC
BB-135	200	N4003J N535E C6- HK-3854X HK-3854W N402RG HK-4236X HP-1598
BB-136	200	N2WC (N2WQ) N92TA N277JB N57FT
BB-137	200	ZP-TKN PP-IKN PP-EOP
BB-138	200	N925B N999DT
BB-139	200	N170SP N810JB
BB-140	200+	C-GPCP
BB-141	200	N977LX N977GT
BB-142	200	YV-426P [w/o 04Feb82 nr Caracas, Venezuela]
BB-143	200$	N1PC N200CJ
BB-144	200	N28S N2883
BB-145	200	N2145L N68JM N6TN N111M N111MT N88CP VH-ZOS
BB-146	200	N32CL N32HB N32HG [w/o 16Jun92 nr Wilmington-New Castle County, DE, USA; canx 19Oct92]
BB-147	200	N88BF N88BK N50MT N550M N777FL N771HC *PR-NKA
BB-148	200	N140S N440S C-GBGW VH-WNH VH-OYH
BB-149	200+	N123ST D-IAHK N982GA
BB-150	200	N203SF N107FL
BB-151	200$	N92ME N98CM N528WG [w/o 12Oct06 Leonardtown-Captain Walter Francis Duke Regional, MD, USA]
BB-152	200	N500CP N500RV N48HB N48HF N1223C N152TW
BB-153	200	N2153L C-GCEV (N502AB) C-GCEV [dbr 28Jan97 Sept Iles, QC, Canada, parts to White Industries, Bates City, MO, USA; location F-12; canx 12May97]
BB-154	200	N67LW N44KS (N771SR) N44KA N44KT
BB-155	200	F-BXSR (N320FJ) SE-GHS OY-GEH 5Y-BMA
BB-156	200	N2156L N69LD N69CD XC-AA79 XC-ADP [dbr Culiacan, Sinaloa, Mexico 21May03, parts to Dodson International Parts, Rantoul, KS, USA]
BB-157	200$	N1200M N93LV N996LM
BB-158	200	N200LM N200LV N200LN N200HW N8198M N81PA N81PF [w/o 27Jan01 nr Strasburg, CO, USA]
BB-159	200$	N47MM (N47MN) (N47MW) N47FH C-FCGT
BB-160	200	N2160L (EI-BGR) OY-CBK EI-BHG N8493D 9Q-CTK EI-BHG G-BLKN (G-ONPA) G-HIGG N65171 YV-665CP YV-2484P XB-KCQ N160WJ [reportedly became XC-LIS after YV-2484P]
BB-161	200	N2161L C-GTIM N131PA N114SB
BB-162	200+	RP-C22 VH-SMT [canx 17Oct05 as exported to USA; last sighting cSep05 in Venezuela]
BB-163	200	TU-TJE [w/o 28Jun96 Boufle, Ivory Coast]
BB-164	200	N70PC N70PQ HP- [canx 16Jun03 as exported to Panama]
BB-165	200	N76MP N76MB VH-XRF VH-SKU
BB-166	200	N2166L N19GR N19GB N89MP N84CA
BB-167	200	D-IFIB F-GJAF N167KA N300DK YV-2703P
BB-168	200	N44GT D-IOVW N10VW C-FOGY
BB-169	200#	N200KA N725MC
BB-170	200+	N720M N720MA N68BC F-GHLM C-FIWH 145202 (Canadian Armed Forces) C-FIWH N869MA C-GPEA
BB-171	200	7T-VRI 7T-WRI
BB-172	200	N100TM N68RR N94KC
BB-173	200$	N55AE N55FG (N205HG) N173RC
BB-174	200	N600CP N66DD N69DD N869 [dbr 12Nov99 Chicago-Meigs Field, IL, USA, parts to White Industries, Bates City, MO, USA; location "Taxiway No"; canx 05May00; restored 08Nov02]
BB-175	200	7T-VRH 7T-WRH
BB-176	200	N2176L N200LJ N62EC N200PJ F-GFMJ N67GA YV [canx 14May04 as exported to Venezuela; reinstated 07Jun04; canx to Venezuela 18Jun04]
BB-177	200+	N456CS
BB-178	200	N3UR N355AF N36CP
BB-179	200	N424BS [stolen 09Sep94 Lake Havasu, AZ, USA; canx 11Jan01; restored 22Jul02; possibly located at Command Aircraft Parts & Recovery, Ormond Beach Municipal, FL, USA]
BB-180	200	5N-AKR G-BHVX PH-SBK G-BHVX PH-SBK HK- [canx 12Sep05 as exported to Colombia]
BB-181	200	C-GPKK N9150R [wfu, parts to White Industries, Bates City, MO, USA; location "Mid Ramp"; canx 17Jan02]
BB-182	200	N155PT N155BT N922JB EC-727 EC-GBB
BB-183	200$	N418GA N175SA
BB-184	200	7T-VRG 7T-WRG
BB-185	200+	C-GWSL VH-WNI N185DA N265EB N503F
BB-186	200	[completed as c/n BT-1]
BB-187	200	N630DB C-GMRS
BB-188	200$	N4288S N417RC

BEECH 200

c/n	Series/Mod	Identities
BB-189	200	N392DM N392K N56CC
BB-190	200+	N2290L N6KA N79PB N190MD C-FCGL N190MD C-FCGL [w/o 28Jul05 Squamish, BC, Canada; canx 07Sep06]
BB-191	200+	N1PC N200TP
BB-192	200$	SE-GRP (EI-BGR) OY-CBV LN-KCI OY-CBV F-OGPQ F-GLIF
BB-193	200$	N31MB N55SC N131MB OB-1468 [wfu; canx 08Feb00]
BB-194	200$	N200PH N300PH N300EH N502EB HB-GIL
BB-195	200$	YV-92CP N161PA YV-92CP N5LE YV1909
BB-196	200	N525BC N625BC SE-IUZ LN-FKF HK-3995X
BB-197	200$	PH-SAT LN-PAE (N12154) ZS-OAK *ZS-PUB
BB-198	200$	N4298S
BB-199	200	N32KA N33DS N83DS OY-AUK LN-PAD F-GNPD
BB-200	200$(WL)	N2PX N2PY
BB-201	200$	YV-42CP (N162PA) N163PA ZS-NRW (5Y-NRW) 5Y-BKS ZS-NRW [w/o 28Jun04 Vilanculos, Mozambique]
BB-202	200	D-IBVW N2425X F-GEXL N4047C
BB-203	200	[completed as c/n BT-2]
BB-204	200	N17530 [w/o 20Oct77 nr Valparaiso, IN, USA; canx 19Feb97]
BB-205	200+(WL)	N6PW N6PX N90KC
BB-206	200$	VR-BDM N200DM N700WE N700WF ZS-NZH N70AJ
BB-207	200$	N111WB N111WH C-FCGW
BB-208	200	SE-GRR EI-BCY 232 (Irish Air Corps) N60MK N188WG N62DL
BB-209	200$	N545GM N5450M EB-001 (Bolivian AF) ZP-PTC ZP-TTC D-IACS F-GPAS G-PSTR
BB-210	200	N5657N G-BMCA G-IBCA G-OAVX G-FRYI
BB-211	200	OY-BTR LN-ASI OY-BTR 5Y-BMC [wfu Nairobi-Wilson, Kenya; CofA exp 31Mar02]
BB-212	200	N79MC N91LP (N190P) N91LP N910P PNC-209 (Colombian Police)
BB-213	200	N4294S C-GBWC F-GHFM [w/o 07May91 La Roche, France]
BB-214	200+	N4291S N441PS C-GMMK N26LE OB-1700
BB-215	200$	N215KA N315KA N215KA 7Q-YTC ZS-NGC N750TT
BB-216	200	N700CP N600LR N600LP OY-AUZ LN-VIU C-FAKN
BB-217	200$	N200SK N200CD C-FCGM
BB-218	200$	N9209Q N575HW N575HA EC-351 EC-ERQ [w/o 09Oct97 Sere Kunda NDing, Gambia]
BB-219	200	N10TT N884CA N200MR [wfu, parts to White Industries, Bates City, MO, USA; location B-39]
BB-220	200	N19LB N70FH N75VF N800HA
BB-221	200$	(N200PB) N20004 N711UE N711FD F-GJEB SE-KYL PH-DDB OK-MAG
BB-222	200$	N23879 ZS-KAA N999GA N999TC F-GIAR F-ODZL ZS-KAA 5Y-BSU
BB-223	200	N17723 YV-O-CVG-5 YV-O-FMO-5 YV-O-SATA-1 YV0101
BB-224	200+	N573M N57BM N215PA OE-FAY N215PA N750KC
BB-225	200	F-GAJP I-PIAO N8534W N917BT XB-ORA XB-JZP
BB-226	200$^6	YV-105CP YV-2359P HK-3699X HK-3699 N717SP N982TM
BB-227	200	N90BR N335S
BB-228	200+	N53G N74ED N79KF N703HT
BB-229	200	N17799 N177AD N60JT N222GL N904CM N911MN N910CA
BB-230	200	G-BEHR F-GDLE [w/o 24Nov01 Moulins, France]
BB-231	200#	N800CP N200FH C-FZVX
BB-232	200$	YV-112CP (N163PA) N162PA [reportedly hijacked in Peru cJun92]
BB-233	200+	N50JD F-GHLD [w/o 17Dec98 Libreville, Gabon; canx 20Jul09]
BB-234	200	N17570 N200JC N80PA N45MF [w/o 06Feb07 Bozeman-Gallatin Field, MT, USA; canx 08Apr09]
BB-235	200	N9BK (N777MW) OY-CBP [std Sindal Flyveplads, Denmark]
BB-236	200$	N17812 N3060C N46KA C-FCGC
BB-237	200	N17640 N7118A N717RM N114JF HP- [canx 11Feb04 as exported to Panama; impounded 19Feb04 in Mexico - fate?]
BB-238	200$	YV-106CP N891MA N200PH
BB-239	200	N17649 N517JM I-ELCO G-BLAE G-WWHL N517JM F-GSIN
BB-240	200$	G-HLUB G-BJBP N62360 N605EE N888EM N888EX XA- [canx 29Jan09 as exported to Mexico]
BB-241	200	N23915 VH-AAZ [dbr 30Nov83 Lord Howe Island, NSW, Australia; canx 18May95]
BB-242	200	N24201 N200RW [dam 25Oct01 Kaiser Lake Ozark-Lee C Fine Memorial, MO, USA and dbr in subsequent landing St.Louis-Spirit of St.Louis, MO, USA; parts to Dodson International Parts, Rantoul, KS, USA cJan02]
BB-243	200$^4	N200PB N234AM N300US N43AJ N932JV
BB-244	200	N631SR [w/o 15Jul81 King Cove, AK, USA; canx cApr82]
BB-245	200	N23930 ZS-KAB A2-ABO VH-AAV [w/o 21Feb80 Sydney-Kingsford Smith, Mascot, NSW, Australia; canx 21Feb80]
BB-246	200+	N30MR (N30MH) N46WC N46WD N200VA (N138CC) N200VA
BB-247	200	N18347 N4000 N400U
BB-248	200+	N925B N825B N60RE N123PM HK-3822X HK-3822 [wfu Palmira Alfonso Bonilla Aragon International, Valle del Cauca, Colombia; canx 06May05]
BB-249	200	C-GQJG [wfu cMar09, parts to MTW Aerospace, Montgomery, AL, USA; canx 24Mar09]
BB-250	200+	N1008J C-FCGX [wfu, parts to Westcan Aircraft Sales & Salvage, Kamloops, BC, Canada; canx 24Jun04]
BB-251	200	N18251 N256TW HB-GGO I-BMPE F-GKCV N147AP
BB-252	200$	N15KA N475U N934SH
BB-253	200	N4200S N999HC N999CY N991SU
BB-254	200$	N1PC N600BW N600BV [w/o 12Sep03 in sea off Madeira, Portugal; canx 05Mar04]
BB-255	200$	N920DY N820DY N32KC N32KD HB-GJM
BB-256	200$	N101PC N101DX (ZS-MRI) ZS-NTM (5Y-NTM) 5Y-BKT
BB-257	200	N200KA N200KE N27BH N27DA N362EA N257NA
BB-258	200+	N18758 N40PS (N2006) N888ET

BEECH 200

c/n	Series/Mod	Identities
BB-259	200$	YV-114CP N3786J N14SU (ZK-CMO) VH-NIB VH-APA VH-LKB VH-ZMP
BB-260	200	N23764 (F-GAME) N1SC N18CJ N152WR
BB-261	200$	YV-O-MMH-9 YV-791CP YV-O-SATA-2 YV0102
BB-262	200	N18762 N92V EC-HHO C-GOMA
BB-263	200	OE-FMW F-GCTP N48Q N2U
BB-264	200$	N24164 N713X C-FCGV HK-3796X HK-3796 N456CJ C-FZNQ
BB-265	200	YV-141CP
BB-266	200$	N18266 ZS-NNS N266EB [w/o 05Feb06 Myrtle Beach-Grand Strand, SC, USA; canx 23Jan07]
BB-267	200#	N813TS N888B N3RC N194WS N96UB N984MC N267TT N8BG TG- [canx 21Jul09 as exported to Guatemala]
BB-268	200$	N20505 N565RA C-GTUC
BB-269	200	N18269 N100SM N180SN N269D D-IICE
BB-270	200	[completed as c/n BT-3]
BB-271	200+	N69BK (N88KE) N131TC
BB-272	200	N272BE N772GS N2000X N202KA N302MB N241CK
BB-273	200	N17743 YV-O-CVG-8 YV-O-FMO-8 YV-O-SATA-3 YV0103
BB-274	200$^4	N18243 (N26MM) N1MM N8AM
BB-275	200	C-GQNJ
BB-276	200+	N205X N130LP EC-FQQ N198SC TF-ELT D-IMON N7GU N865HR
BB-277	200	N17759 N946BF N200AP N593DJ
BB-278	200	N24153 AP-CAD AP-CAA
BB-279	200	N18306 N184SK F-GFJM 4X-ARD N279CA YV [canx 19Nov03 as exported to Venezuela]
BB-280	200$	N76CB F-GJPD N280TT
BB-281	200	N949CW N1865A N1866A N315JW N4AT C-FFAR [dbr 30Oct08 Tadoule Lake, MB, Canada; canx 04Jun09]
BB-283	200$^4	N8100H N200MP F-GPRB (N68AA) N283JP C-FATA
BB-284	200$	N200EA N20BD N25MK N50LT [wfu, parts to White Industries, Bates City, MO, USA; location F-05]
BB-285	200$	C-GQXF C-FKBU
BB-286	200	N23761 ZS-KAO ZS-XGD Z-MRS ZS-XGD 7Q-NXB ZS-XGD 5Y-BVU
BB-287	200	N429E (N71PW) N429E N498AC C-GWWV
BB-288	200$	G-BEST G-ORMC SE-IRP N288SF ZS-NRR 5Y-HHG ZS-NRR
BB-289	200	N7MB N5ST
BB-290	200	YV-161CP N290SJ
BB-291	200	N1HS N286TC N769 N291PA
BB-292	200+	N17739 VR-BDM N393DM N393K N393JW (N393JM) N393JW
BB-293	200	N500CP N200BT (N202QS) N200BT
BB-294	200	N18494 9M-KNS
BB-295	200	(F-GAPV) TU-VBB [w/o 21Jun90 Touba, Ivory Coast]
BB-296	200	N2480A N402CJ N402KA
BB-297	200	N23765 VH-IBD P2-IAH [w/o 12Apr95 Lae-Nadzab, Papua New Guinea]
BB-298	200	N5110 N862DD
BB-299	200	N5111 N6111 N200FV
BB-300	200	N211BB N211PD F-GHLV N86Q HP- [canx 11Feb04 as exported to Panama]
BB-301	200$	YV-78CP N222GA ZK-CGS N611SW C-FCGU
BB-302	200	N600CP N300BW N86Y G-OWAX G-IMEA
BB-303	200	N18345 F-GHCS LX-JDP [dam 30Oct04 Lyon-Bron, France; canx cFeb07]
BB-304	200$	N18421 N483G N451DP N451DB N103PM PR-JSP
BB-305	200$^4	N5000 N50ZY HK-3227X HK-3227W N50ZY N30XY N11AB
BB-306	200(WL)	N274K N500HY N306SS 4X-DZK N230CS *PR-JPG
BB-307	200+	N23687 N921S N703HT HB-GPG F-GMPO
BB-308	200	N90WP N98WP LN-TSA [w/o 19Mar93 Dagali, Norway; canx 13Sep04]
BB-309	200	G-BEUZ D-ILNY OY-PEB 5Y-NUR (OY-FTC) OY-PEB
BB-310	200	N200KA N100DS N100KM N988SC "N705TL" R704 (Guatemalan AF)[intercepted 27Feb05 wearing false marks N705TL; forced to land at Torcoroma, Santander, Colombia & impounded; canx 14Apr05 as exported to Colombia, became R704 with Guatemalan AF]
BB-311	200	N18454 (N370AA) F-GILE N370TC HP-1512
BB-312	200	N77CT N97CT F-GEBC N127GA
BB-313	200$	N23313 N30SE
BB-314	200	N18335 N101BP N767WF
BB-315	200$^6	N89315 N873DB Z-TAB ZS-TAB ZS-PZU
BB-316	200$	YV-168CP YV-2584P
BB-317	200	XC-PGR [w/o 27Oct79 nr San Ysidro, CA, USA]
BB-318	200	N49KC
BB-319	200	N20903 F-GGZV N300WJ N6HU
BB-320	200	N23786 VH-KTE [w/o 28Aug83 5km S of Adavale, QLD, Australia; canx 28Aug83]
BB-321	200	N455TA N38JL N261AC
BB-322	200	N202LJ N715MA N710NC
BB-323	200$	YV-74CP N4430V N811VT PR-GBI
BB-324	200	N88PA N1WV N37GA D-IGME N900VG HA-ACS N107AB N111SF N701NC
BB-325	200	N15KA N15RA N115RA HZ-MW1 (F-GGAK) N7045P F-GGAK N65EB
BB-326	200	N700CP N1PC N1PQ N40BL N944CE N944CF
BB-327	200	N771HM N771HA VH-XRP N327CM ZS-OSB 5Y-BPJ [wfu Nairobi-Wilson, Kenya; CofA exp 09Jan04]
BB-328	200	N6789 (N64783) N6789W N78AM N795PA (D-IDOL) N795PA
BB-329	200	N5112 N202CF C-GLSE N311GA N53CK N587DR HP- [canx 01Dec06 as exported to Panama]
BB-330	200	N5113 N200CE N130PA N127TT HP- [canx 15Oct03 as exported to Panama]
BB-331	200$	N111JW N400WH N111WA N87LP G-FSEU

BEECH 200

c/n	Series/Mod	Identities
BB-332	200$	N23807 N3DE N58DE N307DM
BB-333	200	N308F N3207 C-FANG F-GHLH TC-AUY
BB-334	200	D-IBAH N77SA ZS-NRT D2-EBG
BB-335	200$	N17610 N371TA N327RK N327RB
BB-336	200	N24096 B-129 N51342 N50TW N311AV
BB-337	200	N600AM N400KW
BB-338	200	VR-BGN N689BV
BB-339	200	N93ME N93MF N5UV N339AJ N545LC
BB-340	200	N925B N925BA N7200B N74BJ (N74PF) N74EJ [w/o 14Aug97 nr Dalton-Municipal, GA, USA; canx 27Jan99]
BB-341	200+	N45D N6DY C-FBWX ZS-LWM ST-BBA ZS-LWM ST-BBA
BB-342	200	N23794 794 (Royal Thai Army) 342 (Royal Thai Army) HS-PON
BB-343	200	N4679M N4679M [cvtd to Beech 300 prototype; first flight 06Oct81]
BB-344	200$	YV-82CP N363DA VH-LHK P2-IAG N6297S VH-ITH
BB-345	200	N962JC (N862JC) N250HC F-GHCT D2-ECH [w/o 28Jan95 nr Canfufo, Angola]
BB-346	200$	N200EA XA-JUB N200EA (N15LS) N84LS N747MB YV-2834P
BB-347	200$	N24110 ZS-KCB 3D-ADS ZS-KCB N424CR C-GJLI
BB-348	200	N28J
BB-349	200	G-BFEA G-BRON G-BFEA N80GA D-IEXD F-GHLB (N349JW) F-GHLB
BB-350	200$	N23743 N125BJ N125MS ZS-NTT
BB-351	200$	N6666K N6666C N351FW N68CP G-CEGR
BB-352	200	N84MD YV-806CP HK-3922X HK-3922P
BB-353	200	N4929M SU-AYD SU-BAX
BB-354	200$	(N900CP) N199GH N198GH N550JC N221BG C-GDFT
BB-355	200	C-GSZX VH-SPQ P2-SMB VH-SMB VH-OYE
BB-356	200	N9KA N28KC (N29PL) N79RR
BB-357	200	N200JV N500DE N6069A
BB-358	200	RP-C5129
BB-359	200$	N200PB N300KC N780W N359K N351MA C-GDFN
BB-360	200+^6	N5006M N992FR N9MH N333ET N210PH N18KA
BB-361	200$	N334RR N1HX
BB-362	200	G-BKTI G-SONG N4562P N200TK G-VSEL N506AB HK- [canx 10May04 as exported to Colombia]
BB-363	200	N101AF N101AK HK-3749X N96GA N642TF
BB-364	200$	N18450 XC-DIK (N364MW) N66171 F-GHYV "OY-JRB" OY-JRN EC-KNT
BB-365	200	C-GNOJ VH-AIH P2-SML VH-OYA
BB-366	200	N1230 D-IBHK EC-IUV
BB-367	200$	N100UP F-GINB N100UP ZS-NPO 5Y-NPO ZS-NPO N367RA
BB-368	200	F-GBRP [w/o 17Oct80 Ribeauville, France; canx 28Sep81]
BB-369	200+	N4659M N800L HK-3555X HK-3555 XC-KAY XC-AA48 [wfu, parts to Dodson International Parts, Rantoul, KS, USA]
BB-370	200$	N117WD N80RT
BB-371	200	N4660M N600CP N151E N151EL
BB-372	200	N4937M SX-ECG
BB-373	200$(WL)	N4799M N200FE
BB-374	200	N10HC N24LA N7CR N47CR N7QR N111UT N111UR C-FWWF
BB-375	200+	N24BL N89FC N23ST
BB-376	200+	N4914M EI-BFJ 234 (Irish Air Corps) N409GA N376RC
BB-377	200	N1GT N41GT N52GT HK-4422X HK-4422 [w/o 11Oct07 Bogota-El Dorado, Distrito Capital, Colombia]
BB-378	200	N4826M N482WF N482SW N200AJ N200BP N378SF
BB-379	200	G-VRES G-ONEX 5Y-DDE 5Y-SMB
BB-380	200	(N7GW) N4825M (N380GW) N142SR N187JN N59GS N323RR
BB-381	200$	N4848M ZS-KGW
BB-382	200	(N700E) N92M ZS-PKM
BB-383	200+	N15KA N78FC N384JD N384DB C-GZYO
BB-384	200	N2025M PR-VIP
BB-385	200$	N81RD N381R
BB-386	200$	(D-ILMA) D-IMLL N310GA ZS-NHX
BB-387	200$^6(WL)	G-BFOL N899TB G-BFOL 5N-ALW G-BFOL 5N-BHL ZS-BHK
BB-388	200	N2040D N50FC N50FQ N890MC N388MC N26BE [stolen 30Jan94 - status?]
BB-389	200$	N5082M N510WP N510WR N859CC (OY-FCT) C-GKOS C-GKOX
BB-390	200	N64HC N1000W N1660W (N202MM) N1660W
BB-391	200	N526AP N1969C YV [canx 31Oct03 as exported to Venezuela]
BB-392	200$	C-GOVF N400GM F-GRAN N392CT N392KC
BB-393	200	N2014K HK-2489X HK-2489 [w/o 28Oct85 Bogota, Distrito Capital, Colombia; canx 03Mar03]
BB-394	200$	YV-122CP N49855 N624AL (N200TC) N223TC YV-597CP [w/o 12Nov89 nr Caracas, Venezuela]
BB-395	200	N4912M XA-IIY XB-BRB XA-ASR XB-RHO
BB-396	200$^6	N203R N403R N326AJ (N96HH) N326AJ
BB-397	200#	PH-SLG 5N-ALF PH-SLG F-GFIV D-IAMW LX-GDB F-GOCF
BB-398	200	N621RM N627BM N398HM N429DM N929DM N572M
BB-399	200	(F-GBGI) 9Q-CTE OO-CTE F-GIRM N399BM
BB-400	200	N3030C N3035C G-ONEA G-GATI N164AB N999BT N208MS [w/o 05Oct99 Mount Berlin, Williamstown, MA, USA]
BB-401	200	F-GBLG OY-JAO SX-APJ
BB-402	200	N4000K N4000K N318W N182Z
BB-403	200$	N900CP N7117 N147K C-FGFZ
BB-404	200	C-GPQZ N207P N5TH N5100J N921DT N777PR N315MS
BB-405	200+	N20KQ N19Y N4S N83GB N350AC N367LF

BEECH 200

c/n	Series/Mod	Identities
BB-406	200	N222PA G-OEMS F-GHOC
BB-407	200$	D-IASB LN-NFT F-GFTT ZS-NUC 5Y-BTO ZS-SGP
BB-408	200	[completed as c/n BT-4]
BB-409	200^4	N2044D N220TA N222LA
BB-410	200	N500BW N275Z N200PL
BB-411	200	N1KA [w/o cMar80; canx cJul81]
BB-412	200	N2030P N316MS
BB-413	200$	N2061B N456PF
BB-414	200	N20620 N5VG N600DM [stolen 09Apr90 Palm Beach, FL, USA; canx 21Mar95]
BB-415	200	N2067M P2-PNG P2-PNH P2-CAA
BB-416	200$	N396DP VR-CCI N396DP ZS-KZU
BB-417	200$	G-BFVZ HB-GHF N201KA
BB-418	200	N200MM N208MM CX-BOR N8092D [wfu, parts to White Industries, Bates City, MO, USA; location G-05]
BB-419	200	N555FP N256EN OY-BVB UN454 (United Nations) ZS-PPZ
BB-420	200	N2920A N210SU N420TA
BB-421	200	YV-143CP N4488L A2-AEZ
BB-422	200	N551E N501EB
BB-423	200$^4	N200PB N32CL (N3202) (N122SC) N549BE N300KC N120RJ XB-HDY XB-IHK
BB-424	200	N1KB F-GGBC D-IGRO F-GMCR N470TC
BB-425	200$^6(WL)	N2057S
BB-426	200+	G-BFWH N400TB N11MY N11HY N220CB N70RD
BB-427	200$	N999MC N999MQ N49LD N48LD N101CC N101GQ YV [canx 03May07 as exported to Venezuela]
BB-428	200$	G-BFWI N106PA N106RH
BB-429	200	N2034P N28BF N28BE N74GS N574GS N409RA
BB-430	200$	N9FC N9FQ N156WC N1BS N1YS N316GC
BB-431	200	(F-GBLE) 9Q-CTF OO-CTF 9Q-CTF F-GILH 5U-ABY F-WQUQ N431WJ
BB-432	200	N925B N426PS (N426FS) N22NP N33KM N200AU
BB-433	200	N2053C (F-GIPH) F-GIPK N133GA N94FG
BB-434	200$	N2051P N200EC C-GPOA N107CT N68AA N50AJ
BB-435	200	N2045D XC-BCN XC-GOL XC-BCN
BB-436	200$	N200AB F-GFJT N261GA N83KA N382ME
BB-437	200^4	N711MD N711MB N500MT N503P
BB-438	200$	EI-BFT (G-BLLC) G-LKOW G-BLLC F-GGPT N438BM N438HT N438CR
BB-439	200	N110MJ CF-MCF C-FMCF N500JA F-GGLN
BB-440	200$	YV-238CP YV1730
BB-441	200$^6	N79CF
BB-442	200	N442KA
BB-443	200$	N700Z (N700ZL) N71RG
BB-444	200$	N200KA N8040A N11HK N122BC N50CD N444JE ZS-LZU N444EB N888HT
BB-445	200$	N179KA N5KW N79KA N79CX N79KA N364SB N790RM N55SR
BB-446	200$	N298D N773KA N885HT N232JS (N727KB) N232JS
BB-447	200	N79ED N300CT N356GA HP-010
BB-448	200(WL)	N865M N865W N700HM N411BL
BB-449	200	N2068L B-13152 NA-301 (Taiwanese Government)
BB-450	200	N6028R N52BC N52BQ C-GJCM HK-3923X HK-4095X [wfu, parts to White Industries, Bates City, MO, USA; location Q-03; canx 24Aug99]
BB-451	200$	D-IBOW HB-GJI
BB-452	200$	N730CE N500PR N500PV 9M-ZAA
BB-453	200^4	N1284 N23TC
BB-454	200$	N888DC
BB-455	200	N1128M N555FP N1122M N24SX N900DG C-GYDQ
BB-456	200	N100FB N80NE N80NF (C6-CAA) C6-BFP N124BB N86LD N456CD G-PFFN
BB-457	200+	N111JW N112GM (N141BB) N800LS N15KA
BB-458	200$	N2000F N169DB AN-233 (Ecuadorian Navy)
BB-459	200$	N75X OY-BVC 101002 (Swedish AF) SE-KXM LN-AWE
BB-460	200	0745/5-T-33 (Argentinian Navy) 0745/4-G-43 (Argentinian Navy) 0745/4-F-43 (Argentinian Navy)
BB-461	200$	EI-BFW N116PA N33TG N277RS N313CT
BB-462	200	N2063T N27C N27CD G-MOAT N220TT
BB-463	200#	(F-GBOT) D-IBOH N4248Y P2-NAT N463DP (VH-ITH) N463MX
BB-464	200	N2066T N79SE N561SS
BB-465	200#	N2065P N24SA N31WC *N113MH
BB-466	200	N780BF (N781BF) N200TW N206P
BB-467	200$	N6024E N307G 5Y-SJB 5H-MUN 5Y-SJB
BB-468	200$	N6056T N2KH N204KA TF-ELT TF-ELI OE-LEA N468SM ZS-PBL N9UT C-FEKB
BB-469	200	[completed as c/n BT-5]
BB-470	200	N2070U ZS-KGS N3018C VH-NIA VH-CWE VH-ZMO
BB-471	200	0746/4-G-44 (Argentinian Navy) LV-RTC 0746/6-P-44 (Argentinian Navy)
BB-472	200	YV-247CP N4489A G-WRCF N305JS YV [canx 15Jun09 as exported to Venezuela]
BB-473	200	N510CB N746KF
BB-474	200	C-GCFF
BB-475	200$	N121LB
BB-476	200$	N6040T N6003 N203BS
BB-477	200	N574M N59DF OY-BPG (F-GGAN) F-GILB N57GA
BB-478	200	N6030F N789BT N789DS XA-PMX N789DS N912SM
BB-479	200	N600SC N200UQ C-GNBB
BB-480	200	N380AC N380MC N302AG SE-IVI N988GA ZS-MJH D2-EMX
BB-481	200$^6	N144K HR-ANL TG-KAD N84XP

BEECH 200

c/n	Series/Mod	Identities
BB-482	200$	N6040U N6017 N7166P
BB-483	200+	N5TW N5TK N213BE N213MB OH-WWR N27BG HC-BSR N6296M HC-CAD (N250GV) N250FN N924AC
BB-484	200	N84KA G-WSJE [w/o 12Sep87 Southend, UK; canx 03Oct88]
BB-485	200	N74GP N74GB N74TG N120K N485K
BB-486	200$	N56RA N56DA N213PH
BB-487	200$	N243KA N400N N40QN VH-NIC N40QN PT-OYR N198SC VH-PIL N8PY G-PLAT G-CBFS G-KVIP
BB-488	200	0747/4-G-45 (Argentinian Navy) 0747/6-P-45 (Argentinian Navy)
BB-489	200	[completed as c/n BT-6]
BB-490	200+	YU-BLW HB-GHA LN-PAF F-ODZE (N217CP) N807SC N145CE N908RC N988CC
BB-491	200	N225AD N225AC RP-C243 N622DC N622KM
BB-492	200	N200PD N64DC
BB-493	200	N6040W N6509F
BB-494	200	N1VN N100CH N30FL N942CE N942CF
BB-495	200$(WL)	EV-7910 (Venezuelan Army)
BB-496	200#	N180S N225MS HK-4278X HK-4278W [stolen cJan90; canx 15Jun95; placed on Colombian register 14Feb03]
BB-497	200	N6052B N73CA N72MM
BB-498	200$	N6040Y N23707 N6507B
BB-499	200	N6051C N302PC N6051C N499TT C-GTJZ
BB-500	200	YV-260CP N4561L N13HC F-GHBE [w/o 08Feb91 Mirecourt, France; canx 16May91]
BB-501	200$^4	SE-GHK N571SS N518F G-KBCA G-OADT G-BSEO OK-JKB N120GA N9UN N175BM N175GM N38TJ
BB-502	200$	N94D N94DU N77PA N275X
BB-503	200+	N400GC RP-C304 N503WJ
BB-504	200	F-GCCC [w/o 26Mar84 Bergamo, Italy; canx 24Aug94]
BB-505	200$	N110KA HP-1083 HP-1083P C-GKBP
BB-506	200+	N43RD C-GRDI N945BV N8SV YV [canx 29May09 as exported to Venezuela]
BB-507	200	N66585 (N80BR) N90BR N600RM F-GEJY N507K YV [canx 17Aug06 as exported to Venezuela]
BB-508	200	G-BGHR [w/o 25Sep79 Tremblay-en-France, France; canx 16Nov79]
BB-509	200	N600G N72DD N72RL
BB-510	200	[completed as c/n BT-7]
BB-511	200	YV-256CP N200LW N202AJ
BB-512	200(WL)	N15KA N4913M N1GC N10CY F-GHCU N333TS N512KA PNC-0236 (Colombian Police)
BB-513	200$	C-GMOC N513SA C-GMOC
BB-514	200	N300HM N335TA (N435TA) N335TA
BB-515	200	N200HC F-GKII (F-HADA) F-GKII
BB-516	200$	N6650H N60TC N60TQ XA-CHA (N60TX) N16TX N231JH N281JH N852JP
BB-517	200	YV-257CP [reportedly w/o cMar81]
BB-518	200$	N6050D VH-IBE DQ-FDS VH-MKR N83GA
BB-519	200$	N6647D N979SR N28RY N28RU (N747P) N721SW C-GCLQ
BB-520	200	2840 (Venezuelan AF) [wfu Caracas-La Carlota, Venezuela]
BB-521	200+	OY-CBL SE-GXM OY-CBL LN-PAB LN-AXB SE-IZB (LN-VIR) LN-AXB N220GK N355TW N200QN G-OEAS
BB-522	200	(YV-261CP) 3150 (Venezuelan AF)
BB-523	200$	N95D N94D N240RL N196MP N500DW N508DW
BB-524	200	N6666C N95PM D-ILPC N524MR
BB-525	200$	N200L ZS-MFC 5Y-NKI
BB-526	200$	OE-BBB
BB-527	200	N662L C-FIFO [canx 23Jul09 - status?]
BB-528	200	N103DC N203BC N700BE
BB-529	200	N333SR N80LM N602MC F-GHPR EC-191 EC-FPH F-GIIY N30AH F-GIQV VH-SWP VH-NTE
BB-530	200	[completed as c/n BT-8]
BB-531	200$	N2657 C-GBWO N2657 VH-XFB SE-LDM 5U-ABX (PH-AMW) (F-GSSD) "F-GSSY" TJ-ROF (PH-SKS) ZS-DSL 5Y-XXC 5Y-FDK
BB-532	200	N46WC N46WQ N300JD N300JK (N731RC) N37CB N16PX N912MF
BB-533	200	YV-262CP N58244 LN-PAH N87RK VH-XDB
BB-534	200	N12CF
BB-535	200	C-GOGT
BB-536	200^4	N33FM N777AW
BB-537	200$	N11ER N700BX N5MK
BB-538	200+	N6724N (F-GBPO) 5N-AVH N477JM
BB-539	200	N555SK ST-SFS
BB-540	200$	N65NL N946CE N946CF YV-946CP YV196T
BB-541	200	N6661A N21EH (N23WL) N113GW N923AS
BB-542	200+	N3333X F-GILP N978GA N542KA
BB-543	200	0746/4-G-46 (Argentinian Navy) [w/o 15May86 Punta Mitre, Tierra del Fuego, Argentina]
BB-544	200$	N548WB N711VH N711VM
BB-545	200$	OY-CBY D-ILIN
BB-546	200	0748/4-G-47 (Argentinian Navy) 0748/6-P-47 (Argentinian Navy)
BB-547	200$	N6654B N594DC ZS-NIP 5Y-HHE
BB-548	200^4	N6654A N11VC N12FH N245AG N78SC N706DG
BB-549	200	0749/4-G-48 (Argentinian Navy) 0749/6-P-48 (Argentinian Navy)
BB-550	200	N6062Q VH-TLX P2-MBM VH-TLX
BB-551	200	[completed as c/n BT-9]
BB-552	200	G-BGRD G-IPRA G-BGRD 5Y-GRD G-BGRD N63593

BEECH 200

c/n	Series/Mod	Identities
BB-553	200$	N49KA N83JN N326RT *N831PA
BB-554	200+^4	N15TT N15TF N102WR N204BR N5PX
BB-555	200#	D-IFOR EC-795 EC-GHZ
BB-556	200	C-GQKK N556JK N556JS I-ARBX N79GA YV1591
BB-557	200	N713GH N200E (N2008) N117PA OY-PAM 5Y-JAI
BB-558	200	EI-BGY PH-BGY N105PA N78V F-GJLI N58JR LV-WGP
BB-559	200	N200SG XA-RJV N559BM N795CA
BB-560	200$	N38DD C-FDLO N72GA N200NA LN-MAA F-GTEF C-FRRQ
BB-561	200$	N963JC N36GA G-ECAV G-VICW F-GULJ (F-GZAT) EC-KNP
BB-562	200$	N192W D-IGVB N549JF N70LM N120FS N120FN YV [canx 21Nov07 as exported to Venezuela]
BB-563	200	[completed as c/n BT-10]
BB-564	200	N6063U ZS-KHK (N6063U) N42LJ
BB-565	200$	YV-296CP XA-RSC N335GA (N253TA) N920C N6630C N239PF
BB-566	200+	N58JB N80GH N200ER N300HB
BB-567	200	CN-CDE [w/o 03Nov86 Casablanca, Morocco]
BB-568	200$^6	G-BGRE
BB-569	200GTO+(WL)	N992C N39K N40HE (N977BA) N40HE *N831LS [canx 14Jun07 as exported to Panama; never registered & seized by US Marshals; reinstated to US register 24Sep08]
BB-570	200$	N968T (N919LN) N968T
BB-571	200	N200KA N202KA N444BL N702AS N769MB
BB-572	200$	N66710 N991LL N971LL N972LL N119MC N898CA XA- [canx 04Apr06 as exported to Mexico]
BB-573	200	[completed as c/n BT-11]
BB-574	200	N75WP N75WL C-GZRX
BB-575	200	N6656W N580 N307P OY-PAL VT-SLS D-ISJP D-IFUN N575RA
BB-576	200	N6667T N505SC N81WU N802CA N53SP
BB-577	200	CN-CDF
BB-578	200	N200EW N333NB (N333ND) (N25GQ) N700GB N780GB F-GHXV N578G N303DK N130CT
BB-579	200+	N6064B VH-AKT P2-KCA P2-MML VH-VCB
BB-580	200$	N6750B N67PC AN-234 (Ecuadorian Navy)
BB-581	200$	N14NA N12NG
BB-582	200$	N78LB N47PA LN-MOA SE-LTL
BB-583	200	N6695M N777AG N777AQ
BB-584	200$	N6679H N400WP (N490WP) LN-MOB
BB-585	200	N759K N438P N43PE N143DE
BB-586	200	N6668H ZS-MGG N653TB
BB-587	200$	N925B N200BH N30AB N247AF
BB-588	200+	N200LJ N200RJ N200AJ N200RJ XA-RQQ N132GA N578BM G-OCEG
BB-589	200	N202BE N553R (N37PW) N911ND N811ND TZ-DDG
BB-590	200+	N6669T 9M-UMW N514BV LN-AXC I-ALGH F-GIDV N524FS
BB-591	200	[completed as c/n BT-12]
BB-592	200$	XA-JIM N26SJ N432FA [dbr 30Jun04 Green Bay-Austin Straubel, WI, USA, parts to White Industries, Bates City, MO, USA; location "Ramp East"; canx 23Nov05]
BB-593	200$	N6064M ZS-KJP N593 ZS-NZI (N209JS) N711KB
BB-594	200	N760NB N760NE N760BM ZS-OYP
BB-595	200+(WL)	N6672V RP-C1260 VH-AKT N528JJ N927JC N126JH
BB-596	200$	(N713D) N6673D N667AT N918JN N72SE *N902AC
BB-597	200$	G-BHAN A2-ACO ZS-MSK V5-MSK 5Y-BJC ZS-MSK 5Y-BJC ZS-MSK
BB-598	200$	YV-335CP YV1731
BB-599	200	N48CR N154BA
BB-600	200+	N15KA N500W N200BR CC-COT
BB-601	200+^4	N6687H N976KC
BB-602	200	N6735T N981LL N981LE YV1387 [dbr 28Nov07 Isletas, Honduras]
BB-603	200+	N9FC N9FQ (N123PE) N232WE F-GHTV N91TR TN-ATR N91TR N70RB N515BA
BB-604	200	N75CX N75C N944CC N944LS
BB-605	200	N6066Z VH-MYO VH-MYU N71GA VH-YNE N605EA (N8BG) N485R
BB-606	200$	N6679E N600KP N600KB HC-BRT N29AJ LV-WIO
BB-607	200$	N6725L ZS-LTE D2-FFT
BB-608	200$	N16AS N284K (N281U) (N932JP) N284K
BB-609	200	[completed as c/n BT-13]
BB-610	200$	N545GM N545AW F-GFDM 5Y-CDO N171RD N200VJ XA- [canx 21Jan04 as exported to Mexico]
BB-611	200$	N6687T N108G N41C N41CV N1JP N25MR XA- [canx 22Jun07 as exported to Mexico]
BB-612	200	N506GT
BB-613	200	N700EZ N2TX N613CS (N603JR) N613JR YV [canx 27May05 as exported to Venezuela]
BB-614	200$	N333CR ZS-LKA A2-KAS
BB-615	200$	N16PM RP-C704 N383JP
BB-616	200	N6693F N123AF SE-IUN F-GGMV
BB-617	200$	N6065R (ZK-UPA) VH-FIL N29913 HP-960 HP-960P
BB-618	200	N1857W N1857L HB-GID N269BW XA- [canx 14Feb06 as exported to Mexico]
BB-619	200$	YV-350CP N4255E N10PC LN-MOD OY-CTJ 101003(Swedish AF) SE-KXN 5Y-RJA
BB-620	200	N6735P (N35P) N900MB N40WH N601T F-GILU TR-LEG ZS-OGV D2-FEI [wfu Lanseria, Gauteng Province, South Africa]
BB-621	200	N6757M N207CM N210CM N217CM
BB-622	200$	N7009 N7009J N212BF F-GHSV

BEECH 200

c/n	Series/Mod	Identities
BB-623	200$^4	N6689D PR-EDW
BB-624	200$^4	N52WC D-ILWH (N888EE) N32JP N123SR N202BB N444EG
BB-625	200+^6(WL)	N6682U N302BC N18BH N8SP N8SZ N869AM G-WVIP
BB-626	200	EI-BHA OY-AUM EI-BHA LN-KOA C9-ASS C9-ENH
BB-627	200	[completed as c/n BT-14]
BB-628	200	N6739P N711TN
BB-629	200	N470MA 9Q-CTG
BB-630	200	N67222 ZS-KLH V5-KLH N107AJ N630VB ZS-NZJ
BB-631	200	N6684B
BB-632	200$	YV-1873P YV-2710P YV1871
BB-633	200	N90D N90DF N62AM N299SC N650TJ C-FSSU [dbf 10Jan93 Quebec City, QC, Canada; canx 29Apr93]
BB-634	200$	N6692D N101CP OY-NUK N469JB (N13MX) N469JB
BB-635	200	N6694D N30PM N30PH [wfu c2005, parts to White Industries, Bates City, MO, USA]
BB-636	200+^4	N6693D N806TC N127TA
BB-637	200	N5AJ N961PS N31WJ N3181
BB-638	200	N3D N8DX N220JB
BB-639	200$	C-GBKL N639JK N550E (N660AC) LV-WOS
BB-640	200	N581 N47CF CS-DDU
BB-641	200	G-OSKA G-CNSI G-CUKL F-GGVV N641TC N641TS
BB-642	200+	N20MK N30MK N10BY N801GG
BB-643	200$	HB-GGY I-LLLL N5369J (N116GR) OY-PEH 5Y-NUN 5Y-HHD ZS-OWH ZS-ALE 5Y-THS
BB-644	200	YV-O-CVF-1 N750HG HP- [canx 28Apr05 as exported to Panama]
BB-645	200^4	N6753K N80GB N999VB
BB-646	200$	N200KA N189VB N53GA N646BM N646DR
BB-647	200	[completed as c/n BT-15]
BB-648	200	N6731T N67CG N648MW N17DW N648KA [w/o 10Dec04 Rancho Buena Vista Apt, TX, USA; canx 23Mar07]
BB-649	200	N6742E (N982EC) N360CB N103TF N777JE N649JC
BB-650	200$	N6745A N209PC N33TJ N740GL ZS-PSP
BB-651	200$^6	N202HC N11TE N132GA N141CT N200TG
BB-652	200	N6727C YU-BMF (N88DA) Z3-BAB [w/o 26Feb04 nr Bitonja, Bosnia and Herzegovina]
BB-653	200	N67224 VH-MXK VH-FII
BB-654	200+(WL)	N67353 XB-BXU N93ZC N654FM
BB-655	200	F-GCGX N89GA G-OGAT N655BA
BB-656	200$	(YV-352CP) YV-783P YV-2354P YV-2576P YV-1051P YV-2745P YV1304
BB-657	200^4	N301PS N91MF
BB-658	200	N6738V N601AM F-GILO N127AP N747HN N658JP
BB-659	200	N77CX N77QX C-GGAO
BB-660	200	N988NA N200TK (N60JK) VH-LKF
BB-661	200$	N111JW N777SS
BB-662	200$	N6747D N117WM N119WM [w/o 03Mar97 Salt Lake City, UT, USA; canx 06Jun00]
BB-663	200$	N115CM 5N-AMT 5N-IHS
BB-664	200	N280SC
BB-665	200	[completed as c/n BT-16]
BB-666	200	N15NA N15NG [b/u; canx 12May04]
BB-667	200$^4	N31WE N33GK N33GR N183DW C-GMPO N667NA C-FWWQ
BB-668	200$	D-IKRA N62EA N1MW N196PP N896CM
BB-669	200	G-OGDN N80GA D-IGSW [w/o 22Nov90 Kellerjoch Mountain, nr Schwaz, Germany; canx c1991]
BB-670	200	N37312 N1VA N7VA N17VA
BB-671	200	C-GFSG
BB-672	200	240 (Irish Air Corps)
BB-673	200$	N67470 N600MS N60MD N755RE N673YV N502RH N503RM
BB-674	200	N766D N63HA N851MK N351MK N851MK N51EE
BB-675	200	N6747T N26SD N26AD SE-IUX
BB-676	200	9Y-TGR N1362B G-ONCA N676DP N970AA F-GHVV
BB-677	200	YV-93CP N200KK N721RD
BB-678	200	N4200K N420QK N318CA N811VC N811VG N811FA
BB-679	200	N6747J N256PL N1194C
BB-680	200+	N6750Y N675PC N675PG N919WM N200WX
BB-681	200	N6751T D-ILBO N200NF LN-AXA F-GGPR
BB-682	200+	N6724P ZS-KLM N208JS N425AP
BB-683	200$	SE-IEH OY-ASS N2877K ZS-OTP
BB-684	200$^4	G-BHLC N8511L N27L G-BHLC G-ROWN ZK457 (RAF)
BB-685	200	N29CH N29HF
BB-686	200#	N3663M N54TK
BB-687	200	EI-BIP SE-INI ZS-PLY A2-MED ZS-PLY
BB-688	200+	N858TM N200AJ N711WV N250TR F-GMCS 5R-MGH ZS-OUI
BB-689	200	N3699L N7090T N187MC N187MQ N364EA
BB-690	200	(C-GBUX) C-FCOS (F-ODUA) ZK-WNL VH-SKN VH-DYN
BB-691	200	N40RL N84CC N84CQ
BB-692	200	N3722H RP-C5139 RP-C264
BB-693	200+	N60SC N60SQ N245JS C-GXHN
BB-694	200+	N3666Y N40FC N90FQ PT-OTO EJC-117 (Colombian Army)
BB-695	200	[completed as c/n BT-18]
BB-696	200	N1967S F-GIFD N200GU 5Y-TWB 5Y-HHK N711A *PR-MOG
BB-697	200	N3667G N50N N5UN (N94CP) N5UN
BB-698	200	N440CE N440CF XT-MBA

BEECH 200

c/n	Series/Mod	Identities
BB-699	200	LV-PIF LV-OFT
BB-700	200+^6(WL)	N101SK N101TS N200PY N440WA G-CGAW
BB-701	200	YV-O-BND-1 YV-353CP YV-O-INH-2 YV-O-MAC-1 YV-O-SATA-4 YV0104
BB-702	200	N30PC [w/o 10Apr89 Pensacola, FL, USA; canx 05Jun90]
BB-703	200	(OY-AUY) N703JK N703KH AN-236 (Ecuadorian Navy)
BB-704	200	N6726D ZS-KLO A2-AJK
BB-705	200	G-GKNB D-IBAB OY-BVW
BB-706	200	N25W N25WD ZS-NBO
BB-707	200$	(D-ILGE) (D-IEHD) N715RD N627BC N715RD
BB-708	200$	N3721B YV-352CP N3721B N200SR N313EL N313EE XA- [canx 12Jun09 as exported to Mexico]
BB-709	200	N3668G N70PA N202NC (N202VT) N71VT
BB-710	200$^4	N3669Z N850C (D-IDSF) C-GXHW C-GCYN
BB-711	200	N3729R N133BC N17HM F-GILJ N1162V
BB-712	200	N66SF N501AB SE-IYU N501AB N943CL N77WM (N77WN) N200BM N411RA
BB-713	200	N36741 CN-CDN
BB-714	200	N7CC N500CR
BB-715	200$	9J-AEV ZS-NOC N140GA N813JP
BB-716	200	C-GSPS N200KW F-ODYR N765TC SP-KGW
BB-717	200	N77CA
BB-718	200	N6728N VH-SGV
BB-719	200$	(YV-384CP) N3722Y N372JB
BB-720	200$	N3684F N700RF N186MC N186MQ N694HP N202SW N208SW N597MM
BB-721	200$	N36956 N610HC N8EF
BB-722	200	9Q-CFE 3A-MBD F-HAAG N722WJ
BB-723	200	HC-BHG 723 (Ecuadorian AF) [w/o 24May81 Huey Rapingo Mountain, Ecuador]
BB-724	200$	N604 N804 (N200WB) N804
BB-725	200	XC-SLP TP-209 (Mexican AF) N725RA
BB-726	200	N222JD N522JA N622JA G-BXMA (N50AJ) G-CEGP
BB-727	200#	N3682A N55CC N1955E N522TG C6-ZBB
BB-728	200$	N3715C (N13UF) N56HF C-GBWO (N124GA) C-GTGA N8170J
BB-729	200$	N743R LV-WPM
BB-730	200	N3690B N572AT N103AL N108AL
BB-731	200$	(YV-386CP) (YV-381CP) YV-O-BIV-1 YV-O-SATA-5 YV0105
BB-732	200	N3716D PK-VKA
BB-733	200+(WL)	N444AD
BB-734	200	N3695B N85BC N85BK [w/o 04Dec03 Newnan-Coweta County, GA, USA; canx 06Dec05]
BB-735	200$	N675SF N980PD N500GC N508JA N507BE
BB-736	200#	N577L N45CF PR-AAX
BB-737	200+	PH-ILH F-GHLC N38GM N703X N767LD
BB-738	200+	N66TS N520DD
BB-739	200+^6	OE-FMI D-IDRB N28TL VT-ESR N81RZ
BB-740	200	YV-385CP [w/o 19Sep99 in Atlantic Ocean 9 mls SW of Bimini, Bahamas]
BB-741	200$	N80GS N75AH N368FA *N368JA
BB-742	200$	N562R N56QR G-BPWJ XT-MAX [wfu Ouagadougou, Burkina Faso]
BB-743	200	N30MK N500BR N508BR N538AS N111LP N28VU
BB-744	200	N3702M N152WC (N700CR) (F-GGPJ) F-GGLA
BB-745	200+	N3698S N428P C-FSPN
BB-746	200#	N131T (N707HB) N707BC C-FMPE N925TT [w/o 10Dec07 Salmon-Lemhi County, ID, USA]
BB-747	200$	N117CM N63SK
BB-748	200$	N925B N260KA N200MV I-FSAC N748SA N154PC N154BB Z-WSG
BB-749	200	N100H (N100HD) N100H N41TV G-HFGP N200AB N12KW N269TA [stolen 20Apr96 Nassau, Bahamas; canx 03Jan00]
BB-750	200	N200T N81TF (N750TT) N81TF
BB-751	200$	(TG-UGA) N3723P N699CC N67NC N804KS N2000C N520WS N751EB N92JR
BB-752	200	N927R N3000W N300QW N616GB
BB-753	200$	N3705B F-GERS EC-KPT
BB-754	200$	SE-IEZ C-GBQO N4426L N44KS N42KS C-GBWO N20GZ N242DM N244JS
BB-755	200+	N572 N15GG N572 N82SA N71TB N711AW N983C
BB-756	200	G-BHYU LN-KOB N389GA ZS-LWD N389GA A2-AGB ZS-LWD 5Y-BWD ZS-LWD
BB-757	200$	N53JC N72CA N72GA C-FMPH N948MB C-GBBS
BB-758	200$	N20RE
BB-759	200	(F-GCTC) 7T-VRS 7T-WRS
BB-760	200	N3710A N269ML
BB-761	200$	N3690S N107TM N78CT
BB-762	200+	N37225 RP-C4650 N762KA VH-ZOR
BB-763	200$	N3707T N40PC N50PM N56KA
BB-764	200	LV-PLN LV-ONH ZS-OUT
BB-765	200#	N3737G (N47JR) N73WL N591M N36GA N242LC N765WA
BB-766	200	N51JH N510H N52GP
BB-767	200	N3717T ZS-KMT [w/o 13Apr87 Johannesburg, Transvaal, South Africa]
BB-768	200	N37392 N413DM N219WC
BB-769	200	N38221 ZS-NPY N769AJ (N623VG) N623VP
BB-770	200	(YV-386CP) YV-O-CPI-1 YV-O-SATA-6 [dbr 05Apr01 in Venezuela, parts to Dodson International Parts, Rantoul, KS, USA]
BB-771	200	N38310 AN-231 (Ecuadorian Navy)
BB-772	200	N111F N111PV (N917GP) N111PV
BB-773	200#^4(WL)	OY-BEH N3913U N83JE N500CS
BB-774	200	N3738B N8NX
BB-775	200	(F-GCTD) 7T-VRT 7T-WRT

BEECH 200

c/n	Series/Mod	Identities
BB-776	200$^4	N3710P N707MA N800KC N800PP N500PP N500FP N899SD
BB-777	200	I-PIAH
BB-778	200	N3846J N36CP N266RH N816BS
BB-779	200	N197RB N811CB F-GEPY YV [canx 26Apr07 as exported; possibly to Venezuela c2004]
BB-780	200$	N3719N VH-ANH N7Q G-BNMR TR-LCP F-GIHK N780RC
BB-781	200$	N26JP N67AS N40BN N215CC N215CX N469JW N37NC N550GL
BB-782	200	YV-397CP N4491Z N21MU G-THUR 5Y-BIW G-THUR 5Y-BIW [dbf 21Sep99 Nairobi-Wilson, Kenya]
BB-783	200$	N3714P N25KA
BB-784	200$	N117S N789H PT-OSR [w/o 23Nov08 nr Recife, Pernambuco, Brazil]
BB-785	200$	N38295 RP-C582 (N85FC) RP-C582 N85FC
BB-786	200$	N120P
BB-787	200#	N26G C-FZVW
BB-788	200	N551JL
BB-789	200+	N3802B (N51RL) N7PA N70KM N905GP
BB-790	200	N3814B F-GIAX D-IAMB N64GA YV1240
BB-791	200$	N81TT F-GHNV N54LG TC-DBY TC-ACN N791EB
BB-792	200	N110G
BB-793	200	N68KA [b/u; canx 24Dec97]
BB-794	200	N3720U PK-VKB
BB-795	200	N3713L N202PV N502EB N828JB N825RT N409DH
BB-796	200	YV-401CP
BB-797	200	N84B G-VPLC G-BVMA
BB-798	200	[completed as c/n BT-17]
BB-799	200+	N666RH N666RL N250DL N269LS
BB-800	200	EI-BJY N200GA N1TX
BB-801	200	N3835C N200SR N123WN N244CH
BB-802	200	(YV-402CP) XA-LIG [w/o 05May84 Poza Rica, Veracruz, Mexico]
BB-803	200	N3825S N380TT N3825S G-WPLC 5Y-TWA ZS-SDS
BB-804	200	N3824P N174WB
BB-805	200$	N3812S N501RH [w/o 24Oct04 nr Martinsville-Blue Ridge Apt, VA, USA]
BB-806	200	N117AS LN-FAQ N86GA EC-ESV N975SC PR-ART
BB-807	200	7T-VRO 7T-WRO
BB-808	200$	N205MB N203EB N711EC N808EB N53RT N910EB N775SC
BB-809	200	F-GCVQ 5N-AMU N43676 N991KA
BB-810	200$^4	N768D N711AE N14TF N810KA CC-CDY
BB-811	200	AEE-001 (Ecuadorian Army) AEE-101 (Ecuadorian Army) [w/o 19Mar09 Quito, Ecuador]
BB-812	200	(YV-402CP) YV-134CP YV-1341P N991GA ZS-MNE 3D-AFO 5Y-PLM N991GA C-GYUI C-GJFY
BB-813	200	N3723K VH-KNA VH-KNR VH-IBF ZS-PAM
BB-814	200	N92DG N6VM XA-RMX
BB-815	200	N3813Z N101CG N255AV ZS-MSL [w/o 26Jun98 Lome-Abidjan, Ivory Coast]
BB-816	200$	OY-BEY N4269Z N19SC N71JT N510G N900RH
BB-817	200	N56RT
BB-818	200$	N3828E N800BW N80QB N145JP
BB-819	200	C-GDKT N555GA N201U N201UU C-GDKT N56GA G-DBAR N425P N500KA N404DP
BB-820	200+	N78P N935SJ N369TA N911CM
BB-821	200	F-GDCB N144TM TC-DBY N821RC G-CLOW
BB-822	200	N3844E N3FH F-GIND N250TM
BB-823	200	[completed as c/n BT-19]
BB-824	200	N38454 (F-GHFL) F-GJCF N824TT N919RE
BB-825	200$	XC-FUS N825KA
BB-826	200	N3842H N205SG N204EB N1CB N800CG
BB-827	200	D-IFES N20AE
BB-828	200+	G-BILY G-MCEO G-SIBE G-SWFT (N828AB) G-MCEO G-OLDZ (N142GA) N62GA C-GJJT
BB-829	200	N225HP N225JL C9-SWE SE-KVL N829AJ LN-NOA
BB-830	200	N88P N88MT
BB-831	200$^4	N7801L N78011 N43WB F-ODUA F-OHCP
BB-832	200	N2PW N45BR N200BE [w/o 13Jun04 Big Mountain, nr Rupert, WV, USA; canx 07Sep04]
BB-833	200$	N3845B XA-RZH PNC-221 (Colombian Police) HP-1469 N833RL XA- [canx 12Mar08 as exported to Mexico]
BB-834	200+	N67MD N929SG
BB-835	200$	N3854B N81CH N81CK N81CT N84PA N84PN
BB-836	200	YV-402CP N9591C N66FG HB-GHR S9-NAQ D2-EBF
BB-837	200$	N38301 ZS-LBD A2-LBD ZS-LBD 5Y-NJS
BB-838	200$	N3859D N14MF ZS-NEP [w/o 28Jun93 Aminuis, Namibia; canx 10Jun94]
BB-839	200	N3849B N21FG
BB-840	B200	F-GDCA N149GA N36GS N36QS PT-MPR N200RC N840RC N712GJ
BB-841	200$(WL)	(D-ICCO) XA-LOW N720US N522CC F-GHLG N841K N366EA N65KG N871UB
BB-842	200+	N38473 N204JS
BB-843	200$	N3850K N211CP N843G
BB-844	200	SE-IGV F-GIAL [dbr 09Sep99 Caen-Carpiquet, France, parts to Dodson International Parts, Rantoul, KS, USA]
BB-845	200$	N38535 N486DC OY-GRB EC-JJP
BB-846	200$	N200EM N846MW ZS-MIM 5Y-BKA ZS-MIM
BB-847	200#	HZ-KT2 SE-IUP N635GA OH-BIF N847BA
BB-848	200$	RP-C267 N848NA
BB-849	200$	N3861S N74B N74F N711MZ N3DE *N849BM

BEECH 200

c/n	Series/Mod	Identities
BB-850	200	N3875F XA-SFY N2UH N3CR
BB-851	200	N3859U (N55NS) N500EW N851JP N200E N208F
BB-852	200^4	N46BR
BB-853	200	(LV-) N3832B N44SR C-GADI
BB-854	200	N3872E N521CC N321SF (N800PA) HK-3214X HK-3214G
BB-855	200$	N223HC N199MH
BB-856	200	N1802H N6PE [w/o 08Dec04 Tulsa, OK, USA; canx 05May05]
BB-857	200$	YV-423CP N57AC 5V-MCG
BB-858	200$	C-GDMU N10AC 5V-MCH
BB-859	200	N3832E VH-MZV N4935X N859DD [w/o 23Jun87 Jasper-Walker County/Bevill Field, TX, USA]
BB-860	200+	N201TT N917BB N488CP N488CA N488AD N84PC
BB-861	200$	OY-BEM N27TB N270L N727DD N727BW
BB-862	200$	N40CR N941GL N260G N260F N207DB
BB-863	200$	YV-419CP N44919 N80WM
BB-864	200+	G-UBHL G-OHBD N150GA N12ST N92TC N847TS C-FFAR
BB-865	200$	N38653 N29KG N531BB N32SV *N700LG
BB-866	200$	N3833A ZK-PBG VH-MSZ
BB-867	200+	N200RT N200RB N24AR ZS-PUF
BB-868	200$	N3872K N231RL [stolen & dbr 18Dec95 Ingleside, TX, USA, parts to Dodson International Parts, Rantoul, KS, USA; canx 09Apr97]
BB-869	200+	XA-MIA XA-LUZ N2135J (N747RW) N31FM
BB-870	200$	N200EL LV-WEW
BB-871	200	[completed as c/n BT-20]
BB-872	200$	(YV-429CP) N1850T F-GHMN D-IOAN N872BA N602CN
BB-873	200	N40TG LN-TWG N48BA N117CA N525JA N529JA XB-JYE
BB-874	B200$	N1808M XC-BCN N200GK N4042J
BB-875	B200	N555GK N313SC PT-WEG
BB-876	B200	N52BC F-GHSC 96/F-ZBFK
BB-877	B200+	N3837S N877AJ N4C N4CQ N711BU N508MV N509MV
BB-878	B200	G-BIPP C-GKRL [w/o 10Dec86 Fort McMurray, AB, Canada; canx 14May87]
BB-879	B200$	N4PT
BB-880	B200+	N1804T YV-1006CP N53KA
BB-881	B200	N677SW N813G XU-008 9M-ASH VH-USD N881CS XA- [canx 16Mar09 as exported to Mexico]
BB-882	B200	N9SB N56AY N56AP N882JP
BB-883	B200	N940WT TC-YPI (TC-HCY) N883BB
BB-884	B200$	N1849B N49JG (D-IKFB) C-FLOR N49JG
BB-885	B200$	N38340 N146BC N146MH
BB-886	B200+^6(WL)	N111JW N146MD N479WB
BB-887	B200$	YV-422CP YV-2222P N87699
BB-888	B200	N1821H N804BL N922CR N700U N70CU
BB-889	B200	N3835K ZS-LAW
BB-890	B200$	N1825H N6EA N100PX N100PY
BB-891	B200+	N711WE (N18VG) N888HG C-GHDP
BB-892	B200	(SE-IIS) N9547P N81LT [wfu San Isidro AFB, Dominican Republic]
BB-893	B200	N762NB
BB-894	B200	N1809B N18VG N230GK N609DK N969MA
BB-895		[completed as c/n BT-21]
BB-896	B200	N1811S (N11GE) N367EA N850BK
BB-897	B200	N1837S N200TM D-IEFB
BB-898	B200	C-GEVN N98GA N911SR N212EJ
BB-899	B200$	N18544 N1KA N527CH
BB-900	B200	N18260 [w/o 24Aug01 nr Piqua-Hartzell Field, OH, USA; canx 09Jan02]
BB-901	B200	N26UT N411KC
BB-902	B200$(WL)	N5TW N65TW
BB-903	B200$	N3837U ZS-LBE 7Q-YMP ZS-LBE A2-BHM ZS-ASB
BB-904	B200	N1818P N830 N830LS N430MC (N430MG) (N202KC) N430MC
BB-905	B200	N18112 N80D N202EJ N80D N79GS N185DH N907G
BB-906	B200	YV-437CP YV-2350P ARV-0212 (Venezuelan Navy) ARBV-0212 (Venezuelan Navy)
BB-907	B200	N1860N (N440KC) N789CT
BB-908	B200$	N3835Q VH-KDK N107GA N88BA N1PD N200TJ N999EG
BB-909	B200$	N36784 N171M SE-KDK
BB-910	B200	OY-BET ZS-LJA N910AJ
BB-911	B200#	N73LC N73LX N270CS N411CC N265EJ
BB-912	B200	C-GFSH N912LD
BB-913	B200	N18371 N82DD N501EZ (N501E) N9WR
BB-914	B200$	N18172 (N800BF) N1WH N1XH ZS-MXH 5X-INS ZS-TNY
BB-915	B200+	N3837N ZS-LFT N333RD XA- [canx 23Feb05 as exported to Mexico]
BB-916	B200	N18261 N916HC N770HM N770SF
BB-917	B200$	N61425 N15TT N95TT (N115SB) N95TT
BB-918	B200	N3LL N70JG ZS-NCH N918TC
BB-919	B200	N160AC N160AD N505AM
BB-920	B200$	C-GSCM N83TJ PK-YPS SE-LMM F-GPAC
BB-921	B200$	N76MP N244JB D-IKOB
BB-922	B200$	N18216 N103LC N200LN N80BC N80BT N1926A
BB-923	B200	N1847A N666PC N200MG N316JP
BB-924	B200	N50YR N52YR N107MG 05-52305 (US Army)
BB-925	B200+	N61408 N115D N282SJ
BB-926	B200+	N200MM N61CE N68GK N203LG
BB-927	B200	N18262 927 (Pakistan Army)

BEECH 200

c/n	Series/Mod	Identities
BB-928	B200+	N102P OY-ASN N38342 N555WF N553HC XC-AA81 N553HC N627FB N627FP N880MB
BB-929	B200	N666EW N848J G-OWNR N81AJ N999GA
BB-930	B200$	YV-443CP N990GA (F-GHEY) F-GHMY YV-1001P F-GHMY N930SP N405PT
BB-931	B200+	N6789 (N410GL) N995MS
BB-932	B200$	D-IBCI OY-CCE SE-KKM 101004 (Swedish AF) SE-KKM HB-GJX F-OIAA
BB-933	B200	N200LP D-IAWS OE-FRF D-IDRF
BB-934	B200	N38381 9Q-CCE
BB-935	B200	N19GR N19GB N500CY N935AJ
BB-936	B200$	N200NS VH-OWN
BB-937	B200$	N417EM D-IKFC N937SL C9-ATW D2-ERK
BB-938	B200#	N132K N722TR
BB-939	B200$	N1TW (N41TW) (N33NW) N8PL (N46FC) N175WW N164TC N125KW C-GGJF
BB-940	B200	N711EX N700DE D-IMDA N519SA C-FZPW
BB-941	B200$	N36801 ZS-MIN
BB-942	B200+^6	N6214B N525BC (N565MD) N625MD N707NV N4QL
BB-943	B200	N250YR N280YR
BB-944	B200	HL5260 HB-GHZ N31WL G-FPLA D-ICFI G-COBH
BB-945	B200+	N1849T N3000R RP-C1577 VH-HLJ
BB-946	B200GTO+	N1850X
BB-947	B200$	N1847V G-FOOD N500WF
BB-948	B200$	XA-MAY N690LW (N400JP) N95CG N15RH N150RH N25CS
BB-949	B200	N61415 N567JD N810GW
BB-950	B200#	N8NA
BB-951	B200$	RP-C969 VH-OYC VH-AGB RP-C969 N37HR LX-ALX OY-CKP
BB-952	B200	N1852B N185XP
BB-953	B200#	N1850W N81KC N10EH N953L N24GN
BB-954	B200$	N1839S ZS-LFM
BB-955	B200+	N18481 N666EC N999P G-BOBM G-WILK N933RT
BB-956	B200	N19CK N193K N956WT N72SE D-IAMK PH-ECF N817BA
BB-957	B200	N1847S N7CT N200HW N800TT
BB-958	B200+	XA-MII N82AJ N30EM [w/o 22Dec00 Beaver Mountain nr Rangeley, ME, USA]
BB-959	B200$	N925B N207SB N2SC N28CN N469TA N81TL
BB-960	B200$	N1858E N999KG HK-3470X HK-3470 HK-3470P (N202PT) N125JB N960GK [wfu c2003, parts to White Industries, Bates City, MO, USA; location "Ramp SO A-10"; canx 29Apr09]
BB-961	B200	YV-476CP N5362J ZK-RGA N189GA G-BNZH A2-AHA ZS-ACS
BB-962	B200+	N1851S N721HC N719HC N437WF
BB-963	B200#(WL)	G-BIZX N400GA D-IKFB N37GA RP-C367 VH-WZN
BB-964	B200$	N3456W VH-HTU VH-SBM
BB-965	B200	N1857A N184MC N184MQ N300AJ
BB-966	B200	F-GDCS G-BYCP
BB-967	B200	N18500 N3EP N89GB N75Z N75ZT C-FVCC
BB-968	B200$	N17TW N422TD N42TD N717CD ZK-KAG NZ1885 (Royal New Zealand AF)
BB-969	B200#	N1858W N188W N48N N969WB N96WC
BB-970	B200	N35P N124CS N93NB [wfu cJan97, parts to Dodson International Parts, Rantoul, KS, USA; canx 12Feb97]
BB-971	B200	N1859E N503RH PT-MMB
BB-972	B200	N18409 VT-EHB
BB-973	B200$	N6104A N53TM C-FEVC C-FKCW
BB-974	B200$	N1861B HK-3507X HK-3507 HK-3507W
BB-975	B200$	N1844S RP-C755 (N208DM) RP-C755
BB-976	B200+(WL)	(YV-466CP) N6260M N1843S N1845S N83RH N83PH YV [canx 25Sep08 as exported to Venezuela]
BB-977	B200+	N733NM N607KW N125BK
BB-978	B200	N635MF N877GF N877RF N877RC
BB-979	B200#	N6120C N22TP C-FRMV
BB-980	B200$	YV-466CP GN-8274 (Venezuelan National Guard)
BB-981	B200	N129P N129DB N481BC N404FA
BB-982	B200$	N750YR N703S N703MD N800JR N800PK
BB-983	B200	N6JL N6JE (D-IKFC) N87FE D-ILTO N983EB D-ISAZ N983AJ G-JASS
BB-984	B200$	N6317R N56JA N9RU HI-701SP
BB-985	B200	N1841Z VT-EHK
BB-986	B200	N379BT N481NS (F-GHMH) (F-GIMC) N986TJ PT-WOF
BB-987	B200$	N6118A N358ST N200HD
BB-988	B200	N67LT HP-82LD N67LT (PH-CRT) (PH-IPC) PH-LMC 5Y-HHA
BB-989	B200+	N520D N850AT
BB-990	B200$	N61369 P2-VIC N990RC N990JC N208TC
BB-991		[completed as c/n BT-22]
BB-992	B200	N340BK N340TT N992TJ
BB-993	B200+	N310GT N32TJ N32LJ
BB-994	B200	N25CN (N994RM) N25CN N99LL
BB-995	B200	N11RM XA-RVJ N454DC
BB-996	B200GTO$	N770M N775M N66U N66UA N707CG N247JM N48PA
BB-997	B200$	N7NA
BB-998	B200+	N61474 N76PM N76PT N899MC
BB-999	B200$	N1842P ZS-LFW 9Q-CYS 9Q-CPV ZS-LFW
BB-1000	B200	N82TT JA8857 N51881 N74RG N74RN N580BK
BB-1001	B200#	N1846S HZ-SWC N94GA N94QD N772AF
BB-1002	B200	N6169S N282CT
BB-1003	B200	HB-GGS I-MEPE N58GA

BEECH 200

c/n	Series/Mod	Identities
BB-1004	B200+	N6179A N66DD N64DD N234U F-GKAN RP-C1515 N101AP N104AK N104CX
BB-1005	B200$	D-ICOH OE-FKW D-ICKM
BB-1006	B200$	N6300S (N46CE) N680CB CN-TPH
BB-1007	B200$	G-BJJV N777GA SE-IVZ G-SBAS N514MA C-FSKO
BB-1008	B200+	N6171N ZP-TWN (N331Z) N6171N ZP-TXR N6171N ZK-KAC NZ1882 (Royal New Zealand AF)
BB-1009	B200	N6451D
BB-1010	B200	N6222C N62FC N702MA
BB-1011	B200	N6230V N394GL N22T N22TZ N20SM N843BC
BB-1012	B200	N6239P N14BW N200MJ
BB-1013	B200+	N144C N711BL N623DS N628DS
BB-1014	B200+(WL)	N6308F N239JV
BB-1015	B200	N1842Y ZK-WIL N1842Y ZS-LXW N901EB N216RP
BB-1016	B200$	N6305V (N203TS) N88TS N245CT (N38AJ) N786SR
BB-1017	B200$	N200PH N385MC
BB-1018	B200$	N1842S ZS-LFU 3D-LKK ZS-LFU
BB-1019	B200	N6236U (N5FW) N8FF N5FW VH-ARZ VH-JJR VH-PWK
BB-1020	B200$	YV-488CP (YV-2248P) YV1733
BB-1021	B200	N6235N N195KC N195KA N678SS
BB-1022	B200	N800JD N404BS N404AU N220RJ C-FDGP C-GWGI
BB-1023	B200	N62546 N125NC
BB-1024	B200	F-GDFF N300DK SU-PAA N83RZ HK-4343X HK-4343
BB-1025	B200	N6325E (N2227F) N22F
BB-1026	B200+	(G-BJSN) YV-554CP YV-2251P YV-554CP N153D D2-FFK [w/o 19Jan08 Huambo, Angola]
BB-1027	B200+	N6427S N220DD N200NY N40AB ZS-NAW
BB-1028	B200	N62569 N173TX
BB-1029	B200	N95BD N176M
BB-1030	B200+	N6348H N360SC N843FC
BB-1031	B200$	N6644J
BB-1032	B200$	N6494S I-CUVI F-GJMJ N67FS N800TS
BB-1033	B200	N551TP N551TR [w/o 26Sep86 in Mexico]
BB-1034	B200	N82KA N185MC N185MV
BB-1035	B200+	N62780 N59TD N96ZZ N712GK C-FGAN N7GA N450S
BB-1036	B200GTO(WL)	N6271C N559DW
BB-1037	B200	N6289C N92LC N501TR VH-DAX VH-FDI
BB-1038	B200$	N763D OH-ABE N223MH ZS-MES
BB-1039	B200$	N62828 (N69F) N6572K HB-GHS N124GA
BB-1040	B200$	N6335P N27LJ N27LS N27LJ N47DG
BB-1041	B200	N6277Y N200BK VH-OYD
BB-1042	B200+	N6338T N131LB N400LM N77JT N447AC N142EB
BB-1043	B200	N62881 N79PG (N666JJ) N277JJ
BB-1044	B200$	N62895 N815CE (N815CF) C-GJJT N7061T G-BPPM G-SYGA
BB-1045	B200#	N6290Q N60SM N810V N810K
BB-1046	B200$^5	N6300R ZS-MBN A2-APG ZS-APG Z-APG 9J-MED
BB-1047	B200	N1844A ZS-LIL V5-LIL ZS-LIL N147NA
BB-1048	B200	9Y-TGY N223MD N739MG G-FPLB
BB-1049	B200$	(F-GDFJ) TS-LMB F-GMLP HK-3894X HK-3894W HP-1404 N6144H (HK-4244X)HK-4256X HK-4256W
BB-1050	B200	N925B (N19KA) N925B
BB-1051	B200$	G-BJWG N6912T D-ICIR N910KG
BB-1052		[completed as c/n BT-23]
BB-1053	B200	(C-GPQX) C-GNTU N493S C-FRYL N212DM N132N
BB-1054	B200$	(N77711) N66911 N810V C-GRFN N244SW ZK-KAB NZ1881 (Royal New Zealand AF)
BB-1055	B200	N92BD N200BE N6LD N6UD
BB-1056	B200	N6687T D-IGSY N56GA VH-RFX VH-FDO
BB-1057	B200	N6464S N641MC N999HC N899HC F-GILY N220TB
BB-1058	B200+	N552D N88SR N220DK C-FWXB N250PW
BB-1059	B200+	N50YR N382AG N818PF
BB-1060	B200$	N300BL N250DM ZS-TON D2-FEG
BB-1061	B200+	N1846K JA8830 N188H N50DR N50DY N200JM N200XC
BB-1062	B200$	N6346C N16TX RP-C1887 N985GA PP-CBD
BB-1063	B200$	N256L HK-3504X HK-3504 N4359T HR-ASY N240CT
BB-1064	B200+	N6335U N129DP N129D N824S
BB-1065	B200GTO	D-ICOA N234KW
BB-1066	B200$	N257L N356WC N356WG N50KG
BB-1067	B200	N63286 N47MM N860H
BB-1068	B200	XB-DCT N2157L HK-3554X HK-3554G
BB-1069	B200+	N6393F N87DR N795GB LV-ZSE N828FM N145LG
BB-1070	B200+	OY-BVL SE-KND ZS-NBJ
BB-1071	B200+^6(WL)	N63435 N82BS N14HG
BB-1072	B200	(G-BJXT) CNA-NG (Royal Moroccan AF)
BB-1073	B200	CNA-NH (Royal Moroccan AF)
BB-1074	B200	C-GDTX N74LV [stolen 06Mar87 Fort Lauderdale, FL, USA; canx 09Feb94]
BB-1075	B200$	C-GTDY N75LV
BB-1076	B200	A40-SR N7146C ZS-MTW C9-MTW ZS-MTW C9-PMZ ZS-MTW
BB-1077	B200$	N258L N95TG RP-C7188 (ZS-OGB) ZS-ZXX
BB-1078	B200	N771HM (N781HM) N129TT
BB-1079	B200$	HB-GDI HB-GDL N200NA
BB-1080	B200$	N63688 N200PL (N200PT) D-ILOH N72GG N720MP N430S
BB-1081	B200$	N6531N
BB-1082	B200$	N6354X N917BE N801BC (N807BC) TC-FIR

BEECH 200

c/n	Series/Mod	Identities
BB-1083	B200+	N250YR ZS-NOH N969 VH-ZEK
BB-1084	B200$	N6879W JA8831 N284KW N569SC N569SG N833PS
BB-1085	B200	N63686 N686CF
BB-1086	B200$	(G-BJXT) D-IBVO TC-SDR TC-YSM N86GA N200JM XB-GEC
BB-1087	B200$	N153D N153GC N860MH N65WM ZK-KAD NZ1883 (Royal New Zealand AF) ZK-KAD NZ1883 (Royal New Zealand AF)
BB-1088	B200	C-GGAT N4449A N868HC N68FA
BB-1089	B200$	N85CR N5NR N5NV G-BOMM D-INKA N87SA (N69JH) N87SA
BB-1090	B200$	YV-493CP (YV-2254P) N54SK N49SK
BB-1091	B200	N9NA N529NA
BB-1092	B200	(YV-555CP) (YV-2250P) YV-555CP YV-2352P YV-O-PTJ-2
BB-1093		[completed as c/n BT-24]
BB-1094	B200$	N730P N35EC N1925P N1925L
BB-1095	B200+	N170S N170L N200DA
BB-1096		[completed as c/n BT-25]
BB-1097		[completed as c/n BT-29]
BB-1098		[completed as c/n BT-26]
BB-1099	B200	N63827 N416CS N34LC N349C N127SD (N160TT) N60AA N488JB
BB-1100	B200+	N63791 VH-XDV
BB-1101	B200$	N63802 N48CG N48CE N395AM
BB-1102	B200	N147D HB-GHI D-IWAN (F-GKDO) 98/F-ZBFJ
BB-1103	B200$	N200KA N57SC N361EA
BB-1104	B200	N6914H (F-GDJS) N4000K N400QK (N7010H) N1628 N162Q
BB-1105		[completed as c/n BT-27]
BB-1106	B200	N63882 N1870S [w/o 17Jul87 Crystal Bay, NV, USA]
BB-1107	B200	D-IMCI HB-GHH N737US N564BC N456ES
BB-1108	B200$	N64478 N20SR HK-3587X HK-3587W HK-3587 XC-JAI XC-AA50
BB-1109	B200$	(YV-554CP) N6580B N900FD N900ED F-GLLH C-FSKN
BB-1110	B200	N200MW HZ-MW2 (F-GGAR) N7045C F-GGAR CN-TNB N110GA TR-LDU F-GSEB
BB-1111	B200	N6679H N600SS N600CM ZS-LVK N83KA
BB-1112	B200	N383NA HK-3334X N7144E N1866A N643HD (N7090U) N311MP
BB-1113	B200	N745R N745RL ZS-OTS
BB-1114	B200$	N18466 N9768S N872CA 07-21907 (US Army)
BB-1115	B200$	N6679E N764NB C-FLRM
BB-1116	B200	(D-ILOC) F-GDJS
BB-1117		[completed as c/n BT-28]
BB-1118	B200	N83BA N913PG N586UC
BB-1119	B200	N66104 N1865A N1865D [stolen and w/o 15May96 Treasure Cay, Bahamas; canx 05Jun96]
BB-1120	B200#	N6609K N120NA
BB-1121	B200	N6604L
BB-1122	B200+	N6606R N87CF
BB-1123	B200$	N223LP N1BC N147GA N272CA N272TA (N282TA) N74ML
BB-1124	B200#	N301D N30SL N800RD N200JW ZS-MMO N678EB D-IVHN LX-DUC I-ASMI T7-SMI I-ASMI T7-SMI
BB-1125	B200	N6705F N12L N12LD VH-KCH A32-002 (Royal Australian AF) VH-KCH HS-KCH [wfu cDec08 Don Muang Apt, Bangkok, Thailand]
BB-1126	B200+	N6635L N663SP N13PR N175BC C-GTLT C-GWXH C-FHJO N650JW C-FSKX
BB-1127	B200	N69131 G-BMNF 5Y-JJZ
BB-1128	B200	C-GGGQ
BB-1129	B200+	N66404 CS-DDF C-GDHF
BB-1130	B200$	N6635N N16KK N200QS N209WC N418DN
BB-1131	B200$	N6642Z HP-1180 LV-AIY
BB-1132	B200	(YV-555CP) N66480 N152C N127MJ
BB-1133	B200	N6649P [wfu 1985 and used as a static test airframe]
BB-1134	B200$	N66460 N623WA N98LP N27RC
BB-1135	B200$	N68943 ZS-LIZ (N171SP) N399LA N74GS
BB-1136	B200	N83KA N62KM N62KL D-IDOK LN-VIZ TF-MYX
BB-1137	B200	N66540 N133LJ N333AP
BB-1138	B200+	N6914Z JA8837 N400AJ ZS-SOL N138AJ N29TV
BB-1139	B200	N6661C (N991LL) N961LL N961LE N256BD N690SC
BB-1140	B200	N42KA N888ZX
BB-1141	B200$	N66549 N500LP
BB-1142	B200+	N6659D N23YP N68MY
BB-1143	B200	N6664P ZS-LXF N153GA N158LM N23WS N79B N23WS
BB-1144	B200$	N221P N62BE D-IBHF ZS-NWT N120AJ LN-TWL
BB-1145	B200$	N835E N528JD N72AM N4377D N71GA HP-1213 N94GA C6-TTC N566TC
BB-1146	B200	N6816T N60PC N60FC N194TR
BB-1147	B200$	N6672V N647JM N200BM
BB-1148	B200	N7211B N5SS N885ST N211DG N211DQ N345MB N525SK
BB-1149	B200	N6671Z N8GT N8GL (F-GHXP) TC-SAY N200HF ZS-OED
BB-1150	B200#	N6712H N18DN N103BG VH-URU
BB-1151	B200+	N6685Y XA-MCB N220DL XB-MCB N151WT
BB-1152	B200$	N6723V N555KP ZS-NJM 5Y-BJM ZS-NJM (ZS-DSL) 5Y-HHM [w/o 06Aug07 Garissa, Kenya]
BB-1153	B200$	N7213B N73MP N1891S
BB-1154	B200+^5(WL)	N6683W (N59GJ) N6683W
BB-1155	B200$	N6695L VH-HPA VH-SMZ N155NA N200UW
BB-1156	B200	N66825 N504GF
BB-1157	B200	N2804B N7201K N7255K HB-GIG N126AP RP-C5555 YV2078
BB-1158	B200+	N200KA N200KK (N712PW) N1824S N158TJ N158EF N419TW N66LM G-JOAL *PR-AJK

BEECH 200

c/n	Series/Mod	Identities
BB-1159	B200$(WL)	N6685N N552TP N552TB (D-IRUS) N552TT N17FS
BB-1160	B200#	N66826 N4404Q N388CP N444KA N161GC
BB-1161	B200$	N77CV N27CV
BB-1162	B200	N557D (N71C) N71CS (N71CE) G-MDJI [w/o 19Oct87 Ottley Chevin Hill, UK; canx 08Mar88]
BB-1163	B200$	N6726V N200DB N200EW N960JP
BB-1164	B200	N701NA N801NA
BB-1165	B200	N6922P 1165 (Royal Thai Army) HS-PON 1165 (Royal Thai Army)
BB-1166	B200$^6	N6693D N10HE N717RM D-ITAB N97SZ
BB-1167	B200$(WL)	N999MC N999MR N18CM N35GR ZS-GJV
BB-1168	B200	N33EA N179MC N844MP D2- [canx 16Oct08 as exported to Angola]
BB-1169	B200+	N6695Z N90LP N40BC N750BB
BB-1170	B200$	N6930P N55PC
BB-1171	B200$	N6713L N100MS N86DD N786DD
BB-1172	B200+	N67219 N200LM G-OJGA VH-FDG VH-KFE
BB-1173	B200$	N2842B N3PX
BB-1174	B200$	N67148 N168AC N200MP N730MS
BB-1175	B200	N833E SE-IXA N515CR N515CP
BB-1176	B200	N7205X N11LC N81LC N904DG
BB-1177	B200#	N731P N200LV N200LU N608JR N193JC *N774MR
BB-1178	B200$	N6724N N670CP D-ILTU N46CE C-GDSH N80BT N888FC N96GA ZK-KAF NZ1884 (Royal New Zealand AF)
BB-1179	B200	N6725D N444WB N204WB
BB-1180	B200$	N6726X VR-BNN N221SP N416AT
BB-1181	B200	N6725Y F-GJBS
BB-1182	B200#	N67262 N416CS N241PH
BB-1183	B200+	N67265 N77CT N44MH N91HT
BB-1184	B200	N6726Z N27SE N93NP
BB-1185		[completed as c/n BT-30]
BB-1186	B200	N6727G ZS-NBA N186EB
BB-1187	B200	N545GM N610SW N200SV N502AP
BB-1188	B200	N334D N334DP [w/o 16Nov87 nr Jefferson, WI, USA]
BB-1189	B200	N6728N N843CK VH-KBH A32-001 (Royal Australian AF) VH-KBH ZS-PLL
BB-1190	B200	N6731L N711PH N70AC N75GF N75GE PT-XEG
BB-1191	B200$	N177CN
BB-1192	B200	N6743D N61AP
BB-1193	B200	N6728H (N78GC) N6728H
BB-1194	B200$	N6744Q N66CD N743E N616DR N1JB YV-988CP HK-4297X N585CE
BB-1195	B200$	N6923C ZS-LRE N61AJ ZS-MCC N773VA
BB-1196	B200	N69282 N101EC Z-ZLT 5H-TZX
BB-1197	B200$	N347D
BB-1198	B200	N6929S N9MS (N6929S) VT-JKC N198DM
BB-1199	B200	N7203R PR-BLP
BB-1200	B200+	(N845BE) N6816A N100LA N873AF
BB-1201	B200	N6815X D-IMMM N53GA
BB-1202	B200$^6(WL)	N7207M N44VM D-IHAP G-REBK VP-BYR N5NV M-FSRE N5NV
BB-1203	B200#	D-ILTA N80AJ TC-CHS N877JE N177JE N177LA
BB-1204	B200	N6927C (N347D) B-3551
BB-1205	B200	N6927D B-3552
BB-1206	B200	N6927G B-3553 N107EM
BB-1207	B200+	N7208T N720MC N200GP N200GE (N321SF) N3ZC
BB-1208	B200+	N7213K N200SE
BB-1209	B200$	D-ICID N46GA D-IKBJ N126SP (N53GA) N439KM
BB-1210	B200	N7213J SE-IXC
BB-1211	B200$	N7220C N10EC
BB-1212	B200$	N7221Y N54FB N500FE
BB-1213	B200+	N7234L 5N-BLF N74AL N109MD
BB-1214	B200#	N7225D N200GS
BB-1215	B200(WL)	N7225V G-BPLC F-GICV D-IEEE PH-ACZ N200KP
BB-1216	B200	(N72272) N7227L N55MP N55MV (N210AC) N155AV
BB-1217	B200+	N200KA N300CR N17TJ N85KS D-IMOL N697P (N204GR) N697P
BB-1218	B200	N740P
BB-1219	B200	N123D N123EA N123D N200YB N301HC (N381HC) N301HC
BB-1220	B200+	N72294 ET-AKA N93GA TR-LDM F-OIAN
BB-1221	B200$	N7230U F-GKGH D-IUUU "TF-UUU" TF-FMS
BB-1222	B200	N72303 (N50FC) ZS-LNR N126KA C-FTYO
BB-1223	B200	N7231M N586BC
BB-1224	B200+	N94LC C-GTLA C-FWXI
BB-1225	B200$	N7233Z N40FC N40FQ N848PF N119MC
BB-1226	B200+	N7234U N200HB N501EB G-OJBA N16GA N770AE N225WL
BB-1227	B200+	N7237A HK-3432X HK-3432 HK-3432P
BB-1228	B200+	N7237J N90PR N6LD N69VC D-IMGL N85GA N532SW
BB-1229	B200	D-IBAD
BB-1230	B200	N224P
BB-1231	B200$	N7239T D-IBAC OE-FJB N360EA
BB-1232	B200$	G-BLYB N209CM C-GBYN
BB-1233	B200$	N7246E N600KP N4445T N887T N74AW
BB-1234	B200$	N7246M N991LL N971LL N971LE ZS-FDR
BB-1235	B200+	N7247R G-OAFB D-IZZZ N43CE N95CT
BB-1236	B200	N72473 VT-ENM
BB-1237	B200	N7250T

BEECH 200

c/n	Series/Mod	Identities								
BB-1238	B200$	N72503	(N86GA)	N98BD	(N86GA)	N212JB	N162GC			
BB-1239	B200$	N7250V	N833BK	N895TT	C-GNAG					
BB-1240	B200$	N7251P	N90BL	N200TK						
BB-1241	B200	N7256K	*N184TX							
BB-1242	B200	N72524	N20VP	LV-ZFC	(N242NA)	(N142NA)	N242NA			
BB-1243	B200	N7257E	N914CT	N804CT	N428A	N84CC	N200HX	N430DD		
BB-1244	B200	N72357	N251DL	G-RIOO	F-GSFA	F-OINC	VH-ITA			
BB-1245	B200+(WL)	N7257G	N76RJ	N776RM	N1MU					
BB-1246	B200$	N7257T	N200CP	(N210CM)	N207CM					
BB-1247	B200$	N392D	(N96DF)	(N392EZ)	N392DF	N48CS				
BB-1248	B200	N7256G	VT-ENL							
BB-1249	B200+	N2512R	N879C	N106GB						
BB-1250	B200	N2519Y	N363CA	(N383CA)	N88VN					
BB-1251	B200GTO+(WL)	N2610Y	ZS-LTG	N857EP	N52GT					
BB-1252	B200$	D-IBAF	HB-GIU	N125GA	N634TT					
BB-1253	B200$	N2614X	A2-AEO	ZS-OVX						
BB-1254	B200	N2646K	VT-EPA							
BB-1255	B200$	N2652M	N125CU	PK-HTI	SE-LMN	N200DU	(N86KA)	N152RP		
BB-1256	B200	N2676M	N184JS	N1847S	N230DC	G-FPLE				
BB-1257	B200+	N2678D	G-BMVY	N841TT	N841TF	G-IJJB	N606AJ			
BB-1258	B200+	N2748X	VH-XDW							
BB-1259	B200$	N734P	D-IDSM	N800MG	G-OMGI	G-WNCH				
BB-1260	B200$^6	N2PX	N27GH							
BB-1261	B200	N2997N	N717DC							
BB-1262	B200	N2997T	N90TM	N800NR						
BB-1263	B200	N2997W	N263SW	N20DH						
BB-1264		[completed as c/n BT-31]								
BB-1265	B200$	N29979	N550TP	N550TF	D-IAKK	N544P				
BB-1266	B200	N2999Y	N204MS	PT-WSX						
BB-1267	B200	N3022F	XB-EHC	N67GA	VT-VHL					
BB-1268	B200	N29997								
BB-1269	B200+	N3034W	N877W	N877WA	N9898	N9898Y	N21NV	N412SH		
BB-1270	B200	N30391	F-GJFA							
BB-1271	B200$	N3048U	PT-LPG							
BB-1272	B200	N3043W	VT-EQD	N37GA	N751CC					
BB-1273	B200+	N30486	N466MW							
BB-1274	B200	N30234	N713RH							
BB-1275	B200$	N3215K	PT-WLT	N998PA	N88RY	N98RY	N450WH			
BB-1276	B200$	N738P	N40TD	N14NG						
BB-1277	B200	N7241L	VT-EPY	N200WJ						
BB-1278	B200+	N30625	N1627	N162E	N504EB	D-IAIR	N533P			
BB-1279	B200	N3007C	N58AU	N58AB	N300TP					
BB-1280	B200	D-IBAR								
BB-1281	B200+	N30721	(N521FA)	PK-HPH	(N281WJ)	SE-LMO	N281WJ	N856TC	C-FAMB	
BB-1282	B200	N3082C	N200RR							
BB-1283	B200$	N200KA	N113US	N113UL						
BB-1284	B200	N72410	ZS-LWE	N6321V	D-IBMP	N205TT				
BB-1285	B200+	N36809	N200JR	N280JR	N32WC					
BB-1286	B200	N1525C	N909ST	N908ST	N800GF	N511AS				
BB-1287	B200	N3082X	N713DH	N921AZ						
BB-1288	B200	N30850	VT-EQK							
BB-1289		[completed as c/n BT-32]								
BB-1290	B200	N3185C	JA8859	N3185C	G-VSBC	N788JB	C-GNDR			
BB-1291	B200+^5	N2763B	D-ICRA	N40PT	ZS-	[canx 30Jun09 as exported to South Africa]				
BB-1292	B200$	N3109Y	N333TP							
BB-1293	B200#	N3127K	N122TP							
BB-1294	B200	N3110Y	N294CS	N294WT	N401HC					
BB-1295	B200+(WL)	N3079S	N95MW	N295CP	G-WCCP					
BB-1296	1300	N296YV	PH-DUS	ZS-OSH						
BB-1297	B200$(WL)	N100PL	N21VF	N55FJ	N23WJ					
BB-1298	B200	N2769B	N1558P	HK-3440X	HK-3440W	N734A	N36GS			
BB-1299	B200	N3083Z	JA8861	N3083Z	JA8885	N3083Z	N123ML	N123ME	N115MX	(N315SA)
		N912SV								
BB-1300	B200+	N3082S	JA8862	N3082S	N875EC	N313ES	(N43GJ)	N313HS		
BB-1301		[completed as c/n BT-33]								
BB-1302	1300	N302YV	PT-WYY	C-GXHS						
BB-1303	B200$	N3175T	N555WF	N1932P	N1932H	N940HC				
BB-1304	B200	N3173K	C-FPQQ							
BB-1305	1300	N305YV	N789GA	VT-SAB	OY-GES	5Y-EOB	C-GXHR			
BB-1306	B200	N1553E	N501HC							
BB-1307	B200	N1547V	N611SD							
BB-1308	B200	N1509G	N201NY							
BB-1309	1300#	N309YV	N4277C	C-GACA						
BB-1310	B200	SE-KGK	N310GA	N16TF	N989LA					
BB-1311	B200$	N1553P	N888CS	N887FB	XT-MBD					
BB-1312	B200	(N200KA)	N1530L	N103DW	TC-KOC	N506EB	(N8753B)	N312JC		
BB-1313	B200+(WL)	8P-BAR	N700WP	N138JH	N312SB	N88KE				
BB-1314	1300	N314YV	N4277E	CR843 (Sri Lankan AF)			[w/o 22Oct07 Anuradhapuram, Sri Lanka]			
BB-1315	B200	N15572	HS-AFI	HS-DCF						
BB-1316	B200	N15570	ZS-MFB	S7-SMB						
BB-1317	B200	N1567T	(N545G)	N545GM	ZS-MWA	N591EB	VT-RSB			

BEECH 200

c/n	Series/Mod	Identities
BB-1318	B200	N1557U ZS-MMV N444KA
BB-1319	B200+	N1548B N769WT [dbf 06Sep98 George West, TX, USA; canx 05Nov98]
BB-1320	B200	N1558K N300LX N825ST
BB-1321	B200	N1558N VR-BKX N112TC (F-GJKV) F-GILI N133GA
BB-1322	B200#	N39H N391L N96GP XA-KGH
BB-1323	B200$	N3154S ZS-NZZ N62BT N4KU
BB-1324	B200$	N1541T G-JHAN N7087N VH-MVY
BB-1325	B200+	N15587 V5-BDL G-KMCD OY-LKH ZS-NVP
BB-1326	B200+	N1544G N326PS N38LA N62WC
BB-1327	B200+	N1543Z (N204BF) N67SD LN-BAA
BB-1328	B200	N1553M
BB-1329	B200	N663P VH-SWC VN-B594
BB-1330	B200+	N770M N773M N681PC N92WC
BB-1331	B200+^6	N5530H N88JH
BB-1332	B200(WL)	N1566W D-ICSM N444BK
BB-1333	B200$	SE-KLC N200SR N1101W VH-MVL
BB-1334	B200$	N5545B TC-SKO LN-MOJ
BB-1335	B200	N1567F N335KW (N10SA) N335KW
BB-1336	B200$^5	N1551F N448M N448T N131BP N89UA
BB-1337	B200$	N1550U N330CS N431SC
BB-1338	1300	N338YV N915YW C-GXHD
BB-1339	1300	N339YV N252AF C-GNAM
BB-1340	1300	N340YV N256AF (N132AZ) OY-GMA ZS-PRA
BB-1341	1300	N341YV N41AV VT-SAD OY-GEU ZS-PRC
BB-1342	1300	N342YV N250AF N99DX VT-SAE OY-GEW 5Y-BTV [wfu Nairobi-Wilson, Kenya]
BB-1343	1300	N15710 N343YV N98DX VT-SAF "OY-GEY" OY-GER 5Y-ECO C-GXHF
BB-1344	B200$	N21PS ZS-PAN ZS-PNR
BB-1345	B200$	N93ME N715JH N887JC N754SC
BB-1346	B200#	N800KT
BB-1347	B200	F-GJFC
BB-1348	B200#	N2842B S9-NAO D2-EST OO-SKL YR-RAD
BB-1349	B200$^6	N200KA N200KG D-IBFS N46CE
BB-1350	B200$	N1570F N147VC N1570F A7-AHK N27HK
BB-1351	B200	N1562F N914CT N914CE N777JV N514TB
BB-1352	B200	N5568V OB2 (Botswana Defence Force) OB1 (Botswana Defence Force)
BB-1353	B200	N15599 A2-AGO
BB-1354	B200#	F-GGVH N161A N15JA N875DM
BB-1355	B200	N5595U N404SK SE-LCE OH-WIB N480BR
BB-1356	B200	N5598N N161RC
BB-1357	B200+	N5551E D-IBSY N299MK
BB-1358	B200	N5682P N826JM
BB-1359	B200	N1565D ZS-MWB N35SA RP-C4188 N90GA
BB-1360	B200+^6	N5560D N35AR HK-3703X HK-3703W N326KW
BB-1361	B200$	N5552U N81DC
BB-1362	B200	N1565F D2-ECX
BB-1363	B200$	N5503K 3B-SKY
BB-1364	B200+(WL)	N5510Y N660PB
BB-1365	B200$(WL)	N56562 XA-RVH N963GM N711VV
BB-1366	B200	N5642T N15JA N11LC N11EQ (N777AQ) N777AG N777VG VH-IMP ZK-MAN
BB-1367	B200+	N5657N G-OBAA G-DBAA N367AJ N67JB N55HL N427P
BB-1368	B200	N5584M D-IPWB N981GA C-GCVE N558FM CC-CDN N200EA
BB-1369	B200#	N5649V N778HP D-IVHM (N567DM) D-IKLN LZ-ITV
BB-1370	B200+^6(WL)	N1554K N73LC N75LC N122H N200BM N79JS N798S N222CY
BB-1371	B200	N56616 D2-EOJ
BB-1372	B200+	N5559X N950MB
BB-1373	B200	N5608J N25GE N25GK N246PH
BB-1374	B200+	N5648Y N999HC N899HC N748LB
BB-1375	B200	N5688F TC-MGB M-1375 (Turkish Army) 4006 (Turkish Army)
BB-1376	1300	N376YV N914YW HK-3990X HK-3990 C-GNAK
BB-1377	B200$	(N65N) N56881 HB-GIR F-GNEG N755JB
BB-1378	B200$	N5637Y N618
BB-1379	B200	F-GJFD 97/F-ZBMB
BB-1380	B200	N8039M N200KA N200KY N77HN N200NR (N884VP) N200NR
BB-1381	B200+	N215P N300ET N800ET N151BG
BB-1382	B200+	N5669B N6789 N6780 N678RM N97WC
BB-1383	1300	N383YV N913YW C-GXHG
BB-1384	1300#	N384YV N912YW N575T C-GACN
BB-1385	B200	501/4X-FEA (Israeli DF/AF) 009/4X-FEA (Israeli DF/AF) 501/4X-FEA (Israeli DF/AF)
BB-1386	B200	N2872B 504/4X-FEB (Israeli DF/AF) 008/4X-FEB (Israeli DF/AF) 504/4X-FEB (Israeli DF/AF)
BB-1387	B200	N2876B 507/4X-FEC (Israeli DF/AF) 007/4X-FEC (Israeli DF/AF) 507/4X-FEC (Israeli DF/AF)
BB-1388	B200$	N2878B 510/4X-FED (Israeli DF/AF) 006/4X-FED (Israeli DF/AF) 510/4X-FED (Israeli DF/AF)
BB-1389	B200$	N8049V N330DR N389SA N277GE
BB-1390	B200	N8043B F-ODZK (F-GLOP) F-GMGB
BB-1391	B200$	N8048W D2-ESP
BB-1392	B200+	N8026J HK-3704X HK-3704W
BB-1393	B200	N8064F N73LC N200ZT N200VU
BB-1394	B200$	N8047Y N625W N625N N818BL
BB-1395	B200	N8049H N132MC

BEECH 200

c/n	Series/Mod	Identities
BB-1396	B200	N8093W N362EA N3620M
BB-1397	B200	N8062J N77HD
BB-1398	B200	YV-121CP [stolen 12Feb94 Caracas-La Carlota, Venezuela]
BB-1399	B200	F-GJFE
BB-1400	B200+	N8085D D-ICHG
BB-1401	B200	N81535 JA8879 N273NA VH-YDH A32-003 (Royal Australian AF) VH-YDH ZS-PLJ
BB-1402	B200$	(N206P) N5516Q N91CD N791DC
BB-1403	B200	N8094Q N33BK N147AA
BB-1404	B200$	N41TW N93CD N793DC
BB-1405	B200	N8129A RP-C2100
BB-1406	B200+	N81536 JA8880 N274NA D-IWKB D-IWKA 5B-CJM N212GA
BB-1407	B200	N2763B D2-ESQ OO-SKM
BB-1408	B200	F-OGQK N74RF N764CA
BB-1409	B200	10010 (Turkish Army)
BB-1410	B200	N8241T PP-EJG
BB-1411	B200	10011 (Turkish Army) [w/o 17Feb93 Yenimahalle, Turkey]
BB-1412	B200	N8241J N38V N38VV
BB-1413	B200	10012 (Turkish Army)
BB-1414	B200	10013 (Turkish Army)
BB-1415	B200	10014 (Turkish Army)
BB-1416	B200+	N8254H VH-MSH VH-MWQ
BB-1417	B200$	N8140P N711HA N511HA N203TW LV-BMG
BB-1418	B200+	N8266V ZS-NFE N131GA (LN-TWL) VH-MWU
BB-1419	B200+	N8248W PT-WCB N146SB C-GNAX
BB-1420	B200	N8267Q VH-OXA P2-MBZ N210SA N212LW N200FR
BB-1421	B200	N8230Z N715CG N715CQ (N538KB) N715CQ
BB-1422	B200+	N8225H N35DT N422BW N125TS N125TE
BB-1423	B200$	N82025 VH-OXL P2-MBH N351SA
BB-1424	B200+	N8236K VH-MWX
BB-1425	B200$	N8002J N212SN N292SN N911RX
BB-1426		[completed as c/n BT-34]
BB-1427	B200	N8003U ZS-NOW
BB-1428	B200$	N8265V N660MW C-GFAD
BB-1429	B200+	N8008A RP-C1995 N80BT N604RK *N505HP
BB-1430	B200+	N8013T N773AM VH-MSM VH-MWZ
BB-1431	B200	N82696 JA8705
BB-1432	B200$	N8037J N43TA
BB-1433	B200$	N8043K C-GMEH C-GMEV N43AJ N43CE G-FPLD
BB-1434	B200	N81148 4005 (Turkish Army)
BB-1435	B200$	N8050X PT-ORB
BB-1436	B200	N1564M 93303 (Thai Government)
BB-1437	B200$	N8059Y N34LT
BB-1438	B200+	N8017M
BB-1439	B200	N250KA N200KA N583AT N583AL N423PC N38JV
BB-1440	B200$	N8064H N655JG
BB-1441	B200	N56385 56385 (Thai Government) 93304 (Thai Government)
BB-1442	B200	N128V N128VT
BB-1443	B200	N56379 56379 (Thai Government) 93305 (Thai Government)
BB-1444	B200+^6(WL)	N8087U (N624CS) N663CS N7PA N57PA
BB-1445	B200	N8121M VT-MPG
BB-1446	B200	N5685X PT-WGS
BB-1447	B200	N8138V N70MN
BB-1448	B200	[completed as c/n BT-35]
BB-1449	B200$	N200KA LN-MOC
BB-1450	B200$	N8059Q N213DB
BB-1451	B200	[completed as c/n BT-36]
BB-1452	B200$	N155V N15HV EJC-118 (Colombian Army)
BB-1453	B200	N8153H 7T-VBE
BB-1454	B200	[completed as c/n BT-37]
BB-1455	B200$	N8105Q PT-JUB
BB-1456	B200	N8090U VT-EUJ [w/o 09Jul94 Sunder Nagar, Himachal Pradesh, India]
BB-1457	B200	[completed as c/n BT-38]
BB-1458	B200+	N8258V N883SW N457TC N457TQ N511RZ
BB-1459	B200$	N8163R LN-MOD
BB-1460	B200$	N8164G LN-MOE
BB-1461	B200$	N8261E LN-MOF
BB-1462	B200	N82425 D-IWSH N988MM
BB-1463	B200(WL)	N8242A JA8784 N564GA VH-YEH A32-004 (Royal Australian AF) VH-YEH ZS-PLK VH-LOA
BB-1464	B200+	N200TW N133LC VH-MSM
BB-1465	B200$	N8214T LN-MOG
BB-1466	B200$	N8216Z LN-MOH
BB-1467	B200+	N8056H N124SC C-GMGG N26FF N95GA
BB-1468	B200	N8230E VT-LNT
BB-1469	B200	N82378 VT-CIL
BB-1470	B200$	N8225Z LN-MOI
BB-1471	B200	N5TW
BB-1472	B200	VH-MYO VH-XCB
BB-1473	B200	N8064Q PT-OXG N8210X OO-LET
BB-1474	B200	N82010 ZS-NKC
BB-1475	B200	N8226M ZS-NKE E3-AAJ

BEECH 200

c/n	Series/Mod	Identities
BB-1476	B200	N8291D Z-MKI ZS-ODU N109GE ZS-ODU [canx 25May07 as exported to Republic of Korea; registered in South Africa 05Jun07]
BB-1477	B200+	N8301D N200PU
BB-1478	B200$	N8150N D-IHAN EC-JGB
BB-1479	B200(WL)	N8155L TG-HYD N479AV YV [canx 06Apr07 as exported to Venezuela]
BB-1480	B200$(WL)	N1559G
BB-1481	B200#	N1559W N200RS
BB-1482	B200$	N1559Y N77CX N62FB
BB-1483	B200	N1559Z XA-TFE N572P N500NG
BB-1484	B200	N200KA N6182A
BB-1485	B200	N1509X VT-BSA
BB-1486	B200	N1542Z VT-EBB
BB-1487	B200	N1548S N133K XT-IGB
BB-1488	B200+	N1568E N195CA
BB-1489	B200	N1563M ZS-SMC
BB-1490	B200$	N1563N N122LC (N769WT) VH-SMZ N208AJ N555WF
BB-1491	B200	N15098 JA8614 N700NA
BB-1492	B200+	N44NL
BB-1493	B200$	N3015Q C-GHJF
BB-1494	B200	N3026H N749FF N806LW
BB-1495	B200	N3051K
BB-1496	B200	N3047L TC-OZD
BB-1497	B200	N3065Y N123SA N508BM N18AF *N220PB
BB-1498	B200	N3092S N777AG N777AJ N770PB
BB-1499	B200	N3199A [dbr 12Aug00 Spanish Cay, Bahamas, parts to White Industries, Bates City, MO, USA c2001; location "Ramp North"]
BB-1500	B200	N3199B RP-C1502 OO-INN
BB-1501	B200+(WL)	N3180S N676BB N676BP PR-DPS N145AJ N200EG
BB-1502	B200	N1515E ZS-NXT
BB-1503	B200#	N3203Z N363K N363D
BB-1504	B200#	N3214D VH-HPW N60383 N50NA
BB-1505	B200$	N3197L VH-HPX HB-GJW
BB-1506	B200+(WL)	N3216L N94LL N993WS N202TS N95AN N75SR
BB-1507	B200$	N1567Z LV-PLF LV-WNJ N233JS C-GBBG N454TM
BB-1508	B200^5	N3208T N288KM
BB-1509	B200	N3219G N200KA N109NT N109NB N716TA
BB-1510	B200	N3213G N991WS N208TS N442JR
BB-1511	B200$(WL)	N3231F N507EF N56AY
BB-1512	B200	(N200KA) N1012S HS-ITD VH-ITM N700FT D2-EBB D2-EDD
BB-1513	B200	N3217N N415RB
BB-1514	B200	N214SE N31SV
BB-1515	B200	N3235Z ZS-TOB
BB-1516	B200	N3246S N1CR N1CQ N207HB
BB-1517	B200#	N3217V D-IANA
BB-1518	B200	N3218V SU-ZBA N65LA G-MEGN
BB-1519	B200	N10827 VR-BBK VP-BBK [w/o 23Dec00 Blackbushe, England]
BB-1520	B200#	N3230X N411CC
BB-1521	B200	N3241N LV-PLO LV-WOR
BB-1522	B200$	N3272E ZS-OBB SE-MAZ
BB-1523	B200	N3250V
BB-1524	B200#	N1024A N24CV [w/o 24May00 in Pacific Ocean nr San Diego, CA, USA; canx 11Dec00]
BB-1525	B200	N1015X N260G N196SC
BB-1526	B200#	N3258P N417MC C-FSAT
BB-1527	B200	N1027Y N170S N170W P2-KSA
BB-1528	B200	N3261L PT-WLF N528SA ZS-PEZ
BB-1529	B200	N3261E RP-C8853
BB-1530	B200	336 (Chilean AF)
BB-1531	B200	N1081F N16GF
BB-1532	B200$	N3252X RP-C3885
BB-1533	B200^5	N14HB N114HB
BB-1534	B200	N1074G
BB-1535	B200+	N1135Z D-IBFT
BB-1536	B200$	N10436 N96CE
BB-1537	B200	N3237M ZS-ARL LN-MON SE-LVV
BB-1538	B200$	N3268L PH-VMP N363EA
BB-1539	B200+	N1089S TC-MDE N1089S N220AJ
BB-1540	B200$	N89WA
BB-1541	B200	N1003W N20LB
BB-1542	B200	N202JT ZS-ODI
BB-1543	B200	N1082S PT-WLK
BB-1544	B200+	N1094S F-OHJK
BB-1545	B200	N1070E TC-OZY N286R N722KP
BB-1546	B200	N770M N770U C-GTDF N932JP C-GAEW
BB-1547	B200$	N1117N N180CA N780CA LN-SUZ
BB-1548	B200	OY-EEF
BB-1549	B200	N1069S G-MAMD
BB-1550	B200$^6(WL)	N1079Y N42SC N42SQ N61XP
BB-1551	B200$	N969TS N151CF N911ND
BB-1552	B200	N1080Y ZS-NZN VH-NSN
BB-1553	B200	N10780 ZS-NZK N200ZK N42FC
BB-1554	B200$	N464A N88WV N38WV

BEECH 200

c/n	Series/Mod	Identities						
BB-1555	B200+(WL)	N1089V	N98DA	N288GS				
BB-1556	B200	N1092N	YV-1031CP	N556BA				
BB-1557	B200#	N57TS	N57TL	G-SPOR				
BB-1558	B200	N1108A	PT-WNN					
BB-1559	B200	N1114K						
BB-1560	B200	N1103B	N30VP	N845TC				
BB-1561	B200	N1069F	N432LW	N224RT	N200HW	F-HBRU		
BB-1562	B200	N203JT	ZS-PPG					
BB-1563	B200	N204JT	VT-BAL	N204JT	VT-DAF			
BB-1564	B200#	N205JT	VP-CMA	G-IMGL	EC-KHR	EC-KND		
BB-1565	B200#(WL)	N1094Y	N23FH	D-IMGI	D-IAJK	N685R	OM-FLY	
BB-1566	B200	N1106J	LV-WYC	N566NA				
BB-1567	B200	N1107F	VT-CSK	VT-SDJ				
BB-1568	B200$	N1067V	D-ILLF	TC-TAT	N568TT			
BB-1569	B200	N20505	VP-CHE	EI-WHE	HB-GPH			
BB-1570	B200	N1120Z	N50PM	N1120Z	G-ORJA			
BB-1571	B200$(WL)	N80BC						
BB-1572	B200	N2272H	N149SB	N149SR	VT-TVS			
BB-1573	B200$	N702TA	N690L					
BB-1574	B200$	N703TA	N429PL					
BB-1575	B200	N705TA	N501P	VH-AYC				
BB-1576	B200	N1118G	N87FB					
BB-1577	B200	N1089V	C-FLXM	N33AR	JA121N			
BB-1578	B200$	N1095G	N330DR	PT-FFS				
BB-1579	B200#	N909J	C-GYSC					
BB-1580	B200+	N200KA	N345WK					
BB-1581	B200+(WL)	N12MG	N1119Z	N12MG	N12MY	N613TA		
BB-1582	B200	N1130R	N43TL					
BB-1583	B200	N424RA	N400GW					
BB-1584	B200	N11355	CP-2351	N11355	PT-WNQ			
BB-1585	B200	N1104X	(N257YA)	N200QS	N200EJ			
BB-1586	B200$^6	N3181Q	N97WE					
BB-1587	B200	N3270Q	N123ML					
BB-1588	B200	N3247Q	LV-PNH	LV-YCS				
BB-1589	B200$	N2288B	PT-MJD					
BB-1590	B200$	D-IHUT	LN-MOT					
BB-1591	B200$	N1819H	D-IPSY	N13FJ	PP-JLM			
BB-1592	B200+	N6148X	F-OHJL	[w/o 16Apr04 in sea nr Papeete, Tahiti; canx 17Dec04]				
BB-1593	B200	N1093Z						
BB-1594	B200#	N2132W	N980GB					
BB-1595	B200	N716FP	N713FP	D-IATM	LZ-BIZ			
BB-1596	B200	N82PK						
BB-1597	B200	N718RJ						
BB-1598	B200	N706TA	N523GM	N911MN				
BB-1599	B200	N200V	C-FGWD	C-FGWR				
BB-1600	B200	N480TC						
BB-1601	B200$(WL)	N2303F	C-GLLS					
BB-1602	B200+(WL)	N2302S	N203HC	N203HQ	N77XW			
BB-1603	B200	N2301R	PT-WSW	PT-WRN	PP-ERG			
BB-1604	B200	N1017V	JA01EP					
BB-1605	B200#	N2245P	N923FP	N123AC				
BB-1606	B200	N2326J						
BB-1607	B200	N724TA	ZS-DJA	F-GRLF				
BB-1608	B200+^5(WL)	N2328E						
BB-1609	B200	N524GM	N610TA	(N260AJ)	N610TA			
BB-1610	B200#	N713TA	C-FSAO					
BB-1611	B200	N2287J	HP-1515	N717FM				
BB-1612	B200	N2287L	N200ND					
BB-1613	B200$	N299RJ	N209CM					
BB-1614	B200	N2332Q	N914CT					
BB-1615	B200$	N2331C	N170S	N170L	EJC-119 (Colombian Army)			
BB-1616	B200	N2294B	LV-YTB					
BB-1617	B200+	N688LL	N550DC	N200CY	N200CV	N709X		
BB-1618	B200+	N2225Y	N1650	(N1652)	N827HT			
BB-1619	B200	N719TA	N240AJ	G-CDZT				
BB-1620	B200	N800BS						
BB-1621	B200+	N698P	N83FT					
BB-1622	B200	N30365	N257YA					
BB-1623	B200	N743TA	N816DK	N816DD	(N250AJ)	N603TA	TU-	[canx 01Feb08 as exported to Ivory Coast]
BB-1624	B200	N1624B	N957CB					
BB-1625	B200	N77CV						
BB-1626	B200	N2299W	PR-ACT					
BB-1627	B200	N744TA	N9898					
BB-1628	B200	N808DS	N337MT					
BB-1629	B200+(WL)	N2221Z	N300FL	N53AR				
BB-1630	B200	N929BW						
BB-1631	B200(WL)	N670DF	N670TA	VT-RSN				
BB-1632	B200	N998SR	N500VA	N12KR				
BB-1633	B200$	N2345M	D-IEDI					
BB-1634	B200+	N2351X	N567PK	N567US	PR-SYS			

BEECH 200

c/n	Series/Mod	Identities							
BB-1635	B200(WL)	N567T	N567A	N831TM					
BB-1636	B200$^6(WL)	N771SC	N771SQ	N771MG					
BB-1637	B200	N899RW	N8998W	[dbr 09Aug01 Sandersville, GA, USA, parts to Dodson International Parts, Rantoul, KS, USA; canx 08Jul02; re-registered N8998W 22Oct07]					
BB-1638	B200	N770TP	N777AG	N777AJ	[dbr 02Feb07 nr Cape Girardeau, MO, USA; canx 05Jun08]				
BB-1639	B200+	N23352	VH-IWO						
BB-1640	B200+	N351SC	N25WC						
BB-1641	B200+	N23355	VH-HWO						
BB-1642	B200+	N3051S	N717LW						
BB-1643	B200+	N23356	VH-LWO						
BB-1644	B200	N3055K	PNC-0225 (Colombian Police)						
BB-1645	B200+	N2202D	N615WH	N777HF					
BB-1646	B200	N399CW							
BB-1647	B200+	N3147B	N50PM	N50PU	N467BC				
BB-1648	B200	N788TA	N730HM						
BB-1649	B200#	N154DE	N154DF	N954MS					
BB-1650	B200$	N2299H	N771TP	5X-INS					
BB-1651	B200	N32434	N74RG						
BB-1652	B200	N3152K	LV-PIF	LV-ZRG					
BB-1653	B200	N653ME	N345DG	N346BA					
BB-1654	B200$	N3154J	ZS-OLM	N202DJ	(N702AJ)	ZS-PMM	N771JH	D2-BES	
BB-1655	B200	N1655M							
BB-1656	B200	N706TA	N531SW						
BB-1657	B200$	N300PU							
BB-1658	B200	N602TA	N207CW	N840CP					
BB-1659	B200+	N911SF							
BB-1660	B200+	N40PJ	N511TA						
BB-1661	B200	N2361C	XA-XAL	XC-CTL					
BB-1662	B200+	N3262P	S5-CEC	D-IVAN					
BB-1663	B200	N3163C	N46BM	N720AM					
BB-1664	B200	N3064J	SU-BNJ						
BB-1665	B200$	N111MD	N111MQ						
BB-1666	B200	N444MT	N401CG						
BB-1667	B200$	N600TA	N968MB	VH-KMS					
BB-1668	B200	N3168F	N6WU	N214GB					
BB-1669	B200	N115CT							
BB-1670	B200+(WL)	N3117N	(N780JB)	N327SE	N163JS				
BB-1671	B200$	N3171H	YV-986CP	N3171H	YV-949CP	YV1694			
BB-1672	B200#	N3172M	D-IVIP						
BB-1673	B200	N3173Y	ZS-RAF						
BB-1674	B200+(WL)	N2304F	N404PT	XC-UAT					
BB-1675	B200+	N2355Z	OY-PCL						
BB-1676	B200$^6	N31094							
BB-1677	B200	N200KA	N200HF	N200HK	*N991PS				
BB-1678	B200$	N2287L	HS-ADS	N678FA					
BB-1679	B200	N55MP							
BB-1680	B200	N604TA	N299AV						
BB-1681	B200$	N2301K	XA-TJN	XC-TJN	N680CA				
BB-1682	B200	N3182M	(G-LYNT)	N888FM	N888FV				
BB-1683	B200(WL)	N511SD							
BB-1684	B200T	N32268	[completed as c/n BT-39]						
BB-1685	B200	N808WD	N116TX						
BB-1686	B200	N52SZ							
BB-1687	B200	N3117V	VT-GUJ						
BB-1688	B200	N42LW							
BB-1689	B200#	N203TS	N225TL						
BB-1690	B200	N690LJ	N600DF	LV-ZYB					
BB-1691	B200+	N200NW							
BB-1692	B200	N772TP	N29AH	LN-MOO	SE-LVU				
BB-1693	B200	N773TP	N771SC	G-GBMR					
BB-1694	B200#	N3194U	N317RT						
BB-1695	B200	N40480	N88AF	A6-SSA	ST-HAL	A6-SSA	N800AJ	N915TL	N909DD
BB-1696	B200	N40481	VH-FDF						
BB-1697	B200#	N40483	VH-FDD						
BB-1698	B200	N32287	F-GUFP						
BB-1699	B200	N3199B	N703RM	N703R	C-FSUG				
BB-1700	B200$(WL)	N4300X	N70VP	N403J	(N483J)	VT-REM			
BB-1701	B200	N4301Y	TC-OPM	N85GP	JY-AW2	JY-AWB			
BB-1702	B200$	N4302Q	N581FM	N677JE					
BB-1703	B200	N3203Z	LV-ZTV						
BB-1704	B200	N3204W	N68MN						
BB-1705	B200	N418J							
BB-1706	B200$(WL)	N3206M	YV-494CP	YV1740					
BB-1707	B200#	N4207G	N205TS	YS-111-N					
BB-1708	B200+	N605TA	N711AW						
BB-1709	B200	N865PT	N408RN						
BB-1710	B200(WL)	N3210N	C6-MIP	N68FB					
BB-1711	B200	N606TA	N44KA						
BB-1712	B200$	N3212E	YV-639CP	YV1603					
BB-1713	B200	N3053Q	N96AM						
BB-1714	B200$	N3214D	5Y-ZBK						

BEECH 200

c/n	Series/Mod	Identities
BB-1715	B200	N607TA G-CDFY
BB-1716	B200	N3216G D-IBFE
BB-1717	B200	N44717 [completed as c/n BT-40]
BB-1718	B200$	N3018C N13LY
BB-1719	B200+	N3219G N410H N45RR N45SQ N37XX
BB-1720	B200	N608TA N208CW G-TAGH
BB-1721	B200	N44721 [completed as c/n BT-41]
BB-1722	B200	N773TP
BB-1723	B200+	N3223R N521DG VT-VSM
BB-1724	B200	N44724 [completed as c/n BT-42]
BB-1725	B200	N609TA
BB-1726	B200$	N774TP N515CL N515CK
BB-1727	B200	N42327 [completed as c/n BT-43]
BB-1728	B200	N946CE
BB-1729	B200	N207TS N728AM 5B-CKJ D-IBCB 5A-DUA
BB-1730	B200#	N611TA N204C C-GBON N318CB
BB-1731	B200	N948CL N942CE
BB-1732	B200	N23268 PK-RGI
BB-1733	B200	N3156L 402 (Greek Army)
BB-1734	B200$	N123NA JA200N N123NA G-MOUN EC-KTI N727B
BB-1735	B200#	N612TA N871C [canx 09May06 as exported to Dominican Republic; never registered & reinstated 26May06]
BB-1736	B200	N942CE N948CE
BB-1737	B200	N4437S N263SP N665MW
BB-1738	B200$	N5075C C-GLFN N999TB
BB-1739	B200	N612TA N257CG [w/o 04Apr03 Leominster, MA, USA; canx 19Apr04]
BB-1740	B200#	N170S N170SE
BB-1741	B200$	N2341K D-IIAH OE-FOS
BB-1742	B200(WL)	N4288L ZS-CBL
BB-1743	B200	N4443V N60AR
BB-1744	B200	N3157F 403 (Greek Army)
BB-1745	B200	N615TA N745EA
BB-1746	B200	N520GM N520GN N518GS N510GS
BB-1747	B200	N214FW G-SGEC
BB-1748	B200+(WL)	N50848 C-GSAE
BB-1749	B200$(WL)	N616TA N944C
BB-1750	B200	N4150T N726CB
BB-1751	B200#(WL)	N617TA N805C
BB-1752	B200	N5152G XA-TVO
BB-1753	B200+	N520DG
BB-1754	B200(WL)	N618TA N200WB
BB-1755	B200	N5055Q PR-APJ
BB-1756	B200#	N5056U N264SP
BB-1757	B200$	N4357Y N261BC N777AG N228FS
BB-1758	B200$(WL)	N619TA VT-RSM
BB-1759	B200(WL)	N5159F N541AS N1Z N95UT
BB-1760	B200	N4360N N311G
BB-1761	B200	N4461C N459DF N610RM
BB-1762	B200	N4362F N415TM
BB-1763	B200	N5063K
BB-1764	B200	N4064Z ZS-PGB VT-YUD
BB-1765	B200+(WL)	N3205Z N540MA
BB-1766	B200	N622TA (N4GP) N315N N994HP N215LW N212LW
BB-1767	B200+(WL)	N4467F N806DG N806GG N806G N111JW N111JZ (N4124T) N441AL
BB-1768	B200$	N4268V N637WM
BB-1769	B200+(WL)	N4469Y N520GM N80VP CC-CEK
BB-1770	B200+	N4270Y (N4SQ) N4270Y
BB-1771	B200$	N4271V N818AG PR-AJT
BB-1772	B200	N4472C N28VM
BB-1773	B200+	N623TA N777SW N425BP
BB-1774	B200	N4053H
BB-1775	B200	N5075E VT-MPT
BB-1776	B200+	N4476M N23EH N7000G
BB-1777	B200	N4347X N33LA N33LV
BB-1778	B200	N4368X N1LF
BB-1779	B200$	N624TA N282JD PR-ATC
BB-1780	B200+	N4480Y N46TF C-GSBC
BB-1781	B200	N4081W N34GN N908BS
BB-1782	B200	N4482Z N4NU
BB-1783	B200	N5003K N625TA N360X
BB-1784	B200	N4484W N710JB
BB-1785	B200$	N4455U N101SG (N171SG) N101SG
BB-1786	B200	N626TA (N716GS) N202FF
BB-1787	B200#	N44857 VH-MSH
BB-1788	B200	N314FW N314FH N770M VT-AEL
BB-1789	B200+	N4470B ZS-PEI N800AJ
BB-1790	B200+(WL)	N4470T C-GSAV
BB-1791	B200	N4471C N252CP
BB-1792	B200	N5092K EC-ILE
BB-1793	B200#	N5093X N404J
BB-1794	B200	N4484F N250JJ TG-OIL

BEECH 200

c/n	Series/Mod	Identities				
BB-1795	B200	N4195S				
BB-1796	B200+	N4126T	CC-CPB			
BB-1797	B200	N5097G	N424RA			
BB-1798	B200	N577P	PR-LIA	N330MG	PR-EPS	
BB-1799	B200#	N5099H	N211HV	N102FG		
BB-1800	B200#	N314FW	N600RL	N600RK		
BB-1801	B200	N5001Q	N602MJ	N604MJ		
BB-1802	B200$	N5092S				
BB-1803	B200	N5093G	XA-ZEC			
BB-1804	B200	N5104B	856 (Israeli DF/AF)			
BB-1805	B200$	N4205G	ZS-TIP			
BB-1806	B200	N4476Y	842 (Israeli DF/AF)			
BB-1807	B200	N5007L	N433HC			
BB-1808	B200	N4488N	TG-FYL			
BB-1809	B200	N61369	844 (Israeli DF/AF)			
BB-1810	B200					
BB-1811	B200	N51161	848 (Israeli DF/AF)			
BB-1812	B200+	N62012	VH-MSB	VH-AMR		
BB-1813	B200+	N61913	VH-MVS	VH-AMQ		
BB-1814	B200+	N60914	VH-MVW	VH-AMS		
BB-1815	B200	N5015M	VT-JVL			
BB-1816	B200+	N5016K	N444LP			
BB-1817	B200	N5117M	LV-ZZH			
BB-1818	B200	N5018F	VT-UPR			
BB-1819	B200	N5019H	859 (Israeli DF/AF)			
BB-1820	B200	N6020Z	N47RM	N47RN	N47RM	
BB-1821	B200+	N5021S				
BB-1822	B200	N6022Q	N203RC			
BB-1823	B200+	N6193C	N299AK	N299AL		
BB-1824	B200	N6124A	N277WC			
BB-1825	B200	N4485Z	I-MTOP	OK-TOS		
BB-1826	B200	N826KA	N200KA	N205SP		
BB-1827	B200	N50807	N667CC	C-FAXD		
BB-1828	B200	N61808	N401SK			
BB-1829	B200	N6129N	G-RAFJ	ZK450 (RAF)		
BB-1830	B200	N50130	G-RAFK	ZK451 (RAF)		
BB-1831	B200	N61831	VT-SAZ			
BB-1832	B200	N5032K	G-RAFL	ZK452 (RAF)		
BB-1833	B200	N51283	G-RAFM	ZK453 (RAF)		
BB-1834	B200+	N6034P	N399AE	N1NP		
BB-1835	B200	N60275	G-RAFN	ZK454 (RAF)		
BB-1836	B200	N60476	G-RAFO	*ZK455 (RAF)		
BB-1837	B200	N61037	G-RAFP	*ZK456 (RAF)		
BB-1838	B200	N5138Q	XA-HPS			
BB-1839	B200	N5039X	N712RH			
BB-1840	B200	N6040N	N816LD	EC-IUX		
BB-1841	B200$	N6191N	N69LS	C-FGMG		
BB-1842	B200$	N50152	VH-MVJ			
BB-1843	B200	N6043T	N356CC	N120FS		
BB-1844	B200	N18ST	N99ML	(N88ZC)	N99ML	N888ZC
BB-1845	B200	N5005V	N912JS	N912JZ		
BB-1846	B200$	N10CW	N10QW			
BB-1847	B200$	N61847	N635SF			
BB-1848	B200	N5148Q	N215HC			
BB-1849	B200	N6109A	N924JD	N924JB		
BB-1850	B200+(WL)	N6150Q	N299AK			
BB-1851	B200$	N6151C	C6-MIP			
BB-1852	B200	N6152L	N633HC			
BB-1853	B200+	N6193R	N45RR	N93RR		
BB-1854	B200	N6194S	N927BG			
BB-1855	B200	N6155T	N214TP			
BB-1856	B200$(WL)	N61956	ZS-PCH			
BB-1857	B200	N5157G	N788SF			
BB-1858	B200	N6158Q	N200HF	*N396CT		
BB-1859	B200+	N61592	XA-SUL	N901SF		
BB-1860	B200	N6200G	G-PCOP			
BB-1861	B200	N50478	OY-LLL	[std: CofA exp 10Jul09]		
BB-1862	B200+	N6162X	N225WC			
BB-1863	B200	N6203T	PR-MLG			
BB-1864	B200	N6084C	N766LF	N766LE		
BB-1865	B200	N6165Q	N6300F			
BB-1866	B200#	N6166Q	N922MM			
BB-1867	B200$	N6167R	N119AR			
BB-1868	B200$	N5078Q	N954RM	LN-LTA		
BB-1869	B200	N5109V	N65GP			
BB-1870	B200	N6170G	N4925T			
BB-1871	B200$(WL)	N6171R	(N432LM)	N917CT	N917CB	PR-FRB
BB-1872	B200	N6172W	N510UF	N510UE		
BB-1873	B200+(WL)	N6113P	N267CB			
BB-1874	B200$	N6194V	F-HAMI			
BB-1875	B200	N6175U	VH-WJY			

BEECH 200

c/n	Series/Mod	Identities					
BB-1876	B200#	N716AV					
BB-1877	B200	N61767	LV-AXO				
BB-1878	B200	N6078T	N750MD				
BB-1879	B200+	N36579	N536RB				
BB-1880	B200$	N6180Q	VH-FDW				
BB-1881	B200$	N36801	VH-FDR				
BB-1882	B200$	N37082	VH-FDZ				
BB-1883	B200						
BB-1884	B200	N625GA					
BB-1885	B200	N36585	ZS-DEV	N204RA			
BB-1886	B200	N509FP					
BB-1887	B200	N36987	F-HJPM				
BB-1888	B200#	N6188N	N187JP				
BB-1889	B200	N36739	N351CB				
BB-1890	B200#	N6190F	PR-MCE				
BB-1891	B200	N6191H	N5AE				
BB-1892	B200+(WL)	N3732K	XA-GFM				
BB-1893	B200	N36893	N173TC				
BB-1894	B200	N6194X	N63LB				
BB-1895	B200	N36995	VT-LKK				
BB-1896	B200	N6196P	VT-DDS				
BB-1897	B200(WL)	N6197H	N897BM	N504CE	N97UT		
BB-1898	B200$	N6198P	F-HARR	N199GA	LN-FIX		
BB-1899	B200	N6199Y	N762GP				
BB-1900	B200	N6200C	N323JG	N111LP	N111LZ	4R-	[canx 28May09 as exported to Sri Lanka]
BB-1901	B200	N3301M	N741JR				
BB-1902	B200+	N36972	HA-ACE	OE-FIJ	DQ-LIR		
BB-1903	B200+	N521RS	N203PT				
BB-1904	B200	N36644	N983JB				
BB-1905	B200	N36705	I-REEF	OK-UNO			
BB-1906	B200	N61806	VT-HRA				
BB-1907	B200+(WL)	N37307	XA-RDJ				
BB-1908	B200+(WL)	N37308	N204PT				
BB-1909	B200+	N909RA	N45RR	N613GA			
BB-1910	B200#	N228RC					
BB-1911	B200$(WL)	N36871	ZS-CPM				
BB-1912	B200+	N6132U	PR-EAO				
BB-1913	B200	N29PE					
BB-1914	B200	N5114Z	VT-UAB				
BB-1915	B200#	N37155	PT-MMF				
BB-1916	B200	N36916	N1542				
BB-1917	B200$	N37097	D-IJAH				
BB-1918	B200	N6118V	VT-FAE				
BB-1919	B200+	N205RA					
BB-1920	B200$	N6178A	N700Z				
BB-1921	B200	N716GS	N224LM	(N225LM)	C-FSQD	C-GPNB	
BB-1922	B200	N6178J	N837JM	N837J	N694KM		
BB-1923	B200	N3123J	HS-CNS				
BB-1924	B200(WL)	N51418	N700KB	N780KB			
BB-1925	B200$(WL)	N928KG					
BB-1926	B200	N61726	N776RW				
BB-1927	B200	N840U					
BB-1928	B200+	N3728E	N964RT	F-	[canx 03Aug09 as exported to France]		
BB-1929	B200	N3729J	N402CT				
BB-1930	B200	N5130V	N881MC				
BB-1931	B200	N37101	G-CLCG	G-KLYN	N37101		
BB-1932	B200$	N36782	N737EA	XB-KBC	N277DM	PR-EFN	N277DM
BB-1933	B200	N3103L	M-EGGA				
BB-1934	B200+	N37134	F-OIQM				
BB-1935	B200(WL)	N3735C	N430TW				
BB-1936	B200$	N36566	LN-TRG				
BB-1937	B200	N831KD					
BB-1938	B200	N36788	ZS-TGM	TC-AYK			
BB-1939	B200$(WL)	N3729N	N707HM	VT-BAF			
BB-1940	B200	N999DZ	C-GDVF/208				
BB-1941	B200	N3191V	(N925GA)	N500VA			
BB-1942	B200+	N321GC					
BB-1943	B200	N70143	VT-RJA				
BB-1944	B200$	N37244	N660WM				
BB-1945	B200	N7345S	N739W				
BB-1946	B200	N37046	N31CG	N31CQ	C-GDNH/209		
BB-1947	B200	N73817	VT-CTG				
BB-1948	B200	N36898	N802MJ				
BB-1949	B200$	N660AA					
BB-1950	B200+(WL)	N70150	N128AS				
BB-1951	B200	N7251U	N954BL				
BB-1952	B200+(WL)	N87LN	N381HC				
BB-1953	B200+(WL)	N426WF					
BB-1954	B200#	N7054D	N500HG				
BB-1955	B200	N7055T	N215ML				

BEECH 200

c/n	Series/Mod	Identities		
BB-1956	B200#	N37156	N95LM	
BB-1957	B200	N104AG	N957BA	D-IRAR
BB-1958	B200$(WL)	N37058	XC-CLQ	
BB-1959	B200	N205PA	TG-CBI	
BB-1960	B200+	N7260R	N23HD	N981BB
BB-1961	B200+	N74061	VH-MQZ	
BB-1962	B200$	N7162V	C-GFSD	
BB-1963	B200$	N7063F	C-GFSE	
BB-1964	B200	N50VM	N60VM	N424TT
BB-1965	B200$	N716GS	N68BK	PR-VDQ
BB-1966	B200$	N37066	YV2392	
BB-1967	B200	N481BR		
BB-1968	B200	N70068	PR-BTN	
BB-1969	B200	N3729R	N458TC	PR-FVP
BB-1970	B200	N7270Z	N390SP	
BB-1971	B200	N779BZ		
BB-1972	B200+(WL)	N7022F	C-GSAH	
BB-1973	B200	N74753	D-ITFC	
BB-1974	B200+(WL)	N7074N	C-GSAU	
BB-1975	B200	N7075V	I-MCAP	OM-ALE
BB-1976	B200$	N124AR	N23YR	N3NC
BB-1977	B200$	N7317A	VH-FDB	
BB-1978	B200#	N70118	N410PT	
BB-1979	B200#	N71089	N337TB	
BB-1980	B200+	N980KA	VH-MVW	
BB-1981	B200+	N7481P	PR-LPM	
BB-1982	B200	N7022Y	VT-HIS	
BB-1983	B200+	N70783	9A-BKB	
BB-1984	B200+	N7184M	N629RP	
BB-1985	B200	N71850	ZS-JSC	
BB-1986	B200$	N986KA	VH-FDA	
BB-1987	B200	N987KA	ZS-CCK	
BB-1988	B200	N988KA	HS-ATS	
BB-1989	B200	N989BK	N807SM	
BB-1990	B200$	N990KA	VH-FDT	
BB-1991	B200	N991HB	N205TM	
BB-1992	B200	N992KA	PP-LOV	
BB-1993	B200+	N124EK	N124EU	N125TS
BB-1994	B200+	N994KA	LN-MMM	
BB-1995	B200	N995KA	SP-IKY	
BB-1996	B200	N996KA	N20LH	
BB-1997	B200+(WL)	N999MM		
BB-1998	B200	N998KA	VT-LMW	
BB-1999	B200	N3199Z	D-IPAP	AP-CAB
BB-2000	B200	N3200V	D-INOR	AP-CAC
BB-2001	B200$(WL)	N3501D	LN-LTB	
BB-2002	B200$(WL)	N60102	LN-LTC	
BB-2003	B200+	N3203Q	VH-MWH	
BB-2004	B200$(WL)	N63924	LN-LTK	
BB-2005	B200$(WL)	N6005S	LN-LTL	
BB-2006	B200$(WL)	N61806	LN-LTD	
BB-2007	B200$(WL)	N63007	LN-LTE	
BB-2008	B200$(WL)	N63578	LN-LTF	
BB-2009	B200$(WL)	N62509	LN-LTG	
BB-2010	B200$(WL)	N6010T	LN-LTI	
BB-2011	B200$(WL)	N6011V	LN-LTJ	
BB-2012	B200+	N60312	(LN-LTK)	VH-FDG
BB-2013	B200	(LN-LTL)	N6473E	
BB-2014	B200			
BB-2015	B200			
BB-2016	B200			
BB-2017	B200			
BB-2018	B200			
BB-2019	B200			
BB-2020	B200			
BB-2021	B200			
BB-2022	B200			
BB-2023	B200			
BB-2024	B200			
BB-2025	B200			
BB-2026	B200			
BB-2027	B200			
BB-2028	B200			
BB-2029	B200			
BB-2030	B200			
BB-2031	B200			
BB-2032	B200			
BB-2033	B200			
BB-2034	B200			
BB-2035	B200			
BB-2036	B200			

c/n	Series/Mod	Identities
BB-2037	B200	
BB-2038	B200	
BB-2039	B200	
BB-2040	B200	
BB-2050	B200	
BB-2051	B200	
BB-2052	B200	
BB-2053	B200	
BB-2054	B200	
BB-2055	B200	
BB-2056	B200	
BB-2057	B200	
BB-2058	B200	
BB-2059	B200	
BB-2060	B200	
BB-2061	B200	
BB-2062	B200	
BB-2063	B200	
BB-2064	B200	
BB-2065	B200	
BB-2066	B200	
BB-2067	B200	
BB-2068	B200	
BB-2069	B200	
BB-2070	B200	
BB-2071	B200	
BB-2072	B200	
BB-2073	B200	
BB-2074	B200	
BB-2075	B200	

BEECH 200C/B200C/C-12F SUPER KING AIR

$ = Raisbeck dual aft body strakes fitted
# = Raisbeck nacelle wing lockers fitted
+ = Raisbeck dual aft body strakes and nacelle wing lockers fitted
^ - Blackhawk XP42 engine upgrade fitted
(WL) = Enhanced Aero winglets fitted

c/n	Series/Mod	Identities
BL-1	200C	N24138 (F-GBLT) 5A-DDT
BL-2	200C	N2027B VH-TRS N690G OY-BVE 5Y-EKO
BL-3	200C	N104AW N200HT N141GS N39PH
BL-4	200C	N8VG (D-IDRK) SE-KON V5-AAL ZS-NUF
BL-5	200C+	N289CA N390AC N143LG N14RD N514RD N468SP [may have used clandestine registration N9693U]
BL-6	200C	5A-DDY
BL-7	200C$	N6690E F-GJBJ HB-GJD
BL-8	200C	N6733R ZS-NAX 5Y-NAX ZS-NAX ZS-PNZ [dam 10Jun09 Lanseria, Gauteng Province, South Africa]
BL-9	200C	N6725R VH-KZL VH-NSG VH-KZL VH-NTG
BL-10	200C#	N6726V VH-AKV VH-NSE C-GWSQ VH-NSE C-GWSQ VH-NSE VH-AKV C-FAMB 5Y-BLA
BL-11	200C^	D-INEF N41JK I-MADY F-GIMD PH-SKP (5B-CJM) (F-GYMD) F-GRSO
BL-12	200C	(F-GCMT) TR-LZH F-GILF VH-SWO VH-NTH
BL-13	200C	PH-ILG OY-JAR C-FGPC N817BB
BL-14	200C	N3697F
BL-15	200C+^	N348MJ HK-2700X HK-2700 HK-2700W N159AG N215AA N511DP
BL-16	B200C	N621AW N200RG F-GFAA N62GA LN-TWI N57LM F-GLTX (OO-SKN) OO-LAC
BL-17	200C	N3715W N818 N818DT F-GJMR 5Y-JMR 5H-ABN 5H-TZW
BL-18	200C	3280 (Venezuelan AF)
BL-19	200C	3240 (Venezuelan AF) [wfu c2000 El Libertador AB, Venezuela; pres Museo Aeronautico de la Fuerza Aerea Venezolana, Maracay, Venezuela]
BL-20	200C$	N37KA D-ILDB ZS-LRS 5Y-LRS ZS-LRS
BL-21	200C	N3831T C9-ASV ZS-SBI
BL-22	200C	N3816W P2-PJV P2-HCN P2-KSN
BL-23	200C	YV-403CP
BL-24	B200CT	[completed as c/n BN-1]
BL-25	200C	N97D (N74DD) N97DG N97D N960A C-GTDP N960A OY-CHE 101001 (Swedish AF) [w/o 24Sep90 nr Halmstad, Sweden]
BL-26	200C	N3723B VH-WLH VH-FDB N326AA HP- [canx 14Nov06 as exported to Panama]
BL-27	200C	N3827Z (XA-LOT) N44MR
BL-28	200C	FAB-018 (Bolivian AF)
BL-29	200C$	N3847H N500PH ZS-PEA
BL-30	200C	N3723Y VH-TNQ VH-NTS
BL-31	200C+	N3849A N111TB N200LG VH-KFN
BL-32	200C	N821CA C9-ASX ZS-CVH
BL-33	200C	FAB-002 (Bolivian AF) EB-002 (Bolivian AF)[w/o 26Nov95 Uncia, Bolivia]

BEECH 200C

c/n	Series/Mod	Identities
BL-34	200C	N38314 ZS-LAY 652 (South African AF)
BL-35	200C	C-GDMY N26732 N617MS [w/o 24Jun87 Madisonville-Municipal, KY, USA; canx 09Apr09]
BL-36	200C	N111NS
BL-37	B200C$	N500GP N351BC G-IFTB 5Y-TWC ZS-SFB
BL-38	B200C	N1812B ST-APW N1812B N10PT P2-CCB VH-CBZ
BL-39	B200C+	D-INEL N666TB N75WD (N299CR) N75WR VH-FDR P2-SIA
BL-40	B200C	N3837R VH-OTH N44344 VH-NSR OY-GEB ZS-PRB
BL-41	B200C+	N3836E OY-BER N100QR VH-HEO VH-OYK VH-LNJ
BL-42	B200C#	N500BX N819CD C-GIND
BL-43	B200C	EI-BKV OY-BEP [w/o 18Sep82 Roodt-Syr, Luxembourg; canx 12Oct84]
BL-44	B200C$	N18379 C-GDPB
BL-45	B200C	(YV-465CP) CC-CIJ N90466 ZS-LXS 651 (South African AF)
BL-46	B200C+	XA-MIN N3125J N312ME
BL-47	B200C+	N6334F VH-FMN [w/o 10Dec01 5km N of Mount Gambier, SA, Australia; canx 08Jan02]
BL-48	B200C$	N1860B VH-MSU
BL-49	B200C$(WL)	N3836E (EI-BME) N17KK Z-TAM (D-ICWM) N51CV D-ICWM D-ICWD OK-LFB OO-ASL
BL-50	B200C+	N18451 ZS-LOF N723RK VH-NSF N54HF N58AS N150RL
BL-51	B200C$	(YV-487CP) GN-8270 (Venezuelan National Guard)
BL-52	B200C	N6872X CP-1849 [w/o 14Mar84 Santa Cruz, Bolivia]
BL-53	B200C+	N494AC 9Q-CJT N494AC N320JS N157A [may have used clandestine registrations N9748N & N32535 (both appear on FAA register cards)]
BL-54	B200C	(N6284N) N6563C N654BA
BL-55	B200C	N1844B VH-NSD VH-FDA N356AA YV N356AA [canx 29Apr08 as exported to Venezuela; reinstated 02Jul09]
BL-56	B200C	N1844C VT-EID N389RA
BL-57	B200C	CNA-NI (Royal Moroccan AF)
BL-58	B200CT	[completed as c/n BN-2]
BL-59	B200CT	[completed as c/n BN-4]
BL-60	B200CT	[completed as c/n BN-3]
BL-61	B200C	(N6284N) N6564C N661BA
BL-62	B200C	(N6284N) N6566C N662BA
BL-63	B200C$	N6921D VT-EIE [w/o 29Jul00 nr Mandi, Himachal Pradesh, India]
BL-64	B200C	N6912F N124JS N1240S N188TC ZK-PLK
BL-65	B200C$	N6770G N73555 N9701Y (N9745S) N870CA N399AS [canx 07Jun06; fate unkn]
BL-66	B200C	YV-2323P [canx c1984 - status?]
BL-67	B200C	N2841B TR-LBP N70LG
BL-68	B200C	N12109 LN-TSH N83GA VH-FDS
BL-69	B200C	N2811B N7232R
BL-70	B200C	N6921R ZS-LNT 654 (South African AF) 650 (South African AF)
BL-71	B200C	N6921T ZS-LNV N771D [dbr 10May97 Steynsburg, Eastern Cape Province, South Africa; sold to Dodson International Parts for spares]
BL-72	B200C+	N6740C N43CE VH-CWO
BL-73	C-12F$	84-0143 (US Army)
BL-74	C-12F$	84-0144 (US Army) N5801D 84-0144 (US Army)
BL-75	C-12F$	84-0145 (US Army)
BL-76	C-12F$	84-0146 (US Army)
BL-77	C-12F	84-0147 (USAF)
BL-78	C-12F	84-0148 (USAF)
BL-79	C-12F$	84-0149 (US Army)
BL-80	C-12F$	84-0150 (US Army)
BL-81	C-12F$	84-0151 (US Army)
BL-82	C-12F$	84-0152 (US Army)
BL-83	C-12F$	84-0153 (US Army) N58009 84-0153 (US Army)
BL-84	C-12F$	84-0154 (US Army)
BL-85	C-12F$	84-0155 (US Army)
BL-86	C-12F$	84-0156 (US Army)
BL-87	C-12F$	84-0157 (US Army)
BL-88	C-12F$	84-0158 (US Army) N58022 84-0158 (US Army)
BL-89	C-12F$	84-0159 (US Army)
BL-90	C-12F$	84-0160 (US Army)
BL-91	C-12F$	84-0161 (US Army)
BL-92	C-12F$	84-0162 (US Army)
BL-93	C-12F$	84-0163 (US Army)
BL-94	C-12F$	84-0164 (US Army)
BL-95	C-12F$	84-0165 (US Army)
BL-96	C-12F$	84-0166 (US Army)
BL-97	C-12F$	84-0167 (US Army)
BL-98	C-12F$	84-0168 (US Army)
BL-99	C-12F$	84-0169 (US Army) [w/o 12Aug03 Pyongtaek, Gyeonggi Province, South Korea]
BL-100	C-12F$	84-0170 (US Army)
BL-101	C-12F$	84-0171 (US Army)
BL-102	C-12F$	84-0172 (US Army)
BL-103	C-12F$	84-0173 (US Army)
BL-104	C-12F$	84-0174 (US Army)
BL-105	C-12F$	84-0175 (US Army) N5803F 84-0175 (US Army)
BL-106	C-12F$	84-0176 (US Army) N5819T 84-0176 (US Army)
BL-107	C-12F$	84-0177 (US Army)
BL-108	C-12F$	84-0178 (US Army)
BL-109	C-12F$	84-0179 (US Army)
BL-110	C-12F$	84-0180 (US Army)

c/n	Series/Mod	Identities
BL-111	C-12F$	84-0181 (US Army)
BL-112	C-12F$	84-0182 (US Army)
BL-113	C-12F	[void - airframe not built]
BL-114	C-12F	[void - airframe not built]
BL-115	C-12F	[void - airframe not built]
BL-116	C-12F	[void - airframe not built]
BL-117	C-12F	[void - airframe not built]
BL-118	C-12F$	84-0484 (US Army)
BL-119	C-12F$	84-0485 (US Army)
BL-120	C-12F$	84-0486 (US Army)
BL-121	C-12F$	84-0487 (US Army)
BL-122	C-12F$	84-0488 (US Army)
BL-123	C-12F$	84-0489 (US Army)
BL-124	B200C	N107Z N149Z
BL-125	B200C	N72381 VH-AMM VH-BRF [canx 27Jun06 as exported to Turks & Caicos Islands; never registered VQ-; aircraft has been std at FXE since cJul06]
BL-126	B200C	N72385 VH-AMR VH-AUP [wfu Sydney-Bankstown, NSW, Australia; canx 11Mar04]
BL-127	B200C$(WL)	D2-ESO SE-LKY
BL-128	B200C$	N2804B HKG-8 (Hong Kong Government) VR-HZM B-HZM N128TJ N361TD
BL-129	B200C	N72401 VT-EOA [w/o 27Aug92 New Delhi, India]
BL-130	B200C$	N2766B HKG-9 (Hong Kong Government) VR-HZN B-HZN N130TJ N362TD C-GWXM N130SC
BL-131	B200C	N3228X VH-AMB VH-BQR VQ-TIU [w/o 06Feb07 East Bay Cay, Turks & Caicos Islands]
BL-132	B200C$	SE-KFP
BL-133	B200C	N15588 VH-AMS VH-BRQ VQ-TRS N133US *PR-JBT
BL-134	B200C$	N1563R PK-YPR PK-HSN (N134WJ) SE-LMP N134WJ
BL-135	B200C	N2826B S9-NAP D2-ECY
BL-136	B200C$	N56641 PK-YPW N136BL ZS-SON *N136AJ [valid import on USCAR as N136AJ since 22Jun00]
BL-137	B200C	N5678J 9G-AGC ZS-NSD VH-HPP
BL-138	B200C(WL)	VH-AJM (VH-OXR) VH-HPZ PK-VKI PK-JCA
BL-139	B200C	N82431 SE-LCB N65LW VT-SRC
BL-140	B200C	N82410 PK-CAK
BL-141	B200C	N5141Y N200KA G-ZAPT LN-IDA
BL-142	B200C+	N5002Y N524GM (N840GR) N524GM
BL-143	B200C+	N4456A
BL-144	B200C+	N5139A
BL-145	B200C+	N4489A
BL-146	B200C+	N5155A
BL-147	B200C	
BL-148	B200C+	N36948 F-OIQL
BL-149	B200C+	N36949 F-OIQK
BL-150	B200C+	N6178D G-SASC
BL-151	B200C+	N6178F G-SASD
BL-152	B200C+	N3202W VH-MWK
BL-153	B200C+	N3203R VH-MVX
BL-154	B200C	
BL-155	B200C	
BL-156	B200C	
BL-157	B200C	
BL-158	B200C	
BL-159	B200C	
BL-160	B200C	
BL-161	B200C	
BL-162	B200C	
BL-163	B200C	
BL-164	B200C	
BL-165	B200C	

BEECH B200CT SUPER KING AIR

c/n	Series/Mod	Identities
BN-1	200CT	FAC499 (Chilean AF) CC-EAA CC-PTN CC-DIV
BN-2	200CT	N2830B N6904Q AE571 (Peruvian Navy) [may have been re-serialled AT-571]
BN-3	200CT	N2856B AE572 (Peruvian Navy) [may have been re-serialled AT-572]
BN-4	200CT	N2790B AE573 (Peruvian Navy) [may have been re-serialled AT-573]
BN-5	200CT	N5005M 703 (Israeli DF/AF)
BN-6	200CT	N5106F 709 (Israeli DF/AF)
BN-7	200CT	N5107Z 711 (Israeli DF/AF)
BN-8	200CT	N51488 714 (Israeli DF/AF)
BN-9	200CT	N50969 719 (Israeli DF/AF)

Production complete

BEECH 200T/B200T SUPER KING AIR

$ = Raisbeck dual aft body strakes fitted
^ - Blackhawk XP42 engine upgrade fitted

c/n	Series/Mod	Identities
BT-1	200T	F-GALN
BT-2	200T	F-GALP
BT-3	200T	N2UW
BT-4	200T	N2067D 871 (Uruguayan Navy)
BT-5	200T	N2071C JA8810 N205EC A2-MXI
BT-6	200T	N2071D JA8811 VH-ITA VH-PPJ VH-OYT
BT-7	200T	N2071X JA8812 N853GA ZS-OEB
BT-8	200T	N2071Y JA8813 N858GA ZS-OPR D2-ERO
BT-9	200T	N2071Z JA8814 N120RL
BT-10	200T	N6065D 9M-JPA 9M-CAM [dbr 13Dec93 Ipoh, Perak, Malaysia; wreckage to Sydney-Bankstown, NSW, Australia]
BT-11	200T$^	N60576 JA8815 N857GA
BT-12	200T	N60581 JA8816 N859GA
BT-13	200T	N60587 JA8817 N45E
BT-14	200T$	N6059C (9Q-CTZ) JA8818 N44U
BT-15	200T	N6059D JA8819 N41R N45N
BT-16	200T	N60603 JA8820 N130RL
BT-17	200T	N3718Q JA8824
BT-18	200T$	N64RA N123PW D2-FMD
BT-19	200T	N3718N JA8825 [w/o 17Feb87 Fukuoka, Fukuoka Prefecture, Japan]
BT-20	200T	N1842B F-WKVR 7T-VRY 7T-WRY
BT-21	200T	F-WKVS 7T-VRZ 7T-WRZ
BT-22	200T	N1841K JA8829 N140RL
BT-23	B200T	N312D VH-LAB
BT-24	B200T	N1845W (9M-JPE) 9M-JPD
BT-25	B200T	N2795B AE574 (Peruvian Navy) [may have been re-serialled AT-574]
BT-26	B200T	N2826B AE575 (Peruvian Navy) [may have been re-serialled AT-575]
BT-27	B200T	N2854B (AE576) (Peruvian Navy) N7244N D-CACB
BT-28	B200T	N1846M JA8833 N170RL
BT-29	B200T$	N150BA N120PR
BT-30	B200T	N6923L 4R-HVE CR841 (Sri Lankan AF) CR842 (Sri Lankan AF)
BT-31	B200T	N72392 JA8854
BT-32	B200T	N3184A JA8860
BT-33	B200T	CC-EAG CC-PTS CC-DSS N5111B N600RD HP-1316 N941B *PR-MPJ
BT-34	B200T	N56361 F-GMLT
BT-35	B200T	N15509 M41-01 (Royal Malaysian AF)
BT-36	B200T	N80024 M41-02 (Royal Malaysian AF)
BT-37	B200T	N80027 M41-03 (Royal Malaysian AF)
BT-38	B200T	N80048 M41-04 (Royal Malaysian AF)
BT-39	B200T	N32268 622 (Israeli DF/AF)
BT-40	B200T	N44717 625 (Israeli DF/AF)
BT-41	B200T	N44721 629 (Israeli DF/AF)
BT-42	B200T	N44724 633 (Israeli DF/AF)
BT-43	B200T	N42327 636 (Israeli DF/AF)
BT-44	B200T	N51214 721 (Israeli DF/AF)
BT-45	B200T	N44869 730 (Israeli DF/AF)
BT-46	B200T	N61346 735 (Israeli DF/AF)

Production complete

BEECH C-12C/A200 SUPER KING AIR

$ = Raisbeck dual aft body strakes fitted
^ - Blackhawk XPR61 engine upgrade fitted

c/n	Series/Mod	Identities
BC-1	C-12C	73-22250 (US Army)[wfu c1996 Fort Rucker-Cairns AAF, AL, USA]
BC-2	C-12C	73-22251 (US Army) N7064B N783MC
BC-3	C-12C	73-22252 (US Army) N7247Y
BC-4	C-12C	73-22253 (US Army) N72470
BC-5	C-12C	73-22254 (US Army) N540SP
BC-6	C-12C	73-22255 (US Army) N530SP N34UP
BC-7	C-12C$	73-22256 (US Army) N253AG N380SA N40R
BC-8	C-12C$	73-22257 (US Army) N999SP N9998P [canx 24Jan05 as exported to Colombia; reinstated 18Mar05; never registered in Colombia]
BC-9	C-12C	73-22261 (US Army) N1560
BC-10	C-12C$	73-22262 (US Army)
BC-11	C-12C	73-22263 (US Army) N72472
BC-12	C-12C	73-22264 (US Army) N254AG N48A (N9TW) N48A
BC-13	C-12C	73-22265 (US Army) N7068B
BC-14	C-12C	73-22258 (US Army) N381PD [wfu; canx 30Aug06]
BC-15	C-12C	73-22259 (US Army) N382PD N222DM N851EM
BC-16	C-12C	73-22260 (US Army) N1559
BC-17	C-12C	73-22266 (US Army) N7074G

BEECH C-12

c/n	Series/Mod	Identities
BC-18	C-12C$	73-22267 (US Army)(N12003) N465MC N505FK
BC-19	C-12C	73-22268 (US Army) N634B
BC-20	C-12C	73-22269 (US Army) N1558
BC-21	C-12C	76-22545 (US Army) N1554
BC-22	C-12C	76-22546 (US Army) N138BC N200NG N703JR
BC-23	C-12C	76-22547 (US Army) N200LW N396SA XA- [canx 20Feb08 as exported to Mexico]
BC-24	C-12C	76-22548 (US Army) N716GA N145MJ
BC-25	C-12C$	76-22549 (US Army) N1172J N200NY
BC-26	C-12C	76-22550 (US Army) N72476
BC-27	C-12C	76-22551 (US Army)
BC-28	C-12C$	76-22552 (US Army) N20AU N28AU (ZS-LES) N213UV N42Z
BC-29	C-12C	76-22553 (US Army) N255AG N612SA (N42J) N612SA
BC-30	C-12C	76-22554 (US Army) N1553
BC-31	C-12C	76-22555 (US Army) N41R
BC-32	C-12C	76-22556 (US Army) N2MP N21DZ
BC-33	C-12C	76-22557 (US Army) N225LH
BC-34	C-12C	401 (Greek Army)
BC-35	C-12C$	76-22558 (US Army) N7067B N283B
BC-36	C-12C	76-22559 (US Army)
BC-37	C-12C	76-22560 (US Army) N256AG N391SA "N168D" FAN002 (Nicaraguan AF) [canx 18Oct04 as exported to Venezuela; seized 27Nov04 in Colombia wearing false marks N168D]
BC-38	C-12C	76-22561 (US Army)
BC-39	C-12C	76-22562 (US Army) N1551
BC-40	C-12C$	76-22563 (US Army) N7066D
BC-41	C-12C	76-22564 (US Army) N257AG N101CS
BC-42	C-12C	77-22931 (US Army) N116SP N6SP N1SP
BC-43	C-12C	77-22932 (US Army)
BC-44	C-12C$	77-22933 (US Army) N258AG
BC-45	C-12C	77-22934 (US Army) N1549
BC-46	C-12C	77-22935 (US Army)
BC-47	C-12C$	77-22936 (US Army) N103BN N46X
BC-48	C-12C	77-22937 (US Army) N45A
BC-49	C-12C	77-22938 (US Army) N635B
BC-50	C-12C	77-22939 (US Army) N1547
BC-51	C-12C	77-22940 (US Army) N48JA [missing 10Jan03 on flight between Caracas & Charallave, Venezuela; assumed w/o or stolen]
BC-52	C-12C	77-22941 (US Army)
BC-53	C-12C	77-22942 (US Army)
BC-54	C-12C	77-22943 (US Army) N7069A
BC-55	C-12C	77-22944 (US Army)
BC-56	C-12C+	77-22945 (US Army) N771AK N46L
BC-57	C-12C$	77-22946 (US Army) N118CA N7308B N215HP *N215SB
BC-58	C-12C	77-22947 (US Army) N1546
BC-59	C-12C	77-22948 (US Army) N229EM [wfu cDec02, parts to MTW Aerospace, Montgomery, AL, USA; canx 03Feb06]
BC-60	C-12C	77-22949 (US Army)
BC-61	C-12C	77-22950 (US Army) N636B
BC-62	C-12C$	78-23126 (US Army) N637B
BC-63	C-12C	78-23127 (US Army) N712GA HP- [canx 11Aug04 as exported to Panama]
BC-64	C-12C$	78-23128 (US Army)
BC-65	C-12C$	78-23129 (US Army) N638B PP-LCB
BC-66	C-12C$	78-23130 (US Army) N66000
BC-67	C-12C+^	78-23131 (US Army) N639B N20LM
BC-68	C-12C$	78-23132 (US Army) 823132 (US Navy)
BC-69	C-12C$	78-23133 (US Army) 823133 (US Navy)
BC-70	C-12C$	78-23134 (US Army) N321F
BC-71	C-12C$	78-23135 (US Army)
BC-72	C-12C	78-23136 (US Army) N200EJ N30W N1149W
BC-73	C-12C	78-23137 (US Army) N200ET
BC-74	C-12C#	78-23138 (US Army) N121TD
BC-75	C-12C	78-23139 (US Army) N259AG N900RF N700TG

Production complete

BEECH C-12C/A200 SUPER KING AIR

$ = Raisbeck dual aft body strakes fitted

c/n	Series/Mod	Identities
BD-1	C-12C	73-1205 (USAF) N11
BD-2	C-12C$	N4998Z 73-1206 (US Army) N200EA N390SA N49R
BD-3	C-12C	N49984 73-1207 (USAF) N140MT N311KB
BD-4	C-12C$	73-1208 (US Army)
BD-5	C-12C$	N4999H 73-1209 (US Army) N9008U 9Q-CAJ
BD-6	C-12C	73-1210 (USAF) [std Davis-Monthan AFB, AZ, USA; storage code AACE0005]
BD-7	C-12C	73-1211 (USAF) [w/o 31Jan79 Esfahan, Iran]
BD-8	C-12C	73-1212 (USAF) N12
BD-9	C-12C	73-1213 (USAF) N121CA
BD-10	C-12C	73-1214 (USAF)
BD-11	C-12C	73-1215 (USAF)
BD-12	C-12C	73-1216 (USAF)
BD-13	C-12C	73-1217 (USAF)
BD-14	C-12C	73-1218 (USAF)
BD-15	C-12C	76-0158 (USAF)
BD-16	C-12C$	76-0159 (USAF) N60159 N1184U [b/u; canx 14Mar03]
BD-17	C-12C	76-0160 (USAF)
BD-18	C-12C	76-0161 (USAF)
BD-19	C-12C	76-0162 (USAF)
BD-20	C-12C	76-0163 (USAF) N8079B 76-0163 (USAF)
BD-21	C-12C	76-0164 (USAF)
BD-22	C-12C	76-0165 (USAF)
BD-23	C-12C	76-0166 (USAF)
BD-24	C-12C	76-0167 (USAF) 76-3239 (USAF)
BD-25	C-12C	76-0168 (USAF)
BD-26	C-12C	76-0169 (US Army) N49K
BD-27	C-12C	76-0170 (USAF)
BD-28	C-12C	76-0171 (USAF)
BD-29	C-12C$	76-0172 (USAF) 760172 (US Navy)
BD-30	C-12C	76-0173 (USAF) [std Davis-Monthan AFB, AZ, USA; storage code AACE0007]

Production complete

BEECH C-12B/B200 SUPER KING AIR

c/n	Series/Mod	Identities
BJ-1	UC-12B	161185 (US Navy) [pres Corpus Christi NAS, TX, USA]
BJ-2	UC-12B	161186 (US Navy) [std Davis-Monthan AFB, AZ, USA; storage code AN5G0011]
BJ-3	UC-12B	161187 (US Navy) N528NA
BJ-4	UC-12B	161188 (US Navy) [std Davis-Monthan AFB, AZ, USA; storage code AN5G0019]
BJ-5	UC-12B	161189 (US Navy) [w/o 02Jan82 nr Pensacola, FL, USA]
BJ-6	UC-12B	161190 (US Navy)
BJ-7	UC-12B	161191 (US Navy)
BJ-8	UC-12B	161192 (US Navy) [std Davis-Monthan AFB, AZ, USA; storage code AN5G0020]
BJ-9	UC-12B	161193 (US Navy)
BJ-10	UC-12B	161194 (US Navy) N325AT [std Davis-Monthan AFB, AZ, USA; storage code AN5G0016]
BJ-11	UC-12B	161195 (US Navy)
BJ-12	UC-12B	161196 (US Navy)
BJ-13	UC-12B	161197 (US Navy)
BJ-14	UC-12B	161198 (US Navy) [wfu, parts to Western Int'l Parts, Tuscon, AZ, USA]
BJ-15	TC-12B	161199 (US Navy) N146AW [std Davis-Monthan AFB, AZ, USA; storage code AN5G0015]
BJ-16	TC-12B	161200 (US Navy) N324BS [std Davis-Monthan AFB, AZ, USA; storage code AN5G0021]
BJ-17	TC-12B	161201 (US Navy)
BJ-18	UC-12B	161202 (US Navy) [std Davis-Monthan AFB, AZ, USA; storage code AN5G0003]
BJ-19	UC-12B	161203 (US Navy)
BJ-20	UC-12B	161204 (US Navy) [std Davis-Monthan AFB, AZ, USA; storage code AN5G0022]
BJ-21	UC-12B	161205 (US Navy)
BJ-22	UC-12B	161206 (US Navy)
BJ-23	UC-12B	161306 (US Navy)
BJ-24	UC-12B	161307 (US Navy) [std Davis-Monthan AFB, AZ, USA; storage code AN5G0025]
BJ-25	UC-12B	161308 (US Navy) [std Davis-Monthan AFB, AZ, USA; storage code AN5G0013]
BJ-26	UC-12B	161309 (US Navy)
BJ-27	UC-12B	161310 (US Navy)
BJ-28	UC-12B	161311 (US Navy)
BJ-29	UC-12B	161312 (US Navy)
BJ-30	UC-12B	161313 (US Navy)
BJ-31	UC-12B	161314 (US Navy)
BJ-32	TC-12B	161315 (US Navy)
BJ-33	TC-12B	161316 (US Navy)
BJ-34	UC-12B	161317 (US Navy) [std Davis-Monthan AFB, AZ, USA; storage code AN5G0026]
BJ-35	UC-12B	161318 (US Navy)
BJ-36	UC-12B	161319 (US Navy)
BJ-37	UC-12B	161320 (US Navy)
BJ-38	UC-12B	161321 (US Navy) [std Davis-Monthan AFB, AZ, USA; storage code AN5G0007]
BJ-39	UC-12B	161322 (US Navy) [std Davis-Monthan AFB, AZ, USA; storage code AN5G0014]

c/n	Series/Mod	Identities		
BJ-40	UC-12B	161323 (US Navy)		
BJ-41	UC-12B	161324 (US Navy)		
BJ-42	UC-12B	161325 (US Navy)		
BJ-43	UC-12B	161326 (US Navy)		
BJ-44	UC-12B	161327 (US Navy)	[b/u cSep98 at Western Int'l Air Parts, Tucson, AZ, USA; ex AMARC 5G0006]	
BJ-45	UC-12B	161497 (US Navy)		
BJ-46	TC-12B	161498 (US Navy)		
BJ-47	UC-12B	161499 (US Navy)	[std Davis-Monthan AFB, AZ, USA; storage code AN5G0004]	
BJ-48	UC-12B	161500 (US Navy)		
BJ-49	UC-12B	161501 (US Navy)		
BJ-50	UC-12B	161502 (US Navy)		
BJ-51	UC-12B	161503 (US Navy)	[std Davis-Monthan AFB, AZ, USA; storage code AN5G0024]	
BJ-52	UC-12B	161504 (US Navy)		
BJ-53	UC-12B	161505 (US Navy)		
BJ-54	UC-12B	161506 (US Navy)	[std Davis-Monthan AFB, AZ, USA; storage code AN5G0018; soc 28Feb05]	
BJ-55	UC-12B	161507 (US Navy)		
BJ-56	TC-12B	161508 (US Navy)		
BJ-57	TC-12B	161509 (US Navy)		
BJ-58	TC-12B	161510 (US Navy)	N324PS	[std Davis-Monthan AFB, AZ, USA; storage code AN5G0028]
BJ-59	UC-12B	161511 (US Navy)		
BJ-60	UC-12B	161512 (US Navy)		
BJ-61	UC-12B	161513 (US Navy)		
BJ-62	UC-12B	161514 (US Navy)		
BJ-63	UC-12B	161515 (US Navy)		
BJ-64	UC-12B	161516 (US Navy)	[std Davis-Monthan AFB, AZ, USA; storage code AN5G0012]	
BJ-65	UC-12B	161517 (US Navy)		
BJ-66	TC-12B	161518 (US Navy)		

Production complete

BEECH C-12D/B200 SUPER KING AIR

$ = Raisbeck dual aft body strakes fitted

c/n	Series/Mod	Identities		
BP-1	C-12D$	78-23140 (US Army)		
BP-2	C-12D	[completed as c/n GR-6]		
BP-3	C-12D	[completed as c/n GR-7]		
BP-4	C-12D	[completed as c/n GR-8]		
BP-5	C-12D	[completed as c/n GR-9]		
BP-6	C-12D	[completed as c/n GR-10]		
BP-7	RC-12D	81-23638 (USAF)	974/4X-FSA (Israeli DF/AF)	
BP-8	RC-12D	81-23639 (USAF)	977/4X-FSB (Israeli DF/AF)	
BP-9	RC-12D	81-23640 (USAF)	980/4X-FSC (Israeli DF/AF)	
BP-10	RC-12D	81-23641 (USAF)	982/4X-FSD (Israeli DF/AF)	
BP-11	RC-12D	81-23642 (USAF)	985/4X-FSE (Israeli DF/AF)	
BP-12	C-12D	[completed as c/n GR-2]		
BP-13	C-12D	[completed as c/n FC-3]		
BP-14	C-12D	[completed as c/n GR-4]		
BP-15	C-12D	[completed as c/n GR-12]		
BP-16	C-12D	[completed as c/n GR-5]		
BP-17	C-12D	[completed as c/n GR-11]		
BP-18	C-12D	[completed as c/n GR-3]		
BP-19	C-12D	[completed as c/n GR-13]		
BP-20	C-12D	[completed as c/n FC-1]		
BP-21	C-12D	[completed as c/n FC-2]		
BP-22	C-12D-1$	81-23541 (US Army)		
BP-23	RC-12D	[completed as c/n GR-1]		
BP-24	C-12D-1$	81-23543 (US Army)	N463DF	
BP-25	C-12D-1$	81-23544 (US Army)		
BP-26	C-12D-1$	81-23545 (US Army)	N50515	
BP-27	C-12D-1$	81-23546 (US Army)	N459DF	
BP-28	C-12D-1$	82-23780 (US Army)	N301PT	
BP-29	C-12D-1$	82-23781 (US Army)	N461DF	
BP-30	C-12D$	82-23782 (US Army)	N302PT	N40Y
BP-31	C-12D-1$	82-23783 (US Army)		
BP-32	C-12D-1$	82-23784 (US Army)		
BP-33	C-12D-1$	82-23785 (US Army)		
BP-34	C-12D-1$	83-24145 (US Army)		
BP-35	C-12D-1$	83-24146 (US Army)		
BP-36	C-12D-1$	83-24147 (US Army)		
BP-37	C-12D-1$	83-24148 (US Army)		
BP-38	C-12D-1$	83-24149 (US Army)		
BP-39	C-12D-1$	83-24150 (US Army)		
BP-40	C-12D	83-0494 (USAF)		
BP-41	C-12D	83-0495 (USAF)		
BP-42	C-12D	83-0496 (USAF)		

c/n	Series/Mod	Identities
BP-43	C-12D	83-0497 (USAF)
BP-44	C-12D	83-0498 (USAF)
BP-45	C-12D	83-0499 (USAF)
BP-46	C-12U-2$	84-24375 (US Army)
BP-47	C-12U-2$	84-24376 (US Army)
BP-48	C-12U-2$	84-24377 (US Army)
BP-49	C-12U-2$	84-24378 (US Army)
BP-50	C-12D$	84-24379 (US Army)
BP-51	C-12U-2$	84-24380 (US Army)
BP-52	C-12D	85-1261 (US Army) [w/o 12Nov92 nr Juneau, AK, USA]
BP-53	C-12T-1$	85-1262 (US Army)
BP-54	C-12T-1$	85-1263 (US Army)
BP-55	C-12T-1$	85-1264 (US Army)
BP-56	C-12T-1$	85-1265 (US Army)
BP-57	C-12T-1$	85-1266 (US Army)
BP-58	C-12T-1$	85-1267 (US Army)
BP-59	C-12T-1$	85-1268 (US Army)
BP-60	C-12F	85-1269 (US Army) [w/o 11Jan92 Corumba, Mato Grosso do Sul, Brazil]
BP-61	C-12T-1$	85-1270 (US Army)
BP-62	C-12T-1$	85-1271 (US Army)
BP-63	C-12T-1$	85-1272 (US Army)
BP-64	C-12T-2	86-0084 (US Army)
BP-65	C-12T-2$	86-0085 (US Army)
BP-66	C-12T-2$	86-0086 (US Army)
BP-67	C-12T-2$	86-0087 (US Army)
BP-68	C-12T-2$	86-0088 (US Army)
BP-69	C-12T-2$	86-0089 (US Army)
BP-70	C-12T-2$	87-0160 (US Army)
BP-71	C-12T-2$	87-0161 (US Army)

Production complete

BEECH UC-12F/B200C SUPER KING AIR

c/n	Series/Mod	Identities
BU-1	UC-12F	163553 (US Navy)
BU-2	UC-12F	163554 (US Navy)
BU-3	UC-12F	163555 (US Navy)
BU-4	UC-12F	163556 (US Navy)
BU-5	UC-12F	163557 (US Navy)
BU-6	UC-12F	163558 (US Navy)
BU-7	UC-12F	163559 (US Navy)
BU-8	UC-12F	163560 (USMC)
BU-9	UC-12F	163561 (US Navy)
BU-10	UC-12F	163562 (US Navy)
BU-11	UC-12F	N2392B 163563 (US Navy)
BU-12	UC-12F	163564 (US Navy) [std Davis-Monthan AFB, AZ, USA; storage code AN5G0023]

Production complete

BEECH UC-12M/B200C SUPER KING AIR

c/n	Series/Mod	Identities
BV-1	UC-12M	163836 (US Navy)
BV-2	UC-12M	163837 (US Navy)
BV-3	UC-12M	163838 (US Navy)
BV-4	UC-12M	163839 (US Navy)
BV-5	UC-12M	163840 (US Navy)
BV-6	UC-12M	163841 (US Navy)
BV-7	UC-12M	163842 (US Navy)
BV-8	UC-12M	163843 (US Navy)
BV-9	UC-12M	163844 (US Navy)
BV-10	UC-12M	163845 (US Navy)
BV-11	UC-12M	163846 (US Navy) N4ZB
BV-12	UC-12M	163847 (US Navy) [std Davis-Monthan AFB, AZ, USA; storage code AN5G0017]

Production complete

BEECH C-12R/B200C SUPER KING AIR

c/n	Series/Mod	Identities
BW-1	C-12F$	N2843B 92-3327 (US Army)
BW-2	C-12F$	N2844B 92-3328 (US Army)
BW-3	C-12F$	N2845B 92-3329 (US Army)
BW-4	C-12R$	94-0315 (US Army)
BW-5	C-12R$	94-0316 (US Army)
BW-6	C-12R$	94-0317 (US Army)
BW-7	C-12R$	94-0318 (US Army)
BW-8	C-12R$	94-0319 (US Army)
BW-9	C-12R$	94-0320 (US Army)
BW-10	C-12R$	94-0321 (US Army)
BW-11	C-12R$	94-0322 (US Army)
BW-12	C-12R$	94-0323 (US Army)
BW-13	C-12R$	94-0324 (US Army)
BW-14	C-12R$	94-0325 (US Army)
BW-15	C-12R$	94-0326 (US Army)
BW-16	C-12R$	95-0088 (US Army)
BW-17	C-12R$	95-0089 (US Army)
BW-18	C-12R$	95-0090 (US Army)
BW-19	C-12R$	95-0091 (US Army)
BW-20	C-12R$	95-0092 (US Army)
BW-21	C-12R$	95-0093 (US Army)
BW-22	C-12R$	95-0094 (US Army)
BW-23	C-12R$	95-0095 (US Army)
BW-24	C-12R$	95-0096 (US Army)
BW-25	C-12R$	95-0097 (US Army)
BW-26	C-12R$	95-0098 (US Army)
BW-27	C-12R$	95-0099 (US Army)
BW-28	RC-12R$	95-0100 (US Army)
BW-29	RC-12R$	95-0101 (US Army)

Production complete

BEECH RC-12/B200 SUPER KING AIR

c/n	Series/Mod	Identities
FC-1	RC-12G	80-23379 (US Army)[pres Fort Bliss, TX, USA]
FC-2	JRC-12G$	80-23380 (US Army)
FC-3	RC-12G	80-23372 (US Army)[pres Fort Huachuca, AZ, USA]

Production complete

BEECH RC-12/B200 SUPER KING AIR

c/n	Series/Mod	Identities
FE-1	RC-12K	85-0147 (US Army)
FE-2	RC-12K	85-0148 (US Army)
FE-3	RC-12K	85-0149 (US Army)
FE-4	RC-12K	85-0150 (US Army)
FE-5	RC-12K	85-0151 (US Army) [w/o 06Nov98 Sommerhausen, Germany]
FE-6	RC-12K	85-0152 (US Army)
FE-7	RC-12K	85-0153 (US Army)
FE-8	RC-12K	85-0154 (US Army) [w/o 26Mar01 Nuremberg, Germany]
FE-9	RC-12K	85-0155 (US Army)
FE-10	RC-12N	88-0325 (US Army)
FE-11	RC-12N	88-0326 (US Army)
FE-12	RC-12N	88-0327 (US Army)
FE-13	RC-12N	89-0267 (US Army)
FE-14	RC-12N	89-0268 (US Army)
FE-15	RC-12N	89-0269 (US Army)
FE-16	RC-12N	89-0270 (US Army)
FE-17	RC-12N	89-0271 (US Army)
FE-18	RC-12N	89-0272 (US Army) [w/o 16Apr97 Ossabaw Island, CA, USA]
FE-19	RC-12N	89-0273 (US Army)
FE-20	RC-12N	89-0274 (US Army)
FE-21	RC-12N	89-0275 (US Army)
FE-22	RC-12N	89-0276 (US Army)
FE-23	RC-12N	91-0516 (US Army)
FE-24	RC-12N	91-0517 (US Army)
FE-25	RC-12N	91-0518 (US Army)
FE-26	RC-12P	92-13120 (US Army)
FE-27	RC-12P	92-13121 (US Army)
FE-28	RC-12P	92-13122 (US Army)
FE-29	RC-12P	92-13123 (US Army)

c/n	Series/Mod	Identities
FE-30	RC-12P	92-13124 (US Army)
FE-31	RC-12P	92-13125 (US Army)
FE-32	RC-12P	93-0697 (US Army)
FE-33	RC-12P	93-0698 (US Army)
FE-34	RC-12P	93-0699 (US Army)
FE-35	RC-12P	93-0700 (US Army)
FE-36	RC-12P	93-0701 (US Army)

Production complete

BEECH RC-12/B200 SUPER KING AIR

c/n	Series/Mod	Identities
FG-1	RC-12K	987/4X-FSF (Israeli DF/AF)
FG-2	RC-12K	990/4X-FSG (Israeli DF/AF)

Production complete

BEECH RC-12/A200CT SUPER KING AIR

c/n	Series/Mod	Identities
GR-1	RC-12D	81-23542 (US Army)
GR-2	RC-12D	80-23371 (US Army)
GR-3	RC-12D$	80-23377 (US Army)
GR-4	RC-12D	80-23373 (US Army)
GR-5	RC-12D	80-23375 (US Army)
GR-6	RC-12D	78-23141 (US Army)
GR-7	RC-12D	78-23142 (US Army)
GR-8	RC-12D	78-23143 (US Army)
GR-9	RC-12D	78-23144 (US Army)
GR-10	RC-12D$	78-23145 (US Army) N321P
GR-11	RC-12D	80-23376 (US Army) [std Fort Rucker-Cairns AAF, AL, USA]
GR-12	RC-12D	80-23374 (US Army)
GR-13	RC-12D$	80-23378 (US Army)
GR-14	RC-12H	83-24313 (US Army)
GR-15	RC-12H	83-24314 (US Army)
GR-16	RC-12H	83-24315 (US Army)
GR-17	RC-12H	83-24316 (US Army)
GR-18	RC-12H	83-24317 (US Army)
GR-19	RC-12H	83-24318 (US Army)

Production complete

BEECH 200GT SUPER KING AIR

$ = Raisbeck dual aft body strakes fitted
# = Raisbeck nacelle wing lockers fitted
+ = Raisbeck dual aft body strakes and nacelle wing lockers fitted
(WL) = Enhanced Aero winglets fitted

c/n	Series/Mod	Identities			
BY-1	200GT	N801GT	LV-BMO		
BY-2	200GT#	N802GT	N175PL		
BY-3	200GT	N803GT	SP-DSA		
BY-4	200GT	N404GT	N384GD		
BY-5	200GT	N440WW			
BY-6	200GT	N3206T	XA-	[canx 25Jan08 as exported to Mexico]	
BY-7	200GT	N708WH			
BY-8	200GT	N34008	VH-KGT	9M-WSK	
BY-9	200GT	N909GT	PR-JUB		
BY-10	200GT+	N792BP			
BY-11	200GT	N3311N	N106PA		
BY-12	200GT	N34712	LV-BMS		
BY-13	200GT	N3213L	PR-WIT		
BY-14	200GT	N34004	G-WATJ		
BY-15	200GT+	N33885	PR-TRD		
BY-16	200GT#	N32166	F-HSFA		
BY-17	200GT	N32017	N555MC		
BY-18	200GT#	N24HD			
BY-19	200GT	N3189D	C-52 (Chilean Police)		
BY-20	200GT	N531SC			
BY-21	200GT	N34651	PR-ARN		
BY-22	200GT	N33122	OM-FUN		
BY-23	200GT	N34923	F-HSYN		
BY-24	200GT#	N510LA			
BY-25	200GT	N99ML			
BY-26	200GT#	N3326Q	N22KL		
BY-27	200GT	N626GT			
BY-28	200GT	N32928	N745ML		
BY-29	200GT+(WL)	N32029	YV352T		
BY-30	200GT#	N94CK			
BY-31	200GT	N3331C	PP-PPC		
BY-32	200GT	N32EU	G-RAFD	*ZK458	
BY-33	200GT	N3203T	OM-VPR		
BY-34	200GT	N925GA			
BY-35	200GT#(WL)	N538RB			
BY-36	200GT	N3196N	G-RAFX	*ZK459	
BY-37	200GT	N370LH	N1931C		
BY-38	200GT	N3338H	LV-BPJ		
BY-39	200GT#	N332M			
BY-40	200GT+	N329MH			
BY-41	200GT	N41EU	N225SL		
BY-42	200GT	N142GT	N160AD		
BY-43	200GT	N32643			
BY-44	200GT+	N550EC			
BY-45	200GT$(WL)	N3345Y	PR-BHB		
BY-46	200GT$(WL)	N3196J	ZS-TWP		
BY-47	200GT	N3347J	LV-BRD		
BY-48	200GT#(WL)	N666YC			
BY-49	200GT$	N912JS			
BY-50	200GT$	N3270V	D-IKAH		
BY-51	200GT	N3251Q	PR-DOC		
BY-52	200GT+	N10CW			
BY-53	200GT+	N618HG	N33LA		
BY-54	200GT+	N900VM			
BY-55	200GT$	N3455L	F-HDJM		
BY-56	200GT$	N3486S	(LN-GHN)	(LN-BJG)	N3486S
BY-57	200GT+(WL)	N34857	D-IBSH		
BY-58	200GT	N878GT			
BY-59	200GT+(WL)	N3499U	CC-CFG		
BY-60	200GT	N3400P	VH-YBP		
BY-61	200GT	N47RM	N362SC		
BY-62	200GT$	N62GT			
BY-63	200GT	N3502P	LV-BSP		
BY-64	200GT	N34177	N181MP		
BY-65	200GT	N465GT			
BY-66	200GT	N31CG			
BY-67	200GT+(WL)	N9988C			
BY-68	200GT$	N3308E	(PR-CFA)	G-SYGB	
BY-69	200GT+(WL)	N42SV	N902SH		
BY-70	200GT	N3420J			
BY-71	200GT	N3471T	PR-ESP		
BY-72	200GT	N60322	PT-SBM		
BY-73	200GT	N227MW			
BY-74	200GT(WL)	N174GT	N703RM		
BY-75	200GT+(WL)	N61675	D-IBTA		
BY-76	200GT+	N64276	C-GJDI		

BEECH 200GT

c/n	Series/Mod	Identities		
BY-77	200GT	N227MW	N227MV	
BY-78	200GT	N766LF		
BY-79	200GT	N63799	*PR-UNI	
BY-80	200GT#	N63980		
BY-81	200GT	N63881	AP-	[canx 09Jun09 as exported to Pakistan]
BY-82	200GT	N82EU		
BY-83	200GT	N321BF		
BY-84	200GT	N6184L	*PP-NTX	
BY-85	200GT	N61285		
BY-86	200GT	N63686		
BY-87	200GT			
BY-88	200GT			
BY-89	200GT	N63989		
BY-90	200GT			
BY-91	200GT			
BY-92	200GT			
BY-93	200GT			
BY-94	200GT			
BY-95	200GT			
BY-96	200GT			
BY-97	200GT			
BY-98	200GT			
BY-99	200GT			
BY-100	200GT			
BY-101	200GT			
BY-102	200GT			
BY-103	200GT			
BY-104	200GT			
BY-105	200GT			
BY-106	200GT			
BY-107	200GT			
BY-108	200GT			
BY-109	200GT			
BY-110	200GT			
BY-111	200GT			
BY-112	200GT			
BY-113	200GT			
BY-114	200GT			
BY-115	200GT			
BY-116	200GT			
BY-117	200GT			
BY-118	200GT			
BY-119	200GT			
BY-120	200GT			
BY-121	200GT			
BY-122	200GT			
BY-123	200GT			
BY-124	200GT			
BY-125	200GT			
BY-126	200GT			
BY-127	200GT			
BY-128	200GT			
BY-129	200GT			
BY-130	200GT			
BY-131	200GT			
BY-132	200GT			
BY-133	200GT			
BY-134	200GT			
BY-135	200GT			
BY-136	200GT			
BY-137	200GT			
BY-138	200GT			
BY-139	200GT			
BY-140	200GT			
BY-141	200GT			
BY-142	200GT			
BY-143	200GT			
BY-144	200GT			
BY-145	200GT			
BY-146	200GT			
BY-147	200GT			
BY-148	200GT			
BY-149	200GT			
BY-150	200GT			
BY-151	200GT			
BY-152	200GT			
BY-153	200GT			
BY-154	200GT			
BY-155	200GT			
BY-156	200GT			
BY-157	200GT			

c/n	Series/Mod	Identities
BY-158	200GT	
BY-159	200GT	
BY-160	200GT	
BY-161	200GT	
BY-162	200GT	
BY-163	200GT	
BY-164	200GT	
BY-165	200GT	
BY-166	200GT	
BY-167	200GT	
BY-168	200GT	
BY-169	200GT	
BY-170	200GT	
BY-171	200GT	
BY-172	200GT	
BY-173	200GT	
BY-174	200GT	
BY-175	200GT	
BY-176	200GT	
BY-177	200GT	
BY-178	200GT	
BY-179	200GT	
BY-180	200GT	
BY-181	200GT	
BY-182	200GT	
BY-183	200GT	
BY-184	200GT	
BY-185	200GT	
BY-186	200GT	
BY-187	200GT	
BY-188	200GT	
BY-189	200GT	
BY-190	200GT	
BY-191	200GT	
BY-192	200GT	
BY-193	200GT	
BY-194	200GT	
BY-195	200GT	
BY-196	200GT	
BY-197	200GT	
BY-198	200GT	
BY-199	200GT	
BY-200	200GT	

BEECH 200CGT SUPER KING AIR

c/n	Series/Mod	Identities
BZ-1	200CGT	
BZ-2	200CGT	
BZ-3	200CGT	
BZ-4	200CGT	
BZ-5	200CGT	
BZ-6	200CGT	
BZ-7	200CGT	
BZ-8	200CGT	
BZ-9	200CGT	
BZ-10	200CGT	
BZ-11	200CGT	
BZ-12	200CGT	
BZ-13	200CGT	
BZ-14	200CGT	
BZ-15	200CGT	
BZ-16	200CGT	
BZ-17	200CGT	
BZ-18	200CGT	
BZ-19	200CGT	
BZ-20	200CGT	
BZ-21	200CGT	
BZ-22	200CGT	
BZ-23	200CGT	
BZ-24	200CGT	
BZ-25	200CGT	

BEECH 300/300LW SUPER KING AIR

$ = Raisbeck dual aft body strakes fitted
# = Raisbeck nacelle wing lockers fitted
+ = Raisbeck dual aft body strakes and nacelle wing lockers fitted
(WL) = BLR winglets fitted

c/n	Series/Mod	Identities
FA-1	300#	N6642B [cvtd to Beech 350 prototype; canx 02Mar09]
FA-2	300+	N300KA N300KK C-GPGI N300KK N32323 N124BB N32PB C-GFES N251LL
FA-3	300#	N67683 N135MK
FA-4	300$	N6790W N111SS
FA-5	300+(WL)	N6823M (N101L) N444HC N444HK N224BB N200WB N313SA
FA-6	300+	N104AW N207RP N39FL N64SS N821TB
FA-7	300#	N6923Y ZS-LRG N925AD F-GJCD N800EB N800RE
FA-8	300+(WL)	N300PK N826MA N52LP
FA-9	300$(WL)	N930G N302NC YV [canx 24Dec08 as exported to Venezuela]
FA-10	300	N84BA N85TT (F-GFVY) N7031T F-GFVY N7031T N13PD YV-98CP HK-3828X HK-3828W
FA-11	300	N732P N132CC N300BT
FA-12	300	N7202Y
FA-13	300	N7202Z N6669M N300TJ (N301GC) (N500GC) N300PR
FA-14	300	N7204D N302HC XA-VID XA-POY N450AC XB-HHA
FA-15	300	N505WR [stolen 17Feb96 Deland Municipal-Sidney H Taylor Field, FL, USA]
FA-16	300	N846BE
FA-17	300#	N6804M N71FA N58ES
FA-18	300	N399D N4200K N4200S N63LB N63LP N163BA
FA-19	300	N316KA N101PC N102PG N888BR N300TE
FA-20	300	N7228T
FA-21	300	N7206L N4000K N4600K (N800RD) N914BH
FA-22	300	N72069 HK-4150X "HK-3397-X" FAC5625 (Colombian AF) FAC5750 (Colombian AF) [stolen 02Aug87 Boca Raton, FL, USA; canx 14Jun96 as exported to Colombia; impounded 02Feb98 wearing false reg HK-3397-X & canx 07Oct98]
FA-23	300	N7208H N313MB N313MP N141SM
FA-24	300	N300KA N124CM
FA-25	300LW+	N7225B N7CR N147CC N147CA SE-LCT N856GA ZS-PAZ
FA-26	300	N984CF PJ-TES PT-OLI [stolen 01Jan93 in Brazil; never recovered; canx]
FA-27	300$	N205R N205K N300PE N203RR
FA-28	300	N7215J N481NS N401NS
FA-29	300+	N72146 N300HV N828JC N970KK
FA-30	300$(WL)	N917BH N7178H N70CR N642JL
FA-31	300	N7216A PT-LNJ HK-3689X HK-3689 PT-LNJ PP-EJO
FA-32	300#	N6PW N100BE N100BZ
FA-33	300+	N7224M N85RR N250PD N311RF N262SP
FA-34	300	N865M N100FL
FA-35	300#	N26JP N312DB
FA-36	300#	N206R N206K
FA-37	300+	N7218Y N600LP N2DB
FA-38	300$	N6812W
FA-39	300+	G-SRES HK-3463X HK-3463 N339WD C-GHQG
FA-40	300$(WL)	N72188 N1MC N52C YV [canx 05Mar08 as exported to Venezuela]
FA-41	300	N72180 N300LM HK-3495X HK-3495 FAP-18 (Peruvian AF)
FA-42	300$(WL)	(N852BE) N16TB (N5513E) N16TE N791X N72DK N385KA
FA-43	300+(WL)	N7291Y N85TH N827CC N827CA
FA-44	300	N48HB N48EB N20KW
FA-45	300$	N7220L N223JR
FA-46	300+	N7222U N123AF
FA-47	300	N7221H XA-NAZ N961AA HK-3556X HK-3556P HK-3556W HK-3556P TG-CPG
FA-48	300$	N7221N N271BC
FA-49	300	N7224A N8VF N984SW N312DE
FA-50	300+	N7214W N202RB N85GA N214EC N629LM
FA-51	300$	N7228Z N20NL N20NK YV1675
FA-52	300	N50KA PT-MCM
FA-53	300	N736P
FA-54	300+	N72231 N1HS N663AC N920C
FA-55	300+	N7230K N101AF N40NE N40NB HC-BYY N321EC N333WC
FA-56	300$	N7231P
FA-57	300$	N7231Z N75MC N75ME
FA-58	300	N72323 N90GC N282HC N555WF N7RC N223RC
FA-59	300(WL)	N7233U N528AM
FA-60	300+	N7234B N109DS N285KA HK-3659X HK-3659 HK-3659P HP-1595
FA-61	300	N7234E N301KS [w/o 14Apr04 Daytona Beach-Spruce Creek Apt, FL, USA]
FA-62	300+	N72345 N1WV (N405P) N215P N103AL N103AD
FA-63	300+(WL)	N7235Z ZK-MGP N985GA D-IILG N35LW
FA-64	300	N7232L RP-C1890 RP-C4567 (HK-4081X) N798KA N103CW
FA-65	300	N7232Z (N400N) N332CP N555DX
FA-66	300+	N7237U N600MS N1DE N17ME N29EC N577BA N577BE
FA-67	300+(WL)	N55SC N79TE
FA-68	300+	N7244U N100UF N100Y N10QY N300SE
FA-69	300(WL)	N7245Y N19CK N92WC N300TB N531MB N531ML HK- [canx 15Sep06 as exported to Colombia]
FA-70	300	N72451 N780BF (N66FB) N780BF [w/o 14Jan99 Cullman, AZ, USA; canx 02Mar99]
FA-71	300+	N72302 ZS-LOI N7586Z
FA-72	300$(WL)	N7246K 7P-AAA ZS-MFW N72GA N82LP

BEECH 300

c/n	Series/Mod	Identities
FA-73	300$(WL)	N65558 N403G N408G N699MW
FA-74	300	N72448 G-BPCH N300TJ HK-3519X HK-3519 HK-3519W XC-AA80
FA-75	300	N7247A AN-232 (Ecuadorian Navy)
FA-76	300	N7247Y D-CASA N404SD N1BK
FA-77	300	N72472 N60TC N60TG N678SB N177JW N477JW N917WA
FA-78	300	N72479 N740PC
FA-79	300LW$(WL)	N7274Y D-COMM D-IOMM N427KW N828CA N873CA N27KG N9GS
FA-80	300+	N7249N N51JH N51UH N402NC N300HH (N257BB) PH-ACE
FA-81	300	N7250L (N125JD) N919HP
FA-82	300+(WL)	N72265 I-FIDB N4154G N36MT N788WG N488WG N154PC N15PX (N317BC) N173KS
FA-83	300	N339D XA-PES N952AA HK-3509X HK-3509 XC-AA49 XC-HGV XC-AA49
FA-84	300+	N7251K N121RH N22BD N477AE
FA-85	300	N7252H N92GC N112AB N907DB
FA-86	300	N7228C C-GIRF N955AA HK-3547X HK-3547
FA-87	300	N7253K N301CG XC-AA72 (N899EA) XC-AA72 [reportedly w/o 26Aug00 Ensenada, Baja California Sur, Mexico]
FA-88	300	N7255X N1250
FA-89	300+	N72353 N1948J N194LJ N505BC ZS-PJR N694JB
FA-90	300+(WL)	N917BH N817BH N38H N38HL N77PA (N77PZ) N111M HP-1382 N1115 N544PS N896RJ N898RJ
FA-91	300(WL)	N72583 N990PT N300MC
FA-92	300$	N2503N PT-OSZ PP-EPD
FA-93	300+	N2507U XA-PEE XA-MIX N93GA (N97DA) (N92CC) N93GA
FA-94	300	N25219 I-AZME F-GVPE LX-SEA N94GA C-FDTP
FA-95	300LW	N7259B G-OCHD N125RP HK-3536X HK-3536W XC-AA46 3971/XA-AVJ (Mexican AF)
FA-96	300	N2586E HK-3534X HK-3534W
FA-97	300	N2605L N50NL N97EB
FA-98	300$(WL)	N739P N30SM N306M
FA-99	300$	N7236C N6293V HK-4111X HP-1382 HK-4406X HK-4406
FA-100	300	N2614C HK-3648X HK-3648 [canx 31Oct97 - status?]
FA-101	300LW	G-UBSH G-BSTF HK-3654X HK-3654W HK-3654G
FA-102	300$	C-FPCC N195AL (N886DT) N195AL
FA-103	300$	N2650C N827DL (HP-1289) HP-1298 N827DL
FA-104	300LW$	N2660D ZS-LSU N215GA N310VE D-CFMC [w/o 24Oct00 Blumberg, Germany; canx 19Jun03]
FA-105	300LW	N69264 (ZK-MAB) ZK-KSL N378MF HK-3628X HK-3628W TG-MDN TG-MDN-P
FA-106	300LW+(WL)	N2686L C-GPKP N810CM N855RA N265PA
FA-107	300LW+(WL)	N27353 N365CA I-ADLA (F-GLER) CN-TNC N90GA N538AS N538AM
FA-108	300LW+	N27856 XA-PIF N654S HK-3574X HK-3574 OY-LKT N494MA
FA-109	300LW	N8133 LV-WGJ N364C N398DE [dbr 19Oct00 Concord-Buchanan Field, CA, USA, parts to White Industries, Bates City, MO, USA c2001; location "Sec-1 R-1 02"; canx 24Apr03]
FA-110	300LW+	N3079K 9Q-CKS ZS-NPL N313KY (N886AY) N886AW
FA-111	300LW+	N326F N510WP N510WR N391MT N305SA
FA-112	300LW#	N29970 N324NE F-GJHH N300SV
FA-113	300LW	N2997X N299GS PT-MMC
FA-114	300LW+	N29978 XA-PIE XC-HGI N976EA N239TT
FA-115	300LW+	N2998A N75WD N75WL XC-AA20 N75WL N300CW
FA-116	300LW	N2998X N240S N637JC
FA-117	300LW	N29985 N80X N80BZ
FA-118	300LW	N3087K F-GGFB N3087K ZS-MHK 653 (South African AF)
FA-119	300LW	N666RH N688RL N118GW
FA-120	300LW	N3025Z N365CS
FA-121	300LW+(WL)	N72405 N301TT HB-GIO N42AJ N268CB N92TX
FA-122	300LW	N108SB EC-953 EC-FLX N112HF N88RY
FA-123	300LW	N7241H N1824S N1844S HK-3670X HK-3670W HP-1457
FA-124	300LW$	N30417 N1845C N500FC N802M
FA-125	300LW$	N3042K N488GA N401BL
FA-126	300	[completed as c/n FF-1]
FA-127	300LW#	N737P N92SS N923S N45BT N926PR N327ME
FA-128	300LW	N3029F VT-EQM [w/o 15Jul93 Taloja, Maharashtra, India]
FA-129	300	[completed as c/n FF-2]
FA-130	300LW+	N3067W N35SK N9UP N3AH
FA-131	300LW+	N2673M EC-424 EC-ETM N131HF N87YC N87YQ N886MS N728WP
FA-132	300LW$	N7241K N1845 N184D
FA-133	300LW+	C-GMCI N2203Z N900GB N53PE N153PE
FA-134	300LW	N30296 EC-EGF N134AM N28RY N38RY
FA-135	300LW$	N3072N HB-GHY N540CB
FA-136	300LW#	G-BNZA N600CB N888AS (N82HR) N888AS
FA-137	300LW+	N3055S C-GMBA C-FTLB N467JB YV [canx 01Apr08 as exported to Venezuela]
FA-138	300LW+	N30757 N541SC
FA-139	300LW	N72413 ZS-MLL 7Q-YST N797P N316RS
FA-140	300LW	N3078U N117DR N792JM
FA-141	300LW#	N3080F N632DS
FA-142	300LW+	N3081Z N987BT HB-GIT N27TB N304JS
FA-143	300LW+	N300KA N600KA
FA-144	300LW+	N3085D N950JM N333DV N111EL N2800 N28EL
FA-145	300LW$	N300AV OB-M-1330 OB-1330 N145NA N149CC
FA-146	300LW(WL)	F-GICA
FA-147	300LW$	N3085Z N860CC N11GS N990L N166BA

BEECH 300

c/n	Series/Mod	Identities
FA-148	300LW$	N3086D N30FE
FA-149	300LW+	N3121G N87DC N92DE N92DN N500S N64TR N64TE N998BW
FA-150	300LW	N3107W
FA-151	300LW	N388CM N282PC C-FMHD N1MW
FA-152	300LW$	N7241V D-IMMB D-CIMB N20EW N535PN
FA-153	300LW	N3143W N21CY N24BL
FA-154	300LW$	N1563K PT-OJQ
FA-155	300LW#(WL)	N3109N HK-3918X HK-3918W HK-4178X N155BM N408C N66TG
FA-156	300LW+	N3216G ZS-ZZZ 9Q-CYS N3216G ZS-NJI N360GA N642BL N397WM N75AH
FA-157	300LW+	(N794PA) N89NC N552M (N70DW) N350DW YV-1077CP N350DW
FA-158	300LW#(WL)	N3131U N330DR N330DA YV-325P XC-AA54 N750HL YV-2401P YV1839 [also reported as YV1246 in INAC records]
FA-159	300LW$	HK-3433X HK-3433G PNC-0208 (Colombian Police)
FA-160	300LW	N3084K
FA-161	300LW+	N3113A N221MM
FA-162	300LW	N3122Z [stolen 23Mar94 Nassau, Bahamas; canx 13Jan98]
FA-163	300LW+(WL)	N3237S
FA-164	300LW+	N1524H D-IMMF N1CB N42AJ N90WE
FA-165	300LW(WL)	N31800 VH-KDV N165FA N886CA N4NF
FA-166	300LW	9J-AFI N166SA
FA-167	300LW	N1517K N19MC
FA-168	300LW#	N1517R N300TM N300TN
FA-169	300LW	N1559Z XA-PUD HK-3860X HK-3860W YV1849
FA-170	300LW	HB-GHV [canx 21Apr09 as exported possibly to Libya]
FA-171	300LW	N15591 D-IKWM D-COIL N300PP
FA-172	300LW+	N89KA N871RC N1BS N34BS N28GC
FA-173	300LW	N1558M ZS-MIP 9Q-CYZ 5V-TPH N89GA N325WP N30HV
FA-174	300LW$	N1543H PT-FFN
FA-175	300LW$	N1558Y JA8868 N175NJ F-GOOO OY-CVB
FA-176	300LW$	N1570H XA-ALT N144AB
FA-177	300LW$	N1555N (N25CN) (N350CD) N300RC N906EA
FA-178	300LW	N15585 ZS-MNG N313BA
FA-179	300LW$	N1548K
FA-180	300LW	N1568E HI-578SP [w/o 21Jan90 in Guatemala]
FA-181	300LW+(WL)	N5547K N456Q N458Q
FA-182	300LW	N1548L N834GA N8840A C-FWWK
FA-183	300LW	N1549D N19NC C-FAKW
FA-184	300LW	D-IBER
FA-185	300LW$	N1191K N341DB N369F
FA-186	300LW	N1556F (HI-578SP) N427P N404EW
FA-187	300LW	(D-IMDW) N15591 N307CW N300VY N300MY N89GC N350BF
FA-188	300LW	N5556S N423MK N815D N156CH
FA-189	300LW(WL)	N7241V SE-KOL N2808B SE-KOL
FA-190	300LW	N1538Q N17TW N100AQ
FA-191	300LW$	N1541Q N801AR (N881AR) N914JF N914JA
FA-192	300LW	N1552K N900RB [canx 05Dec01 as exported to Germany; aircraft was stolen 17Nov91 from Fort Pierce, FL, USA]
FA-193	300LW#	N15613
FA-194	300LW+(WL)	N1568T N811LC
FA-195	300LW	N1554U N195AE
FA-196	300LW$(WL)	N1557R N127BB N325JG N825JG
FA-197	300LW	N1551C N59AP N59AH N416DY
FA-198	300LW	N5513E N16TB N603WM
FA-199	300LW	OY-GEL N42GA N30MC N169MC N199CE
FA-200	300LW#	D-ICBW HK-3954X HK-3954W OY-CCZ N61KA
FA-201	300LW+	N300PH N566KB N566KA
FA-202	300LW$	N1553V HB-GIP VP-BMK
FA-203	300LW	N1562V LV-PAN LV-RBM N369MK XB-RZH
FA-204	300LW$	N5662T D-IBNK N29LT SE-KXL N65LW "N29LT" ST-DAL
FA-205	300LW	N5672A OH-BSA
FA-206	300LW	N5672J OH-BSB
FA-207	300LW	CNA-NX (Royal Moroccan AF)
FA-208	300LW	CNA-NY (Royal Moroccan AF)
FA-209	300LW$	N148M HP-1182
FA-210	300LW	N8011Q D-IDLS OE-FEM [w/o 12May96 nr Vienna, Austria; canx cMar90]
FA-211	300LW$	N5666L ZS-MYE N42AJ N701JP N822VK
FA-212	300LW+	N2804B N8241F N8PL (N68PL) N52MW N5070W N54YC
FA-213	300LW#(WL)	N5647Q N83RH N555FD N555FH
FA-214	300LW+	N5666S D-ICHT C-GYUI N393CF (N967JG) N393CF
FA-215	300LW+	N8017G OE-FSO C-GTDB
FA-216	300LW	N82345 N160AC N160AB N312AR
FA-217	300LW+	N8115M N911RB D-IEBM N675P N544JC N507P N79CB N507P
FA-218	300LW	N8188F (D-IHIT) N770GX N193FS
FA-219	300LW	N82039 JA8881 N6080W JA8881
FA-220	300LW	D-IOEB D-IOWB N41GA HB-GPI
FA-221	300LW	N82687 N70FL LV-WLT
FA-222	300LW	N8273L LV-POX LV-WMA
FA-223	300LW	N80775 D-IHHB OK-GTJ
FA-224	300LW	N56449 D-IFFB
FA-225	300LW	N82396 D-IBAB CC-PWA
FA-226	300LW	N80907 F-OHRT F-GPRH

c/n	Series/Mod	Identities				
FA-227	300LW	N81418	D-ICBC	(SP-FNH)	D-ICBC	[w/o 14Feb02 Sansura glacier, 14 mls NW of St.Moritz-Samedan, Switzerland; canx 21Mar02]
FA-228	300LW+	N80806	HB-GJC	(D-CAIR)	OE-FME	
FA-229	300LW	N82446	LV-PHI	LV-WIP		
FA-230	300LW	N80679	VT-UPA			

Production complete

BEECH 300 SUPER KING AIR

c/n	Series/Mod	Identities	
FF-1	300	N66	
FF-2	300	N67	
FF-3	300	N68	
FF-4	300	N69	
FF-5	300	N70	
FF-6	300	N71	
FF-7	300	N72	
FF-8	300	N73	
FF-9	300	N74	
FF-10	300	N75	
FF-11	300	N76	
FF-12	300	N77	
FF-13	300	N78	
FF-14	300	N79	
FF-15	300	N80	
FF-16	300	N81	
FF-17	300	N82	[w/o 26Oct93 Front Royal, VA, USA; canx 05Nov97]
FF-18	300	N83	
FF-19	300	N84	

Production complete

BEECH B300C/300CER SUPER KING AIR

$ = Raisbeck dual aft body strakes fitted
# = Raisbeck nacelle wing lockers fitted
+ = Raisbeck dual aft body strakes and nacelle wing lockers fitted

c/n	Series/Mod	Identities				
FM-1	B300C	N1564D	V5-RTZ	F-GOAE	[w/o 07Jun01 Santiago de Compostela, Spain]	
FM-2	B300C+	N350TW	N749RH	HP-2888		
FM-3	B300C+	N55947	N8230Q	N430JT		
FM-4	B300C+	N8275P	N173S			
FM-5	B300C+	N56016	N7285Y	*N841DE		
FM-6	B300C+	N80605	N5888K			
FM-7	B300C+	N82324	N2789A	N5066N	*N846DJ	
FM-8	B300C	N55684	YV-877CP	YV1498		
FM-9	B300C+	N10024	N4009L			
FM-10	B300C$	N23280	N1667J			
FM-11	B300C+	N6195A	N4466A			
FM-12	B300C	N132TJ	N148AA			
FM-13	B300C	N7033U				
FM-14	B300CER$	N814KA	G-JENC	ZZ416 (RAF)		
FM-15	B300C	N415KA	C-GPNC			
FM-16	B300CER	N816KA	G-NICY	ZZ417 (RAF)		
FM-17	B300CER	N817KA	G-JIMG	*ZZ418 (RAF)		
FM-18	B300CER	N818KA	G-OTCS	*ZZ419 (RAF)		
FM-19	B300CER$	N3419S	HZ-MS71			
FM-20	B300CER$	N3120U	HZ-MS72			
FM-21	B300CER	N68RF				
FM-22	B300CER$	N3222K	HZ-MS73			
FM-23	B300CER$	N3203K	HZ-MS74			
FM-24	B300CER$	N3204K	HZ-MS75			
FM-25	B300CER	N250AA				
FM-26	B300CER	N3276B	CS-DPT			
FM-27	B300CER	N927KA				
FM-28	B300CER	N928KA				
FM-29	B300CER	N6029S				
FM-30	B300CER	N6430B				
FM-31	B300CER	N6211Z				
FM-32	B300CER					
FM-33	B300CER					
FM-34	B300CER					

BEECH B350 SUPER KING AIR

$ = Raisbeck dual aft body strakes fitted
# = Raisbeck nacelle wing lockers fitted
+ = Raisbeck dual aft body strakes and nacelle wing lockers fitted

c/n	Series/Mod	Identities
FL-1	350+	N120SK N552TP N552TR N10TX
FL-2	350	N350KA N350KR N400AL N400AE
FL-3	350+	N350TW N92TW (N350PC) N92TW
FL-4	350$	N5513F N97DR N97DL N10K
FL-5	350+	N5634E N450LM (N264DF) N350TK
FL-6	350	N5643B N100BG N350BS
FL-7	350+	N5668F D-CINA N7350C N711VN
FL-8	350#	N5526V HI-586SP N124BB N770JH
FL-9	350	VR-CSH N350S N2SC N1SC
FL-10	350$	N305P N305RL N350FH D2-FFO
FL-11	350	N3739C N37390
FL-12	350#	N5655K (N419CE) N5655K
FL-13	350+	N2856B N56862 N300JC N301JW C-FWXR C-GJLK
FL-14	350	N207R N996AM N350MR N355MR N350Q
FL-15	350	N300PS N75MC N75NC N25KB 23-050 (JGSDF) [pres inst airframe Utsunomiya Flying School, Tochigi Prefecture, Japan]
FL-16	350	N48HB N48HP N350GA
FL-17	350+	N56872 C-GEAS
FL-18	350	N5611B N80CK HK-3988X HK-4268X HK-4268 N688JB
FL-19	350$	N5532T N44KA (N573P) N933CL
FL-20	350$	N1552Q RP-C1587 N350NJ N99U
FL-21	350	N666RH (N6060) EP-825 (Peruvian Army)
FL-22	350$	N5673Y ZS-NGI N350AJ N350BB
FL-23	350+	N1543Q (F-GKIZ) N391RR N323DB
FL-24	350	N1551A N2SM N1551A [dbr 18May03 West Houston Apt, TX, USA, parts to MTW Aerospace, Montgomery, AL, USA; re-registered N1551A although markings N2SM are still worn on the aircraft]
FL-25	350$	N1551T N769WT N768WT N37TD
FL-26	350+	N903M N59TF C-GNLA
FL-27	350+	N5630Q N14NE N63GB N357BB
FL-28	350	N5655W N203HC N203HG N220CL N300KA
FL-29	350+	N8029Y ZS-NAV VH-PSK N67DW N234KK
FL-30	350+	N56800 PK-NSI PK-TDR PK-RJR N448BC N350DK
FL-31	350+	N8013R N126DS
FL-32	350	N2811B (YV-350CP) N81827 (YV-350CP) YV-42CP YV1497
FL-33	350	N8033J N844TS (N180CA) N555WE N882CA N15WS C-FRLD
FL-34	350+	N8023F N987HT N57SC
FL-35	350	N8035H N550TP N470SC
FL-36	350	N4200K N96KA (N825G) N96KA
FL-37	350	N81604 TC-DHA [w/o 06Dec98 Istanbul, Turkey]
FL-38	350	N350KA N358KA N350SR N600CB
FL-39	350+	N8040A HP-1211 N390TT N395MB
FL-40	350+	N8048U PT-WYO N923JK
FL-41	350+	N8051Q N25CU N350VM
FL-42	350	N315P N17NC PT-FGB
FL-43	350+	N5626Y
FL-44	350$	N5521D N90PR N904MC
FL-45	350	FAP-01 (Paraguayan AF) N350CA (N350FT) N111SF
FL-46	350	N81623 D-CCBW UR-CWB
FL-47	350+	N8069F N1100W N326MA N326MX N350P
FL-48	350+	N8068R N309M N555ZA
FL-49	350+	N8068N N27BH N350EB N999HW
FL-50	350+	N8092F N202PV N300TM
FL-51	350#	N8055J N75WD N519KK
FL-52	350	N81664 B-135 B-00135
FL-53	350	N8061U HS-TFI HS-SLA
FL-54	350+	N8080Q
FL-55	350+	N5692L YV-112CP YV0138
FL-56	350$	N8107N N717CT N917CT N350DK N351GC
FL-57	350+	(N319P) N8148F N15WD (N114JB) N159JB
FL-58	350	N8116N
FL-59	350$	N8110N S9-NAY D2-ECZ N350JJ N964LB
FL-60	350$	N65CR N224CR
FL-61	350+	N8140F N350CS N57KE
FL-62	350$	N82682 C-FPWR
FL-63	350	N319P TC-SAB (TC-DHC) TC-MNK N549BJ N350DR
FL-64	350	D-CAMM UR-CWA
FL-65	350	N40FM N999MC N999MG
FL-66	350	N8266L VR-CRI EI-CRI VP-CRI N199Y
FL-67	350	N8213Q (N520LT) N350TR (N850TR) N487TT
FL-68	350+	N8131E N877W N877V N593MA
FL-69	350+	N8230Q N273TA N293TA N110HC
FL-70	350	N350KA N350KC N850D
FL-71	350+	N56456 N38H
FL-72	350+	N8248M N24FT N3739C (N200MP) N89WC
FL-73	350$	N8270R "G-CCCB" YR-CAA
FL-74	350+	N317P N115TT

BEECH 350

c/n	Series/Mod	Identities					
FL-75	350$	N8097Y	HB-GJB	D-COLA	ZS-LAD		
FL-76	350$	N8274U	D-CFMA	UP-K3501			
FL-77	350#	N82277	N4000K	N988ME			
FL-78	350$	N8291K	N551ES	N598AC	N590AC		
FL-79	350	N8246Q	P2-PNG				
FL-80	350	N8275D	PH-BRN	F-GTEM			
FL-81	350	N8053R	N507EB	*N507WG			
FL-82	350+	N8182C	N4YS				
FL-83	350+	N350AB	OY-CVL	RP-C8300	VH-HPT	N441FP	*N441FR
FL-84	350	N8084J	N614ML				
FL-85	350#	N8080C	AN-235 (Ecuadorian Navy)				
FL-86	350+	N8086L	N35DT	N39DT	N27GE	ZS-MMB	
FL-87	350#	C-FNZO	C-GCSL	C-FMHD			
FL-88	350$	N8288W	N1525C				
FL-89	350+	N8112F	N490TN	N145DC			
FL-90	350$	D-CKRA	VH-FIX	D-CFIX	VH-FIX		
FL-91	350+	N350KA	N227KM	N143CE			
FL-92	350+	N8138E	N141DR	N141DA			
FL-93	350	N82678	N188MC				
FL-94	350$	N8194Q	N861CC	N983TM			
FL-95	350$	N8145E	DF-103 (Bahamas Defence Force)		C6-BDF		
FL-96	350+	N403P	N19GR	N19GD	N60WC		
FL-97	350$	N8297L	D-CFMB				
FL-98	350+	C-FPTQ	N8302N	HK-4043X	N8302N	HP-	[canx 27Dec07 as exported to Panama]
FL-99	350	N8299L	N350MS	N850MS	N30SM		
FL-100	350	N8199W	JA8598	N350AM	C-FABR	N86GA	
FL-101	350	N82311	D-CADN				
FL-102	350$	N8202P	S9-TAP	D2-ECW	S9-TAP	D2-ECW	
FL-103	350+	N8192M	N1865A	N1865N	N350TT	N6103K	N113GF
FL-104	350+	N8207D	N733NM	N74RR			
FL-105	350$	N8215W	VT-MNM	VT-BHL	N193RA		
FL-106	350+	N8221K	N793EM	N223P	C-GLOX		
FL-107	350$	N8257V	N4S	N344L			
FL-108	350	N80663	B-13153	NA-302 (Taiwanese Government)			
FL-109	350$	N8203C	N510WP	N434BW	N470KA		
FL-110	350+	N8279P	VH-MKA	N8248W	N774CC	N721BS	N921BS
FL-111	350	N8139K	B-3581				
FL-112	350+	N82112	VT-IRC	N850SJ	N405J	C-FAFF	
FL-113	350	N8291Y	B-3582				
FL-114	350+	N8288Q	N616CK	N895CA			
FL-115	350+	N1551F	N35DT	N5XM			
FL-116	350#	N1552C	D-CAAA	(N350E)	N350EA	D-CAAA	N711RJ
FL-117	350	N1553V	N43BG				
FL-118	350	N1555E	RP-C1728				
FL-119	350	N1558H	N812PM				
FL-120	350$	N1512H	D-CBBB	F-GPGH			
FL-121	350$	N1529M	D-CSAG	N351EB	N1PD		
FL-122	350#	N1562Z	VH-BTL	VH-OXF	VH-OXE	9M-DSL	VH-EWQ
FL-123	350	N30YR	N350BD				
FL-124	350#	N3198N	D-CKWM	N235PB	D-CFIS		
FL-125	350+	N3026K	VH-KJD	VH-AJZ	N32KQ	N32KC	C-FWPR
FL-126	350#	N3164C	N102CS	N124EB			
FL-127	350$	C-GPPC	N300LS				
FL-128	350#	N3157D	D-CDDD	N128FL	EC-GSQ		
FL-129	350+	N46FL	N827HB				
FL-130	350	D-CSKY					
FL-131	350	N3251S	A6-MHH	801 (UAE AF)		[last sighting cFeb03; 801 also carried by a Learjet 35 so may have been re-serialled after Sep04]	
FL-132	350	N3263Y	825 (UAE AF)		A6-KHZ	802 (UAE AF)	
FL-133	350+	N97DR	N577PW				
FL-134	350+	N3252V	SP-FNS				
FL-135	350#	N3263M	N288CB	N283CB	N73WC		
FL-136	350	N350KA	N35017	N189MC			
FL-137	350	N1067S	RP-C2638				
FL-138	350$	N3245S	LV-PLU	LV-WPG	N350P	N311GM	
FL-139	350+	N60CM					
FL-140	350#	N1070D	N806JW	(N806JN)	N806JW	N140WT	
FL-141	350	N1061Q	PT-WND				
FL-142	350$	N1072S	N991LL				
FL-143	350	N3263X	YV-1030CP	N2392S	N789SB		
FL-144	350+	N1084W	N394S	N397S	N49WC		
FL-145	350$	N1075G	RP-C2850				
FL-146	350	N3268Z	2011 (Royal Thai AF)				
FL-147	350	N3269W	2012 (Royal Thai AF)				
FL-148	350	N3268H	RP-C3500				
FL-149	350$	N350KA	N42EL	N42ED	N726T	[dbr cJan09 during maintenance Little Rock, AR, USA; aircraft was sanded prior to painting however several thousand rivets were damaged during the process]	N149KA
FL-150	350+	N10691	VH-SGQ	VH-SCQ			
FL-151	350	N10817	HS-ITD				
FL-152	350$	N1092S	PT-WSJ				

BEECH 350

c/n	Series/Mod	Identities						
FL-153	350#	N1083N	5N-MAG	N506P	RP-C1807			
FL-154	350+	N1063F	N160AC	N160AR	N57VA			
FL-155	350$	N1105X	N253MS	N253AS				
FL-156	350#	N1093A	N470MM	N470MN	N350KG	N769BJ		
FL-157	350#	N1093Q	N350LL					
FL-158	350$	N1095Q	N10UN					
FL-159	350$	N1100N	PT-WNL					
FL-160	350	N1100A	VT-JNK	N177GA				
FL-161	350	N11176	OY-LEL	N141K				
FL-162	350$	N1112Z	VH-MNG	N1112Z	N40593	N915MK		
FL-163	350$	N1057Q	S9-CAM					
FL-164	350	N1104Y	C-FOIL	N312RL				
FL-165	350+	N1135L	N893CF	N53TM				
FL-166	350	N6786S	VH-HPJ	N166FL	XC-CHI			
FL-167	350	N1130B	OY-GIG	N222PV				
FL-168	350#	N1118W	N109NT	N108NT	N17WC			
FL-169	350	N1099E	PT-WSI					
FL-170	350	N2015G	CN-RLE					
FL-171	350+	N2315A						
FL-172	350+	N511D						
FL-173	350	N350KA	SU-BMW	F-HJPD				
FL-174	350$	C-GFSA						
FL-175	350	N1071S	RP-C7000	N1071S	SE-LLU			
FL-176	350	N11309	23-051 (JGSDF)					
FL-177	350	N2029Z	PT-WAC					
FL-178	350#	N2045Q	N675PC	N675BC	N303RR			
FL-179	350	N2047V	(PT-WVA)	PT-WUA	N379SA	N744WW	N744W	N350S
FL-180	350	N18237	JA861A					
FL-181	350+	N2281S	N6789	N500FC	N710HS			
FL-182	350+	N381MG	(N128MG)	N503LM				
FL-183	350	HB-GJL	F-GNOE					
FL-184	350#	N774A	(N100PX)	N800BJ	N350AF			
FL-185	350	N18269	JA350N	N18269	N2SM			
FL-186	350	N11310	23-052 (JGSDF)					
FL-187	350	N25GE	N319EE	N819EE				
FL-188	350	N18297	JA862A					
FL-189	350	N1562H	N198SV					
FL-190	350	N2290V	LV-YLC					
FL-191	350	N11191	JA863A					
FL-192	350	N2192V	VT-MGJ					
FL-193	350	N11250	JA864A					
FL-194	350	N2314S	VH-KJD	HS-SLC				
FL-195	350	N11278	JA865A					
FL-196	350$	N2296G	RP-C2296					
FL-197	350	N82WU						
FL-198	350+	N2298B	N221G					
FL-199	350	N981AR						
FL-200	350#	N2122M	N76PM					
FL-201	350	N2325Y						
FL-202	350+	N2217C	N350TF					
FL-203	350$	N877W	N877WA	N824ST				
FL-204	350	N2301Q	N204W					
FL-205	350	N23216	(PT-WZC)	PT-WTW				
FL-206	350	N23227	YV-910CP					
FL-207	350	N2308R	N717VL	N717VE				
FL-208	350+	N23086	C-FJOL	N350JW				
FL-209	350#	N2303B	N454LF					
FL-210	350+	N23105	N21DX	N350WH	N111M			
FL-211	350+	N715CG	N11TE					
FL-212	350+	N2341F	PT-MSC	N2341F	N350AB			
FL-213	350	N350JB						
FL-214	350+	N2297P	C-GMEH	C-GMEA	N350WG	N350CS	N350FC	
FL-215	350	N2342F	N160AC	N160SM				
FL-216	350	N898MC	N893MC					
FL-217	350+	N23142	N350FC	N350BG				
FL-218	350	N2352N	JA866A					
FL-219	350#	N276JB						
FL-220	350+	N3120X	S9-BAA					
FL-221	350$	N3030S	OK-YES	N221Z	PT-FSA			
FL-222	350	N23272	JA867A					
FL-223	350+	N3033U	N1WV	N787JB	N558BC			
FL-224	350	N2217C	HB-GPF	N2217C	N2535B	*N4982R		
FL-225	350#	N3052C	N57TS	N57TX				
FL-226	350+	N226K	N42KB					
FL-227	350+	N823EB						
FL-228	350+	N350CV	N272SW	N124DA	N75WZ			
FL-229	350	N9WV	OY-MEN					
FL-230	350+	N3059F	N579MC					
FL-231	350+	N231PK	N103RN	N87CE				
FL-232	350$	N2307T	N816DK	N816DE				
FL-233	350+	N350KA	N700PE	N700PG				

BEECH 350

c/n	Series/Mod	Identities
FL-234	350$	N3234K C-FDTC
FL-235	350+	N325JM
FL-236	350	N2346S C-GTEM
FL-237	350#	N2317N (N350KA) N310TK N115GB PR-MOZ [w/o 22May09 nr Porto Seguro-Terravista Golf Club Apt, Bahia, Brazil]
FL-238	350+	N2341R 5N-MPB
FL-239	350+	N3139C N455SC N455SF N655SC
FL-240	350	N3078T PT-WUT
FL-241	350	N2341S *M-SPEC
FL-242	350#	N983AR
FL-243	350+	N3043S (N3333M) N333M N299AS
FL-244	350#	N2344N N171CP
FL-245	350$	N179SG N350K N328AJ
FL-246	350	N3106P N87YC D-CBIL 5N-FLS
FL-247	350+	N3217H N350TG N516BA N6JL
FL-248	350+	N3078W N28PH
FL-249	350	N3080F
FL-250	350$	N3092K N81PA
FL-251	350	N3151H XA-FCV
FL-252	350#	N3252B N525BC
FL-253	350#	N3253U N525BC N525BA (N64GG) N88WV N350GL
FL-254	350#	N3254A
FL-255	350	N3205M D-COEB EC-KJQ
FL-256	350#	N350WD D-CSKF LN-AWD
FL-257	350$	N3257N HC-CAF N257MM N351DD
FL-258	350#	N3258R N583AT (N583SC) N972SC
FL-259	350	N350KA C-GDKI N327R
FL-260	350+	N3206K N5256S (N350CE) N20EW
FL-261	350	N350GT N506MV
FL-262	350+	N3112K N725BA N771HM N772HM
FL-263	350	N3203K N823SD N823SE N102FL
FL-264	350$	N2344H N961LL
FL-265	350$	N3265T N981LL
FL-266	350	N31379 23-053 (JGSDF)
FL-267	350$	N4167H N971LL
FL-268	350#	N49CL
FL-269	350+	N3169N C-GOGS
FL-270	350	N4170N
FL-271	350+	N350HB (N788MB) XB-MVG N992MA
FL-272	350+	N3172N C-GOIC
FL-273	350+	N4473E OY-JVL C-FVKC
FL-274	350#	N64GG (N350GL) M-SPEX
FL-275	350+	N4475N (N350RC) N275BT
FL-276	350+	N3176T D-CLOG
FL-277	350#	N4477Q XA-RCG
FL-278	350+	N350BW
FL-279	350	N3179Q 9H-ADV D-CIAO 5N-FLY
FL-280	350	N4380Y
FL-281	350	N552TP
FL-282	350$	N350WP FAC5746 (Colombian AF)
FL-283	350+	N4083L N350NY N850NY N980BC
FL-284	350+	N4484A N886AC
FL-285	350#	N3185J C-GRJZ
FL-286	350#	N4486V G-BZNE
FL-287	350	N43870 N555WF N555WQ
FL-288	350$	N168ET N721NB (PP-KKK) PP-KKG
FL-289	350$	N3189T PP-JSC
FL-290	350#	N3178P (N290BT) N969MB (N246DF) PR-LJA
FL-291	350	N701FC
FL-292	350	N3192N JA868A
FL-293	350+	N3253Q 08-2093 (USAF) [cvtd to MC-12W]
FL-294	350$	N3214J S9-CAN
FL-295	350	N3195T JA869A
FL-296	350+	N1668A N4096B N296BT N383AS N877SA N505M N290AS
FL-297	350	N3197N JA870A
FL-298	350	N4298H N151E
FL-299	350$	N3128K N74KS
FL-300	350+	N1CR N18RN LX-MLB F-GVLB
FL-301	350+	N4211V F-GOSB
FL-302	350+	N4302J N42EL N42ED
FL-303	350+	N4303R N551TP
FL-304	350+	N44866 N60YP N60YB
FL-305	350	N3132M N351MP
FL-306	350#	N525DF
FL-307	350	N5007H 23-054 (JGSDF)
FL-308	350+	N825TS N64FB
FL-309	350+	N309BT N385AS N1244J C-GKMS N143DK 08-0309 (USAF) [cvtd to MC-12W]
FL-310	350	N5010R LV-ZXX
FL-311	350$	N5011K D-CUNO [w/o 12Jan06 Freiburg, Germany; canx 14Mar06]
FL-312	350+	N3165M HB-GJN N350JR N511PS
FL-313	350$	N3103L YV-2663P YV-783CP [w/o 24May05 De Irapa, Venezuela]

BEECH 350

c/n	Series/Mod	Identities				
FL-314	350+	N4314X	N350J			
FL-315	350$	N3115K				
FL-316	350+	N3216L	N200VC			
FL-317	350+	N3217V	C-FPCP			
FL-318	350$	N3218Z	(D-CISU)	B-3583		
FL-319	350$	N4319T	N350TV			
FL-320	350+	N4320L	N350MS	N380MS	N355DM	
FL-321	350+	N541GA	N748SB			
FL-322	350$	N3222K	(D-CVVV)	D-CHGS	OK-LFD	
FL-323	350$	N4323W	N350KS			
FL-324	350$	N4424S	N350CB	(N797WB)	N793WB	
FL-325	350$	N5025L	N450DW			
FL-326	350+	N4006K	(N326PK)	N350MS	N363CA	
FL-327	350+	N5027X	N1845			
FL-328	350+	N4328W	EC-IBK			
FL-329	350+	N5129J	N350KA	N668K	08-0329	[cvtd to MC-12W]
FL-330	350+	N5030Y	N350KA	N1253W		
FL-331	350#	N350KA	N350KD	23-055 (JGSDF)		
FL-332	350+	N4332U	N133NL	N291AS		
FL-333	350$	N4483Y	N390MD			
FL-334	350+	N5034F	N350D			
FL-335	350$	N5135N	PR-EDF			
FL-336	350+	N4336P	N360CB	08-0336 (USAF)		[cvtd to MC-12W]
FL-337	350+	N5037A	N707FA			
FL-338	350$	N3238S	N802BS			
FL-339	350+	N5039E	VH-DHP	A32-339 (Royal Australian AF)		
FL-340	350+	N5070M	HB-GJR	N450CR		
FL-341	350$	N4471J	VH-ZKA	N4471J	XA-CAB	
FL-342	350+	N4472S	N512DC			
FL-343	350+	N5043X	VH-JHP	A32-343 (Royal Australian AF)		
FL-344	350+	N5044B	N72RE			
FL-345	350$	N5045L	JA353N	N370NA	PR-MRF	
FL-346	350+	N5046Y	VH-UHP	A32-346 (Royal Australian AF)		
FL-347	350+	N5047F	N350TT	N350TL	N923FP	
FL-348	350+	N5048F	VH-VHP	A32-348 (Royal Australian AF)		
FL-349	350+	N5149F	VH-WHP	A32-349 (Royal Australian AF)		
FL-350	350+	N5150Q	N350BK	VH-XHP	A32-350 (Royal Australian AF)	
FL-351	350+	N5151F	VH-YHP	A32-351 (Royal Australian AF)		
FL-352	350$	N5152H	N675PC			
FL-353	350+	N6153V	C-GMEH	N53LJ	08-0353 (USAF)	[cvtd to MC-12W]
FL-354	350+	N60454	N354H	C-FNIL		
FL-355	350$	N6055H	(N288CB)	N685BC		
FL-356	350+	N5156G	N455SC	N455SE		
FL-357	350$	N61907	F-GKYY			
FL-358	350					
FL-359	350+	N359MB				
FL-360	350+	N5030D	N1880C			
FL-361	350+	N6011W	VH-KDX	VH-OXF		
FL-362	350$	N6162K	N300R	N270AB		
FL-363	350$	N6043M	N700U			
FL-364	350+	N5084V	N447TF			
FL-365	350$	N6165J	N350RR	N350RD		
FL-366	350+	N366SL				
FL-367	350$	N6167K	N160AC			
FL-368	350$	N6068V	OO-SDU			
FL-369	350+	N5009U	N100BE	N103BE	N468BV	
FL-370	350$	N6170D	N74TF			
FL-371	350+	N6171N	N391MT	N708DC		
FL-372	350+	N6172B	VH-PHP	A32-372 (Royal Australian AF)		
FL-373	350$	N6173K	N357RL			
FL-374	350$	N6174N	CN-ANJ			
FL-375	350$	N6175F	N657PP			
FL-376	350+	N6176C	JA376N	N376NA	08-0376 (USAF)	[cvtd to MC-12W]
FL-377	350$	N6177F	PR-AEF			
FL-378	350+	N4478H	N225CM			
FL-379	350+	N61679	N790P	N973SC		
FL-380	350					
FL-381	350+	N350PL	N818WV	PR-JFC		
FL-382	350#	N61942	23-056 (JGSDF)			
FL-383	350+	N6183S	N500VL			
FL-384	350+	N5084Y	N455SC	N465SC	N350PJ	
FL-385	350+	N5085T	C-GEJE			
FL-386	350+	N5086P	N789LL			
FL-387	350+	N5117S	N141CE			
FL-388	350+	N4488H	N15EW			
FL-389	350+	N6089N	VH-WHP	VH-MLG		
FL-390	350+	N777YC	N823SD			
FL-391	350+	N5091G	N142CE			
FL-392	350$	N6192C	N350CB			
FL-393	350+	N6193S	N350HA			
FL-394	350+	N6194U	N246SD	N246SE	N644CB	

BEECH 350

c/n	Series/Mod	Identities				
FL-395	350$	N61185	HP-1555			
FL-396	350+	N6196H	N351CB	N351CR	N613BA	
FL-397	350+	N220CG				
FL-398	350$	N6198N	PR-ADM			
FL-399	350#	N504TF				
FL-400	350+	N40TH	N40GZ			
FL-401	350+	N319EE				
FL-402	350+	N6182Z	N402JL	N459M		
FL-403	350+	N6113X	N100BE			
FL-404	350+	N6204G	HB-GJS	N495DH		
FL-405	350+	N6165Y				
FL-406	350+	N828AJ				
FL-407	350+	N160MW				
FL-408	350+	N6108A	N929BG	N350MR	(N350MT)	PR-XAA
FL-409	350+	N6109U	N409LV			
FL-410	350$	N61740	D-CWKM			
FL-411	350+	N36811	N953PC	N15WS		
FL-412	350+	N6112G	(N626JP)	N6112G		
FL-413	350+	N36813	N350TT			
FL-414	350+	N36814	N19GR			
FL-415	350$	N36715				
FL-416	350+	N6116N				
FL-417	350+	N6117C	N8YN	VN-B444		
FL-418	350+	N888FM				
FL-419	350+	N36919	N810N	419 (Pakistan Ministry of Defence)		
FL-420	350$	N36620	LV-BAN			
FL-421	350+	N350FW				
FL-422	350+	N3722Y	N350K			
FL-423	350+	N3723Q	N5RF			
FL-424	350+	N3724Q	N106ER	D-CFIA		
FL-425	350+	N37025	JA02EP			
FL-426	350+	N3726E	VH-XHP	A32-426 (Royal Australian Army)		
FL-427	350+	N3727Q	(N246DF)	N345DG		
FL-428	350+	N5128X	N400AL			
FL-429	350+	N6129Q	HP-1588			
FL-430	350+	N631ME				
FL-431	350+	N6131Q	N75PX			
FL-432	350+	N536BW	N586BW			
FL-433	350+	N24JJ	N375CP			
FL-434	350+	N727MH	N727MU	PP-LOG		
FL-435	350+	N36635	PR-JDB			
FL-436	350+	N37336	N103AL	N253P	N83KB	N83KE
FL-437	350+	N6137L	VH-YHP	A32-437 (Royal Australian Army)		
FL-438	350+	N61638	G-SERC	N438GC		
FL-439	350+	N6139Z	VH-ZHP	A32-439 (Royal Australian Army)		
FL-440	350+	N3040P	N412CB			
FL-441	350+	N36941	N246SD			
FL-442	350+	N374BH				
FL-443	350+	N37183	VH-KDT	VH-KJD		
FL-444	350+	N36744	444 (Pakistan Army)			
FL-445	350+	N555ZT	N575MX	N140AE		
FL-446	350+	N37246	N60DL			
FL-447	350+	N37247	N961PP	N524PC		
FL-448	350+	N122RG				
FL-449	350+	N6179X	N73WW	N374CH		
FL-450	350+	N6150U	C-GCGB	N45AJ		
FL-451	350+	N36851	JA377N			
FL-452	350+	N36932	CN-RLL			
FL-453	350+	N36953	N62AZ			
FL-454	350+	N660P	FAC5747 (Colombian AF)			
FL-455	350+	N6155U	XA-UET			
FL-456	350+	N316W				
FL-457	350+	N36957	N827CC			
FL-458	350+	N945SH				
FL-459	350+	N36659	ZS-ZAZ			
FL-460	350+	N36860	(OO-GMJ)	D-CGMJ	OO-GMJ	
FL-461	350+	N36561	VH-SGQ			
FL-462	350+	N36962	N900PL	08-0462 (USAF)		[cvtd to MC-12W]
FL-463	350+	N36933	N352BC			
FL-464	350+	N37164	N450CK			
FL-465	350+	N37065	VT-ACD			
FL-466	350+	N35VP				
FL-467	350+	N36767	N350PT			
FL-468	350+	N6048L	N609BG			
FL-469	350+	N37069	UR-HBD			
FL-470	350+	N3070R	N350MS	OB-1881-P		
FL-471	350+	N36946	N865LS	N865LR		
FL-472	350+	N37172				
FL-473	350+	N37173	D-CFMD			
FL-474	350+	N37174	N350SM			
FL-475	350+	N36975	N949PC	N214ML		

BEECH 350

c/n	Series/Mod	Identities			
FL-476	350+	N3726M	SU-MMN		
FL-477	350+	N71837	HB-GJP		
FL-478	350+	N6178N	VT-FIU		
FL-479	350+	N3179V	C-GAEO		
FL-480	350+	N73380			
FL-481	350+	N37318	PR-DAH		
FL-482	350+	N37084			
FL-483	350+	N36999	N910BD		
FL-484	350+	N36984	VH-ZGS		
FL-485	350+	N71885			
FL-486	350+	N36886	TR-AEM		
FL-487	350+	N7087U	N831PT		
FL-488	350+	N36988			
FL-489	350+	N200VJ			
FL-490	350+	N37090	N825TT		
FL-491	350+	N3AW			
FL-492	350+	N7192X	N394S		
FL-493	350+	N30MC			
FL-494	350+	N37094	CN-TWY		
FL-495	350+	N71795	N641MC		
FL-496	350+	N7196M	N900WP		
FL-497	350+	N7197Y	N409D		
FL-498	350+	N36998	N900WS		
FL-499	350+	N7199V	N680CB		
FL-500	350+	N455SC			
FL-501	350+	N7001Z	N2112V		
FL-502	350+	N7102Y	C-GBCE		
FL-503	350+	N37026	(N551BV)	N551VB	
FL-504	350+	N37040	N553CL		
FL-505	350+	N37085	RP-C8300		
FL-506	350+	N7106L	G-POWB		
FL-507	350+	N533GP	HK-4643		
FL-508	350+	N7208N	N883P		
FL-509	350+	N92TH			
FL-510	350+	N7410L	N851TC		
FL-511	350+	N7011Y	C-GKOS		
FL-512	350+	N7212S	N114RG		
FL-513	350+	N7193K	N189CB	YV	[canx 21May08 as exported to Venezuela]
FL-514	350+	N7014X	N350LM	YV	[canx 24Jan08 as exported to Venezuela]
FL-515	350+	N70155	D-CRAO		
FL-516	350+	N350RK			
FL-517	350+	N514LK			
FL-518	350+	N273TA			
FL-519	350+	N3729Y	N373WP		
FL-520	350+	N883GB			
FL-521	350ER+	N7021Z	YI-321 (Iraqi AF)		[unconfirmed serial]
FL-522	350+	N74226			
FL-523	350+	N7233V			
FL-524	350+	N141L			
FL-525	350+	N7185A	VH-PYN		
FL-526	350+	N3726V	VT-LJS		
FL-527	350+	N7017C	N1WV		
FL-528	350+	N7418L	N350MG		
FL-529	350+	N214WL			
FL-530	350+	N7130X			
FL-531	350+	N7131Z			
FL-532	350+	N7262U	ZS-PXF		
FL-533	350+	N71966			
FL-534	350+	N71834	ZS-FML		
FL-535	350+	N7035V			
FL-536	350+	N536MR			
FL-537	350+	N71970	N2VA		
FL-538	350+	N7368X			
FL-539	350+	N350NY			
FL-540	350+	N540BK	N672MM		
FL-541	350+	N7101C	PR-CCB		
FL-542	350+	N304BP			
FL-543	350+	N543KA	ZS-MCO	ZS-SHY	
FL-544	350+	N544KA	N64TR		
FL-545	350+	N545KA			
FL-546	350+	N350AG	08-0546	[cvtd to MC-12W]	
FL-547	350+	N111MD			
FL-548	350+	N548KA	D2-	[canx 12Oct07 as exported to Angola; possibly became D2-EDG]	
FL-549	350+	N21VA	N1VA		
FL-550	350+	N750KA	PR-CVI		
FL-551	350+	N791BP			
FL-552	350+	N552KA	VT-JKK		
FL-553	350+	N775MG			
FL-554	350+	N454TB			
FL-555	350+	N872CT			
FL-556	350+	N556KA	N898CD		

BEECH 350

c/n	Series/Mod	Identities
FL-557	350+	N557KA OK-HLB
FL-558	350+	N558KA
FL-559	350+	N291B
FL-560	350+	N350PX
FL-561	350+	N350EB
FL-562	350+	N628LD
FL-563	350+	N33703 RP-C2226
FL-564	350+	N564KA
FL-565	350+	N971JP
FL-566	350+	N3366K F-OIQY
FL-567	350+	N31967 RP-C2528
FL-568	350ER+	N32148 A6-GJD
FL-569	350+	N569KA M-OORE M-FLYI
FL-570	350+	N268LB
FL-571	350+	N362DB
FL-572	350+	N3272Q N902CE
FL-573	350+	N31973 YV2525
FL-574	350+	N3474P HK-4603
FL-575	350+	N3215G C-GMKW N138CC HK- [canx 14Aug09 as exported to Colombia]
FL-576	350+	N111UT
FL-577	350+	N564BC
FL-578	350+	N32078 N605MJ
FL-579	350+	N3197L PR-DCT
FL-580	350+	N34010 M-FIVE
FL-581	350+	N427BC
FL-582	350+	N3382Z F-HACJ
FL-583	350+	N3483A N350SK
FL-584	350+	N33984 C-FTIU
FL-585	350+	N350RV
FL-586	350+	N466AC
FL-587	350+	N34687 9M-PTA
FL-588	350+	N3188H CN-AMH
FL-589	350+	N123RF
FL-590	350+	N590EU LN-BAB
FL-591	350+	N3191G C-GNLF
FL-592	350+	N150GX
FL-593	350+	N3193E 9M-PTB
FL-594	350+	N3292H N594SC
FL-595	350+	N3195V 7Q-ULC
FL-596	350+	N606MJ
FL-597	350+	N3197D *ZZ500 (Royal Navy)
FL-598	350+	N3198M 9M- [canx 06May09 as exported to Malaysia]
FL-599	350ER	N3496C
FL-600	350+	N48AZ (N85AZ) N480EB
FL-601	350+	N350KA
FL-602	350#	N517DP
FL-603	350+	N3203Z CN-AMI
FL-604	350+	N3292S N110RF
FL-605	350+	N3425W CN-TJC
FL-606	350+	N505SG
FL-607	350+	N336MM
FL-608	350+	N3208K PP-KIA
FL-609	350+	N32154 N350JG
FL-610	350+	N385H
FL-611	350+	N536BW
FL-612	350+	N412KA
FL-613	350+	N3193Q N598AC
FL-614	350+	N614BK EX-00003
FL-615	350+	N510UF
FL-616	350+	N458TB N83KB
FL-617	350+	N846YT
FL-618	350+	N618HB *ZZ501 (Royal Navy)
FL-619	350+	N60819 PK-JBK
FL-620	350+	N60YP
FL-621	350+	N85AZ N7RC
FL-622	350+	N110RF (N622KA) N990GR
FL-623	350+	N452TB
FL-624	350+	N624KA
FL-625	350+	N6425D
FL-626	350+	N61726
FL-627	350$	N6127U D-CFME
FL-628	350+	N6028Z
FL-629	350+	N63699 *ZZ502 (Royal Navy)
FL-630	350+	N6430N
FL-631	350+	N60041 G-KLNB
FL-632	350+	N6232E A6- [canx 06Jul09 as exported to United Arab Emirates]
FL-633	350+	N6433F *ZZ503 (Royal Navy)
FL-634	350+	N6434Y N350RR
FL-635	350+	N64255
FL-636	350+	N6196R
FL-637	350+	N6377L

BEECH 350

c/n	Series/Mod	Identities			
FL-638	350+	N60318	CN-TAD		
FL-639	350+	N63669			
FL-640	350+	N63740			
FL-641	350+	N6441Y			
FL-642	350+	N6412T			
FL-643	350+	N63123	D-CADF	*YU-BTC	
FL-644	350+	N60064			
FL-645	350+	N60125			
FL-646	350+	N64386			
FL-647	350+	N61227			
FL-648	350+	N61788			
FL-649	350+	N6349E			
FL-650	350+	N6350A			
FL-651	350+	N6151N	VH-ZHP	*A32-651	(Royal Australian AF)
FL-652	350+	N6452D			
FL-653	350+	N61353			
FL-654	350+	N60954			
FL-655	350+	N63255			
FL-656	350+	N63560			
FL-657	350+	N6357B	PR-JCC		
FL-658	350+	N6478F	C-FMUN		
FL-659	350	N63769			
FL-660	350	N6160T			
FL-661	350	N63561			
FL-662	350	N60162			
FL-663	350	N63563			
FL-664	350				
FL-665	350	N63815			
FL-666	350	N6366S			
FL-667	350	N63997			
FL-668	350	N6068L			
FL-669	350	N6369D			
FL-670	350	N6470Q			
FL-671	350	N6171U			
FL-672	350	N350HB			
FL-673	350	N6373C			
FL-674	350	N63494			
FL-675	350	N6475T			
FL-676	350				
FL-677	350	N6477Q			
FL-678	350				
FL-679	350				
FL-680	350				
FL-681	350				
FL-682	350				
FL-683	350				
FL-684	350				
FL-685	350				
FL-686	350				
FL-687	350				
FL-688	350				
FL-689	350				
FL-690	350				
FL-691	350				
FL-692	350				
FL-693	350				
FL-694	350				
FL-695	350				
FL-696	350				
FL-697	350				
FL-698	350				
FL-699	350				
FL-700	350				
FL-701	350				
FL-702	350				
FL-703	350				
FL-704	350				
FL-705	350				
FL-706	350				
FL-707	350				
FL-708	350				
FL-709	350				
FL-710	350				
FL-711	350				
FL-712	350				
FL-713	350				
FL-714	350				
FL-715	350				

BEECH 350C SUPER KING AIR

= Raisbeck nacelle wing lockers fitted

c/n	Series/Mod	Identities
FN-1	350C#	N2758B HB-GII T-721 (Swiss AF) N102SK T-721 (Swiss AF)

BEECH 2000/2000A STARSHIP

c/n	Series	Identities
NC-1		N2000S [wfu c1988; tested to destruction & canx 28Feb89]
NC-2		N3042S [wfu Wichita-Beech Field, KS, USA c2002; b/u c2004]
NC-3		N3234S [wfu & b/u c2001; canx 15Feb01]
NC-4		N2000S N75WD N4UB [wfu c2003 Marana-Pinal Airpark, AZ, USA; b/u c2005; canx 05Sep05]
NC-5		N1550S N42SR N1550S [canx 03Apr00; dismantled as spares source for NC-51]
NC-6		N1556S [wfu c2003; pres cDec04 Mid-America Air Museum, Liberal, KS, USA; canx 09May05]
NC-7		N4NV N1548S (N14NV) (N8873) N7388K [wfu c2003 Marana-Pinal Airpark, AZ, USA; b/u c2005; canx 09May05]
NC-8		N1508S OY-GEA N194DB N10TX N10TQ [pres inst airframe Wichita State University National Institute of Aviation Research, Building B40, Wichita-Beech Field, KS, USA; canx 10Sep08]
NC-9		N900DR N2009W N999RF [wfu c2003 Marana-Pinal Airpark, AZ, USA; b/u c2005; canx 09May05]
NC-10		N1563Z N253TA [wfu c2003 Marana-Pinal Airpark, AZ, USA; b/u c2005; canx 09May05]
NC-11		N1569S [wfu c2003 Marana-Pinal Airpark, AZ, USA; b/u c2005; canx 10May05]
NC-12		N1552S [wfu c2003 Marana-Pinal Airpark, AZ, USA; donated to US Army for explosive composite testing; canx 10May05]
NC-13		N1553S (N7388E) N1553S [wfu c2003 Marana-Pinal Airpark, AZ, USA; b/u c2005; canx 10May05]
NC-14		N5674B N214JB [wfu cSep03, pres Southern Museum Of Flight, Birmingham, AL, USA; canx 10May05]
NC-15		N5549B [wfu c2003 Marana-Pinal Airpark, AZ, USA; b/u c2005; canx 10May05]
NC-16		N80KM N80KK N515AC [wfu Wichita-Beech Field, KS, USA; canx 10Sep08]
NC-17		N62KM N62KK N2000S [wfu c2003 Marana-Pinal Airpark, AZ, USA; b/u c2005; canx 10May05]
NC-18		N8246S N638LD [wfu c2003 Marana-Pinal Airpark, AZ, USA; canx 02Dec05; fuselage to Bend Municipal, OR, USA]
NC-19		N8025L N401AS [wfu c2003 Marana-Pinal Airpark, AZ, USA; moved cAug05; pres Salt Lake City Community College, Salt Lake City-International, UT, USA; canx 10Sep08]
NC-20		N8186S N321MK [wfu c2003 Marana-Pinal Airpark, AZ, USA; b/u c2005; canx 10May05]
NC-21		N206R N206RF [wfu c2003 Marana-Pinal Airpark, AZ, USA; b/u c2005; canx 10May05]
NC-22	A	N2000S N14VP N14VR [wfu c2003 Marana-Pinal Airpark, AZ, USA; b/u c2005; canx 14Feb05]
NC-23	A	N8244S N24VP (N24UP) N39TW N39TU [wfu cJul04, pres Pima Air & Space Museum, Tucson, AZ, USA; canx 10May05]
NC-24	A	N1560S (N560SA) N1560S [wfu c2003 Marana-Pinal Airpark, AZ, USA; b/u c2005; canx 10Sep08]
NC-25	A	N1553Y N500CP [wfu c2004 Orange County-John Wayne, CA, USA, parts to Aviation Warehouse, El Mirage, CA, USA; canx 15Nov04]
NC-26	A	N8000Q [wfu c2003 Marana-Pinal Airpark, AZ, USA; b/u c2005; canx 10May05]
NC-27	A	N8225Y N74TF N74TD [wfu c2003 Marana-Pinal Airpark, AZ, USA; moved cNov03; pres Evergreen Museum, McMinnville-Municipal, OR, USA; canx 11May05]
NC-28	A	N82428 N786BP [wfu cApr04 Marana-Pinal Airpark, AZ, USA; moved cOct04; pres Queensland Institute for Aviation Engineering, Caloundra, QLD, Australia; canx 10May05]
NC-29	A	N8244L (N121GV) N8244L
NC-30	A	N8114Q (N53MP) N55MP N55MU [wfu c2003 Marana-Pinal Airpark, AZ, USA; b/u c2005; canx 10May05]
NC-31	A	N1558S N181CE [wfu c2003 Marana-Pinal Airpark, AZ, USA; b/u c2005; canx 10May05]
NC-32	A	N8254Q N23FH N23FL [wfu c2003 Marana-Pinal Airpark, AZ, USA; moved cNov04; pres National Institute for Aviation Research, Wichita, KS, USA; canx 10May05]
NC-33	A	N8074S XB-JTE [wfu c2003 Marana-Pinal Airpark, AZ, USA; canx 10May05; re-appeared c2006 in Mexico]
NC-34	A	N8119S [wfu c2003 Marana-Pinal Airpark, AZ, USA; b/u c2005; canx 09May05]
NC-35	A	N8149S [impounded cSep01 Tampico, Tamaulipas, Mexico]
NC-36	A	N8176S N555KK N555KG XA-TNR N555KG [wfu c2003 Marana-Pinal Airpark, AZ, USA; b/u c2005; canx 09May05]
NC-37	A	N8194S [wfu cNov03 Marana-Pinal Airpark, AZ, USA; canx 20Feb06; later moved to Tucson-Avra Valley, AZ, USA]
NC-38	A	N8280S [wfu cApr03 Marana-Pinal Airpark, AZ, USA; canx 11May05; later moved to Tucson-Avra Valley, AZ, USA]
NC-39	A	N8282S [wfu c2003 Marana-Pinal Airpark, AZ, USA; b/u c2005; canx 09May05]
NC-40	A	N8300S N48FL [wfu cApr03 Marana-Pinal Airpark, AZ, USA; b/u c2005; canx 09May05]
NC-41	A	N8283S [wfu 17Aug03; pres Kansas Aviation Museum, Wichita, KS, USA; canx 09May05]
NC-42	A	N8158X [wfu cMar04, pres Museum of Flight, Snohomish County-Paine Field, WA, USA; canx 29Sep04]
NC-43	A	N2000S N200ZS N999P [wfu c2003 Marana-Pinal Airpark, AZ, USA; canx 09May05; later moved to Tucson-Avra Valley, AZ, USA]
NC-44	A	N8163Q N631DS [wfu c2003 Marana-Pinal Airpark, AZ, USA; canx 09May05; b/u c2006]

BEECH 2000

c/n	Series	Identities
NC-45	A	N8215Q N45FL
NC-46	A	N8170Q N312KJ N641SE [wfu c2003 Marana-Pinal Airpark, AZ, USA; later moved to Tucson-Avra Valley, AZ, USA]
NC-47	A	N8277Q N64GG N64GQ N30LH [wfu c2003 Marana-Pinal Airpark, AZ, USA; canx 06May05; later moved to Tucson-Avra Valley, AZ, USA]
NC-48	A	N8196Q [wfu c2004 Marana-Pinal Airpark, AZ, USA; b/u c2005; canx 09May05]
NC-49	A	N8224Q XA-TQF N8224Q [wfu cSep03, pres Staggerwing Museum, Tullahoma, TN, USA; canx 09May05]
NC-50	A	N8285Q (N500CP) N8285Q
NC-51	A	N8286Q N55TY N6204U N514RS
NC-52	A	N1564Q N515JS [wfu cApr03 Marana-Pinal Airpark, AZ, USA; canx 09May05; later moved to Tucson-Avra Valley, AZ, USA]
NC-53		N1564J N6MF N26RA [wfu c2003 Marana-Pinal Airpark, AZ, USA; canx 09May05]

Production complete

BRITTEN-NORMAN ISLANDER/TRISLANDER

The suffix to the construction numbers listed below denotes where the aircraft was assembled. Those aircraft with no suffix shown were assembled at Bembridge. Regular updates can be found in the section "Islander News" which is a regular feature in Air-Britain News. A wealth of additional information can be obtained from BN Historians, including a full production history with owner/operator information, either as an A4 binder version or a downloadable PDF file at www.bnhistorians.co.uk

Suffixes;
(E) = Assembled at Eastleigh, UK
(G) = Assembled at Gosselies, Belgium
(P) = Assembled at Manila, Philippines
(R) = Assembled at Bucharest, Romania

c/n	Series	Identities
1	BN-2	G-ATCT [w/o 09Nov66 Sneek, Netherlands; canx 27Jan67]
2	BN-2	G-ATWU [cvtd to BN-2A MkII cJul68; cvtd to BN-2A MkIII cSep70; wfu 30Oct70; canx 23Nov70; b/u c1979 Bembridge, UK]
3	BN-2A-8	G-AVCN F-OGHG N290VL G-AVCN [std Bembridge, Isle of Wight, UK]
4	BN-2A-21	G-AVKC (F-BUFX) N43MJ C-FAOU N663SA
5	BN-2	G-AVOS N584JA N589SA N584JA [w/o 13Jan69 San Luis, San Luis Province, Argentina]
6	BN-2A-8	G-AVRA (F-BUFV) F-BUOQ J6-SLW [w/o 12Jul90 Union Island, St.Vincent]
7	BN-2A-26	G-AVRB YV-T-MTM N32JC C-GSAD
8	BN-2A-26	G-AVRC G-51-1 I-TRAM G-4-8 OO-ARI OO-AST G-AVRC (TF-REJ) N28BN HI-653CA HI-653CT HI-653CA [w/o 07Feb08 El Seibo, Dominican Republic]
9	BN-2A-27	G-AVUB (OO-ARI) G-4-9 CF-YZF C-FYZF DQ-FEO [w/o 11May93 Suva, Fiji]
10	BN-2A-26	G-AVUC N671JA N17UP N417UP XB-GUG N14451 C-GOMC [w/o 04Dec87 nr Tuktoyaktuk, BC, Canada; canx 03Jun88]
11	BN-2A-8	G-AVXO N672JA (N141TA) N14KA N65GC N851JA [w/o cDec88 in the Bahamas; canx 14Mar89]
12	BN-2A	G-AVXP N581JA (N681VK) N900RC N900GD [canx cJun86 - status?]
13	BN-2A	(G-AVXR) G-51-2 TR-LNG [w/o 26Nov77 Tchimbele, Gabon]
14	BN-2A	G-51-3 G-AVXS TI-1063C [w/o 08Oct68 Puerto Cortes, Costa Rica]
15	BN-2A-26	G-AVXT VH-AIA (H4-AAH) P2-ISR [w/o 22Dec93 Mount Hagen, Papua New Guinea]
16	BN-2A	(G-AVXU) G-51-4 TR-LNF [w/o cOct74 Port Gentil, Gabon]
17	BN-2A-6	G-AWBY I-LACO
18	BN-2A-8	G-AWBZ VH-ISG [w/o 03Dec75 off Du Motu, Tonga; canx 19Dec75]
19	BN-2A-26	G-AWCA N582JA TF-REH N19BN YV-2244P YV-417C YV-230C [w/o 05Jun87 Ciudad Bolivar, Venezuela]
20	BN-2A	G-AWCB N585JA N555JA
21	BN-2A	G-AWCC D-IOLT [w/o 18May83 Helgoland, West Germany; canx 18Jul83]
22	BN-2A	(G-AWHZ) G-51-5 D-IJAN [w/o 27Jun75 Bremen, West Germany; canx 29Jul75]
23	BN-2A-26	G-AWIA CF-XYK C-FXYK N2233Z C-FXYK N2233Z
24	BN-2A	G-AWIB N586JA XB-WAG XA-CUL XB-EBZ [wfu & canx]
25	BN-2A	G-AWIC N589JA [w/o 21Dec71 Culebra, San Juan, PR]
26	BN-2A	G-AWID 501 (Thai Government) HS-SKB 501 (Thai Government) [pres Golden Jubilee Museum of Agriculture, Khlong Luang, Thailand]
27	BN-2A	G-AWIE N457SA [w/o 19Sep89 Vieques, PR during Hurricane Hugo; canx 07Feb91]
28	BN-2A	VH-ATI P2-ATI P2-DNI [w/o 25Aug85 in Papua New Guinea]
29	BN-2A	VH-ATK [w/o 20Nov69 Bolovip, Papua New Guinea; canx 20Nov69]
30	BN-2A	G-AWNR N30BN HP-1077KN YV-508C [dbr 07Nov90 in Venezuela; canx c1997]
31	BN-2A	(G-AWNS) G-51-6 N676SA N66HA [w/o 26Dec74 Riverton Heights, WA, USA]
32	BN-2A	G-AWNT
33	BN-2A-26	G-AWNU 8P-ASD 8R-GFQ [CofA exp 24Apr86; wfu Barbados-Grantley Adams International]
34	BN-2A	G-AWNV 201 (Abu Dhabi Defence Force) 801 (Abu Dhabi Defence Force) MM60222 (Somalian Aeronautical Corps) [wfu c1991 Mogadishu, Somalia & b/u]
35	BN-2A	(G-AWNW) CF-RDI [w/o 14Jul73 Home Ranch, BC, Canada; canx 16Oct73]
36	BN-2A-26	(G-AWNX) VH-ATS P2-ATS P2-ALC P2-BBC P2-NAS
37	BN-2A	G-AWNY F-OGDR [w/o cMar70 Guayaquil, Ecuador; canx 19Apr73]
38	BN-2A	(G-AWNZ) G-51-7 N589SA [w/o 02Aug84 off Isla de Vieques, PR]
39	BN-2A-8	(G-AWOD) G-51-8 N583JA N67HA C-GPCF [dbr 23May85 Ten Mile Creek, BC, Canada, parts to Upper Valley Aviation for spares use; canx 02Apr86]
40	BN-2A	G-51-9 N587JA [w/o 03Jan69 nr Narsarsuaq, Greenland]
41	BN-2A-9	G-51-10 9M-APD 9M-MDA DQ-FDV [CofA exp 23Jan86; wfu Nadi, Fiji]
42	BN-2A	G-51-11 9V-BBS 9M-ARM 9M-MDB 9M-AYJ ZK-FMS 5W-FAV
43	BN-2A-26	G-51-12 F-OCMN ZK-FWH ZK-REA
44	BN-2A	G-51-13 LV-PLU N595JA HP-839 HP-839KN SAN-209 (Panamanian Government) [dbr cAug96 Panama City, Panama]
45	BN-2A	G-51-14 N588JA [w/o 19Sep89 Vieques, PR during Hurricane Hugo; canx 21Jan93]
46	BN-2A-26	I-TRAL D-IBNB HB-LIC G-BJSA N123NE
47	BN-2A	G-AWVX 202 (Abu Dhabi Defence Force) 802 (Abu Dhabi Defence Force) MM60223 (Somalian Aeronautical Corps) [b/u c1995 Mogadishu, Somalia]
48	BN-2A-26	G-AWVY N48BN G-AWVY SE-IIA ES-PNA
49	BN-2A	N590JA N88MA HP-677 [dbr 08Aug75 Provenir Island, Panama then w/o when dropped by salvage helicopter]
50	BN-2A	CF-XZS [dbr 26Mar73 80 mls SW of Dawson Creek, BC, Canada; canx 06Aug74; parts to Huron Park, ON, Canada, later to Fort Lauderdale-Executive, FL, USA; b/u c1977]
51	BN-2A	G-51-15 G-AXBA F-OGEB (N70733) HC-BDX
52	BN-2A	F-OCMO ZK-FWZ T3-ATH ZK-FWZ
53	BN-2A	CS-AJP S9-TAM [wfu c1982 in Angola]
54	BN-2A	(G-AWYA) 6Y-JFL (HR-LAK) HR-SHD (N48VY) C-GQMG 8P-HEC C-GQMG 8P-DIS 8R-GGL [wfu c1993 Georgetown, Guyana]

ISLANDER

c/n	Series	Identities
55	BN-2A	G-AWYW 5A-BBA 5A-DEA [wfu c1996 Tripoli, Libya]
56	BN-2A-26	I-BATT N351SP YR-BNY YV-920C YV1204
57	BN-2A	N591JA [w/o 24Apr75 Tin City, AK, USA]
58	BN-2A	N592JA CF-DEB C-FDEB HP-1617
59	BN-2A	G-51-16 VQ-GAB N863JA HC-BHC [std Guayaquil, Ecuador]
60	BN-2A-6	N593JA N125JL HP-639 HP-639KN HP-639PS
61	BN-2A	N594JA CF-JPW N405SC HP-987PS HP-987TN HP-987XI [w/o 13Apr98 nr Paitilla, Panama]
62	BN-2A	N290EA N290VL [w/o 19Sep89 Vieques, PR during Hurricane Hugo; canx 11Jul91]
63	BN-2A	9M-APE [w/o 05Dec69 Sarawak, Malaysia]
64	BN-2A	N596JA N126JL HP-659 [w/o 28Jan85 Toboga Island, Panama]
65	BN-2A-8	N291EX N16KA N25DA C-FIAZ V7-0009 YJ-009
66	BN-2A	N598JA
67	BN-2A	VH-ATW P2-ATW P2-DNW [w/o 30Aug85 Kokoda, Papua New Guinea]
68	BN-2A	CS-AJQ [w/o 28Jul76 Covilha, Portugal]
69	BN-2A	N599JA N127JL [w/o 28Nov89 Block Island Sound, nr Block Island, RI, USA; canx 16Mar94]
70	BN-2A	G-AXDH VP-LMG [dam cSep95 Montserrat in Hurricane Luis; parts to Fort Lauderdale-Executive, FL, USA for rebuild]
71	BN-2A	N851JA (N106PC) N851JA [w/o 11Oct80 in the Bahamas]
72	BN-2A	N852JA [missing presumed w/o 11Oct69 between Fort Lauderdale, FL & San Juan, PR; canx]
73	BN-2A	G-51-17 G-AXFL 9H-AAB G-AXFL (VH-AAB) VH-MKN P2-MKN P2-ISI P2-ALI VH-RQW
74	BN-2A	N850JA N68HA N32MN [wfu Homestead Executive, FL, USA]
75	BN-2A-8	G-51-18 G-AXGB HS-SKA VH-TZH (H4-AAI) H4-AAH [destroyed cSep00 Guadalcanal, Solomon Islands]
76	BN-2A-26	G-AXFC (D-IAFC) VH-WGQ P2-WGQ P2-DNB P2-ALD P2-NAM
77	BN-2A-26	N853JA N128JL N112VA C-GGZR N678TA J6-SLZ N678TA
78	BN-2A-27	G-51-19 CF-YZT C-FYZT N200MU 6Y-JLB 6Y-JSX N200MU
79	BN-2A	G-51-20 G-AXIN VH-RTP
80	BN-2A	G-51-21 N854JA VP-LAC V2-LAC G-BNXA N80KM
81	BN-2A-26	G-51-22 (N870JA) G-AXSN VH-ROV P2-ROV P2-PAA P2-ISM (H4-AAI) P2-ISS YJ-RV6 VH-CSU P2- [canx 02Apr09 as exported to Papua New Guinea]
82	BN-2A-26	CF-YZU C-FYZU N100NE PJ-BIW C-
83	BN-2A	G-51-23 TR-LOC [w/o cMay73 in Gabon]
84	BN-2A	D-IAWD SE-INM
85	BN-2A	[void - airframe built as c/n 601]
86	BN-2A	G-AXHE "F-CXFR" 4X-AYV G-AXHE [dbr 05Feb94 Cark, UK, parts to Cormack Aircraft Services, Cumbernauld, UK; canx 31Mar94]
87	BN-2A	G-51-24 N855JA [w/o 09Sep70 Orocovis, PR]
88	BN-2A-26	G-51-25 D-IFDS C-GYMW VP-AAG [dam 02Feb08 Anguilla-Wallblake, Anguilla]
89	BN-2A	VH-FLE (DQ-FBV) P2-ISJ [w/o 18Jul79 Wanuma, Papua New Guinea]
90	BN-2A	G-51-26 N871JA C-GVCJ
91	BN-2A	G-51-27 G-AXLY JA5175 N87877 [w/o 15Nov90 nr Pohnpei, Pacific Ocean; canx 02Jan91]
92	BN-2A	G-51-28 N857JA [w/o 07Oct71 Isla Grande, PR]
93	BN-2A	YR-BNA 93 (Romanian AF) [wfu Bucharest-Otopeni, Romania]
94	BN-2A	G-51-29 VH-ATY P2-ATY P2-DNY P2-SAC
95	BN-2A	G-51-30 G-AXKB N95BN
96	BN-2A	(G-AXNF) G-51-31 4X-AYT 00./4X-FN? (Israeli DF/AF) 4X-AYT
97	BN-2A	(G-AXKC) G-51-32 YR-BNB 97 (Romanian AF) YR-BNB N260AK V2- [canx 06Jan09 as exported to Antigua]
98	BN-2A	G-51-33 CS-AJR HI-663CA
99	BN-2A	G-51-34 A2-ZEV [w/o 26Jan72 80 mls North of Maun, Botswana]
100	BN-2A-26	G-51-35 VH-ATV P2-ATV P2-DNV P2-SAB P2-ALE P2-NAJ
101	BN-2A	G-51-36 4X-AYF (N101BN) TG-REB YS-25C N101WD [wfu cJan00 Fort Lauderdale-Executive, FL, USA]
102	BN-2A	TR-LOD [w/o cJun73 in Gabon]
103	BN-2A	G-51-37 N861JA [w/o 19Sep89 Vieques, PR during Hurricane Hugo; canx 14Feb90]
104	BN-2A-27	F-OCFQ ZK-FLU YJ-RV16
105	BN-2A	G-51-38 G-AXMZ 7Q-YKC G-AXMZ OB-R-1272 OB-T-1272 OB-1272 [w/o 19May86 Puerto Maldonado, Peru; canx 21Dec01]
106	BN-2A	G-51-39 CF-AJL N25JA HP-658 [w/o cDec89 in Panama]
107	BN-2A	G-51-40 4X-AYW 006/4X-FN? (Israeli DF/AF) 001/4X-FMA[wfu cMar78; pres Israeli Defence Force Museum, Beersheba-Hatzerim AB, Israel]
108	BN-2A	N856JA [w/o 20Jul79 Bimini, Bahamas]
109	BN-2A	5W-FAF [w/o 20Aug88 Asau, Samoa; canx cDec88]
110	BN-2A-26	F-OCFR ZK-FXE
111	BN-2A	G-51-41 G-AXPY (PH-KJF) PH-NVA [w/o 30Aug70 Haringvreter Island, Veerse Meer, Netherlands; canx 25Sep70]
112	BN-2A-8	G-51-42 F-OCFS VH-SLM
113	BN-2A-26	VH-EQE P2-DWA
114	BN-2A-7	G-51-43 (CF-AJM) CF-AZM [w/o 18Jul77 Goose River, AB, Canada; canx 27Sep77]
115	BN-2A	N858JA [w/o 19Sep89 Vieques, PR during Hurricane Hugo; canx 29Mar90]
116	BN-2A	(VH-FLF) G-51-46 ST-ADJ G-BGRZ N2905C 6Y-JSM N9699N YV-473C N9699N 8R-GHG [w/o 29May96 Holitipu, Guyana]
117	BN-2A	G-51-44 G-AXPE 203 (Abu Dhabi Defence Force) 803 (Abu Dhabi Defence Force) MM60224 (Somalian Aeronautical Corps) [wfu c1991 Mogadishu, Somalia & b/u]
118	BN-2A-6	G-51-45 8R-GDN G-AYIV CR-AME C9-AME [wfu Maputo, Mozambique]
119	BN-2A	VH-ATU P2-ATU [w/o 05Oct79 Klantina, Papua New Guinea]
120	BN-2A	N869JA [w/o 20Jan78 nr Toksook Bay, between Bethel & Tununak, AK, USA]

ISLANDER

c/n	Series	Identities
121	BN-2A	G-51-47 (N859JA) G-AXUB 5N-AIJ G-AXUB
122	BN-2A	G-51-48 YR-BNC 122 (Romanian AF) [wfu Bucharest-Otopeni, Romania]
123	BN-2A	(N862JA) G-AXRJ [w/o 07Apr70 Rawalpindi, Pakistan; canx 06Jul70]
124	BN-2A	(VH-FLF) G-AXWK VH-EQT P2-NAA P2-ALM
125	BN-2A	G-51-49 (8R-GDQ) G-AYIW CS-AJO [w/o cNov82 Cascais, Portugal]
126	BN-2A	VT-ATX P2-ATX [w/o 14Aug75 Naoro, Papua New Guinea]
127	BN-2A-8	G-51-50 G-AXVP (F-BUIB) F-BUID TN-ADS [w/o cJun81 in Congo]
128	BN-2A-8	G-51-51 G-AXRM N158MA C-GKAW
129	BN-2A-26	G-51-52 G-AXRN C-GGYY (N724JP) N555DM
130	BN-2A	(N863JA) YR-BND 130 (Romanian AF) YR-BND 130 (Romanian AF) [wfu c1993; pres Muzeul Aviatiei, Bucharest-Otopeni, Romania]
131	BN-2A	G-51-53 F-OCOY [CofA exp 29Jan99; wfu Tahiti-Faaa/Papeete, Tahiti; canx 13Mar06]
132	BN-2A	VH-ATZ G-AXUD VH-ATZ P2-ATZ [wfu cApr90 Port Moresby, Papua New Guinea; reportedly b/u]
133	BN-2A	VH-APD P2-APD P2-AND [b/u c1988 Port Moresby, Papua New Guinea]
134	BN-2A-20	G-51-54 G-AXXF VH-BPV P2-BPV VH-BPV P2-ISQ P2-SAA [b/u c1993 Port Moresby, Papua New Guinea]
135	BN-2A	G-51-55 (N862JA) G-AXWG 5N-AIK G-AXWG [w/o 08Aug79 nr Angmagssalik, Greenland; canx 25Jun80]
136	BN-2A-8	G-51-56 F-OCOZ N6522T [dbr 23Sep04, Hallo Bay, AK, USA; canx 22Sep06]
137	BN-2A	G-51-58 (N864JA) G-AXWH 5N-AIL VR-BBI G-AXWH N137MW
138	BN-2A	G-51-57 (YR-BNE) YR-BNF N138LW
139	BN-2A-8	(N865JA) G-51-65 G-AXVR N139BN HR-LAR N139BT 4X-CCO [wfu, parts to Global Aircraft Industries, Edmonton-Villeneuve, AB, Canada]
140	BN-2A	G-51-59 G-AXWO G-4-10 G-AXWO JA5193 VH-UBD P2-CBB [w/o 14Dec02 Finisterre Mountains, Papua New Guinea]
141	BN-2A-7	G-51-61 VH-FLF N28377 [w/o 04Jun81 off Exuma Islands, Bahamas]
142	BN-2A	G-51-60 LN-RTO TF-RTO [w/o 22Sep80 Mount Snjofjoll, Iceland; canx 14Oct80]
143	BN-2A-2	G-51-62 G-AXXG 5X-BEE
144	BN-2A-26	G-51-64 G-AXXH ST-AIY [wfu c1999]
145	BN-2A-3	G-51-63 G-AYBI VH-ISD VH-UQN VH-ISD YJ-RV2 [w/o 19Dec08 nr Espiritu Santo, Vanuatu]
146	BN-2A	VH-EQK [w/o 31Mar78 Landsborough, QLD, Australia; canx 19Apr78]
147	BN-2A	G-51-66 G-AXWP VP-LMH J3-GAI [wfu Kingstown, St.Vincent]
148	BN-2A	G-51-67 G-AXXI 8R-GDJ [wfu c1993 Georgetown, Guyana]
149	BN-2A	G-51-68 G-AXWR YV-921C YV1241
150	BN-2A	G-51-150 G-AXXJ OO-ARI G-AXXJ G-PASW 4X-CAH HH-JEC
151	BN-2A	G-51-151 G-AXXK EI-AUF G-AXXK F-BPTT TR-LXW [w/o cJun85; exact date & location unkn]
152	BN-2A-26	G-51-152 G-AXWS VH-RTV DQ-FEA YJ-RV19 ZK-EVT
153	BN-2A-26	G-51-153 G-AXZK VP-LAD V2-LAD G-AXZK [wfu Bembridge, UK]
154	BN-2A	G-51-154 G-AYBL D-INYL OY-DVJ TI-AIW N154BN VQ-TAH
155	BN-2A	G-51-155 G-AXYL 5Y-DLC 9J-AFK Z-UAS 9J-UAS
156	BN-2A-26	G-51-156 G-AXYM 5N-AIQ G-AXYM G-BSPY HS-RON [w/o 14Jan03 1.5km from Pattaya Airpark, Thailand]
157	BN-2A	G-51-157 G-AXYN 9Q-CRF [w/o date & location unkn]
158	BN-2A	G-51-158 G-AXYP VH-FLD P2-MBD VH-MBK
159	BN-2A-26	G-51-159 G-AXYR VH-ISA DQ-FIN
160	BN-2A	G-51-160 VP-LAE V2-LAE [w/o 20Aug82 Mount Soufriere, St.Vincent]
161	BN-2A-26	G-51-161 VP-LAF V2-LAF G-BNXB EC-843 EC-FIQ [wfu c1998 Barcelona-El Prat, Spain]
162	BN-2A	G-51-162 G-AYBM CR-ALR [b/u; date & location unkn]
163	BN-2A	G-51-163 VP-LAG V2-LAG J3-GAG J8-VBJ
164	BN-2A-26	G-51-164 G-AXYS VH-EQX ZK-DBV
165	BN-2A	G-51-165 G-AXYT VH-RUT
166	BN-2A-26	G-51-166 4X-AYC G-BJWL 5B-CHD
167	BN-2A	G-51-167 G-AYBN CR-ALQ C9-ALQ [canx c1991 - status?]
168	BN-2A	G-51-168 G-AYCD VH-EQY ZK-DBW P2-FHP [w/o 12Jul83 Mount Hagen, Papua New Guinea]
169	BN-2A-27	G-51-169 G-AYCU CF-CMY C-FCMY [w/o 17Dec86 Norman Wells, NT, Canada; canx 27Dec00]
170	BN-2A-26	G-51-170 G-AYCV "VP-LVE" VP-LVD N140FS HP-1284AR HP-1284
171	BN-2A	G-51-171 G-AYCW (N111VA) G-51-171 G-AYCW 4X-AYA N119JE YV [canx 14Apr09 as exported to Venezuela]
172	BN-2A	G-51-172 G-AYCX VH-EQV VP-PAT F-OCXC YJ-RV2 (P2-ISW) YJ-RV2 [wfu 11Sep03 Port Vila-Bauerfield, Vanuatu]
173	BN-2A	G-51-173 G-AYCY VH-EQW VP-PAS H4-AAP YJ-RV5 [wfu cDec89 Port Vila-Bauerfield, Vanuatu]
174	BN-2A-6	G-51-174 G-AYDL CR-ALS C9-ALS
175	BN-2A	G-51-175 N864JA [w/o 10Feb74 off St Thomas, Virgin Islands]
176	BN-2A	G-51-176 N865JA [w/o 03May85 in the Bahamas]
177	BN-2A	G-51-177 VP-HBI V3-HBI [on rebuild Panama City-Marcos A Gelabert, Panama]
178	BN-2A	G-51-178 N859JA N100JL N103NA N403NA HP-986PS HP-986XI HP-986PS [w/o 31Dec97 Rio Sidra, Panama]
179	BN-2A-27	G-51-179 G-AYDM LN-VIW TF-REJ C-GMOW [dbf 15Mar02 Winnipeg, MB, Canada; canx 22Apr02]
180	BN-2A-6	G-51-180 EI-AUL G-BAVT VH-CPN P2-IST [w/o cMay90 Wau, Morobe, Papua New Guinea]
181	BN-2A-6	G-51-181 OH-BNA G-51-181 G-AYRU
182	BN-2A-7	G-51-182 G-AYGS ZS-IJA ZK-IAS [w/o 27Oct80 Stewart Island, New Zealand; canx cMar81; parts to Nandi, Fiji]

ISLANDER

c/n	Series	Identities
183	BN-2A-27	G-51-183 G-AYGT CF-ZUT C-FZUT N7UZ C-GLOD VP-MNI
184	BN-2A-6	G-51-184 N862JA [w/o 19Dec77 off Vieques, PR; canx 07Jan84]
185	BN-2A-6	G-51-185 N866JA
186	BN-2A-6	G-51-186 N867JA F-OGFA HP-676 [w/o cDec89 in Panama]
187	BN-2A-6	G-51-187 N870JA C-GKMJ [dam c1986, parts to Rocky Mountain Aircraft, Calgary-Springbank, AB, Canada; canx 10Jun98]
188	BN-2A-21	G-51-188 OY-DHS G-BAKZ LN-BNI G-BAKZ C-GUAW N8000J P2-MFI VH-CWG
189	BN-2A-6	G-51-189 N44JA N44DW [w/o cSep89 Vieques, PR during Hurricane Hugo]
190	BN-2A-6	G-51-190 G-AYGU XU-BAE [w/o c1975 Phnom Penh, Cambodia]
191	BN-2A-9	G-51-191 G-AYGV N88CA [wfu Culebra, PR & b/u; canx 14Mar89]
192	BN-2A-7	G-51-192 G-AYGW ZS-IJB CR-AMO C9-AMO ZS-IJB G-AYGW VP-WHX Z-WHX 9J-WHX
193	BN-2A-8	G-51-193 G-AYGF VP-LVB J6-SLV N1202S [w/o 07Aug97 Fajardo, PR in mid-air collision with c/n 375; canx 20Oct08]
194	BN-2A-26	G-51-194 G-AYHK VH-RTK P2-RTK (P2-PAB) P2-ISN P2-MBE [w/o 15Dec92 nr Alotau, Papua New Guinea]
195	BN-2A-6	G-51-195 G-AYHL VH-ISB VQ-FBO DQ-FBO [w/o 12Jul79 nr Bua, Vanua Levu, Fiji]
196	BN-2A-6	G-51-196 F-OCPY TU-TFW [w/o 09Jul75 Kabila, Gabon]
197	BN-2A-6	G-51-197 G-AYLR VQ-LAQ F-OGFO N197BN [w/o 19Sep89 Vieques, PR during Hurricane Hugo; canx 18Dec91]
198	BN-2A-6	G-51-198 N31JA N104PC TI-AYU N7079N [wfu Fort Worth-Meacham International, TX, USA still marked as TI-AYU]
199	BN-2A-6	G-51-199 N32JA C-GGIY
200	BN-2A-27	G-51-200 G-AYMB F-BTGO HC-BZF
201	BN-2A-6	G-51-201 N33JA N12JC N101NE
202	BN-2A-6	G-51-202 N34JA N116DW [w/o 20Jul81 San Juan, PR; canx 22Oct81]
203	BN-2A-6	G-51-203 (N35JA) YV-O-MOP-12 YV-O-MAR-6 [w/o 15Jun77 in Venezuela]
204	BN-2A-6	G-51-204 (N36JA) G-AYMC HP-556 HP-556KN [w/o date & location unkn]
205	BN-2A-6	G-51-205 G-AYIS PT-DYL
206	BN-2A-26	G-51-206 SE-FTA G-BNEA PH-PAR G-ISLA VP-AAS
207	BN-2A-3	G-51-207 G-AYKP VH-ISC P2-ISC P2-NAM [w/o 22Dec95 Bagasin, Papua New Guinea]
208	BN-2A-6	G-51-208 SE-FTB PT-KHK [w/o 13May80 nr Jacarepagua, Rio de Janeiro State, Brazil]
209	BN-2A-6	G-51-209 N36JA N712JC N36JA HR-AKR N209BN C6-BHR N209AB N209RG
210	BN-2A-6	G-51-210 N37JA [w/o 29Oct73 Mount Gimie, St.Lucia]
211	BN-2A-6	G-51-211 N38JA [w/o 16Aug73 Dondon, Haiti; canx 25Mar74]
212	BN-2A-27	G-51-212 CF-GAQ C-FGAQ
213	BN-2A-6	G-51-213 (N39JA) G-AYNH CR-AMG C9-AMG [wfu Maputo, Mozambique]
214	BN-2A-21	G-51-214 4X-AYB N51JA C-GNSC N6661A N214TL C6-BAA
215	BN-2A-6	G-51-215 N111VA [w/o 05Sep88 Sitka, AK, USA; canx 05Oct89]
216	BN-2A-7	G-51-216 G-AYNI PT-IAS 8R-GHM
217	BN-2A-2	G-51-217 G-AYKR VH-MIB P2-MIB [w/o 08Dec87 Kanabea, Papua New Guinea]
218	BN-2A-6	G-51-218 OH-BNB D-IAEB
219	BN-2A-6	G-51-219 G-AYYV CR-AMV C9-AMV [w/o 15May85 Chongoene, Mozambique]
220	BN-2A-9	G-51-220 F-OCRG YJ-RV4 [w/o 25Jul91 Espiritu Santo, Vanuatu]
221	BN-2A-6	G-51-221 F-OCRH [w/o 23Oct72 Ile de Tanna, New Hebrides; canx 21Apr75]
222	BN-2A-6	G-51-222 N40JA (HI-217) HI-220 N5450V N67TA [wfu Deland Municipal-Sidney H Taylor Field, FL, USA]
223	BN-2A-26	G-51-223 N41JA C-GTPB [w/o 18Sep87 Caribou Horn Lake, NT, Canada; canx 22Jun89]
224	BN-2A-6	G-51-224 N132JL HK-849
225	BN-2A-6	G-51-225 N131JL
226	BN-2A-6	G-51-226 G-AYON HP-572 HP-572OL HP-572XI [w/o c1989 exact date & location unkn]
227	BN-2A-20	G-51-227 G-AYLS VH-EDI P2-EDI (P2-ISD) VH-EDI P2-ISM
228	BN-2A-6	G-51-228 N42JA XA-PJA N4991X YV [canx 31Dec07 as exported to Venezuela]
229	BN-2A-6	G-51-229 N43JA PJ-WIC N229BN
230	BN-2A-8	G-51-230 8R-GDN 8R-GGR [w/o cOct96 Hampton Court, Guyana]
231	BN-2A-8	G-51-231 8R-GDQ [b/u c1990 Georgetown, Guyana]
232	BN-2A-8	G-51-232 N222TW N120DW [canx 05Feb91; fate unkn]
233	BN-2A-7	G-51-233 (G-AYRV) CF-ZWF [w/o 18Apr75 Fort Simpson, NT, Canada; canx 24Jul89]
234	BN-2A-6	G-51-234 N444TW N122DW [w/o 15Sep75 San Juan, PR]
235	BN-2A-3	G-51-235 G-AYTS 9V-BDT PK-OAN [w/o 21Mar85 Irian Jaya, Indonesia]
236	BN-2A-6	G-51-236 OO-GVS VH-CPG ZK-SFK
237	BN-2A-6	G-51-237 I-BADE [w/o 27Jun80 off Capoliveri, Elba Island, Italy]
238	BN-2A-26	G-51-238 CF-ZVV C-FZVV [w/o 18Sep79 Blinkhorn Point, BC, Canada, canx 11Feb86]
239	BN-2A-26	G-51-239 N130JL N118DW N66HA C-GDFC N143BW N909GD
240	BN-2A-7	G-51-240 "CF-ZVW" CF-ZVY CF-ZVY-X CF-ZVY N13CA [dbr 08Oct79 Crested Butte, CO, USA; canx 23Nov88]
241	BN-2A-7	G-51-241 (CF-QPM) G-AZAX CF-QPM C-FQPM N67HA [w/o date & location unkn]
242	BN-2A-6	G-51-242 LV-PRE LQ-JYV LV-JYV HP-1172KN N4278B HP-1220KN HP-1220PS YV-1116C YV178T YV1996
243	BN-2A-8	G-51-243 G-AYYP N119DW [wfu Culebra, PR]
244	BN-2A-6	G-51-244 N45JA (N28DW) N45JA [wfu cSep77 Dorado Beach, PR]
245	BN-2A MkIII	"G-AYPX" G-51-245 G-AYTU TR-LQL P2-DNN [wfu Boroko, Papua New Guinea]
246	BN-2A-3	G-51-246 9J-ACB
247	BN-2A-3	G-51-247 G-AYOO CR-AMS C9-AMS [wfu in Mozambique; canx cNov80]
248	BN-2A-7R	G-51-248 HP-549 HK-1244X HK-1244
249	BN-2A-6	G-51-249 N46JA N128DW [wfu Isla Grande, PR]
250	BN-2A-7R	G-51-250 N47JA TP-0207 (Mexican AF) TP-207 (Mexican AF) XC-DIS
251	BN-2A-27	G-51-251 5Y-AMU G-FANS G-HGPC 8R-GGU [w/o cSep94 in Guyana]
252	BN-2A-7R	G-51-252 N48JA TP-0208 (Mexican AF) TP-208 (Mexican AF) XB-FNS N158SP
253	BN-2A-3	G-51-253 G-AYPL ZS-IJC G-AYPL C-GZKG [canx 23Nov84 - status?]
254	BN-2A-3	G-51-254 9J-ACC

c/n	Series	Identities
255	BN-2A-7R	G-51-255 N49JA TP-0209 (Mexican AF) XC-FIK PF-209 (Mexican Police)
256	BN-2A-6R	G-51-256 N50JA FAP-208 (Panama AF) HP-786 SAN-208 (Panama AF) [w/o 03Jan08 nr Bahia Pina, Panama]
257	BN-2A-7	G-51-257 HP-571 6Y-JHU [wfu cMay83 Montego Bay, Jamaica]
258	BN-2A-7	G-51-258 PT-DVE [wfu by Jun92 Vera Cruz, Rondonia, Brazil]
259	BN-2A-7	G-51-259 PT-DVN [w/o 04Oct73 Itaituba, Paraguay]
260	BN-2A-3	G-51-260 9J-ACE
261	BN-2A-3	G-51-261 9J-ACF [w/o 27Mar75 Kalengwa, Zambia]
262	BN-2A MkIII-1	G-51-262 G-AYWI G-OCME [w/o 09Feb87 Hale, UK; canx 22Mar89]
263	BN-2A-27	G-51-263 CF-QPN N27JA C-GSAF [w/o 26Jan90 Inuvik, NT, Canada; canx 01Dec99]
264	BN-2A-6	G-51-264 N22JA [w/o 21Jul77 nr Ruby, AK, USA]
265	BN-2A-7R	G-51-265 HP-551 HK-1241X HK-1241 [b/u, parts at Villavicencio, Meta, Colombia]
266	BN-2A-7	G-51-266 HP-570 [w/o c1973; no further details known]
267	BN-2A-7	G-51-267 HP-569 HP-569P TP-310/XC-UPJ (Mexican Government)
268	BN-2A-9	G-51-268 HP-568 N89CA F-OGFY N4259X [wfu Fort Myers, FL, USA]
269	BN-2A-6	G-51-269 OH-BNC BN-1 (Finnish AF) OH-BNC D-IBNA G-51-269 (G-BRZH) 8R-GHB 8R-GHE
270	BN-2A-3	G-51-270 9J-ACG 9J-SKY
271	BN-2A-3	G-51-271 G-AYPX ZS-IRC 7P-IRC 7P-LAD ZS-LKE A2-AJA
272	BN-2A-3	(G-AYRW) G-51-272 TC-KUN [w/o 20Oct89 Hatay Province, Turkey; shot down by Syrian AF MiG21]
273	BN-2A-3	G-51-273 G-AYRX EP-PAC [w/o 17Mar83 Bandar Abbas, Iran]
274	BN-2A-3	G-51-274 HP-548 HP-581 N84CA C-GIPF [w/o 02Sep73 nr Campbell River, BC, Canada; canx 26Jan84]
275	BN-2A-3	G-51-275 "9J-ACH" 9J-ACL G-BASW 5Y-AUA [w/o c1991 in Kenya]
276	BN-2A-3	G-51-276 G-AYWJ (HP-547) CR-LMW D2-FMW
277	BN-2A-6	G-51-277 G-AYYW D-IOLA G-AYYW BDF-05 (Belize Defence Force) [w/o 03Apr07 Gales Point, Belize]
278	BN-2A-27	G-51-278 G-AYYA VH-ISE ZK-DKN VH-ISE N8021M ZK-WNZ [w/o 28Dec06 nr Tauranga, New Zealand; b/u for spares; canx 13Aug09]
279	BN-2A MkIII	G-AYZR N85CA VH-BSG [w/o 17Nov80 Annanberg, Papua New Guinea; canx 17Jun81]
280	BN-2A-3	G-51-280 9J-ACM
281	BN-2A-20	G-51-281 G-AYYB VH-ISF P2-ISF [w/o 23Dec93 Bambu, Papua New Guinea]
282	BN-2A-7	G-51-282 HP-550 [w/o cOct71 in Panama]
283	BN-2A-21	G-51-283 N51JA 4X-AYO N581MA F-OGHL [w/o 28Oct88 Pointe-a-Pitre, Guadeloupe; canx 28Aug91]
284	BN-2A-3	G-51-284 5Y-ANV [wfu Nairobi, Kenya; CofA exp 07Oct98]
285	BN-2A-2	G-51-285 G-AZBV (EI-AVO) 4X-AYK 004/4X-FNP (Israeli DF/AF) 004/4X-FMD [pres Israeli Defence Force Museum, Beersheba-Hatzerim AB, Israel]
286	BN-2A-7R	G-51-286 N52JA TP-0212 (Mexican AF) TP-212 (Mexican AF) XC-GOQ XC-UPK [b/u c1999 Mojave, CA, USA]
287	BN-2A-3	G-51-287 5Y-ANU VQ-SAC [w/o 04Sep76 Praslin Island, Seychelles; forward fuselage pres Chelsea College, Shoreham, UK]
288	BN-2A-3	G-51-288 G-AZCG ZS-IJD A2-ZGK CR-AOK [no reported sightings since 1973; presumed destroyed]
289	BN-2A-2	G-51-289 G-AZEH VQ-SAJ S7-AAJ N4249Y 8R-GFN [w/o 06Jan01 Ebini Mountain, Guyana]
290	BN-2A-3	G-51-290 (N20JL) TC-KUR
291	BN-2A-2	G-51-291 G-AZEI PK-OAB [w/o 13May80 Pit River, Indonesia]
292	BN-2A-9	G-51-292 F-OCSB TU-TLC [wfu Abidjan, Ivory Coast]
293	BN-2A-7R	G-51-293 N35JA TP-0211 (Mexican AF) TP-211/XC-FOJ (Mexican AF)
294	BN-2A-7R	G-51-294 N39JA TP-0210 (Mexican AF) TP-210/XC-FIY (Mexican AF) N933SC [wfu Sarasota-Bradenton, FL, USA; canx 13Aug07]
295	BN-2A-8	G-51-295 N55JA
296	BN-2A-8	G-51-296 (N56JA) F-BOAL G-BEXP F-OGID HR-ALP HP-1209XI HP-1209PS YV-1115C [w/o 31Mar05 Caracas-Simon Bolivar, Venezuela]
297	BN-2A-6	G-51-297 G-AZLI EP-PAE [w/o 11Aug72 Ganaveh, Iran]
298	BN-2A-3	G-51-298 G-AZPU YI-AFZ [status?]
299	BN-2A MkIII-1	G-51-299 G-AZFG N60JA CF-CHZ C-FCHZ N90541 HK-2482X HK-2482 [wfu Villavicencio, Meta, Colombia; canx 02Apr03]
300	BN-2A-3	G-51-300 XA-CIQ [status?]
301	BN-2A-6	G-51-301 N53JA PT-IJF PT-KYA
302	BN-2A-20	G-51-302 (N57JA) G-AZUR JA5195 VH-BSL
303	BN-2A-2	G-51-303 (N58JA) G-AZUS D-IHVH F-OGXB
304	BN-2A-6	G-51-304 N54JA PT-IJE [w/o 12Jun79 Cuiaba, Mato Grosso, Brazil]
305	BN-2A MkIII-1	G-51-305 G-AZJA HP-946 [w/o 30May84 in Panama]
306	BN-2A-8	G-51-306 N80CA C-GPVN 8R-GHC 8R-GAR [wfu c1999 Georgetown, Guyana]
307	BN-2A-9R	G-51-307 N20JA XC-GAU XC-UPJ [w/o c1990 in Mexico]
308	BN-2A-3S	G-51-308 G-BAAE PK-KNA [b/u by May04 in Indonesia]
309	BN-2A-8	G-51-309 G-BADK F-ODYF [wfu Noumea, New Caledonia]
310	BN-2A-8	G-51-310 (N91CA) F-OGGA HP-1079KN YV-522C
311	BN-2A-26	G-BAFE N92CA C-GAPZ N102NE C-FFXS PJ-SEA
312	BN-2A-8	G-51-312 N93CA N121DW
313	BN-2A-8	G-BAJP (N24JA) XC-DAB [status?]
314	BN-2A-9	G-BAJS (N27JA) "PT-EFI" PP-EFI PT-WMY
315	BN-2A-8	G-BALV N94CA [w/o date & location unkn]
316	BN-2A-26	G-BALO 4X-AYL SX-BFC 4X-AYL SX-BFG 4X-AYL G-BJWN ZK-FVD
317	BN-2A-3	G-BANJ ZS-IZZ [w/o 24Aug74 Richards Bay, Natal, South Africa]
318	BN-2A-8	G-BANL RP-C764 [w/o 02Apr09 between Tuguegarao & Maconacon, Philippines]
319	BN-2A MkIII-1	G-51-319 G-AZLJ G-OAVW G-OREG SX-CBN G-OREG G-AZLJ [wfu cJan01 Lydd, UK; canx 01Mar01]

ISLANDER

c/n	Series	Identities
320	BN-2A MkIII-1	G-51-320 5Y-AOY [w/o c1986 in Kenya]
321	BN-2A MkIII	G-AZZM HK-2481X HK-2481 [wfu Villavicencio, Meta, Colombia; canx 07Apr00]
322	BN-2A MkIII	G-BAFF DQ-FBY VH-BGS P2-DNX (VH-CYC) VH-MRJ ZK-LOU
323	BN-2A-8	N96CA XC-COJ XC-UPL XB-JTA YV258T
324	BN-2A-8	N97CA XA-CUJ
325	BN-2A-3	G-51-325 G-BATK (VH-ISH) N2000J [wfu & canx 18Jun91; parts to Invercargill, New Zealand for spares use]
326	BN-2A-8	XA-DEU [w/o c1981 in Mexico]
327	BN-2A-3	G-BATL PT-EFJ PP-EFJ PT-WOU
328	BN-2A-3	G-BAUS N800CA HP-651 HP-680 [w/o c1986 in Panama]
329	BN-2A-21	G-BAUT VH-ISI [w/o 25Nov84 Wilton, NSW, Australia; canx 25Nov84]
330	BN-2A-3	G-BAXA (F-BUFV) 5Y-ARZ 5N-AKL TZ-ACF
331	BN-2A-9R	N98CA XA-DAV N2718W [dbf 21Jul83 Brownwood, TX, USA; canx 26Mar91]
332	BN-2A-9	G-BAXB TR-LRP [wfu cSep79 Port Gentil, Gabon]
333	BN-2A-9	G-BAZW G350 (Ghana AF) N158A [wfu cApr95; on rebuild Kelowna, BC, Canada]
334	BN-2A-26	G-BAXC 4X-AYR SX-BBX 4X-AYR G-BJWO
335	BN-2A-8	G-BAZX (N91CA) B-11107 [w/o 09Sep79 off Lan-Yu Island, Taiwan]
336	BN-2A-9	G-BAZY ZK-MCB P2-FHO [canx cAug86 - status?]
337	BN-2A-9	G-BAZZ G351 (Ghana AF) N164A [wfu Hollywood-North Perry, FL, USA]
338	BN-2A-9	G-BBAL G352 (Ghana AF) N146A N821RR
339	BN-2A-9	G-BBAM G353 (Ghana AF) N149A 6Y-JRC N149A C-FTAM N905GD
340	BN-2A-9	G-BBAN G354 (Ghana AF) N161A (6Y-JRD) N907GD
341	BN-2A-9	G-BBAO G355 (Ghana AF) N153A 6Y-JLA N910GD [wfu c2008 Fort Lauderdale-Executive, FL, USA; undergoing rebuild San Juan, PR]
342	BN-2A-9	G-BBDW G356 (Ghana AF) N148A [wfu Fort Myers, FL, USA]
343	BN-2A-9	G-BBDX G357 (Ghana AF) N4414P N723JM
344	BN-2A-2	G-BBDY JA5218 ZK-PIY
345	BN-2A-9	G-BBDZ (N26JA) YV-T-AEW YV-795P YV-269C [w/o 29Mar88 in Venezuela]
346	BN-2A-9	G-BBGV F-OCUC TL-CUC TL-KAA
347	BN-2A-8	G-51-347 (F-BUTN) N87JA N69HA C6-BFQ
348	BN-2A-9	G-BBIZ (N23JA) N84JA 8R-GEH [w/o 07Nov77 Georgetown, Guyana]
349	BN-2A MkIII	VP-PAO G-51-349 G-BASA VP-PAO H4-AAQ YJ-RV3 [w/o 03Jan90 in Vanuatu]
350 (G)	BN-2A MkIII-1	(N29JA) G-BBNL HK-2412X HK-2412 [wfu Villavicencio, Meta, Colombia; canx 02Apr03]
351	BN-2A-20	G-BBJA PK-VIN
352	BN-2A-20	G-BBJC N24JA C-GCXB N352BN F-OGNV LN-FSK CS-DBO
353	BN-2A-8	N87CA XC-SIB
354	BN-2A-20	G-BBLW JA5227 H4-WPC H4-SIE VH-PNJ VH-WZE
355	BN-2A-9	G-BBLX N355BN H4-AAI
356 (G)	BN-2A-8	G-BANM XA-DEW (P2-FHC) XA-DEW
357 (G)	BN-2A-8	G-BANN N95CA [w/o 19Sep89 Vieques, PR during Hurricane Hugo]
358 (G)	BN-2A-8	G-BATZ N28JA XA-FEQ [status?]
359	BN-2A MkIII	G-BAXD G-XTOR
360 (G)	BN-2A MkIII	(VH-BML) G-BBWO ZS-JJC C-GSZI [w/o 07Sep81 in Canada; canx 10Dec81]
361 (G)	BN-2A MkIII	G-BBWP (N29JA) C-GOXZ RP-C [canx 18Nov08 as exported to Philippines]
362	BN-2A MkIII-1	G-BBWR G-BBYO ZS-KMH G-BBYO [wfu Guernsey, Channel Islands, UK; canx 23Feb95]
363 (G)	BN-2A MkIII-1	G-BCCT 9L-LAQ [w/o 25Aug80 Freetown, Sierra Leone]
364	BN-2A-8	G-BBLY CR-APQ C9-APQ [wfu Maputo, Mozambique]
365	BN-2A-8	G-BBLZ N80JA [w/o 19Sep89 Vieques, PR during Hurricane Hugo]
366	BN-2A MkIII-1	(LN-VIV) G-BCCU 9L-LAR G-BCCU 4X-CCK G-BCCU G-LCOC
367	BN-2A-8	G-BBMA CR-APC C9-APC [wfu Maputo, Mozambique]
368	BN-2A-9	G-BBON N82JA 6Y-JJA 6Y-JQA [wfu Montego Bay, Jamaica]
369	BN-2A-8	G-51-369 F-OGGP HP-1075KN YV-509C YV-2478P YV-1132C
370	BN-2A-3	G-BBRM (N83JA) PT-JZN [status?]
371	BN-2A-9	G-BBRP [dbr 20Feb82 Netheravon, UK; fuselage used as para trainer; canx 27Apr83; b/u c1994]
372	BN-2A MkIII-1	G-BCEG VH-BSP (N38535) P2-DNP VH-BSP ZK-LGR [wfu c2008]
373	BN-2A MkIII-1	(9L-LAR) G-BCJV 5X-UAS [wfu c1980 Entebbe, Uganda]
374 (G)	BN-2A-8	G-BBBG (N91CA) VP-HCD [w/o 22Feb77 Hillbank, Belize]
375	BN-2A-8	G-BBBH N26JA [w/o 07Aug97 Fajardo, PR in mid-air collision with c/n 193; canx 20Oct08]
376 (G)	BN-2A-8	G-BBMC N88JA 4X-AYS (G-BJWL) 4X-AYS
377	BN-2A-8	G-BBUA F-BUTN 5T-TJV G-51-377 G-BBUA D-IHER SE-LGN PJ-SUN
378	BN-2A-9R	G-BBUB N83JA XC-GOA [wfu in Mexico]
379	BN-2A-8	G-BBUC 9M-ATS 9M-JPC
380	BN-2A-8	G-BBWS 9V-BGA B-12202 [w/o 09Dec83 off Lan-Yu Island, Taiwan]
381	BN-2A MkIII-1	G-BCJW (N58JA) C-GNKW VH-NKW ZK-LGC [wfu & canx 02Oct08]
382	BN-2A-8	G-BBWT 382/5R-MSA (Madagascan AF) N361RA VP-AAA
383	BN-2A-27	G-BBWU TF-RED N4261U C-GSGK [dbr 25Jan95 Paungassi, MB, Canada, parts to Penticton, BC, Canada; canx 19Dec08]
384	BN-2A-8	G-BBWV VQ-SAH S7-AAH N42495 8R-GFL J6-SLY J8-VBN N296TA
385	BN-2A-8	G-BBWW (N81JA) PT-JYC [w/o c1987 exact date & location unkn]
386	BN-2A-21	G-BBWX (N86JA) LN-VIV A2-AFM [wfu c1985]
387	BN-2A-9	G-BBYX TR-LSF [w/o 23Aug77 Ngonnon, Gabon]
388 (G)	BN-2A-7R	G-BBWY N85JA (8P-DON) XA-FUA [w/o 03Nov77 San Cristobal, Chiapas, Mexico]
389	BN-2A-26	G-BBZD VP-LVG [wfu Tortola, British Virgin Islands]
390	BN-2A-8	G-BCBS (PT-JZJ) N89JA XA-FIC XB-DVH XA-RRM [wfu c2000]
391	BN-2A MkIII-2	G-BCJX DQ-FCC T3-ATD [wfu cMay94 Tarawa, Kiribati]
392	BN-2A-23	G-BCJY 9V-BGJ 9M-AUD 9V-BGJ PK-VIR [w/o 24Feb87 Banjarmasin, Indonesia]
393 (G)	BN-2A-20	G-BBYY P2-CBT P2-TNT [w/o 25Jul95 Bomia, Papua New Guinea]
394 (G)	BN-2A-20	G-BBYZ P2-MKX P2-ISC [w/o 03Jun93 Kiriwina Island, Papua New Guinea]
395 (G)	BN-2A-26	G-BBZA ZK-MCC P2-FHQ P2-ALF [w/o 19Sep94 Rabaul, Papua New Guinea]

ISLANDER

c/n	Series	Identities
396 (G)	BN-2A-20	G-BBZC HB-LIA 3D-ADO Z-WPR [dbr cOct96 Kariba, Zimbabwe, parts to Harare-Charles Prince, Zimbabwe]
397 (G)	BN-2A-8	G-BCEH F-BVVP F-ODJV TZ-ASC [wfu cSep87 Bamako, Mali]
398 (G)	BN-2A-20	G-BCEI (N56JA) N90PB C-GMOP [dbr 03Dec93 8 mls SE of Tuktoyaktuk, NT, Canada, parts to Global Aircraft Industries, Edmonton-Villeneuve, AB, Canada; canx 28Oct97]
399 (G)	BN-2A-26	G-BCEJ N57JA 4X-AYP SX-BFA 4X-AYP SX-BFD 4X-AYP SX-BFF 4X-AYP G-BJWP F-OGOV N60616 [wfu St.Barthelemy, Guadeloupe; canx 22Nov02]
400 (G)	BN-2A-21	G-BCEK 301 (Omani AF) N7071C XU-MTC XU-MLC ML501 (Cambodian AF)
401 (G)	BN-2A-21	G-BCEL 302 (Omani AF) N7071H XU-MTA XU-MLA [b/u Phnom Penh, Cambodia]
402 (G)	BN-2A-21	(N59JA) G-BCEM 303 (Omani AF) N7071M VH-OIA VH-URJ
403 (G)	BN-2A-26	G-BCEN N90JA 4X-AYG SX-BFB 4X-AYG G-BCEN
404 (G)	BN-2A-20	G-BCKW N81JA C-GIRH [dbr 12Jan87 Lake Ontario, ON, Canada; canx 10Jun98 as exported to Peru]
405 (G)	BN-2A-9	G-BCKX YV-T-AKL YV-C-AKL GN-7432 (Venezuelan National Guard) YV-2384P [w/o 31Dec93 in Venezuela; re-registered YV-2384P; status?]
406 (G)	BN-2A-21	G-BCKY N59JA VH-SBH ZK-SFE [w/o 19Mar89 Northwest Bay, New Zealand; canx 16Mar90]
407 (G)	BN-2A-9	G-BCKZ N91JA PT-KSP
408 (G)	BN-2A-21	G-BCLE RP-C1262
409 (G)	BN-2A-21	G-BCLF RP-C28 (VH-BRC) RP-C28
410 (G)	BN-2A-21	G-BCLH N56JA N94JA HH-CNA 1270 (Haitian Air Corps) HI-551CA [wfu c1997 Haina, Dominican Republic]
411 (G)	BN-2A-21	G-BCMK JA5241 DQ-FES [dbr 23Sep96 Gau Island, Fiji; wfu Nadi, Fiji]
412 (G)	BN-2A-21	G-BCMM ZS-ORD 7213 (Rhodesian AF) 7213 (Zimbabwean AF)
413 (G)	BN-2A-21	G-BCMN 304 (Omani AF) [w/o 03Aug76 nr Muscat, Oman]
414 (G)	BN-2A-21	G-BCMO 305 (Omani AF) N7071N XU-MTB XU-MLB [w/o 30Apr96 in Cambodia]
415 (G)	BN-2A-21	G-BCMP 306 (Omani AF) N7071S VH-HIA [w/o 07Apr96 off Currumbin Beach, Southport, QLD, Australia; canx 08Apr96]
416 (G)	BN-2A-21	G-BCMS N92JA C-GILS
417 (G)	BN-2A-21	G-BCMU 307 (Omani AF) N7071U DQ-FIF ZK-FIF N130PC
418 (G)	BN-2A-21	G-BCMV 308 (Omani AF) [w/o 10Jun87 nr Khasab, Oman]
419 (G)	BN-2T	G-BCMY G-BPBN G-OTVS [wfu c1989 Headcorn, UK; canx 08Apr94; b/u c1999 Gloucester-Staverton, UK]
420 (G)	BN-2A-8R	G-BCSD N23JA TP-0209 (Mexican AF) XC-FIK
421 (G)	BN-2A-20	G-BCSF RP-2131 RP-C2131 P2-FHR P2-MFT VH-UBN VH-WZK
422 (G)	BN-2A-21	G-BCSG RP-C2132
423 (G)	BN-2A-27	G-BCSH (N93JA) C-GPPP [dam c2004 in Canada; remains stored Penticton, BC, Canada pending rebuild]
424 (G)	BN-2A-27R	G-BCSI OO-TOP C-FJJR [w/o 07Jun09 nr Port Hope Simpson, NL, Canada]
425 (G)	BN-2A-21	G-BCSJ D-IELE VH-NTC P2-KAF VH-NTC P2-KAF P2-IAC
426 (G)	BN-2A-21	G-BCTY (9V-BGD) 426 (Philippine Navy) [w/o 19May76 nr Palawan, Philippines]
427 (G)	BN-2A-8	G-BCTZ N21JA XA-CAZ N599MT
428 (G)	BN-2A-21	G-BCUA (N23JA) 428 (Philippine Navy) 301(Philippine Navy)[wfu c1995]
429 (G)	BN-2A-21	G-BCUD (I-CIRS) PK-OBE [w/o 29Apr83 Landitma, Irian Jaya, Indonesia]
430 (G)	BN-2A-21	G-BCUE RP-2133 430 (Philippine Navy) 310(Philippine Navy)
431 (G)	BN-2A-26	G-BCWO LN-MAC SE-LAX G-BCWO G-IOWA N431V 8R- [canx 17Jun09 as exported to Guyana]
432 (G)	BN-2A-21	G-BCWP VH-ISL P2-TFI
433 (G)	BN-2A-20	G-BCWR OY-RPZ G-BCWR [b/u c1994; canx 26Oct94]
434 (G)	BN-2A-8	G-BCWS N94JA PT-KQS
435 (G)	BN-2A-8	G-BCWT N58JA 4X-AYI SX-BBZ 4X-AYI SX-BFE 4X-AYI N721BN [wfu Jacksonville, FL, USA]
436 (G)	BN-2A-27	G-BCWU J8-VAK [w/o 08Jan96 in sea 17 mls off Barbados]
437 (G)	BN-2A-8	G-BCWV D-IEDA [w/o 12Jan79 Juist, West Germany; canx 16Jan79]
438 (G)	BN-2A-21	G-BCWX RP-C2134 P2-CBE [canx c1989 - status?]
439 (G)	BN-2A-21	G-BCWY (I-CIRS) RP-C2135 [w/o 18Jan76 Mactan, Philippines]
440 (G)	BN-2A-21	G-BCWZ RP-C2136 [w/o 21Dec75 Tacloban, Leyte, Philippines]
441 (G)	BN-2A-21	G-BCZS LN-MAF [pres Flyhistorik Museum, Sola, Norway; canx 18Dec85]
442 (G)	BN-2A-21	G-BCZT N95JA HH-CNB [w/o 26Dec78 between South Caicos & Grand Turk, Turks & Caicos Islands]
443 (G)	BN-2A-21	G-BCZU RP-2137 RP-C2137
444 (G)	BN-2A-26	G-BCZV EI-BBA [w/o 16Oct75 Inishmore, Ireland; canx 21Dec76]
445 (G)	BN-2A-21	G-BCZW RP-C2138
446 (G)	BN-2A-21	G-BCZX N93JA 4X-AYH
447 (G)	BN-2A-21	G-BCZY N97JA (PT-KSJ) (ZK-KHB) N97JA [w/o 20Apr78 San Jose-Reid/Hillview, CA, USA]
448 (G)	BN-2A-21	G-BCZZ RP-C2139 VH-FCJ P2-ALL [w/o 10Dec93 Namatanai, Papua New Guinea]
449 (G)	BN-2A-21	G-BDAA N96JA N90PA C-GMND N799MT
450 (G)	BN-2A-21	G-BDAF RP-C2140 VH-USD VH-WZD
451 (G)	BN-2A-27	G-BDDK N21JA XA-MHT [canx; fate unkn]
452 (G)	BN-2A-21	G-BDDL RP-C2141 [wfu Tanauan, Philippines; CofA exp 08Oct05]
453 (P)	BN-2A-21	RP-C2148 453 (Philippine Navy) 302 (Philippine Navy)
454 (G)	BN-2A-8	G-BDDM F-OGHA N454CT [w/o cMay95 in Surinam, parts to Daytona Beach, FL, USA; rebuild abandoned; canx 18Jan06]
455 (G)	BN-2A-21	G-BDDN RP-C2142 455 (Philippine AF) [wfu c1995]
456 (G)	BN-2A-21	G-BDDO (RP-C2143) 456 (Philippine Navy) 304 (Philippine Navy)
457 (G)	BN-2A-21	G-BDDP N29JA N115DW
458 (G)	BN-2A-21	G-BDDR RP-C2144 ZK-JSB VH-OBJ
459 (G)	BN-2A-21	G-BDDU RP-C2145 459 (Philippine AF)
460 (G)	BN-2A-21	RP-C2147 460 (Philippine Navy) 303 (Philippine Navy)

ISLANDER

c/n	Series	Identities
461 (G)	BN-2A-26	G-BDDV SX-BFH G-BDDV (OO-PCM) OO-MPC 9Q-CPT ZS-OSD [w/o 05Oct08 nr Barberton, Mpumalanga Province, South Africa]
462 (G)	BN-2A-21	RP-C2146 RP-2164 462 (Philippine Police) RP-462 RP-2164 RP-4177
463 (G)	BN-2A-21	G-BDDW RP-2169 463 (Philippine Police) RP-463 RP-C2169
464 (G)	BN-2A-20	G-BDIZ HP-768 TI-AKI C-GEVX N634MA [dbr 28Apr07 nr Hamilton-Ravalli Apt, MT, USA; canx 20Jan09]
465 (G)	BN-2A-21	G-BDHE N21JA N21YA C-FWLS N21YA V3-HFO [w/o 19Nov05 Privacion, Belize]
466 (G)	BN-2A-21	G-BDJA B-01 (Belgian Army) 3X-GEF
467 (G)	BN-2A-21	G-BDHF N98JA XA-GEL [dbr date unkn; wreck noted Toluca, Mexico State, Mexico]
468 (G)	BN-2B-21	G-BDHG B-02 (Belgian Army) OO-MMM
469 (G)	BN-2A-21	G-BDHH RP-C850 [w/o 31Jul86 Mount Canlandog, Philippines]
470 (G)	BN-2A-26	G-BDHI N99JA XC-CRM N81567 8R-GGY
471 (P)	BN-2A-21	RP-C2149 471 (Philippine AF) [wfu c1995; b/u cFeb98 Sangley Point, Philippines]
472 (G)	BN-2A-8	G-BDJS (F-BVOE) EI-BBR [w/o 07Aug80 Carnmore, Ireland; canx 12Sep85]
473 (P)	BN-2A-21	(RP-C2150) RP-C471 [w/o 09Jun99 Coron, Philippines; CofR exp 27Sep99]
474 (G)	BN-2A-21	G-BDJT (N56JA) N61JA HH-CNC [w/o 02Jan80 Grande Riviere du Nord, Haiti]
475 (G)	BN-2A-26	G-BDJU C-GIHF
476 (G)	BN-2B-21	G-BDJV B-03/OT-ALC (Belgian Army) G-BDJV [dbr 14Feb03 Brasschaat, Belgium; parts to Cumbernauld, UK for spares use; re-registered G-BDJV 08Aug06]
477 (G)	BN-2T	G-BDJW IN126 (Indian Navy)
478 (G)	BN-2A-21	G-BDJX 8R-GER [wfu Georgetown, Guyana]
479 (G)	BN-2A-27	G-BDJY N4990M A40-DL (N333GM) N8491B (N15AA) N8491B [w/o 19Sep89 Vieques, PR during Hurricane Hugo; canx 27Dec91]
480 (G)	BN-2T	G-BDJZ IN127 (Indian Navy)
481 (G)	BN-2A-21	G-BDKX IN128 (Indian Navy)
482 (G)	BN-2A-27	G-BDKY 8R-GES [w/o 15Dec86 Georgetown, Guyana]
483 (G)	BN-2A-21	G-BDLF F-OCXP YJ-AV3
484 (G)	BN-2A-27	G-BDLG 8R-GET [w/o 25Apr07 Kopinang, Guyana]
485 (P)	BN-2A-21	RP-C2151 G-BEGB PK-VIS
486 (G)	BN-2A-27	G-BDLH XA-GAZ [status?]
487 (P)	BN-2A-21	RP-C2152 [w/o 07Oct78 Sierra Madre Mountains, Philippines]
488 (G)	BN-2A-21	G-BDLI PT-KSJ [canx; fate unkn]
489 (G)	BN-2A-21	G-BDLJ F-GAJA P2-KAE [canx; fate unkn]
490 (G)	BN-2A-20	G-BDLK XA-GUT N138PC C-FVFN HC-CGY
491 (G)	BN-2A-27	G-BDLL PT-KTP
492 (G)	BN-2A-21	G-BDLN 7Q-YAZ [w/o 04Feb77 in Malawi]
493 (G)	BN-2A-27	G-BDNM PT-KTQ [dam 22Sep01 Rio Branco, Acre, Brazil]
494 (P)	BN-2A-21	RP-C2153 G-BEGC VH-SQS T3-JMR
495 (G)	BN-2A-27	G-BDNN PT-KTR
496 (G)	BN-2A-21	G-BDNP [w/o 18Sep81 St Andrews, Guernsey, UK; fuselage used as para-trainer, Headcorn, UK; canx 08Jan82]
497 (G)	BN-2A-26	G-BDPM HP-712 TI-ART N497BN [wfu Castries, St Lucia]
498 (G)	BN-2B-21	G-BDPN B-04/OT-ALD (Belgian Army) G-BDPN G-ECZA
499 (G)	BN-2A-27	G-BDPO PT-KTS [canx; fate unkn]
500 (P)	BN-2A-21	RP-C2154 VH-SBD RP-C1048 [wfu Manila-Ninoy Aquino International, Philippines; CofR exp 15Aug91]
501 (G)	BN-2A-21	G-BDPP B-05/OT-ALE (Belgian Army) [dbf 23Nov88; stored PS Aero, Baarlo, Netherlands pending fate]
502 (P)	BN-2A-21	RP-C2155 502 (Philippine AF) RP-C1323 [wfu Manila-Ninoy Aquino International, Philippines; CofA exp 26Nov99]
503 (P)	BN-2A-21	RP-C2156 G-BEUO VH-IGT P2-KAG [w/o 29Jul95 Fane, Papua New Guinea]
504 (G)	BN-2A-27LN	G-BDPR (N3265N) VH-LRX HI-704CT VQ-TDA
505 (P)	BN-2A-21	RP-C2157 RP-2157 RP-C2157 [wfu Manila-Ninoy Aquino International, Philippines; canx 27Sep06]
506 (G)	BN-2T	G-BDPS IN129 (Indian Navy)
507 (G)	BN-2A-21	G-BDPT IN130 (Indian Navy) [w/o 11Jan83 in sea nr Cochin, India]
508 (P)	BN-2A-21	RP-C2158 508 (Philippine AF) [wfu Sangley Point, Philippines]
509 (P)	BN-2A-21	RP-C2159 G-BFAE RP-C2167 509 (Philippine AF) [wfu Manila-Ninoy Aquino International, Philippines]
510 (G)	BN-2A-21	G-BDPU B-06/OT-ALF (Belgian Army) [dbf 23Nov88 Butzweilerhof, West Germany; pres Musee Royale de L'Armee, Brussels, Belgium]
511 (G)	BN-2A-21	G-BDSW N62JA ZK-KHB DQ-FIC
512 (G)	BN-2A-21	G-BDSX N69JA PT-KUO [w/o 12May77 50km from Curitiba, Parana, Brazil]
513 (G)	BN-2A-21	G-BDSY N63JA C-GVZY HR-AUL
514 (G)	BN-2A-26	G-BDSZ N4564Q N112JC [w/o 19Sep89 Isle Grande, PR during Hurricane Hugo; canx 26Apr91]
515 (G)	BN-2A-21	G-BDUS N65JA N62TA [wfu Saint Thomas-Cyril E King, US Virgin Isles]
516 (G)	BN-2A-21	G-BDUT N66JA [wfu Fort Myers, FL, USA]
517 (G)	BN-2A-26	G-BDTA (C-GUKZ) N400JA N18WA J6-AAC N18WA C6-BGU
518 (G)	BN-2A-26	G-BDUU B-11109 [w/o 28Sep83 Lan-Yu Island, Taiwan]
519 (G)	BN-2A-26	G-BDUV EI-BCE
520 (G)	BN-2A-20	G-BDUW YV-1073P YV-O-GSF-6 YV-O-FDN-1 YV-O-GSF-6 YV-1073P N6561B [dam 15Jul07 Stanley, ID, USA]
521 (G)	BN-2A-20	G-BDVV JA5255 P2-MFW VH-VPC
522 (G)	BN-2A-26	G-BDVW [w/o 01Jun84 Sanday, Orkney, UK; canx 04Feb88]
523 (G)	BN-2B-21	G-BDVX B-07/OT-ALG (Belgian Army) G-BDVX G-OBNL
524 (G)	BN-2A-27	G-BDVY N64JA N19WA (N307SK) N19WA [wfu c2002 Beaver Island-Welke, MI, USA]
525 (G)	BN-2A-20	G-BDVZ N111BN XA-RZV XB-ALD
526 (G)	BN-2A-21	G-BDWD YR-BPA 2451 (Angolan Government) R-201 (Angolan AF) [w/o 31Mar84 in Angola]

ISLANDER

c/n	Series	Identities
527 (P)	BN-2A-21	RP-C2160 527 (Philippine AF) [wfu Sangley Point, Philippines]
528 (P)	BN-2A-21	RP-C2161 528 (Philippine AF) [pres Philippine AF Museum, Manila, Philippines]
529 (G)	BN-2A-9	G-BDWF N20BN N65BA
530 (G)	BN-2A-26	G-BDWG (C-GYUF) (N90255) G-LOTO G-XAXA
531 (G)	BN-2B-21	G-BDZI B-08/OT-ALH (Belgian Army) G-BDZI
532 (G)	BN-2A-27	G-BDZJ N68JA 8P-ASE V2-LDL V4-AAA V2-LDL J8-SLU
533 (G)	BN-2B-21	G-BDZK B-09/OT-ALI (Belgian Army) G-BDZK N21BN YV [canx 14Nov08 as exported to Venezuela]
534 (G)	BN-2A-8	G-BDZL N33MN C-GSUC N946JD EL-YNA EL-RML
535 (G)	BN-2A-27	G-BDZM N70JA C-GBFU
536 (G)	BN-2A-27	G-BDZN N67JA C-GTCL [wfu Fort Nelson, BC, Canada; canx 20Dec91]
537 (G)	BN-2A-21	G-BDZO 5Y-RAJ VH-WZF
538 (P)	BN-2A-21	RP-C2162 538 (Philippine AF) 311 (Philippine Navy)
539 (P)	BN-2A-21	RP-C2163 539 (Philippine AF) RP-C1324
540 (G)	BN-2A-27	G-BDZP S7-AAA [wfu cJul04 Victoria, Seychelles]
541 (G)	BN-2B-21	G-BEDW B-10/OT-ALJ (Belgian Army) G-BEDW
542 (G)	BN-2A-26	G-BEDX N35MN HI-787SP HI-787CA HI-787SP HI-787CA
543 (G)	BN-2A-21	G-BEDY YR-BPC 2453 (Angolan Government) R-203 (Angolan AF)
544 (G)	BN-2A-26	G-BEDZ (C-GYUG) G-BEDZ [w/o 20May96 Tingwall, UK; canx 14Mar97]
545 (G)	BN-2A-21	G-BEEB PK-TRC PK-VIB
546 (G)	BN-2A-8	G-BEEC N36MN [missing, presumed w/o 21Nov77 during a local flight from Kotzebue, AK, USA; canx]
547 (P)	BN-2A-21	RP-C2143 547 (Philippine AF) RP-C1321
548 (P)	BN-2A-21	RP-C2146 548 (Philippine AF) [w/o 01Dec89 in the Philippines]
549 (G)	BN-2B-21	G-BEED B-11/OT-ALK (Belgian Army) [pres Liege-Bierset, Belgium]
550 (G)	BN-2A-26	G-BEEG (C-GYUH) ZK- [canx 18Mar09 as exported to New Zealand]
551 (P)	BN-2A-21	RP-C2147 551 (Philippine AF) [wfu Sangley Point, Philippines]
552 (P)	BN-2A-21	RP-C2148 552 (Philippine AF) 320 (Philippine Navy)
553 (G)	BN-2A-21	G-BEFI B-12/OT-ALL (Belgian Army) G-BEFI OY-CKS
554 (G)	BN-2A-21	G-BEFJ C-GYTC [w/o 22Mar80 Mount Lloyd George, BC, Canada; canx 30Jan92]
555 (G)	BN-2A-26	G-BEFK N70PA N301SK C-GJRL [w/o 02Sep88 Hopedale, NL, Canada; canx 04Oct88]
556 (G)	BN-2A-21	G-BEFL ZS-KAG 7P-LAE [w/o 25Aug81 Tebellong, Lesotho]
557 (G)	BN-2A-27	G-BEFM VP-LCF V2-LCF N143PC [wfu cNov90; std Hollywood-North Perry, FL, USA pending rebuild]
558 (G)	BN-2A-8	G-BEFN N37MN [w/o 07Apr83 Selawik, AK, USA]
559 (P)	BN-2A-21	RP-C2150 559 (Philippine AF) [w/o 28Aug91 Mount Halcon, Philippines]
560 (P)	BN-2A-21	RP-C2151 RP-2151 560 (Philippine AF) [w/o 18Nov92 Zamboanga, Philippines]
561 (P)	BN-2A-21	RP-C2153 561 (Philippine AF) [wfu Sangley Point, Philippines]
562 (G)	BN-2A-21	G-BEGD YR-BPB 2452 (Angolan Government) R-202 (Angolan AF) [w/o date & location unkn]
563 (G)	BN-2A-8	G-BEGE N38MN [w/o 19Sep89 Vieques, PR during Hurricane Hugo; canx 19Apr91]
564 (G)	BN-2A-26	G-BEGF N80PA N304SK N404WB
565 (G)	BN-2A-21	G-BEGH PK-ZAE
566 (G)	BN-2A-8	G-BEGI N39MN [w/o 19Sep89 Vieques, PR during Hurricane Hugo; canx 17Apr91]
567 (P)	BN-2A-21	RP-C2156 567 (Philippine AF) 312 (Philippine Navy)
568 (P)	BN-2A-21	RP-C2165 568 (Philippine AF) 314 (Philippine Navy)
569 (P)	BN-2A-21	RP-C2166 569 (Philippine AF) RP-C1320
570 (G)	BN-2A-26	G-BEGJ N402JA C-GGVJ J3-GAH J8-VBK
571 (G)	BN-2A-27	G-BEIU VP-HCT V3-HCT [dbr 25Nov89 Belize City, Belize]
572 (G)	BN-2A-8	G-BEIV (N69JA) G-51-572 N28MN V3-HEP [wfu Belize-International, Belize]
573 (G)	BN-2A-20	G-BEIW YV-142CP YV-270C
574 (G)	BN-2A-21	G-BEIX 5T-MAY
575 (G)	BN-2A-26	G-BEIY B-11110 (B-17021) B-11110 [static test airframe at China Institute of Technology, Chu-Tung, Taiwan]
576 (G)	BN-2A-21	G-BEJC 5T-MAZ
577 (G)	BN-2A-21	G-BEJF 5T-MAA [w/o in Mauritania; date & location unkn]
578 (G)	BN-2A-26	G-BEJG D-IEDB [wfu cMay98 Emden, Germany; b/u & canx cMay98]
579 (G)	BN-2A-21	G-BEJH YR-BPG D2-EEP
580 (G)	BN-2A-21	G-BEJI YR-BPH D2-EEQ
581 (G)	BN-2A-21	G-BEKP EP-PBE [w/o 03Nov82 Shiraz, Iran]
582 (G)	BN-2A-20	G-BEKU P2-ISD [w/o 08Aug89 nr Manyanya, Papua New Guinea]
583 (G)	BN-2A-8	G-BEKV G-51-583 N29MN ZK-EVK [w/o 08Aug89 Mount Aspiring, New Zealand; canx 22Feb90]
584 (G)	BN-2A-21	G-BEKW N46958 9V-BLM 9M-AXU [w/o 11Aug84 in Malaysia]
585 (G)	BN-2A-8	G-BEKX N31MN YJ-RV20 [w/o 13Sep88 Emae, Vanuatu]
586 (G)	BN-2A-20	G-BEKY N407JA YV-291CP YV-291C
587 (G)	BN-2A-21	G-BEKZ 5T-MAV [w/o in Mauritania; date & location unkn]
588 (G)	BN-2A-27R	G-BELA (N69JA) N405JA HC-BFI [w/o 17Oct78 Quito, Ecuador]
589 (G)	BN-2A-21	G-BELB S7-AAD A2-01M (Seychelles Defence Force) S7-AAU
590 (G)	BN-2A-27R	G-BELC N404JA HC-BFJ [w/o 03Mar82 Quito, Ecuador]
591 (G)	BN-2A-27	G-BENU 9Q-CMJ F-GDHD
592 (G)	BN-2A-26	G-BENV HP-785 TI-ALU XA-IOH N902GD HI-567CA N9SJ N62183 PJ-EZR
593 (P)	BN-2A-21	(G-BENW) RP-C2168 593 (Philippine AF) RP-C1325 [w/o 16Oct04 Mount Tagpao, Barangay Baroc, 5 mls from Coron, Philippines]
594 (P)	BN-2A-21	(G-BENX) RP-C2159 594 (Philippine Navy) [wfu Sangley Point, Philippines]
595 (G)	BN-2A-20	G-BENY 9V-BJN PK-VIT [w/o 24Feb80 Banjarmasin, Indonesia]
596 (G)	BN-2A-21	G-BENZ N331MS C-GSGX PT-MGX C-GSGX
597 (G)	BN-2A-27	G-BEOA N123NP [canx cMar83 - status?]
598 (G)	BN-2A-26	G-BEOB XA-IIM [canx; fate unkn]
599 (G)	BN-2A-26	G-BEOC N20875 N178SC C6-ASA [w/o cJun05 Moss Town, Bahamas; to Tropic Air for spares use]

ISLANDER

c/n	Series	Identities
600	BN-2A	[void - c/n never allocated]
601 (R)	BN-2A	G-AXHY 5Y-AMG [w/o 15May74 Addis Ababa, Ethiopia]
602 (R)	BN-2A-26	G-AXND 9M-APK 9M-MDC DQ-FDW
603 (R)	BN-2A-26	G-AXSS S7-AAE [w/o 30Aug84 Seychelles]
604 (R)	BN-2A	G-AXST 7Q-YKD G-AXST OB-R-1271 [w/o 10Mar89 Lima, Peru; canx 10Aug89]
605 (R)	BN-2A-26	G-AXSU VH-EQZ VP-PAU F-OCXD YJ-RV6 P2-ISU VH-XFI DQ-SLM
606 (R)	BN-2A	G-AXUS VT-DYZ C-GJFT N133RS [dam 27Jun07 Nassau, Bahamas]
607 (R)	BN-2A	G-AXUT 9Q-CTS [w/o 20Jul70 Busira River, Zaire]
608 (R)	BN-2A	G-AXUU VT-EAN
609 (R)	BN-2A-9	G-AXWI F-OCRA ZK-CRA VH-SKG
610 (R)	BN-2A	G-AXWJ 8R-GDS VQ-LAT 8P-ASC VP-HCU V3-HCU YS-51C HH-MSA C6-BAS
611 (R)	BN-2A-9	G-AXZY F-OCRB ZK-FXY DQ-FFF DQ-FHB (N4391A) ZK-FXY T3-ATG ZK-FXY H4-WPF
612 (R)	BN-2A	G-AXZZ 8R-GDT VQ-LAS J6-LAS J6-SLS N9110R J6-SLX HP-1232TN HP-1232XI HP-1232PS
613 (R)	BN-2A	G-AYAX VP-PAM H4-AAC [w/o 22Oct78 off Rennell Island, Polynesia]
614 (R)	BN-2A	G-AYAY VQ-FBP DQ-FBP VH-BRQ ZK-FFL [on rebuild Invercargill, New Zealand]
615 (R)	BN-2A-7	G-AYAZ (9V-BDW) HKG-7 (Hong Kong AAF) (VR-HZO) HKG-7 (Hong Kong AAF) [pres Hong Kong Historic Aviation Society, Hong Kong]
616 (R)	BN-2A-27	G-AYBA 4X-AYN G-51-616 4X-AYN SX-BBY 4X-AYN SX-BBY 4X-AYN N616GL [dbr 18Jan02 nr Havers, British Virgin Islands, parts to Global Aircraft Industries, Edmonton-Villeneuve, AB, Canada; canx 11Dec06]
617 (R)	BN-2A	G-AYBB 9Q-CYA
618 (R)	BN-2A-3	G-AYGH EP-AFQ [status?]
619 (R)	BN-2A	G-AYGI A2-ZFY VP-WEX Z-WEX 9J-MAC 5H-CAM
620 (R)	BN-2A-6	G-AYGJ VH-BAY P2-BAY [wfu c1996 Tabubil, Papua New Guinea]
621 (R)	BN-2A-6	G-AYGK SX-BBS G-AYGK 6Y-JAP
622 (R)	BN-2A-7	G-AYGL SX-BBV G-AYGL C-GKES 8R-GHD
623 (R)	BN-2A	G-AYJE (EI-AVE) CR-CAS G-AYJE EC-844 EC-FIP [wfu - location?]
624 (R)	BN-2A-3	G-AYJF CR-AOV C9-AOV
625 (R)	BN-2A-8	G-AYJG CR-AOH C9-AOH CS-AQP HI-636CA HI-636CT N903GD
626 (R)	BN-2A-7	G-AYJH F-OCQH N66177 TI-AYA N7069Y [wfu Fort Worth-Meacham International, TX, USA still marked as TI-AYA]
627 (R)	BN-2A-7	G-AYJI HP-566 VP-HBX YS-23C YS-24C N627WD
628 (R)	BN-2A-7	G-AYJJ A40-DJ (N628BN) N268BN HP-1016PS HP-1016XI HP-1016PS [w/o 29Dec02 nr Changuinola, Panama]
629 (R)	BN-2A-7	G-AYJK A40-DK N629BN HP-1002KN [w/o during 1989 in Panama]
630 (R)	BN-2A-8	G-AYJL 9Q-CAE 9T-BHB (Zairean AF) 9Q-CAE [status?]
631 (R)	BN-2A-3	G-AYNT 9Q-CRP
632 (R)	BN-2A-3	G-AYNU 9V-BDH 9M-ARQ VH-JUU [w/o 21Mar94 Weipa, QLD, Australia; canx 27May94]
633 (R)	BN-2A-7	G-AYNV 9Q-CYB [w/o 07Aug75 Kasangulu, Congo]
634 (R)	BN-2A-3	G-AYNW 9V-BEB PK-VIM
635 (R)	BN-2A-8	G-AYNX VP-LVA VQ-TAG 8R-GGT [wfu Georgetown, Guyana]
636 (R)	BN-2A-3	G-AYNY CR-AMX C9-AMX [canx; fate unkn]
637 (R)	BN-2A-3	G-AYNZ CR-AMU C9-AMU [canx; fate unkn]
638 (R)	BN-2A-7	G-AYOA 9Q-CYC 9Q-CYC [wfu Kinshasa, Zaire]
639 (R)	BN-2A-3	G-AYOB 9V-BEC PK-OAV [w/o 07Oct75 off Savu Island, Indonesia]
640 (R)	BN-2A-8	G-AYOC CR-CAT G-AYOC 4X-CAY
641 (R)	BN-2A-6	G-AYSM YR-BNG D-IORS HP-1312AR
642 (R)	BN-2A-9	G-AYSN PT-JJI [wfu by Oct86 - status?]
643 (R)	BN-2A-21	G-AYSO D-IOLG G-AYSO C-GPAB N7049T
644 (R)	BN-2A-9	G-AYSP PT-KAC PT-KAC-X PT-KAC [w/o 11Aug80 Rio de Janeiro, Rio de Janeiro State, Brazil]
645 (R)	BN-2A-9	G-AYSR PT-JQF PT-JZJ [wfu by Jan88 - status?]
646 (R)	BN-2A-8	G-AYSS VH-WGT P2-WGT P2-MBF VH-MBF
647 (R)	BN-2A-9	G-AYST (F-OCSB) F-OCTB TL-AAQ TN-ADN
648 (R)	BN-2A-9	G-AYSU 204 (Abu Dhabi Defence Force) 804 (Abu Dhabi Defence Force) MM60225 (Somalian Aeronautical Corps) [b/u c1991 Mogadishu, Somalia]
649 (R)	BN-2A-9	G-AYSV F-BTGH [w/o 15Nov72 Dinard/Pleurtuit-St.Malo, France; canx 08Jul74]
650 (R)	BN-2A-9	G-AYSW PP-FBU PT-FBU
651 (R)	BN-2A-20	G-AYXC CS-AJU LN-SAM SE-GTV F-GBTV 5R-MVF 5R-MLG
652 (R)	BN-2A-9	G-AYXD "PP-FBY" PP-FBV PT-FBV
653 (R)	BN-2A-8	G-AYXE EI-AWM G-OWIN N606NT
654 (R)	BN-2A-3	G-AYXF CS-AGH G-AYXF CS-AGH VH-UWV H4-WPB RP-C1047 [w/o 07Feb07 off Cebu, Philippines; CofR exp 16Mar07]
655 (R)	BN-2A-2	G-AYXG EP-PAF
656 (R)	BN-2A-8	G-AYXH CR-ANJ 7319 (Rhodesian AF) 7319 (Zimbabwean AF)
657 (R)	BN-2A-8	G-AYXI F-BTOY F-OBSN [wfu cNov77 Port Gentil, Gabon; canx 13Oct81]
658 (R)	BN-2A-8	G-AYXJ CR-ANH 7317 (Rhodesian AF) 7317 (Zimbabwean AF)
659 (R)	BN-2A-8	G-AYXK D-IAJW N9857C N40UC N659CM PJ-WEA
660 (R)	BN-2A-21	G-AYXL ZS-VIS A2-VIS VH-OCH P2-SWD VH-AUN V6-03FM
661 (R)	BN-2A-26	G-AZDL ZK-KHA ZK-NNE DQ-FET [wfu Suva, Fiji]
662 (R)	BN-2A-3	G-AZDM 9XR-KA [w/o c1991 Rwanda]
663 (R)	BN-2A-3	G-AZDN PK-KNC [w/o 30Dec76 Mara, Tarakan, Indonesia]
664 (R)	BN-2A-3	G-AZDO 9XR-KG [w/o c1980 Rwanda]
665 (R)	BN-2A-3	G-AZDP EP-PAG
666 (R)	BN-2A-8	G-AZDR HI-213 HI-383 [canx; fate unkn]
667 (R)	BN-2A-8	G-AZDS CS-AJF N65323 [wfu San Jose, Costa Rica; canx 18Dec01]
668 (R)	BN-2A-9	G-AZDT PT-IKA [wfu by Oct85 - status?]
669 (R)	BN-2A-9	G-AZDU PT-ILB PP-ZDD PT-KNM [w/o 02Feb99 in Rondonia State, Brazil]
670 (R)	BN-2A-8	G-AZDV PT-IMI [wfu by Jan89 - status?]

ISLANDER

c/n	Series	Identities
671 (R)	BN-2A-9	G-AZGN PT-ILC [canx; fate unkn]
672 (R)	BN-2A-8	G-AZGO HI-215 HR-AJP HP-1153XI HP-1153PS
673 (R)	BN-2A-3	G-AZGP (5Y-ARZ) F-BUFV CN-TCC HP-1494 HP-1494PS HK-4613
674 (R)	BN-2A-9	G-AZGR F-BUTN 5U-AAN [w/o 02Feb75 Agades, Niger]
675 (R)	BN-2A-21	G-AZGS PK-KNE [w/o 12May85 Maluku, Indonesia]
676 (R)	BN-2A-9	G-AZGT EC-CFX G-AZGT DQ-FCN [w/o 06Aug91 nr Rarotonga, Fiji]
677 (R)	BN-2A-9	G-AZGU EC-CFY G-AZGU 8R-GFI
678 (R)	BN-2A-2	G-AZGV CR-LOQ G-AZGV HP-691 ZS-JZO 7323 (Rhodesian AF) 7323 (Zimbabwean AF)
679 (R)	BN-2A-8	G-AZGW HI-214 N5400C YV-1116P YV-1131C [dam 09Jul03 San Juan de Manapiare, Amazonas, Venezuela]
680 (R)	BN-2A-8	G-AZGX HI-216 F-OGGL [w/o c1979 Martinique; canx 23Jan86]
681 (R)	BN-2A-8	G-AZRJ XA-DIM [wfu c1985]
682 (R)	BN-2A-2	G-AZXN OB-T-1035 OB-1035 [dbr 06Feb89 Campo Verde, Peru; b/u c1991 San Ramon, Peru; canx 21Dec01]
683 (R)	BN-2A-9	G-AZXO CR-APD C9-APD ZS-BLV
684 (R)	BN-2A-8	G-AZXP 9M-ASL 9M-MDD [w/o 06Jul82 Long Semado, Malaysia]
685 (R)	BN-2A-9	G-AZXR CR-CAU G-AZXR N143FS N148ES N902VL
686 (R)	BN-2A-9	G-AZXS DQ-FCA [wfu Nadi, Fiji; canx c2007]
687 (R)	BN-2A-2	G-AZXT CR-APO C9-APO [std Maputo, Mozambique]
688 (R)	BN-2A-9	G-AZXU (F-OCTB) F-BUFX F-OGSM [w/o 21Dec89 Sudan; canx 20Feb90]
689 (R)	BN-2A-9	G-AZXV PT-KAB PT-KAB-X PT-KAB [w/o cDec96 in Brazil]
690 (R)	BN-2A-9	G-AZXW PT-JNT [canx; fate unkn]
691 (R)	BN-2A-8	G-AZXX CR-APT C9-APT G-AZXX EC-DBK CS-DAF [w/o 08May94 Braganca, Portugal]
692 (R)	BN-2A-3	G-AZXY PK-KND RP-C2750
693 (R)	BN-2A-3	G-AZXZ 9M-ATM PK-VIO [w/o 14Feb85 Banjarmasin, Indonesia]
694 (R)	BN-2A-9	G-BAYJ 8P-PAT 8R-GGN 8R-GAC [w/o 03May00 Kurupung, Guyana]
695 (R)	BN-2A-6	G-BAYI PT-JSC [w/o 30Mar80 Cuiaba, Mato Grosso, Brazil]
696 (R)	BN-2A-3	G-BAYH PT-KNE [w/o 11Jan01 in NE Brazil]
697 (R)	BN-2A-21	G-BAYG PK-LAV PK-ESS PK-VIZ [w/o 07Nov02 Tarakan, Indonesia]
698 (R)	BN-2A-3	G-BAYF PT-KCF PT-KCF-X PT-KCF
699 (R)	BN-2A-3	G-BAYE T-2 (Jamaican Defence Force)
700 (R)	BN-2A-9	G-BAYD (TR-LRY) 6V-ADJ F-OCZE 6V-AES TZ-ASM [w/o c1998 in Mali]
701 (R)	BN-2A-8	G-BBFG 9M-ATN B-11108 [w/o 13Jun81 nr Hualien, Taiwan]
702 (R)	BN-2A-9	G-BBFH OY-DZV 5U-ABZ
703 (R)	BN-2A-20	G-BBFI P2-MKV P2-ISA [w/o 15Jun81 Lukanai, Papua New Guinea]
704 (R)	BN-2A-8	G-BBFJ EI-AYN
705 (R)	BN-2A-8	G-BBFK CR-APN C9-APN HP-761 3718 (Rhodesian AF) 3718 (Zimbabwean AF)
706 (R)	BN-2A-6	G-BBFM CR-AQE C9-AQE [canx; fate unkn]
707 (R)	BN-2A-6	G-BBFN CR-AQF 7136 (Rhodesian AF) 7136 (Zimbabwane AF)
708 (R)	BN-2A-9	G-BBFO TN-ACO [w/o 24Jul78 in the Congo]
709 (R)	BN-2A-20	G-BBFP P2-MKW P2-ISB
710 (R)	BN-2A-8	G-BBFR F-BVTD [w/o 23Jun84 Ajaccio, France]
711 (R)	BN-2A-9	G-BBZT YV-C-AJG YV-T-AJG YV-145P YV1641
712 (R)	BN-2A-9	G-BBZU YV-C-MTM YV-T-MTM YV-527P YV1197
713 (R)	BN-2A-27R	G-BBZW A-10021 (Indonesian Army)
714 (R)	BN-2A-27	G-BBZX EC-CKK [wfu Laayoune, Western Sahara]
715 (R)	BN-2A-27	G-BBZY EC-CKL
716 (R)	BN-2A-9	G-BBZZ P2-BAC [w/o cFeb90 Papua New Guinea]
717 (R)	BN-2A-26	G-BCAE 4X-AYE G-BJWM LX-AJH 5V-TTB [wfu Bamako, Mali]
718 (R)	BN-2A-21	G-BCAF RP-C2207 [w/o 20Nov07 Retac, Roxas, Philippines; CofR exp 05Jul08]
719 (R)	BN-2A-26	G-BCAG ZK-MCD
720 (R)	BN-2A-27	(G-BCAL) G-BCHO 8R-GEE [wfu Georgetown, Guyana]
721 (R)	BN-2A-21	G-BCGY RP-C2130 P2-TCP [canx; fate unkn]
722 (R)	BN-2A-26	G-BCGZ HP-709 FAP-207 (Panamanian AF) SAN-207 (Panamanian AF)
723 (R)	BN-2A-21	G-BCHA RP-C684 PCG-684 (Philippine Coast Guard)
724 (R)	BN-2A-26	G-BCHB ZK-MCE
725 (R)	BN-2A-21	G-BCHC RP-C1966 RP-C868 [w/o 12Dec03 between Macanacon & Palanan, Philippines; CofR exp 17Nov04]
726 (R)	BN-2A-21	G-BCHD 5N-AOI I-KIMO (N352SP) I-KIMO [b/u Rome-Urbe, Italy]
727 (R)	BN-2A-21	G-BCHE PK-WBA
728 (R)	BN-2A-21	G-BCHF SU-AYB [status?]
729 (R)	BN-2A-21	G-BCHG 7P-LAC ZS-LKF A2-AKE [wfu Gaborone, Botswana]
730 (R)	BN-2A-21	G-BCHH PK-ZAA [w/o 26Apr94 Mount Saran, Indonesia]
731 (R)	BN-2A-9	G-BCMZ EL-AHX [b/u c1990 Monrovia, Liberia]
732 (R)	BN-2A-21	G-BCNA PK-ZAD [w/o 24Sep77 Lhokseumawe, Indonesia]
733 (R)	BN-2A-9	G-BCNB EL-AHY [b/u c1991 Monrovia, Liberia]
734 (R)	BN-2A-9	G-BCND EL-AHZ [b/u c1994 Monrovia, Liberia]
735 (R)	BN-2A-27	G-BCNE YI-AHF [status?]
736 (R)	BN-2A-21	G-BCNF 5Y-AYE ZS-XGF A2-ZED
737 (R)	BN-2A-27	G-BCNG YI-AHE [status?]
738 (R)	BN-2A-27	G-BCNH YI-AHG [status?]
739 (R)	BN-2A-21	G-BCNI RP-C1801 RP-1801 RP-C1801
740 (R)	BN-2A-9	G-BCNJ TR-LUR F-ODSF [w/o 19Aug85 in Chad; canx 19Aug85]
741 (R)	BN-2A-21	G-BCVK 9M-AUQ RP-C2103 9M-AUQ ZK-FGR N3211Z V2-LDV J6-SLT N196TA N297TA
742 (R)	BN-2A-21	G-BCVL PT-KRO
743 (R)	BN-2A-21	G-BCVM PT-KRP [w/o 10Aug78 Amoreira Mountains, Brazil]
744 (R)	BN-2A-9	G-BCVN 5U-AAS TR-LYU TR-LCN [wfu Duala, Cameroon]
745 (R)	BN-2A-21	G-BCVO PK-KNF [w/o 05Aug83 off Bula, Indonesia]
746 (R)	BN-2A-21	G-BCVP 9Q-CIN [wfu Kinshasa, Zaire]

ISLANDER

c/n	Series	Identities
747 (R)	BN-2A-21	G-BCVR 5T-MAS
748 (R)	BN-2A-21	G-BCVS VQ-SAK S7-AAK 5Y-MAX [w/o 26Apr79 Bakitabu, Kenya]
749 (R)	BN-2A-21	G-BCVT PK-KNG [w/o 26Apr79 Beoga, Indonesia]
750 (R)	BN-2A-27	G-BCVU ST-AFU HP-860 (OB-T-1196) N48VM HP-1133IT [w/o cDec89 in Panama]
751 (R)	BN-2A-9	G-BCYT 9XR-GV [w/o 08Oct90 Kigali, Rwanda]
752 (R)	BN-2A-21	G-BCYU 9V-BGT PK-VIP [w/o 03Sep91 Sampit, Indonesia]
753 (R)	BN-2A-20	G-BCYV VH-TXH P2-ISE P2-CBA
754 (R)	BN-2A-21	G-BCYW 9V-BGV PK-VIQ [w/o 20Oct79 Pangkalan Bun, Philippines]
755 (R)	BN-2A-26	G-BCYX VH-FCP RP-C809
756 (R)	BN-2A-20	G-BCZA VH-TXL P2-ISG [w/o 06Sep84 Star Mountain, Papua New Guinea]
757 (R)	BN-2A-20	G-BCZB (VH-TXL) P2-ISH [w/o 14Jan84 nr Karimui, Papua New Guinea]
758 (R)	BN-2A-20	G-BCZC VH-MET P2-SWB P2-ISA
759 (R)	BN-2A-21	G-BCZD N11216 JA5268 P2-MFZ P2-VAB ZK-KTR [wfu North Shore Airfield, NZ]
760 (R)	BN-2A-21	G-BCZE LN-MAG F-GFID F-OTAG
761 (R)	BN-2A-26	G-BDHN VH-TXC VH-IBS P2-PAC P2-ISO P2-ALH [w/o 04Feb99 New Britain, Papua New Guinea]
762 (R)	BN-2A-20	G-BDHO P2-HAC [w/o 10Mar82 Kopi, Papua New Guinea]
763 (R)	BN-2A-26	G-BDHP VH-TXF P2-PAD P2-ISP VH-XFF [w/o 16Jan99 into Torres Strait, off Coconut Island, QLD, Australia; canx 29Oct99]
764 (R)	BN-2A-9	G-BDHR TR-LWL TN-ADY
765 (R)	BN-2A-21	G-BDHS 5T-MAT [w/o 21Jul78 in Mauritania]
766 (R)	BN-2A-20	G-BDHT TI-AKC C-GTWI N25SA N443S N4438
767 (R)	BN-2A-26	G-BDHU 9L-LAV [w/o 07Nov89 Sinoe, Liberia]
768 (R)	BN-2A-21	G-BDHV VH-TXG P2-COB P2-IAD P2-NCE
769 (R)	BN-2A-20	G-BDHW VH-SYU [wfu c2007]
770 (R)	BN-2A-20	G-BDHX TI-AKD C-GTOP N6365G N442S
771 (R)	BN-2A-9	G-BDMR TR-LWI TR-LCM 5U-ABJ [b/u c1996 Niamey, Niger]
772 (R)	BN-2A-21	G-BDMT OA4 (Botswana Defence Force) [w/o 23Nov99 Gaborone, Botswana]
773 (R)	BN-2A-9	G-BDMU TR-LWO ZS-PDJ 5H-UNT [dam 15Sep06 in forced landing Mangungu, Tanzania]
774 (R)	BN-2A-21	G-BDMV ZS-JXT ZS-XGC N777TG ZS-XGC A2-AGJ N6257X XC-JDK
775 (R)	BN-2A-27	G-BDMX YR-BNH [wfu Bucharest-Baneasa, Romania]
776 (R)	BN-2A-27	G-BDMY YR-BNI [w/o 27Jun77 Nucet, Romania]
777 (R)	BN-2A-27	G-BDMZ YR-BNJ [w/o 26May89 nr Bubocu, Romania]
778 (R)	BN-2A-27	G-BDNA YR-BNK [wfu Bucharest-Baneasa, Romania]
779 (R)	BN-2A-27	G-BDNB YR-BNE N779KS
780 (R)	BN-2A-21	G-BDND (N99358) 9V-BHX PK-ZAL [w/o 10Aug84 Aceh, Indonesia]
781 (R)	BN-2A-21	G-BDRN 9V-BJO (PK-KNH) PK-VIU
782 (R)	BN-2A-21	G-BDRO 9V-BJF (PK-KNI) A6-FFA G-BDRO PK-ZAM [wfu cJan98 Indonesia]
783 (R)	BN-2A-21	G-BDRP OA2 (Botswana Defence Force)
784 (R)	BN-2A-21	G-BDRR D-IFST [w/o 30Oct84 nr Itzehoe, West Germany; canx cDec84]
785 (R)	BN-2A-26	G-BDRS 9V-BJG VH-IBZ 5W-FAQ ZK-EVO
786 (R)	BN-2A-21	G-BDRT 5T-MAQ [w/o 06Sep80 in Mauritania]
787 (R)	BN-2A-21	G-BDRU 5T-MAR [w/o 03Jan77 over Sahara Desert]
788 (R)	BN-2A-26	G-BDRV PH-PFS D-IHUG F-OGXA
789 (R)	BN-2A-27	G-BDRW TF-ORN N4915U (N810RE) N4915U
790 (R)	BN-2A-27	G-BDRX YR-BNL [wfu Bucharest-Baneasa, Romania]
791 (R)	BN-2A-21	G-BDTC OA1 (Botswana Defence Force)
792 (R)	BN-2A-21	G-BDTD 7Q-YAX [w/o 18Mar83 Chikkala Hills, Malawi]
793 (R)	BN-2A-21	G-BDTE 5T-MAU [w/o c1978 in Mauritania]
794 (R)	BN-2A-27	G-BDTF 5N-ASI [b/u c1998 Lagos, Nigeria]
795 (R)	BN-2A-21	G-BDTG OA2 (Botswana Defence Force) [w/o 09May78 in Botswana]
796 (R)	BN-2A-21	G-BDTH T-5 (Jamaican Defence Force) [w/o 30Apr94 Kingston, Jamaica]
797 (R)	BN-2A-21	G-BDTI YR-BPD 2454 (Angolan Government) [w/o date & location unkn]
798 (R)	BN-2A-21	G-BDTJ YR-BPE 2456 (Angolan Government) R-206(Angolan AF)
799 (R)	BN-2A-21	G-BDTK OA3 (Botswana Defence Force) 9J-PLJ
800 (R)	BN-2A-20	G-BDTM VH-TWI P2-KAD [w/o 20Jun87 nr Lae, Papua New Guinea]
801 (R)	BN-2A-21	G-BDYN YR-BPF 2455 (Angolan Government) R-205(Angolan AF)
802 (R)	BN-2A-21	G-BDYO YR-BPG 2457 (Angolan Government) R-207(Angolan AF)
803 (R)	BN-2A-21	G-BDYP YR-BPH 2458 (Angolan Government) R-208(Angolan AF)
804 (R)	BN-2A-27	G-BDYR YR-BNN [wfu Bucharest-Baneasa, Romania]
805 (R)	BN-2A-20	G-BDYS P2-ISK P2-SWA [w/o 09Jun93 Gulgubip, Papua New Guinea]
806 (R)	BN-2A-20	G-BDYT P2-ISL
807 (R)	BN-2A-21	G-BDYU LN-MAY A2-AFN
808 (R)	BN-2A-27	G-BDYV YR-BNM [wfu Bucharest-Baneasa, Romania]
809 (R)	BN-2A-21	G-BDYW 5Y-BBB
810 (R)	BN-2A-21	G-BDYX 5Y-BBC UN-1 (United Nations) 5Y-BBC A2-AGA
811 (R)	BN-2A-21	G-BEGK 9XR-GW
812 (R)	BN-2A-27	G-BEGL YR-BNS [w/o 11Nov92 Tulcea, Romania]
813 (R)	BN-2A-21	G-BEGM P2-COD P2-TND
814 (R)	BN-2A-21	G-BEGN S7-AAC 5Y-BHZ N814WJ 9U-BRV 9Q-CMM
815 (R)	BN-2A-20	G-BEGO VH-TRW P2-HBE [w/o 13Oct93 Jimi Valley, Papua New Guinea]
816 (R)	BN-2A-27	G-BEGP YR-BNT 816 (Romanian AF) YR-BNT HA-BNA YR-RAB
817 (R)	BN-2A-27	G-BEGR YR-BNU [wfu Bucharest-Baneasa, Romania]
818 (R)	BN-2A-21	G-BEGS 5Y-BCS HP-1338 HP-1338MF
819 (R)	BN-2A-27	G-BEGT XA-HIT XC-CII N696WA XA-SKG
820 (R)	BN-2A-21	G-BEGU 5Y-BCR XC-JDN
821 (R)	BN-2A-27	G-BELD YR-BNO ZK-LYP
822 (R)	BN-2A-27	G-BELE YR-BNP [wfu Bucharest-Baneasa, Romania]
823 (R)	BN-2A-26	G-BELF D-IBRA G-BELF G-HEBZ [wfu c2001; pres cFeb05 Scottish Museum of Flight, East Fortune, Scotland]

ISLANDER

c/n	Series	Identities
824 (R)	BN-2A-27	G-BELG YR-BNR [wfu Bucharest-Baneasa, Romania]
825 (R)	BN-2A-21	G-BELH YR-BPI D2-EEO
826 (R)	BN-2A-21	G-BELI YR-BPJ D2-ESE
827 (R)	BN-2A-21	G-BELJ YR-BPK D2-ESI
828 (R)	BN-2A-21	G-BELK N50693
829 (R)	BN-2A-9	YR-BNX G-BELM TR-LXX F-GFDK F-OHFY [w/o 05Sep97 Bondo, Congo]
830 (R)	BN-2A-6	YR-BNY G-BELN [w/o 14Dec78 Bembridge, UK; canx 02Mar81]
831 (R)	BN-2A-26	YR-BNZ G-BEMG 9V-BKQ B-12207 [w/o cFeb87 in Taiwan]
832 (R)	BN-2A-20	G-BEMH VH-EER P2-EER
833 (R)	BN-2A-9	G-BEMJ DQ-FCX
834 (R)	BN-2A-26	G-BEMK HP-813 N834BN ZS-LSE 17(South African AF) ZS-LSE
835 (R)	BN-2A-20	G-BEML VH-WPT VH-AGI P2-SWC [w/o 22Nov94 Tabubil, Papua New Guinea]
836 (R)	BN-2A-21	G-BEMN OA5 (Botswana Defence Force)
837 (R)	BN-2A-21	G-BEMO PK-BIG
838 (R)	BN-2B-27	G-BEMP TR-LYW [wfu c1992 Libreville, Gabon; reportedly on rebuild in Canada]
839 (R)	BN-2A-26	G-BEMR D-IEDC G-BEMR V3-HFA [wfu Philip S.W.Goldson International, Belize]
840 (R)	BN-2A-27	G-BEMS YR-BNV [wfu Bucharest-Baneasa, Romania]
841 (R)	BN-2A-9	YR-BNX G-BESB HP-822 N8536A HK-2687X [w/o 26Apr83 Barranca de Upia, Meta, Colombia; canx 26Aug83]
842 (R)	BN-2A-20	G-BESC VH-IOA
843 (R)	BN-2A-20	YR-BNY G-BESD P2-COG [w/o cDec87 Kanabea, Papua New Guinea]
844 (R)	BN-2A-6	G-BESE [w/o 14Dec78 Bembridge, UK; canx 02Mar81]
845 (R)	BN-2A-8	G-BESF VH-FCO DQ-YIR
846 (R)	BN-2B-26	G-BESG P2-BAB [w/o 21Mar89 Bougainville, Papua New Guinea]
847 (R)	BN-2A-26	G-BESH G-HMCG N29884
848 (R)	BN-2A-26	G-BESI HP-870 HP-870XI HP-870PS [w/o c1996 in Panama]
849 (R)	BN-2A-21	G-BESJ 9J-AEO ZS-LIM A2-AEA HI-640CA HI-789CA HC-CGI
850 (R)	BN-2A-6	G-BESK [w/o 14Dec78 Bembridge, UK; canx 28Oct80]
851 (R)	BN-2A-21	G-BEVZ EV-7911 (Venezuelan Army) [wfu Caracas-Oscar Machado Zuloaga International, Venezuela]
852 (R)	BN-2A-21	G-BEWA PK-VIV [w/o 06Jan94 Kuala Kapuas, Indonesia]
853 (R)	BN-2A-27	G-BEWB YR-BNW N271RS V3-HGK
854 (R)	BN-2A-20	(G-BEWC) G-BEWK ZS-KMD A2-NAA ZS-KMD
855 (R)	BN-2A-8	G-BEWD XA-JEK N901GD
856 (R)	BN-2A-26	G-BEWE JA5265 VH-LHA VH-IFA DQ-JJS
857 (R)	BN-2B-21	G-BEWF ZS-KMG N21LE N129SP VH-LCI P2-DNJ [w/o 05Jul90 nr Port Moresby, Papua New Guinea]
858 (R)	BN-2B-21	G-BEWG I-KUNO VQ-THL N222SC N678CC
859 (R)	BN-2B-26	G-BEWH HP-843 OB-T-1207 OB-1207 [w/o 03Nov90 La Escalera Mountain, nr Tarapoto, Peru; canx 21Dec01]
860 (R)	BN-2A-21	G-BEWI PK-TAR [w/o 16Jul02 East Kalimantan, Indonesia]
861 (R)	BN-2B-21	G-BFCN JY-DCA JY-CAA 330 (Royal Jordanian AF) JY-CAA 5X-EMM
862 (R)	BN-2B-21	G-BFCO ZS-KLK 16 (South African AF) ZS-KLK A2-AJM
863 (R)	BN-2A-27	G-BFCP YV-364CP YV-444C YV-2235P YV-689C
864 (R)	BN-2B-27	G-BFCR XC-DIB XA-RML
865 (R)	BN-2A-9	G-BFCS 5A-DHU [w/o c1984 Sarir, Libya]
866 (R)	BN-2A-26	(G-BFCT) G-BFCM B-12203
867 (R)	BN-2A-21	G-BFCU F-GCMF F-ODHO [w/o 10Jan86, location unkn]
868 (R)	BN-2A-27	G-BFCV (N410JA) C-FSTJ J8-VAW N630VC [w/o 04Sep03 Cayey, PR]
869 (R)	BN-2A-27	G-BFCW TR-LZK ZS-PCJ [w/o 21Aug05 nr Durban, KwaZulu-Natal Province, South Africa]
870 (R)	BN-2A-26	G-BFCX 5B-CHG [dam cFeb92 in Cyprus; to be rebuilt]
871 (R)	BN-2A-6	G-BFNL [w/o 14Dec78 Bembridge, UK; canx 02Mar81]
872 (R)	BN-2A-27	G-BFNN VP-FAY [w/o 01May82 Stanley Airport, Falkland Islands during a Royal Navy Sea Harrier raid; canx 29Mar95; fwd section to Chilbolton, Hampshire, UK]
873 (R)	BN-2A-21	G-BFNO IN131 (Indian Navy) [w/o 07Aug86 Port Blair, India]
874 (R)	BN-2A-21	G-BFNR (YV-377CP) N2742N N341CC
875 (R)	BN-2A-21	G-BFNS IN132 (Indian Navy) [w/o 09Dec87 nr Cochin, India]
876 (R)	BN-2B-26	G-BFNT N425NE N610PA V3-HRT C-GZTP PJ-CIW C-FZXG
877 (R)	BN-2A-21	G-BFNU [wfu cMar90 St.Just, UK; canx 28Jan94]
878 (R)	BN-2A-26	G-BFNV G-BPCD G-PASZ 5B-CHV [wfu c2005 Santorini, Greece]
879 (R)	BN-2B-21	G-BFNW HP-896 HP-1156P HP-1156AR
880 (R)	BN-2T	G-BFNX N413JA (YV-2173P) N73413 N5079R 88-0196 (US Army) N200LQ N121MT
881 (R)	BN-2A-26	G-BFNY XC-DUI N25MR [w/o 31Oct87 Mount Chiriaco, nr Desert Center, CA, USA; canx 25Mar91]
882 (R)	BN-2A-26	G-BFNZ XC-DUL N26MR VH-WRR
883 (R)	BN-2A-26	G-BFOA XC-DUK C-FBCB N220T VR-CII VP-CII N706MC
884 (R)	BN-2A-26	G-BFOB XC-DUN N27MR [dam 17Jun07 Egekik, AK, USA]
885 (R)	BN-2A-26	G-BFOC XC-DUO N29MR C-FDYT PJ-SKY
886 (R)	BN-2T	G-BFTI IN133 (Indian Navy)
887 (R)	BN-2A-21	G-BFTJ IN134 (Indian Navy) [w/o 17May85 Cochin, India]
888 (R)	BN-2T	G-BFTK IN135 (Indian Navy) [w/o 10Nov06 Veloor, India]
889 (R)	BN-2A-21	G-BFTL IN136 (Indian Navy)
890 (R)	BN-2A-21	G-BFTM YR-NBZ R-211 (Angolan AF) I-303 (Angolan AF)
891 (R)	BN-2A-26	G-BFUP XC-DUR N32MR
892 (R)	BN-2A-26	G-BFUR XC-DUJ XA-PIQ
893 (R)	BN-2A-26	G-BFUT XC-DUM N38MR C-GBRB [dbr 15May08 nr Nanuk Polar Bear Lodge, MB, Canada; canx 01Aug08]
894 (R)	BN-2A-26	G-BFUU XC-DUP
895 (R)	BN-2A-26	G-BFUV XC-DUS XC-FNV N76JL
896 (R)	BN-2A-21	G-BFWA YR-NBY R-210 (Angolan AF) I-302 (Angolan AF) [w/o 23Sep85 in Angola]

ISLANDER

c/n	Series	Identities
897 (R)	BN-2A-26	G-BFWV XC-DUU C-GVKE N999SA N684AS
898 (R)	BN-2A-21	G-BFWX YR-BNX R-209 (Angolan AF) I-301 (Angolan AF) 9Q-CJA
899 (R)	BN-2A-21	G-BFWY YR-NBW I-304 (Angolan AF)
900 (R)	BN-2A-26	G-BFWZ XC-DUT N7136K
901 (R)	BN-2A-26	G-BFYR XC-DUW XB-EMA XB-FNU N40JL HR- [canx 18May05 as exported to Honduras]
902 (R)	BN-2A-21	G-BFYS YR-NBU I-305 (Angolan AF)
903 (R)	BN-2A-21	G-BFYT YR-NBV I-306 (Angolan AF) D2-ECE [w/o 16Mar94 Cabinda, Angola]
904 (R)	BN-2A-21	G-BFZZ 5N-AVI N904WA [w/o 17Mar96 nr Keflavik, Iceland; parts to Cormack Aircraft Services, Cumbernauld, UK; canx 10Aug98]
905 (R)	BN-2A-26	G-BGAN HP-998P N70161 YV-475C N6596Z D-IADM N993RA VP-AAE N902GD [w/o 29Sep04 Vega Baja, PR; canx 01Dec04]
906 (R)	BN-2A-26	G-BFYG XC-DUV [canx 28Mar85 - status?]
907 (R)	BN-2A-26	G-BEVM XC-DUY XA-POX N5252L V3-HFB
908 (R)	BN-2A-26	G-BGEJ VP-HDV V3-HDV [wfu - status?]
909 (R)	BN-2B-26	G-BGFU JA5270 [wfu cApr98]
910 (R)	BN-2A-9	G-BGFV TZ-ACS [w/o cMay85 in Mali]
911 (R)	BN-2A-26	G-BGFW XC-GRO C-FOKH HC-BTX N103NE V3-HGE
912 (R)	BN-2A-27	G-BGPV HP-955P [w/o c1996 in Panama]
913 (R)	BN-2A-26	G-BGPW HP-935 N75AJ N851JA [w/o 07Mar97 between Guapiles & Paseo de las Palmas, Costa Rica]
914 (R)	BN-2A-26	G-BGPX HP-945 [w/o 06Apr83 in Panama]
915 (R)	BN-2A-26	G-BGPY N661J AP-BEM
916	BN-2B-21	G-BIUA SAF-001 (Suriname AF)
917	BN-2A	(G-BIUB) [airframe not completed; canx 23Jun83]
918	BN-2A-21	G-BIUC OA6 (Botswana Defence Force)
919	BN-2A-26	G-BIUD N662J V2-LDI VP-AAC
920	BN-2A	(G-BIUE) [airframe not completed; canx 12Dec86]
1001 (G)	BN-2A MkIII-1	G-BCNK (F-OCYP) 5X-UDC [b/u c1986 Paraa, Uganda]
1002 (G)	BN-2A MkIII-1	G-BCNL HK-1711X HK-1711 [w/o 09Jan78 Cienaga Grande, Bolivar, Colombia; canx 16Feb00]
1003 (G)	BN-2A MkIII-1	G-BCNM VH-BPH N3851B N904GD N901TA N901VL [b/u; canx 15Nov05]
1004 (G)	BN-2A MkIII-2	G-BCNN DQ-FCE (N2965T) T3-ATE
1005 (G)	BN-2A MkIII-1	G-BCNO HP-947 [w/o 01Nov82 in Panama]
1006 (G)	BN-2A MkIII-1	G-BCXU PK-KTA [dbr Balikpapan, Indonesia & b/u; date unkn]
1007 (G)	BN-2A MkIII-1	G-BCXV HP-899 HP-899CH HP-899PS YV-1117C [wfu Caracas-Maiquetia, Venezuela]
1008 (G)	BN-2A MkIII-2	G-BCXW DQ-FCF VR-CAA (G-OLPL) G-OCTA G-ITEX G-RLON
1009 (G)	BN-2A MkIII-2	(N29JA) G-BCXX 6Y-JJH VQ-TAJ [w/o cSep86 Grand Turk, Turks & Caicos Islands]
1010 (G)	BN-2A MkIII-2	G-BCXY DQ-FCG N127LB [wfu; canx 02Apr09]
1011 (G)	BN-2A MkIII-1	G-BCYC EL-AIB G-BCYC [dbr 15May79 Aberdeen, UK; b/u ; fuselage on dump at Guernsey, UK; canx 31May83]
1012 (G)	BN-2A MkIII-2	G-BDGC 6Y-JJI N624BN HP-1076KN YV-488C (N902VL) YV-2521P [dbr 03Feb98 Hollywood-North Perry, FL, USA, parts to Deland Municipal-Sidney H Taylor Field, FL, USA]
1013 (G)	BN-2A MkIII-2	(N96JA) G-BDGD F-OGGS N29929 [dbf 21Jul83 Brownwood, TX, USA]
1014 (G)	BN-2A MkIII-2	G-BDGE EL-AIC [w/o 28Oct81 Foya Kamala, Liberia]
1015 (G)	BN-2A MkIII-2	G-BDGF EL-AID [wfu c1990 Monrovia, Liberia]
1016 (G)	BN-2A MkIII-2	G-BDGG C-GSAA G-BDGG G-JOEY
1017 (G)	BN-2A MkIII-2	G-BDKN PK-KTC [w/o 25Oct91 nr Sampit, Indonesia]
1018 (G)	BN-2A MkIII-2	G-BDKO PK-KTD [w/o 10Jan77 Samarinda, Indonesia]
1019 (G)	BN-2A MkIII-2	G-BDKP HK-1704X HK-1704 [wfu nr Villavicencio, Meta, Colombia; canx 23Apr91]
1020 (G)	BN-2A MkIII-3	G-BDKR N26877 N412WA [wfu Fort Lauderdale-International, FL, USA; canx 18Mar05]
1021 (G)	BN-2A MkIII-2	G-BDOJ PK-KTI [w/o 03Apr89 Balikpapan, Indonesia]
1022 (G)	BN-2A MkIII-2	G-BDOK PK-KTH [wfu cMar00; b/u cDec03]
1023 (G)	BN-2A MkIII-2	G-BDOM N411WA
1024 (G)	BN-2A MkIII-2	G-BDOS (4X-CCI) G-OJAV
1025 (G)	BN-2A MkIII-2	G-BDOT VH-BPB N3850K N903GD N900TA ZK-SFF G-BDOT RP-C [canx 28Apr09 as exported to Philippines]
1026 (G)	BN-2A MkIII-2	G-BDTN VQ-SAN S7-AAN G-BDTN [wfu cJan98 Alderney, UK]
1027 (G)	BN-2A MkIII-2	G-BDTO (C-GYOX) 8P-ASC G-BDTO G-OTSB G-RBSI G-BDTO
1028 (G)	BN-2A MkIII-2	G-BDTP 9L-LAU G-BDTP [w/o 14Sep86 Amsterdam-Schiphol, Netherlands; canx 13May87]
1029 (G)	BN-2A MkIII-3	G-BDTR N403JA VQ-TAD N650LP [w/o 15Dec08 off Providenciales, Turks & Caicos Islands]
1030 (G)	BN-2A MkIII-2	G-BDTS VH-EGU [w/o 16Dec80 Blowering, nr Batlow, 18km S of Tumut, NSW, Australia; canx 16Dec80]
1031 (G)	BN-2A MkIII-2	G-BDWR ZS-JYF [w/o 08Oct77 Lanseria, Transvaal, South Africa]
1032 (G)	BN-2A MkIII-2	G-BDWS 5Y-CMC [w/o 24Jul78 Nyeri Hills, Kenya]
1033 (G)	BN-2A MkIII-2	G-BDWT PK-KTJ [b/u by Jun04 in Indonesia]
1034 (G)	BN-2A MkIII-2	G-BDWU N414WA YV-872C YV1416
1035 (G)	BN-2A MkIII-2	G-BDWV 8P-ASF G-BDWV G-RBCI
1036 (G)	BN-2A MkIII-2	G-BEDM B-11112 [wfu cJun93; pres c1997 Taitung City, Taiwan]
1037 (G)	BN-2A MkIII-2	G-BEDN VP-VAG J8-VAG V2-LCI F-OGOI [wfu c1991 Antigua]
1038 (G)	BN-2A MkIII-2	G-BEDO N32650 N199PC [wfu cNov79; fuselage in scrapyard adjacent to Deland Municipal-Sidney H Taylor Field, FL, USA]
1039 (G)	BN-2A MkIII-2	G-BEDP N401JA N1FY N902TA ZK-SFG G-BEDP
1040 (G)	BN-2A MkIII-3	G-BEDR N420WA YV-943CP XA-TYU [dam 22Oct05 Playa del Carmen, Quintana Roo, Mexico during Hurricane Wilma; under rebuild]
1041 (G)	BN-2A MkIII-2	G-BEFO VP-LMB V2-LMB F-BYCJ G-SARN G-BEFO 5H-AZP G-BEFO DQ-TRI [wfu c2005 Nausori, Fiji]
1042 (G)	BN-2A MkIII-2	G-BEFP JA6401 N30WA G-BEFP 4X-CCL G-BEFP 5H-AZD G-WEAC G-RHOP (ZK-CJS) ZK-LGC
1043 (G)	BN-2A MkIII-2	G-BEGX XA-LIZ N143TR [dbr cAug05 by Hurricane Katrina; canx 27Nov07]

ISLANDER

c/n	Series	Identities
1044 (G)	BN-2A MkIII-2	G-BEGY ZS-KME G-BEGY N511WA HP-1157IT YV-487C (N903VL) YV-2523P XA-UBD
1045 (G)	BN-2A MkIII-2	G-BEHA XA-KOQ [w/o cMay84 in Mexico]
1046 (G)	BN-2A MkIII-2	G-BEHB XA-KOP N146TR [dbr cAug05 by Hurricane Katrina; canx 27Nov07]
1047 (G)	BN-2A MkIII-2	G-BEHC (N1348G) HC-BLG HP-1155IT YV-486C (N904VL) YV-486C [reportedly b/u c2001 in Venezuela]
1048 (G)	BN-2A MkIII-2	G-BEHD (XA-HOI) N905GD N905VL
1049 (G)	BN-2A MkIII-2	G-BEHE HC-BLH HP-1113IT F-OGOR [w/o 09Nov97 Farmers Cay, Bahamas]
1050 (G)	BN-2A MkIII-2	G-BEHF (N1348M) N164LG [b/u c1993 Vieques, PR; canx 15Jan93]
1051 (G)	BN-2A MkIII-2	G-BEPG XA-JPE [w/o 05May89 Chichen Itza, Yucatan, Mexico]
1052 (G)	BN-2A MkIII-2	G-BEPH S7-AAG G-BEPH G-PCAM [wfu cJan04 Guernsey, UK]
1053 (G)	BN-2A MkIII-2	G-BEPI G-FTSE
1054 (G)	BN-2A MkIII-2	G-BEPJ OE1 (Botswana Defence Force) A2-AGX Z-AIR SX-CVM [wfu Athens-Hellinikon, Greece]
1055 (G)	BN-2A MkIII-2	G-BEPK OE2 (Botswana Defence Force) A2-AGY Z-UTD SX-CPG YJ-0019
1056 (G)	BN-2A MkIII-2	G-BEVR XA-TEH G-BEVR 6Y-JQE G-BEVR [wfu cOct95, parts to Guernsey, UK; canx 20Mar03]
1057 (G)	BN-2A MkIII-2	G-BEVT
1058 (G)	BN-2A MkIII-2	G-BEVU ZS-KMF G-BEVU N611WA 6Y-JQF [dbr cSep88 Montego Bay, Jamaica]
1059 (G)	BN-2A MkIII-2	G-BEVV G-BNZD 6Y-JQK G-BEVV [wfu cOct95, parts to Cumbernauld, UK; canx 20Mar03]
1060 (G)	BN-2A MkIII-2	G-BEVY (XA-CUC) N906GD N906VL
1061 (G)	BN-2A MkIII-2	G-BFDD B-11118 [wfu c1998 - status?]
1062 (G)	BN-2A MkIII-3	N3265T N299PC [status? incomplete kit was supplied cAug82; aircraft was never completed]
1063 (G)	BN-2A MkIII-3	N3266A N399PC [status? incomplete kit was supplied cAug82; aircraft was never completed]
1064 (G)	BN-2A MkIII-3	N3266B N599PC [status? incomplete kit was supplied cAug82; aircraft was never completed]
1065 (G)	BN-2A MkIII-3	N3266G [incomplete kit was supplied cAug82; aircraft was never completed; used in rebuild of c/n 359]
1066 (G)	BN-2A MkIII-3	N3266H N899PC [incomplete kit was supplied cAug82; aircraft was never completed; fuselage in scrapyard adjacent to Deland Municipal-Sidney H Taylor Field, FL, USA]
1067 (G)	BN-2A MkIII-3	N3266K N279PC [status? incomplete kit was supplied cAug82; aircraft was never completed]
1068 (G)	BN-2A MkIII-3	N3266R N449PC [status? incomplete kit was supplied cAug82; aircraft was never completed]
1069 (G)	BN-2A MkIII-3	N3266T N559PC [incomplete kit was supplied cAug82; aircraft was never completed; fuselage in scrapyard adjacent to Deland Municipal-Sidney H Taylor Field, FL, USA]
1070 (G)	BN-2A MkIII-3	N3266W N629PC [incomplete kit was supplied cAug82; aircraft was never completed; fuselage in scrapyard adjacent to Deland Municipal-Sidney H Taylor Field, FL, USA]
1071 (G)	BN-2A MkIII-3	N3267A N929PC [incomplete kit was supplied cAug82; aircraft was never completed; fuselage in scrapyard adjacent to Deland Municipal-Sidney H Taylor Field, FL, USA]
1072 (G)	BN-2A MkIII-2	N3267J [incomplete kit was supplied cAug82; aircraft was never completed; canx 23Jun97, parts to Anglo-Normandy, Guernsey, UK]
1100	BN-2A MkIII-2	(G-BYSB) [void - airframe not built]
1101	BN-2A MkIII-2	(G-BYSC) [void - airframe not built]
1102	BN-2A MkIII-2	(G-BYSD) [void - airframe not built]
2001 (G)	BN-2A-26	G-BESL B-11111 [w/o cApr87 in Taiwan]
2002 (G)	BN-2B-20	G-BESM N407JA N302SK D-IAOR G-BESM 5Y-JAK ZS-PEF 5X-MHB 5H-KLA
2003 (G)	BN-2A-20	G-BESN G-51-2003 (N408JA) YV-337CP YV-269C [w/o 06Nov79 in Venezuela]
2004 (G)	BN-2A-26	G-BESO SX-DKB [wfu Ikaros, nr Athens, Greece]
2005 (G)	BN-2A-26	G-BESP N417WA HI-566CA N7134A HI-593CA
2006 (G)	BN-2A-26	G-BESR V2-LCL
2007 (G)	BN-2A-26	G-BESX B-11116 [w/o 10Apr92 off Lan-Yu Island, Taiwan]
2008 (G)	BN-2A-27	G-BESU N8055X
2009 (G)	BN-2A-26	G-BESV N68HA [w/o 20Aug91 18 mls from Ketchikan-International, AK, USA; canx 06Jan92]
2010 (G)	BN-2A-26	G-BESW N3835Z
2011 (G)	BN-2A-21	G-BEXA G-DIVE (ZB503) (RAF) G-MALI G-BEXA G-BPCB G-PASY G-CHES EI-IPC G-CHES [w/o 17Oct07 nr Guadalcanal, Spain; canx 17Mar08]
2012 (G)	BN-2A-26	G-BEXB N406JA JA5261 N2132M ZK-PIZ
2013 (G)	BN-2A-26R	G-BEXC XA-IEX HP-1303
2014 (G)	BN-2B-27	G-BEXD YV-365CP N45858 B-12201 P2-KST V6-SFM V6-01FM
2015 (G)	BN-2A-26	G-BEXE N8069X N416WA V3-HIA C-GZVU C6-FYP
2016 (G)	BN-2A-26	G-BEXF N385KG VQ-TAA
2017 (G)	BN-2A-26	G-BEXG G-51-2017 N59360 C-GZGO
2018 (G)	BN-2B-26	G-BEXH 8P-RAD VP-VAH J8-VAH J8-CIW
2019 (G)	BN-2A-26	G-BEXI VQ-TAB N2159X N903VL
2020 (G)	BN-2A-26	G-BEXJ G-51-2020 (N412JA) G-BEXJ N60PA N100DA D-IORF
2021	BN-2B-26	G-BHPE N50PA N415WA J8-VAT 8R-GMM N599MS C6-BHH
2022	BN-2B-27	G-BHPF N17JA XC-FEE
2023	BN-2B-21	G-BHPG N408JA N999JH YV-474C N81KM V3-HFB N81KM YV-2425P YV1987
2024	BN-2B-21	G-BHXH N409JA XC-GEC N21DA VP-AAF
2025	BN-2B-26	G-BHXI G-UERN J3-GAI J8-VBI
2026 (E)	BN-2A-21	G-BIPD PK-VIW
2027 (E)	BN-2A-21	G-BIUF PK-VIX [wfu Jakarta, Indonesia]
2028	BN-2A-26	G-BIUG G-MALB C-FCVK [w/o 07Dec98 Baie-Comeau, QC, Canada; canx 26Oct99]
2029	BN-2A-26	G-BIUH G-BNGA B-11125 [w/o 19Jan88 off Green Island, Taiwan]
2030	BN-2T	G-BIUJ G-KEMZ 9Q-CLW [w/o 29Jun93 Mitwaba, Zaire]
2031	BN-2B-27	G-BIPE XC-FOE [w/o 01May04 nr Vallecillos, Guerrero, Mexico]

ISLANDER

c/n	Series	Identities
2032	BN-2A-26	G-BNAE B-11123 (B-17022) B-11123 [static test airframe at China Institute of Technology, Chu-Tung, Taiwan]
2033	BN-2T	G-BJOG [construction not completed; canx 29Oct86]
2034	BN-2T CC.2A	G-BJOH G-OPBN ZF573 (RAF) G-SRAY ZF573 (RAF)
2035	BN-2A-20	G-BNAF N9745N A6-NHM (AP-BEL) VH-OBL ZK-OBL VH-OBL
2036	BN-2	[construction not completed]
2037	BN-2A-26	G-BNEB JA5284 OY-PPP ZK-MSF
2038	BN-2A-26	G-BNEC JA5285 N8094K 9M-WKC C-FLRB C-GZKG PJ-AIW
2039	BN-2A-26	G-BNMJ B-12232 B-69832
2040	BN-2A-26	G-BOGZ TC-FBL TF-ARA HK-3811 N23US C6-BUS N908GD
2041	BN-2	[construction not completed; fuselage to Queen Mary & Westfield College, London, UK]
2042 (P)	BN-2A-26	RP-C688 T8-A103 VH-BWO
2043 (P)	BN-2A-26	RP-C693 ZK-TSS

Production complete

c/n	Series	Identities
2101 (R)	BN-2B-27	G-BIIN TR-LZY [canx 24Jul93 - status?]
2102 (R)	BN-2T	G-BIIO N660J VP-LMF V2-LDF (OB-T-1282) LX-III LX-KEV
2103 (R)	BN-2B-26	G-BIIP N411JA 6Y-JKJ 6Y-JQJ G-BIIP G-SEIL
2104 (R)	BN-2B-26	G-BIIR XA-MAO [w/o c1987 in Mexico]
2105 (R)	BN-2B-26	G-BIIS XA-MAP N2119V
2106 (R)	BN-2B-21	G-BIXC G-MICV (5B-CFP) 5B-ICV 12106 (Cyprus Defence Force) 5B-ICV 12106 (Cyprus Defence Force)
2107 (R)	BN-2B-26	G-BIXD N414JA (YV-2174P) C-FYPB C-GSGR
2108 (R)	BN-2B-21	G-BIXE SAF-002 (Suriname AF) PZ-TGU
2109 (R)	BN-2B-27	G-BIXF N2643X HK-2822X HK-2822
2110 (R)	BN-2B-26	G-BIXG N663J N663VL
2111 (R)	BN-2B-27	G-BJBD N3235G HK-2890X HK-2890 [w/o 23May94 Loma Linda, Cesar, Colombia; canx 06Oct99]
2112 (R)	BN-2T	G-BJBE G-HOPL 9M-BSS VH-IAE N717MC
2113 (R)	BN-2B-27	G-BJBF HK-2904X HK-2904 "HK-1209" UAP-6 (Peru Police) GC-006(Peru Police) FP-006 (Peru Police) [wfu Lima-Callao, Peru]
2114 (R)	BN-2B-27	G-BJBG G-BLEC SX-DKA 8R-GRC
2115 (R)	BN-2T-4R	G-BJBH G-51-2115 G-RAPA N360WT G-RAPA [wfu cOct98; b/u cNov01 parts at Bembridge, UK; canx 03May02]
2116 (R)	BN-2B-21	G-BJEA SAF-003 (Suriname AF) PZ-TGT
2117 (R)	BN-2B-21	G-BJEB SAF-004 (Suriname AF)
2118 (R)	BN-2T CC.2B	G-BJEC 411 (UAE AF) 318 (UAE AF) G-BJEC G-SELX (ZG998)(RAF) ZH537 (RAF)
2119 (R)	BN-2T	G-BJED G-MAFF
2120 (R)	BN-2T	G-BJEE C9-TAH G-BJEE [on rebuild Cumbernauld, UK; wears false marks "K9-DOG"]
2121 (R)	BN-2T	G-BJEF C9-TAK G-BJEF [std Cumbernauld, UK pending rebuild]
2122 (R)	BN-2T	G-BJEG C9-TAI [w/o 03Nov84 Tete, Mozambique]
2123 (R)	BN-2B-21	G-BJEH IN137 (Indian Navy)
2124 (R)	BN-2T	G-BJEJ C9-TAJ G-BJEJ [std Cumbernauld, UK pending rebuild]
2125 (R)	BN-2B-27	G-BJEK VP-FBF C-GFBF
2126 (R)	BN-2B-26	G-BJOJ VP-FBG [w/o 24Jun87 Brookfield Farm airstip, East Falkland, Falkland Islands; canx 27Jun87]
2127 (R)	BN-2B-27	G-BJOK (9Q-CKR) TR-LBJ [w/o 08Jul95 Medouneu, Gabon]
2128 (R)	BN-2B-26	G-BJOL D-IFLN G-BJOL J8-VAP 8P-ASF 8P-TAC N902VL N904GD
2129 (R)	BN-2B-26	G-BJOM N665J JA5282 VH-BSO
2130 (R)	BN-2B-26	G-BJON VH-AEU
2131 (R)	BN-2B-26	G-BJOO B-12222 P2-MCA VH-ISL ZK-DLA
2132 (R)	BN-2B-26	G-BJOP
2133 (R)	BN-2B-21	G-BJOR PK-VIY [w/o 18Nov00 Datah Dawai, Indonesia]
2134 (R)	BN-2B-21	G-BJOS IN138 (Indian Navy)
2135 (R)	BN-2B-21	G-BJOU IN139 (Indian Navy)
2136 (R)	BN-2A-21	G-BJYP BDF-02 (Belize Defence Force)
2137 (R)	BN-2A-21	G-BJYR BDF-01 (Belize Defence Force) [w/o 19Oct98 in Belize]
2138 (R)	BN-2T	G-BJYS G-IACL G-IAHL 9M-LYG 9M-TIR P2-SIV
2139 (R)	BN-2T	G-BJYT G-WOTG ES-PNW
2140 (R)	BN-2T (Mod)	G-BJYU G-DLRA ZG989 (Army Air Corps) G-DLRA ZG989 (Army Air Corps)
2141 (R)	BN-2T	G-BJYV 7Q-YAW ZS-PKK
2142 (R)	BN-2T	G-BJYW G-ORED
2143 (R)	BN-2T-4R	G-BJYX G-TEMI G-MSSA N360TL
2144 (R)	BN-2T	G-BJYY 5T-BSA G-PASU N770FK
2145 (R)	BN-2T	G-BJYZ G-BOBC N54EW VH-YVH
2146 (R)	BN-2T	G-BKEA G-DEMO G-05/OT-GLA (Belgian AF) LX-REM 6V-AHW
2147 (R)	BN-2T	G-BKEB TN-AEQ [w/o 13Dec85 Accra, Ghana]
2148 (R)	BN-2B-21	G-BKEC IN140 (Indian Navy)
2149 (R)	BN-2B-21	G-BKED IN141 (Indian Navy)
2150 (R)	BN-2B-21	G-BKEE IN142 (Indian Navy)
2151 (R)	BN-2T	G-BKEF 7Q-YAU ZS-PKJ
2152 (R)	BN-2B-21	G-BKEG VP-LMG V2-LDE 8P-ASL 8P-TAD [w/o 17Jul94 Fort de France, Martinique]
2153 (R)	BN-2B-26	G-BKEH EC-EBC N633BB PZ-TBL
2154 (R)	BN-2B-26	G-BKEI N667J JA5281 VH-YIE T3-VIN
2155 (R)	BN-2B-26	G-BKEJ N668J VP-LVP N861JA N861VL
2156 (R)	BN-2B-26	G-BKJG G-LIPP 9H-ADF AS9819 (Armed Forces of Malta) G-51-2156 AS9819 (Armed Forces of Malta)
2157 (R)	BN-2B-21	G-BKJH HC-BNR G-BKJH G-PASV EC- [canx 28Jan08 as exported to Spain; illegally operated under UK marks, impounded 01Mar08 nr Toledo, Spain]

c/n	Series	Identities
2158 (R)	BN-2T	G-BKJI 7Q-YAV ZS-NAT
2159 (R)	BN-2B-26	G-BKJJ G-TWOB 9M-TAD 9H-ACU AS9516 (Armed Forces of Malta)
2160 (R)	BN-2B-26	G-BKJK VP-FBD
2161 (R)	BN-2B-21	G-BKJL TZ-ADN [w/o cOct87 Dogofri, Mali]
2162 (R)	BN-2B-21	G-BKJM HC-BNS G-CIAS
2163 (R)	BN-2B-21	G-BKJN N671J N455JH [w/o cSep86 location unkn]
2164 (R)	BN-2B-26	G-BKJO VH-AEC
2165 (R)	BN-2B-26	G-BKJP N670J J8-VAM
2166 (R)	BN-2B-27	G-BKOC CC-CGE CC-PAC
2167 (R)	BN-2B-26	G-BKOD I-LILY N405RM D-IAAI [w/o 26Dec01 Bremerhaven, Germany; canx 07Feb02]
2168 (R)	BN-2B-27	G-BKOE CC-CGG CC-PQO N2407B ZK-MFN
2169 (R)	BN-2B-27	G-BKOF CC-CGH CC-PGT CX-PGT CC-CYR
2170 (R)	BN-2B-26	G-BKOG N672JA 6Y-JLG 6Y-JLU
2171 (R)	BN-2B-21	G-BKOH OH-BND N856BC
2172 (R)	BN-2B-20	G-BKOI JA5290 YJ-008
2173 (R)	BN-2B-20	G-BKOJ JA5294 N999BR A2-TAU
2174 (R)	BN-2B-27	G-BKOK OY-CFV G-BKOK [w/o 15Jun02 Anholt Island, Denmark (as OY-CFV); registered G-BKOK 30Jul08]
2175 (R)	BN-2B-26	G-BKOL G-OSEA
2176 (R)	BN-2B-27R	G-BLDS EC-DYF G-BLDS FP-15 (Peru Police) PNP-215 (Peru Police)
2177 (R)	BN-2B-21	G-BLDT VH-INB 9M-AZV VH-BNX H4-WPG *YJ-007
2178 (R)	BN-2B-21	G-BLDU N117MC
2179 (R)	BN-2B-26	G-BLDV D-INEY G-BLDV
2180 (R)	BN-2B-27	G-BLDW EC-DYG G-51-2180 G-BLDW N272BN V2-LDM
2181 (R)	BN-2B-26	G-BLDX [w/o 21Aug87 Ainsdale Beach, UK; canx 18Jan94]
2182 (R)	BN-2B-21	G-BLNC TZ-APV
2183 (R)	BN-2T	G-BLND G-LEAP
2184 (R)	BN-2T AL.1	G-BLNE ZG844 (Army Air Corps)
2185 (R)	BN-2B-26	G-BLNF D-IFBN
2186 (R)	BN-2B-26	G-BLNG (D-IEDB) D-IFOX G-BLNG
2187 (R)	BN-2B-26	G-BLNH D-IOLA G-BLNH N728JM
2188 (R)	BN-2B-26	G-BLNI VP-FBI [dbr 19Nov06 West Point Island airstip, West Falkland, Falkland Islands; fuse & wings to Stanley Airport, Falkland Islands cFeb07]
2189 (R)	BN-2B-26	G-BLNJ
2190 (R)	BN-2T	G-BLNK PH-RPM G-BLNK PH-RPM G-BLNK RAN-50 (Royal Nepalese Army)
2191 (R)	BN-2T	G-BLNL PH-RPN G-BLNL PH-RPN G-BLNL RAN-49 (Royal Nepalese Army)
2192 (R)	BN-2B-26	G-BLNM TC-FBK TF-ARB HK-3812 N907VL [dbr 19Nov99 Anguilla during Hurricane Lenny, parts to Wessex Aerospace, UK cMay00; canx 05Jun00]
2193 (R)	BN-2B-27	G-BLNS B-11126 (B-17023) B-11126 [static test airframe at China Institute of Technology, Chu-Tung, Taiwan]
2194 (R)	BN-2T AL.1	G-BLNT ZG845 (Army Air Corps)
2195 (R)	BN-2T AL.1	G-BLNU ZG846 (Army Air Corps)
2196 (R)	BN-2T AL.1	G-BLNV ZG847 (Army Air Corps)
2197 (R)	BN-2B-26	G-BLNW ZK-ZQN
2198 (R)	BN-2B-26	G-BLNX G-BPCA
2199 (R)	BN-2T AL.1	G-BLNY ZG848 (Army Air Corps)
2200 (R)	BN-2B-26	G-BLNZ VP-FBM
2201 (R)	BN-2T	G-BOMC G-51-2201 A40-CT G-51-2201 A40-CT N700FK
2202 (R)	BN-2T AL.1	G-BOMD ZG993 (Army Air Corps)
2203 (R)	BN-2B-20	G-BOME B-3901 (N66AM) (8P-TAF) N628RC A2-ZOO ZS-PAO 5H-MVE
2204 (R)	BN-2B-20	G-BOMF B-3902 N16VM (8P-TAH) N16VM [w/o 02Dec94 off Marshall Islands, Pacific Ocean]
2205 (R)	BN-2B-26	G-BOMG D-IBNF G-BOMG [w/o 15Mar05, Mull of Kintyre, Scotland, UK; canx 20Sep05]
2206 (R)	BN-2T AL.1	G-BPLN ZG994 (RAF) [dbr 30Jun99 Middle Wallop, UK, parts to Bembridge, UK]
2207 (R)	BN-2T	G-BPLO G-CYPP 5B-CPA CP-1 (Cyprus Police Air Wing)
2208 (R)	BN-2B-20	G-BPLP B-3903 N32GM (8P-SCA) 8P-TAG PJ-WEB
2209 (R)	BN-2B-26	G-BPLR JA5298 OY-BNT G-BPLR TF-VEJ
2210 (R)	BN-2B-20	G-BPLS B-3904 N105AM 8P-TAJ N848MA
2211 (R)	BN-2B-20	G-BPXR B-3905 N17EL 8P-TAI V2-LFP N708SA N705SA N887MA
2212 (R)	BN-2B-26	G-BPXS D-ILFH
2213 (R)	BN-2T	G-BPXT CN-TWK
2214 (R)	BN-2T	G-BPXU CN-TWL
2215 (R)	BN-2T	G-BPXV CN-TWM
2216 (R)	BN-2B-26	G-BRFY VP-FBN
2217 (R)	BN-2B-26	G-BRFZ F-ODUR ZK-JQB N26BN
2218 (R)	BN-2B-26	G-BRGA VP-FBO
2219 (R)	BN-2B-26	G-BRGB F-ODUP C-GGJG
2220 (R)	BN-2B-26	G-BRGC F-ODUQ ZK-JQC N27BN
2221 (R)	BN-2B-20	G-BRPA VH-INO HP-1550
2222 (R)	BN-2T	G-BRPB G361 (Ghana AF)
2223 (R)	BN-2T	G-BRPC G362 (Ghana AF)
2224 (R)	BN-2B-26	G-BRPD EC-750 EC-FFZ OY-CAT
2225 (R)	BN-2T	G-BRSR G360 (Ghana AF)
2226 (R)	BN-2B-20	G-BRSS OA7 (Botswana Defence Force)
2227 (R)	BN-2B-20	G-BRST OA8 (Botswana Defence Force)
2228 (R)	BN-2T	G-BRSU CN-TWN
2229 (R)	BN-2T	G-BRSV G363 (Ghana AF)
2230 (R)	BN-2B-26	G-BSAC DQ-FHG
2231 (R)	BN-2T	G-BSAD TC-TKG
2232 (R)	BN-2T	G-BSAE CN-TWO
2233 (R)	BN-2T	G-BSAF CN-TWP

ISLANDER

c/n	Series	Identities
2234 (R)	BN-2B-20	G-BSAG 9M-TAM G-CHEZ
2235 (R)	BN-2T CC.2	G-BSAH ZH536 (RAF)
2236 (R)	BN-2B-26	G-BSPO JA5306
2237 (R)	BN-2T	G-BSPP CN-TWQ
2238 (R)	BN-2T	G-BSPR MP-CG-02 (Mauritius Coast Guard)
2239 (R)	BN-2B-26	G-BSPS JA5305
2240 (R)	BN-2B-26	G-BSPT JA5316 OY-PHY N52WA G-BSPT TF-VEG G-BSPT
2241 (R)	BN-2B-20	G-BSPU D-IFLN (N200BN) G-BSPU B-68802
2242 (R)	BN-2T	G-BSWN 42/AR-NYB (Pakistan Navy)
2243 (R)	BN-2B-26	G-BSWO D-ILFA
2244 (R)	BN-2B-20	G-BSWP G-HPAA N345CP
2245 (R)	BN-2T	G-BSWR
2246 (R)	BN-2T	G-BSWS 46/AR-NYC (Pakistan Navy)
2247 (R)	BN-2B-26	G-BSWT G-SSKY
2248 (R)	BN-2B-26	G-BSWU N203PR
2249 (R)	BN-2B-20	G-BTLU PK-HNG PK-RGP
2250 (R)	BN-2B-20	G-BTLV PK-HNF PK-VIA [w/o 09Sep05 Samarinda, Indonesia]
2251 (R)	BN-2B-20	G-BTLW 9M-TAC V2-LFE F-OHQY
2252 (R)	BN-2B-26	G-BTLX VP-FBR
2253 (R)	BN-2B-26	G-BTLY I-DEPE
2254 (R)	BN-2B-20	G-BTLZ Z-CAA
2255 (R)	BN-2B-26	G-BTVI B-68801
2256 (R)	BN-2B-26	G-BTVJ TL-ABU TL-KAF
2257 (R)	BN-2B-20	G-BTVK OA9 (Botswana Defence Force)
2258 (R)	BN-2B-20	G-BTVL OA10 (Botswana Defence Force)
2259 (R)	BN-2T	G-BTVM CN-TWR
2260 (R)	BN-2B-20	G-BTVN G-NESU G-SICB
2261 (R)	BN-2T	G-BUBD CN-TWS
2262 (R)	BN-2T	G-BUBE CN-TWT
2263 (R)	BN-2B-26	G-BUBF LV-WFR
2264 (R)	BN-2T	G-BUBG G-JSPC VT-SKI
2265 (R)	BN-2A-20	G-BUBH OA11 (Botswana Defence Force)
2266 (R)	BN-2T	G-BUBI CN-TWU
2267 (R)	BN-2B-26	G-BUBJ JA5318 N450PM G-BUBJ G-HEBS
2268 (R)	BN-2B-26	G-BUBK JA5319
2269 (R)	BN-2B-20	G-BUBM JA5320
2270 (R)	BN-2B-26	G-BUBN
2271 (R)	BN-2B-26	G-BUBO D-ILFB [dbr 03Mar07 Ruhnu, Estonia; canx cJun07]
2272 (R)	BN-2B-20	G-BUBP JA5321 D-ILFC
2273 (R)	BN-2T	G-BVFG CN-TWV
2274 (R)	BN-2T	G-BVFH CN-TWW
2275 (R)	BN-2T	G-BVFI CN-TWX
2276 (R)	BN-2T	G-BVFJ A2-MOA
2277 (R)	BN-2T	G-BVFK G-JSAT
2278 (R)	BN-2B-26	G-BVNB HC-BUZ
2279 (R)	BN-2B-20	G-BVNC VH-ZZT
2280 (R)	BN-2B-20	G-BVND VH-ZZU
2281 (R)	BN-2B-20	G-BVNE VH-ZZV
2282 (R)	BN-2B-20	G-BVNF VH-ZZW JA127D
2283 (R)	BN-2B-20	G-BVSG VH-ZZX
2284 (R)	BN-2B-20	G-BVSH VH-ZZY VH-WZP
2285 (R)	BN-2B-20	G-BVSI JA5322 [dbr 07Feb96 nr Kawatana, Nagasaki Prefecture, Japan]
2286 (R)	BN-2B-20	G-BVSJ EP-BFR
2287 (R)	BN-2T	G-BVSK F-OIAR VT-SUN
2288 (R)	BN-2B-26	G-BVSL [wfu; canx 12Oct00; b/u cAug03 Bembridge, UK]
2289 (R)	BN-2B-20	G-BVXX 6Y-JNS
2290 (R)	BN-2B-20	G-BVXY D-IFKU
2291 (R)	BN-2B-20	G-BVYD JA5323 OY-PHS G-BVYD F-OIJU *OY-PHS
2292 (R)	BN-2B-20	G-BVYE [dbr 28Aug96 Bucharest-Baneasa, Romania; canx 27Nov98; b/u c2002 Bembridge, UK]
2293 (R)	BN-2B-20	G-BWYW EI-CUW
2294 (R)	BN-2B-20	G-BWJO VH-CSS F-OIJS
2295 (R)	BN-2B-20	G-BWNE OA12 (Botswana Defence Force)
2296 (R)	BN-2B-20	G-BWNF JA02TY D-ILFD
2297 (R)	BN-2B-20	G-BWNG JA5324
2298 (R)	BN-2B-20	G-BWYX JA5325
2299 (R)	BN-2B-20	G-BWYY D-IFTI
2300 (R)	BN-2B-20	G-BWYZ G-OBNG D-IFUT
2301 (R)	BN-2B-20	G-BWZF G-CZNE
2302 (R)	BN-2B-20	G-CCUX N188AM
2303 (R)	BN-2T	G-CDCJ N2536Y
2304 (R)	BN-2B-20	G-SLAP G-SICA
2305 (R)	BN-2B-20	G-CEUA D-IOLO
2306 (R)	BN-2B-26	G-CEUB *D-IOLK
2307	BN-2B-20	G-CEUC
2308	BN-2B-20	G-CCIM 08/AR-NYD (Pakistan Maritime Security Agency)
2309	BN-2B-20	G-CEUD
2310	BN-2B-20	G-CEUE
2311	BN-2B-20	
2312	BN-2B-20	
2313	BN-2B-20	
2314	BN-2B-20	

c/n	Series	Identities
2315	BN-2B-20	
2316	BN-2B-20	
2317	BN-2B-20	
2318	BN-2B-20	
2319	BN-2B-20	
2320	BN-2B-20	
3000	BN-2B-20	G-OBNC

PADC/BRITTEN-NORMAN ISLANDER

c/n	Series	Identities
3001 (P)	BN-2A-21	RP-C258 3001 (Philippine AF)[dbr 01Dec89 Sangley Point, Philippines; b/u]
3002 (P)	BN-2A-21	RP-C251 RP-251 PCG-251 (Philippine Coast Guard)
3003 (P)	BN-2A-21	RP-C530 3003 (Philippine AF)[w/o 17Mar82 in Philippines]
3004 (P)	BN-2A-26	RP-C662 VH-HPL VH-WRF
3005 (P)	BN-2A-26	RP-C340 9M-BSM VH-BSN [w/o 22May89 56 mls SW of Derby, WA, Australia; canx 14Nov90]
3006 (P)	BN-2A-27	RP-C552 JA5280 N42540 (N9HV) 8R-GRA
3007 (P)	BN-2T	RP-C766 RP-766
3008 (P)	BN-2A-26	RP-C553 G-BLEI V3-HEZ VP-AAB N906GD
3009 (P)	BN-2A-26	RP-C1849 G-BLNR OY-CEG D-IORC (F-OHQW) F-OHQX
3010 (P)	BN-2T	RP-C788
3011 (P)	BN-2A-26	RP-C1850 G-BLYO G-MALN J8-VAN N5891V
3012 (P)	BN-2A-26	RP-C604 G-BMDT [w/o 14Jun86 Walney Island, UK; canx 03Dec86]
3013 (P)	BN-2A-26	RP-C578 G-BMMH G-SBUS
3014 (P)	BN-2A-26	RP-C664 G-BMWO TC-FBI TF-ARG HK-3813 N904VL
3015 (P)	BN-2A-26	RP-C665 VH-CFZ VH-WRM VH-EGE

Production complete

BRITTEN-NORMAN DEFENDER 4000 & MSSA

This is a new c/n series introduced for the BN-2T-4 series aircraft which feature larger engines, a higher AUW wing (common design from the Trislander) and a redesigned tail unit. The BN-2T-4S "Defender 4000" features a stretched fuselage whereas the BN-2T-4R "MSSA" has a standard length fuselage with a larger radar nose. The aircraft is produced in kit form in Romania and shipped to Bembridge, IOW, UK for final completion.

c/n	Series	Identities
4001	BN-2T-4R	
4002	BN-2T-4R	
4003	BN-2T-4R	G-BVHX [wfu Bembridge, UK; canx 05Apr00]
4004	BN-2T-4R	G-BVHY [aircraft incomplete; parts std Bembridge, UK; canx 06Apr04]
4005	BN-2T-4S AL.1	G-BVHZ G-SURV ZG995 (Army Air Corps)
4006	BN-2T-4R	G-BWPK G-SJCH
4007	BN-2T-4S	G-BWPM [aircraft incomplete; parts std Bembridge, UK; canx 19Oct00]
4008	BN-2T-4R	G-BWPN 254 (Irish Air Corps)
4009	BN-2T-4S T.3	G-BWPO 9M-TPS VH-YVH G-BWPO ZH004 (Ministry of Defence)
4010	BN-2T-4S AL.1	G-BWPR ZG996 (Army Air Corps)
4011 (R)	BN-2T-4S	G-BWPU (9M-TPD) G-GMPB
4012	BN-2T-4S AL.2	G-BWPV ZG997 (Army Air Corps)
4013	BN-2T-4S	G-BWPW [aircraft incomplete; parts std Bembridge, UK; canx 12Oct00]
4014	BN-2T-4S AL.2	G-BWPX ZG998 (Army Air Corps)
4015	BN-2T-4S AL.2	G-CEIO ZH001 (Army Air Corps)
4016	BN-2T-4S AL.2	G-CEIP ZH002 (Army Air Corps)
4017	BN-2T-4S AL.2	G-CEIR *ZH003 (Army Air Corps)
4018	BN-2T-4S	
4019	BN-2T-4S	
4020	BN-2T-4S	

CESSNA 425 CORSAIR/CONQUEST I

^ - Blackhawk XP135A engine upgrade fitted

c/n	Mod	Identities
693		N4089L [b/u c1981 Wichita, KS, USA]
425-0001		N2079A [w/o 29May85 Dayton, OH, USA]
425-0002		N425CC N74HR N443H
425-0003		N98751 D-INGA G-KRMA
425-0004		N98817 N425TF N425AT
425-0005		N98820 N6SK N345TP
425-0006		N98830 N734M C-GMSV N757H
425-0007		N98858 C-GJEB N67BA
425-0008		N98876 RP-C574 N811NA C-FKTL
425-0009		N425AC (N98896) N425AC [w/o 18Nov81 Natchez-Hardy Anders Field/Adams County, MS, USA]
425-0010		N6769Z N313JL N813JL N425PL
425-0011		N6770G N6161P A2-AHT
425-0012		N6770M D-IAAS N127DC N127BB
425-0013	^	(N6770S) N93DA (N117EE) N444JV [w/o 06Mar02 nr San Jose, CA, USA; canx 06May04]
425-0014		(N6770W) N425TC
425-0015		N67704 N40RD C-GFDV N40RL N40RD N522WD
425-0016		N6771L ZS-KST HB-LOE N239JP [status? was wfu Zurich-Kloten, Switzerland]
425-0017		N6771U N55CH N58CH N794B
425-0018		N6775L N425EE N425CF N794PF N20PF N784PF
425-0019		N6771Y [w/o 11Feb88 Orlando-Sanford, FL, USA; canx 20Feb91]
425-0020		N6772B (LV-PLT) LN-PAT N110JT N200MT N55AC
425-0021	^	N6772G N666HC N686HC N202MS ZS-LYZ V5-LYZ
425-0022		N6772P
425-0023		N6772S N23AW N707CB
425-0024		(N6772U) (G-BHNW) G-BJET D-IEAT OE-FPS [w/o 08Oct91 Hannover, Germany]
425-0025		N6772V N53MS N83CH
425-0026		N6772Y N17PL N540GA N540GC
425-0027		N67720 N97DA (N711EF) HI-598SP N181AA VR-BNM VP-BNM VP-BJT N425GC
425-0028	^	N67724 YV-450CP N67724 N425WB ZS-PES
425-0029		N67725 N926FS N926ES N425GJ
425-0030		N67726 N425WG
425-0031		N6773A N311TP N355MA C-GBMI [w/o 20Nov88 Larouche, QC, Canada; canx 21Mar89]
425-0032		N6773B F-GFJR N44GB 5R-MGV [w/o 25Oct06 Toliara, Madagascar]
425-0033	^	N6773C ZS-KVX N105TT D-IAJA N425GM (N425GZ) N425GM
425-0034		N6773E N303MC [dbr 18Jan94 nr London, KY, USA, parts to White Industries, Bates City, MO, USA; location Q-06; canx 10Jan98]
425-0035		N6773F N402NC N402NG N480EA OE-FBH
425-0036		(N6773H) F-GCQN N700WJ
425-0037		N6773L N425SF
425-0038		(N6773P) N425AA N3FC N425JP [w/o 05Dec06 Menominee, MI, USA; canx 05Jul07]
425-0039		(N6773T) N33QT N81PE D-INWG N425TX
425-0040		N6775J HB-LLS [w/o 03Mar86 Berne, Switzerland; canx 19Mar86]
425-0041		N6773X N326L ZS-MVW N425AF
425-0042		N67735 N1BM
425-0043		N6774G N550SC N425JB
425-0044		N6774L VH-PTH N555BE N425HS M-MANX
425-0045		N6774R [w/o 12Dec83 Newburgh-Stewart International, NY, USA]
425-0046		N6774T N67DT ZS-NES N425BA
425-0047		N6774X ZS-KXU 5Y-KXU N585PA
425-0048		N6774Z (N425E) N6774Z
425-0049		(N67741) N31AD N67EA N628MR
425-0050		N67743 N744BH N425FB N37PS
425-0051		(N6775C) XA-LOS XA-RLN XB-FMS
425-0052		N6775D N377SC N425SG N922KV
425-0053		N6776L N99TD N4420F (D-IFLY) N4420F
425-0054		(N6776P) (G-BICL) G-NORC N345GA G-YOTT G-LILI N425SM N425LC
425-0055		(N6776T) N425FW N425VC (N425VV) D-ICEK [w/o 10Dec92 Aichstetten, Germany; canx cJan93]
425-0056		(N6776Y) N56DA N502NC
425-0057		N67761 N425BN [w/o 11Jan92 nr Las Vegas, NV, USA]
425-0058		N6777C N67CA N67JE
425-0059		(N6777L) SE-IFM LN-AFB F-GEFZ N425FZ
425-0060	^	N68436 N1222B
425-0061		(N68439) N66QT D-IAGT N425SW 5R- [canx 04Feb08 as exported to Madagascar]
425-0062		N6844D
425-0063		N6844H 9M-AXZ G-BMSH G-DCFB N79MM OE-FGE (D-IACE) N82HB G-FERM N425TY C-GDLG N425EA
425-0064	^	N6844P ZS-MIG N425XP
425-0065		N6844S N81TR N6844S N425AR
425-0066	^	N6844T N425DH
425-0067		N6844V 5N-AMW 3D-IAN ZS-PYD
425-0068		N68446 N1906K (N425PF) N1906K N425TB
425-0069		(N68449) N634M N12NL
425-0070		N6845P N425NW N444JV
425-0071	^	(OO-LFC) N6845R ZS-CPX
425-0072		N6845S (N425TS) N425ET (N425TB) N425ET
425-0073		N6845T N45AC N425HB
425-0074		N6845Y HB-LPU N146GA N10RM OE-FAW

CESSNA 425

c/n	Mod	Identities
425-0075		(N68451) XA-LUL N17EA ZS-PNP ZS-ONZ
425-0076	^	N68455 N14BM
425-0077		N68456 ZS-MJW V5-MJW
425-0078		N6846D (N6844V) N6846D [dbr 31Jan90 Augusta Regional/Bush Field, GA, USA, parts to White Industries, Bates City, MO, USA; location Q-04; canx 28Sep92]
425-0079		(N6846D) N6846K N900MS
425-0080		(N6846R) OE-FED D-IRAA N880EA C-GJHF C-GVCI
425-0081		N6846S
425-0082	^	N6846T N86EA N470RJ
425-0083		(N6846X) N425DD
425-0084		N6846Y N1918W N547GA N547GC
425-0085		N6846Z N602EZ N5HE N71HE
425-0086		N6847C N911RD N717LW N425XP N40RD N40RN N823DB N425DK
425-0087		N6847P (N777MD) N616MG N616CG N616MG
425-0088		N6847S C-GLAD N425BW N35TK N35TY
425-0089		N6847T N74JW N73DW
425-0090		(N68476) G-BHNY N90GA N90YA
425-0091		N68478 (N901CC) XB-FXK
425-0092		N6848D N60JF N89GC (N87GC) N40RD N425LA
425-0093		N6848R N926FS N456JR
425-0094		N6848Y (G-BHNY) N104HW N105FC
425-0095		N68481 N8FR
425-0096		N68489 N425EA N425E
425-0097		N6849D N410VE
425-0098		N6849L N425DM (N425TS) N425DM
425-0099		(N6849S) (N425TH) N425DS N425NF N404EW N425EZ
425-0100		N6849Y N55MS N70HB N425AL
425-0101		(N6849Z) N425AF N543GA N543GC
425-0102		(N68493) YV-414CP YV-2246P YV-414CP N151GA D-ICMF
425-0103		N68496 C-GINT N4276Z
425-0104	^	N68498 N300HS N425NT N425BZ N425MB N425PV
425-0105		N6850K N777UP N425FT N1848T N18481 (N7711B) N18481
425-0106		(N6850M) G-OLEN N425GA N425SX
425-0107		N6850P N1NL N425LG
425-0108		N6850Q D-IAAX N70GM XA- [canx 25Nov08 as exported to Mexico]
425-0109		N6850Y N66LL N818PL
425-0110	^	N6851A N555TP N114HL
425-0111		(N6851C) OE-FCO N50FS N77YP
425-0112		N6851G
425-0113		N6851L N425HD
425-0114		N68803 N847YT
425-0115		N68807 ZS-KSU
425-0116		N6881D N45GP N45GR N45TP N420MA
425-0117		N6881L N123SC N10FB
425-0118		N6881Q HK-3036X HK-3036P HK-3036 HK-3036P HK-3036 HP-1544 TG-SUS
425-0119		N6881T N17RC N7WF
425-0120		N68817 N425R D-IPOS N425TK
425-0121		N6882C N944JV N425D
425-0122		N6882D G-BJYA (N4560L) N6882D N751JT N828SG
425-0123		N6882L N825B
425-0124		N6882M VH-ULX N425DS N425JH
425-0125		(N6882R) N425AJ N425FC N125VE N125PG
425-0126		N6882S ZS-KXL N607DD N425SC [w/o 11Jan86 Granby, CO, USA]
425-0127		N6882V N456FC
425-0128	^	N6882X (N226RH) N444RH N444RR N425JG
425-0129	^	N68822 N520RM N425JT
425-0130	^	N68823 ZS-KXB N68823 N43BH N438H N425WD
425-0131		N6883L N54BC (N489BC) N977MP N385MA OE-FIB OE-FAM D-ILPC N250GM
425-0132		N6883R N83GF (N84GF) N24TW
425-0133		N6883T N425TS N425SR
425-0134	^	N6883X SE-IHM HB-LNT N156GA
425-0135		N6884D N5CE
425-0136		N6884G N125SC
425-0137		N6884L N66LM [w/o 11Feb92 Lakeland Linder Regional, FL, USA; canx 02Sep92]
425-0138	^	N6884Q N39A
425-0139		N6884R N383SS N320SS N881JP
425-0140	^	N6884X N5829J N15ST
425-0141	^	N68844 N77ML N77MF D-IIGA N373LP
425-0142		(N6885L) OH-CIK N101CA
425-0143		N6885P
425-0144		N6885S
425-0145		N6885T N901FD N801ED N440HC
425-0146	^	(N6885V) N146FW N146GW
425-0147		N6885X N425WM N500MC N500WD N425RF
425-0148		(N6885Y) PH-LTW D-IDAM N425EK N701CR N701QR [dbr 29Nov05 nr Bozeman-Gallatin Field, MT, USA; canx 23May08]
425-0149		N6885Z (N77EJ) N425EJ N425LD N441CR
425-0150		(N68854) N425EW [w/o 16Dec96 Bohemia, NY, USA; canx 03Oct05]
425-0151		N68859 VH-HBM N81798 EC-ETH [dbr 04Sep92 off Malaga, Spain, parts to Dodson International Parts, Rantoul, KS, USA; canx 04Sep92]
425-0152		N6886D [w/o 25Feb84 Dryden, NY, USA]

CESSNA 425

c/n	Mod	Identities
425-0153		N6886L (N41JF) C-GAGE N153JM N74RF
425-0154		N6886V
425-0155		N6886X YV-266CP N168MA
425-0156		N6886Z N425BX N857C (N156CC) N17CP
425-0157		(N68860) N425PJ
425-0158		N68863 N25QT N25QL N353ES
425-0159		(N68864) N425BB N813ZM N425CC
425-0160		N68865 N505AK D-IAWG
425-0161		N68867 N707NY N425TW
425-0162		(N68869) YV-547CP YV-2263P YV1957
425-0163		N6887B TF-ELT N66218 D-IBAA [w/o 24Jan96 Hannover Langenhagen, Germany; canx cFeb96]
425-0164		N6887F (N425RJ) D-IJOY N425EM
425-0165		N6887K N517WM N425TA D-IFNA N425SP D-IRGW N49GM
425-0166	^	N6872D N425WL (N802JH) N425SG [w/o 13Aug05 Denver-Centennial/Arapahoe County, CO, USA]
425-0167	^	N6872L C-GRHD
425-0168		(N6872T) G-BJYC PH-JOE
425-0169		N169FW N6872Z PH-VMC ZS-AMC N425HJ
425-0170		N68721 N100CC
425-0171		N6873D D-IBBP N51CU ZK-LHL
425-0172		N6873L N425LS N41054 (N425DS) N41054 [w/o 10Nov00 Idaho Falls, ID, USA; canx 14Nov06]
425-0173		N6873Q G-BKSA G-ONOR N30WF N16P N6873Q N425CQ
425-0174		N6873R G-GLOR N384MA N425KC
425-0175		N6873S N74LD N425WT (D-ILPC) N425WT
425-0176		N6873T ZS-LDR N425TV
425-0177		N6873X N414CW (N435BC) TC-OPN N600TJ C-GRJM (N850GM) C-GSFI C-GSFF (D-IAWG) D-IPCG
425-0178		N6873Y LN-RAE D-IMOD (N90GM) C-FVAX
425-0179		N6873Z N9180K N918CK N333UJ
425-0180		N68731 N425RM
425-0181		N68732 N24QT N24QF N80PM
425-0182		N68734
425-0183		N6874D VH-JEC VH-EGS 5H-SCB [dbr 12Jun00 nr Dar es Salaam, Tanzania, parts to Dodson International Parts, Rantoul, KS, USA]
425-0184		N6874G VH-JER (N127DC) N425SP
425-0185		N6874L N425DC
425-0186		N6874R N444AK N425FG N425Z
425-0187		(N6874Z) N12201 (N425KA) N622MM
425-0188	^	(N68746) N1221C D-ICTB N188EA N188CP N188DF
425-0189	^	N1221F N969ME YV-548CP YV-2767P YV1750 [also quoted as YV1203 in INAC paperwork]
425-0190		N1221K N444RH N444RU C-FKTN
425-0191		N1221N N444KF
425-0192		N1221T C-FSEA *D-IAWE
425-0193	^	N1221X D-IJGW N214KC N425PC
425-0194		N12214 N577PW N577PA
425-0195		(N195RB) N12218 VH-EGR N207RS (N316LR) N207RS
425-0196		N1222G (N196TM) N425TN [dbr 12Jan07 Harbor Springs, MI, USA, parts to Oshkosh-Wittman Regional Apt, WI, USA; canx 26Feb08]
425-0197		N1222K OO-BOS N406MA D-ICOM N10QM N501 N425WL
425-0198		N1222P N425PA N5PP N5PU N425BL
425-0199		(N1223A) G-BLGM VR-BDR VP-BDR N425DR
425-0200	^	N1223C N122MD N17HM N425PG N122MD N425PG
425-0201		N1223G N777UP N37JT (N888TP) N1223B
425-0202		N1223K VH-ICO VH-EGQ N788JL
425-0203		N1223N N122BN N45TP N425KD
425-0204		N1223P N76SJ
425-0205		N1223V N105TC N111SU
425-0206		N12238 N425CL
425-0207		N1224B HK-3518X HK-3518 N425NC
425-0208		N1224J
425-0209		N1224K N13FH N13EB D-IMPC D-IDAX
425-0210	^	N1224N N721VB N425BS
425-0211		N1224S [dbr 17Aug97 Perkasie, PA, USA, parts to Atlanta Air Salvage, Griffin-Spalding County, GA, USA; canx 26Sep98]
425-0212		N1224T [b/u; canx 01Nov94]
425-0213		N12244
425-0214		(N12249) N475JM N425JM D-ISAR N214LA N425PN
425-0215	^	N1225D N888JS
425-0216	^	N1225J VH-EGT N216BJ XA- [canx 15Mar07 as exported to Mexico; unconfirmed reports suggest it became XB-KFK]
425-0217		N1225T N425TM (N526LS) N425TM
425-0218		N1225V N425GV N425N
425-0219		N1225Y N444TH N242GB N232GM
425-0220	^	N12254 N22HS N188RB N425AD N137CD
425-0221		N12256 N410WA N904RM C-GNEP
425-0222		N1226B N1777X D-IAWF
425-0223		N1226G ZP- [canx cMay87 as exported to Paraguay]
425-0224	^	N1226S G-NORS D-IPAS N850GM N425NP

c/n	Mod	Identities
425-0225	^	N6522T N652MC N902DP N225DF (N425KK) N225DF
425-0226		N1226Z N111KU (N264HB) N111KU
425-0227		N12268
425-0228		N1227A D-IEFW [w/o 25Jan94 Lake Constance, off Rorschach, Switzerland; canx cMar94]
425-0229		N1227J
425-0230		N1227V N98EP
425-0231		N12270 N127MC
425-0232		N12271 N50JG N50JN N75HW
425-0233		N1262H EC-DZQ N80938 D-ICHS N377GL
425-0234		N1262K (G-BNDY) N1262K
425-0235		N1262P JA8855
425-0236		N1262T G-BNDY N425SL

Production complete

CESSNA 441 CONQUEST II

c/n	Identities
679	N7185C N441CC [canx cAug81; parts to prototype c/n 698]
682	N404WD [b/u; canx 11May92]
689	N402CW [b/u]
698	N441CC 5N-JBN ZS-ASM [originally built as prototype c/n 679]
441-0001	N9123G N983SM TJ-AHZ N983SM YV [canx 02Feb07 as exported to Venezuela]
441-0002	N9175G (SE-IBI) LN-MAH [dbr 17Jul86, parts to Dodson International Parts, Rantoul, KS, USA; canx 14Sep04]
441-0003	N9449G C-GRYC N2899P N8838T
441-0004	N9456G N555JK N555JJ N716SM
441-0005	N9917G N500CE N441RZ VH-TAZ
441-0006	N9971G (N441SA) N9971G [w/o 15Nov77 nr Greensboro, AL, USA]
441-0007	YV-128CP N107EA ZS-PES N441HH
441-0008	N441CP N441CC
441-0009	N36929 N777ED N87WS
441-0010	N36930 N20HC N903WD N581AT
441-0011	N36931 N222HM N900JT N93HC
441-0012	N36932 N441SC C-FTML
441-0013	(N36933) D-IAAG N703US N441BG N442JA [stolen 20May92 Cat Island, Bahamas; never recovered]
441-0014	(N36934) N441AA N441ST [dbr 10Nov84 nr Grand Chenier, LA, USA]
441-0015	N36936 N90DA N200HW N441HR XA-REF XA-STD N441CE N441TJ N24PT
441-0016	N36938 HK-2390X HK-2390W [canx 17Apr00 - status?]
441-0017	N36939 N30PL (N711DB) N500UW VH-HMZ
441-0018	N36941 [w/o 01Apr80 Butte, MT, USA; canx 30Sep82]
441-0019	N36942 (N55CC) N6VP XC-AA74 XC-UJX
441-0020	(N36943) C-GTCC N4213V N700AB N920C [dbr 10Aug92 Gainesville, GA, USA, parts to Atlanta Air Salvage, Griffin-Spalding County, GA, USA; canx 03Nov92]
441-0021	(N36944) OO-LFJ N411MA XA-SKJ XB-GBN
441-0022	(N36946) YV-136CP N136CP (N441GG) N53GG N889DM YV [canx 31Oct07 as exported to Venezuela]
441-0023	(N36947) N441DA VH-TFW VH-LBY
441-0024	(N36948) (N441CL) N169CA TG-UME YS-111N N441MJ
441-0025	N36949 (N300JC) N36949 N12TV N41AG N441HD VH-XMD
441-0026	N36951 VH-FWA VH-AZW
441-0027	(N36952) OE-FCC N489G N489CE (N29HA) N900HA N922HP
441-0028	N36955 N441DS
441-0029	N36956 N441RB [wfu, parts to Dodson International Parts, Rantoul, KS, USA]
441-0030	(N36957) (XA-LEO) D-IAAN N4813H N441MM VH-OCS
441-0031	(N308F) N36958 N441KH N918FE PNC-204 (Colombian Police)
441-0032	(N36961) N441JA N52WS N30WW N441M N441P
441-0033	N36962 [w/o 12May83 Arkansas City, KS, USA; canx 29Mar84]
441-0034	(N36964) N441CM N441BW
441-0035	SE-GYC G-FRAZ N441DR N441LC
441-0036	N36968 N3AW N441F [dam 26Apr09 Plant City, FL, USA]
441-0037	(N36970) N441TH N81PN
441-0038	N36971 N300FE VH-HWD VH-LBZ
441-0039	N36972 9M-AXL N36972 RP-C685 N36972 N74BY
441-0040	(N36974) N12DT (N441RA) YV [canx 13Dec06 as exported to Venezuela]
441-0041	(N36975) N812KC N123WR N555GB N441FS N458HR N441WL
441-0042	N36984 (N441GA) N46MK N46MR VH-LBA
441-0043	(N36985) D-IAAI N1349N LN-KAP N1349N VH-NIE N445WS N445AE N43GT
441-0044	N36987 XB-EQT N441AD N549GA N549GS N441KM
441-0045	(N36988) N441TA N441JA N441PS N16NW
441-0046	(N36989) N441CA [w/o 18Jun94 Fort Frances, ON, Canada; canx 28Mar95]
441-0047	(N36990) D-IAAE [w/o 11Jun82 Mount Orsa, nr Saltrio, Switzerland; canx cJul82]
441-0048	N36992 N441CT N60FJ N441CT
441-0049	(N36993) N441FW N441EB
441-0050	(N36994) N55FC N83A
441-0051	N36995 N986SG N725SV

CESSNA 441

c/n	Identities
441-0052	(N36997) N441W N441GM N441W [dbr 20Apr96 Walker's Cay, Bahamas, parts to Atlanta Air Salvage, Griffin-Spalding County, GA, USA; canx 15Oct96]
441-0053	N8877N N777BW N887WF N333RF N40KM (N441MJ) N42MJ N2441K
441-0054	(N88791) N887JT C-GRSL N454EA
441-0055	N88792 ZS-KDP N820CA N5UD N5FF HB-LFF N477B
441-0056	(N88795) N56TA N441GT C-GDBB N441MS [w/o 02Jan97 Lakeland Linder Regional, FL, USA; canx 19Aug98]
441-0057	N88796 N441AK N56MS N441AK TF-ORF
441-0058	(N88797) (F-GATZ) 3A-MCR F-GCGG N240DA OY-BHM C-GPSP
441-0059	(N88798) N441CH N441MS HK-3401X HK-3401 [canx 23Nov93 - status?]
441-0060	N88799 N441CF N88598 YV1690
441-0061	N88800 N114EA N111MP (N441DK) N55MS N441MB N903DC
441-0062	(N8881N) N76DA N441KP
441-0063	(N88822) YV-176CP YV-2390P YV1705
441-0064	N88823 N767Z
441-0065	(N88824) N21EH (N60352) N67DM N1220W N1228W N777XW N771XW
441-0066	(N88825) N441RB N66ME N58JJ D-INKA N185GA N385GH N23NW
441-0067	(N88726) YV-225CP YV1753
441-0068	N88827 N3WM
441-0069	(N88830) N441CF N441SE N400BG [w/o 01Oct85 nr Dallas, TX, USA]
441-0070	N88831 VH-KDJ N442WS N326DJ N910EA N621SC N318AK
441-0071	N88832 [w/o cSep79 in Mexico]
441-0072	N88833 5Y-NCA N9306A N550JD N441PL C-FMSP N441TF YV1647
441-0073	N88834 D-IAAC
441-0074	N88836 N888CF N406BE N441RK N1962J N441RK
441-0075	(N88837) LV-PBA LV-MMY
441-0076	(N88838) N441RC C-GPSQ
441-0077	(N88840) LV-PBB LV-MRU
441-0078	(N88842) G-AUTO G-HOSP N441FC N441KW N784RR
441-0079	(N88845) N441Q N441RF N441KR C-FWRL
441-0080	N88846 N441DT N441BL N441LB
441-0081	(N88848) D-ICKH N4490C VH-LEM
441-0082	N88849 LV-PAZ LV-MRT
441-0083	N441MP N420A XA-PEL N467JV XA-RDM XA-TBM N26BJ N441EE
441-0084	N8894N N719AL N48BS N441GN N84LJ
441-0085	N8904N (N312CT) N711MF C-GSJJ N347AR N441HT
441-0086	(N8931N) N441CG N20BF C-GAGE C-GLGE N441BD
441-0087	N8935N N441DW N687AE
441-0088	N8936N VH-EVP VH-OPM
441-0089	N8949N C-GWRA N89VT N90GC N441DZ
441-0090	N8961N C-GVJT N13NW C-GVJT N13NW C-GNWM N13NW C-GNWM N4061K N13NW
441-0091	N8964N N79JE N600SF VH-AZY VH-LBX
441-0092	N8970N
441-0093	(N8971N) N441P N441K N410MF
441-0094	N8972N N555JE N555GD N441A
441-0095	N8975N RP-C346 VH-JEB VH-JFD ZS-JMA V5-AIR
441-0096	N8977N N451WS C-FJVR
441-0097	N3846G YU-BLV N32GA N30RP N434AE YV-2616P YV1906
441-0098	N441DS (N35DD) N441WP
441-0099	(N4106G) N441NC [w/o 11Jan80 in Atlantic Ocean 100mls E of Norfolk, VA, USA]
441-0100	(N4123G) N700RP D-IADC N700GP N388DR N234CC YV228T
441-0101	N4124G N412FW N412PW MT-224 (Mexican Navy)
441-0102	(N4128G) OE-FBD N4246Z VH-OAA [wfu Mount Gambier, SA, Australia]
441-0103	(N4136G) N441CE N441MD
441-0104	N4137G N79TA N214LJ XA-RRV N8194Z N273AZ
441-0105	N4152G N11MM
441-0106	N4180G VH-HXM VH-YOL (N441AF) VH-NAX
441-0107	(N4189G) (G-CARS) G-BHFX G-PRES N455SC N441SC C-FGPK N441WD
441-0108	(N2622Z) N104RD XA-MHA XA-KEY XA-PAH N104RD N108TJ
441-0109	N26226 G-SOFE N26226 VH-FMQ
441-0110	(N26227) N57MK N84CH HP-
441-0111	(N26228) TG-PAF HK-2413X HK-2413W HK-2413P HK-2413 YV-25CP YV-977CP N426AC N59RT
441-0112	N2623A N2484B [w/o 15Nov87 nr Mexicali, Baja California, Mexico]
441-0113	(N2623B) N27TA N990AR VH-XMJ
441-0114	N2623F HK-2538X HK-2538 HK-2538P
441-0115	N2623Q RP-C549 N441VB
441-0116	N2623Y (N444WS) N441GE N711MB
441-0117	(N2623Z) N441CJ
441-0118	N26230 5N-APZ 5N-DOV N14FJ
441-0119	N26231 N22CG
441-0120	(N26232) N441DM N544AL C-FSKG N [canx 31Jul09 as exported to USA]
441-0121	(N26233) C-GRJL N44776 C-GRJL N44776
441-0122	N2624D N441M
441-0123	(N2624L) N441ND (N441JH) N441ND
441-0124	N2624N N441NL N555FT
441-0125	(N2624Z) N100EA N441HH C-GKWT N375K N48BS
441-0126	(N2625C) D-IAMB N98630 N337C
441-0127	N2625D N322AN N825SP
441-0128	N2625H N441TM N128EZ

CESSNA 441

c/n	Identities
441-0129	N2625M C-FETE N900PS N441BJ (N441BD) N420DB
441-0130	N2625N VH-KDN VH-XMG
441-0131	(N2625Y) N441CD [w/o 15Jan86 Columbia Metropolitan, SC, USA]
441-0132	N2625Z N441SS VH-ANJ VH-SMO
441-0133	N26253 N33DS N332S N4441T N744WD
441-0134	(N2626A) N441EW N441DE N441SM
441-0135	(N2626J) N441GP N93RK N502BR
441-0136	N2626X C-GBWD N690GA N441HC N207SS
441-0137	N2626Y N200LD C-FTEE N37DK N301KB N441JA
441-0138	(N2626Z) N141TA C-GAAA N311RR VH-KUZ VH-JLT
441-0139	(N26263) N441E N10CC N441LL C-FSKC C-GWCA XB-KBI [impounded Roatan, Honduras]
441-0140	(N26264) C-GCTA N604RR YV1855
441-0141	N26267 VH-CFD ZK-NFD
441-0142	N2627J XB-FCD XA-PQZ XC-AA11 N142WJ [wfu; canx 26Jun07]
441-0143	N2627K (N66TR) N26PK C-GPSR
441-0144	(N2627N) D-IAAY [w/o 06Nov80 nr Malaga, Spain; canx cDec80]
441-0145	N2627P (N711YK) N31CR N441BH
441-0146	(N2627U) N441GB HB-LMB D-ICRI N146EA N911PJ
441-0147	N2627Y N555HD N441CL N441RL N999PP N999BE N564AC
441-0148	N2627Z N441AS N148GA XB-FVK N170MA N441AR [dbr 30Jan02 Winfield, KS, USA, parts to Dodson International Parts, Rantoul, KS, USA]
441-0149	(N26271) N441CH N441DW N600VT N419SC
441-0150	(N2628B) YU-BMG SL-CAE S5-CAE OE-FUN
441-0151	N2628M N441RJ
441-0152	N2628X HK-3620X HK-3620W [canx 05Jun02 - status?]
441-0153	N2628Y N400CT N86CG (N66ES) C-FMSK N722GA XB-JTJ YV2186
441-0154	(N2628Z) G-BHLN G-MOXY [w/o 25Apr87 Blackbushe, UK; canx 28Jun89]
441-0155	N2629B XB-BON XB-FND HK-2486X HK-2486W XC-AA82 N779CC
441-0156	N2629P N441TC N779DD N789MA N113RF N7RC N829JC N829JQ N441JC
441-0157	N2629Y N51LR VH-YFD (ZS-SMA) VH-YFD
441-0158	(N2629Z) N441R N36EF N3TK
441-0159	N26296 N45FM VH-NFD (ZS-PMA) ZS-TMA N102NA
441-0160	(N26308) D-IAAV N47JR
441-0161	N2721D N383SS
441-0162	(N2721F) N441CF N66CP N477SJ N800AB LN-ABU ZS-PMC
441-0163	N2721U (N38BR) N38AA N441R
441-0164	N2721X N164TG VH-LBC VH-LFD (ZS-TMA) ZS-SMA 5Y-BRZ ZS-SMA N164GP
441-0165	N27214 N140MP EI-DMG
441-0166	(N27216) D-IAAX I-GEFI N624CB
441-0167	N27219 (N78DA) LN-MOA N416MA N312KJ N332DM
441-0168	N2722D
441-0169	(N2722F) N441CN N441CM [w/o 24Dec84 Marble Falls, TX, USA]
441-0170	(N2722H) (D-ICCE) D-IDLW (N8088J) N720JM N783ST N783RS
441-0171	(N2722S) N10FG C-GRSR N441EA C-GKMA N14NW
441-0172	(N2722U) N441VP N441SA
441-0173	N2722Y
441-0174	N27220 N441HW VH-IJQ VH-VEM
441-0175	N2723A N988AE
441-0176	N2723B N877JV N139ML XA-PEZ N139ML N441DK
441-0177	(N2723C) N441T N59MD [w/o 11Nov85 Derry, PA, USA]
441-0178	N2723P VH-CCY (N4555Y) VH-CCY N446WS HK-3614X HK-3614 HK-3614W [canx 06Mar00 - status?]
441-0179	N2723S PK-FKL VH-TLD N415PA N441EC
441-0180	N2723X (N33AR) N2723X
441-0181	(N27237) OE-FCP D-IFCP N62MA N81WS N441W [w/o 05Dec03 Vestavia Hills, AL, USA; canx 22May06]
441-0182	N2724K N15VG OO-NAN N983GA VH-AZB VH-VEZ
441-0183	(N2724L) (N120EA) N23EA N599AS
441-0184	(N2724M) OO-LFL N184VB (N184DF) N184VB
441-0185	(N2724R) N441CM N999DF N797RW
441-0186	N2724S N7NW
441-0187	N27248 N405JB N88GW
441-0188	(N2725A) N441SW (N123K) N441GP N111RC [w/o 30Dec03 Greenacres City, FL, USA; canx 13May04]
441-0189	N2725D (N666AM) N696AM HK-3595X HK-3595 "N670W" XC-AA71
441-0190	N2725N
441-0191	(N2725Q) C-GGMK N117EA [dbr 30Nov86 Erie, PA, USA, parts to White Industries, Bates City, MO, USA; location Q-05; canx 11May94]
441-0192	N2725U N441DW N441VC ZS-TBS
441-0193	(N2725X) D-IBAA OE-FRZ D-IEGA [dbr 02Apr00 Ascheberg, Germany, parts to Dodson International Parts, Rantoul, KS, USA; canx 08May00]
441-0194	N27252 N88TB N808TB N345MP (N311HC) N26RF N441WJ
441-0195	(N2726B) N195FW YV N195FW YV [canx 16May07 as exported to Venezuela]
441-0196	N2726F N992TE N441KM [dbr 22Nov94 St.Louis-Lambert Field, MO, USA, parts to White Industries, Bates City, MO, USA; location "Building 05"; canx 27Apr95]
441-0197	(N2726J) D-IFAA TT-BAS N8108Z N441JK
441-0198	N2726N N10CF N118EA C-FCWZ N447WS XA- [canx 09Aug07 as exported to Mexico]
441-0199	(N2726S) N441DC N441MD N441JG N441AW [w/o 05Jan02 Rio Grande, PR; canx 09Apr02]

CESSNA 441

c/n	Identities
441-0200	(N2726X) F-GCTY N313GA N423TG N441TG
441-0201	N2727A [w/o 29Aug86 Lander-Hunt Field, WY, USA]
441-0202	N2727B N449DR N77ML
441-0203	(N2727F) HB-LMP N9317T N140DR N140BR N1WB C-GLTP N93BA N441Z N60TR N74GL
441-0204	N2727L N441TA [stolen 02May89 Van Nuys, CA, USA]
441-0205	(N2727X) N3330S N295CE
441-0206	(N2728B) (SE-IFU) LN-KAA N7049Y (N499WS) HK-3613X HK-3613 HK-3613P [canx 14Mar03 - status?]
441-0207	N2728D G-BMTZ G-FRAX G-FPLC N440DA
441-0208	N2728F XC-GOO
441-0209	N2728G N711GE M-USHY
441-0210	(N2728N) SE-IBM N790MA N4YA D-IAPW N525MA N441LA
441-0211	N6851T
441-0212	N6851X
441-0213	N6851Y N716CC
441-0214	N6852L N721TD N337RE N837RE N441EW N792KC C-GAGE
441-0215	N6852T ZS-KPB N665TM N441MY
441-0216	N6852X N441DM C-FNWC
441-0217	N6853A N441WM N441BB
441-0218	N6853G N57CC N41TA N846YT N846Y
441-0219	(N6853L) (N441CX) N555WA N553AM
441-0220	N6853T
441-0221	N6853X N76PM N6853X N881GB N881CD N441RS
441-0222	(N68539) N7707C D-IDRJ N500GM N533M
441-0223	(N6854A) (SE-IBS) LN-MOR N52GA N92JC N92JQ
441-0224	N6854B XC-GON
441-0225	N6854D N441VH
441-0226	(N6854L) G-BHLO N226C HK-3546X HK-3546W N6281R N441AD
441-0227	N6854T YV-533P
441-0228	(N6854X) N88QT (N363PD) N88QT
441-0229	N68548 OY-CGM [w/o 11Sep90 80 mls SSW of Sondre Stromfjord, Greenland; canx 18Aug92]
441-0230	(N6855E) N501LC N14P N14PN N441G
441-0231	N6855H N441YA HK-3647X HK-3647 N441YA VH-JVB
441-0232	(N6855L) (SE-IHE) LN-VIB N7023D VH-NIF N443WS HK-3562X HK-3562 XB-ACA XC-AA12 XB-KFC
441-0233	N6855P N112CZ
441-0234	(N6855S) N441CR N42DT N441GA
441-0235	(N6855T) N333GE OY-CTM N333GE XB-EWO
441-0236	N6855X VH-TFG VH-LBC
441-0237	N6855Z N700JE N700JG XA-TLW
441-0238	N68559 N95TD N3NC VH-VEH
441-0239	(N6856L) G-BHLP N3XR N45TP N45TF HK-3615X HK-3615W [canx 05Jun95 - status?]
441-0240	(N6856Q) N54DA N441MA N140CB N10FJ N413PC N441PW
441-0241	(N6856S) N241FW [w/o 23Nov86 Chicago-DuPage County, IL, USA; canx 09Aug88]
441-0242	(N6856U) OE-FCL N3127R N441WT N88598
441-0243	(N6856X) N441HA N916AS N916SJ
441-0244	N6857E [w/o 16Jul86 nr Muskegon County Apt, MI, USA]
441-0245	N6857L XC-LAP N441WF N441EL C-GMSL N441PG
441-0246	N6857S (F-GBPB) (F-GCQO) N6117C N333DP N833DP N246DP D-IMAX N246SP N913DC N913DG
441-0247	N6857T N5HG
441-0248	(N6857X) (SE-IHH) LN-MAM N441JV N441SX
441-0249	N68577 N800BN N911ER VH-VEJ
441-0250	(N6858G) N441AE N441MC C-GLBL N691AC YV [canx 20Sep06 as exported to Venezuela]
441-0251	(N6858L) G-BJGJ N711GF HK-3573X HK-3573 HK-3573P [canx 18Jul03 - status?]
441-0252	(N6858R) N441RW N441CG F-GFHR [w/o 17Nov88 Saclay, France; canx 04Jan89]
441-0253	N6858S [w/o 21Feb87 Flagstaff-Pulliam Apt, AZ, USA; canx 15Jul88]
441-0254	N68586 D-IHAA SE-IPB (D-ITTW) N410MA N441X
441-0255	N68587 N9683N
441-0256	N6859L C-FDYN N256DP N256DD
441-0257	(N6859S) OH-CIE SE-KOM N100YA N505HC
441-0258	(N6859Y) N258VB
441-0259	N68594 N106BC N106BQ N87HT N441CD YV [canx 20Dec06 as exported to Venezuela]
441-0260	N68597 VH-TFB
441-0261	(N68598) N261FW N261DW HK-3512X HK-3512
441-0262	N88731 N489G N489ST N489WC N50MF
441-0263	(N88791) G-BJXO N815MC N233RC
441-0264	N88795 (F-ODJP) G-EVNS F-ODUJ N264WS C-GSKH C-FWCP VH-VEW
441-0265	N88798 N441E C-FHSP
441-0266	N8881N N800YM N441ME
441-0267	N88727
441-0268	N88830 N82CL N17KZ HP-1190 VR-BPH HC-BXH
441-0269	N88834
441-0270	N441AC F-ODUK [w/o 04Dec90 Papeete, Tahiti, French Polynesia]
441-0271	N98418 N228MJ N507DR HK-3456X HK-3456W HK-3456P
441-0272	N98432 N594G N394G VH-VED

CESSNA 441

c/n	Identities
441-0273	N98436 YV-368CP N98436 HK-3009X HK-3009 HK-3009P HK-3009W HK-3009P [canx 24Oct01 - status?]
441-0274	N98468 N322P
441-0275	N98563 (N90AG) XC-HHU XC-AA37 XC-LGE
441-0276	N98599 N40SG HK-3596X HK-3596W HK-3596P YV1482
441-0277	(N98682) N441SA N441HT HP-
441-0278	N98718 N15DB
441-0279	(N98784) G-BJYB LN-VIP [dbr 11Oct85 Skien, Norway, parts to Dodson International Parts, Rantoul, KS, USA; canx 25Mar88]
441-0280	N6831N N986MC N441AE
441-0281	N6832C N689AE
441-0282	N6832M
441-0283	N6833C N456AE N925WS C-GMSL N441EP
441-0284	(N6888C) N441AB
441-0285	N8757K D-IIAA N707MA
441-0286	N8816K N441WM C-FUDY N441MW
441-0287	N8837K N811VC N811VG HK-3540X HK-3540W
441-0288	N8860K OE-FCY N325RT N77R
441-0289	N88638 N377CA
441-0290	N88692
441-0291	N88707 SE-IHX [dbf 24Mar84 Orebro, Sweden; canx 05Apr84]
441-0292	N88716 N666HC N441PP
441-0293	N88723 C-FMHD G-FCAL N293DR N878JL
441-0294	(N88724) G-HSON G-OFHJ N294VB N456GT
441-0295	N6837R N181MD VH-VEY
441-0296	N6838K VH-LBD
441-0297	N6838T N829BB C-GBFM N6838T N441MT VH-XBC
441-0298	N6839C N16EF N245DL C-GCYB
441-0299	N6840T
441-0300	N68439 N441DB
441-0301	N6853A N328VP N441SB
441-0302	N68599 N500RJ N349MP
441-0303	N6860A N441JR [stolen 19Aug90 Aurora, IL, USA; never recovered]
441-0304	N6860C (N304EN) YV-34CP N6860C
441-0305	N42BW N47SW N441FB N441CX
441-0306	N6860S N886BC N45TP N47TP (N441DM) N66BZ N441E
441-0307	N8617K N2NC N2NQ
441-0308	N87494 N33DE
441-0309	N1207G N441MT HK-3568X HK-3568W
441-0310	N1207N N444KE N977MP
441-0311	(N1207Z) N441AF XA-OAC N832AD N102AD
441-0312	(N312SA) N12070 N514MC N331MP
441-0313	(N12072) N313DS N443DW
441-0314	N12076 N710BV N104AG N186EC N894FL XB-CSB C-GCIL C-GCIK
441-0315	N1208A CC-CWZ N441HF
441-0316	(N1208G) G-BLCJ G-LOVX N441KW N405MA N800SR C-FSFI C-GWAM
441-0317	N1208J N1843S
441-0318	N1208M N300NK N441FS
441-0319	N1208T N103AG HK-3542X HK-3542W XC-AA10 XB-ATO N6412Q YV1504 XB-KBX
441-0320	N1209B TR-LBE N189WS HK-3550X HK-3550
441-0321	(N1208D) G-BLCL N321DA LN-VIS N953JH C-FNNC N441PJ N858AC
441-0322	N1209J N727AC N727ST N901CC D-IEWA N536MA N441BL
441-0323	N1209N N323JG N441S
441-0324	N1209P HK-3611X HK-3611 HK-3611W HK-3611
441-0325	N1209S N30FJ N325CM N441DN
441-0326	(N1209T) D-IGGI N171SP N326RS
441-0327	(N1209X) N441AG
441-0328	N12093 HK- [canx cSep83 as exported to Colombia]
441-0329	N12099 N77SA [w/o 28Aug05 Anchorage-International, AK, USA; canx 06Apr06]
441-0330	N1210B N55CH N747JB (N747VB) N441HS
441-0331	N1210D N68HS
441-0332	N1210G G-BLCZ N441MM N888FL HP-1189
441-0333	N1210L HK-3418X HK-3418P
441-0334	(N1210N) N334FW N444AK
441-0335	N1210T HK-3497X HK-3497W HK-3497P
441-0336	N1210U N441JD N441HK [w/o 17Jul08 Sunriver, OR, USA]
441-0337	(N1210V) G-BLIR N9045C XA-PEH N337KC
441-0338	N1210Y [w/o 26Sep87 Maiduguri, Nigeria; canx cNov87]
441-0339	N1210Z (N441CP) N612CC
441-0340	N1211C [stolen 05May90 Miami/Opa-Locka, Florida, USA; canx 18Aug92]
441-0341	(N1211M) N441AJ OB-1337 HK-3549X HK-3549W N341WJ N441PM N441DD
441-0342	N1211N N986SG N986SC N986PC N441DD N30832 N441LS
441-0343	N12114 N835MA
441-0344	N12116 D-ICAR N413MA OO-KNM N169MA N441ML N441UC
441-0346	N782CC N1212C
441-0347	N1212K N441PN
441-0348	N1212N HK-3529X HK-3529 [w/o cSep92 in Mexico; canx 05Jun03]
441-0349	N12125 N274GC
441-0350	N12127 AP-BCY
441-0351	N1213G N117TS N118TS N369PC N441PZ N441EH
441-0352	N1213N AP-BCQ VH-JVL

CESSNA 441

c/n	Identities						
441-0353	N1213R	G-BNDZ	N321AF	5N-ATR	ZS-RGS		
441-0354	N1213S	HK-3337X	HK-3337	[wfu Bogota-El Dorado, Distrito Capital, Colombia]			
441-0355	N1213Y	AP-BCW	N355VB	D-ILYS	G-USAR		
441-0356	(N1213Z)	N441CS	HK-3532X	HK-3532W	HK-3532P	YV-1062CP	YV1857 [impounded 06Nov06 in Honduras wearing false marks YV1372; also quoted in INAC paperwork as YV1854]
441-0357	N1214B	PH-BMP	D-IOHL	N441TL			
441-0358	N1214D	N444RH	N85DJ	D-IJLF	N441FA	N440EH	
441-0359	N12827	N4CS	HK-3457X	HK-3457W	N359BA	N40FJ	N123ME
441-0360	N12829	N441AR	N441RW	N731BH			
441-0361	N1283B	N592G	N592Q				
441-0362	(N12383)	G-BMOA	LX-ETB	D-IAGA	C-GSSK	N36FR	

Production complete

EMBRAER EMB-121 XINGU

c/n	Series	Identities
121001	AA	PP-ZCT PP-ZXI PT-MAA [pres Museu Aerospacial, Rio de Janeiro, Rio de Janeiro State, Brazil; marked as PP-ZXI]
121002	VU-9	2650 (Brazilian AF)
121003	VU-9	2651 (Brazilian AF)
121004	VU-9	2652 (Brazilian AF)
121005	VU-9	2653 (Brazilian AF)
121006	VU-9	2654 (Brazilian AF)
121007	A	PT-MAB
121008	VU-9	2655 (Brazilian AF) [w/o cJan82 in Brazil]
121009	E	PP-ZDK PT-MAC [b/u]
121010	A	PT-MAD
121011	A1	PT-MAE PP-EUW PT-MSA
121012	A1	PT-FAN PP-EOM PT-OUH
121013	A1	PT-MAG
121014	A1	G-BGIE PT-MBN
121015	A1	PT-MAH PP-EGW PT-OZS
121016	E	(PT-MAI) PP-EGT PT-MCD
121017	A	PT-MAJ
121018	A	PT-MAK
121019	A	PT-MAL
121020	A	PT-MAM
121021	A	PT-MAN PP-ACM
121022	A	PT-MAO
121023	A	PT-MAP
121024	A1	PT-MAQ
121025	A	PT-MAR
121026		PT-MAS
121027	AN	PT-MAT PP-EHJ 27 (French Navy)
121028	A	(PT-MAU) PT-MBA PP-EIL PT-OAU
121029	A	PT-MAV
121030	AN	PT-MAW G-XING G-XTWO 30 (French Navy)
121031	A	PT-MAX
121032	A	PT-MAY
121033	A	PT-MAZ
121034	A	PT-MBB
121035	A	(PT-MBC) PP-EMN
121036	A	PT-MBD
121037	VU-9	PT-MBE 2657 (Brazilian AF)
121038		PT-MBF OO-SXA [wfu Kortrijk-Wevelgem, Belgium]
121039	A	PT-MBG (PP-EGA) PP-EIC
121040		PT-MBH OO-SXB
121041	A	PT-MBI HK-2693X HK-2693
121042		PT-MBJ OO-SXC
121043		PT-MBK OO-SXD OO-SXD [wfu 30Nov05 Dinan-Trelivan, France; canx 13Dec05]
121044	A1	PT-MBL PT-FRG
121045		PT-MBM OO-SXE
121046	A1	PT-MBO
121047	AN	PT-MBP 47 (French Navy)
121048		PT-MBQ 5N-ARG
121049	A	PT-MBR PT-FAX
121050	A	PT-MBS
121051	A1	PT-MBT PT-FAY PP-FHE
121052	A	PT-MBU
121053	A	PT-MBV
121054	AA	PP-ZXA PT-MBW 054/YX (French AF)
121055	AN	PP-ZXB PT-MBX 55 (French Navy) 055/YZ (French AF)
121056	AN	PT-MBY 56 (French Navy)
121057	A1	PT-MBZ PT-FEG
121058	A1	PT-MCA
121059	A1	PT-MCB PP-EPE PT-WLV
121060	VU-9	2656 (Brazilian AF)
121061		PT-MCC
121062		[void - aircraft not built]
121063		[void - aircraft not built]
121064	AA	064/YY (French AF)
121065	AN	PP-ZXD 65 (French Navy)
121066	AN	066/ZA (French AF)
121067	AN	67 (French Navy)
121068	AN	PP-ZXU F-YDNC 68 (French Navy)
121069	AN	PP-ZXF 69 (French Navy) 069/ZB (French AF)
121070	AN	PP-ZXG 070/ZC (French AF)
121071	AN	PP-ZXH 71 (French Navy)
121072	AA	PP-ZXJ 072/YA (French AF)
121073	AA	PP-ZXL 073/YB (French AF)
121074	AN	PP-ZXM 74 (French Navy)
121075	AA	PP-ZXN 075/YC (French AF)
121076	AA	PP-ZXO 076/YD (French AF)
121077	AN	PP-ZXP 077 (French AF) 77 (French Navy)
121078	AA	PP-ZXQ 078/YE (French AF)
121079	AN	PP-ZXR 79 (French Navy)
121080	AA	PP-ZXS 080/YF (French AF)

EMB-121 XINGU

c/n	Series	Identities
121081	AN	PP-ZXT 81 (French Navy)
121082	AA	PP-ZXX 082/YG (French AF)
121083	AN	PP-ZXV F-YDNB 83 (French Navy) 083/ZE (French AF)
121084	AA	PP-ZXW 084/YH (French AF)
121085	AN	PP-ZXZ 85 (French Navy)
121086	AA	PP-ZYA 086/YI (French AF)
121087	AN	PP-ZYB 87 (French Navy)
121088	A1	PT-MCG
121089	AA	PP-ZYC 089/YJ (French AF)
121090	AN	PP-ZYD 90 (French Navy) 090/ZF (French AF)
121091	AA	PP-ZYE 091/YK (French AF)
121092	AA	PP-ZYF 092/YL (French AF)
121093	A1	PT-MCF
121094	A1	PP-EIJ PT-MCE
121095	AA	PP-ZYG 095/YM (French AF)
121096	AA	PP-ZYH 096/YN (French AF)
121097	A1	PT-MCI
121098	AA	PP-ZYI 098/YO (French AF)
121099	AA	PP-ZYJ 099/YP (French AF)
121100	A	PP-ZYK PT-MCJ
121101	AA	101/YR (French AF)
121102	AA	102/YS (French AF)
121103	AA	103/YT (French AF)
121104	A1	PT-MCK
121105	AA	105/YU (French AF)
121106		[void - aircraft not built]
121107	AA	107/YV (French AF)
121108	AA	108/YW (French AF)
121109		[void - aircraft not built]
121110		[void - aircraft not built]
121111	AA	111/YQ (French AF)

Production complete

FAIRCHILD-HILLER PC-6 HELI-PORTER

This was a licence-built version of the Pilatus PC-6 with a Garrett TPE-331 turboprop engine

c/n	Series	Identities
2001	B1-H2	N346F [dam 26May05 Sturtevant-Sylvania, WI, USA]
2002	C-H2	N347F HB-FDO N331V [w/o 05Oct77 Oklahoma City-Wiley Post, OK, USA; canx 06Mar78]
2003	C-H2	N3601R [w/o in Peru; exact date unkn]
2004	B1-H2	N3602R [w/o 19Apr72 Deadhorse, AK, USA]
2005	B1-H2	N3603R N120TD [status? reportedly wfu]
2006	B1-H2	N348F N348FH HP-1064 [w/o date & location unkn]
2007	B1-H2	N349FH [w/o 30Jan68 Zephyrhills, FL, USA]
2008	B1-H2	N350FH [dbr 15Mar74 nr Point Lay, AK, USA; canx c1995]
2009	B1-H2	N353F CF-ZIZ C-FZIZ
2010	B2-H2	N354F
2011	B1-H2	N352F XW-PKI N62157 2011 (Royal Thai Army) N511SA [w/o 11Jul92 in Thailand]
2012	C-H2	N351FH [w/o 09Jul74 nr Mount Baldy Airstrip, AZ, USA]
2013	C-H2	N355F [abandoned 29Apr75 Saigon-Tan Son Nhat, South Vietnam]
2014	C-H2	N356F [w/o in Paraguay; exact date unkn]
2015	C-H2	N357F [dbr 12Sep72 nr Vang Vieng, South Vietnam; b/u c1973]
2016	C-H2	N358F [abandoned 29Apr75 Saigon-Tan Son Nhat, South Vietnam]
2017	C-H2	N359F [abandoned 29Apr75 Saigon-Tan Son Nhat, South Vietnam]
2018	C-H2	N360F [abandoned 29Apr75 Saigon-Tan Son Nhat, South Vietnam]
2019	C-H2	N364F N364CL N344CL
2020	AU-23A	N362F 72-1318 (USAF) 72-1318/B.JTh2-13\15 (Royal Thai AF) [w/o c1973 in Thailand]
2021	C-H2	N363F N19H N62524 XC-BIC [w/o c1979 Chiuacha, Mexico]
2022	C-H2	N365F [abandoned 29Apr75 Saigon-Tan Son Nhat, South Vietnam]
2023	C-H2	N366F [abandoned 29Apr75 Saigon-Tan Son Nhat, South Vietnam]
2024	C-H2	N367F [abandoned 29Apr75 Saigon-Tan Son Nhat, South Vietnam]
2025	C-H2	N361F
2026	B2-H2	HK-1378X HK-1378W TG-TEG HK-3207X HK-3207W N5113K XA-TLD XB-GRY N511SK HS-EFS
2027	B2-H2	N3604R HC-ATF [w/o date & location unkn]
2028	B2-H2	N3605R HK-1391X HK-1391W N7391U
2029	B2-H2	N3606R HC-AOG N67265 HC-BGK [w/o 25Jan02 in Ecuador]
2030	B2-H2	N2789R 1601 (Royal Thai Border Police) [wfu c2002]
2031	B2-H2	N2790R 1602 (Royal Thai Border Police) [w/o 05Feb73 in Thailand]
2032	B2-H2	N2791R 1603 (Royal Thai Border Police) [w/o 11Nov95 Bangkok, Thailand; reportedly on rebuild]
2033	C-H2	N3612R [canx 07Mar00; possibly b/u]
2034	B1A-H2	N3611R 0674/6-G-1 (Argentine Navy) [w/o 20Jan78 Trelew, Chubut Province, Argentina]
2035	B2-H2	N3613R HC-ATX [w/o date & location unkn]
2036	B2-H2	N5300F HC-AQV [w/o date & location unkn]
2037	B2-H2	N21428 SAE-T-1540 (Ecuadorian AF) [reportedly w/o c1983]
2038	B2-H2	N21429 SAE-T-1545 (Ecuadorian AF) [dbr & std]
2039	AU-23A	N5301F 72-1317 (USAF) 72-1317/B.JTh2-12\15 (Royal Thai AF)
2040	B1A-H2	N3608R HL5101 N3608R N476XP
2041	B2-H2	N3607R HC-AVL [w/o cMar88 location unkn]
2042	B2-H2	N3609R [fate unkn]
2043	B2-H4	N2792R 1604 (Royal Thai Border Police)
2044	C-H2	N3610R HP-564 [w/o 17Nov73 Cerro Ratan, Panama]
2045	B1A-H2	N21443 0684/4-G-2 (Argentine Navy) [w/o 05Sep86 Trelew, Chubut Province, Argentina]
2046	B1A-H2	N21442 0685/4-G-3 (Argentine Navy) 0684/4-G-1 (Argentine Navy) [w/o 09Nov91 Ciudad de Lobos, Buenos Aires Province, Argentina]
2047	B1A-H2	N21441 0686/4-G-4 (Argentine Navy)
2048	C-H2	N5302F HK-2994X HK-2994 HK-2994P YV-129P YV1912
2049	C-H2	N5304F [w/o 25Nov73 Ban Boua Mu, Laos]
2050	AU-23A	72-1304 (USAF) 72-1304/B.JTh2-1\15 (Royal Thai AF)
2051	AU-23A	72-1305 (USAF) 72-1305/B.JTh2-2\15 (Royal Thai AF) [w/o 05Jan89 Trat Province, Thailand]
2052	AU-23A	72-1306 (USAF) 72-1306/B.JTh2-3\15 (Royal Thai AF) [w/o 26Jul82 Lopburi Province, Thailand]
2053	AU-23A	72-1307 (USAF) 72-1307/B.JTh2-34\20 (Royal Thai AF)
2054	AU-23A	72-1308 (USAF) 72-1308/B.JTh2-4\15 (Royal Thai AF) [wfu c2004]
2055	AU-23A	72-1309 (USAF) [w/o 10May72 Eglin AFB, FL, USA]
2056	AU-23A	72-1310 (USAF) 72-1310/B.JTh2-5\15 (Royal Thai AF) [wfu c2004]
2057	AU-23A	72-1311 (USAF) 72-1311/B.JTh2-6\15 (Royal Thai AF) [w/o cApr77 in Thailand]
2058	AU-23A	72-1312 (USAF) 72-1312/B.JTh2-7\15 (Royal Thai AF) [w/o cApr78 in Thailand]
2059	AU-23A	72-1313 (USAF) 72-1313/B.JTh2-8\15 (Royal Thai AF) [w/o 06Feb73 Khok Krathiam, Thailand]
2060	AU-23A	72-1314 (USAF) 72-1314/B.JTh2-9\15 (Royal Thai AF) [wfu c2004]
2061	AU-23A	72-1315 (USAF) 72-1315/B.JTh2-10\15 (Royal Thai AF)
2062	AU-23A	72-1316 (USAF) 72-1316/B.JTh2-11\15 (Royal Thai AF) [wfu cDec99]
2063	C-H2	N21438 1605 (Royal Thai Border Police)
2064	C-H2	N21441 1606 (Royal Thai Border Police) [wfu c2000]
2065	C-H2	N21442 1607 (Royal Thai Border Police) [w/o 15Sep84 Tambon Nong Bua Tai, Thailand]
2066	C-H2	N21443 1608 (Royal Thai Border Police)

FAIRCHILD-HILLER PC-6

c/n	Series	Identities	
2067	C-H2	(N21444) 1609 (Royal Thai Border Police)	[w/o 20Sep79 Mahanakhon, Thailand]
2068	C-H2	N5308F	
2069	C-H2	N5309F XC-BIB [w/o 20Feb76 Topia, Durango, Mexico]	
2070	C-H2	N5307F FAB-009 (Bolivian AF)	[reportedly w/o; date & location unkn]
2071	B2-H2	N5305F N392CA N392AC F-GRCP	
2072	B2-H2	N5306F FAB-005 (Bolivian AF)	N530RQ F-GHVH
2073	AU-23A	74-2073/B.JTh2-14\19 (Royal Thai AF)	[w/o 18Aug78 in Thailand]
2074	AU-23A	74-2074/B.JTh2-15\19 (Royal Thai AF)	
2075	AU-23A	74-2075/B.JTh2-16\19 (Royal Thai AF)	[pres Saraburi Aero Park, Saraburi, Thailand]
2076	AU-23A	74-2076/B.JTh2-17\19 (Royal Thai AF)	
2077	AU-23A	74-2077/B.JTh2-18\19 (Royal Thai AF)	
2078	AU-23A	74-2078/B.JTh2-19\19 (Royal Thai AF)	
2079	AU-23A	74-2079/B.JTh2-20\19 (Royal Thai AF)	
2080	AU-23A	74-2080/B.JTh2-21\19 (Royal Thai AF)	
2081	AU-23A	74-2081/B.JTh2-22\19 (Royal Thai AF)	
2082	AU-23A	74-2082/B.JTh2-23\19 (Royal Thai AF)	
2083	AU-23A	74-2083/B.JTh2-24\19 (Royal Thai AF)	
2084	AU-23A	74-2084/B.JTh2-25\19 (Royal Thai AF)	[w/o cApr77 in Thailand]
2085	AU-23A	74-2085/B.JTh2-26\19 (Royal Thai AF)	
2086	AU-23A	74-2086/B.JTh2-27\19 (Royal Thai AF)	
2087	AU-23A	74-2087/B.JTh2-28\19 (Royal Thai AF)	
2088	AU-23A	74-2088/B.JTh2-29\19 (Royal Thai AF)	
2089	AU-23A	74-2089/B.JTh2-30\19 (Royal Thai AF)	[w/o cAug78 in Thailand]
2090	AU-23A	74-2090/B.JTh2-31\19 (Royal Thai AF)	[w/o 06Sep05 in Thailand]
2091	AU-23A	74-2091/B.JTh2-32\19 (Royal Thai AF)	[w/o 21Jan79 in Thailand]
2092	AU-23A	74-2092/B.JTh2-33\19 (Royal Thai AF)	

Production complete

GRUMMAN G.159 GULFSTREAM

c/n	Series	Identities
1		N701G ZS-NVG 5Y-EMK 5Y-XXX 3X-GER [std Johannesburg-Rand/Germiston, Gauteng Province, South Africa]
2		N702G N1 N3 N3003 N40CE N42CE N40CE N116GA N39PP 86-0402 (US Army) [b/u 30Sep90]
3		N703G CF-MAR C-FMAR [b/u c1988 Montreal-Dorval, QC, Canada; canx 05Sep91]
4		N704G N704HC N717 N99DE N89DE N371BG [b/u cDec85]
5		N705G N601HK N601HP N700PR N43AS N9EB N159AJ N925WL N159AJ F-GFGT ZS-OOE
6		N2425 S9-NAU N221AP [wfu Jan95 Chicago-Palwaukee, IL, USA; b/u 15Feb96; canx 27Aug97]
7		CF-LOO N5VX (N77EL) N99EL
8		N708G [wfu c1985; fuselage located in yard at Cosgrove Aircraft Services, South of Houston-William P Hobby at 9190 Telephone Road, Houston, TX, USA]
9		N709G N43M N436M N436 N436M G-BNCE [wfu cOct91 Aberdeen-Dyce, Scotland, UK; b/u, fuselage with fire service at Dundee Apt, Scotland, UK; canx 04May93]
10		N710G N1623 N1623Z XB-CIJ [dbr cMay88 in Yucatan State, Mexico; aircraft std and subsequently destroyed by Hurricane Gilbert 14Sep88]
11		N711G N650ST N650BT N100FL N100EL N7SL [wfu Valencia-Arturo Michelena International, Venezuela]
12		N712G N400P N4009 N166NK N91JR N8VB XA-TBT [wfu cSep97, parts to Dodson International Parts, Rantoul, KS, USA still marked as N8VB]
322		N769G N90M N9QM N71RD [originally designated as c/n 13; wfu c2000 Chicago-Palwaukee, IL, USA, parts to White Industries, Bates City, MO, USA; location "Ramp North"]
14		N714G N1607Z N723RA [b/u cAug88 Shreveport Regional, LA, USA; canx 18Nov88]
15		N715G N1501 N1501C N72EZ N26KW XB-ESO [w/o 11Oct90 Zacapu, Michoacan, Mexico]
16		N716G N2998 N707WA N8001J N20NH N202HA N615C [b/u Chicago-Palwaukee, IL, USA; fuselage in use as fire trainer at Joint Fire Training Facility, Buffalo Grove, IL, USA]
17		N717G N199M CF-TPC N9971F [wfu c1985; b/u c1986]
18		N718G N300UP N3UP N48PA [canx 29Sep05 as exported to Venezuela; captured 20Oct05 by Venezuelan Army with 2.5 tons of cocaine on board still marked as N48PA]
19		N719G N80L N80LR N70LR N12GW PK-WWG N12GW [b/u cOct87; canx 16Aug89]
20		N720G N266P N227LS N227LA N250AL N5PC VR-CTN N732US F-GFMH TJ-WIN TU-TDM N19FF [wfu cMar05 Madrid-Barajas, Spain]
21		N721G N361G N361Q XC-BIO N6653Z [b/u 01Aug91 Savannah-Hilton Head International, GA, USA; canx 28Nov95]
22		N722G N80G N8BG C-GKFG [derelict Calgary-International, AB, Canada; canx 12Feb97]
23		N723G N1929Y N1929B OE-BAZ OE-HAZ N193PA N186PA N810CB
24		N724G N1620 N1625 N1625B YV-P-AEA YV-09CP N713US HK-3315X [w/o 06Feb90 El Salado Mountain, nr Ibague, Tolima, Colombia; canx 26Jun90]
25		N725G OK-NEA 4X-ARH 3D-DLN ZS-PHK
26		N726G N726S N505S N120S N348DA YV-82CP N185PA
27	C	N727G N100P N1009 XB-FUB XB-VIW XB-VAD N2150M N80M N114GA N415CA N198PA
28		N728G N900JL N9006L N666ES N11SX N118X N719RA [wfu c1992, parts to Dodson International Parts, Rantoul, KS, USA; listed in Dodson inventory as N719RD]
29		N729G N785GP N1844S N1845S N1925P N222SG N222SE N431G [canx 23Jun99 to Canada; b/u cNov00 Toronto-Pearson International, ON, Canada still marked as N431G]
30		N730G N901G N961G [wfu cApr89; b/u cNov91 Detroit-Willow Run, MI, USA; canx 26Nov91]
31		N731G CF-JFC C-FJFC N715RA [wfu cFeb89; canx 07Jun89; b/u c1999 Shreveport Regional, LA, USA]
32		N732G N734ET N734EB N733EB N297X N300MC [b/u Hanover, PA, USA; canx 16Dec88]
33		N126J N88Y N261L N295SA HR-IAJ TG-TJB (N21AH) N23AH 9Q-CBY
34		N734G N620K N48TE HK-3634X HK-3634 N34LE 5Y-BLR
35		N735G XC-IMS XB-DVG XA-PUA N86MA 9Q-CBD [wfu Kinshasa-N'Djili, DR Congo; canx cMay05]
36		N130A N230E [wfu cNov88 Detroit-Willow Run, MI, USA; canx 14Mar89; b/u, parts to Aviation Warehouse, El Mirage, CA, USA (bare metal fuselage only)]
37		N130G N130B N716RD N716R N20S N91G [w/o 24Sep78 Houston-William P Hobby, TX, USA; canx cJul90]
38		N738G ZS-AAC VQ-ZIP 3D-AAC N7001N N38JK N333AH N717RS [canx 10Jul06 as exported to Mexico; aircraft disappeared 09Jul06 between Manaus, Amazonas, Brazil & Maiquetia, Vargas, Venezuela]
39		N40Y N39TG EC-376 EC-EVJ [std Madrid-Barajas, Spain]
40		N6PG N8ZA N40AG EC-493 EC-FIO N19TZ [std Madrid-Barajas, Spain]
41		N7PG N9ZA N41TG EC-494 EC-EZO [std Madrid-Barajas, Spain]
42		N366P N430H N888PR XA-MAS XC-AA61 ZS-OCA 3D-TRE 3D-DOM TL-ADN
43		N344DJ N140NT C-GNOR N39289 N716RA [wfu cJul88 Shreveport Regional, LA, USA & b/u; canx 25Feb91]
44		N285AA N121NC N717JF N717RW N717RD F-GFGV 5Y-JET [CofA exp 22Jun02; wfu Nairobi-Wilson, Kenya]
45		N745G N7788 N329CT N65CE [pres inst airframe at Des Moines Central Campus Aviation Laboratory, Des Moines-International, IA, USA; canx 25Mar04]
46		N746G [wfu cOct86 & b/u Shreveport Regional, LA, USA]

G.159 GULFSTREAM

c/n	Series	Identities
47		N747G N20CC N20HF [b/u cOct86 Arlington, TX, USA; canx 08Feb90]
48		N748G VR-BBY N302K G-AWYF N213GA [b/u cApr97 Chicago-Palwaukee, IL, USA; canx 13Feb08]
49		N749G N456 F-GFIC [wfu Marseille-Marignane, France; canx 17Apr98]
50		N80J N8BJ N6PA N3100E N8200E N820CE N28CG [wfu & canx 05Jun90; parts to Schweizer Maintenance Training School, Elmira, NY, USA; b/u; fuselage remains present Elmira-Corning Regional, NY, USA]
51		N80K N80KA XC-HYC N90PM I-MGGG [b/u cJun06 Geneva-Cointrin, Switzerland]
52		N752G VH-ASJ N3858H N18TF (N18TZ) N612DT
53		N753G (N701JW) N700JW [wfu, parts to White Industries, Bates City, MO, USA; location R-02; canx 21Jun94]
54		CF-MUR C-FMUR N26AJ N164PA
55		N755G N255AA N1234X N429W N9MH N429W N27L VR-CAE N9446E N118LT [wfu 15Jan87; b/u Abilene-Regional, TX, USA; canx 24Jul91]
56		N756G N220B N510E YV-46CP N168PA [wfu Cartersville, GA, USA; canx 15Mar05]
57		N757G I-CKET N66JD PK-TRM [b/u cJan02]
58		N758G N358AA 5N-AAI N16776 N46TE N47TE XB-FLL XA-TTU XC-VNC [wfu Toluca, Mexico State, Mexico]
59		N759G N205AA N23D N11CZ HK-3316X [w/o 02May90 Los Garzones, Monteria, Colombia; canx 14Dec99]
60		CF-IOM C-FIOM PK-TRL [CofA exp 10Jun98 - status?]
61		N761G N594AR N734HR N191SA [wfu cJun88, parts to Dodson International Parts, Rantoul, KS, USA]
62		N205M [w/o 25Jul67 New Cumberland, PA, USA; bill of sale 19Nov74 as N400NL to salvage broker; still current as such on register]
63		N763G N144NK N580BC [b/u c1999; remains present at Aviation Warehouse, El Mirage, CA, USA; canx 08Jul03]
64		N764G N466P CF-COL C-FCOL N49401 N64TG EC-460 EC-EXS [std Madrid-Barajas, Spain]
65		N765G N345TW N340WB N641B N721RA [b/u cAug88 Shreveport Regional, LA, USA; canx 18Nov88]
66		N766G N623W N65H N65HC N111DR XC-GEI [wfu 04Sep86 & b/u]
67		N767G N376 N48 N806S N5241Z N806W
68		N768G N15GP N4765P N4765C N7ZA N68TG [w/o 15Jul83 Blountville/Tri-Cities, TN, USA]
69		N769G N377 N47 N47R [wfu c1986 to Vocational/Technical School, Rexburg, ID, USA; moved c1998 to Pratt Community College, Pratt, KS, USA]
70		N770G N331H [wfu cJun92, parts to Dodson International Parts, Rantoul, KS, USA]
71		N771G N530AA N60CR VR-BTI N222EF F-GFIB XA-MYR [wfu cMar06 Toluca, Mexico State, Mexico]
72		N772G (N304K) CF-NOC N743G [b/u cApr89]
73		N773G N773WJ N207M N720X [w/o pre-Feb87 buried by sand in Arizona Desert following drug-running flight incident; canx 21Nov88]
74		N774G N212H N5619D N701BN
75		N775G N304K PT-KYF
76		N776G N305K G-BRAL P4-JML
77		N777G N706G N73M N748M N748MN N748M 9Q-CFK G-BOBX [b/u cApr89 Birmingham-International, UK; canx 25Apr89]
78		N778G N1040 N7040 N431H N33CP HK-3681X HK-3681W [canx 04Feb04 - status?]
79		N779G N190DM N79HS (EC-491) N79HS [b/u c1993 Fort Lauderdale-International, FL, USA; canx 03Sep92]
80		N780G N605AA N605AB N20GB N200GJ F-GGGY D2-EXC
81		N781G N22G N2PQ C-GMJS I-TASO "5Y-BMT" 5Y-BMR [dbr 19Feb98 Mogadishu International, Somalia]
82		N782G N789S N98R N798R N629JM (N801CC) SE-LFV SE-LDV N12RW 3C- [std Ras al Khaimah, UAE marked as N12RW; canx 29Mar01 as exported to Guinea]
83	C	N783G N437A N117GA N245CA [wfu, parts to White Industries, Bates City, MO, USA; location R-03]
84		N784G N362G N362GP N184K N183K [shot down 03Jun06 Necocli, Antiochian Uraba, Colombia]
85		N706G N1150S XC-BAU N66534 [wfu 01Aug91; b/u Savannah-Hilton Head International, GA, USA; canx 28Nov95]
86		N786G N678RW N231GR N712MW N712MR N712MP N106GH N106GA N86JK N10TB ZS-ALX
87		N787G N10VM N102PL N711BT N87CH N87CE (N87MK) N845JB [b/u cJun97 Bartow-Municipal, FL, USA; canx 04Sep97]
88		N788G N410AA N1M N357H N857H C-GPTN N195PA
89		N789G
90		N790G N4567 N18N N80R N41JK HK-3330X [wfu cDec92, parts to Dodson International Parts, Rantoul, KS, USA; canx 10Jan96]
91	VC-4A	N791G 1380 (USCG) 02 (USCG) 03 (USCG) [wfu cDec01 Miami/Opa-Locka, FL, USA; b/u cJun02]
92		N710G NASA3 (NASA) N3NA 02 (USCG) N3NA YV [canx 12Sep05 as exported to United Kingdom, reinstated 07Oct05; canx 18Aug06 as exported to Venezuela]
93		N740AA N574DU N574K N674C N137C XA-ILV N137C N197PA N820CB
94		N794G N8E
95		N795G N50UC N500RL N500RN [wfu cAug03; used as cabin trainer Andrews AFB, MD, USA]
96		NASA1 (NASA) N1NA N2NA N444BC

G.159 GULFSTREAM

c/n	Series	Identities
97		N797G N5152 N671NC N49DE YV-85CP N184PA [wfu Cartersville, GA, USA; canx 21Apr09]
98		N798G NASA2 (NASA) N2NA N29AY N98MK [wfu cApr91, parts to White Industries, Bates City, MO, USA; location R-04]
99		N799G N62B N102M N364G N364L N750BR [dbr 13Nov88 Niedenberg, nr Frankfurt, West Germany; canx 19Oct89; fuselage remains to Ingolstadt-Manching, Germany]
100		N715G N116KJ N116K VH-FLO [canx 22May95; fuselage remains at Auckland, New Zealand]
101		N716G N222H N300SB F-GFGU 4X-ARV F-GNGU [b/u c1999 Marseille, France; rear fuselage used as a travelling exhibit]
102		N717G N621A N28CG N48CG N48CQ (N73CG) HA-ACV C6-UNO HA-ACV N11UN [wfu c2004 Kendall-Tamiami Executive, FL, USA]
103		N718G N608RP N608R "N4045" XC-AA57 [canx 05Aug92 on export to Brazil; intercepted wearing false marks "N4045" and impounded; wfu Mexico City-Benito Juarez International, Mexico]
104		N719G CF-HBO C-FHBO [pres Southern Alberta Institute of Technology, Art Smith Aerocentre, Calgary-International, AB, Canada; canx 09Nov06; reinstated 11Jun07]
105		N702G I-TASB [CofA exp 01Jun90; wfu Milan-Linate, Italy; b/u cDec93, fuselage used as a bar at Flight 2000 Resort, Bacong Negros Oriental, Philippines]
106		N706G N780AC N72X N72XL N38CG N64CG C-FAWG 9XR-WR YV1020 [dest 29Sep05 by Colombian AF, nr San Andres, Colombia in anti-drug campaign; aircraft was being prepared to fly 2 tons of cocaine to the USA]
107		N722G N34C N73B N7ZB N71CR N71CJ [wfu Houston-William P Hobby, TX, USA; located in fire service training yard south of Apt perimeter (between Monroe & Telephone Roads); canx 21Mar05]
108		N723G N1707Z N23UG [b/u c1986; canx 12Feb90]
109		N724G N1000 N823GA N2000C N1000 N1091 N804CC N307AT N109P [b/u c1998 Cartersville, GA, USA; canx 02Oct99]
110		N727G N533CS C-GTDL [canx 20May86; b/u c1989]
111		N728G N363G N3630 F-GJGC [b/u c1991 Marseille-Marignane, France]
112		N729G N942PM N300PM N300PE (N300BP) N803CC [wfu cMar88 Detroit-Willow Run, MI, USA; canx 02Aug89; b/u after 1991]
323		N900 N988AA N346DA S9-NAV N22320 "N900TT" N980TT HI-678CA HI-678CT [originally designated as c/n 113]
114		N712G N205M N705M N705RS N9300P VH-WPA N724RA [wfu 01Mar88; b/u c1989; canx 19Jan89]
115		CF-ASC N61SB [wfu c1995 Dallas-Love Field, TX, USA & b/u]
116	C	N706G N26L N5400G N5400C N110GA N159AN N328CA [wfu, parts to White Industries, Bates City, MO, USA; location "Ramp Mid"]
117		N710G N519M N23AK N41KD YV-08CP N167PA [b/u cMar05 Cartersville, GA, USA; canx 15Mar05]
118		N715G [b/u cOct83; canx c1984]
119		N734G YV-P-EPC YV-28CP N165PA [wfu Cartersville, GA, USA; canx 08Mar07]
120		N718G P-9 (Greek AF) [wfu c1995; pres Tatoi-Dekelia AF Base, Greece since c1998]
121		N732G N234MM [wfu cJul92; pres MGM Studio theme park, Orlando, FL, USA]
122		N733G N153SR N152SR N707MP F-GFEF
123	C	N736G N687RW N714MW N714MR N2602M N17CA [wfu, parts to White Industries, Bates City, MO, USA; location "Ramp Mid"]
124		N737G N504C N725MK N476S ZS-NKT D2-EXD
125	C	N738G N205G N10NA N5NA N193PA
126		N739G N913BS N913PS N100TV N63AU N110RB
127		N741G N500S N50LS N717JP XA-TDJ [wfu Merida-International, Yucatan, Mexico]
128		N4567 N122Y N516DM N910BS G-BMSR F-GIIX [dbf 28Jun94 Lyon-Satolas, France; canx 04Aug94]
129		N743G N770AC N770A N834H N812CC N113GA N129AF YV [canx 05Jul07 as exported to Venezuela]
130		N744G N902JL N3416 PK-TRO
131		N750G N730TL N730T N1TX N21TX C-FRTT 5Y-BLF [CofA exp 02Apr87; b/u cMay06 Nairobi-Wilson, Kenya]
132		N120HC N1207C N944H N27G N154SR N154NS N154RH [wfu Cartersville, GA, USA & b/u cApr05; canx 17Nov03]
133		N752G N2010 N7776 TU-VAC N33TF [wfu, parts to White Industries, Bates City, MO, USA; locations R-05 & T-01; canx 19Feb97]
134		N754G N914BS N920BS G-BMPA 4X-ARF 3D-ARF 4X-ARF ZS-ONO 3D-DUE ZS-PHJ
135		N755G G-ASXT [wfu & canx 09Aug82; b/u cSep83 Denver, CO, USA]
136		N756G XB-GAW XA-TBT [wfu Uruapan, Michoacan, Mexico]
137		N757G CF-DLO N36DD N42CA (N811CC) N42CA [wfu c1991 Detroit-Willow Run, MI, USA; b/u & canx 06Jun95]
138		N758G N126K XA-ALK XA-RLK [wfu Guadalajara, Jalisco, Mexico]
139		N759G N42G N7972S N8500N N8500C N157WC N62J C-FRTU N196PA
140		N760G N40G N140A N300A N92K N92SA F-GFCQ [wfu Marseille-Marignane, France; canx 17Apr98]
141		N762G N228H N800PA ZS-NHW
142		N764G N10ZA N142TG EC-461 EC-EXQ [std Madrid-Barajas, Spain]
143		N720G N914P I-MDDD [dbr 22Jun92 Pantelleria, Italy, parts to Dodson International Parts, Rantoul, KS, USA]
144		N766G N860E N70CR N70QR [wfu c1986; b/u cMar91 Lewisville, TX, USA; canx 29Mar91]
145		N767G N233U N149X N7FD N155T HK-3329X HK-3580X HK-3580W

G.159 GULFSTREAM

c/n	Series	Identities
146		N772G N2011 N906F OE-GSN OE-HSN 001/4X-JUD (Israeli DF/AF) N906F [b/u cSep01 Miami/Opa-Locka, FL, USA; fuselage remained for some years after scrapping]
147		N774G N861H [w/o 11Jul67 Le Center, MN, USA; canx]
148		N775G N804CC N120S (N9036P) N107GH N1701L C-FWAM XC-LIE [wfu Toluca, Mexico State, Mexico]
149		N776G N636 N636G N400HT N684FM N192PA
150		N706G N777G YV-121CP [w/o cJun88 in Venezuela]
151		N741G NASA4 (NASA) N4NA [wfu cSep03, std Pima Community College, Tucson, AZ, USA; canx 02Jun04, later moved to Pima Air & Space Museum]
152		N718G N705G HP-799 OB-M-1235 HP-799 N705G [wfu 01May89 & b/u]
153		N733G N733NM N80AC N153TG EC-433 EC-EXB N19BX [std Madrid-Barajas, Spain]
154		N736G N267AA N72B N800PM N800PD N802CC G-BNKO C-GNAK [w/o 19Jul00 Houlton, ME, USA; canx 26Mar01]
155		N778G N992CP N22CP N24CP N900PM N900PA N805CC G-BMOW 9Q-CJB
156		N737G N22AS N41LH (N159KK) 9Q-COE
157		N741G N94SA HK-3663X HK-3663 [canx 12Feb96 - status?]
158		N779G N697A N72CR N2NR N2NC 5Y-MIA 5Y-EMJ [w/o 24Jan03 Busia, Kenya]
159		N751G N287AA N940PM N200PM N200PF N809CC G-BNKN XA-RJB
160		N752G N3 N965CJ N3 N599TR [wfu Lakeland Linder Regional, FL, USA; canx 19Jun06]
161		N790G N307EL N925GC XB-JGR
162		N724G N547Q N547QR N547BN N5470R N31CN N300GP C-GPTA [dbr 19Nov96 Toronto-Pearson International, ON, Canada; canx 28May01 & b/u]
163		N727G N618M N71CR [w/o 11Jul75 Addison, TX, USA]
164		N738G N8PG N83908 N88PP N590AS N590AQ N290AS ZS-PHI
165		N739G N75M N75MT N657PC N657P N500WN N501WN
166		N791G N67CR N20CR N76DM N725RA F-GKES (OO-IBG) HB-IRQ 4X-ARG D2-EXB
167		N794G N908LN C-GDWM N717RA S9- [canx 01May06 as exported to Sao Tome]
168		N754G N209T N722RA [b/u cAug88 Shreveport Regional, LA, USA; canx 18Nov88]
169		N725HG N725HC N400WP N400WF N200AE
170		N790G N89K N189K YV-620CP YV-627CP YV-627C
171		VH-CRA N171LS (N1PC) N728GM YV-621CP YV-628CP YV-628C YV2054
172		N700DB N44MC N11NY N172RD TC-SMA [wfu 05May99 Geneva-Cointrin, Switzerland; b/u cAug08]
173		N360WT N944H N944HL N49CB I-TASC 5Y-BMT YV-988C N173BT YV-903CP [stolen 12Feb06 Valencia-Arturo Michelena International, Venezuela]
174		N774G N7004 N7004B N718RA [b/u c1991 Shreveport Regional, LA, USA; canx 25Feb91]
175		N795G N10CR N55AE N578KB YV-453CP N173PA [b/u cJan05 Cartersville, GA, USA; canx 26Jan05]
176	TC-4C	N798G 155722 (US Navy) [pres National Museum of Naval Aviation, NAS Pensacola, FL, USA]
177		N751G N307K N4PC OY-BEG N12GP G-BRWN PK-CTE PK-CDM [CofA exp c1999; wfu Jakarta-Halim, Indonesia]
178	TC-4C	N778G 155723 (US Navy) [w/o 16Oct75 Cherry Point, NC, USA]
179		N779G N1916M N61UT N60AC N60WK HK-3622X HK-3622 XC-AA53 [dbr Acapulco-International, Guerrero, Mexico and dumped]
180	TC-4C	N786G 155724 (US Navy) [std 24May94 Davis-Monthan AFB, AZ, USA; storage code 4G0002; pres on celebrity row]
181		N759G N966H N966HL N25W N25WL N181TG [w/o 31May85 Nashville, TN, USA]
182	TC-4C	N762G 155725 (US Navy) [std 13Sep95 Davis-Monthan AFB, AZ, USA; storage code 4G0007]
183	TC-4C	N766G 155726 (US Navy) [std 13Sep95 Davis-Monthan AFB, AZ, USA; storage code 4G0006]
184	TC-4C	155727 (US Navy) [std 13Sep94 Davis-Monthan AFB, AZ, USA; storage code 4G0004]
185	TC-4C	155728 (US Navy) [std 13Sep94 Davis-Monthan AFB, AZ, USA; storage code 4G0003]
186	TC-4C	155729 (US Navy) [std 26Apr94 Davis-Monthan AFB, AZ, USA; storage code 4G0001]
187	TC-4C	155730 (US Navy) [std 17Oct94 Davis-Monthan AFB, AZ, USA; storage code 4G0005]
188		N17582 HB-LDT C-FAWE
189		N776G C-GPTG [canx 22Mar01; b/u c2002 Montreal-Dorval, QC, Canada]
190		N1901W HK-3579X HK-3579W HK-4022X N190LE [w/o 02Aug96 Lubi, Sudan whilst on delivery to Kenya; canx 20Sep96]
191		N200P N300P (N300XZ) G-BKJZ VH-JPJ PK-RJA [CofA exp c2000; wfu Jakarta-Halim, Indonesia]
192		N712G N67H YV-76CP N171PA
193		N713G N754G PK-TRN 3D-TRN ZS-JIS 9Q- [dam 16Jan08 Lubumbashi, DR Congo; canx 23Jun08 as exported to DR Congo]
194		N718G N6702 N720E N702EA N81T I-MKKK 4X-CST I-MKKK 5Y-BMS YV-989C YV-1076CP [std Miami/Opa-Locka, FL, USA; still marked as YV-989C]
195		N724G N1900W N190PA
196		N728G N752RB N752R N93AC (N811CC) I-EHAJ N134PA N659PC N100EG
197		N385M N777JS (N725RB) (N811CC) N977JS (N385M) N20H N20HE N197RM N520JG N748AA
198		N740G N1902P N1902D N100C N80RD [w/o 23Aug90 Houston-Intercontinental, TX, USA; canx 24Oct91]
199		N745G XA-RIV N745G YV-83CP N183PA N167PA
200		N750G N255TK N159GS

MITSUBISHI MU-2

Construction numbers bearing the prefix SA were assembled at San Angelo, TX, USA

Each series also has an equivalent model designation sometimes referred to in documentation;

MU-2C = C/LR-1 (used by JGSDF)	MU-2K = MU-2B-25
MU-2D = MU-2B-10	MU-2L = MU-2B-36
MU-2DP = MU-2B-15	MU-2M = MU-2B-26
MU-2E = S/LR-1 (used by JASDF)	MU-2N = MU-2B-36A
MU-2F = MU-2B-20	MU-2P = MU-2B-26A
MU-2G = MU-2B-35	MU-2 Marquise = MU-2B-60
MU-2J = MU-2B-35	MU-2 Solitaire = MU-2B-40

c/n	Series	Identities
001	A	JA8620 [wfu 20Jan65; pres Niigata Science Museum, Niigata Prefecture, Japan]
002	A	JA8625 [wfu 18Oct65; pres Osaka-Itami Internationa, Osaka Prefecture, Japan]
003	A	JA8626 [wfu 14Jul65; pres nr Nagoya Apt, Aichi Prefecture, Japan; canx 14Jul75]
004	B	JA8627 [wfu 12Sep75; fate unkn]
005	B	JA8628 [wfu 12Aug83; pres Museum of Aeronautical Sciences, nr Tokyo-Narita, Chiba Prefecture, Japan]
006	B	JA8629 N3540X N92JR C-GMUA N92JR [dbr 13May81 nr Miami, FL, USA, parts to White Industries, Bates City, MO, USA; location S-03; canx 02Apr96]
007	B	JA8647 N3541X (D-IHFS) N307MA [w/o 23Apr80 Las Vegas-Henderson, NV, USA]
008	B	N3542X N224FW N505SA [wfu c1985; b/u]
009	B	JA8655 D-IBUF HB-LEB CF-QMS C-FQMS [w/o 07Apr80 Athabasca, AB, Canada; canx 03May83]
010	B	N3543X N4MA HK-2532X HK-2532G N4MA [b/u by Turbine Aircraft Marketing, San Angelo Regional-Mathis Field, TX, USA]
011	B	JA8657 D-IBUG HB-LEA SE-EDM N9613 N96MA [b/u; canx cJun85]
012	B	N3544X [b/u; canx 20Oct88]
013	B	N3545X N251M [w/o 09Apr79 Gardner-Municipal, KS, USA; canx 31Mar04]
014	B	N3546X N4WD N155MA [pres Kirtland Community College, Roscommon, MI, USA; trfd cMar06 to Milwaukee Area Technical College, Milwaukee, WI, USA]
015	B-10	N3547X N322GB N879Q N707EB N31CL [wfu cSep95 Detroit-Willow Run, MI, USA; b/u by Turbine Aircraft Marketing, San Angelo Regional-Mathis Field, TX, USA; canx 11Jun96]
016	B	N3548X (N232LJ) N208MA [w/o 03Aug79 Hays-Municipal, KS, USA; canx 28Oct94]
017	B	N269AA N750Q [b/u c1981; canx 16Apr02; reinstated to register as a valid import 15Nov07]
018	B	N3550X [w/o 21Dec68 nr Springfield, MO, USA; canx 25Jun70]
019	B	N3551X N728F
020	B	N3552X N39BC [wfu, parts to White Industries, Bates City, MO, USA; location S-07; canx 11Apr91]
021	B	N3553X N50BR N22JZ [canx 29Jun94 as exported to Honduras; reportedly b/u for spares]
022	B	N3554X N549LK [dbr 13Oct70 Northfield-Welcome, OH, USA, parts to White Industries, Bates City, MO, USA; canx 21Dec70]
023	B	N3555X N555VK N15CC N15VC [b/u by Turbine Aircraft Marketing, San Angelo Regional-Mathis Field, TX, USA; canx 23Aug07]
024	B	N3556X N111FN N154MF [b/u; date & location unkn]
025	B	N3557X N2GT N2GZ [pres inst airframe Tarrant County Junior College, Fort Worth, TX, USA]
026	B	N301LA N301L N121L N482G PT-LMD [canx 01Sep95 - status?]
027	B	N888L N8884 N519T N519TL N261WR N57907 N27GP [w/o 13Jul82 Schellville/Sonoma County, CA, USA]
028	B	HB-LEC SE-FGP LN-DAB SE-FGP N53JL ZP-CCQ CP-1962 N2176D [pres inst airframe at Thief River Falls Technical Institute, MN, USA; canx 11Apr03]
029	B	N3560X [wfu c1985, parts to Dodson International Parts, Rantoul, KS, USA; canx 20Oct93]
030	B	N3561X N302X [wfu c1989; b/u Conroe-Montgomery County, TX, USA; canx 30Jul90]
031	B	JA8671 N38920 N2BC N38920 N222GS (N631BA) N31WM
032	B	N224FW N243RA N229MA N707EB N21MK [wfu c1994; b/u San Angelo Regional-Mathis Field, TX, USA by Turbine Aircraft Marketing; canx 14Mar95]
033	B	N3563X N122G [wfu c1988; b/u by Bounty Aviation, Ypsilanti, MI, USA; canx cAug90]
034	B	N3547X N23HR N28HR XB-FMV XB-EFN [wfu Toluca, Mexico State, Mexico]
035	B	N3564X N601CT N36G
036		[void - aircraft built as c/n 801]
037	B	N3565X CF-CRL C-FCRL N37MU ZK-WAL VH-JWO VH-NYM [pres Darwin Aviation Heritage Museum, Winnellie, NT, Australia; canx 01Sep93]
038	B	N3566X N8BL N706DM [pres inst airframe Tulsa-International, OK, USA]
101	B-10	JA8673 VH-FSE N237MA N75MD N3ED [w/o 06Sep81 nr Riverton, WY, USA]
102	B-10	HB-LED SE-FGO [wfu Nykoping-Skavsta, Sweden; CofA exp 30Dec90]
103	B-10	N3567X N850Q XB-TIM XC-FEL N850Q [wfu, parts to White Industries, Bates City, MO, USA; marked as XC-FEL; location T-11; canx 01Dec94]
104	B-10	N3568X N851Q XA-BUB N170MA N177DM N151JB N377NJ [b/u by Turbine Aircraft Marketing, San Angelo Regional-Mathis Field, TX, USA; canx 20Aug08]
105	B-10	N3569X N852Q N55LC N852Q N2RA N98AL [b/u by Turbine Aircraft Marketing, San Angelo Regional-Mathis Field, TX, USA; canx 10Oct96]
106	B-10	N3570X N853Q N518T N518TQ N28DC [pres Eastern New Mexico University, Roswell, NM]
107	B-10	N3571X N854Q [w/o 07Jan77 Rochester-Municipal, MN, USA; canx 08Aug77]
108	B-10	N3572X N855Q [b/u cSep97 Grand Junction-Regional, CO, USA; canx 30Aug97]
109	B-10	N3573X N856Q N1AN C-GWGP [pres inst airframe Canadore Technical College, ON, Canada; canx 04Aug89]

MITSUBISHI MU-2

c/n	Series	Identities
110	B-10	N3574X N857Q N666RK [wfu: reportedly b/u Miami/Opa-Locka, FL, USA]
111	B-10	N858Q N721FC [wfu Columbus-Golden Triangle Regional, MS, USA]
112		[void - aircraft built as c/n 901]
113	B-10	N859Q
114	B-20	N860Q CF-CEL C-FCEL N9010B N500X [wfu cDec02, parts to Dodson International Parts, Rantoul, KS, USA]
115	B-15	N861Q YV-T-WTI N102MA N4TN [b/u San Angelo Regional-Mathis Field, TX, USA; fuselage remains to Aviation Warehouse, El Mirage, CA, USA]
116	B-10	N862Q N77TM [wfu c1996 Quest Aviation, Lake City, FL; canx 31Mar99]
117	B-10	N863Q [wfu c1990; pres inst airframe Anchorage-Merrill Field, AK, USA; canx 08Oct97]
118	B-15	N864Q N333RK N100KK N400KK [b/u cMay86 Las Vegas-North Air Terminal, NV, USA; canx 20Oct93]
119	B-10	N856Q N333FP N333JE N333BR (N101ES) N333BR [pres Tulsa-International, OK, USA; canx 14Apr83]
120	B-10	JA8725 N284MA N200HL [w/o 20Sep74 New Orleans, LA, USA; canx 10Jul09]
121	B-10	N866Q [dbr 07Dec87 White Plains, NY; b/u by Turbine Aircraft Marketing, San Angelo Regional-Mathis Field, TX, USA; canx 25Nov88]
122	B-20	N867Q CF-MCF N11HR N98MA MT-223 (Mexican Navy)
123	B-20	N868Q CF-HTL C-FHTL N105MA [wfu c1996; canx 03Sep96; b/u by Turbine Aircraft Marketing, San Angelo Regional-Mathis Field, TX, USA]
124	B-20	N100MA N76MD N10UT N987MA
125	B-20	N750Q CF-AMP C-FAMP N71674 N750QQ [b/u c1994 Hermitage, TN, USA; canx 03May94]
126	B-20	N751Q YV-T-ANI YV-07P YV-19P N3917J PT-LOH [reportedly wfu - status?]
127	B-20	N752Q N700DM N700FN [b/u; location unkn; canx 03Mar94]
128		[void - aircraft built as c/n 902]
129	B-20	N753Q N555C
130	B-20	N754Q N22CH N1173Z N531MA [dbr 18Feb76 nr Argyle, NY, USA, parts to White Industries, Bates City, MO, USA; canx 28Oct76]
131	B-20	N755Q C6-BFA N755Q
132	B-20F	N756Q VH-DTV
133	B-20	N488GB N500QX [b/u Aiken-Municipal, SC, USA; canx 03Aug04; reinstated 05Dec07; canx 08Oct08]
134	B-20	N758Q [w/o 15Apr69 Trenton-Mercer, NJ, USA; canx 01Jul69]
135	B-20	HB-LEE N121SF N44MA N66CL N54CK [aircraft possibly demonstrated as "I-SAIF" cJun68]
136	B-20	N759Q PP-EEF N82793 N424AJ N75RJ N115AP
137	B-20	N760Q N304LA N304L [w/o 21Apr79 Marsh Harbour, Bahamas; canx 12Oct79]
138	B-20	N761Q N252DC N703DM [b/u; canx 08Oct08]
139	B-20	N762Q N44JC N40PP N40RP N90SA LV-WME N126AB [b/u by Turbine Aircraft Marketing, San Angelo-Mathis Field, TX, USA; canx 23Aug01]
140	B-20	N763Q CF-GHK C-FGHK N90165 N606MA N333RK N376BT N333RK N900TV N700DA
141	B-20	N753Q N764Q [w/o 16Jan70 Salisbury-Wicomico County Regional, MD, USA; canx 29Jun70]
142	B-20	N766Q N11WF N209MA N23CD [w/o 16Oct85 nr El Paso, TX, USA]
143	B-20	N767Q N700MA N3MU [dbr 12Oct86 Denver-Stapleton, CO, USA, parts to White Industries, Bates City, MO, USA; location S-13; canx 06Feb95]
144	B-20	N768Q CF-CII N12SC (N13FA) N11KR N176BJ [dbr 12Mar99 Knoxville-McGhee Tyson, TN, USA; b/u by Turbine Aircraft Marketing, San Angelo Regional-Mathis Field, TX, USA; canx 01Mar07]
145	B-20	N769Q PT-BOY
146	B-20	N780Q N1MU N100RT N91JR N55PC (N78HC) N55PC [b/u c1993 Las Vegas-North Air Terminal, NV, USA; canx 20Oct93]
147		[void - aircraft built as c/n 903]
148		[void - aircraft built as c/n 904]
149	B-20	N781Q CF-YSU N8527Z N701DM [w/o 28Feb89 off San Diego, CA, USA; canx 12Dec91]
150	B-20	N782Q CF-FER C-FFER N5589S [w/o 15Dec82 Louisville-Bowman Field, KY, USA]
151	B-20	N757Q [w/o 20Nov72 nr Manning, SC, USA]
152		[void - aircraft built as c/n 501]
153		[void - aircraft built as c/n 502]
154	B-20	N783Q N327E (N81LJ) N720JK
155	B-20	N784Q N513DM N512DM
156	B-20	N869Q XB-HOV
157	B-20	N870Q N157CG (N157WP) LV-PAZ LV-RAZ N157AF N711VK
158	B-20	N871Q PT-BPY N22MZ
159	B-20	N872Q N17UC N30MA N888DS [impounded c1997 San Isidro AFB, Dominican Republic]
160	B-20	N873Q [w/o 01Nov79 Nashville-International, TN, USA]
161	B-20	N874Q N11LC N11LQ N400TR [b/u c1999 San Angelo Regional-Mathis Field, TX, USA; canx 06Aug99]
162	B-20	N875Q N573MA
163	B-20	N876Q N74TL N333RB N388RB N388RD N6TN N60BN [pres inst airframe University of Alabama, Birmingham, AL, USA; canx 16Aug91]
164	B-20	N877Q [b/u c1986; canx cNov86]
165	B-20	N878Q N310Y N333KM YV-1067P
166	B-20	N879Q N322GB N322GA N800DH [b/u c1994 Conroe-Montgomery County, TX, USA; canx 18Apr94]
167	B-20	N25UF N549LK N310MA [dbr 07Apr96 Batesville-Panola County, MS, USA, parts to Global Aircraft Industries, Edmonton-Villeneuve, AB, Canada]
168	B-20	N882Q [w/o 03Jun73 nr Cedillos City, Mexico]
169	B-20	N883Q N550MA [wfu c1984 Aiken-Municipal, SC, USA]

MITSUBISHI MU-2

c/n	Series	Identities
170	B-20	N884Q XB-JII N239MA N58CA
171		[void - aircraft built as c/n 905]
172	B-20	N885Q [wfu, parts to White Industries, Bates City, MO, USA; location S-11; canx 17Nov94]
173	B-20	N887Q XC-FAJ N887Q N18BF
174	B-20	N889Q C-FCCD N52CD
175	B-20	N890Q PT-BZW
176		[void - aircraft built as c/n 906]
177	B-20	N891Q N177SA N12RA
178	B-20	N892Q N711SH N9JS [w/o 23Apr81 Alpena, MI, USA]
179	B-20	N103MA N78WC N10FR N4WD N4WQ N777VK
180	B-20	N104MA N10HK N180MA N180SB N711LL [dbr 21May85 San Angelo Regional-Mathis Field, TX, USA; b/u by Turbine Aircraft Marketing, San Angelo Regional-Mathis Field, TX, USA]
181		[void - aircraft built as c/n 907]
182	B-20	N105MA N2100T
183	B-20	JA8183 N350MA N25JB N711FR N967MA N221KP N67SM [b/u 1995 unkn location; canx 04Apr95]
184	B-20	N106MA [w/o 07May91 nr Kenefic, OK, USA in mid-air collision with a Cessna 310; canx 03Sep96]
185	B-20	N107MA [wfu, parts to White Industries, Bates City, MO, USA; location "Ramp Mid"; canx 08Nov95]
186		[void - aircraft built as c/n 908]
187	B-20	N108MA N641KE N508MA OY-DLM N187AF [w/o 10Jun01 nr Cerrillos, NM, USA; canx 04Jun03]
188	B-20	N109MA PT-BZY
189	B-20	N110MA XB-XOI
190	B-20	N111MA N140CM
191	B-20	N112MA N12BC N23BC N99EE SE-GHG HA- [canx 03Aug93 as exported to Hungary; no further details known]
192	B-20	N113MA N900M N907M N770WC N22LC N22EQ [b/u by Turbine Aircraft Marketing, San Angelo Regional-Mathis Field, TX, USA; canx 07Sep95]
193	B-20	N114MA N121JW N1210W N8PC
194	B-20	N115MA N300SM N600K N440EZ N282MS HI- [canx cJul86 as exported to Dominican Republic; possibly became HI-483]
195	B-20	JA8770 [wfu 10Dec85; pres Iwanuma Education Centre, Sendai, Miyagi Prefecture, Japan]
196	B-20	N116MA PT-DTL
197	B-20	N117MA XB-SUR XA-GOL XB-SUR N2406U
198	B-20	N118MA N118CD N118RB N71MF N91MM
199	B-20	N119MA N4SP N3RN N800BR [wfu, parts to Dodson International Parts, Rantoul, KS, USA]
200		[void - aircraft built as c/n 909]
201		[void - aircraft built as c/n 910]
202		[void - aircraft built as c/n 911]
203		[void - aircraft built as c/n 802]
204		[void - aircraft built as c/n 912]
205	B-20	N120MA N200BR [w/o 21Dec79 Provo Municipal, UT, USA; canx 08Oct82]
206	B-20	N121MA [b/u c1994 San Angelo Regional-Mathis Field, TX, USA; canx 06Jan95]
207	B-20	N122MA
208	B-20	N123MA N93BD N15EW N111HF
209	B-20	N124MA N100VC N212CC N92TC (N34LC) N92TC *N35JL
210	B-20	N125MA N34DD N38BE
211	B-20	N126MA N123GS N45EV [wfu Aiken-Municipal, SC, USA]
212	B-20	N127MA N33VM YV-150CP YV-1978P N1978P [status? possibly w/o but not reported]
213	B-20	N128MA N33BK (N128MA) N38BK N100BR PT-LYI
214	B-20	N129MA N123VC [wfu c1990; pres inst airframe FlygTeknikCentrum Hasslo, Vasteras-Hasslo, Sweden; canx 28Mar90]
215	B-20	N181MA PT-ICD [w/o 13Mar93 Goiania, Goias, Brazil]
216	B-20	N182MA N921JG N921RM N922ST N922FM
217	B-20	N183MA [wfu cJul04; b/u by Turbine Aircraft Marketing, San Angelo Regional-Mathis Field, TX, USA; canx 16Feb07]
218	B-20	N184MA [w/o 18Jun87 nr Coral Springs, FL, USA; canx 20Oct94]
219	B-20	N185MA
220	B-20F	N186MA N123JA N123UA N123AX [wfu, parts to White Industries, Bates City, MO, USA; location S-04]
221	B-20	N187MA N13EW N800BR N800BY
222	B-20	N188MA N4PN N5PN N9PN SE-GHH
223	B-20	N189MA N447AB [wfu c1992, parts to Dodson International Parts, Rantoul, KS, USA; canx 02Jun92]
224	B-20	N190MA N500PS [wfu cFeb02; b/u by Turbine Aircraft Marketing, San Angelo Regional-Mathis Field, TX, USA; canx 16Feb07]
225		[void - aircraft built as c/n 913]
226	B-20	N215MA C-GUNG N21722 N31SK N187SB N107SB
227		[void - aircraft built as c/n 914]
228	B-20	N216MA N100TB N963MA N228WP
229	B-20	N217MA N100CF
230		[void - aircraft built as c/n 803]
231	B-20	N218MA N666MA N346VL
232	B-20	N219MA N55LC N55EG N800HR PT-WIX
233	B-20	N220MA N43W N43WU N5HE N5NE N89CR [dbr 20Nov98 Oklahoma City, OK, USA; b/u c1999 San Angelo Regional-Mathis Field, TX, USA; canx 06Aug99]

MITSUBISHI MU-2

c/n	Series	Identities
234		[void - aircraft built as c/n 915]
235		[void - aircraft built as c/n 916]
236		[void - aircraft built as c/n 804]
237		[void - airframe not built]
238		[void - airframe not built]
239	B-25	N221MA N222LR N303AG OK-ATX
240	B-25	N222MA N222HH N222HL N64LG
241	B-25	N223MA N88HL N555MA C-GJAV N700RX
242	B-25	N224MA N48MD N211BA N727DM [b/u c1994 Tulsa-International, OK, USA; canx 14Jun94]
243	B-25	N225MA HK-2060X HK-2060W HK-2060 N250AF
244	B-25	N226MA N400SM PT-LEW
245	B-25	N227MA N256PL N32EC N44F N448F N180SB N722DM [b/u White Industries, Bates City, MO, USA; canx 17Nov94]
246	B-25	N228MA N730SF [b/u c1994 Tulsa-International, OK, USA; canx 19Aug94]
247	B-25	N238MA N5TC N5TQ SE-KBX [wfu Falkoping, Sweden]
248	B-25	N230MA CF-MKK C-FMKK N9036N N105MA N80JM N101QA N725DM N725FN N480AF
249	B-25	N231MA N711PD N711PB N702DM N702FN [b/u c1994 Tulsa-International, OK, USA; canx 17Aug94]
250	B-25	N232MA SE-GHX N232MA N740DM N740FN N500XX
251	B-25	N233MA [w/o 02Sep81 nr McLeod, TX, USA; canx 11Jul84]
252	B-25	N234MA [w/o 26Nov79 nr Post Oak, TX, USA; canx 28Oct94]
253	B-25	N235MA YV-T-AFD YV-05CP N54656 TG-FRD N54656 N430DA N481AF
254	B-25	N236MA N616AF N69QJ [w/o 13Nov75 Morristown/Moore-Murrell, TN, USA]
255	B-25	N275MA [dbr 04Jan85 6 mls W of West Point Municipal, VA, USA, parts to White Industries, Bates City, MO, USA; location S-17]
256	B-25	N276MA HZ-BIN N4594V [wfu Tulsa-International, OK, USA]
257	B-25	N277MA N344K N344KL
258	B-25	N278MA N600TB [b/u by Turbine Aircraft Marketing, San Angelo Regional-Mathis Field, TX, USA]
259	B-25	N279MA XB-LIJ [w/o 30Dec75 Beloit-Moritz Memorial, KS, USA]
260	B-25	N280MA N111GP (N102GP) N290MA N457SC N790CA N444FF N50ET
261	B-25	N281MA
262	B-25	N282MA N212MA [b/u c1984 San Angelo Regional-Mathis Field, TX, USA]
263	B-25	N283MA N99KC N10VU N30RR
264	B-25	N310MA N549LK N50TT N264KW N261KW N38AF *N31FW
265	B-25	N311MA N9WC SE-IOY N121CH N482AF
266	B-25	N312MA [w/o 24May05 nr Portland-Hillsboro, OR, USA; canx 04Jun08]
267	B-25	N313MA N59RW
268	B-25	N314MA PT-JGA
269	B-25	N315MA N315LP N473LP (N473W) N473FW [dbr 20Nov92 Denver Broomfield-Jeffco, CO, USA, parts to White Industries, Bates City, MO, USA; location S-10; canx 17Nov94]
270	B-25	N316MA N45CF N45GE VH-MUO N4284V [b/u cApr95 Augusta Regional/Bush Field, GA, USA; canx 17May95]
271	B-25	N317MA N234BC N879MA N222D N22YD N23HR N708DM N483AF
272	B-25	N318MA N3EE N500BJ (N500BE) N666RL N10BK N272MC
273	B-25	N319MA XB-ZIP N46HK XB-ZIP
274	B-25	N320MA (N10GE) N320MA [b/u San Jose, CA, USA; canx 22Jul94]
275		[void - aircraft built as c/n 805]
276	B-25	N321MA [w/o 04Apr77 Detroit-Willow Run, MI, USA; canx 24Jun77]
277	B-25	N322MA SE-FTS (N322MA) N71959 C-GMUK N390K N3GT
278		[void - aircraft built as c/n 917]
279		[void - aircraft built as c/n 918]
280	B-25	N323MA N1RZ N90SA N322TA N707DM N707FN N54PC N10BK N460FS
281	B-25	N325MA N111PM N666HB [dbr 09Jan90 Jacksonville, FL, USA; b/u Augusta Regional/Bush Field, GA, USA; canx 14Jun94]
282	B-25	N326MA N3MP OB-S-1284 OB-1284 [w/o 14May92 Juanjui, Peru]
283	B-25	N327MA SE-GHA
284	B-25	N328MA N31BN N15JA N726DM N726FN N484AF
285	B-25	N329MA N111JE N11SJ
286	B-25	N330MA N842LC N666SP C-FGEM N666SP N50AF
287	B-25	N331MA SE-GHB
288	B-25	N333MA [w/o 24Mar74 nr Gander, NL, Canada; canx 14Jun74]
289	B-25	N334MA SE-GHC
290	B-25	N450MA N438SP (N51PC) N61DP N61DX VH-MWZ N4186Y N14YS
291	B-25	N451MA CP-1147 N291MB
292	B-25	N452MA N346K [b/u c1993 Las Vegas-North Air Terminal, NV, USA; canx 20Oct93]
293	B-25	N453MA SE-GHD
294	B-25	N454MA SE-GHE
295	B-25	N455MA N21PC [b/u Las Vegas-North Air Terminal, NV, USA; canx 20Oct93]
296	B-25	N456MA N729DM N729FN [b/u Dodson International Parts, Rantoul, KS; canx 24Aug94]
297	B-25	N457MA C-GODA N106GB N7DD
298	B-25	N458MA N188RM PT-OFV N188RM
299	B-25	N459MA SE-GHF
300	B-25	N460MA N724DM N724FN [dbr 20May96 Panama City-Tyndall AFB, FL, USA, parts to White Industries, Bates City, MO, USA; location S-17; canx 10Jan97]
301	B-25	N461MA N10T N461MA
302	B-25	N462MA YV-349P N462MA
303	B-25	N463MA N1US N1UQ (N92BC) N21PB N728DM N728FN
304	B-25	N464MA N15EW N410MA SE-IOU [w/o 16Feb86 Alvdalen, Sweden; canx 30Mar87]

MITSUBISHI MU-2

c/n	Series	Identities
305	B-25	N465MA N50K
306	B-25	N495MA N856JT
307	B-25	N496MA N200TM N321ST [w/o 08Sep91 Campbell River, BC, Canada; canx 20Feb97]
308	B-25	N497MA ZS-MUK N497MA SE-GHU N3750N N111MD N709DM N709FN N485AF
309	B-25	N498MA N44RF N66U [w/o 12Sep82 Hayden-Yampa Valley, CO, USA]
310	B-25	N499MA RP-C575 VH-MUK N290GC N324GM
311	B-25	N501MA N311JB N311RN
312	B-25	N502MA N200NW N444RG N721DM [wfu, parts to White Industries, Bates City, MO, USA; location T-12; canx 17Nov94]
313SA	B-25	N503MA N100KP N100KE
314	B-25	N504MA N18BA N982MA PT-LTC [dbf 10Jul98 Sao Paulo-Congonhas, Sao Paulo State, Brazil; canx 05Mar99]
315	B-25	N505MA N99SR
316	B-25	N506MA N77SS N12EW [wfu c1991, parts to White Industries, Bates City, MO, USA; location T-10; canx 16Nov94]
317		[void - aircraft built as c/n 806]
318		[void - aircraft built as c/n 919]
319	B-26	N507MA N6SG N475CA N54PC
320	B-26	N508MA N14645 N641KE N30EM N641KE SE-IOZ
321SA	B-26A	N509MA N513DC N513DQ N5LJ N893SC
322	B-26	N510MA N20KC N40KC
323	B-26	N511MA N216CD
324	B-26	N512MA N143JA
325	B-26	N513MA N333RB N233RB N440RB N325MA
326	B-26	N514MA N44AG (N44EG) N888CD XA-RLZ N700LW N401JC N165MA
327	B-26	N515MA N375AC
328	B-26	N516MA N388NC N388NG N500HA N767MD N5PC N305DS
329	B-26	N517MA N202AU N35TT N35RR N35VS N60AZ N486AF
330	B-26	N518MA N261WR N261WB
331	B-26	N519MA YV-880P N3982L SE-IOX [w/o 15Mar86 Ringenaes, Sweden; canx 30Mar87]
332	B-26	N520MA N33LS N555LL N555JP N333TX
333	B-26	N521MA N12SJ N487AF
334		[void - aircraft built as c/n 807]
335		[void - aircraft built as c/n 920]
336		[void - aircraft built as c/n 921]
337	B-26	N522MA SE-IOV
338	B-26	N523MA N8PL N79AC N456PS N450FS
339	B-26	N524MA N555DD N60NJ N800ED
340	B-26	N525MA (N912DM) N525MA [b/u c1994 Sandston, VA, USA; canx 17Nov94]
341	B-26	N726MA XB-LIJ
342	B-26	N727MA [dbr 11Jul85 Southbridge-Municipal, MA, USA; b/u c1989 Conroe-Montgomery County, TX, USA]
343	B-26	N728MA C-GFRU [w/o 18Jan82 nr Kelowna, BC, Canada; canx 27Sep83]
344	B-26	N729MA N418CD [wfu cJul91, parts to White Industries, Bates City, MO, USA; location S-17]
345	B-26	N730MA N730MP SE-IUA
346	B-26	N731MA N888RF N10UT (N45PD) N10UT
347	B-26	N732MA (YV-1050P) YV-94CP [w/o 23Jul80 in Venezuela]
348SA	B-26A	N733MA I-NARI N733MA N1KC N522MC D-IEMU N500GK YV-2604P YV2188
349SA	B-26	N734MA N316EN
350SA	B-26A	N735MA N711MZ N958MA PT-OVW
351SA	B-26A	N736MA N67LH (N879RS) N10FR N10MR N500LE
352SA	B-26A	N737MA N234BC N978MA N41WB N41AD D-IAHT
353SA	B-26A	N738MA 6Y-JDB
354SA	B-26A	N739MA PT-OIP
355SA	B-26A	N741MA N54EC N741MA N29WD
356SA	B-26A	N742MA N5NC N5NQ [b/u c1994 Augusta Regional/Bush Field, GA, USA; canx 14Jun94]
357SA	B-26A	N743MA N2HP N21HP
358SA	B-26A	N744MA N8GR C-GIRO N60BT [w/o 06Oct00 Edgartown-Katama Airpark, MA, USA; canx 12Apr01]
359		[void - aircraft built as c/n 808]
360		[void - aircraft built as c/n 922]
361SA	B-26A	N745MA LV-PYI LV-MCV
362SA	B-26A	N746MA N41PC N231LC N231LQ N111GK (N111GD) N78FS N801L N140CP
363SA	B-26A	N748MA N80BR N110GC (N178GV) N110GC
364SA	B-26A	N749MA N547TA
365SA	B-40	N750MA [w/o 19Nov81 nr Fernandina Beach, FL, USA; canx cFeb83]
366SA	B-26A	N751MA N18LR N123JM N123JA N99GR I-MITS N66UP N2RA
367SA	B-26A	N752MA N67GT N2GT [wfu, parts to White Industries, Bates City, MO, USA; location "Ramp North 03"]
368SA	B-26A	N754MA N78WD N16TC N78WD
369SA	B-26A	N755MA N202MC N24PE
370SA	B-26A	(N760MA) HB-LKD F-GDLA N370SA N370AC N370MA
371SA	B-26A	N764MA N399SP VH-XMZ ZK-ECR N30MA
372SA	B-26A	N765MA [w/o 28Aug78 nr Bedford, NH, USA]
373SA	B-26A	N766MA
374SA	B-26A	N767MA N9HA N122CK
375SA	B-26A	N768MA (N6LA) XA-TCS N17JQ N81MF
376		[void - aircraft built as c/n 809]
377		[void - aircraft built as c/n 923]

MITSUBISHI MU-2

c/n	Series	Identities
378		[void - aircraft built as c/n 924]
379SA	B-26A	N769MA N910DA N50VS N500V [w/o 02Jan89 Mansfield-Lahm Regional, OH, USA]
380SA	B-26A	N770MA (N570SS) ZS-NIY N333RK
381SA	B-26A	N771MA N400JH (N350EC) N103RB N356AJ
382SA	B-26A	N772MA
383SA	B-26A	N773MA N10JJ N40JJ
384SA	B-26A	N774MA (N127RM) N774MA
385SA	B-26A	N775MA LV-PAL LV-MLT N808PK N52WM
386SA	B-26A	N778MA N999BE LV-RAC N386TM [w/o 22Jan00 nr San Antonio, TX, USA]
387SA	B-26A	N779MA N8TB N333WF [dbr 11Mar05 Blythe, CA, USA; b/u San Angelo Regional-Mathis Field, TX, USA by Turbine Aircraft Marketing; canx 16Mar07]
388SA	B-26A	N780MA N91CM PT-OOS
389SA	B-26A	N781MA N4LZ N781MA (N10KP) N600KP (N787X) N400ES N543JF
390SA	B-26A	N782MA
391SA	B-26A	N783MA
392SA	B-26	N784MA D-IFMU N392P N892SC
393SA	B-26A	N786MA N9SR N82WC
394		[void - aircraft built as c/n 810]
395SA	B-40	N787MA F-GGRZ [w/o 09May91 in France; canx 05Sep91]
396SA	B-40	N788MA D-IHAN [w/o 09Aug79 Steinhausen, West Germany]
397SA	B-40	N789MA XA-IUC N666SP N777WM
398SA	B-40	N790MA N222MS N61DP N61GJ
399SA	B-40	N960MA YV-70CP N9052Y N1930P
400SA	B-40	N961MA N7UE N666MA C-GBVB N40MZ N700WA
401SA	B-40	N962MA [w/o 23Mar80 New Orleans, LA, USA]
402SA	B-40	N963MA N149JA [dbr 03Feb82 Hayden-Yampa Valley, CO, USA, parts to White Industries, Bates City, MO, USA; location S-05; canx 11Dec82]
403SA	B-40	N964MA N7PW N12LE N264KW
404SA	B-40	N965MA [w/o 29Aug93 South Charleston-Mallory, WV, USA; canx 13Dec96]
405SA	B-40	N966MA N711TF N966MA [w/o 11Mar04 nr Napa County, CA, USA]
406SA	B-40	N967MA F-GCJS [wfu; canx 02Feb00]
407SA	B-40	N968MA N43DC N979MA TG-ASE N979MA N750CA
408SA	B-40	N969MA [w/o 06Dec80 nr Minneapolis/Anoka County-Blaine, MN, USA; canx cJun85]
409SA	B-40	N990MA YV-313CP N990MA N78FS N781H
410SA	B-40	N991MA (N10MH) N329WM N701K [dbr 24May99 nr Parry Sound, ON, Canada, parts to Dodson International Parts, Rantoul, KS, USA; canx 13Apr00]
411SA	B-40	N992MA N8LC N400PS
412SA	B-40	N993MA N88HL N288HL N468MA N814HH N25GM
413SA	B-40	N994MA I-FRUT [dbr Rome-Urbe, Italy c1986; parts to Rotterdam-Zestienhoven, Netherlands; b/u c1987]
414SA	B-40	N102MA XA-JET XB-DVV N72TJ N73MA
415SA	B-40	N108MA 5N-ALP F-ODRZ N860SM N893KB
416SA	B-40	N109MA N44AB N44AX N613CF N44AX
417SA	B-40	N110MA N131SA N42DE N29JS N61JB
418SA	B-40	N140MA (N52RC) N16CG YV-11CP N16CG [w/o 01May01 nr The Woodlands, TX, USA; canx 11Jan02]
419SA	B-40	N153MA N322GB N52MA
420SA	B-40	N154MA N5KD I-SOLT D-IKKY
421		[void - aircraft built as c/n 811]
422		[void - aircraft built as c/n 812]
423SA	B-40	N156MA N100NP
424SA	B-40	N157MA
425SA	B-40	N159MA N111GP N575CA N425TF
426SA	B-40	N161MA N181RS N36AT
427SA	B-40	N166MA N40AM
428SA	B-40	N167MA N124AX PT-LIR
429SA	B-40	N168MA N881BH N1TJ N55DL N77DB N361MA
430SA	B-40F	N170MA N856JC N66FF
431SA	B-40	N171MA [w/o 25Aug06 nr Bunnell, FL, USA; canx 26Jun09]
432SA	B-40	N205MA N15WF N13WF N44VR
433SA	B-40	N209MA D-IMMC N5LC
434SA	B-40	N211MA N127AX N5PC N24MW C-FGEM
435SA	B-40	(N213MA) N104JB (N609HF) N12HF
436SA	B-40	N214MA N32MT N670CA N62CP (N928VF) D-ISTC N62CN
437SA	B-40	N216MA I-SKYL N666AM N145FS
438SA	B-40	N217MA N19RB D-IOSI N4SY N99LC N10VU
439SA	B-40	N218MA VH-MSU N4490U (N100WS) D-IFWR N439SA D-IBBB N439BA N477DD
440SA	B-40	N219MA
441SA	B-40	N220MA N234BC N220MA [w/o 09Jul92 nr Concord, NH, USA; canx 09Nov92]
442		[void - aircraft built as c/n 813]
443		[void - aircraft built as c/n 814]
444		[void - aircraft built as c/n 815]
445		[void - aircraft built as c/n 925]
446SA	B-40	N221MA N81MW N15TR
447SA	B-40	N223MA N1610W N290MA (N348CP) N48NP
448SA	B-40	N226MA N231LC N68CL
449SA	B-40	N227MA N22TG N77DK N449BK
450SA	B-40	N228MA (N100AX) C-GAUR N28PP N220W N220N
451SA	B-40	N229MA N1728S N725JT
452SA	B-40	N230MA N388NC (D-IBBB) N388NC
453SA	B-40	N235MA N80WD N24FJ PT-OIY

MITSUBISHI MU-2

c/n	Series	Identities
454SA	B-40	N236MA I-FRTL N19GA
455		[void - aircraft built as c/n 926]
456		[void - aircraft built as c/n 816]
457		[void - aircraft built as c/n 817]
458SA	B-40	(N237MA) N30SR N88AD N4EW XB-FQM N458BB
459SA	B-40	N238MA N117HR OY-CGW N459SA
460		[void - aircraft built as unkn LR-1 variant]
461		[void - aircraft built as unkn LR-1 variant]
462		[void - aircraft built as unkn LR-1 variant]
463		[void - aircraft built as c/n 819]
464		[void - aircraft built as c/n 927]
465		[void - aircraft built as c/n 818]
466		[void - aircraft built as c/n 820]
501	B-30	JA8737 [b/u; location unkn]
502	B-30	JQ8502 JA8738 N131MA CF-AXP C-FAXP N211RV
503	B-30	JA8739 N132MA [w/o 16Apr72 nr Atlantic City, NJ, USA; canx 15Aug72]
504	B-30	JA8753 [w/o 11Mar81 Kagoshima, Kagoshima Prefecture, Japan]
505	B-30	JA8505 HB-LEF VH-CJP [w/o 15Nov83 Cairns, QLD, Australia; canx 15Nov83]
506	B-30	N133MA [w/o 26Dec75 nr Rollinsville, CO, USA; canx 19Feb76]
507	B-30	N134MA [canx 19Apr99 as exported to Canada; pres Stevenson Aviation Tech Training Centre, Southport, MB, Canada]
508	B-30	N135MA N246W N246WA N246NW N950MA N555CH [b/u; canx 09Dec94]
509	B-30	N136MA N269AS N289AS N154WC C-GBOX N154WC
510	B-30	N137MA N227 [b/u by Turbine Aircraft Marketing, San Angelo Regional-Mathis Field, TX, USA; canx 20Mar01]
511	B-30	N130MA CF-ZJB N5580A N60KC N60KG [b/u; canx 25Jun99]
512	B-30	N138MA XC-EZS N138MA XA-JUC N318MA VH-WMU [w/o 07Nov90 Bathurst, NSW, Australia; canx 01Apr93]
513	B-30	N139MA N88BC ZK-EON VH-UZD N513NA [dbr c1990 in storm at Brisbane Apt, QLD, Australia; parts to Turbine Aircraft Marketing, San Angelo Regional-Mathis Field, TX, USA; registered N513NA 24Mar95; b/u; canx 06Jun95]
514	B-30F	N140MA N777KQ N514WG N999TA [wfu c2001, parts to White Industries, Bates City, MO, USA; location "Ramp South B-14"]
515	B-30	N141MA N155WC N40PP [b/u by Turbine Aircraft Marketing, San Angelo Regional-Mathis Field, TX, USA]
516	B-30F	N142MA VH-JES N881DP VH-JES N516AF VH-AUI VH-JES N516AF VH- [canx 25Mar08 as exported to Australia; possibly for spares]
517	B-30	N143MA N730SS N530SS N89DR N89CR N80CR VH-IAM N119BF [dbr 21Dec94 nr Melbourne-Tullamarine, VIC, Australia; remains exported to USA and registered N119BF; canx 07Sep95]
518	B-30	N144MA N115S [w/o 19Jan78 nr Lewisport-Hancock County/Ron Lewis Field, KY, USA; canx 10Mar84]
519	B-30	N145MA N120S N671MA ZK-EKZ VH-UZC [wfu; canx 10Mar92]
520	B-30	JA8767 [wfu location unkn]
521	B-30F	N146MA N200BD N222JW N100PA VH-JER N771DP VH-WYY VH-KOH ZK-KOH
522	B-30F	N147MA N617BB
523	B-30	N148MA N99UM N711 N711AH [dbr 02Mar74 nr Glenwood Springs, CO, USA; b/u by Turbine Aircraft Marketing, San Angelo Regional-Mathis Field, TX, USA]
524	B-30	N149MA CF-GWF C-FGWF N45591 [wfu, parts to White Industries, Bates City, MO, USA; location S-09; canx cOct87]
525	B-30	N150MA XB-TON N150MA YV-O-CDM-1N360JK C-FTML [pres Southern Alberta Institute of Technology, Art Smith Aero Centre, Calgary-International, AB, Canada; canx 24Nov08]
526	B-30	SE-FGG D-IDEE SE-FGG OO-TBW [w/o 15Aug76 Angouleme, France]
527	B-30F	N151MA N223DD N151MA VH-UZN VH-MNU N527AF [b/u; canx 08Oct08]
528	B-30F	N152MA N100SG N200WG ZK-ESM VH-UZB N528AF [b/u; canx 08Oct08]
529	B-30	N153MA (N115S) N98UM N98CM N3MP N313BB [canx 12Feb90 - status? possibly dbr 22Feb80 Crossville, TN, USA]
530	B-30	N154MA (N120S) N999WB (N999ST) (N999TA) N999WB [dbr 30Dec97 nr Chicago-DuPage County, IL, USA, parts to Dodson International Parts, Rantoul, KS, USA; canx 31Aug98]
531	B-30	N155MA N313PC [b/u; canx 09Nov94]
532	B-30	N156MA N8400E (N444UP) N30SA OH-MIB [wfu Den Helder-De Kooy, Holland, parts to Global Aircraft Industries, Edmonton-Villeneuve, AB, Canada; canx 29Oct00; TT 3724 hours]
533	B-30	N157MA (N130MA) N96UM C-FKCL N618BB [dbr 28Sep96 Chillicothe-Ross County, OH, USA, parts to White Industries, Bates City, MO, USA; location "Taxiway North"; canx 28Jul99]
534	B-30F	N158MA N23DH N158MA N333RB N882MA N920S (N78V) N920S [wfu cJul04; b/u by Turbine Aircraft Marketing, San Angelo Regional-Mathis Field, TX, USA; canx 16Mar07]
535	B-30	N159MA N159RS N21VM [b/u; canx 03May94]
536	B-30	N160MA N123BG N40JT N58BC N255C
537	B-30	N161MA N93UM [wfu cDec02, parts to Aiken-Municipal, SC, USA]
538	B-30	N162MA N4LH N77RZ N713GB [wfu for spares c1987, fuselage remains to Aviation Warehouse, El Mirage, CA, USA; canx 24Oct94]
539	B-30	N163MA N100SW (YV-168P) N100SW [dbr 01Apr77 nr Augusta, GA, USA]
540	B-30	N164MA N164BD N164AH N164MA N869P N869D
541	B-30	N165MA [w/o 20Apr82 Lookout Mountain, GA, USA; canx 21Sep83]
542	B-30	N166MA N888RJ [w/o 05Apr77 nr New York-La Guardia, NY, USA; canx cJan94]

c/n	Series	Identities
543	B-30	N167MA YV-T-QTO YV-61CP YV-1049P N109TW [w/o 22Nov81 nr Pago Pago, American Samoa]
544	B-30F	N168MA N168BB VH-WMW VH-KOF N544AF [b/u; canx 08Oct08]
545	B-30	N169MA N108SC [w/o 24Jun92 nr Alamogordo, NM, USA; canx 15Mar93]
546	B-30	JA8783 [wfu cApr86 location unkn]
547	B-30	N171MA N300BD [wfu c1989 Conroe-Montgomery County, TX, USA, parts to Global Aircraft Industries, Edmonton-Villeneuve, AB, Canada; TT 6698 hours; canx 15Apr94]
548	B-35	N172MA 1521 (Dominican AF) HI-547 N68DA N200RX
549	B-35F	N173MA N50W N173MA N331MM N9MA VH-JMU N65198 C-FTOO
550	B-35	N174MA N220SB N888MA [w/o 12Feb78 Neiva, Huila, Colombia]
551	B-35	N175MA N111WB N111WN N3330K N10DA [b/u cJul01; canx 17Aug01]
552	B-35	N176MA N246W N539MA [wfu c2004; b/u by Turbine Aircraft Marketing, San Angelo Regional-Mathis Field, TX, USA; canx 16Mar07]
553	B-35	N177MA N306H N31LK C-FAMF N7034K N755MA
554	B-35	N178MA [dbr 25Aug78 nr Raton Municipal/Crews Field, NM, USA, parts to White Industries, Bates City, MO, USA]
555	B-35	N179MA N74TL N74TC N74TM N78BK N444AR [w/o 18Nov81 Eagle County Regional/Gypsum, CO, USA]
556	B-35	N191MA N9SS N9043E N33RH N96JP [w/o 06Apr93 Casper/Natrona County International, WY, USA; canx 13Jul94]
557	B-35	N192MA C-GWID N192MA N73MC N314MA OY-CUG OH-MIC (N345SA) [canx 08Oct01; fate unkn; was valid import to US register (I5838) 02Dec92 but ntu.]
558	B-35	N193MA C-GMJS N9179Y N888FS N43SR N45BS [w/o 15Apr02 Carolina, PR; canx 28Aug02]
559	B-35	N194MA N777MA [w/o 18Mar77 nr Austin, TX, USA]
560	B-35	N195MA N776CC C-GUKP
561	B-35	N196MA N123JS N22FL VH-JMZ N561AF [b/u; canx 14Apr04]
562	B-35	N197MA N5DL N100BR N28GS N500MA N580MA N29CY N66CY
563	B-35F	N198MA [b/u by Turbine Aircraft Marketing, San Angelo Regional-Mathis Field, TX, USA; canx 24Jan07]
564	B-35	N199MA N2060M [b/u; canx 03May94]
565	B-35	N209MA N11WF N11WU [wfu, parts to Global Aircraft Industries, Edmonton-Villeneuve, AB, Canada; canx 15Apr94; TT 7517 hours]
566	B-35	N210MA MU-1550/XC-GAR (Mexican Navy)
567	B-35F	N211MA N1VN N1VY [w/o 01Aug01 nr Hilton Head Island, SC, USA; canx 23Jan02]
568	B-35	N212MA N100MK N212MA N99SL N334EB
569	B-35	N213MA N8CC [w/o 02Jun86 nr Bartlett, TX, USA; canx 20Oct93]
570	B-35	N214MA N959L [wfu; canx c1984]
571	B-35	N240MA N4BG N5HE N106DP [b/u; canx 25Jul94]
572	B-35	N241MA N18T N986MA N300RX [wfu cFeb02; b/u by Turbine Aircraft Marketing, San Angelo Regional-Mathis Field, TX, USA; canx 16Mar07]
573	B-35	N242MA YV-T-ADD YV-04CP YV-1860P N3929L N203GA N260CB
574	B-35	N243MA N19GU [pres inst airframe Tennessee Technology Centre, nr Nashville-John C Tune Apt, TN, USA]
575	B-35	N244MA N7PW N254TP [wfu, parts to Global Aircraft Industries, Edmonton-Villeneuve, AB, Canada; canx 15Apr94; TT 5536 hours]
576	B-35	N245MA [pres TSTC Air Academy, Abilene, TX, USA; canx 20Oct93]
577	B-35	N246MA CF-BAN C-FBAN N81601 [b/u; canx 13Nov00]
578	B-35	N247MA N578EH N1MU [wfu Beaumont-Pt.Arthur, TX, USA; canx 02Dec02]
579	B-35	N248MA N441PS N441FS N500GL [w/o 19Apr81 Lajitas-International, TX, USA; canx cMar82]
580	B-35	N249MA N249ME N103BB N103Q CP-2390 N580AF
581	B-35	N285MA N100CW N161WC N93AH
582	B-35	N286MA N155BA N725MA [b/u cJun01 San Angelo Regional-Mathis Field, TX, USA; canx 13Jul01]
583	B-35	N287MA XB-NEB
584	B-35	N288MA N941S N9059Q N791MA N900YH [dbr 05Jan93 nr Nome, AK, USA; canx 24May93]
585	B-35	N289MA [wfu, parts to White Industries, Bates City, MO, USA; location S-08]
586	B-35	N290MA N21AU 9Q-CAZ OO-ENG N21AU N217SB [b/u cJun01; canx 11Jul01]
587	B-35F	N291MA EC-CQL N102BH N212BA N450MA
588	B-35	N292MA ZS-MUZ ZS-TCL 3D-ADF N292MA N32CK N37KK [wfu Pontiac-Oakland County International, MI, USA]
589	B-35	N293MA N155AS [b/u by Turbine Aircraft Marketing, San Angelo Regional-Mathis Field, TX, USA; canx 13Jun06]
590	B-35	N294MA N4HG N7RC N5PA N550K N54US N640MA
591	B-35	N295MA N99BT
592	B-35	N296MA [w/o 09Dec88 in Coral Sea 370 mls ENE from Cairns, QLD, Australia]
593	B-35	N297MA N100BW N297MA N311CE N400RX C-GJAV N400RX
594	B-35	N298MA [b/u cJun01; canx 20Aug01]
595	B-35	N299MA N11LG [b/u Conroe-Montgomery County, TX, USA; canx 28Feb94]
596	B-35	N300MA [w/o 08Feb76 Easton-Municipal, MD, USA; canx 14Jun76]
597	B-35	N301MA N1DC N5MW N5NW N33WD N33ND [dbr 23Jan79 Searcy-Municipal, AR, USA, fuselage remains to Aviation Warehouse, El Mirage, CA, USA; canx cJul92]
598	B-35	N303MA N14GD N28TD C-FMBL N15YS
599	B-35	N304MA N121BA N22XY
600	B-35	N307MA N343MA N100BT (N400BX) N880MA N707TT N113SD
601	B-35	N308MA CF-ROM C-FROM
602	B-35	N309MA [w/o 21Sep95 Smyrna, TN, USA; canx 13Dec96]
603	B-35	N335MA N3311G EC-EDK N4202K [wfu; canx 25Jul94; std Pontiac-Oakland County International, MI, USA; fuselage section to Flint-Bishop International, MI, USA cApr07]

MITSUBISHI MU-2

c/n	Series	Identities
604	B-35F	N336MA N300WT N5AP [b/u; canx 23Aug01]
605	B-35	N337MA XB-ARE N621TA
606	B-35	N338MA C-FOUR [wfu Saskatoon-John G.Diefenbaker, SK, Canada; canx 07Nov00]
607	B-35	N339MA D-IMME N339MA N98630 N339MA [dbr 12Feb88 Philadelphia-International, PA; b/u Augusta Regional/Bush Field, GA, USA; canx 03Mar94]
608	B-35	N340MA XA-DIS [w/o 20Dec83 El Paso, TX, USA]
609	B-35	N341MA N508W N808W [dbr 14Apr85 Patterson-Harry P Williams Memorial, LA, USA, parts to Conroe-Montgomery County, TX, USA; b/u c1990; canx 15Apr91]
610	B-35F	N342MA N92ST N601SD
611	B-35	N344MA N44MR (N8037J) N44MR [dbr 30Nov80 Port Aransas-Mustang Beach, TX, USA, parts to White Industries, Bates City, MO, USA; location S-12; canx cMar82]
612	B-35	N345MA N4TB N65JG N85JG VH-MUT VH-MUG VH-JEJ VH-UUJ N799MA N840MA
613	B-35	N346MA [w/o 14Feb80 Houston-Intercontinental, TX, USA; canx 02Jul80]
614	B-35	N348MA N123JA N128JA N2BQ N998CA N21JA
615	B-35	N349MA YV-T-ABH YV-176P YV-108CP N349MA N940MA
616	B-35	N466MA N80XY N881MA N456DR SE-IUB N110MA
617	B-35	N467MA EI-AWY (N467MA) N8484T [wfu c2004; b/u by Turbine Aircraft Marketing, San Angelo Regional-Mathis Field, TX, USA; canx 31Jul08]
618	B-35	N468MA 9T-MBA (Zaire AF) 9Q-CAA [wfu, parts to Dodson International Parts, Rantoul, KS, USA; listed in Dodson inventory as 9T-MBC]
619	B-35	N469MA XB-NUG
620	B-35	N470MA 9T-MBD (Zaire AF) [w/o date & location unkn]
621	B-35	N471MA ZS-MUZ SE-GHT N20WK HK-2120X HK-2120 HK-2120P
622	B-35	N472MA (N360MC) N616MC ZS-MGF 3D-AFH ZS-MGV ZS-MGF
623	B-35	N473MA N9LP N20TF N367DA (N234RC) N60GS N22YA N912NF N910NF
624	B-35	N474MA C-GLOW [w/o 06Dec81 Edmonton, AB, Canada; canx 27Dec82]
625	B-35	N475MA N95RM C-GSKM N625BF C-GSKM N22522 N770MA [wfu cFeb02; b/u by Turbine Aircraft Marketing, San Angelo Regional-Mathis Field, TX, USA; canx 16Feb07]
626	B-35	N476MA SE-GHY OY-ATZ EC-GLU N80JN [wfu Waterford, Ireland; being b/u for spares; canx 28Jun07]
627	B-35	N477MA N8TB N200EP N500EC ZS-MVK N34MG 5Y-BJX N770RW
628	B-35F	N478MA N69HS EC-EEE N4202M C-FROW
629	B-35	N479MA YV-O-CDA-2 YV-O-MRI-2YV-122CP N122CP ZS-NDM N629MU [wfu, parts to Global Aircraft Industries, Edmonton-Villeneuve, AB, Canada; TT 3465 hours]
630	B-35F	N480MA SE-FTF OY-BIS LN-MAU OY-BIS N630HA [dbr 02Nov03 Bonaire, Netherlands Antilles; b/u by Turbine Aircraft Marketing; canx 31Jul08]
631	B-35	N481MA N781SU N538MA N58BC N629TM (N628TM) N629TM
632	B-35	N482MA YV-T-ANH YV-34CP N995MA XB-AQQ
633	B-35F	N483MA N503AA (N56JS) N503AA [wfu cJan04; b/u by Turbine Aircraft Marketing, San Angelo Regional-Mathis Field, TX, USA; canx 12Sep06]
634	B-35	N484MA C-GODE N400SG [status?]
635	B-35	N485MA XA-DID N485AH OY-ARV LN-MTU OY-ARV EC-GOK
636	B-35	N486MA N20PS N636SW [wfu, parts to White Industries, Bates City, MO, USA; location S-06; canx 16Nov94]
637	B-35F	N487MA XB-RUE N951MA N951MS N637WG
638	B-35	N488MA N8LC N638MA [dbr 31Mar89 Syracuse-Hancock International, NY, USA; b/u & canx 14Jun94]
639	B-35	N489MA N550M N558M [b/u; canx 25Jul94]
640	B-35	N490MA
641	B-35	N491MA XA-DID N291MA XA-DID XB-LVE N114MA N211BE
642	B-35	N492MA N680CA [b/u Aiken-Municipal, SC, USA; canx 02Feb05; reinstated 30Nov07; canx 08Oct08]
643	B-35	N493MA N881DT N375CA
644	B-35	N494MA N494WC LV-WJY
645	B-35	N526MA YV-T-NDD YV-11CP N6569L [w/o 01Sep06 nr Argyle, FL, USA]
646	B-35	N527MA N113P N118P
647	B-35F	N528MA N44KS N44KU (N110SS) N44KU
648	B-35	N529MA N18WP [wfu & b/u c1984]
649	B-35	N530MA C-GODI [w/o 28May77 Portage La Prairie, MB, Canada]
650	B-35	N531MA N900M N990M PT-LFX [w/o 01Jul03 Belem-Vale de Cans, Para, Brazil]
651	B-35	N532MA N55KS N55KV N112SK [wfu, fuselage to Aviation Warehouse, El Mirage, CA, USA; canx 10Nov94]
652	B-35	N533MA N533DM [b/u by Turbine Aircraft Marketing, San Angelo Regional-Mathis Field, TX, USA; canx 12Sep06]
653	B-35	N534MA D-INKI N1024Y N350HE N45CE N129DW
654		[void - aircraft built as c/n 951]
655	B-35	N535MA N535WM
656	B-36	N536MA N77GA N77GF N666D N866D
657	B-36	N537MA N111MV N387MA N111MV N740PC N740PB
658	B-36F	N538MA N654L (N660CA) N741DM N741FN
659	B-36	N540MA ZS-JJK N878MA N5JE N6KF
660	B-36	N541MA N44PR N44RR TF-FHL N4065D
661SA	B-36A	N821MA
662	B-36	N822MA N444CC N444HP C-FFFG N5191B C-FFFG
663	B-36F	N823MA YV-46CP YV-409P N823MA [wfu cFeb02; b/u by Turbine Aircraft Marketing, San Angelo Regional-Mathis Field, TX, USA; canx 16Feb07]
664	B-36	N824MA N555BC N59KS
665	B-36	N825MA SX-AGQ N82MA [w/o 06Sep90 Nashville-International, TN, USA; canx 22Jan93]
666	B-36	N826MA N826RC SE-IVA EC-IJA N207BA
667	B-36F	N827MA N300CW N305CW [wfu Pontiac-Oakland County International, MI, USA]

MITSUBISHI MU-2

c/n	Series	Identities
668	B-36	N828MA N500RM N500PJ
669	B-36	N829MA YV-30CP N4262Z TF-JMC N710CA [wfu, parts to Global Aircraft Industries, Edmonton-Villeneuve, AB, Canada; canx 15Apr94; TT 5326 hours]
670	B-36	N830MA N18JB N181B N670L N742DM N742FN [w/o 18May92 Edwards AFB, CA, USA]
671	B-36	N831MA N17SA N31AT EC-EDE N4203C N950MA
672	B-36F	N832MA N777VM N709US C-FTWO (ZS-ONC) C-FTWO [w/o 20Dec05 Terrace, BC, Canada; canx 16Feb06]
673	B-36	N833MA D-ICVW D-IFAG OH-MIS N4565E N103RC [w/o 23Sep05 West Memphis-Municipal, AR, USA; canx 30Dec05]
674	B-36	N834MA N861E N299HT ZS-ONB
675	B-36F	N835MA N68TN [b/u Aiken-Municipal, SC, USA; canx 02Feb05; reinstated 04Dec07]
676	B-36	N836MA N90BC N999FA [dbr 20Jul96 Scottsdale, AZ, USA; b/u Dodson International Parts, Rantoul, KS, USA; canx 09Apr97]
677	B-36F	N837MA N2ND N915RF [b/u Aiken-Municipal, SC, USA; canx 31Jan05; reinstated 04Dec07]
678	B-36	N838MA HK-2403X HK-2403 HK-2403P HK-2403W N678BK [b/u c2005 Tulsa-International, OK, USA; canx 15May08]
679	B-36	N839MA N333KM N900EE C-FYBN N679BK
680	B-36F	N840MA N201U N201UV [w/o 25Mar04 nr Pittsfield, MA, USA; canx 05Nov08; parts to Anglin Aircraft Recovery Services, Clayton, DE, USA]
681	B-36	N841MA N841SC C-GJWM N361JA
682	B-36F	N842MA N78JS N13PR N13RR [wfu cJan04; b/u by Turbine Aircraft Marketing, San Angelo Regional-Mathis Field, TX, USA; canx 26Apr04]
683	B-36F	N843MA YV-102CP N843MA OY-CEF C-FIFE
684	B-36	N844MA N600TN HK-2245X HK-2245W HK-2245P [dbr & b/u c1988]
685	B-36	N845MA YV-O-BDA-3
686	B-36F	N846MA N23RA N717PS [wfu Pontiac-Oakland County International, MI, USA]
687	B-36	N847MA LV-PVB LV-LZT XB-ARF N687HB
688	B-36F	N848MA N848LM N800HT N848MA N1601A N688MA N688RA [wfu Pontiac-Oakland County International, MI, USA]
689	B-36	N849MA N78HF XA-LER N974MA VH-LMU N974MA C-FTAD N112MA
690	B-36	N850MA (N88DW) N850MA [w/o 09Jun84 Sugar Land Regional, TX, USA; canx 14Jun94]
691	B-36	N851MA N444PA [w/o 20Oct83 Patterson-Harry P Williams Memorial, LA, USA]
692	B-36	N852MA N623DC N869P
693SA	B-36A	N853MA N693FB N87WW "N693SA" F-GHDS N693PA [w/o 15Jan96 nr Malad City, ID, USA]
694	B-36	N854MA (C-FHZK) C-GBTV N800PC N13YS
695	B-36	N855MA YV-174CP [w/o 04Jun81 nr Caracas, Venezuela]
696	B-36	N856MA N301GM N425EW
697SA	B-36A	N857MA N7601L
698SA	B-36A	N858MA N263ND N187SB
699SA	B-36A	N859MA N32EC
700SA	B-60	N860MA
701SA	B-36	N861MA N902M N971MA N468DB F-GERA [w/o 16Apr88 nr St.Etienne, France]
702SA	B-36	N862MA YV-144CP
703SA	B-36A	N863MA N333GM N338CM
704SA	B-36	N864MA LV-PZT LV-MGC
705SA	B-36A	N865MA N24WC
706SA	B-36A	N866MA C-FJEL [wfu 07Nov08 Thunder Bay, ON, Canada; TT 17942 hrs; b/u]
707SA	B-36F	N867MA N15CN VH-NMU N707AF
708SA	B-36A	N868MA (D-IMMU) N51PC N15UD N868MA
709SA	B-36A	N869MA (N600RM) N4SR (N785MA) N869MA N105WM
710SA	B-36	N870MA N65FT N65HT N853MA I-MLST N710G [wfu cJul03; b/u by Turbine Aircraft Marketing, San Angelo Regional-Mathis Field, TX, USA; canx 31Jul08]
711SA	B-36A	N871MA D-IOTG N871MA N171CA PT-WST
712SA	B-36F	N873MA N603SS VH-SSL N80398 [b/u cApr95 Augusta Regional/Bush Field, GA, USA; canx 17May95]
713SA	B-36A	N874MA N89DR
714SA	B-36A	N876MA (OY-CKF) OY-NIR N994PE N222FA
715		[void - aircraft built as c/n 952]
716		[void - aircraft built as c/n 953]
717		[void - aircraft built as c/n 954]
718SA	B-36A	N889MA VH-ENH N715US C-GJSD N150BA OH-WBA OK-HLB N718EE
719SA	B-36A	N890MA (N104AL) OY-SUF LN-HAC N890MA N911JJ (C-GDGP) N911JE N777LP
720SA	B-36A	N891MA VH-MIT N3UN [b/u by Turbine Aircraft Marketing, San Angelo Regional-Mathis Field, TX, USA; canx 31Jul08]
721SA	B-36A	N892MA [b/u; canx 14Jun94]
722SA	B-36	N894MA N87AP N73MC N722BJ F-GFHB N722MU PT-WYT
723SA	B-36A	N895MA
724SA	B-36A	N896MA N79GB N711HK N44MM N44MX N300GM N223JB
725SA	B-36A	N897MA N8SR N888RH C-FKIO
726SA	B-36A	(N89809) N898MA N903BC N2CJ [w/o 28Jun91 nr Santa Barbara Municipal, CA, USA; canx 23Apr99]
727SA	B-36A	N899MA N702H YV-717P N21MU ZS-ONC 5Y-BSR N104DA (PR-UTH) PR-UTI
728SA	B-36A	N900MA N9NC (N9HN) N9NB
729SA	B-36AF	N904MA N25AP C-FHXZ N61BA
730SA	B-36A	N905MA N127BJ OB-M-1219 OB-1219 [w/o 10Jul91 Progreso, Peru]
731SA	B-60	N907MA N222JW N888RH N888PH N81FR N731CJ
732SA	B-60	N909MA N69PC (N30MA) N80HH
733SA	B-60	N910MA N7RC N533MA N142BK N15ET

MITSUBISHI MU-2

c/n	Series	Identities
734SA	B-60	N912MA N9SS N988S N271TW
735SA	B-60	N913MA N72B [w/o 24Mar83 nr Jeffersonville, GA, USA; canx cJun83]
736SA	B-60	N914MA N100KP N711PD N175CA (N175GC) N175CA
737SA	B-60	N915MA HB-LKV N315MA N888RH
738SA	B-60	N916MA N941S
739SA	B-60	N917MA N707EZ N8083A
740SA	B-60	N918MA XA-IUJ XA-RWP XB-EFU N360RA
741SA	B-60	N919MA VH-SMZ N31480 N193AA
742SA	B-60	N920MA LV-PBY LV-MOP [w/o 03May95 nr Bahia Blanca, Buenos Aires Province, Argentina]
743SA	B-60	N940MA XB-BHP XB-PRO [b/u c1995 by Turbine Aircraft Marketing, San Angelo Regional-Mathis Field, TX, USA]
744SA	B-60	N941MA
745SA	B-60F	N942MA (N755EC) N942ST
746SA	B-60	N943MA I-SNAS N943MA VH-MUA [w/o 26Jan90 nr Meekatharra, WA, Australia; canx 27Jan90]
747SA	B-60	N944MA N777ST N64MD [w/o 09Feb90 Rapid City Regional, SD, USA; canx 16Mar90]
748SA	B-60F	N945MA (N3MQ) (N305PC) N102BG N102BX [wfu cFeb09; canx 19Mar09]
749SA	B-60	N946MA N77GA N980MA PT-LIS
750SA	B-60	N947MA N130MS
751SA	B-60	N948MA N117H
752SA	B-60	N173MA N11WF N11WQ N37AL [wfu cSep03, parts to White Industries, Bates City, MO, USA; location "Ramp North B-15"; canx 29Apr09]
753SA	B-60F	N174MA N100BY N174MA
754SA	B-60	N175MA XA-JEA XB-FBY N46AK
755SA	B-60	N176MA OY-CGN SE-KGO N755AF [w/o 14May04 Baltimore/Washington-International, MD, USA; canx 03Feb05]
756SA	B-60	N179MA N179CM N179OM
757SA	B-60	N180MA XB-BLU XA-RRE N43866
758SA	B-60	N186MA N777FL N261MA
759SA	B-60	N188MA LV-PFD LV-ODZ N759AF
760SA	B-60	N190MA N999RC N321RC (N321SJ) N322TA
761SA	B-60	N191MA LV-PEM LV-OAN N94JK N678RH N316PR [w/o 25Jun06 Fort Pierce-St.Lucie County, FL, USA; canx 23May08]
762SA	B-60	N194MA N200NW OY-SUH (D-IHHG) N762JC
763SA	B-60	N195MA N95BD N95BE N26AP C-GEHS [wfu 30May03 Thunder Bay, ON, Canada; TT 9057 hrs; b/u; canx 11Sep03]
764SA	B-60	N196MA
765SA	B-60	N197MA N69PC N984MA N86SD [dbr 19Apr93 nr Dubuque, IA, USA, parts to Atlanta Air Salvage, Griffin-Spalding County, GA, USA; canx 14Jul94]
766SA	B-60	N199MA N6KE
767SA	B-60	N251MA HB-LLP [w/o 22Sep94 Urnasch, Switzerland; canx 21May96]
768SA	B-60	N253MA (N816RB) N31MG N36MF N331MA [wfu cNov04; b/u by Turbine Aircraft Marketing, San Angelo Regional-Mathis Field, TX, USA; canx 12Sep06]
769SA	B-60	N254MA N57MS I-IDMA [w/o 24Oct89 into Tyrrhenian Sea off Sardinia, Italy]
770SA	B-60	N255MA N378RM N74FB [w/o 11Sep92 nr Greenwood Municipal, IN, USA in mid-air collision with PA-32 N82419; canx 03May93]
771SA	B-60	N257MA N246NW N248NW N221MA [b/u by Turbine Aircraft Marketing, San Angelo Regional-Mathis Field, TX, USA; canx 12Sep06]
772SA	B-60	N258MA N17UC N17QC N318CD I-MLPT (N772SA) N772DA PR-FBI
773SA	B-60	N259MA N350RG
774SA	B-60	N260MA TU-TXW N2549C N10HV N15ZM PT-OHK
775SA	B-60	N261MA N93GN N70KC
776SA	B-60	N262MA N53AD [w/o 05Nov81 Saratoga-Shively Field, WY, USA; canx 06Sep89]
777SA	B-60	N263MA XA-KIB XB-DJX XA-RNL XB-RRG
778SA	B-60	N264MA N10HT
779SA	B-60	N266MA D-IJMZ N266MA D-IFTG F-GDHV [w/o 27May94 Papeete, Tahiti]
780SA	B-60	N267MA N77UP N16HA N321TP [b/u c1995 Ventura, CA, USA; canx 16May95]
781SA	B-60	N268MA N711MZ N7HM N7045X N60KC
782SA	B-60	N269MA VH-BBA [w/o 16Dec88 nr Perth, WA, Australia; canx 30Dec88]
783SA	B-60	N270MA N65FT N777PD C-FCLM N81604 C-FFSS
784SA	B-60	(N271MA) N3MP N952MA N9LP N12LP N785MA N50KW [w/o 19Jan96 Columbia Metropolitan, SC, USA; canx 17Dec03]
785SA	B-60	N273MA C-GAMC
786SA	B-60	N274MA [dbr 22Feb91 Tulsa International, OK, USA; b/u Dodson International Parts, Rantoul, KS, USA; canx 13Mar91]
787SA	B-60	N276MA N267PC N984RE
788SA	B-60F	N277MA N610CA
789SA	B-60F	N278MA N21CJ
790SA	B-60	N279MA F-GEQM N999WW
791SA	B-60	N280MA N111LG N888WW
792SA	B-60	N283MA N32WT N82WT OY-SVN F-GGLD N66LA N34AL
793SA	B-60	N284MA HB-LLG F-GDPH HZ-AMA N425EC
794SA	B-60	N285MA N54CE N794MA
795SA	B-60	N287MA N300CW [w/o 14Feb90 nr Putnam, TX, USA; canx 28Mar91]
796SA	B-60	N288MA N903M HZ- N4251F N700MA C-GGDC
797SA	B-60	N271MA [w/o 16Nov88 Chicago, IL, USA; canx 01Dec94]
798SA	B-60	N401MA VH-MIU N661DP
799SA	B-60	N403MA N44TU N928VF N5LN [w/o 04Nov98 nr Rock, KS, USA; canx 01May00]
801	C/LR1	22-001 (JGSDF) [w/o 10May71 in Japan]
802	C/LR1	22-002 (JGSDF) [w/o 14Jun77 Sigappu-to, Hokkaido Prefecture, Japan]

MITSUBISHI MU-2

c/n	Series	Identities
803	C/LR1	22-003 (JGSDF) [pres Tachikawa AFB, Tokyo Prefecture, Japan]
804	C/LR1	22-004 (JGSDF) [pres Mitsu Keki Collection, Awaji-Shi, Hyogo Prefecture, Japan]
805	C/LR1	22-005 (JGSDF) [wfu Sapporo, Hokkaido Prefecture, Japan]
806	C/LR1	22-006 (JGSDF) [wfu Utsunomiya AFB, Tochigi Prefecture, Japan]
807	C/LR1	22-007 (JGSDF)
808	C/LR1	22-008 (JGSDF) [pres Kasumi Nome AFB, Miyagi Prefecture, Japan]
809	C/LR1	22-009 (JGSDF) [pres Misawa Aviation & Science Museum, Aomori Prefecture, Japan]
810	C/LR1	22-010 (JGSDF) [wfu Kasumigaura, Ibaraki Prefecture, Japan]
811	C/LR1	22-011 (JGSDF) [w/o 10Aug81 nr Utsunomiya AB, Tochigi Prefecture, Japan]
812	C/LR1	22-012 (JGSDF) [w/o 07Feb90 nr Miyakojima, Okinawa Prefecture, Japan]
813	C/LR1	22-013 (JGSDF) [pres Kumamoto, Kumamoto Prefecture, Japan]
814	C/LR1	22-014 (JGSDF) [wfu Kasumigaura, Ibaraki Prefecture, Japan]
815	C/LR1	22-015 (JGSDF)
816	C/LR1	22-016 (JGSDF)
817	C/LR1	22-017 (JGSDF) [wfu Kasumigaura, Ibaraki Prefecture, Japan]
818	C/LR1	22-018 (JGSDF)
819	C/LR1	22-019 (JGSDF)
820	C/LR1	22-020 (JGSDF)
901	S/LR1	73-3201 (JASDF) [pres Cafe Hikohjyo, Lake Saharuko, nr Hamamatsu, Shizuoka Prefecture, Japan]
902	S/LR1	73-3202 (JASDF) [wfu location unkn]
903	S/LR1	83-3203 (JASDF) [wfu location unkn]
904	S/LR1	83-3204 (JASDF) [wfu location unkn]
905	S/LR1	93-3205 (JASDF) [w/o 11Apr73 in Japan]
906	S/LR1	93-3206 (JASDF) [wfu Nagoya Komaki AFB, Aichi Prefecture, Japan]
907	S/LR1	03-3207 (JASDF) [w/o 20Sep70 in Japan]
908	S/LR1	03-3208 (JASDF) [wfu Nagoya Komaki AFB, Aichi Prefecture, Japan]
909	S/LR1	13-3209 (JASDF) [pres Hamamatsu-Minami AFB, Shizuoka Prefecture, Japan]
910	S/LR1	13-3210 (JASDF) [wfu Nagoya Komaki AFB, Aichi Prefecture, Japan]
911	S/LR1	13-3211 (JASDF) [wfu Nagoya Komaki AFB, Aichi Prefecture, Japan]
912	S/LR1	13-3212 (JASDF)
913	S/LR1	23-3213 (JASDF)
914	S/LR1	23-3214 (JASDF)
915	S/LR1	33-3215 (JASDF)
916	S/LR1	33-3216 (JASDF)
917	S/LR1	33-3217 (JASDF)
918	S/LR1	43-3218 (JASDF)
919	S/LR1	53-3219 (JASDF) [w/o 19Oct94 into sea 40km SW of Hamamatsu-Minami AB, Shizuoka Prefecture, Japan]
920	S/LR1	63-3220 (JASDF)
921	S/LR1	63-3221 (JASDF)
922	S/LR1	73-3222 (JASDF)
923	S/LR1	83-3223 (JASDF)
924	S/LR1	83-3224 (JASDF)
925	S/LR1	93-3225 (JASDF)
926	S/LR1	23-3226 (JASDF)
927	S/LR1	33-3227 (JASDF)
928	S	63-3228 (JASDF) [pres Hamamatsu-Minami AFB, Shizuoka Prefecture, Japan]
929	S	73-3229 (JASDF) [w/o 14Apr05 Mikagura-dake Mountain nr Aga, Niigata Prefecture, Japan]
951	B-35	53-3271 (JASDF) [wfu Iruma, Saitama Prefecture, Japan]
952	B-35	73-3272 (JASDF) [wfu Iruma, Saitama Prefecture, Japan]
953	B-35	83-3273 (JASDF) [wfu Iruma, Saitama Prefecture, Japan]
954	B-35	93-3274 (JASDF) [wfu Iruma, Saitama Prefecture, Japan]
1501SA	B-60	N405MA N43DC PT-WNS
1502SA	B-60	N406MA VH-MVU N71DP
1503SA	B-60	N407MA [w/o 22Jan93 Beucherling, Germany]
1504SA	B-60	N410MA N541NC N1727S
1505SA	B-60	N411MA YV-438CP N342SC N15EW N101SN N901BF N999ET N321GM
1506SA	B-60	N412MA N81BR N45CF N450FA N15MV N160SP
1507SA	B-60	N413MA N612CC N976MA N888FS (N415HH) PH-BOA N308TC *PR-ILF
1508SA	B-60	N415MA N618RT PT-LHH
1509SA	B-60	N416MA N900M N973MA N973BB
1510SA	B-60	N417MA N17HG
1511SA	B-60	N418MA N27TJ N3MA
1512SA	B-60F	N422MA N25JB HB-LQB N60FL
1513SA	B-60	N423MA F-GDAR VH-ORE N275CA N513DC [w/o 05Mar86 nr Eola, IL, USA]
1514SA	B-60	N424MA N402JH YV-108CP N14VL
1515SA	B-60	N426MA N910DA N802SM LX-TWO (F-HASI) OH-STA LY-ZDV
1516SA	B-60	N428MA N4SB N4SY N89SC
1517SA	B-60	N429MA N429DT C-FNWC N727TP
1518SA	B-60	N430MA N430MC N678KM N303CA [dbr 05Mar92 nr Rifle-Garfield County Regional, CO, USA, parts to White Industries, Bates City, MO, USA; location Q-01; canx 05Jul94]
1519SA	B-60	N434MA N33TW N331W N33EW
1520SA	B-60	N436MA N411JE N777MJ N429WM N924PG
1521SA	B-60	N437MA C-FRWK
1522SA	B-60	N438MA N902M C-GFFH N78PK
1523SA	B-60	N439MA N65JG C-FHMA
1524SA	B-60	N440MA [dbr 27Jan83 Scottsdale, AZ, USA, parts to Aviation Warehouse, El Mirage, CA, USA; wears N282MA on one side]
1525SA	B-60	N442MA N35RR
1526SA	B-60	N443MA N44MM N44MX

MITSUBISHI MU-2

c/n	Series	Identities
1527SA	B-60	N445MA VH-MLU [w/o 23May83 2km E of Bargo, NSW, Australia; canx 24May83]
1528SA	B-60	N446MA HB-LMX F-GMJK OO-CVL D-IBBB N46TT 5Y-BIZ N60NB N466DC
1529SA	B-60	N448MA N818R N132BK
1530SA	B-60	N449MA N555FS N449MA PT-LSQ
1531SA	B-60	N450MA N125AB [b/u c1994 Augusta Regional/Bush Field, GA, USA; canx 14Jun94]
1532SA	B-60	N451MA F-WDHS F-GDHS [w/o 21May91 nr Troyes, France]
1533SA	B-60	N452MA [dbr 09Dec08 Millington-Jetport, TN, USA]
1534SA	B-60	N453MA HB-LQS N667AM N644EM
1535SA	B-60	N454MA [w/o 04Aug05 nr Denver-Centennial/Arapahoe County, CO, USA; canx 18Oct06; parts at Greeley, CO, USA]
1536SA	B-60	N457MA N178CA RP-C585 N157GA N544CB
1537SA	B-60	N459MA OY-BHY N152BK [dbr 11Feb00 nr Lewiston Nez-Perce County, ID, USA, parts to Dodson International Parts, Rantoul, KS, USA; canx 14Jul00]
1538SA	B-60	N463MA N75Z N538MC N538EA [w/o 10Dec04 Denver-Centennial/Arapahoe County, CO, USA; canx 01Dec07]
1539SA	B-60	N465MA N291GS ZS-MRJ N42AF N888YB
1540SA	B-60	N466MA [w/o 19Apr84 Burlington, CT, USA]
1541SA	B-60	N467MA N100TB N888TP [dbr 18Jan96 Allentown-Lehigh Valley International, PA, USA, parts to White Industries, Bates City, MO, USA; location "Ramp North 02"; canx 25Apr97]
1542SA	B-60	N468MA N88HL N4R
1543SA	B-60	N469MA TF-FHM N469MA
1544SA	B-60	N470MA N18T XA-OAC N850CA N222JM N223JS N202DT N215MH
1545SA	B-60	N471MA N900M
1546SA	B-60	N472MA PT-LIK
1547SA	B-60	N473MA [w/o 18Mar83 nr North Adams Harriman-and-West, MA, USA]
1548SA	B-60	N474MA PH-FWM N47RW N8RW
1549SA	B-60	N475MA N888SE
1550SA	B-60	N476MA N64WB C-GZNS
1551SA	B-60	N477MA N444WF
1552SA	B-60	N478MA N246W
1553SA	B-60	N479MA
1554SA	B-60	N480MA
1555SA	B-60	N481MA PH-DRX [w/o 12Sep88 Best, nr Eindhoven-Welschap, Netherlands; canx 11Oct88]
1556SA	B-60	N482MA N277JB N277JR N747SY N511AM
1557SA	B-60	N483MA N988RR N999UP
1558SA	B-60	N484MA N12WF N5PC N5PQ N157CA
1559SA	B-60	N485MA N10FR HB-LQN N880AC
1560SA	B-60	N486MA N513DM
1561SA	B-60	N487MA N64MD
1562SA	B-60	N488MA OY-BPE (F-GFDM) F-GFZM D-ICDG N1164F
1563SA	B-60	N494MA N781SU N10MX (D-IOMX) N7HN
1564SA	B-60	N496MA N5PC N95MJ [dbr 11Jan99 Egelsbach, Germany, parts to Turbine Aircraft Marketing, San Angelo Regional-Mathis Field, TX, USA]
1565SA	B-60	N497MA N100FT N530DP N100BY
1566SA	B-60	N498MA N4CS N64BA 5Y-SPR N468SP (N468SB) N54PE
1567SA	B-60	N499MA PT-LPB N467MA
1568SA	B-60	N501MA PT-LJS
1569SA	B-60	N502MA N222HH
1570SA	B-60	(N503MA) [aircraft incomplete at closure of production in 1986; parts assembled but aircraft never flew; sent to Cheyenne Aero Tech 1986 then moved to Westwood College of Aviation, Denver Broomfield-Jeffco, CO, USA in 1994; pres marked as N86CAT]
1571SA		(N504MA) [void - airframe not built]
1572SA		(N505MA) [void - airframe not built]
1573SA		(N506MA) [void - airframe not built]
1574SA		(N507MA) [void - airframe not built]
1575SA		(N508MA) [void - airframe not built]
1576SA		(N509MA) [void - airframe not built]

Production complete

PACIFIC AEROSPACE CORPORATION 750XL

c/n	Identities
101	ZK-XLA
102	ZK-FNZ
103	ZK-UAC [w/o 26Dec03 in Pacific Ocean 300 mls off the Californian coast on delivery routing Hilo, HI-Oakland, CA, USA]
104	ZK-TTL
105	ZK-JPV VH-XLS
106	ZK-JPP [w/o 21Sep08 Pont-en-Ogoz, nr Ecuvillens, Switzerland; canx 15Jul09]
107	ZK-KAY
108	ZK-JPH N750DZ
109	ZK-JQA N750XL
110	ZK-JQE VH-EAK
111	ZK-JQF N750SD
112	ZK-JPQ "N750XL" N750DV
113	ZK-JGI SE-LYZ
114	ZK-JNV N216PK
115	ZK-JGJ N750SS
116	ZK-JQP N820AB
117	ZK-JPU
118	ZK-JQK
119	ZK-JBC
120	ZK-JAY VH-XLC
121	ZK-JBD [airframe not built; parts used to complete c/n 128]
122	ZK-JAD ZK-XLG VH-NZJ
123	ZK-JQO ZS-BLU
124	ZK-JOA P2-SDB
125	ZK-LAQ ZS-POZ N143AU
126	ZK-JQR VH-ZVM
127	ZK-JQV ZS-MIZ
128	ZK-JQQ OK-SKW
129	ZK-JRB VH-DXQ
130	ZK-JNV ZK-SWA
131	ZK-JNH ZS-AIL
132	ZK-JRQ VH-EAJ
133	ZK-JNA ZS-BDZ
134	ZK-JQO P2-NCA
135	ZK-JNF T7-PAC
136	ZK-JQQ P2-BWC
137	ZK-JRR ZS-PHG
138	ZK-JRS ZS-SBW 5R-MKI
139	ZK-JDQ D-FGOJ
140	ZK-XLB
141	ZK-JFM
142	ZK-JSQ N750SN
143	ZK-JNG P2-TNT
144	ZK-JSE ZS-EPV
145	ZK-SDF
146	ZK-KDF ZS-GCO
147	ZK-JHA N750LH
148	ZK-JSU ZS-SHJ
149	ZK-KAH PK-RCD
150	ZK-KAJ N141DZ
151	ZK-XLE
152	ZK-JHM
153	ZK-JIF VH-YIF N902ST
154	ZK-JJH 9N-AIZ
155	ZK-JZI N155AV
156	ZK-JZL
157	ZK-KAK [dam 27Jul09 in Cambodia]
158	ZK-KAV
159	ZK-KAX
160	
161	
162	
163	
164	
165	
166	
167	
168	
169	
170	
171	
172	
173	
174	
175	
176	
177	
178	
179	
180	

PARTENAVIA P.68/OBSERVER

c/n	Series	Identities
01		I-TWIN
02		I-GAUS
03		I-VICT
04		I-SIGN [w/o 03May75 Vergiate, Italy]
05		HB-LGL [w/o 16Oct86 Mt.Bindino nr Cuneo, Italy; canx 05Nov86]
06		I-PARJ
07		I-SFCC [w/o 20Mar75 Gairo, Sardinia, Italy]
08		I-SEPA
09		4X-IPA 4X-CCV
10		OH-PVA EC-HYF D-GPLA
11		I-ETOS
12		I-LYFE
13	B	OH-PVB G-HPVC G-MOET F-WQHL F-OHCT F-GKBV
14	B	OY-DZR D-GBRD
15	OB	(G-BCDK) D-GERD G-SPOT [w/o 06Jul87 nr Vagar, Faroe Islands; canx 16Jan89]
16	B	I-VICC
17	B	I-ANCP
18	B	VH-FSH
19	B	G-BCFM I-VICV F-GDRY 3A-MOI I-GISG F-WVOX F-BVOX [w/o 11Jul82 Rouen-Boos, France; canx 25Aug82]
21	B	G-BCMB [wfu; CofA expired 01Sep77; canx 04Jul83]
22	B	OY-DJV
23	B	G-BCNT G-UNIT I-UNIT D-GNIT I-UNIT
24	B	SE-FTM G-BFBU
25	B	HB-LGO ZK-LGO D-GERP
26	B	D-GIUT OO-FKT 9Q-CKV
27	B	G-BCPO G-KIMK
28	B	(G-BCPP) I-VICZ ZS-JWA
29	B	P2-DNA VH-DNA P2-DNA P2-GTZ [wfu Cairns-International, QLD, Australia]
30	B	OO-TOF G-BFST OY-CEW [w/o 28Sep91 Lerchenborg Gods, Denmark; canx 10Jun92]
31	B	F-WVVC (F-BVVC) F-ODBZ CN-TBZ [dbf cOct76]
32	B	G-BCDK A6-ALN G-BCDK
33	B	P2-DNK VH-DNK VH-TLQ
34	B	HB-LHN D-GBRS
35	B	D-GITE HB-LOA
36	B	LN-MAD [w/o 05Mar78 in Norway; canx 31Mar80]
37	B	P2-DNC VH-PNC VH-DBF
38	B	N777EW 9Q-CMQ N777EW PH-PNA
39	B	SE-FUK G-BFVO F-OGVX
40	B	I-VICR I-SRAL
41	B	VH-FAO VH-LJR
42	B	VH-FAB ZK-PFT DQ-DNT
43	B	F-BXLI F-GTBY
44	B	OH-PVC OY-CEP HB-LPZ
45	B	VH-FAP
46	B	VH-FAX [w/o 02Jul78 into Bass Strait, off Five Mile Beach, Wilsons Promontory, VIC, Australia; canx 02Jul08]
47	B	D-GERT
48	B	OY-CAA ES-SPA
49	B	D-GERY
50	B	VH-PNN VH-CCR
51	B	VH-PNP
52	B	D-GILA
53	B	I-AVJA VH-FAZ
54	B	(VH-FHH) YV-870P N5379D N568B I-CDSY
55	B	(PH-PAG) D-GINI [w/o 13Feb87 Monchengladbach, West Germany; canx cJul93]
56	B	SE-GFN [w/o 20Apr87 Roenne, Bornholm Island, Denmark; canx 19Jan07]
57	B	LN-LMS D-GIFR (N4412H) G-RVRE
58	B	F-OGHF N? [wfu Montpellier, France; CofA expired 24Nov89; canx 06Jun07 to USA]
59	B	D-GINA
60	B	D-GINO [w/o 26May78 San Giorgio Scarampi, Italy; canx cNov79]
61	B	D-GIGI N590WA
62	B	(N712R) PH-EEO D-GATE OY-CEY G-PART F-GMPT G-PART
63	B	VH-PNQ VH-WZG
64	B	VH-PNR
65	B	VH-PNW [w/o 10Jul78 nr Melbourne-Essendon, VIC, Australia; canx 10Jul78]
66	B	VH-PNX
67	B	I-TIZY EC-IMD
68	B	G-BECJ ZK-DMA [w/o 20Jul01 North Shore Aerodrome, Auckland, North Island, New Zealand]
69	B	D-GIRO HB-LTS
70	B	VH-PNY ZK-LAL
71	B	VH-PNS
72	B	OY-CAB
73	B	VH-PNT
74	B	I-VICZ 5Y-BAO
75	B	(PH-EPB) PH-RVR F-GCCD
76	B	YV-1170P
77	B	VH-PNZ
78	B	VH-PFN [dbr 20Jan88 Norgate Mine, QLD, Australia; canx 09Nov88]
79	B	OY-PRW TF-GTM TF-JVI TF-VEB TF-ISA

c/n	Series	Identities
80	B	5Y-BAV ZS-LMJ VH-FSI
81	B	F-OACR TN-ADD
82	B	D-GATA
83	B	F-BXXC F-OGIN
84	B	VH-PNU
85	B	VH-PNV
86	B	G-BEJX A6-ALO ZK-PLA
87	B	I-IEAA
88	B	OO-TPN [w/o 18Oct82 Breendonk, Belgium]
89	B	F-OAEK TJ-AFJ TR-LAT [b/u; canx cJul88]
90	B	VH-PFO [wfu; canx 01Oct97]
91	B	VH-PFP
92	B	D-GITA
93	B	5Y-BBA [w/o 24Mar80 Guera, Aberdare Mountains, Kenya]
94	B	F-ODAQ TN-ADH [wfu Pointe Noire-Agotino Neto, Congo; CofA exp 17Aug87]
95	B	VH-PFQ [w/o 14Oct88 29 mls ENE of Taroom, QLD, Australia; canx 24Apr03]
96	B	VH-PFR
97	B	G-BEUT [w/o 22Jan79 Lydd, UK; canx 22Aug79]
98	B	PH-RVS
99	B	VH-PFS VH-ECO VH-ABX
100	B	I-RAIL VH-PFU VH-WZQ VH-NKI
101	B	D-GERA CS-AYB D-GERA G-SAMJ
102	B	OY-PRY [w/o 04Mar86 nr Malmo, Sweden; canx 17Aug88]
103	B	I-EEVA G-BMOI
104	B	D-GANE [w/o 27Oct78 nr Leer-Nuttermoor, West Germany; canx 31Oct78]
105	B	D-GISA [w/o 20Sep96 Schoenhagen, Germany; canx 29Oct96]
106	B	5Y-BBE VP-WMT Z-WMT ZS-OWL
107	B	5Y-BBF [wfu; canx 20May91]
108	B	D-GELI
109	B	SE-GUI G-OJOE G-JCTI G-JVMR TF-VEY
110	B	I-IEAB [w/o 22Aug82 nr Cisterna D'Asti, Italy]
111	B	G-BEXM [w/o 26Nov79 Kings Farm, Bulphan, Essex, UK; canx 07Jan80]
112	B	VH-IYJ VH-ZWJ
113	B	OY-AJH G-SVHA G-FJMS
114	B	VH-IYA ZK-NMK
115	B	G-BFBD G-ORVR
116	B	9Q-CBC 9Q-CTS [w/o 16Apr80 in Zaire]
117	B	D-GANA
118	B	VH-IYB
119	B	VH-IYC
120	B	N344EA 9Q-CEW 5H-ZAA 5H-TZO
121	B	G-BFET F-GATX LY-ATD
122	B	D-GERO OE-FGW
123	B	VH-IYD ZK-ERA ZK-MYF
124	B	VH-IYE SP-KWB
125	B	5Y-BBT
126	B	YV-1478P N53695
127	B	9Q-CDB [wfu Goma, Zaire]
128	B	VH-IYF
129	B	G-BFKP G-OPED ZK-ZSP
130	B	YV-1477P YV1762
131	B	5Y-BBY 9Q-CBL 9Q-CAD
132	B	VH-IYG VH-OAP
133	B	F-ODHU ET-A??
134	B	VH-IYH [dbr 05Feb82 Hall's Creek, NT, Australia; canx 05Feb82]
135	B	I-IEAC [wfu Forli-Luigi Ridolfi, Italy; CofA exp 16Apr83]
136	B	VH-IYI
137	B	D-GELA
138	B	VH-IYK [w/o 12Nov06 Rottnest Island, WA, Australia; canx 28Mar07]
139	B	5Y-BCB 6O-SBB [b/u; canx c1981; wreck noted Mogadishu-International, Somalia cFeb93]
140	B	VH-IYL
141	B	G-BFSU G-OROY G-ENCE
142	B	F-ODHV TU-TXQ TU-TLQ F-OPCL N? PZ-
143	B	VH-IYM
144	B	D-GENI [w/o 02Sep92 Schiffdorf-Laven, nr Luneburg, Germany; canx 03Nov92]
145	B	5Y-BCG 9Q-CTL
146	B	VH-IYN
147	B	G-PAUL EI-BKH G-BJOF G-CNIS OY-TLC
148	B	VH-IYO [w/o 23Dec80 7km W of Sydney-Bankstown, NSW, Australia; canx 28Dec80]
149	B	5Y-BCH VP-WLE Z-WLE 5Y-BCH 5H-AZY 5H-TZY
150	B	I-IEAD
151	B	I-IEAE N23MW
152	B	G-KWIK OO-WIK
153	B	5Y-BCI
154	B	VH-IXB VH-JQM
155	B	F-GBLY F-OGVN [dism St.Francois, Guadeloupe cMar95; fuselage later noted at Montpellier, France cMar00]
156	B	PH-RVT OO-RVT G-BMCB [w/o 20Oct90 nr East Midlands Apt, UK; canx 16Jul91]
157	B	YV-1471P YV1898
158	B	D-GFPI (N2084J) N146BK D-GFPI
159	B	G-BGBT G-OLMA

PARTENAVIA P.68

c/n	Series	Identities
160	B	YV-1538P N200VE EC-IVC
161	B	I-IEAF [dbr 25Mar94 Rome-Urbe, Italy; CofA exp 16May94; pres Bentivoglio scrapyard, Bufalotta, Rome, Italy]
162	B	5Y-BCT 9Q-CTO
163	B	(F-ODCX) F-BXCX TR-LZD 9Q-CEZ
164	B	VH-IXC
165	B	G-BGEM [dbf 27Dec90 Staverton, UK; canx 18Feb92]
166	B	D-GFPH [w/o 27Jun83 nr Biberach, West Germany in collision with French AF Mirage IIIR "342"; canx cJul83]
167	B	(N2349L) 5Y-BDK [wfu cJan91 Nairobi-Wilson, Kenya; CofA exp 25Sep87]
168	B	VH-IXD
169	B	G-BGFZ G-WICK F-GNHI
170	B	D-GFPG
171	B	N10485 9Q-CNV
172	B	I-KLUB G-BHJS
173	B	D-GERB
174	B	SE-GEU OY-BSE
175	B	(YV-1834P) D-GEMA
176	B	HB-LKS [w/o 09Feb86 Friedrichshafen, West Germany; canx 26Feb86]
177	B	9Q-CVB
178	B	VH-IXE
179	B	OY-CAC
180	B	D-GEKA PH-SPB OY-OCM
181	B	I-RTAA
182	B	G-BGMY G-OCAL G-LOUP [w/o 07Feb93 Bodmin, UK; canx 29Mar93]
183	B	I-GYAN (D-GEMB) I-AGAE
184	B	EC-DHE [w/o 03Oct81 off Guernsey, Channel Islands]
185	B	YV-1835P YV1323
186	B	VH-IXH [w/o 20Jul98, 7 km S of Wagga Wagga, NSW, Australia; canx 15Sep99]
187	B	PH-RVU N4432M
188	B	D-GEMB
189	B	G-BGXJ N321RT
190	B	F-GCJP
191	B	G-BHBZ
192	B	5Y-BDC [wfu, parts at Nairobi-Wilson, Kenya; CofA exp 13Apr98]
193	B	I-RRPG
194	B	SE-GXL OY-BJH G-HUBB
195	B	D-GITI [w/o 05May80 Glemm Valley, nr Saalbach-Hinterglemm, Austria; canx cJun80]
196	B	G-BHEE OY-CAF
197	B	OO-TPT 9Q-CEZ [w/o 29Nov83 into Zaire River, Zaire]
198	B	YV-920P N920AA
199	B	G-BHEF OY-CAE *LN-AAQ [dbr 08Aug98 Hesselo, Denmark; canx 02Jan01; allocated LN-AAQ for spares use; parts reportedly to Stockholm Bromma cSep09]
200	B	D-GEMC
201	B	TR-LYZ
202	B	OO-TNY 9Q-CFZ
203	B	YV-928P [w/o 28Nov04 Santa Lucia, Venezuela]
204	B	HB-LLV CN-TCD G-BNXN CS-AYQ EC-IFX
205	B	9Q-CAK
206	B	I-GJUL
207	B	9Q-CDV
208-01-TC	TC	I-VITC 9Q-CHV N775MW
209	C	I-MAKT 9Q-CZV
210	C	OO-HJA ZS-LAJ
211	C	D-GEMD OY-CDC
212	C	G-BHJP EI-BWH
213	C	I-VICD I-VCID OY-CFT N468C
214	B	N868C N868SC XB-GDY
215	B	CC-CHK [w/o 23Aug82 La Serena, 30km N of Coquimbo, Chile]
216	C	OO-HJC 9Q- [canx 13Mar81 as exported to Zaire]
217	C	OY-CAD G-DORE G-TELE I-CITT G-ONCM EC-JZJ
218	C	OO-EEC G-BJCR PH-SOK D-GEEK
219	C	G-BHJX G-NEWU G-SITU G-WTBC TF-ETP TF-VEL
220	C	VH-UUP
221	C	D-GEME N2200R (N13PK) EC-FPZ SE-LBZ OE-FFF
222-02-TC	TC	I-GRAD
223	C	G-BHOV G-OJCT C9-ATK ZS-PCU
224	C	I-VIPS HB-LNK [wfu; canx 13Dec83]
225	C	N4234L
226	C	I-KDUE HB-LPW OE-FIL
227	C	VH-UUG ZK-MIR
228	C	VH-AJX (ZK-FCS) VH-WZP VH-XLI
229	C	G-BIFZ EC-IOD
230	C	N9655B N73N (N73NL) N73N
231	C	G-BJRZ G-OAKP G-BJRZ S5-CER
232	C	N1352W [w/o 11Sep87 nr New Orleans-Lakefront, LA, USA; canx 09Apr91]
233	C	N13392 N68FP YV-2357P YV2278
234	C	I-IEAG [wfu cAug84 Naples-Capodichino, Italy]
235	C	VH-PCX
236-01-OB	OB	I-OBSR
237-03-TC	TC	D-GEMF

PARTENAVIA P.68

c/n	Series	Identities
238-04-TC	TC	OO-TZT 9Q-CTN
239-05-TC	TC	VH-TCU SP-KWA EC-ITV
240-06-TC	TC	9Q-CYK ZS-OXT
241-02-OB	OB	OO-HJB ZS-LAK T190 (Bophuthatswana Defence Force) ZS-MJZ C-GYNW N34269
242-07-TC	TC	YV-2085P YV1706
243-03-OB	OB	OY-CAG
244	C	OO-XJF 5N-ATE [w/o 16Jun01 in Nigeria]
245-08-TC	TC	OO-HJD VP-WLL Z-WLL OO-PXL
246-04-OB	OB	D-GEMG OY-SUR
247-09-TC	TC	D-GEMI
248-10-TC	TC	(EC-DOI) I-AGSD
249-05-OB	OB	VH-PGN
250-11-TC	TC	YV-2084P HP-008
251	C	N2670W [w/o 21Apr89 nr Antananarivo, Madagascar; canx 28Jun89]
252	C	OO-TJH 5N-AYC [w/o c1988 in Nigeria]
253	C	(OO-XJG) OO-TJG G-JAJV G-OLES PH-EMC F-GIEV
254-14-TC	TC	I-ATAT
255-13-TC	TC	(OO-HJE) OO-XJE "9Q-XJF" 9Q-CKT [believed to have been w/o c1983]
256-06-OB	OB	N2959B N850H N856H
257-15-TC	TC	D-GEML [w/o 16Dec85 Lake Geneva, Switzerland; canx 10Jan86]
258-16-TC	TC	D-GEMK I-GEMK
259-07-OB	OB	I-VIPV N49579 N321RB N9000V
260-17-TC	TC	N2959C
261-08-OB	OB	I-OBPC
262	C	N2959A N2KY V2-LDR [wreck noted cOct94 Antigua]
263-12-TC	TC	YV-2083P YV1999
264	C	N2956D HC-BTK [w/o 21Dec04 Puerto Villamil, Isla Isabela, Galapagos Islands]
265	C	N2957A YV-2424P YV1375
266	C	N29561 [w/o 11Sep83 Plainview-Hale County, TX, USA; canx 01Jan85]
267-18-TC	TC	N2958W D-GBGK
268	C	VH-PUZ
269	C	I-VIPT N4958K
270	C	(VH-PUE) N3832E [w/o 01May86 Goudeau, LA, USA; canx cOct87]
271	C	(VH-PUG) N3832G N483FW
272	C	N3832K
273	C	N3832P N681KW [w/o 07Nov08 nr Gainesville-Regional, LA, USA]
274	C	N3832Q C-GANW N3832Q
275	C	VH-NAV
276	C	N2855S N51N (N51NL) N51N
277-19-TC	TC	(OO-XJI) OO-TJI ZS-NJV T180 (Bophuthatswana Defence Force) ZS-MJX 7Q-YFZ
278	C	(PH-GRO) D-GOBY OY-BYS G-BMLR PH-GRO N12VK HA-ACD F-HUBG
279	C	D-GIMI OO-LSA N85VK SE-LYG F-GRYA
280	C	V2-LCM (F-OITC) N6244N
281	C	N3236Z N490NR (N10WL) N490NR
282	C	N3927U 5R-MKA N3927U
283	C	N39272 [w/o 19Aug88 into Atlantic Ocean nr Duncan Town, Bahamas]
284	C	OO-TJJ G-BUJC TF-VEN [w/o 30Jun95 nr Geitahlio, Iceland]
285	C	N39273 YV-2380P N3380P N944CC N344CC EC-KBN
286	C	I-RAIO VH-NAI
287	C	N39274 C9-ATO ZS-PCT
288-20-TC	TC	YV-2318P N60CH F-GEQD HB-LSB F-GROG N997JB C- [canx 25Jul07 as exported to Canada]
289-21-TC	TC	9Q-CKW
290	C	N4496M N714G TF-VEJ EC-IMV
291	C	N4496N YV-2418P N291CJ
292	C	N4496P N76L [w/o 25Apr85 Tilden, TX, USA; canx cJul92]
293	C	N39278 I-ELIM
294	C	N4496W N84N N75N (N75NT) N682KW
295	C	N44967 N300LE N300LF
296	C	N5389X HP-1099 [w/o date & location unkn; canx 11Jun90]
297	C	G-BKTD F-GEGT PH-DKI
298	C	VH-LCA
299	C	N5391C YV-2362C YV2005
300-22-TC	TC	I-TCFI N800AT *N383DF
301	C	N5386U CP-2031 N5386U HP-1115 HP-1115P [wfu; canx 16Dec96]
302	C	N5390X YV-804CP V2-LEG (F-OITB) N90UB
303-09-OB	OB	I-ATOP [canx, possibly to Mozambique]
304	C	N5387J CP-2172
305	C	N79N (N79NT) N79N
306	C	N5384Z YV-2274P N6307M I-VICW [wfu Maputo-Mavalane, Mozambique]
307	C	I-VIPX (G-BMTU) C9-MEG ZS-PBP
308	C	G-BMEI G-JVJA ZK-SMB
309		[no details known]
310-10-OB	OB	N4574C CP-(2029?) N4574C [w/o 30Apr06 Kaunakakai-Panda Apt, HI, USA]
311	C	YV-2370P
312	C	N3980B N75N N75NL
313-23-TC	TC	N4497D N766
314-11-OB	OB	N44955 N701 N4450F N708 N708L
315-24-TC	TC	N4497U XA- [canx 19Dec01 as exported to Mexico]
316-12-OB	OB	I-OBSV LN-LML N947MZ
317-25-TC	TC	N4497W

PARTENAVIA P.68

c/n	Series	Identities
318-13-OB	OB	N44956
319-14-OB	OB	N44959
320-26-TC	TC	N4465Y
321-15-OB	OB	N4496B N605
322-27-TC	TC	N44951 HL2004
323-16-OB	OB	N4496D C9-ASO ZS-LSX
324-17-OB	OB	EC-DTS
325-18-OB	OB	I-OBST N801AT N28FG
326-19-OB	OB	I-OBSU VH-OBS N6602L
327	C	G-VJCT ZK-FUZ ZK-KAP
328	C	N70MR
329-20-OB	OB	G-OBSV EC-GHS
330-28-TC	TC	N4682N [wfu; canx cSep84]
331-21-OB	OB	I-OBSW
332	C	N46809 CP-1930
333-22-OB	OB	PS-A94 (Italian Police) [w/o 05May86 Latina, Italy]
334-29-TC	TC	N46810 YV-391P N46810
335	C	I-GIFE
336-23-OB	OB	PS-A95 (Italian Police)
337-24-OB	OB	PS-A96 (Italian Police)
338-25-OB	OB	PS-A97 (Italian Police)
339-26-OB	OB	PS-A98 (Italian Police)
340-02-OTC	OB	N680TC N737 N340PN
341-35-TC	TC	I-FLOT N68PK I-FLOT [wfu; CofA exp 07Oct88]
342-30-TC	TC	D-GANS [w/o 10Feb91 nr Munich- Franz Josef Strauss, Germany; canx cMar91]
343-31-TC	TC	D-GOGO
344-01-OTC	OB	N344TC LN-NAC N246P N246PN HB-LTB N1010
345	C	N223MS N480NR
346-32-TC	TC	N32PV N32NR
347-33-TC	TC	N33PV [w/o 03Jun01 Uttoxeter, UK; canx 05Nov01]
348-34-TC	TC	I-VIPW [reportedly dbr 11Apr01; noted cApr07 Maputo-Mavalane, Mozambique]
349-35-TC	TC	[no details known]
350	C	I-DMPL
351-36-TC	TC	N68PK I-VIPY VH-HUU VH-SLS VH-APH
352-37-TC	TC	N9717N N88N
353	C	YV-2344P YV1303
354	C	PH-VDO [w/o 10Oct94 nr Serres, France]
355	C	N35MT YV-2310P
356	C	VH-ICM VH-ILM
357-38-TC	TC	N42821 N17RA TG-PAF N357PN
358-39-TC	TC	[no details known]
359-40-TC	TC	C9-ATB ZS-PBR
360-41-TC	TC	N360TC D-GAHI HB-LRK D-GITY
361	C	N243BK N14LP N14XT
362-42-TC	TC	D-GITY [w/o 13Mar95 Aschau, Germany; canx cApr95]
363-43-TC	TC	OY-CDG 5Y-BFR
364	C	YV-2222P YV2047
365	C	V2-LDC (F-OITA) N90KB [w/o 15Jan07 Adjuntas, PR]
366	C	G-NVIA G-JACT SE-LKI OY-LKI
367	C	D-GERI HA-ACQ OY-GCM
368	C	YV-2323P YV1980
369-27-OB	OB	C-GJMZ
370	C	C-GISY N80383
371-44-TC	TC	N9719L N17XL ZK-TCP
372-28-OB	OB	OO-TJK
373	C	TL-ABL N69HA
374-29/OB	C	[no details known]
375-45-TC	TC	N9719N
376	C	C-GJSH ZK-TZZ
377-30/OB	C	[no details known]
378-31-OB	OB	PS-A99 (Italian Police)
379-32-OB	OB	[no details known]
380-33-OB	OB	[no details known]
381-34-OB	OB	TS-POB
382-35-OB	OB	PS-B02 (Italian Police) [w/o 11May05 in Italy]
383-36-OB	OB	PS-B03 (Italian Police)
384-01-OB2	OB	I-RAIT I-ODUE N384VP
385-37-OB	OB	PS-B04 (Italian Police)
386-38-OB	OB	PS-B05 (Italian Police)
387	C	I-IEAH
388-39-OB	OB	PS-B06 (Italian Police)
389-02-OB2	OB	I-DOLF N8082Y TF-BMW
390-03-OB2	OB	I-PNCB N390AM N701
391	C	I-THAJ HS-DCH HS-TCE
392-46-TC	TC	OY-CDI 5Y-SRS
393-04-OB2	OB	I-SMTA N76TW
394-05-OB2	OB	N394AM N917J 5Y-GJW
395	C	I-THAK HS-TCL
396	C	5A-DSF
397-06-OB2	OB	5A-DSE 9H-AFF
398-07-OB2	OB	[to Taneja Aerospace and built as c/n OB-1A-001]

PARTENAVIA P.68

c/n	Series	Identities
399-49-TC	TC	D-GABS
400-04-OTC	OB	I-RAIL N737
401-08-OB2	OB	PS-B07 (Italian Police)
402	C	I-RAIZ N402VP F-GPEI
403-09-OB2	OB	PS-B08 (Italian Police)
404-10-OB2	OB	PS-B09 (Italian Police)
405-11-OB2	OB	PS-B10 (Italian Police)
406-12-OB2	OB	PS-B11 (Italian Police)
407-13-OB2	OB	I-STAD [wfu; CofA exp 20Dec07]
408-14-OB2	OB	PS-B12 (Italian Police)
409-15-OB2	OB	PS-B13 (Italian Police)
410-16-OB2	OB	PS-B14 (Italian Police)
411-17-OB2	OB	N68TP N26FG
412	C	(N412VR) EC-IFL
413-18-OB2	OB	N684FW C-FLIR
414	C	I-RAIZ ZK-TZY VH-CFT
415-05-OTC	OB	D-GYRO HB-LTQ
416-06-OTC	OB	D-GHAN 5X-UAF
417	C	ZK-MYO VH-VME
418	C	
419-19-OB2	OB	N419FW
420-20-OB2	OB	I-RAIT I-FINA
421-21-OB2	OB	EC-IPG [w/o 23Jun09 Sant Pere de Vilamajor, Spain]
422-22-OB2	OB	EC-IOQ
423-23-OB2	OB	I-SORV G-RIPA
424-24-OB2	OB	EC-IOP
425-25-OB2	OB	N19WL
426 JET	Jet	I-DJET [prototype with 227HP Turbo Diesel; ff 24Feb05; wfu & canx cSep08]
427-26-OB2	OB	I-ALTM
428-27-OB2	C	EC-JNH
429	C	I-TOPZ D-GVMD
430	R	VH-VRI
431	C	
432-28-OB2	OB	N78AG
433	C	YL-FBI
434	C	N68VR
435	C	VH-VMV
436	C	N68VA VT-JOY [w/o 08Sep07 nr Bangalore, India]
437	C	HB-LUA
438-30-OB2	OB	EC-KBS
439-31-OB2	OB	N87AG
440	C	N68VA
441-32-OB2	C	SE-MBE N821BA
442-07-OTC	OB	N68PV
443	C	VH-OLV
444-08-OTC	OB	EC-KQV
445	C	VH-CJJ
446-33-OB2	OB	N46VA *N37FG
447-09-OTC	OB	EC-KYY
448	C	VH-KBO
449	C	C6-BDF
450	C	N89LT
451-34-OB2	OB	*PP-JJM
452		
453		
454		
455		
456		
457		
458		
459		
460		
461		
462		
463		
464		
465		
466		
467		
468		
469		
470		
471		
472		
473		
474		
475		

PARTENAVIA P.68C (INDIAN PRODUCTION)

Licensed production built by Taneja Aerospace and Aviation Ltd (TAAL) at Hosur, nr Bangalore, India from 1994 onwards

c/n	Series	Identities	
OB-1A-001	OB2	VT-TAA	
1A-002		VT-TAB	ZS-OYN
C-1A-003	C	VT-TAC	
TC-1A-004	TF	VT-TAD	
C-1A-005	C	VT-TAE	
C-3006	C	VT-TAH	
C-3007	C	VT-TAI	
C-3008	OB2	VT-TLA	
C-3009	C	VT-TLB	
C-3010	C	VT-TLC	
C-3011	C	VT-TLD	
C-3012	C	VT-TLE	
C-3013	C	VT-TLF	
C-3014	C	VT-TLH	
C-3015	C		
C-3016	C		
C-3017	C		

PIAGGIO P.166

c/n	Series	Identities
341	A	I-RAIF I-PIAK I-NCAS [prototype; canx & b/u]
342	A	N7650E
354	A	G-APSJ (VH-SMF) VH-ACV [b/u cJun67 Melbourne-Essendon, VIC, Australia; parts used in rebuild of c/n 365; canx 25Nov66]
355	A	G-APVE VH-SMF [b/u, date & location unkn; canx 15Sep75]
356	A	(N7651E) N166Y
357	A	VH-PAP VH-PNC [canx 04Feb75; b/u cNov78; parts to Australian Aviation Museum, Sydney-Bankstown, NSW, Australia]
358	A	(N7652E) N7651E N7661Y
359	A	HB-LAY [wfu Zurich-Kloten, Switzerland; canx cJun80; b/u c1994]
360	A	D-IHAL VH-FSA [canx 30Oct77; pres Uralla Military Museum, NSW, Australia]
361	AL-1	I-MINP [CofA exp 26Mar69 - status?]
362	AL-1	G-APWY [pres Science Museum, Wroughton, UK; canx 20Oct00]
363	AL-1	D-IHAK [w/o 23Feb67 Piz Acletta GR, 5km NW of Disentis, Switzerland; canx 10Apr67]
364	AL-1	G-APXK 5N-ADQ I-PIAG [b/u c1974]
365	AL-1	G-APYP VH-MMP [pres Australia's Museum of Flight, Nowra, NSW, Australia; canx 07Aug02]
366	AL-1	VH-PAU [w/o 08Mar61 Kokoda Gap, Papua New Guinea; canx 01Jun61]
367	AL-1	D-IBID N777Y YV-272P N272P [wfu & canx 05Nov93]
368	AL-1	I-MINT [CofA exp 20Oct78 - status?]
369	AL-1	I-PIAK [CofA exp 06Jan74 - status?]
370	AL-1	VH-BHK "VH-PQA" [canx 22Dec77; pres Queensland Air Museum, Caloundra, QLD, Australia; displayed in false marks VH-PQA]
371	AL-1	I-RAIB I-RAIW I-RAID I-RAIF I-PIAP I-RAIE [CofA exp 18Jun75 - status?]
372	AL-1	I-FINS [status?]
373	AL-1	D-INLE VH-GOE [pres PNG War Museum, Port Moresby, Papua New Guinea; canx 24May76]
374	AL-1	D-INLG VH-PGA [b/u; canx 01Sep85]
375	AL-1	VH-CAC [dbf 15Sep82 Sydney-Bankstown, NSW, Australia; hit whilst parked by TB-10 VH-BXC; canx 15Sep82]
376	AL-1	G-ARUJ [CofA exp 26May71; wfu Yeadon, UK; canx 25Feb72 & b/u]
377	AL-1	VR-NDO 5N-ABE
378	AL-1	VH-GOA [canx 11Nov74; b/u]
379	ML-1	MM61871/36-74 (Italian AF) [wfu c1984; pres Rotondi, Italy]
380	ML-1	MM61872/SP-81 (Italian AF) [wfu c1984; was pres Museo del Volo, Comignago, Italy; presumed b/u after closure of museum]
381	ML-1	MM61873/SP-30 (Italian AF) [pres Latina, Italy]
382	ML-1	MM61874/RM-79 (Italian AF) [pres Museo Storico dell'Aeronautica Militare Italiano, Vigna di Valle, Italy]
383	ML-1	MM61875/303-28 (Italian AF) [wfu Bentivoglio scrapyard, Bufalotta, Rome, Italy]
384	ML-1	MM61876/303-32 (Italian AF) [pres Ditellandia Air Acqua Park, Castel Volturno, Italy]
385	ML-1	MM61877/SP-37 (Italian AF) [pres Ditellandia Air Acqua Park, Castel Volturno, Italy]
386	ML-1	MM61878/SP-35 (Italian AF) [pres Ditellandia Air Acqua Park, Castel Volturno, Italy]
387	ML-1	MM61879/36-75 (Italian AF) [pres Gioia del Colle, Italy]
388	ML-1	MM61880/SP-38 (Italian AF) [w/o 30Mar73 Masseria Mutata, Taranto, Italy]
389	ML-1	MM61881/SP-34 (Italian AF) [pres Ditellandia Air Acqua Park, Castel Volturno, Italy]
390	ML-1	MM61882 (Italian AF) [pres Gallarate, Italy]
391	ML-1	MM61883/36-76 (Italian AF) [wfu Gioia del Colle, Italy]
392	ML-1	MM61884 (Italian AF) [wfu Caserta, Italy]
393	ML-1	MM61885/303-33 (Italian AF) [wfu Rome-Guidonia, Italy]
394	ML-1	I-PIAU MM61886/53-76 (Italian AF) [wfu Cameri, Italy]
395	ML-1	MM61887/36-75 (Italian AF) [b/u after 1989 Rome-Guidonia, Italy]
396	ML-1	MM61888/RM-80 (Italian AF) [wfu Castello di Annone, Piedmont, Italy]
397	ML-1	MM61889/303-31 (Italian AF) [b/u after 1989 Rome-Guidonia, Italy]
398	ML-1	MM61890 (Italian AF) [pres inst airframe Forli, Italy]
399	ML-1	MM61891 (Italian AF) [wfu cNov82; derelict Cameri, Italy]
400	AL-1	VH-GOB [pres Australian Aviation Museum, Sydney-Bankstown, NSW, Australia; canx 20Jul81]
401	AL-1	VH-PAR VH-PND [wfu; canx 19Dec76; b/u cNov83 Sydney-Bankstown, NSW, Australia]
402	AL-1	D-INLF [w/o 15Jul62 nr Oberalpstock, West Germany; canx 19Jul62]
403	AL-1	VH-BBG VH-GOC [w/o 22Feb77 20km NNE of Marulan, NSW, Australia; canx 10May77]
404	ML-1	MM61902/303-36 (Italian AF) [pres Ditellandia Air Acqua Park, Castel Volturno, Italy]
405	ML-1	MM61903/SP-33 (Italian AF) [pres Gioia del Colle, Italy]
406	AL-1	9L-LAF G-AWWJ 5N-ADP [status?]
407	ML-1	MM61904/303-31 (Italian AF) [wfu Rome-Guidonia, Italy]
408	ML-1	MM61905 (Italian AF) [b/u after Sep96 Rome-Guidonia, Italy]
409	B	VH-ASA [b/u c1979 Sydney-Bankstown, NSW, Australia; fuselage to Historic Aircraft Restoration Society, Illawarra Regional Airport, Albion Park Rail, NSW Australia; canx 19Apr79]
410	B	VH-PQA ZK-DAI VH-PQA [wfu; canx 25Feb76; b/u Melbourne-Tullamarine, VIC, Australia]
411	CL-2	I-PIAS [wfu Milan-Bresso, Italy; CofA exp 09Jun89; canx 16Jan09]
412	B	G-ASPC [wfu 08May71 Luton, UK; canx 01Jun72; b/u cSep72]
413	B	SE-EDN D-INTC [wfu cSep73; canx 24Apr75; used as evacuation trainer, Cologne-Bonn Konrad Adenauer, Germany; marked as D-CGN2]
414	CL-2	VH-FSC [wfu Sydney-Bankstown, NSW, Australia; canx 27Sep76 - status?]
415	B	[void - airframe not built]
416	DL-3	G-AVSM I-PJAG [CofA exp 16Nov89; fuselage located at Genoa-Sestri, Italy]
417	S	881 (South African AF) ZU-DFI [pres South African AF Museum, Swartkop, Gauteng Province, South Africa]
418	ML-1	MM61906/53-72 (Italian AF) [pres Ditellandia Air Acqua Park, Castel Volturno, Italy]
419	ML-1	MM61907 (Italian AF) [stored Castello di Annone, Italy]
420	ML-1	MM61908/53-73 (Italian AF) [wfu Rome-Guidonia, Italy]

PIAGGIO P.166

c/n	Series	Identities		
421	ML-1	MM61909/303-28 (Italian AF) [b/u after 1994 Rome-Guidonia, Italy]		
422	ML-1	MM61910/4-4 (Italian AF)	[wfu Viterbo, Italy]	
423	ML-1	I-PIAA MM61911/SP-36 (Italian AF) [wfu San Possidonio, Italy]		
424	ML-APM	MM61912/VV-12 (Italian AF)	[pres Museo Memoriale della Liberta, Bologna, Italy]	
425	ML-APM	MM61913/303-37 (Italian AF)	[pres Parco Tematico - Museo dell'Aviazione, Rimini, Italy]	
426	ML-APM	MM61914/VV-14 (Italian AF)	[wfu Bologna, Italy (stored in a back garden)]	
427	ML-APM	MM61915 (Italian AF)	[b/u Rome-Guidonia, Italy]	
428	ML-APM	MM61916 (Italian AF)	[b/u Rome-Guidonia, Italy]	
429	ML-1	MM61917/SP-37 (Italian AF)		
430	ML-APM	MM61918/303-33 (Italian AF)	[wfu Rome-Guidonia, Italy]	
431	ML-1	MM61919/SP-40 (Italian AF)		
432	ML-1	MM61920/53-35 (Italian AF)	[wfu Rome-Guidonia, Italy]	
433	ML-APM	MM61921/36-66 (Italian AF)	[pres Scuola Sottufficiali, Caserta, Italy]	
434	ML-APM	MM61924/303-10 (Italian AF)	[pres Belricetto di Lugo, Italy]	
435	ML-1	MM61925/36-65 (Italian AF)	[pres Ca di Mari, Italy]	
436	ML-APM	MM61926/VV-26 (Italian AF)	[pres Ca di Mari, Italy]	
437	ML-APM	MM61927/53-34 (Italian AF)	[pres Cameri, Italy]	
438	ML-APM	MM61928/303-39 (Italian AF)	[wfu Rome-Guidonia, Italy]	
439	ML-APM	MM61929/VV-33 (Italian AF)	[pres Polytechnic University of Turin, Turin, Italy]	
440	ML-APM	MM61930/53-35 (Italian AF)	[wfu Rome-Guidonia, Italy]	
441	ML-1	MM61931/RR-05 (Italian AF)	[w/o 04Nov72 Rome-Guidonia, Italy]	
442	ML-APM	MM61932/36-66 (Italian AF)	[wfu Rome-Guidonia, Italy]	
443	ML-1	MM61933/53-34 (Italian AF)	[pres Museo Storico dell'Aeronautica Militare Italiano, Vigna di Valle, Italy]	
444	S	882 (South African AF)	ZU-ABU	ZS-FIN
445	S	883 (South African AF)	ZU-ADO	ZS-NJY
446	S	884 (South African AF)	ZS-NJX	
447	S	885 (South African AF)	ZU-ACI	
448	S	886 (South African AF)	ZS-NJW	
449	S	887 (South African AF)	ZU-ABV	[pres nr Port Elizabeth Apt, Eastern Cape Province, South Africa]
450	S	888 (South African AF)	ZU-ABU	ZS-NJV
451	S	889 (South African AF)	ZU-ABM	[fuselage std Wonderboom, Gauteng Province, South Africa]
452	S	890 (South African AF)	ZS-NJU	
453	S	891 (South African AF)	ZS-NJT	
454	S	892 (South African AF)	ZU-ADD	ZS-NJS
455	S	893 (South African AF)	ZS-NJR	[w/o 01Mar97 Pomona, Gauteng Province, South Africa]
456	S	894 (South African AF)	[w/o 06May76 Cape Town, Cape Province, South Africa]	
457	S	895 (South African AF)	ZS-NJP	
458	S	896 (South African AF)	[pres Ysterplaat, Western Cape Province, South Africa]	
459	S	897 (South African AF)	ZU-AGM	ZS-NKN
460	S	898 (South African AF)	ZU-ABO	ZS-NJZ
461	S	899 (South African AF)	ZU-ABL	ZS-NHR
462	S	900 (South African AF)	ZU-ABN	ZS-MMI
463	DL-2	YI-AHZ [status?]		
464	DL-2	YI-AIA [status?]		
465	DL-3/SEM1	I-PIAC (MM61922) MM25171/GF-01 (Guardia di Finanzia) [prototype P.166-DP1]		
466	DL-3/SEM1	I-PIAE (MM61923) MM25172/GF-02 (Guardia di Finanzia) CSX25172/GF-02 (Guardia di Finanzia) [prototype P.166-DP1]		
467	DL-3	60-SBI MM60210/CC-216 (Somali AF) [wfu & dumped Mogadishu, Somalia]		
468	DL-3	60-SBJ MM60211/CC-215 (Somali AF) [wfu & dumped Mogadishu, Somalia]		
469	DL-3	60-SBK MM60212/CC-214 (Somali AF) [status?]		
470	DL-3	60-SBL MM60213/CC-213 (Somali AF) [wfu & dumped Mogadishu, Somalia]		
471	DL-3	I-PIAQ [CofA exp 26Mar87; b/u]		
472	DL-3/APH	MM25153/303-20 (Italian AF)		
473	DL-3/APH	MM25154/303-21 (Italian AF)		
474	DL-3/APH	MM25155/303-22 (Italian AF)		
475	DL-3/APH	MM25156/303-23 (Italian AF)		
476	DL-3/APH	MM25157/303-24 (Italian AF)	[wfu Pratica Di Mare, Pomezia, Italy]	
477	DL-3/APH	MM25158/303-25 (Italian AF)		
478	DL-3/SEM1	MM25159/8-01 (Italian Coast Guard)		
479	DL-3/SEM1	MM25160/8-02 (Italian Coast Guard)		
480	DL-3/SEM1	MM25161/8-03 (Italian Coast Guard)		
481	DL-3/SEM1	MM25162/8-04 (Italian Coast Guard)		
482	DL-3/SEM1	MM25163/8-05 (Italian Coast Guard)		
483	DL-3/SEM1	MM25164/8-06 (Italian Coast Guard)		
484	DL-3/SEM1	MM25165/8-07 (Italian Coast Guard)		
485	DL-3/SEM1	MM25166/8-08 (Italian Coast Guard)		
486	DL-3/SEM1	MM25167/8-09 (Italian Coast Guard)		
487	DL-3/SEM1	MM25168/8-10 (Italian Coast Guard)		
488	DL-3/SEM1	MM25169/8-11 (Italian Coast Guard)		
489	DL-3/SEM1	MM25170/8-12 (Italian Coast Guard)		
490	DL-3/SEM2	MM25173/GF-03 (Guardia di Finanzia)		
491	DL-3/SEM2	MM25174/GF-04 (Guardia di Finanzia)		
492	DL-3/SEM2	MM25175/GF-05 (Guardia di Finanzia)		
493	DL-3/SEM2	MM25176/GF-06 (Guardia di Finanzia)		
494	DL-3/SEM2	MM25177/GF-07 (Guardia di Finanzia)		
495	DL-3/SEM2	MM25178/GF-08 (Guardia di Finanzia)		
496	DL-3/SEM2	MM25179/GF-09 (Guardia di Finanzia)		

PIAGGIO P.166/P.180

c/n	Series	Identities	
601	DL-3/SEM2	MM25180/GF-10 (Guardia di Finanzia)	[originally built as c/n 497]
602	DL-3/SEM2	MM25181/GF-11 (Guardia di Finanzia)	[originally built as c/n 498]
603	DL-3/SEM2	MM25182/GF-12 (Guardia di Finanzia)	[originally built as c/n 499]

Production complete

PIAGGIO P.180 AVANTI/AVANTI II

c/n	Series	Identities
1001		I-PJAV [CofA exp 07Dec90; restored 03May01; used as flying test platform for P.180 Avanti II]
1002		I-PJAR [CofA exp 03Jun95; restored; used as flying test platform for P.180 Avanti II]
1003		[static test airframe]
1004		I-RAIH N180BP
1005		[fatigue test airframe]
1006		I-RAIH I-PJAS N180PT N34S N111VR
1007		I-RAII C-FNGA
1008		I-RAIP EC-619 EC-FKL LZ-VPC LZ-PIA N94LY N1LY N109MS
1009		I-RAIH D-IHMO C-GLEM
1010		I-ALPV N23SV N589H
1011		N180AB N53MW D-IHOT VP-CRS N130AV N301SL N128SL N8GF
1012		N180TE (D-IMED) D-ITPV N180TE N27KG N500GC N416LF
1013		N180AZ I-PJAP I-FXRA N128PA N155SL
1014		I-ACTC D-IKAI I-ACTC N705PA N330DM N152SL
1015		I-RAIJ I-ALPN N180SH N181BG N990RS
1016		I-PJAT D-IGOB
1017		N180TP N180AV N14P D-IJCL N17PA
1018		LZ-VPA N220TW N180AV
1019		D-IHRA N121WH N40CR N677P
1020		(D-ISAP) F-GNAE (PH-TCN) D-ITCN N113SL
1021		D-IPIA N925TK
1022		I-RAIH F-GMCP N501PM
1023		MM62159 (Italian AF)
1024		(F-GMCP) MM62160 (Italian AF)
1025		MM62161 (Italian AF)
1026		(D-IMED) MM62167 (Italian Army)
1027		(F-GMRM) MM62168 (Italian Army)
1028		MM62162 (Italian AF)
1029		MM62163 (Italian AF)
1030		MM62164 (Italian AF) CSX62164 (Italian AF) MM62164 (Italian AF)
1031		MM62169 (Italian AF)
1032		(D-IMLP) I-DPCR
1033		I-DPCS *D-IPCI
1034		I-RAIH (N180RP) N680JP D-IZZY
1035		I-FXRB
1036		SX-BNC N126PA N785JH
1037		(F-GUAE) VP-BBG (N180UJ) C-GJMM
1038		SX-BND N122PA *N196SL
1039		N120PA N39GK
1040		I-BCOM
1041		MM62199 (Italian AF)
1042		HB-LTE D-IXIE
1043		N122PA N180HM
1044		N128PA N395KT (N503RV) N395KT
1045		I-FXRC
1046		N124PA N29JS
1047		MM62200 (Italian AF)
1048		N133PA N74BJ N629GT N105GP
1049		I-FXRE
1050		(D-IJET) N134PA N50WG
1051		N129PA N61GT
1052		N925GS N139PA N102SL
1053		MM62201 (Italian AF)
1054		N137PA N701GT N153SL
1055		N136PA N925GS C-FSTP
1056		D-IJET
1057		N126PA N333BH C-GBCI C-GPDJ N401WS
1058		MM62202 (Italian AF)
1059		N128PA N103SL
1060		I-FXRF F-HALE OY-TLP
1061		N129PA C-GWRK
1062		N133PA
1063		N137PA C-FFST N130EM
1064		F-GZPE
1065		N126PA C-GFOX
1066		HB-LTN
1067		I-FXRD
1068		N105SL

PIAGGIO P.180

c/n	Series	Identities		
1069		N143PA N320CA C-GJOL		
1070		N106SL		
1071		I-RAII MM62203 (Italian AF)		
1072		N157PA C-GPIA		
1073		N107SL		
1074		N72EE C-GWII N174WA		
1075		MM62205 (Italian AF)		
1076		MM62212/9-01 (Italian Navy)		
1077		N205PA N304SL N149SL		
1078		VF-181 (Italian Government)		
1079		SP-MXH		
1080		G-OESL N23RF		
1081		I-BPAE		
1082		MM62204 (Italian Navy)	MM62204 (Italian AF)	
1083		N305SL N147SL		
1084		N306SL N130SL		
1085		CSX62211 (Italian Navy)	MM62211/9-02 (Italian Navy)	
1086		I-BPAF YV1676 G-CFDW	N108GF	
1087		MM62206 (Italian AF)		
1088		N205PA XA-ANS		
1089		PH-TCN		
1090		CSX62213 (Italian Navy)	MM62213/9-03 (Italian Navy)	
1091		N307SL N146SL		
1092		N136PA N109SL		
1093		N308SL N145SL		
1094		CFS-181/I-CFPA (Italian Government)		
1095		N143PA C-GKWQ		
1096		MM62207 (Italian AF)		
1097		N131SL		
1098		N132SL		
1099		N8870B		
1100		N134SL		
1101		N136SL		
1102		N137SL		
1103		N138SL		
1104		N139SL		
1105	II	I-RAIL HB-LTZ		
1106	II	N780CA		
1107	II	N140SL		
1108	II	N108SL		
1109	II	N143SL		
1110		F-HBAI		
1111		N150SL		
1112		F-HALF I-FXRG		
1113		CSX62247 (Italian Government)		MM62247/PS-B15 (Italian Government)
1114		CSX62246 (Italian Government)		MM62246/CC-112 (Italian Government)
1115		N156SL		
1116		N157SL		
1117		N7PS N179S C-GCOM		
1118		MM62248/GF-18 (Italian Government)		
1119	II	N158SL		
1120		PH-HRK		
1121	II	N159SL		
1122	II	N124PA		
1123		F-GPKN		
1124		SP-MXI		
1125		D-IIVA		
1126	II	CSX62249 (Italian Government)		MM62249/GF-19 (Italian Government)
1127	II	N160SL		
1128	II	N161SL		
1129	II	N5166P		
1130	II	N162SL		
1131	II	N163SL		
1132	II	F-GPKO		
1133	II	N139PA C-GPII		
1134	II	N164SL		
1135	II	N165SL		
1136	II	N167SL		
1137	II	N408SF		
1138	II	I-PREE		
1139	II	N168SL		
1140	II	N169SL		
1141	II	N172SL		
1142	II	VF-182 (Italian Government)		
1143	II	I-DPCL		
1144	II	F-HCPE		
1145	II	N145GS		
1146	II	N173SL		
1147	II	N175SL		
1148	II	N611GT		
1149	II	N24XJ		

PIAGGIO P.180

c/n	Series	Identities		
1150	II	N176SL		
1151	II	N178SL		
1152	II	N179SL	N989BJ	
1153	II	HB-LUR		
1154	II	N161PA	N369LC	
1155	II	N183SL	N80TC	
1156	II	D-IPIA		
1157	II	XB-KSW		
1158	II	N184SL	N327A	
1159	II	I-PDVO	I-FEMA	
1160	II	N134EC		
1161	II	N144PA	VT-RNB	
1162	II	D-INKY		
1163	II	I-DPCB		
1164	II	N187SL		
1165	II	I-PDVO	F-GPKP	
1166	II	I-PDVS	VP-CYA	
1167	II	N90DE		
1168	II	I-DDFG		
1169	II	N7JW		
1170	II	N179SL		
1171	II	(PH-DLN)	I-PDVO	N183SL
1172	II	N184SL	I-PDVP	D-IPPY
1173	II	I-PDVS	N143PA	N327YR
1174	II	I-PDVR	N188SL	
1175	II	I-PDVP	PH-DLN	
1176	II	LX-JFP		
1177	II	I-FXRH		
1178	II	I-PDVR	I-FXRJ	
1179	II	N806J		
1180	II	I-PDVR	I-AVBN	
1181	II	N189SL		
1182	II	N146PA	N228BE	
1183	II	N154PA	VT-TET	
1184	II	I-DARC		
1185	II	I-PDVP	VP-CYC	
1186	II	(LZ-ASP)	F-GPKS	
1187	II	N184SL		
1188	II	I-TIAF		
1189	II	I-PDVO	I-FXRI	
1190	II	N166PA	N166PB	
1191	II	N405KT	N7PA	
1192	II	N146PA	PK-VVX	
1193	II	S2-AEV		
1194	II	N191SL		
1195	II			
1196	II			
1197	II			
1198	II	N166PA		
1199	II	N192SL		
1200	II			
1201	II			
1202	II			
1203	II			
1204	II			
1205	II			
1206	II			
1207	II			
1208	II			
1209	II			
1210	II			
1211	II			
1212	II			
1213	II			
1214	II			
1215	II			
1216	II			
1217	II			
1218	II			
1219	II			
1220	II			
1221	II			
1222	II			
1223	II			
1224	II			
1225	II			
1226	II			
1227	II			
1228	II			
1229	II			
1230	II			

PIAGGIO P.180

c/n	Series	Identities
1231	II	
1232	II	
1233	II	
1234	II	
1235	II	
1236	II	
1237	II	
1238	II	
1239	II	
1240	II	
1241	II	
1242	II	
1243	II	
1244	II	
1245	II	
1246	II	
1247	II	
1248	II	
1249	II	
1250	II	
1251	II	
1252	II	
1253	II	
1254	II	
1255	II	
1256	II	
1257	II	
1258	II	
1259	II	
1260	II	
1261	II	
1262	II	
1263	II	
1264	II	
1265	II	
1266	II	
1267	II	
1268	II	
1269	II	
1270	II	
1271	II	
1272	II	
1273	II	
1274	II	
1275	II	
1276	II	
1277	II	
1278	II	
1279	II	
1280	II	
1281	II	
1282	II	
1283	II	
1284	II	
1285	II	
1286	II	
1287	II	
1288	II	
1289	II	
1290	II	
1291	II	
1292	II	
1293	II	
1294	II	
1295	II	
1296	II	
1297	II	
1298	II	
1299	II	
1300	II	

PILATUS PC-6 PORTER/TURBO PORTER

As with all other types within this book, monthly updates are available in the Biz-Props section of Air-Britain News. Recommended additional reading can be found on the web at www.pc-6.com which is an excellent site by Markus Herzig, dedicated to this ubiquitous aircraft.

c/n	Series	Identities
337		HB-FAN [dbr 05May60 Dambuschpass, Nepal making the world record of the highest landing of a fixed-wing aircraft at over 5200m; canx 16May60]
338	H2	HB-FAO [w/o 25Aug75 in Nepal]
339		HB-FAP [wfu c1967 & b/u; canx 06Mar67]
340		HB-FAR ST-AFR N340N F-GODZ [wfu cAug89 in Sudan; parts to Malta then the USA; to Icarus Aerotechnics, Gap Tallard, Hautes Alpes, France cJul98 and cvtd to PC6/B2-H2]
341	275	HB-FAS OH-POA LN-BEP N4795P
342	H2	HB-FAT F-BIII [w/o 07Oct72 Angouleme, France]
343		HB-FAZ [w/o 02Sep61 Col du Dome du Gouter, nr Mont Blanc, France]
344		HB-FAX [w/o 08Feb67 in Nepal; canx 29Aug68]
345	B2-H2	HB-FAV F-BIEL [w/o 07Feb86 Plateau des Glieres de Roussillon, France; canx 11Jan96]
346		HB-FAU 9N-AAF [w/o 26Aug62 Barse Dhuri, Nepal]
347		HB-FAW 9N-AAG [w/o 09Mar61 Giri, Nepal]
348		D-ENLI [w/o 13Oct62 Hessisch-Lichtenau, nr Kassel, West Germany; canx 18Oct62]
349		HB-FAY FAC160 (Colombian AF) HK-1375X HK-1375P HK-1375E HK-1375P [canx 09Oct00 - status?]
350		HB-FAI UN-1 (United Nations)[may have been registered 9N-AAN cMay69; fate unkn]
513	A-H2	D-EDTF OE-DEM D-EDTF HB-FCG F-BOJJ [w/o 14Aug82 Royan-Medis, France; canx 22Aug94]
514	C-H2	HB-FAE N12450 ST-AHD [wfu Khartoum, Sudan; possibly b/u]
515	A	HB-FAD F-BFAD [prototype PC-6/A; canx 04Dec95]
516	B1-H2	HB-FAF D-ELAV HB-FAF [w/o 03Oct82 Triengen, Switzerland; canx 21Jan83]
517	B2-H2	D-ENLJ HB-FCI XW-PDG N62150 0517 (Royal Thai Army) N617SA F-GOYE
518	B2-H2	PH-OTB N6251U F-GMVS
519	A/C-H2	D-ENLK HB-FBV N391R [w/o 24Apr72 Nyot Mo, Laos]
520		HB-FAH F-OBZJ [canx 26May71; fate unkn]
521	C1-H2	HB-FBD N9444 ST-AGX N9444
522	H2	N1409Z N10058 [b/u after 1990]
523	B1-H2	HB-FBA XW-PCI N62158 0523 (Royal Thai Army) N523SA ZK-PCI
524	B2-H2	F-BKRR OO-POF HB-FHL F-GPRO
525	A-H2	F-BJSZ [w/o 09Oct74 Belleville, France; canx 13May77]
526		HB-FAK N4226G [w/o cDec62 in Laos]
527	350	HB-FAG 5N-ADG ET-ACK [b/u c1992 in Ethiopia]
528		HB-FBE JA3196 [wfu 21Apr71]
529	A	HB-FBB 02/4X-SVV (Israeli DF/AF) [reportedly b/u]
530	C-H2	V-611 (Swiss AF) N392R [w/o 30Oct73 Lam Son, South Vietnam; canx 23Apr74]
531	B1-H2	HB-FBC I-ONDI HB-FFR F-BTCH [w/o 27Sep89 La Ferte-Gaucher, France; canx 15May95]
532		N4227G [w/o cJan63 in Laos]
533		F-OCBD [w/o cJan64 location unkn]
534	B2-H2	F-BKQU
535	A-H2	N1417Z [dbr 12Jul64 Ruby Creek, AK, USA]
536	B2-H2	N4915 F-GMEL
537		HB-FBF I-CONA [w/o 25Apr66 nr Ceva, Italy]
538	H2	HB-FBS PK-NPY [w/o 08Mar66 Genjem, Indonesia]
539	C-H2	HB-FBK N748N [abandoned 29Apr75 Saigon-Tan Son Nhat, South Vietnam]
540	H2	HB-FAL CF-RZZ N17077 CF-BGL C-FBGL N283SW
541	H2	HB-FAM G-ASTO HB-FAM 7T-VBV 7T-VSV [fate unkn]
542	H2	HB-FBR PK-NPX [w/o 31Jan67 Ureb, Indonesia]
543	B2-H2	N4911 F-GOME
544	350	N4912 [w/o 01Oct79 nr Sparrevohn, AK, USA]
545	350	N4913 [w/o 29Jul91 Yakutat, AK, USA, parts to Styles Aviation, Lagrangeville, NY, USA]
546	350	N4914 N3914 [dbf c1975]
547	B-H2	HB-FBU XW-PDC [w/o after 1966 in SE Asia]
548	A-H2	F-BKRQ [w/o 11May80 location unkn; canx 04Dec95]
549	B2-H2	F-BKQY [dbr 09Apr90 in France; reportedly b/u]
550	C-H2	N180K [w/o 29Apr71 nr Muang Kham, Laos in mid-air collision with Cessna U-17A 65-10853]
551	B2-H2	I-SORE F-BTCG (HB-FIR) F-BTCG
552	A-H2	I-ALBO F-BRPJ [w/o 15Dec75 Cluny, France; canx 22Apr76]
553	A	HB-FBG XW-PBI [w/o after Sep65 exact date & location unkn]
554	C-H2	HB-FBH XW-PBQ N152L [w/o 08Apr72 nr Ban Xieng, Laos]
555	A	HB-FBI B-1410 HL5102 [wfu Hankuk Aviation University, South Korea]
556	A-H2	HB-FBL XW-PBL N12235 [dbf 21Dec67 Can Tho, South Vietnam]
557	B2-H2	N184L ST-AGR N184L F-GUAS [dbr 26Jun01; std Challes-les-Eaux, France]
558	H2	JA3201 N62403 C-GHPP [canx 27Jul89; parts used to rebuild c/n 634]
559	H2	JA3202 [wfu 11Mar74; fuselage std at unkn location in Japan]
560	H2	HB-FBP PK-NPZ [w/o 03Oct67 Sentani, Indonesia]
561	B2-H2	N1421Z F-GOMO D-FJMO
562	A-H2	N1422Z [b/u; date & location unkn]
563	C-H2	N185K [abandoned 29Apr75 Saigon-Tan Son Nhat, South Vietnam; canx 19Apr79]
564	B-H2	N187H N777XX N17XX F-GIXX
565	C-H2	HB-FBN N285L ST-AHE N285L [w/o 16Jul91 Ottawa, ON, Canada]
566	A-H2	HB-FBM N185X [w/o 12Jan67 nr Chu Lai, South Vietnam]
567	C-H2	HB-FBO XW-PCB [w/o 21Mar71 Tha Tam Bleung, Laos]
568	A-H1	HB-FBT XW-PCC [w/o date & location unkn]
569	B2-H4	N2851T C-GAAP
570	C-H2	90 (Swedish AF) N9445 [w/o 20Jan72 Ban Tha Si, Laos]

PILATUS PC-6

c/n	Series	Identities
571	A-H2	HB-FBX XW-PCE [w/o 12Feb69 in Laos]
572	B2-H2	N2852T C-GWZO F-GFCC
573	A-H2	I-ROCE I-MIDI F-BTCE [w/o 24Apr88 Loos en Gohelle, France; canx 15May95]
574	B-H2	N2853T [w/o 12Aug69 Chevak, AK, USA]
575	B-H2	N2854T [w/o 08Nov72 Anchorage, AK, USA]
576	C-H2	HB-FBY XW-PCH N153L [abandoned 29Apr75 Saigon-Tan Son Nhat, South Vietnam; canx 17Jul75]
577	H2	PK-NPU [b/u c1979]
578	H2	PK-NPV [b/u c1979]
579	H2	PK-NPW [b/u c1979]
580	B-H2	HB-FBW VH-PNF [w/o 14Dec65 Terapo Mission, Papua New Guinea; canx 14Dec65]
581	B1-H2	N13200 XW-PFB HS-CHE HS-SKE HS-TFD F-GIHM
582	B-H2	N13201 N80XY [w/o 02Jul71 location unkn (possibly in Libya)]
583	B2-H2	N13202 (N1302R) XW-PCL [w/o before Jul71; location unkn]
584	B2-H2	HB-FBZ VH-PNG P2-PNG P2-PNO P2-SEA HB-FBZ F-GIDS
585	B1-H2	HB-FCD LN-VID [dbr 17Dec67 Hamar, Norway]
586	C-H2	N192X [abandoned 29Apr75 Saigon-Tan Son Nhat, South Vietnam; canx 17Apr79]
587	C-H2	N193X [w/o 27Nov68 Old San Soak, Laos; canx 03Feb70]
588	H2	PK-NPT [b/u c1979]
589	H2	PK-NPS [wfu c1975; b/u c1979]
590	H2	PK-NPR [b/u c1979]
591	A-H2	HB-FCA XW-PCK [w/o date & location unkn]
592	C-H2	N194X HK-2993X HK-2993 HK-2993P [wfu Bogota-El Dorado, Distrito Capital, Colombia]
593	C-H2	N195X [w/o 05Apr72 Tin Bong, South Vietnam]
594	B2-H2	HB-FCB XW-PCN [w/o 14Jul73 in Laos]
595	A-H2	HB-FCC XW-PCO [w/o 02Apr71 in Laos]
596	C-H2	N196X [w/o 19Aug69 nr Long Tieng, Laos]
597	C-H2	N197X [dbf 24Dec71 Long Tieng, Laos; canx 15Feb72]
598	A-H2	N393R [w/o 17Mar71 Can Tho, South Vietnam in mid-air collision with AH-1G 67-15676]
599	C-H2	N394R ST-AGW N394R [w/o 28Aug03 Vigo Park, TX, USA; canx 19May05]
600	C-H2	N198X ST-AGY N198X [w/o 28Sep77 100 mls SW of Port Sudan, Sudan; canx 25Aug86; registered N198X 02Nov91 for spares import]
601	C-H2	N199X [w/o 20Apr71 Doi Suthep mountain, 12km WNW of Chiang Mai, Thailand; canx 21Jan71]
602	B-H2	HB-FBD XW-PCQ [w/o date & location unkn]
603	B-H2	HB-FCE XW-PCR [w/o 01Dec71 nr Long Chieng, Laos]
604		[kit provided to Fairchild-Hiller for US production as c/n 2001]
605		[kit provided to Fairchild-Hiller for US production as c/n 2002]
606		[kit provided to Fairchild-Hiller for US production as c/n 2003]
607		[kit provided to Fairchild-Hiller for US production as c/n 2004]
608		[kit provided to Fairchild-Hiller for US production as c/n 2005]
609		[kit provided to Fairchild-Hiller for US production as c/n 2006]
610		[kit provided to Fairchild-Hiller for US production as c/n 2007]
611		[kit provided to Fairchild-Hiller for US production as c/n 2008]
612		[kit provided to Fairchild-Hiller for US production as c/n 2009]
613		[kit provided to Fairchild-Hiller for US production as c/n 2010]
614	B1-H2	HB-FCF
615	B-H2	HB-FCH VH-PNH [w/o 09Mar74 Kanabea, Papua New Guinea; canx 02Jul74]
616	B1-H2	HB-FCK G-AWDS ST-AEU [w/o 17Aug73 Ed Damazin, Sudan]
617	B1-H2	HB-FCL F-GDCT [dam 14Jun89; std pending rebuild]
618	B1-H2	HB-FCM [w/o 26Aug72 Frienisberg, Switzerland; canx cDec72]
619	B1-H2	"619" (British Antarctic Survey) [w/o 01Mar68 nr Miller and Meiklejohn Glaciers, Palmer Land, Antarctica]
620	B1-H2	HB-FCN XW-PDI N62154 C-GXIL N62154 N8217A F-GHXS [w/o 01Nov97 Chambry, France]
621	H2	PK-NPQ [wfu c1975 and b/u]
622	H2	PK-NPP [wfu c1975 and b/u]
623	H2	PK-NPO [wfu c1975 and b/u]
624	B2-H2M-1	V-612 (Swiss AF)
625	8D	HB-KOA [airframe used to rebuild PC-8 Twin Porter c/n 1001; project was abandoned and aircraft b/u]
626	B1-H2	HB-FCP XW-PDJ [w/o cApr71 in South Vietnam]
627	B2-H4	HB-FDE 5Y-AHY HB-FDE 9M-APQ HS-CHV N4229S I-SAEZ F-GLEU
628	B1-H2	HB-FCO VH-FSB ZK-DFJ VH-FSB [dbr in a storm cJan75 Mawson Base, Antarctica; canx 23Jan75]
629	B2-H2	HB-FDF 5Y-AHR HB-FDF D-FDFF
630	B2-H2M-1	V-613 (Swiss AF)
631	B2-H4	HB-FCR XW-PFC (XW-PDK) N62148 0631 (Royal Thai Army) N631SA C-FRAV HB-FLW G-BYNE
632	B1-H2	HB-FCS XW-PFD N62153 0632 (Royal Thai Army) N632SA [wfu, parts stored Sultan-Sky Harbor Apt, WA, USA]
633	B2-H2M-1	V-614 (Swiss AF)
634	B2-H4	HB-FCU LN-VIJ VH-FZB ZK-FZB C-FPZB D-FSCB
635	B2-H2M-1	V-615 (Swiss AF) [w/o 29Jan02 Altenrhein, Switzerland]
636	B2-H4	F-BOSZ D-FCLG
637	B2-H2	HB-FCT
638	B1-H2	HB-FCW ZS-FEM HB-FCW [w/o 22Jun70 in Sahara desert; canx 17Jul70]
639	B2-H2M-1	V-616 (Swiss AF)
640	B2-H2M-1	V-617 (Swiss AF)
641	B2-H2M-1	V-618 (Swiss AF)
642	B1-H2	HB-FDG AM-75 (Somali Government) [wfu; noted derelict cFeb93 Mogadishu-Petrella, Somalia]

PILATUS PC-6

c/n	Series	Identities
643	B2-H2M-1	V-619 (Swiss AF)
644	B2-H2M-1	V-620 (Swiss AF)
645	B1-H2	HB-FCX ST-ADE HB-FCX OO-AER HB-FCX [w/o 09Mar81 Benghazi, Libya; canx 13Nov81]
646	A-H2	HB-FCV 06/4X-SVY (Israeli DF/AF) [pres Israeli Defence Force Museum, Beersheba Hatzerim AB, Israel]
647	B2-H2M-1	V-621 (Swiss AF) [w/o 27Apr93 Finsteraarhorn, Switzerland]
648	B2-H2M-1	V-622 (Swiss AF)
649	B2-H2M-1	V-623 (Swiss AF)
650	B1-H2	HB-FCY ST-ADF HB-FCY (9M-API) HB-FCY [w/o 15Dec69 Bahrain-International; canx 17Jun70]
651	B2-H2	HB-FCZ ST-ADG HB-FCZ OH-POB D-FLEV F-GIBV
652	B1-H2	HB-FDK A14-652 (Royal Australian Army) VH-OWB [pres Museum of Australian Army Flying, Oakey, QLD, Australia; canx 06Jul06]
653	B1-H2	HB-FDL A14-653 (Royal Australian Army) N101CP ZK-JML
654	B2-H4	HB-FDT F-BSTF HB-FDT D-FROH
655	B1-H2	HB-FDA ST-ADH HB-FDA 9M-APJ [w/o 28Mar73 Bario, Sarawak, Borneo]
656	B2-H2	HB-FDC VH-SMA F-OCQV ZK-PTP F-GFDC
657	B1-H2	HB-FDD VH-SMB [w/o 20May76 Polo Flat, NSW, Australia; canx 09Aug76]
658	B2-H2	HB-FDH D-FDHP F-GOAG
659	B2-H2	HB-FEF EC-CHK HB-FEF F-GIMU HB-FEF F-GMJG
660	H2	HB-FDB VH-UIC P2-UIC P2-SEZ [dbr cAug85; parts used to rebuild c/n 551]
661	B2-H2	HB-FDM A14-661 (Royal Australian Army) HB-FKQ F-OIPB
662	B2-H2	HB-FDN A14-662 (Royal Australian Army) C-GROO
663	B2-H2	HB-FDU
664	B2-H4	OE-BBL OE-BIA 3G-EN (Austrian AF)
665	B1-H2	HB-FDI [w/o 05Dec74 Wad Medani, Sudan; canx cDec74]
666	B1-H2	HB-FDP ST-AEV [w/o 07Jan74 in Sudan]
667	B2-H4	HB-FDR XW-PFQ N62156 C-GXIJ SE-IRR HB-FLL F-GOCC
668	B1-H2	HB-FDS XW-PFR [w/o 03May73 Bouam Long, Laos]
669	B2-H2	HB-FEH XW-PFW N62161 0669 (Royal Thai Army) N699SA
670	B2-H4	HB-FES AP-AVU S2-ACD F-GKDM
671	B2-H4	HB-FFI I-MEFA
672	B2-H2	HB-FEI XW-PEF N62149 C-GXIK F-GHAS EC-EMZ
673	B1-H2	HB-FEL [w/o 24Jul69 Tegal, Indonesia; canx 06Aug69]
674	B1-H2	HB-FEM [w/o 02Sep75 Tamanrasset, Algeria; canx 01Oct75]
675	B1-H2	HB-FEN [w/o 28Jun69 Karawang, Indonesia; canx 08Jul69]
676	B2-H2	HB-FEO F-GEEO
677	B2-H2	HB-FEP ZS-LJY EC-KGD
678	B2-H4	HB-FEY I-ALPJ HB-FEY LN-VIT OY-PBA ZS-AFE
679	B1-H2	HB-FFY [w/o 31Dec76 Sion, Switzerland; canx 16Feb77]
680	B1-H2	HB-FDV A14-680 (Royal Australian Army) [w/o 21Sep81 Weipa, QLD, Australia]
681	B1-H2	HB-FDW A14-681 (Royal Australian Army) [w/o 28Nov80 nr Oakey, QLD, Australia]
682	H2	HB-FEK 7P-FDG [w/o 25Nov68 nr Quacha's Nek, Lesotho]
683	B1-H2	HB-FDX A14-683 (Royal Australian Army) [w/o 12Nov91 Jaspers Brush, NSW, Australia]
684	B2-H2	HB-FDY A14-684 (Royal Australian Army) N19TX
685	B2-H2	PH-OTE N4926 HB-FIS [w/o 18Apr87 Casale Monferrato, Italy; canx 12May87]
686	B1-H2	HB-FDZ A14-686 (Royal Australian Army) [w/o 03Dec69 Nui Dat, South Vietnam]
687	B1-H2	HB-FEA A14-687 (Royal Australian Army) N2185M
688	C1-H2	HB-FEG D-FDHM [dam 13Jun00 Bremgarten, Germany; currently under rebuild]
689	B1-H2	HB-FEB A14-689 (Royal Australian Army) VH-MKT F-GKIA
690	B1-H2	HB-FEC A14-690 (Royal Australian Army) [pres Australian War Memorial, Treloar Tech Centre, Canberra, ACT, Australia]
691	B2-H2	HB-FEV SX-AFC HB-FEV F-GLTP [dam 15Aug02 Forte de Mami, Italy]
692	B1-H2	HB-FED A14-692 (Royal Australian Army) [w/o 23Mar77 Buckambool, NSW, Australia]
693	B2-H4	HB-FEE A14-693 (Royal Australian Army) VH-REL ZK-JMP
694	B1-H2	HB-FEW SX-AFB [w/o 22Jul69 in Greece]
695	B1-H2	HB-FEX XW-PEK [w/o 16Aug71 nr Long Cheing, Laos]
696	B1-H2	HB-FFM I-SAER [CofA exp 25Jun88; std, location unkn]
697	B1-H2	HB-FET [dbf 10Mar82]
698	B1-H2	HB-FEU [w/o 02Mar70 Potgietersrus, Transvaal Province, South Africa; canx cJul70]
699	B2-H4	HB-FEZ F-GOSP
700	B2-H4	HB-FFA F-GOBR HB-FMR EC-JXH [w/o 30May08 Lillo, Spain]
701	B1-H2	HB-FER A14-701 (Royal Australian Army) N111FX [w/o 09Jul94 nr Raeford-Municipal, NC, USA; canx 21Apr97]
702	B2-H4	HB-FFK F-GEBS
703	B1-H2	HB-FFN [reportedly w/o; canx 05Nov74]
704	B1-H2	HB-FFF XW-PEO N62160 0704 (Royal Thai Army) N504SA [wfu, parts stored Sultan-Sky Harbor Apt, WA, USA]
705	B1-H2	HB-FFG XW-PGN N62162 HS-CHV 0705 (Royal Thai Army) N705SA F-GZDO EC-JOE [dam 14Apr07 Casas de los Pinos Aerodrome, Spain]
706	B1-H2	HB-FFB [w/o 03Dec71 in Bangladesh; canx 06Jan72]
707	B1-H2	HB-FFC PH-MEN [w/o 30Jul95 Spa-La Sauveniere, Belgium; canx 20Sep95]
708	B2-H2	HB-FFD F-GFFD
709	B1-H2	HB-FFO [w/o 21Dec71 Dhaka, Bangladesh; canx 06Jan72]
710	B2-H4	HB-FFP OO-FWJ HB-FFP OO-NAC (F-GXAC) OO-NAC
711	B1-H2	HB-FFX XW-PHG [w/o 01Jul74 San Thong, Laos]
712	A1-H2	HB-FFH [w/o 22Dec69 Pau, France]
713	B2-H4	HB-FFZ ZS-IHB EC-LAU
714	B2-H2	HA-YDC F-GMMA [dbf 13Nov03 Granville, France]

PILATUS PC-6

c/n	Series	Identities
715	B1-H2	HB-FGE D2- 1723 (Angolan AF) [w/o date & location unkn]
716	B2-H4	HB-FFL 9N-AAW HB-FFL F-GJBP
717	B2-H2	FAP-314 (Peruvian AF) [w/o 17Mar75 in Peru]
718	B2-H2	FAP-316 (Peruvian AF) [w/o 13Sep74 in Peru]
719	B2-H2	FAP-319 (Peruvian AF) [wfu c1984 - fate unkn]
720	B2-H2	FAP-320/OB-1165 (Peruvian AF) [w/o 07Apr08 Iquitos, Peru]
721	B2-H2	HA-YDA F-GJDA
722	B2-H2	FAP-331/OB-1166 (Peruvian AF)
723	B2-H2	(HB-FGK) FAP-337 (Peruvian AF) FAP-332/OB-R-1167 (Peruvian AF) [w/o 22Aug98 Iquitos, Peru]
724	B2-H2	(HB-FFV) N2386 HC-BJS
725	B1-H2	HB-FFE A14-725 (Royal Australian Army) A14-702 (Royal Australian Army) [w/o 07Dec83 Point Cook, VIC, Australia]
726	B2-H4	HB-FGA N30TU F-GAMV HB-FGA PK-YPC [w/o 18Jan02 Bugalaga, Indonesia]
727	B2-H2	9N-AAZ [w/o 31Mar75 Kathmandu, Nepal]
728	B2-H2	9N-ABC [wfu prior to 1992]
729	B2-H4	HB-FFQ (A14-729) (Royal Australian Army) A14-703 (Royal Australian Army) 4X-AIY N24144 N6FU [dam 24Apr99 in Israel & rebuilt in the USA]
730	B1-H2	HB-FFU (A14-730) (Royal Australian Army) A14-704 (Royal Australian Army) [std Museum of Australian Army Flying, Oakey, QLD, Australia]
731	B2-H2	HB-FFS (A14-731) (Royal Australian Army) A14-705 (Royal Australian Army) VH-ZCZ C-GZCZ D-FREE
732	B2-H2	HB-FFT ST-AEW HB-FFT G-BHCR [w/o 15Feb81 Sibson, UK; canx 24May82]
733	B2-H2	HB-FGB 1609 (Royal Thai Border Police)
734	B1-H2	HB-FGC I-SAEP [reportedly wfu - status?]
735	B2-H2	HB-FFW F-HDEY
736	B2-H2	HB-FGD D2- [w/o date & location unkn]
737	B2-H2	FAP-334/OB-1168 (Peruvian AF) [wfu c1984 - fate unkn]
738	B2-H2	FAP-336/OB-1169 (Peruvian AF) [wfu c1984 - fate unkn]
739	B2-H2	FAP-338/OB-1170 (Peruvian AF) [dam 21Nov90 in Peru; std Iquitos awaiting rebuild]
740	B2-H2	HA-YDB F-GFUM
741	B2-H2	A40-AK HB-FIM [w/o 29Jul87 nr Grenchen, Switzerland; canx 12Aug87]
742	B2-H2	HB-FGF [w/o 29Nov74 Stans, Switzerland]
743	B2-H2	HB-FGG T-185 (Ecuadorian AF) E-190 (Ecuadorian AF)
744	B2-H2	(FAP-339) (Peruvian AF) FAP-340 (Peruvian AF) [w/o 16Mar77 in Peru]
745	B2-H2	FAP-341 (Peruvian AF)
746	B2-H2	HB-FGJ 9N-ABJ [w/o 19Nov81 Biratnagar, Nepal]
747	B2-H2M	V-630 (Swiss AF) [w/o 12Nov97 Boltigen, Switzerland]
748	B2-H4	A40-AL HB-FIE D-FEAR [w/o 01Jun02 Breitscheid, Germany; canx 25Jun02]
749	B2-H2M	V-631 (Swiss AF)
750	B2-H2	HB-FGF T-180 (Ecuadorian AF) E-180 (Ecuadorian AF) N8171K [wfu, parts stored Sultan-Sky Harbor Apt, WA, USA]
751	B2-H2M	V-632 (Swiss AF)
752	B2-H2	3G-EA (Austrian AF)
753	B2-H4	HB-FGH 1311 (Thai KASET)
754	B2-H4	HB-FGL 1312 (Thai KASET) [w/o 29Mar06 Tai Mai District, Thailand]
755	B2-H4	HB-FGK 9N-ABK [w/o 19Nov98 Phakding, Nepal]
756	B2-H2	FAP-314/OB-1163 (Peruvian AF)
757	B2-H2M	V-633 (Swiss AF)
758	B2-H2	3G-EB (Austrian AF)
759	B2-H2M	V-634 (Swiss AF)
760	B2-H2	FAP-316/OB-1164 (Peruvian AF) N4113F PK-SDI
761	B2-H2M	V-635 (Swiss AF)
762	B2-H2	HB-FGM TT-KAA [w/o date & location unkn]
763	B2-H2	HB-FGN TT-KAC TT-BAV [w/o c1991; exact date & location unkn]
764	B2-H2	3G-EC (Austrian AF)
765	B2-H2	3G-ED (Austrian AF)
766	B2-H2	3G-EE (Austrian AF)
767	B2-H4	HB-FGO 1313 (Thai KASET) N7895J
768	B2-H4	HB-FGP 1314 (Thai KASET)
769	B2-H2	3G-EF (Austrian AF)
770	B2-H2	3G-EG (Austrian AF)
771	B2-H2	3G-EH (Austrian AF)
772	B2-H2	HB-FGU 4001 (Burmese AF) 4001 (Myanmar AF)
773	B2-H2	HB-FGV 4002 (Burmese AF) 4002 (Myanmar AF)
774	B2-H2	3G-EI (Austrian AF) [w/o 27Jun76 Ebental, Austria]
775	B2-H2	3G-EJ (Austrian AF)
776	B2-H2	3G-EK (Austrian AF)
777	B2-H2	3G-EL (Austrian AF)
778	B2-H4	LV-MAE (D-FHPK) N117SA OY-SFH I-PSFH T7-SFH
779	B2-H4	LV-MAF (D-FACT) N119SA HB-FLK
780	B2-H2	HB-FGW 4003 (Burmese AF) 4003 (Myanmar AF)
781	B2-H2	HB-FGX 4004 (Burmese AF) 4004 (Myanmar AF)
782	B2-H2	HB-FGS 1315 (Thai KASET) [w/o 06Feb91 Doi Suthep, Thailand; parts at Takhli AFB, Thailand]
783	B2-H4	HB-FGT 1316 (Thai KASET)
784	B2-H2	HB-FGR 1317 (Thai KASET) [status? reportedly w/o cFeb92]
785	B2-H2	HB-FGY AG-601 (Indonesian AF) ST-0601 (Indonesian AF)
786	B2-H2	GN-804 (Argentine National Guard)
787	B2-H2	GN-805 (Argentine National Guard)

PILATUS PC-6

c/n	Series	Identities
788	B2-H4	GN-806 (Argentine National Guard) [w/o 31Jul82 Monte Cristo, Cordoba, Argentina]
789	B2-H4	HB-FHH HC-BHL OB-1600
790	B2-H2	LV-MCW (D-FTWO) N181DA
791	B2-H2	LV-MCX (D-FTRI) HB-FNC S5-CMA
792	B2-H2	HB-FGZ AG-602 (Indonesian AF) ST-0602 (Indonesian AF)
793	B2-H2	LV-MIS [rebuilt using frame from c/n 808]
794	B2-H2	HB-FHA TG-BOC [w/o 14Jul82 in Guatemala]
795	B2-H2	HB-FHB 4005 (Burmese AF) 4005 (Myanmar AF)
796	B2-H2	HB-FHC 4006 (Burmese AF) 4006 (Myanmar AF)
797	B2-H2	HB-FHD 4007 (Burmese AF) 4007 (Myanmar AF)
798	B2-H2	HB-FHE AG-603 (Indonesian AF) ST-0603 (Indonesian AF) N12LH F-HFLC
799	B2-H2	HB-FHF AG-604 (Indonesian AF) ST-0604 (Indonesian AF) PK-AFE
800	B2-H2	JA8221 [pres Ishikawa Aviation Plaza, Komatsu Apt, Ishikawa Prefecture, Japan]
801	B2-H2	HB-FHG AG-605 (Indonesian AF) ST-0605 (Indonesian AF) N80LH
802	B2-H2(UV-20A)	79-23253 (US Army)[w/o 15Mar02 nr Marana, AZ, USA]
803	B2-H2(UV-20A)	79-23254 (US Army)
804	B2-H4	LV-MYZ (D-FFOR) D-FLAC
805	B2-H2	GN-807 (Argentine National Guard) [w/o 09Jul00 in Argentina]
806	B2-H2	GN-808 (Argentine National Guard) [dam; currently awaiting repair]
807	B2-H2	GN-809 (Argentine National Guard) [w/o 06Sep03 Las Lomitas, Formosa, Argentina]
808	B2-H2	[fuselage used for rebuild of c/n 793]
809	B2-H4	HB-FHO ZK-MCK
810	B2-H4	HB-FGI EI-IAN
811	B2-H2	HB-FHI HC-BKL [reportedly dam and wfu; fate unkn]
812	B2-H2	G-BIZP [w/o 18Dec83 Yarwell, UK; canx 10Dec84]
813	B2-H2	HB-FHK HC-BKM [reportedly dbr 14Mar89]
814	B2-H2	HA-YDE
815	B2-H4	G-OAPA HB-FKF EC-IBY
816	B2-H2	HB-FHM TG-AKE
817	B2-H4	HB-FFV 9Q-CTH HB-FFV 7T-VNA
818	B2-H2	HB-FHP FAC1110 (Colombian AF) [w/o 19Apr89 in Colombia]
819	B2-H4	HB-FHR FAC1111 (Colombian AF) HB-FMG F-GOMB
820	B2-H2	HB-FHN FAC1115 (Colombian AF) [w/o 29Aug97 Puerto Inirida, Guainia, Colombia]
821	B2-H2	HB-FHS FAC1112 (Colombian AF) [w/o 24Jun93 nr Mitu, Guainia, Colombia]
822	B2-H2	HB-FHT FAC1113 (Colombian AF) [w/o cMar87 in Colombia]
823	B2-H2	HB-FHU FAC1114 (Colombian AF) [w/o 25Jun87 nr Guapi, Cauca, Colombia]
824	B2-H4	HB-FCV ZK-MCN
825	B2-H2	HB-FHV 4-9801 (Iranian AF)
826	B2-H2	HB-FHW 4-9802 (Iranian AF)
827	B2-H2	HB-FHX 4-9803 (Iranian AF) [reportedly wfu]
828	B2-H2	HB-FHY 4-9804 (Iranian AF)
829	B2-H2	HB-FIA 4-9805 (Iranian AF)
830	B2-H2	HB-FIB 4-9806 (Iranian AF)
831	B2-H2	HB-FIC 4-9807 (Iranian AF)
832	B2-H2	HB-FID 4-9808 (Iranian AF)
833	B2-H2	HB-FIF 4-9809 (Iranian AF) [w/o 18Apr95 nr Tehran, Iran]
834	B2-H2	HB-FIG 4-9810 (Iranian AF)
835	B2-H2	HB-FIH 4-9811 (Iranian AF)
836	B2-H2	HB-FII 4-9812 (Iranian AF) [w/o date & location unkn]
837	B2-H2	HB-FIK 4-9813 (Iranian AF)
838	B2-H2	HB-FIL 4-9814 (Iranian AF)
839	B2-H2	HB-FIN 4-9815 (Iranian AF)
840	B2-H4	HB-FHZ ZS-MTP HB-FHZ
841	B2-H4	HB-FIO ZK-MCT
842	B2-H2	HB-FIP [w/o 04Dec85 Al Furt, Yemen; canx 12Dec85]
843	B2-H2	[fuselage used for rebuild of c/n 724]
844	B2-H4	HB-FKC
845	B2-H4	HB-FAB JA8223 D-FELI
846	B2-H4	HB-FKA 5821 (Iraqi Army) [reportedly destroyed]
847	B2-H4	HB-FKB 5822 (Iraqi Army) [reportedly destroyed]
848	B2-H4	OE-ECS G-WGSC
849	B2-H4	HB-FIT 9M-PSE
850	B2-H4	HB-FIU 9M-PSF
851	B2-H4	HB-FIV 9M-PSG
852	B2-H4	HB-FIW 9M-PSH
853	B2-H4	HB-FIX 9M-PSI
854	B2-H4	HB-FIY 9M-PSJ [w/o 17May89 nr Kuala Lumpur, Malaysia]
855	B2-H4	HB-FIZ 9M-PSK
856	B2-H2	3G-EM (Austrian AF)
857	B2-H4	D-FFBZ [w/o 17May89 Hassfurt, West Germany; canx 26May89]
858	B2-H4	HB-FKG TG-TUC
859	B2-H4	HB-FKD T-185 (Ecuadorian AF) E-185 (Ecuadorian AF) N8171E [wfu, parts stored Sultan-Sky Harbor Apt, WA, USA]
860	B2-H4	D-FALL [w/o 30Jun01 Ravenna, Italy; canx 16May02; rebuilt] D-FMTA
861	B2-H4	HB-FKE JA8228 N93JJ
862	B2-H4	G-ITPS D-FAXI
863	B2-H4	HB-FKI 321 (Dubai AF) 321 (UAE AF) 2215 (UAE AF) D-FSWB
864	B2-H4	HB-FKK 322 (Dubai AF) 322 (UAE AF) 2216 (UAE AF) D-FGMG
865	B2-H4	HB-FKH
866	B2-H4	ZS-MSZ
867	B2-H4	HB-FKL

PILATUS PC-6

c/n	Series	Identities
868	B2-H4	F-GJBC
869	B2-H4	D-FFBZ
870	B2-H4	HB-FKN N5CN XA-SXW
871	B2-H4	T320 (Bophuthatswana Defence Force) 2070 (South African AF) ZS-OLO
872	B2-H4	HB-FKR
873	B2-H4	HB-FKM
874	B2-H4	HB-FKO V5-ODH HB-FKO D-FIPS
875	B2-H4	HB-FKS [w/o 21Jun93 Aoussard, 500km SE of Layoune, Sahara Desert; canx 11Mar94]
876	B2-H4	HB-FKT
877	B2-H4	HB-FKP
878	B2-H4	D-FSKY
879	B2-H4	[fuselage used for rebuild of c/n 743]
880	B2-H4	TR-303 (Mexican AF) 3301 (Mexican AF)
881	B2-H4	TR-304 (Mexican AF) 3302 (Mexican AF)
882	B2-H4	D-FSPA OO-PCV
883	B2-H4	TR-301 (Mexican AF) 3303 (Mexican AF)
884	B2-H4	TR-302 (Mexican AF) 3304 (Mexican AF)
885	B2-H4	ZS-NIR
886	B2-H4	ZS-NIS
887	B2-H4	HB-FKU 887/MCA (French Army)
888	B2-H4	HB-FKV 888/MCB (French Army)
889	B2-H4	HB-FKW 889/MCC (French Army)
890	B2-H4	HB-FKX 890/MCD (French Army)
891	B2-H4	HB-FKY 891/MCE (French Army)
892	B2-H4	HB-FKZ I-INOT
893	B2-H4	F-GONE HB-FLI
894	B2-H4	D-FUNY HB-FMH D-FATA
895	B2-H4	HB-FKJ [w/o 26Dec99 nr Turin, Italy; canx 29Jun00]
896	B2-H4	ZS-NIT
897	B2-H4	ZS-NIU
898	B2-H4	ZS-NIV
899	B2-H4	ZS-NIW
900	B2-H4	ZS-NIX
901	B2-H4	F-GRVZ
902	B2-H4	HB-FIJ F-GSAC
903	B2-H4	E-195 (Ecuadorian AF) N1158T N338CC PK-RCZ [w/o 09Aug08 Doorman Mountains, Papua New Guinea]
904	B2-H4	HB-FLC F-GSAT
905	B2-H4	HB-FLA
906	B2-H4	HB-FLB
907	B2-H4	N601ET N68859 95-6039 (US Army) N68859 N106SF N907AW
908	B2-H4	N908PL
909	B2-H4	OO-PKZ PH-JFD TR-LOL
910	B2-H4	HB-FLG
911	B2-H4	OO-JDV PK-RCQ
912	B2-H4	HB-FLE
913	B2-H4	HB-FLD I-BMGF
914	B2-H4	OO-NAP [w/o 09Jun02 Temploux, nr Namur, Belgium; canx 06Aug03]
915	B2-H4	F-OGXM HB-FMI F-GVTF
916	B2-H4	HB-FLF 9Q-CZG [w/o 31Jan98 Durba, Zaire]
917	B2-H4	HB-FLJ 7T-VCG
918	B2-H4	HB-FLH
919	B2-H4	HB-FLM 7T-WLA HB-FLM N919MA D-FICA
920	B2-H4	HB-FLN 7T-WLE
921	B2-H4	(N282HJ) HB-FLU N77D N77DQ
922	B2-H4	HB-FLO PK-RCX
923	B2-H4	HB-FLP PK-RCY
924	B2-H4	F-OHQO
925	B2-H4	HB-FLQ L6-02 (Slovenian AF)
926	B2-H4	HB-FLR L6-03 (Slovenian AF)
927	B2-H4	HB-FLS N927MX PK-UCI
928	B2-H4	HB-FLT HC-CAC HB-FLT OE-EMD
929	B2-H4	HB-FLX 7T-VCH
930	B2-H4	HB-FMA 7T-VCI
931	B2-H4	HB-FLV N7995D (N849B) N7995D
932	B2-H4	HB-FMB
933	B2-H4	HB-FLY 7T-VCJ
934	B2-H4	HB-FLZ 7T-VCK
935	B2-H4	D-FREI HB-FMP F-GYRY
936	B2-H4	HB-FMD N424PS N2TS G-CECI
937	B2-H4	HB-FME 7T-WLD
938	B2-H4	HB-FMC [w/o 08Apr00 Breitscheid, Germany]
939	B2-H4	HB-FMF N939WA HB-FMF F-GTHA
940	B2-H4	HB-FMJ F-GRUB
941	B2-H4	HB-FMK D-FEJE
942	B2-H4	HB-FMM I-CAKE
943	B2-H4	HB-FMN (PK-JAB) PK-UCE
944	B2-H4	F-GOBR
945	B2-H4	HB-FMO PK-UCF
946	B2-H4	(5B-CKS) HB-FMQ N327SC
947	B2-H4	HB-FMS PH-JFL OK-PTP

PILATUS PC-6

c/n	Series	Identities			
948	B2-H4	HB-FMT	PK-RCS		
949	B2-H4	F-HBSF			
950	B2-H4	HB-FMV	YL-CCQ		
951	B2-H4	HB-FMU	F-GVPC		
952	B2-H4	OY-PLC	ZS-PWS		
953	B2-H4	HB-FMW	GN-853	(Argentine National Guard)	N338SB
954	B2-H4	HB-FMX	PH-LLL		
955	B2-H4	HB-FMY	D-FIBE		
956	B2-H4	HB-FMZ			
957	B2-H4	HB-FNA	PK-VVP		
958	B2-H4	HB-FNB	PK-VVK		
959	B2-H4	HB-FND	PK-LTJ	[w/o 17Apr09 Gunung Geraji, Indonesia]	
960	B2-H4	HB-FNE	HC-CGP		
961	B2-H4	HB-FNF	HC-CGQ		
962	B2-H4	HB-FNG	9N-AIU		
963	B2-H4	HB-FNH	9N-AIV		
964	B2-H4	HB-FNI			
965	B2-H4	HB-FNJ	*PK-VVQ		
966	B2-H4				
967	B2-H4				
968	B2-H4				
969	B2-H4				
970	B2-H4				
971	B2-H4				
972	B2-H4				
973	B2-H4				
974	B2-H4				
975	B2-H4				
976	B2-H4				
977	B2-H4				
978	B2-H4				
979	B2-H4				
980	B2-H4				
981					
982					
983					
984					
985					
986					
987					
988					
989					
990					
991					
992					
993					
994					
995					
996					
997					
998					
999					

PILATUS PC-12 (PC-XII)

c/n	Series	Identities							
P01		HB-FOA	[pres Stans, Switzerland; canx 31Dec96]						
P02	Eagle	HB-FOB							
101		HB-FOC	N312BC						
102	45	HB-FOE	VH-NGC	VH-YDO					
103		HB-FOD	N361DB	HB-FOD	ZS-NWZ	HB-FOD	N610GH		
104		HB-FQA	(JA5319)	JA8613	N979GA	N813PC	N5WN	N51WN	N813PA
105		HB-FQB	N269JR	N269JP	(N91MT)	N95NW			
106		HB-FQC	N601BM	N106WA	N82HR	N812PA			
107		HB-FQD	N62JT	PH-ECC					
108	45	N667JJ	(ZS-BBO)	ZS-ONR	D-FANS	LX-SKY			
109		VH-FMC							
110		VH-FMF							
111		HB-FQE	N222CM						
112		HB-FQG	N263AL	N263RS					
113		HB-FQF	JA8204	N562GA	ZS-SMY				
114		HB-FQH	N114SV	N121RF					
115		HB-FQI	N74BE	N398CA	N946JJ				
116		HB-FQJ	N321DH	N491PC	N1JW	N116SK			
117		HB-FQK	N117WF	N12FA					
118		HB-FQL	N802HS						
119	45	HB-FQM	N432CV						
120	45	HB-FQN	N112AF	N15EK					
121		HB-FQO	ZS-PVT	HB-FOT					
122		VH-FMP							
123		VH-FMW							
124	45	HB-FQP	N124BW	HB-FQP	N124PB	N124UV			
125	45	HB-FQQ	N695WF	ZS-ZEN	V5-ZEN				
126		HB-FQR	Z-KEN	VH-JLK					
127		HB-FQS	N33JA	N33JQ	N888CG				
128		HB-FQT	JA8599	TT-AAF	*D-FLIR				
129		HB-FQX	N961PC	N420DW	N426DW	N412KC	N129JW		
130		HB-FQU	N1TC						
131		HB-FOF	N88EL	N100WG	N643BW				
132		HB-FQV	N361DB	N361GB					
133	45	HB-FQW	N133CZ	LV-ZSX					
134	Eagle	HB-FOG							
135		HB-FQY	N12CA	LV-WSN	N29CA	N999EP	VT-MEG		
136		HB-FOH	N79CA	N900HS					
137	45	HB-FQZ	N116AF	(N316WF)	N137SG				
138		VH-FMZ							
139	45	HB-FRA	N96WF	[w/o 18Oct02 Trenton-Mercer, NJ, USA; canx 09Sep03]					
140		HB-FRB	N129DH	N2YF					
141		HB-FRC	N141BL	PT-WKF					
142		HB-FRD	OE-EKD						
143		HB-FRE	ZS-BEL	N6DQ	XB-ILU				
144	45	HB-FRF	N312PC						
145		HB-FRG	8030 (South African AF)						
146	45	HB-FRH	N612PC	N777JF	N146PC				
147		HB-FRI	(ZS-FDS)	ZS-NYM					
148	45	HB-FRJ	N148PC	N2JB	N998JB				
149		HB-FRK	N464WF	N15TP	N74AX				
150		HB-FRL	N150PB	(N696SS)	N950GC	N94FE			
151		HB-FRM	N151PB	C-FKAL	[w/o 18May98 nr Clarenville, NL, Canada; canx 09Jul98]				
152		HB-FRN	N444CM						
153	45	HB-FRO	N153PB						
154	45	HB-FRP	N144PC	N217EB					
155		HB-FRQ	N361FB	N718JP					
156		HB-FRR	N156SB						
157	45	HB-FOI							
158		HB-FOJ	[dbr 26May98 Brno, Czech Republic, parts to Dodson International Parts, Rantoul, KS, USA; canx 07Sep98]						
159	45	HB-FRU	N159PB	C-GBTL					
160	45	HB-FRV	N160PC	N55BK					
161	45	HB-FOK	VH-FAM	N161AJ					
162	45	HB-FRX	N162PB	(N871GM)	(N377AC)	N162PB			
163	45	HB-FRY	N49LM						
164	45	HB-FRZ	(N164PB)	C-FMPA	C-FKGA				
165	45	HB-FSA	N165PD	PT-WZE	N65KW	N10PF			
166	45	HB-FOL	N166PB	XB-IHX					
167	45	HB-FSC	(N167PB)	N774DK					
168	45	HB-FSD	N168WA	N853AL					
169	45	HB-FSE	N696TS	N696SS	N661DT	N912NM			
170	45	HB-FSF	N170PD	C-GBXW					
171	45	HB-FSG	N171PD	N172JS					
172	45	HB-FSH	N172PB						
173	45	HB-FSI	N173KS	N612KC					
174	45	HB-FSJ	N174PC	N562NA					
175	45	HB-FSK	(D-FCJA)	N118AF	N118AP				
176	45	HB-FSL	N176BS	VP-BLS					
177	45	HB-FSM	D-FCJA	EC-JXM					
178	45	HB-FSN	N178PC	C-GKAY					

PILATUS PC-12

c/n	Series	Identities				
179	45	HB-FSO	N340RE	N179SS	N818RA	
180	45	HB-FSP	ZS-BEB			
181	45	HB-FSB	N601BM			
182	45	HB-FSQ	N182PE	C-FKAC	C-FOPD	
183	45	HB-FSR	N183PC			
184	45	HB-FSS	C-GMPE	C-GGWA		
185	45	HB-FST	N185PB			
186	45	HB-FSU	N186WF	(N186PH)	N121PH	
187	45	HB-FSV	N187PC	C-GAWP		
188	45	HB-FSW	N188PC			
189	45	HB-FSX	N977XL			
190	45	HB-FSY	ZS-OFN	HB-FOV	N190PE	
191	45	HB-FSZ	N48PG	(N242PM)	N48PG	
192	45	HB-FQA	N192PC	N418DR		
193	45	HB-FQB	N193PC	C-GDGD		
194	45	HB-FQC	N194PC	N216	N455DK	
195	45	HB-FQD	C-FKAE	N37DA	N721PB	
196	45	HB-FQE	N196PC	C-GRJP		
197	45	HB-FQF	N197PC	N613NA		
198	45	HB-FQG	ZS-DMM			
199	45	HB-FQH	N199WF			
200	45	HB-FQI	N200PD	C-GRMS		
201	45	HB-FOM	N456V			
202	45	(ZS-JEM)	ZS-SRK	C-FSRK		
203	45	(ZS-SWV)	ZS-AMS	VH-VAT		
204	45	ZS-PAY	C-FKUL			
205	45	ZS-OFB				
206		ZS-OFC	[w/o 13Feb98 nr Nairobi-Wilson, Kenya]			
207	45	ZS-OEV	C-GVKC			
208	45	ZS-OFD				
209	45	HB-FQQ	N209PB	N108JC	N108JQ	
210	45	HB-FQR	N210PT			
211	45	ZS-OEW	C-FVPK			
212	45	HB-FQT	N212PB			
213	45	HB-FON	N213WA	N852AL		
214	45	HB-FQV	N214PB	PT-XTG	C-GRDC	
215	45	HB-FQS	N119AF	N321MX		
216	45	HB-FQU	N216PD	N4PC	N216KC	
217	45	HB-FQJ	N124PC	N25EP		
218	45	HB-FQK	N218WA	N777ZK		
219	45	HB-FQL	N219PC			
220	45	ZS-EXC	5H-EXC	N220ED	N224JD	[dam 31Mar06 Bukemba, Tanzania & rebuilt]
221	45	HB-FQM	N221PC			
222	45	HB-FQN	C-FKEN	C-FIJV	N932SP	
223	45	HB-FQO	N223PD	N317NA		
224	45	HB-FQP	N224PB	N400BW		
225	45	HB-FQW	N69FG			
226	45	HB-FQX	N226PC	N308NA	N970NA	
227	45	HB-FQY	N227PB	C-FYZS		
228	45	HB-FQZ	N12JD			
229	45	HB-FRA	C-FMPO			
230	45	HB-FSY	OY-TUS	N230PG		
231	45	VH-PIL	VH-PIU	VH-PID		
232	45	HB-FRC	N242JH			
233	45	HB-FRD	C-FKRB			
234	45	HB-FRE	"C-FAJN"	C-FAJV		
235	45	HB-FRF	N235AH	N105MW		
236	45	HB-FRG	N299AM			
237	45	HB-FRH	C-GBJV			
238	45	HB-FRI	N238PC	C-GRBA		
239	45	HB-FRJ	C-GMPI			
240	45	HB-FRK	N240PD	C-FCJV	N933SP	
241	45	HB-FRL	N241PC	C-FGRE	N316PM	
242	45	ZS-DAT				
243	45	HB-FRN	5Y-MAF			
244	45	HB-FRO	C-GEOW			
245	45	ZS-DET	C-GKPL			
246	45	HB-FRQ	N651CA	N6154F	N642CT	
247	45	HB-FRR	F-GTTT	(PH-CVA)	HB-FPL	V5-TSO
248	45	HB-FRS	N652CA	N40191		
249	45	HB-FRT	(F-GTTT)	N399AM		
250	45	HB-FRU	(F-GUUU)	N250PB	C-FKPI	
251	45	ZS-SRL	VT-DAR			
252	45	ZS-SRM	VT-DAV			
253	45	HB-FRM	N253PC			
254	45	HB-FRP	N254PC	C-FYUT		
255	45	HB-FRV	N401SM			
256	45	HB-FSA	N141VY	F-GJFG		
257	45	HB-FSB	N653CA	HB-FOR	N92AG	
258	45	HB-FSC	N258WC	C-FPCN		
259	45	HB-FSD	N259WA	N62GA		

PILATUS PC-12

c/n	Series	Identities					
260	45	HB-FSE	N260HS	(N472SW)	N260HS		
261	45	HB-FSF	N654CA	N33JA			
262	45	HB-FSG	N199CM				
263	45	HB-FSH	N263PS	N329PA	N65TB		
264	45	HB-FSI	N264WF				
265	45	HB-FSJ	N68PK				
266	45	HB-FSK	N112AF	N913AL	N159GL		
267	45	HB-FSL	N267WF				
268	45	HB-FSM	N268PC	C-GFIL			
269	45	HB-FSN	N269PB				
270	45	HB-FSO	N270PC	N360DA	(N880TR)	N360DA	
271	45	HB-FSP	N555EW				
272	45	HB-FSQ	N272PC	C-GMPZ			
273	45	HB-FSR	N273AF	N37FP			
274	45	HB-FSS	N274PC	C-GMPW			
275	45	HB-FST	N275PC	C-FKPA			
276	45	HB-FSU	N276PC	C-FKPI	C-GMAE	N276CN	C-FPCL
277	45	HB-FSV	N277PC				
278	45	HB-FSW	N278WC				
279	45	HB-FSX	N167AR				
280	45	HB-FSY	N280PC	C-FWAV			
281	45	HB-FSZ	N100YC				
282	45	ZS-SDO					
283	45	HB-FQA	N283PC	C-FMPB			
284	45	HB-FQB	N284LK	N191SP			
285	45	HB-FQC	N1983R	N285PS	N88NT		
286	45	ZS-SDP	N123CF				
287	45	HB-FQD	N287PC				
288	45	HB-FQE	N288PB	N777JF	N777JX	N554VR	
289	45	HB-FQF	N289PB	(N454PR)	N289PB		
290	45	HB-FOO	N565EZ	N6FZ			
291	45	HB-FOP					
292	45	HB-FQG	N292PB	N715HL			
293	45	HB-FQH	N293PC	C-GFLA			
294	Eagle	HB-FQI	GN-810 (Argentine National Guard)				
295	45	HB-FQJ	N295PC	N957ST			
296	45	HB-FQK	C-FMPN				
297	45	HB-FQL	N269AF	N269AB			
298	45	HB-FQM	N64WF	N889DH			
299	45	F-GUUU	HB-FPF	N770G	[w/o 26Mar05 Bellefonte, PA, USA; canx 31May06]		
300	45	HB-FQN	N300PB	C-FNAS	N77ZA		
301	45	VH-YDN					
302	45	HB-FQO	N302PB				
303	45	HB-FQQ	N912RP	N303JD			
304	45	HB-FQR	N304PB	N990PT	N304PT	(N304PR)	N304PT
305	45	HB-FQS	N695PC				
306	45	HB-FQT	N271SS	(N271SF)	N271SS		
307	45	HB-FQU	N307PB	C-FKVL			
308	45	HB-FQV	C-GKNR	N934SP			
309	45	HB-FRG	PH-DIX				
310	45	HB-FQW	N166SB				
311	45	HB-FQX	N311PB	C-GMPY			
312	45	HB-FQY	N142LT	[canx 22Aug07 as exported to Canada; reinstated 16Oct07]			
313	45	ZS-SRH					
314	45	HB-FQZ	C-FMPE				
315	45	HB-FRA	C-FMPW				
316	45	HB-FRH	(ZS-SRO)	N102RR	N388SR		
317	45	ZS-SRP	5H-SRP	ZS-SRP			
318	45	HB-FRB	N318MT				
319	45	ZS-SRR					
320	45	HB-FRC	N605TC	N605TQ			
321	45	HB-FRD	N321PL				
322	45	HB-FRE	N124MK	N444FT			
323	45	HB-FRF	N956PC				
324	45	HB-FRI	N324PC	C-FKSL			
325	45	HB-FRJ	(ZS-SRI)	N325MW			
326	45	HB-FRK	N326PC	PT-TPU	N337TP		
327	45	HB-FRL	N767JT	N327JZ			
328	45	HB-FRM	N328PA	N328AF	N328JP		
329	45	HB-FRN	(ZS-SRJ)	N329NG			
330	45	HB-FRO	N515RP				
331	45	HB-FRP	N331PC	C-FASP			
332	45	VH-FDE					
333	45	HB-FRQ	N488MS	N333PA	XA-UAO		
334	45	HB-FOX					
335	45	HB-FRR	N335PB	N335WH			
336	45	HB-FRS	N336PC	N422MU			
337	45	HB-FSJ	N601HT				
338	45	HB-FRT	N338PC				
339	45	HB-FRU	N339PC	C-FGFL			
340	45	HB-FRV	N343CW				

PILATUS PC-12

c/n	Series	Identities
341	45	HB-FRW N58VS
342	45	(ZS-SRJ) N2JB
343	45	HB-FRM N31DX HB-FVZ
344	45	HB-FRX N411MV
345	45	HB-FRY N345PC N1983R N345RF
346	45	HB-FRZ N377L
347	45	HB-FSA N347KC
348	45	HB-FSB N348PC XB-JDK N348PC
349	45	HB-FOQ (ZS-SRO) HB-FOQ
350	45	HB-FSC N451DM
351	45	HB-FSD N351PC
352	45	(ZS-SRI) (ZS-TLA) HB-FOZ I-TOPS
353	45	HB-FSE N353PC C-FASR
354	45	HB-FSF N354AF N666SF
355	45	HB-FSG N5DM
356	45	HB-FSH N660NR [w/o 08Jul01 in Sea of Okhotsk nr Sakhalin Island, Western Pacific]
357	45	HB-FSI N7725X C-GZGZ
358	45	HB-FSK N358PC C-FVPC
359	45	HB-FSN F-GVJB PR-ECT
360	45	HB-FSL N851RM
361	45	HB-FSX N771KT C-FDMM N717PT C-FIAS
362	45	HB-FSM N326PA
363	45	VH-KWO
364	45	HB-FSP N220CL
365	45	HB-FSQ N365PC C-FMDF C-GSLC
366	45	HB-FOS
367	45	HB-FSR N45PM N45PQ
368	45	HB-FOU N368PC
369	45	N94PP VP-BKD N126GH
370	45	HB-FST N78PG
371	45	HB-FSU N71TP
372	45	HB-FSV N372GT
373	45	HB-FSS N373KM (N373GE) N373KM
374	45	HB-FSY N374PC C-GMPP
375	45	HB-FSO N375PC N933SE
376	45	HB-FSZ N376KC
377	45	HB-FSW N377PC N409DR
378	45	PH-WMC HB-FPA N378HH
379	45	VH-MWO
380	45	HB-FQA N380PB N792SG N380TM
381	45	HB-FSO HB-FPB I-LOAN
382	45	HB-FQB N359CV
383	45	ZS-TLA
384	45	HB-FQC N14RD
385	45	HB-FQD N7ZT
386	45	HB-FOY
387	45	HB-FQJ N387W
388	45	HB-FQE N388PC
389	45	HB-FQN N389W
390	45	HB-FQF N46CE N12DZ
391	45	HB-FQG N391EC
392	45	HB-FQH N392WC
393	45	HB-FQI N393AF
394	45	HB-FQO N395W
395	45	HB-FQP N395PC
396	45	HB-FQQ VH-NWO
397	45	HB-FQK N397WA N854AL
398	45	HB-FQL N398J
399	45	HB-FQM N399PB C-FPCI
400	45	HB-FQR VH-VWO
401	45	HB-FQS N401PD
402	45	HB-FQX N9DC N22LP
403	45	HB-FQT N128CM [w/o 22Mar09 nr Butte-Bert Mooney, MT, USA]
404	45	HB-FQU N420DW
405	45	HB-FQV N405PB XA-PCM
406	45	F-GRAJ
407		VP-BBB HB-FPW
408	45	HB-FQY N408LB N82HR
409	45/U-28A	HB-FQW N922RG 05-0409 (USAF)
410	45	HB-FQZ N10VQ N524CM N524CE N679JB
411	45	HB-FOW
412	45	HB-FRA N412WC HB-FSI N412MD N10778 N412MD G-ILMD N412MD
413	45	HB-FRB N413AF N629SK
414	45	HB-FRC N905B N226N N247N
415	45/U-28A	HB-FRI N415PB
416	45	HB-FRE N416PC C-FASF
417	45	HB-FRF N417KC
418	45	HB-FRG N418PB N507AM N507AZ
419	45/U-28A	HB-FRH N419WA 05-0419 (USAF)
420	45	HB-FRJ N420AF

PILATUS PC-12

c/n	Series	Identities				
421	45	HB-FRN	OY-GSA			
422	45	HB-FRK	VP-BBB	HB-FPC		
423	45	HB-FRM	N423WA			
424	45/U-28A	HB-FRL	N424PB	05-0424 (USAF)		
425	45	HB-FRO	N451ES	[w/o 14Sep02 nr Westphalia, MO, USA]		
426	45	VH-FDC				
427	45	HB-FRP	N427WA			
428	45	VH-FDM				
429	45	HB-FRR	N429PC			
430	45	HB-FRS	N8421E			
431	45	HB-FRT	N431WC			
432	45	HB-FRQ	N432PC	N432MH		
433	45	HB-FRU	N433PC	C-FPCZ		
434	45	VH-FDP				
435	45	HB-FRV	N435PC			
436	45	ZS-COH				
437	45	HB-FRZ	N654JC			
438	45	HB-FRW	VH-FGR			
439	45	HB-FSD	N439WC			
440	45	HB-FRX	VH-FGS			
441	45	HB-FSA	N216TM	N329SK	*N970ME	
442	45	HB-FRY	VH-FGT			
443	45	N466SA	N552TC			
444	45	HB-FSB	N925HW			
445	45	HB-FSC	VT-TSA	HB-FPN	VH-JMU	
446	45/U-28A	HB-FSE	N446PC	N131JN		
447	45/U-28A	HB-FSG	N447PC	05-0447 (USAF)		
448	45	HB-FSP	N712BC			
449	45	HB-FSH	N449BY			
450	45	HB-FSF	N450PC			
451	45	HB-FSJ	C-FKPX			
452	45	HB-FSK	N452MD			
453	45	HB-FSL	N453PC			
454	45	HB-FSM	N454PS			
455	45	HB-FSN	N455WM			
456	45	HB-FSQ	N456PC	XA-	[canx 23Jan09 as exported to Mexico]	
457	45	HB-FSR	N457PC	N327YR	N514NL	
458	45	HB-FSS	N458PC	N458DL		
459	45	HB-FST	N459PC			
460	45	HB-FSU	N460PB			
461	45	HB-FSV	N461PC	XA-TWZ		
462	45	HB-FSW	N462PC			
463	45	HB-FRD	N463JT	(N107DE)	N463JT	
464	45	HB-FSX	N464WC	N769CM		
465	45	HB-FSY	N465PC			
466	45	HB-FSZ	VH-FDK			
467	45	HB-FQM	VH-ZWO			
468	45	HB-FQA	N944BT			
469	45	HB-FQB	N469AF			
470	45	HB-FQC	N470WA	N470AH		
471	45	HB-FQN	ZS-AGI			
472	45	HB-FQO	VT-TAS			
473	45	HB-FQD	N473PC			
474	45	HB-FQE	N57LT			
475	45	HB-FQF	N475PC	C-GLCE		
476	45	HB-FQG	N476D			
477	45	HB-FQH	HB-FPD	(PH-JKS)	PH-JFS	
478	45	HB-FQI	N478PC	N26VW		
479	45	HB-FQJ	HB-FPE	A6-GAK	HB-FPE	ZS-PZB
480	45	HB-FQK	N480WH			
481	45	HB-FQL	N481TL	XA-BLU		
482	45/U-28A	HB-FQP	N482WA	05-0482 (USAF)		
483	45	HB-FQQ	N483PC	N281WB		
484	45	HB-FQR	N484AF	N667RB		
485	45	HB-FQS	N485PC			
486	45	HB-FQT	N486PB			
487	45	HB-FQU	N487PC			
488	45/U-28A	HB-FQV	(SP-KEZ)	N56EZ	[canx 05Feb09 tfd to USAF]	
489	45	HB-FQW	N489JG			
490	45	HB-FPJ	G-IJIM	N324SC		
491	45	HB-FQY	C-GPAI	N491VA	C-GPAI	
492	45	HB-FQZ	N492WA			
493	45	HB-FQX	N493PB	XB-IKO		
494	45	HB-FRA	N494PC	N612J		
495	45	HB-FRB	N495PC	N83AJ		
496	45	HB-FRD	N496DT	OY-SCI		
497	45	HB-FRE	N497PC			
498	45	HB-FPG	EC-ISH			
499	45	HB-FRF	N1056B			
500	45	HB-FRC	N500ZP	N500NK		
501	45	HB-FRG	N501PB	N770FL		

PILATUS PC-12

c/n	Series	Identities				
502	45	HB-FRH	N124PS			
503	45	HB-FRI	N503PB	N503WS		
504	45	HB-FRJ	N504PB	XA-JOS		
505	45	HB-FRK	N505P			
506	45	ZS-MSF				
507	45	HB-FRL	N507PB	N507RC	(N222DP)	N507RC
508	45	ZS-KAL	N508DL	(N118CD)	M-ICKY	
509	45	HB-FRM	N509PB	N4TS		
510	45	HB-FRN	N861PP			
511	45	HB-FRO	N511PB			
512	45	HB-FRP	N512PB	XA-UBA		
513	45	HB-FPK	D-FUEL	EC-KFK	EC-KLP	
514	45	HB-FRQ	N156SW			
515	45	HB-FRR	N515AF			
516	45	HB-FRS	N629MC	N628MC		
517	45	HB-FRT	N487LM			
518	-M	HB-FPH	020 (Bulgarian AF)			
519	45	HB-FRU	N519PC			
520	45	HB-FRV	N234RG			
521	45	HB-FRW	N521PC			
522	45	LX-JFH				
523	45	HB-FRY	N523JL			
524	45	HB-FRZ	N524GT			
525	45	HB-FSA	ZS-PDZ	7Q-YLT	ZS-SFS	
526	45	HB-FSB	N526PB	N269AF	N600WY	
527	45	HB-FSC	N527PB			
528	45	HB-FSD	N528EJ			
529	45	HB-FSE	N529PB	N529PS		
530	45	HB-FSK	N530WC			
531	45	(LX-DOG)	LX-LAB			
532	45	HB-FSF	N532WA	N7YR		
533	45	HB-FSG	N533PC			
534	45	HB-FSH	N353KM			
535	45	HB-FSI	N535MJ	*N535MT		
536	45	HB-FPO	(D-FAPC)	OE-EPC		
537	45	HB-FSJ	N537PC			
538	45	HB-FSL	HB-FPP	S2-AED		
539	45	HB-FPQ	N539PS	N522DJ		
540	45	HB-FSN	N950KM			
541	45	HB-FSO	N541PB			
542	45	HB-FSP	N542PB	N2222C		
543	45	HB-FSQ	N543PB			
544	45	HB-FPR				
545	47E	HB-FPT				
546	45	HB-FSL	N546PB			
547	45	HB-FSS	N547AF			
548	45	HB-FST	N715TL			
549	45	HB-FQE	G-CCPU	EC-JFO		
550	45	PH-XII				
551	45	(N551PB)	VH-PCE	HB-FPI		
552	45	HB-FSU	N152PC	(N777ZA)	N152PC	
553	45	HB-FSV	N553CA			
554	45	ZS-DER				
555	45	HB-FSW	N555PE			
556	45	HB-FSX	N556HL			
557	45	HB-FSR	N557PC	(N557DF)	N4TF	N4LZ 5H-SUZ
558	45	HB-FSY	N558AF			
559	45	HB-FSZ	N559PB			
560	45	ZS-PGX				
561	45	HB-FQA	N561ST			
562	45	HB-FQB	N562PB	VT-ACG		
563	45	HB-FQC	N563TM	N776JT		
564	45	HB-FQD	N564PB	N724HS		
565	45	HB-FSM	N65AF			
566	45	HB-FPX	C-GPLT			
567	45	HB-FQF	N567FH			
568	45	G-CCWY	VT-IOO			
569	45	HB-FQG	N569AF			
570	45	HB-FQH	N570DC	N578DC	[w/o 05Jul09 McCormick Farm, Rockbridge County, VA, USA]	
571	45	HB-FQI	N571PC			
572	45	HB-FQJ	N572PC			
573	45/U-28A	HB-FQK	N666GT	05-0573 (USAF)		
574	45	LX-JFI				
575	45	HB-FQL	N575PC			
576	45	HB-FQM	N576RG			
577	45	HB-FQN	N577BF			
578	45	HB-FQO	N661WP			
579	45	D-FAPC				
580	45	HB-FQR	N150MX	PR-BZE		
581	45	HB-FQY	N581PC			
582	45	HB-FQS	N582DT			

c/n	Series	Identities			
583	45	HB-FQT	N5904A		
584	45	HB-FQU	N584JV		
585	45	HB-FQV	N585PB	XA-UES	
586	45	HB-FQW	N586PB		
587	45	HB-FQZ	N888WG		
588	45	HB-FRA	N588KC		
589	45	HB-FRB	N589AC		
590	45	N629DF			
591	45	N591AF			
592	45	HB-FRD	N26KH		
593	45	HB-FRE	N593PC		
594	45	HB-FRF	N594WA		
595	45	HB-FRG	N212LT		
596	45	HB-FRH	N535BB		
597	45/U-28A	N597CH			
598	45	N598HC	N598MM		
599	45	N599PB			
600	45	HB-FRK	N600PE	N500BG	
601	45	N601PL	N1983R	N154DF	
602	45/U-28A	N901TR	04-0602 (USAF)		[dam 08Jul08 Hurlburt Field, FL, USA]
603	45	HB-FRC	C-GPCO		
604	45	HB-FQG	N604WP	[w/o 11Jan09 nr Hayden, CO, USA]	
605	45	HB-FQQ	N605PC	(N705CC)	N605PC
606	45	HB-FQP	N21AU		
607	45	N607AF			
608	45	HB-FPS			
609	45	HB-FRI	N595PB	HS-SMC	G-INTO
610	45	HB-FRJ	N610NK		
611	45	HB-FRL	N417AR		
612	45	HB-FRM	N120CJ	C-FQMM	
613	45	HB-FRP	N798WC		
614	45	HB-FRQ	N614LD		
615	45	ZS-FTG			
616	45	HB-FRN	N616EL		
617	45	VH-WBI			
618	45	HB-FRR	N618JL	N618JC	
619	45	N619AF			
620	45	HB-FRO	N620WA		
621	45	ZS-YEA			
622	45	HB-FQX	N622WW	N271SM	
623	45	HB-FRS	N623BA		
624	45	N624AF			
625	45	HB-FPU	CS-DIQ		
626	45	HB-FRT	N538BH		
627	45	HB-FRU	N1RH		
628	45	HB-FRV	N452GH		
629	45	HB-FRW	N6971Z		
630	45	HB-FRX	N292P		
631	45	HB-FRY	N631BL		
632	45	HB-FPV	G-PVPC		
633	45	HB-FSL	D-FCGH		
634	45	ZS-PRX			
635	45	N705KC			
636	45	HB-FSA	N942TW		
637	45	HB-FSB	N637PH		
638	45	HB-FSM	VH-ZMM	N638AV	
639	45	HB-FSC	N639KC		
640	45	HB-FRZ	N640MY		
641	45	HB-FSD	N641TK		
642	45	HB-FSE	N642PC		
643	45	HB-FSF	N643PC		
644	45	HB-FSG	N644SD		
645	45	HB-FSH	N645PC		
646	45/U-28A	HB-FSI	N875RJ	05-0646 (USAF)	
647	45	N320PW			
648	45	HB-FSU	G-OLTT	M-YBUB	
649	45	HB-FSJ	N649P		
650	45	HB-FSN	N650MC		
651	45	HB-FSK	N651PB		
652	45	OY-PLA	N133N	PR-AGR	
653	45	HB-FSO	N528PM		
654	45	HB-FSP	N650BG		
655	45	N655PB	PP-BER		
656	45	N656AF			
657	45	HB-FSR	N700PL		
658	45	HB-FSS	N504SR		
659	45	HB-FST	C-GPDJ	OY-MID	
660	45	HB-FSV	N660WA		
661	45	HB-FSW	N755EM		
662	45	HB-FSX	N747KL		
663	45	HB-FQJ	OE-EMC		

PILATUS PC-12

c/n	Series	Identities				
664	45	HB-FSY	N602BM			
665	45	HB-FSZ	N665MC			
666	45	HB-FQA	N672SD			
667	45	N667PE	PR-AGM			
668	45	HB-FQB	N212PK			
669	45	N669AF				
670	45	HB-FQC	N670WH			
671	45	HB-FQD	N671PC			
672	45	HB-FQE	N672PB	N672PP		
673	45	HB-FQF	N673PC			
674	45	HB-FQG	N674KC	XA-	[canx 02Jul09 as exported to Mexico]	
675	45	HB-FQH	C-GCRN			
676	45	HB-FQI	N676PC			
677	45	OY-NUT	D-FFAH			
678	45	LX-JFJ				
679	45	N679PE				
680	45	N680PE	XA-PCA			
681	45	N681GH				
682	45	G-MATX				
683	45	LX-JFK				
684	47	D-FHGN				
685	47	HB-FPY				
686	47	HB-FQM	N686PC			
687	47	N687AF				
688	47/U-28A	HB-FQN	N707KH			
689	47	HB-FQU	N689PE			
690	47	ZS-PRK				
691	47/U-28A	HB-FQO	N691PC	[canx 05Feb09 tfd to USAF]		
692	47	HB-FQP	N692BC			
693	47	HB-FSQ	N693AT			
694	47	HB-FQQ	N909BJ			
695	47	ZS-PTX				
696	47	HB-FQZ	N126BK			
697	47	HB-FRA	(N909PP)	OY-PPP	M-NGSN	
698	47	HB-FQR	N758PC			
699	47	N699AF				
700	47/U-28A	HB-FQS	N600KP	[canx 13Mar09 tfd to USAF]		
701	47	HB-FQK	N701PE	XA-UFN		
702	47	HB-FPZ				
703	47	HB-FQL	N703TL			
704	47	VH-WPE				
705	47	HB-FQT	N569AB	N1CW		
706	47	HB-FQV	N706AG			
707	47	HB-FRI	C-GODE			
708	47	N708AF				
709	47	HB-FQW	N709RB	N709WY		
710	47	HB-FQX	G-TRAT			
711	47/U-28A	HB-FQY	N711PN	[canx 05Feb09 tfd to USAF]		
712	47/U-28A	HB-FRB	N609TW	[canx 05Feb09 tfd to USAF]		
713	47	ZS-AVH				
714	47	HB-FRC	N893WB			
715	47	HB-FRD	N227NS			
716	47	HB-FRE	N768H	[w/o 24Jun06 Big Timber, MT, USA]		
717	47	HB-FRF	N717NC			
718	47/U-28A	HB-FRG	N324BK	N824BK	[canx 13Mar09 tfd to USAF]	
719	47	HB-FRH	N719PC			
720	47	VH-WPY				
721	47	N721AF				
722	47	HB-FRX	N12MC	N623AC		
723	47	HB-FRJ	RA-01510			
724	47	HB-FRK	N624TS			
725	47	VH-YWO				
726	47	HB-FRL	N721SL	N855KC		
727	47	HB-FRM	C-GBMF			
728	47	HB-FRN	I-CNDB			
729	47	N729AF				
730	47	HB-FRO	N950KA			
731	47	HB-FRP	N731PC			
732	47	HB-FRQ	G-ZUMO			
733	47	HB-FRR	N326V			
734	47	HB-FRS	N608SM			
735	47	HB-FRT	N735MD			
736	47/U-28A	HB-FRU	N72EA	07-0736 (USAF)		
737	47	HB-FRV	N52NK			
738	47	N738PE	PR-LJR			
739	47	ZS-CWM				
740	47/U-28A	HB-FRW	N740AF			
741	47	HB-FRY	N531MP	N804ST	N741SD	PT-GAV
742	47	HB-FRZ	N742R			
743	47	HB-FSA	N743AE			
744	47	HB-FSB	N744DA			

c/n	Series	Identities		
745	47	HB-FSC	RA-01509	
746	47	HB-FSD	N325FS	
747	47	HB-FSE	N797GM	
748	47	HB-FSF	N814TB	
749	47	HB-FSG	N749GC	
750	47	ZS-TSW		
751	47	HB-FSN	LX-DNI	D-FFMM
752	47	HB-FSH	N752JS	N516CB
753	47	HB-FSI	N92CA	
754	47	HB-FSJ	N777CQ	
755	47	N755HF		
756	47	HB-FSK	N916AD	
757	47	HB-FSL	N770PW	
758	47	HB-FSM	N56RJ	
759	47	N759PB		
760	47	HB-FSO	N660WB	
761	47	D-FINE		
762	47	HB-FSQ	N500WY	
763	47	HB-FSR	N16VK	
764	47	HB-FSS	N26KR	
765	47	HB-FST	CX-FCS	
766	47	HB-FSU	N214CS	
767	47	HB-FSV	N767PB	TG-ASC
768	47	HB-FSY	C-FMPF	
769	47	N769AF		
770	47	HB-FSW	N35WA	
771	47	ZS-APS		
772	47	VH-HIG		
773	47	HB-FSX	D-FIBI	
774	47	HB-FSZ	N774GW	
775	47	HB-FQA	N775PC	XA-BWA
776	47	N776AF		
777	47	HB-FQJ	N72DZ	
778	47	HB-FVV		
779	47	HB-FQB	N779PC	
780	47	HB-FQC	N48GA	
781	47	HB-FQD	N781PE	
782	47	HB-FQQ	VT-JSL	
783	47	HB-FQE	N783JJ	N783PC
784	47	HB-FQF	N784BK	
785	47	HB-FQG	N785PC	PP-SAM
786	47	HB-FQH	N786WM	
787	47	HB-FQI	N787PB	N220JP
788	47	D-FATN		
789	47	HB-FQK	C-GFLN	
790	47/U-28A	HB-FQL	N757ED	[canx 13Mar09 tfd to USAF]
791	47	ZS-DLB		
792	47	HB-FQM	N775CC	
793	47	HB-FQN	N96MV	
794	47	N794AF		
795	47	HB-FQO	VH-ZKM	PK-UCG
796	47	HB-FQP	N657PC	
797	47	ZS-GMC		
798	47	HB-FQR	N798RG	
799	47	HB-FQS	N1983R	
800	47	HB-FQW	C-FMDF	
801	47	HB-FQT	N801J	
802	47	N802AF		
803	47	OY-PLB	RA-01500	
804	47	HB-FQV	N236WR	
805	47	ZS-JDD		
806	47	HB-FQX	N806PE	N629MC
807	47	HB-FQY	N807D	
808	47	HB-FQZ	N808PC	N531MP
809	47/U-28A	HB-FRA	N36EG	[canx 13Mar09 tfd to USAF]
810	47	HB-FRO	N184TH	D-FGAG
811	47	HB-FRB	N811PC	
812	47	LX-JFM		
813	47	HB-FRC	N527DM	
814	47	HB-FRD	N814PC	PR-DOG
815	47	N815AF		
816	47	HB-FRE	N816PC	
817	47	HB-FRF	N777JZ	
818	47	HB-FRG	N6818R	
819	47	HB-FRH	N434JA	
820	47	HB-FRI	N626MT	
821	47/U-28A	HB-FRJ	N821PE	07-0821 (USAF)
822	47/U-28A	HB-FRK	N822BM	[canx 13Mar09 tfd to USAF]
823	47	HB-FRL	N823PE	N1130D
824	47	HB-FRM	N824SM	
825	47	HB-FRN	N844GT	

PILATUS PC-12

c/n	Series	Identities		
826	47	HB-FRP	N828VV	
827	47	VH-OOU	VH-DQV	VH-OOI
828	47	HB-FRQ	N144MF	
829	47/U-28A	HB-FRS	N829PE	[canx 05Feb09 tfd to USAF]
830	47	G-WINT		
831	47	HB-FRT	N4DF	
832	47	N832PC	XA-GAS	
833	47	HB-FVA		
834	47	HB-FRV	N695QE	
835	47/U-28A	HB-FRW	N100MS	[canx 05Feb09 tfd to USAF; reinstated 08May09]
836	47	HB-FRX	N996KF	
837	47	HB-FSI	(OK-AAA)	VH-ZBD
838	47/U-28A	HB-FRY	N838PE	07-0838 (USAF)
839	47	HB-FRZ	N666M	
840	47/U-28A	HB-FSA	N840PE	07-0840 (USAF)
841	47	HB-FSP	RA-01501	
842	47	VH-ZKM	PK-	[canx 21Nov07 as exported to Indonesia; std Singapore-Seletar still marked as VH-ZKM]
843	47	HB-FSJ	N967AB	D-FCAP
844	47	HB-FSB	N739S	
845	47	ZS-AMS		
846	47	HB-FRR	N846PW	
847	47	D-FFHZ		
848	47	HB-FSD	N848PC	
849	47	HB-FSE	C-GMLF	
850	47	HB-FSF	N850CB	
851	47	HB-FSR	N851AF	
852	47	HB-FSG	N852FR	
853	47	HB-FSH	N853WM	
854	47	HB-FSK	N12AG	
855	47	HB-FSQ	LX-JFN	
856	47	N856PC	PR-GRB	
857	47	HB-FSL	N693PD	
858	47	HB-FSS	ZS-GAA	
859	47	HB-FSM	N859PL	
860	47	HB-FSN	N116TH	
861	47	HB-FST	VH-FDJ	
862	47	HB-FSU	RA-01502	
863	47	HB-FSV	OY-TWO	
864	47	HB-FSO	C-FDLV	
865	47	HB-FSW	LX-PFD	
866	47	HB-FSX	N866PE	PR-ENO
867	47	HB-FSY	G-OCLE	N867PP
868	47	HB-FSZ	N868PE	XA-FFG
869	47	HB-FQA	N869AF	
870	47	HB-FQB	N870KC	
871	47	HB-FQC	N650WC	
872	47	HB-FQD	OY-VIN	
873	47	HB-FQE	N873PC	
874	47	HB-FQF	N874AF	
875	47	HB-FQG	N178MH	
876	47	HB-FQH	LX-JFQ	
877	47	HB-FQI	N877AF	[dam 12Jun09 Bridgeport-Igor I Sikorsky Memorial, CT, USA]
878	47	HB-FQJ	C-FCSC	C-FPXY
879	47	HB-FQK	N879AF	
880	47	HB-FQL	N2UX	
881	47	HB-FQM	N57SG	
882	47	HB-FQN	RA-01503	
883	47	HB-FQO	N883PC	N108JC
884	47	HB-FQP	N884PC	XA-MIC
885	47	HB-FQR	G-DAKI	
886	47	HB-FQS	N886PC	N51DJ
887	47	HB-FQT	F-HANN	
888	47	HB-FVU		
1001	47E	HB-FVB	N47NG	N77SD
1002	47E	HB-FVC		
1003	47E	HB-FQU	N808JS	
1004	47E	HB-FQV	N869TW	
1005	47E	HB-FQW	N939HE	
1006	47E	HB-FQX	N801PB	
1007	47E	HB-FQY	VH-PIL	
1008	47E	HB-FQZ	LX-TAI	
1009	47E	HB-FRA	N2244	
1010	47E	HB-FRB	N421PP	
1011	47E	HB-FRC	N911NG	C-GMPM
1012	47E	HB-FRD	N125BP	
1013	47E	N913AF		
1014	47E	HB-FRF	N71PW	
1015	47E	HB-FRG	N888SK	
1016	47E	HB-FRH	(D-FEIA)	D-FUDA
1017	47E	HB-FRI	N917NG	C-GMPX

c/n	Series	Identities			
1018	47E	HB-FRJ	N443DB		
1019	47E	HB-FRK	N213KP		
1020	47E	HB-FRL	N606SL	[w/o 30Sep08 3 mls N of Santa Fe-Municipal, NM, USA]	
1021	47E	HB-FRM	N921NB	N324BK	
1022	47E	HB-FRN	M-IFLY		
1023	47E	HB-FQI	ZS-KAL		
1024	47E	HB-FRO	I-LGMG		
1025	47E	HB-FRP	N10HS		
1026	47E	HB-FRQ	RA-01504		
1027	47E	HB-FQF	N811DD		
1028	47E	HB-FQG	N928NG		
1029	47E	HB-FQH	RA-01505		
1030	47E	HB-FQJ	ZS-MSG		
1031	47E	HB-FQK	N75WH		
1032	47E	HB-FQL	VH-OWP		
1033	47E	HB-FQM	N605MD		
1034	47E	HB-FQN	N934NG		
1035	47E	HB-FQO	N935NG		
1036	47E	HB-FQP	N614P		
1037	47E	HB-FQQ	ZS-CPD		
1038	47E	HB-FQR	OY-NUS	N227UT	
1039	47E	HB-FQS	N257SE		
1040	47E	HB-FQT	C-GECT		
1041	47E	HB-FQU	N29BY		
1042	47E	HB-FQV	N942NG	XA-	[canx 26Mar09 as exported to Mexico]
1043	47E	HB-FQW	ZS-RVL		
1044	47E	HB-FQX	N944NG	PT-VXJ	
1045	47E	HB-FQY	VH-VTF		
1046	47E	HB-FQZ	N32WK		
1047	47E	HB-FRA	N625MC		
1048	47E	HB-FRB	N387TT		
1049	47E	HB-FRC	N149DL		
1050	47E	HB-FRD	N950NG	N623E	
1051	47E	HB-FRE	N226N		
1052	47E	HB-FRF	VH-OWQ		
1053	47E	HB-FRG	N488PG		
1054	47E	HB-FRH	N52CK	*N62SK	
1055	47E	HB-FRI	N955AF		
1056	47E	HB-FRJ	N988EC		
1057	47E	HB-FRK	N535PC		
1058	47E	HB-FRL	N958NG	N45PM	
1059	47E	HB-FRM	N959AF		
1060	47E	HB-FRN	N852W		
1061	47E	HB-FRO	RA-01506		
1062	47E	HB-FRP	N962NG	N588RS	
1063	47E	HB-FRR	M-OLTT		
1064	47E	HB-FRS	HB-FSQ	RA-01507	
1065	47E	HB-FRT	N184TH		
1066	47E	HB-FRU	N966NG	PP-MVT	
1067	47E	HB-FRV	N967NG	C-GBNG	
1068	47E	HB-FRW	VH-AAD		
1069	47E	HB-FRX	ZS-ZBR		
1070	47E	HB-FRY	(LX-JFR)	N620FB	
1071	47E	HB-FVF			
1072	47E	HB-FVD			
1073	47E	HB-FSB	N973NG	C-GMPE	
1074	47E	HB-FSC	*OY-SKI		
1075	47E	HB-FSD	N2852N		
1076	47E	HB-FSE	N640KC		
1077	47E	HB-FSF	N812FS		
1078	47E	HB-FSG	N978AF		
1079	47E	HB-FSH	N460PM		
1080	47E	HB-FSI	D-FKGI		
1081	47E	HB-FVE			
1082	47E	HB-FSK	VH-OWR		
1083	47E	HB-FSL	N983NG	C-GRXA	
1084	47E	HB-FSM	N600BL	*N600GR	
1085	47E	HB-FSN	N65W		
1086	47E	HB-FSO	N812GS		
1087	47E	HB-FSP	N92DZ		
1088	47E	HB-FSR	N988NG	PR-VZE	
1089	47E	HB-FSS	ZS-PGN		
1090	47E	HB-FST	G-MOLO		
1091	47E	HB-FSU	*LX-JFS		
1092	47E	HB-FSV	N992NG	C-FMPK	
1093	47E	HB-FVG			
1094	47E	HB-FSW	N994NG	C-GRXB	
1095	47E	HB-FSX	N613VW		
1096	47E	HB-FSY	N58WS		
1097	47E	HB-FSZ	N657EZ		
1098	47E	HB-FRZ	N998WA	N948MR	

PILATUS PC-12

c/n	Series	Identities		
1099	47E	HB-FSJ	YR-	[canx 03Aug09 as exported to Romania]
1100	47E	HB-FSA	N147PE	
1101	47E	HB-FQA	*OY-PNG	
1102	47E	HB-FQB	N102AF	
1103	47E	HB-FQC	N103PB	
1104	47E	HB-FQD	*PH-OLS	
1105	47E	HB-FQE	A2-MDM	
1106	47E	HB-FQF	N106PC	C-GRXD
1107	47E	HB-FQG	N107NX	C-FGMQ
1108	47E	HB-FQH	N918NG	C-GLVK
1109	47E	HB-FQI	N109AF	
1110	47E	HB-FQJ	C-GKRY	
1111	47E	HB-FQK	N126TS	
1112	47E	HB-FQL	N83JR	
1113	47E	HB-FQM	ZS-SGJ	
1114	47E	HB-FQN	M-ARTY	
1115	47E	HB-FQR	VH-OWA	
1116	47E	HB-FQO	N47NX	
1117	47E	HB-FQP	N117PZ	C-GRXE
1118	47E	HB-FQQ	N111VK	
1119	47E	HB-FQS	N212JL	
1120	47E	HB-FQT	N120GS	
1121	47E	HB-FQU	PH-PNG	
1122	47E	HB-FQY	VH-YOJ	
1123	47E	HB-FQW	N123NX	
1124	47E	HB-FQZ	N7274L	
1125	47E	HB-FQX	N25NX	
1126	47E			
1127	47E	HB-FRA	N127PE	
1128	47E	HB-FRB	N221XX	
1129	47E	HB-FRC	N129NX	
1130	47E	HB-FRD	PH-RUL	
1131	47E	HB-FRE	N5326S	
1132	47E	HB-FRF		
1133	47E	HB-FRG	*D-FOUR	
1134	47E	HB-FRH	N705MS	
1135	47E	HB-FRI	ZS-LJB	ZS-CTR
1136	47E	HB-FRJ	N136PE	
1137	47E	HB-FRK	N946RB	
1138	47E	HB-FRL		
1139	47E	HB-FRM	N567ER	
1140	47E	HB-FRN		
1141	47E	HB-FRO	N810Z	
1142	47E	HB-FRR	OK-PPP	
1143	47E	HB-FRP	N706MS	
1144	47E	HB-FRQ	M-PRIT	
1145	47E	HB-FRS		
1146	47E	HB-FRT		
1147	47E	HB-FRU	N147PZ	
1148	47E	HB-FRV		
1149	47E	HB-FRW		
1150	47E	HB-FSB		
1151	47E	HB-FRX	N983SC	
1152	47E	HB-FSF		
1153	47E	HB-FSD		
1154	47E	HB-FSH		
1155	47E			
1156	47E	HS-FSE		
1157	47E	HB-FSG		
1158	47E	HB-FSI		
1159	47E	HB-FSK		
1160	47E	*D-FNAH		
1161	47E			
1162	47E			
1163	47E	HB-FRZ	N163NP	
1164	47E			
1165	47E	HB-FSL		
1166	47E			
1167	47E			
1168	47E	HB-FSM		
1169	47E	HB-FSA	N169NP	
1170	47E			
1171	47E			
1172	47E			
1173	47E			
1174	47E			
1175	47E			
1176	47E			
1177	47E			
1178	47E			
1179	47E			

PILATUS PC-12

c/n	Series	Identities
1180	47E	
1181	47E	
1182	47E	
1183	47E	
1184	47E	
1185	47E	
1186	47E	
1187	47E	
1188	47E	
1189	47E	
1190	47E	
1191	47E	
1192	47E	
1193	47E	
1194	47E	
1195	47E	
1196	47E	
1197	47E	
1198	47E	
1199	47E	
1200	47E	
1201	47E	
1202	47E	
1203	47E	
1204	47E	
1205	47E	
1206	47E	
1207	47E	
1208	47E	
1209	47E	
1210	47E	
1211	47E	
1212	47E	
1213	47E	
1214	47E	
1215	47E	
1216	47E	
1217	47E	
1218	47E	
1219	47E	
1220	47E	
1221	47E	
1222	47E	
1223	47E	
1224	47E	
1225	47E	
1226	47E	
1227	47E	
1228	47E	
1229	47E	
1230	47E	
1231	47E	
1232	47E	
1233	47E	
1234	47E	
1235	47E	
1236	47E	
1237	47E	
1238	47E	
1239	47E	
1240	47E	
1241	47E	
1242	47E	
1243	47E	
1244	47E	
1245	47E	
1246	47E	
1247	47E	
1248	47E	
1249	47E	
1250	47E	
1251	47E	
1252	47E	
1253	47E	
1254	47E	
1255	47E	
1256	47E	
1257	47E	
1258	47E	
1259	47E	

PIPER PA-31T CHEYENNE

^ - Blackhawk XP135A engine upgrade fitted

c/n	Identities
31T-1	N7500L [wfu c1987; pres Piper Aviation Museum, Lock Haven, PA, USA]
31T-7400002	N131PT OH-PNS SE-GLB [wfu cMar89; pres inst airframe FlygTeknikCentrum Hasslo, Vasteras-Hasslo, Sweden; canx 06Mar89]
31T-7400003	N231PT (N177PT) N336P
31T-7400004	N331TT N331PT N61DP N88LB [status?]
31T-7400005	N66834 N10BC (N80BC) N10BQ [wfu, parts to Dodson International Parts, Rantoul, KS, USA]
31T-7400006	N66835 YV-146CP YV-2200P [w/o 20Jun90 in sea off New Town, Bahamas]
31T-7400007	N66836 N101FB [wfu, parts to White Industries, Bates City, MO, USA; location H-11]
31T-7400008	N66837 (N424M) N227TM
31T-7400009	N66838 XA-HER N66838 N910HM N910HG
31T-7400010	[completed as c/n 31T-7520001] N300PE N66839
31T-7400011	[completed as c/n 31T-7520002] N66840
31T-7400012	[completed as c/n 31T-7520003] N66841
31T-7400013	[completed as c/n 31T-7520004] N287MN
31T-7400014	[completed as c/n 31T-7520005] N1976J
31T-7400015	[completed as c/n 31T-7520006] N35RT
31T-7400016	[completed as c/n 31T-7520007] N9720N
31T-7400017	[completed as c/n 31T-7520008] N1017T
31T-7400018	[completed as c/n 31T-7520009] N9722N
31T-7520001	N300PE N66839 N668RJ N668DH N234K
31T-7520002	N66840 D-IJET N90589 F-GFLE [CofA exp cOct87; b/u c1989 Paris-Le Bourget, France; canx cAug96]
31T-7520003	N66841 HB-LHT [w/o 12Nov76 Shannon, Ireland; canx cNov76]
31T-7520004	N287MN [wfu, parts to White Industries, Bates City, MO, USA; location F-45]
31T-7520005	N1976J [wfu, parts to Dodson International Parts, Rantoul, KS, USA]
31T-7520006	N35RT N33DT N19NM N49NM
31T-7520007	N9720N N35RT OH-PNT N522AS
31T-7520008	N1017T C-GNKP [wfu cMay02 Regina, SK, Canada; canx 22Jan03]
31T-7520009	N9722N F-BVTC N2645Z (N113KA) N113RC (N117BL) N113RC
31T-7520010	N66843 N431PT XA-JOF N3951F
31T-7520011	N66844 N200RS [w/o 18Jan88 Hazelwood, nr St.Louis-Lambert Field, MO, USA; canx 18Aug97]
31T-7520012	N9706N PT-KME
31T-7520013	N100TN (N7PB) N100TN [wfu, parts to Atlanta Air Salvage, Griffin-Spalding County, GA, USA; canx 13Mar91]
31T-7520014	N66845 N123LV N3TK N8TK FAC5194 (Colombian AF) FAC5739 (Colombian AF)
31T-7520015	N73Z N500ZC N11232 C-FYBV [wfu Calgary-Springbank, AB, Canada; marked as N11232; canx 03Oct08]
31T-7520016	N101T 5N-AUT [wfu cAug94 Groton-New London, CT, USA]
31T-7520017	N66846 N43SP N550T N550F N502RH N707ML (N5RZ) N707ML
31T-7520018	N54961 N300CS N300WT N202JP [wfu, parts to White Industries, Bates City, MO, USA; location F-48]
31T-7520019	N66847 [wfu, parts to White Industries, Bates City, MO, USA; location G-06]
31T-7520020	N66848 N5SM N741P [stolen cOct81 in Jamaica & w/o; canx cJan84]
31T-7520021	N66849 HP-800 N31PT C-GZQD C-GKPC
31T-7520022	N66850 LV-PTS LV-LTV
31T-7520023	N66851 (N711HG) N711HC C-GHMU N314GA N40TT
31T-7520024	N66852 N431LS N431AC C-GPNP
31T-7520025	C-GHSI [wfu, parts to White Industries, Bates City, MO, USA; location H-46; canx 27Oct95]
31T-7520026	N9749N C-GPTP N180JS N181DC
31T-7520027	N9688N YV-TAYA YV-08CP YV-1990P
31T-7520028	N9662N N54975 PK-SYS PK-DYS VH-HMA ZK-PDC VH-HMA N607DD [wfu, parts to White Industries, Bates City, MO, USA; marked as VH-HMA; location F-50]
31T-7520029	N66854 ZS-JLR N43SC N43SQ N770MG
31T-7520030	N54959 N444RC
31T-7520031	N9657N SE-GLA N590DL [wfu Calgary-Springbank, AB, Canada; canx 16Sep92]
31T-7520032	N9658N F-BXLC N4116W
31T-7520033	N54964 I-CGAT
31T-7520034	N54966 I-HYDR
31T-7520035	N54967 N100KR N667JB N66LD N17TU
31T-7520036	N54968 N31DF C-GPCW N60049 HC-BXZ N360LL [w/o 24Jan03 nr Denver, CO, USA in mid-air collision with Cessna 172P N52241; canx 07Aug07]
31T-7520037	N54969 N79ND N85AJ N111RF (N111BF) VH-DXD
31T-7520038	N54970 XA-COJ HP-818 HP-774 N54970 N570AB [wfu, parts to White Industries, Bates City, MO, USA; canx 31Mar89]
31T-7520039	N54990 N531PT C-GJPT
31T-7520040	N54971 N200FD [w/o 20Mar87 nr Lawrence-Municipal, MA, USA; canx 12Jan89]
31T-7520041	N54972 C-GWFM [b/u; canx 18Aug93]
31T-7520042	N54973 C-GSID (N1181L) C-GSID [w/o 18Oct87 Kirkland Lake, ON, Canada; canx 08May89]
31T-7520043	N54974 N54CW N29KL TI-AWN
31T-7520044	[completed as c/n 31T-7620001] N54976
31T-7520045	[completed as c/n 31T-7620002] N54977
31T-7520046	[completed as c/n 31T-7620003] N9661N
31T-7520047	[completed as c/n 31T-7620004] N54978

PA-31T

c/n	Mods	Identities
31T-7620001		N54976 C-GNPT OY-BSB OH-PHA [wfu 24Aug01; pres inst airframe Bardufoss, Norway; canx 24Oct01]
31T-7620002		N54977 N610P
31T-7620003		N9661N LV-PUU LV-DMA LV-LZO
31T-7620004		N54978 C-GAPT [w/o 17Oct84 nr Toronto, ON, Canada; canx 28Dec88]
31T-7620005		N54979 I-PALS
31T-7620006		N54980 C-GDOW F-GDPJ [w/o 12Dec84 Paris-Le Bourget, France; canx 20Jun86]
31T-7620007		N54985 (N76NL) N54985 [wfu, parts to White Industries, Bates City, MO, USA; location H-42]
31T-7620008		N54986 F-BXSA C-FYTK N484PS C-GMEJ C-FPNJ
31T-7620009		N54987 I-GEAR N900TB C-GIVM N4425W [wfu, parts to White Industries, Bates City, MO, USA; location H-43; canx 29Jun91]
31T-7620010		N9748N C-GXBF
31T-7620011		N54988 N76PT F-GFEA [wfu; canx 26May09]
31T-7620012		N54989 ZS-XAT ZS-JTP C9-JTP
31T-7620013		N54992 N931SW CX-BLT N931SW [wfu, parts to White Industries, Bates City, MO, USA; location "Ramp Mid"]
31T-7620014		N54993 (N200JH) N98PT N98AT (N460LC) N98AT
31T-7620015		N54994 9V-BHF PK-PJH [wfu for spares - location?]
31T-7620016		N57524 C-GTFP (N57524) C-GTFP [wfu Calgary-Springbank, AB, Canada; canx 03Oct08]
31T-7620017		N57526 N234K [dbr 23Sep88 Eugene-Mahlon Sweet Field, OR, USA; canx 16Mar89]
31T-7620018		N57528 N69BK N89BK C-GSGC N71588 N941SS N318MA 5B-CJD SX-BFR N232PS SX-BFR N232PS SX-BFR N232PS SX-AVE
31T-7620019		N82000 C-GMDF
31T-7620020		N9662N F-BXSK
31T-7620021		N82002 N131RC N131RG N96JS [wfu, parts to White Industries, Bates City, MO, USA; location "Ramp Mid"]
31T-7620022		N82005 N57MK N57MR LV-BCR
31T-7620023		N82006 N100MP N988TA C-FMHB 5B-CIM SX-ABT C-FMHB [wfu Calgary-Springbank, AB, Canada; moved cOct08 to MTW Aerospace, Montgomery, AL, USA; canx 03Oct08]
31T-7620024		N82009 N176CC [w/o 05Jun78 nr Lamar, CO, USA]
31T-7620025		N82010 (N820YL) N82010 [wfu, parts to White Industries, Bates City, MO, USA; location "Ramp North"; canx 04Dec89]
31T-7620026		N9651N C-GXCD [wfu Calgary-Springbank, AB, Canada; canx 03Oct08]
31T-7620027		N82013 N90BB [wfu, parts to White Industries, Bates City, MO, USA; b/u]
31T-7620028		N82016 N531PT N555PM
31T-7620029		N82017 N97JT C-GMDY N177JE C-GEBA C-GNWD
31T-7620030		N82000 N300CM N35GT [wfu, parts to White Industries, Bates City, MO, USA; location H-09]
31T-7620031		N82019 N35RT N35RR N801HD [w/o 24Nov77 nr Beckley-Raleigh County, WV, USA]
31T-7620032		N9726N F-GALD [dam 14Jan05 Lille-Lesquin, France]
31T-7620033		N82021 D-IHSO (N124AA) C-GQCC N44TC C-FNYM
31T-7620034		N82022 N727PC N7276C N69XX N7276C XA-TAY N7276C XA-PGT
31T-7620035		N82023 N21AR N21AF N21KN N197TA N199ND LV-BCT
31T-7620036		N82025 N73TB C-GNDI
31T-7620037		N82000 C-GFIN N5136V
31T-7620038		N82028 N600WR [wfu c1989, parts to Dodson International Parts, Rantoul, KS, USA]
31T-7620039		N82031 C-FWUT [wfu Calgary-Springbank, AB, Canada; marked as N82031; canx 03Oct08]
31T-7620040		N9663N N400CM
31T-7620041		N82033 D-IOTT D-IMAX N27856 D-IEEA N27856 N67DW
31T-7620042		N9718N F-GAJC N8131F
31T-7620043		N82026 N52BC N62BC [wfu, parts to White Industries, Bates City, MO, USA; location "Ramp North"]
31T-7620044		N82033 N12FC N92FC PT-OPH
31T-7620045		N82053 F-ODEE F-BTEE [CofA exp 16Dec92 - status?]
31T-7620046		N82037 HP-111A FAP-200 (Panamanian AF) HP-1082 N5432V XC-UAT XA-
31T-7620047		N82039 N111CT (N45FN) N111CT
31T-7620048		N82044 N801L N801C (N414VM) N801C [wfu, parts to White Industries, Bates City, MO, USA; location H-05]
31T-7620049		N82045 N22WF N979SW C-FRWW N37TH N37RL XB- [canx 13Feb04 as exported to Mexico]
31T-7620050		N82047 YV-97CP N2FJ (N39RP) N2FJ
31T-7620051		N82048 N111HH N631MC N631WF N788BB
31T-7620052		N82054 N65MC N65MD N737WB N577JE N220FS
31T-7620053		N82055 N8CP N16HA (N717CB) C-GHRM PR-HRM
31T-7620054		N82057 YV-98CP N39518 (N700EM) F-GFBF [b/u; canx 03Dec99]
31T-7620055		N82058 N300BP ZK-ROM N85KA N55R
31T-7620056		N82063 N110DE N319JG [wfu c1993 for spares - location?]
31T-7620057		N9659N SE-GNB N280K N74TC F-GDAL 6V-AGO TJ-TAC N200VE [wfu, parts to Alliance Air Parts, Oklahoma City, OK, USA]
31T-7720001		N82064 N631PT [w/o 24Feb77 Bressler, nr Harrisburg-Capital City, PA, USA; canx cMay77]
31T-7720002		N82065 N771SW N505GP N771SW
31T-7720003		N82071 N333P N82194 N231PT (N82AB) N28AB (YV-46CP) N28FM N34HM
31T-7720004		N82073 N200CM [wfu, parts to White Industries, Bates City, MO, USA; location "Ramp Mid"]
31T-7720005		N82075 N444ET N28BG
31T-7720006		N82076 N77CG N77PR [wfu, parts to White Industries, Bates City, MO, USA; location F-49; canx 03Mar89]
31T-7720007		N82077 N721RB N721RP N99VA
31T-7720008		N82081 N730PT XA-HAY N730PT

PA-31T

c/n	Mods	Identities
31T-7720009		N82084 N500CM N701RG N701RQ C-GRCW (N4378D) N4327X ZK-MPI ZK-POD [sold in USA for spares; canx 06Apr01]
31T-7720010		N82085 N2YP N74NL [w/o 30Dec86 Merrillville, IN, USA]
31T-7720011		N82086 N51BJ TF-VLH N51BJ N20WL
31T-7720012		N82091 (N772SW) N77PK N78PK N79ML (N79ME) N79ML N119EB
31T-7720013		N82092 C-GSWB [dbr 12Nov93 Montreal-Dorval, QC, Canada, parts to White Industries, Bates City, MO, USA; location H-47; canx 30Nov94]
31T-7720014		N82094
31T-7720015		N82096 N775SW N444JW [dbr 03Dec79 San Angelo Regional-Mathis Field, TX, USA, parts to Dodson International Parts, Rantoul, KS, USA; canx cDec81]
31T-7720016		N62825 N82097 N811PM C-FACM N311LM [wfu, parts to White Industries, Bates City, MO, USA; location "Ramp North 01"]
31T-7720017		N82100 C-GXNA N19AC N19AG N12TW C- [canx 05Dec07 as exported to Canada]
31T-7720018		N82102 N500GC OE-FFH 3A-MBA N819MK
31T-7720019		N82105 N772SW C-GSKR (N83GA) N75465 N135CL
31T-7720020		N82109 N35RT N37RT N37HB
31T-7720021		N82112 N200CN N100LB (N234C) N100LB [wfu, parts to White Industries, Bates City, MO, USA; location H-07]
31T-7720022		(N773SW) N831PT N14LW OB-1403 [w/o 16Jan96 Mt Chachani, Peru; canx 21Dec01]
31T-7720023		N82115 C-GGMD N515WB [w/o 02Dec93 nr Norwich, OH, USA; canx 14Jan00]
31T-7720024		N82116 N600CM (N840CM) N600CM [w/o 23Aug85 Flat Rock, NC, USA; canx cNov85]
31T-7720025		N774SW N33HW N741P (N710MA) N741P [wfu, parts to White Industries, Bates City, MO, USA; location H-44]
31T-7720026		N82118 C-GPIP [wfu, parts to Quest Aviation, Lake City, FL, USA; canx 14Dec92]
31T-7720027		N82120 N143RJ XB-HGY N427TA
31T-7720028		N82121 N29JM N171JP
31T-7720029		N82122 F-GAMP [CofA exp 23Apr93 - status?]
31T-7720030		N82123 [wfu, parts to White Industries, Bates City, MO, USA; location "Ramp North"]
31T-7720031		N9725N N82144 HB-LIW F-GEPE [wfu cJun01; pres inst airframe Bodo, Norway; canx 16Jul01]
31T-7720032		N82126 N931PT N301CS N977PC XB-ELW N747RL (N748RL) N747RE
31T-7720033		N9731N N82152 TU-TJL
31T-7720034		N82130 N500HM N777KV (N774KV) N777KV [wfu, parts to White Industries, Bates City, MO, USA; location "Ramp North"]
31T-7720035		N9718N N200NB
31T-7720036		N9733N YV-123CP N1RA N41RC F-GGRV 5R- [canx 11Jun06 as exported to Madagascar]
31T-7720037		N9753N N112BL
31T-7720038		N82136 N77NL [cvtd to Comanchero 750]
31T-7720039		N9738N N1144Z PT-LUJ
31T-7720040		N82139 (N14BW) N82139 [wfu, parts to White Industries, Bates City, MO, USA; location "Ramp North"]
31T-7720041		N9734N N82144 LN-PAE TS-LAZ F-ODGS
31T-7720042		N82148 YU-BKT F-GJPE [wfu c1993 for spares - location? canx 11Jul93]
31T-7720043		N9739N N82152 YV-132CP N4207U N777GA OO-RDW F-GEBH (F-GJDK) N80MA
31T-7720044		N82155 N4015Y N23MV LV-BCU
31T-7720045		N82156
31T-7720046		N9741N N82175 VH-CCW [w/o 03May81 Guildford, Perth, WA, Australia; canx 03May81]
31T-7720047		N9748N YV-124CP YV1226
31T-7720048		N82163 N521PM
31T-7720049		N82161 (N82LS) XA- N82161 XA- [canx 22Feb08 as exported to Mexico; reinstated 14May08; canx to Mexico 12Jun08]
31T-7720050		N9727N YV-193CP YV-2451P
31T-7720051		N82164 N27KM 85-1609 (US Army) 85-1609 (US Navy) N27KM [stored Davis-Monthan AFB, AZ, USA; storage code AN7U0001; canx 01Jun07]
31T-7720052		N82165 C-GXTC
31T-7720053		N82166 N101PT (N799SW) N613HC
31T-7720054		N82167 N30DJ N30DU (N98AS) N30DU
31T-7720055		N82168 N778SW XA-IEQ XB-EGZ N2157A XB-MMR
31T-7720056		N82169 OE-FDS
31T-7720057		N82172 N300BX N31LZ N610RG N61SG C-GGVB N411DL
31T-7720058		N82176 N7WS C-GKMX N167DA C-FFNV
31T-7720059		N82177 LV-PXD LV-MGD N48AR 5R-MIM
31T-7720060		N82178 D-IASG N708US N149BC XB-JIC N160NA N909PW
31T-7720061		N82177 N33BJ [wfu, parts to White Industries, Bates City, MO, USA; location "Ramp Mid"]
31T-7720062		N82182 C-GEAL 5B-CIP SX-ABV C-GEAL N68LM N361JC
31T-7720063		N82125 YV-279CP N3948A F-GFUV SX-FDC
31T-7720064		N9697N (N779SW) N45LS N60DR N211AE
31T-7720065		N82188 LV-PYD LV-MDG
31T-7720066		N82189 N70CW N15PJ N499EH N888JM N993RH
31T-7720067		N82186 N999WS N900SF F-GHJV
31T-7720068		N82190 XA-SBW XB-GGZ N510LC (N69XX) N510LC
31T-7720069	^	(N779SW) N45TX N411LM N950CT

Production complete

PIPER PA-31T CHEYENNE II

Kit-AM indicates kit supplied to Aero Mercantile in Colombia
Kit-CH indicates kit supplied to Chincul SACAIFI in Argentina
^ - Blackhawk XP135A engine upgrade fitted

c/n	Identities
31T-7820001	N78PC N88DC (N88LH) N711FN N115PC (N300PR) N115PC
31T-7820002	N333P C-GCUL C-FRJE
31T-7820003	N82196 N780SW N444ER C-GKMV N547TA N55GD
31T-7820004	N82197 N33LA N33LD N910JP
31T-7820005	N82204 N5MC N131AF [dbr 05Nov92 Medford-Jackson County, OR, USA, parts to White Industries, Bates City, MO, USA; location "Ramp Mid"; canx 14Oct05]
31T-7820006	N9730N N78CA F-GFPV N14EA LV-BCP
31T-7820007	N82207 N700CM [w/o 09Jan86 Jacksonville-International, FL, USA]
31T-7820008	N82209 (N700CM) N77SE N14MR YV-1402P YV-703CP YV-695CP YV1651
31T-7820009	N131PC
31T-7820010	N82211 N333PD D-IFPD F-GGAT 3A-MSB (LX-GPP) F-GRPS
31T-7820011	N82212 N378HC N777TH N88NW (N8RS) N884CA N250CT HA-SIT
31T-7820012	N781SW XB-HVO
31T-7820013	N9657N N21CA N59RB N47NS N20FB (N813AM) N813AR 5V- [canx 12Dec06 as exported to Togo; unconfirmed 5V-TPT]
31T-7820014	N82216 C-GSBC N18ZX
31T-7820015	N82217 N107BK F-GHTA
31T-7820016	N82218 N47CC [w/o 29Jul81 nr Richlands, VA, USA; canx cMay83]
31T-7820017	N82222 HB-LRV
31T-7820018	N82223 N35RT N353T N35RT CC-CIW
31T-7820019	N9748N N82250 D-IASF N9113Y N727SM N521BH N727SM N31ET
31T-7820020	N9661N LV-PZC LV-MHL CC-CZB CC-PZB
31T-7820021	N82225 N231PC N102FL (N182FL) N182ME
31T-7820022	N82226 N9DK N484SC
31T-7820023	N9662N C-GGPS
31T-7820024	N82210 N54MC (F-GGTV) YV-762CP N155CA N771MF
31T-7820025	N82228 N978BC N727BN N888SV N888CV
31T-7820026	N82229 N782SW (N123LC) N59JM N59JN N21TB N36JM (N36JK) N570AB N473GG
31T-7820027	N82231 N22CA N61RA F-GGPJ LX-RST
31T-7820028	N82232 N444BN
31T-7820029	N82233 N783SW C-GGFL N78UA N427DD
31T-7820030	N82236 N700JR N700TR PT-OZY [w/o 12Jan01 Fazenda Independencia, nr Agua Comprida, Minas Gerais, Brazil]
31T-7820031	N82238 (N711TD) N711TB [wfu, parts to White Industries, Bates City, MO, USA; location I-03]
31T-7820032	N82242 N43CE (N43BE) N43CW N700PT XB-ILT YV1031
31T-7820033	TG-ZAZ TG-AVE XB-CMY TG-AVE N50902 I-SAES F-GHNT OO-DGS N63CA
31T-7820034	N82249 N419R *N772MF
31T-7820035	N82246 N6NB N17NM N5MQ CC-CMH
31T-7820036	N82251 N202HC
31T-7820037	N82253 N784SW N24E YV-2365P
31T-7820038	N82255 C-FBCS N2689E N679MM C-GVKK
31T-7820039	N82256 N900JM N131MP 5B-CJC SX-BFQ N233PS SX-BFQ N233PS SX-BFQ N233PS
31T-7820040	N82259 N23CA N300JC (N342DA) N68MB N98TB
31T-7820041	N9733N D-IMTT N82WC D-IMTT [dbr 16Aug89 in Peine-Eddesse, West Germany; parts to Dodson International Parts, Rantoul, KS, USA; canx 23Nov89]
31T-7820042	N82266 N400RT N700RG 4X-CIN
31T-7820043	N82267 N44DT
31T-7820044	N82271 [dbr 13May78 nr Pellston-Emmet County, MI, USA, parts to Dodson International Parts, Rantoul, KS, USA; canx cMar82]
31T-7820045	N9740N N82288 I-CGTT
31T-7820046	N82273 N777LM N688CA PP-LCQ
31T-7820047	N82274 N785SW N374GS N374GA N290T N926LD
31T-7820048	N82275 OE-FOP D-IAKS [w/o 23Jul83 Borkum Island, West Germany; canx cAug83]
31T-7820049	N82276 C-GXMT N9156N C-GXMT N89MC OB-1497 N689AC PT-WFQ
31T-7820050	N82277 F-GGPV N250TT
31T-7820051	N9739N OY-BRL LN-AET D-IGAK OE-FBO SE-LUB
31T-7820052	N6002A YV-194CP YV1137 YV2006
31T-7820053	N9748N N6003A I-GFAW F-GJJF C-GJJE N786AH
31T-7820054	N9748N VH-MWT PK-DYR
31T-7820055	N82282 [dbr 27Apr79 nr Elyria-Lorain County, OH, USA, parts to White Industries, Bates City, MO, USA; b/u]
31T-7820056	N82285 N786SW N123DG N123DE N4NH N51RD N781CK
31T-7820057	N9740N OB-M-1003 [w/o 06Oct81 Cuzco-Teniente Alejandro Velasco Astete International, Peru; canx 03Aug82]
31T-7820058	N82290 TG-GAP
31T-7820059	N82291 N26AC N11BC [wfu location unkn; (may have been in Italy); canx 07Jan87]
31T-7820060	N82293 N89TW XA- N89TW XA-RMT N990LR
31T-7820061	N82294 N161MP (N84WG) N4007 N62286 (N794PL) N303KL N5007
31T-7820062	N82295 N26CA [w/o 12Mar80 Kettleman City, CA, USA; canx 20Oct93]
31T-7820063	N82298 C-GAMJ [w/o 17Apr89 Hall Beach, NT, Canada; canx 22Feb90]
31T-7820064	N6002A N777JM [dbr 21Feb94 Norwood-Memorial, MA, USA, parts to White Industries, Bates City, MO, USA; location I-02; canx 20May94]
31T-7820065	N9662N LV-PAC [w/o 14Jul78 Lima, Peru]
31T-7820066	N9715N N6108A D-IKEW

PA-31T

c/n	Mods	Identities
31T-7820067		N331PC YV-1402P YV1165 [w/o 02Jul08 nr Charallave, Venezuela]
31T-7820068		N6027A N15SS [dbr 30Nov81 nr Madison-Municipal, IN, USA, parts to White Industries, Bates City, MO, USA; location F-15; canx 26Oct82]
31T-7820069		N9691N LV-PAB LV-MLU N25AB HC-BVA HC-BXF N168DA N155MC
31T-7820070		N6033A YV-2331P [w/o 08Feb87 in Venezuela; canx 08May87]
31T-7820071		YV-215CP [w/o 04Jun81 nr Caracas, Venezuela; canx 17Jan82]
31T-7820072		N6038A (N90TW) N6038A [w/o 31Jan92 nr Swanton-Toledo Express, OH, USA; canx 28May92]
31T-7820073		N6039A N788SW C-GVBO N7703L N814W
31T-7820074		N6062A N787SW N274SB
31T-7820075		N6075A N781CW N75TF (N715WA) N75TF
31T-7820076		N9748N YV-133CP N29CA N429AP
31T-7820077		N6080A N87SJ XA- N87SJ
31T-7820078		N91TW [w/o 17Jan82 Delta, UT, USA; canx cOct82]
31T-7820079		N9668N N6109A VH-DRV [wfu; canx 10Dec03]
31T-7820080		N6097A D-IAPE N6097A N5D
31T-7820081		N34CA N2DS N881NA
31T-7820082		N6100A N7FL
31T-7820083		N6102A N53TM N53TA
31T-7820084		N6103A N789SW N22EM TG-LAR N450DA N100WQ
31T-7820085		N9687N D-IOKY N589GA N12HF V5-CCH
31T-7820086		N6104A N44CS N186GA
31T-7820087		N6107A
31T-7820088		N9717N SE-IAB OY-BRV N4491C N345DF [wfu cJun07, parts to MTW Aerospace, Montgomery, AL, USA; canx 24Aug07]
31T-7820089		N6110A N92TW XA-JGS N275CA [b/u; canx 12Dec96]
31T-7820090		N6113A YU-BLU D-IBEU D-IJPG N32KW
31T-7820091		N6121A YV-38CP N100RN [w/o 23Feb85 Utica, MI, USA; canx 26Apr91]
31T-7820092		N6133A N777DL ZS-LUC [dbr 26Apr89 Welkom, Free State Province, South Africa, parts to Dodson International Parts, Rantoul, KS, USA; canx 08Feb90]
31T-7920001		N6150A N333P N123HK I-NANE 3A-MIO
31T-7920002		N6152A N431PC N431Y N400PB N141DT D-IXXX OM-VIP
31T-7920003		N9670N LV-PAS LV-DMO LV-MNU N225WW [wfu cSep07, parts to MTW Aerospace, Montgomery, AL, USA]
31T-7920004		N790SW N790SD [wfu cJul07, parts to MTW Aerospace, Montgomery, AL, USA]
31T-7920005		N6166A N817CJ CC-PLL
31T-7920006		N6167A N778HD [wfu, parts to White Industries, Bates City, MO, USA; location F-39; canx 22Aug08]
31T-7920007		N6171A N791SW N22WF (N53TR) N22WF
31T-7920008		N9715N C-GVKA
31T-7920009		N6174A N90TW N901CC N615PS N723JR N723JP
31T-7920010		N9748N N6196A D-IOTT
31T-7920011		N6175A C-GHXG N6175A
31T-7920012		(N36CA) N6176A N614SC XB-RTG XB-HNA
31T-7920013		N6177A N36CA [w/o 08Feb84 Riviera, AZ, USA; canx cMay85]
31T-7920014		N6178A N792SW N3FH N20MR N792SW D-IDDI [w/o 05Feb93 Cologne, Germany; canx cMar93]
31T-7920015		N6179A N200GF N200GH N200PG
31T-7920016		N6180A (N61SM) N79FB N161XX
31T-7920017	Kit-CH	LV-MNR
31T-7920018		N6185A N165RB N100KR YV-655CP YV1081
31T-7920019		N9738N C-GVKS N619J N20SH N20TV N20TN
31T-7920020		N6187A N866RA N224EC N39EH
31T-7920021		N6188A N20PJ YV-723P YV217T
31T-7920022		N9741N YV-251CP
31T-7920023		N793SW XB-RLM
31T-7920024		N6194A TG-LIA N333KB N10FG N117EW N117EB N111HT N159DG
31T-7920025		N6195A N163SA [dbr 14Aug96 Pottstown-Limerick, PA, USA, parts to White Industries, Bates City, MO, USA; location H-48]
31T-7920026		N900CM VH-LJK VH-TNP [w/o 28Jul04 34km SE of Benalla, VIC, Australia; canx 21Oct04]
31T-7920027		N6198A N71CS N71QS C-GLAG [canx 25Jan05 as exported to UK; actually placed on US register 24Feb05] N31ZS
31T-7920028		N94TW N10MC N123EA
31T-7920029		N23137 N531PC N310WA (N494HL) N494CA TG-VDG N68BJ
31T-7920030		N23138 N38CA N65EL N288DC (N288SB) 4X-CIE N89JA
31T-7920031	Kit-CH	N23138 LV-MOC [w/o 04May80 Buenos Aires Don Torcuato, Buenos Aires Province, Argentina]
31T-7920032		N23139 N88BC
31T-7920033	Kit-CH	N23140 LV-MOD [dbr 10Oct86 Lago Posadas, Santa Cruz Province, Argentina, parts to White Industries, Bates City, MO, USA; location "Taxiway South 1"]
31T-7920034		N23140 N96TW N29KR PT-OFH
31T-7920035		N23152 N80BC N110MP N111KV N774MF
31T-7920036		N23159 N796SW N222 C-GEAS N525CA EC-FOT N81918 N160TR [w/o 12Feb07 Zweibrucken, Germany; canx 27Jun07]
31T-7920037		N23173 N610MW N53AM
31T-7920038		N9734N YV-258CP N4445K SE-IYB N333CE N333XX
31T-7920039		N9739N (N610MW) C-GVON N32745 HB-LOZ 3A-MBT F-GLLG 3A-MTD N524AM
31T-7920040		N23185 N80CP
31T-7920041		N23189 N302HA N66WJ XA-HNG
31T-7920042		N23217 N95TW N711LV (N5CA) (N74WA) N777LE C-GFAM N28CA

PA-31T

c/n	Mods	Identities
31T-7920043		N47CA
31T-7920044		N9735N N23217 D-IAMK N29825 N163MC PT-OTF N90WG
31T-7920045		N23219 N52LS C-FGWA
31T-7920046		N23272 N797SW N700TF N700LT N800EB
31T-7920047		N79CA XA-RWR
31T-7920048		N798SW N404AF N406RS
31T-7920049		N23310 N500FE (N500FC) F-GFVO [wfu cOct01; pres inst airframe Stavanger-Sola, Norway; may be wearing false marks LN-KBV; canx 26Nov01 as exported to Monaco]
31T-7920050	Kit-CH	LV-MOE
31T-7920051		N23340 N9772N N97TW
31T-7920052		N23343 N48MD N789RW N333MX N333MZ N333LM [w/o 29May96 nr Malvern-Municipal, AR, USA; canx 28Apr99]
31T-7920053		N23352 N731PC YV-1082P YV175T N27GD CC-CYT
31T-7920054		N23406 N799SW N23406 C-FBBO N16RK YV-187CP (N690CA) N187CP
31T-7920055		N23407 N620DB
31T-7920056		N9737N F-ODJS 5T-TJY F-ODJS 5T-TJY 5U-ACC ZS-PXB
31T-7920057		N23408 N102TW N102E N52TT
31T-7920058		N23411 N179SW N12GR CC-PJG CC-CAO
31T-7920059		N9731N N23600 PH-CAM N4616T N63SC N25MG
31T-7920060		N23412 N809E N86MP N31WE N81WE
31T-7920061		N23414 N575JM N117FN N44HT
31T-7920062		N23415 YV-307CP N44319 N19HM (F-GIYV) N78CA XA- [canx 22May09 as exported to Mexico]
31T-7920063		N23416 N24AD N31KF N23KF PT-LZB
31T-7920064		N9743N N23477 VH-TNZ [w/o 29Sep88 in hangar Melbourne-Moorabbin, VIC, Australia; canx 23Nov92]
31T-7920065		N23449 (N279SW) LV-PCJ LV-OAP
31T-7920066		N23457 N111AM N444PC
31T-7920067		N23466 N74TW (N4301L) N74TW
31T-7920068		N23475 N40JC N711RD [wfu, parts to Alliance Air Parts, Oklahoma City, OK, USA]
31T-7920069		N9746N F-ODKO TJ-AGS F-GFLN N250KA C-FCEF
31T-7920070		N9730N C-GJPD [dbf 10Jan93 Quebec City, QC, Canada; canx 07Apr94]
31T-7920071		N23591 N379SW N727CM C-FEQB 5B-CIL SX-ABU C-FEQB [wfu Calgary-Springbank, AB, Canada; moved cOct08 to MTW Aerospace, Montgomery, AL, USA; canx 03Oct08]
31T-7920072		N23593 N48CA YV-62CP N620P CC-CZC
31T-7920073		N9733N N23699 EC-DHF
31T-7920074		N23617 N204EF N24DD
31T-7920075		N23627 (N727LK) OB-S-1308 OB-1308 [canx 21Dec01 - status?]
31T-7920076	Kit-AM	N10F HK-2347X HK-2347 HK-2347P HK-2347 YV-2822P YV1153
31T-7920077		N23630 LV-PCM LV-MZA PT-WHI [w/o 30Oct98 Morro do Caju, San Francisco do Sul, Brazil]
31T-7920078		N23646 (PH-BAM) N23646
31T-7920079		N23649 N555RC N789CH N775MF
31T-7920080	Kit-CH	N10F N23661 LV-MTU
31T-7920081		N23665 N62CA N131TC (N701RM) N600RM N602RM (N438BH) N602RM [w/o 01Jul99 nr Deerfield, VA, USA; canx 20Apr00]
31T-7920082		N23667 N222SC N56HF N109TT (N777JM) CC-PNA CC-CCC
31T-7920083		N23676 N31DC PT-LZR
31T-7920084		N23677 (N700JR) N666JL (N505TB) N189GH PK-PTI [also quoted as PK-PCI on register]
31T-7920085	Kit-CH	N10F N23680 LV-MYY [w/o 01Feb80 Buenos Aires, Bueno Aires Province, Argentina]
31T-7920086		N23687 OE-FMR N1183G
31T-7920087		N23718 N396JH
31T-7920088		N2334R N64CA HK-3331X HK-3331W HK-3331P N171DA HK-3331X HK-3331W
31T-7920089		N2344R N579SW N579CW N101AF N171AF [w/o 23Feb09 Pueblo-Memorial, CO, USA; canx 15Jun09]
31T-7920090		N2349R N801L N881L
31T-7920091		N2510R F-GCFG N19GA N26SL
31T-7920092		N2410R N73TW (N2345W) (N38CW) N78TW N108NL
31T-7920093		N2416R N99KF
31T-7920094		SE-ICS OH-PYE F-GPBF
31T-8020001		N2345R N831PC [w/o 01Jun83 in sea nr West Palm Beach, FL, USA; canx 05Sep84]
31T-8020002		N2429R N333P (N4LH) N333P
31T-8020003		N2430R (N73CA) (N83TW) (N870WE) N87TW N122EL N985CA TG-OIL TG-GOL TG-CYC
31T-8020004		N2438R N800SW (N800TW) (N51RL) N23WP
31T-8020005		YV-314CP N4471P (N42WC) N112WC N118WC VH-DXI VH-TTD N25AS N25ND
31T-8020006		N2516R N801CM YU-BPF YU-BLK
31T-8020007		N2529R D-IHVI [w/o 13Mar86 nr Southend-Rochford, UK; canx cApr86]
31T-8020008		N2547R N84TW N84WC N417G (N43WC) N165CA XB-GVI
31T-8020009		N2547R N24HE D-ILRA [w/o 11Aug87 Munich, West Germany; canx cAug87]
31T-8020010		OB-M-1176 OB-S-1176 OB-1176 [w/o 28Feb90 Tocache, Peru; canx 21Dec01]
31T-8020011		N2325W N73CA N90FS
31T-8020012		N2328W YU-BPG
31T-8020013	Kit-CH	N2342W LV-OGF
31T-8020014		N2348W N801SW N801GC N801ST N137JT N137JE
31T-8020015		N2353W HP-809 [canx 14May81 - status?]
31T-8020016		N2355W N801HL
31T-8020017		N2359W N802SW (N100ES) I-APIT N154CA D-IKET N154CA D-IKET
31T-8020018		N2366W N802CM N802HC N108UC
31T-8020019		N2369W N71TW N85CM XC-QET

PA-31T

c/n	Mods	Identities
31T-8020020		N2374W N500TW N113WC N118WC
31T-8020021		N2382W D-IIOO "YU-1100" YU-BMM
31T-8020022		N2427W N38V N38VT
31T-8020023		N2386W N457RS N611LM N970PS
31T-8020024		N2393W N103SP N151GS
31T-8020025		N2407W N135MA N4WF
31T-8020026		N2473W N89CA N155DS SX-AVA
31T-8020027		N2483W (N248WW) N2483W SX-AVB
31T-8020028	Kit-CH	N2542W LV-OGG PT-OAM
31T-8020029		N9746N N2556W YV-363CP N4424W (N661AE) PT-OED
31T-8020030		N2563W HB-LLO I-EJAG N37CA D-IIWB [wfu cFeb96, parts to Atlanta Air Salvage, Griffin-Spalding County, GA, USA; canx 08Feb96]
31T-8020031		N2529W N807SW N9HJ N102AF N102AR N47JF
31T-8020032		N803SW TG-HCR
31T-8020033		N2556W N11WC PT-OCL
31T-8020034		D-IHKC N4241Y N97PC (N313SS) N97PC
31T-8020035		N2566W (N321SS) N2566W [w/o 19Feb81 Pontiac, MI, USA; canx 20Mar81]
31T-8020036		N2570W N30DJ OE-FKG
31T-8020037		N805SW F-GIII
31T-8020038		N804CM N300HP SX-AVC
31T-8020039		N2584W N63CM
31T-8020040	Kit-AM	HK-2451X HK-2451P [canx 06May00 - status?]
31T-8020041		N2312V PT-OHS N198AA N198CC PH-SVY
31T-8020042		N2315V XB-BRR N300TB N716WA (N414CW) N716WA
31T-8020043	Kit-AM	N2326V HK-3472X [canx 22Nov90 - status?]
31T-8020044		N2330V F-GCLH N178SG
31T-8020045		N2334V C-GKKG N75CA TG-EAB [w/o c1996 Rio Dulce, Izabal, Guatemala]
31T-8020046		N2334V N805CM N1879W N1879D N302TA
31T-8020047	Kit-AM	HK-2455X HK-2455 HK-2455P HK-2455W
31T-8020048		N2336V C-GOCR N42EJ PT-WFB
31T-8020049		N2338V N15UE C-GLSW
31T-8020050		N2339V N806SW C-FSRW N91TS
31T-8020051		N2343V N60AW [w/o 16Feb92 7.5 mls SW of Big Bear City Apt, CA, USA; canx 23Jun92]
31T-8020052		OE-FDH D-IAPD N117SB N700CC N700GC OE-FGK [w/o 08Feb92 Friedrichshafen, Germany; canx cDec96]
31T-8020053		N2372V N380CA N141TC N147TC (N200JH) CC-PKU N100QM N440HP N39K C-GTTS
31T-8020054	Kit-CH	LV-OGB PT-LLG
31T-8020055		N2373V PH-TAX N3998Y (N235MB) N3998Y [w/o 31Oct02 Hobbs, NM, USA; canx 06May08]
31T-8020056		N2376V (N82TW) N81TW N804CD N144PL N144RL N314TD
31T-8020057		N2379V N806CM N22DT
31T-8020058		N2384V D-IGKG PT-WME (N203CS) N236SR PT-MGZ
31T-8020059		SE-IDM N457TC N457TG
31T-8020060		N2385V N703CJ N112ED
31T-8020061		N2388V N707CJ N707JC N711DH PT-OZN
31T-8020062		N2388V YV-390CP N5452J N8CF
31T-8020063		N2389V YU-BPH
31T-8020064		N2390V N711WV N711WE N231SY N376WS (N32WS) HK- [canx 09Jun09 as exported to Colombia]
31T-8020065		N2395V N712CJ N118EL C-GNAM C-GPIM [wfu, parts to Westcan Aircraft Sales & Salvage, Kamloops, BC, Canada; canx 06Feb04]
31T-8020066		N2398V N555CG N555HP (F-GHSV) ZP-TYI
31T-8020067		N2466V N83TW N301CH N79JS N793S N42CV (N46CV) N22LD
31T-8020068		N2467V N350ST
31T-8020069		N9746N OB-M-1193 OB-S-1193 OB-1193 CC-CNH CC-PZX
31T-8020070		N2469V
31T-8020071		N2471V N400CP N650RS (N658RS) N650RS
31T-8020072		N2472V N810CM N8100M C-FEVC N83CA
31T-8020073		N2474V N100CM
31T-8020074		N2506V N808SW (N47DR) N62E
31T-8020075		N2507V N36TW
31T-8020076		N2510V N76PM N71PM N777LP N18AF F-GNAC N29LA
31T-8020077	Kit-AM	(N2519V) HK-2585X HK-2585P [canx 29Feb00 - status?]
31T-8020078		N2522V
31T-8020079	Kit-CH	LV-OEU PT-ODR
31T-8020080		N2570V (F-ODMM) N809SW 4X-CBL
31T-8020081		N2579V N814CM N814DM C-GCNO N88CA [dbr 24Aug92 Kendall-Tamiami Executive during Hurricane Andrew; canx 08Oct97]
31T-8020082		N2580V N82PC XA- [canx 25Jan08 as exported to Mexico]
31T-8020083		N2587V N1JB N54JB HB-LNL
31T-8020084		N2592V N9718N F-ODMM
31T-8020085		N2601V D-IIPA N154CA
31T-8020086		N2605V N880SW (N259DB) YV [canx 22Apr08 as exported to Venezuela]
31T-8020087	^	N2319X N48AA N384MC N565JF N500WR N500WP N331BB N26PJ N455MM
31T-8020088		N2320X (F-GCQZ) PH-ALA SE-KDG D-ICAP N58GG N431GW
31T-8020089		N2328X N63DG D-IGEM N333TN
31T-8020090		N2329X C-GPOE N925CA CC-PMZ C-51 (Chilean Police)
31T-8020091		N2331X N40TW N20AM N76SC F-GIPL HB-LTI
31T-8020092	Kit-CH	LV-OIF GN-705 (Argentinian Army) [w/o 06Oct95 General Villegas, Buenos Aires Province, Argentina]

PA-31T

c/n	Mods	Identities
31T-8020093		[completed as c/n 31T-8120002]
31T-8020094		[completed as c/n 31T-8120003]
31T-8020095		[completed as c/n 31T-8120004]
31T-8120001		N2335X N880CA [w/o 10Sep82 Delta-Municipal, UT, USA; canx 19Jul94]
31T-8120002		N2336X VH-IHK N2336X [w/o 20May87 nr Cody-E.E.Faust Regional, WY, USA; canx 18Feb97]
31T-8120003		N2337X N815CM D-IOWA N57KW TG-COB
31T-8120004		N2338X N811SW D-IKKK C-GSSC N139CS
31T-8120005		N2340X (N817CM) N19AC CC-PBP N57656 PT-OLZ
31T-8120006	^	N2366X (N101TR) N998LM
31T-8120007		N2369X (N46TW) N55KW
31T-8120008		N2376X N812SW D-ICBH N778HA PP-CHE
31T-8120009		N2385X N466WP N97MA N21TA N2198T N97MA D-IHMS N85GC *N40HB
31T-8120010		N2387X ZS-KTG OY-BEE N38789 TU-TLW (D-IIKW) N16KW PT-OPC
31T-8120011		N2407X C-GRNJ N31FR PT-WLJ
31T-8120012		N2393X C-FZIH C-FJVB
31T-8120013		N2401X N60WA YV-04CP YV-1995P YV-2800P YV1397
31T-8120014		N2405X N46CE N8DB (N322JD) N636CR
31T-8120015	Kit-AM	N2411X HK-2617X HK-2617P N107TT F-GKRR HB-LUF
31T-8120016		N2414X N241PS N311AC
31T-8120017		EB-004 (Bolivian Army) CP-1678 EB-004 (Bolivian Army) CP-1678
31T-8120018		N2420X N400TM N406TM N794CA [dbr 04Feb02 Hobbs, NM, USA, parts to White Industries, Bates City, MO, USA; location "Taxiway SO 1"; canx 22Apr02]
31T-8120019		N2546X N2425X HC-BIF
31T-8120020		N2443X N813SW CN-TVM N890WA PT-OKS N56MC PT-WNC
31T-8120021		N2457X N80WA N85HB [w/o 24Aug90 nr Boston-General Edward Lawrence Logan, MA, USA]
31T-8120022		N2495X N2459X HK-2607X HK-2607 HK-2607W HK-2607X N127AT N661TC
31T-8120023		N2468X I-CODE [w/o 30Dec86 Malindi, Kenya; parts to Nairobi-Wilson, Kenya]
31T-8120024		N2470X 5T-MAB
31T-8120025		N2476X N290CM D-ICPA N51JK
31T-8120026		N2483X 5T-MAC
31T-8120027		N2485X N815SW N974DC [dbr 04Jul97 Austin Airpark, TX, USA, parts to Dodson International Parts, Rantoul, KS, USA; canx 10Dec03]
31T-8120028		N2499X N820CM N59KG N59KC CC-PCY CC-CYB
31T-8120029		N2495X N129CC (D-IKHK) F-GJPL [w/o 05Jun90 nr Horta, Faial, Azores; canx 10Jul90]
31T-8120030		N2510X XA-LOJ XB-HYP N199RC PT-WOR
31T-8120031		N2516X N71FM N628DE PT-OJE
31T-8120032	Kit-AM	N2531Y HK-2631X HK-2631G
31T-8120033		N2589Z N42TW D-IBSA
31T-8120034		N2565X F-GDCR D-IKKS [w/o 14Jul84 Concord-Buchanan Field, CA, USA; canx cJul84]
31T-8120035		N2567X (D-IKDG) D-ILET OE-FYA D-IFFA N12KW D-IIRR N888LB N888LG PR-DGO
31T-8120036		N2574X N25WA N33MS
31T-8120037	Kit-AM	N2582X HK-2642X HK-2642P [canx 02May03 - status? possibly impounded 22Sep85]
31T-8120038		N806CA N300PV N606DW
31T-8120039		N2589X N47CP [dbr c1987 in California, USA and reportedly b/u; canx 25Jul90]
31T-8120040		N44TW PT-LRT
31T-8120041		N2604X (N818SW) N816SW N8361T (N79CA) N220SC SP-KKH
31T-8120042		N2405Y N131CC PT-ODM
31T-8120043		N2409Y N29WA N40H TG-LIA
31T-8120044		N825CM N444PD N515BA N666JK (N40PD) N666JK
31T-8120045		N2441Y TG-VAL
31T-8120046		N2482Y CC-CFR N101DH N178CD
31T-8120047	Kit-AM	(N2436Y) HK-2674X HK-2674P HK-2674G [wfu Bogota-El Dorado, Distrito Capital, Colombia]
31T-8120048		N2443Y OB-M-1228 OB-S-1228 OB-1228 [impounded Lima-Jorge Chavez International, Peru; canx 08Feb00]
31T-8120049		N2465Y YV-459CP N459CP CC-CNT CC-PJH
31T-8120050		N2476Y N828CM (N51WA) N234SE N194MA N33MC *N39MC
31T-8120051	Kit-AM	(N2525Y) HK-3043X HK-3043W HK-3043P
31T-8120052		N2519Y N43TW D-IFGN N67JG D-IFGN
31T-8120053		N2531Y N49TW N9CH N53TW N87YP *N115BM
31T-8120054		N2551Y (N151CC) (N315JS) ZS-PBS
31T-8120055		N2558Y N19BG (N610L) N49B
31T-8120056		N2572Y N51TW F-GGCH N463DN HB-LUQ
31T-8120057		N9087Y N382MB
31T-8120058		N9114Y N3GF OE-FMO CC-CFP
31T-8120059	^	N2603Y N20WE N18KW
31T-8120060		N9118Y N816JA N31HL
31T-8120061		N831CM PT-LNG
31T-8120062	Kit-AM	(N9129Y) HK-3025X HK-3025 HK-4179
31T-8120063		N9134Y N715CA
31T-8120064	Kit-AM	(N9141Y) HK-2906X HK-2906P F-WFLQ 0064/F-ZBFZ (French Customs) F-GLRP
31T-8120065		N9147Y N182TC [cvtd to c/n 31T-8120103]
31T-8120066		N9153Y N152CC [cvtd to c/n 31T-8120101]
31T-8120067		N9151Y N822SW [cvtd to c/n 31T-8120102]
31T-8120068		N9157Y D-ILIG OE-FSY D-IJOE N43WH
31T-8120069		N9162Y [cvtd to c/n 31T-8120104]
31T-8120070		N9166Y N826SW PT-OJM
31T-8120071		N832CM [airframe not completed]
31T-8120072		N827SW [airframe not completed]

c/n	Mods	Identities		
31T-8120101		N9153Y	N152CC	PT-WGJ
31T-8120102		N9151Y	N822SW	D-INNN
31T-8120103		N9147Y	N182TC	N707WD
31T-8120104		N9162Y	C-FZIC	N777LE

Production complete

PIPER PA-31T1 CHEYENNE I

Kit-CH indicates aircraft kit supplied to Chincul SACAIFI in Argentina
^ - Blackhawk XP135A engine upgrade fitted

c/n	Identities
31T-7804001	N6600A [wfu c1987; b/u; canx 01Feb90]
31T-7804002	N301PT N48GS N94TB N200TS
31T-7804003	N82281 N49AA N21JA N913CR
31T-7804004	N6083A N178SW N500TL N500MT N500MY
31T-7804005	N6095A N97MA N96MA
31T-7804006	N6108A N6134A [w/o 12Nov01 nr Graham-Municipal, TX, USA; canx 03Jan02]
31T-7804007	N51CA N214WG N244GC N22UC N17CE
31T-7804008	N6123A [w/o 22Feb79 nr Baltimore/Washington International, MD, USA; canx 27Jan89]
31T-7804009	(N79LD) N6125A N331KB
31T-7804010	N6127A N93TW N7VR
31T-7804011	D-IOFC [w/o 25Mar84 Borgo Ticino, Italy; canx cMar84]
31T-7904001	N9684N N6183A D-ILOR N195AA
31T-7904002	N9700N N52CA D-IEIS N119RL
31T-7904003	N6172A N800CM N37PJ
31T-7904004	N6173A N131SW OY-BHU
31T-7904005	N6181A N3WE N888PH
31T-7904006	N6182A (N24HE) N6182 N300WP
31T-7904007	N6190A N231SW
31T-7904008	N6191A N31X N409SC N65MS N33HG (N38X) N38HG N528DS C-GTMM
31T-7904009	N6192A [dbr 18Feb93 Pittsfield-Municipal, ME, USA, parts to Atlanta Air Salvage, Griffin-Spalding County, GA, USA; canx 07Feb96]
31T-7904010	N6189A N25BF N212HH
31T-7904011	N23199 N6EA N96MM N6JM [w/o 08Aug98 nr Baker, NV, USA; canx 22Sep98]
31T-7904012	N23203 N331SW N4RX (N204MB) N4RX
31T-7904013	N23215 N18KT N18KP N384CA N104RF YV-171P YV1443
31T-7904014	N23216 N401PT HB-LLK
31T-7904015	N23235 N131DF
31T-7904016	N23236 N431SW C-GBTV N7FL N93CV N503WR
31T-7904017	N23243
31T-7904018	N23250
31T-7904019	N23257 C-GRCL N3NT N504TC N504TQ N70TJ
31T-7904020	N23260 N800MP N187SC [b/u; canx 06Aug92]
31T-7904021	N23263 N232DH
31T-7904022	N23272 N9732N N23358 I-SERV (D-IBWB) N46CR N165KC
31T-7904023	N23285 N23319 (N80F) N52PC N52PF
31T-7904024	N23334
31T-7904025	N23338 N531SW N918FM
31T-7904026	N9746N N23447 XC-CUA N458SC EC-EIM 3A-MSI D-ISVK
31T-7904027	N23363 N98TW N98TG
31T-7904028	N23371 N680CA N711DG N711D N5WC N51FT N688CP
31T-7904029	N23373 N631SW N779JT F-GHTG N29CA N93SH
31T-7904030	N23376 N601PT I-POMO [w/o 06Nov06 nr Piacenza, Italy]
31T-7904031	N23381 (N673BB) (N300CM) N54EZ XB-SCH
31T-7904032	N23384 N65RA N20JS N188CA (N188EC) N60KV
31T-7904033	N23418 N627NB N290RS
31T-7904034	N23424 N23HB C9-ENT N334CA
31T-7904035	N23426
31T-7904036	N24346 N831SW N831LJ N331SY N55EU N149CC N14886
31T-7904037	N9749N N2332R N200FB
31T-7904038	N23493 (N528KL) N888AH
31T-7904039	N23497 N900RB N664RB HC-BNF N939JB
31T-7904040	N9745N YV-239CP YV-O-MAC-2 [w/o 06Nov82 El Tocuyo, Lara, Venezuela]
31T-7904041	N23521 4X-CBS N65CK N301TA
31T-7904042	N23555 C-FCOS N247R N129LC
31T-7904043	N70TW
31T-7904044	N23569 N523PD
31T-7904045 Kit-CH	LV-MYX [w/o 18Dec08 San Fernando, Buenos Aires Province, Argentina]
31T-7904046	N23658 N222SL
31T-7904047	N23680 N479SW
31T-7904048	N23687 N501PT N827LP
31T-7904049	N2368R N22CN (N256RS) N22CN [w/o 29Nov94 15 mls SW of Brockway, MT, USA]
31T-7904050	N9747N N2512R F-GCFI N2512R N222GW (N222QW) N222GW [dbr 18Feb90 Atlanta-DeKalb/Peachtree, GA, USA, parts to Dodson International Parts, Rantoul, KS, USA]
31T-7904051	N2369R N49RW N779SW N49RM N165SW
31T-7904052	N72TW (N418DJ) N137CW

c/n	Mods	Identities
31T-7904053		N2379R (N123FF) XB-FXU
31T-7904054		N2388R CC-PDV CC-CDV CC-PDV CC-CPV CC-PHM
31T-7904055		N66CA [w/o 21Apr83 in Mexico; canx 01Jul91]
31T-7904056		N879SW
31T-7904057		N9742N N2348W
31T-8004001		N2489R N167SL N55HR D-IHJJ N118BW N10CS
31T-8004002		N2499R N300TB (N2499R) N424CM
31T-8004003		N2556R
31T-8004004		N2587R (N77773) N2587R
31T-8004005		N2594R N2594Z N2594R PT-OAJ
31T-8004006		N2604R N108SW N100WT N108WT N611RR
31T-8004007		N2379W PT-OPQ
31T-8004008		N2409W N701PT (N701DH) N701PT [dam 25Jun09 Creve Coeur, MI, USA]
31T-8004009		(N180CA) N2412W N244CA N2412W N98GF [wfu cJun07, parts to MTW Aerospace, Montgomery, AL, USA; canx 16Sep08]
31T-8004010		N2415W N555FR
31T-8004011		N2418W N208SW N707CM N76TG (N803AW) D-IBIW 9A-BOR
31T-8004012		N9745N C-GMGO N4490E N432RR (N400WS) D-IIPN N41PN N400LJ
31T-8004013		N2434W N31MB
31T-8004014		N2436W N308SW N308LH N234PC PT-OVE
31T-8004015		N2442W N244AB
31T-8004016		N2448W N75TW
31T-8004017		N2458W
31T-8004018		N2464W N408SW N4DF N32JP N669WB
31T-8004019		D-ICGD N992TT
31T-8004020		N2316V N803CM N61WM N328AJ N20PT N120ET N700BS N166WT
31T-8004021		N2317V (N231PC) (N150AC) N49AC
31T-8004022		N9744N N2337V G-BHTP N141GA
31T-8004023		N2320V N180CA N4QG N52HL
31T-8004024		N2321V I-SASA [reportedly w/o 15Apr02 in Italy; still current on register]
31T-8004025		N2323V N314DD N20WE
31T-8004026		N2324V N452DP N76CP N314GK
31T-8004027		N9748N N711VN N711VW (N701GP) N73BG
31T-8004028		N2325V C-GTOL N300CE
31T-8004029		N280CA N5WC N49GG N93CN
31T-8004030		N2347V N66TW
31T-8004031		N2349V N60JW
31T-8004032		N2390V N2354V N668JG C-FDDD N800W [wfu, parts to White Industries, Bates City, MO, USA; location H-45; canx 11Apr98]
31T-8004033		N2355V (N179AC) N117WR XB-FDE N935CA N855RM N826RM
31T-8004034		N82TW
31T-8004035		N2369V
31T-8004036		(N508SW) N2371V 9V-BMA ZK-KPH N657DC N121BE [dbr 19May98 Great Falls-International, MT, USA, parts to Dodson International Parts, Rantoul, KS, USA; canx 24Apr00]
31T-8004037		N2477V N54TW N54TD HB-LRA N114JR
31T-8004038		N2478V N608SW N977CP PT-OPF
31T-8004039		N2480V N809CM N500AU N500AQ PT-OLF
31T-8004040		N2484V N444WA N420DW N744WP N219SC
31T-8004041		N2490V N80MB N769MB N768MB
31T-8004042		N2492V N75SK N617DW (N612AM) N617DW
31T-8004043		N2500V N53WM PT-WMU
31T-8004044		N2503V N180SW OO-JMR HB-LQP
31T-8004045		N2504V N85TW N9CH N444AK N26DV N20DL [w/o 13Dec06 Waterloo-Regional, IA, USA; canx 26Jun07]
31T-8004046		N2529V N811CM (N525CA) CX-BRU PT-WNZ N926K
31T-8004047		N2557V N40BT N831CH
31T-8004048		N2592V (N480CA) N14PT N169DC N55JP
31T-8004049		N2596V (N244GW) N5GW D-IKWP [w/o 10Dec88 Blieskastel, West Germany; canx cMar89]
31T-8004050		N2606V N2605V N812CM N896DR
31T-8004051		N2313X N480CA [w/o 02Jan04 nr Toussus-le-Noble, France; canx 14Dec04]
31T-8004052		N2316X I-LIAT D-IRVK N118HB
31T-8004053		N2335X N2372V D-ILCE
31T-8004054		N2334X N176FB N176FE N176CS N51RM
31T-8004055		N2349X N50TW N46HM N849KM N619RB N484AS
31T-8004056		N2347X N8TH XB-GQI
31T-8004057	^	N2350X N280SW N316JP N316WB
31T-8104001		N2351X N181SW
31T-8104002		N2352X N780CA (N50MW) CC-PNS
31T-8104003		N2356X
31T-8104004		N2360X N70WA N707TD N4WP N70GW
31T-8104005		N2365X N76HC N944JD N944JG N199MA [dbr 31Aug07 Madison-Dane County Regional/Truax Field, WI, USA; canx 09Apr08]
31T-8104006		N2367X (N816CM) N37TW
31T-8104007		N2370X N281SW N222BC N1LF N914CR HK-4347X HK-4347P N434R
31T-8104008		N2378X N38TW
31T-8104009		N2386X N816CM
31T-8104010		N2389X N980CA
31T-8104011		N2391X N50WA N40BG N839AB (N839CH) N329KK
31T-8104012		N2396X N39TW N39TL

PA-31T

c/n	Mods	Identities
31T-8104013		N2399X (N707JT) N200HV N212GM N707CV
31T-8104014		N2403X
31T-8104015		N2406X N381SW N105MA
31T-8104016		N2412X N481SW
31T-8104017		N2419X HB-LMT N4494U (N409AC) PT-OTV
31T-8104018		N2422X N801CA
31T-8104019		N2427X N581SW N581B N312CC N323CT N817CT N817QT N191MA
31T-8104020		N2433X N31WM N26JB
31T-8104021		N2455X N633AB (N112BB) N633AB N112BB
31T-8104022		N2457X N77NH (N9107N) N300SR
31T-8104023		N2463X N41TW N124DP N124DF N234SB CC-CWK CC-PWH
31T-8104024		N2464X N818CM SE-IUG N225CA
31T-8104025		N2467X N88QM
31T-8104026		N2480X
31T-8104027		N2481X N681SW N398SP
31T-8104028		N2482X N241AC N38RE
31T-8104029		N2484X (N90WA) N803CA OE-FKH
31T-8104030		N2492X N90WA N71LA N917F N47GW
31T-8104031		N2494X N90JC N90VM (N90FJ) N90VM
31T-8104032		N2496X N821CM N5SL (N5SS) D-IAPA 9A-BZG
31T-8104033		N881SW N23TC N881SW N94EG (D-IHYL) N94EG
31T-8104034		N2511X N100GY PT-WEF
31T-8104035		N2519X
31T-8104036		N2533X N43TX N75BR N633WC
31T-8104037		N822CM N2571X N822CM (N822WC) (N244RP) N919RD [w/o 16Dec99 Santa Fe-Municipal, NM, USA; canx 13Dec01]
31T-8104038		N2539X N130CC N27BF
31T-8104039		N2569X N824CM N824VA (N54EM) N824VA
31T-8104040		N2576X N981SW N981SR N711LD
31T-8104041		N2587X N805CA PT-OKT [wfu cMar97 for spares - location?]
31T-8104042		N2590X D-IJET N12WZ N5RB
31T-8104043		N2603X N45TW N527JC N247LM
31T-8104044		N2607X N817SW [b/u; canx 28Jun96]
31T-8104045		N2402Y N26WA N150BC N514M N855JL
31T-8104046		N2412Y N82KK N478PC N221RC 9A-CZG
31T-8104047		N2420Y N83MG
31T-8104048		N826CM N862RA
31T-8104049		N2435Y
31T-8104050		N2442Y N49WA N515GA
31T-8104051		N2512Y N47TW PT-OVB
31T-8104052		N2459Y N427RP N422DM N422HV (N408SH) N409SH
31T-8104053		N2478Y N2468Y N23ES G-JVAJ N454CA
31T-8104054		N2490Y N818SW N555AT (N555AE) N555AT
31T-8104055		N2491Y N48TW (N880WW) N123AT D-ISIG
31T-8104056		N2495Y N87DM N94JS N711ER (D-IAHM) N711ER
31T-8104057		N134CC (N169KD) N62BW D-IHJK YV2499
31T-8104058		N807CA N527JM N713BH N278HM N999NP N130A N277DB N277DG
31T-8104059		N2537Y N819SW
31T-8104060		N2547Y N51WA N74ML N14PX
31T-8104061		N2552Y (N711QC) N2552Y
31T-8104062		N2560Y PT-WMX
31T-8104063		N2568Y CC-PBT
31T-8104064		N2571Y N502MM PT-XOC
31T-8104065		N2580Y N777G N977G
31T-8104066		N2590Y (N259PC) N600DR (N32LC) N82LC D-IHMM D-IIXX N914AS
31T-8104067		N2608Y N52TW D-IACR LX-ACR D-IACR
31T-8104068		N9088Y N200SL N410NA N138TA XA-RLB (N328PD) N456AC N917TP
31T-8104069		[completed as c/n 31T-8104101]
31T-8104070		N9105Y LN-TEE HB-LPR VR-BKF N17KW D-IIHW N17KW CC-CBD CC-PFD
31T-8104071		N9139Y N122DM (N122LM) CC-CRU CC-CWD
31T-8104072		N9175Y N482TC N800BB
31T-8104073		N9185Y PT-WHN [canx 12Mar97 - status?]
31T-8104101		N136CC N711UP N104MC D-IASW N75WA

Production complete

PIPER PA-31T1 CHEYENNE IA

^ - Blackhawk XP135A engine upgrade fitted

c/n	Identities						
31T-8304001	N9183C	*N31PF					
31T-8304002	N2522Z	N910HM	N810HM				
31T-8304003	N2409W	N71TW	VH-SJJ	N68SF	N26DV	N84CF	
31T-1104004	N2418W	N550AC	N488HA	N15AT	N90WW		
31T-1104005	N2427W	N58AM	(N16NB)	N58AM	*N16NB		
31T-1104006	N2434W	N511PJ					
31T-1104007	N2436W	S3-BHN (Bangladesh Defence Force)					
31T-1104008	N9266Y						
31T-1104009	N9268Y	XB-GAL					
31T-1104010	N9270Y	N426RJ	N426RQ	N804CT	N817CT	(N234PC)	UN-P3101
31T-1104011 ^	N2434V	N371TM					
31T-1104012	N284MC	N284BL	N284BB	N622BB	N14NE		
31T-1104013	N9348T	N347AA	N20MR	N65EZ	N48AM	N601AJ	
31T-1104014	N9382T	D-ILGA					
31T-1104015	N9168T	D-IIAH	S5-CEJ	D-IHJL	D-IEMR		
31T-1104016	N91201	D-IFHZ	9A-BIH				
31T-1104017	N91204	(N715GW)	D-IEPA	EC-HCQ	N65KG	N85KG	

Production complete

PIPER PA-31T2 CHEYENNE IIXL

Kit-AM indicates kit supplied to Aero Mercantile in Colombia
^ - Blackhawk XP135A engine upgrade fitted

c/n	Identities							
31T-8166001	N2446X	N812JJ	(N50FC)	N450CB	VH-RSW	N136SP	N731PB	
31T-8166002	N2322X	C-FKEY	N431CF					
31T-8166003	N2321X	N31XL	[w/o 03Jun01 7 mls S of Jackson-McKellar/Sipes Regional, TN, USA; canx 03Aug04]					
31T-8166004	N2617X	N2571X	(N82BT)	N2517X	[w/o 16Feb82 nr Springfield-Lebanon, KY, USA; canx 23Aug90]			
31T-8166005	N2467Y	(N60TW)	N60XL	N30WE	N41PH	N717SP	N127GP	N410CA
31T-8166006	N2473Y	N38WA	N282PC					
31T-8166007	N2474Y	LN-TEA	N187GA	N491MB	N303TS			
31T-8166008	N2477Y	N132CC	N9VF	N40VF	N93DD	C-GKRS	N35CA	N1380
31T-8166009	N2488Y	N248J						
31T-8166010	N2484Y	N200XL	(N200JH)	N200XL				
31T-8166011	N2494Y	N218SW	N630MW					
31T-8166012	N2580Y	N809CA	N888PT	N321LB				
31T-8166013	N2501Y	C-FCED	G-FCED					
31T-8166014	N2515Y	C-GSFY	N99BH	N77NH	N31KF	N15KW	(N31KP)	N15KW
31T-8166015	N2541Y	C-GSGJ	N131XL	N192TB				
31T-8166016	N2520Y	N120TC	N80DA	CC-CWH	CC-PVO	N400XL	N440S	
31T-8166017	N2536Y	N550MM						
31T-8166018	N2553Y	N170CC	N5VF	N5UB	N22VF	C-FWCP		
31T-8166019 Kit-AM	N2550Y	HK-2749X	HK-2749P	[canx 11Apr00 - status?]				
31T-8166020	N2563Y	N318SW	N711HF	YV-295CP	N11YC	N22YC		
31T-8166021	N2569Y	N300XL	N450HC					
31T-8166022	N2570Y	(N302CA)	N86CM	N81502	N3RK			
31T-8166023	N2577Y	N88B						
31T-8166024	N2586Y	N58PL						
31T-8166025	N2588Y	N53WA	XA-	[canx cApr85 as exported to Mexico]				
31T-8166026	N2597Y	N31X	(N910HM)	N77UH	N28WN			
31T-8166027	N2602Y	N500PB						
31T-8166028	N400XL	N355SS	C-FJAK					
31T-8166029	N2609Y	N418SW	N555CG	N346GA	N346JC	N66JC	N372JM	
31T-8166030	N9084Y	N76TW	C-FCEC					
31T-8166031	N172CC	ZS-LSY	V5-LSY	ZS-LSY				
31T-8166032	N9083Y	N48CP	N107MC	(N107MQ)	N225PT			
31T-8166033	N9092Y	N59WA	N42ND	N42NE	N67PD	G-CHEY		
31T-8166034	N9098Y	N730PC	XA-MCB	N730PC	HK-3603X	HK-3603	N82XL	
31T-8166035 Kit-AM	(N9103Y)	HK-3074X	HK-3074	HK-3047P	[canx 14Aug01 - status?]			
31T-8166036 ^	N9106Y	N618SW						
31T-8166037	N63XL	(D-IESW)	N63XL	[w/o 15Sep89 nr Louisville-Jefferson County, KY, USA; canx 30Jan91]				
31T-8166038	N9107Y	N700CA	N161TC	CC-PVE				
31T-8166039	N9110Y	N10BC	N65TJ	N56DK	N121LH	N121EH	N120SK	
31T-8166040	N9115Y	C-FTRX	N30XL	(N4DF)	N824JH			
31T-8166041	N9120Y	N61WA	C-GFLL	N916RT				
31T-8166042	N9122Y	N500XL	N767DM					
31T-8166043	N9124Y	N820SW	(N117GM)	N711FN				
31T-8166044 ^	N9130Y	VH-IWT	N10XL	OE-FLO	N31KW	N400WS		
31T-8166045	N9138Y	N600BS	N237PC					

c/n	Mods	Identities
31T-8166046		N9140Y (N64XL) C-GTVV N67XL N67TW N92CD N67TW (N18KW) (N9CH) N107PC
31T-8166047		N821SW N457SR XB-FSG
31T-8166048		N9143Y N600XL C-FGSX
31T-8166049		N9148Y N7UF D-ILPG C-GSAM N500XL N57AF HC-BXF PT-WNG
31T-8166050		N9150Y N700XL HB-LNX
31T-8166051		N9155Y N62TW N162PM N37SR N30VB N287CB
31T-8166052		N9156Y N823SW D-IOKA N423JB PR-MSP
31T-8166053	Kit-AM ^	N9159Y N174CC HK-2963 HK-2963W
31T-8166054		N9160Y N824SW N300TM N1234L N176RS N444WC
31T-8166055		N9161Y VH-HXL N410BL (CP-1699) N85EM
31T-8166056		(N715CA) N9165Y N550T N550TL D-ICGA EC-IPZ
31T-8166057		N9168Y N774KV
31T-8166058		N9127Y N825SW
31T-8166059	Kit-AM	HK-2907X HK-2907P (N620AD) HK-2907 [w/o 13Feb00 nr Bocono, Trujillo, Venezuela]
31T-8166060		N9184Y (N716CA) N88XL N66MT N68MT N500EW
31T-8166061		N9169Y N151TC N151FB N983GA TJ-AIM [wfu & dism Doula, Cameroon]
31T-8166062		N9174Y N828SW (N200HF) N59AP N58AP N310JD N31JZ N312MT
31T-8166063		N9186Y N777YP N777YR N776AK N151MP C-GLDZ
31T-8166064		N9194Y N200JE SE-KHM (N689CA) N7194Y HC-BUS N7194Y
31T-8166065		N9160C (N829SW) N222XL N1879W [dbr 29Nov90 Des Moines-International, IA, USA, parts to White Industries, Bates City, MO, USA; location G-04; canx 25Jan91]
31T-8166066		N9170C C-FWPT
31T-8166067		N9179C (N67ER) PT-MFW
31T-8166068		N9185C N612BB N328KK
31T-8166069		N9190Y (N61TW) (N61XL) N511SC C-GBFO
31T-8166070		N9192C N555RT N333X CC-PTA CC-CPR
31T-8166071		N2553Z N81GD N85GD N44FH N8EE N622AJ N444ER
31T-8166072		N2580Z N65XL [cvtd to c/n 31T-1166002]
31T-8166073	Kit-AM	(N2376R) HK-3117X HK-3117 HK-3117W
31T-8166074		[cvtd to c/n 31T-1166003]
31T-8166075	^	N2325W (N66XL) N83XL
31T-8166076		N2342W N51GS N2342W N51GS N516S N57KC
31T-1166001		N2359W HP-1066 HP-1066P N835MW N359GP
31T-1166002		N2580Z N65XL CC-PML [canx 03May99 - status?]
31T-1166003		N2604R (N68TW) D-ICDU D-IXXX EC-JRF
31T-1166004		N6667A N90SC ZS-PBT D-ISEP PH-SVX
31T-1166005		N91296 HB-LRM N395CA
31T-1166006		N2409W N80BC N804C (N42RL) N804C
31T-1166007		N2428V N9CH D-IAQA N285KW TG-SIK
31T-1166008		N2433V N362AB D-IIRC N150RC N150TK

Production complete

PIPER PA-31T3 CHEYENNE T-1040

c/n	Identities
31T-8275001	N2489Y N401VA
31T-8275002	N2605Y N309SC 5Y-UAL ZS-OUP
31T-8275003	N9101Y N4140T HP- [canx 18Jun91 as exported to Panama]
31T-8275004	N9152Y N302SC [w/o 22Dec89 8 mls NW of Beluga Apt, AK, USA; canx 24Jun91]
31T-8275005	N9171Y C-GPBC N219CS [dbr 21Feb00 nr Kotzebue-Ralph Wein Memorial, AK, USA, parts to Westcan Aircraft Sales & Salvage, Kamloops, BC, Canada]
31T-8275006	N9176Y N311SC [wfu, parts to Westcan Aircraft Sales & Salvage, Kamloops, BC, Canada]
31T-8275007	N9180Y N314SC [dbr 11Nov97 Beluga Apt, AK, USA, parts to Westcan Aircraft Sales & Salvage, Kamloops, BC, Canada; canx 21Dec06]
31T-8275008	N9182Y N308SC N315SC N223CS [wfu, parts to Westcan Aircraft Sales & Salvage, Kamloops, BC, Canada; canx 14Jan09]
31T-8275009	N9183Y N9088S N307SC [w/o 13Dec91 Ninilchik, AK, USA; canx 20Aug97]
31T-8275010	N9193Y [w/o 24Sep84 nr Hartsfield-Jackson/Atlanta International, GA, USA; canx cOct85]
31T-8275011	N9189C G-BKGK N303SC 5Y-BIG 5H-MTX N2VZ ZS-OTL
31T-8275012	N9197Y N82HP N82AZ C-GZRJ [dbr 08Mar91 Big Trout Lake, ON, Canada, parts to Atlanta Air Salvage, Griffin-Spalding County, GA, USA; canx 03Sep91]
31T-8275013	N9189Y C-GBDJ N220CS [w/o 18Sep00 Nuiqsut, AK, USA; canx 12Dec00]
31T-8275014	N9094C C-FYPL N217CS [wfu, parts to Westcan Aircraft Sales & Salvage, Kamloops, BC, Canada; canx 14Jan09]
31T-8275015	N9097C HK-2926X HK-2926 HK-2926P [canx 23Feb00 - status?]
31T-8275016	N9183C N83HP N83AZ C-GKIF N218CS [w/o 07Apr97 Stebbins, AK, USA; canx 23Dec98]
31T-8275017	N9096C N304SC [wfu, parts to Westcan Aircraft Sales & Salvage, Kamloops, BC, Canada]
31T-8275018	[cvtd to c/n 31T-8375001] N9174C
31T-8275019	[cvtd to c/n 31T-8375002] N9196C
31T-8275020	[cvtd to c/n 31T-8375003] N2448W
31T-8275021	[built as c/n 31T-8375004] (N2464W)
31T-8275022	[built as c/n 31T-8375005] (N2474W)
31T-8275023	[built as c/n 31T-5575001] (N41202)
31T-8275024	[built as c/n 31T-5575002]
31T-8275025	N9191Y TJ-AGR 3C-JJP TJ-AIQ [w/o 14Feb01 N'Djamena, Chad]

c/n	Mods	Identities
31T-8375001		N9174C 5Y-JJB N1194V [dbr 05Oct93 Nairobi, Kenya; regd N1194V 09Dec96, presumably for spares use]
31T-8375002		N9196C C-FBBR N502WJ 5Y-UAC [w/o 25Jan95 Nairobi National Park, Kenya]
31T-8375003		N2448W C-GBDH [dbr 22Sep89 Sachs Harbour, NT, Canada, parts to Global Aircraft Industries, Edmonton-Villeneuve, AB, Canada; canx 20Jan97; TT 3816 hours]
31T-8375004		[cvtd to c/n 31T-8475001] N2464W
31T-8375005		N2474W PJ-WIG N110JK [dbr 09Feb00 Wales, AK, USA, parts to Westcan Aircraft Sales & Salvage, Kamloops, BC, Canada; canx 11Jun01]
31T-8475001		N2464W ZK-FPL F-OIAV
31T-5575001		N41202 HP-1101 HP-1101P N700RD
31T-5575002		[void - airframe not completed]

Production complete

PIPER PA-31T5 CHEYENNE IIXLa

c/n	Identities
31T-1122001	N2428V [c/n changed to 31T-5522001, cvtd to c/n 31T-1166007]
31T-1122002	N2433V [c/n changed to 31T-5522002, cvtd to c/n 31T-1166008]

Production complete

PIPER PA-42 CHEYENNE III

Kit-AM indicates kit supplied to Aero Mercantile in Colombia

c/n	Identities
42-7800001	N420PA [wfu & std Vero Beach-Municipal, FL, USA]
42-7800002	N420PT VH-KGW N4494E F-GGTV N202VJ N911VJ OB-1803 OB-1803-P
42-7801003	N142PC N64AM N39GR N134KM OB-1633 OB-1633-P
42-7801004	N242PC (N442TW) N96TC XC-UPZ XB-DZV XA-RLW N48RA OY- N48RA [canx 06Jun08 as exported to Denmark; reinstated 14Jul08]
42-7901001	[built as c/n 42-8001001]
42-7901002	(N342PC) [built as c/n 42-8001002]
42-7901003	(N42SW) [built as c/n 42-8001003]
42-8001001	N442PC N662MP N124EL (N124TS) N124EL C-FWCC N51KC
42-8001002	N21PL N610R N61QR C-GIDC D-IONE
42-8001003	N42SW N54GC N423JD N8EA N242RA (N33AX) N242RA
42-8001004	(N290T) (N304EF) N30WA (N304EF) N404EF N59JM (N4WZ) N42WZ N717ES
42-8001005	N700CJ (N942TW) N700WT N609GA N13TT N113WC
42-8001006	N80PC N131RC C-FCAV [wfu, parts to Westcan Aircraft Sales & Salvage, Kamloops, BC, Canada; canx 08Dec05]
42-8001007	N51SM N81SM [w/o 07Feb87 Horseshoe Bay, TX, USA; canx 12Sep95]
42-8001008	N808CA N977XT
42-8001009	C-GNRD N825NW N151PC (N401MD) (OB-1631) OB-1649 N849AM (D-IASB) D-IDSF LV-BEI
42-8001010	YV-134CP YV-O-ICA-1 YV-O-MAC-1YV-O-ICA-1N133FM YV-O-SATA-8 YV0108
42-8001011	N1515H N151XX OE-FHF D-IGAS N795KW N619JB N247WW D-IABA
42-8001012	F-GCQY N25LA N528DS OB-1819-T OB-1819-P N813RA N813CF
42-8001013	LV-PGT LV-OOO N275AB (N827KR) OB-1714
42-8001014	N542PC N710EC N710EQ C-GAKA N373Q
42-8001015	N4505B [stolen 02Dec89 Nassau, Bahamas; never recovered; canx 02Dec91]
42-8001016	(N823SS) N823CM PH-BDV C-GESV N300DK N69PC OB-1687
42-8001017	(N96TC) N342TW XA-SEK N175AA
42-8001018	N19CD OB-1365 [hijacked to Colombia 15Aug90; fate unkn; canx 21Dec01]
42-8001019	N4086R OB-M-1234 OB-S-1234 OB-1234 [w/o 16Sep98 San Rafael, Peru; canx 21Dec01]
42-8001020	N20PT N20PU N328AJ (N4113Q) N332SA N332SM
42-8001021	N142CD C-FWAB N396FW
42-8001022	N180CC I-AFEP (F-GIPV) (N525JM) N145CA OB-1630
42-8001023	N802CA N711DG N717MB N5PF N69PC
42-8001024	C-GRCY N250TJ [w/o 31Oct92 nr Grand Junction, CO, USA]
42-8001025	N727PC (D-IBDV) N727PC
42-8001026	LV-PLR LV-DMP LQ-APF LV-APF
42-8001027	N112BC
42-8001028	N52WA N48GS N190CA
42-8001029	N40PT N811DA N238PC
42-8001030	N40764 ZS-LCA V5-LCA N930CA N21MS F-GOON N855GA C-GPSB
42-8001031	N4088Y N200GF N123CN N123AG
42-8001032	N827CM HP-1097 HP-1097SI N525TG C-GLMO N432R N121CS [w/o 18Oct06 nr Prescott, AZ, USA; canx 05Jan07]
42-8001033	N40880 N582SW VH-WCE
42-8001034	N642PC N777FG (N59RB) N74FB N444SC CN-TJL
42-8001035	N80PC N24CC PT-OSX PP-EPB
42-8001036	C-GSIH N46TW N3JQ N8RY

PA-42

c/n	Identities
42-8001037	N804CA (N222RR) HK-3618X HK-3618W N373CA D-IABE
42-8001038	LV-PMT LV-ONL PT-LZD
42-8001039	N40837 N829CM N45SL F-GHAB D-ICMC XA-TJH
42-8001040	N40889 N456JW N455JW
42-8001041	N4089A G-BWTX N669CA N176FB YR-ANF
42-8001042	N40886 HK-2684X HK-2684 [dam in Colombia c1983; returned to US for rebuild; c/n plate re-used when 42-8001069 exported to Colombia] N54568 N7139B
42-8001043	N4089T N48WA HB-LRI N809AA OY-YES D-IYES F-GXES
42-8001044	I-CGTO N325CA ZP-TYZ LV-WXG
42-8001045	N181CC C-FCJP (N169TC) N444LN
42-8001046	N4089U N99CS OY-CGH N148CA N75AW
42-8001047	N4099U VH-ISW VH-BUW
42-8001048	N830CM N830CB N830CM D-IMIM OE-FIT
42-8001049	N4099V (D-IAPD) (N789WW) N4099V N789MM (N116MS) N789MM N112WC N71MA C-FIZG N95VR
42-8001050	N4098K (N15DE) N4098K N116JP
42-8001051	N40946 N81FX N810L N5PA
42-8001052	N542TW [dbr 28Jun85 Charlotte-Douglas International, NC, USA, parts to White Industries, Bates City, MO, USA; location F-47; canx 11Dec86]
42-8001053	N4098P N158CA N543FM N700VF
42-8001054	(HZ-AMK) N4107K HZ-SN4 TR-LBG N4107K N29HS N94EW
42-8001055	N4088T G-BJIZ PH-JDV C-GESB N190AA N22BD N93BD N937D
42-8001056	N4088Z HR-JFA FAH012 (Honduran AF)
42-8001057	N40844 I-FINE HB-LOV XB-EZL N303PL N158TJ (N821TB) N158TJ
42-8001058	N4098T N157LL
42-8001059 Kit-AM	N4098A HK-2772X HK-2772P
42-8001060	N64WA N631PC OK-OKL
42-8001061	N4100L N821DK
42-8001062	(N642TW) HK-3000X HK-3000G FAC5744 (Colombian AF)
42-8001063	N40980 (N22MV) (N883TC) N22MV N58LC N98LC N18AF N355BC C-FCEH C-GBOT
42-8001064	N40981 N833CM N42SJ N932BF 4X-CBF
42-8001065	N742TW (N888JH) N742RB N395DR
42-8001066	N62WA N62WC VH-NMA
42-8001067	N183CC OB-1629
42-8001068	N4099Y HK-2684X HK-2684 [canx to Colombia cNov84 as replacement for 42-8001042; illegally assumed identity HK-2684]
42-8001069	N4102L N5SS N5SY (N878VP) N5SY
42-8001070	N142TW (HI-409) N721CA N82PG
42-8001071	N834CM N23KW XA-SBU N65MC XA-TIL N108SB N880TC
42-8001072	N63WA N801JW
42-8001073	N982SW N321CF 4X-CIC
42-8001074	N4107U N82KK N82TD CX-ROU N423KC N479MM
42-8001075	(N942TW) HI-409 N4998M ZS-LKL N4998M F-GIBS N4998M HK-3693X HK-3693 [impounded cSep07 Bogota-El Dorado, Distrito Capital, Colombia]
42-8001076	C-GTVV [cvtd to c/n 42-8001101]
42-8001077	N184CC [cvtd to c/n 42-8001102]
42-8001078	(D-IAPD) (D-IMAY) N4101T D-IMAX N22HD N28DA
42-8001079	N711CA N515DW N515M N22UP
42-8001080	N882SW PT-MFL
42-8001081	N4086T N401NC XB-EVU N881AM N802MW
42-8001082	(N782SW) [built as c/n 42-8001103]
42-8001083	(N712CA) [built as c/n 42-8001104]
42-8001084	(N4109W) [built as c/n 42-8001105]
42-8001085	(N842PC) [built as c/n 42-8301001]
42-8001086	(N282TC) (N4109X) [built as c/n 42-8001106]
42-8001087	(N41090) [built as c/n 42-8301005; c/n changed to 42-8301005]
42-8001088	[built as c/n 42-8301002]
42-8001089	(N682SW) [built as c/n 42-8301003]
42-8001090	[built as c/n 42-8301004; c/n changed to 42-5501004]
42-8001091	[built as c/n 42-8301006; c/n changed to 42-5501006]
42-8001092	(N382TC) [built as c/n 42-8301007; c/n changed to 42-5501007]
42-8001093	[built as c/n 42-8301008; c/n changed to 42-5501008]
42-8001094	[built as c/n 42-8301009; c/n changed to 42-5501009]
42-8001095	[built as c/n 42-8301010; c/n changed to 42-5501010]
42-8001096	[built as c/n 42-8301011; c/n changed to 42-5501011]
42-8001101	N4101T N41139 F-GEHR N30MA 9H-ADD N110SC 4X-CIM D-IFSH [w/o 28Oct03 Zurich-Kloten, Switzerland; canx 07Jan04]
42-8001102	N4114A N760MM
42-8001103	N4114D PT-OKL
42-8001104	N712CA N334FP XB-JNC
42-8001105	N4109W N620MW N820BC UP- ? [canx 30Jul07 as exported to Kazakhstan]
42-8001106	N4109X N42PA D-IADI N42KA N933DG PR-BZZ

Production complete

PIPER PA-42-720 CHEYENNE IIIA

c/n	Identities
42-8301001	N842PC JA8869 N842PC D-IHLA
42-8301002	N420PC N420CA N420TS HB-LPV (N830AM) N75FL
42-8301003	(N4088Z) (N111BX) [c/n changed to 42-5501003]
42-5501003	N111BX N29TF (N340BH) N29TF
42-5501004	N41158 D-IEEF N775CA N995SC
42-5501005	N4114K N5381X N2247R OK-MPM
42-5501006	N924PC N809E N236PC
42-5501007	N40833 (N142PC) N142TW N834CM D-ICGB D-IXXX
42-5501008	N41117 N777YP XA-EJS
42-5501009	N4116K N4115J N555RT N555RY N59KG N31GA N124WS N66MT N66MF [dbr 30Jan02 Ames-Municipal, IA, USA, parts to MTW Aerospace, Montgomery, AL, USA; canx 26Oct05]
42-5501010	N4116Q N905LC N720LS SE-KBY D-IFRC N627KW N627PC
42-5501011	N4116W (N35DG) PT-OLT (N288FA) N8887W N888FW N100CS C-GZRP G-GZRP
42-5501012	N4116Q
42-5501013	N40833 N90TW
42-5501014	N4115F N916CM N900MP C-FSOZ N45SL D-IDSF D-IFSH
42-5501015	N942TW D-ILSW N794A
42-5501016	N4118M I-CENT N536CA N94CS N313BB
42-5501017	N4118H N75LS
42-5501018	N4117V N516GA N515RC
42-5501019	N829PC XA-PSG
42-5501020	N4118K N623KW N690L (N690E) (N700LT) N690E G-MHAR
42-5501021	N4115F N9030S N200JH N141TC
42-5501022	N4115K N905LC [stolen 08Apr88 Greenville, SC, USA; never recovered; canx 22Jun88]
42-5501023	N4118X N4190F F-GHPF D6-ECA N449CA N932AK N950MT
42-5501024	N41182 (N9150T) N41182 N9150T [wfu c2002, parts to White Industries, Bates City, MO, USA]
42-5501025	N4118N D-IHVA N444CY
42-5501026	N4118N N300JC N300JQ N31KF N690TW
42-5501027	G-BLRK N9174Z D-IHGO N440CA
42-5501028	N4120K N9159Y
42-5501029	G-BLSA N410LD (N800DG) N700CC D-IDBU
42-5501030	G-BLTB N5022M OE-FMM N627KW N9CH N627KW N637KC N787LB
42-5501031	TC-FAG TC-THK
42-5501032	N9531N N9233T [wfu cFeb03, parts to White Industries, Bates City, MO, USA; location "Ramp South B-29"; canx 29Apr09]
42-5501033	TC-FAH
42-5501034	N9532N N9085U
42-5501035	N9520N N9091J
42-5501036	N9522N N9279A
42-5501037	N9528N N9116Q
42-5501038	N9536N N9142B
42-5501039	N9544N N9126B HK-3381X HK-3381G FAC5743 (Colombian AF)
42-5501040	N41182 N9554N N9127F D-IOSE N561GA N925RM N556BR N95SA
42-5501041	N9578N D-IOSA
42-5501042	D-IOSB
42-5501043	D-IOSC D-IOKP D-IOSC
42-5501044	D-IOSD
42-5501045	I-TREP (D-ITRI) N56MV D-ITRI
42-5501046	I-TREQ D-ITWO
42-5501047	I-TRER D-IAAE
42-5501048	N92264 JA8871 N948TA XB-AIN XB-TYS
42-5501049	N92266 JA8872 N949TA N121LH
42-5501050	N92275 JA8873 N950TA G-GMED
42-5501051	(D-IOSF) N92400 B-3621 *D-IAWD
42-5501052	(D-IOSG) N92402 B-3622 (D-IAWE) B-3622
42-5501053	D-IOSF N425PC N426PC PT-WQA N102AE
42-5501054	N92409 B-3623 D-IAWB
42-5501055	D-IOSG N9198F JA8724 N955TA D-IDIA [w/o 19Jan09 nr Falkenstein, Germany; canx 11Feb09]
42-5501056	N9241D B-3624 [w/o 23Mar95 nr Taiyun, China]
42-5501057	OE-FAA N120GA C-GSAA C-GWCA
42-5501058	N9194X JA8874 N958TA XA-VIP
42-5501059	(OE-FAB) N9094U B-3625
42-5501060	N9115X B-3626

Production complete

PIPER PA-42-1000 CHEYENNE IV

Kit-AM indicates kit supplied to Aero Mercantile in Colombia

c/n	Identities
42-8427001	N400PT [c/n changed to 42-5527001]
42-8427002	N400PS [c/n changed to 42-5527002]
42-8427003	N400PJ [c/n changed to 42-5527003]
42-5527001	N400PT [wfu & stored Vero Beach-Municipal, FL, USA; canx 04Aug98]
42-5527002	N400PS N400VB
42-5527003	N400PJ N70CA N333MX ZS-PHO (N42AJ) N40FK (N77WR) N400LR
42-5527004	N4119B N411BG
42-5527005	N25HE N24HE N25HE PT-OVD HP-2001 N85SL
42-5527006	N98RF HK-3413X HK-3413W (N7MZ) N54DA XB-WWG N158MH
42-5527007	(N844MC) N4118V N400SL N531MC XA- [canx 20Mar07 as exported to Mexico]
42-5527008	N401TW (N234BC) N42MD HK-3423X HK-3423W HK-3423P N408GP (N31WE) N408WG (N950TA) N554DM
42-5527009	N440WH XB-EYZ HK-4110X HK-4110W N941AA YV-991CP YV1391 YV1699
42-5527010	N307CA N100AK C-FHRV N24KW N105LV SE-LYY LN-LYY
42-5527011	N86CR N901MT
42-5527012	N65CR (N87CR) N95CR N42MD N42FT C-GRGE N321LH
42-5527013	(N440WH) N848PC N82KK N32KK N450MW
42-5527014	(N144MC) N33DS (N83ES) N814CM N400SN N144PL
42-5527015	N125EL N42MD ZK-RUR (N42QB) PK-ZGZ
42-5527016	N500LM
42-5527017	N4118Y N410TW N46HL
42-5527018	N4112Z N124DP D-IIAQ EC-IIP D-IYYY D-ISMS
42-5527019	N1515H VH-BUR
42-5527020	N402TW N812BJ
42-5527021	N41125 N500WE N4RP N248DJ N500PM
42-5527022	N41187 N551AC (N322KW) D-IQAS
42-5527023	N429BX C-GMFI N722ER LN-ACV
42-5527024	(N400TM) N41126 D-IMAY [w/o 05May01 Nuremberg, Germany; canx 26Jun01]
42-5527025	N4119A N552AC N325KW (D-IHHH) (N92AG) N332SA
42-5527026	(N429BX) N400WH JA8853
42-5527027	N4119V N721SG HP-1341 N46FD
42-5527028	N4119X HB-LTM
42-5527029	(N743PC) N41191 (N999TJ) N410VB N429MD HL5217 N689CA N38AF N40MV
42-5527030	N41198 "HK-3320W" D-IEXP D-IUCN
42-5527031	N41199 N431MC N47ZG
42-5527032	N4120G XA-CYR N425D 9M-TDM

PA-42

c/n	Identities
42-5527033	N827PC (PH-SLK) HK-3451X HK-3451
42-5527034	N9529N (N404TW) N9099U VH-PTG N7KK JA8878 N448CA *N2UZ
42-5527035	N9295A N9534N G-BMVP N9295A JA8867
42-5527036	N9548N N9095N N742TW TC-SCM TC-EEE D-IONE N34ER
42-5527037 Kit-AM	N9561N HK-3397X HK-3397W LQ-BLU
42-5527038 Kit-AM	N9127N (N518B) HK-3459X HK-3459P HK-3459 (D-IHHH) N438GP D-IGRK [canx 24Jul06 as exported to Venezuela; reinstated 07Dec07; aircraft was impounded Fort Lauderdale-Executive, FL, USA and never took up YV- marks]
42-5527039	N9171R N518B C-FPQA N37KW
42-5527040	N9524N N9219G JA8870 OH-PAY
42-5527041	N9518N N4WE
42-5527042	[void - airframe not built]
42-5527043	N9525N N9226B HL5204 [w/o 20Mar91 Cheju, South Korea; canx 01May91]
42-5527044	N91940 (HL5205) HL5213 N495CA N313PC

Production complete

PIPER PA-46-500TP MALIBU MERIDIAN

c/n	Identities
4697E1	N400PT [proof-of-concept acft cvtd from c/n 4622202; wfu on fire dump Vero Beach-Municipal, FL, USA]
4697E2	[static test airframe]
4697E3	N4137E N403MM [1st prototype; dbr 07Jan00 Ft.Pierce, FL, USA; canx 16Dec05]
4697001	N401MM [2nd prototype; wfu & canx 30Dec05]
4697002	N402MM
4697003	N375RD
4697004	N711HC (N711HQ) N250SA
4697005	N43VM
4697006	N4757S
4697007	N4152R N17LH
4697008	N41842 N62WM N89ST
4697009	N4184K N209KC
4697010	N41851 N333MM (N113WE) N333MM
4697011	N41848 N67BW
4697012	N520HP
4697013	N465SK
4697014	(OY-NEW) N4174V
4697015	N4175D N965SB
4697016	N461BB
4697017	N4170L N123AD N747AW
4697018	N4180T N388TW
4697019	(OY-NEW) N519MM OY-GPT D-EPKD
4697020	N255DW
4697021	N5322M (N555SZ) N532MM
4697022	N999NG
4697023	N938JW
4697024	N524PM
4697025	N4185L
4697026	N184AL N184AE
4697027	N62LT
4697028	N264B
4697029	N529PM
4697030	N117PW
4697031	N4182K N45PJ ZS- [canx 30Jul09 as exported to South Africa]
4697032	N125WZ
4697033	N723KR
4697034	N4189N (ZS-ORM) N154DR
4697035	N77Y OE-KGB
4697036	N767TP
4697037	N999RW
4697038	N5040P N747DN [dbr 09Jul01 Palm Beach County-Glades Apt, FL, USA; canx 08Apr02]
4697039	N5018E N139KC N226DL
4697040	N5020Y N262MM [w/o 09Apr01 Vero Beach-Municipal, FL, USA; canx 20Sep06]
4697041	N5053Y N134G
4697042	N5068P N59WF
4697043	N5077Y N301D
4697044	N5111T N804JH
4697045	N5235B N93LL
4697046	N5113K N46PV
4697047	N9527N SE-ILR LX-ILE N120WW (F-HBZZ) N120WW
4697048	N5156P N32KE
4697049	N215SD
4697050	N5020Y N9531N (G-BZTP) N53308 G-BZTP N123SX LX-FUN D-EALL
4697051	N5320A N901DM
4697052	N5170J N9532N N733P
4697053	N9533N N61PK N155BM [w/o 17Dec03 nr Daytona Beach, FL, USA]
4697054	(PH-EPS) N53263 D-FKAI N46PL
4697055	N9534N (ZS-DCG) N53283 ZS-DCG
4697056	N5319K N76MG
4697057	C-FGDM N120SL
4697058	N50758 N97LL
4697059	N84SH N598AT
4697060	N5320A C-FIPO D-FIPO
4697061	N633RB D-ECRB
4697062	C-GEMO N801WA
4697063	N253MM D-ECBE
4697064	N51151 N164ST
4697065	N5319U N129EJ
4697066	N9535N N5237Y N777MG
4697067	N5053Y N44SK N8UM
4697068	N5215U
4697069	N5321R N310JM
4697070	N9536N N53322 D-FOXI D-ESSS D-ECTP
4697071	N53215 N355PM
4697072	N9537N C-GNSS N135JM
4697073	N282SW
4697074	N5322D
4697075	N711SB
4697076	N5319K
4697077	N5053Y N797BG N19CX

PA-46T

c/n	Identities
4697078	N51151 G-PCAR G-DERI
4697079	N5326C (D-EADK) (D-EARG) D-EPUS
4697080	N5324Q N73YP
4697081	N5326W N71562
4697082	N5326R N262TL N55ZG
4697083	N53235
4697084	N5333N
4697085	N5325P
4697086	N53238
4697087	N184RB
4697088	N53258 N53369
4697089	N5327A N9538N (VH-TPM) N5331N VH-TPM
4697090	N5343C N46WE N46WK N189DB SE-LTM N46WK
4697091	C-FHVM HB-PRG N137KM
4697092	N53362 N14GV
4697093	N53270 N249C N53PK
4697094	N53272 N221FP N337TF
4697095	N5339G
4697096	N455SG
4697097	N5329Q
4697098	N53328 [w/o 19Dec02 Palma, Mallorca, Spain; aircraft was canx 20Dec02 as exported to UK but never registered]
4697099	N9539N N99MZ C-GPDP N199CP
4697100	N5335R
4697101	N5336S N530HP
4697102	N5337N
4697103	N803JH N5338M
4697104	N5338M N104BH
4697105	N429MM D-EVER
4697106	N5322A N2HD N225MA
4697107	N5331N N600NS N5340U N9545N N607MA
4697108	N9540N (OY-LMM) N480M OY-LMM
4697109	N53362 N46JV
4697110	N5339V N9544N N5339V
4697111	N9542N N338DB G-RKJT OE-KDM [w/o 24Nov06 Tartu/Ylenurme, Estonia; canx cSep07]
4697112	N53415 N1RQ
4697113(1)	N5341U N90CP [cvtd to c/n 4697118(2)]
4697113(2)	N5339U N715MA N6DM N26KC *D-EMBK
4697114	N5342Z C-GMYM
4697115(1)	N5339U N715MA [cvtd to c/n 4697113(2)]
4697115(2)	N715MA N1968W
4697116	N53416 ZS-OUO
4697117(1)	N53453 (G-DIPM) N5361C [cvtd to c/n 4697125(2)]
4697117(2)	N53353 N211EZ
4697118(1)	N53353 [cvtd to c/n 4697117(2)]
4697118(2)	N5341U N90CP N500SE N993TM
4697119	N5324Q N522RF [w/o 07Mar03 Double Eagle II Apt, Albuquerque, NM, USA; canx 11Oct03]
4697120(1)	N5345S [cvtd to c/n 4697123(2)]
4697120(2)	N5357M N551S N402GW (N402PS) N91KM
4697121	N5346M N990DP
4697122(1)	N715MA [cvtd to c/n 4697115(2)]
4697122(2)	N9546N (OY-LAW) N53450 N961JM [dbr 31Dec02 Dunkeswell, UK, parts to MTW Aerospace, Montgomery, AL, USA; canx 05Aug04]
4697123(1)	N5341C [cvtd to c/n 4697124(2)]
4697123(2)	N5345S N633P N32CK
4697124(1)	(N5347N) [void - airframe not built]
4697124(2)	N5341C N428DC [w/o 12Jan09 nr Milton, FL, USA]
4697125(1)	[void - airframe not built]
4697125(2)	N53453 (G-DIPM) N5361C D-EICO
4697126	N5347V
4697127	N5341M N527MA
4697128	N53511 N85TK
4697129	N5349F N302MM N395SM
4697130	N5346U N682C
4697131	[void - airframe not built]
4697132	N53516
4697133	N5351G N672C N104ET N3325H
4697134	N5346U N46WE N134KA
4697135	N5346Y N135FL
4697136	N5355S
4697137	[void - airframe not built]
4697138	N9531N OY-LAW OH-SHG
4697139	N5357D N562HP
4697140	N5358J
4697141	N5353V
4697142(1)	N53401 [cvtd to c/n 4697143(2)]
4697142(2)	N5341C
4697143(1)	N53554 [cvtd to c/n 4697146(2)]
4697143(2)	N53401
4697144	N5346A N5361A
4697145	N5352G N5PP

PA-46T

c/n	Identities					
4697146(1)	N5341C	[cvtd to c/n 4697142(2)]				
4697146(2)	N53554	N231CM				
4697147	OY-LDA	UR-CCZV				
4697148	N53199	N802MM				
4697149	N5348S	N303JW				
4697150	N53487	C-GMCM	N241PM			
4697151	N4180A					
4697152	N9533N	N165MA	G-DERK			
4697153	N5320N					
4697154	N5351M	N3055C	N6DM	N995ST		
4697155	N53599	N9534N	N53677	N338DB		
4697156	N5364F	N156SE	N248DA			
4697157	N5363J	N235TW				
4697158	N53667	(N117WT)	N53667			
4697159	N5368H	N870C				
4697160	N5351M	N81BL				
4697161	N5365D					
4697162	N5321C	N563MA	N501AR			
4697163	N53689	N78CC				
4697164	N53705	N54199				
4697165	N3043N	N504SR	N501SR	VH-WMY		
4697166	N3010F	N9536N	N772SE	N166PM	N145DP	
4697167	N30397	(N145TP)	N30397			
4697168	N53599	N9537N	N2HD	N341MM	N844MS	
4697169	N17HP	N134M				
4697170	N3046P	EC-IVZ				
4697171	N5366Q	N477HC				
4697172	N53599	N9541N	N9540N	N821J		
4697173	N30469	N565C				
4697174	N30614	N9541N	N875SH			
4697175	N3064J	N951TB	N951TP			
4697176	N3043N	N9542N	N164DB	N606WC		
4697177	N5365M	N9543N	N62WM	*N621N		
4697178	N3063T	N9545N	(OY-PHD)	N3096P		
4697179	N29LH	*N29LT				
4697180	N30663	N187JD				
4697181	N53705	N175WB				
4697182	N3064K	N152AL				
4697183	N30912	N9546N	N220JM	(N220JN)	N220UM	
4697184	N3063T	N9547N	N294DR			
4697185	N3094W	N556MP	C-GLER			
4697186	N846RD					
4697187	N3095L	N909P				
4697188	N3097Q	N582SE	C-GDLE			
4697189	N30983					
4697190	N30993	N3103A				
4697191	N31008	N28NK				
4697192	N9549N	N752MM				
4697193	N9550N	N3096D	OY-PHD			
4697194	N31122	N234Z	HB-PQX			
4697195	N816BC					
4697196	N30898	N27DK				
4697197	N3099E	N46KH	N343RR	(N281DS)	N343RR	*N268DS
4697198	N3094R	N3115M				
4697199	N3094S	N77400	(ZS-PLG)	N3095Q	ZS-PLG	
4697200	N3095L	N9515N	C-GNSS	N234PM		
4697201	N3095N	N851LC	N428CW			
4697202	N9531N	N30898				
4697203	N3104R	N455LG				
4697204	N31087	N465TP				
4697205	N31098	N43MN				
4697206	N3110T	N9532N	N77400			
4697207	N3106Y	N9533N	N46ME			
4697208	N31062					
4697209	N31061	N209ST				
4697210	N455RS	N30912	N3292C			
4697211	N31064	N3095N	(N777FX)	N565HP		
4697212	N3107V	N812MA	N9537N	N49LG		
4697213	N3113J	N863RB				
4697214	N31136	N9538N	N455RS			
4697215	N31145					
4697216	N3123H	N32CA				
4697217	N3106Y	N142EE				
4697218	N3106Z	N618MA				
4697219	N3106Z	N9539N	N123TS			
4697220	N3124E	N10ST				
4697221	N3110T					
4697222	N3106P	N7778T				
4697223	N3092K	N90ZZ				
4697224	N3106Z	N646KC				
4697225	N3115C	N951TB				

PA-46T

c/n	Identities				
4697226	N3111K	N747BL	N7UJ		
4697227	N3113J	N9540N	N771BL	(N9021A)	N771BL
4697228	N3114P	N186PS			
4697229	N31105	N629KC			
4697230	N3117S				
4697231	N3106Y	N53KB			
4697232	N3111C	N785PJ			
4697233	N3123H	N465ME			
4697234	N3117V				
4697235	N3126W	N118JV			
4697236	N31240	N9542N	N111TN	N930HM	
4697237	N3126Z	N9543N	N237ST		
4697238	N3127G	N911TC			
4697239	N31141	N439KC	N188CE		
4697240	N31278	N9512N	OY-PHO	G-CEJB	N584V
4697241	N3121V	N45FF			
4697242	N3123H				
4697243	N3120L	N725JP			
4697244	N3128S	N210MA	N219GR	N419GR	
4697245	N3131M	N759H			
4697246	N3129X				
4697247	N3130Z	N2QE			
4697248	N3130T	N753C			
4697249	N31141	D-EXTP	N462PJ		
4697250	N3120L	N600YE			
4697251	N3128S				
4697252	N3106Z	N566HP	N168RV		
4697253	N3132B	N253SE	N535JR		
4697254	N3132A				
4697255	N3132V				
4697256	N3129S				
4697257	N3137T				
4697258	N3135Y				
4697259	N3143M	N917CC			
4697260	N3143G	(N650CA)	N9546N	N444RR	N260GF
4697261	N9547N	N9524N	C-GVJV		
4697262	N3150E	N704C	N281PD		
4697263	N3106Z	N172MA			
4697264	N3146G	N477MD	[w/o 28Jun07 nr Wellsville, MO, USA; canx 30Jan08]		
4697265	N3150U	N665KC			
4697266	(ZS-SPD)	N10409	ZS-SPD		
4697267	N267ST	N345WT			
4697268	N1040D	N668KC	C-FMKK		
4697269	N1052L				
4697270	N1052X				
4697271	N1047M	N271SE	N512MM		
4697272	N1063F				
4697273	(OK-VIP)	N10656	OK-VIP		
4697274	N1061T				
4697275	N1042H	N598C	(N222SH)	N598C	
4697276	N10563	D-ERAH	D-FRAH		
4697277	N1063M	N705MA			
4697278	N1040D	N444RR			
4697279	N9532N	N279ST			
4697280	N1063M				
4697281	N1019T	N281SE			
4697282	N9534N	(PH-FHB)	N10803	PH-FHB	
4697283	N9535N	OY-PHZ	YL-CHD		
4697284	N1065G	N219BC			
4697285	N1032G				
4697286	N1066D	N626AR			
4697287	C-GCOL				
4697288	N1075P	N9538N	N424PM		
4697289	N1075F	N9539N	N760C	N58BT	
4697290	N1075N	N568HP	N885DS		
4697291	N1042H	N291ST	D-EAVK	EC-KDV	
4697292	N9540N	C-GUXL			
4697293	N1081P	N4839R			
4697294	N1065G	N299MA			
4697295	N1065Y				
4697296	N296ST				
4697297	N9543N	N10694			
4697298	N1071S				
4697299	N9544N	D-FMOR			
4697300	N1047M	N9545N	N336P	N169CA	[w/o 18Jan08 San Antonio, TX, USA; canx 29Feb08]
4697301	N1032H	N9547N	N490CA	N95KW	
4697302	N1032H				
4697303	N1060X	N9549N	N411HB		
4697304	N9550N	N30953	ZS-TAY		
4697305	N1080G	N9531N	N305DG		
4697306	N3028G	N9533N	N568HP		

PA-46T

c/n	Identities				
4697307	N1047R	N9534N	N153TC		
4697308	N3046N	N308ST			
4697309	N31136	OY-PKB	N31136		
4697310	N717MA	N9536N	N827CM		
4697311	N3014C				
4697312	N1078D	N113T			
4697313	N3088X	N953CM			
4697314	N3090K	N9538N	N168CA	N505HP	N505HB
4697315	N31010	OK-NET			
4697316	N3091F	N401CP			
4697317	N3088U	OY-PKC	[canx 26Feb09; restored 13Mar09]		
4697318	N9540N	N618ST			
4697319	N9541N	N287MA			
4697320	N60182	OK-CTR			
4697321	N1080Q	N891CR			
4697322	N3061J				
4697323	N3088X				
4697324	N3092J	N9542N	N724KC		
4697325	N60419	D-EVTP			
4697326	N3046N	N820DM			
4697327	N3042J	N9544N	N71SE		
4697328	N9545N	N457C	N328SE	N457C	
4697329	N60690	N580HP			
4697330	N3106P	N111RC			
4697331	N546MA				
4697332	N9549N	C-GMHP			
4697333	N63SE				
4697334	N334ST				
4697335	N535KC				
4697336	N3088U	N9550N	N220JL	N220JE	
4697337	N9548N	N194JL			
4697338	N9531N	(SP-NLL)	N60887	SP-NLL	
4697339	N3091F	C-GHVM			
4697340	N3095G	N6101G			
4697341	N9539N	N60910			
4697342	N3051B	N9541N	N342SE	N3975X	
4697343	N3091Y	N9542N	N731JB	N3091Y	N731JB
4697344	N9548W	(OK-TOP)	N60897	OK-TOP	
4697345	N3091F	OE-DMG			
4697346	N9545N	N6002G	N687CA	N558RW	
4697347	N6004U	D-ETVA	D-ESSS		
4697348	N6021L	N723K			
4697349	N60935	OK-DAG			
4697350	N9533N	OY-PKE			
4697351	N9537N	C-GWEL			
4697352	N3092J	N9538N	N999SV		
4697353	N9542N	N684KM			
4697354	N9543N	N40MA			
4697355	N9546N	(OK-TIP)	N60951	OK-TIP	
4697356	N6048L	N541ND			
4697357	N6061K	N499CA	N31LA		
4697358	N3091Y	N9531N	N26DR		
4697359	N9533N	N573MS			
4697360	N6064A	N373LD			
4697361	N3110B	N625JD			
4697362	N3091Y	N9539N	N721MT		
4697363	N9538N	N813S			
4697364	N6105D	N67TE	[w/o 22Nov08 nr Marshfield-Municipal, WI, USA]		
4697365	N697ST				
4697366	N60925	S5-DJC			
4697367	N9540N	N675MA			
4697368	N9541N	N27ER			
4697369	N6026J	N390C			
4697370	N6033Z	N9546N	N175		
4697371	N6043K	N171HP			
4697372	N675CA	N57SE	N796JS		
4697373	N6048Y	D-EXPA			
4697374	N6061K				
4697375	N6064A	N375SE			
4697376	N6071M	N776CA	N776KC		
4697377	N3106Z	N577HP			
4697378	N60964	OK-FLT			
4697379	N6075N				
4697380	N6075U	N380SE	N8755X		
4697381	N61006				
4697382	N351C	N30CX			
4697383	N6077Q				
4697384	N6043K	ZS-MSD			
4697385	N385KC				
4697386	N6072J	N486HP	N119TP		
4697387	OY-PMM				

PA-46T

c/n	Identities	
4697388	N6074J	N388HP
4697389	N61027	
4697390	N6076Z	
4697391	N566MA	
4697392	N808LA	
4697393	N464C	
4697394	N994MA	
4697395	N270PS	
4697396	N3090K	
4697397	N6074J	
4697398	N3046N	N351C
4697399	N926PC	
4697400	N6081E	C-
4697401	N6082Z	
4697402	N9546N	N793CA
4697403	N403KC	
4697404	N19WM	
4697405	N6064A	
4697406	N121MA	
4697407	N6087W	OK-NTG
4697408	C-GPMF	
4697409	N6082J	
4697410	N626AC	
4697411	N32TC	
4697412		
4697413		
4697414		
4697415		
4697416		
4697417		
4697418		
4697419		
4697420		
4697421		
4697422		
4697423		
4697424		
4697425		
4697426		
4697427		
4697428		
4697429		
4697430		
4697431		
4697432		
4697433		
4697434		
4697435		
4697436		
4697437		
4697438		
4697439		
4697440		
4697441		
4697442		
4697443		
4697444		
4697445		
4697446		
4697447		
4697448		
4697449		
4697450		
4697451		
4697452		
4697453		
4697454		
4697455		
4697456		
4697457		
4697458		
4697459		
4697460		
4697461		
4697462		
4697463		
4697464		
4697465		
4697466		
4697467		
4697468		

PIPER PA-46 DLX CONVERSION

Aircraft are listed in conversion order with the registration at the time of conversion highlighted in bold text.

DLX No.	c/n	Identities					
1	4608032	**N9095U**	N712MK				
2	46-8508088	**N2428Q**					
3	46-8408049	**N4360U**	N469CC				
4	4622070	N9183X	**N7876C**	N7876Q			
5	4608099	N9122U	**N87NF**				
6	46-8608040	N9516N	C-FCSP	N69BS	**N68BS**	N788M	
7	4608014	**N9100Z**					
8	46-8608001	N2606Y	N9504N	**N70DL**			
9	46-8508033	N4385P	N9566N	**N85RT**			
10	4636137	N41199	**N648DH**	N123TF	N123ZY		
11	4622102	N919SF	N122SR	(N234DZ)	**N122SR**		
12	4636122	N9293W	**N22SY**				
13	46-8608058	N9535N	F-ODRR	**F-GHRR**			
14	4622141	(HB-PND)	N9222F	**N46WH**			
15	4622196	N646CA	**(N77PK)**	N646CA	[re-converted as #179]		
16	4608134	**N9143B**	[w/o 13Jun02 Osteen, FL, USA; canx 24Apr03]				
17	46-8508061	N4387L	**N221TB**				
18	4608034	N9104Z	N121RF	N121RP	**N87WW**	N302H	C-FTNM
19	468508068	N856M	N9584N	SE-ION	D-EION	**N46PW**	N49PW
20	4636065	N9275N	N965DA	**N4190B**			
21	4608127	**N9GF**					
22	4636141	N4124P	**N146GS**	S5-CGS			
23	4622036	N91716	**N126SR**	N26TF			
24	4622067	C-FHTH	N189PM	N888CD	**N881DB**		
25	4608125	C-FWHV	N188PC	D-ESHF	**N49HF**		
26	4636128	N92929	C-FLER	**N97CX**			
27	4608077	N9121G	**N63PW**				
28	4622106	N91991	N12FA	N12RS	**N90U**		
29	4636092	N9286L	**N429CA**				
30	4636046	N9262L	**N86000**				
31	4636173	**N715LM**					
32	4636158	N41257	**N629DK**				
33	4622163	(N595PM)	**N19500**	[re-converted as #160]			
34	4636063	N92771	**N246PR**				
35	4608114	N9134D	C-FLGB	**N94WM**			
36	4636011	**N595PM**	PH-LUX				
37	46-8408072	N4367L	SE-IXL	**N6214Q**	C-FWEM		
38	4622031	N9167Q	XB-EYL	**N9167Q**			
39	46-8608060	N9095N	**N100GF**				
40	4622118	N7777G	(JA4150)	**N7777G**			
41	4622111	N9211B	**C-GTCB**	[re-converted as #146]			
42	46-8508014	N4379A	N9504N	**N14EV**			
43	46-8508041	N4387L	N9534N	N915MC	**N119CP**		
44	4622176	N92263	**N43CH**				
45	4622032	**N9167R**	N67TG				
46	4636082	N9283N	D-ECBE	**N37RT**			
47	4622159	N92468	(JA4207)	**N94KM**			
48	4622162	N92490	**N423JT**				
49	4636134	N4141T	**N120FW**				
50	4636138	N117NJ	**N117NU**				
51	4622015	**N111MK**					
52	4636135	**N37AT**					
53	4622016	N9155H	**N7777F**				
54	4622003	**N9138Q**					
55	4622181	N9252N	**N9255H**	EC-IQX	[w/o 30Apr07 15 mls N of Ibiza, Spain]		
56	46-8508019	N4380E	VH-LRJ	N79MP	ZS-OMK	**N118AG**	
57	46-8608037	N9082E	**D-EFCH**				
58	4622058	N9176X	D-EHPJ	**N58BC**			
59	4622014	**N9140N**	N99CX	(N89CX)	N99CX		
60	4636104	N92880	**N245S**				
61	4636186	**HB-PKS**					
62	4636080	**N92819**	[re-converted as #147]				
63	4636167	N41270	**N735RC**				
64	4622095	CC-CBD	N640BD	ZS-NTH	**N640BD**		
65	4622110	**N9204C**	[re-converted as #161]				
66	46-8608044	N9084U	N904BM	**N904TM**			
67	4622064	N91782	N350PM	N350KM	N255SW	**D-EOPG**	
68	4636214	**N45WF**					
69	4636070	**N92765**					
70	4622199	N92537	JA4207	**N455MS**			
71	4636199	N4132L	N9502N	**N464JB**			
72	4622054	**N9174N**					
73	4636230	**N41874**					
74	4622146	N9235D	**N194PM**				
75	4608116	C-GWCN	**N788SM**				
76	46-8408017	**N4322Y**					
77	4636165	N4130H	N490CA	N77PK	**N77BK**		
78	4636192	N41270	**N135CC**				
79	4636036	N92671	**N582AS**				

PA-46 DLX

DLX No.	c/n	Identities				
80	4636105	N92832	D-ELEX			
81	4622177	N9252K	N177MA			
82	4622008	N9151X	D-ENII	OE-KFD	D-EKFD	
83	4622100	N9193V	N558RS	D-EKAU		
84	4636084	N92840	N922WD	N122WD		
85	4622066	N9181X	N23LH	N909RB		
86	4622180	N9251R	D-EPOE	[w/o 24Apr08 nr Parma, Italy]		
87	4636112	F-GSJR				
88	46-8508005	N4376B	D-EADC			
89	46-8508085	N23466	VH-BGK			
90	4636284	N4169T	N427LS	(N4075N)	N427LS	
91	4636236	N147BK				
92	4622150	N92380	N88846			
93	4636174	N295SS	N295S			
94	4636238	N41653	N68CP			
95	4636051	N92735	N5EG	N5EQ		
96	4636041	N926SL	N12321			
97	4622061	N9178B	N9517N	N554T	N1AM	[w/o 21Dec06 nr Concord, CA, USA; canx 24Apr07]
98	4622189	N9254X	C-GGMC			
99	4636002	N92552	N9275D	N648T		
100	4636216	N4136U	N463JM	N463JP		
101	4636193	N26TG				
102	4636153	N4124V	N318CW			
103	4636261	N4160T				
104	4608075	N9130N	[w/o 19Oct06 nr Odenton, MD, USA]			
105	4636297	N4170K				
106	4636222	C-FRPX	N529WM			
107	4636200	N399PM	N747TH			
108	4622160	N92474	N146PM	N296J		
109	4636265	N4165P	N829AG	HS-	[canx 29Dec08 as exported to Thailand]	
110	4636127	N9299E	N316JM	N35CX	[w/o 06Aug07 nr Sitka, AK, USA]	
111	4636087	N9284X				
112	4636301	N4183M	N901MA			
113	4622092	N202SE	C-FKKH	[w/o 28Mar08 Wainwright, AB, Canada]		
114	4636005	(HS-RGR)	N9259X	HS-RGR		
115	4636035	C-GNSS	N7WS			
116	4636067	N9278X	N67VK			
117	4636246	N177RD				
118	4636124	N92850	N321CR			
119	4636027	G-HOOP	N71DH			
120	4636055	N92660	N76BF	N7688		
121	4636160	N4177P	N822DK			
122	4636012	N92575	D-EPTC			
123	4636202	N41346	D-EIWM	OE-KAB	N54WT	
124	4636075	N9281J	N313BC	SE-LYL		
125	4636107	N92884				
126	4636061	N92735	N694CM	N305JD		
127	4636171	N4129P	N1RQ	N560MP		
128	4622088	N9193X	N747RC	(N706CC)	N193BD	RA-0216G
129	4636175	C-GMCM	N72VG			
130	4636077	C-GLCE	N234HS	N113MC		
131	4622050	SE-KIP	OY-SVE	N49PK		
132	4622004	N9140F	D-EMDB	[w/o 07Apr04 12km NE of St.Moritz, Switzerland]		
133	46-8608010	N9120Y				
134	4608055	N9119N	N9580N	N777PG	D-EPRA	
135	4636164	N4128K	N964MA	N21PD	N28JK	
136	4622105	N9197B	N350MM			
137	4636201	N4167C				
138	4636143	N81SM	N16CP			
139	4622179	N9252X	N33VM			
140	4622080	N91859	N69DN			
141	46-8608019	N9230T	G-BMMT	I-GHIO	HB-POA	D-ELAO
142	4622174	(OY-JEL)	N92460	N8W	N775RD	N794MM
143	4636300	N4170D				
144	4622200	N9258D	N100VC	(N800RG)	D-ERGC	
145	4622009	N91520	N14EF			
146	4622111	N9211B	C-GTCB			
147	4636080	N92819				
148	4636059	N9272X	N347DW			
149	4636190	N9500N	N922WD			
150	4636071	N896PM	N8686			
151	4636074	N9281B				
152	4636111	N9291S	N92849	(N55WF)	N812MB	
153	4608047	N9114D	N9565N	N86RL		
154	4636106	N797MA	N721BB	N21AG		
155		[not identified]				
156	46-8608002	N9094T	(N193M)	D-ENHP	D-ETPW	[dam 02Aug09 Pula, Croatia]
157	4622194	F-GPKL				
158	4636285	N41865	N462HP			
159	4636210	N9506N	N47PM	OO-PJM		
160	4622163	(N595PM)	N19500			

PA-46 DLX

DLX No.	c/n	Identities				
161	4622110	**N9204C**				
162	4636231	N41469	**N301DM**			
163	4636019	G-DODI	**N352CM**			
164	4636242	N46WE	**N46WD**	N629JJ		
165	46-8608054	N9094Z	N9530N	N719LR	**D-EAAB**	
166	4622041	N9512N	**N90SE**			
167	4636099	(ZS-OHJ)	N92091	ZS-OHJ	**N510RB**	
168	4636047	N9272X	N722EW	**N722ET**		
169	4636123	N9294N	**N9299P**			
170	4636370	N3064K	**N46PW**			
171	4636256	N41760	N4165N	CC-PGO	**N706Z**	
172	4622134	N92263	**N193MM**			
173	4608120	N9136J	N133WW	N183WW	**D-EBKK**	
174	4636162	N4120V	**N25PF**			
175	4636151	N41222	N4165D	**C-FGNG**		
176	4636345	N5354K	N345SE	**N708DP**		
177	4636026	N9264Q	**D-EXTA**	[w/o 18Apr07 Karlsruhe/Baden-Baden, Germany; canx 22Aug07]		
178	4636089	**N389MA**				
179	4622196	N646CA	(N77PK)	**N646CA**		
180	4622072	HB-PMO	**D-EVSM**			
181	4636064	N92660	**N747MF**	N9266R	N557ML	
182	4636211	N4134N	N31BG	XB-JYN	**D-EXRE**	
183	4608031	**N9104N**				
184	4636147	N41212	**N415WR**			
185	4622172	**N195PM**				
186	4636096	**N9282J**	ZS-TWZ			
187	4622087	N321FS	**N816TM**			
188	46-8408087	**N4372L**				
189	4636136	N4124U	LV-ZPG	**N921GG**		
190	4636114	N92880	N722EW	**N5757**		
191	4636085	N9282W	**N727MC**			
192	4636249	N9533N	G-BYSO	**N417RK**		
193	4636015	N92552	**N400TW**			
194	4636132	N9298L	N9898M	**F-GZBC**	OO-NMU	
195	4636212	N951CS				
196	4636208	N4126Z	N9505N	**N516RS**		
197	4636218	N46DX	**N46DV**			
198	4636031	(N962DA)	N9263D	**N962DA**		
199	4636091	G-RMST	G-PALL	**D-ERFC**		
200	4636354	N30908	**N146ST**			
201	4636320	N5324Q	**N461HP**			
202	4622170	N92502	**C-GJJH**			
203	4636235	N9509N	N41653	EC-HIZ	N998AA	**N97AA**
204	4636161	N41244	**N122TM**			
205	4636329	N535457	N103TK	**N280KT**		
206	4636339	N5354K	N318ED	**N955SH**		
207	4622186	N9252X	N666AS	(N526AS)	**N664AE**	N103EN
208	4622075	**N9180X**				
209	4636350	N5370S	N9544N	N303C	**N787RP**	
210	4636361	**N726ED**				
211	4636144	G-CUPN	**N446SB**			
212	4636146	N4125K	**N545JW**			
213	4608025	**N9098U**				
214	4622115	**N9195F**				
215	4636312	N4170T	**N403HP**			
216	4636023	N9263D	**N623MA**			
217	4636277	N4176D	**N887JD**			
218	46-8508096	N2494X	G-MICZ	**N323ML**	N323FL	
219	4608001	OY-CEL	N181CA	D-ETBL	**N350BR**	
220	4622187	N92537	**N118JG**			
221	4636363	N3093B	**N113BP**			
222	4636248	N4137U	N338DB	**N638DB**		
223	4622140	N9288N	**N92156**			
224	46-8608061	**N9095S**				
225	4622148	N9235X	N1221K	D-EMVF	S5-DGN	**D-EMBZ**
226	4622005	N9148V	**D-EEEY**			
227	4636121	N9294G	**N629BC**			
228	4636224	N4145B	**N16TC**			
229		[not identified]				
230	4636154	**N243KF**				
231	4636140	**N4121K**				
232	4636102	N4287X	N7795W	XB-HYM	**N203CA**	
233	4636170	**N296LC**				
234	4622113	**N190RW**				
235	4636204	**N55WH**				
236	4636291	N4189C	(N742JW)	**N4189C**		
237	4636239	N41647	**N225MC**			
238	4622173	N9250J	N463WP	**N195JG**		
239	4636185	N4138A	**N7SA**			
240	4636206	N4132H	N9504N	**N785HC**		

REIMS-CESSNA F.406 CARAVAN II

c/n	Identities
F406-1	F-WZLT F-GFLT F-ZBFA [prototype]
F406-0001	F-WZDD F-GDRK N406CE OO-TIV EC-ESE PH-ALO N17CK
F406-0002	F-WZDD F-GEUF N1986F OO-TIS PH-MNS D2-ECN
F406-0003	F-WZDJ (F-GEUP) OO-TIK PH-ALK 5Y-JJG [w/o 08Aug94 Nairobi-Wilson, Kenya]
F406-0004	F-WDRL (F-GDRL) F-ZBEO F-WIVD V5-EEZ
F406-0005	F-WZDS (SE-IPH) N9751N 5R-MSK ZS-NNA 5H-RAS [dbr 25Nov04 Arusha, Tanzania, parts to Preferred Airparts, Kidron-Stoltzfus, OH, USA]
F406-0006	0006/F-ZBEP (French Customs)
F406-0007	F-WZDT (OO-TIA) OO-TIR PH-FWC EC-ESF PH-FWC LX-LMS TR-LEQ D-IATE
F406-0008	0008/ABM (French Army) F-WQUD N27NW
F406-0009	F-WZDS PH-FWB 5Y-TAL [wfu Skive, Denmark]
F406-0010	0010/ABN (French Army) F-WQAY 5Y-BYX
F406-0011	F-WZDT D-IDAA D2-ECO
F406-0012	F-WZDU OO-TIZ PH-ALE 5Y-WAW ZK-CII ZK-VAA ZK-XLC
F406-0013	F-WZDV OO-TIY 5Y-JJA F-GPRA F-WWSR ZS-MAD V5-MAD F-GRAZ
F406-0014	F-WZDS PH-FWD G-TWIG [w/o 22Oct04 Beinn Dearg, Scotland; canx 13May05]
F406-0015	F-WZDX PH-FWE EC-177 EC-FOH PH-FWE G-TINI OY-PBG OH-OTL
F406-0016	F-WZDY (F-GEUK) PH-LAS D2-ECP
F406-0017	F-ZBES
F406-0018	F-WZDZ OO-TIW PH-ALN EI-CKY G-LEAF
F406-0019	F-WZDR G-CVAN D2-ECQ
F406-0020	F-WZDS PH-FWF (EI-CND) G-TURF
F406-0021	F-WZDT PH-FWG 5Y-BKN
F406-0022	F-WZDT YV-26CP YV-525C YV-990CP YV1187
F406-0023	F-WZDU F-WZIJ N53474 ZS-OEE 5V- ZS-OEE
F406-0024	F-WZDR F-GEUJ PH-PEL G-THAN PH-PEL 5Y-ING [w/o 12Jun95 Nairobi-Wilson, Kenya]
F406-0025	F-WZDV F-GEUL 0025/F-ZBAB (Securite Civile)
F406-0026	F-OGOG
F406-0027	F-WZDX PH-FWH D-ISHY ZS-SSD [w/o 26Sep07 nr Entebbe, Uganda; canx 21Jan09]
F406-0028	F-WZDR N7037C 5H-TWD 5H-TZC [dbr 13Aug02 Muyowasi, Tanzania]
F406-0029	F-WZDS PH-FWI 5H-TZD [w/o 24Apr96 nr Morogoro, Tanzania]
F406-0030	F-WZDT PH-FWJ G-BPSV 5Y-MMJ ZS-NYI 5H-ANS 5H-AWK [w/o 03Apr08 nr Mwanza, Tanzania]
F406-0031	F-WZDR N7035B D-IBOM VT-ASB F-WWSR VT-ASB
F406-0032	F-WZDU G-BPSW N442AB AP-BFA PH-CLE LN-TWH PH-CLE ZS-SSC
F406-0033	F-WZDV F-WZDR N22591 VT-SAC VH-RCB VH-JVN
F406-0034	F-WZDX G-BPSX N443AB AP-BFB PH-PHO OY-PAB (D-ILIM) OO-LMO N861FT
F406-0035	F-WZDY S7-AAM SY-006 (Seychelles Government) S7-IDC S7-IDO ZS-OGY 5H-PAY
F406-0036	F-WZDZ G-DFLT G-MAFA
F406-0037	F-WZDT D-ICAS 5Y-BIS PH-MJM ZS-PPU PR-FAG
F406-0038	F-WZDR PH-ALX 5Y-NAL [reportedly w/o cMar94 in Kenya]
F406-0039	F-WZDS 0039/F-ZBBB (Securite Civile)
F406-0040	F-WZDV PH-ALY OH-ALY PH-ALY 5Y-JJC (5Y-HHJ) ZS-OTT 5H-SXB ZS-OTT [acft was also regd 3D-AAT at some point (date?)]
F406-0041	F-WZDX PH-ALZ 9H-ACI N563GA ZS-OIG [w/o 03Nov01 Johannesburg, Gauteng Province, South Africa]
F406-0042	F-WKRA F-GKRA F-WKRA F-ZBCE
F406-0043	F-WQUD D-INUS F-WQUD ZS-SSE
F406-0044	F-WZDZ PH-ALU OH-ALU PH-ALU (LN-TED) 5Y-MKM
F406-0045	F-WZDT PH-ALV G-FIND 5Y-LAN OY-PEU G-FIND
F406-0046	F-WZDU PH-ALP G-BSRY OY-PED 5H-TZE
F406-0047	F-WZDV (PH-ALN) N6589A D-IAAD TF-ORD
F406-0048	F-WZDX (PH-ALR) N6589C HP-1236 S9-IHD D-ILIB OY-PEZ G-FLYN V5-WAK
F406-0049	N6589E (G-ZAPH) 9M-PMS N406GV
F406-0050	F-WZDS N7148T VT-SAA VH-RCA N406P D-ICCC
F406-0051	N7148P S7-AAI
F406-0052	N6590Y
F406-0053	N6591L [w/o 17Aug03 off Pearl Bay, AK, USA; canx 07Nov06]
F406-0054	N6591R
F406-0055	F-WZDN N65912 5Y-BIX
F406-0056	F-GJLH [w/o 22Sep93 nr Strasbourg, France]
F406-0057	F-WZDP N31226 F-ODYZ ZK-VAF ZK-XLF
F406-0058	F-GEUD F-OGPX PH-GPX ZS-OXE V5-MDA
F406-0059	N3122E AP-BFK
F406-0060	N6660A F-OGUG PH-GUG 5H-WOW
F406-0061	N3121X F-OGVS F-GURA N406CT F-GRAI F-ZBGE
F406-0062	N3125G YS-15C N744C V5-DHL
F406-0063	N3129V F-OGUI PH-GUI N406SD
F406-0064	G-SFPA G-CVXN
F406-0065	G-SFPB
F406-0066	F-WZDT F-ZBCG
F406-0067	F-GEUG 14/Z-DDG (Zimbabwe AF)
F406-0068	F-GIQC 15/Z-DDE (Zimbabwe AF)
F406-0069	F-GIQD 17/Z-DDD (Zimbabwe AF)
F406-0070	F-ZBCI
F406-0071	F-GIQE 16/Z-DDF (Zimbabwe AF)
F406-0072	[void - airframe not built]
F406-0073	G-BVJT F-WQFA G-BVJT
F406-0074	F-ZBCJ
F406-0075	F-ZBCH

REIMS-CESSNA F.406

c/n	Identities			
F406-0076	F-WZDX	VH-ZZE	VH-YZE	
F406-0077	F-WZDZ	F-ZBCF		
F406-0078	F-WZDY	VH-BPH	VH-ZZF	VH-YZF
F406-0079	F-WZDZ	VH-ZZG	VH-YZG	
F406-0080	F-WWSR	G-MAFB		
F406-0081	F-WWSR	98-1001 (South Korean Navy)		
F406-0082	F-WWSS	98-1002 (South Korean Navy)		
F406-0083	F-WWST	98-1003 (South Korean Navy)		
F406-0084	F-WWSU	99-1005 (South Korean Navy)		
F406-0085	F-WWSV	99-1006 (South Korean Navy)		
F406-0086	F-WWSR	F-ZBGA		
F406-0087	F-WWSS	F-GJJK	AC-21 (Greek Navy)	
F406-0088	F-WWST	F-GJJN	AC-22 (Greek Navy)	
F406-0089	F-WWSU	F-GJJO	AC-23 (Greek Navy)	
F406-0090	F-WWSV	(F-ZBGB)	F-WWNP	F-ZBGD
F406-0091	F-OSPJ			
F406-0092	F-WWNP	5A-DKW		
F406-0093	F-WWNP	V5-FMR		
F406-0094	G-SMMA			
F406-0095	G-SMMB			
F406-0096	G-TDSA			
F406-0097				
F406-0098				
F406-0099				
F406-0100				
F406-0101				
F406-0102				
F406-0103				
F406-0104				
F406-0105				
F406-0106				
F406-0107				
F406-0108				
F406-0109				
F406-0110				
F406-0111				
F406-0112				
F406-0113				
F406-0114				
F406-0115				
F406-0116				
F406-0117				
F406-0118				
F406-0119				
F406-0120				
F406-0121				
F406-0122				
F406-0123				
F406-0124				
F406-0125				
F406-0126				
F406-0127				
F406-0128				
F406-0129				
F406-0130				
F406-0131				
F406-0132				
F406-0133				
F406-0134				
F406-0135				
F406-0136				
F406-0137				
F406-0138				
F406-0139				
F406-0140				
F406-0141				
F406-0142				
F406-0143				
F406-0144				
F406-0145				
F406-0146				
F406-0147				
F406-0148				
F406-0149				
F406-0150				

SWEARINGEN (FAIRCHILD) SA.26T MERLIN II

c/n	Series	Identities
T26-001	2	N2601S [wfu c1970 and used as test frame; status?]
T26-002	2A	N2100S N969BJ N500BW N2301N [w/o 22Nov78 nr Memphis-Olive Branch, MS, USA; canx 08Oct82]
T26-003	2A	N100HF N30W N111FL N100MX N100NX [wfu, parts to White Industries, Bates City, MO, USA; location S-14]
T26-004	2A	N2104S N100JB N700SC N76ST [wfu, parts to Dodson International Parts, Rantoul, KS, USA]
T26-005	2A	N400P N201SM [wfu c1985 Winnipeg-St Andrews, MB, Canada]
T26-006	2A	N600P [wfu, parts to Dodson International Parts, Rantoul, KS, USA]
T26-007	2A	N2101S N44BB C-GGFJ N9032H [pres inst airframe Enterprise-Ozark Community College, Ozark Aviation Campus, Ozark, AL, USA; canx 03Feb93]
T26-008	2A	N304M [wfu, parts to White Industries, Bates City, MO, USA; b/u]
T26-009	2A	N2102S N22EM N22EK N400DG
T26-010	2A	[cvtd to Merlin IIB c/n T26-100]
T26-011	2A	N263K N55JM N55ZM [b/u; canx 02Mar89]
T26-012	2A	N1198S C-GRDT N1198S [wfu, parts to White Industries, Bates City, MO, USA; location S-02]
T26-013	2A	[void - airframe not built]
T26-014	2A	N953HF N952HE N711AH [w/o 17May82 Fresno-Air Terminal, CA, USA; canx 21Sep92]
T26-015	2A	N41T N341T N111PT [wfu c1988; b/u; canx 27Apr92]
T26-016	2A	N748G C-GTHN [dbr 20Jun97 Whale Cove Airstrip, NT, Canada, parts to Global Aircraft Industries, Edmonton-Villeneuve, AB, Canada; canx 25Aug97]
T26-017	2A	N340X [wfu, parts to White Industries, Bates City, MO, USA; location Q-24]
T26-018	2A	N136LK N136LE N136EK N200SW N12NA N801BT
T26-019	2A	N1203S N422RK N2JE C-FSVC [w/o 31May99 Churchill, MB, Canada; canx 19Jan00]
T26-020	2A	N425UX N426JX CF-HAD C-FHDA N59TC N77WF C-GLKA [canx 13Jun02 - status?]
T26-021	2A	N1204S N137RD N802AC [wfu, parts to Dodson International Parts, Rantoul, KS, USA]
T26-022	2A	N37D N337H N999DT N737EF [wfu, parts to White Industries, Bates City, MO, USA; location Q-23; canx 18Mar93]
T26-023	2A	N1206S [wfu; b/u c1991; canx 20Oct93]
T26-024	2A	N1207S
T26-025	2A	N1208S
T26-026	2A	N1209S N105EC C-GWKA N269PM
T26-027	2A	N1210S [wfu c1985 Winnipeg-St Andrews, MB, Canada]
T26-028	2A	N1212S N30SG [wfu, parts to White Industries, Bates City, MO, USA; b/u; canx 14Mar91]
T26-029	2A	N22CE N187Z [b/u; canx 15Oct92]
T26-030	2A	N95D N950 [wfu, parts to OK Aircraft Parts, Hayward, CA, USA; b/u c1987; canx 13Jun02]
T26-031	2A	N1214S [w/o 16May73 nr Deadhorse, AK, USA]
T26-032	2A	N742G C-FANF [wfu, parts to White Industries, Bates City, MO, USA; location "Ramp North 05"; canx 08Oct96]
T26-033	2A	N1215S N121KB
T26-034	2A	N96D N106EC [wfu, parts to White Industries, Bates City, MO, USA; location T-03]
T26-035	2A	N1216S N1014T N500DM N508GW [pres inst airframe Northrop University, CA, USA; canx 18Sep89]
T26-036	2A	N739G C-FFYC [w/o 01Jun94 nr Thompson, MB, Canada; canx 25Aug97]
T26-100	2B	N1202S N333F
T26-101	2B	N1217S N101VV N101HK N707SC N505GC N11PM N669SP N699AM VT- [canx 06May08 as exported to India]
T26-102	2B	N1218S N100SM N100SN N160SN C-FBWU N803DJ [b/u; canx 09Sep02]
T26-103	2B	N1219S VH-CAI P2-CAI VH-CAI N136PS N2MP N136SP N171PC [wfu cNov02, parts to White Industries, Bates City, MO, USA; location "Building 04"; canx 29Apr09]
T26-104	2B	N504W
T26-105	2B	N345T
T26-106	2B	N370X
T26-107	2B	N1220S N711SA N642RP C-GMOU N158CA
T26-108	2B	N964WM N122NK N480BC [wfu, parts to White Industries, Bates City, MO, USA; location "Ramp South B-01"]
T26-109	2B	N1221S
T26-110	2B	N941PM N6SP N2295F N20TA N199TA [w/o 19Jun85 Rocksprings, TX, USA]
T26-111	2B	VH-CAH N135SP
T26-112	2B	N1222S N7603 [wfu c2005 parts to White Industries, Bates City, MO, USA; location "Sec-1 R-1 10"; canx 04Feb09]
T26-113	2B	N97D N97N N87WJ N87BS N878SC HP-1136AP
T26-114	2B	N664MC N82DW N97AB N97RD N7HL N485G N5B N78WL N1AQ N963BP
T26-115	2B	N1223S N50KV [dbr 26Apr05 Lawrenceville-Gwinnett County/Briscoe Field, GA, USA, parts to Atlanta Air Salvage, Griffin-Spalding County, GA, USA; canx 26Mar08]
T26-116	2B	N216F N100AW N80RP N100AW N96RL
T26-117	2B	N852AC N1SS N211CC N3HV C-GYLP N802DJ [w/o 21Jun94 Greenville-Donaldson Center Apt, SC, USA; canx 28Mar95]
T26-118	2B	N1224S N12WC
T26-119	2B	VH-CAJ N4468M [dbr 29Dec87 Telluride-Regional, CO, USA, parts to White Industries, Bates City, MO, USA; location Q-20]
T26-120	2B	N1225S N747YC N74YC N58FS N18ZD N58FS [b/u; canx 15Feb90]
T26-121	2B	N4252X N261PL [b/u; canx 14Mar89]
T26-122	2B	N369DR N63SC C-GBZM

MERLIN II

c/n	Series	Identities
T26-123	2B	N1227S N872D N872S [wfu, parts to White Industries, Bates City, MO, USA; location Q-22]
T26-124	2B	N4051X
T26-125	2B	N393W N642WM [wfu, parts to Quest Aviation, Lake City, FL, USA; canx 20Dec93]
T26-126	2B	N411X [dbr 28Mar72 Nashville, TN, USA, parts to Dodson International Parts, Rantoul, KS, USA]
T26-127	2B	N1500X [dbr 14Nov76 King Salmon Apt, AK, USA; canx 24Sep98]
T26-128	2B	N717JB N789X N717JB C-FBVI N20PT [dbr 18Mar94 Winchester-Regional, VA, USA, parts to Dodson International Parts, Rantoul, KS, USA]
T26-129	2B	N398T N517DQ N711SE N711SL N8484 N784AF N100SN RF-14004
T26-130	2B	N66Q N87Y N87YB [wfu, parts to Aviation Warehouse, El Mirage, CA, USA; canx 04May98]
T26-131	2B	N4254X N425DC N4251R N1YC [b/u; canx 13Aug04]
T26-132	2B	N4253X N425MC N72CF HA-SIP
T26-133	2B	N401NW N474U [wfu cDec96, parts to Quest Aviation, Lake City, FL, USA; canx 03Dec99]
T26-134	2B	N1969K N134G N307G N1UA N18SE [w/o 06Sep87 Columbia-Owens Field, SC, USA]
T26-135	2B	N175P N124PS N213SC [wfu, parts to Atlanta Air Salvage, Griffin-Spalding County, GA, USA]
T26-136	2B	N51L N51LF N137CP
T26-137	2B	N192G N192GL N698X [w/o 27Nov03 Jacksonville-Craig Municipal, FL, USA; canx 22Sep04]
T26-138	2B	N52LF N52L N73HC
T26-139	2B	N303WP N12MH N458G C-FCAR N469BL N280AR
T26-140	2B	N218G N1QL N1QD N69ST N699F N718GL N321PH
T26-140E	2B	D-IBMC N65103 [w/o 19Oct79 Palo Alto, CA, USA]
T26-141	2B	N50L N50LF N64MN N690X C-GHWM N690X [w/o 12Oct90 Monongahela, PA, USA; canx 17Dec90]
T26-142	2B	N449WC N400S N111PM N112CW N991CB N226HA YV [canx 08May03 as exported to Venezuela]
T26-143	2B	N4266X VH-KRG N312JC N312RJ N61PH LV-PFP LV-RZB
T26-144	2B	N920DY N920D N600MS N599MS N913DM N558AC
T26-145	2B	N34UA [w/o 10Feb93 Ardmore-Municipal, OK, USA; canx 12Apr93]
T26-146	2B	N939SC N939WB N7WY N501FS [w/o 07Jul98 nr Saint George Apt, AK, USA; canx 21Aug98]
T26-147	2B	N239P [w/o 29Jan70 Willoughby-Cuyahoga County, OH, USA]
T26-148	2B	N4256X N540MC N200MH
T26-149	2B	N25AC N193G N642RB N642PB N329HS (N829HS) EC-202 EC-GJZ
T26-149E	2B	XB-ZAO N200BC N846BB XA- [canx 29Jul08 as exported to Mexico]
T26-150	2B	N4257X N457G
T26-151	2B	N222JC N222JG N30WA N70SC N180HH N396PS C-GSWJ HR- N396PS
T26-152	2B	N4259X N348KN N4ER (N617DM) N939C RF-14424
T26-153	2B	N4262X
T26-154	2B	N4255X CF-GRA C-FGRA N40DK N400VF C-FGRA N71SF N20KV
T26-154E	2B	F-BRSL D-IBMF N90874 N666SE [wfu, parts to White Industries, Bates City, MO, USA; location T-04]
T26-155	2B	N98D N98DB C-GVCO N5307Q [wfu; b/u c1991; canx cFeb92]
T26-156	2B	N112A N30HS
T26-157	2B	N777N N88SC N20ER N20EF [wfu cJun03; pres Western Michigan University, Battle Creek-W.K.Kellogg, MI, USA]
T26-158	2B	N4260X XA- [canx 31Aug04 as exported to Mexico]
T26-158E	2B	D-IKUS N65150 N711FR N256WC N8KT
T26-159	2B	N4261X N14JK N66MD
T26-160	2B	N324CE N300CE N38MJ C-GPWR [wfu, parts to White Industries, Bates City, MO, USA; location Q-21; canx 26Jun89]
T26-161	2B	N22DL N22DE N10WE N10WL N101BU N101BE N59TP N669HS [wfu, parts to White Industries, Bates City, MO, USA; b/u]
T26-162	2B	N4267X N735EB N7603 CF-TEL N30TF [dbr 16Feb03 Cahokia-St.Louis Downtown, IL, USA, parts to White Industries, Bates City, MO, USA; location "Ramp South A-07"; canx 16Mar04]
T26-163	2B	N4268X N111SE N26JB [w/o 13Feb92 Glenwood Springs, CO, USA; canx 21Dec94]
T26-163E	2B	F-BKML D-ILSE [w/o 10Apr73 Stuttgart-Echterdingen, West Germany; canx 14Jun73]
T26-164	2B	N50MA N36PE N164BT N164P
T26-165	2B	N5674M N111GL N111SF N35WB N66RE N67HM C-GMZG N160EA
T26-166	2B	N4270X N226LS N23X N17JJ
T26-167	2B	N4265X N5353M N400DC
T26-167E	2B	D-IBMD I-PEBI D-IDMD N2303P (N841MA) N2303P
T26-168	2B	N4271X N100NL N20DE [w/o 16Oct71 Hot Springs-Ingalls Field, VA, USA]
T26-169	2B	N227CH N22GW N102DY
T26-170	2B	N4273X N19SE N33SE [b/u; canx 23Oct95]
T26-171	2B	[cvtd to Merlin III c/n T-200]
T26-171E	2B	VQ-ZIZ 3D-AAG 9K-ACW N50TF N50AK C-GRBF
T26-172	2B	N5675M N45BB N45MM N120FS N742GR N789RB
T26-172E	2B	VH-CAK N309SP N135SR C-FCAW
T26-173	2B	N49MJ N49MZ N99RK N22NR
T26-174	2B	CF-HYX [w/o 11Oct73 Airport Road, 166 Dempster Highway, Inuvik, NT, Canada; canx 12Feb74]
T26-175	2B	N5678M N60Y XA-RWJ N499SP YV-941CP YV123T
T26-176	2B	N5679M N5117H N777PE N1907W [status?]
T26-177	2B	N5680M N120GW N83RS C-GYMR [w/o 12Oct88 Fort Good Hope, NT, Canada; canx 13Jul89]

c/n	Series	Identities
T26-178	2B	N5682M N210SW N210SN N717CC N542JV N717BD N61775 N717PD
T26-179	2B	N5383M ZS-RTZ N177MF [w/o 02Dec80 Albany, KY, USA; canx 15Oct81]
T26-180E	2B	N5301M ZS-ILA A2-KAM N1039Y [status?]

Production complete

SWEARINGEN (FAIRCHILD) SA.226T MERLIN III

c/n	Series	Identities
T-200	3	[built as Merlin III c/n T-205E]
T-201	3	N5292M N555DB N555AM [w/o 10Jun81 nr Cameron, LA, USA]
T-202	3	N5671M N103PA C-FDAC N103PA [wfu c2000 NAYAK Technical Training, Cologne-Bonn, Germany; canx 14Jan00]
T-203	3	N5273M N97AB
T-204	3	N828C N400CC N486DC N224BA N224SB VH-EGC VH-SSM
T-205	3	N240HM N240CE N200CE N200QE N20GC N555AW N555WW N20GC N970M
T-205E	3	N1226S N4BC
T-206	3	D-IBMG N47074 N11RM N46NA
T-207	3	D-IDHS N88BT N98BZ N500CP N500QP N693PG [w/o 18Sep95 nr Chino, CA, USA]
T-208	3	N5271M N85H VH-EMO N555BR VH-EMO N4470D N969EE N429LC N269DE
T-209	3	N400SJ N400SU N66KS [w/o 09Sep86 in Bahamas]
T-210	3	VH-CAM N173SP VH-SSL
T-211	3	N5272M N45TA TN-ADO 5Y-TNT [w/o 01Oct92 nr Nairobi, Kenya]
T-212	3	N222JC N222JQ VR-BHQ N222MV
T-213	3	VH-CAL N174SP VH-SSD
T-214	3	N664MC N7090 N3RB [w/o 17Sep85 in sea 100 mls off Louisiana Coast, USA]
T-215	3	PT-DUX [w/o 27Sep71 Sao Paulo, Sao Paulo State, Brazil]
T-216	3	N5294M N950M N50PK N26RT [w/o 24Feb89 Helsinki, Finland; canx 07Mar89]
T-217	3	N199Z N224HR
T-218	3	N990M N75MX
T-219	3	N5296M [w/o 10Apr73 Montreal, QC, Canada]
T-220	3	N905P N905RK N14TP XB-JQC
T-221	3	N2649 N264B N22EQ (N18BQ) N22EQ
T-222	3	N5306M F-GEJY [wfu La Roche-sur-Yon, France; b/u cAug87]
T-223	3	N2630 N2630M N263CM
T-224	3	N5307M N12EK N5307M N550BE
T-225	3	N5305M N533AR C-GRTL N950TT [w/o 19Dec97 nr Byers, CO, USA, canx 21Jul98]
T-226	3	VH-BCL P2-BCL N41BA N70FC [wfu c2005, parts to White Industries, Bates City, MO, USA; location "Sec-1 R-2"]
T-227	3	N22DW N22DT C-GTRL N2746Z N142NR N555AM
T-228	3	N5310M N348KN N348KX N92RC N92RQ C-GNJM N188SC C-GURG N610ED N290TA
T-229	3	N5311M N105BB N78CS XA- [canx 31Jan06 as exported to Mexico]
T-230	3	N5312M N10TB N10TF D-IOTF N44264 N789B LV-WLW [dbr 04Jan96 Ushuaia, Tierra del Fuego, Argentina, parts to Dodson International Parts, Rantoul, KS, USA]
T-231	3	N20CN N20QN N46SA (N321TS) N46SA *N321TS
T-232	3	N5313M N500 N5004 C-GSWY N56TA LV-WIR
T-233	3	N5314M N66AL N20CL N84LC N300PT [canx 18Aug05 - status?]
T-234	3	N5316M N531LP N101MC
T-235	3	XC-SIC XC-UTE TP-206 (Mexican AF) N45818
T-236	3	N5317M
T-237	3	N5319M N99ML C-FCPH N633ST
T-238	3	N5321M N130PC XC-HFA
T-239	3	N5323M N333SG N833S C-GPRO N239DR
T-240	3	N5324M N76U N240NM TG- [canx 16May06 as exported to Guatemala]
T-241	3	N5326M N75RD N75RC N73542 N23AE
T-242	3	N5327M N12HH N7UU N770U N241DT [w/o 25May93 5 mls W of Santa Fe County Municipal, NM, USA; canx 03Mar94]
T-243	3	N5329M [w/o 03Mar77 Nassau, Bahamas]
T-244	3	N5330M RP-C203 N244SA
T-245	3	N5331M RP-C1261 N4209S
T-246	3	N5333M N43FC N43FG N43CB [status?]
T-247	3	N5337M C-GSCM N5337M N100T N999PF [reportedly b/u c1992; canx 22Sep93]
T-248	3	N5338M N10WL F-GGGH N120TT OH-ADA N104EM [wfu c2005, parts to White Industries, Bates City, MO, USA; location "Taxiway South"; canx 29Apr09]
T-249	3A	N200ET D-IFWZ N249RL N777HZ XB-KSB
T-250	3A	N5340M N250EH N322BB N656PS N656BS N70X N311RV N85DB N125WG
T-251	3A	N5345M XB-AUV XA-ABB N54574 N711RD C-GDSD [dbr cDec92; b/u; canx 15Dec92]
T-252	3A	(N5347M) YV-T-ART YV-640P YV-500CP N600DL (N600DH) N252RR N600DL D-IBIN N600DL XA- [canx 31Aug07 as exported to Mexico]
T-253	3A	N5358M N959M HK-
T-254	3A	N5363M N959TF N114PA N58018 N25677
T-255	3A	N5349M D-INWK N9NZ
T-256	3A	N234TT N500KK N311GM N699KM (N226JP) N699KM
T-257	3A	N45BB N39MS
T-258	3A	N666LB N15GS N828CM N772SL

MERLIN III

c/n	Series	Identities
T-259	3A	N5374M CF-01 (Belgian AF) LX-NOP
T-260	3A	N5373M CF-02 (Belgian AF) LX-RSO N422GK
T-261	3A	N2601S N300TA OY-ATW [w/o 26Apr78 Gronholt, Denmark; canx 11Oct78]
T-262	3A	N5375M CF-03 (Belgian AF) [w/o 16Apr80 Lille-Lesquin, France; b/u Vilvoorde, Belgium]
T-263	3A	N5377M N34SM [w/o 03Feb77 Beckman, TX, USA]
T-264	3A	N5378M (N100JB) CF-04 (Belgian AF) LX-LAP N422AG F-GZJM
T-265	3A	N5381M CF-05 (Belgian AF) LX-NRJ
T-266	3A	N28SC N99JW N9900 (N97FT) N9900
T-267	3A	N5382M CF-06 (Belgian AF) LX-PIX PH-PIX
T-268	3A	N5383M N19SD N4273X N502WC YV177T
T-269	3A	N5376M N132TA N169GL N500CP N5039F N104BR [w/o 28Aug01 Chicago-DuPage County, IL, USA; canx 17May02]
T-270	3A	N5384M N17SD N953AE N226SR
T-271	3A	N5385M N707DB N707PK 4X-CIZ [wfu Herzeliya, Israel]
T-272	3A	N5388M N49MJ F-GEBK [w/o cApr85 location unkn]
T-273	3A	N5390M YV-179CP N5390M N463DC
T-274	3A	N5391M N600ET N600TA I-SWAA C-FAMF
T-275	3A	N5393M AE176 (Argentinian Army)
T-276	3A	N5477M N5111B N262PC N188SC N132CW F-WQHQ F-GLLO
T-277	3A	N5395M AE177 (Argentinian Army) [w/o c1977-1978 in Argentina]
T-278	3A	N5398M N117PB N475MG N303MA
T-279	3A	N5396M N34SM N279M
T-280	3A	N5397M AE178 (Argentinian Army)
T-281	3A	N5399M AE179 (Argentinian Army) [w/o 28Dec93 Buenos Aires, Buenos Aires Province, Argentina]
T-282	3A	N5477M N958BC N51RX N956DS XA- N956DS XA- [canx 29Jan04 as exported to Mexico; reinstated 28Jan05; canx 11Oct05]
T-283	3A	N5441M D-IFAH OY-CBW SE-GXV N5441M
T-284	3A	N5445M N2GL N36JP N28TA N154L
T-285	3A	N20TA N65P N636SP [dbr 31Mar04 Omaha-Millard, NE, USA, parts to Dodson International Parts, Rantoul, KS, USA; canx 13Nov06]
T-286	3A	N5444M XB-ZAO N226DD N505GM
T-287	3A	N5454M YV-180CP YV-693CP YV-O-IGV-1YV0132
T-288	3A	N5443M TU-TJQ N525SC HP-1069 HP-1069P
T-289	3B	N5449M (F-GBBD) D-IFAL N104TA C-FHWM
T-290	3A	N5450M N75RM YV334T
T-291	3A	N5461M N19SD N800LD
T-292	3B	N5475M LV-PDH LV-MRL N262SA (N1AQ) YV261T
T-293	3B	N5469M D-IBBB F-GGVG
T-294	3B	N800TA N802ME XA-JSC N15KR PH-DYB LN-HTD
T-295	3B	N4442F N4444F N444LM [w/o 03May85 Livermore-Municipal, CA, USA]
T-296	3B	N5491M VH-SWK N245DA F-GFMS [w/o 07Nov87 Vannes, France; canx 06Jan88]
T-297	3B	N5465M N3928G N839KA N92427 N111CZ N127WD
T-298	3B	N5495M VH-AWU F-GLPT
T-299	3B	N81CH N81QH N55ZP N512FS [w/o 28Jun03 Goodnews, AK, USA]
T-300	3B	N29TA N210SW N193CS N699RK
T-301	3B	N5652M N666CP N175WB YV-710CP YV2135
T-302	3B	N5497M G-IIIB 9Q-COI [w/o 06Oct83 in Zaire]
T-303E	3B	N5654M N1011R [dam 31May79 San Marcos, TX, USA; rebuilt as c/n T-303E; w/o 24Mar81 San Marcos-Municipal, TX, USA; canx 13Feb84]
T-304	3B	N37BT N48HH F-GBOP N48HH N76CC [canx 21Jan09 - status?]
T-305	3B	N5658M HK-2438W HK-2438W [wfu cSep97 Bogota-El Dorado, Distrito Capital, Colombia]
T-306	3B	N5661M N226FC N749L
T-307	3B	N5665M N300MT N606PS N307PA
T-308	3B	N900TA N900TX N50MT
T-309	3B	N5668M N999MM N60NH
T-310	3B	N5669M N400FF N49H
T-311	3B	N5670M N27563 N96954
T-312	3B	N90NB (N52SJ) N90NB N84GA F-WRNT F-GRNT
T-313	3B	N5673M RP-C323 N326MS N763LD
T-314	3B	N10053 D-IBBC HZ-OCE N963DC N814SS C-FWXB
T-315	3B	N10058 N700JR N800JR N318AK N315DB N50LG
T-316	3B	N550PC N51DA N616PS
T-317	3B	N10143 N22DW [w/o 31May05 Teterboro, NJ, USA]
T-318	3B	N1006F D-IBBD OE-FOW VH-OVC
T-319	3B	N10057 N808LB N601JT
T-320	3B	N10140 HK-2479X HK-2479
T-321	3B	N1014V N888R N1014V
T-322	3B	N1006K OO-HSA D-IOKG N7031Z N312AC D-IDEA (N330JP) D-IDEA
T-323	3B	N1006M N2GL N28GL N82AB N329HS
T-324	3B	N1006Q N77UU N5805
T-325	3B	N972EK (N254MC) N100DS (N120DS) N900FS HC-BUA N100CE N117CC
T-326	3B	N28TA N19J N300AL
T-327	3B	N1007B
T-328	3B	N1006T N23X XB-EFZ ETE-1328 (Mexican AF) XB-DIP
T-329	3B	N1007S N290T N200KF N300KF N626PS N405SA *N626SS
T-330	3B	N10074 N588FM (N264BL) YV-788CP N113GS
T-331	3B	N1008C VH-UBB N2457X N331TB N331GM N331J
T-332	3B	N1008F N61RJ D-IAMM N841MA N46KC
T-336	3B	N336SA [w/o 19Jan82 Rockport-Aransas County, TX, USA in collision with Grumman AA-5A N26660; canx 21Mar91]

MERLIN III

c/n	Series	Identities
T-339	3B	N1008L D-IBBE HB-LOD N8167Z N15CC N15CN N339RW
T-341	3B	N10063 N61RS N161RS [dbr 16Jan93 Grant County Regional/Ogilvie Field, OR, USA, parts to White Industries, Bates City, MO, USA; location R-19; canx 18Feb97]
T-342	3B	N1008S G-IIIA 9Q-CQP N342NX LN-SFT [w/o 20Jun08 off Sotra Island, Norway; canx 15Jul08]
T-345	3B	N10061 OO-HSC 5A-DHZ [wfu Tripoli, Libya]
T-348	3B	N1009G 348 (Royal Thai Army) [wfu c1992 - status?]
T-351	3B	N1008U [stolen c1980; never recovered; canx 12Aug02]
T-354	3B	N1009C YV-395CP N4130Y N656PS N200SN
T-357	3B	N29TA N30042 YV-242CP
T-360	3B	N1009U ZK-YCL N118BR N387CC
T-363	3B	N40DA N779M (N155AM) N779M
T-366	3B	N366SA N79LP N141GS N141DS N911JZ N500SX
T-369	3B	N1009Y N901MC
T-372	3B	N1010V [reportedly operates for El Salvador AF as "2"]
T-375	3B	N1011G N800MM N98FT N800MM
T-378	3B	N1011P N98UC
T-381	3B	N1008Y N300JE N300NC N123ZZ N80MJ N95AC [wfu cMar06, parts to MTW Aerospace, Montgomery, AL, USA; canx 16Dec05]
T-384	3B	N38DA N71FN YV-2395P YV-770CP
T-387	3B	N10118 N221DT N22NG N203WT N777JE N36LC
T-388	3B	N10119 OO-XSC 5A-DJB [wfu Tripoli, Libya]
T-391	3B	N1012J D-IBBF F-GCTC N391GM
T-394	3B	N1QL N59EZ
T-397	3B	N38TA
T-400	3B	N10126 N350MC
T-403	3B	N1013A OY-BJY SE-IIM N4464V N800AW [w/o 10Jan88 Pontiac-Oakland, MI, USA; canx 28Nov88]
T-405	3B	N1012T N189CC N120TM
T-407	3B	N111AB N402ML YV313T
T-410	3B	N1013N CS-ARU OY-BPM N299EC
T-414	3B	N1013T N271DC N379JG
T-417	3B	N1013U SY-005 (Seychelles Government) S7-AAO N18TA N89RP N12MF

Production complete

SWEARINGEN (FAIRCHILD) SA.227TT MERLIN IIIC

c/n	Series	Identities
TT-421	3C	N1014B N90BJ N75X
TT-424	3C	N39TA N40DG N700JR N900AK N266M
TT-426A	3C	N1014H N4491E VH-UCR N2GL
TT-428A	3C	N444LB
TT-431	3C	N431SA N431S
TT-433	3C	N1014U N808DD C-GFCL C-GFCE N123LH
TT-435	3C	N10127 N39TA N92RC YV-808CP
TT-438	3C	N53DA (N312ST) N53DA
TT-441	3C	N30042 YV-277CP N125RG N6UP N6UP
TT-444A	3C	N3001D VH-UZA N227TT
TT-447	300	N447SA HK-3980X N447SA YV-852CP YV-718CP YV1923
TT-450	3C	N28TA N53PC N99JW
TT-453	3C	N453SA N32SJ N944KR N31JV
TT-456A	3C	N3019U YV-740CP YV1657
TT-459A	3C	N3028L VH-IHJ N3028L OY-BPK YV-292CP YV2045
TT-462A	3C	N30296 YV-453CP N58237 YV-453CP ZP- [canx cJun86 as exported to Paraguay]
TT-465	300	N3038W N79AE OY-CRU YV-695CP (N510CP) N696CP YV-695CP YV1412
TT-468A	3C	N3048V VH-JCB YV-612CP YV2310
TT-471	300	N471SA D-IISA YV-472CP
TT-474	3C	N75SC VH-RCI
TT-477A	3C	N3059Y 6O-SBV N227JT
TT-480	3C	N3021A CN-TOM N500DB N81WS
TT-483A	300	N3059F N190JS N300CV N328AJ N795TB
TT-486A	3C	N3067W N214LS N86SH N1MN
TT-489A	3C	N3066V N655PE N888AY
TT-507	3C	N507SA N212Q N813Q N507TT YV-539CP YV128T
TT-512A	300	N3108G N13JV N927DC N123GM D-IHBL F-GVBJ
TT-515A	3C	N3108L YV-507CP N44287 N66WC N352SM YV-652CP [wfu Caracas-Oscar Machado Zuloaga International, Venezuela]
TT-518A	300	N3072Y N861CG N213PA
TT-521	300	N3109A D-IOOO YV-262CP
TT-527	300	N3109K N40EF N500AK [w/o 01Apr93 5.5 mls NE of Blountville/Tri-Cities Regional, TN, USA; canx 06Oct93]
TT-529A	300	N3109S D-IMWK
TT-534	3C	N345SA N9X N139X N139F N90GT
TT-536	300	N3110P D-IBMW OE-FLU D-IGFD N72WC N17VV
TT-541	3C	N541SA N348KN N112CS
TT-555	3C	N3113C [built as Metro c/n AC-633]

Production complete

SWEARINGEN (FAIRCHILD) SA.227TT MERLIN IV/IVA

c/n	Series	Identities
AT-001	4	N5291M [built as Metro c/n TC-202E]
AT-002	4	D-IBMH OY-DSJ D-IBMH OO-JPN N9112F N39RD C-GTMW YV [canx 24Jul04 as exported to Venezuela]
AT-003	4	N5295M C-GVCY [dbr 06Dec93 Deer Lake, NF, Canada, parts to Dodson International Parts, Rantoul, KS, USA; canx 27May94]
AT-003E	4	N226TC N226AT [cvtd from Metro c/n TC-200; wfu c1985; b/u]
AT-004	4	N55CE N94CE
AT-005	4	N960M [w/o 14Apr75 nr Southern Pines, SC, USA]
AT-006	4	N5297M XC-FUG TP-0207/XC-UTF (Mexican AF) N4679K
AT-007	4	N2610 HZ-SN6
AT-008	4	N5208M N2TF N577KA TR-LZS N577KA [w/o 07May86 nr Billings-Logan International, MT, USA]
AT-009	4	N5315M N49SA C-FJTC N615GA N479VK XA- [canx 21Aug06 as exported to Mexico]
AT-010	4	N600C N600L N603L C-GWSP [b/u; canx 08Oct03]
AT-011	4	N5318M N411JC N400PL C-GSWF N750AA PT-WGH N750AA C-GCPX
AT-012	4	N5320M N111MT N111MV F-GERP
AT-013	4	N5332M N28BP N720R C-GJWW [w/o 12Jan88 Hamilton, ON, Canada; canx 02Aug88]
AT-014	4	N430G OY-AUD C-GSDR N4019
AT-015	4	N5328M N222JC N223JC OY-AUI [dbr 12Nov82 Copenhagen-Kastrup, Denmark; canx 22Apr83; b/u cOct83]
AT-016	4	N5332M N6NC N76MX JA8828
AT-017	4	N5334M N511S N5RT C-GPCL
AT-018	4	N5335M RP-C204 N32MG OY-CCD D-IDEP N636PS N316MW N600TA N427SP
AT-019	4	[built as Metro c/n TC-208E]
AT-020	4	N74NA N747BD I-NARB
AT-021	4	[built as Metro c/n TC-211E]
AT-022	4	[built as Metro c/n TC-211EE]
AT-023	4	[built as Metro c/n TC-211EEE]
AT-024	4	[built as Metro c/n TC-211EEEE]
AT-025	4A	N457SA N11SX N11SK N52LB TN-ADP [w/o 11Mar94 Pointe Noire, Congo]
AT-026	4	[built as Metro c/n TC-212]
AT-027	4A	N5339M C-GSOC N824MD N582JF
AT-028	4A	N5341N C-GWSL [wfu Montreal-St.Hubert, QC, Canada; canx 14Feb02]
AT-029	4A	N5342M N100US N300CE N3753V N19RT N642BA C-GTEM N5135X F-GHLA N294A N78CP [wfu c2004, parts to White Industries, Bates City, MO, USA; location "Ramp East"]
AT-030	4A	N5440F N69ST N430RR
AT-031	4A	N5346M N44AG N5FW N95KY N22KW F-GMTO
AT-032	4A	N51LB N205MB N205MP N44PB N44GL N90NH N133BB
AT-033	4A	N1005Y VH-CFO (ZK-MAA) ZK-SWB VH-SWP [w/o 09Mar94 15km NE of Tamworth, NSW, Australia; canx 10May94]
AT-034	4A	N5348M N807MA N807MF N717CC N54GP
AT-035	4A	N5350M 10 (South African AF) ZS-LJR N90090 I-NARC
AT-036	4A	N5351M 11 (South African AF) N82GA D-ICIT N70315 F-GIAC N70315 N642TS LV-WNC
AT-037	4A	ZS-JMA 9 (South African AF) N85GA F-GHGR N216GA N202WS
AT-038	4A	N536DM 12 (South African AF) N5FJ OO-JPN EC-509 EC-FUX SX-BGT EC-JCV
AT-038E	4	[built as Metro c/n TC-215E]
AT-039	4A	N26GB N28GB N261MC C-GVEJ N439BW N727DP
AT-040	4A	N5361M 16 (South African AF) ZS-JLZ [w/o 14Jul82 Pretoria, Transvaal, South Africa]
AT-041	4A	N5362M 14 (South African AF) N6FJ OO-JPA EC-867 EC-GBI
AT-042	4A	N5354M D-IEWK F-GBBA D-IEWK OE-FTA D-IEWK [w/o 05Feb87 Munich-Riem, West Germany; canx cMar87]
AT-043	4A	N5371M 15 (South African AF) ZS-LID N5371M N814MM F-GGAF EC-975 EC-GDV [w/o 10Oct01 in Mediterranean sea between Barcelona, Spain & Oran, Algeria]
AT-044	4A	N5441F N544FF C-GGPT TC-BPS TC-UPS
AT-045	4	[static test airframe]
AT-046	4	[built as Metro c/n TC-222EE]
AT-047	4	[built as Metro c/n TC-222E]
AT-048	4	[built as Metro c/n TC-223]
AT-049	4	[built as Metro c/n TC-224]
AT-050	4	[built as Metro c/n TC-225]
AT-051	4A	N5386M D-IDEE N5386M (OY-CCW) D-IGEP N4NY C-FTJC TU-TOG ZS-ZOB [cvtd from Metro c/n TC-226]
AT-052	4	[built as Metro c/n TC-227]
AT-053	4	[built as Metro c/n TC-227E]
AT-054	4	[built as Metro c/n TC-228E]
AT-055	4	[built as Metro c/n TC-229]
AT-056	4	[built as Metro c/n TC-229E]
AT-057	4A	N5392M OO-PSM (D-ILKE) D2-EDU N31264 N31AT [dbr 15Dec95 Detroit-Metropolitan Wayne County, MI, USA, parts to White Industries, Bates City, MO, USA; location "Ramp North 06"; canx 22Jan09]
AT-058	4A	N500YM OY-AST D-ICFB I-NARW [pres Museo Italiano Parco Tematico dell'Aviazione, Rimini, Italy]
AT-059	4	[built as Metro c/n TC-234E]
AT-060	4	[built as Metro c/n TC-237E]
AT-061	4	[built as Metro c/n TC-238E]
AT-062 (1)	4	[built as Metro c/n TC-239E]

c/n	Series	Identities
AT-062 (2)	4A	N5446M D-IFAD YU-ALF OO-VGD OY-FFD N548SM EC-125 EC-GFK
AT-062E	4A	21-111 (Royal Thai AF) [cvtd from Metro c/n TC-244; w/o 06Nov78 Sakon Nakhon, Thailand]
AT-063	4A	N5438M TS-01 (Argentinian Army) AE181 (Argentinian Army)
AT-064	4A	N5439M TS-02 (Argentinian Army) AE182 (Argentinian Army)
AT-064E	4A	N21PC OM-M-1146 OB-1146 [cvtd from Metro c/n TC-246]
AT-065	4A	N5442M 29-999 (Royal Thai AF) [w/o 20Sep82 Hat Yai, Thailand]
AT-066	4A	N5455M D-IBAB YU-ALG OO-VGC OY-FFE N5455N C-FTIX N5FY EC-JQC
AT-067	4A	N5459M C-FJTL N120SC
AT-068	4A	N68TA N222JC N223JC N256MT N121DP F-GFPR N836MA [wfu San Antonio-International, TX, USA]
AT-069	4A	N5466M N311RV N63SC C-GDEF N631FA
AT-070	4	N5498M [cvtd to Metro c/n AC-421B]
AT-071	4A	N5650M 60301 (Royal Thai AF) 60501 (Royal Thai AF) [std Bangkok-Don Muang International, Thailand]
AT-071E	4A	N5656M AE180 (Argentinian Army) [cvtd from Metro c/n TC-286]
AT-072	4A	N5496M 60302 (Royal Thai AF) 60502 (Royal Thai AF)
AT-073	4A	N5672M 60303 (Royal Thai AF) 60503 (Royal Thai AF)
AT-074	4A	N1006Y C-GDEF N1006Y OY-CHA EC-702 EC-GDR EC-HBF
AT-075	4A	[built as Metro c/n TC-331E]
AT-076	4A	[built as Metro c/n TC-334E]

Production complete

SWEARINGEN (FAIRCHILD) SA.227AT MERLIN IVC (EXPEDITER)

c/n	Series	Identities
AT-423	4C	N807M N10NB 9Q-CFK F-GHVF
AT-427	4C	N1014L D-CAIR N66GA N629TG N66GA
AT-434	4C	N3110F HZ-SN8 A9C-DHB
AT-439B	4C	N439SA N39PD N41BP N555GB N439AF [w/o 29Nov03 Spokane-Felts Field, WA, USA; canx 14Jul04]
AT-440B	4C	N36JP N56TA N36JP I-FSAD D-CBIN
AT-446B	4C	N3008L N573G
AT-452	4C	N3010Q N45MW N950MD
AT-454	4C	N3013T N807M
AT-455	4C	N3016K N69CS [cvtd to Metro c/n AC-455]
AT-461	4C	N109TA N222JC OY-CHB [cvtd to Metro c/n AC-461B]
AT-464	4C	N30364 N313D
AT-469	4C	N900TA N300ZD N469GM C-GCAU N318DH [w/o 08Feb01 nr Beaver Island, MI, USA; canx 30Jul01]
AT-487	4C	N3068Z N550TP N550TD [cvtd to Metro c/n AC-487]
AT-492	4C	N60TA N30HE C-FJTA N8897Y
AT-493	4C	N3075A CP-2109 N3075A OY-CHC F-GGLH N121FA F-GGLG PH-RAX D-CNAY
AT-495B	4C	N3094T SE-IRM 88002 (Swedish AF) SE-IRM N113GA C-FNAL N9UA N851BC
AT-501	4C	N3051H N999MX
AT-502	4C	N3107W D-CABC OH-FCU OY-CHH VH-UUA VH-UZA
AT-504	4C	N31072 [cvtd to Metro c/n AC-504]
AT-506	4C	N234SA N87FM N370AE [cvtd to Metro c/n AC-506 then reverted cMay93 to Merlin c/n AT-506]
AT-511	4C	N3108F N600L N600N D-CCCC
AT-513	4C	N3108H [cvtd to Metro c/n AC-513]
AT-524	4C	N3109D N4442F [cvtd to Metro c/n AC-524]
AT-528	4C	N3109N N5441F [cvtd to Metro c/n AC-528]
AT-532	4C	N3110B [cvtd to Metro c/n AC-532]
AT-539	4C	N539SA [wfu cMay86; b/u]
AT-543	4C	N31101 D-CKVW [cvtd to Metro c/n AC-543]
AT-544	4C	N68TA N544UP
AT-546	4C	N31108 [cvtd to Metro c/n AC-546]
AT-547	4C	N3111D [cvtd to Metro c/n AC-547]
AT-548	4C	N548SA N548UP
AT-549B	4C	N3111K N525ES N3111K 89-1471 (USAF) N471CD
AT-556	4C	N3113B N556UP
AT-557	4C	N400FA [cvtd to Metro c/n DC-557B]
AT-560	4C	N3113A N560UP
AT-561	4C	N3113F N561UP
AT-563	4C	N3113M N563UP VH-EEN
AT-564	4C	N3114B N564UP VH-EEO
AT-566	4C	N3113N N566UP
AT-567	4C	N3113T N565UP VH-EEP
AT-568	4C	N568SA N568UP [w/o 31Jan85 London-Corbin/Magee Field, KY, USA]
AT-569	4C	N31134 N569UP
AT-570	4C	N31135 N570UP VH-UZI
AT-577	4C	N31136 N120JM
AT-585	4C	N3114Y N111MT N227JW N919CK
AT-602	4C	N3117P N240DH
AT-607B	4C	N3118A N241DH

MERLIN IVC

c/n	Series	Identities	
AT-608B	4C	N3118G	N242DH
AT-609B	4C	N3118H	N243DH
AT-618B	4C	N244DH	
AT-624B	4C	N245DH	
AT-625B	4C	N246DH	
AT-626B	4C	N247DH	
AT-630B	4C	N248DH	
AT-631B	4C	N249DH	
AT-695B	4C	N2709Z	N762VM

Production complete

EXPERIMENTAL & LIMITED PRODUCTION TYPES

AASI JETCRUZER 500

c/n	Identities
001	N102JC "N500JC" [cvt from Jetcruzer 450; wfu; canx 17Jan98]
002	N200JC [wfu]
003	N136JC [wfu; canx 01Mar02]

AMERICAN JET INDUSTRIES HUSTLER 400

c/n	Identities
101	N400AJ [wfu; canx 13Jun86]

AUGUSTA SIAI-MARCHETTI F.600 CANGURO

c/n	Identities
001	I-CANG [w/o 09Feb85 Mt.Tolfa, nr Rome, Italy]
002	I-CNGR [canx; believed b/u]
003	I-KANG [canx; believed b/u; CofA exp 27Oct92]
004	I-CARG [canx; believed b/u]
005	I-CNGS [canx; believed b/u; CofA exp 30Oct97]
006	I-CNGT S5-CAM
007	I-CNGV HL5220
008	I-SLAB I-RAIA I-PADC RP-C1298 [w/o 01Sep97 in sea between Fortune Island, Nasugbu, Batangas and Lubang Island, Philippines; CofR exp 25Apr98]
009	I-SLBB [canx; believed b/u; CofA exp 29Mar89]
010	I-VULA

AVTEK 400

c/n	Identities
POC	N400AV

CESSNA 435

c/n	Identities
435-0001	N435CC [wfu c1986; pres inst airframe Wichita Area Technical College, Wichita, KS, USA]

CIRRUS ST-50

c/n	Identities
001	N50ST [canx 04May95; tfd to Israviation, Israel] 4X-COD

COMP AIR 12

c/n	Identities
701A4412	N54RD

EMBRAER CBA-123 VECTOR

c/n	Identities
123801	PT-ZVE
123802	PT-ZVB

EPIC ESCAPE

c/n	Identities
001	N28RQ

EPIC LT

c/n	Identities
001	N370JP
002	
003	N89CL
004	N3XF
005	
006	N525TT
007	N8XK
008	
009	N900RB
010	N700MM
011	N111DY
012	N468TT
013	
014	C-FJRQ N6XK
015	N603JS
016	N67PT
017	N388AB
018	N181LT
019	N600BD
020	N910MC
021	N53VW
022	N592MG
023	N618P
024	N66MB
025	N653SB
026	N495JJ
027	
028	N491WF
029	N669WR
030	N5Z
031	N850DV
032	N397MY
033	
034	N35PZ
035	
036	
037	
038	N44GB
039	N8H
040	N933RC
041	N395WK
042	
043	
044	
045	
046	
047	
048	
049	
050	
109	N9BE
110	N351BM
111	N454RM
201	
202	N7208N
203	
204	
205	
206	
207	
208	
209	
210	
211	
212	
213	
214	
215	
216	
217	

c/n	Identities
218	
219	
220	
221	
222	
223	
224	
225	
226	
227	C-GOHK N96HK
228	
229	
230	

FARNBOROUGH AIRCRAFT CORP F1 KESTREL

c/n	Identities
0001	N352F

GROB G160T RANGER

c/n	Identities
87000	D-FTGB
87001	D-FTBG

GULFSTREAM AMERICAN HUSTLER 500

c/n	Identities
501	N501GA [wfu; canx 11Apr95]

IBIS AE.270P

c/n	Identities
001	OK-EMA OK-EMA [wfu Odolena Voda, Czech Republic; canx 05Mar04]
002	[static test airframe]
003	OK-SAR OK-SAR [wfu Odolena Voda, Czech Republic; canx 06Dec04]
004	[static test airframe]
005	OK-LIB [wfu, parts to AIDC, Taichung, Taiwan; canx 02Jun08]
006	OK-INA
007	OK-EVA
008	OK-ALE
009	
010	

LEARFAN 2100

c/n	Identities
E-001	N626BL [pres Museum Of Flight, Seattle-Boeing Field, WA, USA]
E-002	[static test airframe]
E-003	N327ML N21LF (N327ML) N21LF [pres Frontiers of Flight Museum, Dallas-Love Field, TX, USA]
E-004	[void - airframe not built]
E-005	[void - airframe not built]
E-006	[void - airframe not built]
E-007	[void - airframe not built]
E-008	[void - airframe not built]
E-009	N98LF [wfu Oklahoma City-Will Rogers World, OK, USA]

MYASISHCHEV M-101T

c/n	Identities
1500001	RA-15001 [w/o 12Sep01 in Russia]
1500002	(RA-15002) [static test airframe]
1500003	RA-15003 [wfu Moscow-Bykovo, Russia]
1500004	RA-15004
1501001	RA-15101
1501002	RA-15102
1501003	RA-15103
1501004	RA-15104
1501005	RA-15105
1501006	RA-15106
1501007	RA-15107
1501008	RA-15108
1501009	RA-15109
1501010	RA-15110
1501011	RA-15111
1501012	RA-15112
1501013	RA-15100
1501014	RA-15114
1501015	
1501016	
1501017	
1501018	
1501019	
1501020	
1501021	
1501022	RA-15122 [unconfirmed c/n]
1501023	RA-15123 [unconfirmed c/n]
1501024	RA-15124 [unconfirmed c/n]
1501025	RA-15125 [unconfirmed c/n]
1501026	RA-15126 [unconfirmed c/n]
1501027	

NAL SARAS

c/n	Identities
SP01	VT-XSD
SP02	VT-XRM [w/o 06Mar09 nr Bangalore, India]

OMAC LASER

c/n	Series	Identities
001	1	N?? [FF 11Dec81; identity & fate unknn]
002	1	N81PH [wfu; canx 14Mar97]
001	300	N301L [wfu Norwalk-Huron County, OH, USA; canx 07May01]

QUEST KODIAK 100

c/n	Identities
K0101	N490KQ
100-0001	N491KQ
100-0002	N838SA
100-0003	N493KQ
100-0004	N494KQ
100-0005	N495KQ
100-0006	N55PY
100-0007	N708
100-0008	N498KQ
100-0009	N525AH
100-0010	N522CM
100-0011	N58NH
100-0012	N500KQ
100-0013	N461JH
100-0014	N974JB
100-0015	N466SP
100-0016	N959WB
100-0017	N102MF
100-0018	N497BH
100-0019	N736
100-0020	N9710M

c/n	Identities
100-0021	N710
100-0022	
100-0023	
100-0024	
100-0025	
100-0026	
100-0027	
100-0028	
100-0029	
100-0030	
100-0031	
100-0032	
100-0033	
100-0034	
100-0035	
100-0036	
100-0037	
100-0038	
100-0039	
100-0040	

VULCANAIR VF600W

c/n	Identities
0001	I-VAVF [prototype single-engined variant of the SF600 Canguro]

MASTER INDEX

Civil-registered aircraft are arranged in order of country registration prefix, with individual aircraft registrations listed in alphabetical or numerical order as appropriate for the registration sequence of that country. For each registration a two-, three- or four-character abbreviation for the aircraft type is given (see table below for decode), followed by the c/n.

All aircraft which are in current use or currently registered are indicated by bold typeface. Reserved marks are shown in the normal typeface.

Aircraft in military use are arranged in alphabetical order of country name.

Code	Type	Code	Type
100	Beechcraft King Air 100 srs	F406	Reims-Cessna F.406 Caravan II
200	Beechcraft King Air 200 srs	F90	Beechcraft King Air F90 srs
200C	Beechcraft King Air B200C srs	FPC6	Fairchild-Hiller PC-6 Heli-Porter
200G	Beechcraft King Air B200GT srs	G1	Grumman G.159 Gulfstream
200T	Beechcraft King Air B200T srs	G160	Grob G160T Ranger
300	Beechcraft King Air 300 srs	G500	Gulfstream American Hustler 500
300C	Beechcraft King Air B300C	H400	American Jet Industries Hustler 400
31T	Piper PA-31T Cheyenne srs	I270	Ibis AE.270P
350	Beechcraft King Air 350 srs	KODK	Quest Kodiak 100
350C	Beechcraft King Air 350C	LFAN	Learfan 2100
425	Cessna 425 Conquest I	M101	Myasishchev M-101T
435	Cessna 435 Conquest	MII	Swearingen SA26T Merlin II
441	Cessna 441 Conquest II	MIIA	Swearingen SA26T Merlin IIA
46D	Piper PA-46 DLX Conversion	MIIB	Swearingen SA26T Merlin IIB
46T	Piper PA-46-500TP Malibu Meridian	MIII	Swearingen SA226T/SA227TT Merlin III
680T	Aero Commander/Rockwell 680T/V	MIV	Swearingen SA226AT Merlin IV
680W	Aero Commander/Rockwell 680W	MIVA	Swearingen SA226AT Merlin IVA
681	Aero Commander/Rockwell 681	MIVC	Swearingen SA227AT Merlin IVC
681B	Aero Commander/Rockwell 681B	MU-2	Mitsubishi MU-2 srs
690	Aero Commander/Rockwell 690	NALS	NAL Saras
690A	Aero Commander/Rockwell 690A	OMAC	OMAC Laser
690B	Aero Commander/Rockwell 690B	P166	Piaggio P.166 srs
690C	Aero Commander/Rockwell 690C	P180	Piaggio P.180 srs
690D	Aero Commander/Rockwell 690D	P68	Partenavia P.68 srs
695	Aero Commander/Rockwell 695	P68T	Aeritalia-Partenavia P.68TP srs
695A	Aero Commander/Rockwell 695A	P750	Pacific Aerospace Corp 750XL
695B	Aero Commander/Rockwell 695B	PA42	Piper PA-42 Cheyenne srs
90	Beechcraft King Air 90 srs	PC12	Pilatus PC-12 srs
A400	Avtek 400	PC6	Pilatus PC-6 srs
AASI	AASI Jetcruzer 500	PT68	Partenavia-Taneja P.68
B100	Beechcraft King Air B100	RC12	Beechcraft King Air 200 (RC-12) srs
BN2	Britten-Norman BN.2 Islander srs	S600	Augusta Siai-Marchetti F.600 Canguro
BN2T	Britten-Norman BN.2T Islander srs	ST50	Cirrus ST-50
CA12	Comp Air 12	STAR	Beechcraft 2000 Starship srs
C-12	Beechcraft King Air 200 (C-12) srs	T-44	Beechcraft King Air H90 (T-44) srs
E121	Embraer Emb.121 Xingu	TBM7	Aerospatiale/SOCATA TBM.700 srs
E123	Embraer CBA-123 Vector	TBM8	Aerospatiale/SOCATA TBM.850 srs
E90	Beechcraft King Air E90	TRIS	Britten-Norman Trislander srs
EPES	Epic Escape	U-21	Beechcraft King Air A90 (U-21) srs
EPIC	Epic LT	UC12	Beechcraft King Air 200 (UC-12) srs
F1	Farnborough Aircraft Corp F1 Kestrel	V600	Vulcanair VF600W

CIVIL INDEX

Nicaragua

AN-ASD 690A 11222
AN-BME E90 LW-195

Pakistan

AP- 200G BY-81
AP-AVU PC6 670
AP-BCQ 441 0352
AP-BCW 441 0355
AP-BCY 441 0350
(AP-BEL) BN2 2035
AP-BEM BN2 915
AP-BFA F406 0032
AP-BFB F406 0034
AP-BFK F406 0059
AP-CAA 200 BB-278
AP-CAB 200 BB-1999
AP-CAC 200 BB-2000
AP-CAD 200 BB-278

Botswana

A2- 90 LJ-1947
A2-ABO 200 BB-245
A2-ABS 100 B-105
A2-ACO 200 BB-597
A2-AEA BN2 849
A2-AEO 200 BB-1253
A2-AEZ 200 BB-421
A2-AFI F90 LA-139
A2-AFM BN2 386
A2-AFN BN2 807
A2-AGA BN2 810
A2-AGB 200 BB-756
A2-AGJ BN2 774
A2-AGO 200 BB-1353
A2-AGX TRIS 1054
A2-AGY TRIS 1055
A2-AHA 200 BB-961
A2-AHT 425 0011
A2-AHV F90 LA-212
A2-AHZ 200 BB-95
A2-AIH 690A 11105
A2-AJA BN2 271
A2-AJK 200 BB-704
A2-AJM BN2 862
A2-AKE BN2 729
A2-APG 200 BB-1046
A2-BHM 200 BB-903
A2-DBH 90 LJ-988
A2-FMB 200 BB-111
A2-JZT 90 LJ-486
A2-KAM MIIB T26-180E
A2-KAS 200 BB-614
A2-LBD 200 BB-837
A2-MDM PC12 1105
A2-MED 200 BB-687
A2-MJM 90 LJ-842
A2-MOA BN2T 2276
A2-MXI 200T BT-5
A2-NAA BN2 854
A2-SID F90 LA-210
A2-TAU BN2 2173
A2-VIS BN2 660
A2-ZED BN2 736
A2-ZEV BN2 99
A2-ZFY BN2 619
A2-ZGK BN2 288
A2-ZGT 90 LJ-484
A2-ZOO BN2 2203

Oman

A40-AK PC6 741
A40-AL PC6 748
A40-CT BN2T 2201
A40-DJ BN2 628
A40-DK BN2 629
A40-DL BN2 479
A40-SL B100 BE-45
A40-SR 200 BB-1076

United Arab Emirates

A6- 350 FL-632
A6-ALN P68 32
A6-ALO P68 86
A6-FAE 90 LJ-1267
A6-FFA BN2 782
A6-GAK PC12 479
A6-GJD 350 FL-568
A6-KHZ 350 FL-132
A6-MHH 350 FL-131
A6-NHM BN2 2035
A6-SKY 90 LJ-397
A6-SSA 200 BB-1695

Qatar

A7-AHK 200 BB-1350

Bahrain

A9C- 90 LJ-301
A9C-DHB MIVC AT-434

China

B-1410 PC6 555
B-3551 200 BB-1204
B-3552 200 BB-1205
B-3553 200 BB-1206
B-3581 350 FL-111
B-3582 350 FL-113
B-3583 350 FL-318
B-3621 PA42 5501051
B-3622 PA42 5501052
B-3623 PA42 5501054
B-3624 PA42 5501056
B-3625 PA42 5501059
B-3626 PA42 5501060
B-7751 90 LJ-1945
B-3901 BN2 2203
B-3902 BN2 2204
B-3903 BN2 2208
B-3904 BN2 2210
B-3905 BN2 2211

Taiwan

B-129 200 BB-336
B-135 350 FL-52
B-00135 350 FL-52
B-11107 BN2 335
B-11108 BN2 701
B-11109 BN2 518
B-11110 BN2 575
B-11111 BN2 2001
B-11112 TRIS 1036
B-11116 BN2 2007
B-11118 TRIS 1061
B-11123 BN2 2032
B-11125 BN2 2029
B-11126 BN2 2193
B-12201 BN2 2014
B-12202 BN2 380
B-12203 BN2 866
B-12207 BN2 831
B-12222 BN2 2131
B-12232 BN2 2039
B-13152 200 BB-449
B-13153 350 FL-108
(B-17021) BN2 575
(B-17022) BN2 2032
(B-17023) BN2 2193
B-68801 BN2 2255
B-68802 BN2 2241
B-69832 BN2 2039

Hong Kong

See also VR-H
B-HZM 200C BL-128
B-HZN 200C BL-130

Canada

C- 100 B-144
C-GAEW 200 BB-1546
C- 31T 7720017
C- 90 LJ-1465
C- P68 288
C-FABR 350 FL-100
C-FACC 690B 11492
C-FACM 31T 7720016
C-FAFD 100 B-42
C-FAFE B100 BE-72
C-FAFF 350 FL-112
C-FAFS B100 BE-31
C-FAFT 200 BB-57
C-FAFZ B100 BE-121
C-FAGA 90 LJ-1040
C-FAIO 100 B-132
C-FAIP 100 B-193
"C-FAJN" PC12 234
C-FAJV PC12 234
C-FAKN 200 BB-216
C-FAKP 690 11040
C-FAKW 300 FA-183
C-FALI 690A 11102
C-FALI 695A 96093
C-FALQ 200 BB-10
C-FAMB 200 BB-1281
C-FAMB 200C BL-10
C-FAMF MIII T-274
C-FAMF MU-2 553
C-FAMP MU-2 125
C-FAMU 100 B-166
C-FANF MIIA T26-032
C-FANG 200 BB-333
C-FAOU BN2 4
C-FAPP 100 B-169
C-FASB 100 B-163
C-FASF PC12 416
C-FASN B100 BE-17
C-FASP PC12 331
C-FASR PC12 353
C-FATA 200 BB-283
C-FATR 681 6020
C-FATW 90 LJ-685
C-FATX E90 LW-147
C-FAWE G1 188
C-FAWG 690D 15037
C-FAWG G1 106
C-FAXD 200 BB-1827
C-FAXE 100 B-41
C-FAXN 680T 1546-9
C-FAXP MU-2 502
C-FBAN MU-2 577
C-FBBO 31T 7920054
C-FBBR 31T 8375002
C-FBCB BN2 883
C-FBCN 200 BB-7
C-FBCO 200 BB-8
C-FBCS 31T 7820038
C-FBCS E90 LW-235
C-FBFP 100 B-35
C-FBGL PC6 540
C-FBGS 100 B-204
C-FBPT 90 LJ-13
C-FBVI MIIB T26-128
C-FBWU MIIB T26-102
C-FBWX 200 BB-341
C-FCAK 100 B-96
C-FCAR MIIB T26-139
C-FCAU 90 LJ-24
C-FCAV PA42 8001006
C-FCAW MIIB T26-172E
C-FCAZ 100 B-44
C-FCBJ 90 LJ-338
C-FCCD MU-2 174
C-FCDF F90 LA-81
C-FCEC 31T 8166030
C-FCED 31T 8166013
C-FCEF 31T 7920069
C-FCEH PA42 8001063
C-FCEL MU-2 114
C-FCGB 200 BB-24
C-FCGC 200 BB-236
C-FCGE 90 LJ-118
C-FCGH 90 LJ-203
C-FCGI 90 LJ-220
C-FCGJ 90 LJ-231
C-FCGL 200 BB-190
C-FCGM 200 BB-217
C-FCGN 90 LJ-313
C-FCGT 200 BB-159
C-FCGU 200 BB-301
C-FCGV 200 BB-264
C-FCGW 200 BB-207
C-FCGX 200 BB-250
C-FCGZ 200 BB-57
C-FCHZ TRIS 299
C-FCJP PA42 8001045
C-FCJV PC12 240
C-FCLH F90 LA-184
C-FCLM MU-2 783SA
C-FCMJ 681B 6054
C-FCMY BN2 169
C-FCOL G1 64
C-FCOS 200 BB-690
C-FCOS 31T 7904042
C-FCPH MIII T-237
C-FCRL MU-2 037
C-FCSC PC12 878
C-FCSD 100 B-75
C-FCSP 46D 6
C-FCVK BN2 2028
C-FCWZ 441 0198
C-FCZZ 690A 11106
C-FDAC MIII T-202
C-FDAM 100 B-8
C-FDDD 31T 8004032
C-FDEB 200 BB-55
C-FDEB BN2 58
C-FDGD 695A 96031
C-FDGP 200 BB-1022
C-FDJQ 100 B-84
C-FDJX 100 B-165
C-FDLO 200 BB-560
C-FDLV PC12 864
C-FDMM PC12 361
C-FDOR 100 B-103
C-FDOS 100 B-106
C-FDOU 100 B-112
C-FDOV 100 B-117
C-FDOY 100 B-120
C-FDTC 350 FL-234
C-FDTP 300 FA-94
C-FDYN 441 0256
C-FDYT BN2 885
C-FEKB 200 BB-468
C-FEQB 31T 7920071
C-FETE 441 0129
C-FEVC 200 BB-973
C-FEVC 31T 8020072
C-FEYP 100 B-206
C-FEYT 100 B-210
C-FFAR 200 BB-281

C-FFAR	200	BB-864
C-FFAS	90	LJ-617
C-FFEO	680T	1693-72
C-FFER	MU-2	150
C-FFFG	MU-2	662
C-FFNV	31T	7720058
C-FFOL	E90	LW-139
C-FFRZ	90	LJ-281
C-FFSS	MU-2	783SA
C-FFST	P180	1063
C-FFXS	BN2	311
C-FFYC	MIIA	T26-036
C-FGAN	200	BB-1035
C-FGAQ	BN2	212
C-FGDM	46T	97057
C-FGEM	MU-2	286
C-FGEM	MU-2	434SA
C-FGFL	PC12	339
C-FGFZ	200	BB-403
C-FGHK	MU-2	140
C-FGIN	100	B-164
C-FGMG	200	BB-1841
C-FGMQ	PC12	1107
C-FGNG	46D	175
C-FGNL	100	B-184
C-FGPC	200C	BL-13
C-FGPK	441	0107
C-FGRA	MIIB	T26-154
C-FGRE	PC12	241
C-FGSX	31T	8166048
C-FGWA	31T	7920045
C-FGWD	200	BB-1599
C-FGWF	MU-2	524
C-FGWR	200	BB-1599
C-FGWT	690D	15042
C-FGXA	90	LJ-1152
C-FGXB	90	LJ-1130
C-FGXC	90	LJ-1111
C-FGXE	90	LJ-1179
C-FGXG	90	LJ-1139
C-FGXH	90	LJ-1162
C-FGXJ	90	LJ-1178
C-FGXL	90	LJ-1189
C-FGXO	90	LJ-1200
C-FGXQ	90	LJ-1192
C-FGXS	90	LJ-1207
C-FGXT	90	LJ-1230
C-FGXU	90	LJ-1140
C-FGXX	90	LJ-1151
C-FGXZ	90	LJ-1177
C-FHBO	G1	104
C-FHBW	90	LJ-336
C-FHDA	MIIA	T26-020
C-FHGG	100	B-207
C-FHJO	200	BB-1126
C-FHKB	100	B-63
C-FHLP	90	LJ-685
C-FHMA	MU-2	1523SA
C-FHNL	690B	11477
C-FHRV	PA42	5527010
C-FHSC	B100	BE-105
C-FHSP	441	0265
C-FHTH	46D	24
C-FHTL	MU-2	123
C-FHVM	46T	97091
C-FHWI	90	LJ-309
C-FHWM	MIII	T-289
C-FHXZ	MU-2	729SA
(C-FHZK)	MU-2	694
C-FIAS	PC12	361
C-FIAZ	BN2	65
C-FIDC	B100	BE-27
C-FIDN	100	B-3
C-FIFE	MU-2	683
C-FIFO	200	BB-527
C-FIIG	680T	1699-76
C-FIIL	690A	11167
C-FIJV	PC12	222
C-FIME	B100	BE-115
C-FIOM	G1	60
C-FIPO	46T	97060
C-FIWH	200	BB-170
C-FIYA	90	LJ-167
C-FIZG	PA42	8001049
C-FJAK	31T	8166028
C-FJDQ	B100	BE-16
C-FJEL	MU-2	706SA
C-FJFC	G1	31
C-FJFH	100	B-171
C-FJHP	90	LJ-325
C-FJJR	BN2	424
C-FJLJ	100	B-58
C-FJOL	350	FL-208
C-FJRQ	EPIC	014
C-FJRT	200	BB-92
C-FJTA	MIVC	AT-492
C-FJTC	MIV	AT-009
C-FJTL	MIVA	AT-067
C-FJTN	90	LJ-1814
C-FJVB	31T	8120012
C-FJVR	441	0096
C-FJWU	E90	LW-332
C-FKAC	PC12	182
C-FKAE	PC12	195
C-FKAL	PC12	151
C-FKBU	200	BB-285
C-FKCL	MU-2	533
C-FKCW	200	BB-973
C-FKEN	PC12	222
C-FKEY	31T	8166002
C-FKGA	PC12	164
C-FKIJ	100	B-52
C-FKIO	MU-2	725SA
C-FKJI	200	BB-105
C-FKKH	46D	113
C-FKPA	PC12	275
C-FKPI	PC12	250
C-FKPI	PC12	276
C-FKPX	PC12	451
C-FKRB	PC12	233
C-FKSL	PC12	324
C-FKTL	425	0008
C-FKTN	425	0190
C-FKUL	PC12	204
C-FKVL	PC12	307
C-FLER	46D	26
C-FLGB	46D	35
C-FLIR	P68	413
C-FLOR	200	BB-884
C-FLRB	100	B-131
C-FLRB	BN2	2038
C-FLRD	100	B-243
C-FLRM	200	BB-1115
C-FLTC	90	LJ-631
C-FLTL	F90	LA-170
C-FLTS	100	B-149
C-FLXM	200	BB-1577
C-FMAI	100	B-145
C-FMAR	G1	3
C-FMBL	MU-2	598
C-FMCF	200	BB-439
C-FMCX	690B	11446
C-FMDF	PC12	365
C-FMDF	PC12	800
C-FMFP	690A	11307
C-FMFQ	90	LJ-1740
C-FMFR	90	LJ-1744
C-FMFS	90	LJ-1745
C-FMFU	90	LJ-1746
C-FMFX	90	LJ-1747
C-FMFY	90	LJ-1749
C-FMFZ	90	LJ-1750
C-FMGL	E90	LW-103
C-FMHB	31T	7620023
C-FMHD	300	FA-151
C-FMHD	350	FL-87
C-FMHD	441	0293
C-FMKD	90	LJ-376
C-FMKK	46T	97268
C-FMKK	MU-2	248
C-FMLC	90	LJ-20
C-FMPA	PC12	164
C-FMPB	PC12	283
C-FMPE	200	BB-746
C-FMPE	PC12	314
C-FMPF	PC12	768
C-FMPH	200	BB-757
C-FMPK	PC12	1092
C-FMPN	PC12	296
C-FMPO	PC12	229
C-FMPW	PC12	315
C-FMSK	441	0153
C-FMSP	441	0072
C-FMUN	350	FL-658
C-FMUR	G1	54
C-FMWM	100	B-59
C-FMXY	100	B-40
C-FNAL	MIVC	AT-495B
C-FNAO	690C	11731
C-FNAS	690	11003
C-FNAS	PC12	300
C-FNCB	E90	LW-287
C-FNCN	90	LJ-468
C-FNED	90	LJ-680
C-FNGA	P180	1007
C-FNIF	100	B-178
C-FNIL	350	FL-354
C-FNNC	441	0321
C-FNRM	690C	11692
C-FNWC	441	0216
C-FNWC	MU-2	1517SA
C-FNWD	690B	11497
C-FNYM	31T	7620033
C-FNZO	350	FL-87
C-FODC	B100	BE-59
C-FOGP	B100	BE-134
C-FOGY	200	BB-168
C-FOIL	350	FL-164
C-FOKH	BN2	911
C-FOLR	90	LJ-256
C-FOMH	F90	LA-48
C-FONY	100	B-154
C-FOPD	PC12	182
C-FOUR	MU-2	606
C-FPAJ	100	B-151
C-FPBC	B100	BE-44
C-FPBL	TBM7	178
C-FPCB	90	LJ-183
C-FPCC	300	FA-102
C-FPCI	PC12	399
C-FPCL	PC12	276
C-FPCN	PC12	258
C-FPCP	350	FL-317
C-FPCZ	PC12	433
C-FPLG	100	B-224
C-FPLZ	90	LJ-1812
C-FPNB	681B	6055
C-FPNJ	31T	7620008
C-FPQA	PA42	5527039
C-FPQQ	200	BB-1304
C-FPTQ	350	FL-98
C-FPWR	350	FL-62
C-FPXY	PC12	878
C-FPZB	PC6	634
C-FQDI	100	B-9
C-FQMM	PC12	612
C-FQMS	MU-2	009
C-FQOV	100	B-38
C-FQPM	BN2	241
C-FRAV	PC6	631
C-FRJE	31T	7820002
C-FRKB	100	B-72
C-FRLD	350	FL-33
"C-FRMP"	695	95074
C-FRMV	200	BB-979
C-FROM	MU-2	601
C-FROW	MU-2	628
C-FRPX	46D	106
C-FRRQ	200	BB-560
C-FRTT	G1	131
C-FRTU	G1	139
C-FRWK	MU-2	1521SA
C-FRWW	31T	7620049
C-FRYL	200	BB-1053
C-FSAO	200	BB-1610
C-FSAT	200	BB-1526
C-FSEA	425	0192
C-FSFI	441	0316
C-FSGZ	90	LJ-1371
C-FSIK	B100	BE-39
C-FSKA	100	B-239
C-FSKC	441	0139
C-FSKG	441	0120
C-FSKN	200	BB-1109
C-FSKO	200	BB-1007
C-FSKQ	200	BB-99
C-FSKX	200	BB-1126
C-FSNA	100	B-227
C-FSOZ	PA42	5501014
C-FSPM	690D	15002
C-FSPN	200	BB-745
C-FSQD	200	BB-1921
C-FSRK	PC12	202
C-FSRW	31T	8020050
C-FSSU	200	BB-633
C-FSTJ	BN2	868
C-FSTP	P180	1055
C-FSUG	200	BB-1699
C-FSVC	MIIA	T26-019
C-FSXG	90	LJ-1305
C-FTAD	MU-2	689
C-FTAM	BN2	339
C-FTEE	441	0137
C-FTIU	350	FL-584
C-FTIX	MIVA	AT-066
C-FTJC	MIVA	AT-051
C-FTLB	300	FA-137
C-FTMA	100	B-174
C-FTML	441	0012
C-FTML	MU-2	525
C-FTNM	46D	18
C-FTOO	MU-2	549
C-FTPE	90	LJ-1342
C-FTRX	31T	8166040
C-FTUA	100	B-61
C-FTWO	MU-2	672
C-FTYO	200	BB-1222
C-FTYZ	100	B-86
C-FUAC	90	LJ-3
C-FUDY	441	0286
C-FUFW	90	LJ-84
C-FUPD	90	LJ-281
C-FUPQ	100	B-162
C-FVAX	425	0178
C-FVCC	200	BB-967
C-FVFN	BN2	490
C-FVKC	350	FL-273
C-FVMH	90	LJ-225
C-FVPC	PC12	358
C-FVPK	PC12	211
C-FWAB	PA42	8001021
C-FWAM	G1	148
C-FWAV	PC12	280
C-FWCC	PA42	8001001
C-FWCP	31T	8166018
C-FWCP	441	0264
C-FWEM	46D	37
C-FWHV	46D	25
C-FWLS	BN2	465
C-FWOL	100	B-84
C-FWPG	100	B-67
C-FWPN	100	B-51
C-FWPR	350	FL-125
C-FWPT	31T	8166066
C-FWRL	441	0079
C-FWRM	100	B-125
C-FWUT	31T	7620039
C-FWWF	200	BB-374
C-FWWK	300	FA-182
C-FWWQ	200	BB-667
C-FWXB	200	BB-1058
C-FWXB	MIII	T-314
C-FWXI	200	BB-1224
C-FWXR	350	FL-13
C-FWYF	100	B-89
C-FWYN	100	B-47
C-FWYO	100	B-28
C-FXAJ	100	B-122
C-FXDE	100	B-176
C-FXNB	90	LJ-257
C-FXRJ	B100	BE-115
C-FXYK	BN2	23
C-FYBN	MU-2	679
C-FYBV	31T	7520015
C-FYCB	E90	LW-275
C-FYPB	BN2	2107

C-FYPL	31T	8275014
C-FYTK	31T	7620008
C-FYUT	PC12	254
C-FYZF	BN2	9
C-FYZS	PC12	227
C-FYZT	BN2	78
C-FYZU	BN2	82
C-FZIC	31T	8120104
C-FZIH	31T	8120012
C-FZIZ	FPC6	2009
C-FZNQ	200	BB-264
C-FZPW	200	BB-940
C-FZRQ	690	11025
C-FZUT	BN2	183
C-FZVV	BN2	238
C-FZVW	200	BB-787
C-FZVX	200	BB-231
C-FZXG	BN2	876
C-GAAA	441	0138
C-GAAL	690A	11104
C-GAAP	PC6	569
C-GACA	200	BB-1309
C-GACN	200	BB-1384
C-GADI	200	BB-853
C-GADI	690A	11102
C-GAEO	350	FL-479
C-GAGE	425	0153
C-GAGE	441	0086
C-GAGE	441	0214
C-GAIK	100	B-104
C-GAJB	690A	11174
C-GAKA	PA42	8001014
C-GAMC	MU-2	785SA
C-GAMJ	31T	7820063
C-GANW	P68	274
C-GAPK	100	B-198
C-GAPT	31T	7620004
C-GAPT	B100	BE-70
C-GAPZ	BN2	311
C-GARM	200	BB-45
C-GARO	200	BB-2
C-GASI	100	B-126
C-GASR	90	LJ-394
C-GAST	100	B-173
C-GASW	100	B-108
C-GAUR	MU-2	450SA
C-GAVI	100	B-201
C-GAWA	90	LJ-1002
C-GAWP	PC12	187
C-GBBG	200	BB-1507
C-GBBS	200	BB-757
(C-GBBY)	F90	LA-174
C-GBCE	350	FL-502
C-GBCI	P180	1057
C-GBCO	TBM7	238
C-GBDH	31T	8375003
C-GBDJ	31T	8275013
C-GBFD	100	B-66
C-GBFF	90	LJ-198
C-GBFM	441	0297
C-GBFO	31T	8166069
C-GBFU	BN2	535
C-GBGW	200	BB-148
C-GBIT	681	6022
C-GBJV	PC12	237
C-GBKL	200	BB-639
C-GBMF	PC12	727
C-GBMI	425	0031
C-GBNG	PC12	1067
C-GBOG	100	B-143
C-GBON	200	BB-1730
C-GBOT	690B	11509
C-GBOT	PA42	8001063
C-GBOX	MU-2	509
C-GBQM	200	BB-45
C-GBQO	200	BB-754
C-GBRB	BN2	893
C-GBTI	90	LJ-352
C-GBTI	E90	LW-111
C-GBTL	F90	LA-58
C-GBTL	PC12	159
C-GBTS	B100	BE-73
C-GBTS	TBM7	19
C-GBTV	31T	7904016
C-GBTV	90	LJ-352
C-GBTV	MU-2	694
(C-GBUX)	200	BB-690
C-GBVB	MU-2	400SA
C-GBVX	B100	BE-99
C-GBWB	B100	BE-120
C-GBWC	200	BB-213
C-GBWD	441	0136
C-GBWF	B100	BE-56
C-GBWO	200	BB-531
C-GBWO	200	BB-728
C-GBWO	200	BB-754
C-GBXW	PC12	170
C-GBYB	90	LJ-920
C-GBYN	200	BB-1232
C-GBZM	MIIB	T26-122
C-GCAU	MIVC	AT-469
C-GCET	200	BB-124
C-GCEV	200	BB-153
C-GCFB	90	LJ-929
C-GCFD	100	B-104
C-GCFF	200	BB-474
C-GCFL	90	LJ-500
C-GCFM	90	LJ-886
C-GCFZ	90	LJ-849
C-GCGB	350	FL-450
C-GCIA	690B	11487
C-GCIK	441	0314
C-GCIL	441	0314
C-GCLQ	200	BB-519
C-GCNO	31T	8020081
C-GCOL	46T	97287
C-GCOM	P180	1117
C-GCPX	MIV	AT-011
C-GCRN	PC12	675
C-GCSL	200	BB-118
C-GCSL	350	FL-87
C-GCTA	441	0140
C-GCUL	31T	7820002
C-GCVE	200	BB-1368
C-GCXB	BN2	352
C-GCYB	441	0298
C-GCYN	200	BB-710
C-GDBB	441	0056
C-GDCL	690A	11192
C-GDEF	MIVA	AT-069
C-GDEF	MIVA	AT-074
C-GDFC	BN2	239
C-GDFJ	B100	BE-15
C-GDFN	200	BB-359
C-GDFT	200	BB-354
C-GDFZ	B100	BE-16
C-GDGD	PC12	193
(C-GDGP)	MU-2	719SA
C-GDHF	200	BB-1129
C-GDKI	350	FL-259
C-GDKT	200	BB-819
C-GDLE	46T	97188
C-GDLG	425	0063
C-GDMN	F90	LA-134
C-GDMU	200	BB-858
C-GDMY	200C	BL-35
C-GDNH	200	BB-1946
C-GDOM	90	LJ-368
C-GDOW	31T	7620006
C-GDPB	200C	BL-44
C-GDPC	90	LJ-671
C-GDPI	100	B-156
C-GDSD	MIII	T-251
C-GDSH	200	BB-1178
C-GDTX	200	BB-1074
C-GDVF	200	BB-1940
C-GDWM	G1	167
C-GEAL	31T	7720062
C-GEAS	31T	7920036
C-GEAS	350	FL-17
C-GEBA	31T	7620029
C-GECT	PC12	1040
C-GEHS	MU-2	763SA
C-GEJE	350	FL-385
C-GEMO	46T	97062
C-GEOS	690A	11279
C-GEOW	PC12	244
C-GERR	690A	11172
C-GESB	PA42	8001055
C-GESV	PA42	8001016
C-GEVN	200	BB-898
C-GEVX	BN2	464
C-GFAB	680T	1601-43
(C-GFAC)	680T	1708-83
C-GFAD	200	BB-1428
C-GFAD	681	6028
C-GFAE	681	6019
C-GFAF	680T	1562-18
C-GFAM	31T	7920042
C-GFBF	BN2	2125
C-GFCE	MIII	TT-433
C-GFCL	MIII	TT-433
C-GFDV	425	0015
C-GFES	300	FA-2
C-GFFH	MU-2	1522SA
C-GFFN	100	B-190
C-GFFY	F90	LA-154
C-GFIL	PC12	268
C-GFIN	31T	7620037
C-GFKS	100	B-247
C-GFLA	PC12	293
C-GFLL	31T	8166041
C-GFLN	PC12	789
C-GFOL	200	BB-27
C-GFOX	P180	1065
C-GFPP	690	11032
C-GFRU	MU-2	343
C-GFSA	350	FL-174
C-GFSB	200	BB-84
C-GFSD	200	BB-1962
C-GFSE	200	BB-1963
C-GFSG	200	BB-671
C-GFSH	200	BB-912
C-GGAO	200	BB-659
C-GGAT	200	BB-1088
C-GGDC	MU-2	796SA
C-GGFJ	MIIA	T26-007
C-GGFL	31T	7820029
C-GGGL	90	LJ-38
C-GGGQ	200	BB-1128
C-GGIY	BN2	199
C-GGJF	200	BB-939
C-GGJG	BN2	2219
C-GGJH	F90	LA-13
C-GGKJ	B100	BE-49
C-GGMC	46D	98
C-GGMD	31T	7720023
C-GGMK	441	0191
C-GGOO	690	11068
C-GGPS	31T	7820023
C-GGPT	MIVA	AT-044
C-GGRS	E90	LW-242
C-GGVB	31T	7720057
C-GGVJ	BN2	570
C-GGWA	PC12	184
C-GGYY	BN2	129
C-GGZR	BN2	77
C-GHDP	200	BB-891
C-GHJF	200	BB-1493
C-GHLA	90	LJ-380
C-GHMD	690A	11237
C-GHMU	31T	7520023
C-GHOC	100	B-194
C-GHOL	200	BB-37
C-GHOP	200	BB-120
C-GHPP	PC6	558
C-GHQG	300	FA-39
C-GHQG	690B	11353
C-GHRM	31T	7620053
C-GHSI	31T	7520025
C-GHUN	F90	LA-231
C-GHVM	46T	97339
C-GHVR	90	LJ-337
C-GHWF	690A	11134
C-GHWM	MIIB	T26-141
C-GHXG	31T	7920011
C-GHYT	100	B-98
C-GIAA	690A	11212
C-GIAB	690A	11305
C-GIAC	690A	11338
C-GIAD	690B	11381
C-GICX	690	11039
C-GIDC	PA42	8001002
C-GIHF	BN2	475
C-GIIT	690C	11691
C-GIIX	E90	LW-220
C-GILM	100	B-124
C-GILS	BN2	416
C-GIND	200C	BL-42
C-GINT	425	0103
C-GIPF	BN2	274
C-GIRF	300	FA-86
C-GIRH	BN2	404
C-GIRO	MU-2	358SA
C-GISH	100	B-152
C-GISY	P68	370
C-GITC	TBM7	223
C-GIVM	31T	7620009
C-GIXF	680T	1577-31
C-GIZX	100	B-172
C-GJAV	MU-2	241
C-GJAV	MU-2	593
C-GJBE	90	LJ-75
C-GJBK	90	LJ-7
C-GJBQ	100	B-191
C-GJBV	100	B-100
C-GJCA	680T	1546-9
C-GJCM	200	BB-450
C-GJDI	200G	BY-76
C-GJEB	425	0007
C-GJEI	695A	96012
C-GJFO	690	11035
C-GJFT	BN2	606
C-GJFY	200	BB-812
C-GJHF	425	0080
C-GJHW	100	B-175
C-GJJE	31T	7820053
C-GJJF	100	B-123
C-GJJH	46D	202
C-GJJT	200	BB-828
C-GJJT	200	BB-1044
C-GJKS	100	B-14
C-GJLI	200	BB-347
C-GJLJ	100	B-235
C-GJLK	350	FL-13
C-GJLP	100	B-148
C-GJMM	P180	1037
C-GJMZ	P68	369
C-GJNH	680T	1587-38
C-GJOL	P180	1069
C-GJPD	31T	7920070
C-GJPT	31T	7520039
C-GJQM	680T	1718-89
C-GJRL	BN2	555
C-GJSD	MU-2	718SA
C-GJSH	P68	376
C-GJSU	100	B-88
C-GJUL	100	B-218
C-GJVC	90	LJ-1111
C-GJVK	100	B-127
C-GJWM	MU-2	681
C-GJWW	MIV	AT-013
C-GKAJ	100	B-232
C-GKAW	BN2	128
C-GKAY	PC12	178
C-GKBB	90	LJ-607
C-GKBN	200	BB-29
C-GKBP	200	BB-505
C-GKBQ	100	B-62
C-GKBZ	100	B-85
C-GKCA	90	LJ-821
C-GKDZ	690	11016
C-GKES	BN2	622
C-GKFG	680W	1842-41
C-GKFG	G1	22
C-GKFR	681	6044
C-GKFV	680T	1704-80
C-GKIF	31T	8275016
C-GKKG	31T	8020045
C-GKMA	441	0171
C-GKMJ	BN2	187
C-GKMS	350	FL-309
C-GKMV	31T	7820003
C-GKMV	680W	1818-32
C-GKMX	31T	7720058
C-GKNP	B100	BE-89

C-GKNR	PC12	308
C-GKOS	200	BB-389
C-GKOS	350	FL-511
C-GKOX	200	BB-389
C-GKPC	31T	7520021
C-GKPL	PC12	245
C-GKRL	200	BB-878
C-GKRS	31T	8166008
C-GKRY	PC12	1110
C-GKSC	F90	LA-113
C-GKWQ	P180	1095
C-GKWT	441	0125
C-GLAD	425	0088
C-GLAG	31T	7920027
C-GLBL	441	0250
C-GLCE	46D	130
C-GLCE	PC12	475
C-GLDZ	31T	8166063
C-GLEB	90	LJ-374
C-GLEM	P180	1009
C-GLER	46T	97185
C-GLFN	200	BB-1738
C-GLGE	441	0086
C-GLKA	MIIA	T26-020
C-GLLS	200	BB-1601
C-GLMC	681	6044
C-GLMO	PA42	8001032
C-GLOD	BN2	183
C-GLOW	MU-2	624
C-GLOX	350	FL-106
C-GLPG	100	B-159
(C-GLRI)	680T	1568-24
C-GLRR	90	LJ-134
C-GLSE	200	BB-329
C-GLSW	31T	8020049
C-GLTP	441	0203
C-GLVK	PC12	1108
C-GMAE	PC12	276
C-GMAG	100	B-229
C-GMBA	300	FA-137
C-GMBC/901	90	LJ-1300
C-GMBD/902	90	LJ-1301
C-GMBG/903	90	LJ-1304
C-GMBH/904	90	LJ-1309
C-GMBW/905	90	LJ-1310
C-GMBX/906	90	LJ-1313
C-GMBY/907	90	LJ-1317
C-GMBZ/908	90	LJ-1319
C-GMCI	300	FA-133
C-GMCM	46D	129
C-GMCM	46T	97150
C-GMDD	690B	11523
C-GMDF	31T	7620019
C-GMDY	31T	7620029
C-GMEA	350	FL-214
C-GMEH	200	BB-1433
C-GMEH	350	FL-214
C-GMEH	350	FL-353
C-GMEJ	31T	7620008
C-GMET	TBM8	355
C-GMEV	200	BB-1433
C-GMFI	PA42	5527023
C-GMGG	200	BB-1467
C-GMGO	31T	8004012
C-GMHJ	90	LJ-300
C-GMHP	46T	97332
C-GMIT	F90	LA-65
C-GMJS	G1	81
C-GMJS	MU-2	558
C-GMKW	350	FL-575
C-GMLF	PC12	849
C-GMMK	200	BB-214
C-GMMO	695A	96034
C-GMNC	680T	1560-17
C-GMND	BN2	449
C-GMOC	200	BB-513
C-GMOP	BN2	398
C-GMOU	MIIB	T26-107
C-GMOW	BN2	179
C-GMPA	90	LJ-570
C-GMPE	PC12	184
C-GMPE	PC12	1073
C-GMPI	PC12	239
C-GMPM	PC12	1011
C-GMPO	200	BB-667
C-GMPP	690C	11732
C-GMPP	PC12	374
C-GMPW	PC12	274
C-GMPX	PC12	1017
C-GMPY	PC12	311
C-GMPZ	PC12	272
C-GMRS	200	BB-187
C-GMSL	441	0245
C-GMSL	441	0283
C-GMSV	425	0006
C-GMTI	F90	LA-65
C-GMUA	MU-2	006
C-GMUK	MU-2	277
C-GMVP	90	LJ-616
C-GMWR	200	BB-68
C-GMYM	46T	97114
C-GMZG	MIIB	T26-165
C-GNAA	100	B-24
C-GNAG	200	BB-1239
C-GNAJ	100	B-107
C-GNAK	200	BB-1376
C-GNAK	G1	154
C-GNAM	200	BB-1339
C-GNAM	31T	8020065
C-GNAR	100	B-190
C-GNAX	100	B-47
C-GNAX	200	BB-1419
C-GNBB	200	BB-479
C-GNCV	100	B-23
C-GNDI	31T	7620036
C-GNDR	200	BB-1290
C-GNEP	425	0221
C-GNEX	100	B-211
C-GNIS	90	LJ-351
C-GNJM	MIII	T-228
C-GNKP	31T	7520008
C-GNKW	TRIS	381
C-GNKX	90	LJ-1439
C-GNLA	350	FL-26
C-GNLF	350	FL-591
C-GNOJ	200	BB-365
C-GNOR	G1	43
C-GNPT	31T	7620001
C-GNRD	PA42	8001009
C-GNSC	B100	BE-102
C-GNSC	BN2	214
C-GNSS	46D	115
C-GNSS	46T	97072
C-GNSS	46T	97200
C-GNTU	200	BB-1053
C-GNUX	90	LJ-49
C-GNVB	100	B-143
C-GNWD	31T	7620029
C-GNWM	441	0090
C-GNYD	680W	1761-7
C-GOCR	31T	8020048
C-GODA	MU-2	297
C-GODE	MU-2	634
C-GODE	PC12	707
C-GODI	MU-2	649
C-GOGS	350	FL-269
C-GOGT	200	BB-535
C-GOHK	EPIC	227
C-GOHK	P750	227
C-GOIC	350	FL-272
C-GOMA	200	BB-262
C-GOMC	BN2	10
C-GOVF	200	BB-392
C-GOVT	690D	15020
C-GOXZ	TRIS	361
C-GPAB	BN2	643
C-GPAI	PC12	491
C-GPBA	100	B-215
C-GPBC	31T	8275005
C-GPCA	690B	11431
C-GPCB	100	B-45
C-GPCD	200	BB-76
C-GPCF	BN2	39
C-GPCL	MIV	AT-017
C-GPCO	PC12	603
C-GPCP	200	BB-140
C-GPCW	31T	7520036
C-GPDJ	P180	1057
C-GPDJ	PC12	659
C-GPDP	46T	97099
C-GPDX	690A	11319
C-GPEA	200	BB-170
C-GPGI	300	FA-2
C-GPIA	P180	1072
C-GPII	P180	1133
C-GPIM	31T	8020065
C-GPIP	31T	7720026
C-GPJL	B100	BE-107
C-GPKK	200	BB-181
C-GPKP	300	FA-106
C-GPLT	PC12	566
C-GPMF	46T	97408
C-GPNB	200	BB-102
C-GPNB	200	BB-1921
C-GPNB	90	LJ-1305
C-GPNC	300C	FM-15
C-GPNP	31T	7520024
C-GPNV	680W	1778-16
C-GPOA	200	BB-434
C-GPOE	31T	8020090
C-GPPA	90	LJ-1653
C-GPPC	350	FL-127
C-GPPK	100	B-35
C-GPPN	90	LJ-389
C-GPPP	BN2	423
C-GPQB	TBM7	335
(C-GPQX)	200	BB-1053
C-GPQZ	200	BB-404
C-GPRO	680T	1609-45
C-GPRO	MIII	T-239
C-GPRU	B100	BE-26
C-GPSB	PA42	8001030
C-GPSP	441	0058
C-GPSQ	441	0076
C-GPSR	441	0143
C-GPTA	G1	162
C-GPTG	G1	189
C-GPTN	G1	88
C-GPTP	31T	7520026
C-GPVE	690C	11635
C-GPVN	BN2	306
C-GPWR	MIIB	T26-160
C-GQCC	31T	7620033
C-GQDD	90	LJ-328
C-GQGA	F90	LA-106
C-GQJG	200	BB-249
C-GQKK	200	BB-556
C-GQMG	BN2	54
C-GQNJ	200	BB-275
C-GQPC	90	LJ-557
C-GQXF	200	BB-285
C-GRBA	PC12	238
C-GRBF	MIIB	T26-171E
C-GRBV	TBM7	191
C-GRCL	31T	7904019
C-GRCN	90	LJ-434
C-GRCW	31T	7720009
C-GRCW	90	LJ-1407
C-GRCY	PA42	8001024
C-GRDC	PC12	214
C-GRDI	200	BB-506
C-GRDT	MIIA	T26-012
C-GREV	695	95074
C-GRFN	200	BB-1054
C-GRGE	PA42	5527012
C-GRHD	425	0167
C-GRJL	441	0121
C-GRJM	425	0177
C-GRJP	PC12	196
C-GRJZ	350	FL-285
C-GRMS	PC12	200
C-GRNJ	31T	8120011
C-GROO	PC6	662
C-GRRO	690A	11166
C-GRSL	441	0054
C-GRSL	90	LJ-609
C-GRSR	441	0171
C-GRTL	MIII	T-225
C-GRVJ	690B	11514
C-GRXA	PC12	1083
C-GRXB	PC12	1094
C-GRXD	PC12	1106
C-GRXE	PC12	1117
C-GRYC	441	0003
C-GSAA	PA42	5501057
C-GSAA	TRIS	1016
C-GSAD	BN2	7
C-GSAE	200	BB-1748
C-GSAF	BN2	263
C-GSAH	200	BB-1972
C-GSAM	100	B-32
C-GSAM	31T	8166049
C-GSAU	200	BB-1974
C-GSAV	200	BB-1790
C-GSAX	90	LJ-697
C-GSBC	200	BB-1780
C-GSBC	31T	7820014
C-GSCM	200	BB-920
C-GSCM	MIII	T-247
C-GSDR	MIV	AT-014
C-GSEP	200	BB-61
C-GSFC	90	LJ-6
C-GSFF	425	0177
C-GSFI	425	0177
C-GSFM	90	LJ-422
C-GSFY	31T	8166014
C-GSGC	31T	7620018
C-GSGJ	31T	8166015
C-GSGK	BN2	383
C-GSGR	BN2	2107
C-GSGX	BN2	596
C-GSID	31T	7520042
C-GSIH	PA42	8001036
C-GSJJ	441	0085
C-GSKH	441	0264
C-GSKM	MU-2	625
C-GSKR	31T	7720019
C-GSLC	PC12	365
C-GSMO	TBM7	130
C-GSNM	E90	LW-194
C-GSOC	MIVA	AT-027
C-GSPS	200	BB-716
C-GSSA	F90	LA-6
C-GSSC	31T	8120004
C-GSSK	441	0362
C-GSUC	BN2	534
C-GSUN	90	LJ-447
C-GSVO	690D	15037
C-GSVQ	680T	1544-8
C-GSWB	31T	7720013
C-GSWF	B100	BE-129
C-GSWF	MIV	AT-011
C-GSWG	B100	BE-131
C-GSWJ	MIIB	T26-151
C-GSWY	MIII	T-232
C-GSYN	100	B-61
C-GSZI	TRIS	360
C-GSZX	200	BB-355
C-GTBM	TBM7	53
C-GTCB	46D	41
C-GTCB	46D	146
C-GTCC	441	0020
C-GTCI	695	95083
C-GTCL	B100	BE-130
C-GTCL	BN2	536
C-GTDB	300	FA-215
C-GTDF	200	BB-1546
C-GTDL	G1	110
C-GTDP	200C	BL-25
C-GTDY	200	BB-1075
C-GTEM	350	FL-236
C-GTEM	MIVA	AT-029
C-GTFP	31T	7620016
C-GTGA	200	BB-728
C-GTHN	MIIA	T26-016
C-GTIM	200	BB-161
C-GTIO	E90	LW-274
C-GTJW	200	BB-29
C-GTJZ	200	BB-499
C-GTLA	100	B-165
C-GTLA	200	BB-1224
C-GTLF	100	B-72
C-GTLS	100	B-35
C-GTLT	200	BB-1126
C-GTMA	90	LJ-348
C-GTMM	31T	7904008

C-GTMW	MIV	AT-002
C-GTOL	31T	8004028
C-GTOP	BN2	770
C-GTPB	BN2	223
C-GTRL	MIII	T-227
C-GTSV	90	LJ-1922
C-GTTS	31T	8020053
C-GTUC	200	BB-268
C-GTVV	31T	8166046
C-GTVV	PA42	8001076
C-GTWI	BN2	766
C-GTWW	90	LJ-657
C-GUAW	BN2	188
C-GUKP	MU-2	560
(C-GUKZ)	BN2	517
C-GUNG	90	LJ-712
C-GUNG	MU-2	226
C-GUPP	100	B-157
C-GURG	MIII	T-228
C-GUXL	46T	97292
C-GVBO	31T	7820073
C-GVCC	90	LJ-414
C-GVCE	100	B-135
(C-GVCF)	680T	1546-9
C-GVCI	425	0080
C-GVCJ	BN2	90
C-GVCO	MIIB	T26-155
C-GVCY	MIV	AT-003
C-GVEJ	MIVA	AT-039
C-GVIK	B100	BE-7
C-GVJT	441	0090
C-GVJV	46T	97261
C-GVKA	31T	7920008
C-GVKC	PC12	207
C-GVKE	BN2	897
C-GVKK	31T	7820038
C-GVKS	31T	7920019
C-GVLH	F90	LA-105
C-GVON	31T	7920039
(C-GVSO)	690D	15037
C-GVZY	BN2	513
C-GWAM	441	0316
C-GWCA	441	0139
C-GWCA	PA42	5501057
C-GWCN	46D	75
C-GWCY	90	LJ-345
C-GWEL	46T	97351
C-GWEW	690	11057
C-GWFM	31T	7520041
C-GWGI	200	BB-1022
C-GWGP	MU-2	109
C-GWGT	90	LJ-373
C-GWID	MU-2	557
C-GWII	P180	1074
C-GWKA	MIIA	T26-026
C-GWLR	100	B-198
C-GWRA	441	0089
C-GWRK	P180	1061
C-GWSL	200	BB-185
C-GWSL	MIVA	AT-028
C-GWSP	MIV	AT-010
C-GWSQ	200C	BL-10
(C-GWSR)	690D	15020
C-GWUY	200	BB-77
C-GWWA	100	B-27
C-GWWN	200	BB-14
C-GWWQ	100	B-76
C-GWWV	200	BB-287
C-GWXH	200	BB-1126
C-GWXM	200C	BL-130
C-GWZO	PC6	572
C-GXBF	31T	7620010
C-GXCD	31T	7620026
C-GXHD	200	BB-1338
C-GXHD	90	LJ-58
C-GXHF	200	BB-1343
C-GXHG	200	BB-1383
C-GXHN	200	BB-693
C-GXHP	100	B-132
C-GXHR	200	BB-1305
C-GXHS	200	BB-1302
C-GXHW	200	BB-710
C-GXIJ	PC6	667
C-GXIK	PC6	672

C-GXIL	PC6	620
C-GXJQ	E90	LW-157
C-GXMT	31T	7820049
C-GXNA	31T	7720017
C-GXRX	100	B-36
C-GXTC	31T	7720052
C-GXVX	100	B-18
C-GXXD	TBM7	75
C-GYDQ	200	BB-455
C-GYLP	MIIB	T26-117
C-GYMR	MIIB	T26-177
C-GYMW	BN2	88
C-GYNW	P68	241
(C-GYOX)	TRIS	1027
C-GYQK	100	B-153
C-GYQT	100	B-189
C-GYSC	200	BB-1579
C-GYSK	200	BB-12
C-GYTC	BN2	554
(C-GYUF)	BN2	530
(C-GYUG)	BN2	544
(C-GYUH)	BN2	550
C-GYUI	200	BB-812
C-GYUI	300	FA-214
C-GZCZ	PC6	731
C-GZGO	BN2	2017
C-GZGZ	PC12	357
C-GZIZ	90	LJ-46
C-GZKG	BN2	253
C-GZKG	BN2	2038
C-GZNS	MU-2	1550SA
(C-GZOA)	690C	11649
C-GZON	690	11020
C-GZQD	31T	7520021
C-GZRJ	31T	8275012
C-GZRP	PA42	5501011
C-GZRX	200	BB-574
C-GZTP	BN2	876
C-GZUZ	100	B-143
C-GZVU	BN2	2015
C-GZYO	200	BB-383
CF-AAP	680T	1568-24
CF-ACB	90	LJ-270
CF-AFD	100	B-42
CF-AJL	BN2	106
(CF-AJM)	BN2	114
CF-ALI	690A	11102
CF-AMP	MU-2	125
CF-ANG	680W	1835-40
CF-ASC	G1	115
CF-ASD	E90	LW-22
CF-AXP	MU-2	502
CF-AZM	BN2	114
CF-BAN	MU-2	577
CF-BCN	200	BB-7
CF-BCO	200	BB-8
CF-BFP	100	B-35
CF-BGL	PC6	540
CF-CAS	90	LJ-23
CF-CAU	90	LJ-24
CF-CEL	MU-2	114
CF-CGE	90	LJ-118
CF-CGH	90	LJ-203
CF-CGI	90	LJ-220
CF-CGJ	90	LJ-231
CF-CGN	90	LJ-313
CF-CHZ	TRIS	299
CF-CII	MU-2	144
CF-CMY	BN2	169
CF-COL	G1	64
CF-CRL	MU-2	037
CF-DCA	90	LJ-374
CF-DEB	BN2	58
CF-DLE	690	11009
CF-DLO	G1	137
CF-DOR	100	B-103
CF-DOS	100	B-106
CF-DOU	100	B-112
CF-DOV	100	B-117
CF-DOY	100	B-120
CF-FAR	90	LJ-391
CF-FAS	90	LJ-617
CF-FDB	681	6003
CF-FEO	680T	1693-72

CF-FER	MU-2	150
CF-GAQ	BN2	212
CF-GHK	MU-2	140
CF-GNL	100	B-184
CF-GRA	MIIB	T26-154
CF-GWF	MU-2	524
CF-HAD	MIIA	T26-020
CF-HAP	680T	1548-10
CF-HBO	G1	104
CF-HBW	90	LJ-336
CF-HTL	MU-2	123
CF-HWI	90	LJ-309
CF-HYX	MIIB	T26-174
CF-IIG	680T	1699-76
CF-IOM	G1	60
CF-JCN	90	LJ-19
CF-JCN	90	LJ-186
CF-JFC	G1	31
CF-JLJ	100	B-58
CF-JPW	BN2	61
CF-KEX	680W	1828-36
CF-LOO	G1	7
CF-MAR	G1	3
CF-MCF	200	BB-439
CF-MCF	MU-2	122
CF-MKK	MU-2	248
CF-MLC	90	LJ-20
CF-MUR	G1	54
CF-NOC	G1	72
CF-PAW	90	LJ-373
CF-PCB	90	LJ-183
CF-PNB	681B	6055
CF-QDI	100	B-9
CF-QMS	MU-2	009
(CF-QPM)	BN2	241
CF-QPM	BN2	241
CF-QPN	BN2	263
CF-RCL	90	LJ-33
CF-RDI	BN2	35
CF-ROM	MU-2	601
CF-RZZ	PC6	540
CF-SIV	90	LJ-212
CF-SVJ	680T	1550-11
CF-TEL	MIIB	T26-162
CF-TPC	G1	17
CF-UAC	90	LJ-3
(CF-VAA)	680T	1575-29
CF-VLR	90	LJ-289
CF-VMH	90	LJ-225
CF-VNX	680T	1698-75
CF-VPM	90	LJ-292
CF-WHV	90	LJ-11
CF-WHV	90	LJ-111
CF-XYK	BN2	23
CF-XZS	BN2	50
CF-YFD	90	LJ-448
CF-YSU	MU-2	149
CF-YZF	BN2	9
CF-YZT	BN2	78
CF-YZU	BN2	82
CF-ZIZ	FPC6	2009
CF-ZJB	MU-2	511
CF-ZUT	BN2	183
CF-ZVV	BN2	238
"CF-ZVW"	BN2	240
CF-ZVY	BN2	240
CF-ZVY-X	BN2	240
CF-ZWF	BN2	233

Chile

CC-CAO	31T	7920058
CC-CBD	31T	8104070
CC-CBD	46D	64
(CC-CBS)	690A	11201
CC-CCC	31T	7920082
CC-CDL	90	LJ-1318
CC-CDN	200	BB-1368
CC-CDV	31T	7904054
CC-CDY	200	BB-810
CC-CEK	200	BB-1769
CC-CFG	200G	BY-59
CC-CFP	31T	8120058
CC-CFR	31T	8120046
CC-CGE	BN2	2166
CC-CGG	BN2	2168
CC-CGH	BN2	2169
CC-CGS	90	LJ-1835
CC-CHK	P68	215
CC-CIH	100	B-79
CC-CII	90	LJ-227
CC-CIJ	200C	BL-45
CC-CIW	31T	7820018
CC-CLY	100	B-79
CC-CMH	31T	7820035
CC-CNH	31T	8020069
CC-CNP	90	LJ-1895
CC-CNT	31T	8120049
CC-COT	200	BB-600
CC-COT	90	LJ-227
CC-CPB	200	BB-1796
CC-CPR	31T	8166070
CC-CPV	31T	7904054
CC-CRE	690A	11155
CC-CRU	31T	8104071
CC-CTE	F90	LA-196
CC-CTW	90	LJ-1389
CC-CVT	90	LJ-1556
CC-CVZ	90	LJ-441
CC-CWD	31T	8104071
CC-CWH	31T	8166016
CC-CWK	31T	8104023
CC-CWZ	441	0315
CC-CYB	31T	8120028
CC-CYR	BN2	2169
CC-CYT	31T	7920053
CC-CZB	31T	7820020
CC-CZC	31T	7920072
CC-DAG	E90	LW-153
CC-DIV	200C	BN-1
CC-DSN	E90	LW-153
CC-DSS	200T	BT-33
CC-EAA	200C	BN-1
CC-EAB	E90	LW-153
CC-EAG	200T	BT-33
CC-ECF	90	LJ-441
CC-ESA	100	B-219
CC-PAC	BN2	2166
CC-PBE	90	LJ-441
CC-PBK	90	LJ-1464
CC-PBP	31T	8120005
CC-PBT	31T	8104063
CC-PBZ	90	LJ-441
CC-PCY	31T	8120028
CC-PDV	31T	7904054
CC-PFD	31T	8104070
CC-PGO	46D	171
CC-PGT	BN2	2169
CC-PHM	31T	7904054
CC-PIE	100	B-79
CC-PIR	90	LJ-227
CC-PJG	31T	7920058
CC-PJH	31T	8120049
CC-PKU	31T	8020053
CC-PLL	31T	7920005
CC-PML	31T	1166002
CC-PMZ	31T	8020090
CC-PNA	31T	7920082
CC-PNS	31T	8104002
CC-PQO	BN2	2168
CC-PTA	31T	8166070
CC-PTN	200C	BN-1
CC-PTQ	E90	LW-153
CC-PTS	200T	BT-33
CC-PTS	90	LJ-1589
CC-PTZ	90	LJ-441
CC-PVE	31T	8166038
CC-PVO	31T	8166016
CC-PWA	300	FA-225
CC-PWH	31T	8104023
CC-PZB	31T	7820020
CC-PZX	31T	8020069

Morocco

CN-AMH	350	FL-588
CN-AMI	350	FL-603
CN-ANJ	350	FL-374
CN-CDE	200	BB-567
CN-CDF	200	BB-577
CN-CDN	200	BB-713
CN-RLE	350	FL-170
CN-RLL	350	FL-452
CN-TAD	350	FL-638
CN-TAX	90	LJ-922
CN-TBZ	P68	31
CN-TCC	BN2	673
CN-TCD	P68	204
CN-TGL	90	LJ-217
CN-TJC	350	FL-605
CN-TJL	PA42	8001034
CN-TNB	200	BB-1110
CN-TNC	300	FA-107
CN-TOM	MIII	TT-480
CN-TPH	200	BB-1006
CN-TVM	31T	8120020
CN-TWK	BN2T	2213
CN-TWL	BN2T	2214
CN-TWM	BN2T	2215
CN-TWN	BN2T	2228
CN-TWO	BN2T	2232
CN-TWP	BN2T	2233
CN-TWQ	BN2T	2237
CN-TWR	BN2T	2259
CN-TWS	BN2T	2261
CN-TWT	BN2T	2262
CN-TWU	BN2T	2266
CN-TWV	BN2T	2273
CN-TWW	BN2T	2274
CN-TWX	BN2T	2275
CN-TWY	350	FL-494

Bolivia

CP-(2029)	P68	310
CP-	680W	1835-40
CP-259_	690B	11463
CP-872	90	LJ-413
CP-894	681	6015
CP-1016	690	11001
CP-1016	690	11053
CP-1017	690	11054
CP-1076	690	11067
CP-1106	690A	11193
CP-1147	MU-2	291
(CP-1335)	690B	11381
CP-1335	690B	11405
CP-1600	90	LJ-905
CP-1600	90	LJ-946
CP-1640	695	95049
CP-1678	31T	8120017
(CP-1699)	31T	8166055
CP-1849	200C	BL-52
CP-1930	P68	332
CP-1962	MU-2	028
CP-1997	P68T	8010
CP-2031	P68	301
CP-2042	681	6025
CP-2050	695A	96055
CP-2078	695	95004
CP-2109	MIVC	AT-493
(CP-2140)	695A	96056
CP-2172	P68	304
CP-2182	690	11055
CP-2183	E90	LW-261
CP-2224	690B	11564
CP-2225	690B	11519
CP-2262	690B	11505
CP-2266	690B	11395
CP-2287	90	LJ-232
CP-2299	690B	11424
CP-2351	200	BB-1584
CP-2390	MU-2	580
CP-2467	690A	11107
CP-2494	E90	LW-314
CP-2526	90	LJ-1543

Mozambique

See also C9-

CR-ALQ	BN2	167
CR-ALR	BN2	162
CR-ALS	BN2	174
CR-AME	BN2	118
CR-AMG	BN2	213
CR-AMO	BN2	192
CR-AMS	BN2	247
CR-AMU	BN2	637
CR-AMV	BN2	219
CR-AMX	BN2	636
CR-ANH	BN2	658
CR-ANJ	BN2	656
CR-AOH	BN2	625
CR-AOI	690	11039
CR-AOK	BN2	288
CR-AOV	BN2	624
CR-APC	BN2	367
CR-APD	BN2	683
CR-APN	BN2	705
CR-APO	BN2	687
CR-APQ	BN2	364
CR-APT	BN2	691
CR-AQE	BN2	706
CR-AQF	BN2	707

Cape Verde

CR-CAS	BN2	623
CR-CAT	BN2	640
CR-CAU	BN2	685

Angola

See also D2-

CR-LAA	690A	11132
"CR-LHL"	690A	11151
CR-LMW	BN2	276
CR-LNX	690A	11151
CR-LOQ	BN2	678

Portugal

(CS-)	690B	11452
CS-AGH	BN2	654
CS-AJF	BN2	667
CS-AJO	BN2	125
CS-AJP	BN2	53
CS-AJQ	BN2	68
CS-AJR	BN2	98
CS-AJU	BN2	651
CS-APV	690A	11171
CS-AQP	BN2	625
CS-ARU	MIII	T-410
CS-ARX	690B	11357
CS-ASA	690B	11465
CS-ASG	690B	11452
CS-AYB	P68	101
CS-AYQ	P68	204
CS-DAF	BN2	691
CS-DBO	BN2	352
CS-DBT	90	LJ-721
CS-DCP	U-21	LM-22
CS-DDF	200	BB-1129
CS-DDU	200	BB-640
CS-DIQ	PC12	625
CS-DPT	300C	FM-26
CS-TFA	E90	LW-102

Uruguay

CX-BLT	31T	7620013
CX-BOE	690	11058
CX-BOR	200	BB-418
CX-BRU	31T	8004046
CX-FCS	PC12	765
CX-PGT	BN2	2169
CX-ROU	PA42	8001074

Bahamas

C6-	200	BB-135
C6-ASA	BN2	599
C6-BAA	BN2	214
C6-BAS	BN2	610
C6-BDF	350	FL-95
C6-BFA	MU-2	131
C6-BFP	200	BB-456
C6-BFQ	BN2	347
C6-BGU	BN2	517
C6-BHH	BN2	2021
C6-BHR	BN2	209
C6-BHV	B100	BE-4
C6-BUS	BN2	2040
(C6-CAA)	200	BB-456
C6-CAM	90	LJ-108
C6-CDF	P68	449
C6-FYP	BN2	2015
C6-MIP	200	BB-1710
C6-MIP	200	BB-1851
C6-SPL	90	LJ-1614
C6-TTC	200	BB-1145
C6-UNO	G1	102
C6-ZBB	200	BB-727

Mozambique

See also CR-

C9-ALQ	BN2	167
C9-ALS	BN2	174
C9-AME	BN2	118
C9-AMG	BN2	213
C9-AMO	BN2	192
C9-AMS	BN2	247
C9-AMU	BN2	637
C9-AMV	BN2	219
C9-AMX	BN2	636
C9-AOH	BN2	625
C9-AOI	690	11039
C9-AOV	BN2	624
C9-APC	BN2	367
C9-APD	BN2	683
C9-APN	BN2	705
C9-APO	BN2	687
C9-APQ	BN2	364
C9-APT	BN2	691
C9-AQE	BN2	706
C9-ASK	90	LJ-954
C9-ASO	P68	323
C9-ASS	200	BB-626
C9-ASV	200C	BL-21
C9-ASX	200C	BL-32
C9-ATB	P68	359
C9-ATK	P68	223
C9-ATO	P68	287
C9-ATQ	P68T	9004
C9-ATW	200	BB-937
C9-ENH	200	BB-626
C9-ENT	31T	7904034
C9-JTP	31T	7620012
C9-MEG	P68	307
C9-MMB	200	BB-72
C9-MTW	200	BB-1076
C9-PMZ	200	BB-1076
C9-SWE	200	BB-829
C9-TAH	BN2T	2120
C9-TAI	BN2T	2122
C9-TAJ	BN2T	2124
C9-TAK	BN2T	2121

Germany

D-CAAA	350	FL-116
D-CABC	MIVC	AT-502
D-CACB	200T	BT-27
D-CADF	350	FL-643
D-CADN	350	FL-101
(D-CAIR)	300	FA-228
D-CAIR	MIVC	AT-427
D-CAMM	350	FL-64
D-CASA	300	FA-76
D-CBBB	350	FL-120
D-CBIL	350	FL-246
D-CBIN	MIVC	AT-440B
D-CCBW	350	FL-46
D-CCCC	MIVC	AT-511
D-CDDD	350	FL-128
D-CFIA	350	FL-424
D-CFIS	350	FL-124
D-CFIX	350	FL-90
D-CFMA	350	FL-76
D-CFMB	350	FL-97
D-CFMC	300	FA-104
D-CFMD	350	FL-473
D-CFME	350	FL-627
D-CGMJ	350	FL-460
"D-CGN2"	P166	413
D-CHGS	350	FL-322
D-CIAO	350	FL-279
D-CIMB	300	FA-152
D-CINA	350	FL-7
(D-CISU)	350	FL-318
D-CKRA	350	FL-90
D-CKVW	MIVC	AT-543
D-CKWM	350	FL-124
D-CLOG	350	FL-276
D-CNAY	MIVC	AT-493
D-COEB	350	FL-255
D-COIL	300	FA-171
D-COLA	350	FL-75
D-COMM	300	FA-79
D-CRAO	350	FL-515
D-CSAG	350	FL-121
D-CSKF	350	FL-256
D-CSKY	350	FL-130
D-CUNO	350	FL-311
(D-CVVV)	350	FL-322
D-CWKM	350	FL-410
D-EAAB	46D	165
D-EADC	46D	88
(D-EADK)	46T	97079
D-EALL	46T	97050
(D-EARG)	46T	97079
D-EAVK	46T	97291
D-EBKK	46D	173
D-ECBE	46D	46
D-ECBE	46T	97063
D-ECRB	46T	97061
D-ECTP	46T	97070
D-EDTF	PC6	513
D-EEEY	46D	226
D-EFCH	46D	57
D-EHPJ	46D	58
D-EICO	46T	97125B
D-EION	46D	19
D-EIWM	46D	123
D-EKAU	46D	83
D-EKFD	46D	82
D-ELAO	46D	141
D-ELAV	PC6	516
D-ELEX	46D	80
*D-EMBK	46T	97113B
D-EMBZ	46D	225
D-EMDB	46D	132
D-EMVF	46D	225
D-ENHP	46D	156
D-ENII	46D	82
D-ENLI	PC6	348
D-ENLJ	PC6	517
D-ENLK	PC6	519
D-EOPG	46D	67
D-EPKD	46T	97019
D-EPOE	46D	86
D-EPRA	46D	134
D-EPTC	46D	122
D-EPUS	46T	97079
D-ERAH	46T	97276
D-ERFC	46D	199
D-ERGC	46D	144
D-ESHF	46D	25
D-ESSS	46T	97070
D-ESSS	46T	97347
D-ETBL	46D	219
D-ETPW	46D	156
D-ETVA	46T	97347
D-EVER	46T	97105

D-EVSM	46D	180
D-EVTP	46T	97325
D-EXPA	46T	97373
D-EXRE	46D	182
D-EXTA	46D	177
D-EXTP	46T	97249
(D-FACT)	PC6	779
(D-FAJS)	TBM7	206
(D-FAJS)	TBM7	271
D-FALF	TBM7	157
D-FALL	PC6	860
D-FANS	PC12	108
(D-FAPC)	PC12	536
D-FAPC	PC12	579
(D-FASC)	TBM7	74
D-FATA	PC6	894
D-FATN	PC12	788
D-FAXI	PC6	862
D-FBFS	TBM7	74
D-FBFS	TBM8	387
D-FBFT	TBM7	302
D-FBOY	TBM7	171
(D-FBOY)	TBM7	172
D-FCAP	PC12	843
D-FCGH	PC12	633
(D-FCJA)	PC12	175
D-FCJA	PC12	177
D-FCLG	PC6	636
D-FDFF	PC6	629
D-FDHM	PC6	688
D-FDHP	PC6	658
D-FEAR	PC6	748
(D-FEIA)	PC12	1016
D-FEIN	TBM7	89
D-FEJE	PC6	941
D-FELI	PC6	845
D-FERY	TBM7	194
D-FFAH	PC12	677
D-FFBU	TBM7	22
D-FFBU	TBM7	175
D-FFBZ	PC6	857
D-FFBZ	PC6	869
D-FFHZ	PC12	847
D-FFMM	PC12	751
(D-FFOR)	PC6	804
D-FGAG	PC12	810
D-FGMG	PC6	864
D-FGOJ	P750	139
D-FGPE	TBM8	413
D-FGYY	TBM7	7
D-FGYY	TBM7	162
D-FHGN	PC12	684
(D-FHPK)	PC6	778
D-FIBE	PC6	955
D-FIBG	TBM8	431
D-FIBI	PC12	773
D-FICA	PC6	919
D-FINE	PC12	761
D-FIPO	46T	97060
D-FIPS	PC6	874
D-FIRE	TBM7	137
D-FIVE	TBM7	186
D-FJMO	PC6	561
D-FKAI	46T	97054
D-FKAI	TBM7	288
D-FKGI	PC12	1080
D-FLAC	PC6	804
D-FLEV	PC6	651
*D-FLIR	PC12	128
D-FMOR	46T	97299
(D-FMOR)	TBM7	148
D-FMTA	PC6	860
*D-FNAH	PC12	1160
D-FNRE	TBM7	142
D-FOOO	TBM7	24
*D-FOUR	PC12	1133
D-FOXI	46T	97070
D-FRAH	46T	97276
D-FREE	PC6	731
D-FREI	PC6	935
D-FROH	PC6	654
D-FSCB	PC6	634
D-FSJP	TBM7	130
D-FSKY	PC6	878
D-FSOC	TBM7	23
D-FSPA	PC6	882
D-FSWB	PC6	863
D-FTAN	TBM7	24
D-FTBG	G160	87001
D-FTBM	TBM7	1
(D-FTBM)	TBM7	258
D-FTGB	G160	87000
(D-FTRI)	PC6	791
(D-FTWO)	PC6	790
D-FUDA	PC12	1016
D-FUEL	PC12	513
D-FUNY	PC6	894
D-FWGJ	TBM7	19
D-FWIR	TBM7	180
D-GABS	P68	399
D-GAHI	P68	360
D-GANA	P68	117
D-GANE	P68	104
D-GANS	P68	342
D-GATA	P68	82
D-GATE	P68	62
D-GBGK	P68	267
D-GBRD	P68	14
D-GBRS	P68	34
D-GEEK	P68	218
D-GEKA	P68	180
D-GELA	P68	137
D-GELI	P68	108
D-GEMA	P68	175
(D-GEMB)	P68	183
D-GEMB	P68	188
D-GEMC	P68	200
D-GEMD	P68	211
D-GEME	P68	221
D-GEMF	P68	237
D-GEMG	P68	246
D-GEMI	P68	247
D-GEMK	P68	258
D-GEML	P68	257
D-GENI	P68	144
D-GERA	P68	101
D-GERB	P68	173
D-GERD	P68	15
D-GERI	P68	367
D-GERO	P68	122
D-GERP	P68	25
D-GERT	P68	47
D-GERY	P68	49
D-GFPG	P68	170
D-GFPH	P68	166
D-GFPI	P68	158
D-GHAN	P68	416
D-GIFR	P68	57
D-GIGI	P68	61
D-GILA	P68	52
D-GIMI	P68	279
D-GINA	P68	59
D-GINI	P68	55
D-GINO	P68	60
D-GIRO	P68	69
D-GISA	P68	105
D-GITA	P68	92
D-GITE	P68	35
D-GITI	P68	195
D-GITY	P68	360
D-GITY	P68	362
D-GIUT	P68	26
D-GNIT	P68	23
D-GOBY	P68	278
D-GOGO	P68	343
D-GPLA	P68	10
D-GVMD	P68	429
D-GYRO	P68	415
D-IAAC	441	0073
D-IAAD	F406	0047
D-IAAE	441	0047
D-IAAE	PA42	5501047
D-IAAG	441	0013
D-IAAH	90	LJ-1247
D-IAAI	441	0043
D-IAAI	BN2	2167
D-IAAK	200	BB-134
D-IAAK	90	LJ-979
D-IAAN	441	0030
D-IAAN	690B	11505
D-IAAS	425	0012
D-IAAV	441	0160
D-IAAX	425	0108
D-IAAX	441	0166
D-IAAY	441	0144
D-IABA	PA42	8001011
D-IABB	90	LJ-1235
D-IABC	680T	1684-65
D-IABE	PA42	8001037
(D-IACE)	425	0063
D-IACR	31T	8104067
D-IACS	200	BB-209
D-IADC	441	0100
D-IADH	690B	11439
D-IADI	PA42	8001106
D-IADM	BN2	905
D-IAEB	BN2	218
D-IAFB	690B	11469
D-IAFC	690B	11479
(D-IAFC)	BN2	76
(D-IAFE)	690B	11488
D-IAFF	90	LJ-1229
D-IAFH	90	LJ-710
D-IAGA	441	0362
D-IAGB	F90	LA-38
D-IAGT	425	0061
D-IAHC	E90	LW-276
D-IAHK	200	BB-149
(D-IAHM)	31T	8104056
D-IAHT	MU-2	352SA
D-IAIR	200	BB-1278
D-IAJA	425	0033
D-IAJK	200	BB-1565
D-IAJW	BN2	659
D-IAKK	200	BB-1265
D-IAKS	31T	7820048
D-IALL	90	LJ-1124
D-IALT	B100	BE-126
D-IAMB	200	BB-790
D-IAMB	441	0126
D-IAMK	200	BB-956
D-IAMK	31T	7920044
D-IAMM	MIII	T-332
D-IAMW	200	BB-397
(D-IAMX)	90	LJ-453
D-IANA	200	BB-1517
D-IAOR	BN2	2002
D-IAPA	31T	8104032
D-IAPD	31T	8020052
(D-IAPD)	PA42	8001049
(D-IAPD)	PA42	8001078
D-IAPE	31T	7820080
D-IAPW	441	0210
D-IAQA	31T	1166007
D-IARF	90	LJ-1034
D-IASB	200	BB-407
(D-IASB)	PA42	8001009
D-IASF	31T	7820019
D-IASG	31T	7720060
D-IASW	31T	8104101
D-IATA	E90	LW-224
D-IATE	F406	0007
D-IATI	680T	1718-89
D-IATM	200	BB-1595
D-IATS	690B	11415
D-IAVI	90	LJ-1583
D-IAVW	100	B-62
D-IAWB	PA42	5501054
D-IAWD	BN2	84
*D-IAWD	PA42	5501051
*D-IAWE	425	0192
(D-IAWE)	PA42	5501052
D-IAWF	425	0222
D-IAWG	425	0160
(D-IAWG)	425	0177
D-IAWK	F90	LA-105
D-IAWS	200	BB-933
D-IAWW	690B	11367
D-IAXX	90	LJ-883
D-IBAA	425	0163
D-IBAA	441	0193
D-IBAB	200	BB-705
D-IBAB	300	FA-225
D-IBAB	MIVA	AT-066
D-IBAC	200	BB-1231
D-IBAD	200	BB-1229
D-IBAF	200	BB-93
D-IBAF	200	BB-1252
D-IBAG	690A	11211
D-IBAH	200	BB-334
(D-IBAI)	690C	11677
D-IBAI	695	95072
(D-IBAP)	690C	11656
D-IBAR	200	BB-1280
D-IBAR	695	95054
D-IBBB	MIII	T-293
D-IBBB	MU-2	439SA
(D-IBBB)	MU-2	452SA
D-IBBB	MU-2	1528SA
D-IBBC	MIII	T-314
D-IBBD	MIII	T-318
D-IBBE	MIII	T-339
D-IBBF	MIII	T-391
(D-IBBI)	90	LJ-926
D-IBBO	F90	LA-185
D-IBBP	425	0171
D-IBBP	90	LJ-1716
D-IBCB	200	BB-1729
D-IBCI	200	BB-932
D-IBDH	90	LJ-1307
(D-IBDV)	PA42	8001025
D-IBEI	690C	11623
D-IBER	300	FA-184
D-IBER	695A	96035
D-IBEU	31T	7820090
D-IBFE	200	BB-1716
D-IBFS	200	BB-1349
D-IBFT	200	BB-1535
D-IBHF	200	BB-1144
D-IBHK	200	BB-366
D-IBIC	200	BB-123
D-IBID	P166	367
D-IBIN	MIII	T-252
D-IBIW	31T	8004011
D-IBMA	690B	11429
D-IBMA	90	LJ-144
D-IBMC	90	LJ-931
D-IBMC	MIIB	T26-140E
D-IBMD	MIIB	T26-167E
D-IBMF	MIIB	T26-154E
D-IBMG	MIII	T-206
D-IBMH	MIV	AT-002
D-IBMP	200	BB-1284
D-IBMW	MIII	TT-536
D-IBNA	BN2	269
D-IBNB	BN2	46
D-IBNF	BN2	2205
D-IBNK	300	FA-204
D-IBOB	690C	11613
D-IBOE	680T	1620-51
D-IBOH	200	BB-463
D-IBOM	F406	0031
(D-IBOS)	690C	11689
(D-IBOS)	695	95036
D-IBOW	200	BB-451
(D-IBOY)	690C	11732
D-IBPD	E90	LW-216
D-IBPE	90	LJ-1115
D-IBPL	90	LJ-775
D-IBRA	BN2	823
D-IBSA	31T	8120033
D-IBSG	90	LJ-1760
D-IBSH	200G	BY-57
D-IBSY	200	BB-1357
D-IBTA	200G	BY-75
D-IBTU	F90	LA-106
D-IBUF	MU-2	009
D-IBUG	MU-2	011
D-IBUR	E90	LW-166
D-IBVO	200	BB-1086
D-IBVW	200	BB-202
(D-IBWB)	31T	7904022
D-ICAP	31T	8020088
D-ICAR	441	0344
D-ICAS	F406	0037
D-ICBA	F90	LA-13

D-ICBC	300	FA-227
D-ICBD	F90	LA-62
D-ICBH	31T	8120008
D-ICBW	300	FA-200
D-ICCC	**F406**	**0050**
(D-ICCE)	441	0170
(D-ICCO)	200	BB-841
D-ICDG	MU-2	1562SA
D-ICDU	31T	1166003
D-ICEK	425	0055
D-ICET	F90	LA-22
D-ICFB	MIVA	AT-058
D-ICFI	200	BB-944
D-ICGA	31T	8166056
D-ICGB	PA42	5501007
D-ICGD	31T	8004019
D-ICHG	**200**	**BB-1400**
D-ICHS	425	0233
D-ICHT	300	FA-214
D-ICID	200	BB-1209
D-ICIL	F90	LA-106
D-ICIR	200	BB-1051
D-ICIT	MIVA	AT-036
D-ICKH	441	0081
(D-ICKH)	690B	11488
D-ICKM	**200**	**BB-1005**
D-ICKS	690	11030
D-ICLE	90	LJ-1002
D-ICMC	PA42	8001039
D-ICMF	**425**	**0102**
D-ICMK	**90**	**LJ-1928**
D-ICMS	690B	11362
D-ICOA	200	BB-1065
D-ICOH	200	BB-1005
D-ICOM	425	0197
D-ICPA	31T	8120025
D-ICPD	90	LJ-150
D-ICRA	200	BB-1291
D-ICRI	441	0146
D-ICSM	200	BB-1332
D-ICSM	690B	11449
D-ICTB	425	0188
D-ICVW	MU-2	673
D-ICWD	200C	BL-49
(D-ICWM)	200C	BL-49
D-ICWM	200C	BL-49
D-IDAA	F406	0011
D-IDAF	690B	11561
D-IDAH	E90	LW-101
D-IDAK	**90**	**LJ-647**
D-IDAM	425	0148
D-IDAX	**425**	**0209**
D-IDBU	**PA42**	**5501029**
D-IDCV	**90**	**LJ-1622**
D-IDDI	31T	7920014
D-IDEA	E90	LW-103
D-IDEA	**MIII**	**T-322**
D-IDEE	MIVA	AT-051
D-IDEE	MU-2	526
D-IDEP	MIV	AT-018
(D-IDGR)	690B	11546
D-IDGR	690B	11554
D-IDHS	MIII	T-207
D-IDIA	PA42	5501055
D-IDIC	F90	LA-47
(D-IDIG)	680T	1718-89
D-IDIW	90	LJ-1263
D-IDIX	90	LJ-1495
D-IDIX	**90**	**LJ-1571**
D-IDKE	**90**	**LJ-1865**
D-IDLS	300	FA-210
D-IDLW	441	0170
D-IDMA	200	BB-75
D-IDMD	MIIB	T26-167E
D-IDOK	200	BB-1136
(D-IDOL)	200	BB-328
D-IDPL	**B100**	**BE-29**
D-IDRB	200	BB-739
D-IDRF	**200**	**BB-933**
D-IDRJ	441	0222
(D-IDRK)	200C	BL-4
(D-IDSB)	90	LJ-628
(D-IDSF)	200	BB-710
D-IDSF	PA42	8001009
D-IDSF	PA42	5501014
D-IDSM	200	BB-1259
D-IDSR	90	LJ-1093
D-IDTB	E90	LW-97
D-IDVK	**F90**	**LA-96**
D-IEAH	**90**	**LJ-1216**
D-IEAT	425	0024
D-IEBE	90	LJ-1267
D-IEBM	300	FA-217
D-IEDA	BN2	437
D-IEDB	BN2	578
(D-IEDB)	BN2	2186
D-IEDC	BN2	839
D-IEDI	**200**	**BB-1633**
(D-IEDI)	F90	LA-147
D-IEEA	31T	7620041
D-IEEE	200	BB-1215
D-IEEE	F90	LA-104
D-IEEF	PA42	5501004
D-IEFB	**200**	**BB-897**
D-IEFW	425	0228
D-IEGA	441	0193
(D-IEHD)	200	BB-707
D-IEHL	90	LJ-158
D-IEIS	31T	7904002
D-IEKG	90	LJ-867
D-IELE	BN2	425
D-IEMR	**31T**	**1104015**
D-IEMU	MU-2	348SA
D-IEPA	31T	1104017
D-IERI	B100	BE-29
(D-IESW)	31T	8166037
D-IEVO	90	LJ-1134
D-IEVV	90	LJ-347
D-IEVW	90	LJ-215
D-IEWA	441	0322
D-IEWK	MIVA	AT-042
D-IEWT	90	LJ-571
D-IEXD	200	BB-349
D-IEXP	PA42	5527030
D-IEXT	90	LJ-1089
D-IFAA	441	0197
D-IFAB	690B	11436
D-IFAC	690B	11444
D-IFAD	MIVA	AT-062-2
D-IFAG	MU-2	673
D-IFAH	MIII	T-283
D-IFAL	MIII	T-289
D-IFBN	**BN2**	**2185**
D-IFCL	90	LJ-829
D-IFCP	441	0181
D-IFDS	BN2	88
D-IFES	200	BB-827
D-IFFA	31T	8120035
D-IFFB	**300**	**FA-224**
D-IFGN	**31T**	**8120052**
D-IFHI	**90**	**LJ-977**
D-IFHZ	31T	1104016
D-IFIB	200	BB-167
(D-IFIP)	90	LJ-959
D-IFIX	690A	11163
D-IFKU	**BN2**	**2290**
D-IFLN	BN2	2128
D-IFLN	BN2	2241
D-IFLU	90	LJ-66
(D-IFLY)	425	0053
D-IFMI	**90**	**LJ-1101**
D-IFMU	MU-2	392SA
D-IFNA	425	0165
(D-IFOC)	90	LJ-1034
(D-IFOM)	90	LJ-867
D-IFOR	200	BB-555
D-IFOX	BN2	2186
D-IFPD	31T	7820010
D-IFRC	PA42	5501010
D-IFSH	PA42	8001101
D-IFSH	**PA42**	**5501014**
D-IFST	BN2	784
D-IFTC	90	LJ-513
D-IFTG	MU-2	779SA
D-IFTI	**BN2**	**2299**
D-IFUN	200	BB-575
D-IFUN	90	LJ-874
D-IFUT	**BN2**	**2300**
D-IFWR	MU-2	439SA
D-IFWZ	MIII	T-249
D-IGAA	690A	11204
(D-IGAB)	690A	11298
D-IGAD	681	6030
D-IGAF	690A	11121
D-IGAH	90	LJ-1539
D-IGAK	31T	7820051
D-IGAS	PA42	8001011
D-IGEL	690C	11616
D-IGEM	31T	8020089
D-IGEP	MIVA	AT-051
D-IGFD	MIII	TT-536
D-IGGI	441	0326
D-IGKG	31T	8020058
D-IGKN	**90**	**LJ-1077**
D-IGLB	690B	11456
D-IGLI	90	LJ-887
D-IGME	200	BB-324
D-IGOB	**P180**	**1016**
D-IGRK	**PA42**	**5527038**
D-IGRO	200	BB-424
D-IGSW	200	BB-669
D-IGSY	200	BB-1056
D-IGTW	90	LJ-266
D-IGVB	200	BB-562
D-IGVW	100	B-2
D-IHAA	441	0254
D-IHAH	90	LJ-1216
D-IHAH	**90**	**LJ-1370**
D-IHAK	P166	363
D-IHAL	P166	360
D-IHAN	200	BB-1478
D-IHAN	MU-2	396SA
D-IHAP	200	BB-1202
D-IHBL	MIII	TT-512A
D-IHBP	90	LJ-1424
D-IHCE	E90	LW-326
D-IHCH	90	LJ-435
D-IHCO	90	LJ-835
D-IHDE	90	LJ-725
(D-IHDM)	690B	11448
D-IHEB	200	BB-75
D-IHEI	100	B-89
D-IHEL	695	95010
D-IHER	BN2	377
(D-IHFS)	MU-2	007
(D-IHGH)	90	LJ-435
D-IHGO	PA42	5501027
D-IHHB	300	FA-223
D-IHHE	**90**	**LJ-1327**
(D-IHHG)	MU-2	762SA
(D-IHHH)	PA42	5527025
(D-IHHH)	PA42	5527038
(D-IHIT)	300	FA-218
D-IHJJ	31T	8004001
D-IHJK	31T	8104057
D-IHJL	31T	1104015
D-IHKC	31T	8020034
D-IHKH	690B	11541
D-IHKM	**90**	**LJ-1158**
D-IHKR	90	LJ-584
D-IHLA	**PA42**	**8301001**
D-IHMM	31T	8104066
D-IHMO	P180	1009
D-IHMS	31T	8120009
D-IHMV	**90**	**LJ-1325**
D-IHMW	90	LJ-1283
D-IHNA	90	LJ-926
D-IHOP	695A	96005
D-IHOT	P180	1011
(D-IHOW)	690C	11666
D-IHRA	P180	1019
D-IHRG	**90**	**LJ-1845**
D-IHSA	90	LJ-1099
D-IHSI	**695**	**95039**
D-IHSO	31T	7620033
D-IHSW	**90**	**LJ-1315**
D-IHUC	695	95069
D-IHUG	BN2	788
D-IHUT	200	BB-1590
D-IHVA	PA42	5501025
D-IHVB	690A	11328
D-IHVB	90	LJ-522
D-IHVF	690B	11391
D-IHVH	BN2	303
D-IHVI	31T	8020007
(D-IHYL)	31T	8104033
D-IIAA	441	0285
D-IIAH	200	BB-1741
D-IIAH	31T	1104015
D-IIAQ	PA42	5527018
D-IIBB	F90	LA-202
D-IIBS	F90	LA-206
D-IICE	**200**	**BB-269**
D-IICL	F90	LA-155
D-IIGA	425	0141
(D-IIGI)	690A	11172
D-IIHA	**90**	**LJ-562**
D-IIHW	31T	8104070
D-IIIS	90	LJ-867
D-IIKM	**90**	**LJ-1120**
(D-IIKW)	31T	8120010
D-IIKY	90	LJ-1334
D-IILG	300	FA-63
(D-IILL)	F90	LA-86
D-IIOO	31T	8020021
D-IIPA	31T	8020085
D-IIPN	31T	8004012
D-IIRC	31T	1166008
D-IIRR	31T	8120035
D-IISA	MIII	TT-471
D-IIVA	**P180**	**1125**
D-IIWB	31T	8020030
D-IIWB	**90**	**LJ-1340**
D-IIWN	90	LJ-887
D-IIXX	31T	8104066
D-IJAH	**200**	**BB-1917**
D-IJAN	BN2	22
D-IJCL	P180	1017
D-IJET	31T	7520002
D-IJET	31T	8104042
(D-IJET)	P180	1050
D-IJET	**P180**	**1056**
D-IJGW	425	0193
D-IJLF	441	0358
D-IJMZ	MU-2	779SA
D-IJOE	31T	8120068
D-IJOY	425	0164
D-IJPG	31T	7820090
D-IKAH	**200G**	**BY-50**
D-IKAH	690B	11506
D-IKAI	P180	1014
(D-IKAO)	680T	1538-5
D-IKAO	90	LJ-68
D-IKBJ	200	BB-1209
D-IKCC	90	LJ-591
(D-IKDG)	31T	8120035
D-IKES	90	LJ-942
D-IKET	**31T**	**8020017**
D-IKEW	**31T**	**7820066**
(D-IKFB)	200	BB-884
D-IKFB	200	BB-963
D-IKFC	200	BB-937
(D-IKFC)	200	BB-983
(D-IKHK)	31T	8120029
D-IKIA	90	LJ-1571
D-IKIM	**90**	**LJ-1324**
D-IKIW	90	LJ-641
D-IKKK	31T	8120004
D-IKKS	31T	8120034
D-IKKY	**MU-2**	**420SA**
D-IKLN	200	BB-1369
D-IKMS	90	LJ-1441
D-IKOA	690B	11496
D-IKOB	**200**	**BB-921**
D-IKOB	690B	11505
D-IKOC	690B	11498
(D-IKOC)	690B	11511
D-IKOM	690C	11672
D-IKOR	100	B-59
D-IKOR	90	LJ-84
D-IKRA	200	BB-668
D-IKUL	100	B-230
D-IKUS	MIIB	T26-158E
D-IKWM	300	FA-171
D-IKWP	31T	8004049
(D-ILAF)	E90	LW-339

D-ILAN	690C	11605
(D-ILAS)	690D	15012
D-ILAS	690D	15022
(D-ILAT)	690B	11429
D-ILBA	90	LJ-1068
D-ILBO	200	BB-681
D-ILCE	31T	8004053
D-ILDB	200C	BL-20
D-ILDB	90	LJ-11
D-ILET	31T	8120035
D-ILFA	BN2	2243
D-ILFB	BN2	2271
D-ILFC	BN2	2272
D-ILFD	BN2	2296
D-ILFH	BN2	2212
D-ILGA	31T	1104014
D-ILGA	90	LJ-900
(D-ILGE)	200	BB-707
D-ILGI	90	LJ-1090
D-ILGK	90	LJ-26
D-ILHA	90	LJ-509
D-ILHB	90	LJ-510
D-ILHC	90	LJ-544
D-ILHD	90	LJ-545
D-ILIB	F406	0048
D-ILIG	31T	8120068
(D-ILIM)	F406	0034
D-ILIM	F90	LA-42
D-ILIN	200	BB-545
D-ILKA	90	LJ-452
D-ILKB	90	LJ-571
(D-ILKC)	90	LJ-211
(D-ILKE)	MIVA	AT-057
D-ILLF	200	BB-1568
(D-ILMA)	200	BB-386
D-ILMA	90	LJ-48
D-ILME	90	LJ-36
D-ILMI	90	LJ-29
D-ILMO	90	LJ-119
(D-ILMO)	90	LJ-775
D-ILMP	E90	LW-289
D-ILMU	90	LJ-7
D-ILMY	90	LJ-58
D-ILNA	90	LJ-121
D-ILNE	90	LJ-68
D-ILNI	90	LJ-116
D-ILNU	90	LJ-178
D-ILNY	200	BB-309
(D-ILNY)	90	LJ-201
D-ILNY	90	LJ-209
(D-ILOC)	200	BB-1116
D-ILOH	200	BB-1080
D-ILOR	31T	7904001
D-ILPC	200	BB-524
D-ILPC	425	0131
(D-ILPC)	425	0175
D-ILPG	31T	8166049
D-ILRA	100	B-34
D-ILRA	31T	8020009
D-ILSE	MIIB	T26-163E
D-ILSW	PA42	5501015
D-ILTA	200	BB-1203
D-ILTA	90	LJ-408
D-ILTE	90	LJ-6
D-ILTI	90	LJ-14
D-ILTO	200	BB-983
D-ILTO	90	LJ-453
D-ILTP	90	LJ-407
D-ILTU	200	BB-1178
D-ILTU	90	LJ-359
D-ILTY	90	LJ-456
D-ILVV	90	LJ-96
D-ILVW	90	LJ-26
D-ILVW	90	LJ-435
D-ILWH	200	BB-624
D-ILYS	441	0355
D-IMAA	E90	LW-235
D-IMAG	690C	11635
D-IMAG	90	LJ-1130
D-IMAG	90	LJ-1833
(D-IMAS)	E90	LW-6
D-IMAX	31T	7620041
D-IMAX	441	0246
D-IMAX	PA42	8001078

(D-IMAY)	PA42	8001078
D-IMAY	PA42	5527024
D-IMBB	690A	11208
D-IMBI	E90	LW-244
D-IMCA	690A	11343
D-IMCI	200	BB-1107
D-IMDA	200	BB-940
D-IMDB	100	B-10
(D-IMDW)	300	FA-187
(D-IMED)	P180	1012
(D-IMED)	P180	1026
D-IMGI	200	BB-1565
D-IMGL	200	BB-1228
D-IMIM	PA42	8001048
D-IMKO	695	95023
D-IMLL	200	BB-386
(D-IMLP)	P180	1032
D-IMMB	300	FA-152
D-IMMC	MU-2	433SA
D-IMME	MU-2	607
D-IMMF	300	FA-164
D-IMMM	200	BB-1201
D-IMMO	F90	LA-76
(D-IMMU)	MU-2	708SA
D-IMOD	425	0178
D-IMOL	200	BB-1217
D-IMOL	695	95058
D-IMON	200	BB-276
D-IMON	680W	1819-33
(D-IMOW)	690C	11666
D-IMPC	425	0209
(D-IMPW)	90	LJ-1202
D-IMSH	100	B-72
D-IMTT	31T	7820041
D-IMTW	90	LJ-128
D-IMUC	90	LJ-797
D-IMWA	E90	LW-59
D-IMWH	F90	LA-114
D-IMWK	MIII	TT-529A
D-IMWT	690B	11488
D-INAC	E90	LW-43
D-INAF	90	LJ-579
D-INAS	90	LJ-1551
D-INAW	90	LJ-140
D-INEF	200C	BL-11
D-INEL	200C	BL-39
D-INEY	BN2	2179
D-INGA	425	0003
D-INIX	690	11013
D-INKA	200	BB-1089
D-INKA	441	0066
D-INKI	MU-2	653
D-INKY	P180	1162
D-INLE	P166	373
D-INLF	P166	402
D-INLG	P166	374
D-INMA	90	LJ-1566
D-INNN	31T	8120102
D-INOR	200	BB-2000
D-INRO	690C	11630
D-INTC	P166	413
D-INUS	F406	0043
D-INWG	425	0039
D-INWK	MIII	T-255
D-INYL	BN2	154
D-IOAN	200	BB-872
D-IOEB	300	FA-220
D-IOEB	695	95036
D-IOET	690A	11142
D-IOFC	31T	7804011
D-IOHL	441	0357
D-IOKA	31T	8166052
D-IOKG	MIII	T-322
D-IOKP	PA42	5501043
D-IOKY	31T	7820085
D-IOLA	BN2	277
D-IOLA	BN2	2187
D-IOLG	BN2	643
*D-IOLK	BN2	2306
D-IOLO	BN2	2305
D-IOLT	BN2	21
D-IOMG	90	LJ-1321
(D-IOMG)	90	LJ-1327
D-IOMM	300	FA-79

(D-IOMX)	MU-2	1563SA
D-IONE	PA42	8001002
D-IONE	PA42	5527036
D-IOOO	MIII	TT-521
D-IOPL	90	LJ-1111
D-IORC	BN2	3009
D-IORF	BN2	2020
D-IORS	BN2	641
D-IOSA	PA42	5501041
D-IOSB	PA42	5501042
D-IOSC	PA42	5501043
D-IOSD	PA42	5501044
D-IOSE	PA42	5501040
(D-IOSF)	PA42	5501051
D-IOSF	PA42	5501053
(D-IOSG)	PA42	5501052
D-IOSG	PA42	5501055
D-IOSI	MU-2	438SA
D-IOTF	MIII	T-230
D-IOTG	MU-2	711SA
(D-IOTO)	90	LJ-910
D-IOTT	31T	7620041
D-IOTT	31T	7920010
D-IOVW	200	BB-168
D-IOWA	31T	8120003
D-IOWB	300	FA-220
D-IPAP	200	BB-1999
D-IPAS	425	0224
D-IPCG	425	0177
*D-IPCI	P180	1033
D-IPEL	90	LJ-1236
D-IPIA	P180	1021
D-IPIA	P180	1156
D-IPOS	425	0120
D-IPPY	P180	1172
D-IPSY	200	BB-1591
D-IPWB	200	BB-1368
D-IQAS	PA42	5527022
D-IRAA	425	0080
D-IRAR	200	BB-1957
D-IREI	F90	LA-219
D-IRGW	425	0165
D-IRIS	F90	LA-229
(D-IRUS)	200	BB-1159
D-IRVK	31T	8004052
D-ISAG	90	LJ-1192
(D-ISAP)	P180	1020
D-ISAR	425	0214
D-ISAZ	200	BB-983
D-ISBC	90	LJ-1935
D-ISEM	90	LJ-1207
D-ISEP	31T	1166004
D-ISHY	F406	0027
D-ISIG	31T	8104055
D-ISIX	90	LJ-1355
D-ISJP	200	BB-575
D-ISMS	PA42	5527018
D-ISTB	F90	LA-227
D-ISTC	MU-2	436SA
D-ISTT	90	LJ-1869
D-ISVK	31T	7904026
D-ITAB	200	BB-1166
D-ITCH	90	LJ-1138
D-ITCN	P180	1020
(D-ITDK)	90	LJ-1865
D-ITEC	200	BB-87
D-ITFC	200	BB-1973
D-ITLL	F90	LA-192
D-ITOP	90	LJ-1606
D-ITPV	P180	1012
(D-ITRI)	PA42	5501045
D-ITRI	PA42	5501045
(D-ITTW)	441	0254
D-ITWO	PA42	5501046
D-IUCN	PA42	5527030
D-IUDE	90	LJ-1323
D-IUTA	690C	11639
(D-IUTA)	690C	11660
D-IUUU	200	BB-1221
(D-IUWM)	90	LJ-1539
D-IVAN	200	BB-1662
D-IVHM	200	BB-1369
D-IVHN	200	BB-1124
D-IVIP	200	BB-1672

D-IVIS	P68T	9002
*D-IWAL	F90	LA-100
D-IWAN	200	BB-1102
D-IWID	90	LJ-1450
D-IWKA	200	BB-1406
D-IWKA	F90	LA-218
D-IWKB	200	BB-1406
D-IWKW	690C	11665
D-IWPF	F90	LA-232
D-IWSH	200	BB-1462
D-IXIE	F90	LA-96
D-IXIE	P180	1042
D-IXXX	31T	7920002
D-IXXX	31T	1166003
D-IXXX	PA42	5501007
D-IYES	PA42	8001043
D-IYYY	PA42	5527018
D-IZAC	B100	BE-29
D-IZZY	P180	1034
D-IZZZ	200	BB-1235

Fiji

See also VQ-F

DQ-DNT	P68	42
DQ-FBO	BN2	195
DQ-FBP	BN2	614
(DQ-FBV)	BN2	89
DQ-FBY	TRIS	322
DQ-FCA	BN2	686
DQ-FCC	TRIS	391
DQ-FCE	TRIS	1004
DQ-FCF	TRIS	1008
DQ-FCG	TRIS	1010
DQ-FCN	BN2	676
DQ-FCX	BN2	833
DQ-FDS	200	BB-518
DQ-FDV	BN2	41
DQ-FDW	BN2	602
DQ-FEA	BN2	152
DQ-FEO	BN2	9
DQ-FES	BN2	411
DQ-FET	BN2	661
DQ-FFF	BN2	611
DQ-FHB	BN2	611
DQ-FHG	BN2	2230
DQ-FIC	BN2	511
DQ-FIF	BN2	417
DQ-FIN	BN2	159
DQ-JJS	BN2	856
DQ-LIR	200	BB-1902
DQ-SLM	BN2	605
DQ-TRI	TRIS	1041
DQ-YIR	BN2	845

Angola

See also CR-L

D2-	200	BB-1168
D2-	350	FL-548
D2-	PC6	715
D2-	PC6	736
D2-ALS	90	LJ-80
D2-BES	200	BB-1654
D2-EAA	690A	11132
D2-EBB	200	BB-1512
D2-EBF	200	BB-836
D2-EBG	200	BB-334
D2-ECE	BN2	903
D2-ECH	200	BB-345
D2-ECL	200	BB-44
D2-ECN	F406	0002
D2-ECO	F406	0011
D2-ECP	F406	0016
D2-ECQ	F406	0019
D2-ECW	350	FL-102
D2-ECX	200	BB-1362
D2-ECY	200C	BL-135
D2-ECZ	350	FL-59
D2-EDD	200	BB-1512
D2-EDU	MIVA	AT-057
D2-EEO	BN2	825
D2-EEP	BN2	579
D2-EEQ	BN2	580

D2-EMX	200	BB-480
D2-EOJ	200	BB-1371
D2-EQC	90	LJ-324
D2-ERK	200	BB-937
D2-ERO	200T	BT-8
D2-ESE	BN2	826
D2-ESI	BN2	827
D2-ESO	200C	BL-127
D2-ESP	200	BB-1391
D2-ESQ	200	BB-1407
D2-EST	200	BB-1348
D2-ETJ	90	LJ-1193
D2-EXB	G1	166
D2-EXC	G1	80
D2-EXD	G1	124
D2-EXW	200	BB-101
D2-FEG	200	BB-1060
D2-FEI	200	BB-620
D2-FFK	200	BB-1026
D2-FFL	200	BB-126
D2-FFO	350	FL-10
D2-FFT	200	BB-607
D2-FMD	200T	BT-18
D2-FMW	BN2	276
D2-LAA	690A	11132

Comores

D6-ECA	PA42	5501023

Spain

(EC-)	681B	6060
EC-	BN2	2157
ECT-014	90	LJ-747
EC-125	MIVA	AT-062-2
EC-177	F406	0015
EC-191	200	BB-529
EC-202	MIIB	T26-149
EC-351	200	BB-218
EC-376	G1	39
EC-424	300	FA-131
EC-433	G1	153
EC-460	G1	64
EC-461	G1	142
(EC-491)	G1	79
EC-493	G1	40
EC-494	G1	41
EC-509	MIVA	AT-038
EC-619	P180	1008
EC-676	690A	11344
EC-702	MIVA	AT-074
EC-727	200	BB-182
EC-750	BN2	2224
EC-795	200	BB-555
EC-843	BN2	161
EC-844	BN2	623
EC-860	90	LJ-382
EC-867	MIVA	AT-041
EC-939	90	LJ-382
EC-953	300	FA-122
EC-975	MIVA	AT-043
EC-BNN	90	LJ-14
EC-CDI	90	LJ-603
EC-CDJ	90	LJ-605
EC-CDK	90	LJ-608
EC-CFX	BN2	676
EC-CFY	BN2	677
EC-CHA	90	LJ-621
EC-CHB	90	LJ-623
EC-CHC	90	LJ-624
EC-CHD	100	B-193
EC-CHE	100	B-195
EC-CHK	PC6	659
EC-CKK	BN2	714
EC-CKL	BN2	715
EC-COI	90	LJ-663
EC-COJ	90	LJ-664
EC-COK	90	LJ-665
EC-COL	90	LJ-666
EC-CQL	MU-2	587
EC-CRB	690A	11252
EC-DBK	BN2	691
EC-DDS	90	LJ-747
EC-DFY	690B	11505
EC-DHE	P68	184
EC-DHF	31T	7920073
(EC-DOI)	P68	248
EC-DSA	680T	1564-20
EC-DTS	P68	324
EC-DXA	690A	11328
EC-DXG	680T	1711-86
EC-DYF	BN2	2176
EC-DYG	BN2	2180
EC-DZQ	425	0233
EC-EAG	680W	1776-14
EC-EAQ	690A	11304
EC-EBC	BN2	2153
EC-EBG	690B	11433
EC-EDE	MU-2	671
EC-EDK	MU-2	603
EC-EEE	MU-2	628
EC-EFH	690A	11130
EC-EFS	690	11034
EC-EGF	300	FA-134
EC-EIH	690A	11212
EC-EIL	690	11007
EC-EIM	31T	7904026
EC-EMZ	PC6	672
EC-ERQ	200	BB-218
EC-ESE	F406	0001
EC-ESF	F406	0007
EC-ESV	200	BB-806
EC-ETH	425	0151
EC-ETM	300	FA-131
EC-EVJ	G1	39
EC-EXB	G1	153
EC-EXQ	G1	142
EC-EXS	G1	64
EC-EZO	G1	41
EC-FFE	690A	11344
EC-FFZ	BN2	2224
EC-FIO	G1	40
EC-FIP	BN2	623
EC-FIQ	BN2	161
EC-FKL	P180	1008
EC-FLX	300	FA-122
EC-FOH	F406	0015
EC-FOT	31T	7920036
EC-FPF	TBM7	12
EC-FPH	200	BB-529
EC-FPZ	P68	221
EC-FQQ	200	BB-276
EC-FRR	690A	11185
EC-FUX	MIVA	AT-038
EC-GBB	200	BB-182
EC-GBI	MIVA	AT-041
EC-GDR	MIVA	AT-074
EC-GDV	MIVA	AT-043
EC-GFK	MIVA	AT-062-2
EC-GHS	P68	329
EC-GHZ	200	BB-555
EC-GIJ	90	LJ-382
EC-GJZ	MIIB	T26-149
EC-GLU	MU-2	626
EC-GOK	MU-2	635
EC-GOY	90	LJ-527
EC-GSQ	350	FL-128
EC-HBF	MIVA	AT-074
EC-HCQ	31T	1104017
EC-HDE	680T	1684-65
EC-HHO	200	BB-262
EC-HIZ	46D	203
EC-HMA	90	LJ-577
EC-HNH	690	11058
EC-HYF	P68	10
EC-IBK	350	FL-328
EC-IBY	PC6	815
EC-IFL	P68	412
EC-IFX	P68	204
EC-IIP	PA42	5527018
EC-IJA	MU-2	666
EC-ILE	200	BB-1792
EC-IMD	P68	67
EC-IMV	P68	290
EC-IOD	P68	229
EC-IOP	P68	424
EC-IOQ	P68	422
EC-IPG	P68	421
EC-IPZ	31T	8166056
EC-IQX	46D	55
EC-ISH	PC12	498
EC-ITV	P68	239
EC-IUV	200	BB-366
EC-IUX	200	BB-1840
EC-IVC	P68	160
EC-IVZ	46T	97170
EC-JCV	MIVA	AT-038
EC-JFO	PC12	549
EC-JGB	200	BB-1478
EC-JJP	200	BB-845
EC-JNH	P68	428
EC-JOE	PC6	705
EC-JQC	MIVA	AT-066
EC-JRF	31T	1166003
EC-JXH	PC6	700
EC-JXM	PC12	177
EC-JZJ	P68	217
EC-KBN	P68	285
EC-KBS	P68	438
EC-KDV	46T	97291
EC-KFK	PC12	513
EC-KGD	PC6	677
EC-KHR	200	BB-1564
EC-KJQ	350	FL-255
EC-KLP	PC12	513
EC-KND	200	BB-1564
EC-KNP	200	BB-561
EC-KNT	200	BB-364
EC-KPT	200	BB-753
EC-KQP	TBM8	453
EC-KQV	P68	444
EC-KTI	200	BB-1734
EC-KYY	P68	447
EC-LAU	PC6	713

Ireland

EI-AUF	BN2	151
EI-AUL	BN2	180
(EI-AVE)	BN2	623
(EI-AVO)	BN2	285
EI-AWM	BN2	653
EI-AWY	MU-2	617
EI-AYN	BN2	704
EI-BAH	681B	6060
EI-BBA	BN2	444
EI-BBL	690A	11119
EI-BBR	BN2	472
EI-BCE	BN2	519
EI-BCY	200	BB-208
EI-BFJ	200	BB-376
EI-BFL	690B	11465
EI-BFT	200	BB-438
EI-BFW	200	BB-461
EI-BGL	690B	11507
(EI-BGR)	200	BB-160
(EI-BGR)	200	BB-192
EI-BGY	200	BB-558
EI-BHA	200	BB-626
EI-BHG	200	BB-160
EI-BHL	E90	LW-321
EI-BIP	200	BB-687
(EI-BJU)	690B	11546
EI-BJY	200	BB-800
EI-BKH	P68	147
EI-BKV	200C	BL-43
EI-BLI	90	LJ-985
(EI-BME)	200C	BL-49
EI-BPC	690B	11546
EI-BWH	P68	212
EI-CCR	690D	15041
EI-CKY	F406	0018
(EI-CND)	F406	0020
EI-CRI	350	FL-66
EI-CUW	BN2	2293
EI-DMG	441	0165
EI-IAN	PC6	810
EI-IPC	BN2	2011
EI-LCM	TBM8	436
EI-TBM	TBM7	232
EI-WHE	200	BB-1569

Liberia

EL-AHX	BN2	731
EL-AHY	BN2	733
EL-AHZ	BN2	734
EL-AIB	TRIS	1011
EL-AIC	TRIS	1014
EL-AID	TRIS	1015
EL-RML	BN2	534
EL-YNA	BN2	534

Iran

EP-AFQ	BN2	618
EP-AGU	681	6012
EP-AGV	690	11045
EP-AGW	690	11047
EP-AHL	690A	11143
EP-AHM	690A	11182
EP-AHN	690A	11147
EP-AKA	681B	6065
EP-AKB	681B	6067
EP-AKI	690	11075
EP-BFR	BN2	2286
EP-FIA	680W	1849-45
EP-FIB	680W	1850-46
EP-FSS	680W	1848-44
EP-KCD	690A	11256
EP-PAC	BN2	273
EP-PAE	BN2	297
EP-PAF	BN2	655
EP-PAG	BN2	665
EP-PBE	BN2	581

Estonia

ES-PNA	BN2	48
ES-PNW	BN2T	2139
ES-SPA	P68	48

Ethiopia

ET-A	P68	133
ET-ACK	PC6	527
ET-AKA	200	BB-1220

Kyrgyzstan

EX-00003	350	FL-614

Eritrea

E3-AAJ	200	BB-1475

France

F-	200	BB-1928
F-ASFA	E90	LW-47
F-BFAD	PC6	515
F-BFRE	90	LJ-136
F-BHLG	100	B-122
F-BIEL	PC6	345
F-BIII	PC6	342
F-BINE	90	LJ-124
F-BJSZ	PC6	525
F-BKML	MIIB	T26-163E
F-BKQU	PC6	534
F-BKQY	PC6	549
F-BKRQ	PC6	548
F-BKRR	PC6	524
F-BNMC	90	LJ-149
F-BOAL	BN2	296
F-BOJJ	PC6	513

F-BOSY	90	LJ-128
F-BOSZ	PC6	636
F-BPPM	100	B-137
(F-BPQQ)	690A	11119
F-BPTT	BN2	151
F-BRNO	90	LJ-482
F-BRPJ	PC6	552
F-BRSL	MIIB	T26-154E
F-BSRP	90	LJ-493
F-BSTF	PC6	654
F-BSTM	680T	1540-6
F-BTAK	90	LJ-206
F-BTCA	90	LJ-518
F-BTCE	PC6	573
F-BTCG	PC6	551
F-BTCH	PC6	531
F-BTDP	90	LJ-560
F-BTEE	31T	7620045
F-BTFG	681B	6060
F-BTGH	BN2	649
F-BTGO	BN2	200
F-BTOK	90	LJ-32
F-BTOY	BN2	657
F-BTQP	90	LJ-40
F-BUFI	90	LJ-4
(F-BUFV)	BN2	6
(F-BUFV)	BN2	330
F-BUFV	BN2	673
(F-BUFX)	BN2	4
F-BUFX	BN2	688
(F-BUFY)	E90	LW-47
(F-BUIB)	BN2	127
F-BUID	BN2	127
F-BUOQ	BN2	6
(F-BUTN)	BN2	347
F-BUTN	BN2	377
F-BUTN	BN2	674
F-BUTS	E90	LW-68
F-BUTV	90	LJ-602
F-BUYS	90	LJ-622
F-BUYZ	E90	LW-91
F-BVET	200	BB-21
F-BVEZ	90	LJ-628
(F-BVOE)	BN2	472
F-BVOX	P68	19
F-BVRD	200	BB-44
F-BVRP	200	BB-38
F-BVRS	E90	LW-116
F-BVTB	90	LJ-579
F-BVTC	31T	7520009
F-BVTD	BN2	710
(F-BVVC)	P68	31
F-BVVM	90	LJ-26
F-BVVP	BN2	397
F-BXAP	90	LJ-522
F-BXAR	90	LJ-658
F-BXAS	690A	11240
F-BXCX	P68	163
F-BXJC	690A	11195
F-BXLC	31T	7520032
(F-BXLE)	200	BB-77
(F-BXLF)	E90	LW-151
F-BXLI	P68	43
F-BXOL	200	BB-87
F-BXOM	90	LJ-672
F-BXON	E90	LW-161
F-BXPK	E90	LW-184
F-BXPL	E90	LW-101
F-BXPU	681B	6045
F-BXPV	681B	6060
F-BXPY	90	LJ-684
F-BXSA	31T	7620008
F-BXSF	90	LJ-29
F-BXSI	200	BB-128
F-BXSK	31T	7620020
F-BXSL	90	LJ-648
F-BXSN	E90	LW-175
F-BXSR	200	BB-155
F-BXXC	P68	83
F-BYCJ	TRIS	1041
"F-CXFR"	BN2	86
F-GABV	E90	LW-102
F-GAJA	BN2	489
F-GAJC	31T	7620042
F-GAJP	200	BB-225
F-GALD	31T	7620032
F-GALN	200T	BT-1
F-GALP	200T	BT-2
F-GALZ	E90	LW-199
(F-GAME)	200	BB-260
(F-GAME)	E90	LW-215
F-GAMP	31T	7720029
F-GAMV	PC6	726
F-GAPO	E90	LW-247
(F-GAPV)	200	BB-295
F-GATR	90	LJ-735
F-GATX	P68	121
(F-GATZ)	441	0058
F-GBBA	MIVA	AT-042
(F-GBBD)	MIII	T-289
F-GBBE	690B	11436
F-GBBF	690B	11444
F-GBDY	90	LJ-795
F-GBDZ	E90	LW-295
(F-GBGI)	200	BB-399
F-GBGL	690A	11343
(F-GBLE)	200	BB-431
F-GBLG	200	BB-401
(F-GBLT)	200C	BL-1
F-GBLU	90	LJ-822
F-GBLV	E90	LW-318
F-GBLY	P68	155
F-GBOP	MIII	T-304
(F-GBOT)	200	BB-463
(F-GBPB)	441	0246
F-GBPB	90	LJ-98
(F-GBPO)	200	BB-538
F-GBPZ	90	LJ-860
F-GBRD	E90	LW-91
F-GBRP	200	BB-368
(F-GBTK)	F90	LA-15
F-GBTV	BN2	651
F-GCCC	200	BB-504
F-GCCD	P68	75
F-GCFG	31T	7920091
F-GCFH	90	LJ-127
F-GCFI	31T	7904050
F-GCGA	90	LJ-894
F-GCGG	441	0058
F-GCGX	200	BB-655
F-GCJN	E90	LW-335
F-GCJP	P68	190
F-GCJS	MU-2	406SA
F-GCJX	690B	11554
F-GCJY	690B	11561
F-GCLD	90	LJ-637
F-GCLH	31T	8020044
F-GCLS	F90	LA-50
F-GCMF	BN2	867
F-GCMJ	690B	11469
(F-GCMT)	200C	BL-12
(F-GCPN)	90	LJ-922
F-GCQK	690B	11444
F-GCQN	425	0036
(F-GCQO)	441	0246
F-GCQY	PA42	8001012
(F-GCQZ)	31T	8020088
F-GCTA	90	LJ-934
F-GCTB	F90	LA-88
(F-GCTC)	200	BB-759
F-GCTC	MIII	T-391
(F-GCTD)	200	BB-775
F-GCTP	200	BB-263
F-GCTR	F90	LA-115
F-GCTY	441	0200
F-GCVQ	200	BB-809
F-GDAK	F90	LA-141
F-GDAL	31T	7620057
F-GDAR	MU-2	1513SA
F-GDCA	200	BB-840
F-GDCB	200	BB-821
F-GDCC	90	LJ-954
F-GDCR	31T	8120034
F-GDCS	200	BB-966
F-GDCT	PC6	617
F-GDFF	200	BB-1024
(F-GDFJ)	200	BB-1049
F-GDHD	BN2	591
F-GDHS	MU-2	1532SA
F-GDHV	MU-2	779SA
(F-GDJS)	200	BB-1104
F-GDJS	200	BB-1116
F-GDLA	MU-2	370SA
F-GDLE	200	BB-230
F-GDMM	90	LJ-54
F-GDPH	MU-2	793SA
F-GDPJ	31T	7620006
F-GDRK	F406	0001
(F-GDRL)	F406	0004
F-GDRT	90	LJ-4
F-GDRY	P68	19
F-GEBC	200	BB-312
F-GEBH	31T	7720043
F-GEBK	MIII	T-272
F-GEBS	PC6	702
F-GECV	100	B-173
F-GEDV	90	LJ-150
F-GEEO	PC6	676
F-GEFR	100	B-220
F-GEFV	100	B-202
F-GEFZ	425	0059
F-GEGT	P68	297
F-GEHR	PA42	8001101
F-GEJV	100	B-129
F-GEJY	200	BB-507
F-GEJY	MIII	T-222
F-GELL	E90	LW-88
F-GELR	100	B-239
F-GEOU	90	LJ-941
F-GEPE	31T	7720031
F-GEPY	200	BB-779
F-GEQD	P68	288
F-GEQM	MU-2	790SA
F-GERA	MU-2	701SA
F-GERH	90	LJ-121
F-GERL	90	LJ-868
F-GERN	90	LJ-854
F-GERP	MIV	AT-012
F-GERS	200	BB-753
F-GESC	90	LJ-554
F-GESJ	E90	LW-97
F-GETI	F90	LA-19
F-GETJ	E90	LW-296
F-GEUD	F406	0058
F-GEUF	F406	0002
F-GEUG	F406	0067
F-GEUJ	F406	0024
(F-GEUK)	F406	0016
F-GEUL	F406	0025
(F-GEUP)	F406	0003
F-GEXK	90	LJ-331
F-GEXL	200	BB-202
F-GEXV	100	B-199
F-GFAA	200C	BL-16
F-GFBF	31T	7620054
F-GFBO	90	LJ-772
F-GFCC	PC6	572
F-GFCO	90	LJ-1098
F-GFCQ	G1	140
F-GFDC	PC6	656
F-GFDF	90	LJ-791
F-GFDJ	E90	LW-86
F-GFDK	BN2	829
F-GFDM	200	BB-610
(F-GFDM)	F90	LA-164
(F-GFDM)	MU-2	1562SA
F-GFDV	100	B-90
F-GFEA	31T	7620011
F-GFEF	G1	122
F-GFEV	100	B-213
F-GFFB	200	BB-124
F-GFFD	PC6	708
F-GFGT	G1	5
F-GFGU	G1	101
F-GFGV	G1	44
F-GFHB	MU-2	722SA
F-GFHC	90	LJ-717
F-GFHQ	90	LJ-347
F-GFHR	441	0252
F-GFIB	G1	71
F-GFIC	G1	49
F-GFID	BN2	760
F-GFIR	90	LJ-434
F-GFIV	200	BB-397
F-GFJD	90	LJ-610
F-GFJF	90	LJ-262
F-GFJM	200	BB-279
F-GFJR	425	0032
F-GFJT	200	BB-436
F-GFLD	90	LJ-741
F-GFLE	31T	7520002
F-GFLN	31T	7920069
F-GFLO	200	BB-106
(F-GFLQ)	90	LJ-496
F-GFLT	F406	1
F-GFLY	90	LJ-1065
F-GFME	90	LJ-828
F-GFMH	G1	20
F-GFMJ	200	BB-176
F-GFMS	MIII	T-296
(F-GFPI)	90	LJ-453
F-GFPR	MIVA	AT-068
F-GFPT	690B	11465
F-GFPV	31T	7820006
F-GFTA	200	BB-52
F-GFTT	200	BB-407
F-GFUM	PC6	740
F-GFUV	31T	7720063
F-GFVM	100	B-168
F-GFVN	F90	LA-166
F-GFVO	31T	7920049
(F-GFVY)	300	FA-10
F-GFVY	300	FA-10
(F-GFYI)	90	LJ-580
F-GFZM	MU-2	1562SA
F-GGAF	MIVA	AT-043
(F-GGAK)	200	BB-325
F-GGAK	200	BB-325
F-GGAM	90	LJ-32
(F-GGAN)	200	BB-477
(F-GGAR)	200	BB-1110
F-GGAR	200	BB-1110
F-GGAT	31T	7820010
F-GGBC	200	BB-424
(F-GGBT)	200	BB-51
F-GGCH	31T	8120056
F-GGDJ	200	BB-102
F-GGFB	300	FA-118
F-GGFE	100	B-63
F-GGGH	MIII	T-248
F-GGGY	G1	80
F-GGLA	200	BB-744
F-GGLD	MU-2	792SA
F-GGLG	MIVC	AT-493
F-GGLH	MIVC	AT-493
F-GGLN	200	BB-439
F-GGLV	100	B-150
F-GGMO	90	LJ-668
F-GGMS	200	BB-80
F-GGMV	200	BB-616
(F-GGPJ)	200	BB-744
F-GGPJ	31T	7820027
F-GGPR	200	BB-681
F-GGPT	200	BB-438
F-GGPV	31T	7820050
F-GGRV	31T	7720036
F-GGRZ	MU-2	395SA
(F-GGTV)	31T	7820024
F-GGTV	PA42	7800002
F-GGVG	MIII	T-293
F-GGVH	200	BB-1354
F-GGVV	200	BB-641
F-GGZV	200	BB-319
F-GHAB	PA42	8001039
(F-GHAF)	F90	LA-15
F-GHAL	200	BB-44
F-GHAS	PC6	672
F-GHAU	90	LJ-460
F-GHBB	90	LJ-510
F-GHBD	90	LJ-545
F-GHBE	200	BB-500
F-GHCS	200	BB-303
F-GHCT	200	BB-345
F-GHCU	200	BB-512
F-GHDO	90	LJ-206
F-GHDS	MU-2	693SA

F-GHEM	90	LJ-760
(F-GHEY)	200	BB-930
(F-GHFC)	90	LJ-544
F-GHFE	90	LJ-544
(F-GHFL)	200	BB-824
F-GHFM	200	BB-213
(F-GHFO)	90	LJ-858
F-GHFS	90	LJ-858
F-GHGP	F90	LA-15
F-GHGR	MIVA	AT-037
F-GHHV	100	B-91
F-GHIV	F90	LA-22
F-GHJV	31T	7720067
F-GHLA	MIVA	AT-029
F-GHLB	200	BB-349
F-GHLC	200	BB-737
F-GHLD	200	BB-233
F-GHLG	200	BB-841
F-GHLH	200	BB-333
F-GHLM	200	BB-170
F-GHLV	200	BB-300
(F-GHMH)	200	BB-986
F-GHMN	200	BB-872
F-GHMY	200	BB-930
F-GHNT	31T	7820033
F-GHNV	200	BB-791
F-GHOA	200	BB-121
F-GHOC	200	BB-406
F-GHPF	PA42	5501023
F-GHPR	200	BB-529
(F-GHRD)	90	LJ-217
F-GHRR	46D	13
F-GHSC	200	BB-876
F-GHSV	200	BB-622
(F-GHSV)	31T	8020066
F-GHTA	31T	7820015
F-GHTG	31T	7904029
F-GHTV	200	BB-603
F-GHUV	E90	LW-278
F-GHVF	MIVC	AT-423
F-GHVH	FPC6	2072
F-GHVV	200	BB-676
(F-GHXP)	200	BB-1149
F-GHXS	PC6	620
F-GHXV	200	BB-578
F-GHYV	200	BB-364
F-GIAC	MIVA	AT-036
F-GIAL	200	BB-844
(F-GIAO)	90	LJ-1303
F-GIAR	200	BB-222
F-GIAT	90	LJ-797
F-GIAX	200	BB-790
F-GIBR	90	LJ-734
F-GIBS	PA42	8001075
F-GIBV	PC6	651
F-GICA	300	FA-146
F-GICE	90	LJ-363
F-GICV	200	BB-1215
F-GIDL	90	LJ-1224
F-GIDS	PC6	584
F-GIDV	200	BB-590
F-GIEV	P68	253
F-GIFB	90	LJ-453
F-GIFC	90	LJ-456
F-GIFD	200	BB-696
F-GIFK	F90	LA-62
F-GIGP	90	LJ-311
F-GIHK	200	BB-780
F-GIHM	PC6	581
F-GIII	31T	8020037
F-GIIX	G1	128
F-GIIY	200	BB-529
F-GIJB	200	BB-13
F-GIJD	90	LJ-649
F-GILB	200	BB-477
F-GILE	200	BB-311
F-GILF	200C	BL-12
F-GILH	200	BB-431
F-GILI	200	BB-1321
F-GILJ	200	BB-711
F-GILO	200	BB-658
F-GILP	200	BB-542
F-GILU	200	BB-620
F-GILY	200	BB-1057

(F-GIMC)	200	BB-986
F-GIMD	200C	BL-11
F-GIMF	200	BB-75
F-GIML	E90	LW-180
F-GIMP	690B	11554
F-GIMU	PC6	659
F-GINB	200	BB-367
F-GIND	200	BB-822
(F-GIPH)	200	BB-433
F-GIPK	200	BB-433
F-GIPL	31T	8020091
(F-GIPV)	PA42	8001022
F-GIQC	F406	0068
F-GIQD	F406	0069
F-GIQE	F406	0071
F-GIQV	200	BB-529
F-GIRM	200	BB-399
F-GIXX	PC6	564
(F-GIYV)	31T	7920062
F-GIZB	90	LJ-955
F-GJAD	E90	LW-3
F-GJAF	200	BB-167
F-GJBC	PC6	868
F-GJBG	E90	LW-329
F-GJBJ	200C	BL-7
F-GJBP	PC6	716
F-GJBS	200	BB-1181
F-GJCD	300	FA-7
F-GJCF	200	BB-824
F-GJCR	E90	LW-251
F-GJDA	PC6	721
(F-GJDK)	31T	7720043
(F-GJDK)	90	LJ-1296
(F-GJDQ)	90	LJ-667
F-GJEB	200	BB-221
F-GJFA	200	BB-1270
F-GJFC	200	BB-1347
F-GJFD	200	BB-1379
F-GJFE	200	BB-1399
F-GJFG	PC12	256
F-GJFL	90	LJ-591
F-GJGC	G1	111
F-GJHH	300	FA-112
F-GJHM	E90	LW-316
F-GJJF	31T	7820053
F-GJJJ	100	B-196
F-GJJK	F406	0087
F-GJJN	F406	0088
F-GJJO	F406	0089
(F-GJKV)	200	BB-1321
F-GJLH	F406	0056
F-GJLI	200	BB-558
F-GJMJ	200	BB-1032
F-GJMR	200C	BL-17
F-GJPA	100	B-247
F-GJPD	200	BB-280
F-GJPE	31T	7720042
F-GJPL	31T	8120029
F-GJPY	TBM7	13
F-GJRD	90	LJ-217
F-GJRK	90	LJ-710
F-GJSD	90	LJ-1261
F-GJTS	TBM7	3
F-GKAN	200	BB-1004
F-GKBV	P68	13
F-GKCV	200	BB-251
(F-GKDG)	90	LJ-1409
(F-GKDJ)	TBM7	13
F-GKDM	PC6	670
(F-GKDO)	200	BB-1102
F-GKEL	100	B-228
F-GKES	G1	166
F-GKGH	200	BB-1221
F-GKGT	90	LJ-1250
F-GKIA	PC6	689
F-GKII	200	BB-515
(F-GKIZ)	350	FL-23
F-GKJD	E90	LW-245
F-GKJV	TBM7	11
F-GKKK	F90	LA-129
F-GKPG	TBM7	02
F-GKPL	200	BB-28
F-GKRA	F406	0042
F-GKRR	31T	8120015

F-GKSP	90	LJ-1409
(F-GKSR)	90	LJ-703
(F-GKTY)	90	LJ-339
F-GKYY	350	FL-357
F-GLBA	TBM7	2
F-GLBB	TBM7	6
F-GLBC	TBM7	18
F-GLBD	TBM7	24
F-GLBE	TBM7	1
F-GLBF	TBM7	23
F-GLBG	TBM7	107
F-GLBH	TBM7	112
F-GLBI	TBM7	118
F-GLBJ	TBM7	122
F-GLBK	TBM7	116
F-GLBL	TBM7	126
F-GLBM	TBM7	22
F-GLBN	TBM7	138
F-GLBP	TBM7	129
F-GLBQ	TBM7	244
F-GLBR	TBM7	23
F-GLBS	TBM7	174
F-GLBT	TBM7	172
F-GLBU	TBM7	217
F-GLBV	TBM7	218
F-GLBX	TBM7	220
F-GLBY	TBM7	229
F-GLBZ	TBM7	32
F-GLED	90	LJ-382
(F-GLER)	300	FA-107
F-GLEU	PC6	627
F-GLIF	200	BB-192
F-GLJD	90	LJ-1035
(F-GLJE)	TBM7	63
F-GLJS	TBM7	63
F-GLLA	90	LJ-1093
F-GLLG	31T	7920039
F-GLLH	200	BB-1109
F-GLLL	TBM7	107
F-GLLO	MIII	T-276
(F-GLOP)	200	BB-1390
F-GLPT	MIII	T-298
F-GLRA	90	LJ-1105
F-GLRP	31T	8120064
F-GLRZ	90	LJ-1296
F-GLTP	PC6	691
F-GLTX	200C	BL-16
F-GMCP	P180	1022
(F-GMCP)	P180	1024
F-GMCR	200	BB-424
F-GMCS	200	BB-688
F-GMEL	PC6	536
F-GMGB	200	BB-1390
F-GMJG	PC6	659
F-GMJK	MU-2	1528SA
F-GMJP	90	LJ-862
F-GMLP	200	BB-1049
F-GMLT	200T	BT-34
F-GMLV	TBM7	219
F-GMMA	PC6	714
F-GMPM	90	LJ-1303
F-GMPO	200	BB-307
F-GMPT	P68	62
(F-GMRM)	P180	1027
F-GMRN	E90	LW-304
F-GMTO	MIVA	AT-031
F-GMVS	PC6	518
F-GNAC	31T	8020076
F-GNAE	P180	1020
(F-GNAK)	100	B-217
F-GNBA	90	LJ-311
(F-GNCY)	90	LJ-822
F-GNEE	90	LJ-1328
F-GNEG	200	BB-1377
F-GNGU	G1	101
F-GNHI	P68	169
F-GNHP	TBM7	102
F-GNMA	90	LJ-1299
F-GNMP	90	LJ-828
F-GNOE	350	FL-183
F-GNPD	200	BB-199
F-GNUV	90	LJ-628
F-GOAE	300C	FM-1
F-GOAG	PC6	658

F-GOBR	PC6	700
F-GOBR	PC6	944
F-GOCC	PC6	667
F-GOCF	200	BB-397
F-GODZ	PC6	340
F-GOMB	PC6	819
F-GOME	PC6	543
F-GOMO	PC6	561
F-GONE	PC6	893
F-GOON	PA42	8001030
F-GOOO	300	FA-175
F-GOSB	350	FL-301
F-GOSP	PC6	699
F-GOYE	PC6	517
F-GPAC	200	BB-920
F-GPAS	200	BB-209
F-GPBF	31T	7920094
F-GPEI	P68	402
F-GPGH	350	FL-120
(F-GPJC)	90	LJ-828
F-GPJD	E90	LW-328
F-GPKL	46D	157
F-GPKN	P180	1123
F-GPKO	P180	1132
F-GPKP	P180	1165
F-GPKS	P180	1186
F-GPLK	90	LJ-1391
F-GPRA	F406	0013
F-GPRB	200	BB-283
(F-GPRG)	90	LJ-1526
F-GPRH	300	FA-226
F-GPRO	PC6	524
F-GQJD	90	LJ-667
F-GRAI	F406	0061
F-GRAJ	PC12	406
F-GRAN	200	BB-392
F-GRAZ	F406	0013
F-GRCP	FPC6	2071
F-GRLF	200	BB-1607
(F-GRLN)	F90	LA-191
F-GRNT	MIII	T-312
F-GROG	P68	288
F-GRPS	31T	7820010
F-GRSO	200C	BL-11
F-GRUB	PC6	940
F-GRVZ	PC6	901
F-GRYA	P68	279
F-GSAC	PC6	902
F-GSAR	100	B-185
F-GSAT	PC6	904
F-GSCF	TBM8	383
F-GSDM	90	LJ-1441
F-GSEB	200	BB-1110
F-GSFA	200	BB-1244
F-GSIN	200	BB-239
(F-GSJL)	90	LJ-393
F-GSJR	46D	87
F-GSLV	TBM8	419
(F-GSSD)	200	BB-531
"F-GSSY"	200	BB-531
F-GTBY	P68	43
F-GTCR	90	LJ-1660
F-GTEF	200	BB-560
F-GTEM	350	FL-80
F-GTHA	PC6	939
F-GTJM	TBM7	145
F-GTRM	90	LJ-1250
F-GTTT	PC12	247
(F-GTTT)	PC12	249
(F-GUAE)	P180	1037
F-GUAS	PC6	557
F-GUFP	200	BB-1698
F-GULJ	200	BB-561
F-GULM	90	LJ-1226
F-GULY	90	LJ-1610
(F-GUPM)	90	LJ-1209
F-GURA	F406	0061
(F-GUUU)	PC12	250
F-GUUU	PC12	299
F-GVBJ	MIII	TT-512A
(F-GVEP)	90	LJ-683
F-GVJB	PC12	359
F-GVJV	F90	LA-88
F-GVLB	350	FL-300

F-GVPC	PC6	951	F-OCTB	BN2	647	F-OHBI	TBM7	68	F-WQUQ	200	BB-431
F-GVPD	90	LJ-1321	(F-OCTB)	BN2	688	F-OHBJ	TBM7	75	F-WQVX	90	LJ-1224
F-GVPE	300	FA-94	F-OCUC	BN2	346	F-OHBK	TBM7	74	F-WRNT	MIII	T-312
F-GVRM	90	LJ-121	F-OCXC	BN2	172	F-OHBL	TBM7	69	F-WSTM	680T	1540-6
F-GVTF	PC6	915	F-OCXD	BN2	605	F-OHBM	TBM7	1	F-WTBM	TBM7	01
F-GXAB	100	B-193	F-OCXP	BN2	483	F-OHBN	TBM7	60	F-WTCR	90	LJ-1660
(F-GXAC)	PC6	710	(F-OCYP)	TRIS	1001	F-OHBP	TBM7	92	F-WVOX	P68	19
F-GXES	PA42	8001043	F-OCZE	BN2	700	F-OHBQ	TBM7	119	F-WVVC	P68	31
F-GYGL	90	LJ-1321	F-ODAQ	P68	94	F-OHBR	TBM7	120	F-WWNP	F406	0090
(F-GYMD)	200C	BL-11	F-ODBZ	P68	31	F-OHBS	TBM7	114	F-WWNP	F406	0092
F-GYRY	PC6	935	(F-ODCX)	P68	163	F-OHBT	TBM7	121	F-WWNP	F406	0093
(F-GZAT)	200	BB-561	F-ODEE	31T	7620045	F-OHBU	TBM7	113	F-WWRD	TBM8	357
F-GZBC	46D	194	F-ODGS	31T	7720041	F-OHBV	TBM7	127	F-WWRE	TBM8	346
F-GZDO	PC6	705	F-ODGU	F90	LA-88	F-OHBY	TBM7	161	F-WWRI	TBM7	196
F-GZJM	MIII	T-264	F-ODHO	BN2	867	F-OHBZ	TBM7	166	F-WWRI	TBM7	220
F-GZPE	P180	1064	F-ODHU	P68	133	F-OHCP	200	BB-831	F-WWRI	TBM7	243
F-GZRA	TBM7	256	F-ODHV	P68	142	F-OHCT	P68	13	F-WWRI	TBM7	244
F-GZRB	TBM7	166	F-ODID	E90	LW-97	F-OHEV	TBM7	52	F-WWRI	TBM7	269
F-GZRC	TBM7	312	(F-ODJP)	441	0264	F-OHFY	BN2	829	F-WWRJ	TBM7	192
*F-GZZB	E90	LW-296	F-ODJS	31T	7920056	F-OHJE	690A	11146	F-WWRJ	TBM7	221
F-HAAA	E90	LW-175	F-ODJV	BN2	397	F-OHJK	200	BB-1544	F-WWRJ	TBM7	246
F-HAAG	200	BB-722	F-ODKO	31T	7920069	F-OHJL	200	BB-1592	F-WWRJ	TBM7	312
(F-HAAG)	F90	LA-62	(F-ODMM)	31T	8020080	F-OHQO	PC6	924	F-WWRJ	TBM8	388
F-HACJ	350	FL-582	F-ODMM	31T	8020084	(F-OHQW)	BN2	3009	F-WWRJ	TBM8	407
(F-HADA)	200	BB-515	F-ODMQ	90	LJ-460	F-OHQX	BN2	3009	F-WWRJ	TBM8	434
F-HADR	90	LJ-1583	F-ODRR	46D	13	F-OHQY	BN2	2251	F-WWRK	TBM7	126
F-HALE	P180	1060	F-ODRZ	MU-2	415SA	F-OHRT	300	FA-226	F-WWRK	TBM7	180
F-HALF	P180	1112	F-ODSF	BN2	740	F-OIAA	200	BB-932	F-WWRK	TBM7	197
F-HAMI	200	BB-1874	(F-ODUA)	200	BB-690	F-OIAN	200	BB-1220	F-WWRK	TBM7	201
F-HANN	PC12	887	F-ODUA	200	BB-831	F-OIAR	BN2T	2287	F-WWRK	TBM7	222
F-HARC	90	LJ-1900	F-ODUJ	441	0264	F-OIAV	31T	8475001	F-WWRK	TBM7	249
F-HARR	200	BB-1898	F-ODUK	441	0270	F-OIJS	BN2	2294	F-WWRK	TBM7	291
(F-HASI)	MU-2	1515SA	F-ODUP	BN2	2219	F-OIJU	BN2	2291	F-WWRK	TBM8	435
*F-HAYP	90	LJ-1334	F-ODUQ	BN2	2220	F-OIKA	TBM7	172	F-WWRL	TBM7	127
F-HBAI	P180	1110	F-ODUR	BN2	2217	F-OIKC	TBM7	199	F-WWRL	TBM7	129
F-HBCF	TBM7	321	F-ODYF	BN2	309	F-OIKD	TBM7	344	F-WWRL	TBM7	205
F-HBGA	TBM8	349	F-ODYR	200	BB-716	F-OIKE	TBM7	208	F-WWRL	TBM7	292
F-HBGB	TBM7	185	F-ODYZ	F406	0057	F-OIKF	TBM7	212	F-WWRL	TBM7	318
F-HBGC	TBM7	3	F-ODZE	200	BB-490	F-OIKG	TBM7	225	F-WWRL	TBM8	408
F-HBGD	TBM8	389	F-ODZK	200	BB-1390	F-OIKH	TBM7	232	F-WWRL	TBM8	432
F-HBGE	TBM8	460	F-ODZL	200	BB-222	(F-OIKI)	TBM7	233	F-WWRM	TBM7	130
F-HBGG	TBM7	166	F-OGDR	BN2	37	F-OIKI	TBM8	397	F-WWRM	TBM7	195
F-HBGH	TBM8	503	F-OGEB	BN2	51	F-OIKJ	TBM7	237	F-WWRM	TBM7	245
F-HBRU	200	BB-1561	F-OGFA	BN2	186	F-OIKL	TBM7	299	F-WWRM	TBM7	248
F-HBSF	PC6	949	F-OGFO	BN2	197	F-OIKM	TBM7	345	F-WWRM	TBM7	326
(F-HBZZ)	46T	97047	F-OGFY	BN2	268	F-OIKN	TBM8	391	F-WWRM	TBM8	385
F-HCPE	P180	1144	F-OGGA	BN2	310	F-OIKQ	TBM8	422	F-WWRN	TBM7	157
F-HDCS	90	LJ-1066	F-OGGL	BN2	680	F-OINC	200	BB-1244	F-WWRN	TBM7	247
F-HDEY	PC6	735	F-OGGP	BN2	369	F-OIPB	PC6	661	F-WWRN	TBM8	365
F-HDGC	90	LJ-1430	F-OGGS	TRIS	1013	F-OIQK	200C	BL-149	F-WWRO	TBM7	124
F-HDJM	200G	BY-55	F-OGHA	BN2	454	F-OIQL	200C	BL-148	F-WWRO	TBM7	132
F-HELO	TBM7	229	F-OGHF	P68	58	F-OIQM	200	BB-1934	F-WWRO	TBM7	176
F-HFLC	PC6	798	F-OGHG	BN2	3	F-OIQY	350	FL-566	F-WWRO	TBM7	232
F-HHAM	90	LJ-1361	F-OGHL	BN2	283	(F-OITA)	P68	365	F-WWRO	TBM7	240
F-HIGH	TBM7	217	F-OGID	BN2	296	(F-OITB)	P68	302	F-WWRO	TBM7	300
F-HJCM	90	LJ-1098	F-OGIN	P68	83	(F-OITC)	P68	280	F-WWRO	TBM8	436
F-HJPD	350	FL-173	F-OGNV	BN2	352	F-OJGL	TBM8	442	F-WWRP	TBM7	128
F-HJPM	200	BB-1887	F-OGOG	F406	0026	F-OPCL	P68	142	F-WWRP	TBM7	133
F-HOPE	TBM7	218	F-OGOI	TRIS	1037	F-ORCE	200	BB-80	F-WWRP	TBM7	171
F-HSFA	200G	BY-16	F-OGOR	TRIS	1049	F-OSPJ	F406	0091	F-WWRP	TBM7	177
F-HSYN	200G	BY-23	F-OGOV	BN2	399	F-OTAG	BN2	760	F-WWRP	TBM7	251
F-HTCR	90	LJ-1887	F-OGOX	90	LJ-668	F-WDHS	MU-2	1532SA	F-WWRP	TBM7	299
F-HUBG	P68	278	F-OGPQ	200	BB-192	F-WDRL	F406	0004	F-WWRP	TBM8	386
F-OACR	P68	81	F-OGPX	F406	0058	F-WFLQ	31T	8120064	F-WWRP	TBM8	430
F-OAEK	P68	89	F-OGQK	200	BB-1408	F-WIVD	F406	0004	F-WWRP	TBM8	437
F-OBSN	BN2	657	F-OGRZ	90	LJ-1296	F-WJRD	90	LJ-217	F-WWRQ	TBM7	253
F-OBZJ	PC6	520	F-OGSM	BN2	688	F-WKDL	TBM7	03	F-WWRQ	TBM8	438
F-OCBD	PC6	533	F-OGUG	F406	0060	F-WKPG	TBM7	02	F-WWRR	TBM7	134
F-OCFQ	BN2	104	F-OGUI	F406	0063	F-WKRA	F406	0042	F-WWRR	TBM7	164
F-OCFR	BN2	110	F-OGUY	90	LJ-1250	F-WKTY	90	LJ-339	F-WWRR	TBM8	374
F-OCFS	BN2	112	F-OGVN	P68	155	F-WKVR	200T	BT-20	F-WWRR	TBM8	387
F-OCMN	BN2	43	F-OGVS	F406	0061	F-WKVS	200T	BT-21	F-WWRR	TBM8	406
F-OCMO	BN2	52	F-OGVX	P68	39	F-WNAK	100	B-217	F-WWRR	TBM8	431
F-OCOY	BN2	131	F-OGXA	BN2	788	F-WNGF	TBM7	118	F-WWSR	F406	0013
F-OCOZ	BN2	136	F-OGXB	BN2	303	F-WNGN	TBM7	114	F-WWSR	F406	0031
F-OCPY	BN2	196	F-OGXM	PC6	915	F-WNGO	TBM7	23	F-WWSR	F406	0080
F-OCQH	BN2	626	F-OHAU	690A	11146	F-WNGU	TBM7	6	F-WWSR	F406	0081
F-OCQV	PC6	656	F-OHBA	TBM7	4	F-WQAY	F406	0010	F-WWSR	F406	0086
F-OCRA	BN2	609	F-OHBB	TBM7	8	F-WQCC	90	LJ-382	F-WWSS	F406	0082
F-OCRB	BN2	611	F-OHBD	TBM7	12	F-WQFA	F406	0073	F-WWSS	F406	0087
F-OCRG	BN2	220	F-OHBE	TBM7	20	F-WQHL	P68	13	F-WWST	F406	0083
F-OCRH	BN2	221	F-OHBF	TBM7	22	F-WQHQ	MIII	T-276	F-WWST	F406	0088
F-OCSB	BN2	292	F-OHBG	TBM7	38	F-WQUD	F406	0008	F-WWSU	F406	0084
(F-OCSB)	BN2	647	F-OHBH	TBM7	52	F-WQUD	F406	0043	F-WWSU	F406	0089

F-WWSV	F406	0085
F-WWSV	F406	0090
F-WXAS	690A	11240
F-WZDD	F406	0001
F-WZDD	F406	0002
F-WZDJ	F406	0003
F-WZDN	F406	0055
F-WZDP	F406	0057
F-WZDR	F406	0019
F-WZDR	F406	0024
F-WZDR	F406	0028
F-WZDR	F406	0031
F-WZDR	F406	0033
F-WZDR	F406	0038
F-WZDS	F406	0005
F-WZDS	F406	0009
F-WZDS	F406	0014
F-WZDS	F406	0020
F-WZDS	F406	0029
F-WZDS	F406	0039
F-WZDS	F406	0050
F-WZDT	F406	0007
F-WZDT	F406	0011
F-WZDT	F406	0021
F-WZDT	F406	0022
F-WZDT	F406	0030
F-WZDT	F406	0037
F-WZDT	F406	0045
F-WZDT	F406	0066
F-WZDU	F406	0012
F-WZDU	F406	0023
F-WZDU	F406	0032
F-WZDU	F406	0046
F-WZDV	F406	0013
F-WZDV	F406	0025
F-WZDV	F406	0033
F-WZDV	F406	0040
F-WZDV	F406	0047
F-WZDX	F406	0015
F-WZDX	F406	0027
F-WZDX	F406	0034
F-WZDX	F406	0041
F-WZDX	F406	0048
F-WZDX	F406	0076
F-WZDY	F406	0016
F-WZDY	F406	0035
F-WZDY	F406	0078
F-WZDZ	F406	0018
F-WZDZ	F406	0036
F-WZDZ	F406	0044
F-WZDZ	F406	0077
F-WZDZ	F406	0079
F-WZIG	E90	LW-97
F-WZIJ	F406	0023
F-WZLT	F406	1
F-YDNB	E121	121083
F-YDNC	E121	121068
F-ZBAB	**F406**	**0025**
F-ZBBB	**F406**	**0039**
F-ZBBF	90	LJ-518
F-ZBCE	**F406**	**0042**
F-ZBCF	**F406**	**0077**
F-ZBCG	**F406**	**0066**
F-ZBCH	**F406**	**0075**
F-ZBCI	**F406**	**0070**
F-ZBCJ	**F406**	**0074**
F-ZBEO	F406	0004
F-ZBEP	**F406**	**0006**
F-ZBES	**F406**	**0017**
F-ZBFA	**F406**	**1**
F-ZBFZ	31T	8120064
F-ZBGA	**F406**	**0086**
(F-ZBGB)	F406	0090
F-ZBGD	**F406**	**0090**
F-ZBGE	**F406**	**0061**
F-ZVMN	**TBM7**	**106**

United Kingdom

G-4-8	BN2	8
G-4-9	BN2	9
G-4-10	BN2	140
G-51-1	BN2	8
G-51-2	BN2	13
G-51-3	BN2	14
G-51-4	BN2	16
G-51-5	BN2	22
G-51-6	BN2	31
G-51-7	BN2	38
G-51-8	BN2	39
G-51-9	BN2	40
G-51-10	BN2	41
G-51-11	BN2	42
G-51-12	BN2	43
G-51-13	BN2	44
G-51-14	BN2	45
G-51-15	BN2	51
G-51-16	BN2	59
G-51-17	BN2	73
G-51-18	BN2	75
G-51-19	BN2	78
G-51-20	BN2	79
G-51-21	BN2	80
G-51-22	BN2	81
G-51-23	BN2	83
G-51-24	BN2	87
G-51-25	BN2	88
G-51-26	BN2	90
G-51-27	BN2	91
G-51-28	BN2	92
G-51-29	BN2	94
G-51-30	BN2	95
G-51-31	BN2	96
G-51-32	BN2	97
G-51-33	BN2	98
G-51-34	BN2	99
G-51-35	BN2	100
G-51-36	BN2	101
G-51-37	BN2	103
G-51-38	BN2	105
G-51-39	BN2	106
G-51-40	BN2	107
G-51-41	BN2	111
G-51-42	BN2	112
G-51-43	BN2	114
G-51-44	BN2	117
G-51-45	BN2	118
G-51-46	BN2	116
G-51-47	BN2	121
G-51-48	BN2	122
G-51-49	BN2	125
G-51-50	BN2	127
G-51-51	BN2	128
G-51-52	BN2	129
G-51-53	BN2	131
G-51-54	BN2	134
G-51-55	BN2	135
G-51-56	BN2	136
G-51-57	BN2	138
G-51-58	BN2	137
G-51-59	BN2	140
G-51-60	BN2	142
G-51-61	BN2	141
G-51-62	BN2	143
G-51-63	BN2	145
G-51-64	BN2	144
G-51-65	BN2	139
G-51-66	BN2	147
G-51-67	BN2	148
G-51-68	BN2	149
G-51-150	BN2	150
G-51-151	BN2	151
G-51-152	BN2	152
G-51-153	BN2	153
G-51-154	BN2	154
G-51-155	BN2	155
G-51-156	BN2	156
G-51-157	BN2	157
G-51-158	BN2	158
G-51-159	BN2	159
G-51-160	BN2	160
G-51-161	BN2	161
G-51-162	BN2	162
G-51-163	BN2	163
G-51-164	BN2	164
G-51-165	BN2	165
G-51-166	BN2	166
G-51-167	BN2	167
G-51-168	BN2	168
G-51-169	BN2	169
G-51-170	BN2	170
G-51-171	BN2	171
G-51-172	BN2	172
G-51-173	BN2	173
G-51-174	BN2	174
G-51-175	BN2	175
G-51-176	BN2	176
G-51-177	BN2	177
G-51-178	BN2	178
G-51-179	BN2	179
G-51-180	BN2	180
G-51-181	BN2	181
G-51-182	BN2	182
G-51-183	BN2	183
G-51-184	BN2	184
G-51-185	BN2	185
G-51-186	BN2	186
G-51-187	BN2	187
G-51-188	BN2	188
G-51-189	BN2	189
G-51-190	BN2	190
G-51-191	BN2	191
G-51-192	BN2	192
G-51-193	BN2	193
G-51-194	BN2	194
G-51-195	BN2	195
G-51-196	BN2	196
G-51-197	BN2	197
G-51-198	BN2	198
G-51-199	BN2	199
G-51-200	BN2	200
G-51-201	BN2	201
G-51-202	BN2	202
G-51-203	BN2	203
G-51-204	BN2	204
G-51-205	BN2	205
G-51-206	BN2	206
G-51-207	BN2	207
G-51-208	BN2	208
G-51-209	BN2	209
G-51-210	BN2	210
G-51-211	BN2	211
G-51-212	BN2	212
G-51-213	BN2	213
G-51-214	BN2	214
G-51-215	BN2	215
G-51-216	BN2	216
G-51-217	BN2	217
G-51-218	BN2	218
G-51-219	BN2	219
G-51-220	BN2	220
G-51-221	BN2	221
G-51-222	BN2	222
G-51-223	BN2	223
G-51-224	BN2	224
G-51-225	BN2	225
G-51-226	BN2	226
G-51-227	BN2	227
G-51-228	BN2	228
G-51-229	BN2	229
G-51-230	BN2	230
G-51-231	BN2	231
G-51-232	BN2	232
G-51-233	BN2	233
G-51-234	BN2	234
G-51-235	BN2	235
G-51-236	BN2	236
G-51-237	BN2	237
G-51-238	BN2	238
G-51-239	BN2	239
G-51-240	BN2	240
G-51-241	BN2	241
G-51-242	BN2	242
G-51-243	BN2	243
G-51-244	BN2	244
G-51-245	TRIS	245
G-51-246	BN2	246
G-51-247	BN2	247
G-51-248	BN2	248
G-51-249	BN2	249
G-51-250	BN2	250
G-51-251	BN2	251
G-51-252	BN2	252
G-51-253	BN2	253
G-51-254	BN2	254
G-51-255	BN2	255
G-51-256	BN2	256
G-51-257	BN2	257
G-51-258	BN2	258
G-51-259	BN2	259
G-51-260	BN2	260
G-51-261	BN2	261
G-51-262	TRIS	262
G-51-263	BN2	263
G-51-264	BN2	264
G-51-265	BN2	265
G-51-266	BN2	266
G-51-267	BN2	267
G-51-268	BN2	268
G-51-269	BN2	269
G-51-270	BN2	270
G-51-271	BN2	271
G-51-272	BN2	272
G-51-273	BN2	273
G-51-274	BN2	274
G-51-275	BN2	275
G-51-276	BN2	276
G-51-277	BN2	277
G-51-278	BN2	278
G-51-280	BN2	280
G-51-281	BN2	281
G-51-282	BN2	282
G-51-283	BN2	283
G-51-284	BN2	284
G-51-285	BN2	285
G-51-286	BN2	286
G-51-287	BN2	287
G-51-288	BN2	288
G-51-289	BN2	289
G-51-290	BN2	290
G-51-291	BN2	291
G-51-292	BN2	292
G-51-293	BN2	293
G-51-294	BN2	294
G-51-295	BN2	295
G-51-296	BN2	296
G-51-297	BN2	297
G-51-298	BN2	298
G-51-299	TRIS	299
G-51-300	BN2	300
G-51-301	BN2	301
G-51-302	BN2	302
G-51-303	BN2	303
G-51-304	BN2	304
G-51-305	TRIS	305
G-51-306	BN2	306
G-51-307	BN2	307
G-51-308	BN2	308
G-51-309	BN2	309
G-51-310	BN2	310
G-51-312	BN2	312
G-51-319	TRIS	319
G-51-320	TRIS	320
G-51-325	BN2	325
G-51-347	BN2	347
G-51-349	TRIS	349
G-51-369	BN2	369
G-51-377	BN2	377
G-51-572	BN2	572
G-51-583	BN2	583
G-51-616	BN2	616
G-51-2003	BN2	2003
G-51-2017	BN2	2017
G-51-2020	BN2	2020
G-51-2115	BN2T	2115
G-51-2156	BN2	2156
G-51-2180	BN2	2180
G-51-2201	BN2T	2201
G-APSJ	P166	354
G-APVE	P166	355
G-APWY	**P166**	**362**
G-APXK	P166	364
G-APYP	P166	365
G-ARUJ	P166	376
G-ASPC	P166	412

G-ASTO	PC6	541
G-ASXT	G1	135
G-ATCT	BN2	1
(G-ATGB)	90	LJ-80
G-ATWU	TRIS	2
G-AUTO	441	0078
G-AVCN	**BN2**	**3**
G-AVKC	BN2	4
G-AVOS	BN2	5
G-AVRA	BN2	6
G-AVRB	BN2	7
G-AVRC	BN2	8
G-AVSM	P166	416
G-AVUB	BN2	9
G-AVUC	BN2	10
G-AVXO	BN2	11
G-AVXP	BN2	12
(G-AVXR)	BN2	13
G-AVXS	BN2	14
G-AVXT	BN2	15
(G-AVXU)	BN2	16
G-AWBY	BN2	17
G-AWBZ	BN2	18
G-AWCA	BN2	19
G-AWCB	BN2	20
G-AWCC	BN2	21
G-AWDS	PC6	616
(G-AWHZ)	BN2	22
G-AWIA	BN2	23
G-AWIB	BN2	24
G-AWIC	BN2	25
G-AWID	BN2	26
G-AWIE	BN2	27
G-AWNR	BN2	30
(G-AWNS)	BN2	31
G-AWNT	**BN2**	**32**
G-AWNU	BN2	33
G-AWNV	BN2	34
(G-AWNW)	BN2	35
(G-AWNX)	BN2	36
G-AWNY	BN2	37
(G-AWNZ)	BN2	38
(G-AWOD)	BN2	39
G-AWPM	90	LJ-417
G-AWVX	BN2	47
G-AWVY	BN2	48
G-AWWJ	P166	406
G-AWWK	90	LJ-446
G-AWXK	680T	1540-6
G-AWXL	680T	1532-2
(G-AWYA)	BN2	54
G-AWYF	G1	48
G-AWYW	BN2	55
G-AXBA	BN2	51
G-AXDH	BN2	70
G-AXFC	BN2	76
G-AXFE	90	LJ-481
G-AXFL	BN2	73
G-AXGB	BN2	75
G-AXHE	BN2	86
G-AXHY	BN2	601
G-AXIN	BN2	79
G-AXKB	BN2	95
(G-AXKC)	BN2	97
G-AXLY	BN2	91
G-AXMZ	BN2	105
G-AXND	BN2	602
(G-AXNF)	BN2	96
G-AXPE	BN2	117
G-AXPY	BN2	111
G-AXRJ	BN2	123
G-AXRM	BN2	128
G-AXRN	BN2	129
G-AXSN	BN2	81
G-AXSS	BN2	603
G-AXST	BN2	604
G-AXSU	BN2	605
G-AXUB	**BN2**	**121**
G-AXUD	BN2	132
G-AXUS	BN2	606
G-AXUT	BN2	607
G-AXUU	BN2	608
G-AXVP	BN2	127
G-AXVR	BN2	139
G-AXWG	BN2	135
G-AXWH	BN2	137
G-AXWI	BN2	609
G-AXWJ	BN2	610
G-AXWK	BN2	124
G-AXWO	BN2	140
G-AXWP	BN2	147
G-AXWR	BN2	149
G-AXWS	BN2	152
G-AXXF	BN2	134
G-AXXG	BN2	143
G-AXXH	BN2	144
G-AXXI	BN2	148
G-AXXJ	BN2	150
G-AXXK	BN2	151
G-AXYL	BN2	155
G-AXYM	BN2	156
G-AXYN	BN2	157
G-AXYP	BN2	158
G-AXYR	BN2	159
G-AXYS	BN2	164
G-AXYT	BN2	165
G-AXZK	**BN2**	**153**
G-AXZY	BN2	611
G-AXZZ	BN2	612
G-AYAX	BN2	613
G-AYAY	BN2	614
G-AYAZ	BN2	615
G-AYBA	BN2	616
G-AYBB	BN2	617
G-AYBI	BN2	145
G-AYBL	BN2	154
G-AYBM	BN2	162
G-AYBN	BN2	167
G-AYCD	BN2	168
G-AYCU	BN2	169
G-AYCV	BN2	170
G-AYCW	BN2	171
G-AYCX	BN2	172
G-AYCY	BN2	173
G-AYDL	BN2	174
G-AYDM	BN2	179
G-AYGF	BN2	193
G-AYGH	BN2	618
G-AYGI	BN2	619
G-AYGJ	BN2	620
G-AYGK	BN2	621
G-AYGL	BN2	622
G-AYGS	BN2	182
G-AYGT	BN2	183
G-AYGU	BN2	190
G-AYGV	BN2	191
G-AYGW	BN2	192
G-AYGY	100	B-79
G-AYHK	BN2	194
G-AYHL	BN2	195
G-AYIS	BN2	205
G-AYIV	BN2	118
G-AYIW	BN2	125
G-AYJE	BN2	623
G-AYJF	BN2	624
G-AYJG	BN2	625
G-AYJH	BN2	626
G-AYJI	BN2	627
G-AYJJ	BN2	628
G-AYJK	BN2	629
G-AYJL	BN2	630
G-AYKP	BN2	207
G-AYKR	BN2	217
G-AYLR	BN2	197
G-AYLS	BN2	227
G-AYLW	100	B-80
G-AYMB	BN2	200
G-AYMC	BN2	204
G-AYNH	BN2	213
G-AYNI	BN2	216
G-AYNT	BN2	631
G-AYNU	BN2	632
G-AYNV	BN2	633
G-AYNW	BN2	634
G-AYNX	BN2	635
G-AYNY	BN2	636
G-AYNZ	BN2	637
G-AYOA	BN2	638
G-AYOB	BN2	639
G-AYOC	BN2	640
G-AYON	BN2	226
G-AYOO	BN2	247
G-AYPL	BN2	253
G-AYPX	BN2	271
"G-AYPX"	TRIS	245
G-AYRU	**BN2**	**181**
(G-AYRV)	BN2	233
(G-AYRW)	BN2	272
G-AYRX	BN2	273
G-AYSM	BN2	641
G-AYSN	BN2	642
G-AYSO	BN2	643
G-AYSP	BN2	644
G-AYSR	BN2	645
G-AYSS	BN2	646
G-AYST	BN2	647
G-AYSU	BN2	648
G-AYSV	BN2	649
G-AYSW	BN2	650
G-AYTS	BN2	235
G-AYTU	TRIS	245
G-AYTX	680T	1709-84
G-AYWI	TRIS	262
G-AYWJ	BN2	276
G-AYXC	BN2	651
G-AYXD	BN2	652
G-AYXE	BN2	653
G-AYXF	BN2	654
G-AYXG	BN2	655
G-AYXH	BN2	656
G-AYXI	BN2	657
G-AYXJ	BN2	658
G-AYXK	BN2	659
G-AYXL	BN2	660
G-AYYA	BN2	278
G-AYYB	BN2	281
G-AYYP	BN2	243
G-AYYV	BN2	219
G-AYYW	BN2	277
G-AYZR	TRIS	279
G-AZAX	BN2	241
G-AZBM	90	LJ-532
G-AZBV	BN2	285
G-AZCG	BN2	288
G-AZDL	BN2	661
G-AZDM	BN2	662
G-AZDN	BN2	663
G-AZDO	BN2	664
G-AZDP	BN2	665
G-AZDR	BN2	666
G-AZDS	BN2	667
G-AZDT	BN2	668
G-AZDU	BN2	669
G-AZDV	BN2	670
G-AZEH	BN2	289
G-AZEI	BN2	291
G-AZFG	TRIS	299
G-AZGG	90	LJ-543
G-AZGN	BN2	671
G-AZGO	BN2	672
G-AZGP	BN2	673
G-AZGR	BN2	674
G-AZGS	BN2	675
G-AZGT	BN2	676
G-AZGU	BN2	677
G-AZGV	BN2	678
G-AZGW	BN2	679
G-AZGX	BN2	680
G-AZJA	TRIS	305
G-AZLI	BN2	297
G-AZLJ	TRIS	319
G-AZPU	BN2	298
G-AZRJ	BN2	681
G-AZUR	BN2	302
G-AZUS	BN2	303
G-AZXN	BN2	682
G-AZXO	BN2	683
G-AZXP	BN2	684
G-AZXR	BN2	685
G-AZXS	BN2	686
G-AZXT	BN2	687
G-AZXU	BN2	688
G-AZXV	BN2	689
G-AZXW	BN2	690
G-AZXX	BN2	691
G-AZXY	BN2	692
G-AZXZ	BN2	693
G-AZZM	TRIS	321
G-BAAE	BN2	308
G-BAAM	E90	LW-28
G-BABW	E90	LW-25
G-BABX	100	B-141
G-BADK	BN2	309
G-BAFE	BN2	311
G-BAFF	TRIS	322
G-BAJP	BN2	313
G-BAJS	BN2	314
G-BAKZ	BN2	188
G-BALO	BN2	316
G-BALV	BN2	315
G-BANJ	BN2	317
G-BANL	BN2	318
G-BANM	BN2	356
G-BANN	BN2	357
G-BASA	TRIS	349
G-BASW	BN2	275
G-BATK	BN2	325
G-BATL	BN2	327
G-BATZ	BN2	358
G-BAUS	BN2	328
G-BAUT	BN2	329
G-BAVE	100	B-171
G-BAVG	E90	LW-59
G-BAVT	BN2	180
G-BAXA	BN2	330
G-BAXB	BN2	332
G-BAXC	BN2	334
G-BAXD	TRIS	359
G-BAYD	BN2	700
G-BAYE	BN2	699
G-BAYF	BN2	698
G-BAYG	BN2	697
G-BAYH	BN2	696
G-BAYI	BN2	695
G-BAYJ	BN2	694
G-BAZW	BN2	333
G-BAZX	BN2	335
G-BAZY	BN2	336
G-BAZZ	BN2	337
G-BBAL	BN2	338
G-BBAM	BN2	339
G-BBAN	BN2	340
G-BBAO	BN2	341
G-BBBG	BN2	374
G-BBBH	BN2	375
G-BBDW	BN2	342
G-BBDX	BN2	343
G-BBDY	BN2	344
G-BBDZ	BN2	345
G-BBFG	BN2	701
G-BBFH	BN2	702
G-BBFI	BN2	703
G-BBFJ	BN2	704
G-BBFK	BN2	705
G-BBFM	BN2	706
G-BBFN	BN2	707
G-BBFO	BN2	708
G-BBFP	BN2	709
G-BBFR	BN2	710
G-BBGV	BN2	346
G-BBIZ	BN2	348
G-BBJA	BN2	351
G-BBJC	BN2	352
G-BBKM	E90	LW-83
G-BBKN	90	LJ-614
G-BBLW	BN2	354
G-BBLX	BN2	355
G-BBLY	BN2	364
G-BBLZ	BN2	365
G-BBMA	BN2	367
G-BBMC	BN2	376
G-BBNL	TRIS	350
G-BBON	BN2	368
G-BBRM	BN2	370
G-BBRP	BN2	371
G-BBUA	BN2	377

G-BBUB	BN2	378	G-BCNF	BN2	736	G-BDGE	TRIS	1014	G-BDTD	BN2	792
G-BBUC	BN2	379	G-BCNG	BN2	737	G-BDGF	TRIS	1015	G-BDTE	BN2	793
G-BBVK	90	LJ-631	G-BCNH	BN2	738	G-BDGG	TRIS	1016	G-BDTF	BN2	794
G-BBVL	100	B-199	G-BCNI	BN2	739	G-BDHE	BN2	465	G-BDTG	BN2	795
G-BBVM	100	B-201	G-BCNJ	BN2	740	G-BDHF	BN2	467	G-BDTH	BN2	796
G-BBWO	TRIS	360	G-BCNK	TRIS	1001	G-BDHG	BN2	468	G-BDTI	BN2	797
G-BBWP	TRIS	361	G-BCNL	TRIS	1002	G-BDHH	BN2	469	G-BDTJ	BN2	798
G-BBWR	TRIS	362	G-BCNM	TRIS	1003	G-BDHI	BN2	470	G-BDTK	BN2	799
G-BBWS	BN2	380	G-BCNN	TRIS	1004	G-BDHN	BN2	761	G-BDTM	BN2	800
G-BBWT	BN2	382	G-BCNO	TRIS	1005	G-BDHO	BN2	762	**G-BDTN**	**TRIS**	**1026**
G-BBWU	BN2	383	G-BCNT	P68	23	G-BDHP	BN2	763	**G-BDTO**	**TRIS**	**1027**
G-BBWV	BN2	384	G-BCPO	P68	27	G-BDHR	BN2	764	G-BDTP	TRIS	1028
G-BBWW	BN2	385	(G-BCPP)	P68	28	G-BDHS	BN2	765	G-BDTR	TRIS	1029
G-BBWX	BN2	386	G-BCSD	BN2	420	G-BDHT	BN2	766	G-BDTS	TRIS	1030
G-BBWY	BN2	388	G-BCSF	BN2	421	G-BDHU	BN2	767	G-BDUS	BN2	515
G-BBYO	TRIS	362	G-BCSG	BN2	422	G-BDHV	BN2	768	G-BDUT	BN2	516
G-BBYX	BN2	387	G-BCSH	BN2	423	G-BDHW	BN2	769	G-BDUU	BN2	518
G-BBYY	BN2	393	G-BCSI	BN2	424	G-BDHX	BN2	770	G-BDUV	BN2	519
G-BBYZ	BN2	394	G-BCSJ	BN2	425	G-BDIZ	BN2	464	G-BDUW	BN2	520
G-BBZA	BN2	395	G-BCTY	BN2	426	G-BDJA	BN2	466	G-BDVV	BN2	521
G-BBZC	BN2	396	G-BCTZ	BN2	427	G-BDJS	BN2	472	G-BDVW	BN2	522
G-BBZD	BN2	389	G-BCUA	BN2	428	G-BDJT	BN2	474	G-BDVX	BN2	523
G-BBZT	BN2	711	G-BCUD	BN2	429	G-BDJU	BN2	475	G-BDVY	BN2	524
G-BBZU	BN2	712	G-BCUE	BN2	430	**G-BDJV**	**BN2**	**476**	G-BDVZ	BN2	525
G-BBZW	BN2	713	G-BCUZ	200	BB-55	G-BDJW	BN2T	477	G-BDWD	BN2	526
G-BBZX	BN2	714	G-BCVK	BN2	741	G-BDJX	BN2	478	G-BDWF	BN2	529
G-BBZY	BN2	715	G-BCVL	BN2	742	G-BDJY	BN2	479	G-BDWG	BN2	530
G-BBZZ	BN2	716	G-BCVM	BN2	743	G-BDJZ	BN2T	480	G-BDWR	TRIS	1031
G-BCAE	BN2	717	G-BCVN	BN2	744	G-BDKN	TRIS	1017	G-BDWS	TRIS	1032
G-BCAF	BN2	718	G-BCVO	BN2	745	G-BDKO	TRIS	1018	G-BDWT	TRIS	1033
G-BCAG	BN2	719	G-BCVP	BN2	746	G-BDKP	TRIS	1019	G-BDWU	TRIS	1034
(G-BCAL)	BN2	720	G-BCVR	BN2	747	G-BDKR	TRIS	1020	G-BDWV	TRIS	1035
G-BCBS	BN2	390	G-BCVS	BN2	748	G-BDKX	BN2T	481	G-BDYN	BN2	801
G-BCCT	TRIS	363	G-BCVT	BN2	749	G-BDKY	BN2	482	G-BDYO	BN2	802
G-BCCU	TRIS	366	G-BCVU	BN2	750	G-BDLF	BN2	483	G-BDYP	BN2	803
(G-BCDK)	P68	15	G-BCWO	BN2	431	G-BDLG	BN2	484	G-BDYR	BN2	804
G-BCDK	**P68**	**32**	G-BCWP	BN2	432	G-BDLH	BN2	486	G-BDYS	BN2	805
G-BCEG	TRIS	372	G-BCWR	BN2	433	G-BDLI	BN2	488	G-BDYT	BN2	806
G-BCEH	BN2	397	G-BCWS	BN2	434	G-BDLJ	BN2	489	G-BDYU	BN2	807
G-BCEI	BN2	398	G-BCWT	BN2	435	G-BDLK	BN2	490	G-BDYV	BN2	808
G-BCEJ	BN2	399	G-BCWU	BN2	436	G-BDLL	BN2	491	G-BDYW	BN2	809
G-BCEK	BN2	400	G-BCWV	BN2	437	G-BDLN	BN2	492	G-BDYX	BN2	810
G-BCEL	BN2	401	G-BCWX	BN2	438	G-BDMR	BN2	771	**G-BDZI**	**BN2**	**531**
G-BCEM	BN2	402	G-BCWY	BN2	439	G-BDMT	BN2	772	G-BDZJ	BN2	532
G-BCEN	**BN2**	**403**	G-BCWZ	BN2	440	G-BDMU	BN2	773	G-BDZK	BN2	533
G-BCFM	P68	19	G-BCXS	690A	11209	G-BDMV	BN2	774	G-BDZL	BN2	534
G-BCGY	BN2	721	G-BCXU	TRIS	1006	G-BDMX	BN2	775	G-BDZM	BN2	535
G-BCGZ	BN2	722	G-BCXV	TRIS	1007	G-BDMY	BN2	776	G-BDZN	BN2	536
G-BCHA	BN2	723	G-BCXW	TRIS	1008	G-BDMZ	BN2	777	G-BDZO	BN2	537
G-BCHB	BN2	724	G-BCXX	TRIS	1009	G-BDNA	BN2	778	G-BDZP	BN2	540
G-BCHC	BN2	725	G-BCXY	TRIS	1010	G-BDNB	BN2	779	G-BECJ	P68	68
G-BCHD	BN2	726	G-BCYC	TRIS	1011	G-BDND	BN2	780	G-BEDM	TRIS	1036
G-BCHE	BN2	727	G-BCYT	BN2	751	G-BDNM	BN2	493	G-BEDN	TRIS	1037
G-BCHF	BN2	728	G-BCYU	BN2	752	G-BDNN	BN2	495	G-BEDO	TRIS	1038
G-BCHG	BN2	729	G-BCYV	BN2	753	G-BDNP	BN2	496	**G-BEDP**	**TRIS**	**1039**
G-BCHH	BN2	730	G-BCYW	BN2	754	G-BDOJ	TRIS	1021	G-BEDR	TRIS	1040
G-BCHO	BN2	720	G-BCYX	BN2	755	G-BDOK	TRIS	1022	**G-BEDW**	**BN2**	**541**
G-BCJV	TRIS	373	G-BCZA	BN2	756	G-BDOM	TRIS	1023	G-BEDX	BN2	542
G-BCJW	TRIS	381	G-BCZB	BN2	757	G-BDOS	TRIS	1024	G-BEDY	BN2	543
G-BCJX	TRIS	391	G-BCZC	BN2	758	G-BDOT	TRIS	1025	G-BEDZ	BN2	544
G-BCJY	BN2	392	G-BCZD	BN2	759	G-BDPM	BN2	497	G-BEEB	BN2	545
(G-BCKE)	E90	LW-126	G-BCZE	BN2	760	G-BDPN	BN2	498	G-BEEC	BN2	546
G-BCKW	BN2	404	G-BCZS	BN2	441	G-BDPO	BN2	499	G-BEED	BN2	549
G-BCKX	BN2	405	G-BCZT	BN2	442	G-BDPP	BN2	501	G-BEEG	BN2	550
G-BCKY	BN2	406	G-BCZU	BN2	443	G-BDPR	BN2	504	G-BEFI	BN2	553
G-BCKZ	BN2	407	G-BCZV	BN2	444	G-BDPS	BN2T	506	G-BEFJ	BN2	554
G-BCLE	BN2	408	G-BCZW	BN2	445	G-BDPT	BN2T	507	G-BEFK	BN2	555
G-BCLF	BN2	409	G-BCZX	BN2	446	G-BDPU	BN2	510	G-BEFL	BN2	556
G-BCLH	BN2	410	G-BCZY	BN2	447	G-BDRN	BN2	781	G-BEFM	BN2	557
G-BCMB	P68	21	G-BCZZ	BN2	448	G-BDRO	BN2	782	G-BEFN	BN2	558
G-BCMK	BN2	411	G-BDAA	BN2	449	G-BDRP	BN2	783	G-BEFO	TRIS	1041
G-BCMM	BN2	412	G-BDAF	BN2	450	G-BDRR	BN2	784	G-BEFP	TRIS	1042
G-BCMN	BN2	413	G-BDDK	BN2	451	G-BDRS	BN2	785	G-BEGB	BN2	485
G-BCMO	BN2	414	G-BDDL	BN2	452	G-BDRT	BN2	786	G-BEGC	BN2	494
G-BCMP	BN2	415	G-BDDM	BN2	454	G-BDRU	BN2	787	G-BEGD	BN2	562
G-BCMS	BN2	416	G-BDDN	BN2	455	G-BDRV	BN2	788	G-BEGE	BN2	563
G-BCMU	BN2	417	G-BDDO	BN2	456	G-BDRW	BN2	789	G-BEGF	BN2	564
G-BCMV	BN2	418	G-BDDP	BN2	457	G-BDRX	BN2	790	G-BEGH	BN2	565
G-BCMY	BN2T	419	G-BDDR	BN2	458	G-BDSW	BN2	511	G-BEGI	BN2	566
G-BCMZ	BN2	731	G-BDDU	BN2	459	G-BDSX	BN2	512	G-BEGJ	BN2	570
G-BCNA	BN2	732	G-BDDV	BN2	461	G-BDSY	BN2	513	G-BEGK	BN2	811
G-BCNB	BN2	733	G-BDDW	BN2	463	G-BDSZ	BN2	514	G-BEGL	BN2	812
G-BCND	BN2	734	G-BDGC	TRIS	1012	G-BDTA	BN2	517	G-BEGM	BN2	813
G-BCNE	BN2	735	G-BDGD	TRIS	1013	G-BDTC	BN2	791	G-BEGN	BN2	814

G-BEGO	BN2	815
G-BEGP	BN2	816
G-BEGR	BN2	817
G-BEGS	BN2	818
G-BEGT	BN2	819
G-BEGU	BN2	820
G-BEGX	TRIS	1043
G-BEGY	TRIS	1044
G-BEHA	TRIS	1045
G-BEHB	TRIS	1046
G-BEHC	TRIS	1047
G-BEHD	TRIS	1048
G-BEHE	TRIS	1049
G-BEHF	TRIS	1050
G-BEHR	200	BB-230
G-BEIU	BN2	571
G-BEIV	BN2	572
G-BEIW	BN2	573
G-BEIX	BN2	574
G-BEIY	BN2	575
G-BEJC	BN2	576
G-BEJF	BN2	577
G-BEJG	BN2	578
G-BEJH	BN2	579
G-BEJI	BN2	580
G-BEJN	690A	11165
G-BEJX	P68	86
G-BEKP	BN2	581
G-BEKU	BN2	582
G-BEKV	BN2	583
G-BEKW	BN2	584
G-BEKX	BN2	585
G-BEKY	BN2	586
G-BEKZ	BN2	587
G-BELA	BN2	588
G-BELB	BN2	589
G-BELC	BN2	590
G-BELD	BN2	821
G-BELE	BN2	822
G-BELF	BN2	823
G-BELG	BN2	824
G-BELH	BN2	825
G-BELI	BN2	826
G-BELJ	BN2	827
G-BELK	BN2	828
G-BELM	BN2	829
G-BELN	BN2	830
G-BEMG	BN2	831
G-BEMH	BN2	832
G-BEMJ	BN2	833
G-BEMK	BN2	834
G-BEML	BN2	835
G-BEMN	BN2	836
G-BEMO	BN2	837
G-BEMP	BN2	838
G-BEMR	BN2	839
G-BEMS	BN2	840
G-BENU	BN2	591
G-BENV	BN2	592
(G-BENW)	BN2	593
(G-BENX)	BN2	594
G-BENY	BN2	595
G-BENZ	BN2	596
G-BEOA	BN2	597
G-BEOB	BN2	598
G-BEOC	BN2	599
G-BEPG	TRIS	1051
G-BEPH	TRIS	1052
G-BEPI	TRIS	1053
G-BEPJ	TRIS	1054
G-BEPK	TRIS	1055
G-BESB	BN2	841
G-BESC	BN2	842
G-BESD	BN2	843
G-BESE	BN2	844
G-BESF	BN2	845
G-BESG	BN2	846
G-BESH	BN2	847
G-BESI	BN2	848
G-BESJ	BN2	849
G-BESK	BN2	850
G-BESL	BN2	2001
G-BESM	BN2	2002
G-BESN	BN2	2003

G-BESO	BN2	2004
G-BESP	BN2	2005
G-BESR	BN2	2006
G-BEST	200	BB-288
G-BESU	BN2	2008
G-BESV	BN2	2009
G-BESW	BN2	2010
G-BESX	BN2	2007
G-BEUO	BN2	503
G-BEUT	P68	97
G-BEUZ	200	BB-309
G-BEVM	BN2	907
G-BEVR	TRIS	1056
G-BEVT	**TRIS**	**1057**
G-BEVU	TRIS	1058
G-BEVV	TRIS	1059
G-BEVY	TRIS	1060
G-BEVZ	BN2	851
G-BEWA	BN2	852
G-BEWB	BN2	853
(G-BEWC)	BN2	854
G-BEWD	BN2	855
G-BEWE	BN2	856
G-BEWF	BN2	857
G-BEWG	BN2	858
G-BEWH	BN2	859
G-BEWI	BN2	860
G-BEWK	BN2	854
G-BEXA	BN2	2011
G-BEXB	BN2	2012
G-BEXC	BN2	2013
G-BEXD	BN2	2014
G-BEXE	BN2	2015
G-BEXF	BN2	2016
G-BEXG	BN2	2017
G-BEXH	BN2	2018
G-BEXI	BN2	2019
G-BEXJ	BN2	2020
G-BEXM	P68	111
G-BEXP	BN2	296
G-BFAE	BN2	509
G-BFBD	P68	115
G-BFBU	**P68**	**24**
G-BFCM	BN2	866
G-BFCN	BN2	861
G-BFCO	BN2	862
G-BFCP	BN2	863
G-BFCR	BN2	864
G-BFCS	BN2	865
(G-BFCT)	BN2	866
G-BFCU	BN2	867
G-BFCV	BN2	868
G-BFCW	BN2	869
G-BFCX	BN2	870
G-BFDD	TRIS	1061
G-BFEA	200	BB-349
G-BFET	P68	121
G-BFKP	P68	129
G-BFNL	BN2	871
G-BFNN	BN2	872
G-BFNO	BN2	873
G-BFNR	BN2	874
G-BFNS	BN2	875
G-BFNT	BN2	876
G-BFNU	BN2	877
G-BFNV	BN2	878
G-BFNW	BN2	879
G-BFNX	BN2T	880
G-BFNY	BN2	881
G-BFNZ	BN2	882
G-BFOA	BN2	883
G-BFOB	BN2	884
G-BFOC	BN2	885
G-BFOL	200	BB-387
G-BFST	P68	30
G-BFSU	P68	141
G-BFTI	BN2T	886
G-BFTJ	BN2	887
G-BFTK	BN2T	888
G-BFTL	BN2	889
G-BFTM	BN2	890
G-BFUP	BN2	891
G-BFUR	BN2	892
G-BFUT	BN2	893

G-BFUU	BN2	894
G-BFUV	BN2	895
G-BFVO	P68	39
G-BFVX	90	LJ-803
G-BFVY	90	LJ-812
G-BFVZ	200	BB-417
G-BFWA	BN2	896
G-BFWH	200	BB-426
G-BFWI	200	BB-428
G-BFWV	BN2	897
G-BFWX	BN2	898
G-BFWY	BN2	899
G-BFWZ	BN2	900
G-BFYG	BN2	906
G-BFYR	BN2	901
G-BFYS	BN2	902
G-BFYT	BN2	903
G-BFZZ	BN2	904
G-BGAN	BN2	905
G-BGBT	P68	159
G-BGEJ	BN2	908
G-BGEM	P68	165
G-BGFU	BN2	909
G-BGFV	BN2	910
G-BGFW	BN2	911
G-BGFZ	P68	169
G-BGHR	200	BB-508
G-BGIE	E121	121014
G-BGMY	P68	182
G-BGNU	E90	LW-304
G-BGPV	BN2	912
G-BGPW	BN2	913
G-BGPX	BN2	914
G-BGPY	BN2	915
G-BGRD	200	BB-552
G-BGRE	200	BB-568
G-BGRZ	BN2	116
G-BGXJ	P68	189
G-BGXM	690B	11374
G-BHAN	200	BB-597
G-BHAP	90	LJ-874
G-BHBZ	**P68**	**191**
G-BHCR	PC6	732
G-BHEE	P68	196
G-BHEF	P68	199
G-BHFX	441	0107
G-BHGT	90	LJ-446
G-BHJP	P68	212
G-BHJS	**P68**	**172**
G-BHJX	P68	219
G-BHKS	E90	LW-333
G-BHLC	200	BB-684
G-BHLI	690B	11546
G-BHLN	441	0154
G-BHLO	441	0226
G-BHLP	441	0239
(G-BHNW)	425	0024
G-BHNY	425	0090
(G-BHNY)	425	0094
G-BHOV	P68	223
G-BHPE	BN2	2021
G-BHPF	BN2	2022
G-BHPG	BN2	2023
G-BHTP	31T	8004022
G-BHUL	E90	LW-83
G-BHUS	F90	LA-80
G-BHUT	F90	LA-81
G-BHVX	200	BB-180
G-BHXH	BN2	2024
G-BHXI	BN2	2025
G-BHYU	200	BB-756
G-BHZC	690C	11602
(G-BICL)	425	0054
G-BIED	F90	LA-100
G-BIEE	90	LJ-944
G-BIEZ	F90	LA-111
G-BIFS	90	LJ-636
G-BIFZ	P68	229
G-BIIN	BN2	2101
G-BIIO	BN2T	2102
G-BIIP	BN2	2103
G-BIIR	BN2	2104
G-BIIS	BN2	2105
G-BILY	200	BB-828

G-BIPD	BN2	2026
G-BIPE	BN2	2031
G-BIPP	200	BB-878
G-BIUA	BN2	916
(G-BIUB)	BN2	917
G-BIUC	BN2	918
G-BIUD	BN2	919
(G-BIUE)	BN2	920
G-BIUF	BN2	2027
G-BIUG	BN2	2028
G-BIUH	BN2	2029
G-BIUJ	BN2T	2030
G-BIXC	BN2	2106
G-BIXD	BN2	2107
G-BIXE	BN2	2108
G-BIXF	BN2	2109
G-BIXG	BN2	2110
G-BIXM	90	LJ-991
G-BIZP	PC6	812
G-BIZX	200	BB-963
G-BJBD	BN2	2111
G-BJBE	BN2T	2112
G-BJBF	BN2	2113
G-BJBG	BN2	2114
G-BJBH	BN2T	2115
G-BJBP	200	BB-240
G-BJCR	P68	218
G-BJEA	BN2	2116
G-BJEB	BN2	2117
G-BJEC	BN2T	2118
G-BJED	BN2T	2119
G-BJEE	**BN2T**	**2120**
G-BJEF	**BN2T**	**2121**
G-BJEG	BN2T	2122
G-BJEH	BN2	2123
G-BJEJ	**BN2T**	**2124**
G-BJEK	BN2	2125
G-BJET	425	0024
G-BJGJ	441	0251
G-BJIZ	PA42	8001055
G-BJJV	200	BB-1007
G-BJMN	90	LJ-554
G-BJOF	P68	147
G-BJOG	BN2T	2033
G-BJOH	BN2T	2034
G-BJOJ	BN2	2126
G-BJOK	BN2	2127
G-BJOL	BN2	2128
G-BJOM	BN2	2129
G-BJON	BN2	2130
G-BJOO	BN2	2131
G-BJOP	**BN2**	**2132**
G-BJOR	BN2	2133
G-BJOS	BN2	2134
G-BJOU	BN2	2135
G-BJRZ	P68	231
G-BJSA	BN2	46
(G-BJSN)	200	BB-1026
G-BJSY	90	LJ-805
G-BJWG	200	BB-1051
G-BJWL	BN2	166
(G-BJWL)	BN2	376
G-BJWM	BN2	717
G-BJWN	BN2	316
G-BJWO	**BN2**	**334**
G-BJWP	BN2	399
G-BJXO	441	0263
(G-BJXS)	F90	LA-198
(G-BJXT)	200	BB-1072
(G-BJXT)	200	BB-1086
G-BJYA	425	0122
G-BJYB	441	0279
G-BJYC	425	0168
G-BJYP	BN2	2136
G-BJYR	BN2	2137
G-BJYS	BN2T	2138
G-BJYT	BN2T	2139
G-BJYU	BN2T	2140
G-BJYV	BN2T	2141
G-BJYW	BN2T	2142
G-BJYX	BN2T	2143
G-BJYY	BN2T	2144
G-BJYZ	BN2T	2145
G-BJZG	200	BB-133

G-BKAK	90	LJ-619
G-BKEA	BN2T	2146
G-BKEB	BN2T	2147
G-BKEC	BN2	2148
G-BKED	BN2	2149
G-BKEE	BN2	2150
G-BKEF	BN2T	2151
G-BKEG	BN2	2152
G-BKEH	BN2	2153
G-BKEI	BN2	2154
G-BKEJ	BN2	2155
G-BKFY	90	LJ-1028
G-BKGK	31T	8275011
G-BKID	90	LJ-604
G-BKIP	90	LJ-1035
G-BKJG	BN2	2156
G-BKJH	BN2	2157
G-BKJI	BN2T	2158
G-BKJJ	BN2	2159
G-BKJK	BN2	2160
G-BKJL	BN2	2161
G-BKJM	BN2	2162
G-BKJN	BN2	2163
G-BKJO	BN2	2164
G-BKJP	BN2	2165
G-BKJZ	G1	191
G-BKNC	90	LJ-848
G-BKOC	BN2	2166
G-BKOD	BN2	2167
G-BKOE	BN2	2168
G-BKOF	BN2	2169
G-BKOG	BN2	2170
G-BKOH	BN2	2171
G-BKOI	BN2	2172
G-BKOJ	BN2	2173
G-BKOK	**BN2**	**2174**
G-BKOL	BN2	2175
G-BKSA	425	0173
G-BKTD	P68	297
G-BKTI	200	BB-362
G-BKUX	90	LJ-1073
G-BKZW	90	LJ-680
G-BLAE	200	BB-239
G-BLCJ	441	0316
G-BLCL	441	0321
G-BLCZ	441	0332
G-BLDS	BN2	2176
G-BLDT	BN2	2177
G-BLDU	BN2	2178
G-BLDV	**BN2**	**2179**
G-BLDW	BN2	2180
G-BLDX	BN2	2181
G-BLEC	BN2	2114
G-BLEI	BN2	3008
G-BLGM	425	0199
G-BLIR	441	0337
G-BLKN	200	BB-160
(G-BLLC)	200	BB-438
G-BLLC	200	BB-438
G-BLNA	90	LJ-446
G-BLNC	BN2	2182
G-BLND	BN2T	2183
G-BLNE	BN2	2184
G-BLNF	BN2	2185
G-BLNG	**BN2**	**2186**
G-BLNH	BN2	2187
G-BLNI	BN2	2188
G-BLNJ	**BN2**	**2189**
G-BLNK	BN2T	2190
G-BLNL	BN2T	2191
G-BLNM	BN2	2192
G-BLNR	BN2	3009
G-BLNS	BN2	2193
G-BLNT	BN2	2194
G-BLNU	BN2	2195
G-BLNV	BN2	2196
G-BLNW	BN2	2197
G-BLNX	BN2	2198
G-BLNY	BN2	2199
G-BLNZ	BN2	2200
G-BLPT	690B	11484
G-BLRK	PA42	5501027
G-BLSA	PA42	5501029
G-BLTB	PA42	5501030

G-BLYB	200	BB-1232
G-BLYO	BN2	3011
G-BMCA	200	BB-210
G-BMCB	P68	156
G-BMDT	BN2	3012
G-BMEF	90	LJ-641
G-BMEI	P68	308
G-BMIC	690B	11437
G-BMKD	**90**	**LJ-1069**
G-BMLR	P68	278
G-BMMH	BN2	3013
G-BMMT	46D	141
G-BMNF	200	BB-1127
G-BMOA	441	0362
G-BMOI	**P68**	**103**
G-BMOW	G1	155
G-BMPA	G1	134
G-BMSH	425	0063
G-BMSR	G1	128
(G-BMTU)	P68	307
G-BMTZ	441	0207
G-BMVP	PA42	5527035
G-BMVY	200	BB-1257
G-BMWO	BN2	3014
G-BMXO	90	LJ-630
G-BMZD	90	LJ-667
G-BNAE	BN2	2032
G-BNAF	BN2	2035
G-BNAT	90	LJ-614
G-BNCE	G1	9
(G-BNDY)	425	0234
G-BNDY	425	0236
G-BNDZ	441	0353
G-BNEA	BN2	206
G-BNEB	BN2	2037
G-BNEC	BN2	2038
G-BNGA	BN2	2029
G-BNKN	G1	159
G-BNKO	G1	154
G-BNMJ	BN2	2039
G-BNMR	200	BB-780
G-BNXA	BN2	80
G-BNXB	BN2	161
G-BNXN	P68	204
G-BNZA	300	FA-136
G-BNZD	TRIS	1059
G-BNZH	200	BB-961
G-BOBC	BN2T	2145
G-BOBM	200	BB-955
G-BOBX	G1	77
G-BOFN	100	B-27
G-BOGZ	BN2	2040
G-BOMC	BN2T	2201
G-BOMD	BN2	2202
G-BOME	BN2	2203
G-BOMF	BN2	2204
G-BOMG	BN2	2205
G-BOMM	200	BB-1089
G-BPBN	BN2T	419
G-BPCA	**BN2**	**2198**
G-BPCB	BN2	2011
G-BPCD	BN2	878
G-BPCH	300	FA-74
G-BPLC	200	BB-1215
G-BPLN	BN2	2206
G-BPLO	BN2T	2207
G-BPLP	BN2	2208
G-BPLR	BN2	2209
G-BPLS	BN2	2210
G-BPPM	200	BB-1044
G-BPSV	F406	0030
G-BPSW	F406	0032
G-BPSX	F406	0034
G-BPWJ	200	BB-742
G-BPXR	BN2	2211
G-BPXS	BN2	2212
G-BPXT	BN2T	2213
G-BPXU	BN2T	2214
G-BPXV	BN2T	2215
G-BRAL	G1	76
G-BRFY	BN2	2216
G-BRFZ	BN2	2217
G-BRGA	BN2	2218
G-BRGB	BN2	2219

G-BRGC	BN2	2220
G-BRON	200	BB-349
G-BRPA	BN2	2221
G-BRPB	BN2T	2222
G-BRPC	BN2T	2223
G-BRPD	BN2	2224
G-BRSR	BN2T	2225
G-BRSS	BN2	2226
G-BRST	BN2	2227
G-BRSU	BN2T	2228
G-BRSV	BN2T	2229
G-BRWN	G1	177
(G-BRZH)	BN2	269
G-BSAC	BN2	2230
G-BSAD	BN2T	2231
G-BSAE	BN2T	2232
G-BSAF	BN2T	2233
G-BSAG	BN2	2234
G-BSAH	BN2T	2235
G-BSEO	200	BB-501
G-BSGA	90	LJ-883
G-BSPO	BN2	2236
G-BSPP	BN2T	2237
G-BSPR	BN2T	2238
G-BSPS	BN2	2239
G-BSPT	**BN2**	**2240**
G-BSPU	BN2	2241
G-BSPY	BN2	156
G-BSRY	F406	0046
G-BSTF	300	FA-101
G-BSWN	BN2T	2242
G-BSWO	BN2	2243
G-BSWP	BN2	2244
G-BSWR	**BN2T**	**2245**
G-BSWS	BN2T	2246
G-BSWT	BN2	2247
G-BSWU	BN2	2248
G-BTLU	BN2	2249
G-BTLV	BN2	2250
G-BTLW	BN2	2251
G-BTLX	BN2	2252
G-BTLY	BN2	2253
G-BTLZ	BN2	2254
G-BTVI	BN2	2255
G-BTVJ	BN2	2256
G-BTVK	BN2	2257
G-BTVL	BN2	2258
G-BTVM	BN2T	2259
G-BTVN	BN2	2260
G-BUBD	BN2T	2261
G-BUBE	BN2T	2262
G-BUBF	BN2	2263
G-BUBG	BN2T	2264
G-BUBH	BN2	2265
G-BUBI	BN2T	2266
G-BUBJ	BN2	2267
G-BUBK	BN2	2268
G-BUBM	BN2	2269
G-BUBN	**BN2**	**2270**
G-BUBO	BN2	2271
G-BUBP	BN2	2272
G-BUJC	P68	284
G-BVFG	BN2T	2273
G-BVFH	BN2T	2274
G-BVFI	BN2T	2275
G-BVFJ	BN2T	2276
G-BVFK	BN2T	2277
G-BVHX	BN2T	4003
G-BVHY	BN2T	4004
G-BVHZ	BN2T	4005
G-BVJT	**F406**	**0073**
G-BVMA	**200**	**BB-797**
G-BVNB	BN2	2278
G-BVNC	BN2	2279
G-BVND	BN2	2280
G-BVNE	BN2	2281
G-BVNF	BN2	2282
G-BVRS	90	LJ-481
G-BVSG	BN2	2283
G-BVSH	BN2	2284
G-BVSI	BN2	2285
G-BVSJ	BN2	2286
G-BVSK	BN2T	2287
G-BVSL	BN2	2288

G-BVXX	BN2	2289
G-BVXY	BN2	2290
G-BVYD	BN2	2291
G-BVYE	BN2	2292
G-BWJO	BN2	2294
G-BWMP	695A	96034
G-BWNE	BN2	2295
G-BWNF	BN2	2296
G-BWNG	BN2	2297
G-BWPK	BN2T	4006
G-BWPM	BN2T	4007
G-BWPN	BN2T	4008
G-BWPO	BN2T	4009
G-BWPR	BN2T	4010
G-BWPU	BN2T	4011
G-BWPV	BN2T	4012
G-BWPW	**BN2T**	**4013**
G-BWPX	BN2T	4014
G-BWTX	PA42	8001041
G-BWYW	BN2	2293
G-BWYX	BN2	2298
G-BWYY	BN2	2299
G-BWYZ	BN2	2300
G-BWZF	BN2	2301
G-BXMA	200	BB-726
G-BXYZ	690C	11620
G-BYCP	**200**	**BB-966**
G-BYNE	**PC6**	**631**
(G-BYSB)	TRIS	1100
(G-BYSC)	TRIS	1101
(G-BYSD)	TRIS	1102
G-BYSO	46D	192
G-BZNE	**350**	**FL-286**
(G-BZTP)	46T	97050
G-BZTP	46T	97050
(G-CARS)	441	0107
G-CBFS	200	BB-487
"G-CCCB"	350	FL-73
G-CCIM	BN2	2308
G-CCPU	PC12	549
G-CCUX	BN2	2302
G-CCWY	PC12	568
G-CDCJ	BN2T	2303
G-CDFY	**200**	**BB-1715**
G-CDZT	**200**	**BB-1619**
G-CECI	**PC6**	**936**
G-CECN	690B	11482
G-CEGP	**200**	**BB-726**
G-CEGR	**200**	**BB-351**
G-CEIO	BN2T	4015
G-CEIP	BN2T	4016
G-CEIR	**BN2T**	**4017**
G-CEJB	46T	97240
G-CEUA	BN2	2305
G-CEUB	**BN2**	**2306**
G-CEUC	**BN2**	**2307**
G-CEUD	**BN2**	**2309**
G-CEUE	**BN2**	**2310**
G-CFBX	**90**	**LJ-1890**
G-CFDW	P180	1086
G-CGAW	**200**	**BB-700**
G-CHES	BN2	2011
G-CHEY	**31T**	**8166033**
G-CHEZ	**BN2**	**2234**
G-CIAS	**BN2**	**2162**
G-CLCG	200	BB-1931
G-CLOW	**200**	**BB-821**
G-CNIS	P68	147
G-CNSI	200	BB-641
G-COBH	**200**	**BB-944**
G-COTE	90	LJ-614
G-COWE	90	LJ-1116
G-CUKL	200	BB-641
G-CUPN	46D	211
G-CVAN	F406	0019
G-CVXN	**F406**	**0064**
G-CYPP	BN2T	2207
G-CZNE	**BN2**	**2301**
G-DAKI	**PC12**	**885**
G-DBAA	200	BB-1367
G-DBAR	200	BB-819
G-DCFB	425	0063
G-DEMO	BN2T	2146
G-DERI	**46T**	**97078**

Registration	Type	c/n
G-DERK	46T	97152
G-DEXY	E90	LW-136
G-DFLT	F406	0036
(G-DIPM)	46T	97117A
(G-DIPM)	46T	97125B
G-DIVE	BN2	2011
G-DLRA	BN2T	2140
G-DODI	46D	163
G-DORE	P68	217
G-ECAV	200	BB-561
G-ECZA	BN2	498
G-ENCE	P68	141
G-ERAD	90	LJ-1565
G-EVNS	441	0264
G-FANS	BN2	251
G-FAVI	E90	LW-59
G-FCAL	441	0293
G-FCED	31T	8166013
G-FERM	425	0063
G-FIND	F406	0045
G-FJMS	P68	113
G-FLTI	F90	LA-59
G-FLYN	F406	0048
G-FOOD	200	BB-947
G-FPLA	200	BB-944
G-FPLB	200	BB-1048
G-FPLC	441	0207
G-FPLD	200	BB-1433
G-FPLE	200	BB-1256
G-FRAX	441	0207
G-FRAZ	441	0035
G-FRYI	200	BB-210
G-FSEU	200	BB-331
G-FTSE	TRIS	1053
G-GATI	200	BB-400
G-GBMR	200	BB-1693
G-GBSC	E90	LW-242
G-GKNB	200	BB-705
G-GLOR	425	0174
G-GMED	PA42	5501050
G-GMPB	BN2T	4011
G-GZRP	PA42	5501011
G-HAMA	200	BB-30
G-HEBS	BN2	2267
G-HEBZ	BN2	823
G-HFGP	200	BB-749
G-HGPC	BN2	251
G-HIGG	200	BB-160
G-HLUB	200	BB-240
G-HMCG	BN2	847
G-HOOP	46D	119
G-HOPL	BN2T	2112
G-HOSP	441	0078
G-HPAA	BN2	2244
G-HPVC	P68	13
G-HSON	441	0294
G-HUBB	P68	194
G-IACL	BN2T	2138
G-IAHL	BN2T	2138
G-IANS	690B	11465
G-IBCA	200	BB-210
G-IBLL	690D	15015
G-IFTB	200C	BL-37
G-IIIA	MIII	T-342
G-IIIB	MIII	T-302
G-IJIM	PC12	490
G-IJJB	200	BB-1257
G-ILMD	PC12	412
G-IMEA	200	BB-302
G-IMGL	200	BB-1564
G-INTO	PC12	609
G-IOOO	695A	96033
G-IOWA	BN2	431
G-IPRA	200	BB-552
G-ISLA	BN2	206
G-ITEX	TRIS	1008
G-ITPS	PC6	862
G-JACT	P68	366
G-JAJV	P68	253
G-JASS	200	BB-983
G-JCTI	P68	109
G-JENC	300C	FM-14
G-JGAL	E90	LW-327
G-JHAN	200	BB-1324
G-JIMG	300C	FM-17
G-JOAL	200	BB-1158
G-JOEY	TRIS	1016
G-JRMM	690B	11530
G-JSAT	BN2T	2277
G-JSPC	BN2T	2264
G-JVAJ	31T	8104053
G-JVJA	P68	308
G-JVMR	P68	109
G-KBCA	200	BB-501
G-KEMW	TBM8	475
G-KEMZ	BN2T	2030
G-KFIT	F90	LA-80
G-KIMK	P68	27
G-KJET	90	LJ-481
G-KLNB	350	FL-631
G-KLYN	200	BB-1931
G-KMCD	200	BB-1325
G-KRMA	425	0003
G-KVIP	200	BB-487
G-KWIK	P68	152
G-LACY	690B	11484
G-LAMB	90	LJ-887
G-LCOC	TRIS	366
G-LEAF	F406	0018
G-LEAP	BN2T	2183
G-LILI	425	0054
G-LIPP	BN2	2156
G-LKOW	200	BB-438
G-LOTO	BN2	530
G-LOUP	P68	182
G-LOVX	441	0316
(G-LYNT)	200	BB-1682
G-MAFA	F406	0036
G-MAFB	F406	0080
G-MAFF	BN2T	2119
G-MALB	BN2	2028
G-MALI	BN2	2011
G-MALN	BN2	3011
G-MAMD	200	BB-1549
G-MATX	PC12	682
G-MCEO	200	BB-828
G-MCMC	TBM7	261
G-MDJI	200	BB-1162
G-MEDI	90	LJ-747
G-MEGN	200	BB-1518
G-MFAL	690D	15033
G-MHAR	PA42	5501020
G-MICV	BN2	2106
G-MICZ	46D	218
G-MOAT	200	BB-462
G-MOET	P68	13
G-MOLO	PC12	1090
G-MOUN	200	BB-1734
G-MOXY	441	0154
G-MSSA	BN2T	2143
G-NATS	690B	11541
(G-NATZ)	690C	11620
G-NESU	BN2	2260
G-NEWU	P68	219
G-NICY	300C	FM-16
G-NISR	690A	11243
G-NORC	425	0054
G-NORS	425	0224
G-NTMN	690D	15015
G-NUIG	90	LJ-1035
G-NVIA	P68	366
G-OADT	200	BB-501
G-OAFB	200	BB-1235
G-OAKL	200	BB-133
G-OAKM	200	BB-55
G-OAKP	P68	231
G-OAKZ	90	LJ-1170
G-OAPA	PC6	815
G-OAVW	TRIS	319
G-OAVX	200	BB-210
G-OBAA	200	BB-1367
G-OBNC	BN2	3000
G-OBNG	BN2	2300
G-OBNL	BN2	523
G-OBSV	P68	329
G-OCAL	P68	182
G-OCEG	200	BB-588
G-OCHD	300	FA-95
G-OCLE	PC12	867
G-OCME	TRIS	262
G-OCTA	TRIS	1008
G-OEAS	200	BB-521
G-OEMS	200	BB-406
G-OESL	P180	1080
G-OFBL	90	LJ-747
G-OFHJ	441	0294
G-OGAT	200	BB-655
G-OGDN	200	BB-669
G-OHBD	200	BB-864
G-OJAV	TRIS	1024
G-OJBA	200	BB-1226
G-OJCT	P68	223
G-OJGA	200	BB-1172
G-OJOE	P68	109
G-OJRO	90	LJ-327
G-OLAF	90	LJ-803
G-OLDZ	200	BB-828
G-OLEN	425	0106
G-OLES	P68	253
G-OLMA	P68	159
(G-OLPL)	TRIS	1008
G-OLTT	PC12	648
G-OMET	90	LJ-614
G-OMGI	200	BB-1259
G-OMNH	200	BB-108
G-ONAL	200	BB-30
G-ONCA	200	BB-676
G-ONCM	P68	217
G-ONEA	200	BB-400
G-ONEX	200	BB-379
G-ONOR	425	0173
(G-ONPA)	200	BB-160
G-OOAG	E90	LW-59
G-OPBN	BN2T	2034
G-OPED	P68	129
G-ORED	BN2T	2142
G-OREG	TRIS	319
G-ORJA	200	BB-1570
G-ORMC	200	BB-288
G-OROY	P68	141
G-ORTH	E90	LW-136
G-ORVR	P68	115
G-OSEA	BN2	2175
G-OSKA	200	BB-641
G-OTCS	300C	FM-18
G-OTSB	TRIS	1027
G-OTVS	BN2T	419
G-OWAX	200	BB-302
G-OWIN	BN2	653
G-OWNR	200	BB-929
G-PALL	46D	199
G-PART	P68	62
G-PASU	BN2T	2144
G-PASV	BN2	2157
G-PASW	BN2	150
G-PASY	BN2	2011
G-PASZ	BN2	878
G-PAUL	P68	147
G-PCAM	TRIS	1052
G-PCAR	46T	97078
G-PCOP	200	BB-1860
G-PFFN	200	BB-456
G-PLAT	200	BB-487
G-PMHT	TBM8	440
G-POWB	350	FL-506
G-PRES	441	0107
G-PSTR	200	BB-209
G-PTER	90	LJ-944
G-PVPC	PC12	632
G-RACI	90	LJ-819
G-RAFD	200G	BY-32
G-RAFJ	200	BB-1829
G-RAFK	200	BB-1830
G-RAFL	200	BB-1832
G-RAFM	200	BB-1833
G-RAFN	200	BB-1835
G-RAFO	200	BB-1836
G-RAFP	200	BB-1837
G-RAFX	200G	BY-36
G-RAPA	BN2T	2115
G-RBCI	TRIS	1035
G-RBSI	TRIS	1027
G-RCCL	90	LJ-824
G-REBK	200	BB-1202
G-RHOP	TRIS	1042
G-RIOO	200	BB-1244
G-RIPA	P68	423
G-RKJT	46T	97111
G-RLON	TRIS	1008
G-RMST	46D	199
G-RNCO	690C	11664
G-ROWN	200	BB-684
G-RVRE	P68	57
G-SALV	90	LJ-991
G-SAMJ	P68	101
G-SANB	E90	LW-304
G-SARN	TRIS	1041
G-SASC	200C	BL-150
G-SASD	200C	BL-151
G-SAXN	200	BB-108
G-SBAS	200	BB-1007
G-SBUS	BN2	3013
G-SEIL	BN2	2103
G-SELX	BN2T	2118
G-SERC	350	FL-438
G-SFPA	F406	0064
G-SFPB	F406	0065
G-SFSG	E90	LW-239
G-SGEC	200	BB-1747
G-SHAM	90	LJ-819
G-SIBE	200	BB-828
G-SICA	BN2	2304
G-SICB	BN2	2260
G-SITU	P68	219
G-SJCH	BN2T	4006
G-SLAP	BN2	2304
G-SMMA	F406	0094
G-SMMB	F406	0095
G-SOFE	441	0109
G-SONG	200	BB-362
G-SPOR	200	BB-1557
G-SPOT	P68	15
G-SPTS	90	LJ-874
G-SRAY	BN2T	2034
G-SRES	300	FA-39
G-SSKY	BN2	2247
G-STYR	F90	LA-81
G-SURV	BN2T	4005
G-SVHA	P68	113
G-SVSS	90	LJ-1170
G-SWAN	690B	11517
G-SWFT	200	BB-828
G-SYGA	200	BB-1044
G-SYGB	200G	BY-68
G-TAGH	200	BB-1720
G-TDSA	F406	0096
G-TELE	P68	217
G-TEMI	BN2T	2143
G-THAN	F406	0024
G-THUR	200	BB-782
G-TINI	F406	0015
G-TRAT	PC12	710
G-TURF	F406	0020
G-TVSA	690B	11530
G-TWIG	F406	0014
G-TWOB	BN2	2159
G-TYME	690B	11512
G-UBHL	200	BB-864
G-UBSH	300	FA-101
G-UERN	BN2	2025
G-UNIT	P68	23
G-USAR	441	0355
G-VICW	200	BB-561
G-VJCT	P68	327
G-VPLC	200	BB-797
G-VRES	200	BB-379
G-VSBC	200	BB-1290
G-VSEL	200	BB-362
G-WATJ	200G	BY-14
G-WCCP	200	BB-1295
G-WEAC	TRIS	1042
G-WELL	E90	LW-198
G-WGSC	PC6	848
G-WICK	P68	169
G-WILK	200	BB-955
G-WINT	PC12	830

G-WLLM	90	LJ-1902
G-WNCH	**200**	**BB-1259**
G-WOTG	BN2T	2139
G-WPLC	200	BB-803
G-WRCF	200	BB-472
G-WSJE	200	BB-484
G-WTBC	P68	219
G-WVIP	**200**	**BB-625**
G-WWHL	200	BB-239
G-XAXA	**BN2**	**530**
G-XING	E121	121030
G-XTOR	**TRIS**	**359**
G-XTWO	E121	121030
G-YABU	695A	96083
G-YOTT	425	0054
(G-ZAPH)	F406	0049
G-ZAPT	200C	BL-141
G-ZUMO	**PC12**	**732**

Hungary

HA-	**MU-2**	**191**
HA-ACD	P68	278
HA-ACE	200	BB-1902
HA-ACQ	P68	367
HA-ACS	200	BB-324
HA-ACV	G1	102
HA-BNA	BN2	816
HA-SIP	**MIIB**	**T26-132**
HA-SIT	**31T**	**7820011**
HA-YDA	PC6	721
HA-YDB	PC6	740
HA-YDC	PC6	714
HA-YDE	**PC6**	**814**

Switzerland

"HB-CPA"	690B	11506
HB-FAB	PC6	845
HB-FAD	PC6	515
HB-FAE	PC6	514
HB-FAF	PC6	516
HB-FAG	PC6	527
HB-FAH	PC6	520
HB-FAI	PC6	350
HB-FAK	PC6	526
HB-FAL	PC6	540
HB-FAM	PC6	541
HB-FAN	PC6	337
HB-FAO	PC6	338
HB-FAP	PC6	339
HB-FAR	PC6	340
HB-FAS	PC6	341
HB-FAT	PC6	342
HB-FAU	PC6	346
HB-FAV	PC6	345
HB-FAW	PC6	347
HB-FAX	PC6	344
HB-FAY	PC6	349
HB-FAZ	PC6	343
HB-FBA	PC6	523
HB-FBB	PC6	529
HB-FBC	PC6	531
HB-FBD	PC6	521
HB-FBD	PC6	602
HB-FBE	PC6	528
HB-FBF	PC6	537
HB-FBG	PC6	553
HB-FBH	PC6	554
HB-FBI	PC6	555
HB-FBK	PC6	539
HB-FBL	PC6	556
HB-FBM	PC6	566
HB-FBN	PC6	565
HB-FBO	PC6	567
HB-FBP	PC6	560
HB-FBR	PC6	542
HB-FBS	PC6	538
HB-FBT	PC6	568
HB-FBU	PC6	547
HB-FBV	PC6	519
HB-FBW	PC6	580
HB-FBX	PC6	571
HB-FBY	PC6	576
HB-FBZ	PC6	584
HB-FCA	PC6	591
HB-FCB	PC6	594
HB-FCC	PC6	595
HB-FCD	PC6	585
HB-FCE	PC6	603
HB-FCF	**PC6**	**614**
HB-FCG	PC6	513
HB-FCH	PC6	615
HB-FCI	PC6	517
HB-FCK	PC6	616
HB-FCL	PC6	617
HB-FCM	PC6	618
HB-FCN	PC6	620
HB-FCO	PC6	628
HB-FCP	PC6	626
HB-FCR	PC6	631
HB-FCS	PC6	632
HB-FCT	**PC6**	**637**
HB-FCU	PC6	634
HB-FCV	PC6	646
HB-FCV	PC6	824
HB-FCW	PC6	638
HB-FCX	PC6	645
HB-FCY	PC6	650
HB-FCZ	PC6	651
HB-FDA	PC6	655
HB-FDB	PC6	660
HB-FDC	PC6	656
HB-FDD	PC6	657
HB-FDE	PC6	627
HB-FDF	PC6	629
HB-FDG	PC6	642
HB-FDH	PC6	658
HB-FDI	PC6	665
HB-FDK	PC6	652
HB-FDL	PC6	653
HB-FDM	PC6	661
HB-FDN	PC6	662
HB-FDO	FPC6	2002
HB-FDP	PC6	666
HB-FDR	PC6	667
HB-FDS	PC6	668
HB-FDT	PC6	654
HB-FDU	**PC6**	**663**
HB-FDV	PC6	680
HB-FDW	PC6	681
HB-FDX	PC6	683
HB-FDY	PC6	684
HB-FDZ	PC6	686
HB-FEA	PC6	687
HB-FEB	PC6	689
HB-FEC	PC6	690
HB-FED	PC6	692
HB-FEE	PC6	693
HB-FEF	PC6	659
HB-FEG	PC6	688
HB-FEH	PC6	669
HB-FEI	PC6	672
HB-FEK	PC6	682
HB-FEL	PC6	673
HB-FEM	PC6	674
HB-FEN	PC6	675
HB-FEO	PC6	676
HB-FEP	PC6	677
HB-FER	PC6	701
HB-FES	PC6	670
HB-FET	PC6	697
HB-FEU	PC6	698
HB-FEV	PC6	691
HB-FEW	PC6	694
HB-FEX	PC6	695
HB-FEY	PC6	678
HB-FEZ	PC6	699
HB-FFA	PC6	700
HB-FFB	PC6	706
HB-FFC	PC6	707
HB-FFD	PC6	708
HB-FFE	PC6	725
HB-FFF	PC6	704
HB-FFG	PC6	705
HB-FFH	PC6	712
HB-FFI	PC6	671
HB-FFK	PC6	702
HB-FFL	PC6	716
HB-FFM	PC6	696
HB-FFN	PC6	703
HB-FFO	PC6	709
HB-FFP	PC6	710
HB-FFQ	PC6	729
HB-FFR	PC6	531
HB-FFS	PC6	731
HB-FFT	PC6	732
HB-FFU	PC6	730
(HB-FFV)	PC6	724
HB-FFV	PC6	817
HB-FFW	PC6	735
HB-FFX	PC6	711
HB-FFY	PC6	679
HB-FFZ	PC6	713
HB-FGA	PC6	726
HB-FGB	PC6	733
HB-FGC	PC6	734
HB-FGD	PC6	736
HB-FGE	PC6	715
HB-FGF	PC6	742
HB-FGF	PC6	750
HB-FGG	PC6	743
HB-FGH	PC6	753
HB-FGI	PC6	810
HB-FGJ	PC6	746
(HB-FGK)	PC6	723
HB-FGK	PC6	755
HB-FGL	PC6	754
HB-FGM	PC6	762
HB-FGN	PC6	763
HB-FGO	PC6	767
HB-FGP	PC6	768
HB-FGR	PC6	784
HB-FGS	PC6	782
HB-FGT	PC6	783
HB-FGU	PC6	772
HB-FGV	PC6	773
HB-FGW	PC6	780
HB-FGX	PC6	781
HB-FGY	PC6	785
HB-FGZ	PC6	792
HB-FHA	PC6	794
HB-FHB	PC6	795
HB-FHC	PC6	796
HB-FHD	PC6	797
HB-FHE	PC6	798
HB-FHF	PC6	799
HB-FHG	PC6	801
HB-FHH	PC6	789
HB-FHI	PC6	811
HB-FHK	PC6	813
HB-FHL	PC6	524
HB-FHM	PC6	816
HB-FHN	PC6	820
HB-FHO	PC6	809
HB-FHP	PC6	818
HB-FHR	PC6	819
HB-FHS	PC6	821
HB-FHT	PC6	822
HB-FHU	PC6	823
HB-FHV	PC6	825
HB-FHW	PC6	826
HB-FHX	PC6	827
HB-FHY	PC6	828
HB-FHZ	**PC6**	**840**
HB-FIA	PC6	829
HB-FIB	PC6	830
HB-FIC	PC6	831
HB-FID	PC6	832
HB-FIE	PC6	748
HB-FIF	PC6	833
HB-FIG	PC6	834
HB-FIH	PC6	835
HB-FII	PC6	836
HB-FIJ	PC6	902
HB-FIK	PC6	837
HB-FIL	PC6	838
HB-FIM	PC6	741
HB-FIN	PC6	839
HB-FIO	PC6	841
HB-FIP	PC6	842
(HB-FIR)	PC6	551
HB-FIS	PC6	685
HB-FIT	PC6	849
HB-FIU	PC6	850
HB-FIV	PC6	851
HB-FIW	PC6	852
HB-FIX	PC6	853
HB-FIY	PC6	854
HB-FIZ	PC6	855
HB-FKA	PC6	846
HB-FKB	PC6	847
HB-FKC	**PC6**	**844**
HB-FKD	PC6	859
HB-FKE	PC6	861
HB-FKF	PC6	815
HB-FKG	PC6	858
HB-FKH	**PC6**	**865**
HB-FKI	PC6	863
HB-FKJ	PC6	895
HB-FKK	PC6	864
HB-FKL	**PC6**	**867**
HB-FKM	**PC6**	**873**
HB-FKN	PC6	870
HB-FKO	PC6	874
HB-FKP	**PC6**	**877**
HB-FKQ	PC6	661
HB-FKR	**PC6**	**872**
HB-FKS	PC6	875
HB-FKT	**PC6**	**876**
HB-FKU	PC6	887
HB-FKV	PC6	888
HB-FKW	PC6	889
HB-FKX	PC6	890
HB-FKY	PC6	891
HB-FKZ	PC6	892
HB-FLA	**PC6**	**905**
HB-FLB	**PC6**	**906**
HB-FLC	PC6	904
HB-FLD	PC6	913
HB-FLE	**PC6**	**912**
HB-FLF	PC6	916
HB-FLG	**PC6**	**910**
HB-FLH	**PC6**	**918**
HB-FLI	**PC6**	**893**
HB-FLJ	PC6	917
HB-FLK	**PC6**	**779**
HB-FLL	PC6	667
HB-FLM	PC6	919
HB-FLN	PC6	920
HB-FLO	PC6	922
HB-FLP	PC6	923
HB-FLQ	PC6	925
HB-FLR	PC6	926
HB-FLS	PC6	927
HB-FLT	PC6	928
HB-FLU	PC6	921
HB-FLV	PC6	931
HB-FLW	PC6	631
HB-FLX	PC6	929
HB-FLY	PC6	933
HB-FLZ	PC6	934
HB-FMA	PC6	930
HB-FMB	**PC6**	**932**
HB-FMC	PC6	938
HB-FMD	PC6	936
HB-FME	PC6	937
HB-FMF	PC6	939
HB-FMG	PC6	819
HB-FMH	PC6	894
HB-FMI	PC6	915
HB-FMJ	PC6	940
HB-FMK	PC6	941
HB-FMM	PC6	942
HB-FMN	PC6	943
HB-FMO	PC6	945
HB-FMP	PC6	935
HB-FMQ	PC6	946
HB-FMR	PC6	700
HB-FMS	PC6	947
HB-FMT	PC6	948
HB-FMU	PC6	951
HB-FMV	PC6	950
HB-FMW	PC6	953

HB-FMX PC6 954
HB-FMY PC6 955
HB-FMZ PC6 956
HB-FNA PC6 957
HB-FNB PC6 958
HB-FNC PC6 791
HB-FND PC6 959
HB-FNE PC6 960
HB-FNF PC6 961
HB-FNG PC6 962
HB-FNH PC6 963
HB-FNI PC6 964
HB-FNJ PC6 965
HB-FOA PC12 P01
HB-FOB PC12 P02
HB-FOC PC12 101
HB-FOD PC12 103
HB-FOE PC12 102
HB-FOF PC12 131
HB-FOG PC12 134
HB-FOH PC12 136
HB-FOI PC12 157
HB-FOJ PC12 158
HB-FOK PC12 161
HB-FOL PC12 166
HB-FOM PC12 201
HB-FON PC12 213
HB-FOO PC12 290
HB-FOP PC12 291
HB-FOQ PC12 349
HB-FOR PC12 257
HB-FOS PC12 366
HB-FOT PC12 121
HB-FOU PC12 368
HB-FOV PC12 190
HB-FOW PC12 411
HB-FOX PC12 334
HB-FOY PC12 386
HB-FOZ PC12 352
HB-FPA PC12 378
HB-FPB PC12 381
HB-FPC PC12 422
HB-FPD PC12 477
HB-FPE PC12 479
HB-FPF PC12 299
HB-FPG PC12 498
HB-FPH PC12 518
HB-FPI PC12 551
HB-FPJ PC12 490
HB-FPK PC12 513
HB-FPL PC12 247
HB-FPN PC12 445
HB-FPO PC12 536
HB-FPP PC12 538
HB-FPQ PC12 539
HB-FPR PC12 544
HB-FPS PC12 608
HB-FPT PC12 545
HB-FPU PC12 625
HB-FPV PC12 632
HB-FPW PC12 407
HB-FPX PC12 566
HB-FPY PC12 685
HB-FPZ PC12 702
HB-FQA PC12 104
HB-FQA PC12 192
HB-FQA PC12 283
HB-FQA PC12 380
HB-FQA PC12 468
HB-FQA PC12 561
HB-FQA PC12 666
HB-FQA PC12 775
HB-FQA PC12 869
HB-FQA PC12 1101
HB-FQB PC12 105
HB-FQB PC12 193
HB-FQB PC12 284
HB-FQB PC12 382
HB-FQB PC12 469
HB-FQB PC12 562
HB-FQB PC12 668
HB-FQB PC12 779
HB-FQB PC12 870
HB-FQB PC12 1102
HB-FQC PC12 106
HB-FQC PC12 194
HB-FQC PC12 285
HB-FQC PC12 384
HB-FQC PC12 470
HB-FQC PC12 563
HB-FQC PC12 670
HB-FQC PC12 780
HB-FQC PC12 871
HB-FQC PC12 1103
HB-FQD PC12 107
HB-FQD PC12 195
HB-FQD PC12 287
HB-FQD PC12 385
HB-FQD PC12 473
HB-FQD PC12 564
HB-FQD PC12 671
HB-FQD PC12 781
HB-FQD PC12 872
HB-FQD PC12 1104
HB-FQE PC12 111
HB-FQE PC12 196
HB-FQE PC12 288
HB-FQE PC12 388
HB-FQE PC12 474
HB-FQE PC12 549
HB-FQE PC12 672
HB-FQE PC12 783
HB-FQE PC12 873
HB-FQE PC12 1105
HB-FQF PC12 113
HB-FQF PC12 197
HB-FQF PC12 289
HB-FQF PC12 390
HB-FQF PC12 475
HB-FQF PC12 567
HB-FQF PC12 673
HB-FQF PC12 784
HB-FQF PC12 874
HB-FQF PC12 1027
HB-FQF PC12 1106
HB-FQG PC12 112
HB-FQG PC12 198
HB-FQG PC12 292
HB-FQG PC12 391
HB-FQG PC12 476
HB-FQG PC12 569
HB-FQG PC12 604
HB-FQG PC12 674
HB-FQG PC12 785
HB-FQG PC12 875
HB-FQG PC12 1028
HB-FQG PC12 1107
HB-FQH PC12 114
HB-FQH PC12 199
HB-FQH PC12 293
HB-FQH PC12 392
HB-FQH PC12 477
HB-FQH PC12 570
HB-FQH PC12 675
HB-FQH PC12 786
HB-FQH PC12 876
HB-FQH PC12 1029
HB-FQH PC12 1108
HB-FQI PC12 115
HB-FQI PC12 200
HB-FQI PC12 294
HB-FQI PC12 393
HB-FQI PC12 478
HB-FQI PC12 571
HB-FQI PC12 676
HB-FQI PC12 787
HB-FQI PC12 877
HB-FQI PC12 1023
HB-FQI PC12 1109
HB-FQJ PC12 116
HB-FQJ PC12 217
HB-FQJ PC12 295
HB-FQJ PC12 387
HB-FQJ PC12 479
HB-FQJ PC12 572
HB-FQJ PC12 663
HB-FQJ PC12 777
HB-FQJ PC12 878
HB-FQJ PC12 1030
HB-FQJ PC12 1110
HB-FQK PC12 117
HB-FQK PC12 218
HB-FQK PC12 296
HB-FQK PC12 397
HB-FQK PC12 480
HB-FQK PC12 573
HB-FQK PC12 701
HB-FQK PC12 789
HB-FQK PC12 879
HB-FQK PC12 1031
HB-FQK PC12 1111
HB-FQL PC12 118
HB-FQL PC12 219
HB-FQL PC12 297
HB-FQL PC12 398
HB-FQL PC12 481
HB-FQL PC12 575
HB-FQL PC12 703
HB-FQL PC12 790
HB-FQL PC12 880
HB-FQL PC12 1032
HB-FQL PC12 1112
HB-FQM PC12 119
HB-FQM PC12 221
HB-FQM PC12 298
HB-FQM PC12 399
HB-FQM PC12 467
HB-FQM PC12 576
HB-FQM PC12 686
HB-FQM PC12 792
HB-FQM PC12 881
HB-FQM PC12 1033
HB-FQM PC12 1113
HB-FQN PC12 120
HB-FQN PC12 222
HB-FQN PC12 300
HB-FQN PC12 389
HB-FQN PC12 471
HB-FQN PC12 577
HB-FQN PC12 688
HB-FQN PC12 793
HB-FQN PC12 882
HB-FQN PC12 1034
HB-FQN PC12 1114
HB-FQO PC12 121
HB-FQO PC12 223
HB-FQO PC12 302
HB-FQO PC12 394
HB-FQO PC12 472
HB-FQO PC12 578
HB-FQO PC12 691
HB-FQO PC12 795
HB-FQO PC12 883
HB-FQO PC12 1035
HB-FQO PC12 1116
HB-FQP PC12 124
HB-FQP PC12 224
HB-FQP PC12 395
HB-FQP PC12 482
HB-FQP PC12 606
HB-FQP PC12 692
HB-FQP PC12 796
HB-FQP PC12 884
HB-FQP PC12 1036
HB-FQP PC12 1117
HB-FQQ PC12 125
HB-FQQ PC12 209
HB-FQQ PC12 303
HB-FQQ PC12 396
HB-FQQ PC12 483
HB-FQQ PC12 605
HB-FQQ PC12 694
HB-FQQ PC12 782
HB-FQQ PC12 1037
HB-FQQ PC12 1118
HB-FQR PC12 126
HB-FQR PC12 210
HB-FQR PC12 304
HB-FQR PC12 400
HB-FQR PC12 484
HB-FQR PC12 580
HB-FQR PC12 698
HB-FQR PC12 798
HB-FQR PC12 885
HB-FQR PC12 1038
HB-FQR PC12 1115
HB-FQS PC12 127
HB-FQS PC12 215
HB-FQS PC12 305
HB-FQS PC12 401
HB-FQS PC12 485
HB-FQS PC12 582
HB-FQS PC12 700
HB-FQS PC12 799
HB-FQS PC12 886
HB-FQS PC12 1039
HB-FQS PC12 1119
HB-FQT PC12 128
HB-FQT PC12 212
HB-FQT PC12 306
HB-FQT PC12 403
HB-FQT PC12 486
HB-FQT PC12 583
HB-FQT PC12 705
HB-FQT PC12 801
HB-FQT PC12 887
HB-FQT PC12 1040
HB-FQT PC12 1120
HB-FQU PC12 130
HB-FQU PC12 216
HB-FQU PC12 307
HB-FQU PC12 404
HB-FQU PC12 487
HB-FQU PC12 584
HB-FQU PC12 689
HB-FQU PC12 1003
HB-FQU PC12 1041
HB-FQU PC12 1121
HB-FQV PC12 132
HB-FQV PC12 214
HB-FQV PC12 308
HB-FQV PC12 405
HB-FQV PC12 488
HB-FQV PC12 585
HB-FQV PC12 706
HB-FQV PC12 804
HB-FQV PC12 1004
HB-FQV PC12 1042
HB-FQW PC12 133
HB-FQW PC12 225
HB-FQW PC12 310
HB-FQW PC12 409
HB-FQW PC12 489
HB-FQW PC12 586
HB-FQW PC12 709
HB-FQW PC12 800
HB-FQW PC12 1005
HB-FQW PC12 1043
HB-FQW PC12 1123
HB-FQX PC12 129
HB-FQX PC12 226
HB-FQX PC12 311
HB-FQX PC12 402
HB-FQX PC12 493
HB-FQX PC12 622
HB-FQX PC12 710
HB-FQX PC12 806
HB-FQX PC12 1006
HB-FQX PC12 1044
HB-FQX PC12 1125
HB-FQY PC12 135
HB-FQY PC12 227
HB-FQY PC12 312
HB-FQY PC12 408
HB-FQY PC12 491
HB-FQY PC12 581
HB-FQY PC12 711
HB-FQY PC12 807
HB-FQY PC12 1007
HB-FQY PC12 1045
HB-FQY PC12 1122
HB-FQZ PC12 137
HB-FQZ PC12 228
HB-FQZ PC12 314
HB-FQZ PC12 410
HB-FQZ PC12 492

HB-FQZ	PC12	587	HB-FRH	PC12	419	HB-FRO	PC12	1061	HB-FRX	PC12	1069
HB-FQZ	PC12	696	HB-FRH	PC12	502	HB-FRO	PC12	1141	HB-FRX	PC12	1151
HB-FQZ	PC12	808	HB-FRH	PC12	596	HB-FRP	PC12	154	HB-FRY	PC12	163
HB-FQZ	PC12	1008	HB-FRH	PC12	719	HB-FRP	PC12	254	HB-FRY	PC12	345
HB-FQZ	PC12	1046	HB-FRH	PC12	819	HB-FRP	PC12	331	HB-FRY	PC12	442
HB-FQZ	PC12	1124	HB-FRH	PC12	1016	HB-FRP	PC12	427	HB-FRY	PC12	523
HB-FRA	PC12	139	HB-FRH	PC12	1054	HB-FRP	PC12	512	HB-FRY	PC12	631
HB-FRA	PC12	229	HB-FRH	PC12	1134	HB-FRP	PC12	613	HB-FRY	PC12	741
HB-FRA	PC12	315	HB-FRI	PC12	147	HB-FRP	PC12	731	HB-FRY	PC12	838
HB-FRA	PC12	412	HB-FRI	PC12	238	HB-FRP	PC12	826	**HB-FRY**	**PC12**	**1070**
HB-FRA	PC12	494	HB-FRI	PC12	324	HB-FRP	PC12	1025	HB-FRZ	PC12	164
HB-FRA	PC12	588	HB-FRI	PC12	415	HB-FRP	PC12	1062	HB-FRZ	PC12	346
HB-FRA	PC12	697	HB-FRI	PC12	503	HB-FRP	PC12	1143	HB-FRZ	PC12	437
HB-FRA	PC12	809	HB-FRI	PC12	609	HB-FRQ	PC12	155	HB-FRZ	PC12	524
HB-FRA	PC12	1009	HB-FRI	PC12	707	HB-FRQ	PC12	246	HB-FRZ	PC12	640
HB-FRA	PC12	1047	HB-FRI	PC12	820	HB-FRQ	PC12	333	HB-FRZ	PC12	742
HB-FRA	PC12	1127	HB-FRI	PC12	1017	HB-FRQ	PC12	432	HB-FRZ	PC12	839
HB-FRB	PC12	140	HB-FRI	PC12	1055	HB-FRQ	PC12	514	HB-FRZ	PC12	1098
HB-FRB	PC12	318	HB-FRI	PC12	1135	HB-FRQ	PC12	614	HB-FRZ	PC12	1163
HB-FRB	PC12	413	HB-FRJ	PC12	148	HB-FRQ	PC12	732	HB-FSA	PC12	165
HB-FRB	PC12	495	HB-FRJ	PC12	239	HB-FRQ	PC12	828	HB-FSA	PC12	256
HB-FRB	PC12	589	HB-FRJ	PC12	325	HB-FRQ	PC12	1026	HB-FSA	PC12	347
HB-FRB	PC12	712	HB-FRJ	PC12	420	HB-FRQ	PC12	1144	HB-FSA	PC12	441
HB-FRB	PC12	811	HB-FRJ	PC12	504	HB-FRR	PC12	156	HB-FSA	PC12	525
HB-FRB	PC12	1010	HB-FRJ	PC12	610	HB-FRR	PC12	247	HB-FSA	PC12	636
HB-FRB	PC12	1048	HB-FRJ	PC12	723	HB-FRR	PC12	335	HB-FSA	PC12	743
HB-FRB	PC12	1128	HB-FRJ	PC12	821	HB-FRR	PC12	429	HB-FSA	PC12	840
HB-FRC	PC12	141	HB-FRJ	PC12	1018	HB-FRR	PC12	515	HB-FSA	PC12	1100
HB-FRC	PC12	232	HB-FRJ	PC12	1056	HB-FRR	PC12	618	HB-FSA	PC12	1169
HB-FRC	PC12	320	HB-FRJ	PC12	1136	HB-FRR	PC12	733	HB-FSB	PC12	181
HB-FRC	PC12	414	HB-FRK	PC12	149	HB-FRR	PC12	846	HB-FSB	PC12	257
HB-FRC	PC12	500	HB-FRK	PC12	240	HB-FRR	PC12	1063	HB-FSB	PC12	348
HB-FRC	PC12	603	HB-FRK	PC12	326	HB-FRR	PC12	1142	HB-FSB	PC12	444
HB-FRC	PC12	714	HB-FRK	PC12	422	HB-FRS	PC12	248	HB-FSB	PC12	526
HB-FRC	PC12	813	HB-FRK	PC12	505	HB-FRS	PC12	336	HB-FSB	PC12	637
HB-FRC	PC12	1011	HB-FRK	PC12	600	HB-FRS	PC12	430	HB-FSB	PC12	744
HB-FRC	PC12	1049	HB-FRK	PC12	724	HB-FRS	PC12	516	HB-FSB	PC12	844
HB-FRC	PC12	1129	HB-FRK	PC12	822	HB-FRS	PC12	623	HB-FSB	PC12	1073
HB-FRD	PC12	142	HB-FRK	PC12	1019	HB-FRS	PC12	734	**HB-FSB**	**PC12**	**1150**
HB-FRD	PC12	233	HB-FRK	PC12	1057	HB-FRS	PC12	829	HB-FSC	PC12	167
HB-FRD	PC12	321	HB-FRK	PC12	1137	HB-FRS	PC12	1064	HB-FSC	PC12	258
HB-FRD	PC12	463	HB-FRL	PC12	150	**HB-FRS**	**PC12**	**1145**	HB-FSC	PC12	350
HB-FRD	PC12	496	HB-FRL	PC12	241	HB-FRT	PC12	249	HB-FSC	PC12	445
HB-FRD	PC12	592	HB-FRL	PC12	327	HB-FRT	PC12	338	HB-FSC	PC12	527
HB-FRD	PC12	715	HB-FRL	PC12	424	HB-FRT	PC12	431	HB-FSC	PC12	639
HB-FRD	PC12	814	HB-FRL	PC12	507	HB-FRT	PC12	517	HB-FSC	PC12	745
HB-FRD	PC12	1012	HB-FRL	PC12	611	HB-FRT	PC12	626	**HB-FSC**	**PC12**	**1074**
HB-FRD	PC12	1050	HB-FRL	PC12	726	HB-FRT	PC12	735	HB-FSD	PC12	168
HB-FRD	PC12	1130	HB-FRL	PC12	823	HB-FRT	PC12	831	HB-FSD	PC12	259
HB-FRE	PC12	143	HB-FRL	PC12	1020	HB-FRT	PC12	1065	HB-FSD	PC12	351
HB-FRE	PC12	234	HB-FRL	PC12	1058	**HB-FRT**	**PC12**	**1146**	HB-FSD	PC12	439
HB-FRE	PC12	322	**HB-FRL**	**PC12**	**1138**	HB-FRU	PC12	159	HB-FSD	PC12	528
HB-FRE	PC12	416	HB-FRM	PC12	151	HB-FRU	PC12	250	HB-FSD	PC12	641
HB-FRE	PC12	497	HB-FRM	PC12	253	HB-FRU	PC12	339	HB-FSD	PC12	746
HB-FRE	PC12	593	HB-FRM	PC12	328	HB-FRU	PC12	433	HB-FSD	PC12	848
HB-FRE	PC12	716	HB-FRM	PC12	343	HB-FRU	PC12	519	HB-FSD	PC12	1075
HB-FRE	PC12	816	HB-FRM	PC12	423	HB-FRU	PC12	627	**HB-FSD**	**PC12**	**1153**
HB-FRE	PC12	1051	HB-FRM	PC12	509	HB-FRU	PC12	736	HB-FSE	PC12	169
HB-FRE	PC12	1131	HB-FRM	PC12	612	HB-FRU	PC12	1066	HB-FSE	PC12	260
HB-FRF	PC12	144	HB-FRM	PC12	727	HB-FRU	PC12	1147	HB-FSE	PC12	353
HB-FRF	PC12	235	HB-FRM	PC12	824	HB-FRV	PC12	160	HB-FSE	PC12	446
HB-FRF	PC12	323	HB-FRM	PC12	1021	HB-FRV	PC12	255	HB-FSE	PC12	529
HB-FRF	PC12	417	HB-FRM	PC12	1059	HB-FRV	PC12	340	HB-FSE	PC12	642
HB-FRF	PC12	499	HB-FRM	PC12	1139	HB-FRV	PC12	435	HB-FSE	PC12	747
HB-FRF	PC12	594	HB-FRN	PC12	152	HB-FRV	PC12	520	HB-FSE	PC12	849
HB-FRF	PC12	717	HB-FRN	PC12	243	HB-FRV	PC12	628	HB-FSE	PC12	1076
HB-FRF	PC12	817	HB-FRN	PC12	329	HB-FRV	PC12	737	**HB-FSE**	**PC12**	**1156**
HB-FRF	PC12	1014	HB-FRN	PC12	421	HB-FRV	PC12	834	HB-FSF	PC12	170
HB-FRF	PC12	1052	HB-FRN	PC12	510	HB-FRV	PC12	1067	HB-FSF	PC12	261
HB-FRF	**PC12**	**1132**	HB-FRN	PC12	616	**HB-FRV**	**PC12**	**1148**	HB-FSF	PC12	354
HB-FRG	PC12	145	HB-FRN	PC12	728	HB-FRW	PC12	341	HB-FSF	PC12	450
HB-FRG	PC12	236	HB-FRN	PC12	825	HB-FRW	PC12	438	HB-FSF	PC12	532
HB-FRG	PC12	309	HB-FRN	PC12	1022	HB-FRW	PC12	521	HB-FSF	PC12	643
HB-FRG	PC12	418	HB-FRN	PC12	1060	HB-FRW	PC12	629	HB-FSF	PC12	748
HB-FRG	PC12	501	**HB-FRN**	**PC12**	**1140**	HB-FRW	PC12	740	HB-FSF	PC12	850
HB-FRG	PC12	595	HB-FRO	PC12	153	HB-FRW	PC12	835	HB-FSF	PC12	1077
HB-FRG	PC12	718	HB-FRO	PC12	244	HB-FRW	PC12	1068	**HB-FSF**	**PC12**	**1152**
HB-FRG	PC12	818	HB-FRO	PC12	330	**HB-FRW**	**PC12**	**1149**	HB-FSG	PC12	171
HB-FRG	PC12	1015	HB-FRO	PC12	425	HB-FRX	PC12	162	HB-FSG	PC12	262
HB-FRG	PC12	1053	HB-FRO	PC12	511	HB-FRX	PC12	344	HB-FSG	PC12	355
HB-FRG	**PC12**	**1133**	HB-FRO	PC12	620	HB-FRX	PC12	440	HB-FSG	PC12	447
HB-FRH	PC12	146	HB-FRO	PC12	730	HB-FRX	PC12	630	HB-FSG	PC12	533
HB-FRH	PC12	237	HB-FRO	PC12	810	HB-FRX	PC12	722	HB-FSG	PC12	644
HB-FRH	PC12	316	HB-FRO	PC12	1024	HB-FRX	PC12	836	HB-FSG	PC12	749

HB-FSG	PC12	852
HB-FSG	PC12	1078
HB-FSG	**PC12**	**1157**
HB-FSH	PC12	172
HB-FSH	PC12	263
HB-FSH	PC12	356
HB-FSH	PC12	449
HB-FSH	PC12	534
HB-FSH	PC12	645
HB-FSH	PC12	752
HB-FSH	PC12	853
HB-FSH	PC12	1079
HB-FSH	**PC12**	**1154**
HB-FSI	PC12	173
HB-FSI	PC12	264
HB-FSI	PC12	357
HB-FSI	PC12	412
HB-FSI	PC12	535
HB-FSI	PC12	646
HB-FSI	PC12	753
HB-FSI	PC12	837
HB-FSI	PC12	1080
HB-FSI	**PC12**	**1158**
HB-FSJ	PC12	174
HB-FSJ	PC12	265
HB-FSJ	PC12	337
HB-FSJ	PC12	451
HB-FSJ	PC12	537
HB-FSJ	PC12	649
HB-FSJ	PC12	754
HB-FSJ	PC12	843
HB-FSJ	PC12	1099
HB-FSK	PC12	175
HB-FSK	PC12	266
HB-FSK	PC12	358
HB-FSK	PC12	452
HB-FSK	PC12	530
HB-FSK	PC12	651
HB-FSK	PC12	756
HB-FSK	PC12	854
HB-FSK	PC12	1082
HB-FSK	**PC12**	**1159**
HB-FSL	PC12	176
HB-FSL	PC12	267
HB-FSL	PC12	360
HB-FSL	PC12	453
HB-FSL	PC12	538
HB-FSL	PC12	546
HB-FSL	PC12	633
HB-FSL	PC12	757
HB-FSL	PC12	857
HB-FSL	PC12	1083
HB-FSL	**PC12**	**1165**
HB-FSM	PC12	177
HB-FSM	PC12	268
HB-FSM	PC12	362
HB-FSM	PC12	454
HB-FSM	PC12	565
HB-FSM	PC12	638
HB-FSM	PC12	758
HB-FSM	PC12	859
HB-FSM	PC12	1084
HB-FSM	**PC12**	**1168**
HB-FSN	PC12	178
HB-FSN	PC12	269
HB-FSN	PC12	359
HB-FSN	PC12	455
HB-FSN	PC12	540
HB-FSN	PC12	650
HB-FSN	PC12	751
HB-FSN	PC12	860
HB-FSN	PC12	1085
HB-FSO	PC12	179
HB-FSO	PC12	270
HB-FSO	PC12	375
HB-FSO	PC12	381
HB-FSO	PC12	541
HB-FSO	PC12	653
HB-FSO	PC12	760
HB-FSO	PC12	864
HB-FSO	PC12	1086
HB-FSP	PC12	180
HB-FSP	PC12	271
HB-FSP	PC12	364

HB-FSP	PC12	448
HB-FSP	PC12	542
HB-FSP	PC12	654
HB-FSP	PC12	841
HB-FSP	PC12	1087
HB-FSQ	PC12	182
HB-FSQ	PC12	272
HB-FSQ	PC12	365
HB-FSQ	PC12	456
HB-FSQ	PC12	543
HB-FSQ	PC12	693
HB-FSQ	PC12	762
HB-FSQ	PC12	855
HB-FSQ	PC12	1064
HB-FSR	PC12	183
HB-FSR	PC12	273
HB-FSR	PC12	367
HB-FSR	PC12	457
HB-FSR	PC12	557
HB-FSR	PC12	657
HB-FSR	PC12	763
HB-FSR	PC12	851
HB-FSR	PC12	1088
HB-FSS	PC12	184
HB-FSS	PC12	274
HB-FSS	PC12	373
HB-FSS	PC12	458
HB-FSS	PC12	547
HB-FSS	PC12	658
HB-FSS	PC12	764
HB-FSS	PC12	858
HB-FSS	PC12	1089
HB-FST	PC12	185
HB-FST	PC12	275
HB-FST	PC12	370
HB-FST	PC12	459
HB-FST	PC12	548
HB-FST	PC12	659
HB-FST	PC12	765
HB-FST	PC12	861
HB-FST	PC12	1090
HB-FSU	PC12	186
HB-FSU	PC12	276
HB-FSU	PC12	371
HB-FSU	PC12	460
HB-FSU	PC12	552
HB-FSU	PC12	648
HB-FSU	PC12	766
HB-FSU	PC12	862
HB-FSU	**PC12**	**1091**
HB-FSV	PC12	187
HB-FSV	PC12	277
HB-FSV	PC12	372
HB-FSV	PC12	461
HB-FSV	PC12	553
HB-FSV	PC12	660
HB-FSV	PC12	767
HB-FSV	PC12	863
HB-FSV	PC12	1092
HB-FSW	PC12	188
HB-FSW	PC12	278
HB-FSW	PC12	377
HB-FSW	PC12	462
HB-FSW	PC12	555
HB-FSW	PC12	661
HB-FSW	PC12	770
HB-FSW	PC12	865
HB-FSW	PC12	1094
HB-FSX	PC12	189
HB-FSX	PC12	279
HB-FSX	PC12	361
HB-FSX	PC12	464
HB-FSX	PC12	556
HB-FSX	PC12	662
HB-FSX	PC12	773
HB-FSX	PC12	866
HB-FSX	PC12	1095
HB-FSY	PC12	190
HB-FSY	PC12	230
HB-FSY	PC12	280
HB-FSY	PC12	374
HB-FSY	PC12	465
HB-FSY	PC12	558
HB-FSY	PC12	664

HB-FSY	PC12	768
HB-FSY	PC12	867
HB-FSY	PC12	1096
HB-FSZ	PC12	191
HB-FSZ	PC12	281
HB-FSZ	PC12	376
HB-FSZ	PC12	466
HB-FSZ	PC12	559
HB-FSZ	PC12	665
HB-FSZ	PC12	774
HB-FSZ	PC12	868
HB-FSZ	PC12	1097
HB-FVA	**PC12**	**833**
HB-FVB	PC12	1001
HB-FVC	**PC12**	**1002**
HB-FVD	**PC12**	**1072**
HB-FVE	**PC12**	**1081**
HB-FVF	**PC12**	**1071**
HB-FVG	**PC12**	**1093**
HB-FVU	**PC12**	**888**
HB-FVV	**PC12**	**778**
HB-FVZ	**PC12**	**343**
(HB-GBK)	90	LJ-7
HB-GBK	90	LJ-45
HB-GCB	90	LJ-14
HB-GCF	90	LJ-32
HB-GCH	90	LJ-40
HB-GCI	90	LJ-4
HB-GCK	90	LJ-99
HB-GCU	90	LJ-121
HB-GCV	90	LJ-264
HB-GCW	90	LJ-88
HB-GDA	90	LJ-996
HB-GDF	90	LJ-136
HB-GDG	90	LJ-206
HB-GDI	200	BB-1079
HB-GDI	90	LJ-265
HB-GDL	200	BB-1079
HB-GDT	90	LJ-423
HB-GDU	90	LJ-434
HB-GDV	90	LJ-433
HB-GDW	90	LJ-132
HB-GEE	90	LJ-482
HB-GEH	690A	11292
HB-GEK	680T	1532-2
HB-GEN	100	B-39
HB-GEP	B100	BE-6
HB-GEV	90	LJ-215
HB-GEZ	90	LJ-518
HB-GFG	E90	LW-6
HB-GFH	690	11055
HB-GFI	E90	LW-39
HB-GFO	690A	11152
HB-GFP	690A	11108
HB-GFQ	690A	11141
HB-GFR	690A	11161
HB-GFS	690A	11243
HB-GFY	690A	11221
HB-GGO	200	BB-251
HB-GGS	200	BB-1003
HB-GGU	E90	LW-315
HB-GGW	90	LJ-741
HB-GGX	F90	LA-15
HB-GGY	200	BB-643
HB-GGY	E90	LW-288
HB-GGZ	F90	LA-84
HB-GHA	200	BB-490
HB-GHB	90	LJ-931
HB-GHC	90	LJ-969
HB-GHD	**F90**	**LA-50**
HB-GHE	690B	11465
HB-GHF	200	BB-417
HB-GHH	200	BB-1107
HB-GHI	200	BB-1102
HB-GHK	695A	96023
HB-GHM	F90	LA-166
HB-GHN	90	LJ-1093
HB-GHO	F90	LA-111
HB-GHP	F90	LA-100
HB-GHR	200	BB-836
HB-GHS	200	BB-1039
HB-GHT	90	LJ-944
HB-GHV	**300**	**FA-170**
HB-GHW	90	LJ-1089

HB-GHY	300	FA-135
HB-GHZ	200	BB-944
HB-GIB	90	LJ-571
HB-GIC	90	LJ-672
HB-GID	200	BB-618
HB-GIE	90	LJ-931
HB-GIF	90	LJ-591
HB-GIG	200	BB-1157
HB-GIH	90	LJ-867
HB-GII	350C	FN-1
HB-GIL	**200**	**BB-194**
HB-GIM	90	LJ-1267
HB-GIN	90	LJ-311
HB-GIO	300	FA-121
HB-GIP	300	FA-202
HB-GIR	200	BB-1377
HB-GIT	300	FA-142
HB-GIU	200	BB-1252
HB-GIW	90	LJ-775
HB-GIY	90	LJ-829
HB-GIZ	90	LJ-1202
HB-GJA	90	LJ-992
HB-GJB	350	FL-75
HB-GJC	300	FA-228
HB-GJD	**200C**	**BL-7**
HB-GJE	90	LJ-1391
HB-GJF	90	LJ-1407
HB-GJH	**90**	**LJ-972**
HB-GJI	**200**	**BB-451**
HB-GJL	350	FL-183
HB-GJM	**200**	**BB-255**
HB-GJN	350	FL-312
HB-GJP	**350**	**FL-477**
HB-GJQ	**F90**	**LA-4**
HB-GJR	350	FL-340
HB-GJS	350	FL-404
HB-GJW	**200**	**BB-1505**
HB-GJX	200	BB-932
HB-GPB	690C	11605
HB-GPF	350	FL-224
HB-GPG	200	BB-307
HB-GPH	**200**	**BB-1569**
HB-GPI	**300**	**FA-220**
HB-GPL	**90**	**LJ-1936**
HB-IRQ	G1	166
HB-KEI	TBM7	3
HB-KFR	**TBM7**	**195**
HB-KHC	**TBM7**	**342**
HB-KHP	TBM8	426
HB-KOA	PC6	625
HB-KOL	**TBM7**	**218**
HB-KOR	**TBM8**	**349**
HB-LAY	P166	359
HB-LDT	G1	188
HB-LEA	MU-2	011
HB-LEB	MU-2	009
HB-LEC	MU-2	028
HB-LED	MU-2	102
HB-LEE	MU-2	135
HB-LEF	MU-2	505
HB-LFF	441	0055
HB-LGL	P68	05
HB-LGO	P68	25
HB-LHN	P68	34
HB-LHT	31T	7520003
HB-LIA	BN2	396
HB-LIC	BN2	46
HB-LIW	31T	7720031
HB-LKD	MU-2	370SA
HB-LKS	P68	176
HB-LKV	MU-2	737SA
HB-LLG	MU-2	793SA
HB-LLK	**31T**	**7904014**
HB-LLO	31T	8020030
HB-LLP	MU-2	767SA
HB-LLS	425	0040
HB-LLV	P68	204
HB-LMB	441	0146
HB-LMP	441	0203
HB-LMT	31T	8104017
HB-LMX	MU-2	1528SA
HB-LNK	P68	224
HB-LNL	**31T**	**8020083**
HB-LNT	425	0134

HB-LNX	**31T**	**8166050**
HB-LOA	**P68**	**35**
HB-LOD	MIII	T-339
HB-LOE	425	0016
HB-LOL	690C	11639
HB-LOV	PA42	8001057
HB-LOZ	31T	7920039
HB-LPR	31T	8104070
HB-LPU	425	0074
HB-LPV	PA42	8301002
HB-LPW	P68	226
HB-LPZ	**P68**	**44**
HB-LQA	695	95069
HB-LQB	MU-2	1512SA
HB-LQN	MU-2	1559SA
HB-LQP	**31T**	**8004044**
HB-LQS	MU-2	1534SA
HB-LQW	P68T	8001
HB-LRA	31T	8004037
HB-LRI	PA42	8001043
HB-LRK	P68	360
HB-LRM	31T	1166005
HB-LRV	31T	7820017
HB-LSB	P68	288
HB-LTB	P68	344
HB-LTE	P180	1042
HB-LTI	**31T**	**8020091**
HB-LTM	PA42	5527028
HB-LTN	**P180**	**1066**
HB-LTQ	**P68**	**415**
HB-LTS	**P68**	**69**
HB-LTZ	**P180**	**1105**
HB-LUA	**P68**	**437**
HB-LUF	**31T**	**8120015**
HB-LUQ	**31T**	**8120056**
HB-LUR	**P180**	**1153**
HB-PKS	**46D**	**61**
HB-PMO	46D	180
(HB-PND)	46D	14
HB-POA	46D	141
HB-PQX	**46T**	**97194**
HB-PRG	46T	97091

Ecuador

HC-	**690D**	**15023**
HC-	**695**	**95026**
HC-	**90**	**LJ-986**
HC-AOG	FPC6	2029
HC-AQV	FPC6	2036
HC-ATF	FPC6	2027
HC-ATX	FPC6	2035
HC-AVL	FPC6	2041
HC-BDX	**BN2**	**51**
HC-BFI	BN2	588
HC-BFJ	BN2	590
HC-BGK	FPC6	2029
HC-BHC	**BN2**	**59**
HC-BHG	200	BB-723
HC-BHL	PC6	789
HC-BHU	690C	11634
HC-BIF	**31T**	**8120019**
HC-BJS	**PC6**	**724**
HC-BKL	**PC6**	**811**
HC-BKM	**PC6**	**813**
HC-BLG	TRIS	1047
HC-BLH	TRIS	1049
HC-BMI	690A	11162
HC-BNF	31T	7904039
HC-BNR	BN2	2157
HC-BNS	BN2	2162
HC-BPF	690A	11235
HC-BPX	690A	11187
HC-BPY	681B	6049
HC-BRT	200	BB-606
HC-BSR	200	BB-483
HC-BTK	P68	264
HC-BTX	BN2	911
HC-BUA	MIII	T-325
HC-BUD	**690C**	**11669**
HC-BUS	31T	8166064
HC-BUZ	**BN2**	**2278**
HC-BVA	31T	7820069
HC-BXF	31T	7820069
HC-BXF	31T	8166049
HC-BXH	**441**	**0268**
HC-BXT	690C	11615
HC-BXZ	31T	7520036
HC-BYY	300	FA-55
HC-BZD	90	LJ-1505
HC-BZF	**BN2**	**200**
HC-CAC	PC6	928
HC-CAD	200	BB-483
HC-CAF	350	FL-257
HC-CGI	**BN2**	**849**
HC-CGP	**PC6**	**960**
HC-CGQ	**PC6**	**961**
HC-CGY	**BN2**	**490**
HC-DAC	**E90**	**LW-178**

Haiti

(HH-)	695A	96009
HH-CNA	BN2	410
HH-CNB	BN2	442
HH-CNC	BN2	474
HH-JEC	**BN2**	**150**
HH-MSA	BN2	610

Dominican Republic

HI-	**MU-2**	**194**
HI-213	BN2	666
HI-214	BN2	679
HI-215	BN2	672
HI-216	BN2	680
(HI-217)	BN2	222
HI-220	BN2	222
HI-366	90	LJ-928
HI-366CT	90	LJ-928
HI-383	BN2	666
(HI-409)	PA42	8001070
HI-409	PA42	8001075
HI-423	690D	15005
HI-446	F90	LA-195
HI-449	F90	LA-207
HI-469	90	LJ-1000
HI-469SP	90	LJ-1000
HI-547	MU-2	548
HI-551CA	**BN2**	**410**
HI-566CA	BN2	2005
HI-567CA	BN2	592
HI-578SP	300	FA-180
(HI-578SP)	300	FA-186
HI-586SP	350	FL-8
HI-593CA	**BN2**	**2005**
HI-598SP	425	0027
HI-605	90	LJ-455
HI-636CA	BN2	625
HI-636CT	BN2	625
HI-640CA	BN2	849
HI-653CA	BN2	8
HI-653CT	BN2	8
HI-663CA	**BN2**	**98**
HI-663SP	100	B-34
HI-678CA	G1	323
HI-678CT	**G1**	**323**
HI-701SP	**200**	**BB-984**
HI-704CT	BN2	504
HI-776SP	**90**	**LJ-1163**
HI-787CA	**BN2**	**542**
HI-787SP	BN2	542
HI-789CA	BN2	849

Colombia

HK-	**441**	**0328**
(HK-)	690B	11400
HK-	**200**	**BB-180**
HK-	**200**	**BB-362**
HK-	**300**	**FA-69**
HK-	**31T**	**8020064**
HK-	**350**	**FL-575**
HK-	**690B**	**11386**
HK-	690C	11602
HK-	690C	11604
HK-	695	95040
HK-	695	95045
HK-	695A	96030
HK-	695A	96035
HK-	**90**	**LJ-248**
HK-	**90**	**LJ-469**
HK-	**90**	**LJ-1873**
HK-	**E90**	**LW-90**
HK-	**MIII**	**T-253**
HK-849	**BN2**	**224**
HK-853P	90	LJ-458
HK-853W	90	LJ-458
HK-853X	90	LJ-458
"HK-1209"	BN2	2113
HK-1241	**BN2**	**265**
HK-1241X	BN2	265
HK-1244	**BN2**	**248**
HK-1244X	BN2	248
HK-1375E	PC6	349
HK-1375P	PC6	349
HK-1375X	PC6	349
HK-1378W	FPC6	2026
HK-1378X	FPC6	2026
HK-1391W	FPC6	2028
HK-1391X	FPC6	2028
HK-1704	**TRIS**	**1019**
HK-1704X	TRIS	1019
HK-1711	TRIS	1002
HK-1711X	TRIS	1002
HK-1770G	**690A**	**11216**
HK-1771G	**690A**	**11217**
HK-1805	90	LJ-329
HK-1805E	90	LJ-329
HK-1805X	90	LJ-329
HK-1844P	**690**	**11056**
HK-1844W	690	11056
HK-1844X	690	11056
HK-1977	**681**	**6035**
HK-1977P	681	6035
HK-1977W	681	6035
HK-1977X	681	6035
HK-1982	690	11014
HK-1982P	690	11014
HK-1982W	**690**	**11014**
HK-1982X	690	11014
HK-2051	690B	11350
HK-2051C	690B	11350
HK-2051W	690B	11350
HK-2051X	690B	11350
HK-2055	**690**	**11005**
HK-2055W	690	11005
HK-2055X	690	11005
HK-2060	MU-2	243
HK-2060W	MU-2	243
HK-2060X	MU-2	243
HK-2120	MU-2	621
HK-2120P	**MU-2**	**621**
HK-2120X	MU-2	621
HK-2217	681B	6053
HK-2217P	681B	6053
HK-2217W	681B	6053
HK-2217X	681B	6053
HK-2218W	**690B**	**11453**
HK-2218X	690B	11453
HK-2245P	MU-2	684
HK-2245W	MU-2	684
HK-2245X	MU-2	684
HK-2281	**690**	**11033**
HK-2281P	690	11033
HK-2281X	690	11033
HK-2282	690A	11128
HK-2282P	**690A**	**11128**
HK-2282W	690A	11128
HK-2282X	690A	11128
HK-2285	680T	1632-57
HK-2285P	680T	1632-57
HK-2285X	680T	1632-57
HK-2291	690B	11364
HK-2291X	690B	11364
HK-2347	31T	7920076
HK-2347P	31T	7920076
HK-2347X	31T	7920076
HK-2376	**681**	**6043**
HK-2376P	681	6043
HK-2376W	681	6043
HK-2376X	681	6043
HK-2390W	**441**	**0016**
HK-2390X	441	0016
HK-2403	MU-2	678
HK-2403P	MU-2	678
HK-2403W	MU-2	678
HK-2403X	MU-2	678
HK-2412	TRIS	350
HK-2412X	TRIS	350
HK-2413	441	0111
HK-2413P	441	0111
HK-2413W	441	0111
HK-2413X	441	0111
HK-2414	690A	11296
HK-2414P	690A	11296
HK-2414X	690A	11296
HK-2415	690A	11100
HK-2415X	690A	11100
HK-2438W	**MIII**	**T-305**
HK-2451P	**31T**	**8020040**
HK-2451X	31T	8020040
HK-2455	31T	8020047
HK-2455P	31T	8020047
HK-2455W	**31T**	**8020047**
HK-2455X	31T	8020047
HK-2478	690C	11609
HK-2478P	690C	11609
HK-2478W	690C	11609
HK-2478X	690C	11609
HK-2479	**MIII**	**T-320**
HK-2479X	MIII	T-320
HK-2481	TRIS	321
HK-2481X	TRIS	321
HK-2482	TRIS	299
HK-2482X	TRIS	299
HK-2484	F90	LA-54
HK-2484X	F90	LA-54
HK-2486W	441	0155
HK-2486X	441	0155
HK-2489	200	BB-393
HK-2489X	200	BB-393
HK-2490	690B	11354
HK-2490P	690B	11354
HK-2490W	690B	11354
HK-2490X	690B	11354
HK-2491	**E90**	**LW-183**
HK-2491X	E90	LW-183
HK-2492	690B	11448
HK-2492P	690B	11448
HK-2492X	690B	11448
HK-2495	690C	11633
HK-2495P	**690C**	**11633**
HK-2495X	690C	11633
HK-2532G	MU-2	010
HK-2532X	MU-2	010
HK-2538	441	0114
HK-2538P	**441**	**0114**
HK-2538X	441	0114
HK-2539G	680T	1563-19
HK-2550	E90	LW-69
HK-2550X	E90	LW-69
HK-2551P	**690B**	**11489**
HK-2551W	690B	11489
HK-2551X	690B	11489
HK-2585P	**31T**	**8020077**
HK-2585X	31T	8020077
HK-2595W	90	LJ-950
HK-2595X	90	LJ-950
HK-2596	**90**	**LJ-957**
HK-2596G	90	LJ-957
HK-2596X	90	LJ-957
HK-2599P	**690C**	**11642**
HK-2599W	690C	11642
HK-2599X	690C	11642
HK-2601	690C	11651
HK-2601P	**690C**	**11651**
HK-2601W	690C	11651
HK-2601X	690C	11651
HK-2607	31T	8120022
HK-2607W	31T	8120022
HK-2607X	31T	8120022

HK-2608	695	95061
HK-2608P	695	95061
HK-2608X	695	95061
HK-2617P	31T	8120015
HK-2617X	31T	8120015
HK-2631G	31T	8120032
HK-2631X	31T	8120032
HK-2642P	31T	8120037
HK-2642X	31T	8120037
HK-2674G	31T	8120047
HK-2674P	31T	8120047
HK-2674X	31T	8120047
HK-2682	695	95066
HK-2682P	695	95066
HK-2682X	695	95066
HK-2684	PA42	8001042
HK-2684	PA42	8001068
HK-2684X	PA42	8001042
HK-2684X	PA42	8001068
HK-2687X	BN2	841
HK-2693	E121	121041
HK-2693X	E121	121041
HK-2700	200C	BL-15
HK-2700W	200C	BL-15
HK-2700X	200C	BL-15
HK-2738	695	95052
HK-2738P	695	95052
HK-2738W	695	95052
HK-2738X	695	95052
HK-2749P	31T	8166019
HK-2749X	31T	8166019
HK-2772P	PA42	8001059
HK-2772X	PA42	8001059
"HK-2784"	690D	15024
HK-2822	BN2	2109
HK-2822X	BN2	2109
HK-2873	90	LJ-994
HK-2873P	90	LJ-994
HK-2873W	90	LJ-994
HK-2873X	90	LJ-994
HK-2888P	F90	LA-181
HK-2888W	F90	LA-181
HK-2888X	F90	LA-181
HK-2890	BN2	2111
HK-2890X	BN2	2111
HK-2904	BN2	2113
HK-2904X	BN2	2113
HK-2906P	31T	8120064
HK-2906X	31T	8120064
HK-2907	31T	8166059
HK-2907P	31T	8166059
HK-2907X	31T	8166059
HK-2908	695A	96044
HK-2908P	695A	96044
HK-2908X	695A	96044
HK-2909	695A	96045
HK-2909P	695A	96045
HK-2909X	695A	96045
HK-2912	695A	96041
HK-2912P	695A	96041
HK-2912X	695A	96041
HK-2926	31T	8275015
HK-2926P	31T	8275015
HK-2926X	31T	8275015
HK-2951	695A	96049
HK-2951P	695A	96049
HK-2951X	695A	96049
HK-2963	31T	8166053
HK-2963W	31T	8166053
HK-2986X	681B	6046
HK-2993	PC6	592
HK-2993P	PC6	592
HK-2993X	PC6	592
HK-2994	FPC6	2048
HK-2994P	FPC6	2048
HK-2994X	FPC6	2048
HK-2996P	690B	11562
HK-2996X	690B	11562
HK-3000G	PA42	8001062
HK-3000X	PA42	8001062
HK-3009	441	0273
HK-3009P	441	0273
HK-3009W	441	0273
HK-3009X	441	0273
HK-3025	31T	8120062
HK-3025X	31T	8120062
HK-3036	425	0118
HK-3036P	425	0118
HK-3036X	425	0118
HK-3043P	31T	8120051
HK-3043W	31T	8120051
HK-3043X	31T	8120051
HK-3047P	31T	8166035
HK-3060	695A	96039
HK-3060P	695A	96039
HK-3060X	695A	96039
HK-3074	31T	8166035
HK-3074X	31T	8166035
HK-3117	31T	8166073
HK-3117W	31T	8166073
HK-3117X	31T	8166073
HK-3118	F90	LA-198
HK-3118W	F90	LA-198
HK-3118X	F90	LA-198
"HK-3147X"	690	11003
HK-3157	695A	96026
HK-3157P	695A	96026
HK-3157W	695A	96026
HK-3157X	695A	96026
HK-3192	695A	96077
HK-3192W	695A	96077
HK-3192X	695A	96077
HK-3193	695A	96086
HK-3193P	695A	96086
HK-3193X	695A	96086
HK-3194	695A	96060
HK-3194W	695A	96060
HK-3194X	695A	96060
HK-3207W	FPC6	2026
HK-3207X	FPC6	2026
HK-3214G	200	BB-854
HK-3214X	200	BB-854
HK-3218	695A	96061
HK-3218X	695A	96061
HK-3221	690C	11660
HK-3221P	690C	11660
HK-3221X	690C	11660
HK-3227W	200	BB-305
HK-3227X	200	BB-305
"HK-3230P"	695	95025
HK-3236P	681B	6046
HK-3236X	681B	6046
HK-3239P	695A	96010
HK-3239W	695A	96010
HK-3239X	695★	96010
HK-3240	695A	96020
HK-3240W	695A	96020
HK-3240X	695A	96020
"HK-3245"	690A	11318
HK-3245G	690A	11318
HK-3253	695A	96074
HK-3253P	695A	96074
HK-3253X	695A	96074
HK-3263	695A	96056
HK-3263P	695A	96056
HK-3263X	695A	96056
HK-3271	695A	96009
HK-3271X	695A	96009
HK-3275	695A	96076
HK-3275P	695A	96076
HK-3275X	695A	96076
HK-3276	90	LJ-804
HK-3276X	90	LJ-804
HK-3277P	90	LJ-892
HK-3277X	90	LJ-892
HK-3278	695A	96073
HK-3278X	695A	96073
HK-3279	695A	96072
HK-3279W	695A	96072
HK-3279X	695A	96072
HK-3283	695A	96099
HK-3283W	695A	96099
HK-3283X	695A	96099
HK-3284	695A	96080
HK-3284G	695A	96080
HK-3284W	695A	96080
HK-3284X	695A	96080
HK-3290	690C	11653
"HK-3290"	690C	11666
HK-3290P	690C	11653
HK-3290X	690C	11653
HK-3291	695A	96088
HK-3291P	695A	96088
HK-3291W	695A	96088
HK-3291X	695A	96088
HK-3314	690A	11255
HK-3314W	690A	11255
HK-3314X	690A	11255
HK-3315X	G1	24
HK-3316X	G1	59
"HK-3320W"	PA42	5527030
HK-3324	695A	96100
HK-3324P	695A	96100
HK-3324X	695A	96100
HK-3328	695A	96013
HK-3328P	695A	96013
HK-3328W	695A	96013
HK-3328X	695A	96013
HK-3329X	G1	145
HK-3330X	G1	90
HK-3331P	31T	7920088
HK-3331W	31T	7920088
HK-3331X	31T	7920088
HK-3334X	200	BB-1112
HK-3337	441	0354
HK-3337X	441	0354
HK-3354W	690B	11518
HK-3354X	690B	11518
HK-3364	695A	96001
HK-3364X	695A	96001
HK-3365	690C	11695
HK-3365P	690C	11695
HK-3365X	690C	11695
HK-3366	695A	96033
HK-3366P	695A	96033
HK-3366X	695A	96033
HK-3367	695A	96018
HK-3367X	695A	96018
HK-3376	695A	96083
HK-3376P	695A	96083
HK-3376X	695A	96083
"HK-3377"	695A	96013
HK-3379	690B	11525
HK-3379P	690B	11525
HK-3379W	690B	11525
HK-3379X	690B	11525
HK-3381G	PA42	5501039
HK-3381X	PA42	5501039
HK-3385	690C	11728
HK-3385P	690C	11728
HK-3385X	690C	11728
HK-3389	695A	96037
HK-3389P	695A	96037
HK-3389X	695A	96037
HK-3390	695A	96047
HK-3390X	695A	96047
HK-3391	695A	96059
HK-3391P	695A	96059
HK-3391W	695A	96059
HK-3391X	695A	96059
"HK-3394X"	695	95080
HK-3397W	PA42	5527037
"HK-3397-X"	300	FA-22
HK-3397X	PA42	5527037
HK-3401	441	0059
HK-3401X	441	0059
HK-3405	695	95074
HK-3405X	695	95074
HK-3406	695	95062
HK-3406X	695	95062
HK-3407	695	95075
HK-3407X	695	95075
HK-3408	695	95050
HK-3408W	695	95050
HK-3408X	695	95050
HK-3409W	695	95068
HK-3409X	695	95068
HK-3412	695	95010
HK-3412W	695	95010
HK-3412X	695	95010
HK-3413W	PA42	5527006
HK-3413X	PA42	5527006
HK-3414	695A	96091
HK-3414X	695A	96091
HK-3417	695A	96084
HK-3417X	695A	96084
HK-3418P	441	0333
HK-3418X	441	0333
HK-3423P	PA42	5527008
HK-3423W	PA42	5527008
HK-3423X	PA42	5527008
HK-3424	690C	11611
HK-3424X	690C	11611
HK-3429	90	LJ-831
HK-3429W	90	LJ-831
HK-3429X	90	LJ-831
HK-3432	200	BB-1227
HK-3432P	200	BB-1227
HK-3432X	200	BB-1227
HK-3433G	300	FA-159
HK-3433X	300	FA-159
HK-3439	695A	96021
HK-3439X	695A	96021
HK-3440W	200	BB-1298
HK-3440X	200	BB-1298
HK-3443	695	95051
HK-3443X	695	95051
HK-3444	695	95057
HK-3444X	695	95057
HK-3447	690C	11722
HK-3447P	690C	11722
HK-3447X	690C	11722
HK-3448	690C	11649
HK-3448W	690C	11649
HK-3448X	690C	11649
HK-3450	695	95083
HK-3450P	695	95083
HK-3450W	695	95083
HK-3450X	695	95083
HK-3451	PA42	5527033
HK-3451X	PA42	5527033
HK-3453	695	95082
HK-3453X	695	95082
HK-3455	695	95065
HK-3455X	695	95065
HK-3456P	441	0271
HK-3456W	441	0271
HK-3456X	441	0271
HK-3457W	441	0359
HK-3457X	441	0359
HK-3459	PA42	5527038
HK-3459P	PA42	5527038
HK-3459X	PA42	5527038
HK-3460	690C	11647
HK-3460P	690C	11647
HK-3460W	690C	11647
HK-3460X	690C	11647
HK-3461	695	95043
HK-3461X	695	95043
HK-3463	300	FA-39
HK-3463X	300	FA-39
HK-3465	690	11059
HK-3465P	690	11059
HK-3465X	690	11059
HK-3466	690A	11165
HK-3466P	690A	11165
HK-3466X	690A	11165
HK-3470	200	BB-960
HK-3470P	200	BB-960
HK-3470X	200	BB-960
HK-3472X	31T	8020043
HK-3473	690D	15007
HK-3473W	690D	15007
HK-3473X	690D	15007
HK-3474	695	95016
HK-3474X	695	95016
HK-3481	695	95079
HK-3481X	695	95079
HK-3484	695	95022
HK-3484P	695	95022
HK-3484X	695	95022
HK-3492	695	95072
HK-3492X	695	95072
HK-3495	300	FA-41
HK-3495X	300	FA-41
HK-3497P	441	0335

HK-3497W 441 0335
HK-3497X 441 0335
"HK-3497X" 695A 96006
HK-3504 200 BB-1063
HK-3504X 200 BB-1063
HK-3505 F90 LA-221
HK-3505P F90 LA-221
HK-3505W F90 LA-221
HK-3505X F90 LA-221
HK-3507 200 BB-974
HK-3507W 200 BB-974
HK-3507X 200 BB-974
HK-3509 300 FA-83
HK-3509X 300 FA-83
HK-3512 441 0261
HK-3512X 441 0261
HK-3514 690A 11221
HK-3514P 690A 11221
HK-3514X 690A 11221
HK-3518 425 0207
HK-3518X 425 0207
HK-3519 300 FA-74
HK-3519W 300 FA-74
HK-3519X 300 FA-74
HK-3529 441 0348
HK-3529X 441 0348
HK-3532P 441 0356
HK-3532W 441 0356
HK-3532X 441 0356
HK-3534W 300 FA-96
HK-3534X 300 FA-96
HK-3536W 300 FA-95
HK-3536X 300 FA-95
HK-3540W 441 0287
HK-3540X 441 0287
HK-3541 690C 11652
HK-3541X 690C 11652
HK-3542W 441 0319
HK-3542X 441 0319
HK-3546W 441 0226
HK-3546X 441 0226
HK-3547 300 FA-86
HK-3547X 300 FA-86
HK-3549W 441 0341
HK-3549X 441 0341
HK-3550 441 0320
HK-3550X 441 0320
HK-3554G 200 BB-1068
HK-3554X 200 BB-1068
HK-3555 200 BB-369
HK-3555X 200 BB-369
HK-3556P 300 FA-47
HK-3556W 300 FA-47
HK-3556X 300 FA-47
HK-3561 690B 11365
HK-3561P 690B 11365
HK-3561X 690B 11365
HK-3562 441 0232
HK-3562X 441 0232
HK-3568W 441 0309
HK-3568X 441 0309
HK-3573 441 0251
HK-3573P 441 0251
HK-3573X 441 0251
HK-3574 300 FA-108
HK-3574X 300 FA-108
HK-3579W G1 190
HK-3579X G1 190
HK-3580W G1 145
HK-3580X G1 145
HK-3587 200 BB-1108
HK-3587W 200 BB-1108
HK-3587X 200 BB-1108
HK-3595 441 0189
HK-3595X 441 0189
HK-3596P 441 0276
HK-3596W 441 0276
HK-3596X 441 0276
HK-3597 690A 11110
HK-3597X 690A 11110
HK-3603 31T 8166034
HK-3603X 31T 8166034
HK-3611 441 0324
HK-3611W 441 0324
HK-3611X 441 0324
HK-3613 441 0206
HK-3613P 441 0206
HK-3613X 441 0206
HK-3614 441 0178
HK-3614W 441 0178
HK-3614X 441 0178
HK-3615W 441 0239
HK-3615X 441 0239
HK-3618W PA42 8001037
HK-3618X PA42 8001037
HK-3620W 441 0152
HK-3620X 441 0152
HK-3622 G1 179
HK-3622X G1 179
HK-3628W 300 FA-105
HK-3628X 300 FA-105
HK-3634 G1 34
HK-3634X G1 34
HK-3647 441 0231
HK-3647X 441 0231
HK-3648 300 FA-100
HK-3648X 300 FA-100
HK-3654G 300 FA-101
HK-3654W 300 FA-101
HK-3654X 300 FA-101
HK-3656 690A 11314
HK-3656P 690A 11314
HK-3656X 690A 11314
HK-3659 300 FA-60
HK-3659P 300 FA-60
HK-3659X 300 FA-60
HK-3663 G1 157
HK-3663X G1 157
HK-3670W 300 FA-123
HK-3670X 300 FA-123
HK-3680 690C 11620
HK-3680X 690C 11620
HK-3681W G1 78
HK-3681X G1 78
HK-3689 300 FA-31
HK-3689X 300 FA-31
HK-3693 PA42 8001075
HK-3693X PA42 8001075
HK-3699 200 BB-226
HK-3699X 200 BB-226
HK-3700 690C 11721
HK-3700X 690C 11721
HK-3703W 200 BB-1360
HK-3703X 200 BB-1360
HK-3704W 200 BB-1392
HK-3704X 200 BB-1392
HK-3705 200 BB-63
HK-3705X 200 BB-63
HK-3749X 200 BB-363
HK-3796 200 BB-264
HK-3796X 200 BB-264
HK-3811 BN2 2040
HK-3812 BN2 2192
HK-3813 BN2 3014
HK-3819 695 95059
HK-3819X 695 95059
HK-3822 200 BB-248
HK-3822X 200 BB-248
HK-3828W 300 FA-10
HK-3828X 300 FA-10
HK-3852 F90 LA-16
HK-3852X F90 LA-16
HK-3854W 200 BB-135
HK-3854X 200 BB-135
HK-3860W 300 FA-169
HK-3860X 300 FA-169
HK-3894W 200 BB-1049
HK-3894X 200 BB-1049
HK-3902X 200 BB-75
HK-3907W E90 LW-39
HK-3907X E90 LW-39
HK-3912 690C 11668
HK-3912P 690C 11668
HK-3912X 690C 11668
HK-3918W 300 FA-155
HK-3918X 300 FA-155
HK-3922P 200 BB-352
HK-3922X 200 BB-352
HK-3923X 200 BB-450
HK-3935W F90 LA-151
HK-3935X F90 LA-151
HK-3936W 200 BB-75
HK-3936X 200 BB-75
HK-3954W 300 FA-200
HK-3954X 300 FA-200
HK-3961X 695A 96069
HK-3975X 680W 1820-34
HK-3980X MIII TT-447
HK-3988X 350 FL-18
HK-3990 200 BB-1376
HK-3990X 200 BB-1376
HK-3995X 200 BB-196
HK-4022X G1 190
HK-4043X 350 FL-98
HK-4063W 690D 15032
HK-4063X 690D 15032
HK-4065W 690C 11673
HK-4065X 690C 11673
(HK-4081X) 300 FA-64
HK-4095X 200 BB-450
HK-4108 200 BB-60
HK-4108X 200 BB-60
HK-4110W PA42 5527009
HK-4110X PA42 5527009
HK-4111X 300 FA-99
HK-4150X 300 FA-22
HK-4178X 300 FA-155
HK-4179 31T 8120062
HK-4236X 200 BB-135
(HK-4244X) 200 BB-1049
HK-4256W 200 BB-1049
HK-4256X 200 BB-1049
HK-4268 350 FL-18
HK-4268X 350 FL-18
HK-4278W 200 BB-496
HK-4278X 200 BB-496
HK-4289X 680W 1820-34
HK-4297X 200 BB-1194
HK-4298 F90 LA-198
HK-4298X F90 LA-198
HK-4323 690B 11354
HK-4323X 690B 11354
HK-4330W 690A 11102
HK-4330X 690A 11102
HK-4343 200 BB-1024
HK-4343X 200 BB-1024
HK-4347P 31T 8104007
HK-4347X 31T 8104007
HK-4357P 90 LJ-668
HK-4357X 90 LJ-668
HK-4358 F90 LA-151
HK-4358X F90 LA-151
HK-4370 695A 96080
HK-4370X 695A 96080
HK-4387 90 LJ-994
HK-4406 300 FA-99
HK-4406X 300 FA-99
HK-4422 200 BB-377
HK-4422X 200 BB-377
HK-4433W F90 LA-191
HK-4433X F90 LA-191
HK-4460W 90 LJ-733
HK-4460X 90 LJ-733
HK-4583 695 95061
HK-4583X 695 95061
HK-4603 350 FL-574
HK-4613 BN2 673
HK-4643 350 FL-507
"HK-268P82" 695 95045

South Korea

HL2004 P68 322
HL5101 FPC6 2040
HL5102 PC6 555
HL5200 90 LJ-1801
HL5204 PA42 5527043
(HL5205) PA42 5527044
HL5213 PA42 5527044
HL5217 PA42 5527029
HL5220 S600 007
HL5223 681B 6057
HL5260 200 BB-944
HL5261 690B 11437

Panama

HP- 441 0110
HP- 441 0277
(HP-) 690A 11314
HP- 200 BB-33
HP- 200 BB-164
HP- 200 BB-237
HP- 200 BB-300
HP- 200 BB-329
HP- 200 BB-330
HP- 200 BB-644
HP- 200C BL-26
HP- 31T 8275003
HP- 350 FL-98
HP- 690 11003
HP- 690 11073
HP- 690B 11565
HP- 690D 15003
HP- 690D 15004
HP- 690D 15009
HP- 690D 15010
HP- 690D 15032
HP- 695A 96017
HP- 695A 96040
HP- 695A 96081
HP- 695A 96082
HP- 90 LJ-55
HP- 90 LJ-184
HP- 90 LJ-384
HP- 90 LJ-455
HP- 90 LJ-520
HP- 90 LJ-1942
HP- 90 LJ-1943
HP- C-12 BC-63
HP-008 P68 250
HP-010 200 BB-447
HP-11GT 695A 96058
HP-77PE 690B 11368
HP-80P F90 LA-57
HP-82LD 200 BB-988
HP-111A 31T 7620046
HP-235 690B 11405
(HP-547) BN2 276
HP-548 BN2 274
HP-549 BN2 248
HP-550 BN2 282
HP-551 BN2 265
HP-556 BN2 204
HP-556KN BN2 204
HP-564 FPC6 2044
HP-566 BN2 627
HP-568 BN2 268
HP-569 BN2 267
HP-569P BN2 267
HP-570 BN2 266
HP-571 BN2 257
HP-572 BN2 226
HP-572OL BN2 226
HP-572XI BN2 226
HP-581 BN2 274
HP-639 BN2 60
HP-639KN BN2 60
HP-639PS BN2 60
HP-651 BN2 328
HP-658 BN2 106
HP-659 BN2 64
HP-676 BN2 186
HP-677 BN2 49
HP-680 BN2 328
HP-691 BN2 678
HP-709 BN2 722
HP-712 BN2 497
HP-752 90 LJ-682
HP-761 BN2 705
HP-768 BN2 464
HP-774 31T 7520038
HP-785 BN2 592
HP-786 BN2 256

HP-799	G1	152
HP-800	31T	7520021
HP-805	F90	LA-57
HP-809	31T	8020015
HP-813	BN2	834
HP-818	31T	7520038
HP-822	BN2	841
HP-823	90	LJ-689
HP-839	BN2	44
HP-839KN	BN2	44
HP-843	BN2	859
HP-860	BN2	750
HP-870	BN2	848
HP-870PS	BN2	848
HP-870XI	BN2	848
HP-896	BN2	879
HP-898	680W	1802-24
HP-899	TRIS	1007
HP-899CH	TRIS	1007
HP-899PS	TRIS	1007
HP-918	90	LJ-601
HP-935	BN2	913
HP-945	BN2	914
HP-946	TRIS	305
HP-947	TRIS	1005
HP-955P	BN2	912
HP-960	200	BB-617
HP-960P	200	BB-617
HP-976	90	LJ-1051
HP-976P	90	LJ-1051
HP-986PS	BN2	178
HP-986XI	BN2	178
HP-987PS	BN2	61
HP-987TN	BN2	61
HP-987XI	BN2	61
HP-998P	BN2	905
HP-1002KN	BN2	629
HP-1016PS	BN2	628
HP-1016XI	BN2	628
HP-1064	FPC6	2006
HP-1066	31T	1166001
HP-1066P	31T	1166001
HP-1069	MIII	T-288
HP-1069P	MIII	T-288
HP-1075KN	BN2	369
HP-1076KN	TRIS	1012
HP-1077KN	BN2	30
"HP-1078"	695A	96058
HP-1078P	695A	96020
HP-1079KN	BN2	310
HP-1082	31T	7620046
HP-1083	200	BB-505
HP-1083P	200	BB-505
HP-1097	PA42	8001032
HP-1097SI	PA42	8001032
HP-1099	P68	296
HP-1101	31T	5575001
HP-1101P	31T	5575001
HP-1108	695A	96006
HP-1113IT	TRIS	1049
HP-1115	P68	301
HP-1115P	P68	301
HP-1118	90	LJ-876
HP-1118P	90	LJ-876
HP-1132P	695	95031
HP-1133IT	BN2	750
HP-1136AP	MIIB	T26-113
HP-1149P	695A	96031
HP-1152P	90	LJ-1073
HP-1153PS	BN2	672
HP-1153XI	BN2	672
HP-1155IT	TRIS	1047
HP-1156AR	BN2	879
HP-1156P	BN2	879
HP-1157IT	TRIS	1044
HP-1172KN	BN2	242
HP-1180	200	BB-1131
HP-1182	300	FA-209
HP-1189	441	0332
HP-1190	441	0268
HP-1203	90	LJ-1272
HP-1209PS	BN2	296
HP-1209XI	BN2	296
HP-1211	350	FL-39
HP-1213	200	BB-1145
HP-1215	F90	LA-152
HP-1220KN	BN2	242
HP-1220PS	BN2	242
HP-1232PS	BN2	612
HP-1232TN	BN2	612
HP-1232XI	BN2	612
HP-1236	F406	0048
HP-1246	E90	LW-218
HP-1252	F90	LA-196
HP-1264	90	LJ-1285
HP-1266	F90	LA-160
HP-1284	BN2	170
HP-1284AR	BN2	170
(HP-1289)	300	FA-103
HP-1298	300	FA-103
HP-1303	BN2	2013
HP-1312AR	BN2	641
HP-1316	200T	BT-33
HP-1336A	100	B-173
HP-1338	BN2	818
HP-1338MF	BN2	818
HP-1341	PA42	5527027
HP-1382	300	FA-90
HP-1382	300	FA-99
HP-1404	200	BB-1049
HP-1411	100	B-66
HP-1411B	100	B-66
HP-1415	690B	11354
HP-1433	680W	1820-34
HP-1457	300	FA-123
HP-1469	200	BB-833
HP-1494	BN2	673
HP-1494PS	BN2	673
HP-1500	90	LJ-1648
HP-1512	200	BB-311
HP-1515	200	BB-1611
HP-1544	425	0118
HP-1550	BN2	2221
HP-1555	350	FL-395
HP-1588	350	FL-429
HP-1591	200	BB-128
HP-1595	300	FA-60
HP-1598	200	BB-135
HP-1607	690A	11209
HP-1608	90	LJ-1500
HP-1617	BN2	58
HP-1635	90	LJ-1663
HP-1888	690C	11621
HP-2001	PA42	5527005
HP-2888	300C	FM-2
HP-5000H	E90	LW-240
HP-8000	90	LJ-1373

Honduras

HR-	BN2	901
HR-	MIIB	T26-151
HR-AAJ	690A	11233
HR-ABN	690B	11364
HR-ADI	690B	11382
HR-AHJ	90	LJ-859
HR-AJP	BN2	672
HR-AKR	BN2	209
HR-ALP	BN2	296
HR-ANL	200	BB-481
HR-ANW	E90	LW-308
HR-ASY	200	BB-1063
HR-ATP	90	LJ-1399
HR-AUL	BN2	513
HR-CEM	690A	11302
HR-IAH	90	LJ-122
HR-IAI	90	LJ-489
HR-IAJ	G1	33
HR-JFA	PA42	8001056
(HR-LAK)	BN2	54
HR-LAR	BN2	139
HR-SHD	BN2	54

Thailand

HS-	46D	109
HS-ADS	200	BB-1678
HS-AFI	200	BB-1315
HS-ATS	200	BB-1988
HS-CHE	PC6	581
HS-CHV	PC6	627
HS-CHV	PC6	705
HS-CNS	200	BB-1923
HS-DCB	200	BB-132
HS-DCF	200	BB-1315
HS-DCH	P68	391
HS-EFS	FPC6	2026
HS-FFI	200	BB-132
HS-ITD	200	BB-1512
HS-ITD	350	FL-151
HS-KCH	200	BB-1125
HS-PBA	TBM7	4
HS-PON	200	BB-342
HS-PON	200	BB-1165
(HS-RGR)	46D	114
HS-RGR	46D	114
HS-RON	BN2	156
HS-SKA	BN2	75
HS-SKB	BN2	26
HS-SKE	PC6	581
HS-SLA	350	FL-53
HS-SLB	90	LJ-1243
HS-SLC	350	FL-194
HS-SMC	PC12	609
HS-TCE	P68	391
HS-TCL	P68	395
HS-TFA	690A	11340
HS-TFB	680T	1573-28
(HS-TFC)	690D	15013
HS-TFD	PC6	581
(HS-TFF)	200	BB-132
HS-TFG	690B	11482
HS-TFH	90	LJ-1243
HS-TFI	350	FL-53

Saudi Arabia

HZ-	MU-2	796SA
HZ-AFC	100	B-214
HZ-AFE	100	B-221
HZ-AMA	MU-2	793SA
(HZ-AMK)	PA42	8001054
HZ-BIN	MU-2	256
HZ-KT2	200	BB-847
HZ-MS71	300C	FM-19
HZ-MS72	300C	FM-20
HZ-MS73	300C	FM-22
HZ-MS74	300C	FM-23
HZ-MS75	300C	FM-24
HZ-MW1	200	BB-325
HZ-MW2	200	BB-1110
HZ-OCE	MIII	T-314
HZ-SN4	PA42	8001054
HZ-SN6	MIV	AT-007
HZ-SN8	MIVC	AT-434
HZ-SS1	690	11006
HZ-SWC	200	BB-1001

Solomon Islands

H4-AAC	BN2	613
(H4-AAH)	BN2	15
H4-AAH	BN2	75
(H4-AAI)	BN2	75
(H4-AAI)	BN2	81
H4-AAI	BN2	355
H4-AAP	BN2	173
H4-AAQ	TRIS	349
H4-SIE	BN2	354
H4-WPB	BN2	654
H4-WPC	BN2	354
H4-WPF	BN2	611
H4-WPG	BN2	2177

Italy

I-ACCT	690B	11513
I-ACLR	690B	11544
I-ACTC	P180	1014
I-ADLA	300	FA-107
I-AESR	TBM7	161
I-AESW	TBM7	225
I-AFEP	PA42	8001022
I-AGAE	P68	183
I-AGSD	P68	248
I-AITE	P68T	9006
I-AITN	P68T	9002
I-AITT	P68T	8011
I-ALBO	PC6	552
I-ALGH	200	BB-590
I-ALPJ	PC6	678
I-ALPN	P180	1015
I-ALPV	P180	1010
I-ALTM	P68	427
I-ANCP	P68	17
I-APIT	31T	8020017
I-ARBO	680T	1564-20
I-ARBX	200	BB-556
I-ASMI	200	BB-1124
I-ATAT	P68	254
I-ATOP	P68	303
I-AVBN	P180	1180
I-AVJA	P68	53
I-AZIO	90	LJ-741
I-AZME	300	FA-94
I-BADE	BN2	237
I-BAML	P68T	9001
I-BATT	BN2	56
I-BCOM	P180	1040
I-BERF	690A	11167
I-BMGF	PC6	913
I-BMPE	200	BB-251
I-BOMY	90	LJ-828
I-BPAE	P180	1081
I-BPAF	P180	1086
I-CAKE	PC6	942
I-CANG	S600	001
I-CARG	S600	004
I-CDSY	P68	54
I-CENT	PA42	5501016
I-CFPA	P180	1094
I-CGAT	31T	7520033
I-CGTO	PA42	8001044
I-CGTT	31T	7820045
(I-CIRS)	BN2	429
(I-CIRS)	BN2	439
I-CITT	P68	217
I-CKET	G1	57
I-CNDB	PC12	728
I-CNGR	S600	002
I-CNGS	S600	005
I-CNGT	S600	006
I-CNGV	S600	007
I-CODE	31T	8120023
I-CONA	PC6	537
I-CUVI	200	BB-1032
I-DARC	P180	1184
I-DDFG	P180	1168
I-DEPE	BN2	2253
I-DJET	P68	426 JET
I-DMPL	P68	350
I-DOLF	P68	389
I-DPCB	P180	1163
I-DPCL	P180	1143
I-DPCR	P180	1032
I-DPCS	P180	1033
I-EEVA	P68	103
I-EHAJ	G1	196
I-EJAG	31T	8020030
I-ELCO	200	BB-239
I-ELIM	P68	293
I-ELTR	E90	LW-37
I-ERRE	90	LJ-14
I-ETOS	P68	11
I-FASJ	E90	LW-106
I-FEMA	P180	1159
I-FIDB	300	FA-82
I-FINA	P68	420

I-FINE	PA42	8001057
I-FINS	P166	372
I-FIRS	90	LJ-931
I-FLOT	P68	341
I-FRTL	MU-2	454SA
I-FRUT	MU-2	413SA
I-FSAB	690A	11139
I-FSAC	200	BB-748
I-FSAD	MIVC	AT-440B
I-FXRA	P180	1013
I-FXRB	P180	1035
I-FXRC	P180	1045
I-FXRD	P180	1067
I-FXRE	P180	1049
I-FXRF	P180	1060
I-FXRG	P180	1112
I-FXRH	P180	1177
I-FXRI	P180	1189
I-FXRJ	P180	1178
I-GAUS	P68	02
I-GEAR	31T	7620009
I-GEBA	690B	11554
I-GEFI	441	0166
I-GEMK	P68	258
I-GFAW	31T	7820053
I-GHIO	46D	141
I-GIFE	P68	335
I-GISG	P68	19
I-GJUL	P68	206
I-GNIS	90	LJ-40
I-GRAD	P68	222
I-GYAN	P68	183
I-HYDR	31T	7520034
I-IDMA	MU-2	769SA
I-IEAA	P68	87
I-IEAB	P68	110
I-IEAC	P68	135
I-IEAD	P68	150
I-IEAE	P68	151
I-IEAF	P68	161
I-IEAG	P68	234
I-IEAH	P68	387
I-INOT	PC6	892
I-INVG	90	LJ-1866
I-KANG	S600	003
I-KDUE	P68	226
I-KIMO	BN2	726
I-KLUB	P68	172
I-KUNO	BN2	858
I-KWYR	90	LJ-873
I-KWYX	90	LJ-775
I-LACO	BN2	17
I-LGMG	PC12	1024
I-LIAT	31T	8004052
I-LILY	BN2	2167
I-LIPO	90	LJ-616
I-LLLL	200	BB-643
I-LOAN	PC12	381
I-LYFE	P68	12
I-MAAA	P68T	8009
I-MADY	200C	BL-11
I-MAGJ	690A	11265
I-MAKT	P68	209
I-MCAP	200	BB-1975
I-MCCC	E90	LW-215
I-MDDD	G1	143
I-MEDI	90	LJ-265
I-MEFA	PC6	671
I-MEPE	200	BB-1003
I-MGGG	G1	51
I-MIDI	PC6	573
I-MINP	P166	361
I-MINT	P166	368
I-MITS	MU-2	366SA
I-MKKK	G1	194
I-MLPT	MU-2	772SA
I-MLST	MU-2	710SA
I-MLWT	680T	1694-73
I-MOFN	E90	LW-283
I-MTOP	200	BB-1825
I-MUDI	90	LJ-265
I-NANE	31T	7920001
I-NARB	MIV	AT-020
I-NARC	MIVA	AT-035

I-NARI	MU-2	348SA
I-NARW	MIVA	AT-058
I-NCAS	P166	341
I-OBPC	P68	261
I-OBSR	P68	236
I-OBST	P68	325
I-OBSU	P68	326
I-OBSV	P68	316
I-OBSW	P68	331
I-ODUE	P68	384
I-ONDI	PC6	531
I-PADC	S600	008
I-PAIR	690B	11444
I-PAIT	P68T	6001
I-PALS	31T	7620005
I-PARJ	P68	06
I-PDVO	P180	1159
I-PDVO	P180	1165
I-PDVO	P180	1171
I-PDVO	P180	1189
I-PDVP	P180	1172
I-PDVP	P180	1175
I-PDVP	P180	1185
I-PDVR	P180	1174
I-PDVR	P180	1178
I-PDVR	P180	1180
I-PDVS	P180	1166
I-PDVS	P180	1173
I-PEBI	MIIB	T26-167E
I-PIAA	P166	423
I-PIAB	E90	LW-52
I-PIAC	P166	465
I-PIAE	P166	466
I-PIAG	P166	364
I-PIAH	200	BB-777
I-PIAK	P166	341
I-PIAK	P166	369
I-PIAO	200	BB-225
I-PIAP	P166	371
I-PIAQ	P166	471
I-PIAS	P166	411
I-PIAU	P166	394
I-PJAG	P166	416
I-PJAP	P180	1013
I-PJAR	P180	1002
I-PJAS	P180	1006
I-PJAT	P180	1016
I-PJAV	P180	1001
I-PNCB	P68	390
I-POMO	31T	7904030
I-PREE	P180	1138
I-PSFH	PC6	778
I-RAIA	S600	008
I-RAIB	P166	371
I-RAID	P166	371
I-RAIE	P166	371
I-RAIF	P166	341
I-RAIF	P166	371
I-RAIH	P180	1004
I-RAIH	P180	1006
I-RAIH	P180	1009
I-RAIH	P180	1022
I-RAIH	P180	1034
I-RAII	P180	1007
I-RAII	P180	1071
I-RAIJ	P180	1015
I-RAIK	P68T	8002
I-RAIL	P180	1105
I-RAIL	P68	100
I-RAIL	P68	400
I-RAIL	P68T	9001
I-RAIL	P68T	9005
I-RAIO	P68	286
I-RAIO	P68T	6002
I-RAIP	P180	1008
I-RAIP	P68T	6003
I-RAIP	P68T	8001
I-RAIS	P68T	9003
I-RAIT	P68	384
I-RAIT	P68	420
I-RAIW	P166	371
I-RAIZ	P68	402
I-RAIZ	P68	414
I-RAIZ	P68T	8006

I-RAIZ	P68T	8011
I-REEF	200	BB-1905
I-ROCE	PC6	573
I-RRPG	P68	193
I-RTAA	P68	181
I-RWWW	E90	LW-220
I-SAEP	PC6	734
I-SAER	PC6	696
I-SAES	31T	7820033
I-SAEZ	PC6	627
I-SASA	31T	8004024
I-SEPA	P68	08
I-SERV	31T	7904022
I-SFCC	P68	07
I-SIGN	P68	04
I-SKYL	MU-2	437SA
I-SLAB	S600	008
I-SLBB	S600	009
I-SMTA	P68	393
I-SNAS	MU-2	746SA
I-SNAT	90	LJ-84
I-SOLT	MU-2	420SA
I-SORE	PC6	551
I-SORV	P68	423
I-SPRS	P68T	8002
I-SPRT	P68T	8003
I-SPRU	P68T	8004
I-SPRV	P68T	8001
I-SPRX	P68T	8008
I-SRAL	P68	40
I-STAD	P68	407
I-SUSE	90	LJ-969
I-SWAA	MIII	T-274
I-TASA	690A	11273
I-TASB	G1	105
I-TASC	G1	173
I-TASE	690A	11260
I-TASO	G1	81
I-TCFI	P68	300
I-TELM	690B	11506
I-THAJ	P68	391
I-THAK	P68	395
I-TIAF	P180	1188
I-TICO	TBM7	345
I-TIZY	P68	67
I-TLRN	P68T	9005
I-TOPS	PC12	352
I-TOPZ	P68	429
I-TRAL	BN2	46
I-TRAM	BN2	8
I-TREP	PA42	5501045
I-TREQ	PA42	5501046
I-TRER	PA42	5501047
I-TWIN	P68	01
I-UNIT	P68	23
I-VAVF	V600	001
I-VCID	P68	213
I-VICC	P68	16
I-VICD	P68	213
I-VICR	P68	40
I-VICT	P68	03
I-VICV	P68	19
I-VICW	P68	306
I-VICZ	P68	28
I-VICZ	P68	74
I-VIPS	P68	224
I-VIPT	P68	269
I-VIPV	P68	259
I-VIPW	P68	348
I-VIPX	P68	307
I-VIPY	P68	351
I-VITC	P68	208
I-VULA	S600	010
I-VULE	P68T	8011

Japan

JA01EP	200	BB-1604
JA01KA	90	LJ-1567
JA02EP	350	FL-425
JA02TY	BN2	2296
JA007C	90	LJ-1350
JA21EG	90	LJ-1591
JA55HA	90	LJ-1198
JA121N	200	BB-1577
JA127D	BN2	2282
JA200N	200	BB-1734
JA350N	350	FL-185
JA353N	350	FL-345
JA376N	350	FL-376
JA377N	350	FL-451
JA860A	695	95078
JA861A	350	FL-180
JA862A	350	FL-188
JA863A	350	FL-191
JA864A	350	FL-193
JA865A	350	FL-195
JA866A	350	FL-218
JA867A	350	FL-222
JA868A	350	FL-292
JA869A	350	FL-295
JA870A	350	FL-297
JA881C	90	LJ-1470
JA3196	PC6	528
JA3201	PC6	558
JA3202	PC6	559
(JA4150)	46D	40
(JA4207)	46D	47
JA4207	46D	70
JA5175	BN2	91
JA5193	BN2	140
JA5195	BN2	302
JA5218	BN2	344
JA5227	BN2	354
JA5241	BN2	411
JA5255	BN2	521
JA5261	BN2	2012
JA5265	BN2	856
JA5268	BN2	759
JA5270	BN2	909
JA5280	BN2	3006
JA5281	BN2	2154
JA5282	BN2	2129
JA5284	BN2	2037
JA5285	BN2	2038
JA5290	BN2	2172
JA5294	BN2	2173
JA5298	BN2	2209
JA5305	BN2	2239
JA5306	BN2	2236
JA5316	BN2	2240
JA5318	BN2	2267
JA5319	BN2	2268
(JA5319)	PC12	104
JA5320	BN2	2269
JA5321	BN2	2272
JA5322	BN2	2285
JA5323	BN2	2291
JA5324	BN2	2297
JA5325	BN2	2298
JA6401	TRIS	1042
JA8183	MU-2	183
JA8204	PC12	113
JA8221	PC6	800
JA8223	PC6	845
JA8228	PC6	861
JA8505	MU-2	505
JA8598	350	FL-100
JA8599	PC12	128
JA8600	695	95070
JA8604	695	95044
JA8613	PC12	104
JA8614	200	BB-1491
JA8620	MU-2	001
JA8625	MU-2	002
JA8626	MU-2	003
JA8627	MU-2	004
JA8628	MU-2	005
JA8629	MU-2	006
JA8647	MU-2	007
JA8655	MU-2	009
JA8657	MU-2	011
JA8671	MU-2	031
JA8673	MU-2	101
JA8705	200	BB-1431
JA8724	PA42	5501055
JA8725	MU-2	120

JA8737 MU-2 501
JA8738 MU-2 502
JA8739 MU-2 503
JA8753 MU-2 504
JA8767 MU-2 520
JA8770 MU-2 195
JA8783 MU-2 546
JA8784 200 BB-1463
JA8810 200T BT-5
JA8811 200T BT-6
JA8812 200T BT-7
JA8813 200T BT-8
JA8814 200T BT-9
JA8815 200T BT-11
JA8816 200T BT-12
JA8817 200T BT-13
JA8818 200T BT-14
JA8819 200T BT-15
JA8820 200T BT-16
JA8822 F90 LA-28
JA8824 200T BT-17
JA8825 200T BT-19
JA8826 695 95078
JA8828 MIV AT-016
JA8829 200T BT-22
JA8830 200 BB-1061
JA8831 200 BB-1084
JA8833 200T BT-28
JA8837 200 BB-1138
JA8838 90 LJ-1097
JA8839 90 LJ-691
JA8840 90 LJ-1139
JA8841 90 LJ-1140
JA8844 90 LJ-1141
JA8845 90 LJ-1142
JA8846 90 LJ-1143
JA8847 90 LJ-1144
JA8848 90 LJ-1145
JA8849 90 LJ-1148
JA8850 90 LJ-1149
JA8851 90 LJ-1150
JA8852 90 LJ-1151
JA8853 PA42 5527026
JA8854 200T BT-31
JA8855 425 0235
JA8856 90 LJ-1160
JA8857 200 BB-1000
JA8859 200 BB-1290
JA8860 200T BT-32
JA8861 200 BB-1299
JA8862 200 BB-1300
(JA8865) F90 LA-211
JA8867 PA42 5527035
JA8868 300 FA-175
JA8869 PA42 8301001
JA8870 PA42 5527040
JA8871 PA42 5501048
JA8872 PA42 5501049
JA8873 PA42 5501050
JA8874 PA42 5501058
JA8878 PA42 5527034
JA8879 200 BB-1401
JA8880 200 BB-1406
JA8881 300 FA-219
JA8882 90 LJ-1290
JA8883 90 LJ-1291
JA8884 90 LJ-1292
JA8885 200 BB-1299
JA8892 TBM7 8
JA8894 TBM7 38
JA8896 TBM7 68
JQ8502 MU-2 502

Jordan

JY-AW2 200 BB-1701
JY-AWB 200 BB-1701
JY-CAA BN2 861
JY-DCA BN2 861

Grenada

See also VQ-G
J3-GAG BN2 163
J3-GAH BN2 570
J3-GAI BN2 147
J3-GAI BN2 2025

Guinea Bissau

J5-GTF 90 LJ-456

St Lucia

See also VQ-L
J6-AAC BN2 517
J6-LAS BN2 612
J6-SLS BN2 612
J6-SLT BN2 741
J6-SLV BN2 193
J6-SLW BN2 6
J6-SLX BN2 612
J6-SLY BN2 384
J6-SLZ BN2 77

St Vincent

See also VP-V
J8-CIW BN2 2018
J8-SLU BN2 532
J8-VAG TRIS 1037
J8-VAH BN2 2018
J8-VAK BN2 436
J8-VAM BN2 2165
J8-VAN BN2 3011
J8-VAP BN2 2128
J8-VAT BN2 2021
J8-VAW BN2 868
J8-VBI BN2 2025
J8-VBJ BN2 163
J8-VBK BN2 570
J8-VBN BN2 384

Norway

LN-AAF 100 B-122
LN-AAG 100 B-190
LN-AAH 100 B-107
*LN-AAQ P68 199
LN-ABU 441 0162
LN-ACE 690A 11121
LN-ACV PA42 5527023
LN-ACY E90 LW-309
LN-AET 31T 7820051
LN-AFB 425 0059
LN-ASG 200 BB-29
LN-ASI 200 BB-211
LN-AWA 100 B-213
LN-AWB 100 B-217
LN-AWD 350 FL-256
LN-AWE 200 BB-459
LN-AXA 200 BB-681
LN-AXB 200 BB-521
LN-AXC 200 BB-590
LN-BAA 200 BB-1327
LN-BAB 350 FL-590
LN-BEP PC6 341
(LN-BJG) 200G BY-56
LN-BNI BN2 188
LN-DAB MU-2 028
LN-FAH 690B 11367
(LN-FAN) 690C 11681
LN-FAQ 200 BB-806
LN-FIX 200 BB-1898
LN-FKF 200 BB-196
LN-FOD 90 LJ-984
LN-FSK BN2 352
LN-FWA 690C 11681
LN-FWB 690C 11613
(LN-GHN) 200G BY-56
LN-HAC 90 LJ-492
LN-HAC MU-2 719SA
LN-HTD MIII T-294
LN-IDA 200C BL-141
LN-KAA 441 0206
LN-KAP 441 0043
LN-KAR 90 LJ-492
LN-KCG 90 LJ-768
LN-KCI 200 BB-192
LN-KCK 100 B-55
LN-KCR 90 LJ-793
LN-KOA 200 BB-626
LN-KOB 200 BB-756
LN-LMF 690A 11215
LN-LML P68 316
LN-LMS P68 57
LN-LMX P68T 8006
LN-LTA 200 BB-1868
LN-LTB 200 BB-2001
LN-LTC 200 BB-2002
LN-LTD 200 BB-2006
LN-LTE 200 BB-2007
LN-LTF 200 BB-2008
LN-LTG 200 BB-2009
LN-LTI 200 BB-2010
LN-LTJ 200 BB-2011
LN-LTK 200 BB-2004
(LN-LTK) 200 BB-2012
LN-LTL 200 BB-2005
(LN-LTL) 200 BB-2013
LN-LYY PA42 5527010
LN-MAA 200 BB-560
LN-MAC BN2 431
LN-MAD P68 36
LN-MAF BN2 441
LN-MAG BN2 760
LN-MAH 441 0002
LN-MAM 441 0248
LN-MAU MU-2 630
LN-MAY BN2 807
LN-MMM 200 BB-1994
LN-MOA 200 BB-582
LN-MOA 441 0167
LN-MOB 200 BB-584
LN-MOC 200 BB-1449
LN-MOD 200 BB-619
LN-MOD 200 BB-1459
LN-MOE 200 BB-1460
LN-MOF 200 BB-1461
LN-MOG 200 BB-1465
LN-MOH 200 BB-1466
LN-MOI 200 BB-1470
LN-MOJ 200 BB-1334
LN-MON 200 BB-1537
LN-MOO 200 BB-1692
LN-MOR 441 0223
LN-MOT 200 BB-1590
LN-MTU MU-2 635
LN-NAC P68 344
LN-NFT 200 BB-407
LN-NLB 100 B-62
LN-NOA 200 BB-829
LN-PAB 200 BB-521
LN-PAD 200 BB-199
LN-PAE 200 BB-197
LN-PAE 31T 7720041
LN-PAF 200 BB-490
LN-PAG 200 BB-119
LN-PAH 200 BB-533
LN-PAJ 100 B-85
LN-PAO 100 B-55
LN-PAT 425 0020
LN-RAE 425 0178
LN-RTO BN2 142
LN-SAE 100 B-246
LN-SAM BN2 651
LN-SFT MIII T-342
LN-SUZ 200 BB-1547
LN-TEA 31T 8166007
(LN-TED) F406 0044
LN-TEE 31T 8104070
LN-TRG 200 BB-1936
LN-TSA 200 BB-308
LN-TSH 200C BL-68
LN-TWG 200 BB-873
LN-TWH F406 0032
LN-TWI 200C BL-16
LN-TWL 200 BB-1144
(LN-TWL) 200 BB-1418
LN-VIB 441 0232
LN-VID PC6 585
LN-VIJ PC6 634
LN-VIP 100 B-42
LN-VIP 441 0279
LN-VIP 90 LJ-271
(LN-VIR) 200 BB-521
LN-VIS 441 0321
LN-VIT 100 B-62
LN-VIT PC6 678
LN-VIU 200 BB-216
LN-VIV BN2 386
(LN-VIV) TRIS 366
LN-VIW BN2 179
LN-VIZ 200 BB-1136

Argentina

LQ-APF PA42 8001026
LQ-BLU PA42 5527037
LQ-JYV BN2 242
LQ-LDB 681B 6064
LQ-ZRB 90 LJ-1552
(LV-) 200 BB-853
LV- 90 LJ-1451
LV-AIY 200 BB-1131
LV-APF PA42 8001026
LV-ARU 90 LJ-1617
LV-AXO 200 BB-1877
LV-AYG E90 LW-135
LV-BAN 350 FL-420
LV-BCJ 690 11022
LV-BCP 31T 7820006
LV-BCR 31T 7620022
LV-BCT 31T 7620035
LV-BCU 31T 7720044
LV-BDG 90 LJ-1730
LV-BDU 90 LJ-489
LV-BEI PA42 8001009
LV-BIC 90 LJ-1819
LV-BLV 90 LJ-1028
LV-BMG 200 BB-1417
LV-BMO 200G BY-1
LV-BMS 200G BY-12
LV-BNA 690B 11419
LV-BNB 690B 11450
LV-BPB 90 LJ-1880
LV-BPJ 200G BY-38
LV-BRD 200G BY-47
LV-BRL 100 B-137
LV-BRS E90 LW-221
LV-BSP 200G BY-63
LV-BXF E90 LW-146
LV-DMA 31T 7620003
LV-DMO 31T 7920003
LV-DMP PA42 8001026
LV-JJW 90 LJ-449
LV-JOJ 681 6007
LV-JYV BN2 242
LV-LDB 681B 6064
LV-LEY 690 11019
LV-LMU 690A 11176
LV-LRF 690A 11228
LV-LRH 690A 11236
LV-LTA 690A 11197
LV-LTB 690A 11238
LV-LTC 690A 11241
LV-LTO 690A 11229
LV-LTU 690A 11261
LV-LTV 31T 7520022
LV-LTW 690A 11310
LV-LTX 690A 11258
LV-LTY 690A 11230
LV-LZL 690A 11246
LV-LZM 690A 11268
LV-LZO 31T 7620003
LV-LZS 690B 11365
LV-LZT MU-2 687
LV-MAE PC6 778
LV-MAF PC6 779
LV-MAG 690B 11392

LV-MAU	690B	11394
LV-MAV	690B	11397
LV-MAW	690B	11398
LV-MBR	690A	11266
LV-MBY	690B	11412
LV-MCV	MU-2	361SA
LV-MCW	PC6	790
LV-MCX	PC6	791
LV-MDG	31T	7720065
LV-MDN	690B	11442
LV-MGC	MU-2	704SA
LV-MGD	31T	7720059
LV-MHL	31T	7820020
LV-MIS	PC6	793
LV-MLT	MU-2	385SA
LV-MLU	31T	7820069
LV-MMY	441	0075
LV-MNR	31T	7920017
LV-MNU	31T	7920003
LV-MOC	31T	7920031
LV-MOD	31T	7920033
LV-MOE	31T	7920050
LV-MOO	690B	11543
LV-MOP	MU-2	742SA
LV-MRL	MIII	T-292
LV-MRN	E90	LW-310
LV-MRT	441	0082
LV-MRU	441	0077
LV-MSR	690B	11451
LV-MTU	31T	7920080
LV-MYA	690B	11558
LV-MYI	690B	11557
LV-MYX	31T	7904045
LV-MYY	31T	7920085
LV-MYZ	PC6	804
LV-MZA	31T	7920077
LV-OAN	MU-2	761SA
LV-OAP	31T	7920065
LV-OBB	E90	LW-330
LV-ODZ	MU-2	759SA
LV-OEI	690C	11612
LV-OEU	31T	8020079
LV-OEV	690C	11628
LV-OFT	200	BB-699
LV-OFX	680T	1681-63
LV-OGB	31T	8020054
LV-OGF	31T	8020013
LV-OGG	31T	8020028
LV-OIF	31T	8020092
LV-ONH	200	BB-764
LV-ONL	PA42	8001038
LV-OOE	695	95051
LV-OOO	PA42	8001013
LV-PAB	31T	7820069
LV-PAC	31T	7820065
LV-PAD	690B	11451
LV-PAJ	90	LJ-1180
LV-PAL	MU-2	385SA
LV-PAN	300	FA-203
LV-PAS	31T	7920003
LV-PAY	E90	LW-310
LV-PAZ	441	0082
LV-PAZ	MU-2	157
LV-PBA	441	0075
LV-PBB	441	0077
LV-PBS	690B	11543
LV-PBY	MU-2	742SA
LV-PCJ	31T	7920065
LV-PCM	31T	7920077
LV-PCZ	690B	11557
LV-PDA	E90	LW-330
LV-PDH	MIII	T-292
LV-PDI	690B	11558
LV-PEM	MU-2	761SA
LV-PFD	MU-2	759SA
LV-PFJ	E90	LW-330
LV-PFP	MIIB	T26-143
LV-PGD	690C	11612
LV-PGE	690A	11145
LV-PGL	90	LJ-1340
LV-PGN	90	LJ-1346
LV-PGT	PA42	8001013
LV-PHH	90	LJ-1381
LV-PHI	300	FA-229
LV-PHJ	690C	11628
LV-PHP	90	LJ-1354
LV-PHZ	90	LJ-1395
LV-PIF	200	BB-699
LV-PIF	200	BB-1652
(LV-PIY)	690C	11646
LV-PIZ	90	LJ-449
LV-PJY	F90	LA-93
LV-PLF	200	BB-1507
LV-PLN	200	BB-764
LV-PLO	200	BB-1521
LV-PLR	PA42	8001026
LV-PLS	695	95051
(LV-PLT)	425	0020
LV-PLU	350	FL-138
LV-PLU	BN2	44
LV-PML	90	LJ-1466
LV-PMT	PA42	8001038
LV-PNH	200	BB-1588
LV-POX	300	FA-222
LV-PRE	BN2	242
LV-PSE	681B	6064
LV-PTC	690A	11176
LV-PTI	690A	11197
LV-PTJ	690A	11228
(LV-PTK)	690A	11224
LV-PTS	31T	7520022
LV-PTT	690A	11236
(LV-PTX)	690A	11230
LV-PTY	690A	11230
LV-PTZ	690A	11229
LV-PUA	690A	11238
LV-PUB	690A	11241
(LV-PUE)	690A	11248
(LV-PUF)	690A	11245
(LV-PUF)	690A	11277
(LV-PUF)	690A	11286
LV-PUF	690A	11310
(LV-PUG)	690A	11246
LV-PUH	690A	11258
LV-PUI	690A	11261
(LV-PUP)	690A	11265
(LV-PUQ)	690A	11266
(LV-PUR)	690A	11268
LV-PUU	31T	7620003
LV-PUV	690A	11266
LV-PUW	690A	11246
LV-PUX	690A	11268
LV-PVA	690B	11365
LV-PVB	MU-2	687
LV-PVH	690B	11392
LV-PVL	690B	11394
LV-PVM	690B	11397
LV-PVN	690B	11398
LV-PXD	31T	7720059
LV-PXN	690B	11412
LV-PYD	31T	7720065
LV-PYH	690B	11419
LV-PYI	MU-2	361SA
LV-PYT	690B	11442
LV-PZC	31T	7820020
LV-PZL	690B	11450
LV-PZT	MU-2	704SA
LV-RAC	MU-2	386SA
LV-RAZ	MU-2	157
LV-RBM	300	FA-203
LV-ROC	90	LJ-1180
LV-RTC	200	BB-471
LV-RZB	MIIB	T26-143
LV-VCU	B100	BE-129
LV-VFC	E90	LW-339
LV-VGS	690A	11145
LV-VHO	90	LJ-428
LV-VHP	681	6014
LV-VHR	90	LJ-323
LV-WCW	90	LJ-1340
LV-WDO	100	B-82
LV-WDP	90	LJ-1346
LV-WEW	200	BB-870
LV-WEY	E90	LW-17
LV-WFB	90	LJ-1414
LV-WFP	E90	LW-129
LV-WFR	BN2	2263
LV-WGJ	300	FA-109
LV-WGP	200	BB-558
LV-WHV	E90	LW-259
LV-WIH	690A	11299
LV-WIO	200	BB-606
LV-WIP	300	FA-229
LV-WIR	MIII	T-232
LV-WIU	90	LJ-1381
LV-WJE	90	LJ-1354
LV-WJP	90	LJ-529
LV-WJY	MU-2	644
LV-WLT	300	FA-221
LV-WLV	90	LJ-1287
LV-WLW	MIII	T-230
LV-WMA	300	FA-222
LV-WMD	90	LJ-493
LV-WME	MU-2	139
LV-WMG	90	LJ-1395
LV-WNC	MIVA	AT-036
LV-WNJ	200	BB-1507
LV-WOR	200	BB-1521
LV-WOS	200	BB-639
LV-WPB	90	LJ-1416
LV-WPG	350	FL-138
LV-WPM	200	BB-729
LV-WRM	90	LJ-333
LV-WSN	PC12	135
LV-WXC	90	LJ-1466
LV-WXG	PA42	8001044
LV-WYC	200	BB-1566
LV-WZR	E90	LW-70
LV-YBP	90	LJ-1489
LV-YCS	200	BB-1588
LV-YLC	350	FL-190
LV-YTB	200	BB-1616
LV-ZFC	200	BB-1242
LV-ZNS	90	LJ-1535
LV-ZPG	46D	189
LV-ZPS	90	LJ-1548
LV-ZPY	F90	LA-89
LV-ZRG	200	BB-1652
LV-ZSE	200	BB-1069
LV-ZSX	PC12	133
LV-ZTO	90	LJ-292
LV-ZTP	90	LJ-1597
LV-ZTV	200	BB-1703
LV-ZXX	350	FL-310
LV-ZXZ	90	LJ-489
LV-ZYB	200	BB-1690
LV-ZZH	200	BB-1817

Luxembourg

LX-ACR	31T	8104067
LX-AJH	BN2	717
LX-ALX	200	BB-951
LX-APB	90	LJ-867
LX-DAK	90	LJ-647
LX-DNI	PC12	751
(LX-DOG)	PC12	531
LX-DUC	200	BB-1124
LX-ETB	441	0362
LX-FRZ	90	LJ-898
LX-FUN	46T	97050
LX-GDB	200	BB-397
LX-GNG	90	LJ-1321
(LX-GPP)	31T	7820010
LX-III	BN2T	2102
LX-ILE	46T	97047
LX-JDP	200	BB-303
LX-JFA	TBM7	63
LX-JFB	TBM7	13
LX-JFC	TBM7	129
LX-JFD	TBM7	199
LX-JFE	TBM7	208
LX-JFF	TBM7	212
LX-JFG	TBM7	244
LX-JFH	PC12	522
LX-JFI	PC12	574
LX-JFJ	PC12	678
LX-JFK	PC12	683
LX-JFL	TBM8	391
LX-JFM	PC12	812
LX-JFN	PC12	855
LX-JFO	TBM8	422
LX-JFP	P180	1176
LX-JFQ	PC12	876
(LX-JFR)	PC12	1070
*LX-JFS	PC12	1091
LX-JFT	TBM8	452
LX-KEV	BN2T	2102
LX-KTY	90	LJ-339
LX-LAB	PC12	531
LX-LAP	MIII	T-264
LX-LLM	90	LJ-1261
LX-LMS	F406	0007
LX-LTX	E90	LW-297
LX-MLB	350	FL-300
LX-NOP	MIII	T-259
LX-NRJ	MIII	T-265
LX-PBL	90	LJ-1539
LX-PFD	PC12	865
LX-PIX	MIII	T-267
LX-PRG	90	LJ-1526
LX-RAD	U-21	LM-126
LX-REM	BN2T	2146
LX-RSO	MIII	T-260
LX-RST	31T	7820027
LX-SEA	300	FA-94
LX-SKY	PC12	108
LX-TAI	PC12	1008
LX-TWO	MU-2	1515SA

Lithuania

LY-ATD	P68	121
LY-ZDV	MU-2	1515SA

Bulgaria

LZ-ADK	90	LJ-1606
(LZ-ASP)	P180	1186
LZ-BIZ	200	BB-1595
LZ-FEO	200	BB-82
LZ-ITV	200	BB-1369
LZ-PIA	P180	1008
LZ-RGP	200	BB-82
LZ-TBM	TBM8	421
LZ-VPA	P180	1018
LZ-VPC	P180	1008
LZ-YUK	200	BB-82

Isle of Man

M-ARTY	PC12	1114
M-EGGA	200	BB-1933
M-FIVE	350	FL-580
M-FLYI	350	FL-569
M-FSRE	200	BB-1202
M-GLAS	90	LJ-1734
M-ICKY	PC12	508
M-IFLY	PC12	1022
M-MANX	425	0044
M-NGSN	PC12	697
M-OLTT	PC12	1063
M-ONTI	90	LJ-1699
M-OORE	350	FL-569
M-OTOR	90	LJ-1733
M-PRIT	PC12	1144
M-SHEP	TBM8	467
*M-SPEC	350	FL-241
M-SPEX	350	FL-274
M-TSRI	90	LJ-1795
M-USCA	TBM8	456
M-USHY	441	0209
M-WLLM	90	LJ-1902
M-YBUB	PC12	648

United States of America

N	P68	58
N	P68	142
N1	G1	2
N1AM	46D	97

N1AM	E90	LW-328	N1MU	MU-2	578	N1WH	200	BB-914	N2SC	200	BB-959
N1AN	MU-2	109	N1MW	200	BB-668	N1WJ	100	B-174	N2SC	350	FL-9
N1AQ	MIIB	T26-114	N1MW	300	FA-151	N1WJ	90	LJ-60	N2SM	350	FL-24
(N1AQ)	MIII	T-292	N1MW	E90	LW-176	N1WV	100	B-174	N2SM	350	FL-185
N1BA	680T	1684-65	N1MX	90	LJ-616	N1WV	200	BB-324	N2SN	690A	11148
N1BC	200	BB-1123	N1NA	G1	96	N1WV	300	FA-62	N2TF	680T	1687-67
N1BC	690B	11428	N1NG	690B	11510	N1WV	350	FL-223	N2TF	MIV	AT-008
N1BK	300	FA-76	N1NL	425	0107	N1WV	350	FL-527	N2TS	PC6	936
N1BM	425	0042	N1NL	90	LJ-100	N1XH	200	BB-914	N2TX	200	BB-613
N1BS	200	BB-430	N1NP	200	BB-1834	N1YC	MIIB	T26-131	N2TX	B100	BE-103
N1BS	300	FA-172	N1NP	90	LJ-1289	N1YS	200	BB-430	N2U	200	BB-263
N1CB	200	BB-826	N1NR	680W	1818-32	N1Z	200	BB-1759	N2UH	200	BB-850
N1CB	300	FA-164	N1NR	690	11024	N1ZA	90	LJ-137	N2UL	680T	1677-60
N1CB	E90	LW-128	N1NR	690	11048	N2	90	LJ-156	N2UV	90	LJ-480
N1CN	690A	11168	N1NR	690B	11413	N2AC	690B	11468	N2UW	200T	BT-3
N1CQ	200	BB-1516	N1NR	690C	11654	N2AE	90	LJ-177	N2UX	PC12	880
N1CR	200	BB-1516	N1NT	690C	11654	N2AK	90	LJ-49	N2UX	TBM7	343
N1CR	350	FL-300	N1PB	90	LJ-438	N2AS	200	BB-50	*N2UZ	PA42	5527034
N1CR	90	LJ-1268	N1PC	200	BB-16	N2AS	E90	LW-41	N2VA	350	FL-537
N1CR	90	LJ-1295	N1PC	200	BB-81	N2BC	MU-2	031	N2VA	690	11043
N1CW	PC12	705	N1PC	200	BB-109	N2BQ	MU-2	614	(N2VA)	690	11063
N1DA	B100	BE-51	N1PC	200	BB-143	N2CJ	MU-2	726SA	N2VA	695A	96062
N1DC	MU-2	597	N1PC	200	BB-191	N2DB	300	FA-37	N2VQ	690	11043
N1DE	200	BB-117	N1PC	200	BB-254	N2DB	690	11028	N2VZ	31T	8275011
N1DE	300	FA-66	N1PC	200	BB-326	N2DD	E90	LW-308	N2WC	200	BB-136
N1DE	F90	LA-4	N1PC	E90	LW-40	N2DF	F90	LA-207	N2WC	90	LJ-643
N1DK	90	LJ-676	N1PC	E90	LW-93	N2DF	TBM7	14	N2WF	TBM7	220
N1ER	690B	11399	(N1PC)	G1	171	N2DS	31T	7820081	(N2WQ)	200	BB-136
N1FC	90	LJ-468	N1PD	200	BB-908	N2EP	90	LJ-284	N2WX	90	LJ-643
N1FV	200	BB-79	N1PD	350	FL-121	N2ES	690A	11159	N2XZ	E90	LW-28
N1FY	TRIS	1039	N1PN	B100	BE-32	N2FA	100	B-60	N2YF	PC12	140
N1GC	200	BB-512	N1PQ	200	BB-326	N2FJ	31T	7620050	N2YP	31T	7720010
N1GC	90	LJ-604	N1PT	90	LJ-505	N2GG	90	LJ-462	N2ZC	E90	LW-80
N1GF	90	LJ-1031	N1PT	90	LJ-507	N2GL	MIII	T-284	N2ZN	90	LJ-347
N1GT	100	B-109	N1QA	90	LJ-479	N2GL	MIII	T-323	N3	G1	2
N1GT	200	BB-377	N1QD	MIIB	T26-140	N2GL	MIII	TT-426A	N3	G1	160
N1GV	100	B-210	N1QL	690A	11312	N2GT	MU-2	025	N3AH	300	FA-130
N1GV	90	LJ-604	N1QL	B100	BE-93	N2GT	MU-2	367SA	N3AT	90	LJ-933
N1GX	100	B-109	N1QL	MIIB	T26-140	N2GZ	MU-2	025	N3AW	350	FL-491
N1HE	F90	LA-4	N1QL	MIII	T-394	N2HD	46T	97106	N3AW	441	0036
N1HP	E90	LW-32	N1RA	31T	7720036	N2HD	46T	97168	N3CC	680T	1680-62
N1HR	690B	11493	N1RH	PC12	627	N2HP	MU-2	357SA	N3CG	680T	1680-62
N1HR	E90	LW-27	N1RQ	46D	127	N2JB	PC12	148	N3CR	200	BB-850
N1HS	200	BB-291	N1RQ	46T	97112	N2JB	PC12	342	N3CR	90	LJ-592
N1HS	300	FA-54	N1RZ	MU-2	280	N2JE	MIIA	T26-019	N3CR	90	LJ-626
N1HS	90	LJ-440	N1SA	90	LJ-66	N2JJ	90	LJ-11	N3D	100	B-162
N1HT	E90	LW-32	N1SC	100	B-69	N2JR	90	LJ-459	N3D	200	BB-638
N1HX	200	BB-361	N1SC	200	BB-260	N2KA	E90	LW-12	N3D	90	LJ-254
N1JB	200	BB-1194	N1SC	350	FL-9	N2KC	690A	11148	N3DE	200	BB-332
N1JB	31T	8020083	N1SP	C-12	BC-42	N2KH	200	BB-468	N3DE	200	BB-849
N1JG	690B	11510	N1SS	690	11031	N2KN	690A	11148	N3DF	90	LJ-36
N1JP	200	BB-50	N1SS	690A	11210	N2KQ	90	LJ-769	(N3DF)	90	LJ-783
N1JP	200	BB-611	N1SS	MIIB	T26-117	N2KS	680T	1704-80	N3DG	100	B-162
N1JW	690	11006	N1TC	PC12	130	N2KS	690A	11104	N3DG	680T	1718-89
N1JW	PC12	116	N1TJ	MU-2	429SA	N2KY	P68	262	(N3DG)	90	LJ-144
N1KA	100	B-102	N1TP	90	LJ-104	N2MF	90	LJ-96	N3DS	690C	11614
N1KA	200	BB-85	N1TP	90	LJ-1490	N2MP	90	LJ-1561	N3DS	90	LJ-36
N1KA	200	BB-411	N1TQ	E90	LW-88	N2MP	C-12	BC-32	N3ED	MU-2	101
N1KA	200	BB-899	N1TR	100	B-238	N2MP	MIIB	T26-103	N3EE	MU-2	272
N1KB	200	BB-424	N1TV	90	LJ-347	N2NA	G1	96	N3EP	100	B-231
N1KC	690B	11444	N1TW	200	BB-939	N2NA	G1	98	N3EP	200	BB-967
N1KC	B100	BE-5	N1TX	200	BB-800	N2NC	441	0307	(N3FA)	100	B-65
N1KC	MU-2	348SA	N1TX	G1	131	N2NC	90	LJ-1855	N3FC	425	0038
N1KG	690A	11235	N1U	90	LJ-414	N2NC	G1	158	N3FH	200	BB-822
N1KQ	100	B-102	N1UA	90	LJ-414	N2ND	MU-2	677	N3FH	31T	7920014
N1LC	90	LJ-12	N1UA	MIIB	T26-134	N2NQ	441	0307	N3GC	90	LJ-576
N1LC	E90	LW-88	N1UC	90	LJ-210	N2NQ	690A	11309	N3GF	31T	8120058
N1LF	200	BB-1778	N1UC	E90	LW-140	N2NR	681B	6066	N3GS	B100	BE-36
N1LF	31T	8104007	N1UM	90	LJ-903	N2NR	690A	11309	N3GT	100	B-94
N1LQ	E90	LW-88	N1UQ	MU-2	303	N2NR	G1	158	N3GT	200	BB-42
N1LY	P180	1008	N1US	200	BB-69	N2PC	90	LJ-209	N3GT	MU-2	277
N1M	G1	88	N1US	MU-2	303	N2PQ	100	B-146	N3GW	100	B-94
N1MA	F90	LA-3	N1UT	680T	1684-65	N2PQ	G1	81	N3GY	200	BB-42
N1MB	90	LJ-616	N1UV	90	LJ-511	N2PW	100	B-146	N3HV	MIIB	T26-117
N1MB	90	LJ-806	N1VA	200	BB-670	N2PW	200	BB-832	N3JQ	PA42	8001036
N1MB	F90	LA-65	N1VA	350	FL-549	N2PX	200	BB-200	N3KF	90	LJ-530
N1MC	300	FA-40	N1VA	90	LJ-381	N2PX	200	BB-1260	(N3KS)	690A	11104
N1MG	B100	BE-5	N1VN	200	BB-494	N2PY	200	BB-200	N3KT	90	LJ-595
N1MM	200	BB-274	N1VN	MU-2	567	N2QE	46T	97247	N3LK	E90	LW-117
N1MN	MIII	TT-486A	N1VQ	690B	11369	N2QE	B100	BE-120	N3LL	200	BB-918
N1MT	100	B-126	N1VY	MU-2	567	N2RA	MU-2	105	N3LL	B100	BE-78
N1MT	90	LJ-824	N1WB	441	0203	N2RA	MU-2	366SA	(N3LL)	B100	BE-126
N1MU	200	BB-1245	N1WB	90	LJ-885	N2RR	90	LJ-163	N3LS	E90	LW-245
N1MU	MU-2	146	N1WD	100	B-67	N2SC	100	B-69	N3MA	MU-2	1511SA

Reg	Type	S/N
N3MP	MU-2	282
N3MP	MU-2	529
N3MP	MU-2	784SA
(N3MQ)	MU-2	748SA
N3MU	MU-2	143
N3NA	G1	92
N3NC	**200**	**BB-1976**
N3NC	441	0238
N3NR	681	6043
(N3NR)	690A	11167
N3NT	31T	7904019
N3PC	90	LJ-96
N3PC	90	LJ-210
N3PR	90	LJ-600
N3PX	**200**	**BB-1173**
N3RA	680W	1818-32
N3RB	MIII	T-214
N3RC	100	B-2
N3RC	200	BB-267
N3RK	**31T**	**8166022**
N3RN	MU-2	199
N3SK	680W	1820-34
N3TH	90	LJ-506
(N3TJ)	690B	11400
N3TJ	690B	11471
N3TK	31T	7520014
N3TK	**441**	**0158**
N3U	100	B-153
N3U	695	95041
N3UA	90	LJ-376
N3UL	B100	BE-78
N3UN	MU-2	720SA
N3UP	G1	18
N3UR	200	BB-178
N3UT	90	LJ-595
N3WE	31T	7904005
N3WM	**441**	**0068**
N3WU	690A	11336
N3XB	**90**	**LJ-234**
N3XF	**EPIC**	**004**
N3XR	441	0239
N3XY	690C	11638
N3ZC	**200**	**BB-1207**
N3ZC	E90	LW-80
N4	200	BB-88
N4AT	200	BB-281
N4B	90	LJ-851
N4B	90	LJ-1077
N4BC	**MIII**	**T-205E**
N4BG	MU-2	571
N4C	200	BB-877
N4C	90	LJ-816
N4CH	90	LJ-1077
N4CQ	200	BB-877
N4CS	441	0359
N4CS	MU-2	1566SA
N4DF	31T	8004018
(N4DF)	31T	8166040
N4DF	**PC12**	**831**
N4ER	MIIB	T26-152
N4EW	MU-2	458SA
N4F	680T	1688-68
N4FB	**680T**	**1688-68**
N4GC	90	LJ-1001
(N4GC)	B100	BE-126
N4GN	E90	LW-38
(N4GP)	200	BB-1766
N4GT	100	B-135
(N4GU)	90	LJ-1001
N4HC	90	LJ-494
N4HG	MU-2	590
N4KT	100	B-209
N4KU	**200**	**BB-1323**
(N4LH)	31T	8020002
N4LH	MU-2	538
N4LZ	MU-2	389SA
N4LZ	PC12	557
N4MA	MU-2	010
N4MD	TBM7	153
N4MD	**TBM8**	**500**
N4ME	681B	6058
N4MF	681B	6058
N4MR	E90	LW-184
N4NA	G1	151
N4NB	681	6044
N4NF	**300**	**FA-165**
N4NH	31T	7820056
N4NH	690B	11531
N4NR	681	6044
N4NR	690B	11531
N4NT	690D	15040
N4NU	**200**	**BB-1782**
N4NV	STAR	NC-7
N4NY	MIVA	AT-051
N4PC	90	LJ-66
N4PC	E90	LW-58
N4PC	G1	177
N4PC	PC12	216
N4PN	MU-2	222
N4PS	90	LJ-572
N4PT	**200**	**BB-879**
N4PT	E90	LW-70
N4PZ	**690A**	**11269**
N4QG	31T	8004023
N4QL	**200**	**BB-942**
N4R	90	LJ-8
N4R	**MU-2**	**1542SA**
N4RG	E90	LW-147
N4RP	PA42	5527021
N4RS	90	LJ-671
N4RT	90	LJ-671
N4RX	**31T**	**7904012**
N4RY	**90**	**LJ-8**
N4S	200	BB-405
N4S	350	FL-107
N4SB	690A	11178
N4SB	MU-2	1516SA
N4SP	MU-2	199
(N4SQ)	200	BB-1770
N4SR	MU-2	709SA
N4SY	MU-2	438SA
N4SY	MU-2	1516SA
N4TB	MU-2	612
N4TF	PC12	557
N4TJ	**200**	**BB-40**
N4TN	**MU-2**	**115**
N4TS	90	LJ-541
N4TS	**PC12**	**509**
N4TX	690B	11353
N4UB	STAR	NC-4
(N4UC)	F90	LA-206
N4WD	MU-2	014
N4WD	MU-2	179
N4WE	**PA42**	**5527041**
N4WF	**31T**	**8020025**
N4WP	31T	8104004
N4WQ	MU-2	179
(N4WZ)	PA42	8001004
N4YA	441	0210
N4YF	90	LJ-1658
N4YS	**350**	**FL-82**
N4ZB	**UC12**	**BV-11**
N5	90	LJ-902
N5AE	**200**	**BB-1891**
N5AH	**F90**	**LA-53**
N5AJ	200	BB-637
N5AJ	E90	LW-100
N5AP	MU-2	604
N5AX	E90	LW-100
N5B	MIIB	T26-114
N5BA	100	B-123
N5BR	**TBM7**	**89**
N5BW	90	LJ-245
(N5CA)	200	BB-12
(N5CA)	31T	7920042
(N5CE)	100	B-234
N5CE	425	0135
N5CJ	90	LJ-2
N5CN	PC6	870
N5D	**31T**	**7820080**
N5DL	MU-2	562
N5DM	**PC12**	**355**
N5E	680W	1788-18
N5EG	46D	95
N5EQ	**46D**	**95**
N5EQ	680W	1788-18
N5ER	680W	1760-6
N5ER	690B	11521
N5EV	680W	1788-18
N5FF	441	0055
N5FJ	MIVA	AT-038
(N5FW)	200	BB-1019
N5FW	200	BB-1019
N5FW	MIVA	AT-031
N5FY	MIVA	AT-066
N5GA	90	LJ-528
N5GC	90	LJ-635
N5GW	31T	8004049
N5HE	425	0085
N5HE	MU-2	233
N5HE	MU-2	571
N5HG	**441**	**0247**
N5HT	**TBM7**	**9**
N5JE	MU-2	659
N5JP	690A	11168
N5JR	90	LJ-273
N5KD	MU-2	420SA
N5KW	200	BB-445
N5KW	690A	11149
N5LC	**MU-2**	**433SA**
N5LE	200	BB-195
N5LJ	MU-2	321SA
N5LN	MU-2	799SA
N5MC	31T	7820005
N5MK	**200**	**BB-537**
N5MQ	31T	7820035
N5MW	MU-2	597
N5NA	G1	125
N5NC	MU-2	356SA
N5NE	MU-2	233
N5NK	690C	11603
N5NM	E90	LW-123
N5NM	E90	LW-237
N5NP	681	6042
N5NQ	MU-2	356SA
N5NR	200	BB-1089
N5NR	681	6042
(N5NR)	690	11048
N5NR	690A	11167
N5NR	690C	11603
N5NV	200	BB-1089
N5NV	**200**	**BB-1202**
N5NV	E90	LW-123
N5NW	F90	LA-199
N5NW	MU-2	597
N5NZ	690A	11167
N5PA	MU-2	590
N5PA	**PA42**	**8001051**
N5PC	200	BB-9
N5PC	90	LJ-6
N5PC	E90	LW-156
N5PC	G1	20
N5PC	MU-2	328
N5PC	MU-2	434SA
N5PC	MU-2	1558SA
N5PC	MU-2	1564SA
N5PF	PA42	8001023
N5PN	MU-2	222
N5PP	425	0198
N5PP	**46T**	**97145**
N5PQ	90	LJ-6
N5PQ	90	LJ-36
N5PQ	MU-2	1558SA
(N5PT)	690	11041
N5PT	90	LJ-507
N5PU	425	0198
N5PX	**200**	**BB-554**
N5RB	**31T**	**8104042**
N5RE	**680W**	**1818-32**
N5RE	E90	LW-103
N5RF	**350**	**FL-423**
N5RT	MIV	AT-017
(N5RZ)	31T	7520017
N5SL	31T	8104032
N5SM	31T	7520020
N5SS	200	BB-1148
(N5SS)	31T	8104032
N5SS	PA42	8001069
N5ST	100	B-196
N5ST	**200**	**BB-289**
N5SY	**PA42**	**8001069**
N5TA	**90**	**LJ-724**
N5TC	MU-2	247
N5TH	200	BB-404
N5TK	200	BB-483
N5TQ	MU-2	247
N5TW	200	BB-483
N5TW	200	BB-902
N5TW	**200**	**BB-1471**
N5TW	90	LJ-724
N5UB	200	BB-69
N5UB	31T	8166018
N5UD	441	0055
N5UL	90	LJ-1502
N5UN	**200**	**BB-697**
N5UT	F90	LA-152
N5UV	200	BB-339
N5VF	31T	8166018
N5VG	200	BB-414
N5VK	90	LJ-1334
N5VK	90	LJ-1502
N5VN	90	LJ-1334
N5VX	G1	7
N5WC	31T	7904028
N5WC	31T	8004029
N5WF	90	LJ-689
N5WG	**90**	**LJ-289**
N5WN	PC12	104
N5WU	90	LJ-635
N5XM	**350**	**FL-115**
N5Y	90	LJ-21
N5Y	**90**	**LJ-272**
N5Z	**EPIC**	**030**
N6B	690A	11174
N6B	690A	11260
N6BZ	690D	15008
N6DM	46T	97113B
N6DM	46T	97154
N6DQ	PC12	143
N6DY	200	BB-341
N6E	**681**	**6002**
N6EA	200	BB-890
N6EA	31T	7904011
N6EA	E90	LW-239
(N6EL)	690C	11610
N6ES	200	BB-53
N6FJ	MIVA	AT-041
N6FU	**PC6**	**729**
N6FZ	**PC12**	**290**
N6GT	90	LJ-73
N6HF	90	LJ-165
N6HU	**200**	**BB-319**
N6JE	200	BB-983
N6JL	200	BB-983
N6JL	**350**	**FL-247**
N6JM	31T	7904011
N6KA	200	BB-190
N6KE	**MU-2**	**766SA**
N6KF	**MU-2**	**659**
N6KZ	**90**	**LJ-238**
(N6LA)	MU-2	375SA
N6LD	200	BB-1055
N6LD	200	BB-1228
N6LD	90	LJ-853
N6MF	STAR	NC-53
N6NB	31T	7820035
N6NC	MIV	AT-016
N6PA	G1	50
N6PE	200	BB-856
N6PG	G1	40
N6PW	200	BB-205
N6PW	300	FA-32
N6PX	200	BB-205
N6RU	90	LJ-914
N6SG	MU-2	319
N6SK	425	0005
N6SP	C-12	BC-42
N6SP	MIIB	T26-110
N6TN	200	BB-145
N6TN	MU-2	163
N6UD	**200**	**BB-1055**
N6UM	E90	LW-39
N6UP	**MIII**	**TT-441**
N6VJ	**F90**	**LA-88**
N6VM	200	BB-814
N6VP	441	0019

N6WU	200	BB-1668	N7ZA	G1	68	N8TB	MU-2	627	N9UG	100	B-130
N6XK	EPIC	014	N7ZB	G1	107	N8TH	31T	8004056	N9UN	200	BB-501
N7AR	690B	11352	N7ZP	E90	LW-227	N8TK	31T	7520014	N9UP	300	FA-130
N7BF	90	LJ-107	N7ZT	PC12	385	N8TZ	90	LJ-773	N9UT	200	BB-468
N7BF	90	LJ-350	N7ZU	E90	LW-251	N8UM	46T	97067	N9UZ	90	LJ-641
N7BQ	90	LJ-107	N7ZU	F90	LA-196	N8VB	G1	12	N9VC	90	LJ-763
N7CC	200	BB-714	N7ZW	E90	LW-262	N8VF	300	FA-49	N9VF	31T	8166008
N7CJ	90	LJ-6	N8AD	690A	11314	N8VG	200C	BL-4	N9WC	MU-2	265
N7CJ	E90	LW-62	N8AF	90	LJ-561	N8VL	690C	11732	N9WR	200	BB-913
N7CQ	90	LJ-6	N8AH	90	LJ-561	N8W	46D	142	N9WV	350	FL-229
N7CR	200	BB-374	N8AM	200	BB-274	N8XK	EPIC	007	N9WW	90	LJ-174
N7CR	300	FA-25	N8BG	200	BB-267	N8YK	F90	LA-219	(N9WZ)	695	95043
N7CT	200	BB-957	(N8BG)	200	BB-605	N8YN	350	FL-417	N9X	MIII	TT-534
N7DD	MU-2	297	N8BG	90	LJ-578	N8ZA	G1	40	N9ZA	G1	41
N7EG	200	BB-97	N8BG	G1	22	N9AN	90	LJ-777	N10AC	200	BB-858
N7EV	690A	11139	N8BJ	G1	50	N9BE	EPIC	109	N10AC	90	LJ-506
N7FD	G1	145	N8BL	MU-2	038	N9BK	200	BB-17	N10AG	B100	BE-100
N7FL	31T	7820082	N8CA	90	LJ-1223	N9BK	200	BB-235	N10AT	90	LJ-88
N7FL	31T	7904016	N8CC	MU-2	569	N9BX	F90	LA-149	(N10AT)	B100	BE-51
N7GA	100	B-119	N8CF	31T	8020062	N9CH	31T	8120053	N10AU	90	LJ-1054
N7GA	200	BB-1035	N8CP	31T	7620053	N9CH	31T	8004045	N10AV	90	LJ-1054
N7GU	200	BB-276	N8DB	31T	8120014	(N9CH)	31T	8166046	N10AY	90	LJ-88
(N7GW)	200	BB-380	N8DX	200	BB-638	N9CH	31T	1166007	N10BC	31T	7400005
N7HD	90	LJ-238	N8E	G1	94	N9CH	PA42	5501030	N10BC	31T	8166039
N7HG	90	LJ-1907	N8EA	PA42	8001003	N9CJ	200	BB-91	N10BK	MU-2	272
N7HL	90	LJ-155	N8EE	31T	8166071	N9CR	90	LJ-626	N10BK	MU-2	280
N7HL	MIIB	T26-114	N8EF	200	BB-721	N9DA	90	LJ-944	N10BQ	31T	7400005
N7HM	MU-2	781SA	N8EG	TBM7	34	N9DC	90	LJ-1668	N10BY	200	BB-642
N7HN	MU-2	1563SA	N8FC	690A	11254	N9DC	PC12	402	N10CC	441	0139
N7HU	90	LJ-155	N8FF	200	BB-1019	N9DF	681	6020	N10CF	441	0198
N7JW	P180	1169	N8FR	425	0095	N9DF	E90	LW-294	N10CR	G1	175
N7KK	PA42	5527034	N8GF	90	LJ-164	N9DK	31T	7820022	N10CS	31T	8004001
N7KS	690B	11521	N8GF	P180	1011	N9EB	G1	5	N10CW	200	BB-1846
N7LH	90	LJ-222	N8GL	200	BB-1149	N9EE	TBM7	286	N10CW	200G	BY-52
N7LR	E90	LW-51	N8GR	MU-2	358SA	N9EN	90	LJ-580	N10CW	90	LJ-832
N7MA	E90	LW-292	N8GT	200	BB-1149	N9FC	200	BB-430	N10CY	200	BB-512
N7MB	200	BB-289	N8GT	90	LJ-164	N9FC	200	BB-603	N10DA	MU-2	551
N7MC	F90	LA-225	N8GT	90	LJ-1103	N9FC	E90	LW-248	N10DH	F90	LA-111
(N7MZ)	PA42	5527006	N8GU	90	LJ-1103	N9FQ	200	BB-430	N10DM	200	BB-63
N7NA	200	BB-997	N8H	EPIC	039	N9FQ	200	BB-603	(N10DR)	F90	LA-149
N7NW	441	0186	N8JG	100	B-31	N9GC	E90	LW-120	N10EC	200	BB-1211
N7P	F90	LA-59	N8KF	TBM7	304	N9GF	46D	21	N10EC	B100	BE-30
N7PA	200	BB-789	N8KF	TBM8	466	N9GS	300	FA-79	N10EH	200	BB-953
N7PA	200	BB-1444	N8KG	690A	11190	N9HA	MU-2	374SA	N10F	31T	7920076
N7PA	P180	1191	N8KT	MIIB	T26-158E	N9HJ	31T	8020031	N10F	31T	7920080
(N7PB)	31T	7520013	N8KU	TBM7	304	(N9HN)	MU-2	728SA	N10F	31T	7920085
N7PB	90	LJ-438	N8LB	690	11032	(N9HV)	BN2	3006	N10FB	425	0117
(N7PB)	E90	LW-198	(N8LB)	690B	11389	N9HW	90	LJ-459	N10FG	31T	7920024
N7PB	F90	LA-6	N8LB	690B	11389	N9JS	MU-2	178	N10FG	441	0171
N7PD	B100	BE-26	N8LB	695	95002	N9KA	200	BB-356	N10FJ	441	0240
N7PG	G1	41	N8LB	695A	96009	N9KG	690B	11426	(N10FL)	200	BB-94
N7PS	P180	1117	N8LB	695A	96054	N9LD	90	LJ-580	N10FR	MU-2	179
N7PW	MU-2	403SA	N8LC	MU-2	411SA	N9LE	TBM7	224	N10FR	MU-2	351SA
N7PW	MU-2	575	N8LC	MU-2	638	N9LP	MU-2	623	N10FR	MU-2	1559SA
N7Q	200	BB-780	N8LD	690	11032	N9LP	MU-2	784SA	N10GA	F90	LA-15
N7QR	200	BB-374	N8LN	695	95002	N9LV	690B	11550	(N10GE)	MU-2	274
N7RB	690A	11134	N8LV	695A	96009	N9MA	100	B-156	N10GP	E90	LW-291
N7RC	300	FA-58	N8LX	690B	11389	N9MA	MU-2	549	N10HC	200	BB-374
N7RC	350	FL-621	N8MG	90	LJ-747	N9MH	200	BB-360	N10HC	681	6025
N7RC	441	0156	N8NA	200	BB-950	N9MH	G1	55	N10HE	200	BB-1166
N7RC	MU-2	590	N8NM	90	LJ-401	N9MS	200	BB-1198	N10HE	90	LJ-1020
N7RC	MU-2	733SA	N8NP	100	B-52	N9MU	90	LJ-1503	N10HG	681	6025
N7RW	200	BB-31	N8NP	90	LJ-401	N9NA	200	BB-1091	N10HK	MU-2	180
N7SA	46D	239	N8NX	200	BB-774	N9NB	681B	6066	N10HS	PC12	1025
N7SL	G1	11	N8PC	E90	LW-64	N9NB	MU-2	728SA	N10HT	MU-2	778SA
N7SP	90	LJ-534	N8PC	E90	LW-110	N9NC	MU-2	728SA	N10HV	MU-2	774SA
N7TD	E90	LW-276	N8PC	MU-2	193	N9NR	695	95043	N10HY	90	LJ-1020
N7TW	90	LJ-478	N8PG	G1	164	N9NZ	MIII	T-255	N10J	90	LJ-10
N7UE	MU-2	400SA	N8PL	200	BB-939	N9PN	MU-2	222	N10J	E90	LW-50
N7UF	31T	8166049	N8PL	300	FA-212	N9PU	F90	LA-57	N10JE	90	LJ-10
N7UJ	46T	97226	N8PL	MU-2	338	N9QM	G1	322	N10JJ	MU-2	383SA
N7UM	E90	LW-223	N8PY	200	BB-487	N9RN	680W	1775-13	N10JP	E90	LW-81
N7UP	680W	1790-20	N8QD	680T	1677-60	N9RU	200	BB-984	N10JQ	E90	LW-50
N7UU	MIII	T-242	N8RA	681	6044	N9SA	90	LJ-41	N10K	350	FL-4
N7UZ	BN2	183	(N8RS)	31T	7820011	N9SB	200	BB-882	N10K	F90	LA-55
N7VA	200	BB-670	N8RW	MU-2	1548SA	N9SJ	BN2	592	N10KF	90	LJ-460
N7VR	31T	7804010	N8RY	PA42	8001036	N9SR	MU-2	393SA	(N10KP)	MU-2	389SA
N7WF	425	0119	N8SD	E90	LW-261	N9SS	MU-2	556	N10MC	31T	7920028
N7WS	31T	7720058	N8SP	200	BB-625	N9SS	MU-2	734SA	N10MD	90	LJ-750
N7WS	46D	115	N8SP	E90	LW-261	N9TN	90	LJ-803	(N10MH)	MU-2	410SA
N7WS	E90	LW-142	N8SR	MU-2	725SA	N9TW	90	LJ-379	N10MR	MU-2	351SA
N7WU	E90	LW-142	N8SV	200	BB-506	(N9TW)	C-12	BC-12	N10MX	MU-2	1563SA
N7WY	MIIB	T26-146	N8SZ	200	BB-625	N9UA	MIVC	AT-495B	N10NA	G1	125
N7YR	PC12	532	N8TB	MU-2	387SA	N9UE	TBM7	224	N10NB	MIVC	AT-423

N10NW	90	LJ-41
N10PC	200	BB-619
N10PF	PC12	165
N10PP	690A	11302
N10PT	200C	BL-38
N10QM	425	0197
N10QW	200	BB-1846
N10QW	90	LJ-832
N10QY	300	FA-68
N10QZ	680T	1685-66
N10RM	425	0074
N10RN	681	6021
(N10SA)	200	BB-1335
N10SA	E90	LW-273
N10ST	46T	97220
N10T	MU-2	301
N10TB	G1	86
N10TB	MIII	T-230
N10TF	MIII	T-230
N10TG	680T	1684-65
N10TM	200	BB-45
N10TM	90	LJ-476
N10TN	681	6037
N10TQ	STAR	NC-8
N10TT	200	BB-219
N10TX	350	FL-1
N10TX	STAR	NC-8
N10UN	350	FL-158
N10UT	MU-2	124
N10UT	MU-2	346
N10VG	690A	11326
N10VM	G1	87
N10VQ	PC12	410
N10VU	MU-2	263
N10VU	MU-2	438SA
N10VW	200	BB-168
N10WE	MIIB	T26-161
N10WG	E90	LW-310
N10WL	MIIB	T26-161
N10WL	MIII	T-248
(N10WL)	P68	281
N10XH	90	LJ-887
N10XJ	E90	LW-117
N10XL	31T	8166044
N10XL	90	LJ-311
N10YP	90	LJ-265
N10ZA	G1	142
N11	C-12	BD-1
N11AB	200	BB-305
N11AB	90	LJ-266
(N11AB)	90	LJ-672
N11AG	100	B-21
N11BC	31T	7820059
N11CK	680T	1701-77
N11CT	680W	1773-11
N11CZ	G1	59
N11DT	E90	LW-11
N11DW	90	LJ-759
(N11EA)	90	LJ-783
N11EQ	200	BB-1366
N11ER	200	BB-537
N11ER	90	LJ-58
(N11EX)	690B	11527
N11EX	690C	11623
N11FL	90	LJ-301
N11FT	90	LJ-958
(N11FX)	90	LJ-829
(N11GE)	200	BB-896
N11GE	E90	LW-111
N11GS	300	FA-147
N11HK	200	BB-444
N11HM	680T	1620-51
N11HR	MU-2	122
N11HY	200	BB-426
N11HY	690B	11403
N11JJ	100	B-2
N11JP	90	LJ-58
N11KR	MU-2	144
N11LA	90	LJ-479
N11LC	200	BB-1176
N11LC	200	BB-1366
N11LC	MU-2	161
N11LG	MU-2	595
N11LQ	MU-2	161
N11LS	90	LJ-825
N11MC	680T	1685-66
N11MM	441	0105
N11MY	200	BB-426
N11NP	690A	11232
N11NY	G1	172
N11PA	200	BB-110
N11PA	90	LJ-479
N11PM	MIIB	T26-101
N11RM	200	BB-995
N11RM	MIII	T-206
N11SJ	MU-2	285
N11SK	MIVA	AT-025
N11SN	90	LJ-1036
N11SX	G1	28
N11SX	MIVA	AT-025
N11T	90	LJ-1893
N11T	TBM8	420
N11TE	200	BB-651
N11TE	350	FL-211
N11TE	90	LJ-419
N11TE	90	LJ-713
N11TN	90	LJ-419
N11UC	90	LJ-210
N11UN	G1	102
N11VA	90	LJ-381
N11VC	200	BB-548
N11VS	690	11058
N11WC	31T	8020033
N11WC	90	LJ-414
N11WF	MU-2	142
N11WF	MU-2	565
N11WF	MU-2	752SA
N11WN	F90	LA-177
N11WQ	MU-2	752SA
N11WU	MU-2	565
N11YC	31T	8166020
N12	C-12	BD-8
N12AB	90	LJ-45
N12AC	90	LJ-554
N12AG	PC12	854
N12AK	E90	LW-79
N12AM	90	LJ-454
N12AQ	100	B-94
N12AQ	90	LJ-454
N12AU	E90	LW-293
N12AW	90	LJ-677
N12AX	E90	LW-293
N12BC	MU-2	191
(N12BU)	690	11028
N12CA	PC12	135
N12CF	200	BB-534
N12DE	690B	11501
N12DT	441	0040
N12DZ	PC12	390
N12EK	MIII	T-224
(N12EN)	TBM7	192
N12EW	MU-2	316
N12FA	46D	28
N12FA	PC12	117
N12FC	31T	7620044
N12FH	200	BB-548
(N12FL)	200	BB-94
N12GJ	E90	LW-12
N12GP	G1	177
N12GR	31T	7920058
N12GW	G1	19
N12HF	31T	7820085
N12HF	MU-2	435SA
N12HH	MIII	T-242
N12JC	BN2	201
N12JD	PC12	228
N12JG	90	LJ-437
N12KA	200	BB-50
N12KA	E90	LW-41
N12KR	200	BB-1632
N12KV	680T	1675-58
N12KW	200	BB-749
N12KW	31T	8120035
N12KW	680T	1675-58
N12L	200	BB-94
N12L	200	BB-1125
N12LA	90	LJ-979
N12LA	E90	LW-49
N12LB	200	BB-94
N12LD	200	BB-1125
N12LE	90	LJ-1751
N12LE	MU-2	403SA
N12LH	PC6	798
N12LP	MU-2	784SA
N12MA	TBM7	318
N12MC	PC12	722
N12MF	MIII	T-417
N12MG	200	BB-1581
N12MH	MIIB	T26-139
N12MU	681B	6051
N12MU	90	LJ-1398
N12MY	200	BB-1581
N12NA	MIIA	T26-018
N12NG	200	BB-581
N12NL	425	0069
N12Q	690A	11201
N12RA	MU-2	177
N12RF	90	LJ-575
N12RS	46D	28
(N12RS)	690B	11358
N12RW	G1	82
N12SC	MU-2	144
N12SJ	MU-2	333
N12ST	200	BB-864
N12TA	90	LJ-883
N12TV	441	0025
N12TW	31T	7720017
N12VA	695A	96062
N12VK	P68	278
N12WC	MIIB	T26-118
N12WF	MU-2	1558SA
N12WY	TBM7	112
N12WZ	31T	8104042
N12ZA	695A	96098
N12ZM	TBM8	474
N13	F90	LA-124
N13BJ	695	95000
N13CA	BN2	240
N13DB	E90	LW-94
N13DR	B100	BE-80
N13EB	425	0209
N13EW	MU-2	221
(N13FA)	MU-2	144
N13FH	425	0209
N13FJ	200	BB-1591
N13GZ	90	LJ-1590
N13HC	200	BB-500
N13JV	F90	LA-20
N13JV	MIII	TT-512A
N13K	100	B-101
N13KA	B100	BE-23
N13LY	200	BB-1718
(N13MX)	200	BB-634
N13NW	441	0090
N13PA	90	LJ-992
N13PD	300	FA-10
N13PF	690B	11455
(N13PK)	P68	221
N13PR	200	BB-1126
N13PR	B100	BE-80
N13PR	MU-2	682
N13RR	MU-2	682
N13ST	90	LJ-162
N13TT	PA42	8001005
N13TV	680W	1776-14
N13TV	690A	11148
(N13UF)	200	BB-728
N13WF	MU-2	432SA
N13YS	MU-2	694
N14	F90	LA-131
N14AD	690A	11314
N14BH	690	11022
N14BM	425	0076
N14BU	690B	11514
N14BW	200	BB-1012
(N14BW)	31T	7720040
N14C	E90	LW-62
N14CE	90	LJ-144
N14CE	E90	LW-44
N14CF	100	B-209
N14CN	695	95069
N14CP	90	LJ-585
N14CV	690	11020
N14CX	695	95069
N14EA	31T	7820006
N14EF	46D	145
N14EV	46D	42
N14FJ	441	0118
(N14FS)	690A	11107
(N14GA)	695A	96100
N14GA	90	LJ-434
N14GD	MU-2	598
N14GG	690A	11107
N14GG	90	LJ-1412
N14GH	690A	11255
N14GV	46T	97092
N14HB	200	BB-1533
N14HG	200	BB-1071
N14JK	MIIB	T26-159
N14KA	90	LJ-688
N14KA	BN2	11
N14KA	F90	LA-202
N14LP	P68	361
N14LW	31T	7720022
N14M	681B	6051
N14MF	200	BB-838
N14MR	31T	7820008
N14MW	E90	LW-10
N14NA	200	BB-581
N14NE	31T	1104012
N14NE	350	FL-27
N14NG	200	BB-1276
N14NM	E90	LW-35
(N14NV)	STAR	NC-7
N14NW	441	0171
N14P	441	0230
N14P	P180	1017
N14PC	100	B-74
N14PN	441	0230
N14PT	31T	8004048
N14PX	31T	8104060
N14RA	90	LJ-474
N14RD	200C	BL-5
N14RD	PC12	384
N14SB	E90	LW-214
N14SU	200	BB-259
N14TF	200	BB-810
N14TG	90	LJ-226
N14TK	90	LJ-255
N14TP	MIII	T-220
N14TT	F90	LA-23
N14V	100	B-65
N14V	200	BB-121
N14V	90	LJ-365
N14V	90	LJ-411
N14VB	100	B-51
N14VK	90	LJ-365
N14VL	MU-2	1514SA
N14VP	STAR	NC-22
N14VR	STAR	NC-22
N14VT	200	BB-121
(N14WL)	90	LJ-692
N14XT	P68	361
N14YS	MU-2	290
N15	F90	LA-138
(N15AA)	BN2	479
N15AJ	690B	11371
N15AT	31T	1104004
N15CC	MIII	T-339
N15CC	MU-2	023
N15CD	690A	11177
N15CN	MIII	T-339
N15CN	MU-2	707SA
N15CT	90	LJ-192
N15DB	441	0278
(N15DE)	PA42	8001050
N15EK	PC12	120
N15ES	680W	1818-32
N15ET	MU-2	733SA
N15EW	350	FL-388
N15EW	MU-2	208
N15EW	MU-2	304
N15EW	MU-2	1505SA
N15GA	90	LJ-656
N15GG	200	BB-755
N15GP	G1	68

N15GS	MIII	T-258	N16P	425	0173	N17TW	200	BB-968	N19CK	300	FA-69
N15GZ	90	LJ-1586	N16PM	200	BB-615	N17TW	300	FA-190	N19CM	90	LJ-524
N15HV	200	BB-1452	N16PX	200	BB-532	N17UC	MU-2	159	N19CX	46T	97077
N15JA	200	BB-1354	N16RK	31T	7920054	N17UC	MU-2	772SA	N19DA	B100	BE-87
N15JA	200	BB-1366	N16SM	100	B-224	N17UP	BN2	10	N19EG	F90	LA-17
N15JA	MU-2	284	N16SW	100	B-51	N17VA	200	BB-670	N19FF	G1	20
N15JW	690	11006	N16TB	300	FA-42	N17VV	MIII	TT-536	N19GA	31T	7920091
N15JW	90	LJ-728	N16TB	300	FA-198	N17WC	350	FL-168	N19GA	MU-2	454SA
N15KA	200	BB-252	N16TB	690A	11177	N17WD	B100	BE-17	N19GB	200	BB-166
N15KA	200	BB-325	N16TB	E90	LW-344	N17WT	90	LJ-86	N19GB	200	BB-935
N15KA	200	BB-383	N16TC	46D	228	N17XL	P68	371	N19GD	350	FL-96
N15KA	200	BB-457	N16TC	MU-2	368SA	N17XX	PC6	564	N19GR	200	BB-166
N15KA	200	BB-512	N16TE	300	FA-42	N17ZD	695A	96017	N19GR	200	BB-935
N15KA	200	BB-600	N16TE	680W	1761-7	N18	90	LJ-902	N19GR	350	FL-96
N15KR	MIII	T-294	N16TE	E90	LW-188	N18	F90	LA-145	N19GR	350	FL-414
N15KW	31T	8166014	(N16TE)	E90	LW-344	N18AF	200	BB-1497	N19GR	90	LJ-383
N15L	100	B-212	N16TF	200	BB-1310	N18AF	31T	8020076	N19GU	MU-2	574
(N15LM)	90	LJ-494	N16TG	690A	11177	N18AF	PA42	8001063	N19H	FPC6	2021
N15LR	100	B-229	N16TG	690C	11619	N18AH	100	B-118	N19HC	690B	11521
(N15LS)	200	BB-346	N16TX	200	BB-516	N18BA	MU-2	314	N19HM	31T	7920062
N15MR	90	LJ-321	N16TX	200	BB-1062	N18BF	MU-2	173	N19HM	90	LJ-744
N15MV	MU-2	1506SA	N16VK	PC12	763	N18BG	90	LJ-801	N19HS	90	LJ-440
N15NA	200	BB-666	N16VM	BN2	2204	N18BH	200	BB-625	N19HT	90	LJ-736
N15NG	200	BB-666	N16WG	F90	LA-226	N18BL	F90	LA-13	N19J	90	LJ-296
N15NM	TBM8	458	N16WL	690A	11307	(N18BQ)	MIII	T-221	N19J	MIII	T-326
N15PJ	31T	7720066	N17	90	LJ-896	N18CD	90	LJ-584	N19JX	90	LJ-296
(N15PT)	90	LJ-1187	N17AE	F90	LA-80	N18CJ	200	BB-260	(N19KA)	200	BB-1050
N15PX	300	FA-82	(N17AK)	90	LJ-998	N18CM	200	BB-1167	N19LB	200	BB-220
N15RA	200	BB-325	N17BC	90	LJ-11	N18CM	F90	LA-42	N19LW	90	LJ-595
N15RH	200	BB-948	N17CA	G1	123	N18CM	F90	LA-219	N19LW	90	LJ-991
N15SB	TBM7	247	N17CD	90	LJ-329	N18DN	200	BB-81	N19M	90	LJ-222
N15SF	690B	11528	N17CE	31T	7804007	N18DN	200	BB-1150	N19MC	300	FA-167
N15SL	90	LJ-886	N17CG	695A	96003	N18DN	E90	LW-245	N19MK	90	LJ-330
N15SS	31T	7820068	N17CK	F406	0001	N18DV	E90	LW-245	N19MU	681B	6051
N15ST	425	0140	N17CP	100	B-243	N18EA	F90	LA-11	N19NC	300	FA-183
N15TF	200	BB-554	N17CP	425	0156	N18EH	F90	LA-11	N19NM	31T	7520006
N15TP	PC12	149	N17CP	E90	LW-60	N18EL	680T	1565-21	N19P	90	LJ-870
N15TR	MU-2	446SA	N17DW	200	BB-648	N18JB	MU-2	670	N19R	90	LJ-8
N15TT	200	BB-554	N17EA	425	0075	N18KA	200	BB-360	N19R	90	LJ-634
N15TT	200	BB-917	N17EE	695A	96091	N18KA	90	LJ-137	N19R	F90	LA-12
N15UB	90	LJ-1776	N17EL	90	LJ-1101	N18KK	681B	6055	N19RB	MU-2	438SA
N15UD	MU-2	708SA	N17EL	BN2	2211	N18KP	31T	7904013	N19RK	F90	LA-12
N15UE	31T	8020049	N17EN	90	LJ-998	N18KT	31T	7904013	N19RT	MIVA	AT-029
N15VC	MU-2	023	N17FL	90	LJ-1101	N18KW	31T	8120059	N19SC	200	BB-816
N15VG	441	0182	N17FS	200	BB-1159	(N18KW)	31T	8166046	N19SD	MIII	T-268
N15VZ	690	11035	N17GD	E90	LW-31	N18LP	90	LJ-278	N19SD	MIII	T-291
N15WD	350	FL-57	N17GG	690C	11636	N18LR	MU-2	366SA	N19SE	MIIB	T26-170
N15WD	690B	11503	N17GR	90	LJ-383	N18MB	90	LJ-919	N19SG	TBM7	194
N15WF	MU-2	432SA	N17HF	690A	11127	N18N	G1	90	N19TX	PC6	684
N15WN	E90	LW-78	N17HG	MU-2	1510SA	(N18RC)	100	B-230	N19TZ	G1	40
N15WS	350	FL-33	N17HM	200	BB-94	N18RN	350	FL-300	N19UM	90	LJ-524
N15WS	350	FL-411	N17HM	200	BB-711	N18S	90	LJ-241	N19UW	90	LJ-595
N15YS	MU-2	598	N17HM	425	0200	N18SE	MIIB	T26-134	N19WA	BN2	524
N15ZM	MU-2	774SA	N17HP	46T	97169	N18SF	F90	LA-236	N19WL	P68	425
N16	90	LJ-893	N17JA	BN2	2022	N18SR	TBM7	161	N19WM	46T	97404
N16AS	200	BB-608	N17JG	680W	1802-24	N18SS	690A	11322	N19Y	200	BB-405
N16BF	200	BB-89	N17JJ	MIIB	T26-166	N18ST	200	BB-1844	N19Y	90	LJ-331
N16BM	F90	LA-23	N17JQ	MU-2	375SA	N18T	MU-2	572	N20	90	LJ-912
(N16CG)	90	LJ-8	N17KA	90	LJ-1138	N18T	MU-2	1544SA	N20AE	200	BB-827
N16CG	MU-2	418SA	N17KK	200C	BL-49	N18TA	MIII	T-417	N20AM	31T	8020091
N16CP	46D	138	N17KK	90	LJ-1318	N18TF	G1	52	N20AM	F90	LA-13
N16CS	90	LJ-113	N17KW	31T	8104070	(N18TG)	690C	11619	N20AS	690A	11331
N16EF	441	0298	N17KZ	441	0268	(N18TZ)	G1	52	N20AU	C-12	BC-28
N16FA	100	B-172	N17LH	46T	97007	N18U	100	B-57	N20BD	200	BB-284
N16GA	200	BB-1226	N17ME	300	FA-66	(N18VG)	200	BB-891	N20BF	441	0086
N16GA	E90	LW-235	N17NC	350	FL-42	N18VG	200	BB-894	N20BL	90	LJ-163
N16GF	200	BB-1531	N17NM	31T	7820035	N18WA	BN2	517	N20BM	680T	1698-75
N16GG	690A	11135	N17NM	E90	LW-237	N18WP	MU-2	648	N20BN	BN2	529
(N16GG)	690D	15019	N17PA	P180	1017	N18X	100	B-57	N20BP	690A	11341
N16GL	690A	11336	N17PL	425	0026	N18X	90	LJ-137	N20CC	G1	47
N16GM	200	BB-121	(N17QC)	695A	96017	N18XJ	90	LJ-1500	N20CL	MIII	T-233
(N16GM)	90	LJ-610	N17QC	MU-2	772SA	N18ZD	MIIB	T26-120	N20CN	MIII	T-231
N16HA	31T	7620053	N17RA	P68	357	N18ZX	31T	7820014	N20CR	G1	166
N16HA	MU-2	780SA	N17RC	425	0119	N19	90	LJ-909	N20DE	MIIB	T26-168
N16KA	BN2	65	N17RM	690A	11104	N19AC	31T	7720017	N20DH	200	BB-1263
N16KK	200	BB-1130	N17SA	90	LJ-164	N19AC	31T	8120005	N20DL	31T	8004045
N16KM	90	LJ-961	N17SA	MU-2	671	N19AG	31T	7720017	N20EB	690A	11282
N16KW	31T	8120010	N17SD	MIII	T-270	N19AP	TBM7	10	N20EF	MIIB	T26-157
N16KW	90	LJ-1435	N17SE	E90	LW-169	N19BG	31T	8120055	N20EG	100	B-179
N16LH	E90	LW-217	(N17TJ)	200	BB-17	N19BK	90	LJ-1294	N20ER	695	95065
(N16NB)	31T	1104005	N17TJ	200	BB-1217	N19BN	BN2	19	N20ER	MIIB	T26-157
*N16NB	31T	1104005	N17TS	F90	LA-192	N19BX	G1	153	N20EW	300	FA-152
N16NM	E90	LW-62	N17TU	31T	7520035	N19CD	PA42	8001018	N20EW	350	FL-260
N16NW	441	0045	(N17TV)	B100	BE-34	N19CK	200	BB-956	N20FB	31T	7820013

N20FD	90	LJ-1213	N21BN	BN2	533	N22EQ	MU-2	192	N23EF	690D	15007
N20FD	90	LJ-1528	N21CA	31T	7820013	N22ER	E90	LW-18	N23EH	200	BB-1776
N20FL	B100	BE-72	N21CH	90	LJ-500	N22ET	680W	1793-23	N23ES	31T	8104053
N20FS	100	B-246	N21CJ	MU-2	789SA	N22F	200	BB-1025	N23EW	E90	LW-168
N20GB	G1	80	N21CT	90	LJ-476	N22FL	MU-2	561	N23FH	200	BB-1565
N20GC	MIII	T-205	N21CY	300	FA-153	N22FR	F90	LA-139	N23FH	STAR	NC-32
N20GM	E90	LW-309	N21DA	BN2	2024	N22FS	90	LJ-1452	N23FL	STAR	NC-32
N20GT	695A	96036	N21DE	200	BB-117	N22G	G1	81	N23HB	31T	7904034
(N20GT)	90	LJ-826	N21DJ	E90	LW-13	N22GW	MIIB	T26-169	N23HD	200	BB-1960
N20GZ	200	BB-754	N21DX	350	FL-210	N22HD	90	LJ-1720	N23HD	90	LJ-1760
N20H	G1	197	N21DZ	C-12	BC-32	N22HD	PA42	8001078	N23HF	90	LJ-1760
N20HC	441	0010	N21EH	200	BB-541	N22HP	690A	11319	N23HR	MU-2	034
N20HE	G1	197	N21EH	441	0065	N22HS	425	0220	N23HR	MU-2	271
N20HF	G1	47	N21EH	E90	LW-228	N22HS	90	LJ-151	(N23JA)	BN2	348
N20HG	695	95022	N21FG	200	BB-839	N22JA	BN2	264	N23JA	BN2	420
N20JA	BN2	307	N21HA	90	LJ-918	N22JJ	90	LJ-391	(N23JA)	BN2	428
(N20JL)	BN2	290	N21HC	681B	6054	N22JR	100	B-28	N23KA	90	LJ-373
N20JS	31T	7904032	N21HP	MU-2	357SA	N22JW	F90	LA-18	N23KF	31T	7920063
N20KC	MU-2	322	N21J	100	B-2	N22JZ	MU-2	021	N23KW	PA42	8001071
N20KQ	200	BB-405	N21JA	31T	7804003	(N22KD)	E90	LW-89	N23LF	90	LJ-901
N20KV	MIIB	T26-154	N21JA	BN2	427	N22KF	E90	LW-89	N23LH	46D	85
N20KW	300	FA-44	N21JA	BN2	451	N22KL	200G	BY-26	N23LS	690B	11372
N20LA	90	LJ-369	N21JA	BN2	465	N22KW	B100	BE-7	N23MV	31T	7720044
N20LB	200	BB-1541	N21JA	MU-2	614	N22KW	E90	LW-89	N23MW	P68	151
N20LB	90	LJ-1121	N21KE	E90	LW-174	N22KW	MIVA	AT-031	N23MY	TBM8	483
N20LH	200	BB-1996	N21KN	31T	7620035	N22LC	MU-2	192	N23NW	441	0066
N20LH	E90	LW-80	N21LE	90	LJ-1682	N22LD	31T	8020067	N23Q	90	LJ-842
(N20LK)	90	LJ-1121	N21LE	BN2	857	N22LP	PC12	402	N23RA	MU-2	686
N20LM	C-12	BC-67	N21LF	LFAN	E-003	N22LY	680T	1563-19	N23RF	P180	1080
N20MA	690B	11514	N21MK	MU-2	032	(N22MV)	PA42	8001063	N23ST	200	BB-375
N20MB	680W	1843-42	N21MS	PA42	8001030	N22MV	PA42	8001063	N23SV	P180	1010
N20ME	680W	1843-42	N21MU	200	BB-782	N22MY	TBM8	443	N23TC	200	BB-453
N20ME	690B	11440	N21MU	MU-2	727SA	N22MZ	MU-2	158	N23TC	31T	8104033
N20MK	200	BB-642	N21NM	E90	LW-336	N22N	E90	LW-48	(N23TJ)	690B	11400
N20MR	31T	7920014	N21NV	200	BB-1269	N22NG	MIII	T-387	(N23TX)	690C	11621
N20MR	31T	1104013	N21PB	MU-2	303	N22NL	90	LJ-707	N23UG	G1	108
N20NH	G1	16	N21PC	MIVA	AT-064E	N22NP	200	BB-432	N23US	BN2	2040
N20NK	300	FA-51	N21PC	MU-2	295	N22NR	MIIB	T26-173	N23UT	90	LJ-17
N20NL	300	FA-51	N21PD	46D	135	(N22QC)	690B	11501	N23W	90	LJ-168
N20NT	681	6043	N21PL	PA42	8001002	N22RJ	90	LJ-321	N23W	E90	LW-230
N20PF	425	0018	N21PS	200	BB-1344	N22RT	680W	1793-23	N23WE	F90	LA-9
N20PJ	31T	7920021	N21RX	100	B-156	N22RT	681	6001	N23WJ	200	BB-1297
N20PS	MU-2	636	N21SP	90	LJ-630	N22SN	F90	LA-211	(N23WL)	200	BB-541
N20PT	31T	8004020	N21TA	31T	8120009	N22SY	46D	12	N23WP	31T	8020004
N20PT	MIIB	T26-128	N21TB	31T	7820026	N22T	100	B-115	N23WS	200	BB-1143
N20PT	PA42	8001020	N21TX	G1	131	N22T	200	BB-1011	N23X	MIIB	T26-166
N20PU	PA42	8001020	N21VA	350	FL-549	N22TE	100	B-115	N23X	MIII	T-328
N20QD	E90	LW-49	N21VF	200	BB-1297	N22TG	MU-2	449SA	N23Y	90	LJ-207
N20QN	MIII	T-231	N21VM	MU-2	535	N22TL	E90	LW-334	N23YP	200	BB-1142
N20RE	200	BB-758	N21WB	90	LJ-583	N22TP	200	BB-979	N23YR	200	BB-1976
N20RF	E90	LW-85	N21WF	90	LJ-536	N22TZ	200	BB-1011	N24A	690C	11627
(N20RT)	100	B-26	N21WF	F90	LA-105	N22UC	31T	7804007	(N24A)	695A	96034
N20RT	90	LJ-117	(N21WY)	90	LJ-1472	N22UP	PA42	8001079	N24AD	31T	7920063
N20S	E90	LW-267	N21XE	E90	LW-62	N22VF	31T	8166018	N24AR	200	BB-867
N20S	G1	37	N21XL	E90	LW-62	N22VF	690B	11368	N24BL	200	BB-375
N20SH	31T	7920019	N21YA	BN2	465	N22VK	90	LJ-1334	N24BL	300	FA-153
N20SM	200	BB-1011	N22	90	LJ-156	N22WC	90	LJ-214	N24BL	90	LJ-590
N20SR	200	BB-1108	N22AS	G1	156	N22WE	90	LJ-321	N24BT	690A	11289
N20TA	MIIB	T26-110	N22BB	90	LJ-241	N22WF	31T	7620049	N24CC	690A	11201
N20TA	MIII	T-285	N22BD	300	FA-84	N22WF	31T	7920007	N24CC	PA42	8001035
N20TF	MU-2	623	N22BD	PA42	8001055	(N22WG)	680T	1601-43	N24CP	G1	155
N20TN	31T	7920019	N22BJ	100	B-133	N22WK	681	6024	N24CV	200	BB-1524
N20TV	31T	7920019	N22BM	90	LJ-630	(N22WL)	90	LJ-707	N24DA	E90	LW-216
N20TX	695A	96089	N22CA	31T	7820027	N22WZ	TBM7	173	N24DD	31T	7920074
N20UN	F90	LA-21	N22CC	690B	11501	N22X	100	B-163	N24DS	90	LJ-1616
N20VP	200	BB-1242	N22CE	MIIA	T26-029	N22XW	B100	BE-7	N24E	31T	7820037
N20WC	90	LJ-500	N22CG	441	0119	N22XY	MU-2	599	N24EM	B100	BE-6
N20WE	31T	8120059	N22CH	MU-2	130	N22YA	MU-2	623	N24FH	90	LJ-1754
N20WE	31T	8004025	N22CK	690B	11524	N22YC	31T	8166020	N24FJ	MU-2	453SA
N20WK	MU-2	621	N22CN	31T	7904049	N22YD	MU-2	271	N24FT	350	FL-72
N20WL	31T	7720011	N22CP	G1	155	N23AD	690	11010	N24GJ	90	LJ-769
N20WP	90	LJ-738	N22CR	90	LJ-1811	N23AE	E90	LW-150	N24GN	200	BB-953
N20WS	E90	LW-30	N22DE	MIIB	T26-161	N23AE	MIII	T-241	N24GT	690A	11254
N20Z	90	LJ-331	N22DL	MIIB	T26-161	N23AH	G1	33	N24HD	200G	BY-18
N20Z	90	LJ-412	N22DT	31T	8020057	N23AK	G1	117	N24HE	31T	8020009
N21	90	LJ-902	N22DT	MIII	T-227	N23AW	425	0023	(N24HE)	31T	7904006
N21AF	31T	7620035	N22DW	MIII	T-227	N23BC	MU-2	191	N24HE	PA42	5527005
N21AG	46D	154	N22DW	MIII	T-317	N23BW	100	B-126	(N24JA)	BN2	313
(N21AH)	G1	33	N22EE	681B	6061	N23CA	31T	7820040	N24JA	BN2	352
N21AK	90	LJ-476	N22EH	E90	LW-18	N23CD	MU-2	142	N24JJ	350	FL-433
(N21AM)	90	LJ-67	N22EK	MIIA	T26-009	N23D	G1	59	N24KW	PA42	5527010
N21AR	31T	7620035	N22EM	31T	7820084	N23DB	E90	LW-94	N24LA	200	BB-374
N21AU	MU-2	586	N22EM	MIIA	T26-009	N23DH	MU-2	534	N24MK	100	B-75
N21AU	PC12	606	N22EQ	MIII	T-221	N23EA	441	0183	N24MK	200	BB-91

N24MK	F90	LA-4	N25PF	690B	11378	N27DA	200	BB-257	N28JK	46D	135
N24MW	MU-2	434SA	N25QL	425	0158	N27DK	46T	97196	N28KC	200	BB-356
N24PE	MU-2	369SA	N25QT	425	0158	N27ER	46T	97368	N28KC	90	LJ-845
N24PL	90	LJ-137	(N25RE)	690A	11320	N27G	G1	132	N28KP	90	LJ-845
N24PR	90	LJ-137	N25RT	E90	LW-307	N27GD	31T	7920053	N28LR	690B	11424
N24PT	441	0015	N25RT	F90	LA-173	N27GE	350	FL-86	N28M	E90	LW-147
N24QF	425	0181	N25RZ	690B	11518	N27GH	200	BB-1260	(N28MM)	90	LJ-1063
N24QT	425	0181	N25SA	BN2	766	N27GP	MU-2	027	N28MN	BN2	572
(N24RE)	690A	11320	(N25SM)	690B	11477	(N27GS)	100	B-169	N28MS	E90	LW-100
N24RE	690C	11627	N25ST	90	LJ-507	N27GT	E90	LW-291	N28NK	46T	97191
N24S	90	LJ-214	N25TG	E90	LW-238	N27HK	200	BB-1350	N28PH	350	FL-248
N24SA	200	BB-465	N25TN	695	95013	N27JA	BN2	263	N28PH	B100	BE-105
N24SM	E90	LW-239	N25UF	MU-2	167	(N27JA)	BN2	314	N28PP	MU-2	450SA
N24SP	200	BB-3	N25W	200	BB-706	N27JE	100	B-28	N28RQ	EPES	001
N24SX	200	BB-455	N25W	G1	181	N27JJ	100	B-28	N28RU	200	BB-519
(N24TF)	E90	LW-30	N25WA	31T	8120036	(N27JT)	690A	11289	N28RY	200	BB-519
N24TL	F90	LA-89	N25WC	200	BB-1640	N27KG	300	FA-79	N28RY	300	FA-134
N24TW	425	0132	N25WD	200	BB-706	N27KG	690D	15016	N28S	200	BB-144
(N24UP)	STAR	NC-23	N25WL	G1	181	N27KG	P180	1012	N28S	90	LJ-239
N24VP	STAR	NC-23	N26AC	31T	7820059	N27KM	31T	7720051	N28SC	MIII	T-266
N24WC	MU-2	705SA	N26AD	200	BB-675	N27L	200	BB-684	N28SE	690B	11401
N24XJ	P180	1149	N26AJ	G1	54	N27L	E90	LW-69	N28SE	90	LJ-239
N24YC	90	LJ-1484	N26AP	MU-2	763SA	N27L	G1	55	N28TA	MIII	T-284
N25AB	31T	7820069	N26BE	200	BB-388	N27LJ	200	BB-1040	N28TA	MIII	T-326
N25AC	MIIB	T26-149	N26BJ	441	0083	N27LR	90	LJ-111	N28TA	MIII	TT-450
N25AE	90	LJ-1116	N26BN	BN2	2217	N27LS	100	B-169	N28TC	690B	11449
N25AJ	90	LJ-1019	N26CA	31T	7820062	N27LS	200	BB-1040	N28TD	MU-2	598
N25AP	E90	LW-309	N26CH	90	LJ-1	N27MH	B100	BE-105	N28TL	200	BB-739
N25AP	MU-2	729SA	N26CS	90	LJ-661	N27MR	BN2	884	N28TM	90	LJ-1029
N25AS	31T	8020005	N26DR	46T	97358	N27MT	690B	11533	N28VM	200	BB-1772
N25AW	90	LJ-871	N26DV	31T	8004045	N27MW	690D	15015	N28VM	90	LJ-1193
N25BD	690	11009	N26DV	31T	8304003	N27NW	F406	0008	N28VU	200	BB-743
N25BE	681	6041	N26E	E90	LW-62	N27PA	F90	LA-231	(N28WL)	100	B-20
N25BF	31T	7904010	N26EH	E90	LW-228	N27RC	200	BB-1134	N28WN	31T	8166026
N25BL	200	BB-27	N26FF	200	BB-1467	N27RF	90	LJ-856	N28WR	690B	11505
N25BL	90	LJ-457	N26FG	P68	411	N27SE	200	BB-1184	N28XJ	90	LJ-1505
N25BW	90	LJ-561	N26G	200	BB-787	N27SE	F90	LA-194	(N29AA)	690A	11304
N25CA	90	LJ-119	N26GB	MIVA	AT-039	N27TA	441	0113	N29AA	90	LJ-110
N25CE	690B	11400	(N26JA)	BN2	345	N27TB	200	BB-861	N29AH	200	BB-1692
N25CJ	B100	BE-127	N26JA	BN2	375	N27TB	300	FA-142	N29AJ	200	BB-606
N25CL	690B	11501	N26JB	31T	8104020	N27TJ	MU-2	1511SA	N29AY	G1	98
N25CN	200	BB-994	N26JB	MIIB	T26-163	N27UU	90	LJ-241	N29BY	PC12	1041
(N25CN)	300	FA-177	N26JP	200	BB-781	N27VE	690B	11553	N29CA	31T	7820076
N25CS	200	BB-948	N26JP	300	FA-35	N27VE	695B	96202	N29CA	31T	7904029
N25CU	350	FL-41	N26KC	46T	97113B	N27VG	690B	11553	N29CA	PC12	135
N25CU	90	LJ-862	N26KH	PC12	592	N27WH	F90	LA-23	N29CH	200	BB-685
N25CU	F90	LA-183	N26KR	PC12	764	N27WT	B100	BE-8	N29CY	MU-2	562
N25DA	BN2	65	N26KW	100	B-67	N28AB	31T	7720003	N29DE	680T	1699-76
N25DC	90	LJ-227	N26KW	G1	15	N28AB	90	LJ-151	N29DS	690C	11732
N25DC	90	LJ-382	N26L	G1	116	N28AD	690	11010	N29EB	90	LJ-871
N25DL	90	LJ-716	N26LE	200	BB-214	N28AD	690A	11291	N29EC	300	FA-66
N25EG	B100	BE-99	(N26MM)	200	BB-274	N28AH	200	BB-94	N29GA	690D	15025
N25EN	E90	LW-239	N26MR	BN2	882	N28AU	C-12	BC-28	N29GB	F90	LA-224
N25EP	PC12	217	N26PJ	31T	8020087	N28BE	200	BB-429	N29GD	690D	15035
N25ES	690A	11320	N26PK	441	0143	(N28BE)	90	LJ-871	(N29HA)	441	0027
N25GA	90	LJ-1284	N26RA	STAR	NC-53	N28BF	200	BB-429	N29HF	200	BB-685
N25GE	200	BB-1373	N26RE	90	LJ-676	N28BF	690D	15026	N29HS	PA42	8001054
N25GE	350	FL-187	N26RF	441	0194	N28BG	31T	7720005	N29JA	BN2	457
N25GK	200	BB-1373	N26RT	MIII	T-216	N28BN	BN2	8	(N29JA)	TRIS	350
N25GM	MU-2	412SA	N26SD	200	BB-675	N28BP	690A	11159	(N29JA)	TRIS	361
(N25GQ)	200	BB-578	N26SE	E90	LW-147	N28BP	MIV	AT-013	(N29JA)	TRIS	1009
(N25GW)	90	LJ-871	N26SJ	200	BB-592	N28C	100	B-216	N29JM	31T	7720028
N25HB	90	LJ-761	N26SL	31T	7920091	N28CA	31T	7920042	N29JS	MU-2	417SA
N25HB	90	LJ-1453	N26TC	90	LJ-708	(N28CC)	E90	LW-249	N29JS	P180	1046
(N25HE)	90	LJ-1453	N26TF	46D	23	N28CG	G1	50	N29KG	200	BB-865
N25HE	PA42	5527005	N26TG	46D	101	N28CG	G1	102	N29KG	690B	11548
N25JA	BN2	106	N26TP	90	LJ-1847	N28CN	200	BB-959	N29KL	31T	7520043
N25JB	MU-2	183	N26UT	200	BB-901	N28DA	PA42	8001078	N29KR	31T	7920034
N25JB	MU-2	1512SA	N26VW	PC12	478	N28DC	MU-2	106	N29LA	31T	8020076
N25JL	100	B-70	N26WA	31T	8104045	(N28DW)	BN2	244	N29LH	46T	97179
(N25JM)	690A	11306	N27BF	31T	8104038	N28EL	300	FA-144	"N29LT"	300	FA-204
N25KA	200	BB-783	N27BG	200	BB-483	N28FG	P68	325	N29LT	300	FA-204
N25KB	350	FL-15	N27BH	200	BB-257	N28FM	31T	7720003	*N29LT	46T	97179
N25KW	200	BB-114	N27BH	350	FL-49	N28G	690	11061	N29M	E90	LW-88
N25KW	90	LJ-716	N27BM	90	LJ-1288	N28GA	690C	11730	N29MN	BN2	583
N25LA	PA42	8001012	N27BM	E90	LW-107	N28GB	MIVA	AT-039	N29MR	BN2	885
N25LS	690B	11545	N27BN	BN2	2220	N28GC	300	FA-172	(N29N)	100	B-212
N25MG	31T	7920059	N27C	100	B-166	N28GL	MIII	T-323	N29PE	200	BB-1913
N25MK	200	BB-284	N27C	200	BB-462	N28GS	MU-2	562	(N29PL)	200	BB-356
N25MR	200	BB-611	N27CD	200	BB-462	N28HF	U-21	LM-82	N29PR	681	6018
N25MR	BN2	881	N27CE	100	B-166	N28HR	MU-2	034	N29S	90	LJ-208
N25ND	31T	8020005	N27CG	90	LJ-641	N28J	200	BB-348	N29SA	695	95055
N25NX	PC12	1125	N27CS	B100	BE-63	N28J	90	LJ-166	N29SA	90	LJ-208
N25PF	46D	174	N27CV	200	BB-1161	N28JA	BN2	358	N29TA	MIII	T-300

N29TA MIII T-357
N29TB 90 LJ-846
N29TC 90 LJ-417
N29TF PA42 5501003
N29TV 200 BB-1138
N29WA 31T 8120043
N29WD MU-2 355SA
N30A E90 LW-281
N30AA 90 LJ-274
N30AB 200 BB-587
N30AB 690B 11522
(N30AG) 690B 11522
N30AH 200 BB-529
N30BG 681B 6059
N30BM 690B 11566
(N30BM) 90 LJ-1192
N30BN BN2 30
N30BY 90 LJ-861
N30CN 90 LJ-1415
N30CV E90 LW-252
N30CW E90 LW-136
N30CX 46T 97382
N30DJ 31T 7720054
N30DJ 31T 8020036
N30DU 31T 7720054
N30EH 90 LJ-296
N30EM 200 BB-958
N30EM MU-2 320
N30FE 300 FA-148
N30FJ 441 0325
N30FL 200 BB-494
N30FL 90 LJ-741
N30GC 100 B-177
N30GK 90 LJ-923
N30GT F90 LA-37
N30HE MIVC AT-492
N30HF 90 LJ-506
N30HS MIIB T26-156
N30HV 300 FA-173
N30KC E90 LW-241
N30KC E90 LW-249
N30KS 90 LJ-115
N30LH STAR NC-47
N30LT TBM7 201
N30MA MU-2 159
N30MA MU-2 371SA
(N30MA) MU-2 732SA
N30MA PA42 8001101
N30MC 300 FA-199
N30MC 350 FL-493
N30MD E90 LW-143
(N30MH) 200 BB-246
N30MK 200 BB-642
N30MK 200 BB-743
N30MR 200 BB-246
N30MR E90 LW-143
N30NH F90 LA-48
N30PC 200 BB-702
N30PC 90 LJ-316
N30PH 200 BB-635
N30PL 441 0017
N30PM 200 BB-635
N30PQ 90 LJ-316
N30RP 441 0097
N30RR MU-2 263
N30RS 681 6043
N30SA 100 B-246
N30SA 695 95061
N30SA MU-2 532
N30SE 200 BB-313
N30SG MIIA T26-028
N30SL 200 BB-1124
N30SM 300 FA-98
N30SM 350 FL-99
N30SR MU-2 458SA
N30TF MIIB T26-162
N30TU PC6 726
N30VB 31T 8166051
N30VP 200 BB-1560
N30W C-12 BC-72
N30W MIIA T26-003
N30WA MIIB T26-151
N30WA PA42 8001004
N30WA TRIS 1042
N30WE 31T 8166005
N30WF 425 0173
N30WW 441 0032
N30XL 31T 8166040
N30XY 200 BB-305
N30XY 90 LJ-380
N30XY 90 LJ-861
N30YR 350 FL-123
N31A E90 LW-281
N31AD 425 0049
(N31AS) 100 B-177
N31AT MIVA AT-057
N31AT MU-2 671
N31BG 46D 182
N31BH 100 B-118
N31BN MU-2 284
N31CG 200 BB-1946
N31CG 200G BY-66
N31CL MU-2 015
N31CN G1 162
N31CP 90 LJ-195
N31CQ 200 BB-1946
N31CR 441 0145
N31DC 31T 7920083
N31DF 31T 7520036
N31DV 690A 11154
N31DX PC12 343
N31EE E90 LW-117
N31ET 31T 7820019
N31FM 200 BB-869
N31FM E90 LW-100
N31FN E90 LW-100
N31FR 31T 8120011
*N31FW MU-2 264
N31GA 695A 96056
N31GA E90 LW-124
N31GA PA42 5501009
N31GH 690B 11550
N31GM 90 LJ-1254
N31HL 31T 8120060
N31JA BN2 198
N31JJ E90 LW-99
N31JL 100 B-244
N31JN 90 LJ-1774
N31JV MIII TT-453
N31JZ 31T 8166062
N31KA E90 LW-202
N31KF 31T 7920063
N31KF 31T 8166014
N31KF PA42 5501026
(N31KP) 31T 8166014
N31KW 31T 8166044
N31LA 46T 97357
N31LA 90 LJ-1003
N31LK MU-2 553
N31LZ 31T 7720057
N31MB 200 BB-193
N31MB 31T 8004013
N31MG MU-2 768SA
N31MN BN2 585
N31MT 90 LJ-787
N31NC 90 LJ-177
*N31PF 31T 8304001
N31PT 31T 7520021
N31SK MU-2 226
N31SN 90 LJ-362
N31SV 200 BB-1514
N31SV 90 LJ-362
N31SV 90 LJ-480
N31TL F90 LA-133
N31WB 90 LJ-536
N31WC 200 BB-465
N31WD 690B 11353
N31WE 200 BB-667
N31WE 31T 7920060
(N31WE) PA42 5527008
N31WJ 200 BB-637
N31WL 200 BB-944
N31WM 31T 8104020
N31WM MU-2 031
N31WP E90 LW-99
N31X 31T 7904008
N31X 31T 8166026
N31XL 200 BB-101
N31XL 31T 8166003
N31ZS 31T 7920027
N32BA 90 LJ-475
N32BG F90 LA-168
N32BW 690A 11123
N32BW 690B 11545
N32CA 46T 97216
N32CC 90 LJ-506
N32CK 46T 97123B
N32CK MU-2 588
N32CL 200 BB-146
N32CL 200 BB-423
N32CM 90 LJ-881
N32DF 680T 1624-53
N32EC MU-2 245
N32EC MU-2 699SA
N32EU 200G BY-32
N32FH 90 LJ-74
N32GA 441 0097
N32GA 690A 11215
N32GM BN2 2208
N32HB 200 BB-146
(N32HF) 90 LJ-707
N32HF F90 LA-171
N32HG 200 BB-146
N32JA BN2 199
N32JC BN2 7
N32JP 200 BB-624
N32JP 31T 8004018
N32JP 90 LJ-1172
N32KA 200 BB-199
N32KC 100 B-94
N32KC 200 BB-255
N32KC 350 FL-125
N32KD 200 BB-255
N32KE 46T 97048
N32KG 100 B-94
N32KK PA42 5527013
N32KQ 350 FL-125
N32KW 31T 7820090
(N32LC) 31T 8104066
N32LJ 200 BB-993
N32MA 90 LJ-1023
N32MG MIV AT-018
N32MN BN2 74
N32MR BN2 891
N32MT 90 LJ-1155
N32MT MU-2 436SA
N32NR P68 346
N32NS E90 LW-209
N32P U-21 LM-31
N32PB 300 FA-2
N32PH 690C 11691
N32PM F90 LA-23
N32PR 690A 11332
N32PV P68 346
N32RL B100 BE-43
N32RL B100 BE-117
N32RT B100 BE-43
N32SJ 90 LJ-881
N32SJ MIII TT-453
N32SV 200 BB-865
N32SV 90 LJ-374
N32TC 46T 97411
N32TC 681 6032
N32TJ 200 BB-993
N32TP 200 BB-57
N32WC 200 BB-1285
N32WK PC12 1046
(N32WS) 31T 8020064
N32WS 690A 11339
N32WT MU-2 792SA
N32WZ TBM8 400
N33AR 200 BB-1577
(N33AR) 441 0180
(N33AR) 690 11006
N33AS 90 LJ-385
(N33AX) PA42 8001003
N33BB 90 LJ-111
N33BJ 31T 7720061
N33BK 200 BB-1403
N33BK MU-2 213
N33CP G1 78
N33CS 90 LJ-410
N33DE 441 0308
(N33DF) TBM7 14
N33DS 200 BB-199
N33DS 441 0133
N33DS PA42 5527014
N33DT 31T 7520006
N33DW 690B 11401
N33EA 200 BB-1168
N33EW MU-2 1519SA
"N33FL" 90 LJ-741
N33FM 200 BB-536
N33FM 90 LJ-341
N33FR E90 LW-299
N33GB 90 LJ-584
N33GB 90 LJ-903
(N33GG) 200 BB-63
N33GK 200 BB-667
N33GK B100 BE-8
N33GR 200 BB-667
N33HC 90 LJ-649
N33HG 31T 7904008
N33HW 31T 7720025
N33JA BN2 201
N33JA PC12 127
N33JA PC12 261
N33JC 90 LJ-79
N33JQ PC12 127
N33KA 90 LJ-517
N33KA F90 LA-82
N33KM 200 BB-432
N33LA 200 BB-1777
N33LA 200G BY-53
N33LA 31T 7820004
N33LA 90 LJ-1572
N33LD 31T 7820004
N33LS MU-2 332
N33LV 200 BB-1777
N33MC 31T 8120050
N33MN BN2 534
N33MS 31T 8120036
N33ND MU-2 597
(N33NW) 200 BB-939
N33PV P68 347
N33QT 425 0039
N33RH MU-2 556
N33SB 90 LJ-252
N33SE MIIB T26-170
N33TF G1 133
N33TG 200 BB-461
N33TJ 200 BB-650
N33TW 90 LJ-709
N33TW MU-2 1519SA
N33VM 46D 139
N33VM MU-2 212
N33WD MU-2 597
N33WG 690 11038
N34AL MU-2 792SA
N34BS 300 FA-172
N34BS E90 LW-242
N34C G1 107
N34CA 31T 7820081
N34CE 90 LJ-932
N34DD MU-2 210
N34EF 690B 11486
N34ER PA42 5527036
N34F 90 LJ-119
N34FF 690B 11493
N34GA 695A 96057
N34GN 200 BB-1781
N34HA 90 LJ-315
N34HM 31T 7720003
N34JA BN2 202
N34LC 200 BB-1099
(N34LC) MU-2 209
N34LE G1 34
N34LT 200 BB-1437
N34MF E90 LW-163
N34MG MU-2 627
N34RF 90 LJ-1371
N34RT 690A 11315
N34S P180 1006
N34SC 690A 11315
N34SM MIII T-263
N34SM MIII T-279

N34TM	90	LJ-996
N34UA	MIIB	T26-145
N34UP	C-12	BC-6
N34W	90	LJ-31
N34WW	E90	LW-242
N35	200	BB-88
N35AR	200	BB-1360
N35BH	E90	LW-103
N35CA	31T	8166008
N35CG	E90	LW-51
N35CM	E90	LW-51
N35CX	46D	110
(N35DD)	441	0098
(N35DG)	PA42	5501011
N35DR	690C	11611
N35DT	200	BB-1422
N35DT	350	FL-86
N35DT	350	FL-115
N35EC	200	BB-1094
N35GR	200	BB-1167
N35GT	31T	7620030
N35HC	90	LJ-1375
N35HD	90	LJ-1731
N35HM	90	LJ-260
N35HP	90	LJ-722
(N35JA)	BN2	203
N35JA	BN2	293
*N35JL	MU-2	209
N35KA	E90	LW-96
N35KD	200	BB-35
N35LW	300	FA-63
N35MN	BN2	542
N35MT	P68	355
(N35P)	200	BB-620
N35P	200	BB-970
N35P	90	LJ-289
N35PZ	EPIC	034
N35RR	31T	7620031
N35RR	MU-2	329
N35RR	MU-2	1525SA
N35RT	31T	7400015
N35RT	31T	7520006
N35RT	31T	7520007
N35RT	31T	7620031
N35RT	31T	7720020
N35RT	31T	7820018
N35SA	200	BB-1359
N35SA	695	95070
N35SK	300	FA-130
N35TK	425	0088
N35TT	200	BB-40
N35TT	MU-2	329
N35TV	90	LJ-572
N35TY	425	0088
N35VP	350	FL-466
N35VS	MU-2	329
N35WA	681	6005
N35WA	690A	11252
N35WA	690B	11444
N35WA	PC12	770
N35WB	MIIB	T26-165
(N36A)	680T	1532-2
(N36A)	680T	1704-80
(N36A)	680T	1709-84
(N36A)	680T	1711-86
(N36A)	680T	1713-87
(N36A)	680T	1719-90
(N36A)	680W	1721-1
(N36AD)	200	BB-60
N36AG	695A	96058
N36AT	MU-2	426SA
N36BA	690A	11167
N36BB	90	LJ-111
N36BE	90	LJ-643
(N36CA)	31T	7920012
N36CA	31T	7920013
N36CP	200	BB-52
N36CP	200	BB-178
N36CP	200	BB-778
(N36CW)	90	LJ-643
N36DD	90	LJ-464
N36DD	G1	137
N36EF	441	0158
N36EG	PC12	809
N36FR	441	0362
N36G	MU-2	035
N36GA	200	BB-561
N36GA	200	BB-765
N36GA	690D	15029
N36GS	200	BB-840
N36GS	200	BB-1298
N36GS	E90	LW-162
(N36JA)	BN2	204
N36JA	BN2	209
(N36JC)	90	LJ-708
N36JF	690B	11478
N36JF	90	LJ-643
(N36JK)	31T	7820026
N36JM	31T	7820026
(N36JP)	200	BB-52
N36JP	MIII	T-284
N36JP	MIVC	AT-440B
N36JT	695	95024
N36LC	MIII	T-387
N36MF	MU-2	768SA
N36MK	90	LJ-442
N36MN	BN2	546
N36MT	300	FA-82
N36PE	MIIB	T26-164
N36PR	90	LJ-442
N36QS	200	BB-840
N36SW	690B	11505
N36TW	31T	8020075
N36WH	B100	BE-26
N36WR	690	11066
N37AL	MU-2	752SA
N37AT	46D	52
N37BT	F90	LA-41
N37BT	MIII	T-304
N37BW	690A	11129
N37CA	31T	8020030
N37CB	200	BB-532
N37CN	90	LJ-745
N37CP	E90	LW-299
N37D	E90	LW-20
N37D	MIIA	T26-022
N37DA	90	LJ-286
N37DA	PC12	195
N37DC	E90	LW-20
N37DK	441	0137
*N37FG	P68	446
N37FP	PC12	273
N37GA	200	BB-324
N37GA	200	BB-963
N37GA	200	BB-1272
N37GA	690D	15031
N37GP	90	LJ-15
N37H	U-21	LM-48
N37HB	31T	7720020
N37HC	E90	LW-108
N37HR	200	BB-951
N37JA	BN2	210
N37JT	425	0201
N37JT	F90	LA-41
N37KA	200C	BL-20
N37KH	90	LJ-676
N37KK	MU-2	588
N37KW	PA42	5527039
N37LA	90	LJ-134
N37LP	690C	11636
N37MC	E90	LW-115
N37MN	BN2	558
N37MU	MU-2	037
N37NC	200	BB-781
N37PC	B100	BE-66
N37PJ	31T	7904003
N37PP	90	LJ-104
N37PS	425	0050
N37PT	90	LJ-731
(N37PW)	200	BB-589
N37PW	90	LJ-731
N37RL	31T	7620049
N37RR	690B	11552
N37RT	31T	7720020
N37RT	46D	46
(N37SA)	695	95080
N37SB	690C	11724
N37SM	200	BB-39
N37SR	31T	8166051
N37SV	TBM8	358
N37SV	TBM8	441
N37T	690	11057
N37T	90	LJ-734
N37TB	690	11057
N37TD	350	FL-25
N37TH	100	B-173
N37TH	31T	7620049
N37TW	31T	8104006
N37UT	F90	LA-41
N37X	E90	LW-108
N37XX	200	BB-1719
N37XX	90	LJ-1112
N38AA	441	0163
N38AA	695	95070
N38AF	MU-2	264
N38AF	PA42	5527029
(N38AJ)	200	BB-1016
N38B	200	BB-1
N38BA	90	LJ-609
N38BE	MU-2	210
N38BK	MU-2	213
(N38BR)	441	0163
N38CA	31T	7920030
N38CA	90	LJ-649
N38CG	G1	106
N38CR	E90	LW-316
(N38CW)	31T	7920092
N38DA	MIII	T-384
N38DD	200	BB-560
(N38DG)	90	LJ-615
N38GK	B100	BE-8
N38GM	200	BB-737
N38GP	690A	11242
N38GP	90	LJ-46
N38H	300	FA-90
N38H	350	FL-71
N38H	90	LJ-1158
N38HB	100	B-31
N38HG	31T	7904008
N38HL	300	FA-90
N38HL	90	LJ-1914
N38JA	BN2	211
N38JK	G1	38
N38JL	200	BB-321
N38JV	200	BB-1439
N38KJ	TBM7	130
N38LA	200	BB-1326
N38LA	90	LJ-134
N38LM	690B	11424
N38LR	690B	11424
N38MJ	MIIB	T26-160
N38MN	BN2	563
N38MR	BN2	893
N38P	100	B-231
N38RE	31T	8104028
N38RH	90	LJ-347
N38RP	90	LJ-722
N38RY	300	FA-134
(N38SA)	690C	11665
(N38SA)	690C	11686
N38TA	MIII	T-397
N38TJ	200	BB-501
N38TR	90	LJ-908
N38TW	31T	8104008
N38V	200	BB-1412
N38V	31T	8020022
N38V	90	LJ-221
N38V	U-21	LM-105
N38VT	31T	8020022
N38VV	200	BB-1412
N38WA	31T	8166006
N38WA	690A	11169
N38WV	200	BB-1554
(N38X)	31T	7904008
N38XJ	90	LJ-1512
N39A	425	0138
N39AS	680W	1721-1
N39BC	MU-2	020
(N39CG)	690B	11486
N39DT	350	FL-86
N39EH	31T	7920020
N39FB	90	LJ-1165
N39FL	300	FA-6
N39GA	695A	96059
N39GK	P180	1039
N39GR	PA42	7801003
N39H	200	BB-1322
(N39JA)	BN2	213
N39JA	BN2	294
N39K	200	BB-569
N39K	31T	8020053
*N39MC	31T	8120050
N39MN	BN2	566
N39MS	MIII	T-257
N39PD	MIVC	AT-439B
N39PH	200C	BL-3
N39PP	G1	2
N39Q	U-21	LM-106
N39RD	MIV	AT-002
(N39RP)	31T	7620050
N39SA	690C	11675
N39TA	MIII	TT-424
N39TA	MIII	TT-435
N39TE	90	LJ-281
N39TG	G1	39
N39TL	31T	8104012
N39TU	STAR	NC-23
N39TW	31T	8104012
N39TW	STAR	NC-23
N39U	E90	LW-109
(N39U)	U-21	LM-21
N39YV	200	BB-39
N40AB	200	BB-1027
(N40AC)	690A	11198
N40AG	G1	40
N40AM	MU-2	427SA
N40BA	90	LJ-444
N40BC	200	BB-1169
N40BG	31T	8104011
N40BL	200	BB-326
N40BN	200	BB-781
N40BR	F90	LA-27
N40BT	31T	8004047
N40CE	G1	2
N40CK	90	LJ-358
N40CR	200	BB-862
N40CR	P180	1019
N40DA	MIII	T-363
N40DG	MIII	TT-424
N40DK	MIIB	T26-154
(N40DN)	TBM7	153
N40DN	TBM7	153
N40DR	690B	11460
N40EF	MIII	TT-527
N40FC	200	BB-19
N40FC	200	BB-694
N40FC	200	BB-1225
N40FJ	441	0359
N40FK	PA42	5527003
N40FM	350	FL-65
N40FQ	200	BB-1225
N40G	G1	140
N40GZ	350	FL-400
N40H	31T	8120043
*N40HB	31T	8120009
N40HE	200	BB-569
N40JA	BN2	222
N40JC	31T	7920068
N40JJ	MU-2	383SA
N40JL	BN2	901
N40JT	90	LJ-801
N40JT	MU-2	536
N40KC	MU-2	322
N40KM	441	0053
N40KW	690C	11665
N40MA	46T	97354
N40MB	90	LJ-787
N40MH	90	LJ-1258
N40MP	690A	11116
N40MV	PA42	5527029
N40MZ	MU-2	400SA
N40NB	300	FA-55
N40NE	300	FA-55
N40PC	200	BB-763
(N40PD)	31T	8120044
N40PJ	200	BB-1660

N40PP	MU-2	139
N40PP	MU-2	515
N40PS	200	BB-258
N40PS	90	LJ-816
N40PT	200	BB-1291
N40PT	PA42	8001029
N40QN	200	BB-487
N40R	**C-12**	**BC-7**
N40RA	**200**	**BB-104**
N40RD	425	0015
N40RD	425	0086
N40RD	425	0092
N40RL	200	BB-691
N40RL	425	0015
N40RM	90	LJ-155
N40RN	425	0086
N40RP	MU-2	139
N40SG	441	0276
N40SM	**690B**	**11559**
N40TD	200	BB-1276
N40TE	**90**	**LJ-281**
N40TG	100	B-14
N40TG	200	BB-873
N40TH	350	FL-400
N40TT	**31T**	**7520023**
N40TW	31T	8020091
N40UC	BN2	659
N40VF	31T	8166008
N40WG	**690B**	**11459**
N40WH	200	BB-620
N40WS	90	LJ-478
N40XJ	**90**	**LJ-1640**
N40Y	**C-12**	**BP-30**
N40Y	G1	39
N41AA	90	LJ-476
N41AD	MU-2	352SA
N41AG	441	0025
N41AJ	90	LJ-898
N41AK	F90	LA-188
N41AV	200	BB-1341
N41BA	MIII	T-226
N41BE	100	B-245
N41BP	100	B-245
N41BP	MIVC	AT-439B
N41C	200	BB-611
N41CK	F90	LA-188
N41CV	200	BB-611
N41CV	90	LJ-592
N41DZ	**90**	**LJ-269**
N41DZ	90	LJ-412
N41EU	200G	BY-41
N41GA	300	FA-220
N41GT	200	BB-377
N41HH	E90	LW-146
N41J	**U-21**	**LM-89**
N41JA	BN2	223
(N41JF)	425	0153
N41JK	200C	BL-11
N41JK	G1	90
N41JR	200	BB-28
N41KA	B100	BE-1
N41KD	G1	117
N41LH	90	LJ-425
N41LH	G1	156
N41LZ	90	LJ-79
(N41PC)	B100	BE-7
N41PC	MU-2	362SA
N41PH	31T	8166005
N41PN	31T	8004012
N41PS	90	LJ-956
N41R	200T	BT-15
N41R	**C-12**	**BC-31**
N41RC	31T	7720036
N41SC	90	LJ-167
N41T	**690**	**11001**
N41T	MIIA	T26-015
N41TA	441	0218
N41TG	G1	41
N41TV	200	BB-749
(N41TW)	200	BB-939
N41TW	200	BB-1404
N41TW	31T	8104023
N41VC	90	LJ-242
N41VY	690C	11627
N41WB	MU-2	352SA
N41WC	**90**	**LJ-430**
N41WE	E90	LW-280
N41WL	F90	LA-60
N42AF	MU-2	1539SA
N42AJ	300	FA-121
N42AJ	300	FA-164
N42AJ	300	FA-211
(N42AJ)	PA42	5527003
N42B	90	LJ-101
N42BP	100	B-84
N42BW	441	0305
N42CA	G1	137
N42CC	90	LJ-245
N42CC	90	LJ-834
N42CC	B100	BE-97
N42CE	G1	2
N42CG	90	LJ-160
N42CQ	**90**	**LJ-245**
N42CV	31T	8020067
N42DE	MU-2	417SA
N42DK	690B	11460
N42DT	441	0234
N42ED	350	FL-149
N42ED	**350**	**FL-302**
N42EJ	31T	8020048
N42EL	350	FL-149
N42EL	350	FL-302
N42FC	**200**	**BB-1553**
N42FT	PA42	5527012
N42G	G1	139
N42GA	300	FA-199
N42GA	F90	LA-203
(N42GG)	690C	11636
(N42J)	C-12	BC-29
N42JA	BN2	228
N42KA	200	BB-1140
N42KA	90	LJ-920
N42KA	E90	LW-158
N42KA	PA42	8001106
N42KB	**350**	**FL-226**
N42KS	200	BB-754
N42LJ	**200**	**BB-564**
N42LW	**200**	**BB-1688**
N42MD	PA42	5527008
N42MD	PA42	5527012
N42MD	PA42	5527015
N42MJ	441	0053
N42MJ	90	LJ-1790
N42MM	690A	11152
N42MP	E90	LW-28
N42MS	690B	11492
N42ND	31T	8166033
N42NE	31T	8166033
N42PA	PA42	8001106
N42PC	**E90**	**LW-85**
(N42QB)	PA42	5527015
N42QC	90	LJ-834
(N42RL)	31T	1166006
N42SC	200	BB-1550
N42SC	F90	LA-131
N42SJ	PA42	8001064
N42SL	690D	15013
N42SQ	200	BB-1550
N42SR	STAR	NC-5
N42SV	200G	BY-69
(N42SW)	PA42	7901003
N42SW	PA42	8001003
N42SY	F90	LA-131
N42TD	200	BB-968
(N42TE)	680T	1687-67
N42TF	680T	1687-67
N42TW	31T	8120033
(N42WC)	31T	8020005
N42WZ	PA42	8001004
N42Z	**C-12**	**BC-28**
N43AJ	200	BB-243
N43AJ	200	BB-1433
N43AS	G1	5
(N43BE)	31T	7820032
N43BG	**350**	**FL-117**
N43BH	425	0130
N43CB	**MIII**	**T-246**
N43CC	200	BB-106
N43CE	200	BB-1235
N43CE	200	BB-1433
N43CE	200C	BL-72
N43CE	31T	7820032
N43CH	**46D**	**44**
N43CQ	200	BB-106
N43CW	31T	7820032
N43DC	MU-2	407SA
N43DC	MU-2	1501SA
N43DT	90	LJ-6
(N43EA)	TBM8	521
N43EC	690A	11331
N43FC	100	B-237
N43FC	MIII	T-246
N43FG	MIII	T-246
N43GA	690C	11731
(N43GJ)	200	BB-1300
N43GT	**441**	**0043**
N43GT	90	LJ-652
N43JA	BN2	229
N43JT	**90**	**LJ-286**
N43KA	B100	BE-2
N43KM	90	LJ-1345
N43LA	F90	LA-168
N43M	G1	9
N43MB	**90**	**LJ-463**
N43ME	690C	11731
N43MJ	BN2	4
N43MN	**46T**	**97205**
N43PC	**E90**	**LW-253**
N43PE	200	BB-585
N43PS	F90	LA-42
N43RD	200	BB-506
N43RE	90	LJ-463
N43RJ	B100	BE-97
N43SC	31T	7520029
N43SP	31T	7520017
N43SQ	31T	7520029
N43SR	MU-2	558
N43TA	**200**	**BB-1432**
N43TC	90	LJ-363
N43TL	**200**	**BB-1582**
N43TT	90	LJ-210
N43TW	31T	8120052
N43TX	31T	8104036
N43VM	**46T**	**97005**
N43W	680W	1792-22
N43W	MU-2	233
N43WA	**90**	**LJ-501**
N43WB	200	BB-831
(N43WC)	31T	8020008
N43WH	**31T**	**8120068**
N43WL	680W	1792-22
N43WS	**E90**	**LW-16**
N43WS	F90	LA-34
N43WU	MU-2	233
(N44AB)	E90	LW-28
N44AB	MU-2	416SA
*N44AF	MU-2	790SA
N44AG	MIVA	AT-031
N44AG	MU-2	326
N44AX	**MU-2**	**416SA**
N44BB	MIIA	T26-007
N44CS	31T	7820086
N44DT	**31T**	**7820043**
N44DW	BN2	189
N44EC	E90	LW-4
(N44EG)	MU-2	326
N44F	90	LJ-106
N44F	MU-2	245
N44FH	31T	8166071
N44FL	90	LJ-106
N44GB	425	0032
N44GB	**EPIC**	**038**
N44GK	**E90**	**LW-298**
N44GL	MIVA	AT-032
N44GP	90	LJ-1185
N44GP	**90**	**LJ-1208**
N44GT	200	BB-168
N44HP	**90**	**LJ-702**
N44HT	200	BB-124
N44HT	**31T**	**7920061**
N44JA	BN2	189
N44JC	MU-2	139
N44KA	200	BB-154
N44KA	**200**	**BB-1711**
N44KA	350	FL-19
N44KA	90	LJ-1051
N44KA	E90	LW-134
N44KA	F90	LA-51
N44KS	200	BB-154
N44KS	200	BB-754
N44KS	MU-2	647
N44KT	**200**	**BB-154**
N44KU	**MU-2**	**647**
N44MA	MU-2	135
N44MC	G1	172
N44MH	200	BB-1183
N44MM	MU-2	724SA
N44MM	MU-2	1526SA
N44MR	**200C**	**BL-27**
N44MR	MU-2	611
N44MV	**E90**	**LW-107**
N44MX	MU-2	724SA
N44MX	**MU-2**	**1526SA**
N44NC	**690B**	**11387**
N44NL	**200**	**BB-1492**
N44PA	**F90**	**LA-149**
N44PB	MIVA	AT-032
N44PR	MU-2	660
N44QM	90	LJ-1036
N44RF	MU-2	309
N44RG	**90**	**LJ-417**
N44RR	MU-2	660
N44SD	695A	96096
N44SF	695A	96096
N44SK	46T	97067
N44SR	200	BB-853
N44SR	F90	LA-27
N44TC	31T	7620033
N44TF	90	LJ-873
N44TG	90	LJ-873
N44TU	MU-2	799SA
N44TW	31T	8120040
N44U	**200T**	**BT-14**
N44UE	100	B-140
N44UF	100	B-140
N44UF	**200**	**BB-36**
N44US	**200**	**BB-56**
N44US	90	LJ-257
N44VC	90	LJ-766
N44VM	200	BB-1202
N44VP	F90	LA-60
N44VR	**MU-2**	**432SA**
N44WC	90	LJ-490
N44WL	E90	LW-107
N44WV	690A	11250
N45A	**C-12**	**BC-48**
N45AC	425	0073
N45AJ	**350**	**FL-450**
(N45AW)	90	LJ-833
N45AZ	**690B**	**11383**
N45BA	90	LJ-511
N45BB	MIIB	T26-172
N45BB	MIII	T-257
N45BC	90	LJ-490
N45BE	90	LJ-546
N45BR	200	BB-832
N45BS	MU-2	558
N45BT	300	FA-127
N45BT	B100	BE-46
N45CE	MU-2	653
N45CF	200	BB-736
N45CF	MU-2	270
N45CF	MU-2	1506SA
N45D	100	B-119
N45D	200	BB-341
N45DZ	100	B-119
N45E	**200T**	**BT-13**
N45EL	90	LJ-804
N45EV	**MU-2**	**211**
N45FF	**46T**	**97241**
N45FL	**STAR**	**NC-45**
N45FM	441	0159
(N45FN)	31T	7620047
N45GA	690D	15036
N45GE	MU-2	270
N45GP	425	0116

N45GR	425	0116	N46DV	46D	197	(N47MW)	200	BB-159	N48V	E90	LW-236
N45GT	100	B-55	N46DX	46D	197	N47NG	PC12	1001	N48VB	B100	BE-110
N45JA	BN2	244	(N46FC)	200	BB-939	N47NS	31T	7820013	N48VL	E90	LW-16
N45LG	695A	96050	N46FD	PA42	5527027	N47NX	PC12	1116	N48VM	BN2	750
N45LS	31T	7720064	N46FL	350	FL-129	N47PA	200	BB-582	(N48VY)	BN2	54
N45LU	B100	BE-8	N46G	90	LJ-280	N47PE	F90	LA-42	N48VZ	E90	LW-221
N45MC	90	LJ-442	N46GA	200	BB-1209	N47PM	46D	159	N48W	90	LJ-93
N45MF	100	B-202	N46GA	695A	96065	N47R	G1	69	N48W	E90	LW-254
N45MF	200	BB-234	N46HA	690B	11381	N47RM	200	BB-1820	N48WA	PA42	8001043
N45MM	MIIB	T26-172	N46HK	MU-2	273	N47RM	200G	BY-61	N48XP	90	LJ-109
N45MN	100	B-202	N46HL	PA42	5527017	N47RN	200	BB-1820	N49AA	31T	7804003
N45MW	MIVC	AT-452	N46HM	31T	8004055	N47RW	MU-2	1548SA	N49AC	31T	8004021
N45N	200T	BT-15	N46HM	E90	LW-316	N47SW	441	0305	N49B	31T	8120055
(N45PD)	MU-2	346	N46JA	BN2	249	N47SW	90	LJ-1057	N49BB	690C	11622
N45PE	90	LJ-830	N46JC	681	6038	N47TE	F90	LA-96	N49CB	G1	173
N45PF	90	LJ-1703	N46JC	690B	11352	N47TE	G1	58	N49CH	F90	LA-2
N45PJ	46T	97031	N46JK	100	B-154	N47TP	441	0306	N49CL	350	FL-268
N45PK	90	LJ-830	N46JK	200	BB-45	N47TT	690C	11600	N49CM	90	LJ-418
(N45PL)	100	B-136	N46JV	46T	97109	N47TW	31T	8104051	(N49CN)	90	LJ-418
N45PL	90	LJ-546	N46JW	F90	LA-171	N47WM	E90	LW-307	N49D	90	LJ-179
N45PM	PC12	367	N46JX	F90	LA-171	N47WY	90	LJ-1903	N49DE	G1	97
N45PM	PC12	1058	N46KA	200	BB-236	N47ZG	PA42	5527031	N49E	90	LJ-146
N45PM	TBM7	62	N46KA	90	LJ-1089	N48	G1	67	N49E	B100	BE-47
N45PQ	PC12	367	N46KA	F90	LA-131	N48A	90	LJ-93	N49EL	90	LJ-146
N45PR	90	LJ-145	N46KC	MIII	T-332	N48A	90	LJ-381	N49FA	90	LJ-936
N45Q	680T	1542-7	N46KH	46T	97197	N48A	C-12	BC-12	N49FD	90	LJ-364
N45Q	690A	11185	N46L	C-12	BC-56	N48AA	31T	8020087	N49FR	90	LJ-1929
N45Q	690C	11623	N46ME	46T	97207	(N48AD)	680T	1473-1	N49GA	690D	15033
N45QA	690A	11185	N46MJ	90	LJ-1860	N48AF	B100	BE-75	N49GG	31T	8004029
N45QC	680T	1542-7	N46MK	441	0042	N48AF	B100	BE-110	N49GM	425	0165
N45RF	695A	96089	N46MR	441	0042	N48AM	31T	1104013	N49GN	90	LJ-381
(N45RJ)	100	B-119	N46NA	MIII	T-206	N48AR	31T	7720059	N49GW	100	B-20
N45RL	90	LJ-565	N46NH	690B	11485	N48AZ	350	FL-600	N49H	MIII	T-310
N45RM	E90	LW-174	N46PL	46T	97054	N48AZ	690A	11307	N49HF	46D	25
N45RR	200	BB-1719	N46PV	46T	97046	N48AZ	90	LJ-859	N49JA	BN2	255
N45RR	200	BB-1853	N46PW	46D	19	N48BA	200	BB-873	N49JG	200	BB-884
N45RR	200	BB-1909	N46PW	46D	170	N48BA	690C	11665	N49K	C-12	BD-26
N45SA	90	LJ-903	N46RF	90	LJ-572	N48BN	BN2	48	(N49K)	U-21	LM-11
N45SC	90	LJ-322	N46RP	E90	LW-193	N48BS	441	0084	N49KA	200	BB-553
N45SL	PA42	8001039	N46SA	MIII	T-231	N48BS	441	0125	N49KC	200	BB-318
N45SL	PA42	5501014	N46TE	G1	58	N48CA	31T	7920072	N49LD	200	BB-427
N45SQ	200	BB-1719	N46TF	200	BB-1780	N48CE	200	BB-1101	N49LD	90	LJ-364
N45ST	690A	11105	N46TT	MU-2	1528SA	N48CG	200	BB-1101	N49LG	46T	97212
N45ST	690B	11369	(N46TW)	31T	8120007	N48CG	G1	102	N49LL	90	LJ-1316
N45TA	MIII	T-211	N46TW	PA42	8001036	N48CP	31T	8166032	N49LM	PC12	163
N45TF	441	0239	N46VA	P68	446	N48CQ	G1	102	N49M	90	LJ-383
N45TP	425	0116	N46WA	90	LJ-65	N48CR	200	BB-599	N49MJ	MIIB	T26-173
N45TP	425	0203	N46WC	200	BB-246	N48CS	200	BB-1247	N49MJ	MIII	T-272
N45TP	441	0239	N46WC	200	BB-532	N48DA	90	LJ-607	N49MZ	MIIB	T26-173
N45TP	441	0306	N46WD	200	BB-246	N48EB	300	FA-44	N49NM	31T	7520006
N45TT	90	LJ-312	N46WD	46D	164	N48FL	STAR	NC-40	N49PH	F90	LA-33
N45TW	31T	8104043	N46WE	46D	164	N48GA	695A	96064	N49PK	46D	131
N45TX	31T	7720069	N46WE	46T	97090	N48GA	PC12	780	N49PW	46D	19
N45US	90	LJ-1004	N46WE	46T	97134	N48GS	31T	7804002	N49R	90	LJ-179
N45V	100	B-45	N46WH	46D	14	N48GS	PA42	8001028	N49R	C-12	BD-2
N45V	100	B-126	N46WK	46T	97090	N48HB	200	BB-152	N49RM	31T	7904051
N45V	200	BB-69	N46WQ	200	BB-532	N48HB	300	FA-44	N49RW	31T	7904051
N45V	90	LJ-414	N46X	C-12	BC-47	N48HB	350	FL-16	N49SA	MIV	AT-009
N45VT	690A	11134	N47	G1	69	N48HF	200	BB-152	N49SK	200	BB-1090
N45VV	200	BB-69	(N47AP)	B100	BE-57	N48HH	MIII	T-304	N49SS	B100	BE-37
N45WF	46D	68	N47AW	E90	LW-130	N48HP	350	FL-16	N49TW	31T	8120053
N45WL	F90	LA-71	N47BH	E90	LW-275	N48JA	BN2	252	N49UC	90	LJ-218
N46A	90	LJ-317	N47CA	31T	7920043	N48JA	C-12	BC-51	N49WA	31T	8104050
N46AE	90	LJ-1582	N47CC	31T	7820016	N48LD	200	BB-427	N49WC	350	FL-144
N46AK	MU-2	754SA	N47CF	200	BB-640	N48MB	B100	BE-110	N50AB	90	LJ-625
N46AX	90	LJ-317	N47CF	690B	11440	N48MD	31T	7920052	N50AC	100	B-144
(N46AZ)	690A	11307	N47CK	681B	6058	N48MD	MU-2	242	N50AF	MU-2	286
N46BA	690A	11235	N47CP	31T	8120039	N48N	200	BB-969	N50AJ	200	BB-434
(N46BA)	695A	96026	N47CR	200	BB-374	N48N	90	LJ-109	(N50AJ)	200	BB-726
(N46BA)	F90	LA-188	N47DG	200	BB-1040	N48NP	MU-2	447SA	N50AK	MIIB	T26-171E
N46BE	100	B-214	(N47DR)	31T	8020074	N48PA	200	BB-996	N50AW	F90	LA-142
N46BM	200	BB-1663	N47EP	690B	11520	N48PA	G1	18	N50BR	MU-2	021
N46BM	E90	LW-198	N47FH	200	BB-159	N48PG	PC12	191	N50BS	B100	BE-22
N46BR	200	BB-852	N47GW	31T	8104030	N48Q	200	BB-263	N50CD	200	BB-444
N46CB	90	LJ-218	N47HM	680T	1691-70	N48RA	PA42	7801004	N50DR	200	BB-1061
(N46CE)	200	BB-1006	N47JA	BN2	250	N48T	690A	11167	N50DX	690A	11227
N46CE	200	BB-1178	N47JF	31T	8020031	N48T	E90	LW-230	N50DY	200	BB-1061
N46CE	200	BB-1349	(N47JR)	200	BB-765	N48TA	E90	LW-283	N50EB	E90	LW-128
N46CE	31T	8120014	N47JR	441	0160	N48TB	90	LJ-2	N50ES	90	LJ-111
N46CE	PC12	390	(N47KS)	B100	BE-59	N48TE	E90	LW-230	N50ET	MU-2	260
N46CR	31T	7904022	N47LC	E90	LW-64	N48TE	G1	34	N50FC	200	BB-388
N46CR	90	LJ-1048	N47MM	200	BB-159	N48TL	690A	11167	(N50FC)	200	BB-1222
(N46CV)	31T	8020067	N47MM	200	BB-1067	N48TW	31T	8104055	(N50FC)	31T	8166001
N46DT	90	LJ-7	(N47MN)	200	BB-159	N48V	E90	LW-16	N50FQ	200	BB-388

N50FS	425	0111	N51GS	31T	8166076	N52WS	441	0032	N54MG	100	B-150
N50GH	90	LJ-140	N51JA	BN2	214	N52YR	200	BB-924	(N54MH)	690	11041
N50GH	F90	LA-7	N51JA	BN2	283	N53AD	MU-2	776SA	N54PC	MU-2	280
N50JA	BN2	256	N51JH	200	BB-60	N53AM	31T	7920037	N54PC	MU-2	319
N50JD	200	BB-233	N51JH	200	BB-766	N53AR	200	BB-1629	N54PE	MU-2	1566SA
N50JG	425	0232	N51JH	300	FA-80	(N53AR)	690A	11280	N54PT	E90	LW-331
N50JJ	90	LJ-290	N51JK	31T	8120025	N53BB	E90	LW-228	(N54RC)	E90	LW-313
N50JN	425	0232	N51K	90	LJ-16	N53CC	681	6022	N54RD	CA12	701A4412
N50JP	90	LJ-290	N51K	F90	LA-6	N53CC	690A	11123	N54SK	200	BB-1090
N50K	MU-2	305	N51KA	200	BB-2	N53CE	E90	LW-160	N54TD	31T	8004037
N50KA	300	FA-52	N51KA	90	LJ-16	N53CK	200	BB-329	(N54TF)	90	LJ-1425
N50KA	B100	BE-55	N51KA	E90	LW-108	N53DA	MIII	TT-438	N54TK	200	BB-686
N50KG	200	BB-1066	N51KC	PA42	8001001	N53EC	90	LJ-552	N54TW	31T	8004037
N50KJ	90	LJ-858	N51L	MIIB	T26-136	N53G	200	BB-228	N54UM	695	95025
N50KK	90	LJ-55	N51LB	MIVA	AT-032	N53G	F90	LA-178	N54US	B100	BE-122
N50KV	MIIB	T26-115	N51LF	MIIB	T26-136	N53GA	200	BB-646	N54US	MU-2	590
N50KW	90	LJ-858	N51LG	TBM8	423	N53GA	200	BB-1201	N54WT	46D	123
N50KW	MU-2	784SA	N51LR	441	0157	(N53GA)	200	BB-1209	N54WW	90	LJ-209
N50L	MIIB	T26-141	N51MF	690B	11479	(N53GA)	690D	15037	N54YC	300	FA-212
N50LF	MIIB	T26-141	N51MT	E90	LW-290	N53GG	441	0022	N55AC	425	0020
N50LG	MIII	T-315	N51N	P68	276	N53JA	BN2	301	N55AE	200	BB-173
N50LS	G1	127	(N51NL)	P68	276	N53JC	200	BB-757	N55AE	G1	175
N50LT	200	BB-284	(N51PC)	MU-2	290	N53JC	B100	BE-80	N55B	680T	1587-38
N50M	100	B-123	N51PC	MU-2	708SA	N53JJ	690A	11185	N55BH	200	BB-56
N50MA	MIIB	T26-164	N51RD	31T	7820056	N53JK	100	B-153	N55BK	PC12	160
N50MB	E90	LW-282	(N51RL)	200	BB-789	N53JL	MU-2	028	N55BN	200	BB-56
N50MF	441	0262	(N51RL)	31T	8020004	N53JQ	B100	BE-80	N55BP	200	BB-39
(N50MG)	690B	11522	N51RM	31T	8004054	N53KA	100	B-149	N55CC	200	BB-727
N50MP	690A	11219	N51RX	MIII	T-282	N53KA	200	BB-880	(N55CC)	441	0019
N50MS	690B	11522	N51SD	200	BB-94	N53KB	46T	97231	(N55CD)	690A	11155
N50MT	200	BB-147	N51SG	E90	LW-7	N53LG	690B	11523	N55CE	MIV	AT-004
N50MT	E90	LW-290	N51SM	PA42	8001007	N53LJ	350	FL-353	N55CH	425	0017
N50MT	MIII	T-308	N51TW	31T	8120056	N53MD	100	B-86	N55CH	441	0330
(N50MW)	31T	8104002	N51UH	300	FA-80	N53MF	690C	11669	N55CM	690A	11155
N50MW	F90	LA-118	N51V	100	B-109	(N53MP)	STAR	NC-30	N55DL	MU-2	429SA
N50N	200	BB-697	N51VK	100	B-109	N53MS	425	0025	N55EG	MU-2	232
N50NA	200	BB-1504	N51VW	100	B-244	N53MW	P180	1011	N55EP	90	LJ-1520
N50NE	B100	BE-26	(N51WA)	31T	8120050	N53PB	90	LJ-1678	N55EU	31T	7904036
N50NL	300	FA-97	N51WA	31T	8104060	N53PC	MIII	TT-450	N55FC	441	0050
N50PA	BN2	2021	N51WF	690C	11684	N53PE	300	FA-133	(N55FF)	100	B-123
N50PC	100	B-19	N51WN	PC12	104	N53PK	46T	97093	N55FG	200	BB-173
N50PD	90	LJ-1704	N52BC	200	BB-450	N53RF	690A	11153	N55FJ	200	BB-1297
N50PK	MIII	T-216	N52BC	200	BB-876	N53RT	200	BB-808	N55FR	B100	BE-123
N50PM	200	BB-763	N52BC	31T	7620043	N53SP	200	BB-576	N55FW	90	LJ-194
N50PM	200	BB-1570	N52BG	90	LJ-1732	N53TA	31T	7820083	N55FY	90	LJ-194
N50PM	200	BB-1647	N52BQ	200	BB-450	N53TD	B100	BE-53	N55GD	31T	7820003
N50PT	690B	11526	N52BW	90	LJ-77	N53TJ	90	LJ-1209	N55GM	90	LJ-266
N50PU	200	BB-1647	N52C	300	FA-40	N53TM	200	BB-973	N55GM	90	LJ-610
N50RD	E90	LW-94	N52C	90	LJ-219	N53TM	31T	7820083	N55GP	90	LJ-49
N50RM	90	LJ-175	N52CA	31T	7904002	N53TM	350	FL-165	N55HC	E90	LW-134
N50RP	90	LJ-200	(N52CB)	E90	LW-133	(N53TR)	31T	7920007	N55HL	200	BB-1367
N50RV	E90	LW-338	N52CD	MU-2	174	N53TT	90	LJ-256	N55HR	31T	8004001
N50SS	B100	BE-22	N52CK	PC12	1054	N53TW	31T	8120053	N55JA	BN2	295
N50ST	690A	11201	N52EL	90	LJ-204	N53VW	EPIC	021	N55JM	90	LJ-53
N50ST	ST50	001	N52GA	441	0223	N53WA	31T	8166025	N55JM	MIIA	T26-011
N50ST	TBM7	20	N52GA	690C	11732	N53WM	31T	8004043	N55JP	31T	8004048
N50TF	MIIB	T26-171E	N52GP	200	BB-766	(N53WT)	B100	BE-80	N55JS	690A	11195
N50TT	MU-2	264	N52GT	200	BB-377	N54AM	90	LJ-1506	N55K	F90	LA-184
N50TW	200	BB-336	N52GT	200	BB-1251	N54BC	425	0131	N55KA	E90	LW-55
N50TW	31T	8004055	N52HL	31T	8004023	N54CE	MU-2	794SA	N55KS	MU-2	651
N50UC	G1	95	N52JA	BN2	286	N54CF	90	LJ-374	N55KV	MU-2	651
N50VM	200	BB-1964	N52KA	E90	LW-42	N54CK	B100	BE-73	N55KW	31T	8120007
N50VP	90	LJ-1185	N52L	MIIB	T26-138	N54CK	MU-2	135	N55LC	90	LJ-1103
N50VS	MU-2	379SA	N52LB	MIVA	AT-025	N54CW	31T	7520043	N55LC	MU-2	105
N50W	MU-2	549	N52LF	MIIB	T26-138	N54DA	441	0240	N55LC	MU-2	232
N50WA	31T	8104011	N52LP	300	FA-8	N54DA	PA42	5527006	N55LH	90	LJ-266
N50WF	690C	11701	N52LS	31T	7920045	N54EC	90	LJ-526	N55LM	90	LJ-460
N50WG	P180	1050	N52MA	MU-2	419SA	N54EC	MU-2	355SA	N55MG	90	LJ-303
N50YR	200	BB-924	N52MW	300	FA-212	(N54EM)	31T	8104039	N55MG	90	LJ-391
N50YR	200	BB-1059	N52NK	PC12	737	N54EW	BN2T	2145	(N55MJ)	90	LJ-529
N50ZY	200	BB-305	N52PB	690A	11196	N54EZ	31T	7904031	N55MN	90	LJ-974
N51BJ	31T	7720011	N52PC	31T	7904023	N54FB	200	BB-1212	N55MP	200	BB-1216
N51BL	100	B-150	N52PF	31T	7904023	N54GA	695A	96066	N55MP	200	BB-1679
N51CA	31T	7804007	N52PY	690A	11196	N54GA	90	LJ-158	N55MP	90	LJ-303
N51CT	90	LJ-1780	(N52RC)	MU-2	418SA	N54GC	PA42	8001003	N55MP	90	LJ-529
N51CU	425	0171	N52SF	200	BB-106	(N54GP)	695	95016	N55MP	B100	BE-96
N51CV	200C	BL-49	(N52SJ)	MIII	T-312	N54GP	MIVA	AT-034	N55MP	STAR	NC-30
N51DA	MIII	T-316	N52SZ	200	BB-1686	N54HF	200C	BL-50	N55MS	425	0100
N51DJ	PC12	886	N52TT	31T	7920057	N54JA	BN2	304	N55MS	441	0061
N51DM	695A	96014	N52TW	31T	8104067	N54JB	31T	8020083	N55MU	STAR	NC-30
N51DN	E90	LW-7	N52WA	BN2	2240	N54JW	100	B-60	N55MV	200	BB-1216
N51EE	200	BB-674	N52WA	PA42	8001028	N54KA	100	B-150	(N55NS)	200	BB-851
N51FT	31T	7904028	N52WC	200	BB-624	N54LG	200	BB-791	N55PC	200	BB-1170
N51GA	690D	15035	N52WM	MU-2	385SA	N54MC	31T	7820024	N55PC	MU-2	146

N55PP	690A	11196
N55PY	KODK	0006
N55R	31T	7620055
N55SC	200	BB-193
N55SC	300	FA-67
N55SC	90	LJ-527
N55SG	90	LJ-527
N55SR	200	BB-445
(N55SR)	690A	11312
N55TJ	B100	BE-96
N55TY	STAR	NC-51
N55UA	90	LJ-399
N55US	B100	BE-77
N55V	90	LJ-257
(N55WF)	46D	152
N55WF	90	LJ-1114
N55WH	46D	235
N55WJ	690B	11427
N55ZG	46T	97082
N55ZM	MIIA	T26-011
N55ZP	MIII	T-299
N56AP	200	BB-882
N56AY	200	BB-882
N56AY	200	BB-1511
N56CC	200	BB-189
N56CD	200	BB-64
N56DA	200	BB-486
N56DA	425	0056
N56DK	31T	8166039
N56DL	90	LJ-732
N56EZ	PC12	488
N56FL	B100	BE-74
N56GA	200	BB-819
N56GA	200	BB-1056
N56GA	690C	11733
N56GR	200	BB-59
N56HF	200	BB-728
N56HF	31T	7920082
N56HT	E90	LW-215
N56JA	200	BB-984
(N56JA)	BN2	296
(N56JA)	BN2	398
N56JA	BN2	410
(N56JA)	BN2	474
(N56JS)	MU-2	633
N56K	90	LJ-412
N56KA	200	BB-763
N56KA	E90	LW-46
N56MC	31T	8120020
N56MC	681B	6050
N56MC	E90	LW-28
N56ME	E90	LW-28
(N56MF)	E90	LW-28
N56MQ	681B	6050
N56MS	441	0057
N56MV	PA42	5501045
N56QR	200	BB-742
N56RA	200	BB-486
N56RJ	PC12	758
N56RT	200	BB-817
N56SC	90	LJ-77
N56SC	B100	BE-32
N56SQ	90	LJ-77
N56TA	441	0056
N56TA	MIII	T-232
N56TA	MIVC	AT-440B
N56TJ	E90	LW-61
N56TW	F90	LA-173
N56WF	TBM7	8
N57AC	200	BB-857
N57AC	690B	11415
N57AF	31T	8166049
N57AG	90	LJ-343
(N57AJ)	90	LJ-343
N57AK	B100	BE-57
N57BM	200	BB-224
N57CC	441	0218
(N57CC)	90	LJ-688
N57EC	690A	11178
N57EG	690A	11178
N57EM	90	LJ-295
N57FM	200	BB-26
N57FM	90	LJ-295
N57FT	200	BB-136
N57GA	200	BB-477
(N57GA)	690D	15038
N57HC	TBM7	90
N57HQ	TBM7	90
N57HT	B100	BE-7
(N57JA)	BN2	302
N57JA	BN2	399
N57JB	90	LJ-794
N57KA	90	LJ-577
N57KC	31T	8166076
N57KE	350	FL-61
N57KW	31T	8120003
N57LM	200C	BL-16
N57LT	PC12	474
N57MA	90	LJ-414
N57MK	31T	7620022
N57MK	441	0110
N57MM	90	LJ-126
N57MR	31T	7620022
N57MS	E90	LW-316
N57MS	MU-2	769SA
N57PA	200	BB-1444
N57RS	690A	11149
N57SC	200	BB-1103
N57SC	350	FL-34
N57SC	90	LJ-532
N57SE	46T	97372
N57SG	PC12	881
N57SL	TBM7	57
N57TJ	B100	BE-102
N57TL	200	BB-1557
N57TM	F90	LA-34
N57TS	200	BB-1557
N57TS	350	FL-225
N57TX	350	FL-225
N57V	90	LJ-268
N57VA	350	FL-154
(N57VS)	200	BB-29
N57WR	90	LJ-1678
N58AB	200	BB-1279
N58AB	F90	LA-2
N58AC	90	LJ-77
N58AM	31T	1104005
N58AP	31T	8166062
N58AS	200C	BL-50
N58AU	200	BB-1279
N58AU	F90	LA-2
(N58B)	680T	1701-77
N58BC	46D	58
N58BC	MU-2	536
N58BC	MU-2	631
N58BT	46T	97289
N58CA	MU-2	170
N58CC	681	6022
N58CH	425	0017
(N58DC)	690B	11382
N58DE	200	BB-332
N58ES	300	FA-17
N58EZ	F90	LA-97
N58FS	MIIB	T26-120
N58GA	200	BB-1003
N58GG	31T	8020088
N58GG	90	LJ-1728
N58GP	90	LJ-578
N58HP	TBM7	170
(N58JA)	BN2	303
N58JA	BN2	435
(N58JA)	TRIS	381
N58JB	200	BB-566
N58JJ	441	0066
N58JR	200	BB-558
N58KA	90	LJ-58
N58KA	90	LJ-578
N58LC	PA42	8001063
N58NH	KODK	0011
N58PL	31T	8166024
N58PP	681	6022
N58VS	PC12	341
N58WB	690B	11408
N58WS	PC12	1096
N58XJ	90	LJ-1522
N59AH	300	FA-197
N59AP	300	FA-197
N59AP	31T	8166062
N59DF	200	BB-477
N59EK	F90	LA-58
N59EZ	MIII	T-394
N59GA	695A	96067
N59GG	90	LJ-1734
(N59GJ)	200	BB-1154
N59GS	200	BB-380
(N59JA)	BN2	402
N59JA	BN2	406
N59JM	31T	7820026
N59JM	PA42	8001004
N59JN	31T	7820026
N59KA	90	LJ-589
N59KC	31T	8120028
N59KG	31T	8120028
N59KG	PA42	5501009
N59KS	MU-2	664
N59MD	441	0177
N59MS	90	LJ-1405
N59RB	31T	7820013
(N59RB)	PA42	8001034
N59RT	441	0111
N59RW	MU-2	267
(N59SS)	B100	BE-106
N59T	100	B-8
N59TC	MIIA	T26-020
N59TD	200	BB-1035
N59TF	350	FL-26
N59TP	MIIB	T26-161
N59WA	31T	8166033
N59WF	46T	97042
(N59WP)	90	LJ-1036
N60AA	200	BB-1099
N60AC	G1	179
N60AR	200	BB-1743
N60AW	31T	8020051
N60AZ	MU-2	329
N60B	690A	11172
N60BA	E90	LW-79
N60BC	681	6013
N60BM	690A	11172
N60BN	MU-2	163
N60BT	MU-2	358SA
N60C	U-21	LM-11
N60CH	P68	288
N60CM	350	FL-139
N60CR	690B	11471
N60CR	G1	71
N60CW	90	LJ-1081
N60DB	690B	11420
(N60DC)	E90	LW-6
N60DL	350	FL-446
N60DR	31T	7720064
N60DR	690C	11669
N60FC	200	BB-1146
N60FJ	441	0048
N60FL	MU-2	1512SA
N60FR	90	LJ-1935
N60FR	90	LJ-1954
N60GS	MU-2	623
N60HT	90	LJ-358
N60JA	TRIS	299
N60JE	90	LJ-636
N60JF	425	0092
(N60JK)	200	BB-660
N60JT	200	BB-229
N60JT	90	LJ-636
N60JW	31T	8004031
N60KA	90	LJ-586
N60KC	90	LJ-821
N60KC	MU-2	511
N60KC	MU-2	781SA
N60KG	MU-2	511
N60KV	31T	7904032
N60KW	90	LJ-800
N60MD	200	BB-673
N60MH	E90	LW-290
N60MK	200	BB-208
N60NB	MU-2	1528SA
N60NH	MIII	T-309
N60NJ	MU-2	339
N60PA	BN2	2020
N60PC	200	BB-58
N60PC	200	BB-1146
N60PD	200	BB-58
N60RE	200	BB-248
N60RJ	90	LJ-86
N60SC	200	BB-693
N60SM	200	BB-50
N60SM	200	BB-1045
N60SQ	200	BB-693
N60TA	MIVC	AT-492
N60TC	200	BB-516
N60TC	300	FA-77
N60TG	300	FA-77
N60TJ	B100	BE-21
N60TQ	200	BB-516
N60TR	441	0203
(N60TW)	31T	8166005
(N60TX)	200	BB-516
N60VM	200	BB-1964
N60VP	90	LJ-1516
N60VS	690C	11683
N60WA	31T	8120013
N60WC	350	FL-96
N60WK	G1	179
N60XL	31T	8166005
N60Y	MIIB	T26-175
N60YB	350	FL-304
N60YP	350	FL-304
N60YP	350	FL-620
N61AJ	200	BB-1195
N61AP	200	BB-1192
N61BA	MU-2	729SA
N61CE	200	BB-926
N61DH	F90	LA-185
N61DP	31T	7400004
N61DP	MU-2	290
N61DP	MU-2	398SA
N61DX	MU-2	290
N61GA	690D	15039
N61GA	90	LJ-797
N61GJ	MU-2	398SA
N61GN	90	LJ-1421
N61GT	P180	1051
N61HB	90	LJ-1219
N61HT	90	LJ-358
N61JA	BN2	474
N61JB	MU-2	417SA
N61KA	300	FA-200
N61KA	90	LJ-587
N61MR	100	B-34
N61NA	E90	LW-40
N61PH	MIIB	T26-143
N61PK	46T	97053
N61PS	E90	LW-40
N61Q	U-21	LM-92
N61QR	PA42	8001002
N61RA	31T	7820027
N61RJ	MIII	T-332
N61RR	200	BB-31
N61RS	MIII	T-341
N61SB	G1	115
N61SG	31T	7720057
(N61SM)	31T	7920016
N61TS	690B	11510
(N61TW)	31T	8166069
N61UT	G1	179
N61WA	31T	8166041
N61WA	690A	11139
N61WM	31T	8004020
(N61XL)	31T	8166069
N61XP	200	BB-1550
N62AM	200	BB-633
N62AZ	350	FL-453
N62B	G1	99
N62BB	90	LJ-965
N62BC	31T	7620043
N62BE	200	BB-1144
N62BL	E90	LW-272
N62BT	200	BB-1323
N62BW	31T	8104057
N62BW	90	LJ-351
N62CA	31T	7920081
N62CE	690C	11721
N62CN	MU-2	436SA
N62CP	MU-2	436SA
N62CS	E90	LW-308

N62DL	200	BB-208
N62DW	690B	11401
N62E	31T	8020074
N62EA	200	BB-668
N62EC	200	BB-176
N62FB	200	BB-1482
N62FC	200	BB-1010
N62GA	200	BB-828
N62GA	200C	BL-16
N62GA	690D	15037
N62GA	695A	96068
N62GA	PC12	259
N62GC	B100	BE-127
N62GT	200G	BY-62
N62HB	90	LJ-610
N62J	G1	139
N62JA	BN2	511
N62JT	PC12	107
N62KA	100	B-158
N62KK	STAR	NC-17
N62KL	200	BB-1136
N62KM	200	BB-1136
N62KM	STAR	NC-17
N62LM	TBM7	67
N62LT	46T	97027
N62MA	441	0181
N62MA	690A	11168
N62MR	200	BB-27
N62NC	100	B-158
N62SK	90	LJ-784
*N62SK	PC12	1054
N62TA	BN2	515
N62TW	31T	8166051
N62V	U-21	LM-74
N62WA	PA42	8001066
N62WC	200	BB-1326
N62WC	PA42	8001066
N62WM	46T	97008
N62WM	46T	97177
N63AU	G1	126
N63BV	E90	LW-256
N63BW	90	LJ-419
N63BW	E90	LW-256
N63CA	31T	7820033
N63CB	200	BB-79
N63CM	31T	8020039
N63DG	31T	8020089
N63DL	690C	11601
N63DL	TBM8	409
N63DU	690C	11601
N63EC	E90	LW-191
N63GA	90	LJ-383
N63GB	350	FL-27
N63GB	90	LJ-383
N63HA	200	BB-674
N63JA	BN2	513
N63JR	200	BB-39
N63KA	100	B-170
N63LB	200	BB-1894
N63LB	300	FA-18
N63LB	90	LJ-1020
N63LP	300	FA-18
*N63LW	E90	LW-191
N63PG	690	11018
N63PW	46D	27
N63RB	690C	11639
N63SC	31T	7920059
N63SC	MIIB	T26-122
N63SC	MIVA	AT-069
N63SE	46T	97333
N63SJ	100	B-243
N63SK	200	BB-747
N63TH	90	LJ-506
N63TP	TBM7	128
N63WA	PA42	8001072
N63XL	31T	8166037
N64AM	PA42	7801003
N64BA	MU-2	1566SA
N64C	U-21	LM-32
N64CA	31T	7920088
N64CG	G1	106
N64DC	200	BB-492
N64DD	200	BB-1004
N64EZ	690B	11526
N64FB	350	FL-308
N64GA	200	BB-790
(N64GG)	350	FL-253
N64GG	350	FL-274
N64GG	STAR	NC-47
N64GQ	STAR	NC-47
N64GT	90	LJ-1765
N64HC	200	BB-390
N64JA	BN2	524
N64JB	F90	LA-4
N64JT	695B	96203
N64KA	100	B-165
N64KA	90	LJ-606
N64LG	MU-2	240
N64MD	MU-2	747SA
N64MD	MU-2	1561SA
N64MN	MIIB	T26-141
N64PS	690C	11702
N64RA	200T	BT-18
N64RA	E90	LW-1
N64RJ	E90	LW-1
N64SS	300	FA-6
N64TE	300	FA-149
N64TG	G1	64
N64TR	300	FA-149
N64TR	350	FL-544
N64TW	TBM7	31
N64WA	PA42	8001060
N64WB	MU-2	1550SA
N64WF	PC12	298
(N64XL)	31T	8166046
N65AF	PC12	565
N65BA	BN2	529
N65CE	G1	45
N65CK	31T	7904041
N65CL	90	LJ-1306
N65CR	350	FL-60
N65CR	PA42	5527012
N65EB	200	BB-325
N65EL	31T	7920030
N65EZ	31T	1104013
N65FT	MU-2	710SA
N65FT	MU-2	783SA
N65GA	690D	15040
N65GC	BN2	11
(N65GE)	90	LJ-1320
N65GH	90	LJ-617
N65GP	200	BB-1869
N65GP	90	LJ-1320
N65H	G1	66
N65HC	G1	66
N65HT	MU-2	710SA
N65JA	BN2	515
N65JA	U-21	LM-34
N65JG	MU-2	612
N65JG	MU-2	1523SA
N65JL	90	LJ-746
N65KA	90	LJ-611
N65KG	200	BB-841
N65KG	31T	1104017
N65KW	PC12	165
N65L	U-21	LM-73
N65LA	200	BB-1518
N65LC	100	B-152
N65LG	100	B-152
N65LW	200C	BL-139
N65LW	300	FA-204
N65MC	31T	7620052
N65MC	PA42	8001071
N65MD	31T	7620052
N65MM	F90	LA-125
N65MS	31T	7904008
N65MS	E90	LW-202
N65MT	F90	LA-38
N65MV	90	LJ-1870
(N65N)	200	BB-1377
N65NL	200	BB-540
N65NL	90	LJ-90
N65P	MIII	T-285
N65RA	31T	7904032
N65RT	200	BB-97
N65SF	F90	LA-18
N65TA	90	LJ-538
N65TB	PC12	263
N65TD	100	B-50
N65TJ	31T	8166039
N65TW	200	BB-902
N65U	U-21	LM-79
N65U	U-21	LM-87
N65V	U-21	LM-113
N65W	PC12	1085
(N65WL)	200	BB-111
N65WM	200	BB-1087
N65XL	31T	8166072
N65XL	31T	1166002
N65Y	690C	11646
N66	300	FF-1
N66AD	90	LJ-380
N66AL	MIII	T-233
(N66AM)	BN2	2203
N66BP	E90	LW-187
N66BS	F90	LA-40
N66BZ	441	0306
N66CA	31T	7904055
N66CD	200	BB-1194
N66CD	90	LJ-366
N66CK	90	LJ-1529
N66CL	MU-2	135
N66CN	90	LJ-644
N66CP	441	0162
N66CP	681	6001
N66CY	MU-2	562
N66DD	200	BB-174
N66DD	200	BB-1004
(N66ES)	441	0153
(N66FB)	300	FA-70
N66FF	MU-2	430SA
N66FG	200	BB-836
N66FP	695	95024
(N66FS)	90	LJ-250
N66FV	680T	1676-59
N66GA	MIVC	AT-427
N66GS	90	LJ-237
N66GW	690A	11174
N66HA	BN2	31
N66HA	BN2	239
N66JA	BN2	516
N66JC	31T	8166029
N66JD	G1	57
N66KA	90	LJ-582
N66KS	MIII	T-209
N66LA	MU-2	792SA
N66LD	31T	7520035
N66LL	425	0109
N66LM	200	BB-1158
N66LM	425	0137
N66LM	90	LJ-1112
N66LP	F90	LA-21
N66MB	EPIC	024
N66MD	MIIB	T26-159
N66ME	441	0066
N66MF	PA42	5501009
N66MR	90	LJ-54
N66MS	90	LJ-54
N66MS	90	LJ-330
N66MT	31T	8166060
N66MT	PA42	5501009
N66PC	90	LJ-214
N66Q	MIIB	T26-130
N66QT	425	0061
N66RA	690C	11725
N66RE	90	LJ-307
N66RE	MIIB	T26-165
N66SF	200	BB-712
N66TG	300	FA-155
N66TJ	200	BB-42
N66TL	90	LJ-636
(N66TR)	441	0143
N66TS	200	BB-738
N66TW	31T	8004030
N66U	200	BB-996
N66U	MU-2	309
N66UA	200	BB-996
N66UP	MU-2	366SA
N66W	U-21	LM-68
N66WB	90	LJ-160
N66WC	90	LJ-54
N66WC	MIII	TT-515A
N66WJ	31T	7920041
(N66XL)	31T	8166075
N67	300	FF-2
N67AS	200	BB-781
(N67AS)	90	LJ-806
N67B	U-21	LM-59
N67BA	425	0007
N67BS	B100	BE-104
N67BW	46T	97011
N67CA	425	0058
N67CC	90	LJ-1619
N67CG	200	BB-648
N67CG	690B	11540
N67CL	90	LJ-1154
N67CQ	90	LJ-1619
N67CR	G1	166
N67DM	441	0065
N67DT	425	0046
N67DW	31T	7620041
N67DW	350	FL-29
N67EA	425	0049
(N67ER)	31T	8166067
N67FE	690C	11729
N67FS	200	BB-1032
N67GA	200	BB-176
N67GA	200	BB-1267
N67GA	695A	96070
N67GT	MU-2	367SA
N67H	G1	192
N67HA	BN2	39
N67HA	BN2	241
N67HC	100	B-167
N67HM	MIIB	T26-165
N67JA	BN2	536
N67JB	200	BB-1367
N67JE	425	0058
N67JG	31T	8120052
N67K	U-21	LM-24
N67KA	100	B-167
N67KA	B100	BE-104
N67LC	100	B-152
(N67LF)	TBM7	50
(N67LG)	100	B-152
N67LH	MU-2	351SA
N67LT	200	BB-988
N67LW	200	BB-154
N67MD	200	BB-834
N67NC	200	BB-751
N67PC	200	BB-580
N67PC	90	LJ-566
N67PD	31T	8166033
N67PL	90	LJ-566
N67PS	E90	LW-112
N67PT	EPIC	016
N67RP	F90	LA-7
N67SA	690C	11632
N67SD	200	BB-1327
N67SM	MU-2	183
N67TA	BN2	222
N67TC	690A	11233
N67TE	46T	97364
N67TG	46D	45
N67TM	F90	LA-58
N67TW	31T	8166046
N67V	100	B-148
N67V	E90	LW-306
N67VK	46D	116
N67X	U-21	LM-14
N67XL	31T	8166046
N68	300	FF-3
(N68AA)	200	BB-283
N68AA	200	BB-434
N68AJ	90	LJ-1071
N68AM	F90	LA-172
N68BC	200	BB-170
N68BJ	31T	7920029
N68BK	200	BB-1965
N68BS	46D	6
N68CC	E90	LW-249
N68CD	90	LJ-366
N68CL	MU-2	448SA
N68CP	200	BB-351
N68CP	46D	94
N68DA	B100	BE-14

N68DA	MU-2	548
N68DK	90	LJ-696
N68DK	F90	LA-45
N68DK	F90	LA-56
N68DR	90	LJ-696
N68FA	200	BB-1088
N68FB	200	BB-1710
N68FP	P68	233
N68GA	690D	15041
N68GK	200	BB-926
N68HA	BN2	74
N68HA	BN2	2009
N68HL	690B	11408
N68HS	441	0331
N68JA	BN2	532
N68JM	200	BB-145
N68KA	200	BB-793
N68KA	90	LJ-591
N68LM	31T	7720062
N68MB	31T	7820040
N68MN	200	BB-1704
N68MT	31T	8166060
N68MU	B100	BE-37
N68MY	200	BB-1142
N68PC	90	LJ-1007
N68PK	P68	341
N68PK	P68	351
N68PK	PC12	265
(N68PL)	300	FA-212
N68PM	E90	LW-188
N68PV	P68	442
N68QR	690B	11471
N68RF	300C	FM-21
N68RR	200	BB-172
N68RT	90	LJ-405
N68SA	690C	11636
N68SF	31T	8304003
N68TA	MIVA	AT-068
N68TA	MIVC	AT-544
(N68TC)	680W	1790-20
N68TD	690	11066
N68TG	G1	68
N68TN	MU-2	675
N68TP	P68	411
(N68TW)	31T	1166003
N68TW	90	LJ-1200
N68VA	P68	436
N68VA	P68	440
N68VH	681	6007
N68VR	P68	434
N69	300	FF-4
N69AD	F90	LA-143
N69AM	E90	LW-69
N69BK	200	BB-271
N69BK	31T	7620018
N69BS	46D	6
N69BS	TBM7	10
N69CD	200	BB-156
N69CS	MIVC	AT-455
N69DD	200	BB-174
N69DN	46D	140
(N69F)	200	BB-1039
N69FG	PC12	225
(N69FR)	TBM7	179
N69GA	695A	96071
N69GT	90	LJ-1950
N69HA	BN2	347
N69HA	P68	373
N69HS	MU-2	628
N69J	90	LJ-337
N69JA	BN2	512
(N69JA)	BN2	572
(N69JA)	BN2	588
(N69JH)	200	BB-1089
N69LD	200	BB-156
N69LS	200	BB-1841
N69PC	MU-2	732SA
N69PC	MU-2	765SA
N69PC	PA42	8001016
N69PC	PA42	8001023
(N69PS)	90	LJ-1113
N69QJ	MU-2	254
N69ST	MIIB	T26-140
N69ST	MIVA	AT-030

N69TD	200	BB-81
N69TM	690A	11322
(N69TX)	90	LJ-826
N69VC	200	BB-1228
N69XX	31T	7620034
(N69XX)	31T	7720068
N70	300	FF-5
N70AB	90	LJ-712
N70AC	200	BB-1190
N70AC	690B	11488
N70AJ	200	BB-206
N70BA	B100	BE-43
N70CA	PA42	5527003
N70CM	90	LJ-1670
N70CR	300	FA-30
N70CR	G1	144
N70CS	90	LJ-445
N70CU	200	BB-888
N70CU	90	LJ-369
N70CW	31T	7720066
N70DL	46D	8
(N70DW)	300	FA-157
N70DW	E90	LW-230
N70EA	E90	LW-176
N70ES	690B	11471
N70FC	MIII	T-226
N70FE	90	LJ-750
N70FG	90	LJ-660
N70FH	200	BB-220
N70FH	90	LJ-692
N70FL	300	FA-221
N70GM	425	0108
N70GW	31T	8104004
N70HB	425	0100
N70JA	BN2	535
N70JG	200	BB-918
N70JL	100	B-87
N70KA	B100	BE-69
N70KC	E90	LW-316
N70KC	MU-2	775SA
N70KM	200	BB-789
N70LA	200	BB-75
N70LG	200C	BL-67
N70LM	200	BB-562
N70LR	G1	19
N70LR	TBM7	225
N70LS	E90	LW-194
N70LT	TBM7	151
N70MD	690A	11210
N70MN	100	B-154
N70MN	200	BB-1447
N70MR	P68	328
N70MT	90	LJ-525
N70MV	E90	LW-48
N70PA	200	BB-709
N70PA	90	LJ-1195
N70PA	BN2	555
N70PC	200	BB-164
N70PH	TBM7	172
N70PJ	90	LJ-1093
N70PQ	200	BB-164
N70Q	90	LJ-380
N70Q	90	LJ-861
N70QR	G1	144
N70QZ	90	LJ-521
N70RB	200	BB-603
N70RD	200	BB-426
N70RF	681	6013
N70RR	690A	11259
N70SC	MIIB	T26-151
N70SM	90	LJ-396
N70SW	E90	LW-101
N70TG	90	LJ-130
N70TJ	31T	7904019
N70TM	200	BB-45
N70TQ	90	LJ-130
N70TW	31T	7904043
N70U	U-21	LM-51
N70UA	90	LJ-130
N70VM	90	LJ-300
N70VP	200	BB-1700
N70VP	90	LJ-1459
N70VR	90	LJ-1651
N70WA	31T	8104004

N70WA	690	11072
N70X	MIII	T-250
N70YC	E90	LW-316
N71	300	FF-6
N71AF	680W	1814-31
N71BX	E90	LW-74
(N71C)	200	BB-1162
(N71CE)	200	BB-1162
N71CJ	G1	107
N71CR	G1	107
N71CR	G1	163
N71CS	200	BB-1162
N71CS	31T	7920027
N71DH	46D	119
N71DP	MU-2	1502SA
N71EE	TBM7	192
N71EE	TBM7	343
N71EN	90	LJ-632
N71FA	300	FA-17
N71FF	TBM7	192
N71FM	31T	8120031
N71FN	90	LJ-632
N71FN	MIII	T-384
N71GA	200	BB-605
N71GA	200	BB-1145
N71GA	690D	15042
N71HE	425	0085
N71JT	200	BB-816
N71KA	90	LJ-578
N71LA	31T	8104030
N71MA	690B	11451
N71MA	PA42	8001049
N71MF	MU-2	198
N71MR	695A	96054
N71NB	690A	11245
N71NH	F90	LA-219
N71PM	31T	8020076
(N71PW)	200	BB-287
N71PW	PC12	1014
N71QS	31T	7920027
N71RD	G1	322
N71RG	200	BB-443
N71SE	46T	97327
N71SF	MIIB	T26-154
N71SL	90	LJ-1020
N71TB	200	BB-755
N71TP	PC12	371
N71TW	31T	8020019
N71TW	31T	8304003
N71TZ	200	BB-105
N71VE	690	11043
N71VG	90	LJ-1279
N71VT	200	BB-709
N71VT	690	11043
N71WB	E90	LW-127
N71WH	90	LJ-495
N71WW	100	B-156
N71WW	90	LJ-1088
N72	300	FF-7
(N72AB)	690A	11329
N72AB	690A	11332
N72AM	200	BB-1145
(N72AM)	90	LJ-1104
N72B	G1	154
N72B	MU-2	735SA
N72BS	100	B-113
N72CA	200	BB-757
N72CF	MIIB	T26-132
N72CR	G1	158
N72DD	200	BB-509
N72DK	300	FA-42
N72DZ	PC12	777
N72EA	PC12	736
N72EE	P180	1074
N72EH	100	B-243
N72EZ	G1	15
N72GA	200	BB-560
N72GA	200	BB-757
N72GA	300	FA-72
N72GA	695A	96072
N72GC	200	BB-34
N72GG	200	BB-1080
N72GL	90	LJ-1261
N72HB	100	B-206

N72J	U-21	LM-72
N72KA	F90	LA-203
N72L	U-21	LM-19
N72LT	100	B-25
N72LT	200	BB-34
N72MM	200	BB-497
N72PK	90	LJ-1449
N72RD	90	LJ-127
N72RE	350	FL-344
N72RF	690B	11431
N72RL	200	BB-509
N72SE	200	BB-596
N72SE	200	BB-956
N72SR	TBM8	493
N72TA	100	B-202
N72TB	690C	11619
N72TG	90	LJ-1252
N72TJ	MU-2	414SA
N72TT	690	11003
N72TW	31T	7904052
N72VF	690A	11242
N72VG	46D	129
N72VT	690A	11242
N72WC	MIII	TT-536
N72WE	90	LJ-367
N72X	100	B-104
N72X	G1	106
N72XL	G1	106
N73	300	FF-8
N73AC	680T	1632-57
N73B	G1	107
N73BF	90	LJ-400
N73BG	31T	8004027
N73CA	200	BB-497
(N73CA)	31T	8020003
N73CA	31T	8020011
(N73CG)	G1	102
N73DC	695	95053
N73DC	695A	96095
N73DQ	695	95053
N73DW	425	0089
N73EF	690C	11617
N73H	695A	96030
N73HC	MIIB	T26-138
N73JC	B100	BE-26
(N73JC)	E90	LW-72
N73KA	100	B-73
N73LC	200	BB-80
N73LC	200	BB-911
N73LC	200	BB-1370
N73LC	200	BB-1393
N73LC	90	LJ-379
N73LK	90	LJ-584
N73LX	200	BB-911
N73M	G1	77
N73MA	690B	11391
N73MA	MU-2	414SA
N73MC	90	LJ-600
N73MC	MU-2	557
N73MC	MU-2	722SA
N73MH	90	LJ-570
N73MP	200	BB-1153
N73MW	200	BB-22
N73N	P68	230
(N73NL)	P68	230
(N73PD)	100	B-73
N73PG	90	LJ-1607
N73PH	90	LJ-875
(N73Q)	U-21	LM-68
(N73SJ)	681	6041
N73TB	31T	7620036
N73TW	31T	7920092
N73WC	350	FL-135
N73WL	200	BB-765
N73WL	B100	BE-81
N73WW	350	FL-449
N73YP	46T	97080
N73Z	31T	7520015
N74	300	FF-9
N74AL	200	BB-1213
N74AW	200	BB-1233
N74AX	PC12	149
N74B	200	BB-849
N74B	90	LJ-1611

N74B	90	LJ-1680
N74B	90	LJ-1766
N74BE	PC12	115
N74BJ	200	BB-340
N74BJ	P180	1048
N74BL	200	BB-34
N74BY	441	0039
N74CC	90	LJ-620
N74CD	695	95043
(N74DD)	200C	BL-25
(N74DE)	90	LJ-529
N74ED	200	BB-228
N74EF	690C	11614
N74EJ	200	BB-340
N74F	200	BB-849
N74FB	MU-2	770SA
N74FB	PA42	8001034
(N74GA)	690D	15043
N74GB	200	BB-485
N74GB	690A	11206
N74GL	441	0203
N74GP	200	BB-485
N74GP	90	LJ-428
N74GR	90	LJ-428
N74GS	200	BB-429
N74GS	200	BB-1135
N74HR	425	0002
N74JV	100	B-74
N74JW	425	0089
N74KA	100	B-197
N74KS	350	FL-299
N74LD	425	0175
N74LV	200	BB-1074
N74MA	90	LJ-479
N74MA	TBM8	385
N74ML	200	BB-1123
N74ML	31T	8104060
N74NA	MIV	AT-020
N74NL	31T	7720010
(N74PF)	200	BB-340
N74RF	200	BB-1408
N74RF	425	0153
N74RF	690C	11614
N74RG	200	BB-1000
N74RG	200	BB-1651
N74RN	200	BB-1000
N74RR	350	FL-104
N74RR	690A	11208
N74RR	690C	11614
N74RR	B100	BE-122
N74SA	690C	11678
N74TC	31T	7620057
N74TC	MU-2	555
N74TD	STAR	NC-27
N74TF	100	B-26
N74TF	350	FL-370
N74TF	STAR	NC-27
N74TG	200	BB-485
N74TL	MU-2	163
N74TL	MU-2	555
N74TM	MU-2	555
N74TW	31T	7920067
N74VR	E90	LW-135
(N74WA)	31T	7920042
N74WA	690B	11513
N74YC	MIIB	T26-120
N75	300	FF-10
N75A	90	LJ-210
N75AH	200	BB-741
N75AH	300	FA-156
N75AJ	BN2	913
N75AP	B100	BE-57
N75AW	PA42	8001046
N75BR	31T	8104036
N75C	200	BB-604
N75CA	31T	8020045
N75CF	E90	LW-212
N75CX	200	BB-604
N75CY	P68T	8001
N75D	680T	1546-9
N75D	90	LJ-235
N75DA	E90	LW-91
N75FL	PA42	8301002
N75G	U-21	LM-83
N75GA	695A	96073
N75GA	90	LJ-803
N75GC	90	LJ-727
N75GE	200	BB-1190
N75GF	200	BB-1190
N75GM	681	6032
N75GP	90	LJ-489
N75GR	100	B-210
(N75HW)	100	B-204
N75HW	425	0232
N75JP	E90	LW-158
N75KA	200	BB-100
N75KC	E90	LW-130
N75LA	100	B-75
N75LC	200	BB-1370
N75LS	PA42	5501017
N75LV	200	BB-1075
N75LW	E90	LW-75
N75M	G1	165
N75MC	300	FA-57
N75MC	350	FL-15
N75MD	MU-2	101
N75ME	300	FA-57
N75MS	F90	LA-204
N75MT	G1	165
N75MX	MIII	T-218
N75N	P68	294
N75N	P68	312
N75N	U-21	LM-57
N75NC	350	FL-15
N75NL	P68	312
(N75NT)	P68	294
N75PD	690A	11235
N75PG	90	LJ-1390
N75PX	350	FL-431
N75RC	MIII	T-241
N75RD	MIII	T-241
N75RJ	MU-2	136
N75RM	MIII	T-290
N75RR	690A	11206
N75RS	90	LJ-533
N75SC	MIII	TT-474
N75SK	31T	8004042
N75SR	200	BB-1506
N75TF	31T	7820075
N75TW	31T	8004016
N75U	690A	11218
N75V	U-21	LM-103
N75VF	200	BB-220
N75WA	31T	8104101
N75WA	690B	11557
N75WD	200C	BL-39
N75WD	300	FA-115
N75WD	350	FL-51
N75WD	STAR	NC-4
N75WH	PC12	1031
N75WL	200	BB-574
N75WL	300	FA-115
N75WP	200	BB-574
N75WR	200C	BL-39
N75WZ	350	FL-228
N75X	200	BB-459
N75X	90	LJ-50
N75X	MIII	TT-421
N75XA	90	LJ-50
N75Z	100	B-210
N75Z	200	BB-967
N75Z	90	LJ-389
N75Z	MU-2	1538SA
N75Z	U-21	LM-61
N75ZT	200	BB-967
N75ZZ	100	B-210
N76	300	FF-11
N76AE	B100	BE-73
N76AS	100	B-170
N76AS	90	LJ-347
N76BF	46D	120
N76BF	B100	BE-73
N76BT	680T	1567-23
N76CB	200	BB-280
N76CB	90	LJ-211
N76CC	MIII	T-304
N76CP	31T	8004026
N76CP	690A	11205
N76CV	90	LJ-211
N76D	680T	1567-23
N76DA	441	0062
N76DM	G1	166
N76DS	90	LJ-1063
N76DT	690B	11542
N76EC	690A	11208
N76EC	690A	11316
N76EC	690B	11495
(N76GA)	690D	15044
N76GM	90	LJ-498
N76HC	31T	8104005
N76HC	F90	LA-159
N76HH	695	95076
N76JL	BN2	895
N76L	P68	292
N76LB	E90	LW-24
N76MB	200	BB-165
N76MD	MU-2	124
N76MG	46T	97056
N76MP	200	BB-165
N76MP	200	BB-921
N76MX	MIV	AT-016
(N76NA)	690D	15040
(N76NL)	31T	7620007
N76PM	200	BB-998
N76PM	31T	8020076
N76PM	350	FL-200
N76PM	441	0221
N76PT	200	BB-998
N76PT	31T	7620011
N76PW	E90	LW-117
N76Q	U-21	LM-15
N76RJ	200	BB-1245
N76RJ	90	LJ-347
N76RJ	90	LJ-1116
N76RU	90	LJ-1116
N76SC	31T	8020091
N76SG	200	BB-101
N76SJ	425	0204
N76SK	E90	LW-115
N76ST	MIIA	T26-004
N76TG	31T	8004011
N76TW	31T	8166030
N76TW	E90	LW-76
N76TW	P68	393
N76U	MIII	T-240
N76WA	690A	11342
N77	300	FF-12
N77A	E90	LW-219
N77AG	E90	LW-219
N77AK	90	LJ-1023
N77AK	F90	LA-114
N77BE	90	LJ-592
N77BK	46D	77
N77CA	200	BB-717
N77CA	90	LJ-266
N77CA	E90	LW-141
N77CE	E90	LW-257
N77CG	31T	7720006
N77CJ	F90	LA-76
N77CT	200	BB-312
N77CT	200	BB-1183
N77CT	90	LJ-566
N77CV	200	BB-1161
N77CV	200	BB-1625
N77CX	200	BB-659
N77CX	200	BB-1482
N77D	PC6	921
N77DA	90	LJ-146
N77DB	MU-2	429SA
N77DE	90	LJ-592
N77DK	MU-2	449SA
N77DQ	PC6	921
N77EC	690A	11138
(N77EC)	690A	11316
N77EC	690A	11316
(N77EJ)	425	0149
(N77EL)	G1	7
N77GA	MU-2	656
N77GA	MU-2	749SA
N77GF	MU-2	656
N77HD	200	BB-1397
N77HE	90	LJ-969
N77HN	200	BB-1380
N77HS	690A	11166
N77HS	690D	15041
N77JL	680W	1791-21
N77JT	200	BB-1042
N77JT	F90	LA-98
N77JX	E90	LW-54
N77M	E90	LW-223
N77M	F90	LA-213
N77MF	425	0141
N77MF	680W	1814-31
N77ML	425	0141
N77ML	441	0202
N77NB	90	LJ-818
N77NH	31T	8104022
N77NH	31T	8166014
N77NL	31T	7720038
N77P	E90	LW-227
N77P	F90	LA-214
N77PA	200	BB-502
N77PA	300	FA-90
N77PA	690B	11368
N77PA	E90	LW-89
N77PA	F90	LA-89
N77PE	690B	11368
N77PF	100	B-70
N77PH	690D	15038
N77PK	31T	7720012
(N77PK)	46D	15
N77PK	46D	77
(N77PK)	46D	179
N77PK	690D	15038
N77PK	F90	LA-91
N77PR	31T	7720006
(N77PR)	690	11038
N77PV	F90	LA-68
(N77PZ)	300	FA-90
N77QX	200	BB-659
N77R	441	0288
N77RC	90	LJ-524
N77RQ	90	LJ-524
N77RZ	MU-2	538
N77SA	200	BB-334
N77SA	441	0329
N77SD	PC12	1001
N77SE	31T	7820008
N77SS	90	LJ-230
N77SS	MU-2	316
N77TM	MU-2	116
N77UA	690B	11422
N77UH	31T	8166026
N77UP	MU-2	780SA
N77UU	MIII	T-324
N77VF	690B	11520
N77W	E90	LW-262
N77WD	90	LJ-649
N77WF	E90	LW-4
N77WF	MIIA	T26-020
N77WM	100	B-35
N77WM	200	BB-712
N77WM	90	LJ-1133
(N77WN)	200	BB-712
N77WN	690A	11177
(N77WR)	PA42	5527003
N77WW	F90	LA-235
N77WZ	E90	LW-316
N77XW	200	BB-1602
N77Y	46T	97035
N77YP	425	0111
N77ZA	PC12	300
N78	300	FF-13
N78AG	P68	432
N78AM	200	BB-328
N78AM	90	LJ-529
N78AM	90	LJ-574
(N78AW)	690B	11494
N78BA	690A	11166
N78BA	90	LJ-1529
N78BK	MU-2	555
N78CA	100	B-109
N78CA	31T	7820006
N78CA	31T	7920062
N78CC	46T	97163
N78CH	681	6038

N78CP	MIVA	AT-029
N78CS	MIII	T-229
N78CT	200	BB-761
N78D	680T	1580-33
(N78D)	680T	1610-46
N78D	U-21	LM-78
(N78DA)	441	0167
N78DA	B100	BE-11
N78DV	200	BB-67
N78FB	F90	LA-231
N78FC	100	B-6
N78FC	200	BB-383
N78FQ	100	B-6
N78FS	MU-2	362SA
N78FS	MU-2	409SA
N78GA	695A	96074
(N78GC)	200	BB-1193
(N78HC)	MU-2	146
N78HF	MU-2	689
N78JD	90	LJ-763
N78JS	MU-2	682
N78K	E90	LW-263
N78K	U-21	LM-17
N78L	100	B-167
N78LB	200	BB-582
N78LC	200	BB-80
N78MK	100	B-109
N78NA	690B	11401
N78NW	F90	LA-76
N78P	200	BB-820
N78PC	31T	7820001
N78PG	PC12	370
N78PK	31T	7720012
N78PK	MU-2	1522SA
(N78SA)	690C	11647
(N78SA)	690C	11650
N78SC	200	BB-548
N78SE	90	LJ-529
N78SR	90	LJ-1078
N78TT	690B	11509
N78TW	31T	7920092
N78UA	31T	7820029
N78V	200	BB-558
(N78V)	MU-2	534
N78WC	MU-2	179
N78WD	MU-2	368SA
N78WL	MIIB	T26-114
N78XJ	90	LJ-1524
N79	200	BB-88
N79	300	FF-14
N79AC	MU-2	338
N79AE	MIII	TT-465
N79B	200	BB-1143
N79BE	690B	11408
N79BJ	680T	1610-46
N79BT	680T	1610-46
N79CA	31T	7920047
(N79CA)	31T	8120041
N79CA	PC12	136
N79CB	300	FA-217
N79CF	200	BB-441
N79CT	90	LJ-566
N79CT	E90	LW-303
N79CX	200	BB-445
N79D	680T	1610-46
(N79D)	680T	1628-55
N79DS	90	LJ-1063
N79EC	F90	LA-74
N79ED	200	BB-447
N79FB	31T	7920016
N79GA	200	BB-556
N79GA	695A	96076
N79GB	MU-2	724SA
N79GS	200	BB-905
N79HS	G1	79
N79JE	441	0091
N79JS	200	BB-1370
N79JS	31T	8020067
N79KA	200	BB-445
N79KF	200	BB-228
(N79LD)	31T	7804009
N79LP	MIII	T-366
N79MC	200	BB-212
(N79ME)	31T	7720012
N79ML	31T	7720012
N79MM	425	0063
N79MP	46D	56
N79N	P68	305
N79NB	100	B-166
N79ND	31T	7520037
N79NS	E90	LW-290
(N79NT)	P68	305
N79P	90	LJ-534
N79PB	200	BB-190
N79PE	90	LJ-1724
N79PG	200	BB-1043
N79PH	695A	96029
N79RA	TBM7	75
N79RR	200	BB-356
N79SA	690C	11693
N79SE	200	BB-464
N79SZ	690D	15024
N79TA	441	0104
N79TE	300	FA-67
N79W	U-21	LM-77
N79Z	TBM7	19
N79Z	U-21	LM-22
N80	300	FF-15
N80AC	G1	153
N80AJ	200	BB-1203
N80AM	90	LJ-643
N80BC	200	BB-922
N80BC	200	BB-1571
(N80BC)	31T	7400005
N80BC	31T	7920035
N80BC	31T	1166006
(N80BR)	200	BB-507
N80BR	MU-2	363SA
N80BT	200	BB-922
N80BT	200	BB-1178
N80BT	200	BB-1429
N80BT	E90	LW-148
N80BZ	300	FA-117
N80CA	BN2	306
N80CK	350	FL-18
N80CK	90	LJ-1258
N80CK	F90	LA-120
N80CM	90	LJ-561
N80CP	31T	7920040
N80CR	MU-2	517
N80D	200	BB-905
N80DA	31T	8166016
N80DB	B100	BE-31
N80DG	90	LJ-131
(N80F)	31T	7904023
(N80FE)	690A	11298
N80G	G1	22
N80GA	200	BB-349
N80GA	200	BB-669
N80GB	200	BB-645
N80GH	200	BB-566
N80GP	90	LJ-137
N80GS	200	BB-741
N80HH	MU-2	732SA
N80J	G1	50
N80JA	BN2	365
N80JM	MU-2	248
N80JN	MU-2	626
N80K	G1	51
N80KA	90	LJ-1862
N80KA	G1	51
N80KK	STAR	NC-16
N80KM	BN2	80
N80KM	STAR	NC-16
N80L	G1	19
(N80LG)	690B	11459
N80LH	PC6	801
N80LM	200	BB-529
N80LP	690A	11298
N80LR	G1	19
N80M	F90	LA-150
N80M	G1	27
N80MA	31T	7720043
N80MB	31T	8004041
N80MC	200	BB-24
N80MD	100	B-218
N80MJ	MIII	T-381
N80NC	E90	LW-16
N80NE	200	BB-456
N80NF	200	BB-456
N80PA	200	BB-234
N80PA	BN2	564
N80PC	PA42	8001006
N80PC	PA42	8001035
N80PM	425	0181
N80QB	200	BB-818
N80R	G1	90
N80R	U-21	LM-21
N80RD	G1	198
N80RE	90	LJ-697
N80RP	MIIB	T26-116
N80RT	200	BB-370
N80SS	680T	1573-28
N80TB	690A	11300
N80TB	90	LJ-690
N80TC	P180	1155
N80VP	200	BB-1769
N80WA	31T	8120021
N80WA	90	LJ-540
N80WD	MU-2	453SA
N80WM	200	BB-863
N80WP	E90	LW-115
N80WP	E90	LW-240
N80WP	F90	LA-228
N80X	200	BB-115
N80X	300	FA-117
N80XC	200	BB-115
N80XY	200	BB-115
N80XY	MU-2	616
N80XY	PC6	582
N80Y	U-21	LM-79
N81	300	FF-16
N81AJ	200	BB-929
N81AS	E90	LW-157
N81AT	90	LJ-490
N81BL	46T	97160
N81BR	MU-2	1506SA
N81CC	100	B-185
N81CC	90	LJ-42
N81CH	200	BB-835
N81CH	MIII	T-299
N81CK	200	BB-835
N81CT	200	BB-835
N81D	680T	1684-65
N81DC	200	BB-1361
N81DD	90	LJ-929
N81FR	MU-2	731SA
N81FX	PA42	8001051
N81GC	F90	LA-73
N81GD	31T	8166071
N81HK	690B	11565
N81HP	E90	LW-72
(N81JA)	BN2	385
N81JA	BN2	404
N81JN	690C	11660
N81KC	200	BB-953
N81KM	BN2	2023
N81LC	200	BB-1176
N81LC	680W	1835-40
(N81LJ)	MU-2	154
N81LT	200	BB-892
N81MD	100	B-203
N81MF	MU-2	375SA
N81MT	90	LJ-787
N81MV	90	LJ-1899
N81MW	MU-2	446SA
N81NA	90	LJ-993
N81P	B100	BE-102
N81PA	200	BB-158
N81PA	350	FL-250
N81PA	90	LJ-53
N81PA	90	LJ-395
N81PE	425	0039
N81PF	200	BB-158
N81PG	90	LJ-395
N81PH	OMAC	002
N81PL	E90	LW-90
N81PN	441	0037
N81PS	90	LJ-53
N81PS	E90	LW-40
N81PS	F90	LA-74
N81QH	MIII	T-299
N81RD	200	BB-385
N81RZ	200	BB-739
N81SD	F90	LA-130
N81SF	E90	LW-216
N81SM	46D	138
N81SM	PA42	8001007
N81T	G1	194
N81TF	200	BB-750
N81TL	200	BB-959
N81TR	425	0065
N81TR	690C	11690
N81TT	200	BB-791
N81TW	31T	8020056
N81WE	31T	7920060
N81WS	441	0181
N81WS	MIII	TT-480
N81WU	200	BB-576
N82	300	FF-17
(N82AB)	31T	7720003
N82AB	MIII	T-323
N82AJ	200	BB-958
N82AZ	31T	8275012
(N82BA)	690C	11649
N82BA	690D	15001
N82BA	690D	15041
N82BS	200	BB-1071
(N82BT)	31T	8166004
N82CL	441	0268
N82DD	200	BB-913
N82DD	F90	LA-121
N82DW	MIIB	T26-114
N82EU	200G	BY-82
N82GA	MIVA	AT-036
N82HB	425	0063
N82HP	31T	8275012
(N82HR)	300	FA-136
N82HR	F90	LA-178
N82HR	PC12	106
N82HR	PC12	408
N82JA	BN2	368
N82KA	200	BB-1034
N82KK	31T	8104046
N82KK	PA42	8001074
N82KK	PA42	5527013
N82LC	31T	8104066
N82LP	300	FA-72
(N82LS)	31T	7720049
N82MA	MU-2	665
N82P	90	LJ-940
N82PC	31T	8020082
N82PG	PA42	8001070
N82PK	200	BB-1596
N82SA	200	BB-755
N82SA	690C	11615
N82TC	100	B-199
N82TD	PA42	8001074
N82TT	200	BB-1000
(N82TW)	31T	8020056
N82TW	31T	8004034
N82WC	31T	7820041
N82WC	F90	LA-183
N82WC	MU-2	393SA
N82WT	MU-2	792SA
N82WU	350	FL-197
N82XL	31T	8166034
N83	300	FF-18
N83A	441	0050
N83AJ	PC12	495
N83AZ	31T	8275016
N83BA	200	BB-1118
N83CA	31T	8020072
N83CH	425	0025
N83CK	200	BB-63
N83DS	200	BB-199
N83ED	B100	BE-63
(N83ES)	PA42	5527014
N83FE	E90	LW-219
N83FM	90	LJ-341
N83FT	200	BB-1621
N83G	690	11064
N83GA	200	BB-518
N83GA	200C	BL-68
(N83GA)	31T	7720019
N83GA	695A	96077

N83GB	200	BB-405
N83GF	425	0132
N83HP	31T	8275016
(N83JA)	BN2	370
N83JA	BN2	378
N83JE	200	BB-773
N83JH	690D	15012
N83JN	200	BB-553
N83JR	PC12	1112
N83KA	200	BB-436
N83KA	200	BB-1111
N83KA	200	BB-1136
N83KA	F90	LA-223
N83KB	350	FL-436
N83KB	350	FL-616
N83KE	350	FL-436
N83KK	90	LJ-1388
(N83LS)	90	LJ-1461
N83MA	200	BB-13
N83MC	690A	11124
N83MG	31T	8104047
N83P	90	LJ-1027
N83PH	200	BB-976
N83RH	200	BB-976
N83RH	300	FA-213
N83RH	E90	LW-311
N83RS	MIIB	T26-177
(N83RV)	690A	11124
N83RZ	200	BB-1024
(N83SA)	690C	11700
(N83SA)	695	95027
N83SF	90	LJ-174
(N83SS)	690	11031
N83TC	690	11055
N83TC	90	LJ-483
N83TJ	200	BB-920
N83TM	100	B-130
(N83TW)	31T	8020003
N83TW	31T	8020067
N83VB	F90	LA-207
N83WA	695A	96063
N83WE	E90	LW-289
N83XL	31T	8166075
N84	300	FF-19
N84B	100	B-134
N84B	200	BB-797
N84BA	300	FA-10
N84CA	200	BB-166
N84CA	BN2	274
N84CC	200	BB-691
N84CC	200	BB-1243
N84CF	31T	8304003
N84CH	441	0110
N84CQ	200	BB-691
N84D	681	6013
N84DT	690	11031
N84G	U-21	LM-33
N84GA	695A	96079
N84GA	E90	LW-136
N84GA	MIII	T-312
(N84GF)	425	0132
N84GU	690B	11522
N84H	695A	96013
N84HS	TBM7	50
N84JA	BN2	348
N84JH	90	LJ-578
N84JL	F90	LA-18
N84KA	200	BB-484
N84LC	MIII	T-233
N84LG	690D	15035
N84LJ	441	0084
N84LS	200	BB-346
N84LS	E90	LW-20
N84MD	200	BB-352
N84N	P68	294
N84P	90	LJ-1045
N84PA	200	BB-835
N84PC	200	BB-860
N84PN	200	BB-835
N84SH	46T	97059
N84TP	90	LJ-911
N84TW	31T	8020008
N84WA	690B	11554
N84WC	31T	8020008

(N84WG)	31T	7820061
N84XP	200	BB-481
N85AB	690A	11167
N85AJ	31T	7520037
(N85AZ)	350	FL-600
N85AZ	350	FL-621
N85BC	100	B-6
N85BC	200	BB-734
N85BH	100	B-6
N85BK	200	BB-734
N85BX	90	LJ-830
N85CA	TRIS	279
N85CC	200	BB-52
N85CM	31T	8020019
N85CR	200	BB-1089
N85D	680T	1697-74
(N85D)	680T	1699-76
N85DB	MIII	T-250
N85DH	E90	LW-289
N85DJ	441	0358
N85DJ	695A	96073
N85DR	90	LJ-767
N85EM	31T	8166055
(N85FC)	200	BB-785
N85FC	200	BB-785
N85GA	200	BB-1228
N85GA	300	FA-50
N85GA	90	LJ-636
N85GA	MIVA	AT-037
N85GC	31T	8120009
N85GD	31T	8166071
N85GP	200	BB-1701
N85GW	90	LJ-712
N85H	MIII	T-208
N85HB	31T	8120021
N85JA	BN2	388
N85JE	TBM8	396
N85JE	TBM8	469
(N85JG)	F90	LA-20
N85JG	MU-2	612
N85KA	31T	7620055
N85KA	B100	BE-86
N85KG	31T	1104017
N85KS	200	BB-1217
N85LF	B100	BE-62
N85LG	90	LJ-1487
N85NL	90	LJ-90
N85NM	695A	96078
N85PH	90	LJ-1157
N85PJ	F90	LA-163
N85RR	300	FA-33
N85RT	46D	9
N85SL	PA42	5527005
N85TB	90	LJ-833
N85TH	300	FA-43
N85TK	46T	97128
N85TT	300	FA-10
N85TW	31T	8004045
N85VK	P68	279
N85WA	695A	96078
N85Z	U-21	LM-9
N85ZG	TBM8	480
N86AT	E90	LW-90
N86BD	90	LJ-331
N86BM	100	B-206
N86BP	690B	11503
"N86CAT"	MU-2	1570SA
N86CG	441	0153
N86CM	31T	8166022
N86CR	PA42	5527011
N86D	680T	1677-60
N86DA	200	BB-76
N86DD	200	BB-1171
N86EA	425	0082
N86FD	B100	BE-14
N86GA	200	BB-806
N86GA	200	BB-1086
(N86GA)	200	BB-1238
N86GA	350	FL-100
N86GA	695A	96080
(N86JA)	BN2	386
N86JG	90	LJ-1076
N86JK	G1	86
N86JR	90	LJ-264

(N86KA)	200	BB-1255
N86LD	200	BB-456
N86LD	90	LJ-1631
N86MA	G1	35
N86MG	90	LJ-264
N86MP	31T	7920060
N86MP	690B	11470
N86PA	100	B-206
N86Q	200	BB-300
N86Q	E90	LW-345
N86RL	46D	153
N86SD	MU-2	765SA
N86SH	MIII	TT-486A
(N86SS)	690A	11210
N86ST	690C	11619
N86TR	B100	BE-22
N86TR	E90	LW-57
N86Y	200	BB-302
(N87AG)	F90	LA-3
N87AG	P68	439
N87AP	MU-2	722SA
N87BP	200	BB-34
N87BS	MIIB	T26-113
N87BT	680T	1705-81
N87CA	100	B-240
N87CA	BN2	353
N87CE	350	FL-231
N87CE	G1	87
N87CF	200	BB-1122
N87CH	E90	LW-20
N87CH	G1	87
(N87CR)	PA42	5527012
N87D	680T	1705-81
N87DC	300	FA-149
N87DM	31T	8104056
N87DR	200	BB-1069
N87E	U-21	LM-5
N87FB	200	BB-1576
N87FE	200	BB-983
N87FM	MIVC	AT-506
N87GA	200	BB-87
N87GA	695A	96081
(N87GC)	425	0092
N87HB	90	LJ-1251
N87HT	441	0259
N87JA	BN2	347
N87JE	B100	BE-27
N87JR	200	BB-70
N87LN	200	BB-1952
N87LP	200	BB-331
(N87MK)	G1	87
N87MM	90	LJ-415
N87NF	46D	5
N87NW	B100	BE-42
N87Q	U-21	LM-60
N87RK	200	BB-533
N87SA	200	BB-1089
N87SA	695	95033
N87SJ	31T	7820077
N87TC	690B	11551
N87TW	31T	8020003
N87V	U-21	LM-130
N87WJ	MIIB	T26-113
N87WS	441	0009
N87WW	46D	18
N87WW	MU-2	693SA
N87WZ	690B	11511
N87XX	B100	BE-105
N87Y	MIIB	T26-130
N87YB	MIIB	T26-130
N87YC	300	FA-131
N87YC	350	FL-246
N87YP	31T	8120053
N87YQ	300	FA-131
N88AD	MU-2	458SA
N88AF	200	BB-1695
N88AP	90	LJ-1023
N88AT	90	LJ-419
N88B	31T	8166023
N88BA	200	BB-908
N88BC	31T	7920032
N88BC	MU-2	513
N88BF	200	BB-147
N88BJ	690C	11627

N88BK	200	BB-147
N88BT	MIII	T-207
N88BW	100	B-100
N88CA	31T	8020081
N88CA	BN2	191
N88CG	90	LJ-770
N88CP	200	BB-145
N88CR	90	LJ-514
N88CV	90	LJ-111
N88CW	90	LJ-1092
(N88DA)	200	BB-652
N88DC	31T	7820001
N88DW	90	LJ-1855
N88DW	90	LJ-1920
(N88DW)	MU-2	690
N88EL	90	LJ-1001
N88EL	PC12	131
N88FA	B100	BE-74
N88GC	E90	LW-50
N88GL	90	LJ-945
N88GW	441	0187
N88HL	MU-2	241
N88HL	MU-2	412SA
N88HL	MU-2	1542SA
N88HM	90	LJ-502
N88JA	BN2	376
N88JH	200	BB-1331
(N88KE)	200	BB-271
N88KE	200	BB-1313
N88LB	31T	7400004
(N88LH)	31T	7820001
N88MA	BN2	49
N88MT	200	BB-830
N88N	P68	352
N88NT	PC12	285
N88NW	31T	7820011
N88NW	695A	96047
N88P	200	BB-830
N88PA	200	BB-324
N88PD	690C	11696
N88PD	90	LJ-1242
N88PP	G1	164
N88QM	31T	8104025
N88QT	441	0228
N88RB	90	LJ-491
N88RB	90	LJ-884
N88RC	690D	15023
N88RG	E90	LW-211
N88RK	681	6014
N88RP	90	LJ-491
N88RY	200	BB-1275
N88RY	300	FA-122
N88SC	MIIB	T26-157
N88SD	90	LJ-661
N88SP	90	LJ-116A
N88SR	200	BB-1058
N88TB	441	0194
N88TL	B100	BE-113
N88TR	E90	LW-57
N88TS	200	BB-1016
N88TW	F90	LA-29
N88U	TBM7	135
N88VN	200	BB-1250
N88WF	TBM7	102
N88WV	200	BB-1554
N88WV	350	FL-253
N88WZ	680T	1713-87
N88XJ	90	LJ-1525
N88XL	31T	8166060
N88Y	G1	33
(N88ZC)	200	BB-1844
N89BC	E90	LW-57
N89BF	90	LJ-529
N89BK	31T	7620018
N89CA	31T	8020026
N89CA	BN2	268
N89CA	F90	LA-152
N89CL	EPIC	003
N89CR	MU-2	233
N89CR	MU-2	517
N89CU	690B	11355
(N89CX)	46D	59
N89D	680T	1702-78
N89DA	680T	1702-78

N89DE	G1	4
N89DR	MU-2	517
N89DR	MU-2	713SA
N89F	U-21	LM-124
N89FC	200	BB-375
N89FF	90	LJ-671
N89FN	E90	LW-239
N89GA	200	BB-655
N89GA	300	FA-173
N89GA	695A	96082
N89GB	200	BB-967
N89GC	300	FA-187
N89GC	425	0092
N89JA	31T	7920030
N89JA	BN2	390
N89JM	100	B-125
N89JR	90	LJ-185
N89K	G1	170
N89KA	300	FA-172
N89KA	90	LJ-1227
N89L	E90	LW-114
N89LT	P68	450
N89MC	31T	7820049
N89MP	200	BB-166
N89N	U-21	LM-34
N89NC	300	FA-157
N89RP	MIII	T-417
(N89SA)	690C	11707
N89SC	MU-2	1516SA
N89ST	46T	97008
N89TM	90	LJ-610
N89TW	31T	7820060
N89UA	200	BB-1336
N89VT	441	0089
N89WA	200	BB-1540
N89WC	350	FL-72
N90AF	E90	LW-29
(N90AG)	441	0275
(N90AJ)	90	LJ-760
N90AL	E90	LW-215
N90AT	690A	11272
N90AW	90	LJ-697
N90BA	690D	15037
N90BB	31T	7620027
N90BC	MU-2	676
N90BD	F90	LA-134
N90BE	90	LJ-209
N90BE	E90	LW-333
N90BF	E90	LW-124
N90BJ	90	LJ-1228
N90BJ	E90	LW-22
N90BJ	MIII	TT-421
N90BL	200	BB-1240
N90BL	695	95026
N90BL	90	LJ-52
N90BL	F90	LA-162
N90BN	F90	LA-10
N90BP	90	LJ-718
N90BR	200	BB-227
N90BR	200	BB-507
N90BR	90	LJ-575
N90BT	90	LJ-289
N90BU	90	LJ-425
N90BW	90	LJ-375
N90BW	90	LJ-575
N90C	100	B-131
N90C	200	BB-18
N90CA	E90	LW-24
N90CB	90	LJ-473
N90CC	100	B-131
N90CD	90	LJ-810
N90CE	90	LJ-842
(N90CE)	90	LJ-932
N90CH	690B	11389
N90CH	90	LJ-1445
N90CJ	E90	LW-88
N90CL	200	BB-18
N90CN	90	LJ-1410
N90CP	46T	97113A
N90CP	46T	97118
N90CP	TBM7	285
N90CR	690B	11413
N90CT	90	LJ-645
N90D	200	BB-633
N90D	90	LJ-289
N90D	U-21	LU-10
N90DA	441	0015
N90DA	681	6003
N90DA	E90	LW-22
N90DE	P180	1167
N90DF	200	BB-633
N90DJ	90	LJ-1130
N90DL	90	LJ-1003
N90DN	90	LJ-437
(N90DS)	90	LJ-1194
N90EA	E90	LW-274
N90EJ	90	LJ-749
N90EL	90	LJ-592
N90EM	B100	BE-5
N90EP	90	LJ-1124
N90ET	F90	LA-20
N90FA	90	LJ-133
N90FD	F90	LA-5
N90FH	90	LJ-86
(N90FJ)	31T	8104031
(N90FL)	90	LJ-741
N90FL	F90	LA-33
N90FP	F90	LA-163
N90FQ	200	BB-694
N90FS	31T	8020011
N90GA	200	BB-1359
N90GA	300	FA-107
N90GA	425	0090
(N90GA)	695A	96083
N90GB	90	LJ-469
N90GC	300	FA-58
N90GC	441	0089
N90GD	E90	LW-138
N90GE	90	LJ-1795
N90GH	90	LJ-1056
N90GK	E90	LW-124
(N90GM)	425	0178
N90GN	90	LJ-157
N90GP	90	LJ-1795
N90GP	90	LJ-1885
N90GS	F90	LA-91
N90GT	F90	LA-28
N90GT	F90	LA-159
N90GT	MIII	TT-534
N90HB	90	LJ-904
N90HB	90	LJ-1328
N90HK	F90	LA-176
N90JA	BN2	403
N90JC	31T	8104031
N90JR	90	LJ-211
N90JS	90	LJ-772
N90KA	90	LJ-506
N90KA	90	LJ-593
N90KA	90	LJ-1228
N90KA	90	LJ-1256
N90KA	90	LJ-1288
N90KA	90	LJ-1323
(N90KA)	90	LJ-1413
N90KA	90	LJ-1493
N90KA	90	LJ-1517
N90KA	90	LJ-1571
N90KA	90	LJ-1694
N90KB	90	LJ-1288
N90KB	P68	365
N90KC	200	BB-205
N90KH	90	LJ-542
N90KP	90	LJ-1699
N90KS	90	LJ-1517
N90KU	90	LJ-1703
N90LB	90	LJ-573
N90LF	90	LJ-852
N90LG	90	LJ-351
N90LJ	90	LJ-701
N90LL	F90	LA-28
N90LL	F90	LA-174
N90LM	F90	LA-146
N90LP	200	BB-36
N90LP	200	BB-1169
N90M	G1	322
N90MB	E90	LW-148
N90ME	90	LJ-661
N90MH	F90	LA-78
N90MK	90	LJ-708
N90ML	200	BB-65
N90ML	90	LJ-679
N90MM	90	LJ-676
N90MR	90	LJ-12
N90MT	90	LJ-404
N90MT	90	LJ-1223
N90MT	F90	LA-19
N90MU	90	LJ-679
N90MV	90	LJ-701
N90NA	F90	LA-104
N90NB	MIII	T-312
N90NH	MIVA	AT-032
N90NM	90	LJ-404
N90NS	F90	LA-19
N90NY	90	LJ-73
N90PA	BN2	449
N90PB	200	BB-125
N90PB	BN2	398
N90PE	90	LJ-1181
N90PH	E90	LW-60
N90PM	G1	51
N90PR	200	BB-1228
N90PR	350	FL-44
N90PR	90	LJ-722
N90PR	90	LJ-1437
N90PU	90	LJ-1046
N90PW	90	LJ-681
(N90QH)	690B	11389
N90RG	90	LJ-546
N90RK	90	LJ-1136
N90RK	90	LJ-1554
N90RT	F90	LA-146
N90RW	90	LJ-375
N90RW	90	LJ-772
N90RZ	90	LJ-489
N90SA	90	LJ-133
N90SA	MU-2	139
N90SA	MU-2	280
N90SB	F90	LA-154
N90SC	31T	1166004
N90SD	90	LJ-1548
N90SE	46D	166
N90SE	F90	LA-72
N90SG	90	LJ-1000
N90SJ	90	LJ-177
N90SK	F90	LA-72
N90SM	90	LJ-323
N90SR	E90	LW-306
N90TD	F90	LA-183
N90TM	200	BB-1262
N90TM	F90	LA-146
N90TP	F90	LA-66
N90TT	690A	11316
N90TT	E90	LW-274
(N90TW)	31T	7820072
N90TW	31T	7920009
N90TW	PA42	5501013
N90TX	F90	LA-146
N90U	46D	28
N90UB	90	LJ-847
N90UB	P68	302
N90VF	90	LJ-1619
N90VM	31T	8104031
N90VP	90	LJ-276
"N90VU"	90	LJ-3
(N90WA)	31T	8104029
N90WA	31T	8104030
N90WC	90	LJ-987
N90WE	300	FA-164
N90WE	690C	11687
N90WG	31T	7920044
N90WJ	90	LJ-525
N90WL	90	LJ-461
N90WP	200	BB-68
N90WP	200	BB-308
N90WP	90	LJ-1383
N90WT	E90	LW-31
N90WW	31T	1104004
N90WW	E90	LW-138
N90XP	90	LJ-1644
N90XS	E90	LW-342
N90XY	E90	LW-326
N90YA	425	0090
N90ZH	90	LJ-594
N90ZZ	46T	97223
N91BM	TBM7	20
N91BM	TBM7	128
(N91CA)	BN2	310
(N91CA)	BN2	335
(N91CA)	BN2	374
N91CD	200	BB-1402
N91CM	MU-2	388SA
N91CR	90	LJ-1295
N91CS	690B	11428
N91CT	690B	11428
N91CT	90	LJ-1521
N91CU	690B	11428
N91D	100	B-159
N91D	680T	1589-40
N91D	680W	1762-8
N91DE	100	B-159
N91DT	90	LJ-381
N91G	G1	37
N91HM	90	LJ-908
N91HT	200	BB-1183
N91JA	BN2	407
N91JR	G1	12
N91JR	MU-2	146
N91KA	90	LJ-1232
N91KM	46T	97120B
(N91L)	B100	BE-102
N91LE	90	LJ-832
N91LP	100	B-125
N91LP	200	BB-212
N91LR	100	B-125
N91LW	90	LJ-1001
N91LY	90	LJ-1295
N91MF	200	BB-657
N91MK	90	LJ-341
N91ML	90	LJ-341
N91MM	MU-2	198
(N91MT)	PC12	105
N91NC	90	LJ-341
N91P	F90	LA-10
N91PD	90	LJ-1806
N91RK	100	B-226
N91S	U-21	LU-15
N91SA	695	95038
N91SF	E90	LW-216
N91TJ	90	LJ-744
N91TR	200	BB-603
N91TR	90	LJ-1092
N91TS	31T	8020050
N91TW	31T	7820078
N91U	100	B-130
(N92AG)	PA42	5527025
N92AG	PC12	257
N92AM	90	LJ-618
N92B	U-21	LM-132
N92BA	200	BB-6
N92BA	90	LJ-480
(N92BC)	MU-2	303
N92BD	200	BB-1055
N92BD	90	LJ-745
N92BE	90	LJ-745
N92BK	90	LJ-1381
N92CA	BN2	311
N92CA	PC12	753
(N92CC)	300	FA-93
N92CD	31T	8166046
N92CD	90	LJ-1252
N92D	100	B-175
N92DE	300	FA-149
N92DG	200	BB-814
N92DL	100	B-175
N92DN	300	FA-149
N92DV	E90	LW-292
N92DZ	PC12	1087
N92FC	31T	7620044
N92FC	90	LJ-1235
N92GC	300	FA-85
N92J	U-21	LU-12
N92JA	BN2	416
N92JC	441	0223
N92JQ	441	0223
N92JR	200	BB-751
N92JR	MU-2	006
N92K	G1	140

N92LC	200	BB-1037
N92M	200	BB-382
N92ME	200	BB-151
N92MT	695	95062
N92P	90	LJ-885
N92P	F90	LA-160
N92PL	90	LJ-528
N92RC	MIII	T-228
N92RC	MIII	TT-435
N92RQ	MIII	T-228
N92S	U-21	LU-5
N92SA	G1	140
N92SS	300	FA-127
N92ST	MU-2	610
N92TA	200	BB-136
N92TC	200	BB-864
(N92TC)	690A	11141
N92TC	MU-2	209
N92TH	350	FL-509
N92TW	31T	7820089
N92TW	350	FL-3
N92TX	300	FA-121
N92UK	F90	LA-87
N92V	200	BB-262
N92W	90	LJ-182
N92WC	200	BB-1330
N92WC	300	FA-69
N92WG	90	LJ-182
N93A	E90	LW-63
N93AC	G1	196
N93AH	MU-2	581
N93AJ	B100	BE-18
N93BA	441	0203
N93BA	90	LJ-230
N93BA	90	LJ-749
N93BA	90	LJ-1065
N93BB	90	LJ-695
N93BC	100	B-41
N93BD	90	LJ-749
N93BD	MU-2	208
N93BD	PA42	8001055
N93BN	TBM7	74
N93CA	BN2	312
N93CD	200	BB-1404
N93CN	31T	8004029
N93CV	31T	7904016
N93D	680W	1722-2
N93D	B100	BE-23
N93DA	425	0013
N93DC	90	LJ-862
N93DD	31T	8166008
N93EJ	90	LJ-388
N93GA	200	BB-1220
N93GA	300	FA-93
N93GA	695A	96084
N93GN	MU-2	775SA
N93HA	90	LJ-388
N93HC	441	0011
N93J	U-21	LM-128
(N93JA)	BN2	423
N93JA	BN2	446
N93JJ	PC6	861
N93KA	F90	LA-24
N93LL	46T	97045
N93LP	90	LJ-901
N93LV	200	BB-157
N93MA	695A	96035
N93ME	200	BB-339
N93ME	200	BB-1345
N93ME	690B	11414
N93MF	200	BB-339
N93NB	200	BB-970
N93NM	695A	96020
N93NP	200	BB-1184
N93QR	90	LJ-1696
N93RA	680W	1722-2
N93RK	441	0135
N93RM	690B	11457
N93RR	200	BB-1853
N93RY	90	LJ-174
N93SA	690B	11463
N93SF	90	LJ-174
N93SF	B100	BE-13
N93SH	31T	7904029
N93TW	31T	7804010
N93UM	MU-2	537
N93V	U-21	LU-3
N93WB	90	LJ-425
N93WT	B100	BE-80
N93WW	690	11031
N93ZC	200	BB-654
N94AC	690B	11486
N94AM	90	LJ-640
N94BA	90	LJ-388
N94CA	BN2	315
N94CD	90	LJ-939
N94CE	MIV	AT-004
N94CK	200G	BY-30
N94CP	100	B-94
(N94CP)	200	BB-697
N94CS	PA42	5501016
N94D	200	BB-502
N94D	200	BB-523
N94DU	200	BB-502
N94EA	695A	96094
N94EG	31T	8104033
N94EW	PA42	8001054
N94FE	PC12	150
N94FG	200	BB-433
N94GA	200	BB-1001
N94GA	200	BB-1145
N94GA	300	FA-94
N94GA	695A	96086
N94HB	90	LJ-904
N94HC	680W	1811-28
N94HD	680W	1811-28
N94JA	BN2	410
N94JA	BN2	434
N94JD	F90	LA-139
N94JK	MU-2	761SA
N94JP	690B	11468
N94JS	31T	8104056
N94KC	200	BB-172
N94KM	46D	47
N94LC	200	BB-1224
N94LL	200	BB-1506
N94LY	P180	1008
(N94MA)	695	95046
N94MG	90	LJ-1229
N94N	U-21	LU-4
N94PA	695A	96005
N94PG	F90	LA-205
N94PP	PC12	369
N94QD	200	BB-1001
N94S	U-21	LM-133
N94SA	690B	11468
N94SA	G1	157
N94SC	90	LJ-975
N94SR	90	LJ-1221
N94TB	31T	7804002
N94TK	90	LJ-1358
N94TW	31T	7920028
N94U	F90	LA-124
N94WM	46D	35
N95AB	695A	96012
N95AC	MIII	T-381
N95AN	200	BB-1506
N95BD	200	BB-1029
N95BD	90	LJ-637
N95BD	MU-2	763SA
N95BE	MU-2	763SA
N95BM	TBM7	20
N95BN	BN2	95
N95CA	BN2	357
N95CG	200	BB-948
N95CM	B100	BE-18
N95CR	PA42	5527012
N95CT	200	BB-1235
N95D	200	BB-523
N95D	MIIA	T26-030
N95DD	90	LJ-637
(N95DW)	TBM7	60
N95GA	100	B-137
N95GA	200	BB-1467
N95GA	695A	96087
N95GR	690B	11411
N95GR	90	LJ-363
N95JA	BN2	442
N95JJ	B100	BE-18
N95JM	690A	11289
(N95KA)	E90	LW-242
N95KW	46T	97301
N95KY	MIVA	AT-031
N95LB	E90	LW-24
N95LF	690A	11290
N95LM	200	BB-1956
N95MJ	MU-2	1564SA
N95MW	200	BB-1295
N95NW	PC12	105
N95PC	90	LJ-1109
N95PM	200	BB-524
N95RB	E90	LW-24
N95RM	MU-2	625
N95S	U-21	LM-125
N95SA	PA42	5501040
N95TD	441	0238
N95TG	200	BB-1077
N95TT	200	BB-917
N95TW	31T	7920042
N95UF	90	LJ-78
N95UT	200	BB-1759
N95VR	PA42	8001049
N95WC	200	BB-85
N96AG	90	LJ-260
N96AH	90	LJ-643
N96AL	100	B-162
N96AM	100	B-162
N96AM	200	BB-1713
N96BW	690A	11104
N96CA	BN2	323
N96CE	200	BB-1536
N96D	MIIA	T26-034
N96DA	E90	LW-62
N96DC	90	LJ-814
(N96DF)	200	BB-1247
N96DQ	90	LJ-814
N96FA	90	LJ-1111
N96GA	200	BB-363
N96GA	200	BB-1178
N96GA	695A	96088
N96GJ	100	B-96
N96GM	100	B-143
N96GM	200	BB-64
N96GP	200	BB-1322
(N96HH)	200	BB-396
N96HK	EPIC	227
N96JA	BN2	449
(N96JA)	TRIS	1013
N96JF	90	LJ-1429
N96JP	MU-2	556
N96JS	31T	7620021
N96KA	350	FL-36
N96LF	690A	11336
N96MA	31T	7804005
N96MA	695	95072
N96MA	MU-2	011
N96MM	31T	7904011
N96MR	90	LJ-1068
N96MV	PC12	793
N96NA	F90	LA-96
N96QM	100	B-143
N96QM	200	BB-64
N96RE	90	LJ-94
N96RL	MIIB	T26-116
N96S	U-21	LU-13
N96TB	E90	LW-107
N96TC	PA42	7801004
(N96TC)	PA42	8001017
N96TH	90	LJ-1382
N96TT	F90	LA-26
N96TW	31T	7920034
N96UB	200	BB-267
N96UM	MU-2	533
N96WC	200	BB-969
N96WF	PC12	139
N96Y	U-21	LU-8
N96ZZ	200	BB-1035
N97AA	46D	203
N97AB	681B	6050
N97AB	MIIB	T26-114
N97AB	MIII	T-203
N97CA	BN2	324
N97CT	200	BB-312
N97CV	90	LJ-1492
N97CX	46D	26
N97D	200C	BL-25
N97D	MIIB	T26-113
N97D	U-21	LM-137
(N97DA)	300	FA-93
N97DA	425	0027
N97DA	90	LJ-1755
N97DG	200C	BL-25
N97DL	350	FL-4
N97DR	350	FL-4
N97DR	350	FL-133
N97EB	300	FA-97
(N97FT)	MIII	T-266
N97GA	695A	96089
N97JA	BN2	447
N97JT	31T	7620029
N97KA	90	LJ-1469
N97KE	90	LJ-1469
N97LL	46T	97058
N97MA	31T	8120009
N97MA	31T	7804005
N97N	MIIB	T26-113
N97PC	31T	8020034
N97RD	MIIB	T26-114
N97SF	90	LJ-818
N97SZ	200	BB-1166
N97T	U-21	LM-127
N97TW	31T	7920051
N97UT	200	BB-1897
N97WC	200	BB-1382
N97WD	B100	BE-97
N97WE	200	BB-1586
N97WT	690C	11709
N98AG	P68T	8011
N98AJ	690B	11458
N98AL	MU-2	105
N98AR	90	LJ-829
(N98AS)	31T	7720054
N98AT	31T	7620014
N98B	90	LJ-87
N98BD	200	BB-1238
N98BK	90	LJ-1522
N98BZ	MIII	T-207
N98CA	BN2	331
N98CH	100	B-173
N98CM	200	BB-151
N98CM	MU-2	529
N98D	B100	BE-49
N98D	MIIB	T26-155
N98DA	200	BB-1555
N98DB	MIIB	T26-155
N98DD	90	LJ-195
N98DX	200	BB-1343
N98EP	425	0230
N98FT	MIII	T-375
N98GA	200	BB-898
N98GA	690D	15030
N98GF	31T	8004009
N98HB	90	LJ-285
N98HF	100	B-23
N98HF	E90	LW-89
N98JA	BN2	467
N98KS	90	LJ-1502
N98LC	PA42	8001063
N98LF	LFAN	E-009
N98LP	200	BB-1134
N98MA	MU-2	122
N98ME	E90	LW-94
N98MK	G1	98
N98MR	690	11022
N98NF	TBM7	133
N98PC	E90	LW-131
N98PJ	690A	11320
N98PM	E90	LW-131
N98PT	31T	7620014
N98R	G1	82
(N98RF)	90	LJ-1034
N98RF	PA42	5527006
N98RY	200	BB-1275
N98TA	B100	BE-56
N98TB	31T	7820040
N98TG	31T	7904027

N98TR	100	B-101
N98TW	31T	7904027
N98UC	100	B-23
N98UC	MIII	T-378
N98UM	MU-2	529
N98WP	200	BB-308
N98WP	90	LJ-1493
N98XK	90	LJ-1500
N99AC	E90	LW-120
N99AF	680T	1697-74
N99AK	695A	96011
N99BH	31T	8166014
N99BT	MU-2	591
N99BW	100	B-50
N99CD	90	LJ-601
N99CS	PA42	8001046
N99CX	46D	59
N99DE	200	BB-65
N99DE	G1	4
N99DX	200	BB-1342
N99EE	MU-2	191
N99EL	G1	7
N99G	U-21	LM-129
N99GR	MU-2	366SA
N99HE	100	B-233
N99JA	BN2	470
N99JW	MIII	T-266
N99JW	MIII	TT-450
N99KA	100	B-80
N99KA	90	LJ-373
N99KC	MU-2	263
N99KF	31T	7920093
N99LC	MU-2	438SA
N99LL	200	BB-994
N99LM	90	LJ-671
N99LM	F90	LA-68
N99ML	200	BB-1844
N99ML	200G	BY-25
N99ML	90	LJ-1460
N99ML	90	LJ-1537
N99ML	MIII	T-237
N99MN	90	LJ-1460
N99MZ	46T	97099
N99RK	MIIB	T26-173
N99SL	MU-2	568
N99SR	MU-2	315
N99TC	E90	LW-40
N99TD	425	0053
N99U	350	FL-20
N99UM	MU-2	523
N99VA	31T	7720007
N99W	90	LJ-13
N99WC	690A	11308
(N100AK)	690A	11125
N100AK	PA42	5527010
N100AM	690B	11361
N100AN	100	B-209
N100AN	90	LJ-76
N100AQ	300	FA-190
N100AW	MIIB	T26-116
(N100AX)	MU-2	450SA
N100BE	100	B-221
N100BE	300	FA-32
N100BE	350	FL-369
N100BE	350	FL-403
N100BG	350	FL-6
N100BP	100	B-60
N100BP	680T	1538-5
N100BR	MU-2	213
N100BR	MU-2	562
N100BT	90	LJ-686
N100BT	MU-2	600
N100BW	100	B-13
N100BW	MU-2	593
(N100BX)	100	B-177
N100BX	90	LJ-686
N100BY	MU-2	753SA
N100BY	MU-2	1565SA
N100BZ	300	FA-32
N100C	G1	198
N100CC	425	0170
N100CE	MIII	T-325
N100CF	MU-2	229
N100CH	200	BB-494
N100CH	90	LJ-498
N100CH	90	LJ-987
N100CL	690A	11127
N100CM	31T	8020073
N100CQ	90	LJ-498
N100CS	PA42	5501011
N100CT	680T	1618-50
N100CU	E90	LW-119
N100CU	F90	LA-182
N100CW	MU-2	581
N100DA	BN2	2020
N100DG	690	11033
N100DS	200	BB-310
N100DS	MIII	T-325
N100EA	441	0125
N100EC	E90	LW-150
N100EG	G1	196
N100EJ	690A	11202
N100EL	G1	11
(N100ES)	31T	8020017
N100FB	200	BB-456
N100FB	90	LJ-570
N100FF	90	LJ-570
N100FL	300	FA-34
N100FL	G1	11
N100FT	MU-2	1565SA
N100GB	90	LJ-277
N100GF	46D	39
N100GJ	100	B-99
N100GL	681	6028
N100GM	100	B-88
N100GV	100	B-116
N100GY	31T	8104034
N100H	200	BB-749
N100HC	100	B-229
N100HC	200	BB-98
N100HC	90	LJ-150
(N100HD)	200	BB-749
N100HF	MIIA	T26-003
N100HM	90	LJ-292
N100HS	90	LJ-949
N100HT	90	LJ-233
N100HW	B100	BE-60
N100JB	90	LJ-752
N100JB	MIIA	T26-004
(N100JB)	MIII	T-264
N100JD	90	LJ-555
N100JD	90	LJ-1472
N100JF	90	LJ-292
(N100JJ)	100	B-58
N100JJ	690A	11290
N100JL	BN2	178
(N100JW)	90	LJ-552
N100JW	E90	LW-61
N100K	90	LJ-277
N100KA	100	B-11
N100KB	90	LJ-820
N100KE	MU-2	313SA
N100KK	MU-2	118
N100KM	200	BB-310
N100KP	MU-2	313SA
N100KP	MU-2	736SA
N100KR	31T	7520035
N100KR	31T	7920018
N100KU	90	LJ-568
N100LA	200	BB-1200
N100LB	100	B-54
N100LB	31T	7720021
N100LJ	100	B-173
N100LS	690	11025
N100MA	MU-2	124
N100MB	690	11055
N100MF	690B	11404
N100MK	MU-2	568
N100MP	31T	7620023
N100MS	200	BB-1171
N100MS	PC12	835
N100MW	E90	LW-2
N100MX	100	B-118
N100MX	MIIA	T26-003
"N100ND"	200	BB-26
N100NE	BN2	82
N100NL	MIIB	T26-168
N100NP	MU-2	423SA
N100NS	200	BB-39
N100NS	E90	LW-49
N100NW	690C	11647
N100NX	MIIA	T26-003
N100P	B100	BE-58
N100P	G1	27
N100PA	100	B-8
N100PA	100	B-88
N100PA	100	B-124
N100PA	MU-2	521
N100PB	TBM7	2
N100PH	F90	LA-119
N100PL	100	B-124
N100PL	200	BB-1297
N100PL	F90	LA-119
N100PX	200	BB-890
(N100PX)	350	FL-184
N100PY	200	BB-890
N100QM	31T	8020053
N100QR	100	B-215
N100QR	200C	BL-41
N100QT	90	LJ-689
N100RN	31T	7820091
N100RT	MU-2	146
N100RU	90	LJ-1433
N100S	100	B-100
(N100S)	200	BB-32
N100SA	100	B-54
N100SA	100	B-123
N100SC	90	LJ-138
N100SC	E90	LW-162
N100SF	200	BB-32
N100SG	MU-2	528
N100SJ	100	B-124
N100SK	E90	LW-162
N100SM	200	BB-269
N100SM	90	LJ-1561
N100SM	MIIB	T26-102
N100SN	MIIB	T26-102
N100SN	MIIB	T26-129
N100SW	MU-2	539
N100T	MIII	T-247
N100TB	90	LJ-117
N100TB	MU-2	228
N100TB	MU-2	1541SA
N100TK	695	95004
N100TM	200	BB-172
N100TN	31T	7520013
N100TT	690A	11159
N100TT	695	95004
N100TV	G1	126
N100TW	B100	BE-51
N100UB	90	LJ-147
N100UE	90	LJ-138
N100UF	300	FA-68
N100UF	90	LJ-138
N100UP	200	BB-367
N100UP	90	LJ-147
N100US	MIVA	AT-029
N100UT	100	B-12
N100V	90	LJ-796
N100VC	46D	144
N100VC	MU-2	209
N100VM	90	LJ-631
N100WB	90	LJ-139
N100WC	690A	11330
N100WC	690B	11360
N100WG	PC12	131
N100WL	90	LJ-148
N100WQ	31T	7820084
(N100WS)	MU-2	439SA
N100WT	31T	8004006
N100Y	300	FA-68
N100YA	441	0257
N100YC	PC12	281
N100ZM	100	B-88
N101AF	100	B-7
N101AF	200	BB-363
N101AF	300	FA-55
N101AF	31T	7920089
N101AK	200	BB-363
N101AP	100	B-7
N101AP	200	BB-1004
N101BE	MIIB	T26-161
(N101BN)	BN2	101
N101BP	200	BB-314
N101BS	90	LJ-375
N101BU	90	LJ-1107
N101BU	MIIB	T26-161
N101CA	425	0142
N101CC	200	BB-427
N101CG	200	BB-815
N101CG	90	LJ-557
N101CG	E90	LW-225
N101CJ	100	B-55
N101CP	200	BB-634
N101CP	PC6	653
N101CS	C-12	BC-41
N101DH	31T	8120046
N101DX	200	BB-256
N101EC	200	BB-1196
(N101ES)	MU-2	119
N101ET	F90	LA-172
N101FB	31T	7400007
N101FC	90	LJ-144
N101GA	90	LJ-11
N101GG	90	LJ-557
N101GQ	200	BB-427
N101HK	MIIB	T26-101
N101KJ	690C	11694
(N101L)	300	FA-5
N101LR	90	LJ-802
N101MC	MIII	T-234
N101NE	BN2	201
N101NK	90	LJ-142
N101NX	TBM7	309
N101PC	200	BB-256
N101PC	300	FA-19
N101PC	E90	LW-44
(N101PF)	100	B-44
N101PT	31T	7720053
N101QA	MU-2	248
N101RF	690B	11531
N101RG	690B	11463
N101RQ	690	11017
N101RW	690	11017
N101RW	690B	11517
N101RW	690B	11564
N101RZ	690B	11564
N101SE	100	B-107
N101SG	200	BB-1785
N101SG	90	LJ-908
N101SG	90	LJ-1231
N101SG	90	LJ-1496
N101SK	200	BB-700
N101SN	B100	BE-118
N101SN	MU-2	1505SA
N101SQ	90	LJ-1231
N101SQ	90	LJ-1496
N101SS	90	LJ-537
N101SZ	90	LJ-908
N101T	31T	7520016
(N101TR)	31T	8120006
N101TS	200	BB-700
N101UA	100	B-3
N101UC	690A	11194
N101VV	MIIB	T26-101
N101WD	BN2	101
N101WL	E90	LW-72
N101WR	90	LJ-934
N101XC	90	LJ-219
N102AD	441	0311
N102AE	PA42	5501053
N102AF	31T	8020031
N102AF	PC12	1102
N102AJ	90	LJ-649
N102AR	31T	8020031
N102BG	MU-2	748SA
N102BH	MU-2	587
N102BX	MU-2	748SA
N102CS	350	FL-126
N102CU	E90	LW-119
N102DE	681	6001
N102DY	MIIB	T26-169
N102E	31T	7920057
N102EP	90	LJ-968
N102FG	100	B-131
N102FG	200	BB-1799

N102FK	90	LJ-982
N102FL	31T	7820021
N102FL	350	FL-263
N102FL	90	LJ-982
N102GP	100	B-143
(N102GP)	MU-2	260
N102JC	AASI	001
N102JK	690A	11145
N102JK	690A	11154
N102LF	100	B-65
N102M	G1	99
N102MA	MU-2	115
N102MA	MU-2	414SA
N102MC	E90	LW-72
N102ME	100	B-140
N102MF	KODK	0017
N102NA	441	0159
N102NE	BN2	311
N102P	200	BB-928
N102PC	E90	LW-149
N102PG	300	FA-19
N102PL	G1	87
N102RB	E90	LW-19
N102RC	90	LJ-147
N102RR	PC12	316
N102RS	100	B-65
N102SK	350C	FN-1
N102SL	P180	1052
N102TW	31T	7920057
(N102US)	680W	1802-24
N102VF	690D	15020
N102WB	B100	BE-50
N102WK	F90	LA-36
N102WR	200	BB-554
N103AD	300	FA-62
N103AG	441	0319
N103AL	200	BB-730
N103AL	300	FA-62
N103AL	350	FL-436
N103AL	E90	LW-176
N103AP	E90	LW-126
N103BB	MU-2	580
N103BE	350	FL-369
N103BG	200	BB-1150
N103BL	90	LJ-650
N103BN	C-12	BC-47
N103CB	F90	LA-98
N103CW	300	FA-64
N103DC	100	B-148
N103DC	200	BB-528
N103DQ	100	B-148
N103DW	200	BB-1312
N103EN	46D	207
N103FG	90	LJ-631
N103FL	90	LJ-650
N103HC	E90	LW-259
N103LC	200	BB-922
N103LC	90	LJ-892
N103MA	MU-2	179
N103NA	BN2	178
N103NE	BN2	911
N103PA	MIII	T-202
N103PB	PC12	1103
N103PM	200	BB-304
N103Q	MU-2	580
N103RB	MU-2	381SA
N103RC	MU-2	673
N103RH	100	B-8
N103RN	350	FL-231
N103SB	E90	LW-49
N103SL	P180	1059
N103SP	31T	8020024
N103TF	200	BB-649
N103TK	46D	205
(N104AG)	200	BB-80
N104AG	200	BB-1957
N104AG	441	0314
N104AJ	90	LJ-1164
N104AK	200	BB-1004
(N104AL)	MU-2	719SA
N104AW	200C	BL-3
N104AW	300	FA-6
N104BH	46T	97104
N104BR	MIII	T-269
N104CX	200	BB-1004
N104DA	MU-2	727SA
N104DT	695A	96010
N104EM	MIII	T-248
N104ET	46T	97133
N104HW	425	0094
N104JB	MU-2	435SA
(N104JM)	690B	11443
N104LC	90	LJ-757
N104LS	B100	BE-115
N104MA	MU-2	180
N104MC	31T	8104101
N104PC	BN2	198
(N104RA)	100	B-75
N104RD	441	0108
N104RF	31T	7904013
N104RG	690B	11443
(N104RG)	690B	11448
N104TA	MIII	T-289
N104TB	100	B-79
N104TM	200	BB-51
N104TT	695A	96010
N104TT	90	LJ-622
N104Z	90	LJ-472
N105AM	BN2	2210
N105AW	90	LJ-892
N105BB	MIII	T-229
N105CG	90	LJ-806
N105EC	MIIA	T26-026
N105FC	425	0094
N105FL	90	LJ-1215
N105GP	P180	1048
N105K	90	LJ-113
N105K	90	LJ-351
N105LV	PA42	5527010
N105MA	31T	8104015
N105MA	MU-2	123
N105MA	MU-2	182
N105MA	MU-2	248
N105MW	PC12	235
N105PA	200	BB-558
N105RG	90	LJ-454
N105RJ	90	LJ-454
N105SL	P180	1068
N105SS	681B	6052
N105TC	425	0205
N105TC	90	LJ-1086
N105TT	425	0033
N105VY	B100	BE-109
N105WM	MU-2	709SA
(N105WW)	E90	LW-138
N106AJ	90	LJ-1041
N106BC	441	0259
N106BQ	441	0259
N106DD	90	LJ-1738
N106DP	MU-2	571
N106EC	MIIA	T26-034
N106ER	350	FL-424
N106GA	G1	86
N106GB	200	BB-1249
N106GB	MU-2	297
N106GH	G1	86
N106MA	MU-2	184
N106ML	90	LJ-1757
N106PA	100	B-66
N106PA	200	BB-428
N106PA	200G	BY-11
(N106PC)	BN2	71
N106PC	PC12	1106
N106RH	200	BB-428
(N106SA)	690B	11484
N106SA	690B	11504
N106SB	B100	BE-135
N106SF	PC6	907
N106SL	P180	1070
N106SP	B100	BE-135
(N106TB)	E90	LW-66
N106TC	690A	11319
N106TT	690C	11630
N106WA	PC12	106
N107AB	200	BB-324
N107AJ	200	BB-630
N107AJ	F90	LA-189
N107B	E90	LW-7
N107BK	31T	7820015
N107BP	TBM7	5
N107CT	200	BB-434
N107DC	680W	1777-15
(N107DE)	PC12	463
N107EA	441	0007
N107EM	200	BB-1206
N107FL	200	BB-150
N107GA	100	B-246
N107GA	200	BB-908
N107GA	90	LJ-408
N107GH	G1	148
N107GL	690B	11554
N107JJ	690A	11209
N107K	90	LJ-911
N107MA	MU-2	185
N107MC	31T	8166032
N107MG	200	BB-924
(N107MQ)	31T	8166032
N107NX	PC12	1107
N107PC	31T	8166046
(N107RP)	TBM7	12
N107SB	MU-2	226
N107SC	90	LJ-788
N107SL	P180	1073
N107TB	E90	LW-87
N107TM	200	BB-761
N107TT	31T	8120015
N107VM	90	LJ-331
N107Z	200C	BL-124
N108AL	200	BB-730
N108BM	200	BB-108
N108EB	B100	BE-108
N108G	200	BB-611
N108GF	P180	1086
N108JC	PC12	209
N108JC	PC12	883
N108JD	90	LJ-555
N108JD	90	LJ-923
N108JL	100	B-204
N108JQ	PC12	209
N108KU	90	LJ-568
N108MA	MU-2	187
N108MA	MU-2	415SA
N108NL	31T	7920092
N108NT	350	FL-168
N108RJ	90	LJ-159
N108SA	690B	11416
N108SB	300	FA-122
N108SB	PA42	8001071
N108SC	MU-2	545
N108SL	P180	1108
N108SW	31T	8004006
N108TJ	441	0108
N108TT	90	LJ-591
N108TT	90	LJ-950
N108UC	31T	8020018
N108WT	31T	8004006
N109AF	PC12	1109
N109DS	300	FA-60
N109DT	90	LJ-1102
N109GE	200	BB-1476
(N109JB)	90	LJ-581
N109KH	90	LJ-425
N109MA	MU-2	188
N109MA	MU-2	416SA
N109MD	200	BB-1213
N109MS	P180	1008
N109NB	200	BB-1509
N109NT	200	BB-1509
N109NT	350	FL-168
N109P	G1	109
N109SL	P180	1092
N109TA	MIVC	AT-461
N109TM	200	BB-124
N109TT	31T	7920082
N109TW	MU-2	543
(N110AS)	90	LJ-17
N110BM	200	BB-110
N110BP	100	B-60
N110BS	90	LJ-375
N110CE	B100	BE-120
N110DE	31T	7620056
N110EC	90	LJ-315
N110EC	B100	BE-30
N110EL	90	LJ-71
N110G	200	BB-792
N110GA	200	BB-1110
N110GA	G1	116
N110GC	MU-2	363SA
N110GM	690A	11184
N110HC	350	FL-69
N110JJ	100	B-108
N110JK	31T	8375005
(N110JM)	TBM7	86
N110JT	425	0020
N110KA	200	BB-505
N110KF	100	B-159
N110LT	90	LJ-729
N110MA	MU-2	189
N110MA	MU-2	417SA
N110MA	MU-2	616
N110MJ	200	BB-439
N110MP	31T	7920035
N110PC	680T	1687-67
(N110PG)	681	6004
N110PM	90	LJ-1481
N110RB	G1	126
N110RF	350	FL-604
N110RF	350	FL-622
N110RK	F90	LA-28
N110RS	690C	11664
N110SC	PA42	8001101
N110SE	90	LJ-685
N110SF	90	LJ-685
N110SL	90	LJ-364
N110SM	90	LJ-425
(N110SS)	MU-2	647
N110TA	200	BB-128
N110TD	100	B-199
(N110VU)	100	B-176
N110WE	690C	11681
N111AA	90	LJ-721
N111AA	F90	LA-6
N111AB	MIII	T-407
N111AM	31T	7920066
N111AT	100	B-41
(N111BF)	31T	7520037
N111BN	BN2	525
(N111BX)	PA42	8301003
N111BX	PA42	5501003
N111CT	31T	7620047
N111CZ	MIII	T-297
N111DR	G1	66
N111DY	EPIC	011
N111EL	300	FA-144
N111EL	F90	LA-230
N111EN	F90	LA-230
N111ER	90	LJ-144
N111F	200	BB-772
N111FF	690A	11138
N111FL	690A	11163
N111FL	MIIA	T26-003
N111FN	MU-2	024
N111FV	E90	LW-105
N111FW	E90	LW-105
N111FX	PC6	701
(N111GD)	MU-2	362SA
(N111GF)	90	LJ-888
N111GK	MU-2	362SA
N111GL	MIIB	T26-165
N111GP	MU-2	260
N111GP	MU-2	425SA
N111HF	MU-2	208
N111HH	31T	7620051
N111HR	90	LJ-514
N111HT	31T	7920024
N111JA	E90	LW-45
N111JA	E90	LW-84
N111JA	E90	LW-147
N111JE	MU-2	285
N111JW	100	B-115
N111JW	200	BB-331
N111JW	200	BB-457
N111JW	200	BB-661
N111JW	200	BB-886
N111JW	200	BB-1767
N111JW	90	LJ-514

N111JW	E90	LW-4
N111JW	E90	LW-119
N111JZ	200	BB-1767
N111KA	90	LJ-256
N111KA	90	LJ-1051
N111KC	90	LJ-1258
N111KU	425	0226
N111KV	31T	7920035
N111LA	690A	11324
N111LG	MU-2	791SA
N111LP	200	BB-743
N111LP	200	BB-1900
N111LS	200	BB-124
N111LZ	200	BB-1900
N111M	200	BB-145
N111M	300	FA-90
N111M	350	FL-210
N111MA	MU-2	190
N111MD	200	BB-1665
N111MD	350	FL-547
N111MD	90	LJ-1367
N111MD	MU-2	308
N111ME	90	LJ-262
N111MK	46D	51
N111MP	441	0061
N111MQ	200	BB-1665
N111MT	200	BB-145
N111MT	MIV	AT-012
N111MT	MIVC	AT-585
N111MU	90	LJ-1367
N111MV	MIV	AT-012
N111MV	MU-2	657
N111NS	200C	BL-36
N111PC	E90	LW-101
N111PM	MIIB	T26-142
N111PM	MU-2	281
N111PT	MIIA	T26-015
N111PV	200	BB-772
N111QL	690A	11312
(N111QP)	90	LJ-728
(N111RA)	681B	6063
N111RA	681B	6063
N111RC	441	0188
N111RC	46T	97330
N111RF	31T	7520037
N111RG	681B	6063
N111RL	90	LJ-816
N111SE	MIIB	T26-163
N111SF	200	BB-324
N111SF	350	FL-45
N111SF	MIIB	T26-165
N111SK	680T	1710-85
N111SS	300	FA-4
N111ST	680T	1710-85
N111SU	425	0205
N111TB	200C	BL-31
N111TC	E90	LW-305
N111TN	46T	97236
N111UR	200	BB-374
N111US	90	LJ-455
N111UT	200	BB-374
N111UT	350	FL-576
(N111VA)	BN2	171
N111VA	BN2	215
N111VK	PC12	1118
N111VR	P180	1006
N111VS	690A	11130
N111VY	695A	96100
N111WA	200	BB-331
N111WA	90	LJ-492
N111WA	E90	LW-73
N111WB	200	BB-207
N111WB	MU-2	551
N111WE	680T	1593-41
N111WH	200	BB-207
N111WN	MU-2	551
N111XE	90	LJ-160
N111XL	90	LJ-160
N111XP	B100	BE-37
N111XT	E90	LW-101
N111YF	B100	BE-30
N112A	MIIB	T26-156
N112AB	300	FA-85
N112AF	PC12	120

N112AF	PC12	266
N112AR	E90	LW-168
(N112BB)	31T	8104021
N112BB	31T	8104021
N112BC	PA42	8001027
(N112BG)	690A	11313
N112BL	31T	7720037
N112BM	100	B-164
(N112CA)	100	B-240
N112CE	690A	11105
N112CE	695A	96097
(N112CM)	E90	LW-163
N112CS	MIII	TT-541
N112CW	MIIB	T26-142
N112CZ	441	0233
N112ED	31T	8020060
N112EF	690A	11123
N112EM	690A	11330
N112GA	690D	15032
N112GM	200	BB-457
N112HF	300	FA-122
N112J	100	B-127
N112JC	BN2	514
N112LS	E90	LW-4
N112MA	MU-2	191
N112MA	MU-2	689
N112SA	690B	11428
N112SB	E90	LW-232
N112SK	MU-2	651
N112TC	200	BB-1321
N112VA	BN2	77
N112WC	31T	8020005
N112WC	PA42	8001049
N113AP	90	LJ-898
N113BP	46D	221
N113CT	681	6006
N113GA	690D	15034
N113GA	G1	129
N113GA	MIVC	AT-495B
N113GF	350	FL-103
N113GS	MIII	T-330
N113GW	200	BB-541
(N113KA)	31T	7520009
(N113LY)	90	LJ-1921
N113MA	MU-2	192
N113MC	46D	130
*N113MH	200	BB-465
N113P	MU-2	646
N113RC	31T	7520009
N113RF	441	0156
N113RL	200	BB-133
N113SA	690B	11434
(N113SB)	E90	LW-237
(N113SB)	E90	LW-304
N113SD	90	LJ-454
N113SD	MU-2	600
(N113SF)	B100	BE-13
N113SL	P180	1020
N113T	46T	97312
N113TC	90	LJ-22
N113TP	90	LJ-1233
N113TT	90	LJ-460
N113UL	200	BB-1283
N113US	200	BB-1283
N113WC	31T	8020020
N113WC	PA42	8001005
(N113WE)	46T	97010
N114AT	E90	LW-90
N114CM	90	LJ-709
N114CW	90	LJ-114
N114CW	F90	LA-97
N114DB	90	LJ-1097
N114EA	441	0061
N114FC	90	LJ-292
N114GA	G1	27
N114HB	200	BB-1533
N114HL	425	0110
N114J	90	LJ-713
(N114JB)	350	FL-57
N114JF	200	BB-237
N114JR	31T	8004037
N114K	E90	LW-122
N114K	E90	LW-157
N114KA	90	LJ-114

N114MA	MU-2	193
N114MA	MU-2	641
N114MR	681	6020
N114NB	90	LJ-689
N114PA	MIII	T-254
N114RG	350	FL-512
N114SA	690B	11437
N114SB	200	BB-161
N114SV	90	LJ-311
N114SV	PC12	114
N114WA	E90	LW-346
N115AB	690A	11231
N115AP	MU-2	136
N115BH	690A	11231
*N115BM	31T	8120053
N115CM	200	BB-663
N115CT	200	BB-1669
N115CW	690A	11107
N115D	100	B-212
N115D	200	BB-925
N115DT	100	B-212
N115DW	BN2	457
(N115GA)	695A	96090
N115GA	695B	96201
N115GB	350	FL-237
N115KC	TBM7	239
N115KU	90	LJ-1040
N115MA	MU-2	194
N115MX	200	BB-1299
N115MX	90	LJ-1040
N115MX	90	LJ-1203
N115MZ	90	LJ-1203
N115PA	90	LJ-117
N115PC	31T	7820001
N115RA	200	BB-325
N115S	MU-2	518
(N115S)	MU-2	529
N115SA	690B	11440
(N115SB)	200	BB-917
N115SB	690B	11452
N115TT	200	BB-107
N115TT	350	FL-74
N115YS	E90	LW-126
N116AC	B100	BE-116
N116AF	PC12	137
N116DG	B100	BE-116
N116DW	BN2	202
N116GA	G1	2
(N116GR)	200	BB-643
N116JP	PA42	8001050
N116K	G1	100
N116KA	100	B-247
N116KJ	G1	100
N116MA	MU-2	196
(N116MS)	PA42	8001049
N116PA	200	BB-461
N116RJ	100	B-96
N116SA	690B	11443
N116SK	PC12	116
N116SP	C-12	BC-42
N116TH	PC12	860
N116TX	200	BB-1685
N116VL	TBM7	116
N117AS	200	BB-806
(N117BL)	31T	7520009
N117CA	200	BB-873
N117CC	MIII	T-325
(N117CM)	100	B-243
N117CM	200	BB-747
N117CP	U-21	LM-68
N117D	90	LJ-1021
N117DR	300	FA-140
N117EA	441	0191
N117EB	31T	7920024
(N117EE)	425	0013
N117EP	B100	BE-24
N117EW	31T	7920024
N117FH	E90	LW-194
N117FN	31T	7920061
N117FS	B100	BE-70
N117GA	G1	83
(N117GM)	31T	8166043
N117H	MU-2	751SA
(N117HP)	90	LJ-1345

N117HR	MU-2	459SA
N117JM	F90	LA-196
N117K	90	LJ-113
N117KL	90	LJ-113
N117MA	MU-2	197
N117MC	100	B-190
N117MC	BN2	2178
N117MF	90	LJ-779
N117NJ	46D	50
N117NU	46D	50
N117PA	200	BB-557
N117PB	MIII	T-278
N117PW	46T	97030
N117PZ	PC12	1117
N117S	200	BB-784
N117SA	690B	11446
N117SA	PC6	778
N117SB	31T	8020052
N117SH	100	B-94
N117TJ	F90	LA-17
N117TP	200	BB-117
N117TS	441	0351
N117VA	90	LJ-381
N117W	F90	LA-20
N117WD	200	BB-370
N117WF	PC12	117
N117WM	200	BB-662
N117WR	31T	8004033
(N117WT)	46T	97158
N118AF	PC12	175
N118AG	46D	56
N118AP	PC12	175
N118BR	MIII	T-360
N118BW	31T	8004001
N118CA	C-12	BC-57
N118CD	MU-2	198
(N118CD)	PC12	508
N118CR	690A	11276
N118DW	BN2	239
N118EA	441	0198
N118EL	31T	8020065
N118GW	300	FA-119
N118HB	31T	8004052
N118HC	90	LJ-648
N118JG	46D	220
N118JV	46T	97235
N118LT	G1	55
N118MA	MU-2	198
N118MB	90	LJ-1470
N118MF	90	LJ-1383
N118MJ	F90	LA-199
N118NL	B100	BE-111
N118P	MU-2	646
N118RB	MU-2	198
N118SA	690B	11449
N118SA	690C	11618
(N118SB)	E90	LW-298
N118TS	441	0351
N118WC	31T	8020005
N118WC	31T	8020020
N118X	G1	28
N119AF	PC12	215
N119AR	200	BB-1867
N119BF	MU-2	517
N119CP	46D	43
N119DW	BN2	243
N119EB	31T	7720012
N119FJ	F90	LA-70
N119GA	695A	96091
N119JE	BN2	171
N119LW	90	LJ-595
N119MA	MU-2	199
N119MC	200	BB-572
N119MC	200	BB-1225
N119RL	31T	7904002
N119SA	690B	11452
N119SA	690C	11624
N119SA	90	LJ-1196
N119SA	PC6	779
N119TP	46T	97386
N119WM	200	BB-662
N120AJ	200	BB-1144
N120AS	100	B-153
N120CJ	PC12	612

N120DA	200	BB-123
N120DP	200	BB-27
N120DP	90	LJ-69
(N120DS)	MIII	T-325
N120DW	BN2	232
(N120EA)	441	0183
N120EK	690D	15026
N120ET	31T	8004020
N120FN	200	BB-562
N120FS	200	BB-562
N120FS	200	BB-1843
N120FS	MIIB	T26-172
N120FW	46D	49
N120GA	200	BB-501
N120GA	695A	96062
N120GA	PA42	5501057
N120GR	E90	LW-61
N120GS	PC12	1120
N120GW	MIIB	T26-177
N120HC	G1	132
N120JJ	90	LJ-534
N120JM	90	LJ-125
N120JM	MIVC	AT-577
N120K	200	BB-485
N120LG	90	LJ-339
N120MA	MU-2	205
N120MG	B100	BE-70
N120NA	200	BB-1120
N120P	200	BB-786
N120PA	P180	1039
N120PR	200T	BT-29
N120RC	F90	LA-117
N120RJ	200	BB-423
N120RL	200T	BT-9
N120RL	90	LJ-1148
N120RP	90	LJ-1075
N120S	G1	26
N120S	G1	148
N120S	MU-2	519
(N120S)	MU-2	530
N120SC	MIVA	AT-067
N120SK	31T	8166039
N120SK	350	FL-1
N120SL	46T	97057
N120TC	31T	8166016
N120TD	FPC6	2005
N120TM	MIII	T-405
N120TT	90	LJ-1073
N120TT	MIII	T-248
N120VE	200	BB-105
N120WW	46T	97047
N121AB	680W	1776-14
N121B	E90	LW-21
N121BA	MU-2	599
N121BE	31T	8004036
N121CA	C-12	BD-9
N121CH	MU-2	265
N121CS	PA42	8001032
N121DA	200	BB-57
(N121DK)	690A	11299
N121DP	MIVA	AT-068
N121DW	BN2	312
(N121EB)	90	LJ-1372
N121EB	90	LJ-1534
N121EG	E90	LW-71
N121EH	31T	8166039
N121FA	MIVC	AT-493
N121FM	690A	11257
(N121GV)	STAR	NC-29
N121GW	E90	LW-123
N121HC	90	LJ-392
N121JW	690A	11206
N121JW	690A	11299
N121JW	MU-2	193
N121KB	MIIA	T26-033
N121L	MU-2	026
(N121LA)	695	95018
N121LB	200	BB-475
N121LH	31T	8166039
N121LH	PA42	5501049
N121MA	46T	97406
N121MA	MU-2	206
N121ML	690B	11526
N121MT	BN2T	880

N121NC	G1	44
N121P	90	LJ-970
N121PH	PC12	186
N121RF	46D	18
N121RF	PC12	114
N121RH	300	FA-84
N121RL	90	LJ-1139
N121RP	46D	18
N121SF	MU-2	135
N121SP	681B	6047
N121TD	C-12	BC-74
N121WH	P180	1019
(N122AS)	90	LJ-55
N122AV	690A	11235
N122BC	200	BB-444
N122BN	425	0203
N122BW	E90	LW-329
N122CK	MU-2	374SA
N122CP	MU-2	629
N122DM	31T	8104071
N122DW	BN2	234
N122EL	31T	8020003
N122G	MU-2	033
N122GA	F90	LA-84
N122H	100	B-32
N122H	200	BB-1370
N122HC	E90	LW-145
(N122K)	690A	11248
N122K	90	LJ-707
N122LA	690A	11290
N122LC	200	BB-1490
(N122LM)	31T	8104071
N122MA	MU-2	207
N122MD	425	0200
N122MM	E90	LW-329
N122NC	E90	LW-125
N122NK	MIIB	T26-108
N122NM	680W	1775-13
N122NN	E90	LW-125
N122PA	P180	1038
N122PA	P180	1043
N122PG	690A	11123
N122RF	200	BB-122
N122RG	350	FL-448
(N122RG)	90	LJ-746
N122SA	690B	11471
(N122SC)	200	BB-423
N122SC	F90	LA-158
N122SR	46D	11
N122TJ	200	BB-122
N122TM	46D	204
N122TP	200	BB-1293
N122U	100	B-32
N122WD	46D	84
N122Y	G1	128
N122ZZ	100	B-6
N123A	200	BB-85
N123AC	200	BB-1605
N123AD	46T	97017
N123AF	200	BB-616
N123AF	300	FA-46
N123AG	PA42	8001031
N123AT	31T	8104055
N123AT	90	LJ-1224
N123AX	MU-2	220
N123BG	MU-2	536
N123BL	B100	BE-83
N123CF	690	11069
N123CF	PC12	286
N123CH	F90	LA-32
N123CN	PA42	8001031
N123CS	100	B-157
N123D	200	BB-1219
N123DE	31T	7820056
N123DG	31T	7820056
N123EA	200	BB-1219
N123EA	31T	7920028
(N123FF)	31T	7904053
N123G	690A	11225
N123GM	F90	LA-158
N123GM	MIII	TT-512A
N123GS	MU-2	211
N123GT	681	6014
N123HK	31T	7920001

N123JA	MU-2	220
N123JA	MU-2	366SA
N123JA	MU-2	614
N123JB	90	LJ-41
N123JM	MU-2	366SA
N123JS	MU-2	561
(N123K)	441	0188
N123KA	90	LJ-189
N123LA	695	95018
(N123LC)	31T	7820026
N123LH	MIII	TT-433
N123LL	90	LJ-885
N123LN	E90	LW-271
N123LV	31T	7520014
N123MA	MU-2	208
N123ME	200	BB-1299
N123ME	441	0359
N123ME	90	LJ-1121
N123MH	E90	LW-104
N123ML	200	BB-1299
N123ML	200	BB-1587
N123ML	90	LJ-1121
(N123MZ)	695	95074
N123NA	200	BB-1734
N123NA	90	LJ-150
N123NA	90	LJ-1006
N123NE	BN2	46
N123NP	BN2	597
N123NX	PC12	1123
(N123PE)	200	BB-603
N123PM	200	BB-248
N123PP	90	LJ-53
N123PP	E90	LW-32
N123PW	200T	BT-18
(N123RC)	695	95007
N123RF	350	FL-589
N123SA	200	BB-1497
N123SC	425	0117
N123SK	90	LJ-540
N123SR	200	BB-624
N123ST	100	B-70
N123ST	200	BB-149
N123SX	46T	97050
N123TF	46D	10
N123TS	46T	97219
N123UA	MU-2	220
N123V	90	LJ-258
N123VC	MU-2	214
N123WH	B100	BE-126
N123WN	200	BB-801
N123WR	441	0041
N123YV	200	BB-123
N123ZC	TBM7	229
N123ZY	46D	10
N123ZZ	MIII	T-381
(N124AA)	31T	7620033
N124AJ	200	BB-124
N124AR	200	BB-1976
N124AX	MU-2	428SA
N124BB	200	BB-456
N124BB	300	FA-2
N124BB	350	FL-8
N124BK	F90	LA-15
N124BW	PC12	124
N124CM	300	FA-24
N124CM	B100	BE-115
N124CN	B100	BE-115
N124CS	200	BB-970
N124DA	350	FL-228
N124DF	31T	8104023
N124DP	31T	8104023
N124DP	PA42	5527018
N124EB	350	FL-126
N124EK	200	BB-1993
N124EL	PA42	8001001
N124EU	200	BB-1993
(N124GA)	200	BB-728
N124GA	200	BB-1039
N124H	690A	11162
N124HQ	690A	11162
N124J	90	LJ-155
N124JS	200C	BL-64
N124LL	90	LJ-1695
N124MA	MU-2	209

N124MB	90	LJ-1088
N124MK	PC12	322
N124PA	P180	1046
N124PA	P180	1122
N124PB	PC12	124
N124PC	PC12	217
N124PS	MIIB	T26-135
N124PS	PC12	502
N124RC	90	LJ-1125
N124SA	690B	11477
N124SA	90	LJ-306
N124SB	690A	11178
N124SC	200	BB-1467
(N124TS)	PA42	8001001
N124UV	PC12	124
N124WS	PA42	5501009
N125A	90	LJ-360
N125AB	MU-2	1531SA
(N125AR)	90	LJ-1655
N125AR	90	LJ-1790
N125BJ	200	BB-350
N125BK	200	BB-977
N125BP	PC12	1012
N125CU	200	BB-1255
N125D	B100	BE-114
N125DB	100	B-87
N125DC	695	95058
N125EL	PA42	5527015
N125GA	200	BB-1252
N125JB	200	BB-960
(N125JD)	300	FA-81
N125JL	BN2	60
N125KW	200	BB-939
N125L	E90	LW-276
N125MA	MU-2	210
N125MM	690C	11605
N125MS	200	BB-350
N125NC	200	BB-1023
N125PG	425	0125
N125RG	MIII	TT-441
N125RP	300	FA-95
N125SC	425	0136
N125TE	200	BB-1422
N125TS	200	BB-1422
N125TS	200	BB-1993
N125TS	F90	LA-182
N125U	B100	BE-25
N125VE	425	0125
N125VH	B100	BE-25
N125WG	MIII	T-250
N125WZ	46T	97032
N126AB	MU-2	139
N126AP	200	BB-1157
(N126AT)	90	LJ-265
N126BK	PC12	696
N126C	90	LJ-205
N126DS	350	FL-31
N126GH	PC12	369
N126HU	B100	BE-115
N126J	G1	33
N126JH	200	BB-595
N126JL	BN2	64
N126JW	681	6016
N126K	G1	138
N126KA	200	BB-1222
N126M	695	95033
N126MA	MU-2	211
N126MM	90	LJ-1669
N126PA	P180	1036
N126PA	P180	1057
N126PA	P180	1065
N126RD	E90	LW-230
N126RL	90	LJ-1151
N126SA	690B	11481
N126SP	200	BB-1209
N126SR	46D	23
N126TS	PC12	1111
N126WA	90	LJ-1093
N127	E90	LW-202
N127AA	690B	11403
N127AP	200	BB-658
N127AT	31T	8120022
N127AX	MU-2	434SA
N127BB	300	FA-196

N127BB	425	0012
N127BB	E90	LW-299
N127BJ	MU-2	730SA
N127DC	425	0012
(N127DC)	425	0184
N127DC	F90	LA-177
N127EC	E90	LW-299
N127GA	200	BB-312
N127GA	695A	96092
N127GP	31T	8166005
N127HT	90	LJ-215
N127JL	BN2	69
N127LB	TRIS	1010
N127MA	MU-2	212
N127MC	425	0231
N127MJ	200	BB-1132
N127P	90	LJ-687
N127PE	PC12	1127
(N127RM)	MU-2	384SA
(N127RS)	90	LJ-184
N127SA	690B	11486
N127SD	200	BB-1099
N127TA	200	BB-636
N127TT	200	BB-330
N127WD	MIII	T-297
N127Z	100	B-179
N127ZW	90	LJ-1369
N128AS	200	BB-1950
N128CM	PC12	403
N128DW	BN2	249
N128EZ	441	0128
N128F	100	B-127
N128FL	350	FL-128
N128JA	MU-2	614
N128JL	BN2	77
N128JP	F90	LA-25
N128JV	90	LJ-1520
N128L	100	B-3
(N128MA)	MU-2	213
N128MA	MU-2	213
(N128MG)	350	FL-182
N128PA	P180	1013
N128PA	P180	1044
N128PA	P180	1059
N128PC	TBM7	128
N128RC	100	B-3
(N128SA)	690B	11493
N128SB	90	LJ-1503
N128SL	P180	1011
N128ST	100	B-70
N128TJ	200C	BL-128
N128V	200	BB-1442
N128VT	200	BB-1442
N129AF	G1	129
N129AG	TBM7	171
N129C	E90	LW-61
N129CC	31T	8120029
N129CP	B100	BE-39
N129D	100	B-134
N129D	200	BB-1064
N129DB	200	BB-981
N129DH	PC12	140
N129DP	200	BB-1064
N129DW	MU-2	653
N129EJ	46T	97065
N129GA	695A	96093
N129GP	90	LJ-216
N129GP	90	LJ-306
N129JS	F90	LA-231
N129JW	PC12	129
N129LA	90	LJ-129
N129LC	31T	7904042
N129MA	MU-2	214
N129NX	PC12	1129
N129P	200	BB-981
N129PA	P180	1051
N129PA	P180	1061
N129RP	90	LJ-1075
N129RW	90	LJ-369
N129SP	BN2	857
N129TB	690C	11676
N129TT	200	BB-1078
N130A	31T	8104058
N130A	G1	36
N130AT	B100	BE-88
N130AV	P180	1011
N130B	G1	37
N130CC	31T	8104038
N130CT	200	BB-578
N130DM	90	LJ-385
N130EM	P180	1063
N130G	G1	37
N130GA	690C	11734
N130JL	BN2	239
N130LP	200	BB-276
N130MA	90	LJ-1075
N130MA	MU-2	511
(N130MA)	MU-2	533
N130MS	MU-2	750SA
N130PA	200	BB-330
N130PC	BN2	417
N130PC	MIII	T-238
N130RL	200T	BT-16
N130S	E90	LW-104
N130S	E90	LW-228
N130SB	E90	LW-104
N130SC	200C	BL-130
N130SL	P180	1084
N130TJ	200C	BL-130
N130TT	681B	6052
N130TT	690B	11495
N131AF	31T	7820005
N131BP	200	BB-1336
N131CC	31T	8120042
N131CD	F90	LA-82
N131CL	90	LJ-1268
N131CR	90	LJ-1268
N131DF	31T	7904015
N131GA	200	BB-1418
N131GA	695A	96094
N131HF	300	FA-131
N131JL	BN2	225
N131JN	690A	11227
N131JN	PC12	446
N131KS	690D	15002
N131LB	200	BB-1042
N131MA	MU-2	502
N131MB	200	BB-193
N131MP	31T	7820039
N131PA	200	BB-161
N131PC	31T	7820009
N131PT	31T	7400002
N131RC	31T	7620021
N131RC	PA42	8001006
N131RG	31T	7620021
N131SA	690B	11498
N131SA	90	LJ-1318
N131SA	MU-2	417SA
N131SJ	200	BB-131
N131SL	P180	1097
N131SP	F90	LA-206
N131SW	31T	7904004
N131T	200	BB-746
N131TC	200	BB-271
N131TC	31T	7920081
N131XL	31T	8166015
N132AS	90	LJ-928
N132AS	F90	LA-13
N132AT	680T	1620-51
(N132AZ)	200	BB-1340
N132B	E90	LW-8
N132BK	MU-2	1529SA
N132CC	300	FA-11
N132CC	31T	8166008
N132CW	MIII	T-276
N132DD	E90	LW-308
N132GA	200	BB-588
N132GA	200	BB-651
N132GA	695A	96095
N132HS	E90	LW-8
N132JH	690A	11126
N132JL	BN2	224
N132K	200	BB-938
N132MA	MU-2	503
N132MC	200	BB-1395
N132N	200	BB-1053
N132PR	695A	96021
N132RD	690A	11221
N132S	E90	LW-228
N132SL	P180	1098
N132TA	MIII	T-269
N132TJ	300C	FM-12
N133BB	MIVA	AT-032
N133BC	200	BB-711
N133CZ	PC12	133
N133DL	690C	11616
N133E	90	LJ-759
N133FM	PA42	8001010
N133GA	200	BB-433
N133GA	200	BB-1321
(N133GA)	695A	96096
(N133GA)	B100	BE-59
N133K	200	BB-1487
N133K	90	LJ-759
N133K	E90	LW-70
N133LA	90	LJ-537
N133LC	200	BB-1464
N133LJ	200	BB-1137
N133MA	MU-2	506
N133N	PC12	652
N133NL	350	FL-332
N133PA	P180	1048
N133PA	P180	1062
N133PL	E90	LW-104
N133RS	BN2	606
N133US	200C	BL-133
N133WW	46D	173
N134AM	300	FA-134
N134CA	90	LJ-17
N134CC	31T	8104057
N134EC	P180	1160
N134G	46T	97041
N134G	MIIB	T26-134
N134GA	695A	96097
N134KA	46T	97134
N134KM	PA42	7801003
N134M	46T	97169
N134MA	MU-2	507
N134PA	G1	196
N134PA	P180	1050
N134SL	P180	1100
N134W	90	LJ-52
(N134WJ)	200C	BL-134
N134WJ	200C	BL-134
N135AA	90	LJ-1112
N135AR	B100	BE-135
N135CC	46D	78
N135CL	31T	7720019
N135FL	46T	97135
N135GA	695A	96098
(N135JA)	90	LJ-944
N135JM	46T	97072
N135MA	31T	8020025
N135MA	MU-2	508
N135MK	300	FA-3
(N135NK)	90	LJ-2
N135SP	MIIB	T26-111
N135SR	MIIB	T26-172E
*N136AJ	200C	BL-136
N136AR	695	95025
N136BL	200C	BL-136
N136CC	31T	8104101
N136CP	441	0022
N136EK	MIIA	T26-018
(N136GA)	690D	15045
N136J	90	LJ-373
N136JC	AASI	003
N136JH	100	B-25
N136K	E90	LW-257
N136LE	MIIA	T26-018
N136LK	MIIA	T26-018
N136MA	MU-2	509
N136MB	B100	BE-50
N136PA	90	LJ-662
N136PA	P180	1055
N136PA	P180	1092
N136PE	PC12	1136
N136PS	MIIB	T26-103
N136SL	P180	1101
N136SP	31T	8166001
N136SP	MIIB	T26-103
N137AL	F90	LA-218
N137B	90	LJ-562
N137BW	690B	11446
N137C	G1	93
N137CD	425	0220
N137CP	MIIB	T26-136
N137CW	31T	7904052
N137D	B100	BE-128
(N137GA)	695A	96099
N137JE	31T	8020014
N137JP	F90	LA-218
N137JT	31T	8020014
N137KM	46T	97091
N137MA	MU-2	510
N137MW	BN2	137
N137PA	P180	1054
N137PA	P180	1063
N137RD	MIIA	T26-021
N137SG	PC12	137
N137SL	P180	1102
N138AJ	200	BB-1138
N138BC	C-12	BC-22
(N138CC)	200	BB-246
N138CC	350	FL-575
N138GA	E90	LW-276
N138JH	200	BB-1313
N138JM	TBM7	7
N138LW	BN2	138
N138MA	MU-2	512
N138PC	BN2	490
*N138RB	F90	LA-111
N138SL	P180	1103
N138TA	31T	8104068
N139B	90	LJ-563
N139BN	BN2	139
N139BT	BN2	139
N139CS	31T	8120004
N139F	MIII	TT-534
N139KC	46T	97039
N139MA	MU-2	513
N139ML	441	0176
N139PA	P180	1052
N139PA	P180	1133
N139SC	90	LJ-868
N139SL	P180	1104
N139X	MIII	TT-534
N140A	G1	140
N140AE	350	FL-445
N140BR	441	0203
N140CA	690B	11563
N140CB	441	0240
N140CM	MU-2	190
N140CN	90	LJ-205
N140CP	MU-2	362SA
N140DR	441	0203
N140FS	BN2	170
N140GA	200	BB-715
N140GL	90	LJ-277
N140MA	MU-2	418SA
N140MA	MU-2	514
N140MP	441	0165
N140MT	C-12	BD-3
N140NT	G1	43
N140PA	90	LJ-297
N140RL	200T	BT-22
N140S	200	BB-148
N140SL	P180	1107
N140SP	90	LJ-890
N140TT	90	LJ-1111
(N140WJ)	690C	11660
N140WT	350	FL-140
(N141BB)	200	BB-457
N141BL	PC12	141
N141CE	350	FL-387
N141CT	200	BB-651
N141DA	350	FL-92
N141DA	E90	LW-146
N141DR	350	FL-92
N141DS	MIII	T-366
N141DT	31T	7920002
N141DZ	P750	150
N141GA	31T	8004022
N141GS	200C	BL-3
N141GS	MIII	T-366
N141JW	F90	LA-172

N141K	350	FL-161
N141L	350	FL-524
N141MA	MU-2	515
N141RR	90	LJ-38
N141SM	300	FA-23
N141TA	441	0138
(N141TA)	BN2	11
N141TC	31T	8020053
N141TC	PA42	5501021
N141VY	PC12	256
N142BK	MU-2	733SA
N142CD	PA42	8001021
N142CE	350	FL-391
N142EB	200	BB-1042
N142EE	46T	97217
(N142GA)	200	BB-828
N142GT	200G	BY-42
N142JC	B100	BE-93
N142LM	90	LJ-28
N142LT	PC12	312
N142MA	MU-2	516
(N142NA)	200	BB-1242
N142NR	MIII	T-227
N142PC	PA42	7801003
(N142PC)	PA42	5501007
N142SR	200	BB-380
N142TG	G1	142
N142TW	PA42	8001070
N142TW	PA42	5501007
N142WJ	441	0142
N143AU	P750	125
N143BW	BN2	239
N143CE	350	FL-91
N143CP	200	BB-129
N143DE	200	BB-585
N143DK	350	FL-309
N143FS	BN2	685
N143JA	MU-2	324
N143KB	90	LJ-339
N143LG	200C	BL-5
N143MA	MU-2	517
N143PA	P180	1069
N143PA	P180	1095
N143PA	P180	1173
N143PC	BN2	557
N143RJ	31T	7720027
N143SL	P180	1109
N143TR	TRIS	1043
N144AB	300	FA-176
N144C	200	BB-1013
N144JB	690D	15039
N144JT	TBM7	144
N144K	200	BB-481
N144MA	MU-2	518
(N144MC)	PA42	5527014
N144MF	PC12	828
N144NK	G1	63
N144PA	P180	1161
N144PC	PC12	154
N144PL	31T	8020056
N144PL	PA42	5527014
N144RL	31T	8020056
(N144SL)	90	LJ-501
N144TM	200	BB-821
(N144WA)	90	LJ-696
N145AF	90	LJ-1721
N145AJ	200	BB-1501
N145CA	PA42	8001022
N145CE	200	BB-490
N145DC	350	FL-89
N145DP	46T	97166
N145FS	MU-2	437SA
N145GS	P180	1145
N145JP	200	BB-818
N145LG	200	BB-1069
N145MA	MU-2	519
N145MC	200	BB-107
N145MJ	C-12	BC-24
N145MR	F90	LA-125
N145NA	300	FA-145
N145SL	P180	1093
(N145TP)	46T	97167
N146A	BN2	338
N146AW	C-12	BJ-15
N146B	90	LJ-564
N146BC	200	BB-885
N146BK	P68	158
N146BT	B100	BE-46
N146D	F90	LA-206
N146E	680T	1544-8
N146EA	441	0146
N146FL	F90	LA-59
N146FW	425	0146
N146GA	425	0074
N146GS	46D	22
N146GW	425	0146
N146MA	MU-2	521
N146MD	200	BB-886
N146MH	200	BB-885
N146PA	P180	1182
N146PA	P180	1192
N146PC	PC12	146
N146PM	46D	108
(N146RT)	90	LJ-1655
N146SB	200	BB-1419
N146SL	P180	1091
N146ST	46D	200
N146TR	TRIS	1046
N147AA	200	BB-1403
N147AP	200	BB-251
N147BK	46D	91
N147CA	300	FA-25
N147CC	300	FA-25
N147D	200	BB-1102
(N147DA)	690A	11185
N147E	E90	LW-35
N147GA	200	BB-1123
N147K	200	BB-403
N147MA	MU-2	522
N147NA	200	BB-1047
N147PE	PC12	1100
N147PZ	PC12	1147
N147RP	695A	96099
N147SL	P180	1083
N147TA	90	LJ-1553
N147TC	31T	8020053
N147VC	200	BB-1350
N148A	BN2	342
N148AA	300C	FM-12
N148CA	PA42	8001046
N148CP	200	BB-129
N148ES	BN2	685
N148GA	441	0148
N148M	300	FA-209
N148MA	MU-2	523
N148PC	PC12	148
N148X	90	LJ-284
N148Z	90	LJ-472
N149A	BN2	339
N149BC	31T	7720060
N149CC	300	FA-145
N149CC	31T	7904036
N149CF	90	LJ-925
N149CM	90	LJ-1184
N149DL	PC12	1049
N149GA	200	BB-840
N149JA	MU-2	402SA
(N149KA)	100	B-149
N149KA	350	FL-149
N149MA	MU-2	524
N149SB	200	BB-1572
N149SL	P180	1077
N149SR	200	BB-1572
N149X	G1	145
N149Z	200C	BL-124
(N150AC)	31T	8004021
N150BA	200T	BT-29
N150BA	F90	LA-159
N150BA	MU-2	718SA
N150BC	31T	8104045
N150BZ	F90	LA-159
N150GA	200	BB-864
N150GW	90	LJ-1531
N150GX	350	FL-592
N150MA	MU-2	525
N150MX	PC12	580
N150PB	PC12	150
N150RC	31T	1166008
N150RH	200	BB-948
N150RL	200C	BL-50
N150SL	P180	1111
N150SP	690B	11555
N150TH	90	LJ-996
N150TJ	B100	BE-3
N150TK	31T	1166008
N150TW	E90	LW-50
N150VE	90	LJ-678
N150W	690	11006
N150YA	B100	BE-124
N150YR	B100	BE-124
N150YR	B100	BE-132
N151A	100	B-174
N151BG	200	BB-1381
N151BU	90	LJ-183
(N151CC)	31T	8120054
N151CF	200	BB-1551
N151E	100	B-143
N151E	200	BB-371
N151E	350	FL-298
N151EL	200	BB-371
N151FB	31T	8166061
N151GA	425	0102
N151GS	31T	8020024
N151JB	MU-2	104
N151JL	90	LJ-1372
N151MA	MU-2	527
N151MP	31T	8166063
N151PB	PC12	151
N151PC	PA42	8001009
N151TC	31T	8166061
N151U	100	B-143
N151WT	200	BB-1151
N151XX	PA42	8001011
N152AL	46T	97182
N152BK	MU-2	1537SA
N152C	200	BB-1132
N152CC	31T	8120066
N152CC	31T	8120101
N152D	E90	LW-119
N152L	PC6	554
N152MA	MU-2	528
N152PC	PC12	552
N152RP	200	BB-1255
N152SL	P180	1014
N152SR	G1	122
N152TW	200	BB-152
N152WC	200	BB-744
N152WE	F90	LA-152
N152WR	200	BB-260
N152WW	90	LJ-654
N152X	100	B-12
N152X	690C	11692
N153A	BN2	341
N153D	200	BB-1026
N153D	200	BB-1087
N153GA	200	BB-1143
N153GC	200	BB-1087
N153JA	100	B-53
N153JM	425	0153
N153JW	100	B-53
N153L	PC6	576
N153MA	MU-2	419SA
N153MA	MU-2	529
N153ML	200	BB-23
N153PB	PC12	153
N153PE	300	FA-133
N153PM	90	LJ-876
N153SL	P180	1054
N153SR	G1	122
N153TC	100	B-247
N153TC	46T	97307
N153TG	G1	153
N154AJ	F90	LA-163
N154BA	200	BB-599
N154BB	200	BB-748
N154BN	BN2	154
N154CA	31T	8020017
N154CA	31T	8020085
N154DE	200	BB-1649
N154DF	200	BB-1649
N154DF	PC12	601
N154DR	46T	97034
N154L	MIII	T-284
N154MA	MU-2	420SA
N154MA	MU-2	530
N154MF	MU-2	024
N154NS	G1	132
N154PA	P180	1183
N154PC	200	BB-748
N154PC	300	FA-82
N154RH	G1	132
N154SR	G1	132
N154TC	100	B-239
N154WC	MU-2	509
N155A	90	LJ-1257
(N155AM)	MIII	T-363
N155AS	MU-2	589
N155AV	200	BB-1216
N155BA	MU-2	582
N155BM	300	FA-155
N155BM	46T	97053
N155BT	200	BB-182
N155CA	31T	7820024
N155CG	E90	LW-40
N155DS	31T	8020026
N155GA	F90	LA-155
N155GB	90	LJ-1107
N155LS	E90	LW-286
N155MA	MU-2	014
N155MA	MU-2	531
N155MC	31T	7820069
N155NA	200	BB-1155
N155NK	90	LJ-2
N155PM	TBM8	461
N155PT	100	B-73
N155PT	200	BB-182
N155QS	200	BB-79
(N155RG)	90	LJ-1009
N155RG	90	LJ-1219
N155RG	90	LJ-1782
N155RJ	200	BB-79
N155S	90	LJ-14
N155SL	P180	1013
N155T	100	B-73
N155T	G1	145
N155TA	690A	11155
N155V	200	BB-1452
N155VV	P750	155
N155WC	200	BB-79
N155WC	MU-2	515
N155WP	690C	11649
(N156CC)	425	0156
N156CH	300	FA-188
N156G	690A	11269
N156GA	425	0134
N156MA	MU-2	423SA
N156MA	MU-2	532
N156MG	90	LJ-1615
N156SB	PC12	156
N156SC	90	LJ-689
N156SE	46T	97156
N156SL	P180	1115
N156SW	PC12	514
N156WC	200	BB-430
N157A	200C	BL-53
N157AF	MU-2	157
N157CA	90	LJ-107
N157CA	MU-2	1558SA
N157CB	90	LJ-758
N157CG	MU-2	157
N157EA	90	LJ-1757
N157GA	MU-2	1536SA
N157JB	TBM7	6
N157LL	PA42	8001058
N157MA	MU-2	424SA
N157MA	MU-2	533
N157PA	P180	1072
N157SL	P180	1116
N157TA	690A	11102
N157WC	G1	139
(N157WP)	MU-2	157
N158A	BN2	333
N158CA	MIIB	T26-107
N158CA	PA42	8001053
N158D	E90	LW-123
N158EF	200	BB-1158

N158G	90	LJ-98
N158GD	90	LJ-98
N158J	90	LJ-1859
N158LM	200	BB-1143
N158MA	BN2	128
N158MA	MU-2	534
N158MH	PA42	5527006
N158SL	P180	1119
N158SP	BN2	252
N158TJ	200	BB-1158
N158TJ	PA42	8001057
N159AG	200C	BL-15
N159AJ	G1	5
N159AN	G1	116
N159B	E90	LW-30
N159DG	31T	7920024
N159G	90	LJ-643
N159GL	PC12	266
N159GS	G1	200
N159JB	350	FL-57
(N159KK)	G1	156
N159MA	MU-2	425SA
N159MA	MU-2	535
N159PB	PC12	159
N159RS	MU-2	535
N159SL	P180	1121
N160AB	300	FA-216
N160AC	200	BB-919
N160AC	300	FA-216
N160AC	350	FL-154
N160AC	350	FL-215
N160AC	350	FL-367
N160AC	90	LJ-743
N160AD	200	BB-919
N160AD	200G	BY-42
N160AR	350	FL-154
N160EA	MIIB	T26-165
N160G	690A	11135
N160H	90	LJ-492
N160MA	MU-2	536
N160MW	350	FL-407
N160NA	31T	7720060
N160PC	PC12	160
N160S	F90	LA-38
N160SF	200	BB-32
N160SL	P180	1127
N160SM	350	FL-215
N160SN	MIIB	T26-102
N160SP	MU-2	1506SA
N160TR	31T	7920036
(N160TT)	200	BB-1099
N160TT	E90	LW-309
N160WJ	200	BB-160
N161A	200	BB-1354
N161A	BN2	340
N161AC	90	LJ-743
N161AJ	PC12	161
N161G	690A	11296
N161GC	200	BB-1160
N161JB	690A	11249
N161MA	MU-2	426SA
N161MA	MU-2	537
N161MP	31T	7820061
N161PA	200	BB-195
N161PA	P180	1154
N161RC	200	BB-1356
N161RS	MIII	T-341
N161SL	P180	1128
N161TC	31T	8166038
N161WC	690A	11271
N161WC	MU-2	581
N161X	680T	1703-79
N161X	690A	11296
N161XX	31T	7920016
N161XX	680T	1703-79
N162E	200	BB-1278
N162GC	200	BB-1238
N162MA	MU-2	538
(N162PA)	200	BB-201
N162PA	200	BB-232
N162PB	PC12	162
N162PM	31T	8166051
N162Q	200	BB-1104
N162RB	681B	6051
N162SL	P180	1130
N163AJ	F90	LA-163
N163BA	300	FA-18
N163D	680T	1701-77
N163JS	200	BB-1670
N163MA	MU-2	539
N163MC	31T	7920044
N163ME	690A	11254
N163NP	PC12	1163
N163PA	200	BB-201
(N163PA)	200	BB-232
N163SA	31T	7920025
N163SL	P180	1131
N164A	BN2	337
N164AB	200	BB-400
N164AH	MU-2	540
N164BD	MU-2	540
N164BT	MIIB	T26-164
N164DB	46T	97176
N164GP	441	0164
N164LG	TRIS	1050
N164MA	MU-2	540
N164P	MIIB	T26-164
N164PA	G1	54
(N164PB)	PC12	164
N164PG	TBM7	164
N164RA	100	B-164
N164SL	P180	1134
N164ST	46T	97064
N164TC	200	BB-939
N164TG	441	0164
N164WS	90	LJ-1736
N165BC	690C	11646
N165CA	31T	8020008
N165CB	90	LJ-687
N165FA	300	FA-165
N165KC	31T	7904022
N165MA	46T	97152
N165MA	MU-2	326
N165MA	MU-2	541
N165NL	90	LJ-90
N165PA	G1	119
N165PD	PC12	165
N165RB	31T	7920018
N165SL	P180	1135
N165SW	31T	7904051
N165U	90	LJ-204
N166A	E90	LW-44
N166BA	300	FA-147
N166FL	350	FL-166
N166MA	MU-2	427SA
N166MA	MU-2	542
N166NK	G1	12
N166PA	P180	1190
N166PA	P180	1198
N166PB	P180	1190
N166PB	PC12	166
N166PM	46T	97166
N166SA	300	FA-166
N166SB	PC12	310
N166SM	90	LJ-619
N166TR	100	B-50
N166WT	31T	8004020
N166Y	P166	356
N167AR	PC12	279
N167BB	90	LJ-1054
N167CA	E90	LW-141
N167DA	31T	7720058
(N167JR)	E90	LW-141
N167KA	200	BB-167
N167MA	MU-2	428SA
N167MA	MU-2	543
N167PA	G1	117
N167PA	G1	199
(N167PB)	PC12	167
N167R	690B	11437
N167SL	31T	8004001
N167SL	P180	1136
N168AC	200	BB-1174
N168BB	MU-2	544
N168CA	46T	97314
"N168D"	C-12	BC-37
N168DA	31T	7820069
N168ET	350	FL-288
N168MA	425	0155
N168MA	MU-2	429SA
N168MA	MU-2	544
N168PA	G1	56
N168RV	46T	97252
N168SL	P180	1139
N168WA	PC12	168
N169B	E90	LW-27
N169CA	441	0024
N169CA	46T	97300
N169CR	695A	96079
N169DB	200	BB-458
N169DC	31T	8004048
N169DR	90	LJ-1205
N169FW	425	0169
N169GL	MIII	T-269
(N169KD)	31T	8104057
N169MA	441	0344
N169MA	MU-2	545
N169MC	300	FA-199
N169MM	100	B-6
N169NP	PC12	1169
N169P	90	LJ-1647
N169RA	100	B-89
N169SL	P180	1140
(N169TC)	PA42	8001045
(N169TM)	100	B-192
(N169WD)	90	LJ-610
N170AJ	90	LJ-1298
N170CC	31T	8166018
N170DB	90	LJ-787
N170L	200	BB-1095
N170L	200	BB-1615
N170MA	441	0148
N170MA	MU-2	104
N170MA	MU-2	430SA
N170PD	PC12	170
(N170RE)	90	LJ-779
N170RL	200T	BT-28
N170S	200	BB-1095
N170S	200	BB-1527
N170S	200	BB-1615
N170S	200	BB-1740
N170S	90	LJ-1708
N170SE	200	BB-1740
N170SP	200	BB-139
N170W	200	BB-1527
N171AF	31T	7920089
N171AT	680T	1616-49
N171CA	MU-2	711SA
N171CP	350	FL-244
N171CP	695	95006
N171CT	695	95006
N171DA	31T	7920088
N171DR	690C	11683
N171HP	46T	97371
N171JP	31T	7720028
N171LS	G1	171
N171M	200	BB-909
N171MA	MU-2	431SA
N171MA	MU-2	547
N171PA	G1	192
N171PC	MIIB	T26-103
N171PD	PC12	171
N171RD	200	BB-610
(N171SG)	200	BB-1785
(N171SP)	200	BB-1135
N171SP	441	0326
N171TE	90	LJ-180
N171TT	690	11007
N171VA	90	LJ-492
N172CC	31T	8166031
N172JS	PC12	171
N172MA	46T	97263
N172MA	MU-2	548
N172PB	PC12	172
N172RD	G1	172
N172SL	P180	1141
N173A	90	LJ-161
N173AL	690	11018
N173AS	E90	LW-345
N173BT	G1	173
N173DB	690B	11485
N173KS	300	FA-82
N173KS	PC12	173
N173LP	690	11018
N173MA	MU-2	549
N173MA	MU-2	752SA
N173PA	G1	175
N173PL	F90	LA-106
N173RC	200	BB-173
N173S	300C	FM-4
N173SL	P180	1146
N173SP	MIII	T-210
N173TC	200	BB-1893
N173TX	200	BB-1028
N174CC	31T	8166053
N174GT	200G	BY-74
N174MA	MU-2	550
N174MA	MU-2	753SA
N174PC	PC12	174
N174PW	200	BB-64
N174SP	MIII	T-213
N174WA	P180	1074
N174WB	200	BB-804
N175	46T	97370
N175AA	PA42	8001017
N175AZ	90	LJ-1006
N175BC	200	BB-1126
N175BC	90	LJ-907
N175BM	200	BB-501
N175CA	MU-2	736SA
N175DB	680T	1519-95
(N175GC)	MU-2	736SA
N175GM	200	BB-501
N175MA	MU-2	551
N175MA	MU-2	754SA
N175NJ	300	FA-175
N175P	MIIB	T26-135
N175PL	200G	BY-2
N175SA	200	BB-183
N175SL	P180	1147
N175WB	46T	97181
N175WB	MIII	T-301
N175WW	200	BB-939
N176BJ	MU-2	144
N176BS	PC12	176
N176CC	31T	7620024
N176CS	31T	8004054
N176FB	31T	8004054
N176FB	PA42	8001041
N176FE	31T	8004054
N176JR	E90	LW-115
N176K	90	LJ-157
N176M	200	BB-1029
N176MA	MU-2	552
N176MA	MU-2	755SA
N176RS	31T	8166054
N176SL	P180	1150
N176TW	E90	LW-76
N177AD	200	BB-229
N177CN	200	BB-1191
N177DC	680W	1760-6
N177DM	MU-2	104
N177EM	690B	11471
N177G	90	LJ-106
N177G	90	LJ-437
N177GA	350	FL-160
N177JE	200	BB-1203
N177JE	31T	7620029
N177JW	300	FA-77
N177KA	E90	LW-149
N177LA	200	BB-1203
N177MA	46D	81
N177MA	MU-2	553
N177MF	MIIB	T26-179
N177MK	E90	LW-149
(N177PT)	31T	7400003
N177RD	46D	117
N177SA	MU-2	177
N178CA	MU-2	1536SA
N178CD	31T	8120046
N178EJ	90	LJ-1818
(N178GV)	MU-2	363SA
N178JM	90	LJ-1430
N178LA	F90	LA-178
N178MA	MU-2	554
N178MH	PC12	875

N178NC	B100	BE-17
(N178NQ)	B100	BE-17
N178PC	PC12	178
N178RC	90	LJ-762
N178SC	BN2	599
N178SG	31T	8020044
N178SL	P180	1151
N178SW	31T	7804004
N178WM	100	B-35
(N179AC)	31T	8004033
N179CA	E90	LW-292
N179CM	MU-2	756SA
N179D	90	LJ-1091
N179KA	200	BB-445
(N179KC)	690A	11313
N179MA	MU-2	555
N179MA	MU-2	756SA
N179MC	200	BB-1168
N179MD	90	LJ-1091
N179RC	90	LJ-1179
N179S	P180	1117
N179SG	350	FL-245
N179SL	P180	1152
N179SL	P180	1170
N179SS	PC12	179
N179SW	31T	7920058
N180AB	P180	1011
N180AV	P180	1017
N180AV	P180	1018
N180AZ	P180	1013
N180B	90	LJ-569
N180BP	P180	1004
N180CA	200	BB-1547
(N180CA)	31T	8004009
N180CA	31T	8004023
(N180CA)	350	FL-33
N180CC	PA42	8001022
N180CH	90	LJ-987
N180HH	MIIB	T26-151
N180HM	P180	1043
N180JS	31T	7520026
N180K	90	LJ-7
N180K	PC6	550
N180MA	MU-2	180
N180MA	MU-2	757SA
N180PT	P180	1006
(N180RP)	P180	1034
N180S	200	BB-496
N180SB	MU-2	180
N180SB	MU-2	245
N180SH	P180	1015
N180SN	200	BB-269
N180SW	31T	8004044
N180TE	P180	1012
N180TP	P180	1017
(N180UJ)	P180	1037
N180VW	681	6005
N181AA	425	0027
N181B	MU-2	670
N181BG	P180	1015
N181CA	46D	219
N181CC	PA42	8001045
N181CE	STAR	NC-31
N181CG	E90	LW-225
N181DA	PC6	790
N181DC	31T	7520026
N181GA	90	LJ-882
N181JH	90	LJ-966
N181LL	90	LJ-440
N181LT	EPIC	018
N181MA	MU-2	215
N181MD	441	0295
N181MP	200G	BY-64
N181NK	90	LJ-142
N181PC	TBM7	261
N181RS	MU-2	426SA
N181SW	31T	8104001
N181TG	G1	181
N181Z	E90	LW-52
N182	690	11048
N182CA	F90	LA-121
(N182FL)	31T	7820021
N182MA	MU-2	216
N182ME	31T	7820021

N182PE	PC12	182
N182TC	31T	8120065
N182TC	31T	8120103
N182Z	200	BB-402
N183CC	PA42	8001067
N183DW	200	BB-667
N183K	G1	84
N183MA	MU-2	217
N183MC	200	BB-24
N183PA	G1	199
N183PC	PC12	183
N183SA	90	LJ-571
N183SL	P180	1155
N183SL	P180	1171
N183WW	46D	173
N184AE	46T	97026
N184AL	46T	97026
N184BB	695A	96061
N184CC	PA42	8001077
N184D	300	FA-132
(N184DF)	441	0184
N184JS	200	BB-1256
N184JS	E90	LW-263
N184K	G1	84
N184L	PC6	557
N184MA	MU-2	218
N184MC	200	BB-965
N184MQ	200	BB-965
N184PA	G1	97
N184RB	46T	97087
N184RL	690	11022
N184SK	200	BB-279
N184SL	P180	1158
N184SL	P180	1172
N184SL	P180	1187
N184TH	PC12	810
N184TH	PC12	1065
*N184TX	200	BB-1241
N184VB	441	0184
N185DA	200	BB-185
N185DH	200	BB-905
N185G	90	LJ-680
N185GA	441	0066
N185K	PC6	563
N185MA	MU-2	219
N185MC	200	BB-1034
N185MV	200	BB-1034
N185PA	G1	26
N185PB	PC12	185
N185X	PC6	566
N185XP	200	BB-952
N186DD	F90	LA-83
N186E	690B	11566
N186EB	200	BB-1186
N186EC	441	0314
N186EC	690B	11566
N186GA	31T	7820086
N186MA	MU-2	220
N186MA	MU-2	758SA
N186MC	200	BB-720
N186MQ	200	BB-720
N186PA	G1	23
(N186PH)	PC12	186
N186PS	46T	97228
N186WF	PC12	186
N187AF	MU-2	187
N187CP	31T	7920054
N187GA	31T	8166007
N187H	PC6	564
N187J	B100	BE-24
N187JD	46T	97180
N187JN	200	BB-380
N187JP	200	BB-1888
N187MA	MU-2	221
N187MC	200	BB-689
N187MQ	200	BB-689
N187PC	PC12	187
N187SB	MU-2	226
N187SB	MU-2	698SA
N187SC	31T	7904020
N187SL	P180	1164
N187Z	MIIA	T26-029
N188	690A	11210
N188AM	BN2	2302

N188BF	F90	LA-105
N188CA	31T	7904032
N188CE	46T	97239
N188CP	425	0188
N188DF	425	0188
N188EA	425	0188
(N188EC)	31T	7904032
N188H	200	BB-1061
N188JB	B100	BE-50
N188JB	F90	LA-107
N188LL	B100	BE-119
N188MA	MU-2	222
N188MA	MU-2	759SA
N188MC	350	FL-93
N188PC	46D	25
N188PC	PC12	188
N188RB	425	0220
N188RM	MU-2	298
N188SC	MIII	T-228
N188SC	MIII	T-276
N188SL	P180	1174
N188TC	200C	BL-64
N188W	200	BB-969
N188WG	200	BB-208
N189B	100	B-133
N189CB	350	FL-513
N189CC	MIII	T-405
N189DB	46T	97090
N189GA	200	BB-961
N189GH	31T	7920084
N189JR	F90	LA-61
N189K	G1	170
N189MA	MU-2	223
N189MC	350	FL-136
N189PM	46D	24
N189SL	P180	1181
N189VB	200	BB-646
N189WS	441	0320
N190AA	PA42	8001055
N190BT	90	LJ-59
N190CA	100	B-57
N190CA	90	LJ-1180
N190CA	PA42	8001028
N190CB	90	LJ-1374
N190CC	90	LJ-862
N190DB	E90	LW-216
N190DM	G1	79
N190EF	90	LJ-1122
N190EU	90	LJ-1935
N190FD	F90	LA-42
N190GM	F90	LA-140
N190JL	90	LJ-69
N190JS	90	LJ-1228
N190JS	MIII	TT-483A
N190K	90	LJ-46
N190LE	G1	190
N190MA	MU-2	224
N190MA	MU-2	760SA
N190MD	200	BB-190
N190N	90	LJ-46
(N190P)	200	BB-212
N190PA	G1	195
N190PE	PC12	190
N190RF	90	LJ-238
N190RL	E90	LW-1
N190RM	E90	LW-1
N190RW	46D	234
N190SS	90	LJ-1298
N190TC	E90	LW-176
N190TT	90	LJ-735
(N190WA)	100	B-226
N191A	90	LJ-765
N191DM	90	LJ-100
N191FL	200	BB-107
N191MA	31T	8104019
N191MA	MU-2	556
N191MA	MU-2	761SA
N191SA	G1	61
N191SL	P180	1194
(N191SP)	90	LJ-1282
N191SP	90	LJ-1285
N191SP	PC12	284
N191TP	90	LJ-1223
N191WB	90	LJ-1295

N192G	MIIB	T26-137
N192GL	MIIB	T26-137
N192MA	MU-2	557
N192MH	680W	1789-19
N192PA	G1	149
N192PC	PC12	192
N192SA	200	BB-92
N192SL	P180	1199
N192TB	31T	8166015
N192W	200	BB-562
N192X	PC6	586
N193A	90	LJ-503
N193AA	MU-2	741SA
N193BD	46D	128
N193CS	MIII	T-300
N193FS	300	FA-218
N193G	MIIB	T26-149
N193GA	200	BB-12
N193GM	F90	LA-193
N193JC	200	BB-1177
N193K	200	BB-956
(N193M)	46D	156
N193MA	MU-2	558
N193MM	46D	172
N193PA	G1	23
N193PA	G1	125
N193PC	PC12	193
N193RA	350	FL-105
(N193SF)	90	LJ-174
N193SS	690C	11734
N193X	PC6	587
N194DB	STAR	NC-8
N194JL	46T	97337
N194KA	E90	LW-194
N194LJ	300	FA-89
N194MA	31T	8120050
N194MA	MU-2	559
N194MA	MU-2	762SA
N194PC	PC12	194
N194PM	46D	74
N194TR	200	BB-1146
N194WS	200	BB-267
N194X	PC6	592
N195AA	31T	7904001
N195AE	300	FA-195
N195AL	300	FA-102
N195B	E90	LW-195
N195BV	E90	LW-195
N195CA	200	BB-1488
N195D	90	LJ-89
N195DP	90	LJ-89
N195DR	90	LJ-89
N195DR	90	LJ-226
N195FW	441	0195
N195JG	46D	238
N195KA	200	BB-1021
N195KC	200	BB-1021
N195KC	90	LJ-688
N195KQ	90	LJ-688
N195MA	100	B-20
N195MA	MU-2	560
N195MA	MU-2	763SA
N195PA	G1	88
N195PM	46D	185
(N195RB)	425	0195
N195WF	E90	LW-195
N195X	PC6	593
N196B	100	B-128
N196HA	90	LJ-1436
N196HA	F90	LA-199
N196JP	F90	LA-196
(N196KC)	680T	1632-57
N196LA	90	LJ-1436
N196MA	MU-2	561
N196MA	MU-2	764SA
N196MP	200	BB-523
N196PA	G1	139
N196PC	PC12	196
N196PP	200	BB-668
N196SC	200	BB-1525
*N196SL	P180	1038
N196TA	BN2	741
(N196TM)	425	0196
N196WC	F90	LA-196

N196X	PC6	596
N197AS	F90	LA-116
N197BN	BN2	197
N197CC	90	LJ-783
N197MA	MU-2	562
N197MA	MU-2	765SA
N197PA	G1	93
N197PC	PC12	197
N197RB	200	BB-779
N197RM	G1	197
N197SC	90	LJ-783
N197SC	90	LJ-1490
N197TA	31T	7620035
N197X	PC6	597
N198AA	31T	8020041
N198BC	90	LJ-147
N198CC	31T	8020041
N198DM	200	BB-1198
N198FM	F90	LA-198
N198GH	200	BB-354
N198KA	90	LJ-162
N198MA	MU-2	563
N198PA	G1	27
N198PP	90	LJ-1314
N198SC	200	BB-276
N198SC	200	BB-487
N198SV	350	FL-189
N198T	90	LJ-162
N198X	PC6	600
N198X	TBM7	138
N199BC	F90	LA-30
N199CE	300	FA-199
N199CG	90	LJ-1661
N199CM	PC12	262
N199CP	46T	97099
N199DW	E90	LW-338
N199GA	200	BB-1898
N199GH	200	BB-354
N199M	G1	17
N199MA	31T	8104005
N199MA	MU-2	564
N199MA	MU-2	766SA
N199MH	200	BB-855
N199ND	31T	7620035
N199PC	TRIS	1038
N199PL	E90	LW-167
N199RC	31T	8120030
N199TA	MIIB	T26-110
N199TD	90	LJ-864
N199TT	E90	LW-157
N199WF	PC12	199
N199WP	690A	11127
N199X	PC6	601
N199Y	350	FL-66
N199Z	MIII	T-217
N200AB	200	BB-436
N200AB	200	BB-749
N200AE	G1	169
N200AF	200	BB-102
N200AJ	100	B-146
N200AJ	200	BB-378
N200AJ	200	BB-588
N200AJ	200	BB-688
N200AL	200	BB-80
N200AP	200	BB-277
N200AU	200	BB-432
N200BC	200	BB-55
N200BC	MIIB	T26-149E
N200BD	695	95062
N200BD	MU-2	521
N200BE	200	BB-832
N200BE	200	BB-1055
N200BH	200	BB-587
N200BK	200	BB-1041
N200BM	200	BB-712
N200BM	200	BB-1147
N200BM	200	BB-1370
N200BM	F90	LA-49
(N200BN)	BN2	2241
N200BP	200	BB-378
N200BR	200	BB-600
N200BR	MU-2	205
N200BT	200	BB-293
N200BX	90	LJ-717
N200CA	200	BB-30
N200CD	200	BB-217
N200CE	200	BB-330
N200CE	MIII	T-205
N200CG	F90	LA-177
N200CJ	200	BB-143
N200CL	E90	LW-63
N200CM	31T	7720004
N200CN	31T	7720021
N200CP	200	BB-1246
N200CT	680T	1563-19
N200CT	680W	1834-39
N200CU	E90	LW-5
N200CU	F90	LA-177
N200CV	200	BB-1617
N200CY	200	BB-1617
N200DA	200	BB-1095
N200DB	200	BB-1163
N200DK	695A	96019
N200DM	200	BB-206
N200DT	680W	1763-9
N200DU	200	BB-1255
N200E	200	BB-557
N200E	200	BB-851
N200E	680T	1626-54
N200E	E90	LW-162
N200E	F90	LA-12
N200EA	200	BB-284
N200EA	200	BB-346
N200EA	200	BB-1368
N200EA	C-12	BD-2
N200EC	200	BB-134
N200EC	200	BB-434
N200EG	200	BB-1501
N200EJ	200	BB-50
N200EJ	200	BB-1585
N200EJ	C-12	BC-72
N200EK	90	LJ-769
N200EL	200	BB-870
N200EM	200	BB-846
N200EP	MU-2	627
N200ER	200	BB-566
N200ET	C-12	BC-73
N200ET	MIII	T-249
N200EW	200	BB-578
N200EW	200	BB-1163
N200EZ	200	BB-9
N200FA	F90	LA-9
N200FB	31T	7904037
N200FD	31T	7520040
N200FE	200	BB-373
N200FH	200	BB-231
N200FM	200	BB-81
N200FR	200	BB-1420
N200FV	200	BB-299
N200GA	200	BB-800
N200GE	200	BB-1207
(N200GE)	690A	11234
N200GF	31T	7920015
N200GF	PA42	8001031
N200GH	31T	7920015
N200GJ	G1	80
N200GK	200	BB-874
N200GP	200	BB-1207
N200GS	200	BB-1214
N200GU	200	BB-696
N200HB	200	BB-1226
N200HC	200	BB-515
N200HD	200	BB-987
N200HF	200	BB-1149
N200HF	200	BB-1677
N200HF	200	BB-1858
(N200HF)	31T	8166062
N200HK	200	BB-1677
N200HL	MU-2	120
N200HT	200C	BL-3
N200HT	690B	11408
N200HV	31T	8104013
N200HV	90	LJ-1262
N200HV	90	LJ-1478
N200HW	200	BB-158
N200HW	200	BB-957
N200HW	200	BB-1561
N200HW	441	0015
N200HX	200	BB-1243
N200JC	200	BB-234
N200JC	AASI	002
N200JE	31T	8166064
(N200JH)	31T	7620014
(N200JH)	31T	8020053
(N200JH)	31T	8166010
N200JH	PA42	5501021
N200JL	200	BB-127
(N200JL)	B100	BE-82
N200JM	200	BB-1061
N200JM	200	BB-1086
N200JN	690A	11224
N200JN	695	95035
N200JQ	690A	11224
N200JR	200	BB-1285
N200JV	200	BB-357
N200JW	200	BB-1124
N200KA	200	BB-2
N200KA	200	BB-42
N200KA	200	BB-169
N200KA	200	BB-257
N200KA	200	BB-310
N200KA	200	BB-444
N200KA	200	BB-571
N200KA	200	BB-646
N200KA	200	BB-1103
N200KA	200	BB-1158
N200KA	200	BB-1217
N200KA	200	BB-1283
(N200KA)	200	BB-1312
N200KA	200	BB-1349
N200KA	200	BB-1380
N200KA	200	BB-1439
N200KA	200	BB-1449
N200KA	200	BB-1484
N200KA	200	BB-1509
(N200KA)	200	BB-1512
N200KA	200	BB-1580
N200KA	200	BB-1677
N200KA	200	BB-1826
N200KA	200C	BL-141
N200KE	200	BB-5
N200KE	200	BB-257
N200KF	MIII	T-329
N200KG	200	BB-1349
N200KK	200	BB-677
N200KK	200	BB-1158
N200KP	200	BB-2
N200KP	200	BB-1215
N200KW	200	BB-716
N200KY	200	BB-1380
N200L	200	BB-525
N200LD	441	0137
N200LG	200C	BL-31
N200LJ	200	BB-176
N200LJ	200	BB-588
N200LM	200	BB-158
N200LM	200	BB-1172
N200LN	200	BB-4
N200LN	200	BB-158
N200LN	200	BB-922
N200LP	200	BB-933
N200LQ	BN2T	880
N200LU	200	BB-1177
N200LV	200	BB-158
N200LV	200	BB-1177
N200LW	200	BB-511
N200LW	C-12	BC-23
N200M	681B	6051
N200M	690A	11115
N200M	690A	11146
N200M	690A	11234
N200M	690B	11435
N200M	695	95013
N200MB	690A	11115
N200MB	B100	BE-71
N200MG	200	BB-923
N200MH	MIIB	T26-148
N200MJ	200	BB-1012
N200ML	690A	11234
N200MM	200	BB-11
N200MM	200	BB-26
N200MM	200	BB-418
N200MM	200	BB-926
N200MN	200	BB-26
N200MP	200	BB-283
N200MP	200	BB-1174
(N200MP)	350	FL-72
N200MR	200	BB-219
N200MT	425	0020
N200MU	BN2	78
N200MV	200	BB-748
N200MW	200	BB-1110
N200MW	F90	LA-137
N200NA	200	BB-560
N200NA	200	BB-1079
N200NB	31T	7720035
N200ND	200	BB-1612
N200NF	200	BB-681
N200NG	C-12	BC-22
N200NR	200	BB-1380
N200NS	200	BB-936
N200NW	200	BB-1691
N200NW	MU-2	312
N200NW	MU-2	762SA
N200NY	200	BB-1027
N200NY	C-12	BC-25
N200P	G1	191
N200PB	200	BB-13
N200PB	200	BB-67
(N200PB)	200	BB-221
N200PB	200	BB-243
N200PB	200	BB-359
N200PB	200	BB-423
N200PD	200	BB-492
N200PD	PC12	200
N200PF	G1	159
N200PG	31T	7920015
N200PH	200	BB-194
N200PH	200	BB-238
N200PH	200	BB-1017
N200PJ	200	BB-176
N200PL	200	BB-410
N200PL	200	BB-1080
N200PM	G1	159
N200PR	690D	15029
(N200PT)	200	BB-1080
N200PT	695A	96067
N200PU	200	BB-1477
N200PY	200	BB-700
N200QE	MIII	T-205
N200QN	200	BB-521
N200QS	200	BB-1130
N200QS	200	BB-1585
N200QT	680W	1834-39
N200RA	F90	LA-153
N200RB	200	BB-867
N200RC	200	BB-840
N200RE	E90	LW-164
N200RG	200C	BL-16
N200RJ	200	BB-588
N200RM	E90	LW-45
N200RR	200	BB-1282
N200RS	200	BB-1481
N200RS	31T	7520011
N200RT	200	BB-867
N200RW	200	BB-242
N200RX	MU-2	548
N200SB	200	BB-130
N200SC	90	LJ-863
N200SC	90	LJ-1227
N200SC	F90	LA-87
N200SE	200	BB-1208
N200SF	E90	LW-216
N200SG	200	BB-559
N200SK	200	BB-217
N200SL	31T	8104068
N200SL	90	LJ-1189
N200SN	MIII	T-354
N200SR	200	BB-708
N200SR	200	BB-801
N200SR	200	BB-1333
N200SV	200	BB-1187
N200SW	90	LJ-34
N200SW	MIIA	T26-018
N200SY	90	LJ-1227
N200T	200	BB-750

N200TB	680T	1708-83
(N200TC)	200	BB-394
N200TE	690B	11370
N200TG	200	BB-651
N200TG	90	LJ-583
N200TJ	200	BB-908
N200TK	200	BB-45
N200TK	200	BB-362
N200TK	200	BB-660
N200TK	200	BB-1240
N200TM	200	BB-117
N200TM	200	BB-897
N200TM	MU-2	307
N200TN	200	BB-117
N200TP	200	BB-191
N200TR	90	LJ-1067
N200TS	31T	7804002
N200TT	690B	11370
N200TT	695	95073
N200TV	B100	BE-36
N200TW	200	BB-466
N200TW	200	BB-1464
N200U	690A	11251
N200U	90	LJ-1389
N200UP	90	LJ-148
N200UQ	200	BB-479
N200UW	200	BB-1155
N200V	200	BB-1599
N200VA	200	BB-246
N200VC	350	FL-316
N200VE	31T	7620057
N200VE	P68	160
N200VJ	200	BB-610
N200VJ	350	FL-489
N200VU	200	BB-1393
(N200WB)	200	BB-724
N200WB	200	BB-1754
N200WB	300	FA-5
N200WB	E90	LW-284
N200WG	MU-2	528
N200WJ	200	BB-1277
N200WX	200	BB-680
N200WZ	200	BB-89
N200XC	200	BB-1061
N200XL	31T	8166010
N200YB	200	BB-1219
N200YY	200	BB-35
N200ZC	200	BB-41
N200ZK	200	BB-1553
N200ZS	STAR	NC-43
N200ZT	200	BB-1393
N201CH	200	BB-103
N201KA	200	BB-417
N201KA	90	LJ-764
N201LB	200	BB-6
N201NY	200	BB-1308
N201SM	MIIA	T26-005
N201TT	200	BB-6
N201TT	200	BB-860
N201U	200	BB-819
N201U	MU-2	680
N201UU	200	BB-819
N201UV	MU-2	680
N202AD	200	BB-60
N202AJ	200	BB-511
N202AU	MU-2	329
N202BB	200	BB-624
N202BE	200	BB-589
N202CC	E90	LW-198
N202CF	200	BB-329
N202DB	200	BB-110
N202DJ	200	BB-1654
N202DT	MU-2	1544SA
N202EJ	200	BB-905
N202FF	200	BB-1786
N202FG	90	LJ-1507
N202HA	G1	16
N202HC	200	BB-651
N202HC	31T	7820036
N202JP	31T	7520018
N202JT	200	BB-1542
N202KA	200	BB-272
N202KA	200	BB-571
N202KA	E90	LW-252
(N202KC)	200	BB-904
N202LJ	200	BB-322
N202MC	MU-2	369SA
(N202MM)	200	BB-390
N202MS	425	0021
N202NC	200	BB-709
(N202PT)	200	BB-960
N202PV	200	BB-795
N202PV	350	FL-50
(N202QS)	200	BB-293
N202RB	300	FA-50
N202RW	90	LJ-248
N202SE	46D	113
N202SW	200	BB-720
N202TS	200	BB-1506
N202VJ	PA42	7800002
(N202VT)	200	BB-709
(N202W)	90	LJ-583
N202WS	MIVA	AT-037
N203AJ	100	B-6
N203BC	200	BB-528
N203BS	200	BB-476
N203CA	46D	232
(N203CS)	31T	8020058
N203EB	200	BB-808
N203GA	MU-2	573
N203HC	200	BB-1602
N203HC	350	FL-28
N203HG	350	FL-28
N203HQ	200	BB-1602
N203JT	200	BB-1562
N203KA	B100	BE-34
N203LG	200	BB-926
N203PC	E90	LW-258
N203PR	BN2	2248
N203PT	200	BB-1903
N203R	200	BB-396
N203RC	200	BB-1822
N203RD	E90	LW-203
N203RR	300	FA-27
N203SF	200	BB-150
(N203SL)	90	LJ-1189
(N203TS)	200	BB-1016
N203TS	200	BB-1689
N203TW	200	BB-1417
N203WT	MIII	T-387
N204AJ	100	B-10
(N204BF)	200	BB-1327
N204BR	200	BB-554
N204C	200	BB-1730
N204CA	200	BB-34
N204CS	100	B-24
N204CS	200	BB-34
N204CS	200	BB-119
N204EA	90	LJ-1111
N204EB	200	BB-826
N204EF	31T	7920074
(N204FW)	90	LJ-472
(N204GR)	200	BB-1217
N204JS	200	BB-69
N204JS	200	BB-842
N204JT	200	BB-1563
N204KA	200	BB-468
(N204MB)	31T	7904012
N204MS	200	BB-1266
N204PT	200	BB-1908
N204RA	200	BB-1885
N204W	350	FL-204
N204WB	200	BB-1179
N205AA	G1	59
N205AB	695A	96085
N205BC	F90	LA-14
N205BL	690B	11404
N205BN	690B	11404
N205CA	E90	LW-105
N205EC	200T	BT-5
N205G	G1	125
(N205HG)	200	BB-173
N205JT	200	BB-1564
N205K	300	FA-27
N205M	G1	62
N205M	G1	114
N205MA	MU-2	432SA
N205MB	200	BB-808
N205MB	MIVA	AT-032
N205MP	MIVA	AT-032
N205MS	90	LJ-948
N205P	90	LJ-1474
N205PA	200	BB-1959
N205PA	P180	1077
N205PA	P180	1088
N205PC	F90	LA-14
N205R	300	FA-27
N205RA	200	BB-1919
N205SG	200	BB-826
N205SM	F90	LA-205
N205SP	200	BB-1826
N205SP	90	LJ-965
N205ST	90	LJ-965
N205TM	200	BB-1991
N205TS	200	BB-1707
N205TT	200	BB-1284
N205X	200	BB-276
N206BN	690B	11455
N206K	300	FA-36
N206P	200	BB-466
(N206P)	200	BB-1402
N206R	300	FA-36
N206R	STAR	NC-21
N206RF	STAR	NC-21
N207BA	MU-2	666
N207CM	200	BB-621
N207CM	200	BB-1246
N207CP	E90	LW-296
N207CW	200	BB-1658
N207DB	200	BB-862
N207E	90	LJ-936
N207HB	200	BB-1516
N207M	G1	73
N207P	200	BB-404
N207P	90	LJ-1406
N207R	350	FL-14
N207R	90	LJ-936
N207RC	90	LJ-1207
N207RP	300	FA-6
N207RS	425	0195
N207SB	100	B-69
N207SB	200	BB-959
N207SS	441	0136
N207TS	200	BB-1729
N208AJ	100	B-6
N208AJ	200	BB-126
N208AJ	200	BB-1490
N208CL	690A	11297
N208CW	200	BB-1720
(N208DM)	200	BB-975
N208F	200	BB-851
N208JS	200	BB-682
N208MA	MU-2	016
N208MM	200	BB-418
N208MS	200	BB-400
N208PC	F90	LA-46
N208PP	F90	LA-46
N208RC	F90	LA-46
N208SB	100	B-146
N208SR	100	B-208
N208SW	200	BB-720
N208SW	31T	8004011
N208TC	200	BB-990
N208TS	200	BB-1510
N209AB	BN2	209
N209BN	BN2	209
N209CM	200	BB-1232
N209CM	200	BB-1613
(N209DM)	E90	LW-302
(N209JS)	200	BB-593
N209KC	46T	97009
N209MA	MU-2	142
N209MA	MU-2	433SA
N209MA	MU-2	565
N209P	90	LJ-1445
N209PB	PC12	209
N209PC	200	BB-650
N209RG	BN2	209
N209ST	46T	97209
N209T	G1	168
N209WC	200	BB-1130
(N210AC)	200	BB-1216
N210AJ	200	BB-8
N210AJ	F90	LA-131
N210CL	TBM7	303
N210CM	200	BB-621
(N210CM)	200	BB-1246
N210EC	690B	11452
N210EC	90	LJ-1070
N210ED	690B	11358
(N210JM)	90	LJ-956
N210K	90	LJ-483
N210MA	46T	97244
N210MA	90	LJ-573
N210MA	MU-2	566
N210PH	200	BB-360
N210PP	F90	LA-14
N210PT	PC12	210
N210SA	200	BB-1420
N210SN	MIIB	T26-178
N210SU	200	BB-420
N210SW	MIIB	T26-178
N210SW	MIII	T-300
N210X	90	LJ-415
*N210YS	E90	LW-268
N211AD	695A	96092
N211AE	31T	7720064
N211BA	MU-2	242
N211BB	200	BB-300
N211BE	MU-2	641
N211BT	90	LJ-448
N211CC	MIIB	T26-117
N211CG	E90	LW-101
N211CP	200	BB-843
N211DG	200	BB-1148
N211DG	E90	LW-154
N211DQ	200	BB-1148
N211EC	F90	LA-123
N211EZ	46T	97117B
N211HV	200	BB-1799
N211JB	200	BB-18
N211JB	200	BB-30
N211MA	MU-2	434SA
N211MA	MU-2	567
N211MH	E90	LW-179
N211NA	F90	LA-199
N211NK	690B	11401
N211PC	90	LJ-910
N211PD	200	BB-300
N211RV	MU-2	502
N211SC	90	LJ-339
N211TT	681	6027
N211VP	100	B-2
N211WT	90	LJ-455
N211X	90	LJ-279
N212BA	MU-2	587
N212BF	200	BB-622
N212CC	MU-2	209
N212CM	680T	1626-54
N212CW	680T	1626-54
N212D	90	LJ-234
N212DM	200	BB-1053
N212EJ	200	BB-898
N212GA	200	BB-1406
N212GM	31T	8104013
N212H	G1	74
N212HH	31T	7904010
N212JB	200	BB-1238
N212JL	PC12	1119
N212LT	PC12	595
N212LW	200	BB-1420
N212LW	200	BB-1766
N212MA	MU-2	262
N212MA	MU-2	568
N212PB	PC12	212
N212PK	PC12	668
N212Q	100	B-28
N212Q	90	LJ-22
N212Q	MIII	TT-507
N212SN	200	BB-1425
N212WP	90	LJ-62
N213BE	200	BB-483
N213CT	90	LJ-1028
N213DB	200	BB-1450
N213DS	E90	LW-64
N213GA	G1	48

N213KP	PC12	1019	N217EB	PC12	154	N221KP	MU-2	183	N222WJ	90	LJ-1106
(N213MA)	MU-2	435SA	N217GA	90	LJ-910	N221MA	MU-2	239	N222XL	31T	8166065
N213MA	MU-2	569	N217GS	200	BB-37	N221MA	MU-2	446SA	N223CG	90	LJ-1069
N213MB	200	BB-483	N217MA	MU-2	229	N221MA	MU-2	771SA	N223CH	90	LJ-321
N213NC	90	LJ-1565	N217MA	MU-2	438SA	N221MA	TBM8	502	N223CS	31T	8275008
N213PA	MIII	TT-518A	N217SB	MU-2	586	N221MJ	90	LJ-512	N223DD	MU-2	527
N213PH	200	BB-486	N217TM	TBM7	217	(N221ML)	90	LJ-245	N223DG	B100	BE-136
*N213RJ	B100	BE-22	N218BA	F90	LA-218	N221MM	300	FA-161	N223EA	TBM7	323
N213RW	E90	LW-167	N218CS	31T	8275016	N221NC	90	LJ-393	N223GA	695B	96203
N213SC	MIIB	T26-135	N218G	MIIB	T26-140	N221P	200	BB-1144	N223HC	200	BB-855
N213UV	200	BB-35	N218MA	MU-2	231	N221PC	PC12	221	N223JB	MU-2	724SA
N213UV	C-12	BC-28	N218MA	MU-2	439SA	N221RC	31T	8104046	N223JC	MIV	AT-015
N213WA	PC12	213	N218MS	695	95041	N221SP	200	BB-1180	N223JC	MIVA	AT-068
N214B	90	LJ-732	N218Q	100	B-28	N221SS	100	B-166	N223JG	TBM8	406
N214B	E90	LW-10	N218SW	31T	8166011	N221SV	690B	11388	N223JR	300	FA-45
N214CK	100	B-191	N218TG	TBM8	487	N221TB	46D	17	N223JS	MU-2	1544SA
N214CS	PC12	766	N218WA	PC12	218	N221TC	B100	BE-136	N223K	90	LJ-306
N214D	90	LJ-750	N219BC	46T	97284	N221TM	90	LJ-672	N223KD	90	LJ-181
N214EC	300	FA-50	N219CS	31T	8275005	N221XX	PC12	1128	N223LH	100	B-223
N214FW	200	BB-1747	(N219D)	680W	1820-34	N221Z	350	FL-221	N223LP	200	BB-1123
N214GA	695	95009	(N219DM)	200	BB-66	N222	31T	7920036	N223MA	MU-2	241
N214GB	200	BB-1668	N219GR	46T	97244	N222AG	F90	LA-159	N223MA	MU-2	447SA
N214JB	STAR	NC-14	N219GR	TBM8	494	N222BC	31T	8104007	N223MD	200	BB-1048
N214K	E90	LW-34	N219MA	MU-2	232	N222BE	690B	11378	N223MD	90	LJ-85
N214KA	F90	LA-14	N219MA	MU-2	440SA	(N222BF)	690B	11378	N223MH	200	BB-1038
N214KC	425	0193	N219PC	PC12	219	N222BJ	90	LJ-636	N223MS	P68	345
N214KF	90	LJ-1570	N219SC	31T	8004040	N222CM	PC12	111	N223P	350	FL-106
N214LA	425	0214	N219WC	200	BB-768	N222CY	200	BB-1370	N223P	90	LJ-1134
N214LJ	441	0104	N220AA	B100	BE-5	N222D	MU-2	271	N223PD	PC12	223
N214LS	MIII	TT-486A	N220AJ	200	BB-1539	N222DM	C-12	BC-15	N223RC	300	FA-58
N214MA	MU-2	436SA	N220B	E90	LW-61	(N222DP)	PC12	507	N223TC	200	BB-394
N214MA	MU-2	570	N220B	G1	56	N222EA	690B	11503	N224BA	MIII	T-204
N214ML	350	FL-475	N220CB	200	BB-426	N222EF	G1	71	N224BB	300	FA-5
N214P	90	LJ-1293	N220CG	350	FL-397	N222FA	MU-2	714SA	N224BH	90	LJ-676
N214PB	PC12	214	N220CL	350	FL-28	N222GA	200	BB-301	N224CC	90	LJ-1218
N214RW	E90	LW-167	N220CL	PC12	364	N222GL	200	BB-229	N224CR	350	FL-60
N214SC	E90	LW-96	N220CS	31T	8275013	N222GS	MU-2	031	N224EC	31T	7920020
N214SE	200	BB-1514	N220DD	200	BB-1027	N222GW	31T	7904050	N224EZ	695B	96206
N214TL	BN2	214	N220DK	200	BB-1058	N222H	G1	101	N224FW	MU-2	008
N214TP	200	BB-1855	N220DL	200	BB-1151	N222HH	MU-2	240	N224FW	MU-2	032
N214WG	31T	7804007	N220ED	PC12	220	N222HH	MU-2	1569SA	(N224GA)	695B	96204
N214WL	350	FL-529	N220F	90	LJ-981	N222HL	MU-2	240	N224HR	MIII	T-217
N215AA	200C	BL-15	N220FS	31T	7620052	N222HM	441	0011	N224JD	PC12	220
(N215AM)	E90	LW-215	N220GK	200	BB-521	N222JC	MIIB	T26-151	N224JE	90	LJ-1629
N215BA	690A	11215	N220HC	690A	11320	N222JC	MIII	T-212	N224JV	90	LJ-1629
N215CC	200	BB-781	N220JB	100	B-10	N222JC	MIV	AT-015	N224LB	100	B-162
N215CX	200	BB-781	N220JB	200	BB-638	N222JC	MIVA	AT-068	N224LM	200	BB-1921
N215GA	300	FA-104	N220JE	46T	97336	N222JC	MIVC	AT-461	N224MA	MU-2	242
N215HC	200	BB-1848	N220JL	46T	97336	N222JD	200	BB-726	N224P	200	BB-1230
N215HC	E90	LW-266	N220JM	46T	97183	N222JD	E90	LW-197	N224P	90	LJ-1067
N215HP	C-12	BC-57	N220JM	TBM7	289	N222JG	MIIB	T26-151	N224PB	PC12	224
N215KA	200	BB-215	N220JM	TBM8	388	(N222JK)	680T	1570-25	N224RT	200	BB-1561
N215LW	200	BB-1766	(N220JN)	46T	97183	N222JM	MU-2	1544SA	N224SB	MIII	T-204
N215MA	MU-2	226	N220JP	PC12	787	N222JP	690A	11273	N225AC	200	BB-491
N215MH	MU-2	1544SA	N220KW	100	B-185	N222JQ	MIII	T-212	N225AD	100	B-130
N215ML	200	BB-1955	N220MA	MU-2	233	N222JW	MU-2	521	N225AD	200	BB-491
N215P	200	BB-1381	N220MA	MU-2	441SA	N222JW	MU-2	731SA	(N225AS)	TBM7	150
N215P	300	FA-62	N220MA	TBM7	248	N222KA	200	BB-49	N225AT	90	LJ-956
N215PA	200	BB-224	N220N	MU-2	450SA	N222LA	200	BB-409	N225CA	31T	8104024
*N215SB	C-12	BC-57	*N220PB	200	BB-1497	N222LP	B100	BE-85	(N225CF)	90	LJ-430
N215SD	46T	97049	N220PB	E90	LW-168	N222LR	MU-2	239	N225CM	350	FL-378
N216	PC12	194	N220RJ	200	BB-1022	N222MA	MU-2	240	N225DF	425	0225
N216AJ	90	LJ-190	N220SB	MU-2	550	N222MB	90	LJ-300	N225HP	200	BB-829
N216BJ	425	0216	N220SC	31T	8120041	N222MC	E90	LW-289	N225JL	200	BB-829
N216CD	MU-2	323	N220T	BN2	883	N222ME	690A	11338	N225LH	C-12	BC-33
N216F	MIIB	T26-116	N220TA	200	BB-409	N222ML	F90	LA-104	(N225LM)	200	BB-1921
N216GA	MIVA	AT-037	N220TB	200	BB-1057	N222MQ	E90	LW-289	N225MA	46T	97106
N216K	90	LJ-583	N220TM	90	LJ-799	N222MS	MU-2	398SA	N225MA	MU-2	243
N216KA	90	LJ-779	N220TT	200	BB-462	N222MT	690A	11155	N225MC	46D	237
N216KC	PC12	216	N220TW	P180	1018	N222MV	MIII	T-212	N225MM	690B	11462
N216LJ	90	LJ-190	N220UM	46T	97183	N222NF	90	LJ-1446	N225MS	200	BB-496
N216MA	MU-2	228	N220W	MU-2	450SA	N222PA	200	BB-406	N225PT	31T	8166032
N216MA	MU-2	437SA	N220Y	E90	LW-220	N222PV	350	FL-167	N225S	90	LJ-695
N216PD	PC12	216	N221AP	G1	6	(N222QW)	31T	7904050	N225SL	200G	BY-41
N216PK	P750	114	N221B	200	BB-19	N222RL	E90	LW-154	N225TL	200	BB-1689
(N216PL)	690A	11332	N221BG	200	BB-354	(N222RR)	PA42	8001037	N225WC	200	BB-1862
N216RP	200	BB-1015	N221CH	90	LJ-436	N222SC	31T	7920082	N225WL	200	BB-1226
N216TM	PC12	441	(N221DR)	F90	LA-147	N222SC	BN2	858	N225WW	31T	7920003
N217CM	200	BB-621	N221DT	MIII	T-387	N222SE	G1	29	N226AT	MIV	AT-003E
(N217CP)	200	BB-490	N221FP	46T	97094	N222SG	G1	29	N226B	E90	LW-14
N217CS	200	BB-37	N221G	350	FL-198	(N222SH)	46T	97275	N226BP	690B	11529
N217CS	31T	8275014	(N221GA)	695B	96202	N222SL	31T	7904046	N226C	441	0226
N217DC	TBM7	88	N221K	695	95077	N222TR	E90	LW-5	N226DD	MIII	T-286
N217DH	TBM7	243	N221KA	E90	LW-272	N222TW	BN2	232	N226DL	46T	97039

N226FC	MIII	T-306
(N226GA)	695B	96205
N226GS	TBM7	226
N226HA	MIIB	T26-142
(N226JP)	MIII	T-256
N226JW	90	LJ-406
N226K	350	FL-226
N226LS	MIIB	T26-166
N226MA	MU-2	244
N226MA	MU-2	448SA
N226N	PC12	414
N226N	PC12	1051
N226PB	TBM7	226
N226PC	PC12	226
N226RA	TBM8	364
N226RA	TBM8	482
N226RC	TBM8	364
(N226RH)	425	0128
N226SR	MIII	T-270
N226TC	MIV	AT-003E
N226W	E90	LW-14
N227	MU-2	510
~~N227BC~~	~~100~~	~~B-227~~
N227CH	MIIB	T26-169
N227DC	90	LJ-876
(N227GA)	695B	96206
N227GA	90	LJ-1927
N227JT	MIII	TT-477A
N227JW	MIVC	AT-585
N227KM	350	FL-91
N227LA	G1	20
N227LS	G1	20
N227MA	MU-2	245
N227MA	MU-2	449SA
N227MV	200G	BY-77
N227MW	200G	BY-73
N227MW	200G	BY-77
N227NS	PC12	715
N227PB	PC12	227
N227TM	31T	7400008
N227TT	MIII	TT-444A
N227US	200	BB-92
N227UT	PC12	1038
N228BE	P180	1182
N228CF	90	LJ-277
N228CX	TBM7	84
N228FS	200	BB-1757
(N228GA)	695C	98001
N228H	G1	141
N228MA	MU-2	246
N228MA	MU-2	450SA
N228MJ	441	0271
N228RA	E90	LW-197
N228RC	200	BB-1910
N228W	680T	1720-91
N228WP	MU-2	228
N229BN	BN2	229
N229C	90	LJ-302
N229CH	90	LJ-302
N229EM	C-12	BC-59
(N229GA)	695B	96207
(N229J)	90	LJ-1629
N229MA	MU-2	032
N229MA	MU-2	451SA
N230CS	200	BB-306
N230DC	200	BB-1256
N230E	G1	36
(N230GA)	695B	96208
N230GK	200	BB-894
N230JS	90	LJ-1263
N230MA	MU-2	248
N230MA	MU-2	452SA
N230PG	PC12	230
(N230RM)	F90	LA-236
N230TW	90	LJ-445
N231CM	46T	97146B
N231GR	G1	86
N231JH	200	BB-516
N231LC	MU-2	362SA
N231LC	MU-2	448SA
N231LQ	MU-2	362SA
N231MA	MU-2	249
N231PC	31T	7820021
(N231PC)	31T	8004021
N231PK	350	FL-231
N231PT	31T	7400003
N231PT	31T	7720003
N231RL	200	BB-868
N231SW	31T	7904007
N231SY	31T	8020064
N232A	90	LJ-237
N232AL	100	B-222
N232BG	90	LJ-1881
N232BS	90	LJ-1881
N232CL	E90	LW-232
N232DH	31T	7904021
(N232GA)	695C	98002
N232GM	425	0219
N232JS	200	BB-446
(N232LJ)	MU-2	016
N232MA	MU-2	250
N232PS	31T	7620018
N232WE	200	BB-603
N233AL	100	B-223
N233JS	200	BB-1507
N233MA	MU-2	251
N233MW	100	B-74
N233MW	200	BB-17
N233MW	90	LJ-404
N233PS	31T	7820039
N233PT	F90	LA-60
N233RB	MU-2	325
N233RC	441	0263
(N233SA)	90	LJ-1585
N233U	G1	145
N234AM	200	BB-243
N234BC	MU-2	271
N234BC	MU-2	352SA
N234BC	MU-2	441SA
(N234BC)	PA42	5527008
(N234C)	31T	7720021
N234CC	441	0100
N234CW	F90	LA-236
N234DP	90	LJ-908
(N234DZ)	46D	11
N234HS	46D	130
N234K	31T	7520001
N234K	31T	7620017
N234KK	350	FL-29
N234KW	200	BB-1065
N234MA	MU-2	252
N234MM	90	LJ-57
N234MM	G1	121
N234PC	31T	8004014
(N234PC)	31T	1104010
N234PM	46T	97200
(N234RC)	MU-2	623
N234RG	PC12	520
N234SA	MIVC	AT-506
N234SB	31T	8104023
N234SE	31T	8120050
N234ST	90	LJ-1447
N234TK	B100	BE-24
N234TT	MIII	T-256
N234U	200	BB-1004
N234Z	46T	97194
N235AH	PC12	235
N235B	100	B-129
(N235GA)	695B	96209
N235HM	90	LJ-162
N235MA	MU-2	253
N235MA	MU-2	453SA
(N235MB)	31T	8020055
N235PB	350	FL-124
N235TW	46T	97157
N236CP	B100	BE-9
(N236GA)	695C	98003
N236JS	F90	LA-90
N236MA	MU-2	254
N236MA	MU-2	454SA
N236ML	F90	LA-236
N236PC	PA42	5501006
N236SC	690A	11245
N236SR	31T	8020058
N236WR	PC12	804
N237JS	F90	LA-15
N237MA	MU-2	101
(N237MA)	MU-2	458SA
N237PC	31T	8166045
N237SC	690B	11433
N237ST	46T	97237
(N238GA)	695B	96210
N238MA	MU-2	247
N238MA	MU-2	459SA
N238MW	90	LJ-404
N238PC	PA42	8001029
N238PC	PC12	238
N239B	E90	LW-13
N239C	90	LJ-738
N239CT	90	LJ-167
N239DR	MIII	T-239
N239JP	425	0016
N239JV	200	BB-1014
N239K	90	LJ-227
N239MA	MU-2	170
N239MW	100	B-74
N239P	MIIB	T26-147
N239PF	200	BB-565
N239TT	300	FA-114
N240AC	681	6043
N240AJ	200	BB-1619
N240CE	MIII	T-205
N240CT	200	BB-1063
N240DA	441	0058
N240DH	MIVC	AT-602
(N240GA)	695C	98004
N240HM	MIII	T-205
N240K	90	LJ-340
N240MA	MU-2	571
N240NM	MIII	T-240
N240PD	PC12	240
N240RE	90	LJ-570
N240RL	200	BB-523
N240RL	90	LJ-570
N240S	300	FA-116
N241AC	31T	8104028
N241B	E90	LW-11
N241CK	200	BB-272
N241CW	B100	BE-54
N241DH	MIVC	AT-607B
N241DT	MIII	T-242
N241FW	441	0241
N241GA	690C	11735
N241MA	MU-2	572
N241PC	PC12	241
N241PH	200	BB-1182
N241PM	46T	97150
N241PS	31T	8120016
N241Q	90	LJ-403
N241TL	TBM7	150
N242A	680W	1761-7
N242CA	TBM7	230
N242DA	90	LJ-484
N242DH	MIVC	AT-608B
N242DM	200	BB-754
N242GB	425	0219
N242JH	PC12	232
N242LC	200	BB-765
N242LF	F90	LA-86
N242MA	MU-2	573
(N242NA)	200	BB-1242
N242NA	200	BB-1242
N242NS	90	LJ-1271
N242PC	PA42	7801004
(N242PM)	PC12	191
N242RA	PA42	8001003
N242TC	690A	11219
N243AR	695	95058
N243BK	P68	361
N243D	90	LJ-200
N243DH	MIVC	AT-609B
N243JB	90	LJ-1243
N243KA	200	BB-487
N243KF	46D	230
N243L	90	LJ-590
N243MA	MU-2	574
N243Q	90	LJ-64
N243RA	MU-2	032
N243TC	90	LJ-584
N244AB	31T	8004015
N244CA	31T	8004009
N244CH	200	BB-801
N244DH	MIVC	AT-618B
N244GC	31T	7804007
(N244GW)	31T	8004049
N244J	F90	LA-44
N244JB	200	BB-30
N244JB	200	BB-921
N244JP	200	BB-109
N244JS	200	BB-754
N244MA	MU-2	575
N244MP	690B	11531
(N244RP)	31T	8104037
N244SA	MIII	T-244
N244SW	200	BB-1054
N245AG	200	BB-548
N245CA	G1	83
N245CF	690A	11313
N245CT	200	BB-1016
N245CT	690A	11313
N245DA	MIII	T-296
N245DH	MIVC	AT-624B
N245DL	441	0298
N245E	680T	1565-21
N245JS	200	BB-693
N245K	200	BB-37
N245KK	695	95016
N245MA	MU-2	576
N245S	46D	60
N246B	100	B-164
N246CA	F90	LA-27
N246CK	90	LJ-694
N246DA	90	LJ-564
(N246DF)	350	FL-290
(N246DF)	350	FL-427
N246DH	MIVC	AT-625B
N246DP	441	0246
N246K	200	BB-62
N246MA	MU-2	577
N246MC	690B	11448
N246NW	MU-2	508
N246NW	MU-2	771SA
N246P	P68	344
N246PH	200	BB-1373
N246PN	P68	344
N246PR	46D	34
N246SD	350	FL-394
N246SD	350	FL-441
N246SE	350	FL-394
N246SP	441	0246
N246W	MU-2	508
N246W	MU-2	552
N246W	MU-2	1552SA
N246WA	MU-2	508
N247AF	200	BB-587
N247B	100	B-139
N247CH	90	LJ-1754
N247DH	MIVC	AT-626B
N247JM	200	BB-996
N247LM	31T	8104043
N247MA	MU-2	578
N247MD	90	LJ-1244
N247N	PC12	414
N247R	31T	7904042
N247WW	PA42	8001011
N248DA	46T	97156
N248DH	MIVC	AT-630B
N248DJ	PA42	5527021
N248J	31T	8166009
N248JH	B100	BE-126
N248JM	200	BB-63
N248MA	MU-2	579
N248MC	90	LJ-872
N248NW	MU-2	771SA
(N248SB)	90	LJ-1433
(N248WW)	31T	8020027
N249C	46T	97093
N249CP	90	LJ-841
N249DA	90	LJ-20
N249DH	MIVC	AT-631B
N249MA	MU-2	580
N249ME	MU-2	580
N249PA	90	LJ-21
N249RC	F90	LA-86
N249RL	MIII	T-249
N249WM	E90	LW-139

N250AA	300C	FM-25
N250AC	681	6022
N250AF	200	BB-1342
N250AF	MU-2	243
(N250AJ)	200	BB-1623
N250AL	G1	20
N250CT	31T	7820011
N250DL	200	BB-799
N250DM	200	BB-1060
N250EH	MIII	T-250
N250FN	200	BB-483
N250GM	425	0131
(N250GV)	200	BB-483
N250HC	200	BB-345
N250HP	E90	LW-58
N250JJ	200	BB-1794
N250KA	200	BB-1439
N250KA	31T	7920069
N250MM	E90	LW-63
N250PB	PC12	250
N250PD	300	FA-33
N250PW	200	BB-1058
N250SA	46T	97004
N250TJ	PA42	8001024
N250TM	200	BB-822
N250TR	200	BB-688
N250TT	31T	7820050
N250U	90	LJ-213
N250YR	200	BB-943
N250YR	200	BB-1083
N251B	680T	1587-38
N251CM	E90	LW-160
N251DA	B100	BE-56
N251DL	200	BB-1244
N251ES	690A	11251
N251LL	300	FA-2
N251M	MU-2	013
N251MA	MU-2	767SA
N251SR	E90	LW-160
N252AF	200	BB-1339
N252CM	E90	LW-205
N252CP	200	BB-1791
N252DC	MU-2	138
N252RC	90	LJ-1152
N252RR	MIII	T-252
N253AG	C-12	BC-7
N253AS	350	FL-155
N253JM	690B	11551
N253MA	MU-2	768SA
N253MM	46T	97063
N253MS	350	FL-155
N253MZ	90	LJ-124
N253P	350	FL-436
N253PC	PC12	253
N253SE	46T	97253
(N253TA)	200	BB-565
N253TA	STAR	NC-10
N253ZM	90	LJ-124
N254AG	C-12	BC-12
N254MA	MU-2	769SA
(N254MC)	MIII	T-325
N254P	90	LJ-1901
N254PC	PC12	254
N254PW	690A	11275
N254TP	MU-2	575
N255AA	G1	55
N255AG	C-12	BC-29
N255AV	200	BB-815
N255C	MU-2	536
N255DF	90	LJ-1197
N255DW	46T	97020
N255MA	MU-2	770SA
N255SW	46D	67
N255TK	G1	200
N256AF	200	BB-1340
N256AG	C-12	BC-37
N256BD	200	BB-1139
N256DD	441	0256
N256DJ	B100	BE-73
N256DP	441	0256
N256EN	200	BB-419
N256K	100	B-36
N256L	200	BB-1063
N256MT	MIVA	AT-068
N256PL	200	BB-679
N256PL	MU-2	245
N256RR	690A	11272
(N256RS)	31T	7904049
N256TA	90	LJ-256
N256TM	200	BB-96
N256TW	200	BB-251
N256WC	MIIB	T26-158E
N257AG	C-12	BC-41
(N257BB)	300	FA-80
N257CG	200	BB-1739
N257CG	90	LJ-1419
N257CQ	90	LJ-1419
N257JM	TBM8	356
N257L	200	BB-1066
N257MA	MU-2	771SA
N257MM	350	FL-257
N257NA	200	BB-257
N257SE	PC12	1039
(N257YA)	200	BB-1585
N257YA	200	BB-1622
N258AG	C-12	BC-44
N258D	E90	LW-255
N258JC	E90	LW-191
N258L	200	BB-1077
N258MA	MU-2	772SA
N258VB	441	0258
N258WC	PC12	258
N259AG	C-12	BC-75
(N259DB)	31T	8020086
N259MA	MU-2	773SA
(N259PC)	31T	8104066
N259SC	E90	LW-17
N259WA	PC12	259
(N260AJ)	200	BB-1609
N260AK	BN2	97
N260CB	MU-2	573
N260F	200	BB-862
N260G	200	BB-862
N260G	200	BB-1525
N260GF	46T	97260
N260HS	PC12	260
N260KA	200	BB-748
N260MA	MU-2	774SA
(N260RC)	680W	1789-19
N260WE	690B	11536
N261AC	200	BB-321
N261BC	200	BB-1757
N261DW	441	0261
N261FW	441	0261
N261GA	200	BB-436
N261GB	90	LJ-1119
N261GB	90	LJ-1550
N261KW	MU-2	264
N261L	G1	33
N261MA	MU-2	758SA
N261MA	MU-2	775SA
N261MC	MIVA	AT-039
N261PL	MIIB	T26-121
N261WB	MU-2	330
N261WR	690A	11168
N261WR	MU-2	027
N261WR	MU-2	330
N262J	TBM7	292
N262MA	MU-2	776SA
N262MM	46T	97040
N262PC	MIII	T-276
N262SA	MIII	T-292
N262SP	300	FA-33
N262TL	46T	97082
N263AL	PC12	112
N263CM	MIII	T-223
N263CW	TBM7	263
N263DC	B100	BE-45
N263K	MIIA	T26-011
N263MA	MU-2	777SA
N263ND	MU-2	698SA
N263PS	PC12	263
N263RS	PC12	112
N263SP	200	BB-1737
N263SW	200	BB-1263
N264B	46T	97028
N264B	MIII	T-221
(N264BL)	MIII	T-330
(N264DF)	350	FL-5
(N264HB)	425	0226
N264KW	MU-2	264
N264KW	MU-2	403SA
N264MA	MU-2	778SA
N264PA	B100	BE-86
N264SP	200	BB-1756
N264WF	PC12	264
N264WS	441	0264
N265EB	200	BB-185
N265EJ	200	BB-911
N265EX	695	95032
N265JH	690C	11689
N265K	100	B-66
N265K	100	B-79
N265PA	300	FA-106
N266EB	200	BB-266
N266F	90	LJ-1330
N266M	MIII	TT-424
N266MA	MU-2	779SA
N266P	G1	20
N266RD	90	LJ-1633
N266RH	200	BB-778
N267AA	G1	154
N267CB	200	BB-1873
N267MA	MU-2	780SA
N267PC	MU-2	787SA
N267R	690B	11456
N267RD	690B	11456
N267ST	46T	97267
N267TT	200	BB-267
N267WF	PC12	267
N268BN	BN2	628
N268CB	300	FA-121
*N268DS	46T	97197
N268LB	350	FL-570
N268MA	MU-2	781SA
N268P	90	LJ-1534
N268PC	PC12	268
(N268PS)	90	LJ-1113
N269AA	MU-2	017
N269AB	PC12	297
N269AF	PC12	297
N269AF	PC12	526
N269AS	MU-2	509
N269BW	200	BB-618
(N269CA)	681B	6052
N269D	200	BB-269
N269DE	MIII	T-208
N269JB	E90	LW-259
N269JG	90	LJ-949
N269JP	PC12	105
N269JR	PC12	105
N269LS	200	BB-799
N269M	695A	96098
N269MA	MU-2	782SA
N269ML	200	BB-760
N269PB	PC12	269
N269PM	MIIA	T26-026
N269RR	90	LJ-321
N269SC	90	LJ-683
N269TA	200	BB-749
N270AB	350	FL-362
N270CS	200	BB-911
N270DP	690B	11541
N270FS	E90	LW-95
N270L	200	BB-861
N270M	90	LJ-288
N270MA	MU-2	783SA
N270PC	PC12	270
N270PS	46T	97395
N270SE	90	LJ-480
N270SF	90	LJ-480
N270TC	90	LJ-858
N271	E90	LW-69
N271AK	90	LJ-1856
N271BC	300	FA-48
N271DC	MIII	T-414
(N271MA)	MU-2	784SA
N271MA	MU-2	797SA
N271MB	90	LJ-106
N271RS	BN2	853
N271SC	100	B-7
N271SE	46T	97271
(N271SF)	PC12	306
N271SG	100	B-7
N271SM	PC12	622
N271SS	PC12	306
N271TW	MU-2	734SA
N271W	90	LJ-2
N271WN	90	LJ-226
N272BE	200	BB-272
N272BN	BN2	2180
N272CA	200	BB-1123
N272E	680T	1563-19
N272EA	90	LJ-1686
N272MA	TBM7	272
N272MC	MU-2	272
N272P	P166	367
N272PC	PC12	272
N272SW	350	FL-228
N272TA	200	BB-1123
N273AF	PC12	273
N273AZ	441	0104
N273MA	MU-2	785SA
N273NA	200	BB-1401
N273NA	E90	LW-273
N273TA	350	FL-69
N273TA	350	FL-518
N274GC	441	0349
N274K	200	BB-306
N274KA	E90	LW-274
N274MA	MU-2	786SA
N274NA	200	BB-1406
N274PC	PC12	274
N274SB	31T	7820074
N274T	200	BB-99
N275AB	PA42	8001013
N275BT	350	FL-275
N275CA	31T	7820089
N275CA	MU-2	1513SA
N275CA	TBM7	200
N275DP	90	LJ-34
N275FA	90	LJ-1403
N275L	90	LJ-728
N275LA	90	LJ-1275
N275LE	90	LJ-373
N275MA	MU-2	255
N275PC	PC12	275
(N275TT)	90	LJ-1275
N275X	200	BB-502
N275X	90	LJ-728
N275Z	200	BB-410
N275Z	90	LJ-728
N276CN	PC12	276
N276H	690A	11175
N276JB	350	FL-219
N276MA	MU-2	256
N276MA	MU-2	787SA
N276PC	PC12	276
N276VM	90	LJ-81
N277DB	31T	8104058
N277DG	31T	8104058
N277DM	200	BB-1932
N277F	90	LJ-73
N277GE	200	BB-1389
N277GM	TBM7	178
N277JB	200	BB-136
N277JB	MU-2	1556SA
N277JJ	200	BB-1043
N277JR	MU-2	1556SA
N277MA	MU-2	257
N277MA	MU-2	788SA
N277PC	PC12	277
N277RS	200	BB-461
N277SP	F90	LA-77
N277SW	90	LJ-968
N277WC	200	BB-1824
N278AB	90	LJ-1012
N278DU	90	LJ-243
N278HM	31T	8104058
N278MA	MU-2	258
N278MA	MU-2	789SA
N278SW	90	LJ-1011
N278WC	PC12	278
N279CA	200	BB-279
N279DD	690B	11373
N279M	MIII	T-279

N279MA	MU-2	259
N279MA	MU-2	790SA
N279PC	TRIS	1067
N279ST	46T	97279
(N279SW)	31T	7920065
N280AR	MIIB	T26-139
N280CA	31T	8004029
N280JR	200	BB-1285
N280K	31T	7620057
N280K	90	LJ-338
(N280KA)	90	LJ-143
N280KT	46D	205
N280MA	MU-2	260
N280MA	MU-2	791SA
N280PC	PC12	280
N280RA	100	B-5
N280RA	200	BB-53
(N280RE)	90	LJ-697
N280SC	200	BB-664
N280SW	31T	8004057
N280TT	200	BB-280
N280YR	200	BB-943
(N281DS)	46T	97197
N281JH	200	BB-516
N281MA	MU-2	261
N281PD	46T	97262
N281SE	46T	97281
N281SW	31T	8104007
(N281U)	200	BB-608
N281WB	PC12	483
(N281WJ)	200	BB-1281
N281WJ	200	BB-1281
N282AC	695A	96029
N282CT	200	BB-1002
N282DB	E90	LW-209
N282HC	300	FA-58
(N282HJ)	PC6	921
N282JD	200	BB-1779
N282MA	MU-2	262
N282MS	MU-2	194
N282PC	300	FA-151
N282PC	31T	8166006
N282SJ	200	BB-925
N282SW	46T	97073
(N282TA)	200	BB-1123
N282TC	E90	LW-311
(N282TC)	PA42	8001086
N283B	C-12	BC-35
N283BS	TBM7	16
N283CB	350	FL-135
N283DP	90	LJ-1037
N283JP	200	BB-283
N283KA	200	BB-83
N283MA	MU-2	263
N283MA	MU-2	792SA
N283PC	PC12	283
N283PM	100	B-46
N283SW	PC6	540
N284BB	31T	1104012
N284BL	31T	1104012
N284K	200	BB-608
N284KW	200	BB-1084
N284LK	PC12	284
N284MA	MU-2	120
N284MA	MU-2	793SA
N284MC	31T	1104012
N284PM	90	LJ-734
N285AA	G1	44
N285JE	TBM8	469
N285KA	300	FA-60
N285KW	31T	1166007
N285L	PC6	565
N285MA	MU-2	581
N285MA	MU-2	794SA
N285PS	PC12	285
N286AF	690A	11286
N286MA	MU-2	582
N286R	200	BB-1545
N286TC	200	BB-291
(N286WA)	90	LJ-1574
N287AA	G1	159
N287CB	31T	8166051
N287GS	B100	BE-105
N287MA	46T	97319
N287MA	MU-2	583
N287MA	MU-2	795SA
N287MN	31T	7400013
N287MN	31T	7520004
N287PC	PC12	287
N288CB	350	FL-135
(N288CB)	350	FL-355
N288CB	E90	LW-269
N288CC	TBM8	369
N288CR	E90	LW-269
N288DC	31T	7920030
(N288FA)	PA42	5501011
N288GS	200	BB-1555
N288HH	90	LJ-157
N288HL	MU-2	412SA
N288KM	200	BB-1508
N288MA	MU-2	584
N288MA	MU-2	796SA
N288MT	90	LJ-1157
N288PB	PC12	288
N288RA	100	B-5
N288RG	90	LJ-159
(N288SB)	31T	7920030
N288SF	200	BB-288
(N288W)	680T	1720-91
N289AS	MU-2	509
N289CA	200C	BL-5
N289MA	MU-2	585
N289PB	PC12	289
N289RP	90	LJ-1665
N290AJ	90	LJ-871
N290AS	350	FL-296
N290AS	G1	164
(N290BT)	350	FL-290
N290CC	90	LJ-132
N290CM	31T	8120025
N290DK	F90	LA-90
N290DP	90	LJ-529
N290EA	BN2	62
N290GC	MU-2	310
(N290JS)	90	LJ-1500
N290K	E90	LW-337
N290KA	E90	LW-59
N290KA	F90	LA-2
N290MA	MU-2	260
N290MA	MU-2	447SA
N290MA	MU-2	586
N290MC	E90	LW-206
N290PA	90	LJ-519
N290PF	690A	11290
N290RD	90	LJ-167
N290RS	31T	7904033
N290SA	90	LJ-1637
N290SJ	200	BB-290
N290T	31T	7820047
N290T	MIII	T-329
(N290T)	PA42	8001004
N290TA	MIII	T-228
N290TC	E90	LW-339
N290VL	BN2	3
N290VL	BN2	62
N290WL	90	LJ-374
N291AS	350	FL-332
N291AV	E90	LW-291
N291B	350	FL-559
N291CC	90	LJ-728
N291CJ	P68	291
N291DF	90	LJ-1534
N291EX	BN2	65
N291GS	MU-2	1539SA
N291MA	MU-2	587
N291MA	MU-2	641
N291MB	MU-2	291
N291MM	E90	LW-32
N291PA	200	BB-291
N291RB	690A	11161
N291ST	46T	97291
N292A	90	LJ-99
N292MA	MU-2	588
N292P	PC12	630
N292PB	PC12	292
N292RG	TBM7	14
N292SN	200	BB-1425
N292Z	680T	1566-22
N293D	B100	BE-59
N293DR	441	0293
N293MA	MU-2	589
N293PC	PC12	293
N293TA	350	FL-69
N293WX	90	LJ-169
N294A	MIVA	AT-029
N294BC	690A	11130
N294CS	200	BB-1294
N294DR	46T	97184
N294MA	MU-2	590
N294PJ	TBM8	438
N294TT	90	LJ-1098
N294VB	441	0294
N294WT	200	BB-1294
(N295AW)	90	LJ-1798
N295BC	690A	11145
N295CE	441	0205
N295CP	200	BB-1295
N295MA	MU-2	591
N295NM	690B	11384
N295PC	PC12	295
N295S	46D	93
N295SA	G1	33
N295SS	46D	93
N295X	90	LJ-244
N296A	90	LJ-208
N296AS	90	LJ-704
N296BT	350	FL-296
N296J	46D	108
N296LC	46D	233
N296MA	MU-2	592
N296ST	46T	97296
N296TA	BN2	384
N296YV	200	BB-1296
N297D	F90	LA-152
N297LE	90	LJ-454
N297MA	MU-2	593
N297PT	90	LJ-454
(N297SL)	B100	BE-27
N297TA	BN2	741
N297W	90	LJ-454
N297X	G1	32
N298D	200	BB-446
N298D	90	LJ-1603
N298MA	MU-2	594
N298S	90	LJ-588
N299AK	200	BB-1823
N299AK	200	BB-1850
N299AL	200	BB-1823
N299AM	PC12	236
N299AS	350	FL-243
N299AV	200	BB-1680
(N299CR)	200C	BL-39
N299D	90	LJ-257
N299DE	680W	1721-1
N299EC	MIII	T-410
N299ED	680W	1721-1
N299F	680T	1703-79
N299F	690A	11112
N299FL	680T	1703-79
N299GS	300	FA-113
N299HT	MU-2	674
N299K	90	LJ-115
N299K	90	LJ-839
N299KA	90	LJ-1125
N299KP	F90	LA-218
N299MA	46T	97294
N299MA	MU-2	595
N299MK	200	BB-1357
N299MS	90	LJ-457
N299MT	B100	BE-58
N299PC	TRIS	1062
N299RJ	200	BB-1613
N299RP	90	LJ-1537
N299SC	200	BB-633
N299VM	90	LJ-1125
(N300A)	90	LJ-463
N300A	G1	140
N300AA	F90	LA-221
N300AE	TBM7	97
N300AJ	200	BB-965
N300AL	MIII	T-326
N300AV	300	FA-145
N300AW	90	LJ-1570
N300AZ	TBM7	300
N300BA	E90	LW-143
N300BD	MU-2	547
(N300BF)	F90	LA-144
N300BJ	E90	LW-191
N300BL	200	BB-1060
N300BP	31T	7620055
(N300BP)	G1	112
N300BT	300	FA-11
N300BW	200	BB-302
N300BX	31T	7720057
N300CE	31T	8004028
N300CE	MIIB	T26-160
N300CE	MIVA	AT-029
N300CF	680W	1843-42
N300CH	690A	11189
(N300CH)	690B	11385
N300CH	E90	LW-148
N300CK	90	LJ-703
N300CK	90	LJ-1126
N300CM	31T	7620030
(N300CM)	31T	7904031
N300CP	200	BB-77
N300CP	690B	11374
N300CR	200	BB-1217
N300CS	31T	7520018
N300CT	200	BB-447
N300CT	680W	1834-39
N300CT	90	LJ-393
N300CV	MIII	TT-483A
N300CW	300	FA-115
N300CW	MU-2	667
N300CW	MU-2	795SA
N300CX	TBM7	327
N300DA	100	B-76
N300DD	90	LJ-196
N300DG	B100	BE-15
N300DK	200	BB-167
N300DK	200	BB-1024
N300DK	PA42	8001016
N300DM	F90	LA-165
N300EH	200	BB-194
N300EH	E90	LW-307
N300ET	200	BB-1381
N300FE	441	0038
N300FL	200	BB-1629
N300FL	90	LJ-1066
N300FN	90	LJ-1066
N300GC	90	LJ-701
N300GC	F90	LA-55
N300GM	MU-2	724SA
N300GN	200	BB-62
N300GP	G1	162
N300HB	200	BB-566
N300HC	90	LJ-94
N300HC	E90	LW-272
N300HG	90	LJ-94
N300HH	300	FA-80
N300HH	680T	1546-9
N300HH	90	LJ-1133
N300HM	200	BB-514
N300HP	31T	8020038
N300HS	425	0104
N300HV	300	FA-29
N300JC	31T	7820040
N300JC	350	FL-13
(N300JC)	441	0025
N300JC	PA42	5501026
N300JD	200	BB-532
N300JE	MIII	T-381
N300JK	200	BB-532
N300JQ	PA42	5501026
N300KA	300	FA-2
N300KA	300	FA-24
N300KA	300	FA-143
N300KA	350	FL-28
N300KC	200	BB-359
N300KC	200	BB-423
N300KC	680T	1709-84
N300KD	E90	LW-148
N300KF	MIII	T-329
N300KK	300	FA-2
N300KQ	680T	1709-84

N300L	OMAC	001
N300LE	B100	BE-15
N300LE	P68	295
N300LF	P68	295
N300LM	300	FA-41
N300LS	350	FL-127
N300LX	200	BB-1320
(N300M)	690B	11361
N300MA	MU-2	596
N300MC	300	FA-91
N300MC	G1	32
N300MP	B100	BE-44
N300MT	B100	BE-58
N300MT	E90	LW-143
N300MT	MIII	T-307
N300MV	B100	BE-73
N300MY	300	FA-187
N300NC	MIII	T-381
N300NK	441	0318
N300P	G1	191
N300PB	PC12	300
N300PE	300	FA-27
N300PE	31T	7400010
N300PE	31T	7520001
N300PE	G1	112
N300PH	200	BB-194
N300PH	300	FA-201
N300PK	300	FA-8
N300PM	G1	112
N300PP	300	FA-171
N300PR	300	FA-13
(N300PR)	31T	7820001
N300PS	350	FL-15
N300PS	E90	LW-92
N300PT	MIII	T-233
N300PU	200	BB-1657
N300PV	31T	8120038
N300PW	200	BB-114
N300PW	TBM7	1
N300PW	TBM7	85
N300QW	200	BB-752
N300R	350	FL-362
N300R	B100	BE-110
N300RC	300	FA-177
N300RK	E90	LW-284
N300RV	90	LJ-376
N300RX	MU-2	572
N300SB	G1	101
N300SE	300	FA-68
N300SM	MU-2	194
N300SP	E90	LW-166
N300SR	31T	8104022
N300SV	300	FA-112
N300TA	F90	LA-9
N300TA	MIII	T-261
N300TB	300	FA-69
N300TB	31T	8020042
N300TB	31T	8004002
N300TE	300	FA-19
N300TJ	300	FA-13
N300TJ	300	FA-74
N300TM	300	FA-168
N300TM	31T	8166054
N300TM	350	FL-50
N300TN	300	FA-168
N300TN	B100	BE-84
N300TP	200	BB-1279
N300TR	200	BB-6
N300UP	G1	18
N300US	200	BB-243
N300VA	90	LJ-877
N300VY	300	FA-187
N300WC	TBM7	82
N300WJ	200	BB-319
N300WP	31T	7904006
N300WT	31T	7520018
N300WT	MU-2	604
N300XL	31T	8166021
(N300XZ)	G1	191
N300ZD	MIVC	AT-469
N301CG	300	FA-87
N301CH	31T	8020067
N301CS	31T	7720032
N301D	200	BB-1124

N301D	46T	97043
N301DK	90	LJ-372
N301DM	46D	162
N301ER	90	LJ-1286
(N301GC)	300	FA-13
N301GM	MU-2	696
N301HC	200	BB-1219
(N301HC)	E90	LW-272
N301JW	350	FL-13
N301KB	441	0137
N301KS	300	FA-61
N301L	MU-2	026
N301L	OMAC	001
N301LA	MU-2	026
N301MA	MU-2	597
(N301MP)	695	95047
N301PS	200	BB-657
N301PT	31T	7804002
N301PT	C-12	BP-28
N301SK	BN2	555
N301SL	P180	1011
N301TA	31T	7904041
N301TS	90	LJ-372
N301TS	B100	BE-76
(N301TT)	200	BB-6
N301TT	300	FA-121
N302AG	200	BB-480
N302BA	690A	11302
N302BC	200	BB-625
(N302CA)	31T	8166022
N302DK	90	LJ-907
N302H	46D	18
N302HA	31T	7920041
N302HC	300	FA-14
N302K	G1	48
N302MB	200	BB-272
N302MM	46T	97129
N302NC	300	FA-9
N302PB	PC12	302
N302PC	200	BB-499
N302PT	C-12	BP-30
N302RJ	TBM8	425
N302SC	31T	8275004
N302SK	BN2	2002
N302TA	31T	8020046
(N302TS)	90	LJ-372
N302WB	690	11003
N302WC	690B	11399
N302X	MU-2	030
N302YV	200	BB-1302
N303AG	MU-2	239
N303C	46D	209
N303CA	90	LJ-1134
N303CA	MU-2	1518SA
N303CB	100	B-84
N303D	90	LJ-1055
N303DK	200	BB-578
N303E	695	95000
N303G	690B	11355
N303GM	695A	96042
N303JD	PC12	303
N303JW	46T	97149
N303KL	31T	7820061
N303MA	MIII	T-278
N303MA	MU-2	598
N303MC	425	0034
(N303MF)	E90	LW-59
N303NH	90	LJ-260
N303PL	PA42	8001057
N303QC	90	LJ-754
N303RR	350	FL-178
N303SC	31T	8275011
N303TS	31T	8166007
N303WB	TBM7	25
N303WJ	90	LJ-363
N303WP	MIIB	T26-139
N303X	90	LJ-329
N304BP	350	FL-542
(N304EF)	PA42	8001004
(N304EN)	441	0304
N304HC	690A	11304
N304JS	300	FA-142
(N304K)	G1	72
N304K	G1	75

N304L	MU-2	137
N304LA	MU-2	137
N304LG	E90	LW-231
N304M	MIIA	T26-008
N304MA	MU-2	599
N304PB	PC12	304
(N304PR)	PC12	304
N304PT	PC12	304
N304SC	31T	8275017
N304SK	BN2	564
N304SL	P180	1077
(N304TC)	100	B-222
N304TC	90	LJ-1719
N305AS	90	LJ-773
N305BC	E90	LW-17
N305CW	MU-2	667
N305DG	46T	97305
N305DS	MU-2	328
N305JD	46D	126
N305JS	200	BB-472
N305K	G1	76
N305P	350	FL-10
N305PC	E90	LW-17
(N305PC)	MU-2	748SA
N305RL	350	FL-10
N305SA	300	FA-111
N305SL	P180	1083
N305TT	90	LJ-992
N305TZ	100	B-169
N305YV	200	BB-1305
N306BC	100	B-225
N306H	MU-2	553
N306M	300	FA-98
N306SL	P180	1084
N306SS	200	BB-306
(N306TC)	100	B-223
N307AT	G1	109
N307CA	PA42	5527010
N307CL	690B	11508
N307CW	300	FA-187
N307DM	200	BB-332
N307EL	G1	161
N307G	200	BB-467
N307G	MIIB	T26-134
N307K	G1	177
N307LW	90	LJ-140
N307MA	MU-2	007
N307MA	MU-2	600
N307P	200	BB-575
N307PA	MIII	T-307
N307PB	PC12	307
N307SC	31T	8275009
(N307SK)	BN2	524
N307SL	P180	1091
N308CF	680W	1843-42
N308F	200	BB-333
(N308F)	441	0031
N308LH	31T	8004014
N308MA	MU-2	601
N308MD	90	LJ-1246
N308NA	PC12	226
N308PS	E90	LW-92
N308RH	200	BB-109
N308RM	90	LJ-628
N308SC	31T	8275008
N308SL	P180	1093
N308ST	46T	97308
N308SW	31T	8004014
N308TC	MU-2	1507SA
N309BT	350	FL-309
N309D	E90	LW-87
N309L	90	LJ-436
N309M	350	FL-48
N309MA	MU-2	602
N309P	90	LJ-1253
N309SC	31T	8275002
N309SP	MIIB	T26-172E
N309YV	200	BB-1309
N310GA	200	BB-386
N310GA	200	BB-1310
N310GA	690B	11422
N310GF	E90	LW-72
N310GT	200	BB-993
N310JD	31T	8166062

N310JM	46T	97069
N310KR	90	LJ-300
N310KR	90	LJ-797
N310MA	MU-2	167
N310MA	MU-2	264
N310TK	350	FL-237
N310VE	300	FA-104
N310WA	31T	7920029
N310Y	MU-2	165
N311AC	31T	8120016
N311AV	200	BB-336
N311CE	MU-2	593
N311CK	90	LJ-1126
N311CM	B100	BE-101
N311DB	F90	LA-55
N311DS	F90	LA-41
N311G	200	BB-1760
N311GA	200	BB-329
N311GC	F90	LA-55
N311GM	350	FL-138
N311GM	MIII	T-256
(N311HC)	441	0194
N311JB	MU-2	311
N311KB	C-12	BD-3
N311LM	31T	7720016
N311MA	MU-2	265
N311MH	680T	1616-49
N311MP	200	BB-1112
N311PB	PC12	311
N311PD	680T	1616-49
N311RF	300	FA-33
N311RN	MU-2	311
N311RR	441	0138
N311RV	MIII	T-250
N311RV	MIVA	AT-069
N311SC	31T	8275006
N311SR	90	LJ-107
N311TJ	90	LJ-1121
N311TP	425	0031
N311UE	100	B-67
N311UL	100	B-67
N312AC	MIII	T-322
N312AR	300	FA-216
N312BC	PC12	101
N312CC	31T	8104019
(N312CT)	441	0085
N312D	200T	BT-23
N312DB	300	FA-35
N312DE	300	FA-49
(N312DS)	90	LJ-36
N312JC	200	BB-1312
N312JC	MIIB	T26-143
N312KJ	441	0167
N312KJ	STAR	NC-46
N312MA	MU-2	266
N312ME	200C	BL-46
(N312MH)	90	LJ-299
N312MP	E90	LW-85
N312MT	31T	8166062
N312P	90	LJ-708
N312PC	PC12	144
N312RF	90	LJ-299
N312RJ	MIIB	T26-143
N312RL	350	FL-164
(N312SA)	441	0312
N312SB	200	BB-1313
(N312ST)	MIII	TT-438
N312VF	90	LJ-299
N313BA	300	FA-178
N313BB	MU-2	529
N313BB	PA42	5501016
N313BC	46D	124
N313BH	F90	LA-114
N313BP	TBM8	434
N313CT	200	BB-461
N313D	MIVC	AT-464
N313DS	441	0313
N313DW	90	LJ-1434
N313EE	200	BB-708
N313EL	200	BB-708
N313ES	200	BB-1300
N313GA	441	0200
N313HS	200	BB-1300
N313JL	425	0010

N313KY	300	FA-110
N313LC	P68T	8001
N313MA	MU-2	267
N313MB	300	FA-23
N313MK	90	LJ-1460
N313MP	300	FA-23
N313PC	MU-2	531
N313PC	PA42	5527044
*N313PT	90	LJ-1662
N313SA	300	FA-5
N313SC	200	BB-875
(N313SS)	31T	8020034
N314DD	31T	8004025
N314EB	B100	BE-125
N314FH	200	BB-1788
N314FW	200	BB-1788
N314FW	200	BB-1800
(N314G)	90	LJ-104
N314GA	31T	7520023
N314GK	31T	8004026
N314MA	MU-2	268
N314MA	MU-2	557
N314MR	E90	LW-184
N314P	F90	LA-170
N314SC	31T	8275007
N314TD	31T	8020056
N314YV	200	BB-1314
(N315B)	90	LJ-1020
N315DB	MIII	T-315
(N315JS)	31T	8120054
N315JW	200	BB-281
N315KA	200	BB-215
N315LP	MU-2	269
N315MA	MU-2	269
N315MA	MU-2	737SA
N315MS	200	BB-404
N315N	200	BB-1766
N315P	350	FL-42
(N315SA)	200	BB-1299
N315SC	31T	8275008
N316AF	90	LJ-214
N316EN	MU-2	349SA
N316GC	200	BB-430
N316JM	46D	110
N316JP	200	BB-923
N316JP	31T	8004057
N316KA	300	FA-19
(N316LR)	425	0195
N316M	90	LJ-12
N316MA	MU-2	270
N316MS	200	BB-412
N316MW	MIV	AT-018
N316PM	PC12	241
N316PR	MU-2	761SA
N316RS	300	FA-139
N316W	350	FL-456
N316WB	31T	8004057
(N316WF)	PC12	137
(N317BC)	300	FA-82
N317EC	90	LJ-847
(N317EC)	90	LJ-848
N317MA	MU-2	271
N317NA	PC12	223
N317P	350	FL-74
N317RT	200	BB-1694
N318AK	441	0070
N318AK	MIII	T-315
N318CA	200	BB-678
N318CB	200	BB-1730
N318CD	MU-2	772SA
N318CW	46D	102
N318DH	MIVC	AT-469
N318DS	90	LJ-873
N318EA	TBM8	366
N318ED	46D	206
N318F	90	LJ-574
(N318FE)	695A	96031
N318LA	90	LJ-892
N318MA	31T	7620018
N318MA	MU-2	272
N318MA	MU-2	512
N318MT	PC12	318
N318SW	31T	8166020
N318TK	690A	11136
N318W	200	BB-402
N318WA	690B	11444
N319BF	690C	11675
*N319D	90	LJ-350
N319D	90	LJ-760
N319EE	350	FL-187
N319EE	350	FL-401
N319FB	680W	1820-34
N319FB	690A	11315
N319JG	31T	7620056
N319MA	MU-2	273
N319MB	90	LJ-1126
N319MP	E90	LW-90
(N319P)	350	FL-57
N319P	350	FL-63
N319P	E90	LW-90
N319PB	680W	1820-34
N319SF	200	BB-9
N319TB	TBM7	319
N320CA	P180	1069
N320E	90	LJ-378
N320F	90	LJ-234
(N320FJ)	200	BB-155
N320JS	200C	BL-53
N320LB	200	BB-60
N320LH	E90	LW-329
N320M	690A	11104
N320MA	MU-2	274
N320PW	PC12	647
N320SS	425	0139
N321AF	441	0353
N321AV	90	LJ-942
N321BF	200G	BY-83
N321CF	PA42	8001073
N321CR	46D	118
N321CW	TBM7	155
N321DA	441	0321
N321DB	690A	11218
N321DH	E90	LW-61
N321DH	PC12	116
N321DM	E90	LW-250
N321DZ	90	LJ-367
N321EC	300	FA-55
N321F	C-12	BC-70
N321FJ	90	LJ-862
N321FS	46D	187
N321GC	200	BB-1942
(N321GM)	690A	11105
N321GM	MU-2	1505SA
N321JG	F90	LA-41
N321LB	31T	8166012
N321LH	PA42	5527012
N321M	690A	11336
N321MA	MU-2	276
N321MC	690B	11541
(N321MD)	695	95014
N321MG	690	11069
N321MK	STAR	NC-20
N321MT	690A	11286
N321MX	PC12	215
N321P	RC12	GR-10
N321PH	MIIB	T26-140
N321PL	PC12	321
N321RB	P68	259
N321RC	MU-2	760SA
N321RT	P68	189
N321SF	200	BB-854
(N321SF)	200	BB-1207
(N321SJ)	MU-2	760SA
(N321SS)	31T	8020035
N321ST	MU-2	307
N321TH	B100	BE-104
N321TP	MU-2	780SA
(N321TS)	MIII	T-231
*N321TS	MIII	T-231
N322AN	441	0127
N322BB	MIII	T-250
N322BR	90	LJ-1222
N322GA	MU-2	166
N322GB	MU-2	015
N322GB	MU-2	166
N322GB	MU-2	419SA
N322GK	F90	LA-64
(N322JD)	31T	8120014
(N322KW)	PA42	5527022
(N322MA)	MU-2	277
N322MA	MU-2	277
N322MR	90	LJ-1611
N322P	441	0274
N322R	90	LJ-746
N322TA	MU-2	280
N322TA	MU-2	760SA
N322TC	90	LJ-1302
N323CT	31T	8104019
N323DB	350	FL-23
N323DB	F90	LA-83
N323FL	46D	218
N323HA	E90	LW-323
N323JG	200	BB-1900
N323JG	441	0323
N323KA	E90	LW-323
N323MA	MU-2	280
N323MB	200	BB-130
N323MC	90	LJ-1000
N323ML	46D	218
N323RR	200	BB-380
N324AB	90	LJ-1270
N324B	100	B-151
N324BK	PC12	718
N324BK	PC12	1021
N324BS	C-12	BJ-16
N324BT	690A	11260
N324CE	MIIB	T26-160
N324EC	100	B-99
N324GM	MU-2	310
N324JP	90	LJ-1921
N324JS	TBM7	230
N324NE	300	FA-112
N324PC	PC12	324
N324PS	C-12	BJ-58
N324SC	PC12	490
(N325A)	90	LJ-1165
N325AT	C-12	BJ-10
N325CA	PA42	8001044
N325CM	441	0325
N325FS	PC12	746
N325JG	300	FA-196
N325JM	350	FL-235
N325KW	PA42	5527025
N325MA	MU-2	281
N325MA	MU-2	325
N325MM	695A	96015
N325MW	PC12	325
N325RT	441	0288
N325WP	300	FA-173
N325WP	F90	LA-10
N325WR	F90	LA-10
N326AA	200C	BL-26
N326AJ	200	BB-396
"N326BA"	200	BB-92
N326DJ	441	0070
N326F	300	FA-111
N326KW	200	BB-1360
N326L	425	0041
N326MA	350	FL-47
N326MA	MU-2	282
N326MS	MIII	T-313
N326MX	350	FL-47
N326PA	PC12	362
N326PC	PC12	326
(N326PK)	350	FL-326
N326PS	200	BB-1326
N326PT	90	LJ-1581
N326RS	441	0326
N326RT	200	BB-553
N326V	PC12	733
N327A	P180	1158
N327CM	200	BB-327
N327E	MU-2	154
N327JZ	PC12	327
N327MA	MU-2	283
N327ME	300	FA-127
(N327ML)	LFAN	E-003
N327ML	LFAN	E-003
N327R	350	FL-259
N327RB	200	BB-335
N327RK	200	BB-335
N327SC	PC6	946
N327SE	200	BB-1670
N327YR	P180	1173
N327YR	PC12	457
N328AF	PC12	328
N328AJ	31T	8004020
N328AJ	350	FL-245
N328AJ	MIII	TT-483A
N328AJ	PA42	8001020
N328CA	G1	116
N328JP	PC12	328
N328KK	31T	8166068
N328MA	MU-2	284
N328PA	PC12	328
(N328PD)	31T	8104068
N328SE	46T	97328
N328TB	E90	LW-136
N328VP	441	0301
N329CT	G1	45
N329H	90	LJ-309
N329HS	MIIB	T26-149
N329HS	MIII	T-323
N329KK	31T	8104011
N329MA	MU-2	285
N329MH	200G	BY-40
N329NG	PC12	329
N329PA	PC12	263
N329SK	PC12	441
N329WM	MU-2	410SA
N330BR	200	BB-115
N330CB	90	LJ-27
N330CS	200	BB-1337
N330DA	300	FA-158
N330DB	90	LJ-1542
N330DM	P180	1014
N330DR	200	BB-1389
N330DR	200	BB-1578
N330DR	300	FA-158
N330DR	90	LJ-1237
N330ES	690B	11476
(N330JP)	MIII	T-322
N330LC	680T	1679-61
N330MA	MU-2	286
N330MG	200	BB-1798
N330PE	90	LJ-1917
N330PM	90	LJ-157
N330RC	90	LJ-1130
N330V	90	LJ-811
N330VP	F90	LA-227
N331AM	90	LJ-144
N331BB	31T	8020087
(N331BB)	B100	BE-60
N331GB	B100	BE-16
N331GM	MIII	T-331
N331H	G1	70
N331J	MIII	T-331
N331JA	690A	11310
N331JP	90	LJ-1756
N331KB	31T	7804009
N331MA	MU-2	287
N331MA	MU-2	768SA
N331MM	MU-2	549
N331MP	441	0312
N331MS	BN2	596
N331NF	695	95063
N331PC	31T	7820067
N331PC	PC12	331
N331PT	31T	7400004
N331RC	690A	11137
N331SC	690C	11635
N331SW	31T	7904012
N331SY	31T	7904036
N331TB	MIII	T-331
N331TT	31T	7400004
N331V	FPC6	2002
N331W	MU-2	1519SA
(N331Z)	200	BB-1008
N332CP	300	FA-65
N332DE	90	LJ-674
N332DM	441	0167
N332K	90	LJ-79
N332M	200G	BY-39
N332MS	90	LJ-1023
N332S	441	0133
N332SA	PA42	8001020

N332SA	PA42	5527025
N332SM	PA42	8001020
N333AH	G1	38
N333AP	200	BB-1137
N333AS	E90	LW-230
N333BH	P180	1057
N333BM	90	LJ-1504
N333BR	MU-2	119
N333CA	690A	11117
N333CA	690A	11136
N333CE	31T	7920038
N333CR	200	BB-614
N333CS	90	LJ-44
N333DP	441	0246
N333DV	300	FA-144
N333EB	F90	LA-139
(N333EC)	690B	11477
N333ET	200	BB-360
N333F	MIIB	T26-100
(N333FJ)	90	LJ-562
N333FP	MU-2	119
N333G	90	LJ-101
N333GC	690B	11441
N333GC	695	95009
N333GE	441	0235
N333GG	90	LJ-129
(N333GM)	BN2	479
N333GM	MU-2	703SA
N333HC	690A	11150
N333JA	90	LJ-882
N333JE	MU-2	119
N333JJ	90	LJ-347
N333KB	31T	7920024
N333KD	690B	11459
N333KM	MU-2	165
N333KM	MU-2	679
N333LE	E90	LW-223
N333LM	31T	7920052
N333LT	90	LJ-125
N333M	350	FL-243
N333MA	MU-2	288
N333MM	46T	97010
N333MW	90	LJ-644
N333MX	31T	7920052
N333MX	PA42	5527003
N333MZ	31T	7920052
N333NB	200	BB-130
N333NB	200	BB-578
N333NB	90	LJ-644
N333NB	B100	BE-29
(N333ND)	200	BB-578
N333P	31T	7720003
N333P	31T	7820002
N333P	31T	7920001
N333P	31T	8020002
N333PA	690B	11523
N333PA	PC12	333
N333PD	31T	7820010
N333RB	MU-2	163
N333RB	MU-2	325
N333RB	MU-2	534
N333RD	200	BB-915
N333RF	441	0053
N333RK	681B	6059
N333RK	MU-2	118
N333RK	MU-2	140
N333RK	MU-2	380SA
N333SG	MIII	T-239
N333SR	200	BB-529
N333TE	680W	1842-41
N333TK	90	LJ-1783
N333TL	90	LJ-999
N333TN	31T	8020089
N333TP	200	BB-1292
N333TP	90	LJ-999
N333TS	200	BB-512
N333TX	MU-2	332
N333UJ	425	0179
N333UP	690	11016
N333UP	690B	11435
N333UP	695A	96001
N333UP	695A	96015
N333UR	690	11016
N333WC	300	FA-55
N333WF	MU-2	387SA
N333WM	46T	97010
N333WT	F90	LA-91
N333X	31T	8166070
N333X	90	LJ-248
N333XX	31T	7920038
N334	680T	1694-73
N334CA	31T	7904034
N334D	200	BB-1188
N334DP	200	BB-1188
N334DP	90	LJ-908
N334EB	MU-2	568
N334FP	PA42	8001104
N334FW	441	0334
N334JG	680T	1694-73
N334JR	TBM7	334
N334LS	200	BB-76
N334MA	MU-2	289
N334RR	200	BB-361
N334ST	46T	97334
N334TP	680T	1694-73
N335AP	90	LJ-1919
N335GA	200	BB-565
N335H	680T	1709-84
N335KW	200	BB-1335
N335MA	MU-2	603
N335MA	TBM7	235
N335PB	PC12	335
N335R	F90	LA-160
N335S	200	BB-227
N335TA	200	BB-514
N335TM	200	BB-115
N335WH	PC12	335
N336JM	E90	LW-345
N336MA	MU-2	604
N336MM	350	FL-607
N336P	31T	7400003
N336P	46T	97300
N336PC	PC12	336
N336SA	MIII	T-336
N337C	441	0126
N337DR	690D	15007
N337FG	681B	6048
N337H	MIIA	T26-022
N337K	100	B-185
N337KC	441	0337
N337MA	MU-2	605
N337MT	200	BB-1628
N337RE	441	0214
N337TB	200	BB-1979
N337TF	46T	97094
N337TP	PC12	326
N338	90	LJ-307
N338AS	90	LJ-493
N338CC	PC6	903
N338CM	MU-2	703SA
N338DB	46D	222
N338DB	46T	97111
N338DB	46T	97155
N338DR	90	LJ-1237
N338GW	90	LJ-234
N338MA	MU-2	606
N338PC	PC12	338
N338SB	PC6	953
N338UP	690B	11435
N338X	90	LJ-248
N338YV	200	BB-1338
N339AJ	200	BB-339
N339D	300	FA-83
N339JG	B100	BE-130
N339KA	E90	LW-339
N339MA	MU-2	607
N339PC	PC12	339
N339RW	MIII	T-339
N339W	TBM7	39
N339WD	300	FA-39
N339YV	200	BB-1339
(N340BH)	PA42	5501003
N340BK	200	BB-992
N340BK	680W	1820-34
N340BK	690	11020
N340BP	690	11020
N340MA	MU-2	608
N340N	PC6	340
N340PN	P68	340
N340RE	PC12	179
N340TT	200	BB-992
N340WB	G1	65
N340X	MIIA	T26-017
N340YV	200	BB-1340
N341CC	BN2	874
N341DB	300	FA-185
N341MA	MU-2	609
N341MH	E90	LW-341
N341MM	46T	97168
N341T	MIIA	T26-015
N341WJ	441	0341
N341YV	200	BB-1341
N342CF	90	LJ-1156
(N342DA)	31T	7820040
N342MA	MU-2	610
N342NX	MIII	T-342
N342P	90	LJ-1616
(N342PC)	PA42	7901002
N342SC	MU-2	1505SA
N342SE	46T	97342
N342TW	PA42	8001017
N342YV	200	BB-1342
N343CL	200	BB-8
N343CP	200	BB-8
N343CW	PC12	340
N343MA	MU-2	600
N343RR	46T	97197
N343YV	200	BB-1343
(N344)	680T	1694-73
(N344)	680T	1713-87
(N344)	680T	1714-88
(N344AC)	681	6016
N344CC	P68	285
N344CL	FPC6	2019
N344DJ	G1	43
N344DP	90	LJ-1414
N344EA	P68	120
N344K	MU-2	257
N344KL	MU-2	257
N344L	350	FL-107
N344MA	MU-2	611
(N344MD)	TBM7	153
N344T	200	BB-124
N344TC	P68	344
N344W	E90	LW-344
N345BH	90	LJ-1645
N345CA	680W	1842-41
N345CM	690B	11402
N345CP	BN2	2244
N345CS	90	LJ-432
N345DF	31T	7820088
N345DG	200	BB-1653
N345DG	350	FL-427
N345GA	425	0054
N345HB	TBM7	155
N345KA	E90	LW-139
N345LL	90	LJ-432
N345MA	MU-2	612
N345MB	200	BB-1148
N345MB	E90	LW-230
N345MP	441	0194
N345PC	PC12	345
N345RC	90	LJ-352
N345RD	TBM7	76
N345RF	PC12	345
N345SA	MIII	TT-534
(N345SA)	MU-2	557
N345SE	46D	176
(N345SP)	690A	11126
N345T	MIIB	T26-105
N345TP	425	0005
N345TT	680W	1791-21
N345TW	G1	65
N345V	E90	LW-23
N345WK	200	BB-1580
N345WT	46T	97267
N346BA	200	BB-1653
N346CM	200	BB-18
N346DA	G1	323
N346F	FPC6	2001
N346GA	31T	8166029
N346JC	31T	8166029
N346K	MU-2	292
N346MA	MU-2	613
N346VL	MU-2	231
N347AA	31T	1104013
N347AR	441	0085
N347D	200	BB-1197
(N347D)	200	BB-1204
N347DW	46D	148
N347F	FPC6	2002
N347KC	PC12	347
N348AC	90	LJ-196
N348BP	680T	1616-49
(N348CP)	MU-2	447SA
N348D	90	LJ-871
N348DA	G1	26
N348F	FPC6	2006
N348FH	FPC6	2006
N348KN	MIIB	T26-152
N348KN	MIII	T-228
N348KN	MIII	TT-541
N348KX	MIII	T-228
N348MA	MU-2	614
N348MJ	200C	BL-15
N348PC	PC12	348
N349AC	690	11032
N349C	200	BB-1099
N349D	200	BB-68
N349FH	FPC6	2007
(N349JW)	200	BB-349
N349MA	MU-2	615
N349MP	441	0302
N350AB	350	FL-83
N350AB	350	FL-212
N350AC	200	BB-405
N350AF	350	FL-184
N350AG	350	FL-546
N350AJ	350	FL-22
N350AM	350	FL-100
N350AT	E90	LW-58
N350BA	F90	LA-186
N350BB	350	FL-22
N350BD	350	FL-123
N350BF	300	FA-187
N350BG	350	FL-217
N350BK	350	FL-350
N350BR	46D	219
N350BS	350	FL-6
N350BW	350	FL-278
N350CA	350	FL-45
N350CB	350	FL-324
N350CB	350	FL-392
(N350CD)	300	FA-177
(N350CE)	350	FL-260
N350CS	350	FL-61
N350CS	350	FL-214
N350CV	350	FL-228
N350D	350	FL-334
N350DK	350	FL-30
N350DK	350	FL-56
N350DR	350	FL-63
N350DW	300	FA-157
(N350E)	350	FL-116
N350EA	350	FL-116
N350EB	350	FL-49
N350EB	350	FL-561
(N350EC)	MU-2	381SA
N350FC	350	FL-214
N350FC	350	FL-217
N350FH	350	FL-10
N350FH	FPC6	2008
(N350FT)	350	FL-45
N350FW	350	FL-421
N350GA	350	FL-16
N350GL	350	FL-253
(N350GL)	350	FL-274
N350GT	350	FL-261
N350HA	350	FL-393
N350HB	350	FL-271
N350HB	350	FL-672
N350HE	MU-2	653
N350J	350	FL-314
N350JB	350	FL-213
N350JG	350	FL-609
N350JJ	350	FL-59

N350JR	350	FL-312	N351C	46T	97382	N359F	FPC6	2017	N364UZ	90	LJ-805
N350JW	350	FL-208	N351C	46T	97398	N359GP	31T	1166001	N364WA	690B	11439
N350K	350	FL-245	N351CB	200	BB-1889	N359JT	90	LJ-1136	N365CA	300	FA-107
N350K	350	FL-422	N351CB	350	FL-396	N359K	200	BB-359	N365CS	300	FA-120
N350KA	350	FL-2	N351CK	TBM8	351	N359MB	350	FL-359	N365F	FPC6	2022
N350KA	350	FL-38	N351CR	350	FL-396	(N360BA)	B100	BE-9	N365G	90	LJ-132
N350KA	350	FL-70	N351DD	350	FL-257	N360BT	100	B-30	N365K	90	LJ-442
N350KA	350	FL-91	N351EB	350	FL-121	N360C	100	B-21	N365PC	PC12	365
N350KA	350	FL-136	N351FH	FPC6	2012	N360CB	200	BB-649	N366EA	200	BB-841
N350KA	350	FL-149	N351FW	200	BB-351	N360CB	350	FL-336	N366F	FPC6	2023
N350KA	350	FL-173	N351GC	350	FL-56	N360D	90	LJ-240	N366FG	690B	11410
N350KA	350	FL-233	N351GR	E90	LW-324	N360DA	PC12	270	N366GW	E90	LW-320
(N350KA)	350	FL-237	N351MA	200	BB-359	N360EA	200	BB-1231	N366JM	E90	LW-320
N350KA	350	FL-259	N351MH	E90	LW-95	N360F	FPC6	2018	N366NC	90	LJ-1444
N350KA	350	FL-329	N351MK	200	BB-674	N360GA	300	FA-156	N366P	G1	42
N350KA	350	FL-330	N351MP	350	FL-305	N360GK	90	LJ-727	N366SA	MIII	T-366
N350KA	350	FL-331	N351PC	PC12	351	N360JK	MU-2	525	N366SL	350	FL-366
N350KA	350	FL-601	N351SA	200	BB-1423	N360LL	31T	7520036	N366SP	F90	LA-53
N350KC	350	FL-70	N351SC	200	BB-1640	N360M	90	LJ-218	N367AJ	200	BB-1367
N350KD	350	FL-331	N351SP	BN2	56	(N360MC)	MU-2	622	N367DA	MU-2	623
N350KG	350	FL-156	N351SS	690D	15001	N360MP	90	LJ-1085	N367DF	90	LJ-42
N350KM	46D	67	N352BC	350	FL-463	N360RA	MU-2	740SA	N367EA	200	BB-896
N350KR	350	FL-2	N352BN	BN2	352	N360SC	200	BB-1030	N367EA	90	LJ-1219
N350KS	350	FL-323	N352CM	46D	163	N360SC	B100	BE-111	N367EA	TBM8	410
N350LL	350	FL-157	N352F	F1	0001	N360TC	P68	360	N367F	FPC6	2024
N350LM	350	FL-514	N352F	FPC6	2011	N360TL	BN2T	2143	N367LF	200	BB-405
N350MA	MU-2	183	N352GR	E90	LW-93	N360WT	BN2T	2115	N367RA	200	BB-367
N350MC	MIII	T-400	N352NR	100	B-25	N360WT	G1	173	N368FA	200	BB-741
N350MG	350	FL-528	N352SM	MIII	TT-515A	N360X	200	BB-1783	*N368JA	200	BB-741
N350MH	E90	LW-95	(N352SP)	BN2	726	N360X	680T	1589-40	(N368L)	690A	11146
N350MM	46D	136	N353ES	425	0158	N360X	90	LJ-422	N368PC	PC12	368
N350MR	350	FL-14	N353F	FPC6	2009	N360XL	90	LJ-422	N368RK	90	LJ-1267
N350MR	350	FL-408	N353KM	PC12	534	N361D	B100	BE-9	N368T	690A	11146
N350MS	350	FL-99	N353PC	PC12	353	N361DB	PC12	103	N369B	90	LJ-1226
N350MS	350	FL-320	N353T	31T	7820018	N361DB	PC12	132	N369BR	F90	LA-73
N350MS	350	FL-326	N353Z	90	LJ-1605	N361EA	200	BB-1103	N369CD	E90	LW-162
N350MS	350	FL-470	N354AF	PC12	354	N361F	FPC6	2025	N369DP	100	B-160
(N350MT)	350	FL-408	N354F	FPC6	2010	N361FB	PC12	155	N369DR	MIIB	T26-122
N350NJ	350	FL-20	N354H	350	FL-354	N361G	G1	21	N369F	300	FA-185
N350NY	350	FL-283	N355AF	200	BB-178	N361GB	PC12	132	N369GA	90	LJ-934
N350NY	350	FL-539	N355BC	PA42	8001063	N361JA	MU-2	681	N369GM	690B	11369
N350P	350	FL-47	N355BN	BN2	355	N361JC	31T	7720062	N369LC	P180	1154
N350P	350	FL-138	N355CL	90	LJ-1520	N361MA	MU-2	429SA	N369MK	300	FA-203
(N350PC)	350	FL-3	N355DM	350	FL-320	N361Q	G1	21	N369PC	441	0351
N350PJ	350	FL-384	N355F	FPC6	2013	N361RA	BN2	382	N369RC	90	LJ-1626
N350PL	350	FL-381	(N355HC)	681	6001	N361SC	B100	BE-111	N369TA	200	BB-820
N350PM	46D	67	N355JS	E90	LW-257	N361TD	200C	BL-128	(N370AA)	200	BB-311
N350PT	350	FL-467	N355MA	425	0031	N361WR	690A	11168	N370AC	MU-2	370SA
N350PX	350	FL-560	N355MR	350	FL-14	N362AB	31T	1166008	N370AE	MIVC	AT-506
N350Q	350	FL-14	N355PM	46T	97071	N362D	E90	LW-265	N370JP	EPIC	001
(N350RC)	350	FL-275	N355SS	31T	8166028	N362DB	350	FL-571	N370K	680T	1570-25
N350RD	350	FL-365	N355TW	200	BB-521	N362EA	200	BB-257	N370LH	200G	BY-37
N350RG	MU-2	773SA	N355VB	441	0355	N362EA	200	BB-1396	N370MA	MU-2	370SA
N350RK	350	FL-516	N356AA	200C	BL-55	N362F	FPC6	2020	N370NA	350	FL-345
N350RR	350	FL-365	N356AJ	MU-2	381SA	N362G	G1	84	N370SA	MU-2	370SA
N350RR	350	FL-634	N356CC	200	BB-1843	N362GP	G1	84	N370TC	200	BB-311
N350RV	350	FL-585	N356F	FPC6	2014	N362MC	90	LJ-760	N370U	90	LJ-1428
N350S	350	FL-9	N356F	TBM7	207	N362SC	200G	BY-61	N370V	90	LJ-41
N350S	350	FL-179	N356GA	200	BB-447	N362SH	690A	11316	N370X	MIIB	T26-106
N350SK	350	FL-583	N356M	TBM7	32	N362TD	200C	BL-130	N371BG	G1	4
N350SM	350	FL-474	N356WC	200	BB-1066	N363CA	200	BB-1250	N371CP	F90	LA-97
N350SR	350	FL-38	N356WG	200	BB-1066	N363CA	350	FL-326	N371CW	TBM8	371
N350ST	31T	8020068	N357BB	350	FL-27	N363CB	90	LJ-429	(N371DG)	681	6020
N350TC	B100	BE-62	(N357CA)	90	LJ-1177	N363D	200	BB-1503	N371DR	681	6020
N350TF	350	FL-202	N357CC	F90	LA-180	N363DA	200	BB-344	N371H	100	B-173
N350TG	350	FL-247	N357CY	90	LJ-1178	N363DB	90	LJ-429	N371TA	200	BB-335
N350TJ	B100	BE-125	N357F	FPC6	2015	N363EA	200	BB-1538	N371TM	31T	1104011
N350TK	350	FL-5	N357H	G1	88	N363EA	B100	BE-134	N372GT	PC12	372
N350TL	350	FL-347	N357HP	90	LJ-1030	N363F	FPC6	2021	N372JB	200	BB-719
N350TR	350	FL-67	N357JR	90	LJ-5	N363G	G1	111	N372JM	31T	8166029
N350TT	350	FL-103	N357PN	P68	357	N363K	200	BB-1503	N373CA	PA42	8001037
N350TT	350	FL-347	N357RL	350	FL-373	N363K	90	LJ-1617	(N373GE)	PC12	373
N350TT	350	FL-413	N357ST	695	95074	N363N	90	LJ-236	N373KM	PC12	373
N350TV	350	FL-319	N357X	680T	1544-8	(N363PD)	441	0228	N373LD	46T	97360
N350TW	300C	FM-2	N358AA	G1	58	N364BC	B100	BE-35	N373LP	425	0141
N350TW	350	FL-3	N358F	FPC6	2016	N364C	300	FA-109	N373Q	PA42	8001014
N350VM	350	FL-41	N358HF	690B	11551	N364CL	FPC6	2019	N373WP	350	FL-519
N350WA	90	LJ-762	N358K	90	LJ-1231	N364D	90	LJ-837	N374BH	350	FL-442
N350WD	350	FL-256	N358KA	350	FL-38	N364EA	200	BB-689	N374CH	350	FL-449
N350WG	350	FL-214	N358PC	PC12	358	N364F	FPC6	2019	N374GA	31T	7820047
N350WH	350	FL-210	N358ST	200	BB-987	N364G	G1	99	N374GS	31T	7820047
N350WP	350	FL-282	N359BA	441	0359	N364L	G1	99	N374PC	PC12	374
N351BC	200C	BL-37	N359CV	PC12	382	(N364MW)	200	BB-364	N375A	680T	1692-71
N351BM	EPIC	110	N359D	90	LJ-810	N364SB	200	BB-445	N375A	680T	1699-76

N375AA	690A	11179
N375AC	MU-2	327
N375BZ	TBM8	472
N375CA	MU-2	643
N375CP	350	FL-433
N375EM	E90	LW-309
N375K	441	0125
N375PC	PC12	375
N375RD	46T	97003
N375SE	46T	97375
N376	G1	67
N376BT	MU-2	140
N376D	90	LJ-42
N376KC	PC12	376
N376NA	350	FL-376
N376RC	200	BB-376
N376RF	690B	11533
N376TC	690	11057
N376WS	31T	8020064
N376YV	200	BB-1376
N377	G1	69
(N377AC)	PC12	162
N377CA	441	0289
N377GL	425	0233
N377L	PC12	346
N377NJ	MU-2	104
N377P	90	LJ-1087
N377PC	PC12	377
N377SC	425	0052
N378FC	TBM8	378
N378HC	31T	7820011
N378HH	PC12	378
N378MF	300	FA-105
N378RM	MU-2	770SA
N378SF	200	BB-378
N379BT	200	BB-986
N379D	F90	LA-114
N379JG	MIII	T-414
N379SA	350	FL-179
N379SW	31T	7920071
N379VM	E90	LW-27
N380AA	90	LJ-883
N380AC	200	BB-480
N380CA	31T	8020053
(N380GW)	200	BB-380
N380M	90	LJ-218
N380MC	200	BB-480
N380MS	350	FL-320
N380PB	PC12	380
N380SA	C-12	BC-7
N380SC	90	LJ-862
N380SE	46T	97380
N380TM	PC12	380
N380TT	200	BB-803
N380W	100	B-145
(N381HC)	200	BB-1219
N381HC	200	BB-1952
N381MG	350	FL-182
N381PD	C-12	BC-14
N381R	200	BB-385
N381SC	90	LJ-1381
N381SW	31T	8104015
N382AC	690D	15016
N382AG	200	BB-1059
N382MB	31T	8120057
N382ME	200	BB-436
N382PD	C-12	BC-15
(N382TC)	PA42	8001092
N382TW	E90	LW-141
N382WC	100	B-24
N383AA	E90	LW-13
N383AS	200	BB-106
N383AS	350	FL-296
(N383CA)	200	BB-1250
N383DA	90	LJ-592
*N383DF	P68	300
N383JC	90	LJ-207
N383JP	200	BB-615
N383NA	200	BB-1112
N383SS	425	0139
N383SS	441	0161
N383YV	200	BB-1383
N384CA	31T	7904013
N384DB	200	BB-383
N384GD	200G	BY-4
N384H	90	LJ-745
N384JB	90	LJ-697
N384JD	200	BB-383
(N384LS)	200	BB-76
N384MA	425	0174
N384MC	31T	8020087
N384VP	P68	384
N384YV	200	BB-1384
N385AS	350	FL-309
N385GA	200	BB-15
N385GH	441	0066
N385H	350	FL-610
N385KA	300	FA-42
N385KC	46T	97385
N385KG	BN2	2016
(N385M)	G1	197
N385M	G1	197
N385MA	425	0131
N385MC	200	BB-1017
N386CP	90	LJ-1119
N386CP	TBM7	335
(N386CP)	TBM8	477
N386CP	TBM8	477
N386GA	90	LJ-775
N386MA	TBM7	286
N386TH	90	LJ-1777
N386TM	MU-2	386SA
N387AS	90	LJ-1417
N387CC	MIII	T-360
N387GA	90	LJ-726
N387GC	90	LJ-1655
N387MA	MU-2	657
N387TT	PC12	1048
N387W	PC12	387
N388AB	EPIC	017
N388AS	90	LJ-493
N388CC	200	BB-126
N388CM	300	FA-151
N388CP	200	BB-1160
(N388CP)	E90	LW-231
N388DR	441	0100
N388HP	46T	97388
N388MC	200	BB-388
N388MC	90	LJ-383
N388MC	90	LJ-442
N388NC	MU-2	328
N388NC	MU-2	452SA
N388NG	MU-2	328
N388PC	PC12	388
N388RB	MU-2	163
N388RD	MU-2	163
N388SC	E90	LW-109
N388SR	PC12	316
N388TW	46T	97018
N389AS	90	LJ-1438
N389GA	200	BB-756
N389MA	46D	178
N389RA	200C	BL-56
N389SA	200	BB-1389
N389W	PC12	389
N390AC	200C	BL-5
N390AM	P68	390
N390C	46T	97369
N390D	F90	LA-216
N390GT	90	LJ-1758
N390K	MU-2	277
N390KA	100	B-240
N390L	90	LJ-987
N390MD	350	FL-333
N390MT	E90	LW-279
N390PS	E90	LW-279
N390SA	C-12	BD-2
N390SP	200	BB-1970
N390TT	350	FL-39
(N390YH)	90	LJ-740
N391BT	90	LJ-983
N391EC	PC12	391
N391GM	MIII	T-391
N391L	200	BB-1322
N391MT	300	FA-111
N391MT	350	FL-371
N391R	PC6	519
N391RR	350	FL-23
N391SA	C-12	BC-37
N392AC	FPC6	2071
N392CA	90	LJ-392
N392CA	FPC6	2071
N392CT	200	BB-392
N392D	200	BB-1247
N392DF	200	BB-1247
N392DM	200	BB-189
(N392EZ)	200	BB-1247
N392K	200	BB-189
N392KC	200	BB-392
N392P	MU-2	392SA
N392R	PC6	530
N392TW	90	LJ-392
N392WC	PC12	392
N393AF	PC12	393
N393CE	F90	LA-230
N393CF	300	FA-214
N393CF	F90	LA-230
N393DM	200	BB-292
(N393JM)	200	BB-292
N393JW	200	BB-292
N393K	200	BB-292
N393R	PC6	598
N393W	MIIB	T26-125
N394AL	90	LJ-394
N394AM	P68	394
N394B	90	LJ-1553
N394G	441	0272
N394GL	200	BB-1011
N394R	PC6	599
N394S	350	FL-144
N394S	350	FL-492
N395AM	200	BB-1101
N395AS	90	LJ-1575
N395CA	31T	1166005
N395DA	90	LJ-495
N395DR	PA42	8001065
N395KT	P180	1044
N395MB	350	FL-39
N395P	90	LJ-1591
N395PC	PC12	395
N395SM	46T	97129
N395W	PC12	394
N395WK	EPIC	041
N396AS	90	LJ-1540
N396AW	TBM7	279
N396CA	90	LJ-1035
*N396CT	200	BB-1858
N396DP	200	BB-81
N396DP	200	BB-416
N396DP	90	LJ-115
N396DP	90	LJ-401
N396DR	90	LJ-401
N396FW	PA42	8001021
N396JH	31T	7920087
N396PS	MIIB	T26-151
N396SA	C-12	BC-23
N397CA	90	LJ-1031
N397MY	EPIC	032
N397S	350	FL-144
N397SA	200	BB-4
N397WA	PC12	397
N397WM	300	FA-156
N398CA	PC12	115
N398D	90	LJ-1082
N398DE	300	FA-109
N398DP	200	BB-81
N398HM	200	BB-398
N398J	PC12	398
N398SP	31T	8104027
N398T	MIIB	T26-129
N399AE	200	BB-1834
N399AM	PC12	249
N399AS	200C	BL-65
N399BM	200	BB-399
N399CW	200	BB-1646
N399D	300	FA-18
N399GM	690	11030
N399GT	90	LJ-73
N399LA	200	BB-1135
N399MB	90	LJ-1591
N399PB	PC12	399
N399PC	TRIS	1063
N399PM	46D	107
N399SA	200	BB-5
N399SP	MU-2	371SA
N399T	680T	1532-2
N399TW	F90	LA-203
N399WS	90	LJ-1547
N400AC	B100	BE-12
N400AE	350	FL-2
N400AJ	200	BB-52
N400AJ	200	BB-1138
N400AJ	H400	101
N400AL	350	FL-2
N400AL	350	FL-428
N400AM	90	LJ-354
N400AV	A400	POC
N400BE	100	B-10
N400BG	441	0069
N400BW	PC12	224
N400BX	90	LJ-686
(N400BX)	MU-2	600
N400CC	MIII	T-204
N400CE	90	LJ-209
N400CM	31T	7620040
N400CP	31T	8020071
N400CT	441	0153
N400DB	200	BB-67
N400DC	MIIB	T26-167
N400DG	MIIA	T26-009
N400DK	695	95041
N400DS	690B	11512
N400DW	695	95041
N400ES	MU-2	389SA
N400FA	MIVC	AT-557
N400FF	MIII	T-310
N400G	680T	1563-19
N400GA	200	BB-963
N400GC	200	BB-503
N400GC	B100	BE-25
N400GM	200	BB-392
N400GW	200	BB-1583
N400GW	90	LJ-1221
N400HT	G1	149
N400JA	BN2	517
N400JH	MU-2	381SA
N400JJ	690	11034
(N400JP)	200	BB-948
(N400JW)	690B	11537
N400KK	MU-2	118
N400KW	200	BB-337
N400LJ	31T	8004012
N400LM	200	BB-1042
N400LP	680T	1697-74
N400LR	680T	1697-74
N400LR	PA42	5527003
N400N	200	BB-487
(N400N)	300	FA-65
N400N	690A	11156
N400N	90	LJ-653
N400P	G1	12
N400P	MIIA	T26-005
N400PB	31T	7920002
N400PC	90	LJ-27
N400PJ	PA42	8427003
N400PJ	PA42	5527003
N400PL	MIV	AT-011
N400PQ	90	LJ-27
N400PS	MU-2	411SA
N400PS	PA42	8427002
N400PS	PA42	5527002
N400PT	46T	97E1
N400PT	PA42	8427001
N400PT	PA42	5527001
N400QE	90	LJ-209
N400QK	200	BB-402
N400QK	200	BB-1104
N400RK	B100	BE-49
N400RT	31T	7820042
N400RV	90	LJ-853
N400RX	MU-2	593
N400S	MIIB	T26-142
N400SF	E90	LW-221
N400SG	MU-2	634
N400SJ	MIII	T-209
N400SL	PA42	5527007

N400SM	MU-2	244
N400SN	PA42	5527014
(N400SR)	90	LJ-1096
N400ST	TBM7	16
N400SU	MIII	T-209
N400TB	200	BB-426
N400TG	90	LJ-1591
N400TJ	B100	BE-111
N400TM	31T	8120018
(N400TM)	PA42	5527024
N400TR	MU-2	161
N400TW	46D	193
N400U	200	BB-247
N400V	90	LJ-157
N400VB	PA42	5527002
N400VF	MIIB	T26-154
N400WF	G1	169
N400WH	100	B-232
N400WH	200	BB-331
N400WH	PA42	5527026
N400WP	200	BB-584
N400WP	G1	169
(N400WS)	31T	8004012
N400WS	31T	8166044
N400XL	31T	8166016
N400XL	31T	8166028
N401AS	STAR	NC-19
N401BL	300	FA-125
N401CG	200	BB-1666
N401CP	46T	97316
N401EM	90	LJ-950
N401HC	200	BB-1294
N401HT	90	LJ-49
N401JA	TRIS	1039
N401JC	MU-2	326
N401MA	MU-2	798SA
(N401MD)	PA42	8001009
N401MM	46T	97001
N401NC	PA42	8001081
N401NS	300	FA-28
N401NW	MIIB	T26-133
N401PD	PC12	401
N401PT	31T	7904014
N401SK	200	BB-1828
N401SM	PC12	255
N401SP	690B	11564
N401TJ	100	B-84
N401TS	90	LJ-1501
N401TT	90	LJ-1501
N401TW	PA42	5527008
N401VA	31T	8275001
N401WS	P180	1057
N402AB	690C	11659
N402BL	F90	LA-130
N402CE	200	BB-81
N402CJ	200	BB-296
N402CT	200	BB-1929
N402CW	441	689
N402EM	90	LJ-914
N402G	100	B-14
N402GW	46T	97120B
N402JA	BN2	570
N402JH	MU-2	1514SA
N402JL	350	FL-402
N402KA	200	BB-296
N402MD	90	LJ-1831
N402ML	MIII	T-407
N402MM	46T	97002
N402NC	300	FA-80
N402NC	425	0035
N402NG	425	0035
(N402PS)	46T	97120B
N402RG	200	BB-135
N402ST	690B	11358
N402TW	PA42	5527020
N402VP	P68	402
N403EM	90	LJ-1000
N403G	300	FA-73
N403HP	46D	215
N403J	200	BB-1700
N403JA	TRIS	1029
N403KC	46T	97403
N403MA	MU-2	799SA
N403MM	46T	97E3
N403MP	200	BB-121
N403N	90	LJ-27
N403NA	BN2	178
N403NW	90	LJ-27
N403P	350	FL-96
N403R	200	BB-396
N404AF	31T	7920048
N404AU	200	BB-1022
N404BS	200	BB-1022
N404DP	200	BB-819
N404EF	PA42	8001004
N404EW	300	FA-186
N404EW	425	0099
N404FA	200	BB-981
N404G	90	LJ-202
N404GT	200G	BY-4
N404J	200	BB-1793
N404JA	BN2	590
N404JP	90	LJ-1039
N404PT	200	BB-1674
(N404RW)	E90	LW-314
N404SC	90	LJ-843
N404SD	300	FA-76
N404SK	200	BB-1355
(N404TW)	PA42	5527034
N404VW	90	LJ-530
N404WB	BN2	564
N404WD	441	682
N404X	90	LJ-330
N405BC	90	LJ-457
N405DD	90	LJ-1748
N405EM	90	LJ-726
N405J	350	FL-112
N405JA	BN2	588
N405JB	441	0187
N405KT	P180	1191
N405MA	441	0316
N405MA	MU-2	1501SA
(N405P)	300	FA-62
N405PB	PC12	405
N405PT	200	BB-930
N405RM	BN2	2167
N405SA	MIII	T-329
N405SC	BN2	61
N406BE	441	0074
N406CE	F406	0001
N406CP	690C	11655
N406CT	F406	0061
N406GV	F406	0049
N406JA	BN2	2012
N406MA	425	0197
N406MA	MU-2	1502SA
N406P	F406	0050
N406RL	90	LJ-1574
N406RS	31T	7920048
N406SD	F406	0063
N406SF	E90	LW-218
N406TM	31T	8120018
N407CF	90	LJ-1849
N407GW	90	LJ-1221
N407JA	BN2	586
N407JA	BN2	2002
N407MA	MU-2	1503SA
N408C	300	FA-155
N408G	300	FA-73
N408GP	PA42	5527008
(N408JA)	BN2	2003
N408JA	BN2	2023
N408LB	PC12	408
N408RN	200	BB-1709
N408SF	P180	1137
(N408SH)	31T	8104052
N408SW	31T	8004018
N408WG	PA42	5527008
(N409AC)	31T	8104017
N409D	350	FL-497
N409DH	200	BB-795
N409DR	PC12	377
N409GA	200	BB-376
N409JA	BN2	2024
N409LV	350	FL-409
N409ND	90	LJ-985
N409RA	200	BB-429
N409SC	31T	7904008
N409SH	31T	8104052
N410AA	G1	88
N410BL	31T	8166055
N410CA	31T	8166005
N410CP	F90	LA-127
(N410GL)	200	BB-931
N410H	200	BB-1719
(N410JA)	BN2	868
N410LD	PA42	5501029
N410MA	441	0254
N410MA	MU-2	304
N410MA	MU-2	1504SA
N410MC	90	LJ-761
N410MF	441	0093
N410NA	31T	8104068
N410PB	E90	LW-86
N410PD	90	LJ-389
N410PD	E90	LW-86
N410PT	200	BB-1978
N410PT	90	LJ-1662
N410RE	200	BB-4
N410SB	100	B-146
N410SH	200	BB-117
N410SP	100	B-146
N410SP	U-21	LM-136
N410TH	680W	1790-20
N410TW	PA42	5527017
N410VB	PA42	5527029
N410VE	425	0097
N410W	90	LJ-39
N410WA	100	B-75
N410WA	425	0221
N410WA	90	LJ-39
N410WB	100	B-75
N410WC	90	LJ-883
N411BG	PA42	5527004
N411BL	200	BB-448
N411CC	200	BB-911
N411CC	200	BB-1520
N411DL	31T	7720057
N411FT	90	LJ-443
N411HA	100	B-21
N411HB	46T	97303
N411JA	BN2	2103
N411JC	MIV	AT-011
N411JE	MU-2	1520SA
N411KC	200	BB-901
N411LM	31T	7720069
N411MA	441	0021
N411MA	MU-2	1505SA
N411MV	PC12	344
N411RA	200	BB-712
N411RJ	F90	LA-108
N411RS	90	LJ-106
N411WA	TRIS	1023
N411X	MIIB	T26-126
N412AC	690B	11375
N412CB	350	FL-440
(N412FB)	690	11015
N412FC	B100	BE-83
N412FS	690	11015
N412FS	B100	BE-83
N412FW	441	0101
(N412JA)	BN2	2020
N412KA	350	FL-612
N412KA	90	LJ-1412
N412KC	PC12	129
N412M	B100	BE-84
N412MA	90	LJ-214
N412MA	MU-2	1506SA
N412MD	PC12	412
(N412PD)	90	LJ-389
N412PW	441	0101
N412Q	90	LJ-22
N412SH	200	BB-1269
N412SR	E90	LW-2
(N412VR)	P68	412
N412WA	TRIS	1020
N412WC	90	LJ-1916
N412WC	PC12	412
N413AF	PC12	413
N413AP	E90	LW-139
N413DM	200	BB-768
N413JA	BN2T	880
N413MA	441	0344
N413MA	MU-2	1507SA
N413PC	441	0240
N414AF	90	LJ-835
(N414CW)	31T	8020042
N414CW	425	0177
(N414EA)	690	11034
N414GC	E90	LW-57
N414GN	90	LJ-36
N414GN	E90	LW-156
N414GQ	E90	LW-57
N414JA	BN2	2107
N414MG	690A	11211
(N414VM)	31T	7620048
N414WA	TRIS	1034
N415CA	G1	27
N415GN	F90	LA-175
(N415HH)	MU-2	1507SA
N415HS	F90	LA-210
N415KA	300C	FM-15
N415MA	90	LJ-900
N415MA	MU-2	1508SA
N415P	90	LJ-1345
N415PA	441	0179
N415PB	PC12	415
N415RB	200	BB-1513
N415RB	F90	LA-210
N415TM	200	BB-1762
N415WA	BN2	2021
N415WR	46D	184
N416AT	200	BB-1180
N416BK	90	LJ-816
N416CS	200	BB-1099
N416CS	200	BB-1182
N416CS	90	LJ-205
N416DY	300	FA-197
N416DY	F90	LA-177
N416LF	90	LJ-267
N416LF	P180	1012
N416MA	441	0167
N416MA	MU-2	1509SA
N416MR	90	LJ-267
N416P	90	LJ-1221
N416P	F90	LA-67
N416PC	PC12	416
N416WA	BN2	2015
N417AR	PC12	611
N417CS	90	LJ-213
N417EM	200	BB-937
N417G	31T	8020008
N417KC	PC12	417
N417MA	MU-2	1510SA
N417MC	200	BB-1526
N417RC	200	BB-188
N417RK	46D	192
N417SH	90	LJ-1789
N417UP	BN2	10
N417VN	90	LJ-1202
N417WA	BN2	2005
N418CD	MU-2	344
N418CS	200	BB-14
(N418DJ)	31T	7904052
N418DN	200	BB-1130
N418DR	PC12	192
N418DY	F90	LA-177
N418GA	100	B-61
N418GA	200	BB-183
N418J	200	BB-1705
N418LA	100	B-61
N418MA	MU-2	1511SA
N418PB	PC12	418
N418SP	U-21	LM-138
N418SW	31T	8166029
(N419CE)	350	FL-12
N419D	90	LJ-401
N419FW	P68	419
N419GR	46T	97244
(N419HM)	E90	LW-225
N419R	31T	7820034
N419S	680T	1560-17
N419SC	441	0149
N419TW	200	BB-1158
N419WA	PC12	419
N420A	441	0083

N420AF	PC12	420	N425BP	200	BB-1773	N425PJ	425	0157	N428SJ	690	11016
N420CA	PA42	8301002	N425BS	425	0210	N425PL	425	0010	N428TB	E90	LW-22
N420DB	441	0129	N425BW	425	0088	N425PN	425	0214	N428V	E90	LW-188
N420DW	31T	8004040	N425BX	425	0156	N425PV	425	0104	N429AP	31T	7820076
N420DW	PC12	129	N425BZ	425	0104	N425R	425	0120	N429BX	PA42	5527023
N420DW	PC12	404	N425CC	425	0002	N425RF	425	0147	(N429BX)	PA42	5527026
N420G	90	LJ-33	N425CC	425	0159	(N425RJ)	425	0164	N429CA	46D	29
N420J	680T	1698-75	N425CF	425	0018	N425RM	425	0180	N429DM	200	BB-398
N420M	90	LJ-12	N425CL	425	0206	N425RR	690A	11259	N429DM	90	LJ-804
N420MA	425	0116	N425CQ	425	0173	N425SC	425	0126	N429DM	E90	LW-221
N420MA	681	6039	N425D	425	0121	N425SF	425	0037	N429DM	F90	LA-102
N420PA	PA42	7800001	N425D	PA42	5527032	N425SG	425	0052	N429DT	MU-2	1517SA
N420PC	PA42	8301002	N425DC	425	0185	N425SG	425	0166	N429DW	E90	LW-221
N420PT	PA42	7800002	N425DC	MIIB	T26-131	N425SL	425	0236	N429E	200	BB-287
N420QK	200	BB-678	N425DD	425	0083	N425SM	425	0054	N429K	690A	11282
N420TA	200	BB-420	N425DH	425	0066	N425SP	425	0165	N429K	90	LJ-389
N420TS	PA42	8301002	N425DK	425	0086	N425SP	425	0184	N429K	90	LJ-1771
N420WA	TRIS	1040	N425DM	425	0098	N425SR	425	0133	(N429K)	E90	LW-86
N420X	90	LJ-33	N425DR	425	0199	N425SV	90	LJ-1159	N429LC	MIII	T-208
N421HV	90	LJ-1266	N425DS	425	0099	N425SW	425	0061	N429MA	MU-2	1517SA
N421PP	PC12	1010	N425DS	425	0124	N425SX	425	0106	N429MD	PA42	5527029
N422AG	MIII	T-264	(N425DS)	425	0172	N425TA	425	0165	N429MM	46T	97105
N422AS	90	LJ-1714	N425DT	690B	11519	N425TB	425	0068	N429PC	PC12	429
N422BW	200	BB-1422	(N425E)	425	0048	(N425TB)	425	0072	N429PL	200	BB-1574
N422D	100	B-84	N425E	425	0096	N425TC	425	0014	N429W	G1	55
N422DM	31T	8104052	N425EA	425	0063	N425TF	425	0004	N429WM	MU-2	1520SA
N422GK	MIII	T-260	N425EA	425	0096	N425TF	MU-2	425SA	N430C	90	LJ-273
N422HV	31T	8104052	N425EC	MU-2	793SA	(N425TH)	425	0099	N430DA	MU-2	253
N422MA	MU-2	1512SA	N425EE	425	0018	N425TK	425	0120	N430DD	200	BB-1243
N422MU	PC12	336	N425EJ	425	0149	N425TM	425	0217	N430G	MIV	AT-014
N422P	100	B-84	N425EK	425	0148	N425TN	425	0196	N430H	G1	42
N422P	90	LJ-1574	N425EM	425	0164	(N425TS)	425	0072	N430JT	300C	FM-3
N422PM	90	LJ-1412	N425ET	425	0072	(N425TS)	425	0098	N430MA	MU-2	1518SA
N422RJ	90	LJ-1229	N425EW	425	0150	N425TS	425	0133	N430MC	200	BB-904
N422RJ	90	LJ-1306	N425EW	MU-2	696	N425TV	425	0176	N430MC	MU-2	1518SA
N422RK	MIIA	T26-019	N425EZ	425	0099	N425TW	425	0161	(N430MG)	200	BB-904
N422TD	200	BB-968	N425FB	425	0050	N425TX	425	0039	N430RR	MIVA	AT-030
N422TW	90	LJ-1229	N425FC	425	0125	N425TY	425	0063	N430S	200	BB-1080
N422X	100	B-84	N425FG	425	0186	N425UX	MIIA	T26-020	N430TW	200	BB-1935
N422Z	F90	LA-135	N425FT	425	0105	N425VC	425	0055	N431AC	31T	7520024
N423JB	31T	8166052	N425FW	425	0055	(N425VV)	425	0055	N431BT	90	LJ-689
N423JD	E90	LW-129	N425FZ	425	0059	N425WB	425	0028	N431CF	31T	8166002
N423JD	PA42	8001003	N425GA	425	0106	N425WD	425	0130	N431G	G1	29
N423JT	46D	48	N425GC	425	0027	N425WG	425	0030	N431GW	31T	8020088
N423KC	PA42	8001074	N425GJ	425	0029	N425WL	425	0166	N431H	G1	78
"N423M"	90	LJ-503	N425GM	425	0033	N425WL	425	0197	N431JS	690B	11551
N423MA	MU-2	1513SA	N425GV	425	0218	N425WM	425	0147	N431LS	31T	7520024
N423MK	300	FA-188	(N425GZ)	425	0033	N425WT	425	0175	N431MC	PA42	5527031
N423PC	200	BB-1439	N425HB	425	0073	N425XP	425	0064	N431MS	690C	11635
N423TG	441	0200	N425HD	425	0113	N425XP	425	0086	N431PC	31T	7920002
N423TJ	90	LJ-1029	N425HJ	425	0169	N425Z	425	0186	N431PT	31T	7520010
N423WA	PC12	423	N425HS	425	0044	N426AC	441	0111	N431R	100	B-71
N424AJ	MU-2	136	N425JB	425	0043	N426DW	PC12	129	N431S	MIII	TT-431
N424BS	200	BB-179	N425JG	425	0128	N426EM	90	LJ-1352	N431SA	MIII	TT-431
N424CM	31T	8004002	N425JH	425	0124	(N426FS)	200	BB-432	N431SC	200	BB-1337
N424CP	F90	LA-182	N425JM	425	0214	N426HM	90	LJ-1709	N431SW	31T	7904016
N424CR	200	BB-347	N425JP	425	0038	N426JX	90	LJ-263	N431U	90	LJ-463
N424EM	90	LJ-1351	N425JT	425	0129	N426JX	MIIA	T26-020	N431V	BN2	431
(N424M)	31T	7400008	N425K	90	LJ-318	N426MA	MU-2	1515SA	N431WC	PC12	431
N424MA	MU-2	1514SA	(N425KA)	425	0187	N426PC	PA42	5501053	N431WJ	200	BB-431
N424MF	90	LJ-1403	N425KC	425	0174	N426PS	200	BB-432	N431Y	31T	7920002
N424PB	PC12	424	N425KD	425	0203	N426RJ	31T	1104010	N432CV	PC12	119
N424PM	46T	97288	(N425KK)	425	0225	N426RQ	31T	1104010	N432DA	F90	LA-81
N424PP	680W	1821-35	N425LA	425	0092	N426WF	200	BB-1953	N432FA	200	BB-592
N424PS	PC6	936	N425LC	425	0054	N427BC	350	FL-581	(N432LM)	200	BB-1871
N424RA	200	BB-1583	N425LD	425	0149	N427DD	31T	7820029	N432LW	200	BB-1561
N424RA	200	BB-1797	N425LG	425	0107	N427DM	90	LJ-804	N432MH	PC12	432
N424SW	100	B-80	N425LS	425	0172	N427KW	300	FA-79	N432PC	PC12	432
N424TT	200	BB-1964	N425MB	425	0104	N427LS	46D	90	N432R	PA42	8001032
N424TV	90	LJ-1057	N425MC	MIIB	T26-132	N427P	200	BB-1367	N432RR	31T	8004012
N425AA	425	0038	N425MM	690C	11699	N427P	300	FA-186	(N432TL)	90	LJ-1574
N425AC	425	0009	N425N	425	0218	N427PA	F90	LA-231	N433HC	200	BB-1807
N425AD	425	0220	N425NC	425	0207	N427RB	90	LJ-1208	N433PC	PC12	433
N425AF	425	0041	N425NE	BN2	876	N427RP	31T	8104052	N434AE	441	0097
N425AF	425	0101	N425NF	425	0099	N427SE	90	LJ-1797	N434BW	350	FL-109
N425AJ	425	0125	N425NP	425	0224	N427SP	MIV	AT-018	N434CC	690B	11537
N425AL	425	0100	N425NT	425	0104	N427TA	31T	7720027	N434EM	90	LJ-726
N425AP	200	BB-682	N425NW	425	0070	N427WA	PC12	427	N434JA	PC12	819
N425AR	425	0065	N425P	200	BB-819	N428A	200	BB-1243	N434MA	MU-2	1519SA
N425AT	425	0004	N425PA	425	0198	N428CW	46T	97201	N434R	31T	8104007
N425BA	425	0046	N425PC	425	0193	N428DC	46T	97124B	N435A	90	LJ-229
N425BB	425	0159	N425PC	PA42	5501053	N428DN	90	LJ-448	(N435BC)	425	0177
N425BL	425	0198	(N425PF)	425	0068	N428MA	MU-2	1516SA	N435CC	435	-0001
N425BN	425	0057	N425PG	425	0200	N428P	200	BB-745	N435DM	TBM7	154

N435PC	PC12	435
(N435TA)	200	BB-514
N436	G1	9
N436CB	TBM7	338
N436CB	TBM8	465
N436M	G1	9
N436MA	MU-2	1520SA
N437A	G1	83
N437CF	90	LJ-140
N437JB	90	LJ-1687
N437MA	MU-2	1521SA
N437WF	200	BB-962
N438	90	LJ-406
(N438BH)	31T	7920081
N438BM	200	BB-438
N438CA	90	LJ-1541
N438CR	200	BB-438
N438GC	350	FL-438
N438GP	PA42	5527038
N438H	425	0130
N438HT	200	BB-438
N438MA	MU-2	1522SA
N438P	200	BB-585
N438SP	90	LJ-692
N438SP	90	LJ-1108
N438SP	MU-2	290
N439AF	MIVC	AT-439B
N439BA	MU-2	439SA
N439BW	MIVA	AT-039
N439CB	TBM7	338
N439EE	E90	LW-98
N439KC	46T	97239
N439KM	200	BB-1209
N439MA	MU-2	1523SA
N439PW	90	LJ-1589
N439SA	MIVC	AT-439B
N439SA	MU-2	439SA
N439WA	E90	LW-216
N439WC	PC12	439
N440A	200	BB-66
(N440CA)	100	B-209
N440CA	690A	11187
N440CA	PA42	5501027
N440CC	690A	11191
N440CE	200	BB-698
N440CF	200	BB-698
N440D	90	LJ-235
N440DA	441	0207
(N440EA)	TBM8	445
N440EA	TBM8	447
N440EH	441	0358
N440EZ	MU-2	194
N440HC	425	0145
N440HP	31T	8020053
N440KA	90	LJ-1499
(N440KC)	200	BB-907
N440KC	90	LJ-878
N440KF	90	LJ-878
N440M	90	LJ-1036
N440MA	MU-2	1524SA
N440RB	MU-2	325
N440S	200	BB-148
N440S	31T	8166016
N440SM	100	B-44
N440ST	200	BB-65
N440TC	90	LJ-332
N440TP	90	LJ-17
N440WA	200	BB-700
N440WH	PA42	5527009
(N440WH)	PA42	5527013
N440WW	200G	BY-5
N441A	441	0094
N441AA	441	0014
N441AB	441	0284
N441AC	441	0270
N441AD	441	0044
N441AD	441	0226
N441AE	441	0250
N441AE	441	0280
(N441AF)	441	0106
N441AF	441	0311
N441AG	441	0327
N441AJ	441	0341
N441AK	441	0057
N441AL	200	BB-1767
N441AR	441	0148
N441AR	441	0360
N441AS	441	0148
N441AW	441	0199
N441BB	441	0217
N441BD	441	0086
(N441BD)	441	0129
N441BG	441	0013
N441BH	441	0145
N441BJ	441	0129
N441BL	441	0080
N441BL	441	0322
N441BW	441	0034
N441CA	441	0046
N441CC	441	679
N441CC	441	698
N441CC	441	0008
N441CD	441	0131
N441CD	441	0259
N441CE	441	0015
N441CE	441	0103
N441CF	441	0060
N441CF	441	0069
N441CF	441	0162
N441CG	441	0086
N441CG	441	0252
N441CG	90	LJ-1398
N441CH	441	0059
N441CH	441	0149
N441CJ	441	0117
(N441CL)	441	0024
N441CL	441	0147
N441CM	441	0034
N441CM	441	0169
N441CM	441	0185
N441CN	441	0169
N441CP	441	0008
(N441CP)	441	0339
N441CR	425	0149
N441CR	441	0234
N441CS	441	0356
N441CT	441	0048
(N441CX)	441	0219
N441CX	441	0305
N441DA	441	0023
N441DB	441	0300
N441DC	441	0199
N441DD	441	0341
N441DD	441	0342
N441DE	441	0134
(N441DK)	441	0061
N441DK	441	0176
N441DM	441	0120
N441DM	441	0216
(N441DM)	441	0306
N441DN	441	0325
N441DR	441	0035
N441DS	441	0028
N441DS	441	0098
N441DT	441	0080
N441DW	441	0087
N441DW	441	0149
N441DW	441	0192
N441DZ	441	0089
N441E	441	0139
N441E	441	0265
N441E	441	0306
N441EA	441	0171
N441EB	441	0049
N441EC	441	0179
N441EE	441	0083
N441EH	441	0351
N441EL	441	0245
N441EP	441	0283
N441EW	441	0134
N441EW	441	0214
N441F	441	0036
N441FA	441	0358
N441FB	441	0305
N441FC	441	0078
N441FP	350	FL-83
*N441FR	350	FL-83
N441FS	441	0041
N441FS	441	0318
N441FS	MU-2	579
N441FW	441	0049
N441G	441	0230
(N441GA)	441	0042
N441GA	441	0234
N441GB	441	0146
N441GE	441	0116
(N441GG)	441	0022
N441GM	441	0052
N441GN	441	0084
N441GP	441	0135
N441GP	441	0188
N441GT	441	0056
N441HA	441	0243
N441HC	441	0136
N441HD	441	0025
N441HF	441	0315
N441HH	441	0007
N441HH	441	0125
N441HK	441	0336
N441HR	441	0015
N441HS	441	0330
N441HT	441	0085
N441HT	441	0277
N441HW	441	0174
N441JA	441	0032
N441JA	441	0045
N441JA	441	0137
N441JC	441	0156
N441JD	441	0336
N441JG	441	0199
(N441JH)	441	0123
N441JK	441	0197
N441JR	441	0303
N441JV	441	0248
N441K	441	0093
N441KH	441	0031
N441KM	441	0044
N441KM	441	0196
N441KP	441	0062
N441KR	441	0079
N441KW	441	0078
N441KW	441	0316
N441LA	441	0210
N441LB	441	0080
N441LC	441	0035
N441LL	441	0139
N441LM	680T	1534-3
(N441LM)	690A	11304
N441LS	441	0342
N441M	441	0032
N441M	441	0122
N441MA	441	0240
N441MB	441	0061
N441MC	441	0250
N441MD	441	0103
N441MD	441	0199
N441ME	441	0266
N441MJ	441	0024
(N441MJ)	441	0053
N441ML	441	0344
N441MM	441	0030
N441MM	441	0332
N441MP	441	0083
N441MS	441	0056
N441MS	441	0059
N441MT	441	0297
N441MT	441	0309
N441MW	441	0286
N441MY	441	0215
N441NC	441	0099
N441ND	441	0123
N441NL	441	0124
N441P	441	0032
N441P	441	0093
N441PG	441	0245
N441PJ	441	0321
N441PL	441	0072
N441PM	441	0341
N441PN	441	0347
N441PP	441	0292
N441PS	200	BB-214
N441PS	441	0045
N441PS	MU-2	579
N441PW	441	0240
N441PZ	441	0351
N441Q	441	0079
N441R	441	0158
N441R	441	0163
(N441RA)	441	0040
N441RB	441	0029
N441RB	441	0066
N441RC	441	0076
N441RF	441	0079
N441RJ	441	0151
N441RK	441	0074
N441RL	441	0147
N441RS	441	0221
N441RW	441	0252
N441RW	441	0360
N441RZ	441	0005
N441S	441	0323
(N441SA)	441	0006
N441SA	441	0172
N441SA	441	0277
N441SB	441	0301
N441SC	441	0012
N441SC	441	0107
N441SE	441	0069
N441SM	441	0134
N441SS	441	0132
N441ST	441	0014
N441SW	441	0188
N441SX	441	0248
N441T	441	0177
N441TA	441	0045
N441TA	441	0204
N441TC	441	0156
N441TF	441	0072
N441TG	441	0200
N441TH	441	0037
N441TJ	441	0015
N441TL	441	0357
N441TM	441	0128
N441UC	441	0344
N441VB	441	0115
N441VC	441	0192
N441VH	441	0225
N441VP	441	0172
N441W	441	0052
N441W	441	0181
N441WD	441	0107
N441WF	441	0245
N441WJ	441	0194
N441WL	441	0041
N441WM	441	0217
N441WM	441	0286
N441WP	441	0098
N441WT	441	0242
N441X	441	0254
N441YA	441	0231
N441Z	441	0203
N442AB	F406	0032
N442DS	TBM7	96
N442JA	441	0013
N442JR	200	BB-1510
N442KA	200	BB-442
N442MA	MU-2	1525SA
N442PC	PA42	8001001
N442S	BN2	770
N442TC	90	LJ-332
(N442TW)	PA42	7801004
N442WS	441	0070
N443AB	F406	0034
N443CL	E90	LW-318
N443DB	PC12	1018
N443DW	441	0313
N443H	425	0002
N443MA	MU-2	1526SA
N443S	BN2	766
N443TC	B100	BE-20
N443WS	441	0232
N444AD	200	BB-733
N444AK	31T	8004045
N444AK	425	0186
N444AK	441	0334
N444AR	MU-2	555

N444BC	G1	96	N445DW	90	LJ-838	*N455AL	90	LJ-1268	N459SA	MU-2	459SA
N444BK	200	BB-1332	N445MA	MU-2	1527SA	N455DK	PC12	194	N460CR	200	BB-37
N444BL	200	BB-571	N445WS	441	0043	N455JH	BN2	2163	N460FS	MU-2	280
N444BN	31T	7820028	N446AS	90	LJ-1446	N455JW	PA42	8001040	N460K	690B	11392
N444CC	MU-2	662	N446JB	690A	11160	N455LG	46T	97203	N460KA	90	LJ-460
N444CM	PC12	152	N446MA	MU-2	1528SA	N455MA	MU-2	295	(N460LC)	31T	7620014
N444CY	PA42	5501025	N446PC	PC12	446	N455MM	31T	8020087	N460MA	MU-2	300
N444DC	90	LJ-887	N446SB	46D	211	N455MS	46D	70	N460PB	PC12	460
N444EB	200	BB-444	N446WS	441	0178	N455PM	100	B-130	N460PM	PC12	1079
N444EG	200	BB-624	N447AB	MU-2	223	N455RS	46T	97210	N461BB	46T	97016
(N444EM)	F90	LA-22	N447AC	200	BB-1042	N455RS	46T	97214	N461DF	C-12	BP-29
N444ER	31T	7820003	N447DB	90	LJ-1656	N455SC	350	FL-239	N461EP	90	LJ-1697
N444ER	31T	8166071	N447PC	PC12	447	N455SC	350	FL-356	N461HP	46D	201
(N444ES)	90	LJ-1677	N447SA	MIII	TT-447	N455SC	350	FL-384	N461JH	KODK	0013
N444ET	31T	7720005	N447TF	350	FL-364	N455SC	350	FL-500	N461LM	TBM7	122
N444EW	B100	BE-63	N447WS	441	0198	N455SC	441	0107	N461MA	MU-2	301
N444FF	MU-2	260	N448BC	350	FL-30	N455SE	350	FL-356	N461PC	PC12	461
N444FT	PC12	322	N448CA	PA42	5527034	N455SF	350	FL-239	N462HP	46D	158
N444GA	E90	LW-170	N448CP	E90	LW-232	N455SG	46T	97096	N462MA	MU-2	302
N444GB	680T	1565-21	N448F	MU-2	245	N455TA	200	BB-321	N462PC	PC12	462
N444GP	680T	1565-21	N448M	200	BB-1336	N455WM	PC12	455	N462PJ	46T	97249
N444H	690B	11402	N448MA	MU-2	1529SA	N456	G1	49	N463AL	90	LJ-226
N444HC	300	FA-5	N448T	200	BB-1336	(N456A)	680W	1842-41	N463CP	90	LJ-1878
N444HK	300	FA-5	N449BK	MU-2	449SA	N456AC	31T	8104068	N463DC	MIII	T-273
N444HP	MU-2	662	N449BY	PC12	449	N456AE	441	0283	N463DF	C-12	BP-24
N444JB	681	6016	N449CA	PA42	5501023	N456CD	200	BB-456	N463DN	31T	8120056
N444JE	200	BB-444	N449CA	TBM7	150	N456CJ	200	BB-264	N463DP	200	BB-463
N444JV	425	0013	N449DR	441	0202	N456CS	200	BB-177	N463JB	90	LJ-1310
N444JV	425	0070	N449LC	690A	11187	N456DR	MU-2	616	N463JM	46D	100
N444JV	TBM7	180	N449MA	MU-2	1530SA	N456ES	200	BB-1107	N463JP	46D	100
N444JW	31T	7720015	N449PC	TRIS	1068	N456FC	425	0127	N463JT	PC12	463
N444KA	200	BB-1160	N449WC	MIIB	T26-142	N456GT	441	0294	N463MA	MU-2	303
N444KA	200	BB-1318	N450AC	300	FA-14	N456JR	425	0093	N463MA	MU-2	1538SA
N444KA	E90	LW-128	N450CB	31T	8166001	N456JW	PA42	8001040	N463MX	200	BB-463
N444KE	441	0310	N450CK	350	FL-464	N456L	200	BB-112	N463RD	TBM8	463
N444KF	425	0191	N450CR	350	FL-340	N456MA	MU-2	296	N463WP	46D	238
N444KK	F90	LA-209	N450DA	31T	7820084	N456PC	PC12	456	N464A	200	BB-1554
N444KU	90	LJ-1040	N450DW	350	FL-325	N456PF	200	BB-413	N464AB	90	LJ-224
N444LB	MIII	TT-428A	N450FA	MU-2	1506SA	N456PH	90	LJ-233	N464AL	90	LJ-224
N444LM	MIII	T-295	N450FS	MU-2	338	N456PP	90	LJ-1699	N464AL	E90	LW-230
N444LN	PA42	8001045	N450HC	31T	8166021	N456PS	MU-2	338	N464C	46T	97393
N444LP	200	BB-1816	N450LM	350	FL-5	N456Q	300	FA-181	N464G	90	LJ-202
N444LR	90	LJ-1447	N450MA	MU-2	290	N456Q	90	LJ-675	N464JB	46D	71
N444MF	F90	LA-81	N450MA	MU-2	587	N456V	PC12	201	N464MA	MU-2	304
N444MS	690A	11110	N450MA	MU-2	1531SA	N456VC	90	LJ-552	N464WC	PC12	464
N444MT	200	BB-1666	N450MW	PA42	5527013	N457C	46T	97328	N464WF	PC12	149
N444NC	690B	11549	N450PC	PC12	450	N457CP	90	LJ-275	N465GT	200G	BY-65
N444NR	690B	11549	N450PM	BN2	2267	N457G	MIIB	T26-150	N465JB	90	LJ-1304
N444PA	MU-2	691	N450S	200	BB-1035	N457MA	MU-2	297	N465KC	90	LJ-1824
N444PC	31T	7920066	N450WH	200	BB-1275	N457MA	MU-2	1536SA	N465MA	MU-2	305
N444PD	31T	8120044	N451A	90	LJ-1348	N457PC	PC12	457	N465MA	MU-2	1539SA
N444PS	90	LJ-615	N451DB	200	BB-304	N457RS	31T	8020023	N465MC	C-12	BC-18
N444RC	31T	7520030	N451DM	PC12	350	N457SA	BN2	27	N465ME	46T	97233
N444RG	MU-2	312	N451DP	200	BB-304	N457SA	MIVA	AT-025	N465P	90	LJ-1629
N444RH	425	0128	N451ES	PC12	425	N457SC	MU-2	260	N465PC	PC12	465
N444RH	425	0190	N451MA	MU-2	291	N457SR	31T	8166047	N465SC	350	FL-384
N444RH	441	0358	N451MA	MU-2	1532SA	N457SR	90	LJ-275	N465SK	46T	97013
N444RK	B100	BE-77	N451WS	441	0096	N457TC	200	BB-1458	N465TP	46T	97204
N444RK	B100	BE-137	N452DP	31T	8004026	N457TC	31T	8020059	N466AC	350	FL-586
N444RL	B100	BE-77	N452GH	PC12	628	N457TG	31T	8020059	N466DC	MU-2	1528SA
N444RR	425	0128	N452MA	MU-2	292	N457TQ	200	BB-1458	N466MA	MU-2	616
N444RR	46T	97260	N452MA	MU-2	1533SA	N458BB	MU-2	458SA	N466MA	MU-2	1540SA
N444RR	46T	97278	N452MD	PC12	452	N458DL	PC12	458	N466MW	200	BB-1273
N444RS	F90	LA-61	N452TB	350	FL-623	N458G	MIIB	T26-139	N466P	G1	64
N444RU	425	0190	N452TT	90	LJ-452	N458HR	441	0041	N466SA	PC12	443
N444SA	90	LJ-117	N453MA	MU-2	293	(N458HW)	100	B-192	N466SC	90	LJ-1466
N444SC	PA42	8001034	N453MA	MU-2	1534SA	N458MA	MU-2	298	N466SP	KODK	0015
N444SR	90	LJ-416	N453PC	PC12	453	N458P	90	LJ-958	N466WP	31T	8120009
N444TH	425	0219	N453SA	MIII	TT-453	N458PC	PC12	458	N467BC	200	BB-1647
N444TW	200	BB-80	N453SR	90	LJ-461	N458Q	300	FA-181	N467BW	100	B-130
N444TW	BN2	234	N454CA	31T	8104053	N458Q	90	LJ-675	N467JB	300	FA-137
(N444UP)	690A	11110	N454CT	BN2	454	(N458S)	90	LJ-1004	N467JM	200	BB-94
(N444UP)	MU-2	532	N454DC	200	BB-995	N458SC	31T	7904026	N467JV	441	0083
N444WA	31T	8004040	N454EA	441	0054	N458TB	350	FL-616	(N467MA)	MU-2	617
N444WB	200	BB-1179	N454GC	F90	LA-39	N458TC	200	BB-1969	N467MA	MU-2	617
N444WC	31T	8166054	N454LF	350	FL-209	N459CA	TBM7	238	N467MA	MU-2	1541SA
N444WD	695A	96006	N454MA	MU-2	294	N459CP	31T	8120049	N467MA	MU-2	1567SA
N444WF	MU-2	1551SA	N454MA	MU-2	1535SA	N459DF	200	BB-1761	N468BV	350	FL-369
N444WG	90	LJ-455	N454P	90	LJ-1372	N459DF	C-12	BP-27	N468C	P68	213
(N444WS)	441	0116	(N454PR)	PC12	289	N459M	350	FL-402	N468DB	MU-2	701SA
N445AE	441	0043	N454PS	PC12	454	N459MA	MU-2	299	*N468M	90	LJ-1017
N445CR	90	LJ-838	N454RM	EPIC	111	N459MA	MU-2	1537SA	N468MA	MU-2	412SA
N445D	90	LJ-1603	N454TB	350	FL-554	N459MA	TBM7	259	N468MA	MU-2	618
N445DR	90	LJ-838	N454TM	200	BB-1507	N459PC	PC12	459	N468MA	MU-2	1542SA

(N468SB)	MU-2	1566SA
N468SC	E90	LW-267
N468SM	200	BB-468
N468SP	200C	BL-5
N468SP	MU-2	1566SA
N468TT	EPIC	012
N469AF	PC12	469
N469B	90	LJ-803
N469BL	MIIB	T26-139
N469CC	46D	3
N469GM	MIVC	AT-469
N469JB	200	BB-634
N469JK	90	LJ-274
N469JW	200	BB-781
N469MA	MU-2	619
N469MA	MU-2	1543SA
(N469PC)	90	LJ-726
N469TA	200	BB-959
N470AH	PC12	470
N470KA	350	FL-109
N470MA	200	BB-629
N470MA	MU-2	620
N470MA	MU-2	1544SA
N470MM	350	FL-156
N470MN	350	FL-156
N470RJ	425	0082
N470SC	350	FL-35
N470TC	200	BB-424
N470WA	PC12	470
N471CD	MIVC	AT-549B
(N471HP)	690B	11520
N471JS	690D	15031
N471MA	MU-2	621
N471MA	MU-2	1545SA
N471SA	MIII	TT-471
N471SC	690	11044
N471SC	690A	11119
N471SC	690A	11300
N471SC	690D	15031
N471SQ	690A	11119
N472MA	MU-2	622
N472MA	MU-2	1546SA
(N472SW)	PC12	260
N473BP	90	LJ-732
N473FW	MU-2	269
N473GG	31T	7820026
N473L	90	LJ-405
N473LP	90	LJ-732
N473LP	MU-2	269
N473MA	MU-2	623
N473MA	MU-2	1547SA
N473PC	PC12	473
(N473W)	MU-2	269
N474DP	90	LJ-202
N474H	90	LJ-474
N474L	90	LJ-405
N474MA	MU-2	624
N474MA	MU-2	1548SA
N474U	MIIB	T26-133
N475CA	MU-2	319
N475JA	90	LJ-1147
N475JM	425	0214
N475K	100	B-140
N475MA	MU-2	625
N475MA	MU-2	1549SA
N475MG	MIII	T-278
N475PC	PC12	475
N475U	200	BB-252
N476D	PC12	476
N476JA	90	LJ-1161
N476MA	MU-2	626
N476MA	MU-2	1550SA
N476S	G1	124
N476XP	FPC6	2040
N477AE	300	FA-84
N477B	441	0055
N477DD	MU-2	439SA
N477HC	46T	97171
N477JA	90	LJ-1162
N477JM	200	BB-538
N477JW	300	FA-77
N477MA	MU-2	627
N477MA	MU-2	1551SA
N477MD	46T	97264
N477P	90	LJ-1550
N477PT	90	LJ-1600
N477SJ	441	0162
N478CR	90	LJ-1474
N478DC	690B	11489
N478JA	90	LJ-1163
N478MA	MU-2	628
N478MA	MU-2	1552SA
N478PC	31T	8104046
N478PC	PC12	478
N479AV	200	BB-1479
N479JA	90	LJ-1177
N479MA	MU-2	629
N479MA	MU-2	1553SA
N479MM	PA42	8001074
N479SA	90	LJ-215
(N479SJ)	90	LJ-504
N479SW	31T	7904047
N479VK	MIV	AT-009
N479WB	200	BB-886
N480AF	MU-2	248
N480BC	MIIB	T26-108
N480BR	200	BB-1355
(N480CA)	31T	8004048
N480CA	31T	8004051
N480EA	425	0035
N480EB	350	FL-600
N480JA	90	LJ-1178
N480K	690B	11543
N480K	90	LJ-439
N480M	46T	97108
N480MA	MU-2	630
N480MA	MU-2	1554SA
N480NR	P68	345
N480TC	200	BB-1600
N480WH	PC12	480
N481AF	MU-2	253
N481BC	200	BB-981
N481BR	200	BB-1967
N481JA	90	LJ-1179
N481MA	MU-2	631
N481MA	MU-2	1555SA
N481NS	200	BB-986
N481NS	300	FA-28
N481SA	90	LJ-408
N481SW	31T	8104016
N481TL	PC12	481
N482AF	MU-2	265
N482G	MU-2	026
N482JA	90	LJ-1183
N482MA	MU-2	632
N482MA	MU-2	1556SA
N482SW	200	BB-378
N482TC	31T	8104072
N482WA	PC12	482
N482WF	200	BB-378
N483	E90	LW-251
N483	F90	LA-163
N483AF	MU-2	271
N483D	90	LJ-212
N483FW	P68	271
N483G	200	BB-304
N483G	90	LJ-212
(N483J)	200	BB-1700
N483JA	90	LJ-1184
N483JM	90	LJ-147
(N483JM)	F90	LA-30
N483K	F90	LA-163
N483MA	MU-2	633
N483MA	MU-2	1557SA
N483PC	PC12	483
N484AF	MU-2	284
N484AF	PC12	484
N484AS	31T	8004055
N484BW	90	LJ-1883
N484JA	90	LJ-1196
N484MA	MU-2	634
N484MA	MU-2	1558SA
N484PS	31T	7620008
N484RJ	TBM7	333
N484SC	31T	7820022
N485AF	MU-2	308
N485AH	MU-2	635
N485AT	90	LJ-1203
N485G	MIIB	T26-114
N485JA	90	LJ-1197
(N485JA)	90	LJ-1200
(N485JA)	90	LJ-1208
N485JD	90	LJ-1197
N485K	200	BB-485
N485MA	MU-2	635
N485MA	MU-2	1559SA
N485PC	PC12	485
N485R	200	BB-605
N486AF	MU-2	329
N486DC	200	BB-845
N486DC	B100	BE-74
N486DC	MIII	T-204
N486HP	46T	97386
N486JA	90	LJ-1198
(N486JA)	90	LJ-1201
N486JD	90	LJ-1198
N486MA	MU-2	636
N486MA	MU-2	1560SA
N486PB	PC12	486
N487AF	MU-2	333
N487JA	90	LJ-1199
(N487JA)	90	LJ-1203
N487JD	90	LJ-1199
N487JH	B100	BE-43
N487LM	PC12	517
N487MA	MU-2	637
N487MA	MU-2	1561SA
N487PC	PC12	487
N487TT	350	FL-67
N488A	B100	BE-74
N488AD	200	BB-860
N488CA	200	BB-860
N488CP	200	BB-860
N488FT	F90	LA-137
N488GA	300	FA-125
N488GB	MU-2	133
N488HA	31T	1104004
N488JB	200	BB-1099
N488JD	90	LJ-1305
N488JR	90	LJ-1305
N488LL	90	LJ-1458
N488MA	MU-2	638
N488MA	MU-2	1562SA
N488MS	PC12	333
N488PG	PC12	1053
N488WG	300	FA-82
N488XJ	90	LJ-1527
(N489BC)	425	0131
N489CE	441	0027
N489G	441	0027
N489G	441	0262
N489GA	690B	11530
N489JD	90	LJ-1311
N489JG	PC12	489
N489JS	90	LJ-1311
N489MA	MU-2	639
N489SC	690C	11635
N489ST	441	0262
N489WC	441	0262
N490CA	46D	77
N490CA	46T	97301
N490J	90	LJ-1312
N490JD	90	LJ-1312
N490JT	90	LJ-1312
N490K	90	LJ-470
N490KC	690A	11300
N490KQ	KODK	K0101
N490MA	MU-2	640
(N490N)	690A	11156
N490NR	P68	281
N490TN	350	FL-89
N490W	90	LJ-1649
(N490WP)	200	BB-584
(N491BF)	90	LJ-983
N491BT	90	LJ-983
N491JV	90	LJ-1349
N491KA	E90	LW-313
N491KD	E90	LW-313
N491KQ	KODK	0001
N491MA	MU-2	641
N491MB	31T	8166007
N491PC	PC12	116
N491VA	PC12	491
N491WF	EPIC	028
(N492B)	TBM8	452
N492B	TBM8	455
N492JW	90	LJ-1350
N492MA	MU-2	642
N492PA	90	LJ-492
N492WA	PC12	492
N493DT	B100	BE-32
N493JX	90	LJ-1351
N493KQ	KODK	0003
N493MA	MU-2	643
N493PB	PC12	493
N493S	200	BB-1053
N494AC	200C	BL-53
*N494AL	F90	LA-152
N494CA	31T	7920029
(N494HL)	31T	7920029
N494JY	90	LJ-1352
N494KQ	KODK	0004
N494MA	300	FA-108
N494MA	MU-2	644
N494MA	MU-2	1563SA
N494PC	PC12	494
N494WC	MU-2	644
N495CA	PA42	5527044
N495DH	350	FL-404
N495JJ	EPIC	026
N495KQ	KODK	0005
N495MA	MU-2	306
N495NM	90	LJ-781
N495PC	PC12	495
N495TM	90	LJ-1495
N495Y	90	LJ-1707
N496DT	PC12	496
(N496MA)	695A	96006
N496MA	MU-2	307
N496MA	MU-2	1564SA
N497BH	KODK	0018
N497BN	BN2	497
N497MA	MU-2	308
N497MA	MU-2	1565SA
N497P	90	LJ-1126
N497PC	PC12	497
(N497SL)	B100	BE-64
N498AC	200	BB-287
N498KQ	KODK	0008
N498MA	MU-2	309
N498MA	MU-2	1566SA
N499CA	46T	97357
N499EH	31T	7720066
N499M	90	LJ-918
N499MA	MU-2	310
N499MA	MU-2	1567SA
N499MC	F90	LA-221
N499N	680T	1534-3
N499SP	MIIB	T26-175
N499SW	B100	BE-89
N499TT	200	BB-499
N499WC	690B	11499
(N499WS)	441	0206
N500	MIII	T-232
N500AK	MIII	TT-527
(N500AL)	690A	11129
N500AQ	31T	8004039
N500AU	31T	8004039
(N500BE)	MU-2	272
N500BG	PC12	600
N500BJ	MU-2	272
N500BR	200	BB-743
N500BW	200	BB-410
N500BW	MIIA	T26-002
N500BX	200C	BL-42
N500CE	441	0005
N500CM	31T	7720009
N500CP	200	BB-152
N500CP	200	BB-293
N500CP	MIII	T-207
N500CP	MIII	T-269
N500CP	STAR	NC-25
(N500CP)	STAR	NC-50
N500CR	200	BB-714
N500CR	690B	11525
N500CS	200	BB-773

N500CT	200	BB-43	N500PR	200	BB-452	N501TR	200	BB-1037	N505P	90	LJ-1569
N500CT	E90	LW-168	N500PR	E90	LW-148	N501WN	G1	165	N505P	PC12	505
N500CY	200	BB-935	N500PS	MU-2	224	(N502AB)	200	BB-153	N505RG	E90	LW-252
N500DB	100	B-138	N500PV	200	BB-452	N502AP	200	BB-1187	N505RP	E90	LW-311
N500DB	MIII	TT-480	N500QE	680W	1812-29	N502BR	441	0135	N505RT	680W	1752-5
N500DC	E90	LW-288	N500QP	MIII	T-207	N502CW	100	B-41	N505S	G1	26
N500DE	200	BB-357	N500QT	90	LJ-1322	N502DT	690B	11413	N505SA	MU-2	008
N500DM	MIIA	T26-035	N500QX	MU-2	133	N502EB	200	BB-194	N505SC	200	BB-576
N500DR	200	BB-76	N500R	690	11051	N502EB	200	BB-795	N505SG	350	FL-606
N500DW	200	BB-523	N500RJ	441	0302	N502LA	90	LJ-1019	(N505TB)	31T	7920084
N500DY	90	LJ-1111	N500RK	90	LJ-475	(N502M)	90	LJ-479	N505WR	300	FA-15
N500EA	E90	LW-240	N500RL	G1	95	N502MA	MU-2	312	N506AB	200	BB-362
N500EC	MU-2	627	N500RM	MU-2	668	N502MA	MU-2	1569SA	N506EB	200	BB-1312
N500ED	90	LJ-1387	N500RN	G1	95	N502MM	31T	8104064	N506F	90	LJ-1129
N500EH	100	B-41	N500RV	200	BB-152	N502MS	90	LJ-996	N506GT	200	BB-612
N500EQ	90	LJ-1387	N500S	300	FA-149	N502NC	425	0056	(N506M)	90	LJ-354
N500EW	200	BB-851	N500S	G1	127	N502RH	200	BB-673	N506MA	MU-2	316
N500EW	31T	8166060	N500SE	46T	97118	N502RH	31T	7520017	(N506MA)	MU-2	1573SA
N500FC	300	FA-124	(N500SR)	690A	11209	N502SC	E90	LW-281	N506MV	350	FL-261
(N500FC)	31T	7920049	N500SX	MIII	T-366	N502SE	90	LJ-740	N506P	350	FL-153
N500FC	350	FL-181	N500TB	100	B-10	N502SM	B100	BE-46	N507AM	PC12	418
N500FE	200	BB-50	N500TH	695	95013	N502SP	F90	LA-4	N507AZ	PC12	418
N500FE	200	BB-1212	N500TL	31T	7804004	N502W	90	LJ-287	N507BC	TBM8	382
N500FE	31T	7920049	N500TL	E90	LW-170	N502WC	MIII	T-268	N507BE	200	BB-735
N500FF	TBM7	141	N500TM	90	LJ-394	N502WJ	31T	8375002	N507DR	441	0271
N500FP	200	BB-776	N500TR	E90	LW-121	N503AA	MU-2	633	N507EB	350	FL-81
N500GC	200	BB-735	N500TS	690A	11209	N503AB	100	B-18	N507EF	200	BB-1511
(N500GC)	300	FA-13	N500TW	31T	8020020	N503B	690B	11503	N507K	200	BB-507
N500GC	31T	7720018	N500UR	200	BB-43	N503CB	90	LJ-997	(N507M)	90	LJ-327
N500GC	E90	LW-288	N500UW	441	0017	N503F	200	BB-185	N507MA	MU-2	319
N500GC	E90	LW-305	N500V	MU-2	379SA	N503LA	90	LJ-267	(N507MA)	MU-2	1574SA
N500GC	P180	1012	N500VA	200	BB-1632	N503LM	350	FL-182	N507P	300	FA-217
N500GK	MU-2	348SA	N500VA	200	BB-1941	N503M	90	LJ-158	N507PB	PC12	507
N500GL	MU-2	579	N500VA	90	LJ-1519	N503MA	MU-2	313SA	N507RC	PC12	507
N500GM	441	0222	N500VL	350	FL-383	(N503MA)	MU-2	1570SA	N507SA	MIII	TT-507
N500GN	200	BB-62	N500W	200	BB-600	N503P	200	BB-437	N507TT	MIII	TT-507
N500GP	200C	BL-37	N500WD	425	0147	N503PB	PC12	503	N507W	90	LJ-269
N500GT	200	BB-43	N500WE	PA42	5527021	N503RH	200	BB-971	*N507WG	350	FL-81
N500HA	MU-2	328	N500WF	200	BB-947	N503RM	200	BB-673	N508AB	695A	96034
N500HG	200	BB-1954	N500WN	G1	165	(N503RV)	P180	1044	N508BM	200	BB-1497
N500HJ	E90	LW-176	N500WP	31T	8020087	N503WJ	200	BB-503	N508BR	200	BB-743
N500HM	31T	7720034	N500WR	200	BB-59	N503WR	31T	7904016	N508CB	90	LJ-1715
N500HY	200	BB-306	N500WR	31T	8020087	N503WS	PC12	503	N508DL	PC12	508
N500HY	680T	1708-83	N500WY	PC12	762	N504AB	90	LJ-991	N508DW	200	BB-523
N500JA	200	BB-439	N500X	90	LJ-199	N504C	G1	124	N508GA	90	LJ-868
N500JE	B100	BE-79	N500X	MU-2	114	N504CB	E90	LW-125	N508GT	90	LJ-1775
N500JP	681	6003	N500XL	31T	8166042	N504CE	200	BB-1897	N508GW	MIIA	T26-035
N500KA	200	BB-819	N500XL	31T	8166049	N504EB	200	BB-1278	N508JA	200	BB-735
N500KB	200	BB-29	N500XX	MU-2	250	N504EC	90	LJ-1130	N508MA	MU-2	187
N500KD	B100	BE-79	N500Y	100	B-86	N504GF	200	BB-1156	N508MA	MU-2	320
N500KK	MIII	T-256	N500YM	MIVA	AT-058	(N504M)	90	LJ-97	(N508MA)	MU-2	1575SA
N500KQ	KODK	0012	N500ZC	31T	7520015	N504MA	MU-2	314	N508MV	200	BB-877
N500KR	90	LJ-708	N500ZP	PC12	500	(N504MA)	MU-2	1571SA	(N508SW)	31T	8004036
N500KS	200	BB-59	N501	425	0197	N504PB	PC12	504	N508T	90	LJ-546
N500KS	90	LJ-708	N501AB	200	BB-712	N504SA	PC6	704	N508W	MU-2	609
N500LE	MU-2	351SA	N501AR	46T	97162	N504SR	46T	97165	N509FP	200	BB-1886
N500LM	PA42	5527016	N501DU	F90	LA-82	N504SR	PC12	658	N509MA	MU-2	321SA
N500LP	200	BB-1141	(N501E)	200	BB-913	N504TC	31T	7904019	(N509MA)	MU-2	1576SA
N500LR	100	B-41	N501EB	200	BB-422	N504TF	350	FL-399	N509MV	200	BB-877
N500MA	MU-2	562	N501EB	200	BB-1226	N504TQ	31T	7904019	N509PB	PC12	509
N500MB	90	LJ-870	N501EZ	200	BB-913	N504W	MIIB	T26-104	(N509W)	90	LJ-243
N500MB	E90	LW-58	N501FS	MIIB	T26-146	N504WR	200	BB-59	N510CB	200	BB-473
N500MC	425	0147	N501GA	G500	501	N505AK	425	0160	N510CH	690A	11168
N500ML	B100	BE-78	N501GS	90	LJ-964	N505AM	200	BB-919	(N510CP)	MIII	TT-465
N500MM	690B	11422	N501HC	200	BB-1306	N505BC	300	FA-89	N510E	G1	56
N500MS	90	LJ-626	(N501KS)	100	B-69	N505BG	E90	LW-312	N510G	200	BB-816
N500MS	E90	LW-123	N501LA	90	LJ-1018	N505EB	90	LJ-1203	N510GS	200	BB-1746
N500MT	200	BB-437	N501LC	441	0230	N505FK	C-12	BC-18	N510H	200	BB-60
N500MT	31T	7804004	N501M	90	LJ-175	N505GA	E90	LW-155	N510H	200	BB-766
N500MT	690B	11529	N501MA	MU-2	311	N505GC	MIIB	T26-101	(N510L)	90	LJ-187
N500MT	90	LJ-958	N501MA	MU-2	1568SA	N505GM	MIII	T-286	N510LA	200G	BY-24
N500MY	31T	7804004	N501MC	690A	11173	N505GP	31T	7720002	N510LC	31T	7720068
N500N	B100	BE-110	N501MQ	690A	11173	N505HB	46T	97314	N510MA	MU-2	322
N500NA	90	LJ-401	N501MS	90	LJ-626	N505HC	441	0257	N510ME	E90	LW-312
N500NG	200	BB-1483	N501NB	695	95003	*N505HP	200	BB-1429	N510RB	46D	167
N500NK	PC12	500	N501P	200	BB-1575	N505HP	46T	97314	N510UE	200	BB-1872
N500NR	680W	1812-29	N501P	90	LJ-1732	N505JC	680W	1811-28	N510UF	200	BB-1872
N500PB	31T	8166027	N501PB	PC12	501	N505M	350	FL-296	N510UF	350	FL-615
N500PH	200C	BL-29	N501PM	P180	1022	(N505M)	90	LJ-31	N510WP	200	BB-389
N500PJ	MU-2	668	N501PP	90	LJ-400	N505MA	MU-2	315	N510WP	300	FA-111
N500PM	PA42	5527021	N501PT	31T	7904048	(N505MA)	MU-2	1572SA	N510WP	350	FL-109
(N500PN)	90	LJ-1111	N501RH	200	BB-805	N505MT	90	LJ-958	N510WR	200	BB-389
N500PP	200	BB-776	N501SR	46T	97165	N505MW	E90	LW-155	N510WR	300	FA-111
N500PP	90	LJ-400	N501TD	F90	LA-82	(N505N)	E90	LW-86	N511AM	MU-2	1556SA

N511AS	200	BB-1286	N515PC	90	LJ-247	N522MJ	E90	LW-80	N528N	90	LJ-109
N511BF	90	LJ-179	N515RC	PA42	5501018	N522RF	46T	97119	N528NA	C-12	BJ-3
N511D	350	FL-172	N515RP	PC12	330	N522SC	90	LJ-1022	N528PM	PC12	653
N511D	90	LJ-951	N515WB	31T	7720023	N522TG	200	BB-727	N528SA	200	BB-1528
N511DP	200C	BL-15	N515WC	690B	11515	N522WD	425	0015	N528WG	200	BB-151
N511HA	200	BB-1417	N516AF	MU-2	516	N523CJ	E90	LW-40	N529JA	200	BB-873
N511J	E90	LW-6	N516BA	350	FL-247	N523CR	90	LJ-523	N529JC	681	6044
N511KV	90	LJ-1422	N516CB	PC12	752	N523GM	200	BB-1598	N529JH	90	LJ-747
N511MA	MU-2	323	N516DM	90	LJ-251	N523JL	PC12	523	N529JM	90	LJ-1470
N511PB	PC12	511	N516DM	G1	128	N523MA	MU-2	338	N529M	90	LJ-487
N511PJ	31T	1104006	N516GA	PA42	5501018	N523P	90	LJ-1414	N529MA	MU-2	648
N511PS	350	FL-312	N516MA	MU-2	328	N523PD	31T	7904044	N529N	90	LJ-112
N511RZ	200	BB-1458	N516RS	46D	196	N523SA	PC6	523	N529NA	200	BB-1091
N511S	MIV	AT-017	N516S	31T	8166076	N523TH	90	LJ-1219	N529PB	PC12	529
N511SA	FPC6	2011	N516SW	90	LJ-511	N524AM	31T	7920039	N529PM	46T	97029
N511SC	31T	8166069	N516SW	90	LJ-736	N524BA	B100	BE-99	N529PS	PC12	529
N511SD	200	BB-1683	N516W	90	LJ-70	N524CE	PC12	410	N529V	90	LJ-487
N511SK	FPC6	2026	N516WB	90	LJ-70	N524CM	PC12	410	N529WM	46D	106
N511TA	200	BB-1660	N517AB	F90	LA-176	N524FS	200	BB-590	N530AA	G1	71
N511WA	TRIS	1044	N517DP	350	FL-602	N524GM	200	BB-1609	N530AC	90	LJ-1611
N511WM	E90	LW-57	N517DQ	MIIB	T26-129	N524GM	200C	BL-142	N530AG	90	LJ-1611
N512DC	350	FL-342	(N517DW)	690B	11355	N524GT	PC12	524	N530CH	90	LJ-1322
N512DM	MU-2	155	N517HP	690B	11517	N524MA	MU-2	339	N530D	90	LJ-256
(N512DS)	B100	BE-126	N517JM	200	BB-239	N524MR	200	BB-524	N530DP	MU-2	1565SA
N512FS	MIII	T-299	N517LF	90	LJ-209	N524PC	350	FL-447	N530HP	46T	97101
N512G	90	LJ-64	N517MA	MU-2	329	N524PM	46T	97024	N530JA	200	BB-60
N512JC	680T	1584-36	N517PC	90	LJ-813	N524SC	100	B-37	N530M	90	LJ-361
(N512JC)	690	11003	N517WM	425	0165	N524TS	90	LJ-1187	N530MA	MU-2	649
N512JD	680T	1584-36	(N518B)	PA42	5527038	N525AH	KODK	0009	N530N	90	LJ-141
N512KA	200	BB-512	N518B	PA42	5527039	N525BA	350	FL-253	N530RQ	FPC6	2072
N512MA	MU-2	324	N518DM	90	LJ-251	N525BC	200	BB-196	N530SP	C-12	BC-6
N512MM	46T	97271	N518F	200	BB-501	N525BC	200	BB-942	N530SS	MU-2	517
N512PB	PC12	512	N518GS	200	BB-1746	N525BC	350	FL-252	N530WC	PC12	530
N512PC	90	LJ-324	N518MA	MU-2	330	N525BC	350	FL-253	N531BB	200	BB-865
N512Q	90	LJ-64	N518NA	U-21	LM-80	N525CA	31T	7920036	N531CB	B100	BE-133
N512RR	90	LJ-832	N518T	MU-2	106	(N525CA)	31T	8004046	N531CM	B100	BE-133
N512W	90	LJ-62	N518TQ	MU-2	106	N525DF	350	FL-306	N531CS	90	LJ-549
N512WP	90	LJ-62	N518TS	90	LJ-1130	N525ES	MIVC	AT-549B	N531DF	100	B-116
N513BT	90	LJ-1798	N519CC	695A	96068	N525JA	200	BB-873	N531DS	F90	LA-82
N513DC	MU-2	321SA	N519HB	695	95013	N525JK	90	LJ-305	N531GK	690B	11394
N513DC	MU-2	1513SA	N519KK	350	FL-51	(N525JM)	PA42	8001022	N531LP	MIII	T-234
N513DM	MU-2	155	N519M	G1	117	N525KA	E90	LW-266	N531M	100	B-116
N513DM	MU-2	1560SA	N519MA	MU-2	331	N525MA	441	0210	N531MA	MU-2	130
N513DQ	MU-2	321SA	N519MM	46T	97019	N525MA	MU-2	340	N531MA	MU-2	650
N513JM	90	LJ-1274	N519PC	PC12	519	N525P	90	LJ-1268	N531MB	300	FA-69
N513KL	F90	LA-123	N519SA	200	BB-940	(N525PC)	90	LJ-696	N531MC	PA42	5527007
N513MA	MU-2	325	N519T	MU-2	027	N525SC	MIII	T-288	N531ML	300	FA-69
N513NA	MU-2	513	N519TL	MU-2	027	N525SK	200	BB-1148	N531MP	PC12	741
N513RB	F90	LA-219	(N520AM)	90	LJ-1490	N525TG	PA42	8001032	N531MP	PC12	808
N513SA	200	BB-513	N520CS	681B	6061	N525TT	EPIC	006	N531N	90	LJ-164
N513SC	90	LJ-422	N520D	200	BB-989	N525WE	B100	BE-20	N531PC	31T	7920029
N514BV	200	BB-590	N520DD	200	BB-738	N525ZS	100	B-66	N531PT	31T	7520039
N514GP	690A	11297	N520DG	200	BB-1753	N526AP	200	BB-391	N531PT	31T	7620028
N514LK	350	FL-517	N520GM	200	BB-1746	(N526AS)	46D	207	N531SC	200G	BY-20
N514LM	F90	LA-53	N520GM	200	BB-1769	N526BT	90	LJ-263	N531SW	200	BB-1656
N514M	31T	8104045	N520GN	200	BB-1746	(N526LS)	425	0217	N531SW	31T	7904025
N514MA	200	BB-1007	N520HP	46T	97012	N526MA	MU-2	645	N532	690B	11388
N514MA	MU-2	326	N520JA	90	LJ-1519	N526PB	PC12	526	N532EB	B100	BE-33
N514MC	441	0312	N520JG	G1	197	N526RR	90	LJ-263	N532M	100	B-151
N514NA	680W	1772-10	N520JK	90	LJ-1898	N527AF	MU-2	527	N532MA	MU-2	651
N514NL	PC12	457	(N520LT)	350	FL-67	N527CC	F90	LA-87	N532SW	200	BB-1228
N514RD	200C	BL-5	N520MA	MU-2	332	N527CH	200	BB-899	N532WA	PC12	532
N514RS	STAR	NC-51	N520MC	200	BB-43	N527DM	PC12	813	N533AR	MIII	T-225
N514TB	200	BB-1351	N520RM	425	0129	N527JC	31T	8104043	N533CS	G1	110
N514WG	MU-2	514	N520WS	200	BB-751	(N527JD)	90	LJ-883	N533DM	MU-2	652
N515AC	STAR	NC-16	N521BH	31T	7820019	N527JM	31T	8104058	N533GP	350	FL-507
N515AF	PC12	515	N521CC	200	BB-854	N527MA	46T	97127	N533M	441	0222
N515AM	695	95008	N521DG	200	BB-1723	N527MA	MU-2	646	N533MA	MU-2	652
(N515AP)	690	11006	(N521FA)	200	BB-1281	N527PB	PC12	527	N533MA	MU-2	733SA
N515AR	690	11006	N521LB	E90	LW-249	N527PM	90	LJ-1897	N533P	200	BB-1278
N515AS	100	B-90	N521MA	MU-2	333	N527SE	90	LJ-1850	N533PC	PC12	533
N515BA	200	BB-603	N521PC	PC12	521	N527TS	TBM7	184	N533SS	E90	LW-197
N515BA	31T	8120044	N521PM	31T	7720048	N528AF	MU-2	528	N534H	90	LJ-372
N515BC	E90	LW-121	N521RS	200	BB-1903	N528AM	300	FA-59	N534MA	MU-2	653
N515CK	200	BB-1726	N522AS	31T	7520007	N528BE	690B	11413	N535BB	PC12	596
N515CL	200	BB-1726	N522CC	200	BB-841	N528DS	31T	7904008	N535DM	TBM8	486
N515CP	200	BB-1175	(N522CC)	F90	LA-87	N528DS	PA42	8001012	N535E	200	BB-135
N515CR	200	BB-1175	N522CF	B100	BE-67	N528EJ	PC12	528	N535JR	200	BB-101
N515DW	PA42	8001079	N522CM	KODK	0010	N528GM	90	LJ-1894	N535JR	46T	97253
N515GA	31T	8104050	N522DJ	PC12	539	N528JD	200	BB-1145	N535KC	46T	97335
N515JS	STAR	NC-52	N522JA	200	BB-726	N528JJ	200	BB-595	N535MA	MU-2	655
N515KJ	90	LJ-566	N522JP	90	LJ-1289	(N528KL)	31T	7904038	N535MJ	PC12	535
N515M	PA42	8001079	N522MA	MU-2	337	N528MA	MU-2	647	*N535MT	PC12	535
N515MA	MU-2	327	N522MC	MU-2	348SA	N528MD	TBM8	462	N535PC	PC12	1057

N535PN	300	FA-152	N545AW	200	BB-610	N551GA	90	LJ-795	N555JE	441	0094
N535SM	680T	1711-86	N545C	90	LJ-1654	N551JL	200	BB-788	N555JJ	441	0004
N535WM	MU-2	655	N545D	90	LJ-1040	N551M	E90	LW-328	N555JK	441	0004
N536	690A	11155	(N545G)	200	BB-1317	N551MA	TBM8	516	N555JP	MU-2	332
N536BW	350	FL-432	N545GM	100	B-188	N551MS	E90	LW-311	N555KG	STAR	NC-36
N536BW	350	FL-611	N545GM	200	BB-209	(N551PB)	PC12	551	N555KK	STAR	NC-36
N536CA	PA42	5501016	N545GM	200	BB-610	N551S	46T	97120B	N555KP	200	BB-1152
N536DM	MIVA	AT-038	N545GM	200	BB-1187	N551SS	90	LJ-430	*N555LD	F90	LA-48
N536MA	441	0322	N545GM	200	BB-1317	N551TP	200	BB-1033	N555LL	MU-2	332
N536MA	MU-2	656	N545JW	46D	212	N551TP	350	FL-303	N555LW	E90	LW-184
N536MR	350	FL-536	N545KA	350	FL-545	N551TR	200	BB-1033	N555MA	MU-2	241
N536RB	200	BB-1879	N545LC	200	BB-339	N551VB	350	FL-503	N555MC	200G	BY-17
N537EC	90	LJ-537	N545RC	200	BB-106	N552AC	PA42	5527025	N555MS	90	LJ-872
N537JH	90	LJ-610	N546BZ	B100	BE-55	N552D	200	BB-1058	N555MT	690B	11418
N537MA	MU-2	657	N546C	90	LJ-1713	N552E	90	LJ-1662	N555PE	PC12	555
N537PC	PC12	537	N546C	90	LJ-1723	N552GA	100	B-215	N555PM	31T	7620028
N538AM	300	FA-107	N546MA	46T	97331	N552JF	TBM7	184	N555RA	90	LJ-974
N538AS	200	BB-743	N546PB	PC12	546	N552KA	350	FL-552	N555RC	31T	7920079
N538AS	300	FA-107	N547AF	PC12	547	N552M	300	FA-157	N555RH	90	LJ-516
N538BH	PC12	626	N547BN	G1	162	N552R	90	LJ-749	N555RT	31T	8166070
N538EA	MU-2	1538SA	N547GA	425	0084	N552TB	200	BB-1159	N555RT	PA42	5501009
(N538KB)	200	BB-1421	N547GA	90	LJ-1559	N552TC	PC12	443	N555RY	PA42	5501009
N538M	100	B-189	N547GC	425	0084	N552TP	200	BB-1159	N555SK	200	BB-539
N538M	90	LJ-30	N547Q	G1	162	N552TP	350	FL-1	(N555SZ)	46T	97021
N538MA	MU-2	631	N547QR	G1	162	N552TP	350	FL-281	N555TB	90	LJ-364
N538MA	MU-2	658	N547TA	31T	7820003	N552TR	350	FL-1	N555TB	E90	LW-273
N538MC	MU-2	1538SA	N547TA	MU-2	364SA	N552TT	200	BB-1159	N555TP	425	0110
N538RB	200G	BY-35	N548GQ	681	6027	N553AM	441	0219	N555TT	E90	LW-170
N539DP	90	LJ-53	N548JG	90	LJ-1452	N553CA	PC12	553	N555TZ	F90	LA-189
N539MA	MU-2	552	N548KA	350	FL-548	N553CL	350	FL-504	N555VE	690B	11546
N539PS	PC12	539	N548SA	MIVC	AT-548	N553HC	200	BB-928	N555VK	MU-2	023
N539SA	MIVC	AT-539	N548SM	MIVA	AT-062-2	N553MA	E90	LW-147	N555VW	90	LJ-1330
N540BK	350	FL-540	N548UP	MIVC	AT-548	N553R	200	BB-589	N555WA	441	0219
N540CB	300	FA-135	N548WB	200	BB-544	N553Z	90	LJ-211	N555WE	350	FL-33
N540GA	425	0026	N549BE	200	BB-423	*N554CA	TBM7	21	N555WF	200	BB-928
N540GA	90	LJ-1557	N549BJ	350	FL-63	N554CF	E90	LW-66	N555WF	200	BB-1303
N540GC	425	0026	N549BR	90	LJ-809	N554DM	PA42	5527008	N555WF	200	BB-1490
N540MA	200	BB-1765	N549GA	441	0044	N554T	46D	97	N555WF	300	FA-58
N540MA	MU-2	659	N549GA	90	LJ-1613	N554VR	PC12	288	N555WF	350	FL-287
N540MC	MIIB	T26-148	N549GS	441	0044	(N555AE)	31T	8104054	N555WF	90	LJ-677
N540SP	C-12	BC-5	N549JF	200	BB-562	N555AL	90	LJ-1268	N555WF	F90	LA-71
N540WJ	F90	LA-54	N549LK	MU-2	022	N555AM	MIII	T-201	N555WQ	350	FL-287
N541AA	90	LJ-1041	N549LK	MU-2	167	N555AM	MIII	T-227	N555WW	MIII	T-205
N541AM	690A	11167	N549LK	MU-2	264	N555AN	90	LJ-610	N555XY	90	LJ-1488
N541AS	200	BB-1759	N550AC	31T	1104004	N555AT	31T	8104054	N555ZA	350	FL-48
N541F	680T	1609-45	N550BE	MIII	T-224	N555AW	MIII	T-205	N555ZT	350	FL-445
N541GA	350	FL-321	N550CP	TBM8	477	N555BC	MU-2	664	N556BA	200	BB-1556
N541MA	MU-2	660	N550DC	200	BB-1617	N555BE	425	0044	N556BR	PA42	5501040
N541MC	U-21	LM-39	N550E	200	BB-639	N555BR	MIII	T-208	N556HL	PC12	556
N541MM	F90	LA-71	N550EC	200G	BY-44	N555C	MU-2	129	N556JK	200	BB-556
N541NC	MU-2	1504SA	N550F	31T	7520017	N555CB	90	LJ-189	N556JS	200	BB-556
N541ND	46T	97356	N550GL	200	BB-781	N555CG	31T	8020066	N556KA	350	FL-556
N541PB	PC12	541	N550JB	690C	11660	N555CG	31T	8166029	N556MP	46T	97185
N541RK	90	LJ-1779	N550JC	200	BB-354	N555CH	MU-2	508	N556UP	MIVC	AT-556
N541SA	MIII	TT-541	N550JD	441	0072	N555CK	90	LJ-677	N557CA	TBM7	306
N541SC	300	FA-138	N550K	MU-2	590	N555DB	MIII	T-201	N557D	200	BB-1162
N541W	680T	1554-13	N550M	200	BB-147	N555DD	MU-2	339	(N557DF)	PC12	557
N541X	680T	1601-43	N550M	MU-2	639	N555DM	BN2	129	N557KA	350	FL-557
N542JV	MIIB	T26-178	N550MA	MU-2	169	N555DX	300	FA-65	N557ML	46D	181
N542KA	200	BB-542	N550MM	31T	8166017	N555EW	PC12	271	N557P	90	LJ-1689
N542PB	PC12	542	N550NP	690A	11234	N555FD	300	FA-213	N557PC	PC12	557
N542PC	PA42	8001014	N550P	E90	LW-301	N555FH	300	FA-213	(N557SA)	90	LJ-1557
N542TW	PA42	8001052	N550PC	MIII	T-316	N555FP	200	BB-419	N558AC	MIIB	T26-144
N543FM	PA42	8001053	N550SC	425	0043	N555FP	200	BB-455	N558AF	PC12	558
N543GA	425	0101	N550SW	90	LJ-1700	N555FR	31T	8004010	N558BC	350	FL-223
N543GA	90	LJ-1558	N550T	31T	7520017	N555FS	MU-2	1530SA	N558DB	90	LJ-354
N543GC	425	0101	N550T	31T	8166056	N555FT	441	0124	N558FM	200	BB-1368
N543HC	90	LJ-1620	N550TD	MIVC	AT-487	N555FW	E90	LW-248	N558KA	350	FL-558
N543JF	MU-2	389SA	N550TF	200	BB-1265	N555GA	200	BB-819	N558M	MU-2	639
N543KA	350	FL-543	N550TL	31T	8166056	N555GA	E90	LW-242	N558RS	46D	83
N543MB	E90	LW-125	N550TP	200	BB-1265	N555GB	441	0041	N558RW	46T	97346
N543PB	PC12	543	N550TP	350	FL-35	N555GB	MIVC	AT-439B	N559BM	200	BB-559
N543S	680T	1556-14	N550TP	MIVC	AT-487	N555GD	441	0094	N559CA	TBM7	213
N544AF	MU-2	544	N550TS	90	LJ-345	N555GG	690A	11159	N559CG	690B	11530
N544AL	441	0120	N550Z	90	LJ-211	N555GG	690C	11721	N559DW	200	BB-1036
N544CB	MU-2	1536SA	N550Z	E90	LW-89	N555GG	695	95004	N559MC	90	LJ-1863
N544FD	B100	BE-43	N551AC	PA42	5527022	N555GK	200	BB-875	N559PB	PC12	559
N544FF	MIVA	AT-044	N551AT	90	LJ-399	N555HD	441	0147	N559PC	TRIS	1069
N544GA	690D	15015	(N551BV)	350	FL-503	N555HJ	90	LJ-1378	N560MP	46D	127
N544JC	300	FA-217	N551CN	90	LJ-1347	(N555HN)	TBM7	108	(N560SA)	STAR	NC-24
N544KA	350	FL-544	N551E	200	BB-422	N555HP	31T	8020066	N560UP	MIVC	AT-560
N544P	200	BB-1265	N551E	90	LJ-399	N555HP	TBM7	108	N561AF	MU-2	561
N544PS	300	FA-90	N551ES	350	FL-78	N555HP	TBM8	402	N561GA	PA42	5501040
N544UP	MIVC	AT-544	N551F	90	LJ-399	N555JA	BN2	20	N561SS	200	BB-464

N561ST	PC12	561
N561TC	690A	11315
N561UP	MIVC	AT-561
N562CC	TBM8	512
N562GA	PC12	113
N562HP	46T	97139
N562NA	PC12	174
N562P	90	LJ-248
N562PB	PC12	562
N562R	200	BB-742
N562R	90	LJ-248
N563AC	90	LJ-1289
N563GA	F406	0041
N563MA	46T	97162
N563MC	90	LJ-384
N563TM	PC12	563
N563UP	MIVC	AT-563
N564AC	441	0147
N564BC	200	BB-1107
N564BC	350	FL-577
N564BC	B100	BE-35
N564CA	B100	BE-58
N564GA	200	BB-1463
N564KA	350	FL-564
N564PB	PC12	564
N564UP	MIVC	AT-564
N565C	46T	97173
N565EZ	PC12	290
N565HP	46T	97211
N565JF	31T	8020087
(N565MD)	200	BB-942
N565RA	100	B-25
N565RA	200	BB-268
N565RA	90	LJ-176
N565RP	100	B-25
N565UP	MIVC	AT-567
N566CA	90	LJ-184
N566HP	46T	97252
N566KA	300	FA-201
N566KB	300	FA-201
N566MA	46T	97391
N566NA	200	BB-1566
N566TC	200	BB-1145
N566UP	MIVC	AT-566
N567A	200	BB-1635
N567CS	90	LJ-390
N567DC	100	B-185
(N567DM)	200	BB-1369
N567ER	PC12	1139
N567FH	PC12	567
N567GJ	E90	LW-95
N567H	690A	11330
N567JD	200	BB-949
N567MD	90	LJ-1231
N567PK	200	BB-1634
N567R	690	11051
N567T	200	BB-1635
N567T	TBM7	49
N567US	200	BB-1634
N568B	P68	54
N568C	B100	BE-32
N568H	690	11027
N568H	690B	11386
N568HP	46T	97290
N568HP	46T	97306
N568K	B100	BE-106
N568SA	90	LJ-1568
N568SA	MIVC	AT-568
N568TT	200	BB-1568
N568UP	MIVC	AT-568
N569AB	PC12	705
N569AF	PC12	569
N569GR	90	LJ-1447
N569H	690	11029
N569KA	350	FL-569
N569SC	200	BB-1084
N569SG	200	BB-1084
N569UP	MIVC	AT-569
N570	100	B-20
N570AB	31T	7520038
N570AB	31T	7820026
N570DC	PC12	570
N570DU	100	B-20
N570GB	690A	11209
N570H	690A	11130
N570M	200	BB-29
N570M	90	LJ-126
(N570SS)	MU-2	380SA
N570UP	MIVC	AT-570
N570VS	200	BB-29
N570WA	690A	11209
N571L	90	LJ-135
N571M	200	BB-59
N571M	90	LJ-135
N571PC	PC12	571
N571SS	200	BB-501
N572	100	B-48
N572	200	BB-755
N572AT	200	BB-730
N572BB	90	LJ-1320
N572DU	100	B-48
N572M	200	BB-94
N572M	200	BB-398
N572M	90	LJ-177
N572P	200	BB-1483
N572PC	PC12	572
N573DU	90	LJ-430
N573G	MIVC	AT-446B
N573M	200	BB-224
N573M	90	LJ-268
N573MA	MU-2	162
N573ML	90	LJ-268
N573MS	46T	97359
(N573P)	350	FL-19
(N573P)	90	LJ-430
N573P	90	LJ-1413
N574DU	G1	93
N574GS	200	BB-429
N574K	G1	93
N574M	200	BB-477
N574M	90	LJ-276
N574P	90	LJ-1548
N575C	90	LJ-532
N575CA	MU-2	425SA
N575HA	200	BB-218
N575HC	E90	LW-67
N575HW	200	BB-218
N575HW	E90	LW-67
N575JM	31T	7920061
N575MX	350	FL-445
N575NM	90	LJ-1776
N575PC	PC12	575
N575RA	200	BB-575
N575T	200	BB-1384
N576D	90	LJ-85
N576DU	90	LJ-85
(N576P)	F90	LA-71
N576RG	PC12	576
N577BA	300	FA-66
N577BE	300	FA-66
N577BF	PC12	577
N577D	100	B-22
N577DC	90	LJ-308
N577DU	100	B-22
N577HP	46T	97377
N577JE	31T	7620052
N577KA	MIV	AT-008
N577L	100	B-22
N577L	200	BB-736
N577LM	F90	LA-149
N577NK	90	LJ-80
N577P	200	BB-1798
N577PA	425	0194
N577PW	350	FL-133
N577PW	425	0194
N577RH	680T	1601-43
N577RW	B100	BE-5
N577VM	680T	1601-43
N577VM	F90	LA-149
N578BM	200	BB-588
N578DC	PC12	570
N578DU	90	LJ-243
N578EH	MU-2	578
N578G	200	BB-578
N578KA	681B	6049
N578KB	G1	175
N578P	90	LJ-1207
N579B	90	LJ-59
N579B	90	LJ-289
N579CW	31T	7920089
N579DU	90	LJ-350
N579MC	350	FL-230
N579NC	TBM7	102
N579PS	90	LJ-496
N579SW	31T	7920089
N580	200	BB-575
N580AC	90	LJ-1388
N580AF	MU-2	580
N580BC	G1	63
N580BK	200	BB-1000
N580C	90	LJ-823
N580HP	46T	97329
N580M	680T	1676-59
N580MA	MU-2	562
N580PA	F90	LA-158
N580RA	90	LJ-580
N580S	B100	BE-77
N581	200	BB-640
N581AT	441	0010
N581B	31T	8104019
N581B	90	LJ-1170
N581FM	200	BB-1702
N581JA	BN2	12
N581M	E90	LW-133
N581MA	BN2	283
N581MW	200	BB-107
N581PC	PC12	581
(N581RA)	90	LJ-1581
N581RJ	F90	LA-14
N581SW	31T	8104019
(N581VP)	90	LJ-581
N581WC	90	LJ-219
N582AS	46D	79
N582C	TBM7	274
N582DT	PC12	582
N582JA	BN2	19
N582JF	MIVA	AT-027
N582SE	46T	97188
N582SW	PA42	8001033
N583AL	200	BB-1439
N583AT	200	BB-1439
N583AT	350	FL-258
N583JA	BN2	39
(N583SC)	350	FL-258
N584JA	BN2	5
N584JV	PC12	584
N584NR	90	LJ-848
N584PM	90	LJ-848
N584SK	90	LJ-1581
N584V	46T	97240
N585CE	200	BB-1194
N585FL	200	BB-107
N585JA	BN2	20
N585PA	425	0047
N585PB	PC12	585
N585R	90	LJ-1169
N585S	90	LJ-273
N585TC	90	LJ-653
N586BC	200	BB-1223
N586BW	350	FL-432
N586DV	690B	11553
N586JA	BN2	24
N586PB	PC12	586
N586TC	90	LJ-653
N586UC	200	BB-1118
N587DR	200	BB-329
N587JA	BN2	40
N587KA	681B	6049
N587M	90	LJ-361
N587PB	90	LJ-1408
N588FM	MIII	T-330
N588JA	BN2	45
N588KC	PC12	588
N588KM	90	LJ-1871
N588RS	PC12	1062
N588SA	90	LJ-1588
N588SD	90	LJ-1663
N588XJ	90	LJ-1530
N589AC	PC12	589
N589GA	31T	7820085
N589H	P180	1010
N589JA	BN2	25
N589SA	BN2	5
N589SA	BN2	38
N590AC	350	FL-78
N590AQ	G1	164
N590AS	G1	164
N590DL	31T	7520031
N590EU	350	FL-590
N590GM	90	LJ-1594
N590GT	90	LJ-1759
N590HB	90	LJ-1934
N590JA	BN2	49
N590PS	90	LJ-1733
N590SA	90	LJ-401
N590WA	P68	61
N591AF	PC12	591
N591EB	200	BB-1317
N591JA	BN2	57
N591M	200	BB-765
N592DC	680T	1552-12
N592DC	90	LJ-165
N592DQ	90	LJ-165
N592G	441	0361
N592JA	BN2	58
N592MG	EPIC	022
N592Q	441	0361
N593	200	BB-593
N593DJ	200	BB-277
N593JA	BN2	60
N593MA	350	FL-68
N593PC	PC12	593
N594AR	G1	61
N594DC	200	BB-547
N594G	441	0272
N594JA	BN2	61
N594SC	350	FL-594
N594WA	PC12	594
N595A	200	BB-13
N595AF	90	LJ-378
(N595AS)	90	LJ-595
N595JA	BN2	44
N595MG	90	LJ-55
N595PB	PC12	609
N595PC	90	LJ-964
(N595PM)	46D	33
N595PM	46D	36
(N595PM)	46D	160
N595RC	90	LJ-964
N595TM	90	LJ-1255
N596CU	90	LJ-721
N596JA	BN2	64
N597CH	PC12	597
N597DM	90	LJ-1111
N597MM	200	BB-720
N597P	90	LJ-1597
N598AC	350	FL-78
N598AC	350	FL-613
N598AT	46T	97059
N598C	46T	97275
N598HC	PC12	598
N598JA	BN2	66
N598MM	PC12	598
N599AS	441	0183
N599G	TBM8	491
N599HL	90	LJ-1762
N599JA	BN2	69
N599MS	BN2	2021
N599MS	MIIB	T26-144
N599MT	BN2	427
N599PB	PC12	599
N599PC	TRIS	1064
N599TR	G1	160
N600AC	100	B-199
N600AC	E90	LW-185
(N600AL)	90	LJ-495
N600AM	200	BB-337
N600BD	EPIC	019
N600BF	90	LJ-193
N600BG	F90	LA-211
N600BL	PC12	1084
N600BM	690C	11691
N600BM	690C	11734
N600BM	695A	96081
N600BN	90	LJ-372
N600BS	31T	8166045

N600BV	200	BB-254
N600BW	200	BB-254
N600BW	90	LJ-193
N600C	MIV	AT-010
N600CB	100	B-36
N600CB	300	FA-136
N600CB	350	FL-38
N600CB	690A	11198
N600CF	90	LJ-1513
N600CM	200	BB-1111
N600CM	31T	7720024
N600CM	690D	15020
N600CP	200	BB-174
N600CP	200	BB-302
N600CP	200	BB-371
N600CX	E90	LW-43
N600DC	200	BB-126
N600DF	200	BB-1690
(N600DH)	MIII	T-252
N600DJ	90	LJ-549
N600DK	100	B-138
N600DL	MIII	T-252
N600DM	200	BB-414
N600DR	31T	8104066
N600EF	E90	LW-250
N600ET	MIII	T-274
N600FC	E90	LW-322
N600FE	90	LJ-935
N600FL	90	LJ-935
N600FL	90	LJ-1540
N600G	200	BB-509
N600GC	100	B-220
*N600GR	PC12	1084
N600K	MU-2	194
N600KA	300	FA-143
N600KB	200	BB-606
N600KC	E90	LW-169
N600KP	200	BB-606
N600KP	200	BB-1233
N600KP	MU-2	389SA
N600KP	PC12	700
N600KW	200	BB-31
N600L	MIV	AT-010
N600L	MIVC	AT-511
N600LP	200	BB-216
N600LP	300	FA-37
N600LR	200	BB-216
N600MM	695	95029
N600MS	200	BB-673
N600MS	300	FA-66
N600MS	MIIB	T26-144
N600N	MIVC	AT-511
N600NS	46T	97107
N600NW	90	LJ-372
N600P	MIIA	T26-006
N600PB	690A	11202
N600PC	90	LJ-656
N600PE	PC12	600
N600RD	200T	BT-33
N600RK	200	BB-1800
N600RL	200	BB-1800
N600RM	200	BB-507
N600RM	31T	7920081
(N600RM)	MU-2	709SA
N600SB	90	LJ-996
N600SC	100	B-231
N600SC	200	BB-479
N600SC	E90	LW-169
N600SF	441	0091
N600SF	F90	LA-186
N600SS	200	BB-1111
N600TA	200	BB-1667
N600TA	MIII	T-274
N600TA	MIV	AT-018
N600TB	MU-2	258
N600TC	695	95016
N600TJ	425	0177
N600TN	MU-2	684
N600VT	441	0149
N600VW	690A	11198
N600WA	F90	LA-71
N600WM	F90	LA-75
N600WR	31T	7620038
N600WS	690B	11435
N600WY	PC12	526
N600XL	31T	8166048
N600YE	46T	97250
N601AJ	31T	1104013
N601AM	200	BB-658
N601BM	PC12	106
N601BM	PC12	181
N601CF	200	BB-25
N601CT	MU-2	035
N601DM	90	LJ-825
N601ET	PC6	907
N601G	680T	1605-44
N601HK	G1	5
N601HP	G1	5
N601HT	PC12	337
N601JT	MIII	T-319
N601LM	100	B-116
N601PA	200	BB-51
N601PC	100	B-225
N601PL	PC12	601
N601PT	31T	7904030
N601R	90	LJ-217
N601SC	90	LJ-753
N601SD	MU-2	610
N601T	100	B-90
N601T	200	BB-620
N601T	90	LJ-120
N601TA	90	LJ-120
N601U	100	B-90
N601WT	690D	15016
N602	90	LJ-232
N602BM	PC12	664
N602CA	690B	11374
N602CN	200	BB-872
N602E	90	LJ-232
N602EB	F90	LA-5
N602EZ	425	0085
N602MC	200	BB-529
N602MJ	200	BB-1801
N602PA	680T	1534-3
N602RM	31T	7920081
N602TA	200	BB-1658
N603H	90	LJ-358
(N603JR)	200	BB-613
N603JS	EPIC	015
N603L	MIV	AT-010
N603PA	90	LJ-403
(N603RE)	90	LJ-403
N603SS	MU-2	712SA
N603TA	200	BB-1623
N603WM	300	FA-198
N604	200	BB-724
N604	90	LJ-395
N604B	90	LJ-395
N604DK	F90	LA-193
N604MJ	200	BB-1801
N604RK	200	BB-1429
N604RR	441	0140
N604TA	200	BB-1680
N604WP	PC12	604
N605	P68	321
N605AA	G1	80
N605AB	G1	80
N605CC	F90	LA-170
N605CW	90	LJ-843
N605DK	90	LJ-676
N605EA	200	BB-605
N605EA	F90	LA-129
N605EE	200	BB-240
N605KC	690A	11198
N605MD	PC12	1033
N605MJ	350	FL-578
N605PC	PC12	605
N605TA	200	BB-1708
N605TC	PC12	320
N605TQ	PC12	320
N605W	E90	LW-305
N606AJ	200	BB-1257
N606DW	31T	8120038
N606MA	MU-2	140
N606MJ	350	FL-596
N606MM	90	LJ-457
N606NT	BN2	653
N606PS	MIII	T-307
N606SF	TBM7	180
N606SL	PC12	1020
N606TA	200	BB-1711
N606WC	46T	97176
N607AB	90	LJ-383
N607AE	90	LJ-383
N607AF	PC12	607
N607DD	31T	7520028
N607DD	425	0126
N607DK	F90	LA-140
N607KW	200	BB-977
N607MA	46T	97107
N607TA	200	BB-1715
N608DK	200	BB-64
N608JR	200	BB-1177
N608P	90	LJ-1632
N608R	G1	103
N608RP	G1	103
N608SM	PC12	734
N608SW	31T	8004038
N608TA	200	BB-1720
N609BG	350	FL-468
N609DK	200	BB-894
N609GA	PA42	8001005
(N609HF)	MU-2	435SA
N609SA	90	LJ-1609
N609TA	200	BB-1725
N609TW	PC12	712
N610CA	MU-2	788SA
N610ED	MIII	T-228
N610GH	PC12	103
N610HC	200	BB-721
N610JM	100	B-26
N610K	100	B-52
N610K	90	LJ-187
N610K	90	LJ-386
N610KR	100	B-26
(N610L)	31T	8120055
N610MW	31T	7920037
(N610MW)	31T	7920039
N610NK	PC12	610
N610P	31T	7620002
N610PA	BN2	876
N610R	PA42	8001002
N610RG	31T	7720057
N610RM	200	BB-1761
N610SC	90	LJ-1817
N610SW	200	BB-1187
N610TA	200	BB-1609
N610W	90	LJ-180
N610W	90	LJ-890
N611	680W	1772-10
N611	690D	15018
N611AY	90	LJ-601
N611CC	100	B-138
N611CF	90	LJ-1198
N611CR	90	LJ-1234
N611DD	90	LJ-806
N611EP	90	LJ-334
N611ER	90	LJ-334
N611GT	P180	1148
N611KA	90	LJ-1279
N611LM	31T	8020023
N611MA	TBM7	330
N611MF	680W	1772-10
N611MT	690B	11537
N611ND	U-21	LM-11
N611R	E90	LW-244
N611RR	31T	8004006
N611SD	200	BB-1307
N611SW	200	BB-301
N611TA	200	BB-1730
N611VP	90	LJ-171
N611WA	TRIS	1058
(N612AM)	31T	8004042
N612BB	31T	8166068
N612CC	441	0339
N612CC	MU-2	1507SA
(N612DM)	690A	11277
N612DT	G1	52
N612J	PC12	494
N612KC	PC12	173
N612MR	90	LJ-1031
N612PC	PC12	146
N612SA	C-12	BC-29
N612TA	200	BB-1735
N612TA	200	BB-1739
N613BA	350	FL-396
N613BR	90	LJ-9
N613CF	MU-2	416SA
N613CS	200	BB-613
N613GA	200	BB-1909
N613HC	31T	7720053
N613JR	200	BB-613
N613M	90	LJ-47
N613M	90	LJ-173
N613NA	PC12	197
N613RF	90	LJ-1068
N613TA	200	BB-1581
N613VW	PC12	1095
N614BK	350	FL-614
N614LD	PC12	614
N614ME	F90	LA-67
N614ML	350	FL-84
N614ML	90	LJ-552
N614ML	F90	LA-67
N614P	PC12	1036
N614RG	F90	LA-80
N614SA	90	LJ-1614
N614SC	31T	7920012
N615	680W	1772-10
N615	690A	11317
N615AA	90	LJ-298
N615C	G1	16
N615DP	690A	11317
N615GA	MIV	AT-009
N615JB	690D	15031
N615PS	31T	7920009
N615SB	690B	11457
N615TA	200	BB-1745
N615WH	200	BB-1645
N616AF	MU-2	254
N616AS	90	LJ-160
N616BH	F90	LA-25
N616CG	425	0087
N616CK	350	FL-114
N616CP	F90	LA-25
(N616DD)	E90	LW-168
N616DR	200	BB-1194
N616E	680T	1707-82
N616EL	PC12	616
N616F	90	LJ-165
N616GB	200	BB-752
N616GL	BN2	616
N616MC	680T	1707-82
N616MC	MU-2	622
N616MG	425	0087
N616PA	90	LJ-511
N616PS	MIII	T-316
N616SC	90	LJ-1192
N616SD	690A	11191
N616TA	200	BB-1749
N617BB	MU-2	522
(N617DM)	MIIB	T26-152
N617DW	31T	8004042
N617KM	90	LJ-1095
N617LM	90	LJ-1012
N617MM	90	LJ-1587
N617MS	200C	BL-35
N617RM	90	LJ-1095
N617SA	PC6	517
N617TA	200	BB-1751
N618	200	BB-1378
N618	690A	11232
N618B	690A	11232
N618BB	MU-2	533
N618DB	90	LJ-1024
N618HB	350	FL-618
N618HG	200G	BY-53
N618HG	90	LJ-1831
N618JC	PC12	618
N618JL	PC12	618
N618M	G1	163
N618MA	46T	97218
N618P	EPIC	023
N618RD	E90	LW-301
N618RT	MU-2	1508SA
N618ST	46T	97318

N618SW	31T	8166036
N618TA	200	BB-1754
N619AF	PC12	619
N619GS	90	LJ-84
N619J	31T	7920019
N619JB	PA42	8001011
N619RB	31T	8004055
N619SH	90	LJ-1737
N619TA	200	BB-1758
(N620AD)	31T	8166059
N620DB	31T	7920055
N620HM	90	LJ-273
N620K	G1	34
N620MW	PA42	8001105
N620P	31T	7920072
N620WA	PC12	620
N620WE	90	LJ-743
N621A	G1	102
N621AW	200C	BL-16
(N621CF)	90	LJ-369
*N621N	46T	97177
N621RM	200	BB-398
N621SC	441	0070
N621TA	MU-2	605
N621TB	90	LJ-334
N621TD	90	LJ-1123
N621WP	90	LJ-1208
N622AJ	31T	8166071
(N622AM)	B100	BE-111
N622BB	31T	1104012
N622DC	200	BB-491
(N622HC)	690B	11471
N622JA	200	BB-726
(N622KA)	350	FL-622
N622KM	200	BB-491
N622MM	425	0187
N622RP	B100	BE-111
N622TA	200	BB-1766
N622WW	PC12	622
N623AC	PC12	722
N623AW	90	LJ-282
N623BA	PC12	623
N623BB	90	LJ-277
N623DC	MU-2	692
N623DS	200	BB-1013
N623DT	90	LJ-1858
N623E	PC12	1050
N623KW	PA42	5501020
N623MA	46D	216
N623R	90	LJ-173
N623RT	TBM7	217
N623TA	200	BB-1773
(N623VG)	200	BB-769
N623VP	200	BB-769
N623W	G1	66
N623WA	200	BB-1134
N624AF	PC12	624
N624AL	200	BB-394
N624B	90	LJ-610
N624BN	TRIS	1012
N624CB	441	0166
(N624CS)	200	BB-1444
N624KA	350	FL-624
N624LF	F90	LA-143
(N624PA)	B100	BE-86
N624TA	200	BB-1779
N624TS	PC12	724
N625BC	200	BB-196
N625BF	MU-2	625
N625GA	200	BB-1884
N625JD	46T	97361
N625MC	PC12	1047
N625MD	200	BB-942
N625N	200	BB-1394
N625PP	E90	LW-58
N625TA	200	BB-1783
N625W	200	BB-1394
N625W	90	LJ-295
N625W	E90	LW-305
N626AC	46T	97410
N626AR	46T	97286
N626BL	LFAN	E-001
N626GT	200G	BY-27
(N626JP)	350	FL-412
N626MT	PC12	820
N626PS	MIII	T-329
N626RM	100	B-177
N626SA	100	B-78
*N626SS	MIII	T-329
N626TA	200	BB-1786
N627AC	F90	LA-108
N627BC	200	BB-707
N627BM	200	BB-398
N627DB	TBM7	328
N627FB	200	BB-928
N627FP	200	BB-928
N627KP	90	LJ-812
N627KW	PA42	5501010
N627KW	PA42	5501030
N627L	100	B-37
N627NB	31T	7904033
N627PC	PA42	5501010
N627WD	BN2	627
(N628BN)	BN2	628
N628DE	31T	8120031
N628DS	200	BB-1013
N628LD	350	FL-562
N628MC	PC12	516
N628MR	425	0049
N628RC	BN2	2203
(N628TM)	MU-2	631
N628VK	90	LJ-1533
N629BC	46D	227
N629BN	BN2	629
N629CD	90	LJ-173
N629DF	PC12	590
N629DK	46D	32
N629GT	P180	1048
N629JG	90	LJ-1688
N629JJ	46D	164
N629JM	G1	82
N629KC	46T	97229
N629LM	300	FA-50
N629MC	PC12	516
N629MC	PC12	806
N629MU	MU-2	629
N629PC	TRIS	1070
N629RP	200	BB-1984
N629SC	100	B-137
N629SK	PC12	413
N629TG	MIVC	AT-427
N629TM	MU-2	631
N630AM	E90	LW-309
N630DB	200	BB-187
N630HA	MU-2	630
N630M	90	LJ-101
N630MW	31T	8166011
N630RH	690A	11234
N630VB	200	BB-630
N630VC	BN2	868
(N631BA)	MU-2	031
N631BL	PC12	631
N631DS	STAR	NC-44
N631FA	MIVA	AT-069
N631MC	31T	7620051
N631ME	350	FL-430
N631PC	PA42	8001060
N631PT	31T	7720001
N631SA	PC6	631
N631SR	200	BB-244
N631SW	31T	7904029
N631WF	31T	7620051
N632DS	300	FA-141
N632RR	F90	LA-111
N632SA	PC6	632
N633AB	31T	8104021
N633BB	BN2	2153
N633D	90	LJ-759
N633EB	200	BB-111
N633HC	200	BB-1852
N633P	46T	97123B
N633RB	46T	97061
N633ST	MIII	T-237
N633WC	31T	8104036
N634B	C-12	BC-19
N634KA	90	LJ-634
N634M	425	0069
N634MA	BN2	464
N634TT	200	BB-1252
N635AF	90	LJ-736
N635B	C-12	BC-49
N635DS	TBM7	19
N635GA	200	BB-847
N635MF	200	BB-978
N635SF	200	BB-1847
N636	90	LJ-1268
N636	G1	149
N636B	C-12	BC-61
N636CR	31T	8120014
N636G	G1	149
N636GW	E90	LW-332
N636JM	E90	LW-332
N636PS	MIV	AT-018
N636SC	90	LJ-163
N636SP	MIII	T-285
N636SQ	90	LJ-163
N636SW	MU-2	636
N637B	C-12	BC-62
N637JC	300	FA-116
N637KC	PA42	5501030
N637PH	PC12	637
N637WG	MU-2	637
N637WM	200	BB-1768
N638AV	PC12	638
N638B	C-12	BC-65
N638D	90	LJ-424
N638DB	46D	222
N638LD	STAR	NC-18
N638MA	MU-2	638
N639B	C-12	BC-67
N639JK	200	BB-639
N639KC	PC12	639
N640BD	46D	64
N640DF	90	LJ-1312
N640KC	PC12	1076
N640MA	MU-2	590
N640MY	PC12	640
N641B	G1	65
N641KE	MU-2	187
N641KE	MU-2	320
N641MC	200	BB-1057
N641MC	350	FL-495
N641PE	F90	LA-91
N641SE	STAR	NC-46
N641TC	200	BB-641
N641TK	PC12	641
N641TS	200	BB-641
N642BA	MIVA	AT-029
N642BL	300	FA-156
N642CT	PC12	246
N642DH	90	LJ-420
N642JL	300	FA-30
N642PB	MIIB	T26-149
N642PC	PA42	8001034
N642PC	PC12	642
N642RB	MIIB	T26-149
N642RP	MIIB	T26-107
N642TD	90	LJ-766
N642TF	200	BB-363
N642TS	MIVA	AT-036
(N642TW)	PA42	8001062
N642WM	MIIB	T26-125
N643BW	PC12	131
N643EA	90	LJ-1643
N643HD	200	BB-1112
N643JA	90	LJ-180
N643PC	PC12	643
N643PU	90	LJ-1002
N644CB	350	FL-394
N644EM	MU-2	1534SA
N644PU	90	LJ-1046
N644S	90	LJ-858
N644SD	PC12	644
N644SP	90	LJ-696
N645PC	PC12	645
N646BM	200	BB-646
N646CA	46D	15
N646CA	46D	179
N646DR	200	BB-646
N646KC	46T	97224
N647JM	200	BB-1147
N648DH	46D	10
N648JG	90	LJ-1706
N648KA	200	BB-648
N648MW	200	BB-648
N648T	46D	99
N649JC	200	BB-649
N649MC	90	LJ-9
N649P	PC12	649
(N650)	690C	11627
N650BG	PC12	654
N650BT	G1	11
(N650CA)	46T	97260
N650DM	TBM7	85
N650JT	B100	BE-60
N650JW	200	BB-1126
N650LP	TRIS	1029
N650MC	PC12	650
N650RS	31T	8020071
N650ST	G1	11
N650TJ	200	BB-633
N650TJ	B100	BE-60
(N650UT)	B100	BE-60
N650WC	PC12	871
N651CA	PC12	246
N651PB	PC12	651
N652CA	PC12	248
N652L	E90	LW-329
N652MC	425	0225
N653CA	PC12	257
N653LP	F90	LA-201
N653ME	200	BB-1653
N653PC	690B	11356
N653SB	EPIC	025
N653TB	200	BB-586
N653TF	90	LJ-1653
N654BA	200C	BL-54
N654C	90	LJ-12
N654CA	PC12	261
N654CW	TBM8	418
N654CW	TBM8	439
N654FM	200	BB-654
N654JC	PC12	437
N654L	MU-2	658
N654MT	90	LJ-388
N654P	90	LJ-1641
N654S	300	FA-108
N655BA	200	BB-655
N655F	E90	LW-93
N655GG	690A	11159
N655JG	200	BB-1440
N655PB	PC12	655
N655PC	695	95015
N655PE	MIII	TT-489A
N655SC	350	FL-239
N656A	90	LJ-304
N656AF	PC12	656
N656BS	MIII	T-250
N656PS	MIII	T-250
N656PS	MIII	T-354
N656SA	90	LJ-1656
N657DC	31T	8004036
N657EZ	PC12	1097
N657P	G1	165
N657PC	G1	165
N657PC	PC12	796
N657PP	350	FL-375
N658JP	200	BB-658
(N658RS)	31T	8020071
N659CM	BN2	659
N659H	90	LJ-512
N659PC	G1	196
N660AA	200	BB-1949
(N660AC)	200	BB-639
(N660CA)	MU-2	658
N660CB	100	B-213
N660GW	90	LJ-673
N660J	BN2T	2102
(N660JC)	681B	6048
N660JM	90	LJ-673
N660L	E90	LW-60
N660M	200	BB-10
N660MW	200	BB-1428
N660NR	PC12	356
N660P	350	FL-454
N660PB	200	BB-1364

N660PC	90	LJ-174
N660RB	690A	11305
N660WA	PC12	660
N660WB	PC12	760
N660WM	200	BB-1944
(N661AE)	31T	8020029
N661BA	200C	BL-61
N661DP	MU-2	798SA
N661DT	PC12	169
N661DW	TBM7	61
N661J	BN2	915
N661JB	90	LJ-54
N661TC	31T	8120022
N661WP	PC12	578
N662BA	200C	BL-62
N662DM	690	11015
N662J	BN2	919
N662JS	E90	LW-176
N662L	200	BB-527
N662MP	PA42	8001001
N663AC	300	FA-54
N663CS	200	BB-1444
N663J	BN2	2110
N663LS	E90	LW-134
N663P	200	BB-1329
N663SA	BN2	4
N663SP	200	BB-1126
N663VL	BN2	2110
N664AE	46D	207
N664MC	MIIB	T26-114
N664MC	MIII	T-214
N664RB	31T	7904039
N665CF	90	LJ-1424
N665D	100	B-215
N665J	BN2	2129
N665JK	90	LJ-665
N665KC	46T	97265
N665MC	PC12	665
N665MW	200	BB-1737
N665TM	441	0215
(N666A)	690B	11564
N666AC	B100	BE-127
(N666AM)	441	0189
N666AM	MU-2	437SA
N666AS	46D	207
N666CP	MIII	T-301
N666D	MU-2	656
N666DA	100	B-26
N666DC	100	B-26
N666DC	E90	LW-44
N666EC	200	BB-955
N666ES	G1	28
N666EW	200	BB-929
N666FG	90	LJ-121
N666GT	PC12	573
N666GW	90	LJ-1082
N666HB	90	LJ-571
N666HB	MU-2	281
N666HC	425	0021
N666HC	441	0292
(N666JJ)	200	BB-1043
N666JK	31T	8120044
N666JL	31T	7920084
N666JM	90	LJ-673
N666K	690A	11105
N666K	690A	11316
N666LB	MIII	T-258
N666LW	690A	11330
N666M	PC12	839
N666MA	MU-2	231
N666MA	MU-2	400SA
N666MN	680T	1568-24
N666PC	200	BB-923
N666PC	681	6014
N666PC	90	LJ-738
N666PC	90	LJ-785
N666PC	90	LJ-1068
N666PD	90	LJ-785
N666RH	100	B-225
N666RH	200	BB-799
N666RH	300	FA-119
N666RH	350	FL-21
N666RK	MU-2	110
N666RL	200	BB-799
N666RL	MU-2	272
N666SE	MIIB	T26-154E
N666SF	PC12	354
N666SP	MU-2	286
N666SP	MU-2	397SA
N666TB	200C	BL-39
N666YC	200G	BY-48
N666ZT	E90	LW-315
N667AM	MU-2	1534SA
N667AT	200	BB-596
N667CC	200	BB-1827
N667HE	F90	LA-29
N667J	BN2	2154
N667JB	31T	7520035
N667JJ	PC12	108
N667NA	200	BB-667
N667PE	PC12	667
N667RB	PC12	484
N668DH	31T	7520001
N668J	BN2	2155
N668JG	31T	8004032
N668K	350	FL-329
N668KC	46T	97268
N668RJ	31T	7520001
N668WJ	90	LJ-668
N669AF	PC12	669
N669CA	PA42	8001041
N669HS	MIIB	T26-161
N669SP	MIIB	T26-101
N669WB	31T	8004018
N669WR	EPIC	029
N670AT	90	LJ-481
N670CA	MU-2	436SA
N670CP	200	BB-1178
N670DF	200	BB-1631
N670J	BN2	2165
N670L	MU-2	670
N670TA	200	BB-1631
"N670W"	441	0189
N670WH	PC12	670
N671J	BN2	2163
N671JA	BN2	10
N671L	100	B-174
N671L	90	LJ-148
N671LL	90	LJ-148
N671MA	MU-2	519
N671NC	G1	97
N671PC	PC12	671
N672C	46T	97133
N672JA	BN2	11
N672JA	BN2	2170
(N672KA)	90	LJ-672
N672LS	90	LJ-369
N672MM	350	FL-540
N672PB	PC12	672
N672PP	PC12	672
N672SD	PC12	666
(N673BB)	31T	7904031
N673PC	PC12	673
N673YV	200	BB-673
N674C	G1	93
N674KC	PC12	674
N674NM	690A	11226
N675BC	350	FL-178
N675CA	46T	97372
N675J	E90	LW-336
N675MA	46T	97367
N675P	300	FA-217
N675PC	200	BB-680
N675PC	350	FL-178
N675PC	350	FL-352
N675PG	200	BB-680
N675SF	200	BB-735
N675SP	90	LJ-312
N676BB	200	BB-1501
N676BP	200	BB-1501
N676DM	681B	6048
N676DP	200	BB-676
N676J	E90	LW-179
N676MA	TBM8	525
N676MB	680T	1597-42
N676PC	PC12	676
N676SA	BN2	31
N677BC	200	BB-86
N677J	E90	LW-294
N677JE	200	BB-1702
N677JM	690A	11102
N677KA	680T	1677-60
N677P	P180	1019
N677PV	680T	1616-49
(N677PV)	680T	1713-87
(N677PV)	680W	1721-1
N677SW	200	BB-881
N677W	90	LJ-110
N677WA	690A	11243
N677WP	90	LJ-110
N678BK	MU-2	678
N678CC	BN2	858
N678DW	F90	LA-195
(N678DW)	F90	LA-199
N678EB	200	BB-1124
N678FA	200	BB-1678
N678GP	90	LJ-607
N678KM	MU-2	1518SA
N678RH	MU-2	761SA
N678RM	100	B-46
N678RM	200	BB-1382
N678RW	G1	86
N678SB	300	FA-77
N678SB	90	LJ-955
N678SS	200	BB-1021
N678TA	BN2	77
(N678WA)	690A	11273
N679BK	MU-2	679
N679FS	90	LJ-996
N679JB	PC12	410
N679MM	31T	7820038
N679PE	PC12	679
N680AD	690	11073
N680CA	200	BB-1681
N680CA	31T	7904028
N680CA	MU-2	642
N680CB	200	BB-1006
N680CB	350	FL-499
N680FS	680T	1687-67
N680JD	680W	1792-22
N680JP	P180	1034
N680KM	680W	1812-29
N680MH	680T	1620-51
N680PD	680T	1620-51
N680PE	PC12	680
N680RH	690A	11234
(N680SJ)	680W	1774-12
N680TC	P68	340
N680W	680W	1776-14
N680WA	690C	11680
N680X	680W	1778-16
N681AC	680T	1572-27
N681AS	681	6027
N681DC	681	6036
N681EV	90	LJ-1228
N681FV	681B	6051
N681GH	PC12	681
N681HV	681B	6049
N681KW	P68	273
(N681NR)	681B	6059
N681PC	200	BB-1330
N681PC	B100	BE-7
N681SM	681	6014
N681SP	681	6027
N681SW	31T	8104027
(N681VK)	BN2	12
N682C	46T	97130
N682DR	200	BB-130
N682KA	90	LJ-682
N682KW	P68	294
(N682SW)	PA42	8001089
N682TA	90	LJ-1102
N683GW	90	LJ-1683
N684AS	BN2	897
N684FM	G1	149
N684FW	P68	413
N684KM	46T	97353
N685BC	350	FL-355
N685R	200	BB-1565
N686AC	B100	BE-127
N686CF	200	BB-1085
N686GW	90	LJ-1082
N686HC	425	0021
N686LD	F90	LA-165
N686N	680T	1473-1
N686PC	PC12	686
N687AE	441	0087
N687AF	PC12	687
N687CA	46T	97346
N687HB	MU-2	687
N687L	680T	1560-17
N687RW	G1	123
N688CA	31T	7820046
N688CC	100	B-31
N688CP	31T	7904028
N688CQ	100	B-31
N688CW	100	B-31
N688DC	680T	1612-47
N688DS	B100	BE-8
N688JB	350	FL-18
N688LL	200	BB-1617
N688LL	90	LJ-1451
N688MA	MU-2	688
N688NA	680T	1593-41
N688P	90	LJ-1611
N688RA	MU-2	688
N688RL	300	FA-119
N688SH	680T	1597-42
N688TM	680T	1687-67
N689AC	31T	7820049
N689AE	441	0281
N689BV	200	BB-338
(N689CA)	31T	8166064
N689CA	PA42	5527029
N689EB	90	LJ-689
N689PE	PC12	689
N690AC	690A	11103
N690AC	690B	11527
N690AE	690A	11125
N690AG	690B	11551
N690AH	690A	11119
N690AJ	690A	11319
N690AR	690A	11155
(N690AR)	690A	11252
N690AS	690A	11277
N690AT	690A	11202
N690AX	690B	11384
N690AZ	690A	11104
N690AZ	690A	11168
N690BA	690B	11513
N690BA	690C	11709
N690BB	690B	11487
N690BD	690B	11541
N690BE	690B	11544
N690BG	690B	11381
(N690BG)	690B	11403
N690BH	690B	11361
N690BK	690B	11508
N690BM	690A	11311
N690BT	690A	11212
N690BW	690	11018
(N690BW)	690B	11433
(N690CA)	31T	7920054
N690CA	690B	11475
N690CA	690C	11697
N690CB	690A	11104
N690CB	690B	11387
N690CB	690B	11477
N690CC	690B	11379
N690CE	690A	11103
N690CF	690A	11168
N690CH	690B	11542
N690CL	690A	11153
N690CM	690	11040
N690CP	690B	11425
N690CP	690B	11451
(N690CR)	690C	11600
N690DA	690A	11104
N690DB	690A	11226
N690DC	690	11040
N690DD	690A	11159
N690DD	690A	11195
N690DE	690A	11316
N690DM	690A	11269
(N690DM)	690B	11426
N690DM	690B	11528

N690DS	690A	11262	N690PT	690A	11252	N695CT	695A	96096	(N700BN)	90	LJ-734
N690DS	690B	11525	N690RA	690	11010	N695DA	695A	96077	N700BN	TBM7	203
N690DT	690B	11413	(N690RB)	690B	11560	N695EC	695	95069	N700BQ	TBM7	298
(N690DT)	690B	11542	N690RC	690A	11251	N695EE	695B	96205	N700BS	31T	8004020
(N690DW)	690A	11134	N690RC	690A	11271	N695FA	695A	96077	N700BS	TBM7	11
(N690E)	PA42	5501020	N690RC	690A	11310	N695GG	695A	96036	N700BU	TBM7	263
N690E	PA42	5501020	(N690RC)	690B	11491	N695GH	695A	96078	N700BX	200	BB-537
N690EA	690B	11550	N690RD	690B	11350	N695GJ	695A	96011	N700BY	TBM7	223
N690EC	690A	11138	N690RE	690A	11271	N695HT	695A	96038	N700CA	31T	8166038
(N690EC)	690A	11242	N690RK	690A	11138	N695JC	695A	96009	N700CB	690	11001
(N690EE)	690B	11429	N690RP	690B	11493	N695JJ	90	LJ-695	N700CB	TBM7	176
N690EH	690A	11309	N690RT	690B	11357	N695KG	695B	96207	N700CC	31T	8020052
N690EL	690B	11503	(N690RW)	690A	11164	N695LD	690D	15007	N700CC	PA42	5501029
N690EM	690A	11125	(N690SA)	690B	11408	N695MG	695B	96204	N700CC	TBM7	113
N690EM	690A	11171	N690SB	690B	11477	N695MM	695A	96050	N700CD	690A	11312
N690ES	690B	11388	N690SC	200	BB-1139	N695NC	695A	96032	N700CF	TBM7	123
N690EX	690B	11517	N690SC	690B	11476	N695P	695B	96202	N700CJ	PA42	8001005
N690FD	690B	11393	(N690SC)	690B	11484	N695PA	695A	96007	N700CL	TBM7	266
N690FP	690A	11102	N690SC	690B	11546	N695PC	PC12	305	N700CM	31T	7820007
N690FR	690B	11436	N690SD	690A	11287	(N695PR)	695A	96071	(N700CM)	31T	7820008
N690G	200C	BL-2	N690SE	690B	11529	N695QE	PC12	834	N700CP	200	BB-16
N690G	E90	LW-34	N690SG	690A	11146	N695RC	695A	96087	N700CP	200	BB-216
N690GA	441	0136	N690SH	690B	11528	N695V	90	LJ-110	N700CP	200	BB-326
N690GF	690B	11357	N690SM	690A	11337	N695WF	PC12	125	N700CP	90	LJ-700
N690GG	690B	11411	N690SP	690	11006	N695WR	695	95015	(N700CR)	200	BB-744
N690GH	690B	11357	N690SS	690B	11550	N695YP	695A	96070	N700CS	90	LJ-445
N690GK	690	11031	N690TB	690A	11109	N696AB	100	B-101	N700CS	TBM7	109
N690GM	690B	11444	(N690TB)	690A	11220	N696AM	441	0189	N700CT	TBM7	16
N690GS	690B	11363	N690TC	690B	11385	N696CP	MIII	TT-465	N700CT	TBM7	236
N690GT	90	LJ-1727	N690TD	690A	11307	N696JB	100	B-13	N700CV	TBM7	221
N690GZ	690A	11319	N690TG	690B	11444	N696JB	100	B-26	N700CZ	TBM7	301
N690HB	690A	11205	N690TH	690B	11487	N696MM	90	LJ-457	N700DA	MU-2	140
N690HC	690B	11352	N690TL	690B	11509	N696RA	F90	LA-87	N700DB	G1	172
N690HC	690C	11625	(N690TL)	690B	11510	N696RH	100	B-225	N700DC	E90	LW-209
N690HF	690A	11298	(N690TL)	690B	11545	(N696SA)	680T	1536-4	N700DC	E90	LW-225
N690HM	690A	11159	N690TP	690A	11218	(N696SS)	PC12	150	N700DD	E90	LW-288
N690HS	690B	11431	N690TP	690D	15001	N696SS	PC12	169	N700DE	200	BB-940
N690HT	690B	11467	N690TR	690	11034	N696TS	PC12	169	N700DE	TBM7	4
N690HV	690A	11228	N690TW	PA42	5501026	N696WA	BN2	819	N700DH	E90	LW-114
N690JB	690A	11185	N690VM	690A	11218	N696WW	90	LJ-1371	N700DH	E90	LW-165
N690JB	690B	11363	N690WC	690	11017	N697A	G1	158	N700DM	MU-2	127
N690JC	690	11058	N690WC	690A	11150	N697D	200	BB-81	N700DM	TBM7	305
N690JC	690B	11479	N690WD	690A	11176	N697JM	690A	11102	N700DN	TBM7	163
N690JH	690B	11529	N690WM	690B	11399	N697MB	90	LJ-554	N700DN	TBM7	305
N690JJ	690A	11171	N690WP	690B	11561	N697MP	90	LJ-554	N700DQ	TBM7	271
N690JK	690B	11480	N690WS	690A	11194	N697P	200	BB-1217	N700DT	TBM7	134
N690JL	690B	11455	N690X	MIIB	T26-141	N697ST	46T	97365	N700DY	TBM7	165
N690JM	690	11072	N690XT	690B	11467	N698CE	690A	11234	(N700DY)	TBM7	244
N690JP	690B	11382	N690XY	690B	11433	N698GN	680T	1589-40	N700DZ	TBM7	295
N690JP	90	LJ-690	N691AC	441	0250	N698P	200	BB-1621	(N700E)	200	BB-382
N690JT	690A	11271	N691AC	690A	11254	N698X	MIIB	T26-137	N700EF	TBM7	21
N690JT	690B	11353	N691AS	90	LJ-1240	N699AF	PC12	699	(N700EF)	TBM7	238
N690KC	690A	11161	N691CL	690	11058	N699AM	MIIB	T26-101	N700EG	TBM7	284
N690KC	690B	11384	N691CP	690B	11457	N699CC	200	BB-751	N700EJ	TBM7	291
(N690KG)	690B	11513	N691PA	690B	11526	N699CP	690B	11472	N700EK	TBM7	304
*N690KM	690A	11210	N691PC	PC12	691	N699F	MIIB	T26-140	N700EL	TBM7	209
N690L	200	BB-1573	N691SM	690B	11492	N699GN	680T	1589-40	(N700EM)	31T	7620054
N690L	PA42	5501020	N691TP	690B	11522	N699GN	690B	11393	(N700EN)	TBM7	195
N690LB	690B	11552	N691WM	690B	11522	N699GN	695A	96098	N700EN	TBM7	329
N690LH	690B	11487	(N692AC)	90	LJ-1076	N699KM	MIII	T-256	N700ER	TBM7	198
N690LJ	200	BB-1690	N692BC	PC12	692	N699MW	300	FA-73	(N700EV)	TBM7	148
N690LJ	690A	11302	N692M	E90	LW-228	N699RK	MIII	T-300	(N700EV)	TBM7	265
N690LL	690B	11384	(N692T)	690B	11551	N699SA	PC6	669	N700EV	TBM7	287
N690LL	690B	11544	N692T	690B	11555	N699SB	690A	11280	N700EZ	200	BB-613
N690LN	690B	11415	N692W	90	LJ-1692	N700AB	441	0020	N700EZ	TBM7	307
N690LP	690A	11165	N693AT	PC12	693	(N700AB)	E90	LW-49	N700FC	90	LJ-700
N690LS	690B	11475	N693FB	MU-2	693SA	N700AC	E90	LW-225	N700FK	BN2T	2201
N690LW	200	BB-948	N693MA	TBM7	293	N700AD	TBM7	250	N700FN	MU-2	127
(N690MC)	690A	11124	N693PA	MU-2	693SA	N700AJ	TBM7	185	N700FT	200	BB-1512
N690MF	690A	11103	N693PD	PC12	857	N700AN	TBM7	132	N700FT	TBM7	267
N690MG	690B	11423	N693PG	MIII	T-207	N700AP	TBM7	130	N700GB	200	BB-578
N690MH	690B	11357	"N693SA"	MU-2	693SA	N700AP	TBM7	190	N700GB	TBM7	27
N690ML	690A	11252	N693VM	690A	11234	N700AQ	TBM7	252	N700GC	31T	8020052
N690MS	690B	11510	N694AB	200	BB-78	N700AR	TBM7	23	N700GC	90	LJ-796
N690MT	690B	11529	N694CM	46D	126	N700AT	100	B-136	N700GC	B100	BE-70
N690NA	690B	11359	N694CT	90	LJ-1694	N700AU	TBM7	185	N700GE	TBM7	255
N690NH	690	11039	N694FC	200	BB-78	N700AZ	TBM7	254	N700GJ	TBM7	102
(N690PB)	690A	11316	N694HP	200	BB-720	N700BA	B100	BE-84	N700GJ	TBM7	241
N690PC	690A	11341	N694JB	300	FA-89	N700BD	TBM7	320	N700GK	TBM7	320
N690PC	690B	11356	N694KM	200	BB-1922	N700BE	200	BB-528	N700GM	90	LJ-1283
(N690PG)	690	11018	N695AB	695A	96055	N700BF	TBM7	53	N700GN	TBM7	246
N690PG	690B	11467	N695AM	695A	96007	N700BH	TBM7	253	N700GP	441	0100
N690PJ	690	11058	N695BA	695A	96012	N700BK	F90	LA-107	N700GQ	TBM7	289
N690PR	690B	11487	N695BE	695B	96208	N700BK	TBM7	262	N700GT	TBM7	276

N700GV	TBM7	290
N700GY	TBM7	302
N700HD	TBM7	313
N700HK	TBM7	60
N700HL	TBM7	281
N700HM	200	BB-448
N700HM	TBM7	297
N700HN	TBM7	204
(N700HS)	TBM7	270
N700HY	TBM7	278
N700JD	TBM7	264
N700JE	441	0237
N700JG	441	0237
N700JJ	TBM7	2
N700JJ	TBM7	242
N700JP	90	LJ-760
N700JR	31T	7820030
(N700JR)	31T	7920084
N700JR	MIII	T-315
N700JR	MIII	TT-424
N700JV	TBM7	245
N700JW	G1	53
N700K	100	B-220
N700KB	200	BB-1924
(N700KB)	90	LJ-1602
N700KB	90	LJ-1615
(N700KD)	TBM7	305
N700KD	TBM7	322
N700KH	TBM7	210
N700KK	TBM7	243
N700KL	TBM7	88
N700KM	TBM7	158
(N700KN)	TBM7	102
N700KP	TBM7	228
N700KV	TBM7	296
N700KW	200	BB-115
N700L	695A	96034
N700LF	TBM7	270
*N700LG	200	BB-865
N700LL	TBM7	86
N700LT	31T	7920046
(N700LT)	PA42	5501020
N700LW	MU-2	326
N700MA	E90	LW-278
N700MA	MU-2	143
N700MA	MU-2	796SA
N700MB	90	LJ-233
N700MK	TBM7	251
N700MM	695	95029
N700MM	EPIC	010
N700MP	690A	11198
N700MV	TBM7	13
N700MX	TBM7	14
N700MZ	TBM7	264
N700NA	200	BB-1491
N700NC	100	B-138
N700ND	TBM7	217
(N700NE)	TBM7	218
N700NE	TBM7	218
N700NS	E90	LW-49
N700PC	690B	11389
N700PC	690B	11537
N700PC	690D	15027
N700PC	695	95023
N700PE	350	FL-233
N700PG	350	FL-233
N700PK	TBM7	52
N700PL	PC12	657
N700PP	TBM7	59
N700PQ	690B	11389
N700PQ	690B	11537
N700PR	G1	5
N700PT	31T	7820032
N700PT	TBM7	268
N700PU	TBM7	15
N700PV	TBM7	215
N700PW	TBM7	29
N700PW	TBM7	211
N700PX	TBM7	249
(N700QB)	TBM7	335
N700QD	TBM7	174
N700QQ	TBM7	277
N700QT	TBM7	324
N700QT	TBM7	337

N700R	690B	11434
N700RD	31T	5575001
N700RE	TBM7	52
N700RF	200	BB-720
N700RF	90	LJ-1262
(N700RF)	TBM7	20
N700RG	31T	7820042
N700RK	TBM7	253
N700RL	F90	LA-150
N700RP	441	0100
N700RX	MU-2	241
N700S	90	LJ-131
N700S	TBM7	193
N700SB	90	LJ-1433
N700SB	B100	BE-42
N700SC	MIIA	T26-004
N700SF	F90	LA-57
N700SF	TBM7	26
N700SL	TBM7	257
N700SN	TBM7	277
N700SP	100	B-92
N700SP	TBM7	98
N700SR	690A	11164
N700SS	690B	11415
N700SX	TBM7	325
N700SY	TBM7	283
N700TB	100	B-154
N700TB	TBM7	123
N700TB	TBM7	148
N700TB	TBM7	256
N700TF	31T	7920046
N700TF	B100	BE-18
N700TG	C-12	BC-75
N700TJ	B100	BE-105
N700TJ	TBM7	25
N700TJ	TBM7	27
N700TK	TBM7	311
N700TL	TBM7	227
N700TR	31T	7820030
N700U	200	BB-888
N700U	350	FL-363
N700U	90	LJ-369
N700US	90	LJ-190
N700VA	TBM7	233
N700VB	TBM7	237
N700VD	TBM7	190
N700VF	PA42	8001053
N700VJ	TBM7	163
N700VM	TBM7	72
N700VP	TBM7	180
N700VV	TBM7	164
N700VX	TBM7	118
N700WA	MU-2	400SA
N700WB	TBM7	324
N700WD	E90	LW-218
N700WD	TBM7	27
N700WE	200	BB-206
N700WE	TBM7	214
N700WF	200	BB-206
N700WH	TBM7	245
N700WJ	425	0036
N700WK	TBM7	175
N700WP	200	BB-1313
N700WS	TBM7	172
N700WT	PA42	8001005
N700WT	TBM7	91
N700XL	31T	8166050
(N700XL)	TBM7	6
N700XL	TBM7	23
N700XL	TBM7	224
N700XS	TBM7	260
N700YB	TBM7	50
N700YN	TBM7	222
N700Z	200	BB-443
N700Z	200	BB-1920
N700Z	90	LJ-521
N700ZA	TBM7	317
(N700ZB)	TBM7	321
N700ZB	TBM7	326
N700ZC	TBM7	328
N700ZE	TBM7	335
N700ZF	TBM7	336
(N700ZL)	200	BB-443
N700ZL	TBM7	6

N700ZM	TBM7	315
N700ZP	TBM7	322
N700ZR	TBM7	87
N700ZZ	TBM7	116
N701	P68	314
N701	P68	390
N701AR	TBM7	209
N701AT	90	LJ-390
N701AV	TBM7	179
N701BN	G1	74
N701CB	690	11040
N701CN	TBM7	260
N701CR	425	0148
(N701DH)	31T	8004008
N701DM	MU-2	149
N701ES	TBM7	46
N701FC	350	FL-291
N701G	G1	1
(N701GP)	31T	8004027
N701GT	P180	1054
N701JF	TBM7	331
N701JP	300	FA-211
(N701JW)	G1	53
N701K	MU-2	410SA
N701LT	TBM7	107
N701MA	TBM7	331
N701MK	TBM7	124
N701MR	TBM7	4
N701NA	200	BB-1164
N701NC	200	BB-324
N701NC	F90	LA-55
N701PE	PC12	701
N701PF	TBM7	31
N701PP	TBM7	124
N701PT	31T	8004008
N701QD	TBM7	126
N701QR	425	0148
N701RG	31T	7720009
N701RJ	100	B-23
(N701RM)	31T	7920081
N701RQ	31T	7720009
N701X	E90	LW-165
N701XP	90	LJ-826
N702AA	TBM7	216
(N702AJ)	200	BB-1654
N702AR	TBM7	275
N702AS	200	BB-571
N702AV	TBM7	182
N702BM	TBM7	2
N702DK	90	LJ-1259
N702DM	MU-2	249
N702EA	G1	194
N702FN	MU-2	249
N702G	G1	2
N702G	G1	105
N702GS	TBM7	177
N702H	MU-2	727SA
N702H	TBM7	112
N702JL	100	B-59
N702JL	B100	BE-110
N702JP	TBM7	85
N702K	90	LJ-5
N702MA	200	BB-1010
N702MB	TBM7	314
N702QD	TBM7	165
N702R	B100	BE-110
(N702RM)	TBM7	241
N702RW	TBM7	256
(N702SB)	TBM7	278
N702TA	200	BB-1573
N702TD	B100	BE-110
N702US	E90	LW-318
N702XP	E90	LW-266
N702Z	200	BB-51
N702Z	B100	BE-51
(N702ZA)	200	BB-51
N703AV	TBM7	214
N703CA	TBM7	273
N703CJ	31T	8020060
N703DM	MU-2	138
N703G	G1	3
N703HT	200	BB-228
N703HT	200	BB-307
N703JK	200	BB-703

N703JR	C-12	BC-22
N703JT	F90	LA-39
N703K	90	LJ-188
N703KH	200	BB-703
N703LW	E90	LW-317
N703MA	690B	11433
N703MD	200	BB-982
N703QD	TBM7	129
N703R	200	BB-1699
N703RM	200	BB-1699
N703RM	200G	BY-74
N703S	200	BB-982
N703TA	200	BB-1574
N703TL	PC12	703
N703US	441	0013
N703WC	90	LJ-188
N703X	200	BB-737
N704C	46T	97262
N704G	G1	4
N704HC	G1	4
N704K	90	LJ-110
N704QD	TBM7	188
N704S	100	B-45
N705AV	TBM7	190
(N705CC)	PC12	605
N705G	G1	5
N705G	G1	152
N705KC	PC12	635
N705M	G1	114
N705MA	46T	97277
N705MS	PC12	1134
N705PA	P180	1014
N705QD	TBM7	231
N705RS	G1	114
N705S	100	B-8
N705SA	BN2	2211
N705SA	PC6	705
N705TA	200	BB-1575
"N705TL"	200	BB-310
N706AG	PC12	706
N706AV	TBM7	191
N706CA	TBM7	285
(N706CC)	46D	128
N706DG	200	BB-548
N706DG	90	LJ-508
N706DM	MU-2	038
N706G	G1	77
N706G	G1	85
N706G	G1	106
N706G	G1	116
N706G	G1	150
N706K	90	LJ-175
N706KC	690A	11343
N706MC	BN2	883
N706MS	PC12	1143
N706TA	200	BB-1598
N706TA	200	BB-1656
N706US	690A	11343
N706Z	46D	171
N707AF	MU-2	707SA
N707AV	TBM7	197
N707BC	200	BB-746
N707BC	E90	LW-238
N707BP	690A	11326
N707CB	425	0023
N707CB	90	LJ-760
N707CE	90	LJ-314
N707CG	200	BB-996
N707CJ	31T	8020061
N707CM	31T	8004011
N707CV	31T	8104013
N707CV	90	LJ-844
N707DB	MIII	T-271
N707DC	E90	LW-238
N707DM	MU-2	280
N707DR	F90	LA-149
N707EB	90	LJ-232
N707EB	MU-2	015
N707EB	MU-2	032
N707EZ	MU-2	739SA
N707FA	350	FL-337
N707FF	90	LJ-1381
N707FN	MU-2	280
(N707HB)	200	BB-746

N707HM	200	BB-1939
N707JC	31T	8020061
(N707JT)	31T	8104013
N707KH	PC12	688
N707MA	200	BB-776
N707MA	441	0285
N707ML	31T	7520017
N707MP	690A	11198
N707MP	G1	122
N707NV	200	BB-942
N707NY	425	0161
N707PC	90	LJ-1703
N707PK	MIII	T-271
N707PR	90	LJ-205
N707RW	90	LJ-573
N707SC	695	95050
N707SC	MIIB	T26-101
N707SS	100	B-81
N707TD	31T	8104004
N707TL	E90	LW-173
N707TS	695A	96038
N707TT	MU-2	600
N707WA	G1	16
N707WD	31T	8120103
N708	KODK	0007
N708	P68	314
N708AF	PC12	708
(N708AV)	TBM7	210
N708DC	350	FL-371
N708DG	90	LJ-508
N708DM	MU-2	271
N708DP	46D	176
N708EF	TBM7	21
N708G	G1	8
N708K	90	LJ-235
N708L	P68	314
N708PW	TBM7	29
N708SA	BN2	2211
N708US	31T	7720060
N708WH	200G	BY-7
N709AV	TBM7	202
N709DB	E90	LW-253
N709DM	MU-2	308
(N709DM)	TBM7	140
(N709DM)	TBM7	143
N709EA	90	LJ-1309
N709FN	MU-2	308
N709G	G1	9
N709K	90	LJ-97
N709MC	TBM7	168
N709RB	PC12	709
N709US	MU-2	672
N709WY	PC12	709
N709X	200	BB-1617
N710	KODK	0021
N710AS	100	B-127
N710BV	441	0314
N710CA	MU-2	669
N710EC	PA42	8001014
N710EQ	PA42	8001014
N710G	G1	10
N710G	G1	92
N710G	G1	117
N710G	MU-2	710SA
N710HS	350	FL-181
N710JB	200	BB-1784
N710JK	680T	1680-62
N710K	90	LJ-104
N710KC	B100	BE-69
N710M	TBM7	326
(N710MA)	31T	7720025
N710NC	200	BB-322
N710TK	90	LJ-22
N710TK	E90	LW-2
N711	100	B-23
N711	MU-2	523
N711A	200	BB-696
N711AE	100	B-206
N711AE	200	BB-810
N711AH	MIIA	T26-014
N711AH	MU-2	523
N711AR	200	BB-123
N711AU	100	B-23
N711AV	100	B-35
N711AW	200	BB-755
N711AW	200	BB-1708
N711BL	200	BB-1013
N711BL	90	LJ-588
N711BL	E90	LW-257
N711BN	90	LJ-588
N711BP	E90	LW-146
N711BT	G1	87
N711BU	200	BB-877
N711BU	90	LJ-55
N711BX	E90	LW-257
N711CA	PA42	8001079
N711CC	90	LJ-773
N711CF	90	LJ-179
N711CQ	90	LJ-773
N711CR	200	BB-16
N711D	31T	7904028
(N711DB)	441	0017
N711DG	31T	7904028
N711DG	PA42	8001023
N711DH	31T	8020061
N711DW	690D	15001
N711EC	200	BB-808
(N711EF)	425	0027
N711EK	E90	LW-10
N711ER	31T	8104056
N711EX	200	BB-940
N711FC	90	LJ-516
N711FD	200	BB-221
N711FN	31T	7820001
N711FN	31T	8166043
N711FR	MIIB	T26-158E
N711FR	MU-2	183
N711G	G1	11
N711GD	90	LJ-330
N711GE	441	0209
N711GF	441	0251
N711GH	TBM7	14
N711GM	100	B-31
N711GT	695A	96058
N711HA	200	BB-1417
N711HA	E90	LW-168
N711HC	31T	7520023
N711HC	46T	97004
N711HF	31T	8166020
(N711HG)	31T	7520023
N711HK	MU-2	724SA
(N711HQ)	46T	97004
N711HS	90	LJ-440
N711HV	E90	LW-246
N711KA	90	LJ-42
N711KB	200	BB-593
N711KP	90	LJ-692
N711KW	F90	LA-99
N711L	F90	LA-222
N711LD	31T	8104040
N711LL	MU-2	180
N711LV	31T	7920042
N711LV	690A	11110
N711MB	200	BB-437
N711MB	441	0116
N711MC	100	B-63
N711MD	200	BB-437
N711MD	90	LJ-565
N711MF	441	0085
N711MP	90	LJ-565
(N711MV)	681	6003
N711MZ	200	BB-849
N711MZ	MU-2	350SA
N711MZ	MU-2	781SA
N711NV	E90	LW-246
N711PB	690B	11356
N711PB	MU-2	249
N711PD	MU-2	249
N711PD	MU-2	736SA
N711PH	200	BB-1190
N711PJ	B100	BE-34
N711PM	TBM7	234
N711PN	PC12	711
(N711QC)	31T	8104061
N711QP	690C	11632
N711RD	31T	7920068
N711RD	MIII	T-251
N711RE	100	B-233
N711RJ	350	FL-116
N711RP	E90	LW-127
N711RQ	E90	LW-127
N711SA	MIIB	T26-107
N711SB	46T	97075
N711SD	F90	LA-65
N711SE	MIIB	T26-129
N711SH	MU-2	178
N711SL	MIIB	T26-129
N711TB	31T	7820031
(N711TD)	31T	7820031
N711TF	MU-2	405SA
N711TN	200	BB-628
N711TT	681	6027
N711TT	690	11007
N711TT	690B	11362
N711TZ	E90	LW-226
N711UE	200	BB-221
N711UG	100	B-138
N711UP	31T	8104101
N711VC	90	LJ-729
N711VH	200	BB-544
N711VK	MU-2	157
N711VM	200	BB-544
N711VN	31T	8004027
N711VN	350	FL-7
N711VP	90	LJ-257
N711VV	200	BB-1365
N711VW	31T	8004027
N711WE	200	BB-891
N711WE	31T	8020064
(N711WT)	90	LJ-808
N711WV	200	BB-688
N711WV	31T	8020064
N711WW	90	LJ-830
(N711YK)	441	0145
N712AS	100	B-198
N712BC	PC12	448
(N712CA)	PA42	8001083
N712CA	PA42	8001104
N712CE	690A	11105
N712CJ	31T	8020065
N712D	90	LJ-854
N712DB	90	LJ-311
N712G	G1	12
N712G	G1	114
N712G	G1	192
N712GA	C-12	BC-63
N712GJ	200	BB-840
N712GK	200	BB-1035
N712J	90	LJ-455
N712JC	90	LJ-1259
N712JC	BN2	209
N712K	90	LJ-104
N712K	90	LJ-455
N712K	90	LJ-694
N712KA	90	LJ-455
N712MA	B100	BE-32
N712MK	46D	1
N712MP	G1	86
N712MR	G1	86
N712MW	G1	86
(N712PW)	200	BB-1158
(N712R)	P68	62
N712RH	200	BB-1839
N713BH	31T	8104058
(N713D)	200	BB-596
N713D	90	LJ-1002
N713DB	F90	LA-225
N713DH	200	BB-1287
N713DH	F90	LA-225
N713EA	90	LJ-1713
N713FP	200	BB-1595
N713G	G1	193
N713GB	MU-2	538
N713GH	200	BB-557
(N713JF)	90	LJ-426
N713K	90	LJ-364
(N713PA)	90	LJ-774
N713RH	200	BB-1274
N713SP	680W	1805-27
N713TA	200	BB-1610
(N713US)	90	LJ-1703
N713US	90	LJ-1727
N713US	G1	24
N713X	200	BB-264
N713X	E90	LW-74
N714D	F90	LA-62
N714F	E90	LW-237
N714G	G1	14
N714G	P68	290
N714K	90	LJ-129
N714KL	90	LJ-129
N714MR	G1	123
N714MW	G1	123
N715AT	90	LJ-913
N715CA	31T	8120063
(N715CA)	31T	8166056
N715CG	200	BB-1421
N715CG	350	FL-211
N715CQ	200	BB-1421
N715DM	90	LJ-546
N715G	G1	15
N715G	G1	100
N715G	G1	118
(N715GW)	31T	1104017
N715GW	F90	LA-118
N715HL	PC12	292
N715JH	200	BB-1345
N715JT	F90	LA-210
N715K	90	LJ-418
N715LM	46D	31
N715MA	200	BB-322
N715MA	46T	97113B
N715MA	46T	97115A
N715MA	46T	97115B
N715MA	46T	97122A
N715MC	TBM7	30
N715RA	G1	31
N715RD	200	BB-707
N715TL	PC12	548
N715US	MU-2	718SA
N715V	TBM7	108
N715WA	100	B-168
(N715WA)	31T	7820075
N716AV	200	BB-1876
(N716CA)	31T	8166060
N716CC	441	0213
N716CC	695	95075
N716FP	200	BB-1595
N716G	G1	16
N716G	G1	101
N716GA	C-12	BC-24
(N716GS)	200	BB-1786
N716GS	200	BB-1921
N716GS	200	BB-1965
N716K	90	LJ-323
N716MA	TBM7	310
N716R	G1	37
N716RA	G1	43
N716RD	G1	37
N716SM	441	0004
N716TA	200	BB-1509
N716WA	31T	8020042
N717	G1	4
N717A	90	LJ-1279
N717AP	690A	11226
N717BD	MIIB	T26-178
(N717CB)	31T	7620053
N717CC	MIIB	T26-178
N717CC	MIVA	AT-034
N717CD	200	BB-968
N717CT	350	FL-56
N717D	B100	BE-91
N717DC	200	BB-1261
N717DC	E90	LW-308
N717DW	90	LJ-1129
N717EP	F90	LA-7
N717ES	PA42	8001004
N717FM	200	BB-1611
N717G	G1	17
N717G	G1	102
N717HT	200	BB-133
N717JB	MIIB	T26-128
N717JF	G1	44
N717JG	90	LJ-672
N717JP	G1	127
N717K	90	LJ-325

N717LW 200 BB-1642
N717LW 425 0086
N717MA 46T 97310
N717MB PA42 8001023
N717MC BN2T 2112
N717NC PC12 717
N717PD MIIB T26-178
N717PP E90 LW-74
N717PS MU-2 686
N717PT PC12 361
N717RA G1 167
N717RD 90 LJ-1199
N717RD G1 44
N717RM 200 BB-237
N717RM 200 BB-1166
N717RS G1 38
N717RW G1 44
N717SP 200 BB-226
N717SP 31T 8166005
N717TM E90 LW-210
N717US E90 LW-288
N717VE 350 FL-207
N717VL 350 FL-207
N717W F90 LA-20
N717X 90 LJ-581
N717XP 90 LJ-581
N717Y TBM7 17
N718BE 90 LJ-1835
N718EE MU-2 718SA
N718G G1 18
N718G G1 103
N718G G1 120
N718G G1 152
N718G G1 194
N718GL MIIB T26-140
N718JP PC12 155
N718K 90 LJ-371
N718MB 90 LJ-1287
N718RA G1 174
N718RJ 200 BB-1597
N718VA 90 LJ-214
N718VN 90 LJ-214
N719AL 441 0084
N719EA 90 LJ-1319
N719G G1 19
N719G G1 104
N719HC 200 BB-31
N719HC 200 BB-962
N719K 90 LJ-324
N719LR 46D 165
N719PC PC12 719
N719RA G1 28
N719TA 200 BB-1619
N719W 90 LJ-119
N720AF 90 LJ-1718
N720AM 200 BB-1663
N720AM 90 LJ-1490
N720C 100 B-171
N720CT 90 LJ-1085
N720DK 90 LJ-1093
N720E G1 194
N720G G1 20
N720G G1 143
N720HC 90 LJ-438
N720JK MU-2 154
N720JM 441 0170
N720K 90 LJ-37
N720LS PA42 5501010
N720M 200 BB-170
N720MA 200 BB-170
N720MC 200 BB-1207
N720MP 200 BB-1080
N720R 90 LJ-306
N720R MIV AT-013
N720RD 90 LJ-720
N720RL 90 LJ-306
N720US 200 BB-841
(N720US) 690B 11484
N720X 90 LJ-175
N720X G1 73
N721AF PC12 721
N721BB 46D 154
N721BN BN2 435
N721BS 350 FL-110
N721BU 690A 11146
N721CA PA42 8001070
N721DM MU-2 312
N721DR F90 LA-203
N721FC MU-2 111
N721G G1 21
N721HC 200 BB-962
N721K 90 LJ-43
N721ML 690D 15002
N721MR 690D 15002
N721MT 46T 97362
N721NB 350 FL-288
N721PB PC12 195
N721RA G1 65
N721RB 31T 7720007
N721RD 200 BB-677
N721RP 31T 7720007
N721SG PA42 5527027
N721SL PC12 726
N721SR TBM7 181
N721SW 200 BB-519
N721TB 690B 11352
N721TD 441 0214
N721VB 425 0210
N722BJ MU-2 722SA
N722DM MU-2 245
N722DR F90 LA-147
N722EJ 690A 11175
N722ER PA42 5527023
N722ET 46D 168
N722EW 46D 168
N722EW 46D 190
N722G G1 22
N722G G1 107
N722GA 441 0153
N722JM 90 LJ-1652
N722K 90 LJ-146
N722KP 200 BB-1545
N722KR 90 LJ-1065
N722LJ 680T 1538-5
N722M E90 LW-6
N722MU MU-2 722SA
(N722NM) 90 LJ-305
N722PM 90 LJ-1820
N722PT F90 LA-235
N722RA G1 168
N722S 90 LJ-448
N722SG 695A 96087
N722SR TBM7 49
N722TR 200 BB-938
N722TS 90 LJ-334
N722VB 90 LJ-987
(N722WB) 90 LJ-885
N722WJ 200 BB-722
N723AC 690A 11249
N723G G1 23
N723G G1 108
N723JM BN2 343
N723JP 31T 7920009
N723JR 31T 7920009
N723K 46T 97348
N723K 90 LJ-142
N723KR 46T 97033
N723RA G1 14
N723RK 200C BL-50
N723T 90 LJ-234
N723W 100 B-225
N724DM MU-2 300
N724DM TBM7 143
N724DR 90 LJ-1612
N724FN MU-2 300
N724G G1 24
N724G G1 109
N724G G1 162
N724G G1 195
N724HS PC12 564
(N724JP) BN2 129
N724KC 46T 97324
N724KH 90 LJ-1426
N724KW 90 LJ-1426
N724N 90 LJ-82
N724RA G1 114
N724RN TBM7 202
N724TA 200 BB-1607
N724TD 90 LJ-824
N725AR 90 LJ-879
N725BA 350 FL-262
N725DM MU-2 248
N725F 90 LJ-374
N725FN MU-2 248
N725G G1 25
N725HC G1 169
N725HG G1 169
N725JP 46T 97243
N725JT MU-2 451SA
N725K 100 B-2
N725K 90 LJ-197
N725K 90 LJ-318
N725K 90 LJ-418
N725KR 90 LJ-978
N725MA MU-2 582
N725MC 200 BB-169
N725MK G1 124
N725RA 200 BB-725
N725RA G1 166
(N725RB) G1 197
N725SF 680T 1577-31
N725SV 441 0051
N726A 690B 11564
N726CB 200 BB-1750
N726DM MU-2 284
N726ED 46D 210
N726FN MU-2 284
N726G G1 26
N726K 90 LJ-367
N726MA MU-2 341
N726S G1 26
N726T 350 FL-149
N727AC 441 0322
N727B 200 BB-1734
N727BN 31T 7820025
N727BW 200 BB-861
N727CC 690A 11319
N727CC 695A 96027
N727CM 31T 7920071
N727CQ 690A 11319
N727DD 200 BB-861
N727DM MU-2 242
N727DP MIVA AT-039
N727G G1 27
N727G G1 110
N727G G1 163
N727JA 690B 11399
N727K 90 LJ-259
N727K 90 LJ-378
N727K 90 LJ-491
(N727KB) 200 BB-446
N727LE 100 B-207
(N727LK) 31T 7920075
N727MA MU-2 342
N727MC 46D 191
N727MH 350 FL-434
N727MT E90 LW-271
N727MU 350 FL-434
N727PC 31T 7620034
N727PC PA42 8001025
N727RS B100 BE-112
N727SM 31T 7820019
N727ST 441 0322
N727TP MU-2 1517SA
N727X 90 LJ-127
N728AM 200 BB-1729
N728DM MU-2 303
N728DS 90 LJ-773
N728F MU-2 019
N728FN MU-2 303
N728G G1 28
N728G G1 111
N728G G1 196
N728GM G1 171
N728JM BN2 2187
N728K 90 LJ-252
N728MA MU-2 343
N728WP 300 FA-131
N729AF PC12 729
N729CC 690B 11539
N729DM MU-2 296
N729FN MU-2 296
N729G G1 29
N729G G1 112
N729K 90 LJ-376
N729MA MU-2 344
N729MS B100 BE-2
N730BR B100 BE-73
N730CE 200 BB-452
N730EB 90 LJ-1774
N730EB 90 LJ-1808
N730EJ 100 B-217
N730EZ 90 LJ-1808
N730G G1 30
N730HM 200 BB-1648
N730K 90 LJ-78
N730K 90 LJ-328
N730K E90 LW-5
N730MA MU-2 345
N730MP MU-2 345
N730MS 200 BB-1174
N730P 200 BB-1094
N730PC 31T 8166034
N730PT 31T 7720008
N730SF MU-2 246
N730SS 690B 11415
N730SS MU-2 517
N730T G1 131
N730TL G1 131
N730WB 90 LJ-730
N731BH 441 0360
N731CA TBM7 332
N731CJ MU-2 731SA
N731G G1 31
N731JB 46T 97343
N731KA 90 LJ-731
N731MA MU-2 346
N731P 200 BB-1177
N731PB 31T 8166001
N731PC 31T 7920053
N731PC PC12 731
(N731RC) 200 BB-532
N731RJ 90 LJ-1023
N731TM TBM7 5
N731TM TBM8 450
N732C TBM7 327
N732G G1 32
N732G G1 121
N732K 90 LJ-379
N732MA MU-2 347
N732NM 90 LJ-305
N732P 300 FA-11
N732US G1 20
N732WJ 90 LJ-869
N733DY 200 BB-78
N733EB G1 32
N733G G1 122
N733G G1 153
N733K 100 B-172
N733K 90 LJ-15
N733K 90 LJ-517
N733KA 90 LJ-517
N733KL 90 LJ-15
N733KY 100 B-172
N733MA MU-2 348SA
N733NM 200 BB-977
N733NM 350 FL-104
N733NM G1 153
N733P 46T 97052
N734A 200 BB-1298
N734EB G1 32
N734ET G1 32
N734G G1 34
N734G G1 119
N734HR G1 61
N734K 90 LJ-383
N734M 425 0006
N734MA MU-2 349SA
N734P 200 BB-1259
N735EB MIIB T26-162
N735G G1 35
N735K 90 LJ-35
N735MA MU-2 350SA
N735MD PC12 735
N735RC 46D 63
N735TD E90 LW-61

N736	KODK	0019
N736EA	90	LJ-1288
N736G	G1	123
N736G	G1	154
N736K	90	LJ-384
N736MA	MU-2	351SA
N736P	300	FA-53
N737	P68	340
N737	P68	400
N737E	690A	11189
N737EA	200	BB-1932
N737EF	MIIA	T26-022
N737G	G1	124
N737G	G1	156
N737K	90	LJ-191
N737L	90	LJ-1112
N737LC	E90	LW-145
N737MA	MU-2	352SA
N737MG	B100	BE-89
N737P	300	FA-127
N737US	200	BB-1107
N737WB	31T	7620052
N738C	TBM7	260
N738G	G1	38
N738G	G1	125
N738G	G1	164
N738K	90	LJ-380
N738MA	MU-2	353SA
N738P	200	BB-1276
N738PE	PC12	738
N738R	90	LJ-517
N738RH	90	LJ-517
N738W	90	LJ-738
N739G	G1	126
N739G	G1	165
N739G	MIIA	T26-036
N739K	90	LJ-533
N739MA	MU-2	354SA
N739MG	200	BB-1048
N739P	300	FA-98
N739S	PC12	844
N739W	200	BB-1945
N740AA	G1	93
N740AF	PC12	740
N740DM	MU-2	250
N740E	90	LJ-64
N740ES	681	6004
N740F	90	LJ-64
N740FN	MU-2	250
N740G	G1	198
N740GL	200	BB-650
N740K	90	LJ-195
N740P	200	BB-1218
N740PB	MU-2	657
N740PC	300	FA-78
N740PC	MU-2	657
N740R	90	LJ-31
N741DM	MU-2	658
N741E	90	LJ-278
N741EB	100	B-123
N741FN	MU-2	658
N741G	G1	127
N741G	G1	151
N741G	G1	157
N741JP	90	LJ-1756
N741JR	200	BB-1901
N741K	90	LJ-390
N741KA	E90	LW-52
N741L	90	LJ-278
N741MA	MU-2	355SA
N741P	31T	7520020
N741P	31T	7720025
N741SD	PC12	741
N742DM	MU-2	670
N742FN	MU-2	670
N742G	MIIA	T26-032
N742GR	MIIB	T26-172
(N742JW)	46D	236
N742K	90	LJ-69
N742MA	MU-2	356SA
N742R	PC12	742
N742RB	PA42	8001065
N742TW	PA42	8001065
N742TW	PA42	5527036
N742UT	90	LJ-69
N743AE	PC12	743
N743E	200	BB-1194
(N743EC)	E90	LW-73
N743G	G1	72
N743G	G1	129
N743JA	E90	LW-73
N743K	90	LJ-187
N743K	90	LJ-386
N743MA	MU-2	357SA
(N743PC)	PA42	5527029
N743R	200	BB-729
N743TA	200	BB-1623
N744BH	425	0050
N744C	F406	0062
N744CH	690B	11470
N744DA	PC12	744
N744G	G1	130
N744JD	690A	11135
N744K	90	LJ-334
N744MA	MU-2	358SA
N744P	90	LJ-1709
N744TA	200	BB-1627
N744W	350	FL-179
N744WD	441	0133
N744WP	31T	8004040
N744WW	350	FL-179
N745EA	200	BB-1745
N745G	G1	45
N745G	G1	199
N745JB	90	LJ-389
N745K	90	LJ-385
N745LP	90	LJ-442
N745MA	MU-2	361SA
N745ML	200G	BY-28
N745R	200	BB-1113
N745RL	200	BB-1113
N745T	690B	11482
N746G	G1	46
N746K	90	LJ-403
N746KF	200	BB-473
N746MA	MU-2	362SA
N747AW	46T	97017
N747BD	MIV	AT-020
N747BL	46T	97226
N747DN	46T	97038
N747G	G1	47
N747HN	200	BB-658
N747JB	441	0330
N747K	90	LJ-51
N747KF	200	BB-70
N747KL	PC12	662
N747MB	200	BB-346
(N747MC)	690A	11213
N747MF	46D	181
(N747P)	200	BB-519
N747RC	46D	128
N747RE	31T	7720032
N747RL	31T	7720032
(N747RW)	200	BB-869
N747SF	90	LJ-1003
N747SY	MU-2	1556SA
N747TH	46D	107
(N747VB)	441	0330
N747YC	MIIB	T26-120
N748AA	G1	197
N748G	G1	48
N748G	MIIA	T26-016
N748GM	690C	11687
N748GM	F90	LA-45
N748LB	200	BB-1374
N748M	G1	77
N748MA	MU-2	363SA
N748MN	G1	77
N748N	PC6	539
(N748RL)	31T	7720032
N748SA	200	BB-748
N748SB	350	FL-321
N749FF	200	BB-1494
N749G	G1	49
N749GC	PC12	749
N749K	90	LJ-406
N749L	MIII	T-306
N749MA	MU-2	364SA
N749RH	300C	FM-2
N749RH	90	LJ-1408
N749RN	90	LJ-1408
N750AA	MIV	AT-011
N750AB	TBM7	4
N750BB	200	BB-1169
N750BR	G1	99
N750CA	MU-2	407SA
N750DC	E90	LW-136
N750DV	P750	112
N750DZ	P750	108
N750FC	100	B-58
N750G	G1	131
N750G	G1	200
N750HG	200	BB-644
N750HL	200	BB-48
N750HL	300	FA-158
N750K	90	LJ-230
N750KA	350	FL-550
N750KC	200	BB-224
N750LH	P750	147
N750MA	MU-2	365SA
N750MD	200	BB-1878
N750P	90	LJ-489
N750Q	MU-2	017
N750Q	MU-2	125
N750QQ	MU-2	125
N750RC	90	LJ-640
N750S	100	B-239
N750SD	P750	111
N750SN	P750	142
N750SS	P750	115
N750TJ	B100	BE-51
N750TT	200	BB-215
(N750TT)	200	BB-750
N750XL	P750	109
"N750XL"	P750	112
N750YR	200	BB-982
N751BR	690B	11436
N751CC	200	BB-1272
N751CM	TBM7	339
N751EB	200	BB-751
N751G	G1	159
N751G	G1	177
N751J	TBM7	25
N751JB	TBM7	25
N751JT	425	0122
N751K	90	LJ-405
N751KC	90	LJ-887
N751MA	MU-2	366SA
N751PC	90	LJ-143
N751Q	MU-2	126
N752G	G1	52
N752G	G1	133
N752G	G1	160
N752HB	90	LJ-691
N752JS	PC12	752
N752MA	MU-2	367SA
N752MM	46T	97192
N752Q	MU-2	127
N752R	G1	196
N752RB	G1	196
N753C	46T	97248
N753D	B100	BE-98
N753DB	100	B-172
N753G	G1	53
N753K	90	LJ-412
N753P	90	LJ-1766
N753Q	MU-2	129
N753Q	MU-2	141
(N753SR)	90	LJ-461
N754D	F90	LA-20
N754G	G1	134
N754G	G1	168
N754G	G1	193
N754K	90	LJ-425
N754MA	MU-2	368SA
N754Q	MU-2	130
N754SC	200	BB-1345
N754TW	90	LJ-754
N755AF	MU-2	755SA
N755DM	TBM7	101
(N755EC)	MU-2	745SA
N755EM	PC12	661
N755G	G1	55
N755G	G1	135
N755HF	PC12	755
N755JB	200	BB-1377
N755K	90	LJ-171
N755MA	MU-2	369SA
N755MA	MU-2	553
N755N	690A	11297
N755PG	TBM7	1
N755Q	MU-2	131
N755RE	200	BB-673
N756G	G1	56
N756G	G1	136
N756P	90	LJ-1619
N756Q	MU-2	132
N756TW	TBM8	519
N757AL	90	LJ-721
N757ED	PC12	790
N757G	G1	57
N757G	G1	137
N757H	425	0006
N757K	90	LJ-393
N757Q	MU-2	151
N758D	90	LJ-897
N758G	G1	58
N758G	G1	138
N758K	90	LJ-316
N758PC	PC12	698
N758Q	MU-2	134
N759AF	MU-2	759SA
N759FS	F90	LA-110
N759G	G1	59
N759G	G1	139
N759G	G1	181
N759H	46T	97245
N759K	200	BB-585
N759K	90	LJ-420
N759KX	90	LJ-420
(N759LP)	E90	LW-124
N759PB	PC12	759
N759Q	MU-2	136
N760BM	200	BB-594
N760C	46T	97289
N760EB	90	LJ-933
N760G	G1	140
(N760MA)	MU-2	370SA
N760MM	PA42	8001102
N760NB	200	BB-46
N760NB	200	BB-594
N760NE	200	BB-594
N760NP	200	BB-46
N760Q	MU-2	137
N761D	F90	LA-182
N761G	G1	61
N761K	90	LJ-426
N761Q	MU-2	138
N762G	G1	141
N762G	G1	182
N762GP	200	BB-1899
N762GT	90	LJ-1762
N762JC	MU-2	762SA
N762JK	TBM7	62
N762KA	200	BB-762
N762NB	200	BB-893
N762Q	MU-2	139
N762RS	TBM7	199
N762VM	MIVC	AT-695B
N763D	200	BB-1038
N763G	G1	63
N763K	100	B-174
N763K	90	LJ-60
N763LD	MIII	T-313
N763Q	MU-2	140
N764CA	200	BB-1408
N764G	G1	64
N764G	G1	142
N764K	100	B-178
N764K	90	LJ-61
N764MA	MU-2	371SA
N764NB	200	BB-1115
N764Q	MU-2	141
N765G	G1	65
N765MA	MU-2	372SA
N765TC	200	BB-716

N765WA	200	BB-765
N766	P68	313
N766D	200	BB-674
N766G	G1	66
N766G	G1	144
N766G	G1	183
N766K	90	LJ-339
N766LE	200	BB-1864
N766LF	200	BB-1864
N766LF	200G	BY-78
N766MA	MU-2	373SA
N766Q	MU-2	142
N766RB	F90	LA-176
N767CW	TBM7	96
N767DM	31T	8166042
N767G	G1	67
N767G	G1	145
N767HP	TBM7	152
N767JT	PC12	327
N767K	90	LJ-170
N767LD	200	BB-737
N767LD	90	LJ-425
N767MA	MU-2	374SA
N767MC	90	LJ-595
N767MD	MU-2	328
N767PB	PC12	767
N767Q	MU-2	143
N767TP	46T	97036
N767WF	200	BB-314
N767Z	441	0064
N768D	200	BB-810
N768G	G1	68
N768H	PC12	716
N768MA	MU-2	375SA
N768MB	31T	8004041
N768Q	MU-2	144
N768SB	90	LJ-955
N768WT	350	FL-25
N769	200	BB-291
N769	90	LJ-185
N769AF	PC12	769
N769AJ	200	BB-769
N769AM	E90	LW-69
N769BJ	350	FL-156
N769CM	PC12	464
N769D	F90	LA-52
N769G	G1	322
N769G	G1	69
N769GR	90	LJ-1509
N769JS	TBM7	187
N769K	90	LJ-185
N769MA	MU-2	379SA
N769MB	200	BB-571
N769MB	31T	8004041
N769Q	MU-2	145
N769WT	200	BB-1319
(N769WT)	200	BB-1490
N769WT	350	FL-25
N770A	G1	129
N770AB	B100	BE-121
N770AC	G1	129
N770AE	200	BB-1226
N770AJ	90	LJ-1272
N770D	B100	BE-90
N770DC	TBM7	183
N770FK	BN2T	2144
N770FL	PC12	501
N770G	G1	70
N770G	PC12	299
N770GX	300	FA-218
N770HM	200	BB-916
N770JH	350	FL-8
N770K	90	LJ-6
N770M	200	BB-996
N770M	200	BB-1330
N770M	200	BB-1546
N770M	200	BB-1788
N770M	90	LJ-326
N770MA	MU-2	380SA
N770MA	MU-2	625
N770MG	31T	7520029
(N770MT)	E90	LW-315
N770PB	200	BB-1498
N770PW	PC12	757
N770RL	100	B-46
N770RW	MU-2	627
N770SD	F90	LA-72
N770SF	200	BB-916
N770TJ	90	LJ-721
N770TP	200	BB-1638
N770U	200	BB-1546
N770U	MIII	T-242
N770VF	90	LJ-1254
N770VF	90	LJ-1641
N770WA	90	LJ-1770
N770WC	MU-2	192
N771AK	C-12	BC-56
N771AW	90	LJ-1219
N771BA	690B	11429
N771BL	46T	97227
N771CP	90	LJ-671
N771CW	B100	BE-52
N771D	200C	BL-71
N771DP	MU-2	521
N771FF	690D	15014
N771G	G1	71
N771HA	200	BB-327
N771HC	200	BB-147
N771HM	200	BB-327
N771HM	200	BB-1078
N771HM	350	FL-262
N771HM	90	LJ-392
N771HM	E90	LW-54
N771JB	90	LJ-1676
N771JB	90	LJ-1848
N771JB	F90	LA-83
N771JC	90	LJ-1676
N771JH	200	BB-1654
N771KT	PC12	361
N771MA	MU-2	381SA
N771MF	31T	7820024
N771MG	200	BB-1636
N771PA	90	LJ-1055
N771PD	90	LJ-1635
N771PS	90	LJ-744
N771S	B100	BE-52
N771SC	200	BB-1636
N771SC	200	BB-1693
N771SC	90	LJ-1410
N771SC	90	LJ-1463
N771SG	90	LJ-1410
N771SQ	200	BB-1636
N771SQ	90	LJ-1463
(N771SR)	200	BB-154
N771SW	31T	7720002
N771TP	200	BB-1650
N771WW	690B	11467
N771XW	441	0065
N772AF	200	BB-1001
N772CB	681B	6050
N772DA	MU-2	772SA
N772G	G1	72
N772G	G1	146
N772GS	200	BB-272
N772HM	350	FL-262
N772JB	90	LJ-1652
N772K	90	LJ-310
N772MA	MU-2	382SA
*N772MF	31T	7820034
(N772SA)	MU-2	772SA
N772SE	46T	97166
N772SL	MIII	T-258
(N772SW)	31T	7720012
N772SW	31T	7720019
N772TP	200	BB-1692
N773	F90	LA-214
N773AM	200	BB-1430
N773CA	690B	11418
N773G	G1	73
N773K	90	LJ-400
N773KA	200	BB-446
N773M	200	BB-1330
N773MA	MU-2	383SA
N773PW	90	LJ-864
N773S	90	LJ-283
N773SD	90	LJ-1413
N773SK	100	B-196
(N773SW)	31T	7720022
N773TC	TBM7	312
N773TP	200	BB-1693
N773TP	200	BB-1722
N773VA	200	BB-1195
N773WJ	G1	73
N774A	350	FL-184
N774CC	350	FL-110
N774DK	PC12	167
N774EA	90	LJ-1776
(N774EM)	90	LJ-914
N774G	G1	74
N774G	G1	147
N774G	G1	174
N774GW	PC12	774
N774K	90	LJ-80
(N774KV)	31T	7720034
N774KV	31T	8166057
N774MA	MU-2	384SA
N774MF	31T	7920035
*N774MR	200	BB-1177
N774SW	31T	7720025
(N774T)	200	BB-99
N774TP	200	BB-1726
N774WW	690B	11467
N775CA	PA42	5501004
N775CC	PC12	792
N775D	90	LJ-1579
N775DM	90	LJ-764
N775G	G1	75
N775G	G1	148
N775M	200	BB-996
N775MA	MU-2	385SA
N775MF	31T	7920079
N775MG	350	FL-553
N775MW	P68	208
N775PC	PC12	775
N775RD	46D	142
N775SC	200	BB-808
N775SR	90	LJ-1813
N775SW	31T	7720015
N776AF	PC12	776
N776AK	31T	8166063
N776CA	46T	97376
N776CC	MU-2	560
N776DC	E90	LW-235
N776G	G1	76
N776G	G1	149
N776G	G1	189
N776JT	PC12	563
N776K	90	LJ-56
N776KC	46T	97376
N776L	100	B-54
N776RM	200	BB-1245
N776RM	TBM7	98
N776RW	200	BB-1926
N777AG	200	BB-583
N777AG	200	BB-1366
N777AG	200	BB-1498
N777AG	200	BB-1638
N777AG	200	BB-1757
N777AG	90	LJ-41
N777AG	F90	LA-56
N777AJ	200	BB-1498
N777AJ	200	BB-1638
N777AJ	E90	LW-49
N777AQ	200	BB-583
(N777AQ)	200	BB-1366
N777AQ	F90	LA-56
N777AS	F90	LA-202
N777AT	90	LJ-166
N777AW	200	BB-536
N777BW	441	0053
N777CQ	PC12	754
N777CR	B100	BE-27
N777DC	B100	BE-59
N777DL	31T	7820092
N777DQ	B100	BE-59
N777EB	90	LJ-863
N777EC	E90	LW-37
N777EC	E90	LW-308
N777ED	441	0009
N777EL	690B	11538
N777EQ	E90	LW-308
N777EW	P68	38
N777FG	PA42	8001034
N777FL	200	BB-147
N777FL	MU-2	758SA
(N777FX)	46T	97211
N777FX	TBM7	294
N777G	31T	8104065
N777G	G1	77
N777G	G1	150
N777GA	200	BB-1007
N777GA	31T	7720043
N777GF	100	B-241
N777GF	90	LJ-564
N777GS	100	B-241
N777HE	690A	11287
N777HF	200	BB-1645
N777HF	90	LJ-1048
N777HZ	MIII	T-249
N777J	90	LJ-1163
N777JE	200	BB-649
N777JE	MIII	T-387
N777JF	PC12	146
N777JF	PC12	288
N777JJ	90	LJ-721
N777JM	31T	7820064
(N777JM)	31T	7920082
N777JN	690B	11444
N777JS	G1	197
N777JV	200	BB-1351
N777JX	PC12	288
N777JZ	PC12	817
N777KA	E90	LW-285
N777KD	690B	11366
N777KQ	MU-2	514
N777KU	90	LJ-377
N777KV	31T	7720034
N777LE	31T	7920042
N777LE	31T	8120104
N777LM	31T	7820046
N777LP	31T	8020076
N777LP	MU-2	719SA
N777MA	MU-2	559
(N777MD)	425	0087
N777MG	46T	97066
N777MJ	MU-2	1520SA
N777MN	90	LJ-1657
(N777MW)	200	BB-235
N777N	MIIB	T26-157
N777NG	90	LJ-979
N777NG	E90	LW-49
N777NP	90	LJ-67
N777NQ	90	LJ-979
N777NR	100	B-191
N777NR	100	B-241
N777NR	90	LJ-67
N777NV	690C	11680
N777NW	90	LJ-561
N777PD	MU-2	783SA
N777PE	MIIB	T26-176
N777PG	46D	134
N777PR	200	BB-404
N777PR	90	LJ-809
N777RD	690B	11366
N777SB	90	LJ-347
N777SD	100	B-102
N777SJ	90	LJ-644
N777SS	200	BB-661
N777SS	E90	LW-45
N777ST	100	B-102
N777ST	MU-2	747SA
N777SW	200	BB-1773
(N777SZ)	100	B-102
N777T	690A	11166
(N777T)	695A	96080
N777TE	690A	11162
N777TG	90	LJ-49
N777TG	BN2	774
N777TH	31T	7820011
N777UP	425	0105
N777UP	425	0201
N777VG	200	BB-1366
N777VH	90	LJ-979
N777VK	MU-2	179
N777VM	MU-2	672
N777W	90	LJ-328

N777WC	90	LJ-592
N777WJ	200	BB-126
N777WM	MU-2	397SA
(N777WN)	90	LJ-385
N777WY	690C	11673
N777XS	200	BB-126
N777XW	441	0065
N777XX	PC6	564
N777XZ	200	BB-126
N777Y	P166	367
N777YC	350	FL-390
N777YN	90	LJ-1657
N777YP	31T	8166063
N777YP	PA42	5501008
N777YR	31T	8166063
(N777ZA)	PC12	552
N777ZK	PC12	218
N778C	TBM7	205
(N778C)	TBM7	229
N778DB	90	LJ-1647
N778G	G1	78
N778G	G1	155
N778G	G1	178
N778HA	31T	8120008
N778HD	31T	7920006
N778HP	200	BB-1369
N778K	90	LJ-432
N778MA	MU-2	386SA
N778SW	31T	7720055
N779AF	E90	LW-51
N779BZ	200	BB-1971
N779CC	441	0155
N779DD	441	0156
N779DD	90	LJ-1297
N779G	G1	79
N779G	G1	158
N779G	G1	179
(N779JM)	90	LJ-1127
N779JM	90	LJ-1183
N779JT	31T	7904029
N779KS	BN2	779
N779M	MIII	T-363
N779MA	MU-2	387SA
N779MJ	90	LJ-1197
N779PC	PC12	779
(N779SW)	31T	7720064
(N779SW)	31T	7720069
N779SW	31T	7904051
N779VF	90	LJ-1254
N780AC	G1	106
N780BF	200	BB-466
N780BF	300	FA-70
N780BP	690	11052
N780CA	200	BB-1547
N780CA	31T	8104002
N780CA	P180	1106
N780G	G1	80
N780GB	200	BB-578
(N780JB)	200	BB-1670
N780K	90	LJ-67
N780KB	200	BB-1924
N780MA	MU-2	388SA
N780Q	MU-2	146
N780RC	200	BB-780
N780SW	31T	7820003
N780W	200	BB-359
(N781BF)	200	BB-466
N781CK	31T	7820056
N781CW	31T	7820075
N781G	G1	81
N781GT	90	LJ-1781
N781H	MU-2	409SA
(N781HM)	200	BB-1078
N781JT	90	LJ-254
N781MA	MU-2	389SA
N781PE	PC12	781
N781Q	MU-2	149
N781SU	MU-2	631
N781SU	MU-2	1563SA
N781SW	31T	7820012
N781TM	TBM7	5
N781VC	F90	LA-76
N782CC	441	0346
N782EA	90	LJ-1782
N782G	G1	82
N782MA	MU-2	390SA
N782P	90	LJ-1607
N782Q	MU-2	150
N782SW	31T	7820026
(N782SW)	PA42	8001082
(N783CB)	690A	11198
N783DJ	TBM7	83
N783DY	200	BB-78
N783G	G1	83
N783JJ	PC12	783
N783K	90	LJ-396
N783MA	MU-2	391SA
N783MC	C-12	BC-2
N783PC	PC12	783
N783Q	MU-2	154
N783RS	441	0170
N783ST	441	0170
N783SW	31T	7820029
N784AF	MIIB	T26-129
N784BK	PC12	784
N784G	G1	84
N784K	90	LJ-427
N784MA	MU-2	392SA
N784PF	425	0018
N784Q	MU-2	155
N784RR	441	0078
N784SW	31T	7820037
N785GP	G1	29
N785HC	46D	240
N785JH	P180	1036
N785JP	90	LJ-1710
N785K	90	LJ-440
(N785MA)	MU-2	709SA
N785MA	MU-2	784SA
(N785MA)	TBM7	268
N785MA	TBM7	280
N785P	90	LJ-1712
N785PC	PC12	785
N785PJ	46T	97232
N785SW	31T	7820047
N786AH	31T	7820053
N786BP	STAR	NC-28
N786CB	B100	BE-4
N786DD	200	BB-1171
N786G	G1	86
N786G	G1	180
N786MA	MU-2	393SA
N786P	90	LJ-1678
N786RM	90	LJ-1545
N786SR	200	BB-1016
N786SW	31T	7820056
N786WM	PC12	786
N787CA	TBM7	338
N787G	G1	87
N787JB	350	FL-223
N787K	90	LJ-102
N787LB	PA42	5501030
N787MA	MU-2	395SA
N787PB	PC12	787
N787RP	46D	209
N787SW	31T	7820074
N787TT	90	LJ-787
(N787X)	MU-2	389SA
N788AA	200	BB-82
N788BB	31T	7620051
N788G	G1	88
N788JB	200	BB-1290
N788JL	425	0202
N788JM	90	LJ-1868
N788K	90	LJ-269
N788KC	90	LJ-1662
N788M	46D	6
N788MA	MU-2	396SA
(N788MB)	350	FL-271
N788RB	TBM7	167
N788RB	TBM8	395
N788RR	TBM7	167
N788SF	200	BB-1857
N788SM	46D	75
N788SW	31T	7820073
N788SW	E90	LW-327
N788TA	200	BB-1648
N788W	90	LJ-298
N788WG	300	FA-82
N789B	MIII	T-230
N789BT	200	BB-478
N789CH	31T	7920079
N789CT	200	BB-907
N789DS	200	BB-478
N789G	G1	89
N789GA	200	BB-1305
N789H	200	BB-784
N789KP	90	LJ-1664
N789LL	350	FL-386
N789MA	441	0156
N789MA	MU-2	397SA
N789MM	PA42	8001049
N789RB	MIIB	T26-172
N789RW	31T	7920052
N789S	G1	82
N789SB	350	FL-143
N789SW	31T	7820084
N789TW	90	LJ-167
N789WA	90	LJ-1407
(N789WW)	PA42	8001049
N789X	MIIB	T26-128
N790A	90	LJ-1016
N790CA	MU-2	260
N790CA	TBM7	341
N790G	G1	90
N790G	G1	161
N790G	G1	170
N790GT	90	LJ-1761
N790K	90	LJ-4
N790MA	441	0210
N790MA	MU-2	398SA
N790P	350	FL-379
N790RB	E90	LW-262
N790RM	200	BB-445
N790RV	90	LJ-1830
N790SD	31T	7920004
N790SW	31T	7920004
N790TB	TBM7	148
N790W	90	LJ-1680
N791BP	350	FL-551
N791DC	200	BB-1402
N791EB	200	BB-791
N791G	G1	91
N791G	G1	166
N791K	90	LJ-253
N791MA	MU-2	584
N791RC	90	LJ-791
N791SW	31T	7920007
N791X	300	FA-42
N792BP	200G	BY-10
N792CA	TBM7	285
N792JM	300	FA-140
N792K	90	LJ-192
N792KC	441	0214
N792SG	PC12	380
N792SW	31T	7920014
N793CA	46T	97402
N793DC	200	BB-1404
N793EM	350	FL-106
N793K	90	LJ-293
N793MA	90	LJ-703
N793P	90	LJ-1836
N793PA	90	LJ-1158
N793S	31T	8020067
N793SW	31T	7920023
N793WB	350	FL-324
N794A	PA42	5501015
N794AF	PC12	794
N794B	425	0017
N794CA	31T	8120018
(N794CA)	TBM7	344
N794CE	B100	BE-69
N794G	G1	94
N794G	G1	167
N794K	90	LJ-535
N794MA	MU-2	794SA
N794MM	46D	142
N794P	90	LJ-1704
(N794PA)	300	FA-157
N794PF	425	0018
(N794PL)	31T	7820061
N794WB	B100	BE-69
N795CA	200	BB-559
N795G	G1	95
N795G	G1	175
N795GB	200	BB-1069
N795K	90	LJ-95
N795KW	PA42	8001011
N795PA	200	BB-328
N795TB	MIII	TT-483A
N796JS	46T	97372
N796K	90	LJ-443
N796SW	31T	7920036
N797BG	46T	97077
N797CF	90	LJ-797
N797G	G1	97
N797GM	PC12	747
N797MA	46D	154
N797P	300	FA-139
N797PA	E90	LW-328
N797RW	441	0185
N797SW	31T	7920046
(N797WB)	350	FL-324
N798G	G1	98
N798G	G1	176
N798K	90	LJ-178A
N798KA	300	FA-64
N798R	G1	82
N798RG	PC12	798
N798S	200	BB-1370
N798SW	31T	7920048
N798WC	PC12	613
N799DD	100	B-102
N799G	G1	99
N799GK	90	LJ-799
N799K	90	LJ-2
N799MA	MU-2	612
N799MT	BN2	449
(N799SW)	31T	7720053
N799SW	31T	7920054
N799V	690B	11407
N800AB	441	0162
N800AC	E90	LW-273
N800AJ	200	BB-1695
N800AJ	200	BB-1789
N800AT	P68	300
N800AW	MIII	T-403
N800BB	31T	8104072
(N800BF)	200	BB-914
N800BF	E90	LW-87
N800BJ	350	FL-184
N800BK	F90	LA-119
N800BM	690C	11691
N800BN	441	0249
N800BP	90	LJ-234
N800BR	MU-2	199
N800BR	MU-2	221
N800BS	200	BB-1620
N800BW	200	BB-818
N800BY	MU-2	221
(N800C)	E90	LW-119
(N800C)	F90	LA-119
N800CA	BN2	328
N800CG	200	BB-826
N800CM	31T	7904003
N800CP	200	BB-231
N800CT	90	LJ-393
(N800DG)	PA42	5501029
N800DH	MU-2	166
N800EB	300	FA-7
N800EB	31T	7920046
N800ED	MU-2	339
N800ET	200	BB-1381
N800GF	200	BB-1286
N800GS	TBM7	5
N800GS	TBM7	149
N800HA	200	BB-220
(N800HA)	680T	1546-9
N800HA	680T	1546-9
N800HH	680T	1546-9
N800HR	MU-2	232
N800HT	MU-2	688
N800JD	200	BB-1022
N800JF	90	LJ-1505
N800JF	90	LJ-1519
N800JR	200	BB-982

N800JR	MIII	T-315
N800KA	90	LJ-372
N800KC	200	BB-776
(N800KD)	90	LJ-628
N800KT	200	BB-1346
N800L	200	BB-369
N800LD	MIII	T-291
N800LS	200	BB-457
N800MD	100	B-7
N800MG	200	BB-1259
N800MK	90	LJ-1460
N800MM	MIII	T-375
N800MP	31T	7904020
N800NR	200	BB-1262
(N800PA)	200	BB-854
N800PA	G1	141
N800PC	MU-2	694
N800PD	G1	154
N800PG	90	LJ-1286
N800PK	200	BB-982
N800PM	G1	154
N800PP	200	BB-776
N800PW	90	LJ-548
N800Q	90	LJ-301
N800RD	200	BB-1124
(N800RD)	300	FA-21
N800RE	300	FA-7
(N800RG)	46D	144
N800RP	90	LJ-628
N800S	90	LJ-249
N800SR	441	0316
N800SW	31T	8020004
N800TA	MIII	T-294
N800TB	90	LJ-175
N800TS	200	BB-1032
N800TT	200	BB-957
(N800TW)	31T	8020004
N800VT	90	LJ-249
N800W	31T	8004032
N800YM	441	0266
N801AR	300	FA-191
N801AT	P68	325
N801BC	200	BB-1082
N801BS	90	LJ-1601
N801BT	MIIA	T26-018
N801C	31T	7620048
N801CA	31T	8104018
(N801CC)	G1	82
N801CM	31T	8020006
N801EB	690A	11111
N801ED	425	0145
N801GC	31T	8020014
N801GG	200	BB-642
N801GT	200G	BY-1
N801HD	31T	7620031
N801HL	31T	8020016
N801J	PC12	801
N801JW	PA42	8001072
N801K	90	LJ-86
N801KM	90	LJ-218
N801L	31T	7620048
N801L	31T	7920090
N801L	MU-2	362SA
N801MF	680T	1710-85
N801MP	90	LJ-508
N801NA	200	BB-1164
N801PB	PC12	1006
N801RA	680T	1620-51
N801ST	31T	8020014
N801SW	31T	8020014
N801WA	46T	97062
N802AC	MIIA	T26-021
N802AF	PC12	802
N802AT	P68T	8002
N802BS	350	FL-338
N802CA	200	BB-576
N802CA	PA42	8001023
N802CC	G1	154
N802CM	31T	8020018
N802DG	90	LJ-807
N802DJ	MIIB	T26-117
N802GC	B100	BE-96
N802GT	200G	BY-2
N802HC	31T	8020018
N802HS	PC12	118
(N802JH)	425	0166
N802K	90	LJ-238
N802M	300	FA-124
N802ME	MIII	T-294
N802MJ	200	BB-1948
N802MM	46T	97148
N802MW	PA42	8001081
N802RD	B100	BE-96
N802SM	MU-2	1515SA
N802SW	31T	8020017
(N803AW)	31T	8004011
N803CA	31T	8104029
N803CC	G1	112
N803CM	31T	8004020
N803DJ	MIIB	T26-102
N803GT	200G	BY-3
N803HC	F90	LA-99
N803JH	46T	97103
N803K	90	LJ-394
N803RA	690A	11165
N803SM	90	LJ-495
N803SW	31T	8020032
N804	200	BB-724
N804BL	200	BB-888
N804C	31T	1166006
N804CA	PA42	8001037
N804CC	G1	109
N804CC	G1	148
N804CD	31T	8020056
N804CM	31T	8020038
N804CT	200	BB-1243
N804CT	31T	1104010
N804GT	90	LJ-1804
N804JH	46T	97044
N804K	90	LJ-254
N804KS	200	BB-751
N804RM	F90	LA-15
N804ST	PC12	741
N805C	200	BB-1751
N805CA	31T	8104041
N805CC	G1	155
N805CM	31T	8020046
N805K	90	LJ-348
N805SW	31T	8020037
N806CA	31T	8120038
N806CM	31T	8020057
N806DG	200	BB-1767
(N806DR)	100	B-160
N806G	200	BB-1767
N806GG	200	BB-1767
N806J	P180	1179
(N806JN)	350	FL-140
N806JW	350	FL-140
N806K	90	LJ-455
N806LW	200	BB-1494
N806PE	PC12	806
N806S	G1	67
N806SW	31T	8020050
N806TC	200	BB-636
N806W	G1	67
N806WB	90	LJ-699
(N807BC)	200	BB-1082
N807CA	31T	8104058
N807D	PC12	807
N807K	90	LJ-411
N807M	MIVC	AT-423
N807M	MIVC	AT-454
N807MA	MIVA	AT-034
N807MF	MIVA	AT-034
N807RS	90	LJ-1602
N807SC	200	BB-490
N807SM	200	BB-1989
N807SW	31T	8020031
N808CA	PA42	8001008
N808CC	B100	BE-70
N808DD	MIII	TT-433
N808DP	90	LJ-111
N808DS	200	BB-1628
(N808DS)	F90	LA-172
N808EB	200	BB-808
N808GA	E90	LW-63
N808GC	B100	BE-70
N808GU	680T	1579-32
N808JS	PC12	1003
N808K	90	LJ-20
N808LA	46T	97392
N808LB	MIII	T-319
N808NC	695A	96085
N808NT	695	95081
N808PC	PC12	808
N808PK	MU-2	385SA
N808S	90	LJ-20
N808SW	31T	8020074
N808SW	90	LJ-801
N808TB	441	0194
N808TC	F90	LA-211
N808W	90	LJ-1114
N808W	MU-2	609
N808WD	200	BB-1685
N808Y	90	LJ-111
N809AA	PA42	8001043
N809AM	P68T	8009
N809CA	31T	8166012
N809CC	G1	159
N809CM	31T	8004039
N809E	31T	7920060
N809E	PA42	5501006
N809K	90	LJ-461
N809P	90	LJ-1849
N809SW	31T	8020080
N810CB	G1	23
N810CM	300	FA-106
N810CM	31T	8020072
N810CM	F90	LA-20
N810EC	695	95071
N810GF	690B	11358
N810GW	200	BB-949
N810HM	31T	8304002
N810JB	200	BB-139
N810K	200	BB-1045
N810K	690B	11487
N810K	695	95082
N810K	90	LJ-53
N810KA	200	BB-810
N810KM	690B	11487
N810L	PA42	8001051
N810N	350	FL-419
N810P	690D	15009
(N810RE)	BN2	789
N810V	200	BB-1045
N810V	200	BB-1054
N810V	E90	LW-344
N810Z	PC12	1141
N811AA	90	LJ-429
N811CB	200	BB-779
(N811CC)	G1	137
(N811CC)	G1	196
(N811CC)	G1	197
N811CM	31T	8004046
N811CU	100	B-165
N811DA	PA42	8001029
N811DD	PC12	1027
N811EC	690C	11615
N811FA	200	BB-678
N811GA	90	LJ-810
N811JB	E90	LW-35
N811KC	90	LJ-869
N811LC	300	FA-194
N811LC	690C	11615
(N811LT)	90	LJ-307
N811MM	E90	LW-345
N811NA	425	0008
N811ND	200	BB-589
N811PC	PC12	811
N811PM	31T	7720016
N811R	90	LJ-1131
N811SV	TBM7	234
N811SW	31T	8120004
N811SW	TBM7	126
N811SW	TBM7	234
N811SW	TBM7	240
N811VC	200	BB-678
N811VC	441	0287
N811VG	200	BB-678
N811VG	441	0287
N811VT	200	BB-323
N812AC	90	LJ-123
N812BJ	PA42	5527020
N812CC	G1	129
N812CM	31T	8004050
N812CP	F90	LA-127
N812DP	200	BB-69
N812FS	PC12	1077
N812G	90	LJ-366
N812GS	PC12	1086
N812JJ	31T	8166001
N812KB	E90	LW-144
N812KC	441	0041
N812LP	90	LJ-1600
N812M	90	LJ-366
N812M	B100	BE-84
N812MA	46T	97212
N812MB	46D	152
N812NB	90	LJ-511
N812P	90	LJ-2
N812PA	PC12	106
N812PM	350	FL-119
N812PS	90	LJ-242
N812Q	90	LJ-2
N812SW	31T	8120008
N812WJ	B100	BE-76
N813AA	90	LJ-214
(N813AM)	31T	7820013
N813AR	31T	7820013
N813AW	690B	11420
N813BL	B100	BE-55
N813CF	PA42	8001012
N813G	200	BB-881
N813JB	90	LJ-899
N813JL	425	0010
N813JP	200	BB-715
N813K	90	LJ-464
N813NH	690A	11299
N813PA	PC12	104
N813PC	PC12	104
N813PR	690A	11107
N813Q	100	B-204
N813Q	MIII	TT-507
N813RA	PA42	8001012
N813S	46T	97363
N813SW	31T	8120020
N813TS	200	BB-267
N813ZM	425	0159
N814CM	31T	8020081
N814CM	PA42	5527014
N814CP	90	LJ-1127
N814DM	31T	8020081
N814G	90	LJ-104
N814GT	B100	BE-75
N814HH	MU-2	412SA
N814K	90	LJ-460
N814K	90	LJ-490
N814KA	200	BB-23
N814KA	300C	FM-14
N814MM	MIVA	AT-043
N814PC	PC12	814
N814SS	MIII	T-314
N814SW	90	LJ-186
N814TB	PC12	748
N814W	31T	7820073
N814WJ	BN2	814
N815AF	PC12	815
N815BC	690C	11731
N815CC	690B	11404
N815CE	200	BB-26
N815CE	200	BB-1044
N815CE	90	LJ-134
(N815CF)	200	BB-1044
N815CL	200	BB-26
N815CM	31T	8120003
N815D	300	FA-188
N815K	90	LJ-123
(N815MA)	690A	11185
N815MC	441	0263
N815RD	TBM7	338
N815S	695A	96005
N815SW	31T	8120027
N816BC	46T	97195
N816BS	200	BB-778
N816C	90	LJ-42
(N816CM)	31T	8104006

N816CM	31T	8104009
N816DD	200	BB-1623
N816DE	350	FL-232
N816DK	200	BB-1623
N816DK	350	FL-232
N816EP	E90	LW-187
N816EP	F90	LA-78
N816JA	31T	8120060
N816KA	300C	FM-16
N816LD	200	BB-1840
N816PC	690B	11395
N816PC	PC12	816
N816RB	200	BB-36
(N816RB)	MU-2	768SA
N816RL	E90	LW-187
N816SW	31T	8120041
N816TM	46D	187
N817BA	200	BB-956
N817BB	200C	BL-13
N817BH	300	FA-90
N817CJ	31T	7920005
(N817CM)	31T	8120005
N817CT	31T	8104019
N817CT	31T	1104010
N817DP	90	LJ-1156
N817F	90	LJ-1129
N817KA	300C	FM-17
N817M	90	LJ-77
N817QT	31T	8104019
N817SW	31T	8104044
N818	200C	BL-17
N818	680T	1558-16
N818	690B	11388
N818AG	200	BB-1771
N818AS	100	B-185
N818BL	200	BB-1394
N818CM	31T	8104024
N818DT	200C	BL-17
N818EC	680T	1558-16
N818EK	690C	11695
N818HT	690B	11513
N818KA	300C	FM-18
N818L	680T	1558-16
N818MS	90	LJ-53
N818PA	B100	BE-18
N818PF	200	BB-1059
N818PL	425	0109
N818R	MU-2	1529SA
N818RA	PC12	179
(N818SW)	31T	8120041
N818SW	31T	8104054
N818WV	350	FL-381
(N819C)	90	LJ-104
N819CD	200C	BL-42
N819EE	350	FL-187
N819K	100	B-7
N819MH	90	LJ-735
N819MK	31T	7720018
N819SW	31T	8104059
N820AB	P750	116
N820BC	PA42	8001105
N820CA	441	0055
N820CB	G1	93
N820CE	G1	50
N820CM	31T	8120028
N820DM	46T	97326
N820DY	200	BB-255
N820K	90	LJ-176
N820RD	E90	LW-82
N820SL	90	LJ-583
N820SM	TBM7	316
N820SW	31T	8166043
(N820YL)	31T	7620025
N821AD	E90	LW-299
N821BA	P68	441
N821CA	200C	BL-32
N821CB	B100	BE-35
N821CM	31T	8104032
N821CS	90	LJ-1674
N821CT	90	LJ-821
N821DK	PA42	8001061
N821J	46T	97172
N821K	90	LJ-462
N821MA	MU-2	661SA
N821MC	690B	11541
N821PE	PC12	821
N821RC	200	BB-821
N821RR	BN2	338
N821SW	31T	8166047
N821TB	300	FA-6
(N821TB)	PA42	8001057
N821U	90	LJ-19
N821U	90	LJ-186
N822BA	F90	LA-191
N822BM	PC12	822
N822CM	31T	8104037
N822DK	46D	121
N822MA	MU-2	662
N822MS	690C	11699
N822SW	31T	8120067
N822SW	31T	8120102
N822TJ	90	LJ-692
N822VK	300	FA-211
(N822WC)	31T	8104037
N823CM	PA42	8001016
N823DB	425	0086
N823EB	350	FL-227
N823FC	90	LJ-1436
N823GA	G1	109
N823K	90	LJ-287
N823MA	MU-2	663
N823PE	PC12	823
N823PW	E90	LW-245
N823SB	690A	11304
N823SB	U-21	LM-16
N823SD	350	FL-263
N823SD	350	FL-390
N823SE	350	FL-263
(N823SS)	PA42	8001016
N823SW	31T	8166052
N824AC	E90	LW-291
N824BK	PC12	718
N824CM	31T	8104039
N824JH	31T	8166040
N824K	90	LJ-387
N824MA	MU-2	664
N824MD	MIVA	AT-027
N824RH	TBM7	279
N824RH	TBM8	448
N824S	200	BB-1064
N824SM	PC12	824
N824ST	350	FL-203
N824SW	31T	8166054
N824TT	200	BB-824
N824VA	31T	8104039
N825B	200	BB-248
N825B	425	0123
N825CM	31T	8120044
(N825G)	350	FL-36
N825JG	300	FA-196
N825K	90	LJ-91
N825KA	200	BB-825
(N825KM)	TBM7	329
N825MA	MU-2	665
N825NW	PA42	8001009
N825P	90	LJ-1793
N825RT	200	BB-795
N825SD	90	LJ-1449
N825SP	441	0127
N825ST	200	BB-1320
N825SW	31T	8166058
N825T	90	LJ-404
N825TL	90	LJ-1876
N825TS	350	FL-308
N825TT	350	FL-490
(N825U)	90	LJ-1776
N826CM	31T	8104048
N826JM	200	BB-1358
N826K	90	LJ-493
N826KA	200	BB-1826
N826MA	300	FA-8
N826MA	MU-2	666
N826P	90	LJ-1813
N826RC	MU-2	666
N826RM	31T	8004033
N826SW	31T	8120070
N826TM	90	LJ-1857
N827CA	300	FA-43
N827CC	300	FA-43
N827CC	350	FL-457
N827CM	46T	97310
N827CM	PA42	8001032
N827DL	300	FA-103
N827DP	F90	LA-77
N827FM	90	LJ-292
N827HB	350	FL-129
N827HT	200	BB-1618
N827K	90	LJ-327
(N827KR)	PA42	8001013
N827LP	31T	7904048
N827MA	MU-2	667
N827PC	PA42	5527033
N827RM	B100	BE-123
N827SW	31T	8120072
N827T	90	LJ-83
N827VG	TBM7	242
(N828AB)	200	BB-828
N828AJ	350	FL-406
N828C	MIII	T-204
N828CA	300	FA-79
N828CM	31T	8120050
N828CM	MIII	T-258
N828FC	90	LJ-1436
N828FM	200	BB-1069
N828JB	200	BB-795
N828JC	300	FA-29
N828MA	MU-2	668
N828SG	425	0122
N828SW	31T	8166062
N828VV	PC12	826
N829AG	46D	109
N829AJ	200	BB-829
N829BB	441	0297
N829BC	TBM7	31
N829CM	PA42	8001039
N829DF	90	LJ-324
N829FC	90	LJ-829
(N829HS)	MIIB	T26-149
N829JC	441	0156
N829JQ	441	0156
N829K	90	LJ-389
N829MA	MU-2	669
N829PC	PA42	5501019
N829PE	PC12	829
(N829SW)	31T	8166065
N830	200	BB-904
N830	680T	1704-80
N830	690	11064
(N830AM)	PA42	8301002
N830CB	PA42	8001048
N830CE	200	BB-16
N830CM	PA42	8001048
N830EM	100	B-29
N830LS	200	BB-904
N830MA	MU-2	670
N830WM	680T	1704-80
N831CH	31T	8004047
N831CM	31T	8120061
N831E	90	LJ-1650
N831EB	90	LJ-1831
N831K	90	LJ-468
N831KD	200	BB-1937
N831LJ	31T	7904036
*N831LS	200	BB-569
N831MA	MU-2	671
*N831PA	200	BB-553
N831PC	31T	8020001
N831PT	31T	7720022
N831PT	350	FL-487
N831SW	31T	7904036
N831TM	200	BB-1635
N832AD	441	0311
N832CM	31T	8120071
N832K	90	LJ-445
N832MA	MU-2	672
N832PC	PC12	832
N833	90	LJ-307
N833BK	200	BB-1239
N833BK	90	LJ-727
N833CM	PA42	8001064
N833DP	441	0246
N833E	200	BB-1175
N833K	90	LJ-365
N833MA	MU-2	673
N833PS	200	BB-1084
N833RL	200	BB-833
N833S	MIII	T-239
N834BN	BN2	834
N834CM	PA42	8001071
N834CM	PA42	5501007
N834GA	300	FA-182
N834H	G1	129
N834MA	MU-2	674
N835BG	90	LJ-404
*N835BL	90	LJ-1835
N835CC	690C	11730
N835E	200	BB-1145
N835MA	441	0343
N835MA	MU-2	675
N835MW	31T	1166001
N836K	90	LJ-469
N836MA	MIVA	AT-068
N836MA	MU-2	676
N837J	200	BB-1922
N837JM	200	BB-1922
N837MA	MU-2	677
N837RE	441	0214
N838GT	90	LJ-1838
(N838JW)	TBM7	71
N838K	90	LJ-410
N838MA	MU-2	678
N838PE	PC12	838
N838RA	TBM7	71
N838SA	KODK	0002
N839AB	31T	8104011
(N839CH)	31T	8104011
N839K	90	LJ-297
N839KA	MIII	T-297
N839MA	MU-2	679
N840AA	690C	11610
N840AA	690C	11697
N840AC	690C	11614
N840AS	690C	11683
N840BC	690C	11663
N840BC	690C	11685
N840BM	690C	11683
N840CC	690C	11658
N840CF	690C	11624
N840CL	690C	11653
(N840CM)	31T	7720024
N840CM	690C	11601
N840CP	200	BB-1658
N840CR	690C	11654
N840DA	690C	11731
N840DC	690C	11661
N840DW	690C	11687
N840EA	690C	11607
(N840EE)	690C	11727
N840FK	690C	11658
N840G	690C	11683
N840GB	690C	11601
N840GH	690C	11615
(N840GR)	200C	BL-142
N840JC	690C	11643
N840JK	690C	11697
N840JP	690C	11601
(N840JP)	690C	11651
N840JW	690C	11658
N840KB	690C	11640
N840LC	690C	11617
N840LE	690C	11709
N840MA	MU-2	612
N840MA	MU-2	680
N840MD	690C	11693
N840MG	690C	11638
N840NB	690C	11663
N840NK	690C	11734
N840PE	PC12	840
N840PH	690C	11649
N840PN	690C	11679
N840PS	690C	11672
N840R	690C	11602
N840RC	200	BB-840
N840RC	690C	11600
N840SA	690C	11607
N840SB	F90	LA-202

N840SE	690C	11610
N840SF	690C	11638
N840SM	690C	11700
N840SW	90	LJ-630
N840TC	690C	11661
N840TC	690C	11688
N840TW	690C	11689
N840U	200	BB-1927
N840V	690C	11727
N840VB	690C	11640
N840VB	690C	11679
N840VM	690C	11607
(N840WZ)	690C	11660
N840XL	690C	11624
(N841BA)	200	BB-15
*N841DE	300C	FM-5
N841K	200	BB-841
N841K	90	LJ-477
(N841MA)	MIIB	T26-167E
N841MA	MIII	T-332
N841MA	MU-2	681
N841SC	MU-2	681
N841TB	90	LJ-1841
N841TF	200	BB-1257
N841TT	200	BB-1257
N842DS	100	B-244
N842KA	90	LJ-1842
N842LC	MU-2	286
N842MA	MU-2	682
N842MA	TBM8	424
(N842PC)	PA42	8001085
N842PC	PA42	8301001
N843BC	200	BB-1011
N843BH	TBM7	196
N843CK	200	BB-1189
N843CP	90	LJ-843
N843FC	200	BB-1030
N843G	200	BB-843
N843K	90	LJ-459
N843KA	90	LJ-1843
N843MA	MU-2	683
N843MC	90	LJ-843
N843RM	90	LJ-1877
N844C	90	LJ-866
(N844CH)	90	LJ-1420
N844GT	PC12	825
N844MA	690C	11669
N844MA	MU-2	684
(N844MC)	PA42	5527007
N844MP	200	BB-1168
N844MS	46T	97168
N844N	200	BB-68
N844S	TBM7	46
N844SC	690C	11701
N844TS	350	FL-33
N844TS	F90	LA-107
(N845BE)	200	BB-1200
N845JB	G1	87
N845K	90	LJ-319
N845KA	90	LJ-1845
N845MA	MU-2	685
N845MC	E90	LW-283
N845TC	200	BB-1560
N846BB	MIIB	T26-149E
N846BE	300	FA-16
N846CM	200	BB-18
*N846DJ	300C	FM-7
N846K	100	B-37
N846KA	90	LJ-1846
N846MA	MU-2	686
N846MW	200	BB-846
N846PW	PC12	846
N846RD	46T	97186
N846Y	441	0218
N846YT	350	FL-617
N846YT	441	0218
N847	690A	11140
N847BA	200	BB-847
N847CE	680W	1834-39
N847CE	690A	11223
N847D	B100	BE-91
N847K	90	LJ-480
N847MA	MU-2	687
N847MA	TBM8	434
N847TS	200	BB-864
N847YT	425	0114
N848CE	690A	11303
N848J	200	BB-929
N848K	90	LJ-303
N848LM	MU-2	688
N848MA	BN2	2210
N848MA	MU-2	688
N848NA	200	BB-848
N848PC	PA42	5527013
N848PC	PC12	848
N848PF	200	BB-1225
N849AM	PA42	8001009
(N849B)	PC6	931
*N849BM	200	BB-849
N849KM	31T	8004055
N849MA	MU-2	689
N849MA	TBM8	412
N850AA	TBM8	399
N850AB	TBM8	381
N850AC	TBM8	426
N850AD	TBM8	444
N850AG	TBM8	414
N850AP	TBM8	379
N850AR	TBM8	386
N850AT	200	BB-989
N850AZ	TBM8	348
N850AZ	TBM8	384
N850BD	TBM8	446
N850BE	90	LJ-1095
N850BG	TBM8	367
N850BK	200	BB-896
*N850BL	TBM8	420
N850BN	TBM8	517
N850BQ	TBM8	420
N850BT	TBM8	433
N850BU	TBM8	508
N850BZ	TBM8	427
N850C	200	BB-710
N850CA	MU-2	1544SA
N850CA	TBM8	367
N850CB	PC12	850
N850CD	TBM8	504
N850CE	90	LJ-1095
N850CW	TBM8	376
N850D	350	FL-70
N850DB	100	B-53
N850DB	TBM8	432
N850DD	TBM8	370
*N850DK	TBM8	496
N850DL	TBM8	354
N850DP	TBM8	423
N850DV	EPIC	031
N850DX	TBM8	484
N850EA	TBM8	501
N850ED	TBM8	473
N850EE	TBM8	409
N850FA	TBM8	471
N850FC	TBM8	490
N850GA	690C	11641
N850GC	TBM8	441
N850GG	TBM8	479
(N850GM)	425	0177
N850GM	425	0224
N850GS	TBM8	359
N850GX	TBM8	435
N850H	P68	256
N850HM	TBM8	355
N850JA	BN2	74
N850JB	TBM8	365
N850JD	TBM8	362
N850JD	TBM8	523
N850JE	TBM8	492
N850JM	TBM8	375
N850JR	TBM8	348
N850JS	TBM8	436
N850JT	TBM8	362
N850KK	TBM8	413
N850KL	TBM8	398
N850KM	TBM8	407
N850KP	TBM8	476
N850L	TBM8	347
N850LA	TBM8	369
N850LD	TBM8	417
N850LE	TBM8	511
N850LH	TBM8	374
N850LK	TBM8	437
N850LL	TBM8	350
N850LR	TBM8	488
N850LW	TBM8	403
N850MA	MU-2	690
N850MA	TBM8	350
N850MB	TBM8	454
N850MD	TBM8	401
N850MF	TBM8	459
N850MK	TBM8	403
N850MS	350	FL-99
N850MT	TBM8	489
N850MV	TBM8	518
N850MW	TBM8	408
N850MY	TBM8	478
N850NW	TBM8	450
N850NW	TBM8	496
N850NY	350	FL-283
N850PB	TBM8	473
N850PC	TBM8	457
N850PD	TBM8	485
N850PL	TBM8	388
N850PT	TBM8	506
N850PW	TBM8	390
N850Q	MU-2	103
N850RB	TBM8	395
N850RB	TBM8	524
N850RT	TBM8	520
N850SB	TBM8	357
N850SC	TBM8	361
N850SC	TBM8	481
N850SD	TBM8	498
N850SF	TBM8	495
N850SJ	350	FL-112
(N850SJ)	TBM8	416
N850SJ	TBM8	447
N850SL	TBM8	358
N850TB	TBM8	346
N850TD	TBM8	461
N850TG	TBM8	361
N850TG	TBM8	449
(N850TL)	TBM8	361
N850TM	TBM8	388
(N850TR)	350	FL-67
N850TT	TBM8	470
N850TV	TBM8	513
N850TX	TBM8	357
N850TX	TBM8	468
N850U	TBM8	380
N850VM	TBM8	507
*N850VT	TBM8	389
(N850WC)	TBM8	426
N850WC	TBM8	426
(N850WC)	TBM8	514
N850WC	TBM8	522
N850WE	TBM8	411
(N850WM)	TBM8	352
N850WM	TBM8	353
N850WT	TBM8	430
N850WW	TBM8	505
N850WZ	TBM8	372
N850XS	TBM8	352
(N850XX)	TBM8	356
N850ZM	TBM8	493
N850ZZ	TBM8	510
N851AF	PC12	851
N851BC	MIVC	AT-495B
N851CM	90	LJ-1731
N851EM	C-12	BC-15
N851GA	90	LJ-1278
N851GC	TBM8	442
N851HB	90	LJ-1851
N851JA	BN2	11
N851JA	BN2	71
N851JA	BN2	913
N851JP	200	BB-851
N851K	90	LJ-475
N851KA	90	LJ-851
N851LC	46T	97201
N851MA	MU-2	691
N851MA	TBM8	392
N851MK	200	BB-674
N851MK	90	LJ-561
N851Q	MU-2	104
N851RM	PC12	360
N851SB	TBM8	497
N851SH	TBM8	438
N851TB	TBM8	373
N851TC	350	FL-510
N851WA	TBM8	394
N852AC	MIIB	T26-117
N852AL	PC12	213
(N852BE)	300	FA-42
N852FR	PC12	852
N852HB	90	LJ-1852
N852JA	BN2	72
N852JP	200	BB-516
N852K	90	LJ-492
N852MA	MU-2	692
N852Q	MU-2	105
N852W	PC12	1060
N853AL	PC12	168
N853CP	690	11061
N853GA	200T	BT-7
N853JA	BN2	77
N853K	90	LJ-282
N853MA	MU-2	693SA
N853MA	MU-2	710SA
N853MA	TBM8	371
N853Q	MU-2	106
N853WM	PC12	853
N854AL	PC12	397
N854JA	BN2	80
N854K	90	LJ-538
N854MA	MU-2	694
N854MA	TBM8	368
N854Q	MU-2	107
N855GA	PA42	8001030
N855JA	BN2	87
N855JL	31T	8104045
N855K	90	LJ-457
N855KC	PC12	726
N855MA	690A	11299
N855MA	MU-2	695
N855MA	TBM8	402
N855Q	MU-2	108
N855RA	300	FA-106
N855RM	31T	8004033
N856BC	BN2	2171
N856GA	300	FA-25
N856H	P68	256
N856JA	BN2	108
N856JC	MU-2	430SA
N856JT	MU-2	306
N856K	100	B-65
N856M	46D	19
N856MA	690A	11299
N856MA	MU-2	696
N856P	90	LJ-1877
N856PC	PC12	856
N856Q	MU-2	109
N856Q	MU-2	119
N856TC	200	BB-1281
N857C	425	0156
N857EP	200	BB-1251
N857GA	200T	BT-11
N857H	G1	88
N857JA	BN2	92
N857MA	MU-2	697SA
N857Q	MU-2	110
N857WC	TBM8	494
N858AC	441	0321
N858B	100	B-81
N858GA	200T	BT-8
N858JA	BN2	115
N858K	90	LJ-184
N858MA	MU-2	698SA
N858Q	MU-2	111
N858TM	200	BB-688
N859CA	TBM8	509
N859CC	200	BB-389
N859DD	200	BB-859
N859GA	200T	BT-12
(N859JA)	BN2	121
N859JA	BN2	178
N859LB	E90	LW-124

N859LP	E90	LW-124
N859MA	MU-2	699SA
N859MB	E90	LW-124
N859PL	PC12	859
N859Q	MU-2	113
N860CC	300	FA-147
N860E	G1	144
N860H	200	BB-1067
N860K	90	LJ-122
N860MA	MU-2	700SA
N860MH	200	BB-1087
N860MH	E90	LW-210
N860Q	MU-2	114
N860SM	MU-2	415SA
N861CC	350	FL-94
N861CG	MIII	TT-518A
N861E	MU-2	674
N861FT	F406	0034
N861H	G1	147
N861JA	BN2	103
N861JA	BN2	2155
N861K	90	LJ-471
N861MA	MU-2	701SA
N861PP	PC12	510
N861Q	MU-2	115
N861VL	BN2	2155
N862CC	90	LJ-1499
N862DD	200	BB-298
(N862JA)	BN2	123
(N862JA)	BN2	135
N862JA	BN2	184
(N862JC)	200	BB-345
N862K	100	B-69
N862MA	MU-2	702SA
N862Q	MU-2	116
N862RA	31T	8104048
N863JA	BN2	59
(N863JA)	BN2	130
N863MA	MU-2	703SA
N863Q	MU-2	117
N863RB	46T	97213
N864DM	TBM8	386
(N864JA)	BN2	137
N864JA	BN2	175
N864MA	MU-2	704SA
N864Q	MU-2	118
N865HR	200	BB-276
(N865JA)	BN2	139
N865JA	BN2	176
N865LR	350	FL-471
N865LS	350	FL-471
N865M	200	BB-448
N865M	300	FA-34
N865M	90	LJ-501
N865MA	90	LJ-501
N865MA	MU-2	705SA
N865PT	200	BB-1709
N865W	200	BB-448
N866A	90	LJ-201
N866D	MU-2	656
N866JA	BN2	185
N866K	90	LJ-76
N866MA	MU-2	706SA
N866PE	PC12	866
N866Q	MU-2	121
N866RA	31T	7920020
N867JA	BN2	186
N867K	90	LJ-211
N867MA	F90	LA-65
N867MA	MU-2	707SA
N867P	90	LJ-1666
N867PP	PC12	867
N867Q	MU-2	122
N868AT	TBM7	232
N868C	P68	214
N868HC	200	BB-1088
N868K	90	LJ-267
N868MA	MU-2	708SA
N868PE	PC12	868
N868Q	MU-2	123
N868SC	P68	214
N869	200	BB-174
N869AF	PC12	869
N869AM	200	BB-625

N869D	90	LJ-362
N869D	MU-2	540
N869JA	BN2	120
N869K	90	LJ-416
N869MA	200	BB-170
N869MA	MU-2	709SA
N869P	MU-2	540
N869P	MU-2	692
N869Q	MU-2	156
N869TW	PC12	1004
N869U	90	LJ-362
N870B	90	LJ-557
(N870BB)	E90	LW-120
N870C	46T	97159
N870CA	200C	BL-65
N870D	90	LJ-557
(N870JA)	BN2	81
N870JA	BN2	187
N870K	90	LJ-183
N870KC	PC12	870
N870MA	100	B-109
N870MA	MU-2	710SA
N870Q	MU-2	157
(N870WE)	31T	8020003
N871C	200	BB-1735
(N871GM)	PC12	162
N871JA	BN2	90
N871K	100	B-27
N871KS	90	LJ-1277
N871MA	MU-2	711SA
N871Q	MU-2	158
N871RC	300	FA-172
N871RC	F90	LA-89
N871UB	200	BB-841
N872BA	200	BB-872
N872CA	200	BB-1114
N872CT	350	FL-555
N872D	MIIB	T26-123
N872Q	MU-2	159
N872S	MIIB	T26-123
N873AF	200	BB-1200
N873CA	300	FA-79
N873DB	200	BB-315
N873K	90	LJ-344
N873MA	MU-2	712SA
N873PC	PC12	873
N873Q	MU-2	160
N874AF	PC12	874
N874CA	TBM8	360
N874MA	MU-2	713SA
N874Q	MU-2	161
N874RJ	TBM7	87
N875DA	F90	LA-25
N875DM	200	BB-1354
N875EC	200	BB-1300
N875K	100	B-90
N875K	100	B-115
N875K	100	B-140
N875K	100	B-168
N875Q	MU-2	162
N875RJ	PC12	646
N875SH	46T	97174
N876K	90	LJ-277
N876L	90	LJ-342
N876MA	MU-2	714SA
N876MC	690A	11137
N876NA	90	LJ-876
N876Q	MU-2	163
N877AF	PC12	877
N877AG	90	LJ-41
N877AJ	200	BB-877
N877AQ	90	LJ-41
N877GF	200	BB-978
N877JE	200	BB-1203
N877JV	441	0176
N877K	90	LJ-321
N877PC	TBM7	11
N877Q	MU-2	164
N877RC	200	BB-978
N877RF	200	BB-978
N877SA	350	FL-296
N877V	350	FL-68
N877W	200	BB-1269
N877W	350	FL-68

N877W	350	FL-203
N877W	90	LJ-807
N877W	F90	LA-174
N877WA	200	BB-1269
N877WA	350	FL-203
N877WL	90	LJ-807
N878GT	200G	BY-58
N878JL	441	0293
N878K	90	LJ-496
N878K	90	LJ-1513
N878MA	MU-2	659
N878MS	690B	11435
N878Q	MU-2	165
N878RA	200	BB-34
N878SC	MIIB	T26-113
N878T	90	LJ-246
(N878VP)	PA42	8001069
N879AF	PC12	879
N879C	200	BB-1249
N879K	100	B-53
N879MA	MU-2	271
N879PC	F90	LA-120
N879Q	MU-2	015
N879Q	MU-2	166
(N879RS)	MU-2	351SA
N879SW	31T	7904056
N880AC	MU-2	1559SA
N880CA	31T	8120001
N880EA	425	0080
N880H	90	LJ-596
N880K	90	LJ-54
N880M	90	LJ-520
N880MA	MU-2	600
N880MB	200	BB-928
N880SW	31T	8020086
N880TC	PA42	8001071
(N880TR)	PC12	270
(N880WW)	31T	8104055
N880X	90	LJ-343
N881AM	PA42	8001081
(N881AR)	300	FA-191
N881BH	MU-2	429SA
N881CA	TBM8	526
N881CD	441	0221
N881CS	200	BB-881
N881DB	46D	24
N881DP	MU-2	516
N881DT	MU-2	643
N881GB	441	0221
N881JP	425	0139
N881JT	90	LJ-1287
N881K	90	LJ-502
N881L	31T	7920090
N881LT	90	LJ-490
N881M	90	LJ-186
N881M	90	LJ-490
N881MA	MU-2	616
N881MC	200	BB-1930
N881MX	90	LJ-490
N881NA	31T	7820081
N881SW	31T	8104033
N882AC	690B	11375
N882CA	350	FL-33
N882GS	690	11035
N882JP	200	BB-882
N882K	90	LJ-476
N882MA	MU-2	534
N882Q	MU-2	168
N882SW	PA42	8001080
N883AC	E90	LW-124
N883AV	90	LJ-528
N883BB	200	BB-883
N883CA	100	B-149
N883CA	TBM7	83
N883CA	TBM7	294
N883CR	TBM7	83
N883GB	350	FL-520
N883K	100	B-33
N883P	350	FL-508
N883PC	PC12	883
N883Q	MU-2	169
N883SW	200	BB-1458
(N883TC)	PA42	8001063
N884CA	200	BB-219

N884CA	31T	7820011
N884D	690C	11696
N884EA	90	LJ-1824
N884K	90	LJ-494
N884PC	PC12	884
N884PG	200	BB-91
N884Q	MU-2	170
(N884VP)	200	BB-1380
N885CA	TBM8	363
N885DS	46T	97290
N885HT	200	BB-446
N885K	90	LJ-116A
N885Q	MU-2	172
N885RA	690	11012
N885ST	200	BB-1148
N885W	90	LJ-419
N886AC	350	FL-284
N886AT	90	LJ-1485
N886AW	300	FA-110
(N886AY)	300	FA-110
N886BC	441	0306
N886BD	90	LJ-331
N886CA	300	FA-165
(N886DT)	300	FA-102
N886J	90	LJ-513
N886K	90	LJ-505
N886MS	300	FA-131
N886PC	PC12	886
N886T	90	LJ-300
N887CF	90	LJ-887
N887FB	200	BB-1311
N887JC	200	BB-1345
N887JD	46D	217
N887JT	441	0054
N887K	90	LJ-357
N887KU	90	LJ-357
N887MA	BN2	2211
N887PE	100	B-49
N887PL	100	B-49
N887Q	MU-2	173
N887T	200	BB-1233
N887TC	TBM7	306
N887WF	441	0053
N888AH	31T	7904038
N888AS	300	FA-136
N888AY	MIII	TT-489A
N888B	200	BB-267
N888BH	E90	LW-3
N888BK	90	LJ-727
N888BR	300	FA-19
N888CD	46D	24
N888CD	MU-2	326
N888CF	441	0074
N888CG	PC12	127
N888CS	200	BB-1311
N888CV	31T	7820025
N888DC	200	BB-454
N888DD	680T	1679-61
N888DE	200	BB-106
N888DR	90	LJ-644
N888DS	MU-2	159
(N888EE)	200	BB-624
N888EM	200	BB-240
N888EM	F90	LA-38
N888ET	200	BB-258
N888EX	200	BB-240
N888FC	200	BB-1178
N888FL	441	0332
N888FM	200	BB-1682
N888FM	350	FL-418
N888FS	MU-2	558
N888FS	MU-2	1507SA
N888FV	200	BB-1682
N888FW	PA42	5501011
N888GD	90	LJ-1713
N888GN	90	LJ-667
N888HG	200	BB-891
N888HT	200	BB-444
(N888JH)	PA42	8001065
N888JM	31T	7720066
N888JS	425	0215
(N888KN)	690	11029
N888KN	690C	11735
N888L	MU-2	027

N888LB	31T	8120035
N888LF	TBM8	445
N888LG	31T	8120035
N888MA	90	LJ-656
N888MA	MU-2	550
(N888MW)	90	LJ-644
N888NT	695	95081
N888PB	690A	11272
N888PH	31T	7904005
N888PH	MU-2	731SA
N888PR	G1	42
N888PT	31T	8166012
N888R	690A	11272
N888R	MIII	T-321
N888RA	TBM7	71
N888RE	F90	LA-89
N888RF	MU-2	346
N888RH	MU-2	725SA
N888RH	MU-2	731SA
N888RH	MU-2	737SA
N888RJ	MU-2	542
N888RK	B100	BE-29
N888RK	B100	BE-134
N888RT	E90	LW-344
N888SE	MU-2	1549SA
N888SF	695	95023
N888SK	PC12	1015
N888SL	690B	11552
N888SV	31T	7820025
N888TB	100	B-171
N888TB	690B	11367
N888TF	TBM7	178
(N888TP)	425	0201
N888TP	MU-2	1541SA
N888TR	200	BB-50
N888VG	200	BB-39
N888WG	PC12	587
N888WW	MU-2	791SA
N888YB	MU-2	1539SA
N888ZC	200	BB-1844
N888ZT	E90	LW-315
N888ZX	200	BB-1140
N889DH	PC12	298
N889DM	441	0022
N889K	90	LJ-189
N889MA	MU-2	718SA
N889Q	MU-2	174
N890CA	F90	LA-113
N890E	200	BB-65
N890GA	F90	LA-113
N890GT	90	LJ-1879
N890HB	90	LJ-1935
N890HB	90	LJ-1944
N890K	90	LJ-114
N890LG	90	LJ-1854
N890MA	MU-2	719SA
N890MC	200	BB-388
N890Q	MU-2	175
N890WA	31T	8120020
N891AA	90	LJ-1221
N891CR	46T	97321
N891K	90	LJ-333
N891MA	200	BB-238
N891MA	MU-2	720SA
N891PC	E90	LW-40
N891Q	MU-2	177
(N891WA)	690A	11260
N892CA	TBM8	408
N892MA	MU-2	721SA
N892Q	MU-2	178
N892SC	MU-2	392SA
(N892WA)	690A	11273
N892WA	690A	11273
N893CA	TBM8	393
N893CF	350	FL-165
N893KB	MU-2	415SA
N893MC	350	FL-216
N893SC	MU-2	321SA
N893WB	PC12	714
N894EA	TBM8	416
N894FL	441	0314
N894K	100	B-85
N894MA	MU-2	722SA
N895CA	350	FL-114
N895FK	90	LJ-759
N895K	90	LJ-25
N895MA	MU-2	723SA
N895TT	200	BB-1239
N896CM	200	BB-668
N896DR	100	B-160
N896DR	31T	8004050
N896K	90	LJ-451
N896MA	MU-2	724SA
N896P	90	LJ-1755
N896PM	46D	150
N896RJ	300	FA-90
N896SB	100	B-160
N897AW	680T	1710-85
N897BM	200	BB-1897
N897CA	TBM8	377
N897K	90	LJ-554
N897MA	MU-2	725SA
N898CA	200	BB-572
N898CA	TBM8	515
N898CD	350	FL-556
N898CM	90	LJ-898
N898F	90	LJ-529
N898K	90	LJ-198
N898MA	MU-2	726SA
N898MC	350	FL-216
N898RJ	300	FA-90
N898SR	100	B-125
N898ST	100	B-125
N898WW	E90	LW-103
N899D	90	LJ-386
(N899EA)	300	FA-87
N899GP	E90	LW-184
N899HC	200	BB-1057
N899HC	200	BB-1374
N899K	100	B-52
N899K	90	LJ-115
N899MA	MU-2	727SA
N899MC	200	BB-998
N899PC	TRIS	1066
N899RW	200	BB-1637
N899SD	200	BB-776
N899TB	200	BB-387
N900	G1	323
N900AB	690D	15013
N900AC	E90	LW-282
N900AK	MIII	TT-424
N900BE	690D	15010
N900BE	90	LJ-907
(N900BK)	F90	LA-104
N900BP	90	LJ-61
N900BR	90	LJ-491
N900BT	90	LJ-1285
N900CA	90	LJ-250
(N900CD)	690D	15005
N900CF	90	LJ-85
N900CK	90	LJ-85
N900CM	31T	7920026
N900CP	200	BB-17
(N900CP)	200	BB-354
N900CP	200	BB-403
N900CP	690D	15016
N900CV	200	BB-17
N900DG	200	BB-455
N900DG	90	LJ-618
*N900DG	TBM7	225
N900DH	100	B-170
N900DJ	690D	15034
N900DN	100	B-170
N900DR	STAR	NC-9
N900DS	690A	11307
N900DS	690D	15035
N900DZ	90	LJ-618
N900EC	695A	96050
N900ED	200	BB-1109
N900EE	MU-2	679
N900ET	690D	15037
N900EZ	695A	96074
N900FD	200	BB-1109
(N900FP)	90	LJ-325
N900FS	MIII	T-325
N900FT	690A	11344
N900GB	300	FA-133
N900GD	BN2	12
N900HA	441	0027
N900HC	690D	15030
N900HM	F90	LA-119
N900HS	PC12	136
N900HV	690D	15032
(N900JA)	90	LJ-404
N900JL	G1	28
N900JM	31T	7820039
N900JP	690B	11457
N900JP	695A	96040
N900JT	441	0011
(N900KW)	90	LJ-1475
N900LC	695	95020
N900LD	90	LJ-325
N900LE	90	LJ-1065
N900LL	690C	11687
N900LS	90	LJ-438
N900M	MU-2	192
N900M	MU-2	650
N900M	MU-2	1509SA
N900M	MU-2	1545SA
N900MA	690D	15002
N900MA	MU-2	728SA
N900MB	200	BB-620
N900MH	E90	LW-187
N900MP	PA42	5501014
N900MS	425	0079
N900MT	90	LJ-1048
N900NE	690D	15008
N900PA	G1	155
N900PL	350	FL-462
N900PM	G1	155
N900PS	441	0129
N900R	690B	11457
N900RB	300	FA-192
N900RB	31T	7904039
N900RB	EPIC	009
N900RC	BN2	12
N900RD	B100	BE-33
N900RF	C-12	BC-75
N900RH	200	BB-816
N900RH	690D	15003
N900RJ	680T	1572-27
N900SC	90	LJ-712
N900SC	90	LJ-758
N900SF	31T	7720067
N900SR	690D	15027
N900TA	MIII	T-308
N900TA	MIVC	AT-469
N900TA	TRIS	1025
N900TB	31T	7620009
N900TB	90	LJ-532
N900TJ	90	LJ-907
N900TJ	B100	BE-5
N900TN	690D	15021
"N900TT"	G1	323
N900TV	MU-2	140
N900TX	MIII	T-308
N900VA	90	LJ-1002
N900VG	200	BB-324
N900VM	200G	BY-54
N900W	90	LJ-150
N900WC	90	LJ-907
(N900WM)	90	LJ-158
N900WP	350	FL-496
N900WS	350	FL-498
N900YH	MU-2	584
N901AJ	90	LJ-829
N901AS	695A	96083
(N901AS)	90	LJ-222
(N901AT)	100	B-18
N901BF	MU-2	1505SA
N901BK	90	LJ-521
(N901BR)	200	BB-65
N901CC	31T	7920009
(N901CC)	425	0091
N901CC	441	0322
N901DM	46T	97051
N901EB	200	BB-1015
N901FD	425	0145
N901G	G1	30
N901GD	BN2	855
N901GS	F90	LA-235
N901JA	90	LJ-694
N901JB	90	LJ-1030
N901JS	90	LJ-1726
N901MA	46D	112
N901MC	MIII	T-369
N901MT	PA42	5527011
N901NB	F90	LA-51
N901PC	90	LJ-1505
N901PS	F90	LA-5
N901R	90	LJ-153
N901SA	90	LJ-66
N901SA	F90	LA-208
N901SF	200	BB-1859
N901TA	TRIS	1003
N901TC	90	LJ-173
N901TE	690D	15031
N901TM	E90	LW-227
N901TP	P68T	9001
N901TR	PC12	602
N901TS	90	LJ-1458
N901UC	90	LJ-173
N901VL	TRIS	1003
N901W	90	LJ-72
N901WL	90	LJ-410
N901WP	F90	LA-51
(N901XP)	90	LJ-1136
*N902AC	200	BB-596
N902CE	350	FL-572
N902DB	90	LJ-1202
N902DP	425	0225
N902GD	BN2	592
N902GD	BN2	905
N902JL	G1	130
N902LT	90	LJ-1480
N902M	MU-2	701SA
N902M	MU-2	1522SA
N902PL	90	LJ-1583
N902SH	200G	BY-69
N902ST	P750	153
N902TA	TRIS	1039
N902TP	P68T	9002
N902TS	90	LJ-1459
N902VL	BN2	685
N902VL	BN2	2128
(N902VL)	TRIS	1012
N902W	90	LJ-75
N902WW	90	LJ-327
N902XP	90	LJ-1136
N903BC	MU-2	726SA
N903DC	441	0061
N903GD	BN2	625
N903GD	TRIS	1025
N903GP	90	LJ-861
N903HC	E90	LW-155
N903K	90	LJ-169
N903L	695	95026
N903M	350	FL-26
N903M	MU-2	796SA
(N903MA)	TBM7	303
N903MA	TBM7	308
N903MD	U-21	LM-98
N903P	90	LJ-1344
N903SE	90	LJ-1403
N903TP	P68T	9003
N903TS	90	LJ-1601
N903TT	90	LJ-1910
N903VL	BN2	2019
(N903VL)	TRIS	1044
N903WD	441	0010
N904BM	46D	66
N904CM	200	BB-229
N904DG	200	BB-1176
N904DJ	90	LJ-561
N904DK	90	LJ-1089
N904GD	BN2	2128
N904GD	TRIS	1003
(N904GM)	90	LJ-1665
N904GT	90	LJ-1946
N904HB	90	LJ-1256
N904JG	90	LJ-1764
N904JP	90	LJ-1121
N904JS	90	LJ-856
N904K	90	LJ-274
N904MA	MU-2	729SA
N904MC	350	FL-44

N904P	90	LJ-1181
N904PA	90	LJ-1792
N904RB	90	LJ-1088
N904RM	425	0221
N904TD	90	LJ-1172
N904TH	90	LJ-1172
N904TH	90	LJ-1680
N904TM	46D	66
N904TP	P68T	9004
N904US	90	LJ-856
N904VL	BN2	3014
(N904VL)	TRIS	1047
N904W	90	LJ-1903
N904WA	BN2	904
N905B	PC12	414
(N905BL)	695	95002
N905DR	90	LJ-1236
N905GD	BN2	339
N905GD	TRIS	1048
N905GP	200	BB-789
N905GP	90	LJ-861
N905K	90	LJ-275
N905LC	PA42	5501010
N905LC	PA42	5501022
N905MA	MU-2	730SA
N905P	MIII	T-220
N905RK	MIII	T-220
N905TF	E90	LW-6
N905VL	TRIS	1048
(N906BB)	E90	LW-17
N906EA	300	FA-177
N906F	G1	146
N906GD	BN2	3008
N906GD	TRIS	1060
N906GP	90	LJ-660
N906HF	U-21	LM-140
N906RS	90	LJ-668
N906TS	90	LJ-1604
N906VL	TRIS	1060
N907AW	PC6	907
N907DB	300	FA-85
N907G	200	BB-905
N907GD	BN2	340
N907K	90	LJ-413
N907M	MU-2	192
N907MA	MU-2	731SA
N907VL	BN2	2192
N908BS	200	BB-1781
N908CM	E90	LW-233
N908EF	90	LJ-1888
N908G	90	LJ-958
N908GD	BN2	2040
N908GR	90	LJ-861
N908K	90	LJ-504
N908LN	G1	167
N908PL	PC6	908
N908R	200	BB-109
N908RC	200	BB-490
N908ST	200	BB-1286
N908TN	690D	15021
N909BJ	PC12	694
N909DD	200	BB-1695
N909EA	90	LJ-1909
N909GA	90	LJ-1160
N909GD	BN2	239
N909GT	200G	BY-9
N909HC	90	LJ-643
N909HH	690D	15035
N909J	200	BB-1579
N909K	90	LJ-311
N909K	F90	LA-13
N909MA	MU-2	732SA
N909P	46T	97187
(N909PP)	PC12	697
N909PW	31T	7720060
N909RA	200	BB-1909
N909RB	46D	85
N909ST	200	BB-1286
N910AJ	200	BB-910
N910BD	350	FL-483
N910BS	G1	128
N910CA	200	BB-229
N910DA	MU-2	379SA
N910DA	MU-2	1515SA
N910E	90	LJ-438
N910EA	441	0070
N910EB	200	BB-808
N910EC	690C	11682
N910FC	690C	11682
*N910GD	BN2	341
N910HG	31T	7400009
N910HM	31T	7400009
N910HM	31T	8304002
(N910HM)	31T	8166026
N910JP	31T	7820004
N910JS	F90	LA-48
N910KG	200	BB-1051
N910MA	MU-2	733SA
N910MC	EPIC	020
N910NF	MU-2	623
N910P	200	BB-212
N911AC	690B	11373
N911AE	690D	15037
N911AZ	E90	LW-300
N911BB	690C	11606
N911BB	690D	15002
N911BP	690C	11606
N911CB	100	B-165
N911CE	100	B-165
N911CF	F90	LA-13
N911CM	200	BB-820
N911CX	90	LJ-830
(N911DR)	90	LJ-830
N911ER	441	0249
N911FG	90	LJ-774
N911FN	90	LJ-688
N911JE	MU-2	719SA
N911JJ	MU-2	719SA
N911JM	681B	6048
N911JW	690B	11537
N911JZ	MIII	T-366
N911KA	90	LJ-254
N911LR	200	BB-123
N911MM	E90	LW-345
N911MN	200	BB-229
N911MN	200	BB-1598
N911ND	200	BB-589
N911ND	200	BB-1551
N911ND	90	LJ-774
N911NG	PC12	1011
N911PJ	441	0146
N911RB	300	FA-217
N911RD	425	0086
N911RL	100	B-55
N911RX	200	BB-1425
(N911RX)	690A	11243
N911SF	200	BB-1659
N911SR	200	BB-898
N911TC	46T	97238
N911UM	90	LJ-769
N911VJ	PA42	7800002
N911WC	200	BB-45
(N912AZ)	E90	LW-300
N912BH	90	LJ-936
(N912DM)	MU-2	340
N912JS	200	BB-1845
N912JS	200G	BY-49
N912JZ	200	BB-1845
N912K	100	B-12
N912LD	200	BB-912
N912MA	MU-2	734SA
N912MF	200	BB-532
N912NF	MU-2	623
N912NM	PC12	169
N912RP	PC12	303
N912SM	200	BB-478
(N912SM)	90	LJ-685
N912SV	200	BB-1299
N912YW	200	BB-1384
N913AF	PC12	1013
N913AL	PC12	266
N913BS	G1	126
N913CR	31T	7804003
N913DC	441	0246
N913DG	441	0246
N913DM	MIIB	T26-144
N913K	90	LJ-513
N913MA	MU-2	735SA
N913PG	200	BB-1118
N913PS	G1	126
N913RM	690D	15031
N913RM	90	LJ-125
N913VS	E90	LW-200
N913YW	200	BB-1383
N914AS	31T	8104066
N914BH	300	FA-21
N914BS	G1	134
N914CE	200	BB-1351
N914CR	31T	8104007
N914CT	200	BB-1243
N914CT	200	BB-1351
N914CT	200	BB-1614
N914D	E90	LW-138
N914JA	300	FA-191
N914JF	300	FA-191
N914K	90	LJ-345
N914MA	MU-2	736SA
N914P	G1	143
N914TT	90	LJ-914
N914YW	200	BB-1376
N915BD	100	B-18
N915BD	90	LJ-258
N915CD	90	LJ-748
N915MA	MU-2	737SA
N915MC	46D	43
N915MK	350	FL-162
N915MP	90	LJ-1637
N915MR	90	LJ-1637
N915RF	MU-2	677
N915TL	200	BB-1695
N915WA	90	LJ-1915
N915YW	200	BB-1338
N916AD	PC12	756
N916AS	441	0243
N916CM	PA42	5501014
N916HC	200	BB-916
N916K	100	B-86
N916MA	MU-2	738SA
N916MP	200	BB-63
N916PA	E90	LW-313
N916RT	31T	8166041
N916SJ	441	0243
N917BA	F90	LA-210
N917BB	200	BB-860
N917BE	200	BB-1082
N917BH	300	FA-30
N917BH	300	FA-90
N917BH	90	LJ-936
N917BH	90	LJ-1123
N917BH	F90	LA-210
N917BT	200	BB-225
N917CB	200	BB-1871
N917CC	46T	97259
N917CT	200	BB-1871
N917CT	350	FL-56
N917F	31T	8104030
(N917GP)	200	BB-772
N917J	P68	394
N917K	100	B-83
N917K	90	LJ-654
N917MA	MU-2	739SA
N917NG	PC12	1017
N917RG	680T	1576-30
N917TP	31T	8104068
N917WA	300	FA-77
N917WP	690A	11191
N918CK	425	0179
N918FE	441	0031
N918FM	31T	7904025
N918JN	200	BB-596
N918K	90	LJ-498
N918MA	MU-2	740SA
N918NG	PC12	1108
N918SA	90	LJ-918
N918TC	200	BB-918
N918VS	E90	LW-200
N919AG	90	LJ-432
N919CK	MIVC	AT-585
N919CL	90	LJ-1160
N919GT	90	LJ-376
N919HP	300	FA-81
N919JP	100	B-202
N919K	90	LJ-332
(N919LN)	200	BB-570
N919MA	MU-2	741SA
N919MA	PC6	919
(N919MD)	690	11025
N919RD	31T	8104037
N919RE	200	BB-824
N919SA	90	LJ-1495
N919SF	46D	11
N919WM	100	B-154
N919WM	200	BB-680
N920AA	P68	198
N920AU	690A	11109
N920BS	G1	134
N920C	200	BB-565
N920C	300	FA-54
N920C	441	0020
N920D	MIIB	T26-144
N920DY	200	BB-255
N920DY	MIIB	T26-144
N920K	90	LJ-260
N920K	90	LJ-375
N920MA	MU-2	742SA
N920P	90	LJ-366
N920S	MU-2	534
N920TT	90	LJ-1300
N920WJ	690C	11621
N921AC	690A	11138
N921AZ	200	BB-1287
N921BS	350	FL-110
N921DT	200	BB-404
N921ER	B100	BE-63
N921GG	46D	189
N921HB	690	11012
N921JG	MU-2	216
N921K	100	B-14
N921KA	90	LJ-1921
N921NB	PC12	1021
N921RA	90	LJ-1867
N921RM	MU-2	216
N921S	200	BB-307
N921SA	100	B-101
N921ST	690A	11200
N922AA	90	LJ-1022
N922CR	200	BB-888
N922DT	90	LJ-809
N922FM	MU-2	216
N922HP	441	0027
N922JB	200	BB-182
N922K	90	LJ-382
N922KV	425	0052
N922MM	200	BB-1866
N922RG	PC12	409
N922ST	MU-2	216
N922WA	90	LJ-1922
N922WD	46D	84
N922WD	46D	149
N923AS	200	BB-541
N923CR	90	LJ-1074
N923FP	200	BB-1605
N923FP	350	FL-347
N923JK	350	FL-40
N923K	100	B-40
N923P	90	LJ-1700
N923S	300	FA-127
N923WS	200	BB-8
N924AC	200	BB-483
N924BB	TBM8	405
N924JB	200	BB-1849
N924JD	200	BB-1849
N924JP	TBM7	277
N924K	90	LJ-1
N924MC	690A	11342
N924PC	690	11041
N924PC	PA42	5501006
N924PG	MU-2	1520SA
N924RM	B100	BE-63
N924TT	90	LJ-1301
N924WS	B100	BE-63
N925AD	300	FA-7
N925B	100	B-4
N925B	100	B-35
N925B	100	B-75
N925B	100	B-94

N925B	100	B-136
N925B	100	B-160
N925B	200	BB-6
N925B	200	BB-39
N925B	200	BB-80
N925B	200	BB-138
N925B	200	BB-248
N925B	200	BB-340
N925B	200	BB-432
N925B	200	BB-587
N925B	200	BB-748
N925B	200	BB-959
N925B	200	BB-1050
N925B	90	LJ-286
N925B	90	LJ-340
N925B	90	LJ-402
N925BA	200	BB-340
N925BA	90	LJ-402
N925BB	100	B-94
N925BC	100	B-136
N925BC	90	LJ-925
N925BD	100	B-4
N925BS	90	LJ-1604
N925CA	31T	8020090
N925ES	90	LJ-906
N925G	90	LJ-242
(N925G)	90	LJ-925
(N925GA)	200	BB-1941
N925GA	200G	BY-34
N925GC	G1	161
N925GS	90	LJ-925
N925GS	P180	1052
N925GS	P180	1055
N925HB	680T	1538-5
N925HW	PC12	444
N925JW	90	LJ-692
N925K	100	B-16
N925MC	690A	11213
N925MM	90	LJ-925
N925RM	PA42	5501040
N925S	90	LJ-431
N925TK	P180	1021
N925TT	200	BB-746
N925WL	G1	5
N925WS	441	0283
N925X	90	LJ-1
N925X	90	LJ-125
N926ES	425	0029
N926FS	425	0029
N926FS	425	0093
N926HS	B100	BE-70
N926K	100	B-60
N926K	31T	8004046
N926KA	90	LJ-1926
N926LD	31T	7820047
N926PC	46T	97399
N926PR	300	FA-127
N926S	200	BB-40
N926S	90	LJ-447
N926SC	690C	11622
N926SL	46D	96
N927BG	200	BB-1854
N927DC	MIII	TT-512A
N927JC	200	BB-595
N927JJ	90	LJ-1263
N927JT	90	LJ-1263
N927K	90	LJ-552
N927K	F90	LA-67
N927KA	300C	FM-27
N927MX	PC6	927
N927R	200	BB-752
N927SM	690D	15013
N928JR	90	LJ-734
N928K	90	LJ-528
N928K	90	LJ-552
N928K	90	LJ-1632
N928KA	300C	FM-28
N928KG	200	BB-1925
N928KG	90	LJ-1632
N928NG	PC12	1028
(N928P)	90	LJ-1208
N928RD	90	LJ-680
N928RS	F90	LA-186
N928TT	90	LJ-1313
N928US	90	LJ-1604
(N928VF)	MU-2	436SA
N928VF	MU-2	799SA
N929BG	350	FL-408
N929BW	200	BB-1630
N929DM	200	BB-398
N929FD	90	LJ-1585
N929K	90	LJ-263
N929P	90	LJ-1923
N929PC	TRIS	1071
N929SG	200	BB-834
N929TT	90	LJ-1317
N930CA	PA42	8001030
N930CA	TBM7	309
N930G	300	FA-9
N930HM	46T	97236
N930K	90	LJ-294
N930MA	TBM7	340
N930MC	90	LJ-1463
N930SP	200	BB-930
N930SU	TBM7	89
N931AJ	90	LJ-1231
N931GG	90	LJ-1572
N931K	100	B-74
N931KA	90	LJ-931
N931M	100	B-38
N931PT	31T	7720032
N931SW	31T	7620013
N931WC	90	LJ-1231
N932	680T	1588-39
N932	690A	11304
N932AK	PA42	5501023
N932BF	PA42	8001064
N932E	680T	1588-39
N932G	F90	LA-96
(N932JP)	200	BB-608
N932JP	200	BB-1546
N932JV	200	BB-243
N932K	E90	LW-17
N932SP	PC12	222
N933CL	350	FL-19
N933DG	PA42	8001106
N933K	90	LJ-489
N933KA	90	LJ-1933
N933RC	EPIC	040
N933RT	200	BB-955
N933SC	BN2	294
N933SE	PC12	375
N933SP	PC12	240
N934DC	E90	LW-202
N934K	E90	LW-1
N934LD	90	LJ-358
N934NG	PC12	1034
N934SH	200	BB-252
N934SP	PC12	308
N935AJ	200	BB-935
N935CA	31T	8004033
N935K	90	LJ-286
N935NG	PC12	1035
N935SJ	200	BB-820
N936K	90	LJ-539
N937BC	90	LJ-1118
N937D	PA42	8001055
N937K	90	LJ-548
N937SL	200	BB-937
N938JW	46T	97023
N938K	90	LJ-508
N938P	90	LJ-1250
N939C	MIIB	T26-152
N939HE	PC12	1005
N939JB	31T	7904039
N939K	90	LJ-349
N939RK	90	LJ-725
N939SC	MIIB	T26-146
N939WA	PC6	939
N939WB	MIIB	T26-146
N940AC	690C	11629
N940BR	690C	11721
N940HC	200	BB-1303
N940K	90	LJ-315
N940MA	MU-2	615
N940MA	MU-2	743SA
N940PM	G1	159
N940SR	E90	LW-158
N940U	680W	1843-42
N940WT	200	BB-883
N941AA	PA42	5527009
N941B	200T	BT-33
N941GL	200	BB-862
N941JD	200	BB-18
N941K	100	B-111
N941MA	MU-2	744SA
N941PM	MIIB	T26-110
N941S	MU-2	584
N941S	MU-2	738SA
N941SS	31T	7620018
N942CE	200	BB-494
N942CE	200	BB-1731
N942CE	200	BB-1736
N942CF	200	BB-494
N942DS	100	B-244
N942K	100	B-26
N942M	90	LJ-640
N942MA	MU-2	745SA
N942NG	PC12	1042
N942PM	G1	112
N942RM	E90	LW-305
N942ST	MU-2	745SA
(N942TW)	PA42	8001005
(N942TW)	PA42	8001075
N942TW	PA42	5501015
N942TW	PC12	636
(N943CA)	TBM7	273
N943CL	200	BB-712
N943CL	E90	LW-318
N943CL	F90	LA-118
N943K	90	LJ-474
N943MA	MU-2	746SA
N944BT	PC12	468
N944C	200	BB-1749
N944CA	TBM7	206
N944CC	200	BB-604
N944CC	P68	285
N944CE	200	BB-326
N944CF	200	BB-326
N944H	G1	132
N944H	G1	173
N944HL	G1	173
N944JD	31T	8104005
N944JG	31T	8104005
N944JV	425	0121
N944K	90	LJ-467
N944KR	MIII	TT-453
N944LS	200	BB-604
N944MA	MU-2	747SA
N944NG	PC12	1044
N944RS	E90	LW-177
N944TT	90	LJ-944
N944WH	680T	1587-38
N945BV	200	BB-506
N945K	100	B-49
N945K	100	B-81
N945M	E90	LW-17
N945MA	MU-2	748SA
N945SH	350	FL-458
N945WS	100	B-94
N946AM	90	LJ-815
N946BF	200	BB-277
N946CE	200	BB-540
N946CE	200	BB-1728
N946CF	200	BB-540
N946JD	BN2	534
N946JJ	PC12	115
N946K	90	LJ-228
N946MA	MU-2	749SA
N946RB	PC12	1137
N946TS	90	LJ-1591
N946V	200	BB-36
N947AM	90	LJ-1238
N947K	100	B-15
N947MA	MU-2	750SA
N947MZ	P68	316
N948AM	90	LJ-1210
(N948C)	TBM7	342
N948CC	E90	LW-236
N948CE	200	BB-1736
N948CL	200	BB-1731
N948HB	B100	BE-98
N948K	90	LJ-526
N948MA	MU-2	751SA
N948MB	200	BB-757
N948MR	PC12	1098
N948RM	90	LJ-121
N948TA	PA42	5501048
N948V	E90	LW-127
N949CW	200	BB-281
N949ET	680T	1685-66
N949PC	350	FL-475
N949SW	B100	BE-34
N949TA	PA42	5501049
N950	MIIA	T26-030
N950CT	31T	7720069
N950GC	PC12	150
N950JM	300	FA-144
N950K	90	LJ-81
N950K	90	LJ-495
N950KA	PC12	730
N950KM	PC12	540
N950M	690A	11173
N950M	MIII	T-216
N950MA	MU-2	508
N950MA	MU-2	671
N950MB	200	BB-1372
N950MD	MIVC	AT-452
N950MT	PA42	5501023
N950NG	PC12	1050
N950TA	PA42	5501050
(N950TA)	PA42	5527008
N950TJ	690D	15016
N950TT	MIII	T-225
(N950WA)	TBM7	151
N950WA	TBM8	404
N951CS	46D	195
N951HE	680W	1751-4
N951HF	680W	1751-4
N951HF	690B	11493
N951K	100	B-17
N951MA	MU-2	637
N951MS	MU-2	637
N951TB	46T	97175
N951TB	46T	97225
N951TP	46T	97175
N952AA	300	FA-83
N952HE	690A	11275
N952HE	MIIA	T26-014
N952HF	690A	11275
N952MA	MU-2	784SA
N953AE	MIII	T-270
N953CM	46T	97313
N953HF	690A	11194
N953HF	MIIA	T26-014
N953JH	441	0321
N953K	90	LJ-515
N953L	200	BB-953
N953PC	350	FL-411
N953RC	B100	BE-33
N954BL	200	BB-1951
N954BL	90	LJ-1681
N954BS	90	LJ-1681
N954HE	680W	1721-1
N954HF	680W	1721-1
N954HF	690B	11486
N954MS	200	BB-1649
N954RM	200	BB-1868
N954TG	90	LJ-713
N955AA	300	FA-86
N955AF	PC12	1055
N955FC	B100	BE-50
N955RA	F90	LA-201
N955SH	46D	206
N955TA	PA42	5501055
N956DS	MIII	T-282
N956PC	PC12	323
N956WT	200	BB-956
N957BA	200	BB-1957
N957CB	200	BB-1624
N957JF	90	LJ-906
N957JF	F90	LA-236
N957MC	E90	LW-210
N957ST	PC12	295
N958BC	MIII	T-282
N958JH	90	LJ-1108

N958MA	MU-2	350SA
N958NG	PC12	1058
N958TA	PA42	5501058
N959AF	PC12	1059
N959B	90	LJ-363
N959CM	90	LJ-971
N959GM	90	LJ-971
N959L	MU-2	570
N959M	MIII	T-253
N959MC	90	LJ-821
N959TF	MIII	T-254
N959WB	KODK	0016
N960A	200C	BL-25
N960AC	695A	96080
N960GK	200	BB-960
N960JP	200	BB-1163
N960M	MIV	AT-005
N960MA	MU-2	399SA
N960V	F90	LA-31
N961AA	300	FA-47
N961DM	E90	LW-256
N961G	G1	30
N961JM	46T	97122B
N961K	90	LJ-410
N961LE	200	BB-1139
N961LL	200	BB-1139
N961LL	350	FL-264
N961MA	MU-2	400SA
N961PC	PC12	129
N961PP	350	FL-447
N961PS	200	BB-637
N962AT	90	LJ-207
N962BL	680T	1562-18
(N962DA)	46D	198
N962DA	46D	198
(N962HB)	90	LJ-305
N962JC	200	BB-345
N962M	90	LJ-94
N962M	90	LJ-561
N962MA	MU-2	401SA
N962NG	PC12	1062
N962R	100	B-44
N962TT	90	LJ-962
N963BP	MIIB	T26-114
N963DC	MIII	T-314
(N963E)	90	LJ-609
N963GM	200	BB-1365
N963JC	200	BB-561
N963KA	E90	LW-242
N963M	90	LJ-458
N963M	90	LJ-609
N963MA	MU-2	228
N963MA	MU-2	402SA
N963P	90	LJ-1806
N964GB	90	LJ-1007
N964LB	350	FL-59
N964MA	46D	135
N964MA	MU-2	403SA
N964RT	200	BB-1928
N964WM	MIIB	T26-108
N965CJ	G1	160
N965DA	46D	20
N965J	90	LJ-856
N965LC	E90	LW-204
N965LG	E90	LW-204
N965MA	MU-2	404SA
N965SB	46T	97015
(N965TT)	90	LJ-965
N966CY	90	LJ-307
N966H	G1	181
N966HL	G1	181
N966MA	MU-2	405SA
N966NG	PC12	1066
N967AB	PC12	843
(N967JG)	300	FA-214
N967MA	MU-2	183
N967MA	MU-2	406SA
N967NG	PC12	1067
N967WJ	90	LJ-967
N968MA	MU-2	407SA
N968MB	200	BB-1667
N968T	200	BB-570
N969	200	BB-1083
(N969BH)	90	LJ-661

N969BJ	MIIA	T26-002
N969CL	E90	LW-252
N969EE	MIII	T-208
N969MA	200	BB-894
N969MA	MU-2	408SA
N969MB	350	FL-290
N969MC	F90	LA-32
N969ME	425	0189
N969RF	TBM7	9
N969TS	200	BB-1551
N969WB	200	BB-969
N970AA	200	BB-676
N970GA	90	LJ-308
N970KK	300	FA-29
N970M	MIII	T-205
*N970ME	PC12	441
N970NA	PC12	226
N970P	90	LJ-1487
*N970P	90	LJ-1923
N970PS	31T	8020023
N970V	90	LJ-851
N971AM	90	LJ-983
N971CF	90	LJ-971
N971EL	90	LJ-314
N971JP	350	FL-565
N971LE	200	BB-1234
N971LL	200	BB-572
N971LL	200	BB-1234
N971LL	350	FL-267
N971LL	90	LJ-314
N971MA	MU-2	701SA
N971P	90	LJ-1575
N971SC	90	LJ-1343
N972AM	90	LJ-1003
N972EK	MIII	T-325
N972LL	200	BB-572
N972SC	350	FL-258
N973AC	90	LJ-786
N973BB	MU-2	1509SA
N973GA	90	LJ-675
N973MA	MU-2	1509SA
N973NG	PC12	1073
N973SC	350	FL-379
N974C	90	LJ-1708
N974DC	31T	8120027
N974GA	90	LJ-748
N974JB	KODK	0014
N974MA	MU-2	689
N975SC	200	BB-806
N975TB	TBM7	75
N976	E90	LW-226
N976EA	300	FA-114
N976JT	90	LJ-699
N976KC	200	BB-601
N976MA	MU-2	1507SA
N977AA	90	LJ-555
(N977BA)	200	BB-569
N977CP	31T	8004038
N977DG	690A	11237
N977FC	90	LJ-733
N977G	31T	8104065
N977GT	200	BB-141
N977JC	690C	11641
N977JS	G1	197
N977LX	200	BB-141
N977LX	90	LJ-450
N977MP	425	0131
N977MP	441	0310
N977PC	31T	7720032
N977QA	90	LJ-254
N977SB	E90	LW-10
N977XL	PC12	189
N977XT	PA42	8001008
N978AF	PC12	1078
N978BC	31T	7820025
N978GA	200	BB-542
N978MA	MU-2	352SA
N979C	90	LJ-945
N979GA	PC12	104
N979LX	90	LJ-450
N979MA	MU-2	407SA
N979MC	90	LJ-1001
N979SR	200	BB-519
N979SW	31T	7620049

N980AA	695	95001
N980AB	695	95030
(N980AC)	695	95028
N980AD	695	95040
N980AK	690C	11636
(N980AN)	695	95001
N980BC	350	FL-283
N980BC	695	95010
N980BH	695	95002
N980BM	695	95056
N980CA	31T	8104010
N980CF	695	95028
(N980CT)	695	95059
(N980DB)	200	BB-10
N980DT	695	95048
N980DW	695	95074
N980E	695	95040
N980EA	695	95031
N980EC	695	95011
N980GB	200	BB-1594
N980GC	695	95056
(N980GK)	695	95074
N980GM	695	95034
N980GM	695	95063
N980GR	695	95049
N980GZ	695	95063
(N980H)	100	B-173
N980H	695	95020
N980HB	695	95006
(N980JC)	695	95019
N980JC	695	95084
(N980JD)	695	95056
(N980JP)	695	95001
N980JP	695	95083
N980JS	695	95065
N980KA	200	BB-1980
N980KA	B100	BE-87
N980MA	MU-2	749SA
N980MD	695	95030
N980MH	695	95078
N980PD	200	BB-735
N980R	695	95002
N980RC	695	95000
N980SA	695	95012
N980TT	G1	323
N980WJ	695	95061
N980WM	695	95034
N981AR	350	FL-199
N981BB	200	BB-1960
N981GA	200	BB-1368
N981LE	200	BB-602
N981LE	90	LJ-65
N981LL	200	BB-602
N981LL	350	FL-265
N981LL	90	LJ-65
N981SR	31T	8104040
N981SW	31T	8104040
N981WJ	695	95045
N982BA	90	LJ-1031
(N982EC)	200	BB-649
N982FA	90	LJ-1000
N982GA	200	BB-149
N982MA	MU-2	314
N982SA	F90	LA-160
N982SB	90	LJ-1518
N982SS	90	LJ-1523
N982SW	PA42	8001073
N982TM	200	BB-226
N983AJ	200	BB-983
N983AR	350	FL-242
N983C	200	BB-755
N983EB	200	BB-983
N983GA	31T	8166061
N983GA	441	0182
N983JB	200	BB-1904
N983K	90	LJ-169
N983NG	PC12	1083
N983SC	PC12	1151
N983SM	441	0001
N983TM	350	FL-94
N984AA	90	LJ-429
N984CF	300	FA-26
N984GA	F90	LA-47
N984K	90	LJ-274

N984MA	90	LJ-883
N984MA	MU-2	765SA
N984MC	200	BB-267
N984RE	MU-2	787SA
N984SW	300	FA-49
N985AA	90	LJ-214
N985CA	31T	8020003
N985GA	200	BB-1062
N985GA	300	FA-63
N985K	90	LJ-275
N986KA	200	BB-1986
N986MA	MU-2	572
N986MC	441	0280
N986PC	441	0342
N986SC	441	0342
N986SG	441	0051
N986SG	441	0342
N986TJ	200	BB-986
N987B	B100	BE-81
N987BT	300	FA-142
N987GM	E90	LW-65
N987GM	E90	LW-98
N987HT	350	FL-34
N987KA	200	BB-1987
N987MA	MU-2	124
N988AA	G1	323
N988AE	441	0175
N988AS	690B	11493
N988C	TBM7	282
N988CC	200	BB-490
N988EC	PC12	1056
N988GA	200	BB-480
N988JR	B100	BE-46
N988KA	200	BB-1988
N988ME	350	FL-77
N988MM	200	BB-1462
N988NA	200	BB-660
N988NG	PC12	1088
N988P	90	LJ-1506
N988RR	MU-2	1557SA
N988S	MU-2	734SA
N988SC	200	BB-310
N988SL	90	LJ-438
N988TA	31T	7620023
N988V	TBM8	429
N988XJ	90	LJ-1566
N989BJ	P180	1152
N989BK	200	BB-1989
N989GA	90	LJ-672
N989GM	E90	LW-109
N989GT	90	LJ-1863
N989LA	200	BB-1310
N989W	90	LJ-1888
N990AR	441	0113
N990BM	F90	LA-70
N990BT	B100	BE-112
N990CB	90	LJ-1362
N990CF	E90	LW-107
N990CH	690C	11615
N990DA	90	LJ-753
N990DP	46T	97121
N990DW	90	LJ-1668
N990F	F90	LA-164
N990GA	200	BB-930
N990GR	350	FL-622
N990GT	90	LJ-1768
N990JC	200	BB-990
N990JC	690D	15011
N990JM	U-21	LM-17
N990KA	200	BB-1990
N990KB	90	LJ-1046
N990L	300	FA-147
N990LR	31T	7820060
N990LS	90	LJ-677
N990M	MIII	T-218
N990M	MU-2	650
N990MA	MU-2	409SA
N990PT	300	FA-91
N990PT	B100	BE-112
N990PT	PC12	304
N990QH	690C	11615
N990RC	200	BB-990
N990RS	P180	1015
N990SA	90	LJ-261

N990SV	B100	BE-112	N998PA	200	BB-1275	N999WS	31T	7720067	N1061T	46T	97274
N990TF	90	LJ-1548	N998RC	100	B-98	N999WT	680T	1694-73	N1063F	350	FL-154
N991CB	MIIB	T26-142	N998SR	200	BB-1632	N999WW	690	11073	N1063F	46T	97272
N991DM	B100	BE-62	N998VB	90	LJ-785	N999WW	MU-2	790SA	N1063M	46T	97277
N991GA	200	BB-812	N998WA	PC12	1098	N1000	G1	109	N1063M	46T	97280
N991GC	F90	LA-224	N999BE	441	0147	N1000C	90	LJ-182	N1065G	46T	97284
N991GT	90	LJ-1805	N999BE	MU-2	386SA	N1000W	200	BB-390	N1065G	46T	97294
N991HB	200	BB-1991	N999BR	BN2	2173	N1000W	90	LJ-354	N1065Y	46T	97295
N991KA	200	BB-809	N999BT	200	BB-400	N1002B	90	LJ-277	N1066D	46T	97286
N991LL	200	BB-572	N999CR	100	B-12	N1003W	200	BB-1541	N1067K	90	LJ-1460
(N991LL)	200	BB-1139	N999CY	200	BB-253	N1005Y	MIVA	AT-033	N1067L	90	LJ-1437
N991LL	200	BB-1234	N999DF	441	0185	N1006F	MIII	T-318	N1067S	350	FL-137
N991LL	350	FL-142	N999DT	200	BB-138	N1006K	MIII	T-322	N1067V	200	BB-1568
N991LL	90	LJ-65	N999DT	MIIA	T26-022	N1006M	MIII	T-323	N1068K	90	LJ-1448
N991LL	90	LJ-314	N999DZ	200	BB-1940	N1006Q	MIII	T-324	N1069F	200	BB-1561
N991MA	MU-2	410SA	N999EF	695A	96080	N1006T	MIII	T-328	N1069F	90	LJ-1489
*N991PS	200	BB-1677	N999EG	200	BB-908	N1006Y	MIVA	AT-074	N1069S	200	BB-1549
N991SA	90	LJ-1691	N999EP	PC12	135	N1007B	MIII	T-327	N1070D	350	FL-140
N991SU	200	BB-253	N999ES	90	LJ-612	N1007S	MIII	T-329	N1070E	200	BB-1545
N991WS	200	BB-1510	N999ES	E90	LW-27	N1008C	MIII	T-331	N1070F	90	LJ-1440
N992C	200	BB-569	N999ET	MU-2	1505SA	N1008F	MIII	T-332	N1071S	350	FL-175
N992C	90	LJ-1122	N999FA	MU-2	676	N1008G	100	B-6	N1071S	46T	97298
N992CP	G1	155	N999FE	695	95026	N1008J	100	B-6	N1072G	90	LJ-1442
N992FR	200	BB-360	N999FG	690B	11535	N1008J	200	BB-250	N1072S	350	FL-142
N992KA	200	BB-1992	N999G	100	B-144	N1008L	MIII	T-339	N1074G	200	BB-1534
N992LJ	90	LJ-992	N999GA	200	BB-222	N1008S	MIII	T-342	N1075F	46T	97289
N992MA	350	FL-271	N999GA	200	BB-929	N1008U	MIII	T-351	N1075G	350	FL-145
N992MA	E90	LW-59	N999GP	E90	LW-184	N1008Y	MIII	T-381	N1075N	46T	97290
N992MA	MU-2	411SA	N999HC	200	BB-253	N1009	G1	27	N1075P	46T	97288
N992NG	PC12	1092	N999HC	200	BB-1057	N1009C	90	LJ-182	N1076K	90	LJ-1461
N992TE	441	0196	N999HC	200	BB-1374	N1009C	MIII	T-354	N1078	90	LJ-908
N992TJ	200	BB-992	N999HC	90	LJ-643	N1009G	MIII	T-348	N1078D	46T	97312
N992TT	31T	8004019	N999HE	E90	LW-318	N1009U	MIII	T-360	N1079D	90	LJ-1462
N992WS	90	LJ-1458	N999HW	350	FL-49	N1009Y	MIII	T-369	N1079Y	200	BB-1550
N993CB	90	LJ-1550	N999JH	BN2	2023	N1010	P68	344	N1080G	46T	97305
N993M	F90	LA-134	N999KG	200	BB-960	N1010M	680T	1624-53	N1080Q	46T	97321
N993MA	MU-2	412SA	(N999KH)	90	LJ-1230	N1010V	MIII	T-372	N1080Y	200	BB-1552
N993RA	BN2	905	N999KK	F90	LA-180	N1011G	MIII	T-375	N1081F	200	BB-1531
N993RC	90	LJ-1089	N999LK	90	LJ-1124	N1011P	MIII	T-378	N1082S	200	BB-1543
N993RH	31T	7720066	N999LL	90	LJ-302	N1011R	MIII	T-303E	N1083K	90	LJ-1464
N993TM	46T	97118	N999MC	200	BB-427	N1012J	MIII	T-391	N1083N	350	FL-153
N993WS	200	BB-1506	N999MC	200	BB-1167	N1012S	200	BB-1512	N1083S	90	LJ-1443
N994DF	TBM7	22	N999MC	350	FL-65	N1012T	MIII	T-405	N1084N	90	LJ-1444
N994HP	200	BB-1766	N999MC	E90	LW-84	N1013A	MIII	T-403	N1084W	350	FL-144
N994KA	200	BB-1994	N999MG	350	FL-65	N1013N	MIII	T-410	N1085V	90	LJ-1455
N994MA	46T	97394	(N999MJ)	90	LJ-645	N1013T	MIII	T-414	N1086Z	90	LJ-1446
N994MA	MU-2	413SA	N999MK	E90	LW-84	N1013U	MIII	T-417	N1089L	90	LJ-1439
N994NG	PC12	1094	N999MM	200	BB-1997	N1014B	MIII	TT-421	N1089S	200	BB-1539
N994PE	MU-2	714SA	N999MM	MIII	T-309	N1014H	MIII	TT-426A	N1089V	200	BB-1555
N994RD	E90	LW-119	N999MQ	200	BB-427	N1014L	MIVC	AT-427	N1089V	200	BB-1577
N994RD	F90	LA-119	N999MR	200	BB-1167	N1014T	MIIA	T26-035	N1090W	90	LJ-581
(N994RM)	200	BB-994	N999MX	MIVC	AT-501	N1014U	MIII	TT-433	N1090X	90	LJ-1473
N994ST	F90	LA-83	N999NG	46T	97022	N1014V	MIII	T-321	N1091	G1	109
N994WS	90	LJ-1459	N999NH	90	LJ-1712	N1015X	200	BB-1525	N1092G	90	LJ-1453
N995GT	90	LJ-1816	N999NP	31T	8104058	N1017T	31T	7400017	N1092H	90	LJ-1454
N995HP	690D	15026	N999P	200	BB-955	N1017T	31T	7520008	N1092N	200	BB-1556
N995KA	200	BB-1995	N999P	STAR	NC-43	N1017V	200	BB-1604	N1092S	350	FL-152
N995MA	MU-2	632	N999PF	MIII	T-247	N1018P	46T	97293	N1093A	350	FL-156
N995MS	200	BB-931	N999PP	441	0147	N1019T	46T	97281	N1093Q	350	FL-157
N995PA	90	LJ-1355	N999RC	F90	LA-208	N1020K	100	B-5	N1093Z	200	BB-1593
N995SA	100	B-246	N999RC	MU-2	760SA	N1024A	200	BB-1524	N1094S	200	BB-1544
N995SC	PA42	5501004	N999RF	STAR	NC-9	N1024Y	MU-2	653	N1094Y	200	BB-1565
N995ST	46T	97154	N999RW	46T	97037	N1027Y	200	BB-1527	N1095G	200	BB-1578
N995TA	90	LJ-1441	N999SA	BN2	897	N1031Y	90	LJ-1431	N1095M	90	LJ-1435
N996AB	690B	11425	N999SE	E90	LW-5	N1032G	46T	97285	N1095Q	350	FL-158
N996AM	350	FL-14	N999SE	E90	LW-344	N1032H	46T	97301	N1095W	90	LJ-1456
N996BL	90	LJ-1864	N999SF	E90	LW-5	N1032H	46T	97302	N1097B	90	LJ-1452
N996KA	200	BB-1996	N999SP	C-12	BC-8	N1039Y	MIIB	T26-180E	(N1097S)	90	LJ-574
N996KF	PC12	836	N999ST	695	95080	N1040	G1	78	N1099D	90	LJ-1471
N996LM	200	BB-157	(N999ST)	MU-2	530	N1040D	46T	97268	N1099E	350	FL-169
N996TT	90	LJ-1398	N999SV	46T	97352	N1040D	46T	97278	N1099K	90	LJ-1463
N997JB	P68	288	N999TA	MU-2	514	N1042H	46T	97275	N1099L	90	LJ-1472
N997JM	TBM7	244	(N999TA)	MU-2	530	N1042H	46T	97291	N1099Z	90	LJ-1470
N997MA	200	BB-102	N999TB	100	B-144	N1042W	100	B-200	N1100A	100	B-41
N997ME	B100	BE-135	N999TB	200	BB-1738	N1047M	46T	97271	N1100A	350	FL-160
N997RC	100	B-97	N999TB	E90	LW-60	N1047M	46T	97300	N1100D	90	LJ-368
N998AA	46D	203	N999TC	200	BB-15	N1047R	46T	97307	N1100M	681	6016
N998BW	300	FA-149	N999TC	200	BB-222	N1052L	46T	97269	N1100M	690A	11271
N998CA	MU-2	614	(N999TJ)	PA42	5527029	N1052X	46T	97270	(N1100M)	690B	11360
N998GT	90	LJ-1892	N999UP	MU-2	1557SA	N1056B	PC12	499	N1100M	690B	11370
N998JB	PC12	148	N999VB	200	BB-645	N1057L	90	LJ-1457	N1100M	E90	LW-25
N998KA	200	BB-1998	N999VB	90	LJ-785	N1057Q	350	FL-163	N1100N	350	FL-159
N998LM	31T	8120006	N999WB	MU-2	530	N1060X	46T	97303	N1100W	350	FL-47
N998P	90	LJ-1526	N999WP	200	BB-117	N1061Q	350	FL-141	N1100X	90	LJ-71

N1101U	90	LJ-1481	N1186Z	680T	1532-2	N1221S	MIIB	T26-109	N1421Z	TBM7	140
N1101W	200	BB-1333	N1187K	F90	LA-93	N1221T	425	0192	N1422Z	PC6	562
N1102K	90	LJ-1465	(N1187Z)	680T	1556-14	N1221X	425	0193	N1444C	680T	1538-5
N1103B	200	BB-1560	N1187Z	680T	1576-30	N1222B	425	0060	N1500X	MIIB	T26-127
N1103G	90	LJ-1475	N1188A	90	LJ-722	N1222G	425	0196	N1501	G1	15
N1104X	200	BB-1585	N1188Z	680T	1558-16	N1222K	425	0197	N1501C	G1	15
N1104Y	350	FL-164	N1191K	300	FA-185	N1222P	425	0198	N1508S	STAR	NC-8
N1105X	350	FL-155	N1192Z	680T	1566-22	N1222S	MIIB	T26-112	N1509G	200	BB-1308
N1105X	E90	LW-108	N1194C	200	BB-679	(N1223A)	425	0199	N1509X	200	BB-1485
N1106J	200	BB-1566	N1194V	31T	8375001	N1223B	425	0201	N1512H	350	FL-120
N1106M	90	LJ-1476	(N1195Z)	680T	1563-19	N1223C	200	BB-152	N1515E	200	BB-1502
N1107F	200	BB-1567	N1195Z	680T	1575-29	N1223C	425	0200	N1515H	PA42	8001011
N1107W	90	LJ-1477	N1198S	MIIA	T26-012	N1223G	425	0201	N1515H	PA42	5527019
N1108A	200	BB-1558	N1199Z	680T	1564-20	N1223K	425	0202	N1515T	90	LJ-139
N1108K	90	LJ-1466	N1200M	200	BB-157	N1223N	425	0203	N1517K	300	FA-167
N1108M	90	LJ-1478	N1200Z	100	B-133	N1223P	425	0204	N1517R	300	FA-168
N1110K	90	LJ-1486	N1202S	BN2	193	N1223S	MIIB	T26-115	N1523L	100	B-222
N1110M	690B	11443	N1202S	MIIB	T26-100	N1223V	425	0205	N1524H	300	FA-164
N1112Z	350	FL-162	N1203S	MIIA	T26-019	N1224B	425	0207	N1524L	100	B-223
N1114K	200	BB-1559	N1204S	MIIA	T26-021	N1224J	425	0208	N1525C	200	BB-1286
N1114Z	90	LJ-1514	N1205S	E90	LW-319	N1224K	425	0209	N1525C	350	FL-88
N1115	300	FA-90	N1206S	MIIA	T26-023	N1224N	425	0210	N1528L	100	B-132
N1117N	200	BB-1547	N1207C	G1	132	N1224S	425	0211	N1528L	200	BB-132
N1118G	200	BB-1576	N1207G	441	0309	N1224S	MIIB	T26-118	N1528T	90	LJ-1193
N1118W	350	FL-168	N1207N	441	0310	N1224T	425	0212	N1529M	350	FL-121
N1119U	90	LJ-1479	N1207S	MIIA	T26-024	N1225D	425	0215	N1530L	200	BB-1312
N1119Z	200	BB-1581	(N1207Z)	441	0311	N1225J	425	0216	N1534T	90	LJ-1363
N1120Z	200	BB-1570	N1208A	441	0315	N1225S	MIIB	T26-120	N1537H	90	LJ-1188
N1122M	200	BB-455	(N1208D)	441	0321	N1225T	425	0217	N1538Q	300	FA-190
N1123V	680T	1713-87	(N1208G)	441	0316	N1225V	425	0218	N1540Y	680T	1675-58
N1125M	100	B-127	N1208J	441	0317	N1225Y	425	0219	N1541Q	300	FA-191
N1126J	90	LJ-1483	N1208M	441	0318	N1226B	425	0222	N1541T	200	BB-1324
N1127D	90	LJ-223	N1208S	MIIA	T26-025	N1226G	425	0223	N1542	200	BB-1916
N1127M	90	LJ-223	N1208T	441	0319	N1226S	425	0224	N1542Z	200	BB-1486
N1127U	90	LJ-1490	N1209B	441	0320	N1226S	MIII	T-205E	N1543H	300	FA-174
N1128B	90	LJ-38	N1209J	441	0322	N1226Z	425	0226	N1543Q	350	FL-23
N1128M	100	B-127	N1209N	441	0323	N1227A	425	0228	N1543Z	200	BB-1327
N1128M	200	BB-455	N1209P	441	0324	N1227J	425	0229	N1544G	200	BB-1326
N1128M	90	LJ-38	N1209S	441	0325	N1227S	MIIB	T26-123	N1544V	90	LJ-1366
N1129M	100	B-127	N1209S	MIIA	T26-026	N1227V	425	0230	N1546	C-12	BC-58
N1129M	100	B-164	(N1209T)	441	0326	N1228W	441	0065	N1546U	90	LJ-1200
N1130B	350	FL-167	(N1209X)	441	0327	N1230	200	BB-366	N1547	C-12	BC-50
N1130D	PC12	823	N1210B	441	0330	N1230D	690	11052	N1547A	690A	11337
N1130J	90	LJ-1467	N1210D	441	0331	N1234L	31T	8166054	N1547V	200	BB-1307
N1130R	200	BB-1582	N1210G	441	0332	N1234X	G1	55	N1548B	200	BB-1319
N1134D	90	LJ-1484	N1210L	441	0333	N1240S	200C	BL-64	N1548K	300	FA-179
N1134G	90	LJ-1468	(N1210N)	441	0334	N1244J	350	FL-309	N1548L	300	FA-182
N1135G	90	LJ-1488	N1210S	MIIA	T26-027	N1250	300	FA-88	N1548S	200	BB-1487
N1135K	90	LJ-1495	N1210T	441	0335	N1250	90	LJ-360	N1548S	STAR	NC-7
N1135L	350	FL-165	N1210U	441	0336	N1250	B100	BE-25	N1549	C-12	BC-45
N1135X	90	LJ-1494	(N1210V)	441	0337	N1250B	90	LJ-360	N1549D	300	FA-183
N1135Z	200	BB-1535	N1210W	MU-2	193	N1253W	350	FL-330	N1550S	STAR	NC-5
N1144Z	31T	7720039	N1210Y	441	0338	N1262H	425	0233	N1550U	200	BB-1337
(N1147W)	90	LJ-1147	N1210Z	441	0339	N1262K	425	0234	N1551	C-12	BC-39
N1149W	C-12	BC-72	N1211C	441	0340	N1262P	425	0235	N1551A	350	FL-24
N1150S	G1	85	(N1211M)	441	0341	N1262T	425	0236	N1551C	300	FA-197
N1151S	90	LJ-150	N1211N	441	0342	N1282	200	BB-89	N1551C	90	LJ-1365
N1152S	90	LJ-160	N1212C	441	0346	(N1282)	680T	1585-37	N1551F	200	BB-1336
N1153S	90	LJ-107	N1212K	441	0347	N1283	200	BB-90	N1551F	350	FL-115
N1153S	90	LJ-438	N1212N	441	0348	N1283B	441	0361	N1551H	90	LJ-1211
N1154S	90	LJ-108	N1212S	MIIA	T26-028	N1284	100	B-3	N1551J	90	LJ-1212
N1154Z	680T	1585-37	N1213G	441	0351	N1284	200	BB-453	N1551T	350	FL-25
N1156Z	680T	1534-3	N1213N	441	0352	(N1284)	680T	1587-38	N1552C	350	FL-116
N1157R	90	LJ-1191	N1213P	90	LJ-962	N1287F	200	BB-66	N1552D	90	LJ-1204
N1158T	PC6	903	N1213R	441	0353	N1290A	90	LJ-30	N1552F	90	LJ-1205
N1161Z	680T	1519-95	N1213S	441	0354	N1290B	90	LJ-362	N1552G	90	LJ-1206
N1162V	200	BB-711	N1213W	690A	11206	(N1301L)	90	LJ-332	N1552K	300	FA-192
N1163Z	680T	1560-17	N1213Y	441	0355	(N1302R)	PC6	583	N1552Q	350	FL-20
N1164F	MU-2	1562SA	(N1213Z)	441	0356	N1310T	90	LJ-617	N1552S	STAR	NC-12
N1168Z	680T	1542-7	N1214B	441	0357	N1346N	90	LJ-844	N1553	C-12	BC-30
(N1171Z)	680T	1544-8	N1214D	441	0358	(N1347J)	90	LJ-1262	N1553D	90	LJ-1210
N1171Z	680T	1557-15	N1214S	MIIA	T26-031	N1347Z	100	B-114	N1553E	200	BB-1306
N1172J	C-12	BC-25	N1215S	MIIA	T26-033	(N1348G)	TRIS	1047	N1553G	90	LJ-1214
N1173Z	MU-2	130	N1216S	MIIA	T26-035	(N1348M)	TRIS	1050	N1553M	200	BB-1328
N1176W	690A	11184	N1217S	MIIB	T26-101	N1349N	441	0043	N1553N	90	LJ-1238
N1178Z	680T	1577-31	N1218S	MIIB	T26-102	N1352W	P68	232	N1553P	200	BB-1311
N1179Z	680T	1573-28	N1219S	MIIB	T26-103	N1362B	200	BB-676	N1553S	STAR	NC-13
(N1181L)	31T	7520042	N1220S	MIIB	T26-107	N1362N	100	B-230	N1553V	300	FA-202
(N1181Z)	680T	1584-36	N1220W	441	0065	N1362W	690B	11554	N1553V	350	FL-117
N1183G	31T	7920086	N1221C	425	0188	N1380	31T	8166008	N1553Y	STAR	NC-25
N1183S	90	LJ-107	N1221F	425	0189	N1409Z	PC6	522	N1554	C-12	BC-21
(N1183Z)	680T	1562-18	N1221K	425	0190	N1413B	90	LJ-144	N1554K	200	BB-1370
N1184U	C-12	BD-16	N1221K	46D	225	N1417Z	PC6	535	N1554U	300	FA-195
N1185Z	680T	1548-10	N1221N	425	0191	N1421Z	PC6	561	N1555E	350	FL-118

N1555L	B100	BE-5
N1555N	200	BB-25
N1555N	300	FA-177
N1556F	300	FA-186
N1556G	90	LJ-1227
N1556S	STAR	NC-6
N1556Z	90	LJ-1224
N1557R	300	FA-196
N1557U	200	BB-1318
N1558	C-12	BC-20
N1558H	350	FL-119
N1558K	200	BB-1320
N1558M	300	FA-173
N1558N	200	BB-1321
N1558P	200	BB-1298
N1558S	STAR	NC-31
N1558Y	300	FA-175
N1559	C-12	BC-16
N1559G	200	BB-1480
N1559T	90	LJ-1213
N1559W	200	BB-1481
N1559Y	200	BB-1482
N1559Z	200	BB-1483
N1559Z	300	FA-169
N1560	C-12	BC-9
N1560S	STAR	NC-24
N1560T	90	LJ-1357
N1560U	90	LJ-1360
N1562F	200	BB-1351
N1562H	350	FL-189
N1562V	300	FA-203
N1562V	90	LJ-1372
N1562Z	350	FL-122
N1562Z	90	LJ-1216
N1563K	300	FA-154
N1563M	200	BB-1489
N1563N	200	BB-1490
N1563R	200C	BL-134
N1563U	90	LJ-1221
N1563Z	STAR	NC-10
N1564D	300C	FM-1
N1564J	STAR	NC-53
N1564M	200	BB-1436
N1564M	90	LJ-1225
N1564M	90	LJ-1273
N1564P	90	LJ-1230
N1564Q	90	LJ-1232
N1564Q	STAR	NC-52
N1564W	90	LJ-1234
N1565D	200	BB-1359
N1565F	200	BB-1362
N1565L	90	LJ-704
N1565X	90	LJ-1240
N1566W	200	BB-1332
N1567F	200	BB-1335
N1567G	90	LJ-1217
N1567T	200	BB-1317
N1567Z	200	BB-1507
N1568E	200	BB-1488
N1568E	300	FA-180
N1568T	300	FA-194
N1568X	90	LJ-1368
N1569N	90	LJ-1235
N1569S	STAR	NC-11
N1570C	90	LJ-1370
N1570F	200	BB-1350
N1570H	300	FA-176
N1570L	E90	LW-170
N1571T	90	LJ-1209
N1573L	E90	LW-173
N1574L	E90	LW-174
N1575W	E90	LW-5
N1580L	90	LJ-680
N1581L	90	LJ-681
N1583L	90	LJ-683
N1585L	90	LJ-685
N1590B	90	LJ-428
N1601A	MU-2	688
N1602C	90	LJ-743
N1607Z	G1	14
N1610W	MU-2	447SA
N1620	G1	24
N1623	G1	10
N1623Z	G1	10
N1624B	200	BB-1624
N1625	G1	24
N1625B	G1	24
N1627	200	BB-1278
N1628	200	BB-1104
N1631W	E90	LW-6
N1650	200	BB-1618
(N1652)	200	BB-1618
N1653H	100	B-30
N1653H	90	LJ-492
N1655M	200	BB-1655
N1660W	200	BB-390
N1667J	300C	FM-10
N1668A	350	FL-296
N1679E	E90	LW-36
N1685S	90	LJ-1685
N1701L	G1	148
N1707Z	G1	108
N1716W	E90	LW-19
N1727S	MU-2	1504SA
N1728S	MU-2	451SA
N1739W	E90	LW-29
N1741W	E90	LW-31
N1762K	E90	LW-222
N1769W	E90	LW-26
N1776L	100	B-54
N1777X	425	0222
N1788W	100	B-148
N1790M	MU-2	756SA
N1790W	90	LJ-568
N1800W	100	B-145
N1801B	90	LJ-634
N1802H	200	BB-856
N1803P	F90	LA-133
N1804T	200	BB-880
N1807H	B100	BE-119
N1808L	B100	BE-8
N1808M	200	BB-874
N1809B	200	BB-894
N1811L	100	B-230
N1811S	200	BB-896
N1811W	90	LJ-571
N1812B	200C	BL-38
N1813P	90	LJ-977
N1814P	B100	BE-120
N1815T	F90	LA-142
N1818P	200	BB-904
N1818W	100	B-118
N1818W	90	LJ-882
N1818W	90	LJ-1086
N1819H	200	BB-1591
N1820P	90	LJ-982
N1821H	200	BB-888
N1822D	F90	LA-113
N1823A	90	LJ-984
N1823B	90	LJ-181
N1824S	200	BB-1158
N1824S	300	FA-123
N1824S	E90	LW-218
N1824T	F90	LA-146
N1825H	200	BB-890
N1826P	F90	LA-148
N1827F	F90	LA-156
N1828W	100	B-147
N1829H	F90	LA-139
N1830H	90	LJ-975
N1834H	90	LJ-987
N1836H	90	LJ-990
N1837F	90	LJ-993
N1837S	200	BB-897
N1837V	F90	LA-155
N1837W	E90	LW-37
N1838H	B100	BE-123
N1839D	90	LJ-1038
N1839G	F90	LA-158
N1839S	200	BB-954
N1840S	E90	LW-263
N1841G	90	LJ-965
N1841K	200T	BT-22
N1841Z	200	BB-985
N1842A	90	LJ-1008
N1842B	200T	BT-20
N1842N	F90	LA-172
N1842P	200	BB-999
N1842S	200	BB-1018
N1842Y	200	BB-1015
N1843S	200	BB-976
N1843S	441	0317
N1844A	200	BB-1047
N1844B	200C	BL-55
N1844B	90	LJ-1844
N1844C	200C	BL-56
N1844K	90	LJ-1031
N1844S	200	BB-975
N1844S	300	FA-123
N1844S	G1	29
N1845	300	FA-132
N1845	350	FL-327
N1845C	300	FA-124
N1845L	F90	LA-162
N1845S	200	BB-976
N1845S	G1	29
N1845W	200T	BT-24
N1845W	90	LJ-597
N1846B	90	LJ-1043
N1846D	90	LJ-1044
N1846F	90	LJ-1047
N1846K	200	BB-1061
N1846M	200T	BT-28
N1846S	200	BB-1001
N1846W	90	LJ-598
N1846W	F90	LA-174
N1847A	200	BB-923
N1847S	200	BB-957
N1847S	200	BB-1256
N1847V	200	BB-947
N1847W	90	LJ-599
N1848S	90	LJ-1455
N1848T	425	0105
N1849B	200	BB-884
N1849T	200	BB-945
N1850T	200	BB-872
N1850W	200	BB-953
N1850X	200	BB-946
N1851S	200	BB-962
N1851T	90	LJ-260
N1852B	200	BB-952
N1853D	F90	LA-163
N1853T	90	LJ-260
N1853T	90	LJ-997
N1853X	90	LJ-998
N1854S	B100	BE-125
N1855H	90	LJ-995
N1857A	200	BB-965
N1857A	90	LJ-525
N1857F	F90	LA-167
N1857L	200	BB-618
N1857W	200	BB-618
N1857W	90	LJ-525
N1858E	200	BB-960
N1858W	200	BB-969
N1859E	200	BB-971
N1860B	200C	BL-48
N1860C	F90	LA-164
N1860N	200	BB-907
N1861B	200	BB-974
N1861D	B100	BE-126
N1865A	200	BB-281
N1865A	200	BB-1119
N1865A	350	FL-103
N1865D	200	BB-1119
N1865N	350	FL-103
N1866A	200	BB-281
N1866A	200	BB-1112
N1869	90	LJ-520
N1870S	200	BB-1106
N1870S	90	LJ-675
N1875C	90	LJ-1626
N1875Z	90	LJ-1060
N1876S	90	LJ-675
N1876Z	90	LJ-1061
N1879D	31T	8020046
N1879W	31T	8020046
N1879W	31T	8166065
N1880C	350	FL-360
N1883M	B100	BE-113
N1888M	B100	BE-113
N1891S	200	BB-1153
N1899	90	LJ-369
N1899	90	LJ-636
N1900W	G1	195
N1901W	G1	190
N1902D	G1	198
N1902P	G1	198
N1905L	90	LJ-133
N1906K	425	0068
N1907L	B100	BE-7
N1907W	MIIB	T26-176
N1909R	90	LJ-59
N1910L	B100	BE-10
N1911L	B100	BE-11
N1916M	G1	179
N1918W	425	0084
N1920H	90	LJ-34
N1925L	200	BB-1094
N1925P	200	BB-1094
N1925P	G1	29
N1926A	200	BB-922
N1928H	680W	1789-19
N1929B	G1	23
N1929J	690C	11652
N1929Y	G1	23
N1930P	MU-2	399SA
N1931C	200G	BY-37
N1931S	690C	11734
N1932H	200	BB-1303
N1932P	200	BB-1303
N1948J	300	FA-89
N1952	200	BB-28
N1952	90	LJ-194
N1952L	90	LJ-194
N1955E	200	BB-727
N1962	90	LJ-1553
N1962J	441	0074
N1963R	680T	1697-74
N1965M	90	LJ-124
N1967H	TBM7	46
N1967S	200	BB-696
N1968W	46T	97115B
N1969C	200	BB-391
N1969K	MIIB	T26-134
N1970T	90	LJ-616
N1974H	90	LJ-630
N1975G	E90	LW-252
N1975L	90	LJ-242
N1976J	31T	7400014
N1976J	31T	7520005
N1976M	F90	LA-81
N1978P	MU-2	212
(N1981B)	B100	BE-17
N1981S	695	95047
N1983R	PC12	285
N1983R	PC12	345
N1983R	PC12	601
N1983R	PC12	799
N1986F	F406	0002
N1999G	90	LJ-319
N2000C	200	BB-751
N2000C	G1	109
N2000E	90	LJ-172
N2000F	200	BB-458
N2000F	90	LJ-172
N2000F	E90	LW-152
N2000J	BN2	325
N2000M	B100	BE-127
N2000S	STAR	NC-1
N2000S	STAR	NC-4
N2000S	STAR	NC-17
N2000S	STAR	NC-22
N2000S	STAR	NC-43
N2000X	200	BB-272
N2000X	90	LJ-403
(N2006)	200	BB-258
N2006	E90	LW-162
(N2008)	200	BB-557
N2009W	STAR	NC-9
N2010	G1	133
N2011	G1	146
N2014K	200	BB-393
N2015G	350	FL-170
N2016L	90	LJ-789
N2016T	B100	BE-51

N2017M	100	B-229
N2017N	E90	LW-292
N2017Y	E90	LW-291
N2019U	90	LJ-792
N2025G	100	B-244
N2025M	200	BB-384
N2025S	B100	BE-54
N2027B	200C	BL-2
N2029N	90	LJ-798
N2029X	E90	LW-298
N2029Z	350	FL-177
N2029Z	90	LJ-1492
(N2030B)	100	B-245
N2030P	200	BB-412
N2030W	90	LJ-788
N2032N	90	LJ-800
N2034P	200	BB-429
N2035C	E90	LW-300
N2035N	E90	LW-302
N2035S	90	LJ-791
N2037C	B100	BE-53
N2038Q	100	B-202
N2038Z	90	LJ-807
N2039B	90	LJ-806
N2040D	200	BB-388
N2040E	90	LJ-1464
N2040S	100	B-24
N2041Y	E90	LW-307
N2043C	E90	LW-324
N2043W	E90	LW-306
N2044C	E90	LW-308
N2044D	200	BB-409
N2045D	200	BB-435
N2045N	E90	LW-309
N2045Q	350	FL-178
N2046D	90	LJ-290
N2047V	350	FL-179
N2048K	E90	LW-311
N2050A	**90**	**LJ-813**
N2051P	200	BB-434
N2052B	B100	BE-52
N2053C	200	BB-433
N2057C	**90**	**LJ-827**
N2057N	90	LJ-815
N2057S	200	BB-425
N2060M	MU-2	564
N2060Y	B100	BE-60
N2061B	200	BB-413
N2062A	E90	LW-317
N2063A	90	LJ-819
N2063T	200	BB-462
N2065D	E90	LW-320
N2065K	E90	LW-319
N2065P	200	BB-465
N2066C	B100	BE-56
N2066T	200	BB-464
N2067D	200T	BT-4
N2067M	200	BB-415
N2068L	200	BB-449
N2068W	90	LJ-805
N2069B	690	11058
N2070U	200	BB-470
N2071C	200T	BT-5
N2071D	200T	BT-6
N2071X	200T	BT-7
N2071Y	200T	BT-8
N2071Z	200T	BT-9
N2073X	B100	BE-61
N2074M	B100	BE-129
N2075L	90	LJ-705
N2077L	200	BB-77
N2079A	425	0001
(N2084J)	P68	158
N2085W	90	LJ-91
N2085W	90	LJ-320
N2090L	90	LJ-690
N2097W	90	LJ-1507
N2100E	90	LJ-351
N2100S	MIIA	T26-002
N2100T	100	B-31
N2100T	**MU-2**	**182**
N2101S	MIIA	T26-007
N2102S	MIIA	T26-009
N2104S	MIIA	T26-004
N2111L	E90	LW-179
N2112V	**350**	**FL-501**
N2114L	200	BB-114
N2115L	200	BB-115
N2119V	**BN2**	**2105**
N2122M	350	FL-200
N2123Y	90	LJ-1422
N2127L	200	BB-127
N2132M	BN2	2012
N2132W	200	BB-1594
N2133L	200	BB-133
N2135J	200	BB-869
N2141B	**690B**	**11484**
N2145L	200	BB-145
N2150M	G1	27
N2153L	200	BB-153
N2155B	**690**	**11046**
N2156L	200	BB-156
N2157A	31T	7720055
N2157L	200	BB-1068
N2159X	BN2	2019
N2160L	200	BB-160
N2161L	200	BB-161
N2162L	E90	LW-162
N2164L	**F90**	**LA-79**
N2166L	200	BB-166
N2173Z	**680T**	**1704-80**
N2176D	MU-2	028
N2176L	200	BB-176
N2177L	E90	LW-177
N2178A	90	LJ-1542
N2178F	**90**	**LJ-1508**
N2180L	E90	LW-180
N2181L	**E90**	**LW-181**
N2185M	**PC6**	**687**
N2186L	**E90**	**LW-186**
N2187J	90	LJ-1540
N2187L	E90	LW-187
N2188L	E90	LW-188
N2191L	E90	LW-191
N2192L	**E90**	**LW-192**
N2192V	350	FL-192
N2194L	E90	LW-194
N2195L	E90	LW-195
N2198T	31T	8120009
N2200R	P68	221
N2202D	200	BB-1645
N2203Z	300	FA-133
N2217C	350	FL-202
N2217C	350	FL-224
N2217Q	90	LJ-1539
N2221Z	200	BB-1629
N2222C	**PC12**	**542**
N2225H	100	B-34
N2225Y	200	BB-1618
(N2227F)	200	BB-1025
N2227L	100	B-227
N2233Z	**BN2**	**23**
N2244	**PC12**	**1009**
N2245P	200	BB-1605
N2247R	PA42	5501005
N2267U	695A	96007
N2269L	E90	LW-196
N2270B	90	LJ-658
N2270T	695A	96011
N2272H	200	BB-1572
N2273A	90	LJ-1528
N2274L	**E90**	**LW-213**
N2281S	350	FL-181
N2287J	200	BB-1611
N2287L	200	BB-1612
N2287L	200	BB-1678
N2288B	200	BB-1589
N2290C	90	LJ-1518
N2290L	200	BB-190
N2290V	350	FL-190
N2291F	90	LJ-1521
N2292Z	690A	11174
N2294B	200	BB-1616
N2295F	MIIB	T26-110
N2296G	350	FL-196
N2296W	90	LJ-438
(N2296Y)	E90	LW-274
N2297C	**90**	**LJ-1497**
N2297L	90	LJ-697
N2297P	350	FL-214
N2298B	350	FL-198
N2299H	200	BB-1650
N2299W	200	BB-1626
N2300Z	100	B-172
N2301K	200	BB-1681
N2301N	MIIA	T26-002
N2301Q	350	FL-204
N2301R	200	BB-1603
N2302S	200	BB-1602
N2303B	350	FL-209
N2303F	200	BB-1601
N2303P	**MIIB**	**T26-167E**
N2304F	200	BB-1674
N2307T	350	FL-232
N2308R	350	FL-207
N2310K	**90**	**LJ-1510**
N2311J	90	LJ-1511
N2312V	31T	8020041
N2313K	90	LJ-1513
N2313X	31T	8004051
N2314S	350	FL-194
N2315A	**350**	**FL-171**
N2315L	**90**	**LJ-1515**
N2315V	31T	8020042
N2316H	90	LJ-1491
N2316V	31T	8004020
N2316X	31T	8004052
N2317N	350	FL-237
N2317V	31T	8004021
N2319X	31T	8020087
N2320V	31T	8004023
N2320X	31T	8020088
N2321V	31T	8004024
N2321X	31T	8166003
N2322X	31T	8166002
N2323V	31T	8004025
N2324V	31T	8004026
N2325G	E90	LW-232
N2325L	90	LJ-1534
N2325V	31T	8004028
N2325W	31T	8020011
N2325W	31T	8166075
N2325Y	**350**	**FL-201**
N2326J	**200**	**BB-1606**
N2326V	31T	8020043
N2328E	**200**	**BB-1608**
N2328Q	300C	FM-10
N2328W	31T	8020012
N2328X	31T	8020089
N2329X	31T	8020090
N2330V	31T	8020044
N2331C	200	BB-1615
N2331X	31T	8020091
N2332Q	200	BB-1614
N2332R	31T	7904037
N2334R	31T	7920088
N2334V	31T	8020045
N2334V	31T	8020046
N2334X	31T	8004054
N2335X	31T	8120001
N2335X	31T	8004053
N2336V	31T	8020048
N2336X	31T	8120002
N2337V	31T	8004022
N2337X	31T	8120003
N2338V	31T	8020049
N2338X	31T	8120004
N2339V	31T	8020050
N2340M	90	LJ-57
N2340X	31T	8120005
N2341F	350	FL-212
N2341K	200	BB-1741
N2341R	350	FL-238
N2341S	350	FL-241
N2342F	350	FL-215
N2342N	90	LJ-1548
N2342W	31T	8020013
N2342W	31T	8166076
N2343V	31T	8020051
N2344H	350	FL-264
N2344N	350	FL-244
N2344R	31T	7920089
N2345M	200	BB-1633
N2345R	31T	8020001
(N2345W)	31T	7920092
N2346S	350	FL-236
N2347V	31T	8004030
N2347X	31T	8004056
N2348W	31T	8020014
N2348W	**31T**	**7904057**
(N2349L)	P68	167
N2349R	31T	7920090
N2349V	31T	8004031
N2349X	31T	8004055
N2350X	31T	8004057
N2351X	200	BB-1634
N2351X	31T	8104001
N2352N	350	FL-218
N2352X	31T	8104002
N2353W	31T	8020015
N2354V	31T	8004032
N2354Y	**90**	**LJ-1532**
N2355V	31T	8004033
N2355W	31T	8020016
N2355Z	200	BB-1675
N2356X	**31T**	**8104003**
N2359W	31T	8020017
N2359W	31T	1166001
N2360X	31T	8104004
N2361C	200	BB-1661
N2365X	31T	8104005
N2366W	31T	8020018
N2366X	31T	8120006
N2367X	31T	8104006
N2368R	31T	7904049
N2369R	31T	7904051
N2369V	**31T**	**8004035**
N2369W	31T	8020019
N2369X	31T	8120007
N2370X	31T	8104007
N2371V	31T	8004036
N2372V	31T	8020053
N2372V	31T	8004053
N2373V	31T	8020055
N2374W	31T	8020020
(N2376R)	31T	8166073
N2376V	31T	8020056
N2376X	31T	8120008
N2378X	31T	8104008
N2379R	31T	7904053
N2379V	31T	8020057
N2379W	31T	8004007
N2382W	31T	8020021
N2384V	31T	8020058
N2385V	31T	8020060
N2385X	31T	8120009
N2386	PC6	724
N2386W	31T	8020023
N2386X	31T	8104009
N2387X	31T	8120010
N2388R	31T	7904054
N2388V	31T	8020061
N2388V	31T	8020062
N2389V	31T	8020063
N2389X	31T	8104010
N2390V	31T	8020064
N2390V	31T	8004032
N2391X	31T	8104011
N2392B	UC12	BU-11
N2392S	350	FL-143
N2393W	31T	8020024
N2393X	31T	8120012
N2395V	31T	8020065
N2396X	31T	8104012
N2398V	31T	8020066
N2399X	31T	8104013
N2400E	100	B-29
N2400X	90	LJ-18
N2401X	31T	8120013
N2402Y	31T	8104045
N2403X	**31T**	**8104014**
N2405X	31T	8120014
N2405Y	31T	8120042
N2406U	**MU-2**	**197**
N2406X	31T	8104015
N2407B	BN2	2168

N2407W	31T	8020025	N2474Y	31T	8166007	N2549C	MU-2	774SA	N2623Q	441	0115
N2407X	31T	8120011	N2476X	31T	8120025	N2549E	680T	1546-9	N2623Y	441	0116
N2409W	31T	8004008	N2476Y	31T	8120050	N2550Y	31T	8166019	(N2623Z)	441	0117
N2409W	31T	8304003	N2477V	31T	8004037	N2551Y	31T	8120054	N2624D	441	0122
N2409W	31T	1166006	N2477Y	31T	8166008	**N2552Y**	**31T**	**8104061**	(N2624L)	441	0123
N2409Y	31T	8120043	N2478V	31T	8004038	N2553Y	31T	8166018	N2624N	441	0124
N2410R	31T	7920092	N2478Y	31T	8104053	N2553Z	31T	8166071	(N2624Z)	441	0125
N2411A	B100	BE-45	N2480A	200	BB-296	**N2556R**	**31T**	**8004003**	(N2625C)	441	0126
N2411X	31T	8120015	N2480V	31T	8004039	N2556W	31T	8020029	N2625D	441	0127
N2412W	31T	8004009	**N2480X**	**31T**	**8104026**	N2556W	31T	8020033	N2625H	441	0128
N2412X	31T	8104016	N2481X	31T	8104027	N2557V	31T	8004047	N2625M	441	0129
N2412Y	31T	8104046	N2482X	31T	8104028	N2558Y	31T	8120055	N2625N	441	0130
N2414X	31T	8120016	N2482Y	31T	8120046	N2560Y	31T	8104062	(N2625Y)	441	0131
N2415W	31T	8004010	N2483W	31T	8020027	N2563W	31T	8020030	N2625Z	441	0132
N2416R	31T	7920093	N2483X	31T	8120026	N2563Y	31T	8166020	(N2626A)	441	0134
N2418W	31T	8004011	N2484B	441	0112	N2565X	31T	8120034	(N2626J)	441	0135
N2418W	31T	1104004	N2484V	31T	8004040	N2566W	31T	8020035	N2626X	441	0136
N2419X	31T	8104017	N2484X	31T	8104029	N2567X	31T	8120035	N2626Y	441	0137
N2420M	F90	LA-134	N2484Y	31T	8166010	N2568Y	31T	8104063	(N2626Z)	441	0138
N2420X	31T	8120018	N2485X	31T	8120027	N2569X	31T	8104039	N2627J	441	0142
N2420Y	31T	8104047	N2488Y	31T	8166009	N2569Y	31T	8166021	N2627K	441	0143
N2422X	31T	8104018	N2489R	31T	8004001	N2570V	31T	8020080	(N2627N)	441	0144
N2425	G1	6	N2489Y	31T	8275001	N2570W	31T	8020036	N2627P	441	0145
~~N2425J~~	~~B100~~	~~BE-72~~	N2490V	31T	8004041	N2570Y	31T	8166022	(N2627U)	441	0146
N2425X	200	BB-202	N2490Y	31T	8104054	N2571X	31T	8104037	N2627Y	441	0147
N2425X	31T	8120019	N2491Y	31T	8104055	N2571X	31T	8166004	N2627Z	441	0148
N2427W	31T	8020022	N2492V	31T	8004042	N2571Y	31T	8104064	(N2628B)	441	0150
N2427W	31T	1104005	N2492X	31T	8104030	N2572Y	31T	8120056	N2628M	441	0151
N2427X	31T	8104019	N2494X	31T	8104031	N2574X	31T	8120036	N2628X	441	0152
N2428Q	**46D**	**2**	N2494X	46D	218	N2576X	31T	8104040	N2628Y	441	0153
N2428V	31T	1122001	N2494Y	31T	8166011	N2577Y	31T	8166023	(N2628Z)	441	0154
N2428V	31T	1166007	N2495X	31T	8120022	N2579V	31T	8020081	N2629B	441	0155
N2429R	31T	8020002	N2495X	31T	8120029	N2580V	31T	8020082	N2629P	441	0156
N2430R	31T	8020003	N2495Y	31T	8104056	N2580Y	31T	8104065	N2629Y	441	0157
N2433V	31T	1122002	N2496X	31T	8104032	N2580Y	31T	8166012	(N2629Z)	441	0158
N2433V	31T	1166008	(N2499R)	31T	8004002	N2580Z	31T	8166072	N2630	MIII	T-223
N2433X	31T	8104020	N2499R	31T	8004002	N2580Z	31T	1166002	N2630M	MIII	T-223
N2434V	31T	1104011	N2499X	31T	8120028	N2582X	31T	8120037	N2637M	680T	1568-24
N2434W	31T	8004013	N2500V	31T	8004043	N2584W	31T	8020039	**N2643B**	**681B**	**6060**
N2434W	31T	1104006	N2501Y	31T	8166013	N2586E	300	FA-96	N2643X	BN2	2109
N2435Y	**31T**	**8104049**	N2503N	300	FA-92	N2586Y	31T	8166024	N2645Z	31T	7520009
N2436W	31T	8004014	N2503V	31T	8004044	**N2587R**	**31T**	**8004004**	N2646K	200	BB-1254
N2436W	31T	1104007	N2504V	31T	8004045	N2587V	31T	8020083	**N2646W**	**690B**	**11496**
(N2436Y)	31T	8120047	N2506V	31T	8020074	N2587X	31T	8104041	N2647C	690C	11602
N2438R	31T	8020004	N2507U	300	FA-93	N2588Y	31T	8166025	N2648M	90	LJ-1136
N2441K	**441**	**0053**	N2507V	31T	8020075	N2589X	31T	8120039	N2649	MIII	T-221
N2441Y	31T	8120045	N2510L	90	LJ-197	N2589Z	31T	8120033	N2650C	300	FA-103
N2442W	31T	8004015	N2510R	31T	7920091	N2590X	31T	8104042	N2652M	200	BB-1255
N2442Y	31T	8104050	N2510V	31T	8020076	N2590Y	31T	8104066	N2655	680T	1565-21
N2443X	31T	8120020	N2510X	31T	8120030	N2592V	31T	8020084	N2657	200	BB-531
N2443Y	31T	8120048	N2511X	31T	8104034	N2592V	31T	8004048	N2660D	300	FA-104
N2446X	31T	8166001	N2512R	200	BB-1249	N2594R	31T	8004005	N2670W	P68	251
N2448W	31T	8004016	N2512R	31T	7904050	N2594Z	31T	8004005	N2673M	300	FA-131
N2448W	31T	8275020	N2512Y	31T	8104051	N2596V	31T	8004049	N2676M	200	BB-1256
N2448W	31T	8375003	N2515Y	31T	8166014	N2597Y	31T	8166026	N2678D	200	BB-1257
N2455X	31T	8104021	N2516R	31T	8020006	N2601S	MII	T26-001	N2686L	300	FA-106
N2457X	31T	8120021	N2516X	31T	8120031	N2601S	MIII	T-261	N2687W	90	LJ-824
N2457X	31T	8104022	N2517X	31T	8166004	N2601V	31T	8020085	N2689E	31T	7820038
N2457X	MIII	T-331	(N2519V)	31T	8020077	N2602M	90	LJ-1135	N2706E	90	LJ-1138
N2458W	**31T**	**8004017**	**N2519X**	**31T**	**8104035**	N2602M	G1	123	N2709J	90	LJ-1531
N2459X	31T	8120022	N2519Y	200	BB-1250	N2602Y	31T	8166027	N2709Z	MIVC	AT-695B
N2459Y	31T	8104052	N2519Y	31T	8120052	N2603X	31T	8104043	**N2711E**	**TBM8**	**396**
N2463X	31T	8104023	N2520Y	31T	8166016	N2603Y	31T	8120059	N2718W	BN2	331
N2464W	31T	8004018	**N2522V**	**31T**	**8020078**	N2604R	31T	8004006	N2721D	441	0161
(N2464W)	31T	8275021	N2522Z	31T	8304002	N2604R	31T	1166003	(N2721F)	441	0162
N2464W	31T	8375004	(N2525Y)	31T	8120051	N2604X	31T	8120041	N2721U	441	0163
N2464W	31T	8475001	N2529R	31T	8020007	N2605L	300	FA-97	N2721X	441	0164
N2464X	31T	8104024	N2529V	31T	8004046	N2605V	31T	8020086	**N2722D**	**441**	**0168**
N2465Y	31T	8120049	N2529W	31T	8020031	N2605V	31T	8004050	(N2722F)	441	0169
N2466V	31T	8020067	N2531Y	31T	8120032	N2605Y	31T	8275002	(N2722H)	441	0170
N2467V	31T	8020068	N2531Y	31T	8120053	N2606V	31T	8004050	(N2722S)	441	0171
N2467X	31T	8104025	N2533X	31T	8104036	N2606Y	46D	8	(N2722U)	441	0172
N2467Y	31T	8166005	**N2535B**	**350**	**FL-224**	N2607X	31T	8104044	**N2722Y**	**441**	**0173**
N2468X	31T	8120023	N2536Y	31T	8166017	N2608Y	31T	8104067	N2723A	441	0175
N2468Y	31T	8104053	**N2536Y**	**BN2T**	**2303**	N2609Y	31T	8166029	N2723B	441	0176
N2469V	**31T**	**8020070**	N2536Z	90	LJ-124	N2610	MIV	AT-007	(N2723C)	441	0177
N2470X	31T	8120024	N2537Y	31T	8104059	N2610Y	200	BB-1251	N2723P	441	0178
N2471V	31T	8020071	N2539X	31T	8104038	N2614C	300	FA-100	N2723S	441	0179
N2472V	31T	8020072	N2541Y	31T	8166015	N2614X	200	BB-1253	**N2723X**	**441**	**0180**
N2473W	31T	8020026	N2542W	31T	8020028	N2617X	31T	8166004	N2724K	441	0182
N2473Y	31T	8166006	N2546X	31T	8120019	(N2622Z)	441	0108	(N2724L)	441	0183
N2474V	31T	8020073	N2547R	31T	8020008	N2623A	441	0112	(N2724M)	441	0184
(N2474W)	31T	8275022	N2547R	31T	8020009	(N2623B)	441	0113	(N2724R)	441	0185
N2474W	31T	8375005	N2547Y	31T	8104060	N2623F	441	0114	N2724S	441	0186

(N2725A)	441	0188	N2905C	BN2	116	N3051S	200	BB-1642	N3092J	46T	97324
N2725B	681	6006	N2920A	200	BB-420	N3052C	350	FL-225	N3092J	46T	97327
N2725D	441	0189	N2930A	90	LJ-808	N3053Q	200	BB-1713	N3092J	46T	97352
N2725N	**441**	**0190**	N2937A	690C	11670	N3053W	90	LJ-613	N3092K	350	FL-250
(N2725Q)	441	0191	N2950L	690B	11384	N3055C	46T	97154	N3092K	46T	97223
N2725U	441	0192	N2956D	P68	264	N3055K	200	BB-1644	N3092S	200	BB-1498
(N2725X)	441	0193	N2957A	P68	265	N3055S	300	FA-137	N3093B	46D	221
(N2726B)	441	0195	N2958W	P68	267	N3059F	350	FL-230	N3094R	46T	97198
N2726F	441	0196	N2959A	P68	262	N3059F	MIII	TT-483A	N3094S	46T	97199
(N2726J)	441	0197	N2959B	P68	256	N3059Y	MIII	TT-477A	N3094T	MIVC	AT-495B
N2726N	441	0198	**N2959C**	**P68**	**260**	N3060C	100	B-225	N3094W	46T	97185
(N2726S)	441	0199	(N2965T)	TRIS	1004	N3060C	200	BB-236	N3094W	90	LJ-594
(N2726X)	441	0200	N2997N	200	BB-1261	**N3061J**	**46T**	**97322**	N3095G	46T	97340
N2727A	441	0201	N2997Q	300	FA-112	N3061W	E90	LW-61	N3095L	46T	97187
N2727B	441	0202	N2997T	200	BB-1262	N3063T	46T	97178	N3095L	46T	97200
(N2727F)	441	0203	N2997W	200	BB-1263	N3063T	46T	97184	N3095N	46T	97201
N2727L	441	0204	N2997X	300	FA-113	N3063W	E90	LW-63	N3095N	46T	97211
(N2727X)	441	0205	N2998	G1	16	N3064J	200	BB-1664	N3095Q	46T	97199
(N2728B)	441	0206	N2998A	300	FA-115	N3064J	46T	97175	N3095W	90	LJ-595
N2728D	441	0207	N2998X	300	FA-116	N3064K	46D	170	N3096D	46T	97193
N2728F	441	0208	N2999Y	200	BB-1266	N3064K	46T	97182	**N3096P**	**46T**	**97178**
N2728G	441	0209	N3000C	90	LJ-245	N3065W	E90	LW-65	N3097Q	46T	97188
(N2728N)	441	0210	N3000R	200	BB-945	N3065Y	200	BB-1497	N3099E	46T	97197
N2736D	90	LJ-1141	N3000R	90	LJ-196	N3066U	90	LJ-1586	N3100E	G1	50
N2742N	BN2	874	N3000W	200	BB-752	N3066V	MIII	TT-489A	**N3100K**	**100**	**B-1**
N2746Z	MIII	T-227	N3000W	90	LJ-117	**N3066W**	**90**	**LJ-1536**	N3100W	90	LJ-1166
N2748X	200	BB-1258	N3000W	E90	LW-49	N3067W	300	FA-130	**N3103A**	**46T**	**97190**
N2755B	680W	1762-8	N3001D	MIII	TT-444A	N3067W	MIII	TT-486A	N3103L	200	BB-1933
N2755H	680T	1628-55	**N3002S**	**90**	**LJ-103**	**N3068Z**	**90**	**LJ-1544**	N3103L	350	FL-313
N2758B	350C	FN-1	N3003	G1	2	N3068Z	MIVC	AT-487	N3104R	46T	97203
N2763B	200	BB-1291	N3007C	200	BB-1279	N3070R	350	FL-470	N3106P	350	FL-246
N2763B	200	BB-1407	N3008L	MIVC	AT-446B	N3070S	90	LJ-1126	N3106P	46T	97222
N2766B	200C	BL-130	N3010F	46T	97166	N3071H	90	LJ-1546	N3106P	46T	97330
N2769B	200	BB-1298	N3010Q	MIVC	AT-452	N3072N	300	FA-135	N3106P	90	LJ-1404
N2785A	90	LJ-1139	N3013T	MIVC	AT-454	N3072Y	MIII	TT-518A	N3106Y	46T	97207
N2789A	300C	FM-7	**N3014C**	**46T**	**97311**	N3075A	MIVC	AT-493	N3106Y	46T	97217
N2789B	90	LJ-1201	N3014R	90	LJ-1554	N3075W	E90	LW-75	N3106Y	46T	97231
N2789R	FPC6	2030	N3015Q	200	BB-1493	N3076U	90	LJ-1154	N3106Y	90	LJ-1412
N2790B	200C	BN-4	N3016K	MIVC	AT-455	N3076U	90	LJ-1549	N3106Z	46T	97218
N2790B	90	LJ-1257	N3018C	200	BB-470	N3076W	100	B-176	N3106Z	46T	97219
N2790R	FPC6	2031	N3018C	200	BB-1718	N3077Y	90	LJ-1155	N3106Z	46T	97224
N2791R	FPC6	2032	N3019U	MIII	TT-456A	N3078D	90	LJ-1159	N3106Z	46T	97252
N2792R	FPC6	2043	N3019W	90	LJ-639	N3078T	350	FL-240	N3106Z	46T	97263
N2795B	200T	BT-25	N3021A	MIII	TT-480	N3078U	300	FA-140	N3106Z	46T	97377
N2800	300	FA-144	N3022F	200	BB-1267	N3078W	100	B-178	N3107V	46T	97212
N2804B	200	BB-1157	N3025Z	300	FA-120	N3078W	350	FL-248	**N3107W**	**300**	**FA-150**
N2804B	200C	BL-128	N3026H	200	BB-1494	N3078W	90	LJ-61	N3107W	MIVC	AT-502
N2804B	300	FA-212	N3026K	350	FL-125	N3079K	300	FA-110	N3108F	MIVC	AT-511
N2808B	300	FA-189	N3026W	E90	LW-84	N3079S	200	BB-1295	N3108G	MIII	TT-512A
N2809B	200	BB-48	N3028G	46T	97306	N3079Z	90	LJ-1164	N3108H	MIVC	AT-513
N2811B	200C	BL-69	N3028L	MIII	TT-459A	N3080F	300	FA-141	N3108K	90	LJ-1176
N2811B	350	FL-32	N3029F	300	FA-128	**N3080F**	**350**	**FL-249**	N3108L	MIII	TT-515A
N2826B	200C	BL-135	N3030C	200	BB-30	N3081K	90	LJ-1165	N3109A	MIII	TT-521
N2826B	200T	BT-26	N3030C	200	BB-400	N3081Z	300	FA-142	N3109D	MIVC	AT-524
N2830B	200C	BN-2	N3030C	90	LJ-754	N3082C	200	BB-1282	N3109K	MIII	TT-527
N2830B	B100	BE-72	N3030C	90	LJ-1117	N3082S	200	BB-1300	N3109N	300	FA-155
N2830S	**B100**	**BE-48**	N3030C	90	LJ-1209	N3082W	90	LJ-1168	N3109N	MIVC	AT-528
N2841B	200C	BL-67	**N3030G**	**90**	**LJ-1117**	N3082X	200	BB-1287	N3109S	MIII	TT-529A
N2842B	200	BB-1173	N3030S	350	FL-221	N3083E	90	LJ-1181	N3109Y	200	BB-1292
N2842B	200	BB-1348	N3033U	350	FL-223	N3083K	90	LJ-1378	N3110B	46T	97361
N2843B	UC12	BW-1	N3034W	200	BB-1269	N3083Z	200	BB-1299	N3110B	MIVC	AT-532
N2844B	UC12	BW-2	N3034W	E90	LW-112	N3084B	90	LJ-1203	N3110F	MIVC	AT-434
N2845B	UC12	BW-3	N3035C	200	BB-400	**N3084K**	**300**	**FA-160**	N3110P	MIII	TT-536
N2851T	PC6	569	N3035P	90	LJ-1535	N3085D	300	FA-144	N3110T	46T	97206
N2852N	**PC12**	**1075**	**N3035T**	**90**	**LJ-1482**	N3085Y	90	LJ-1170	**N3110T**	**46T**	**97221**
N2852T	PC6	572	N3038W	MIII	TT-465	N3085Z	300	FA-147	N3110Y	200	BB-1294
N2853T	PC6	574	N3040P	350	FL-440	N3086D	300	FA-148	N3111C	46T	97232
N2854B	200T	BT-27	N3042K	300	FA-125	N3086G	90	LJ-1171	N3111D	MIVC	AT-547
N2854B	90	LJ-1226	N3042K	90	LJ-1377	N3087K	300	FA-118	N3111K	46T	97226
N2854T	PC6	575	N3042S	STAR	NC-2	N3088U	46T	97317	N3111K	90	LJ-1551
N2855B	90	LJ-1250	N3043N	46T	97165	N3088U	46T	97336	N3111K	MIVC	AT-549B
N2855S	P68	276	N3043N	46T	97176	N3088X	46T	97313	N3112K	350	FL-262
N2856B	200C	BN-3	N3043S	350	FL-243	**N3088X**	**46T**	**97323**	N3112K	90	LJ-1379
N2856B	350	FL-13	N3043W	200	BB-1272	N3090A	90	LJ-1152	N3112W	90	LJ-612
N2860A	90	LJ-1142	N3046N	46T	97308	N3090C	200	BB-30	N3113A	300	FA-161
N2872B	200	BB-1386	N3046N	46T	97326	N3090K	46T	97314	N3113A	MIVC	AT-560
N2872B	90	LJ-1013	N3046N	46T	97398	**N3090K**	**46T**	**97396**	N3113B	MIVC	AT-556
N2876B	200	BB-1387	N3046P	46T	97170	N3090W	E90	LW-60	N3113C	MIII	TT-555
N2877K	200	BB-683	N3047L	200	BB-1496	N3091F	46T	97316	N3113F	MIVC	AT-561
N2878B	200	BB-1388	N3048U	200	BB-1271	N3091F	46T	97339	N3113J	46T	97213
N2883	**200**	**BB-144**	N3048V	MIII	TT-468A	N3091F	46T	97345	N3113J	46T	97227
N2888A	690B	11415	N3051B	46T	97342	N3091Y	46T	97343	N3113M	MIVC	AT-563
N2896W	90	LJ-596	N3051H	MIVC	AT-501	N3091Y	46T	97358	N3113N	MIVC	AT-566
N2899P	441	0003	**N3051K**	**200**	**BB-1495**	N3091Y	46T	97362	N3113T	MIVC	AT-567

N3114B	MIVC	AT-564
N3114P	46T	97228
N3114Y	MIVC	AT-585
N3115C	46T	97225
N3115K	350	FL-315
N3115M	46T	97198
N3116C	P68T	8007
N3117N	200	BB-1670
N3117P	MIVC	AT-602
N3117S	46T	97230
N3117V	200	BB-1687
N3117V	46T	97234
N3118A	MIVC	AT-607B
N3118G	MIVC	AT-608B
N3118H	MIVC	AT-609B
N3120L	46T	97243
N3120L	46T	97250
N3120U	300C	FM-20
N3120U	90	LJ-1382
N3120X	350	FL-220
N3121G	300	FA-149
N3121V	46T	97241
N3121X	F406	0061
N3122E	F406	0059
N3122Z	300	FA-162
N3123H	46T	97216
N3123H	46T	97233
N3123H	46T	97242
N3123J	200	BB-1923
N3124E	46T	97220
N3125G	F406	0062
N3125J	200C	BL-46
N3125W	E90	LW-85
N3126W	46T	97235
N3126W	E90	LW-86
N3126Z	46T	97237
N3127G	46T	97238
N3127K	200	BB-1293
N3127R	441	0242
N3128K	350	FL-299
N3128K	90	LJ-1380
N3128S	46T	97244
N3128S	46T	97251
N3129S	46T	97256
N3129V	F406	0063
N3129X	46T	97246
N3130T	46T	97248
N3130Z	46T	97247
N3131M	46T	97245
N3131U	300	FA-158
N3132A	46T	97254
N3132B	46T	97253
N3132D	90	LJ-1552
N3132M	350	FL-305
N3132V	46T	97255
N3133L	90	LJ-1533
N3133L	90	LJ-1873
N3135Y	46T	97258
N3137T	46T	97257
N3138B	90	LJ-1538
N3139C	350	FL-239
N3139T	90	LJ-1175
N3141G	46T	97260
N3143M	46T	97259
N3143T	90	LJ-1543
N3143W	300	FA-153
N3145F	90	LJ-1545
N3146G	46T	97264
N3147B	200	BB-1647
N3150E	46T	97262
N3150U	46T	97265
N3151H	350	FL-251
N3151P	90	LJ-1599
N3151P	90	LJ-1615
N3152K	200	BB-1652
N3154J	200	BB-1654
N3154S	200	BB-1323
N3156F	90	LJ-1556
N3156L	200	BB-1733
N3157D	350	FL-128
N3157F	200	BB-1744
N3160G	690B	11509
N3160P	90	LJ-1560
N3163C	200	BB-1663
N3164C	350	FL-126
N3164R	90	LJ-1564
N3165M	350	FL-312
N3165M	90	LJ-1386
N3166W	E90	LW-66
N3168F	200	BB-1668
N3169N	350	FL-269
N3171A	90	LJ-1561
N3171H	200	BB-1671
N3172M	200	BB-1672
N3172N	350	FL-272
N3173K	200	BB-1304
N3173Y	200	BB-1673
N3175T	200	BB-1303
N3176T	350	FL-276
N3177W	E90	LW-77
N3178H	90	LJ-1648
N3178P	350	FL-290
N3178R	90	LJ-1578
N3179Q	350	FL-279
N3179V	350	FL-479
N3180S	200	BB-1501
N3181	200	BB-637
N3181Q	200	BB-1586
N3182M	200	BB-1682
N3184A	200T	BT-32
N3184F	90	LJ-1584
N3184W	90	LJ-1884
N3185C	200	BB-1290
N3185J	350	FL-285
N3186W	90	LJ-1886
N3188H	350	FL-588
N3188W	90	LJ-1928
N3189D	200G	BY-19
N3189T	350	FL-289
N3189W	E90	LW-89
N3190S	90	LJ-1190
N3190W	E90	LW-90
N3191E	90	LJ-1891
N3191G	350	FL-591
N3191V	200	BB-1941
N3192M	90	LJ-1912
N3192N	350	FL-292
N3193E	350	FL-593
N3193Q	350	FL-613
N3194K	90	LJ-1375
N3194U	200	BB-1694
N3195B	90	LJ-1895
N3195Q	90	LJ-1595
N3195T	350	FL-295
N3195V	350	FL-595
N3195W	E90	LW-95
N3196J	200G	BY-46
N3196K	90	LJ-1384
N3196N	200G	BY-36
N3197A	90	LJ-1897
N3197D	350	FL-597
N3197L	200	BB-1505
N3197L	350	FL-579
N3197L	90	LJ-1597
N3197N	350	FL-297
N3198K	90	LJ-1385
N3198M	350	FL-598
N3198N	350	FL-124
N3199A	200	BB-1499
N3199B	200	BB-1500
N3199B	200	BB-1699
N3199Z	200	BB-1999
N3200V	200	BB-2000
N3201W	90	LJ-1901
(N3202)	200	BB-423
N3202A	90	LJ-1602
N3202A	90	LJ-1902
N3202W	200C	BL-152
N3203K	300C	FM-23
N3203K	350	FL-263
N3203L	90	LJ-1573
N3203P	681	6019
N3203Q	200	BB-2003
N3203R	200C	BL-153
N3203T	200G	BY-33
N3203Z	200	BB-1503
N3203Z	200	BB-1703
N3203Z	350	FL-603
N3204K	300C	FM-24
N3204K	90	LJ-1389
N3204W	200	BB-1704
N3204Y	90	LJ-1904
N3205M	350	FL-255
N3205W	90	LJ-1555
N3205Z	200	BB-1765
N3206K	350	FL-260
N3206M	200	BB-1706
N3206T	200G	BY-6
N3207	200	BB-333
N3208K	350	FL-608
N3208T	200	BB-1508
N3208T	90	LJ-1908
N3210N	200	BB-1710
N3211Z	BN2	741
N3212A	695	95074
N3212E	200	BB-1712
N3212Y	90	LJ-1399
N3212Y	90	LJ-1612
N3213G	200	BB-1510
N3213L	200G	BY-13
N3214D	200	BB-1504
N3214D	200	BB-1714
N3214J	350	FL-294
N3215G	350	FL-575
N3215K	200	BB-1275
N3216G	200	BB-1716
N3216G	300	FA-156
N3216K	90	LJ-1392
N3216L	200	BB-1506
N3216L	350	FL-316
N3216U	90	LJ-1397
N3217H	350	FL-247
N3217K	90	LJ-1394
N3217M	90	LJ-1393
N3217N	200	BB-1513
N3217P	90	LJ-1617
N3217V	200	BB-1517
N3217V	350	FL-317
N3217X	90	LJ-1417
N3218K	90	LJ-1396
N3218P	90	LJ-1411
N3218V	200	BB-1518
N3218X	90	LJ-1418
N3218Z	350	FL-318
N3219G	200	BB-1509
N3219G	200	BB-1719
N3220E	90	LJ-1620
N3220L	90	LJ-1420
N3221M	90	LJ-1621
N3222K	300C	FM-22
N3222K	350	FL-322
N3222K	90	LJ-1369
N3223H	90	LJ-1425
N3223R	200	BB-1723
N3225V	90	LJ-1925
N3228M	90	LJ-1628
N3228V	90	LJ-1182
N3228X	200C	BL-131
N3230X	200	BB-1520
N3231F	200	BB-1511
(N3232U)	200	BB-44
N3234K	350	FL-234
N3234K	90	LJ-1402
N3234S	STAR	NC-3
N3234X	90	LJ-1414
N3235G	BN2	2111
N3235U	200	BB-44
N3235Z	200	BB-1515
N3236T	90	LJ-946
N3236Z	P68	281
N3237K	90	LJ-1390
N3237M	200	BB-1537
N3237S	300	FA-163
N3238K	90	LJ-1398
N3238S	350	FL-338
N3239K	90	LJ-1400
N3241N	200	BB-1521
N3242L	90	LJ-1413
N3242Q	90	LJ-1924
N3242V	90	LJ-1422
N3242Z	90	LJ-1428
N3245S	350	FL-138
N3245Y	90	LJ-1410
N3246S	200	BB-1516
N3246S	90	LJ-1576
N3247Q	200	BB-1588
N3250V	200	BB-1523
N3251E	90	LJ-1427
N3251H	90	LJ-1673
N3251Q	200G	BY-51
N3251Q	90	LJ-1429
N3251S	350	FL-131
N3251U	90	LJ-1430
N3252B	350	FL-252
N3252B	90	LJ-1421
N3252J	90	LJ-1424
N3252V	350	FL-134
N3252W	90	LJ-1570
N3252X	200	BB-1532
N3253Q	350	FL-293
N3253Q	90	LJ-1423
N3253U	350	FL-253
N3253U	680T	1718-89
N3254A	350	FL-254
N3254A	90	LJ-1433
N3254E	90	LJ-1416
N3257N	350	FL-257
N3258P	200	BB-1526
N3258P	90	LJ-1558
N3258R	350	FL-258
N3261E	200	BB-1529
N3261L	200	BB-1528
N3262P	200	BB-1662
N3262R	90	LJ-1562
N3263C	90	LJ-1432
N3263M	350	FL-135
N3263N	90	LJ-1563
N3263X	350	FL-143
N3263Y	350	FL-132
N3263Y	690C	11617
N3264N	90	LJ-1434
N3265K	90	LJ-1450
(N3265N)	BN2	504
N3265Q	TRIS	1038
N3265T	350	FL-265
N3265T	TRIS	1062
N3266A	TRIS	1063
N3266B	TRIS	1064
N3266G	TRIS	1065
N3266H	TRIS	1066
N3266K	TRIS	1067
N3266R	TRIS	1068
N3266T	TRIS	1069
N3266W	TRIS	1070
N3267A	TRIS	1071
N3267J	TRIS	1072
N3268H	350	FL-148
N3268L	200	BB-1538
N3268M	90	LJ-1438
N3268Z	350	FL-146
N3269W	350	FL-147
N3270K	90	LJ-1401
N3270Q	200	BB-1587
N3270T	90	LJ-1870
N3270V	200G	BY-50
N3270V	90	LJ-1451
N3271S	90	LJ-1441
N3272E	200	BB-1522
N3272Q	350	FL-572
N3276B	300C	FM-26
N3279Y	690A	11104
N3289T	90	LJ-1879
N3289Z	90	LJ-1889
N3290A	90	LJ-347
N3292C	46T	97210
N3292H	350	FL-594
N3292S	350	FL-604
N3296J	90	LJ-1896
N3298D	90	LJ-1918
N3301M	200	BB-1901
N3305E	90	LJ-1905
N3306X	90	LJ-1906
N3308E	200G	BY-68
N3311G	MU-2	603
N3311N	200G	BY-11
N3325H	46T	97133

N3326Q	200G	BY-26
N3330K	MU-2	551
N3330S	441	0205
N3331C	200G	BY-31
N3333D	90	LJ-259
(N3333M)	350	FL-243
N3333X	200	BB-542
N3333X	90	LJ-259
N3338H	200G	BY-38
N3345Y	200G	BY-45
N3347J	200G	BY-47
N3366K	350	FL-566
N3380P	P68	285
N3382Z	350	FL-582
N3388C	90	LJ-1913
N3400H	90	LJ-1890
N3400P	200G	BY-60
N3400T	90	LJ-1900
N3416	G1	130
N3419S	300C	FM-19
N3420J	200G	BY-70
N3425W	350	FL-605
N3455L	200G	BY-55
N3456W	200	BB-964
N3471T	200G	BY-71
N3474P	350	FL-574
N3483A	350	FL-583
N3486S	200G	BY-56
N3496C	350	FL-599
N3499U	200G	BY-59
N3500E	100	B-74
N3500E	90	LJ-1899
N3500F	E90	LW-48
N3500P	100	B-74
N3500P	200	BB-15
N3500P	90	LJ-132
N3500R	90	LJ-400
N3501B	90	LJ-1911
N3501D	200	BB-2001
N3502P	200G	BY-63
N3540X	MU-2	006
N3541X	MU-2	007
N3542X	MU-2	008
N3543X	MU-2	010
N3544X	MU-2	012
N3545X	MU-2	013
N3546X	MU-2	014
N3547X	MU-2	015
N3547X	MU-2	034
N3548X	MU-2	016
N3550X	MU-2	018
N3551X	MU-2	019
N3552X	MU-2	020
N3553X	MU-2	021
N3554X	MU-2	022
N3555X	MU-2	023
N3556X	MU-2	024
N3557X	MU-2	025
N3560X	MU-2	029
N3561X	MU-2	030
N3563X	MU-2	033
N3564X	MU-2	035
N3565X	MU-2	037
N3566X	MU-2	038
N3567X	MU-2	103
N3568X	MU-2	104
N3569X	MU-2	105
N3570X	MU-2	106
N3571X	MU-2	107
N3572X	MU-2	108
N3573X	MU-2	109
N3574X	MU-2	110
N3600A	100	B-30
N3601R	FPC6	2003
N3602R	FPC6	2004
N3603R	FPC6	2005
N3604R	FPC6	2027
N3605R	FPC6	2028
N3606R	FPC6	2029
N3606T	100	B-30
N3607R	FPC6	2041
N3608R	FPC6	2040
N3609R	FPC6	2042
N3610R	FPC6	2044
N3611R	FPC6	2034
N3612R	FPC6	2033
N3613R	FPC6	2035
N3620M	200	BB-1396
N3630	G1	111
N3634K	U-21	LM-22
N3650	90	LJ-132
N3650P	90	LJ-132
N3663B	B100	BE-94
N3663M	200	BB-686
N3666Y	200	BB-694
N3667G	200	BB-697
N3667U	F90	LA-53
N3668G	200	BB-709
N3668P	B100	BE-95
N3669U	B100	BE-96
N3669Z	200	BB-710
N3675B	B100	BE-97
N3679A	F90	LA-55
N3680A	F90	LA-60
N3682A	200	BB-727
N3682E	E90	LW-338
N3684F	200	BB-720
N3684P	F90	LA-56
N3685C	F90	LA-48
N3685G	F90	LA-57
N3685P	F90	LA-49
N3686B	F90	LA-75
N3686V	F90	LA-63
N3687S	F90	LA-70
N3688F	B100	BE-100
N3688P	90	LJ-915
N3690B	200	BB-730
N3690F	90	LJ-921
N3690S	200	BB-761
N3694C	F90	LA-61
N3694F	F90	LA-73
N3695A	B100	BE-101
N3695B	200	BB-734
N3695W	90	LJ-924
N3697F	200C	BL-14
N3697P	F90	LA-85
N3698H	F90	LA-64
N3698S	200	BB-745
N3699B	B100	BE-107
N3699L	200	BB-689
N3699P	B100	BE-99
N3699T	B100	BE-103
N3699U	F90	LA-87
N3700M	E90	LW-340
N3701B	F90	LA-83
N3701F	681B	6053
N3701F	90	LJ-927
N3702M	200	BB-744
N3703L	90	LJ-925
N3704S	F90	LA-77
N3705B	200	BB-753
N3706F	F90	LA-89
N3707T	200	BB-763
N3709B	F90	LA-91
N3709S	90	LJ-933
N3709W	90	LJ-935
N3710A	200	BB-760
N3710P	200	BB-776
N3710Y	E90	LW-343
N3711H	90	LJ-74
N3711M	90	LJ-74
N3713L	200	BB-795
N3714P	200	BB-783
N3715C	200	BB-728
N3715T	F90	LA-92
N3715W	200C	BL-17
N3716D	200	BB-732
N3717E	F90	LA-86
N3717J	90	LJ-930
N3717T	200	BB-767
N3718N	200T	BT-19
N3718Q	200T	BT-17
N3719N	200	BB-780
N3720U	200	BB-794
N3720W	F90	LA-66
N3721B	200	BB-708
N3721Z	F90	LA-117
N3722G	E90	LW-341
N3722H	200	BB-692
N3722Y	200	BB-719
N3722Y	350	FL-422
N3723B	200C	BL-26
N3723K	200	BB-813
N3723N	F90	LA-122
N3723P	200	BB-751
N3723Q	350	FL-423
N3723Y	200C	BL-30
N3724Q	350	FL-424
N3726E	350	FL-426
N3726M	350	FL-476
N3726V	350	FL-526
N3726Y	90	LJ-1826
N3727Q	350	FL-427
N3728E	200	BB-1928
N3729J	200	BB-1929
N3729N	200	BB-1939
N3729R	200	BB-711
N3729R	200	BB-1969
N3729Y	350	FL-519
N3731V	90	LJ-1731
N3732K	200	BB-1892
N3734Y	90	LJ-1834
N3735C	200	BB-1935
N3735D	F90	LA-90
N3735H	B100	BE-105
N3735M	90	LJ-1815
N3735W	F90	LA-94
N3737G	200	BB-765
(N3737G)	B100	BE-81
N3738B	200	BB-774
N3738J	681	6027
N3739C	350	FL-11
N3739C	350	FL-72
N3739C	F90	LA-96
N3741M	E90	LW-342
N3741U	F90	LA-99
N3750N	MU-2	308
N3753V	MIVA	AT-029
N3754C	681	6027
(N3754C)	690B	11512
N3754V	90	LJ-156
N3786J	200	BB-259
N3802B	200	BB-789
N3802F	F90	LA-103
N3804C	90	LJ-941
N3804F	90	LJ-947
N3805E	90	LJ-943
N3806N	B100	BE-110
N3806U	F90	LA-109
N3809C	F90	LA-112
N3810Q	B100	BE-113
N3811F	B100	BE-109
N3812S	200	BB-805
N3813C	E90	LW-196
N3813Z	200	BB-815
N3814B	200	BB-790
N3816W	200C	BL-22
N3817H	90	LJ-938
N3818C	B100	BE-112
N3818C	E90	LW-196
N3818H	E90	LW-344
N3821S	E90	LW-346
N3824H	F90	LA-104
N3824P	200	BB-804
N3824V	F90	LA-110
N3825E	F90	LA-116
N3825S	200	BB-803
N3826T	F90	LA-119
N3827Z	200C	BL-27
N3828E	200	BB-818
N3831Q	200	BB-771
N3831T	200C	BL-21
N3832B	200	BB-853
N3832E	200	BB-859
N3832E	P68	270
N3832G	90	LJ-976
N3832G	P68	271
N3832K	90	LJ-980
N3832K	P68	272
N3832P	P68	273
N3832Q	P68	274
N3832X	90	LJ-967
N3833A	200	BB-866
N3833P	680W	1761-7
N3834P	90	LJ-651
N3835C	200	BB-801
N3835K	200	BB-889
N3835Q	200	BB-908
N3835Z	90	LJ-978
N3835Z	BN2	2010
N3836E	200C	BL-41
N3836E	200C	BL-49
N3836H	B100	BE-121
N3837N	200	BB-915
N3837R	200C	BL-40
N3837S	200	BB-877
N3837U	200	BB-903
N3838S	F90	LA-153
N3841V	E90	LW-347
N3842H	200	BB-826
N3844E	200	BB-822
N3845B	200	BB-833
N3845S	F90	LA-125
N3846G	441	0097
N3846J	200	BB-778
N3847H	200C	BL-29
N3848V	F90	LA-126
N3849A	200C	BL-31
N3849B	200	BB-839
N3850H	90	LJ-956
N3850K	200	BB-843
N3850K	TRIS	1025
N3851B	TRIS	1003
N3852V	B100	BE-116
N3854B	200	BB-835
N3855K	F90	LA-224
N3858H	G1	52
N3859D	200	BB-838
N3859U	200	BB-851
N3861H	90	LJ-960
N3861S	200	BB-849
N3866B	B100	BE-118
N3867A	F90	LA-128
N3867N	681	6010
N3869F	690A	11141
N3872E	200	BB-854
N3872K	200	BB-868
N3875F	200	BB-850
N3913U	200	BB-773
N3914	PC6	546
N3917J	MU-2	126
N3926M	90	LJ-151
N3927U	P68	282
N3928G	MIII	T-297
N3929G	E90	LW-55
N3929L	MU-2	573
N3948A	31T	7720063
N3951F	31T	7520010
N3969P	90	LJ-115
N3975X	46T	97342
N3980B	P68	312
N3980D	90	LJ-682
N3980U	690B	11380
N3981Y	90	LJ-817
N3982C	695	95049
N3982L	MU-2	331
N3998Y	31T	8020055
N4000	200	BB-247
N4000	90	LJ-138
N4000D	100	B-66
N4000K	200	BB-402
N4000K	200	BB-1104
N4000K	300	FA-21
N4000K	350	FL-77
N4003J	200	BB-135
N4005J	90	LJ-1605
N4006K	350	FL-326
N4007	31T	7820061
N4009	G1	12
N4009L	300C	FM-9
N4015Y	31T	7720044
N4019	MIV	AT-014
N4031K	90	LJ-1631
N4042J	200	BB-874
"N4045"	G1	103
N4047C	200	BB-202

N4051X	MIIB	T26-124
N4053H	200	BB-1774
N4060Z	90	LJ-1590
N4061K	441	0090
N4064Z	200	BB-1764
N4065D	MU-2	660
N4072S	90	LJ-652
(N4075N)	46D	90
N4081W	200	BB-1781
N4083L	350	FL-283
N4086R	PA42	8001019
N4086T	PA42	8001081
N4088T	PA42	8001055
N4088Y	PA42	8001031
N4088Z	PA42	8001056
(N4088Z)	PA42	8301003
N4089A	PA42	8001041
N4089L	425	693
N4089T	PA42	8001043
N4089U	PA42	8001046
N4095S	90	LJ-655
N4096B	350	FL-296
N4098A	PA42	8001059
N4098K	PA42	8001050
N4098P	PA42	8001053
N4098T	PA42	8001058
N4099U	PA42	8001047
N4099V	PA42	8001049
N4099Y	PA42	8001068
N4100B	680W	1803-25
N4100H	100	B-44
N4100L	PA42	8001061
N4101T	PA42	8001078
N4101T	PA42	8001101
N4102L	PA42	8001069
(N4106G)	441	0099
N4107K	PA42	8001054
N4107U	PA42	8001074
N4107W	E90	LW-238
(N4109W)	PA42	8001084
N4109W	PA42	8001105
(N4109X)	PA42	8001086
N4109X	PA42	8001106
N4112Z	PA42	5527018
N4113F	PC6	760
(N4113Q)	PA42	8001020
N4114A	PA42	8001102
N4114D	PA42	8001103
N4114K	PA42	5501005
N4115F	PA42	5501014
N4115F	PA42	5501021
N4115H	90	LJ-1645
N4115J	PA42	5501009
N4115K	PA42	5501022
N4116K	PA42	5501009
N4116Q	PA42	5501010
N4116Q	PA42	5501012
N4116W	31T	7520032
N4116W	PA42	5501011
N4117V	PA42	5501018
N4118H	PA42	5501017
N4118K	PA42	5501020
N4118M	PA42	5501016
N4118N	PA42	5501025
N4118N	PA42	5501026
N4118V	PA42	5527007
N4118X	PA42	5501023
N4118Y	PA42	5527017
N4119A	PA42	5527025
N4119B	PA42	5527004
N4119V	PA42	5527027
N4119X	PA42	5527028
N4120G	PA42	5527032
N4120K	PA42	5501028
N4120V	46D	174
N4121K	46D	231
(N4123G)	441	0100
N4124G	441	0101
N4124P	46D	22
(N4124T)	200	BB-1767
N4124U	46D	189
N4124V	46D	102
N4125K	46D	212
N4126T	200	BB-1796

N4126Z	46D	196
(N4128G)	441	0102
N4128K	46D	135
N4129P	46D	127
N4130H	46D	77
N4130Y	MIII	T-354
N4131S	90	LJ-1170
N4132H	46D	240
N4132L	46D	71
N4134N	46D	182
(N4136G)	441	0103
N4136U	46D	100
N4137E	46T	97E3
N4137G	441	0104
N4137U	46D	222
N4138A	46D	239
N4138S	E90	LW-142
N4139S	E90	LW-139
N4140S	90	LJ-661
N4140T	31T	8275003
N4141T	46D	49
N4145B	46D	228
N4146S	90	LJ-646
N4150T	200	BB-1750
N4152G	441	0105
N4152R	46T	97007
N4154G	300	FA-82
N4160T	46D	103
N4165D	46D	175
N4165N	46D	171
N4165P	46D	109
N4167C	46D	137
N4167H	350	FL-267
N4167P	100	B-55
N4169T	46D	90
N4170D	46D	143
N4170K	46D	105
N4170L	46T	97017
N4170N	350	FL-270
N4170T	46D	215
N4172Q	90	LJ-1622
N4174V	46T	97014
N4175D	46T	97015
N4176D	46D	217
N4177P	46D	121
N4180A	46T	97151
N4180G	441	0106
N4180T	46T	97018
N4182K	46T	97031
N4183M	46D	112
N4184K	46T	97009
N4185L	46T	97025
N4186Y	MU-2	290
N4189C	46D	236
(N4189G)	441	0107
N4189N	46T	97034
N4190B	46D	20
N4190F	PA42	5501023
N4195S	200	BB-1795
N4200A	100	B-64
N4200K	200	BB-678
N4200K	300	FA-18
N4200K	350	FL-36
N4200S	200	BB-253
N4200S	300	FA-18
N4201S	200	BB-43
N4202K	MU-2	603
N4202M	MU-2	628
N4202S	200	BB-51
N4203C	MU-2	671
N4204S	E90	LW-204
N4205G	200	BB-1805
N4205S	200	BB-105
N4206S	200	BB-106
N4206U	90	LJ-1606
N4207G	200	BB-1707
N4207S	E90	LW-207
N4207U	31T	7720043
N4209L	100	B-89
N4209S	100	B-229
N4209S	MIII	T-245
N4210S	E90	LW-200
N4211S	200	BB-111
N4211V	350	FL-301

N4213S	B100	BE-13
N4213V	441	0020
N4214S	B100	BE-14
N4216S	E90	LW-211
N4218S	B100	BE-18
N4224U	690B	11482
N4226G	PC6	526
N4227G	PC6	532
N4229S	PC6	627
N4234L	P68	225
N4237M	F90	LA-107
N4241Y	31T	8020034
N4246Z	441	0102
N4248Y	200	BB-463
N4249Y	BN2	289
N4251F	MU-2	796SA
N4251R	MIIB	T26-131
N4252X	MIIB	T26-121
N4253X	MIIB	T26-132
N4254X	MIIB	T26-131
N4255E	200	BB-619
N4255X	MIIB	T26-154
N4256X	MIIB	T26-148
N4257X	MIIB	T26-150
N4259X	BN2	268
N4259X	MIIB	T26-152
N4260X	MIIB	T26-158
N4261U	BN2	383
N4261X	MIIB	T26-159
N4262X	MIIB	T26-153
N4262Z	MU-2	669
N4264D	E90	LW-69
N4265X	MIIB	T26-167
N4266X	MIIB	T26-143
N4267X	MIIB	T26-162
N4268V	200	BB-1768
N4268X	MIIB	T26-163
N4269Y	F90	LA-22
N4269Z	200	BB-816
N4270	90	LJ-380
N4270X	MIIB	T26-166
N4270Y	200	BB-1770
N4271V	200	BB-1771
N4271X	MIIB	T26-168
N4273X	MIIB	T26-170
N4273X	MIII	T-268
N4276Z	425	0103
N4277C	200	BB-1309
N4277E	200	BB-1314
N4278B	BN2	242
N4283R	E90	LW-261
N4284S	E90	LW-210
N4284V	MU-2	270
N4287X	46D	232
N4288L	200	BB-1742
N4288S	200	BB-188
N4291S	200	BB-214
N4292S	90	LJ-692
N4294S	200	BB-213
N4297S	200	BB-97
N4298H	350	FL-298
N4298S	200	BB-198
N4298X	90	LJ-1598
N4299S	200	BB-26
N4300X	200	BB-1700
(N4301L)	31T	7920067
N4301Y	200	BB-1701
N4302J	350	FL-302
N4302Q	200	BB-1702
N4303R	350	FL-303
N4314X	350	FL-314
N4318S	100	B-218
N4318W	90	LJ-618
N4319T	350	FL-319
N4320L	350	FL-320
N4322Y	46D	76
N4323W	350	FL-323
N4324K	90	LJ-1624
N4327X	31T	7720009
N4328W	350	FL-328
N4332U	350	FL-332
N4333W	90	LJ-588
N4336P	350	FL-336
N4345R	680T	1676-59

N4347X	200	BB-1777
N4357Y	200	BB-1757
N4359T	200	BB-1063
N4360N	200	BB-1760
N4360U	46D	3
N4362F	200	BB-1762
N4367L	46D	37
N4368X	200	BB-1778
N4368Y	90	LJ-1599
N4372L	46D	188
N4376B	46D	88
N4377D	200	BB-1145
(N4378D)	31T	7720009
N4378W	E90	LW-78
N4379A	46D	42
N4380E	46D	56
N4380Y	350	FL-280
N4385P	46D	9
N4387L	46D	17
N4387L	46D	43
(N4391A)	BN2	611
N4391W	100	B-191
N4392K	90	LJ-1642
N4392W	100	B-192
N4398W	E90	LW-98
N4400W	E90	LW-67
N4404Q	200	BB-1160
N4406W	E90	LW-25
N4408U	90	LJ-1608
N4409U	90	LJ-1659
(N4412H)	P68	57
N4414P	BN2	343
N4415F	90	LJ-1675
N4415L	B100	BE-67
N4420F	425	0053
N4423W	E90	LW-102
N4424S	350	FL-324
N4424V	E90	LW-296
N4424W	31T	8020029
N4425W	31T	7620009
N4425W	90	LJ-625
N4426L	200	BB-754
N4428V	F90	LA-153
N4430V	200	BB-323
N4432M	P68	187
N4432W	690A	11274
N4437S	200	BB-1737
N4438	BN2	766
N4441T	441	0133
N4442F	MIII	T-295
N4442F	MIVC	AT-524
N4443V	200	BB-1743
N4444F	MIII	T-295
N4445K	31T	7920038
N4445T	200	BB-1233
N4446D	90	LJ-1646
N4447W	90	LJ-627
N4449A	200	BB-1088
N4449Q	90	LJ-895
N4450F	P68	314
N4455U	200	BB-1785
N4456A	200C	BL-143
N4461C	200	BB-1761
N4463W	90	LJ-633
N4464V	MIII	T-403
N4465F	90	LJ-1665
N4465Y	P68	320
N4466A	300C	FM-11
N4467F	200	BB-1767
N4467M	E90	LW-146
N4468F	695	95006
N4468F	90	LJ-1668
N4468M	MIIB	T26-119
N4469Y	200	BB-1769
N4469Z	90	LJ-1669
N4470B	200	BB-1789
N4470D	MIII	T-208
N4470H	680T	1550-11
N4470K	90	LJ-1670
N4470M	90	LJ-1660
N4470T	200	BB-1790
N4471C	200	BB-1791
N4471J	350	FL-341
N4471M	90	LJ-1671

N4471P 31T 8020005
N4472C 200 BB-1772
N4472S 350 FL-342
N4473E 350 FL-273
N4473M 90 LJ-1633
N4473W 200 BB-12
N4474Y 90 LJ-1644
N4475N 350 FL-275
N4475W 100 B-208
N4476M 200 BB-1776
N4476Y 200 BB-1806
N4477N 90 LJ-1577
N4477Q 350 FL-277
N4478H 350 FL-378
N4479M 90 LJ-1679
N4479W 90 LJ-1649
N4480Y 200 BB-1780
N4481P 90 LJ-1681
N4482A 90 LJ-1662
N4482Z 200 BB-1782
N4483Y 350 FL-333
N4484A 350 FL-284
N4484F 200 BB-1794
N4484T 90 LJ-1674
N4484W 200 BB-1784
N4484W 90 LJ-640
N4485Z 200 BB-1825
N4486V 350 FL-286
N4487W E90 LW-107
N4488H 350 FL-388
N4488L 200 BB-421
N4488L 90 LJ-1423
N4488N 200 BB-1808
N4488N F90 LA-197
N4488W 90 LJ-626
N4489A 200 BB-472
N4489A 200C BL-145
N4490C 441 0081
N4490E 31T 8004012
N4490L 90 LJ-952
N4490M B100 BE-64
N4490U MU-2 439SA
N4491C 31T 7820088
N4491E MIII TT-426A
N4491Z 200 BB-782
N4492D 90 LJ-927
N4494E PA42 7800002
N4494U 31T 8104017
N4495N E90 LW-14
N4495U 90 LJ-948
N4496B P68 321
N4496D P68 323
N4496M P68 290
N4496N P68 291
N4496P P68 292
N4496W P68 294
N4497D P68 313
N4497U P68 315
N4497W P68 317
N4505B PA42 8001015
N4517E 680T 1675-58
N4527E 680T 1622-52
N4545S 100 B-215
N4549E 680T 1683-64
(N4555Y) 441 0178
N4556E 680T 1614-48
N4557E 680T 1703-79
(N4558E) 680T 1624-53
N4560E 690A 11250
(N4560L) 425 0122
N4561 680W 1763-9
N4561L 200 BB-500
N4562P 200 BB-362
N4564Q BN2 514
N4565E MU-2 673
(N4566E) 680T 1718-89
N4567 G1 90
N4567 G1 128
N4571M 90 LJ-752
N4574C P68 310
N4576E 680T 1616-49
N4581U 690A 11318
N4585E 680T 1691-70
(N4594E) 680T 1620-51
N4594V MU-2 256
(N4598E) 680T 1612-47
(N4599E) 680T 1698-75
N4600A 100 B-63
N4600K 300 FA-21
N4601L 690A 11322
N4603E 680T 1708-83
N4616T 31T 7920059
N4622E 680W 1723-3
(N4633E) 680T 1677-60
N4638E 680T 1692-71
N4638E 680T 1699-76
N4646S 90 LJ-150
(N4648E) 680T 1693-72
N4648E 680T 1701-77
N4659M 200 BB-369
N4660M 200 BB-371
(N4664E) 680T 1694-73
(N4664E) 680T 1702-78
(N4669E) 680T 1697-74
N4676U 695A 96036
N4679K MIV AT-006
N4679M 200 BB-343
N4682E 680T 1630-56
N4682N P68 330
N4693E 680T 1618-50
(N4700E) 680T 1681-63
N4700K B100 BE-118
(N4704E) 680T 1713-87
N4704E 680W 1763-9
N4710E 680T 1679-61
N4712W 695 95063
N4717V 690A 11220
N4718C E90 LW-59
N4725M E90 LW-275
N4730E 680W 1772-10
N4742M 90 LJ-774
N4751W 695B 96204
N4757C E90 LW-278
N4757S 46T 97006
N4763M E90 LW-279
N4764A 90 LJ-1161
N4765C G1 68
N4765P G1 68
N4770M 90 LJ-770
N4773M 90 LJ-773
N4774M 90 LJ-771
N4776M 90 LJ-776
N4795P PC6 341
N4798M 681 6044
N4799M 200 BB-373
N4813H 441 0030
N4820M E90 LW-280
N4821M E90 LW-281
N4825M 200 BB-380
N4826M 200 BB-378
N4839R 46T 97293
N4841M B100 BE-45
N4847M 90 LJ-784
N4848M 200 BB-381
N4852E 680W 1773-11
(N4857M) 100 B-246
(N4859E) 680T 1685-66
(N4859E) 680T 1691-70
(N4860E) 680T 1689-69
(N4860E) 680W 1774-12
N4875E 680T 1626-54
N4884M TBM8 451
N4900W 90 LJ-17
N4901E 680T 1632-57
N4908M 90 LJ-790
N4911 PC6 543
N4912 PC6 544
N4912M 200 BB-395
N4913 PC6 545
N4913M 200 BB-512
N4914 PC6 546
N4914M 200 BB-376
N4915 PC6 536
N4915M E90 LW-283
N4915U BN2 789
N4920Y TBM7 169
N4925T 200 BB-1870
N4926 PC6 685
(N4928E) 680T 1714-88
N4928E 680W 1721-1
N4929M 200 BB-353
(N4930E) 680T 1687-67
(N4930E) 680W 1775-13
N4935X 200 BB-859
N4937M 200 BB-372
N4938E 680T 1688-68
N4947E 680T 1710-85
N4947M 90 LJ-780
N4948W 90 LJ-31
N4950C 90 LJ-629
N4953M 90 LJ-781
N4954S E90 LW-231
N4958K P68 269
N4975M B100 BE-43
N4977M E90 LW-277
*N4982R 350 FL-224
N4988E 680W 1776-14
N4990M BN2 479
N4990Y 90 LJ-49
N4991X BN2 228
(N4992E) 680T 1718-89
N4992E 680W 1777-15
N4992M E90 LW-284
N4996M B100 BE-47
N4998M PA42 8001075
N4998Z C-12 BD-2
N4999H C-12 BD-5
N5000 200 BB-305
N5000 90 LJ-143
N5000T E90 LW-38
N5001Q 200 BB-1801
N5002Y 200C BL-142
N5003K 200 BB-1783
N5004 MIII T-232
N5005M 200C BN-5
N5005V 200 BB-1845
N5006 90 LJ-143
N5006M 200 BB-360
N5007 31T 7820061
N5007 690A 11271
N5007H 350 FL-307
N5007L 200 BB-1807
N5007X B100 BE-70
N5008M B100 BE-49
N5009M B100 BE-48
N5009U 350 FL-369
N5010R 350 FL-310
N5011K 350 FL-311
N5013J 90 LJ-1613
N5015M 200 BB-1815
N5016H 690B 11452
N5016K 200 BB-1816
N5017E 680W 1811-28
N5018E 46T 97039
N5018F 200 BB-1818
N5019H 200 BB-1819
N5020Y 46T 97040
N5020Y 46T 97050
N5021E 680W 1788-18
N5021S 200 BB-1821
N5022E 680W 1778-16
N5022M PA42 5501030
N5023T 90 LJ-1623
N5024W 90 LJ-1618
N5025L 350 FL-325
N5025R 90 LJ-1625
N5026C 90 LJ-1626
N5027V 90 LJ-1627
N5027X 350 FL-327
N5028E 690 11030
N5029E 680W 1812-29
N5030D 350 FL-360
N5030Y 350 FL-330
(N5031E) 680W 1813-30
N5032K 200 BB-1832
N5034F 350 FL-334
N5035M 90 LJ-1635
(N5036E) 680W 1814-31
N5037A 350 FL-337
N5037W 90 LJ-1630
N5039E 350 FL-339
N5039F MIII T-269
N5039X 200 BB-1839
N5040P 46T 97038
N5043X 350 FL-343
N5044B 350 FL-344
N5045L 350 FL-345
N5046Y 350 FL-346
N5047F 350 FL-347
N5048F 350 FL-348
N5049E 680W 1760-6
N5051E 680W 1752-5
N5052E 680W 1751-4
N5053Y 46T 97041
N5053Y 46T 97067
N5053Y 46T 97077
N5055Q 200 BB-1755
N5056U 200 BB-1756
N5057E 680W 1761-7
N5058E 680W 1787-17
N5061E 680W 1790-20
N5061X 90 LJ-1661
N5062E 680W 1791-21
N5063K 200 BB-1763
N5064C 680W 1792-22
N5064E 680W 1792-22
N5064L 90 LJ-1664
N5066N 300C FM-7
N5066N 90 LJ-1706
N5067L 90 LJ-1667
N5068P 46T 97042
N5069E 680W 1793-23
N5070M 350 FL-340
N5070W 300 FA-212
N5072R 90 LJ-1672
N5075C 200 BB-1738
N5075E 200 BB-1775
N5076G 90 LJ-1676
N5077Y 46T 97043
N5078E 680W 1802-24
N5078Q 200 BB-1868
N5079E 680W 1803-25
N5079K U-21 LT-1
N5079L U-21 LT-2
N5079R BN2T 880
N5081E 680W 1804-26
N5082E 680W 1805-27
N5082M 200 BB-389
N5083M 90 LJ-783
N5084J 90 LJ-1684
N5084V 350 FL-364
N5084Y 350 FL-384
N5085T 350 FL-385
N5086P 350 FL-386
N5091G 350 FL-391
N5092K 200 BB-1792
N5092S 200 BB-1802
N5093G 200 BB-1803
N5093X 200 BB-1793
N5095K 90 LJ-928
N5097G 200 BB-1797
N5099H 200 BB-1799
N5100J 200 BB-404
N5104 90 LJ-154
N5104B 200 BB-1804
N5105 90 LJ-155
N5106F 200C BN-6
N5107Z 200C BN-7
N5109V 200 BB-1869
N5110 200 BB-298
N5111 200 BB-299
N5111 90 LJ-154
N5111B 200T BT-33
N5111B MIII T-276
N5111C 90 LJ-444
N5111T 46T 97044
N5111U 90 LJ-154
N5112 200 BB-329
N5112 90 LJ-155
N5113 200 BB-330
N5113 90 LJ-255
N5113K 46T 97046
N5113K FPC6 2026
N5114 90 LJ-256
N5114Z 200 BB-1914
N5115 90 LJ-261

N5115D	90	LJ-261	N5321C	46T	97162	N5355S	46T	97136	N5442M	MIVA	AT-065
N5115H	90	LJ-1705	N5321M	MIII	T-238	N5356M	695	95036	N5443M	MIII	T-288
N5116	90	LJ-262	N5321R	46T	97069	N5357D	46T	97139	N5444M	MIII	T-286
N5117H	MIIB	T26-176	N5322A	46T	97106	N5357M	46T	97120B	N5445M	MIII	T-284
N5117M	200	BB-1817	N5322D	46T	97074	N5358J	46T	97140	N5446M	MIVA	AT-062-2
N5117S	350	FL-387	N5322M	46T	97021	N5358M	MIII	T-253	N5449M	MIII	T-289
N5128X	350	FL-428	N5323M	MIII	T-239	N5361A	46T	97144	N5450J	695A	96024
N5129J	350	FL-329	N5324M	MIII	T-240	N5361C	46T	97117A	N5450M	200	BB-209
N5130V	200	BB-1930	N5324Q	46D	201	N5361C	46T	97125B	N5450M	MIII	T-290
N5133W	90	LJ-1663	N5324Q	46T	97080	N5361M	MIVA	AT-040	N5450V	BN2	222
N5134S	90	LJ-1701	N5324Q	46T	97119	N5362J	200	BB-961	N5452J	31T	8020062
N5135N	350	FL-335	N5325P	46T	97085	N5362M	MIVA	AT-041	N5454M	MIII	T-287
N5135X	MIVA	AT-029	N5326C	46T	97079	N5363J	46T	97157	N5455M	MIVA	AT-066
N5136V	31T	7620037	N5326M	MIII	T-241	N5363M	MIII	T-254	N5455N	MIVA	AT-066
N5138Q	200	BB-1838	N5326R	46T	97082	N5364F	46T	97156	N5459M	MIVA	AT-067
N5139A	200C	BL-144	N5326S	PC12	1131	N5365D	46T	97161	N5461M	MIII	T-291
N5141G	90	LJ-1641	N5326W	46T	97081	N5365M	46T	97177	N5462G	E90	LW-69
N5141Y	200C	BL-141	N5327A	46T	97089	N5366Q	46T	97171	N5465M	MIII	T-297
N5148Q	200	BB-1848	N5327M	MIII	T-242	N5368H	46T	97159	N5466M	MIVA	AT-069
N5149F	350	FL-349	N5328M	MIV	AT-015	N5369J	200	BB-643	N5469M	MIII	T-293
N5150K	90	LJ-1650	N5329M	MIII	T-243	N5370S	46D	209	N5470R	G1	162
N5150Q	350	FL-350	N5329Q	46T	97097	N5371	90	LJ-906	N5475M	MIII	T-292
N5151F	350	FL-351	N5330M	MIII	T-244	N5371M	MIVA	AT-043	N5476R	100	B-72
N5152	G1	97	N5331M	MIII	T-245	N5373M	MIII	T-260	N5477M	MIII	T-276
N5152G	200	BB-1752	N5331N	46T	97089	N5374M	MIII	T-259	N5477M	MIII	T-282
N5152H	350	FL-352	N5331N	46T	97107	N5375M	MIII	T-262	N5491M	MIII	T-296
N5153V	90	LJ-1653	N5332M	MIV	AT-013	N5376M	MIII	T-269	N5495M	MIII	T-298
N5154E	90	LJ-1655	N5332M	MIV	AT-016	N5377C	100	B-27	N5496M	MIVA	AT-072
N5155A	200C	BL-146	N5333M	MIII	T-246	N5377M	MIII	T-263	N5497M	MIII	T-302
N5156G	350	FL-356	N5333N	46T	97084	N5378M	MIII	T-264	N5498M	MIV	AT-070
N5156P	46T	97048	N5334M	MIV	AT-017	N5379D	P68	54	N5500F	E90	LW-48
N5157G	200	BB-1857	N5335M	MIV	AT-018	N5381M	MIII	T-265	N5500S	90	LJ-345
N5159F	200	BB-1759	N5335R	46T	97100	N5381X	PA42	5501005	N5502D	90	LJ-1233
N5166P	P180	1129	N5336S	46T	97101	N5382M	MIII	T-267	N5503K	200	BB-1363
N5170J	46T	97052	N5337M	MIII	T-247	N5383M	MIIB	T26-179	N5510Y	200	BB-1364
N5191B	MU-2	662	N5337N	46T	97102	N5383M	MIII	T-268	N5511A	90	LJ-399
N5208M	MIV	AT-008	N5338M	46T	97103	N5384M	MIII	T-270	(N5513E)	300	FA-42
N5215U	46T	97068	N5338M	46T	97104	N5384Z	P68	306	N5513E	300	FA-198
N5235B	46T	97045	N5338M	MIII	T-248	N5385M	MIII	T-271	N5513F	350	FL-4
N5237Y	46T	97066	N5339G	46T	97095	N5386M	MIVA	AT-051	N5516Q	200	BB-1402
N5241Z	G1	67	N5339M	MIVA	AT-027	N5386U	P68	301	N5519C	90	LJ-1202
N5245F	90	LJ-92	N5339U	46T	97113B	N5387J	P68	304	N5519V	90	LJ-1219
N5252L	BN2	907	N5339U	46T	97115A	N5387V	690B	11405	N5520X	90	LJ-1220
N5256S	350	FL-260	N5339V	46T	97110	N5388M	MIII	T-272	N5521D	350	FL-44
N5271M	MIII	T-208	N5340M	MIII	T-250	N5389X	P68	296	N5521T	90	LJ-1361
N5272M	MIII	T-211	N5340U	46T	97107	N5390M	MIII	T-273	N5522X	90	LJ-1223
N5273M	MIII	T-203	N5341C	46T	97123A	N5390X	P68	302	N5526V	350	FL-8
N5291M	MIV	AT-001	N5341C	46T	97124B	N5391C	P68	299	N5530H	200	BB-1331
N5292M	MIII	T-201	N5341C	46T	97142B	N5391M	MIII	T-274	N5532T	350	FL-19
N5294M	MIII	T-216	N5341C	46T	97146A	N5392M	MIVA	AT-057	N5537W	90	LJ-1237
N5295M	MIV	AT-003	N5341M	46T	97127	N5393M	MIII	T-275	N5545B	200	BB-1334
N5296M	MIII	T-219	N5341N	MIVA	AT-028	N5395M	MIII	T-277	N5546K	100	B-44
N5297M	MIV	AT-006	N5341U	46T	97113A	N5396M	MIII	T-279	N5547K	300	FA-181
N5300F	FPC6	2036	N5341U	46T	97118	N5397M	MIII	T-280	N5547Y	90	LJ-1229
N5301F	FPC6	2039	N5342M	MIVA	AT-029	N5397W	90	LJ-848	N5549B	STAR	NC-15
N5301M	MIIB	T26-180E	N5342Z	46T	97114	N5398M	MIII	T-278	N5551E	200	BB-1357
N5302F	FPC6	2048	N5343C	46T	97090	N5399M	MIII	T-281	N5552U	200	BB-1361
N5304F	FPC6	2049	N5345M	MIII	T-251	N5400C	BN2	679	N5555L	E90	LW-250
N5305F	FPC6	2071	N5345S	46T	97120A	N5400C	G1	116	N5556S	300	FA-188
N5305M	MIII	T-225	N5345S	46T	97123B	N5400G	G1	116	N5559X	200	BB-1372
N5306F	FPC6	2072	N5346A	46T	97144	N5401U	90	LJ-227	N5560D	200	BB-1360
N5306M	MIII	T-222	N5346M	46T	97121	N5410	681	6043	N5568V	200	BB-1352
N5307F	FPC6	2070	N5346M	MIVA	AT-031	N5411	680T	1687-67	N5580A	MU-2	511
N5307M	MIII	T-224	N5346U	46T	97130	N5411	681	6044	N5582K	90	LJ-1243
N5307Q	MIIB	T26-155	N5346U	46T	97134	(N5412)	681B	6066	N5584M	200	BB-1368
N5308F	FPC6	2068	N5346Y	46T	97135	N5413	680T	1609-45	N5589S	MU-2	150
N5309F	FPC6	2069	(N5347M)	MIII	T-252	(N5415)	680T	1554-13	N5590L	90	LJ-1228
N5310M	MIII	T-228	(N5347N)	46T	97124A	N5415U	90	LJ-281	N5595K	90	LJ-1231
N5311M	MIII	T-229	N5347V	46T	97126	N5416	680W	1774-12	N5595U	200	BB-1355
N5312M	MIII	T-230	N5348M	MIVA	AT-034	N5417	680W	1775-13	N5598L	90	LJ-1236
N5313M	MIII	T-232	N5348S	46T	97149	N5418	680T	1601-43	N5598N	200	BB-1356
N5314M	MIII	T-233	N5349F	46T	97129	(N5418)	680T	1622-52	N5607X	90	LJ-1251
N5315M	MIV	AT-009	N5349M	MIII	T-255	N5418	680W	1818-32	N5608J	200	BB-1373
N5316M	MIII	T-234	N5350M	MIVA	AT-035	N5419	680T	1554-13	N5611B	350	FL-18
N5317M	MIII	T-236	N5351G	46T	97133	(N5420)	680T	1622-52	N5618Z	90	LJ-1260
N5318M	MIV	AT-011	N5351M	46T	97154	N5422P	695A	96011	N5619D	G1	74
N5319K	46T	97056	N5351M	46T	97160	N5431M	90	LJ-1673	N5626Y	350	FL-43
N5319K	46T	97076	N5351M	MIVA	AT-036	N5432V	31T	7620046	N5630Q	350	FL-27
N5319M	MIII	T-237	N5352G	46T	97145	N5438M	MIVA	AT-063	N5634E	350	FL-5
N5319U	46T	97065	N5353M	MIIB	T26-167	N5439M	MIVA	AT-064	N5637Y	200	BB-1378
N5320A	46T	97051	N5353V	46T	97141	N5440F	MIVA	AT-030	N5639K	90	LJ-1239
N5320A	46T	97060	N5354K	46D	176	N5441F	MIVA	AT-044	N5641X	90	LJ-1241
N5320M	MIV	AT-012	N5354K	46D	206	N5441F	MIVC	AT-528	N5642T	200	BB-1366
N5320N	46T	97153	N5354M	MIVA	AT-042	N5441M	MIII	T-283	N5643B	350	FL-6

N5644E	90	LJ-1244
N5647Q	300	FA-213
N5648Y	200	BB-1374
N5649F	100	B-25
N5649V	200	BB-1369
N5650M	MIVA	AT-071
N5651J	90	LJ-1247
N5652K	90	LJ-8
N5652M	MIII	T-301
N5654E	90	LJ-1245
N5654M	MIII	T-303E
N5655K	**350**	**FL-12**
N5655W	350	FL-28
N5656A	90	LJ-176
N5656M	MIVA	AT-071E
N5657N	200	BB-210
N5657N	200	BB-1367
N5658M	MIII	T-305
N5661M	MIII	T-306
N5662T	300	FA-204
N5665M	MIII	T-307
N5666L	300	FA-211
N5666S	300	FA-214
N5668F	350	FL-7
N5668M	MIII	T-309
N5669B	200	BB-1382
N5669M	MIII	T-310
N5670D	90	LJ-1302
N5670M	MIII	T-311
N5671M	MIII	T-202
N5672A	300	FA-205
N5672J	300	FA-206
N5672M	MIVA	AT-073
N5673M	MIII	T-313
N5673Y	350	FL-22
N5674B	STAR	NC-14
N5674M	MIIB	T26-165
N5675M	MIIB	T26-172
N5678J	200C	BL-137
N5678M	MIIB	T26-175
N5679M	MIIB	T26-176
N5680M	MIIB	T26-177
N5680S	90	LJ-1263
N5682M	MIIB	T26-178
N5682P	200	BB-1358
N5685K	90	LJ-1270
N5685X	200	BB-1446
N5688F	200	BB-1375
N5690K	90	LJ-1
N5692L	350	FL-55
N5724M	90	LJ-36
N5727	**100**	**B-48**
N5757	**46D**	**190**
N5760U	90	LJ-85
N5767K	90	LJ-33
N5776P	690A	11249
N5779N	690D	15001
(N5798)	90	LJ-350
N5799	90	LJ-59
N5801D	200C	BL-74
N5803F	200C	BL-105
N5805	**MIII**	**T-324**
N5819T	200C	BL-106
N5829J	425	0140
N5831A	100	B-202
N5833N	690C	11606
N5833N	690D	15002
N5836N	690D	15003
N5838N	690D	15004
N5841N	690D	15005
(N5852K)	690C	11601
N5852K	695B	96205
N5852N	690D	15006
(N5853K)	690C	11602
N5854K	690C	11603
N5855K	690C	11604
N5855N	690D	15007
N5856K	690C	11605
N5858K	690C	11606
(N5859K)	690C	11607
N5860K	690C	11608
N5860N	690D	15008
N5861K	690C	11609
(N5862)	690C	11610

(N5862K)	690C	11610
N5862N	690D	15009
N5863K	690C	11611
N5863N	690D	15010
(N5864K)	690C	11612
N5865K	690C	11613
N5865N	690D	15011
(N5866K)	690C	11614
N5866N	690D	15012
(N5867K)	690C	11615
N5867N	690D	15013
N5868K	690C	11616
N5869K	690C	11617
N5869N	690D	15014
(N5870K)	690C	11618
N5871K	690C	11619
N5872K	690C	11620
(N5873K)	690C	11621
(N5874K)	690C	11622
N5874N	690D	15015
(N5875K)	690C	11623
(N5876K)	690C	11624
(N5876N)	690D	15016
N5877K	690C	11625
N5878K	**690C**	**11626**
N5879K	690C	11627
(N5880K)	690C	11628
N5880N	690D	15017
N5881K	690C	11629
(N5882K)	690C	11630
N5883K	690C	11631
(N5884K)	690C	11632
N5885K	690C	11633
N5886K	690C	11634
(N5886N)	690D	15018
(N5887K)	690C	11635
N5888K	**300C**	**FM-6**
(N5888K)	690C	11636
N5889K	690C	11637
N5889N	690D	15019
N5890K	690C	11638
(N5891K)	690C	11639
N5891V	**BN2**	**3011**
N5892K	690C	11640
(N5893K)	690C	11641
N5894K	690C	11642
N5894N	690D	15020
N5896K	690C	11644
N5896N	690D	15021
(N5897K)	690C	11645
N5898K	690C	11646
N5900K	**690C**	**11648**
(N5901K)	690C	11649
N5902K	690C	11650
N5903K	690C	11651
N5904A	**PC12**	**583**
N5904K	690C	11652
N5905K	690C	11653
N5905N	690D	15022
N5906K	690C	11654
N5906N	690D	15023
(N5907K)	690C	11655
(N5908K)	690C	11656
(N5909K)	690C	11657
N5910K	690C	11658
N5911K	690C	11659
N5911N	690D	15024
N5911P	E90	LW-70
N5912K	690C	11660
(N5912N)	690D	15025
(N5913K)	690C	11661
N5913K	690C	11663
(N5913K)	690C	11679
N5914K	690C	11662
N5914N	690D	15026
N5915K	690C	11661
N5915N	690D	15027
N5916K	690C	11664
N5916N	690D	15028
N5917K	690C	11665
(N5918K)	690C	11666
N5919K	690C	11667
(N5919N)	690D	15029
N5920C	680T	1552-12

(N5920K)	690C	11668
(N5920N)	690D	15030
N5921K	690C	11669
N5922K	690C	11670
(N5922N)	690D	15031
(N5923K)	690C	11671
(N5924K)	690C	11672
(N5924N)	690D	15032
N5925K	690C	11673
(N5925N)	690D	15033
N5926K	690C	11674
(N5926N)	690D	15034
N5928K	690C	11676
(N5929K)	690C	11677
(N5931K)	690C	11679
N5931K	690C	11679
(N5932K)	690C	11680
N5933K	690C	11681
N5934K	690C	11682
N5935K	690C	11683
N5936K	690C	11684
N5937K	690C	11685
N5938K	690C	11686
N5939K	690C	11687
(N5940K)	690C	11688
N5941K	690C	11689
N5942K	690C	11690
N5943K	690C	11691
(N5944K)	690C	11692
N5946K	690C	11694
N5947K	690C	11695
N5948K	690C	11696
N5949K	690C	11697
N5950K	690C	11698
N5951K	690C	11699
N5952K	690C	11700
N5953K	690C	11701
N5954K	690C	11702
N5955K	**690C**	**11703**
(N5956K)	690C	11704
N5956K	**690C**	**11719**
(N5957K)	690C	11705
N5957K	690C	11720
(N5958K)	690C	11706
N5958K	690C	11721
(N5959K)	690C	11707
N5959K	690C	11722
(N5960K)	690C	11708
N5960K	690C	11723
N5961K	690C	11709
(N5961K)	690C	11724
N5962K	690C	11724
N5963H	90	LJ-267
N5963K	690C	11725
N5964K	690C	11726
N5965K	690C	11727
N5966K	690C	11728
N5967K	690C	11729
(N5968K)	690C	11730
(N5969K)	690C	11731
(N5970K)	690C	11732
N6000	90	LJ-174
N6002A	31T	7820052
N6002A	31T	7820064
N6002G	46T	97346
N6003	200	BB-476
N6003A	31T	7820053
N6004U	46T	97347
N6005S	200	BB-2005
N6005Y	90	LJ-1945
N6010T	200	BB-2010
N6011V	200	BB-2011
N6011W	350	FL-361
N6017	200	BB-482
N6020Z	200	BB-1820
N6021L	46T	97348
N6022Q	200	BB-1822
N6023R	90	LJ-823
N6023Y	90	LJ-830
N6024E	200	BB-467
N6026J	46T	97369
N6026K	90	LJ-826
N6026R	90	LJ-829
N6027A	31T	7820068

N6028P	B100	BE-63
N6028R	200	BB-450
N6028Y	90	LJ-1728
N6028Z	**350**	**FL-628**
N6029H	90	LJ-1929
N6029M	90	LJ-831
N6029S	**300C**	**FM-29**
N6030F	200	BB-478
N6030K	**90**	**LJ-1930**
N6031W	90	LJ-1160
N6032E	B100	BE-66
N6032F	**90**	**LJ-1932**
N6032L	90	LJ-832
N6033A	31T	7820070
N6033Z	46T	97370
N6034D	90	LJ-834
N6034P	200	BB-1834
N6034Z	90	LJ-839
N6035H	B100	BE-67
N6037C	90	LJ-828
N6038A	31T	7820072
N6039A	31T	7820073
N6040M	90	LJ-840
N6040N	200	BB-1840
N6040T	200	BB-476
N6040U	200	BB-482
N6040W	200	BB-493
N6040Y	200	BB-498
N6042K	90	LJ-1942
N6043K	46T	97371
N6043K	46T	97384
N6043M	350	FL-363
N6043T	200	BB-1843
N6043Z	90	LJ-1943
N6044B	B100	BE-62
N6045S	**B100**	**BE-65**
N6048L	350	FL-468
N6048L	46T	97356
N6048Y	46T	97373
N6050D	200	BB-518
N6050F	E90	LW-322
N6051C	200	BB-499
N6052B	200	BB-497
N6052C	B100	BE-68
N6052F	90	LJ-842
N6053H	90	LJ-843
N6055H	350	FL-355
N6055W	**90**	**LJ-1955**
N6056T	200	BB-468
N6059C	200T	BT-14
N6059D	200T	BT-15
(N6060)	350	FL-21
N6061K	46T	97357
N6061K	**46T**	**97374**
N6061L	**90**	**LJ-1961**
N6062A	31T	7820074
N6062Q	200	BB-550
N6062X	90	LJ-855
(N6063U)	200	BB-564
N6063U	200	BB-564
N6064A	46T	97360
N6064A	46T	97375
N6064A	**46T**	**97405**
N6064A	90	LJ-857
N6064B	200	BB-579
N6064M	200	BB-593
N6065D	200T	BT-10
N6065L	F90	LA-28
N6065R	200	BB-617
N6066Z	200	BB-605
N6068L	**350**	**FL-668**
N6068V	350	FL-368
N6069A	**200**	**BB-357**
N6069C	**90**	**LJ-291**
N6071M	46T	97376
N6072J	46T	97386
N6074J	46T	97388
N6074J	**46T**	**97397**
N6075A	31T	7820075
N6075N	**46T**	**97379**
N6075U	46T	97380
N6076Z	**46T**	**97390**
N6077Q	**46T**	**97383**
N6077X	90	LJ-1677

N6078T	200	BB-1878	N6161P	425	0011	N6195A	31T	7920025	N6350A	350	FL-650
N6080A	31T	7820077	N6162K	350	FL-362	N6196A	31T	7920010	N6351S	200	BB-70
N6080W	300	FA-219	N6162X	200	BB-1862	N6196H	350	FL-396	N6352J	90	LJ-1952
N6081E	46T	97400	N6165J	350	FL-365	N6196P	200	BB-1896	N6354H	B100	BE-131
N6082A	90	LJ-1682	N6165Q	200	BB-1865	N6196R	350	FL-636	N6354X	200	BB-1082
N6082J	46T	97409	N6165Y	350	FL-405	N6196S	90	LJ-1721	N6356C	90	LJ-1052
N6082Z	46T	97401	N6166A	31T	7920005	N6197H	200	BB-1897	N6356V	90	LJ-1956
N6083A	31T	7804004	N6166Q	200	BB-1866	N6197V	90	LJ-1767	N6357B	350	FL-657
N6084C	200	BB-1864	N6167A	31T	7920006	N6198A	31T	7920027	N6359U	680T	1536-4
N6087W	46T	97407	N6167K	350	FL-367	N6198N	350	FL-398	(N6361U)	695A	96007
N6089N	350	FL-389	N6167R	200	BB-1867	N6198P	200	BB-1898	N6364H	90	LJ-1026
N6095A	31T	7804005	N6168T	90	LJ-1968	N6199P	90	LJ-1016	N6365G	BN2	770
N6097A	31T	7820080	N6169S	200	BB-1002	N6199Y	200	BB-1899	N6366S	350	FL-666
N6100A	31T	7820082	N6170D	350	FL-370	N6200B	90	LJ-250	N6369D	350	FL-669
N6100K	100	B-2	N6170G	200	BB-1870	N6200C	200	BB-1900	N6373C	350	FL-673
N6101G	46T	97340	N6171A	31T	7920007	N6200D	90	LJ-250	N6377L	350	FL-637
N6102A	31T	7820083	N6171N	200	BB-1008	N6200G	200	BB-1860	N6378E	B100	BE-134
N6103A	31T	7820084	N6171N	350	FL-371	N6203T	200	BB-1863	N6381U	680T	1473-1
N6103K	350	FL-103	N6171R	200	BB-1871	N6204G	350	FL-404	N6382H	90	LJ-1037
N6104A	200	BB-973	N6171U	350	FL-671	N6204U	90	LJ-1964	N6382U	680T	1538-5
N6104A	31T	7820086	N6172A	31T	7904003	N6204U	STAR	NC-51	(N6387U)	680T	1550-11
N6105D	46T	97364	N6172B	350	FL-372	N6207F	90	LJ-1017	N6393F	200	BB-1069
N6107A	31T	7820087	N6172W	200	BB-1872	N6211J	90	LJ-1931	N6406S	E90	LW-206
N6108A	31T	7820066	N6172Y	90	LJ-1714	N6211Z	300C	FM-31	(N6410X)	E90	LW-193
N6108A	31T	7804006	N6173A	31T	7904004	N6214B	200	BB-942	N6411E	F90	LA-183
N6108A	350	FL-408	N6173C	90	LJ-1014	N6214Q	46D	37	N6412Q	441	0319
N6109A	200	BB-1849	N6173K	350	FL-373	N6222C	200	BB-1010	N6412T	350	FL-642
N6109A	31T	7820079	N6174A	31T	7920009	N6228Q	90	LJ-280	N6416P	F90	LA-187
N6109U	350	FL-409	N6174N	350	FL-374	N6230V	200	BB-1011	N6420H	90	LJ-1028
N6110A	31T	7820089	N6175A	31T	7920011	N6232E	350	FL-632	N6424Q	90	LJ-1024
N6111	200	BB-299	N6175F	350	FL-375	N6234M	90	LJ-1934	N6425D	350	FL-625
N6111S	90	LJ-1004	N6175U	200	BB-1875	N6235N	200	BB-1021	N6427S	200	BB-1027
N6111V	90	LJ-1711	N6176A	31T	7920012	N6236U	200	BB-1019	N6429M	F90	LA-188
N6112G	350	FL-412	N6176A	F90	LA-173	N6238N	90	LJ-124	N6430B	300C	FM-30
N6113A	31T	7820090	N6176C	350	FL-376	N6239P	200	BB-1012	N6430N	350	FL-630
N6113P	200	BB-1873	N6177A	31T	7920013	N6241P	B100	BE-130	N6433F	350	FL-633
N6113X	350	FL-403	N6177F	350	FL-377	N6244N	P68	280	N6434Y	350	FL-634
N6116N	350	FL-416	N6178A	200	BB-1920	N6251U	PC6	518	N6436U	90	LJ-1936
N6117C	350	FL-417	N6178A	31T	7920014	N6253B	90	LJ-1953	N6439R	90	LJ-1939
N6117C	441	0246	N6178D	200C	BL-150	N6253V	F90	LA-178	N6441Y	350	FL-641
N6118A	200	BB-987	N6178F	200C	BL-151	N6257X	BN2	774	N6445N	90	LJ-1046
N6118V	200	BB-1918	N6178J	200	BB-1922	N6260M	200	BB-976	N6446Q	90	LJ-1946
N6120C	200	BB-979	N6178N	350	FL-478	N6260Q	90	LJ-1960	N6449B	90	LJ-1949
N6121A	31T	7820091	N6178V	90	LJ-1777	N6261C	F90	LA-180	N6451D	200	BB-1009
N6123A	31T	7804008	N6179A	200	BB-1004	N6262B	F90	LA-177	N6452D	350	FL-652
N6124A	200	BB-1824	N6179A	31T	7920015	N6262M	90	LJ-1023	N6464S	200	BB-1057
N6125A	31T	7804009	N6179X	350	FL-449	N6271C	200	BB-1036	N6466G	90	LJ-1966
N6127A	31T	7804010	N6180A	31T	7920016	N6272C	90	LJ-1025	N6470Q	350	FL-670
N6127U	350	FL-627	N6180P	90	LJ-1780	N6277Y	200	BB-1041	N6473E	200	BB-2013
N6128P	F90	LA-168	N6180Q	200	BB-1880	N6280E	90	LJ-1015	N6473V	90	LJ-1048
N6129C	B100	BE-127	N6181A	31T	7904005	N6280P	90	LJ-1022	N6475T	350	FL-675
N6129N	200	BB-1829	N6182	31T	7904006	N6281R	441	0226	N6477Q	350	FL-677
N6129Q	350	FL-429	N6182A	200	BB-1484	(N6284N)	200C	BL-54	N6478F	350	FL-658
N6131Q	350	FL-431	N6182A	31T	7904006	(N6284N)	200C	BL-61	N6492C	90	LJ-1050
N6132U	200	BB-1912	N6182Z	350	FL-402	(N6284N)	200C	BL-62	N6494S	200	BB-1032
N6133A	31T	7820092	N6183A	31T	7904001	N6289C	200	BB-1037	(N6503V)	680T	1580-33
N6133H	F90	LA-166	N6183A	90	LJ-1683	N6290Q	200	BB-1045	N6504H	90	LJ-1030
N6134A	31T	7804006	N6183S	350	FL-383	N6292H	F90	LA-175	N6506V	680T	1572-27
N6135Z	90	LJ-1010	N6184L	200G	BY-84	N6293V	300	FA-99	N6507B	200	BB-498
N6137	90	LJ-47	N6185A	31T	7920018	N6296M	200	BB-483	N6507V	680T	1588-39
N6137L	350	FL-437	N6187A	31T	7920020	N6297S	200	BB-344	N6509F	200	BB-493
N6139U	90	LJ-1011	N6187L	90	LJ-1687	N6300	680T	1540-6	(N6509V)	680T	1554-13
N6139Z	350	FL-439	N6187U	B100	BE-129	N6300F	200	BB-1865	N6514V	680T	1581-34
N6144H	200	BB-1049	N6188A	31T	7920021	N6300R	200	BB-1046	(N6517V)	680W	1818-32
N6148X	200	BB-1592	N6188N	200	BB-1888	N6300S	200	BB-1006	N6519V	680T	1568-24
N6148Z	90	LJ-1948	N6189A	31T	7904010	N6305V	200	BB-1016	(N6520V)	680T	1597-42
N6150A	31T	7920001	N6190A	31T	7904007	N6307M	P68	306	(N6520V)	680W	1819-33
N6150Q	200	BB-1850	N6190F	200	BB-1890	N6308	90	LJ-101	N6522T	425	0225
N6150U	350	FL-450	N6190S	90	LJ-1702	N6308F	200	BB-1014	N6522T	BN2	136
N6151A	90	LJ-1951	N6191A	31T	7904008	N6317R	200	BB-984	N6523V	680T	1583-35
N6151C	200	BB-1851	N6191H	200	BB-1891	N6321V	200	BB-1284	(N6525V)	680W	1820-34
N6151N	350	FL-651	N6191N	200	BB-1841	N6325E	200	BB-1025	N6530B	F90	LA-201
N6151T	695A	96069	N6192A	31T	7904009	N6331Q	F90	LA-192	N6530E	F90	LA-203
N6151W	695A	96075	N6192C	350	FL-392	N6334F	200C	BL-47	N6531N	200	BB-1081
N6151X	695A	96078	N6193C	200	BB-1823	N6335F	F90	LA-190	(N6532V)	680T	1601-43
N6152A	31T	7920002	N6193J	90	LJ-1693	N6335P	200	BB-1040	N6532V	680W	1821-35
N6152L	200	BB-1852	N6193R	200	BB-1853	N6335U	200	BB-1064	N6536V	680T	1579-32
N6152U	90	LJ-1752	N6193S	350	FL-393	N6338C	B100	BE-133	N6537V	680T	1605-44
N6153V	350	FL-353	N6194A	31T	7920024	N6338P	90	LJ-1938	N6539V	680T	1562-18
N6154F	PC12	246	N6194S	200	BB-1854	N6338T	200	BB-1042	N6540V	680T	1571-26
N6155T	200	BB-1855	N6194U	350	FL-394	N6344H	F90	LA-176	N6541V	680T	1593-41
N6155U	350	FL-455	N6194V	200	BB-1874	N6346C	200	BB-1062	N6543V	680T	1587-38
N6158Q	200	BB-1858	N6194X	200	BB-1894	N6348H	200	BB-1030	N6555C	90	LJ-1078
N6160T	350	FL-660	N6195A	300C	FM-11	N6349E	350	FL-649	N6561B	BN2	520

N6563C	200C	BL-54	N6671M	E90	LW-327	N6731A	F90	LA-23	(N6776P)	425	0054
N6563K	90	LJ-1032	N6671Z	200	BB-1149	N6731L	200	BB-1190	(N6776T)	425	0055
N6564C	200C	BL-61	N6671Z	F90	LA-27	N6731T	200	BB-648	(N6776Y)	425	0056
N6566C	200C	BL-62	N6672N	90	LJ-875	N6732V	90	LJ-899	N6777C	425	0058
N6567C	90	LJ-1029	N6672V	200	BB-595	N6733	680W	1814-31	(N6777L)	425	0059
N6569H	F90	LA-204	N6672V	200	BB-1147	N6733H	680W	1814-31	N6780	100	B-46
N6569L	MU-2	645	N6673D	200	BB-596	N6733H	B100	BE-83	N6780	200	BB-1382
N6571S	E90	LW-171	N6673R	90	LJ-878	N6733R	200C	BL-8	N6781W	F90	LA-218
N6572K	200	BB-1039	N6673V	F90	LA-29	N6735P	200	BB-620	N6786S	350	FL-166
N6574C	90	LJ-1056	N6675W	F90	LA-31	N6735T	200	BB-602	N6788	90	LJ-285
N6580B	200	BB-1109	N6679E	200	BB-606	N6736C	F90	LA-36	N6789	100	B-46
N6581B	90	LJ-1059	N6679E	200	BB-1115	N6736L	90	LJ-884	N6789	100	B-92
N6583K	90	LJ-1074	N6679H	200	BB-584	N6736S	B100	BE-81	N6789	200	BB-328
N6586K	90	LJ-1058	N6679H	200	BB-1111	N6737C	B100	BE-89	N6789	200	BB-931
N6589A	F406	0047	N6681S	90	LJ-850	N6738V	200	BB-658	N6789	200	BB-1382
N6589C	F406	0048	N6682U	200	BB-625	N6739	100	B-92	N6789	350	FL-181
N6589E	F406	0049	N6683W	200	BB-1154	N6739H	F90	LA-34	N6789	90	LJ-285
N6590Y	F406	0052	N6684B	200	BB-631	N6739P	200	BB-628	N6789W	200	BB-328
N6591L	F406	0053	N6685H	B100	BE-79	N6740C	200C	BL-72	N6790F	F90	LA-236
N6591R	F406	0054	N6685H	F90	LA-200	N6740D	B100	BE-91	N6790W	300	FA-4
N6596Z	BN2	905	N6685N	200	BB-1159	N6742E	200	BB-649	N6794W	90	LJ-908
N6599A	B100	BE-15	N6685P	F90	LA-194	N6743D	200	BB-1192	N6804M	300	FA-17
N6600A	31T	7804001	N6685Y	200	BB-1151	N6743V	90	LJ-904	N6812W	300	FA-38
N6602L	P68	326	N6685Y	90	LJ-886	N6744Q	200	BB-1194	N6815X	200	BB-1201
N6604L	200	BB-1121	N6686A	F90	LA-19	N6745A	200	BB-650	N6816A	200	BB-1200
N6606R	200	BB-1122	N6687H	200	BB-601	N6746S	90	LJ-1039	N6816T	200	BB-1146
N6607H	690A	11110	N6687T	200	BB-611	N6747D	200	BB-662	N6818R	PC12	818
N6609K	200	BB-1120	N6687T	200	BB-1056	N6747J	200	BB-679	N6821W	F90	LA-219
N6619B	100	B-101	N6689D	200	BB-623	N6747T	200	BB-675	N6823M	300	FA-5
N6619B	90	LJ-54	N6690C	90	LJ-1106	N6748P	F90	LA-40	N6831N	441	0280
N6623D	90	LJ-1000	N6690C	F90	LA-30	N6749C	90	LJ-907	N6832C	441	0281
N6630C	200	BB-565	N6690E	200C	BL-7	N6749E	F90	LA-43	N6832M	441	0282
N6635L	200	BB-1126	N6690L	90	LJ-892	N6750B	200	BB-580	N6833C	441	0283
N6635N	200	BB-1130	N6690L	F90	LA-226	N6750C	F90	LA-11	N6833S	E90	LW-165
N6642B	300	FA-1	N6690N	90	LJ-1137	N6750Y	200	BB-680	N6837C	F90	LA-220
N6642B	F90	LA-6	N6690R	F90	LA-205	N6751T	200	BB-681	N6837R	441	0295
N6642Z	200	BB-1131	N6691L	90	LJ-1053	N6752C	F90	LA-45	N6838K	441	0296
N6643D	F90	LA-170	N6692D	200	BB-634	N6753K	200	BB-645	N6838T	441	0297
N6644J	200	BB-1031	N6692D	90	LJ-1072	N6754H	90	LJ-891	N6839C	441	0298
N6645B	B100	BE-73	N6693D	200	BB-636	N6756L	F90	LA-217	N6840T	441	0299
N6645P	B100	BE-75	N6693D	200	BB-1166	N6756P	B100	BE-92	N6842D	TBM7	192
N6646R	90	LJ-836	N6693F	200	BB-616	N6757M	200	BB-621	N6843S	E90	LW-137
N6647D	200	BB-519	N6694D	200	BB-635	N6759J	90	LJ-913	N6844D	425	0062
N6647P	90	LJ-849	N6695L	200	BB-1155	N6759P	E90	LW-336	N6844H	425	0063
N6649P	200	BB-1133	N6695L	B100	BE-84	N6763K	90	LJ-1064	N6844P	425	0064
N6650H	200	BB-516	N6695M	200	BB-583	N6767M	695A	96064	N6844S	425	0065
N6651H	F90	LA-17	N6695Z	200	BB-1169	N6769Z	425	0010	N6844T	425	0066
N6652G	90	LJ-856	N6702	G1	194	N6770G	200C	BL-65	N6844V	425	0067
N6653Z	G1	21	N6705F	200	BB-1125	N6770G	425	0011	(N6844V)	425	0078
N6654A	200	BB-548	N6712H	200	BB-1150	N6770M	425	0012	N6845L	F90	LA-221
N6654B	200	BB-547	N6713L	200	BB-1171	(N6770S)	425	0013	N6845P	425	0070
N6654Q	200	BB-1137	N6717T	90	LJ-1033	(N6770W)	425	0014	N6845R	425	0071
N6654V	F90	LA-208	N6720Y	TBM7	245	N6771L	425	0016	N6845S	425	0072
N6656D	90	LJ-879	N6720Y	TBM7	265	N6771U	425	0017	N6845T	425	0073
N6656W	200	BB-575	N6723T	B100	BE-85	N6771Y	425	0019	N6845Y	425	0074
N6659D	200	BB-1142	N6723V	200	BB-1152	N6772B	425	0020	N6846D	425	0078
N6659V	F90	LA-86	N6723Y	90	LJ-1013	N6772G	425	0021	(N6846D)	425	0079
N6660A	F406	0060	N6724D	90	LJ-917	N6772P	425	0022	N6846K	425	0079
N6661A	200	BB-541	N6724N	200	BB-538	N6772S	425	0023	(N6846R)	425	0080
N6661A	BN2	214	N6724N	200	BB-1178	(N6772U)	425	0024	N6846S	425	0081
N6661C	200	BB-1139	N6724P	200	BB-682	N6772V	425	0025	N6846T	425	0082
N6661J	90	LJ-1005	N6725D	200	BB-1179	N6772Y	425	0026	(N6846X)	425	0083
N6662D	90	LJ-869	N6725L	200	BB-607	N6773A	425	0031	N6846Y	425	0084
N6663A	90	LJ-864	N6725R	200C	BL-9	N6773B	425	0032	N6846Z	425	0085
N6663Y	90	LJ-863	N6725T	F90	LA-16	N6773C	425	0033	N6847C	425	0086
N6664P	200	BB-1143	N6725Y	200	BB-1181	N6773E	425	0034	N6847P	425	0087
N6664P	90	LJ-866	N6726D	200	BB-704	N6773F	425	0035	N6847S	425	0088
N6666C	200	BB-351	N6726P	F90	LA-212	(N6773H)	425	0036	N6847T	425	0089
N6666C	200	BB-524	N6726V	200	BB-1163	N6773L	425	0037	N6848D	425	0092
N6666K	100	B-44	N6726V	200C	BL-10	(N6773P)	425	0038	N6848R	425	0093
N6666K	200	BB-70	N6726X	200	BB-1180	N6773S	200	BB-120	N6848Y	425	0094
N6666K	200	BB-351	N6726Z	200	BB-1184	(N6773T)	425	0039	N6849D	425	0097
N6666K	B100	BE-106	N6726Z	F90	LA-33	N6773X	425	0041	N6849L	425	0098
N6666N	E90	LW-205	N6727C	200	BB-652	N6774G	425	0043	(N6849S)	425	0099
N6666Q	200	BB-70	N6727C	F90	LA-69	N6774L	425	0044	N6849Y	425	0100
N6667A	31T	1166004	N6727G	200	BB-1186	N6774R	425	0045	(N6849Z)	425	0101
N6667K	F90	LA-25	N6727L	90	LJ-1065	N6774T	425	0046	N6850K	425	0105
N6667T	200	BB-576	N6727M	90	LJ-1066	N6774X	425	0047	(N6850M)	425	0106
N6668C	F90	LA-26	N6727U	F90	LA-209	N6774Z	425	0048	N6850P	425	0107
N6668H	200	BB-586	N6728H	200	BB-1193	(N6775C)	425	0051	N6850Q	425	0108
N6668U	90	LJ-872	N6728N	200	BB-718	N6775D	425	0052	N6850Y	425	0109
N6669M	300	FA-13	N6728N	200	BB-1189	N6775J	425	0040	N6851A	425	0110
N6669T	200	BB-590	N6730S	B100	BE-74	N6775L	425	0018	(N6851C)	425	0111
N6670C	90	LJ-873	N6730S	F90	LA-215	N6776L	425	0053	N6851G	425	0112

N6851L	425	0113	N6883X	425	0134	N7031L	U-21	LM-21	N7101C	350	FL-541
N6851T	441	0211	N6884D	425	0135	N7031T	300	FA-10	N7101L	695	95027
N6851X	441	0212	N6884G	425	0136	N7031Z	MIII	T-322	N7102V	90	LJ-1802
N6851Y	441	0213	N6884L	425	0137	N7033U	300C	FM-13	N7102Y	350	FL-502
N6852L	441	0214	N6884Q	425	0138	N7034K	MU-2	553	N7106L	350	FL-506
N6852T	441	0215	N6884R	425	0139	N7034K	U-21	LM-22	N7111H	90	LJ-205
N6852X	441	0216	N6884X	425	0140	N7035B	F406	0031	N7112M	U-21	LM-87
N6853A	441	0217	(N6885L)	425	0142	N7035B	U-21	LM-24	N7112T	U-21	LM-88
N6853A	441	0301	N6885P	425	0143	N7035V	350	FL-535	N7113Z	U-21	LM-89
N6853G	441	0218	N6885S	425	0144	N7036L	U-21	LM-26	N7114E	100	B-138
(N6853L)	441	0219	N6885T	425	0145	N7037C	F406	0028	N7117	200	BB-403
N6853T	441	0220	(N6885V)	425	0146	N7038Y	U-21	LM-28	N7117	90	LJ-137
N6853X	441	0221	N6885X	425	0147	N7039T	U-21	LM-30	N7118A	200	BB-237
(N6854A)	441	0223	(N6885Y)	425	0148	N7040	G1	78	N7120P	U-21	LM-90
N6854B	441	0224	N6885Z	425	0149	N7040J	U-21	LM-31	N7123C	U-21	LM-92
N6854D	441	0225	N6886D	425	0152	N7040V	U-21	LM-32	N7125Y	90	LJ-1825
(N6854L)	441	0226	N6886L	425	0153	N7041M	U-21	LM-33	N7126U	U-21	LM-93
N6854T	441	0227	N6886S	90	LJ-1062	N7041N	90	LJ-328	N7127	90	LJ-332
(N6854X)	441	0228	N6886V	425	0154	N7042R	U-21	LM-34	N7128H	90	LJ-641
(N6855E)	441	0230	N6886X	425	0155	N7043D	U-21	LM-35	N7128H	U-21	LM-94
N6855H	441	0231	N6886Z	425	0156	N7043G	U-21	LM-37	N7128J	90	LJ-619
(N6855L)	441	0232	N6887B	425	0163	N7043N	U-21	LM-38	N7130X	350	FL-530
N6855P	441	0233	N6887F	425	0164	N7043Y	U-21	LM-39	N7131Z	350	FL-531
(N6855S)	441	0234	N6887K	425	0165	N7045C	200	BB-1110	N7132Z	U-21	LM-95
(N6855T)	441	0235	(N6888C)	441	0284	N7045P	200	BB-325	N7134A	BN2	2005
N6855X	441	0236	N6900K	690B	11441	N7045X	MU-2	781SA	N7134J	E90	LW-24
N6855Z	441	0237	N6904Q	200C	BN-2	N7047D	U-21	LM-41	N7136K	BN2	900
(N6856L)	441	0239	N6912F	200C	BL-64	N7049T	BN2	643	N7136M	U-21	LM-98
(N6856Q)	441	0240	N6912T	200	BB-1051	N7049U	90	LJ-1073	N7137G	U-21	LM-99
(N6856S)	441	0241	N6914H	200	BB-1104	N7049Y	441	0206	N7138C	90	LJ-446
(N6856U)	441	0242	N6914Z	200	BB-1138	N7050J	E90	LW-251	N7138E	90	LJ-680
(N6856X)	441	0243	N6921D	200C	BL-63	N7051K	U-21	LM-44	N7138N	90	LJ-338
N6857E	441	0244	N6921R	200C	BL-70	N7052J	690C	11680	N7139B	PA42	8001042
N6857L	441	0245	N6921T	200C	BL-71	N7052X	U-21	LM-45	N7139Z	U-21	LM-101
N6857S	441	0246	N6922P	200	BB-1165	N7052Y	U-21	LM-47	N7143Y	U-21	LM-103
N6857T	441	0247	N6923C	200	BB-1195	N7054D	200	BB-1954	N7144E	200	BB-1112
(N6857X)	441	0248	N6923L	200T	BT-30	N7055T	200	BB-1955	N7146C	200	BB-1076
(N6858G)	441	0250	N6923Y	300	FA-7	N7057A	690C	11664	N7146X	U-21	LM-104
(N6858L)	441	0251	N6923Z	90	LJ-1083	N7059H	U-21	LM-48	N7148A	U-21	LM-105
(N6858R)	441	0252	N6927C	200	BB-1204	N7061T	200	BB-1044	N7148P	F406	0051
N6858S	441	0253	N6927D	200	BB-1205	N7062W	U-21	LM-49	N7148T	F406	0050
N6859L	441	0256	N6927G	200	BB-1206	N7063D	U-21	LM-50	N7154W	U-21	LM-106
(N6859S)	441	0257	(N6929S)	200	BB-1198	N7063F	200	BB-1963	N7155P	U-21	LM-107
(N6859Y)	441	0258	N6929S	200	BB-1198	N7063W	U-21	LM-51	N7155S	U-21	LM-112
N6860A	441	0303	N6930L	F90	LA-225	N7064B	C-12	BC-2	N7156J	U-21	LM-113
N6860C	441	0304	N6930P	200	BB-1170	N7064Q	U-21	LM-52	N7157K	U-21	LM-115
N6860S	441	0306	N6931W	90	LJ-1080	N7066D	C-12	BC-40	N7162V	200	BB-1962
N6868C	TBM8	415	N6969B	680T	1597-42	N7066X	U-21	LM-54	N7165J	U-21	LM-119
N6872D	425	0166	N6971Z	PC12	629	N7067B	C-12	BC-35	N7165Y	U-21	LM-120
N6872L	425	0167	N7000B	U-21	LM-1	N7067S	U-21	LM-55	N7166P	200	BB-482
(N6872T)	425	0168	N7000G	200	BB-1776	N7068B	C-12	BC-13	N7169U	U-21	LM-122
N6872X	200C	BL-52	N7000H	680T	1707-82	N7069A	C-12	BC-54	N7169Z	U-21	LM-123
N6872Z	425	0169	N7000Z	90	LJ-829	N7069F	U-21	LM-56	N7170A	U-21	LM-125
N6873D	425	0171	N7001L	E90	LW-61	N7069Y	BN2	626	N7171A	U-21	LM-126
N6873L	425	0172	N7001N	G1	38	N7070Z	U-21	LM-57	N7173K	U-21	LM-127
N6873Q	425	0173	N7001Z	350	FL-501	N7071C	BN2	400	N7173Y	U-21	LM-128
N6873R	425	0174	N7004	G1	174	N7071H	BN2	401	N7174J	U-21	LM-129
N6873S	425	0175	N7004B	G1	174	N7071H	U-21	LM-58	N7177	90	LJ-207
N6873T	425	0176	N7007	100	B-18	N7071M	BN2	402	N7178H	300	FA-30
N6873X	425	0177	N7007G	U-21	LM-2	N7071N	BN2	414	N7181E	U-21	LM-132
N6873Y	425	0178	N7007Q	U-21	LM-5	N7071N	U-21	LM-59	N7181H	U-21	LM-134
N6873Z	425	0179	N7007Y	90	LJ-1807	N7071S	BN2	415	N7181J	U-21	LM-135
N6874D	425	0183	N7009	200	BB-622	N7071U	BN2	417	N7181Z	U-21	LM-136
N6874G	425	0184	N7009	90	LJ-31	N7074G	C-12	BC-17	N7182H	U-21	LM-137
N6874L	425	0185	N7009J	200	BB-622	N7074N	200	BB-1974	N7184M	200	BB-1984
N6874R	425	0186	(N7010H)	200	BB-1104	N7075V	200	BB-1975	N7185A	350	FL-525
(N6874Z)	425	0187	N7010L	U-21	LM-7	N7076X	U-21	LM-60	N7185C	441	679
N6879W	200	BB-1084	N7010N	90	LJ-308	N7077N	90	LJ-359	N7185C	90	LJ-1835
N6881D	425	0116	N7011Y	350	FL-511	N7078J	U-21	LM-67	N7191N	90	LJ-1791
N6881L	425	0117	N7014L	U-21	LM-10	N7078L	U-21	LM-69	N7191W	U-21	LM-138
N6881Q	425	0118	N7014X	350	FL-514	N7078S	90	LJ-159	N7192X	350	FL-492
N6881S	90	LJ-450	N7017C	350	FL-527	N7079N	BN2	198	N7193K	350	FL-513
N6881T	425	0119	N7018F	U-21	LM-13	N7079S	U-21	LM-70	N7193M	U-21	LM-139
N6882C	425	0121	N7021Z	350	FL-521	N7081L	U-21	LM-72	N7193Q	90	LJ-1823
N6882D	425	0122	N7022F	200	BB-1972	(N7084B)	E90	LW-245	N7194P	U-21	LM-140
N6882L	425	0123	N7022Y	200	BB-1982	N7086V	90	LJ-1786	N7194Y	31T	8166064
N6882M	425	0124	N7023D	441	0232	N7087N	200	BB-1324	N7196M	350	FL-496
(N6882R)	425	0125	N7026H	U-21	LM-15	N7087U	350	FL-487	N7197Y	350	FL-497
N6882S	425	0126	N7028M	P68T	9004	N7087U	U-21	LM-74	N7198B	U-21	LM-141
N6882V	425	0127	N7029P	680T	1699-76	N7089Q	U-21	LM-77	N7198S	U-21	LU-1
N6882X	425	0128	N7030B	90	LJ-1830	N7090	MIII	T-214	N7198Y	U-21	LU-2
N6883L	425	0131	N7031F	U-21	LM-19	N7090T	200	BB-689	N7199B	U-21	LU-5
N6883R	425	0132	N7031J	695A	96006	(N7090U)	200	BB-1112	N7199D	U-21	LU-6
N6883T	425	0133	N7031K	695A	96009	N7092K	U-21	LM-83	N7199H	U-21	LU-7

N7199J	U-21	LU-8	N7233U	300	FA-59	N7300R	200	BB-22	N8022Q	90	LJ-1314
N7199L	U-21	LU-9	N7233V	350	FL-523	N7308B	C-12	BC-57	N8023F	350	FL-34
N7199N	U-21	LU-10	N7233Z	200	BB-1225	N7309R	E90	LW-130	N8025L	STAR	NC-19
N7199S	U-21	LU-11	N7234B	300	FA-60	N7311R	90	LJ-637	N8026J	200	BB-1392
N7199V	350	FL-499	N7234E	300	FA-61	N7312R	90	LJ-642	N8029Y	350	FL-29
N7200B	200	BB-340	N7234H	90	LJ-1117	N7317A	200	BB-1977	N8033J	350	FL-33
N7200R	100	B-206	N7234L	200	BB-1213	N7328B	90	LJ-1828	N8035H	350	FL-35
N7200R	90	LJ-1086	N7234U	200	BB-1226	N7332	100	B-34	N8037J	200	BB-1432
N7200U	90	LJ-1081	N7234Z	90	LJ-1118	N7338R	90	LJ-641	(N8037J)	MU-2	611
N7201K	200	BB-1157	N7235Z	300	FA-63	N7345S	200	BB-1945	N8039M	200	BB-1380
N7201S	U-21	LM-61	N7236C	300	FA-99	N7350C	350	FL-7	N8040A	200	BB-444
N7201Z	U-21	LM-100	N7237A	200	BB-1227	N7368X	350	FL-538	N8040A	350	FL-39
N7202D	U-21	LM-133	N7237J	200	BB-1228	N7373R	100	B-203	N8042N	680T	1720-91
N7202L	90	LJ-129	N7237K	90	LJ-1120	N7374R	100	B-204	N8043B	200	BB-1390
N7202Y	300	FA-12	N7237U	300	FA-66	N7377	90	LJ-115	N8043K	200	BB-1433
N7202Z	300	FA-13	N7238B	90	LJ-1121	N7387R	E90	LW-117	N8045T	90	LJ-1272
N7203R	200	BB-1199	N7238J	90	LJ-1110	(N7388E)	STAR	NC-13	N8047Y	200	BB-1394
N7204D	300	FA-14	N7239S	90	LJ-1143	N7388K	STAR	NC-7	N8048U	350	FL-40
N7204V	90	LJ-1093	N7239T	200	BB-1231	N7391U	FPC6	2028	N8048W	200	BB-1391
N7205X	200	BB-1176	N7239U	90	LJ-1144	N7400V	E90	LW-152	N8049H	200	BB-1395
N7206E	F90	LA-234	N7239Y	90	LJ-1145	N7410L	350	FL-510	N8049R	90	LJ-1287
N7206L	300	FA-21	N7240D	90	LJ-1148	N7418L	350	FL-528	N8049V	200	BB-1389
N7206N	F90	LA-228	N7240E	90	LJ-1149	N7481P	200	BB-1981	N8050X	200	BB-1435
N7206Z	F90	LA-227	N7240K	90	LJ-1150	N7500L	31T	1	N8051Q	350	FL-41
N7207M	200	BB-1202	N7240L	90	LJ-1151	N7529N	90	LJ-370	N8053R	350	FL-81
N7207M	90	LJ-1827	N7241H	300	FA-123	N7586Z	300	FA-71	N8053U	90	LJ-1307
N7208H	300	FA-23	N7241K	300	FA-132	N7601L	MU-2	697SA	N8055J	350	FL-51
N7208L	90	LJ-1125	N7241L	200	BB-1277	N7603	MIIB	T26-112	N8055X	BN2	2008
N7208N	350	FL-508	N7241V	300	FA-152	N7603	MIIB	T26-162	N8056H	200	BB-1467
N7208N	EPIC	202	N7241V	300	FA-189	N7610U	680T	1548-10	N8059Q	200	BB-1450
N7208T	200	BB-1207	N7242V	90	LJ-1160	N7644R	90	LJ-335	N8059Y	200	BB-1437
N7209Z	F90	LA-229	N7243R	100	B-213	N7649J	690C	11636	N8059Y	690A	11222
N7210H	90	LJ-1090	N7244J	90	LJ-1122	N7650E	P166	342	N8061Q	680W	1833-38
N7210R	200	BB-10	N7244N	200T	BT-27	(N7651E)	P166	356	N8061Q	90	LJ-1329
N7211B	200	BB-1148	N7244U	300	FA-68	N7651E	P166	358	N8061U	350	FL-53
N7212D	90	LJ-1092	N7245Y	300	FA-69	(N7652E)	P166	358	N8062J	200	BB-1397
N7212S	350	FL-512	N7245Z	90	LJ-1123	N7661Y	P166	358	N8064A	90	LJ-1330
N7213B	200	BB-1153	N7246B	90	LJ-1124	N7688	46D	120	N8064F	200	BB-1393
N7213J	200	BB-1210	N7246E	200	BB-1233	N7701L	690B	11489	N8064H	200	BB-1440
N7213K	200	BB-1208	N7246K	300	FA-72	N7702	90	LJ-326	N8064Q	200	BB-1473
N7214W	300	FA-50	N7246M	200	BB-1234	N7703L	31T	7820073	N8065R	90	LJ-1276
N7215C	F90	LA-230	N7247A	300	FA-75	N7707C	441	0222	N8068N	350	FL-49
N7215J	300	FA-28	N7247R	200	BB-1235	(N7711B)	425	0105	N8068R	350	FL-48
N7215L	90	LJ-1094	N7247Y	300	FA-76	N7725X	PC12	357	N8069F	350	FL-47
N7216A	300	FA-31	N7247Y	C-12	BC-3	N7729B	B100	BE-29	N8069S	E90	LW-140
N7216H	90	LJ-1096	N7248G	90	LJ-1128	N7736M	90	LJ-1645	N8069X	BN2	2015
N7218V	90	LJ-1098	N7248M	90	LJ-1129	N7771R	100	B-71	N8074S	STAR	NC-33
N7218Y	300	FA-37	N7249N	300	FA-80	N7775	F90	LA-117	N8079B	C-12	BD-20
N7218Y	90	LJ-1818	N7249R	90	LJ-649	N7776	G1	133	N8080C	350	FL-85
N7219D	90	LJ-1099	N7250L	300	FA-81	N7777	90	LJ-477	N8080Q	350	FL-54
N7219G	F90	LA-232	N7250T	200	BB-1237	N7777F	46D	53	N8082Y	P68	389
N7219K	90	LJ-1100	N7250V	200	BB-1239	N7777G	46D	40	N8083A	MU-2	739SA
N7220C	200	BB-1211	N7251H	90	LJ-1132	N7778T	46T	97222	N8084J	350	FL-84
N7220L	300	FA-45	N7251K	300	FA-84	N7782	90	LJ-119	N8085D	200	BB-1400
N7220T	F90	LA-231	N7251P	200	BB-1240	(N7787)	690A	11166	N8086L	350	FL-86
N7221H	300	FA-47	N7251U	200	BB-1951	N7788	G1	45	N8087U	200	BB-1444
N7221N	300	FA-48	N7252H	300	FA-85	N7795W	46D	232	N8087V	90	LJ-1279
N7221Y	200	BB-1212	N7252S	90	LJ-1087	N7801L	200	BB-831	(N8088J)	441	0170
N7221Y	90	LJ-1821	N7253K	300	FA-87	N7801L	90	LJ-883	N8088V	90	LJ-538
N7222U	300	FA-46	N7254B	90	LJ-1127	N7812	695A	96089	N8089J	90	LJ-1331
N7223X	90	LJ-1104	N7255K	200	BB-1157	N7872L	690B	11374	N8090U	200	BB-1456
N7224A	300	FA-49	N7255X	300	FA-88	N7876C	46D	4	N8092D	200	BB-418
N7224M	300	FA-33	N7256G	200	BB-1248	N7876Q	46D	4	N8092F	350	FL-50
N7225B	300	FA-25	N7256K	200	BB-1241	N7895J	PC6	767	N8093W	200	BB-1396
N7225D	200	BB-1214	N7256R	90	LJ-651	N7896G	695A	96070	N8093W	90	LJ-412
N7225K	F90	LA-235	N7257E	200	BB-1243	N7931D	90	LJ-1049	N8094K	BN2	2038
N7225V	200	BB-1215	N7257G	200	BB-1245	N7972S	G1	139	N8094Q	200	BB-1403
N7227L	200	BB-1216	N7257P	90	LJ-1133	N7995D	PC6	931	N8096U	90	LJ-1326
N7227R	90	LJ-1108	N7257T	200	BB-1246	N8000	90	LJ-249	N8097Y	350	FL-75
N7228C	300	FA-86	N7259B	300	FA-95	N8000J	BN2	188	N8099G	90	LJ-1274
N7228T	300	FA-20	N7260R	200	BB-1960	N8000Q	STAR	NC-26	N8100D	100	B-51
N7228Y	90	LJ-1111	N7262U	350	FL-532	N8001J	G1	16	N8100H	100	B-51
N7228Z	300	FA-51	N7270Z	200	BB-1970	N8001V	90	LJ-1265	N8100H	200	BB-283
N7229Z	90	LJ-1112	N7274L	PC12	1124	N8002J	200	BB-1425	N8100M	31T	8020072
N7230H	90	LJ-1113	N7274Y	300	FA-79	N8003U	200	BB-1427	N8100R	100	B-55
N7230K	300	FA-55	N7275R	E90	LW-135	N8008A	200	BB-1429	N8103E	90	LJ-1315
N7230U	200	BB-1221	N7276C	31T	7620034	N8011Q	300	FA-210	N8105D	90	LJ-1355
N7231M	200	BB-1223	N7277F	90	LJ-1837	N8012U	90	LJ-1277	N8105Q	200	BB-1455
N7231P	300	FA-56	N7282X	90	LJ-1832	N8013R	350	FL-31	N8107N	350	FL-56
N7231Z	300	FA-57	N7285Y	300C	FM-5	N8013T	200	BB-1430	N8108E	90	LJ-1275
N7232L	300	FA-64	N7291Y	300	FA-43	N8017G	300	FA-215	N8108Z	441	0197
N7232R	200C	BL-69	N7295T	90	LJ-1795	N8017M	200	BB-1438	N8108Z	90	LJ-1283
N7232U	90	LJ-1114	(N7300K)	90	LJ-651	N8021M	BN2	278	N8109J	T-44	LL-30
N7232Z	300	FA-65	N7300N	90	LJ-651	N8021P	90	LJ-1269	N8109N	90	LJ-1099

N8110N	350	FL-59
N8112F	350	FL-89
N8114P	90	LJ-1316
N8114Q	STAR	NC-30
N8115M	300	FA-217
N8116N	**350**	**FL-58**
N8117N	200	BB-92
N8118R	**E90**	**LW-118**
N8119N	90	LJ-1320
N8119S	STAR	NC-34
N8121C	90	LJ-1322
N8121M	200	BB-1445
N8129A	200	BB-1405
N8131E	350	FL-68
N8131F	**31T**	**7620042**
N8133	300	FA-109
N8133	90	LJ-322
N8135M	90	LJ-1325
N8138E	350	FL-92
N8138V	200	BB-1447
N8139K	350	FL-111
N8140F	350	FL-61
N8140P	200	BB-1417
N8141K	90	LJ-1278
N8145E	350	FL-95
N8148F	350	FL-57
N8148N	90	LJ-1334
N8149S	**STAR**	**NC-35**
N8150N	200	BB-1478
N8153H	200	BB-1453
N8154G	90	LJ-1282
N8155L	200	BB-1479
N8156E	90	LJ-134
N8156Z	**90**	**LJ-1333**
N8157R	100	B-198
N8158X	STAR	NC-42
N8159G	695A	96011
N8163Q	STAR	NC-44
N8163R	200	BB-1459
N8164G	200	BB-1460
N8167Z	MIII	T-339
N8170J	**200**	**BB-728**
N8170Q	STAR	NC-46
N8171E	**PC6**	**859**
N8171K	**PC6**	**750**
N8176S	STAR	NC-36
N8178W	90	LJ-1291
N8180	90	LJ-152
N8181Z	100	B-122
N8182C	350	FL-82
N8186S	STAR	NC-20
N8188F	300	FA-218
N8192M	350	FL-103
N8194Q	350	FL-94
N8194S	STAR	NC-37
N8194Z	441	0104
N8196Q	STAR	NC-48
N8198M	200	BB-158
N8199W	350	FL-100
N8200E	G1	50
N8202P	350	FL-102
N8203C	350	FL-109
N8203C	90	LJ-1390
N8207D	350	FL-104
N8208C	90	LJ-1343
N8210C	90	LJ-1347
N8210X	200	BB-1473
N8213Q	350	FL-67
N8214T	200	BB-1465
N8215Q	STAR	NC-45
N8215W	350	FL-105
N8216Z	200	BB-1466
N8217A	PC6	620
N8220V	90	LJ-1344
N8221K	350	FL-106
N8224Q	STAR	NC-49
N8225H	200	BB-1422
N8225Y	STAR	NC-27
N8225Z	200	BB-1470
N8226M	200	BB-1475
N8227P	90	LJ-1327
N8230E	200	BB-1468
N8230Q	300C	FM-3
N8230Q	350	FL-69

N8230Z	200	BB-1421
N8232L	90	LJ-1321
N8236B	90	LJ-1436
N8236K	200	BB-1424
N8239Q	90	LJ-1297
N8241F	300	FA-212
N8241J	200	BB-1412
N8241T	200	BB-1410
N8242A	200	BB-1463
N8244L	**STAR**	**NC-29**
N8244S	STAR	NC-23
N8246Q	350	FL-79
N8246S	STAR	NC-18
N8248H	90	LJ-1295
N8248M	350	FL-72
N8248W	200	BB-1419
N8248W	350	FL-110
N8250K	90	LJ-1328
N8253D	90	LJ-1299
N8254H	200	BB-1416
N8254Q	STAR	NC-32
N8255A	90	LJ-1257
N8257V	350	FL-107
N8258V	200	BB-1458
N8259Q	90	LJ-1332
N8261E	200	BB-1461
N8264G	90	LJ-1298
N8265V	200	BB-1428
N8266L	350	FL-66
N8266V	200	BB-1418
N8267Q	200	BB-1420
N8270R	350	FL-73
N8273L	300	FA-222
N8274U	350	FL-76
N8275D	350	FL-80
N8275P	300C	FM-4
N8277Q	STAR	NC-47
N8279P	350	FL-110
N8280K	90	LJ-1359
N8280S	STAR	NC-38
N8282S	STAR	NC-39
N8283S	STAR	NC-41
N8285Q	**STAR**	**NC-50**
N8286Q	STAR	NC-51
N8287E	**90**	**LJ-1356**
N8288Q	350	FL-114
N8288W	350	FL-88
N8290T	90	LJ-1306
N8291D	200	BB-1476
N8291K	350	FL-78
N8291Y	350	FL-113
N8292Y	90	LJ-1353
N8294Z	90	LJ-1354
N8297L	350	FL-97
N8299L	350	FL-99
N8300C	90	LJ-949
N8300E	100	B-29
N8300S	STAR	NC-40
N8301D	200	BB-1477
N8302N	350	FL-98
N8361T	31T	8120041
N8400E	MU-2	532
N8415B	200	BB-15
N8416B	200	BB-76
N8416B	680W	1843-42
N8421E	**PC12**	**430**
N8473N	90	LJ-377
N8479Y	100	B-94
N8482N	90	LJ-397
N8484	MIIB	T26-129
N8484T	MU-2	617
N8491B	BN2	479
N8493D	200	BB-160
N8500B	90	LJ-132
N8500C	G1	139
N8500N	G1	139
N8511L	200	BB-684
N8514B	B100	BE-6
N8520L	90	LJ-156
N8527Z	MU-2	149
N8534W	200	BB-225
N8534Z	695	95010
N8535	690A	11131
N8536A	BN2	841

N8554R	E90	LW-122
N8570R	100	B-202
N8594R	E90	LW-124
N8617K	441	0307
N8686	**46D**	**150**
(N8753B)	200	BB-1312
N8755X	**46T**	**97380**
N8757K	441	0285
N8774P	695	95033
(N8798R)	200	BB-33
N8798R	200	BB-33
N8816K	441	0286
N8837K	441	0287
N8838T	**441**	**0003**
N8840A	300	FA-182
N8841	90	LJ-1140
N8860K	441	0288
N8870B	**P180**	**1099**
(N8873)	STAR	NC-7
N8877N	441	0053
(N8881N)	441	0062
N8881N	441	0266
N8884	MU-2	027
N8887B	**90**	**LJ-1148**
N8887W	PA42	5501011
N8894N	441	0084
N8897Y	**MIVC**	**AT-492**
N8904N	441	0085
N8912B	690A	11146
(N8931N)	441	0086
N8935N	441	0087
N8936N	441	0088
N8949N	441	0089
N8961N	441	0090
N8964N	441	0091
N8970N	**441**	**0092**
(N8971N)	441	0093
N8972N	441	0094
N8975N	441	0095
N8977N	441	0096
N8998W	**200**	**BB-1637**
N8999A	90	LJ-145
N9000V	**P68**	**259**
N9001N	690	11000
N9003N	680W	1828-36
N9004N	680W	1829-37
N9006L	G1	28
N9006N	680T	1565-21
N9007	690A	11205
(N9008N)	680W	1833-38
N9008U	C-12	BD-5
N9009N	680W	1834-39
N9010B	MU-2	114
N9010N	680W	1835-40
N9012N	681	6023
N9015P	690A	11128
N9017N	680W	1842-41
N9018N	680W	1843-42
(N9018W)	680W	1843-42
N9019N	680W	1844-43
N9019Q	90	LJ-497
N9020N	681	6024
(N9021A)	46T	97227
N9021J	100	B-80
(N9023N)	680W	1848-44
N9023N	681	6025
N9023R	200	BB-20
(N9024N)	680W	1849-45
N9024N	681	6026
N9024R	E90	LW-114
(N9025N)	680W	1850-46
N9025N	681	6027
N9026R	90	LJ-644
N9027R	90	LJ-645
N9028N	681	6028
N9029R	**E90**	**LW-132**
N9030R	90	LJ-657
N9030S	PA42	5501021
N9030V	90	LJ-537
N9031R	E90	LW-131
N9031X	680T	1546-9
N9031Y	90	LJ-295
N9032H	MIIA	T26-007
N9035N	681	6030

N9036N	MU-2	248
(N9036P)	G1	148
N9043E	MU-2	556
N9045C	441	0337
N9046G	E90	LW-152
N9049X	690B	11364
N9050V	100	B-91
N9051N	681	6001
N9051S	E90	LW-129
N9052N	681	6002
N9052S	E90	LW-152
N9052Y	MU-2	399SA
N9053N	681	6003
N9053S	90	LJ-653
N9054F	690B	11517
N9054N	681	6004
N9055N	681	6005
N9056N	681	6006
N9057N	681	6007
N9057S	E90	LW-193
N9058N	**681**	**6008**
N9059N	681	6009
N9059Q	MU-2	584
N9059S	**E90**	**LW-159**
N9060N	681	6011
N9060S	90	LJ-660
N9061N	681	6012
N9061S	90	LJ-691
(N9062N)	681	6013
N9063N	681	6014
N9063S	E90	LW-163
N9064S	90	LJ-761
N9065D	100	B-130
N9065N	681	6010
N9065S	E90	LW-145
N9066N	681	6015
N9066N	90	LJ-557
(N9067N)	681	6016
N9067N	681B	6050
N9067S	90	LJ-667
N9068N	681	6018
N9068S	E90	LW-168
N9069N	681	6019
N9069S	90	LJ-668
N9070N	681	6020
N9071N	681	6021
N9071S	90	LJ-671
N9073N	681	6022
N9073S	90	LJ-673
N9074N	681	6029
N9074S	90	LJ-674
N9075S	90	LJ-647
N9076S	**90**	**LJ-715**
N9077S	90	LJ-650
N9078S	90	LJ-754
N9079N	681	6032
N9079S	F90	LA-1
N9080S	E90	LW-160
N9081R	90	LJ-859
N9081S	E90	LW-266
N9082E	46D	57
N9082S	90	LJ-682
N9083Y	31T	8166032
N9084U	46D	66
N9084Y	31T	8166030
N9085S	90	LJ-755
N9085U	**PA42**	**5501034**
N9086N	681	6033
N9087N	681	6034
N9087Y	31T	8120057
N9088N	681	6035
N9088S	31T	8275009
N9088Y	31T	8104068
N9089N	681	6036
N9090N	681	6037
N9090S	F90	LA-3
N9091J	**PA42**	**5501035**
N9091N	681	6038
N9091S	90	LJ-678
N9092N	681	6039
N9092S	90	LJ-767
N9092Y	31T	8166033
N9093S	E90	LW-143
N9094C	31T	8275014

N9094T	46D	156
N9094U	PA42	5501059
N9094Z	46D	165
N9095N	46D	39
N9095N	PA42	5527036
N9095S	**46D**	**224**
N9095S	E90	LW-155
N9095U	46D	1
N9096C	31T	8275017
N9097C	31T	8275015
N9097N	681	6040
N9097S	E90	LW-167
N9098U	**46D**	**213**
N9098Y	31T	8166034
N9099U	PA42	5527034
N9100N	690	11001
N9100S	100	B-238
N9100Z	**46D**	**7**
N9101F	690A	11152
N9101N	681	6041
N9101Y	31T	8275003
N9102N	681	6042
N9103S	B100	BE-3
(N9103Y)	31T	8166035
N9104N	**46D**	**183**
N9104S	B100	BE-4
N9104Z	46D	18
(N9105N)	681	6043
N9105Y	31T	8104070
N9106Y	31T	8166036
(N9107N)	31T	8104022
N9107N	681B	6045
N9107Y	31T	8166038
N9108N	681B	6046
N9109N	681B	6047
N9110N	681B	6048
N9110R	BN2	612
N9110Y	31T	8166039
N9111N	681B	6049
N9112F	MIV	AT-002
N9113Y	31T	7820019
N9114D	46D	153
N9114S	90	LJ-676
N9114Y	31T	8120058
N9115X	PA42	5501060
N9115Y	31T	8166040
N9116Q	**PA42**	**5501037**
N9116S	B100	BE-6
N9117N	681B	6051
(N9118N)	681B	6052
N9118Y	31T	8120060
N9119N	46D	134
N9120Y	31T	8166041
N9120Y	**46D**	**133**
N9121G	46D	27
N9121N	681B	6053
N9122U	46D	5
N9122Y	31T	8166042
N9123G	441	0001
N9123S	200	BB-123
N9124N	681B	6054
N9124Y	31T	8166043
N9126B	PA42	5501039
N9126N	690	11057
N9126S	100	B-226
N9127F	PA42	5501040
N9127N	681B	6055
N9127N	PA42	5527038
N9127Y	31T	8166058
N9129N	681B	6056
N9129S	100	B-232
(N9129Y)	31T	8120062
N9130N	**46D**	**104**
N9130N	681B	6057
N9130Y	31T	8166044
N9131N	690	11059
(N9132N)	690	11052
N9134D	46D	35
N9134Y	31T	8120063
N9136J	46D	173
N9137N	681B	6058
N9138N	681B	6059
N9138Q	100	B-76
N9138Q	**46D**	**54**
N9138Y	31T	8166045
N9139Y	31T	8104071
N9140F	46D	132
N9140N	46D	59
N9140N	690	11073
N9140Y	31T	8166046
(N9141Y)	31T	8120064
N9142B	**PA42**	**5501038**
N9142N	681B	6060
N9143B	46D	16
(N9143N)	681B	6061
(N9143N)	690	11043
N9143Y	31T	8166048
(N9144N)	681B	6062
N9144N	690	11044
N9146N	681B	6063
N9147N	690	11062
N9147Y	31T	8120065
N9147Y	31T	8120103
N9148N	690	11058
N9148V	46D	226
N9148Y	31T	8166049
(N9149N)	681B	6064
(N9149N)	690	11072
N9149N	690A	11196
N9150N	690	11063
N9150R	200	BB-181
(N9150T)	PA42	5501024
N9150T	**PA42**	**5501024**
N9150Y	31T	8166050
(N9151N)	681B	6065
N9151N	690	11051
N9151X	46D	82
N9151Y	31T	8120067
N9151Y	31T	8120102
N9152Q	46D	145
N9152Y	31T	8275004
(N9153N)	681B	6066
N9153Y	31T	8120066
N9153Y	31T	8120101
(N9154N)	681B	6065
N9154N	690	11064
N9155H	46D	53
N9155Y	31T	8166051
N9156N	31T	7820049
N9156N	690	11056
N9156Y	31T	8166052
N9157Y	31T	8120068
N9159Y	31T	8166053
N9159Y	**PA42**	**5501028**
N9160C	31T	8166065
N9160Y	31T	8166054
(N9161N)	681B	6067
N9161Y	31T	8166055
(N9162N)	681B	6068
(N9162N)	690	11055
N9162Y	31T	8120069
N9162Y	31T	8120104
(N9163N)	681B	6069
(N9164N)	681B	6070
N9164N	690A	11172
(N9165N)	681B	6071
(N9165N)	690	11065
N9165N	690A	11212
N9165Y	31T	8166056
(N9166N)	681B	6072
N9166N	690	11066
N9166Y	31T	8120070
N9167Q	**46D**	**38**
N9167R	46D	45
N9168N	690	11068
N9168T	31T	1104015
N9168Y	31T	8166057
N9169N	690A	11231
N9169Y	31T	8166061
N9170C	31T	8166066
N9171R	PA42	5527039
N9171S	690B	11437
N9171Y	31T	8275005
N9174C	31T	8275018
N9174C	31T	8375001
N9174N	**46D**	**72**
N9174P	90	LJ-1490
N9174Y	31T	8166062
N9174Z	PA42	5501027
N9175G	441	0002
N9175N	**690**	**11071**
N9175Y	31T	8104072
N9176X	46D	58
N9176Y	31T	8275006
N9177N	690B	11541
N9178B	46D	97
N9179C	31T	8166067
N9179Y	MU-2	558
N9180K	425	0179
N9180X	**46D**	**208**
N9180Y	31T	8275007
N9181N	690A	11300
N9181X	46D	85
N9182Y	31T	8275008
N9183C	**31T**	**8304001**
N9183C	31T	8275016
N9183X	46D	4
N9183Y	31T	8275009
N9184Y	31T	8166060
N9185C	31T	8166068
N9185Y	31T	8104073
N9186Y	31T	8166063
(N9187N)	690	11075
N9187N	690A	11294
N9189C	31T	8275011
N9189Y	31T	8275013
N9190Y	31T	8166069
N9191Y	31T	8275025
N9192C	31T	8166070
(N9192N)	690	11074
N9192N	690A	11233
(N9193N)	690A	11216
N9193N	690A	11238
N9193V	46D	83
N9193X	46D	128
N9193Y	31T	8275010
N9194X	PA42	5501058
N9194Y	31T	8166064
N9195F	**46D**	**214**
N9196C	31T	8275019
N9196C	31T	8375002
(N9196N)	690	11067
N9196Q	690B	11561
N9197B	46D	136
N9197N	690A	11197
N9197Y	31T	8275012
N9198F	PA42	5501055
N9200N	690A	11100
N9201N	690	11008
N9202N	690	11002
N9203N	690	11003
N9204C	46D	65
N9204C	**46D**	**161**
N9204N	690	11004
(N9205N)	690	11005
N9206N	690	11006
N9207N	690	11007
N9209N	690	11009
N9209Q	200	BB-218
N9209Q	90	LJ-507
N9210N	690	11010
N9211B	46D	41
N9211B	46D	146
N9211N	690	11011
(N9212N)	690	11012
N9214N	690	11014
N9215N	690	11015
N9216N	690	11016
N9217N	690	11017
N9218N	690	11018
N9219G	PA42	5527040
N9219N	690	11019
N9220N	690	11020
N9222F	46D	14
N9222N	690	11022
N9223N	**690**	**11023**
N9225N	690	11025
N9226B	PA42	5527043
N9226N	690	11026
(N9227N)	690	11076
N9227N	690A	11217
N9228N	690	11028
(N9229N)	690	11077
N9229N	690A	11218
N9229Y	690A	11122
N9230T	46D	141
(N9231N)	690	11078
N9231N	690A	11236
(N9232N)	690	11079
(N9232N)	690A	11240
N9232N	690A	11312
N9233N	690	11033
N9233T	PA42	5501032
N9234N	690	11034
N9235D	46D	74
N9235N	690	11035
N9235X	46D	225
(N9237N)	690A	11241
(N9237N)	690A	11298
(N9237N)	690B	11517
N9238N	690	11038
N9238Q	46D	92
N9239N	690	11039
N9240N	690	11040
N9240Q	PA42	5501051
N9241D	PA42	5501056
N9241N	690	11041
N9246Q	46D	142
N9249Q	46D	48
N9250J	46D	238
N9251R	46D	86
N9252K	46D	81
N9252N	46D	55
N9252X	46D	139
N9252X	46D	207
N9254X	46D	98
N9255H	46D	55
N9258D	46D	144
N9258Q	90	LJ-523
N9259X	46D	114
N9262L	46D	30
N9263D	46D	198
N9263D	46D	216
N9264Q	46D	177
N9266R	46D	181
N9266Y	**31T**	**1104008**
N9268Y	31T	1104009
N9270Y	31T	1104010
N9272X	46D	148
N9272X	46D	168
N9275D	46D	99
N9275N	46D	20
N9278X	46D	116
N9279A	**PA42**	**5501036**
N9281B	**46D**	**151**
N9281J	46D	124
N9282J	46D	186
N9282W	46D	191
N9283N	46D	46
N9284Q	46D	84
N9284X	**46D**	**111**
N9285Q	46D	118
N9286L	46D	29
N9288N	46D	223
N9291S	46D	152
N9293W	46D	12
N9294G	46D	227
N9294N	46D	169
N9295A	PA42	5527035
N9296Z	E90	LW-141
N9298L	46D	194
N9298Q	90	LJ-540
N9299E	46D	110
N9299P	**46D**	**169**
N9300P	100	B-26
N9300P	G1	114
N9306A	441	0072
N9314Q	90	LJ-541
N9317T	441	0203
N9324Q	100	B-105
N9348T	31T	1104013
N9355Q	100	B-107
N9366Q	100	B-108
N9369Q	100	B-93
N9376Q	90	LJ-551
N9378Q	100	B-78

N9379S	200	BB-27	N9537N	46T	97351	N9662N	31T	7820023	N9751N	F406	0005
N9382T	31T	1104014	N9538N	46T	97089	N9662N	31T	7820065	N9753N	31T	7720037
N9390C	90	LJ-473	N9538N	46T	97214	N9663N	31T	7620040	N9755S	200	BB-55
N9397S	90	LJ-669	N9538N	46T	97288	N9668N	31T	7820079	**N9756S**	**695**	**95003**
N9399S	90	LJ-670	N9538N	46T	97314	N9670N	31T	7920003	N9757S	695	95004
N9412Q	100	B-104	N9538N	46T	97352	(N9670N)	681	6020	(N9757S)	695	95026
N9426	**90**	**LJ-421**	N9538N	46T	97363	**N9683N**	**441**	**0255**	N9758S	695	95005
N9439Q	100	B-113	N9539N	46T	97099	N9684N	31T	7904001	N9759S	695	95006
N9442Q	90	LJ-542	N9539N	46T	97219	N9687N	31T	7820085	N9760S	695	95007
N9444	**PC6**	**521**	N9539N	46T	97289	N9688N	31T	7520027	N9761S	695	95008
N9445	PC6	570	N9539N	46T	97341	(N9690B)	90	LJ-1447	(N9762S)	695	95009
N9446E	G1	55	N9539N	46T	97362	N9691N	31T	7820069	(N9763S)	695	95010
N9449G	441	0003	N9540N	46T	97108	N9697N	31T	7720064	N9764S	695	95011
N9449Q	90	LJ-549	N9540N	46T	97172	N9699N	BN2	116	(N9765S)	695	95012
N9450Q	**90**	**LJ-550**	N9540N	46T	97227	N9700N	31T	7904002	N9766S	695	95013
N9456G	441	0004	N9540N	46T	97292	N9701Y	200C	BL-65	**N9767S**	**695**	**95014**
N9456Q	90	LJ-556	N9540N	46T	97318	N9704S	E90	LW-141	N9768S	200	BB-1114
N9456T	695A	96007	N9540N	46T	97367	N9706N	31T	7520012	N9768S	695	95015
N9457Q	90	LJ-557	N9541N	46T	97172	**N9710M**	**KODK**	**0020**	N9769S	690A	11163
N9477Q	100	B-77	N9541N	46T	97174	N9711B	90	LJ-367	N9769S	695	95016
N9491Y	F90	LA-154	N9541N	46T	97319	N9715N	31T	7820066	N9770S	695	95017
N9493Q	E90	LW-3	N9541N	46T	97342	N9715N	31T	7920008	N9771S	695	95018
N9494Q	100	B-119	N9541N	46T	97368	N9716G	F90	LA-76	N9772N	31T	7920051
N9498Q	90	LJ-555	N9542N	46T	97111	N9717N	31T	7820088	N9772S	695	95019
N9500N	46D	149	N9542N	46T	97176	N9717N	P68	352	(N9773S)	695	95020
N9502N	46D	71	N9542N	46T	97236	N9718N	31T	7620042	(N9774S)	695	95021
N9502Q	90	LJ-22	N9542N	46T	97324	N9718N	31T	7720035	N9775S	695	95022
N9502Q	E90	LW-2	N9542N	46T	97343	N9718N	31T	8020084	(N9776S)	695	95023
N9504N	46D	8	N9542N	46T	97353	N9719L	P68	371	(N9778S)	695	95024
N9504N	46D	42	N9543N	46T	97177	**N9719N**	**P68**	**375**	N9779S	695	95025
N9504N	46D	240	N9543N	46T	97237	N9720N	31T	7400016	N9780S	695	95026
N9505N	46D	196	N9543N	46T	97297	N9720N	31T	7520007	N9781S	695	95028
N9506N	46D	159	N9543N	46T	97354	N9722N	31T	7400018	(N9782S)	695	95029
N9507Q	90	LJ-247	N9544N	46D	209	N9722N	31T	7520009	(N9783S)	695	95030
N9509N	46D	203	N9544N	46T	97110	N9725N	31T	7720031	N9784S	695	95031
N9512N	46D	166	N9544N	46T	97299	N9726N	31T	7620032	N9785S	695	95032
N9512N	46T	97240	N9544N	46T	97327	N9727N	31T	7720050	N9786S	695	95034
N9515N	46T	97200	N9544N	PA42	5501039	N9728S	200	BB-72	N9787S	695	95035
N9516N	46D	6	N9545N	46T	97107	N9730N	31T	7820006	(N9788S)	695	95036
N9517N	46D	97	N9545N	46T	97178	N9730N	31T	7920070	N9789S	695	95037
N9518N	PA42	5527041	N9545N	46T	97300	N9730S	200	BB-74	(N9790S)	690C	11639
N9520N	PA42	5501035	N9545N	46T	97328	N9731N	31T	7720033	N9790S	695	95039
N9522N	PA42	5501036	N9545N	46T	97346	N9731N	31T	7920059	(N9792S)	695	95027
N9524N	46T	97261	N9546N	46T	97122B	N9731S	100	B-210	N9793S	695	95041
N9524N	PA42	5527040	N9546N	46T	97183	N9732N	31T	7904022	N9794S	695	95042
N9525N	PA42	5527043	N9546N	46T	97260	N9733N	31T	7720036	N9795S	695	95043
N9527N	46T	97047	N9546N	46T	97355	N9733N	31T	7820041	N9796S	695	95044
N9528N	PA42	5501037	N9546N	46T	97370	N9733N	31T	7920073	N9797S	695	95045
N9529N	PA42	5527034	N9546N	46T	97402	N9734N	31T	7720041	N9798S	695	95046
N9530N	46D	165	N9547N	46T	97184	N9734N	31T	7920038	N9799S	695	95047
N9531N	46T	97050	N9547N	46T	97261	N9735N	31T	7920044	N9800S	695	95048
N9531N	46T	97138	N9547N	46T	97301	N9737N	31T	7920056	(N9801S)	695	95049
N9531N	46T	97202	N9547P	200	BB-892	N9738N	31T	7720039	N9802S	695	95050
N9531N	46T	97305	N9548N	46T	97337	N9738N	31T	7920019	(N9803S)	695	95051
N9531N	46T	97338	N9548N	PA42	5527036	N9739N	31T	7720043	N9804S	695	95052
N9531N	46T	97358	N9548W	46T	97344	N9739N	31T	7820051	N9805S	695	95053
N9531N	PA42	5501032	N9549N	46T	97192	N9739N	31T	7920039	(N9806S)	695	95054
N9532N	46T	97052	N9549N	46T	97303	N9740N	31T	7820045	(N9807S)	695	95055
N9532N	46T	97206	N9549N	46T	97332	N9740N	31T	7820057	N9808S	695	95056
N9532N	46T	97279	N9550N	46T	97193	N9741N	31T	7720046	N9809S	695	95057
N9532N	PA42	5501034	N9550N	46T	97304	N9741N	31T	7920022	(N9810S)	695	95058
N9533N	46D	192	N9550N	46T	97336	N9741S	200	BB-95	N9811S	695	95059
N9533N	46T	97053	N9551Q	90	LJ-337	N9742N	31T	7904057	**N9812S**	**695**	**95060**
N9533N	46T	97152	N9554N	PA42	5501040	N9743N	31T	7920064	(N9813S)	695	95061
N9533N	46T	97207	N9561N	PA42	5527037	N9744N	31T	8004022	N9814S	695	95062
N9533N	46T	97306	N9565N	46D	153	N9745N	31T	7904040	(N9814S)	695	95063
N9533N	46T	97350	N9566N	46D	9	N9745N	31T	8004012	(N9815S)	695	95063
N9533N	46T	97359	N9578N	PA42	5501041	N9745N	BN2	2035	(N9816S)	695	95064
N9534N	46D	43	N9580N	46D	134	(N9745S)	200C	BL-65	N9817S	695	95065
N9534N	46T	97055	N9584N	46D	19	N9746N	31T	7920069	(N9818S)	695	95061
N9534N	46T	97155	N9591C	200	BB-836	N9746N	31T	8020029	N9818S	695	95066
N9534N	46T	97282	N9613	MU-2	011	N9746N	31T	8020069	(N9819S)	695	95067
N9534N	46T	97307	N9636	90	LJ-458	N9746N	31T	7904026	N9820	90	LJ-370
N9534N	PA42	5527035	N9651N	31T	7620026	N9747N	31T	7904050	N9820S	695	95068
N9535N	46D	13	N9655B	P68	230	N9748N	31T	7620010	N9821S	695	95069
N9535N	46T	97066	N9657N	31T	7520031	N9748N	31T	7720047	(N9822S)	695	95070
N9535N	46T	97283	N9657N	31T	7820013	N9748N	31T	7820019	(N9823S)	695	95071
N9536N	46T	97070	N9658N	31T	7520032	N9748N	31T	7820053	(N9824S)	695	95072
N9536N	46T	97166	N9659N	31T	7620057	N9748N	31T	7820054	N9825S	695	95073
N9536N	46T	97310	N9661N	31T	7520046	N9748N	31T	7820076	N9826S	695	95074
N9536N	PA42	5501038	N9661N	31T	7620003	N9748N	31T	7920010	N9827S	695	95075
N9537N	46T	97072	N9661N	31T	7820020	N9748N	31T	8004027	N9828S	695	95076
N9537N	46T	97168	N9662N	31T	7520028	N9749N	31T	7520026	N9829S	695	95077
N9537N	46T	97212	N9662N	31T	7620020	N9749N	31T	7904037	N9830S	695	95078

N9831S	695	95079
(N9832S)	695	95080
N9833S	695	95081
N9834S	695	95082
(N9835S)	695	95083
(N9836S)	695	95084
N9838Z	**90**	**LJ-435**
N9857C	BN2	659
N9872C	**90**	**LJ-698**
N9898	200	BB-1269
N9898	**200**	**BB-1627**
N9898	B100	BE-57
N9898M	46D	194
N9898Y	200	BB-1269
N9900	**MIII**	**T-266**
N9900S	695A	96001
N9901	**90**	**LJ-93**
N9902S	695A	96002
N9906S	**695A**	**96003**
(N9907S)	695A	96004
(N9910S)	695A	96005
N9913S	695A	96006
(N9915S)	695A	96007
N9915S	695B	96206
N9917G	441	0005
N9917S	695A	96008
(N9924S)	695A	96009
(N9926S)	695A	96010
(N9928S)	695A	96011
(N9931S)	695A	96012
N9933E	90	LJ-956
N9933E	90	LJ-1035
(N9933S)	695A	96013
N9933S	B100	BE-56
N9934S	695A	96014
(N9935S)	695A	96015
(N9936S)	695A	96016
N9937S	695A	96017
(N9938S)	695A	96018
(N9939S)	695A	96018
(N9939S)	695A	96019
N9940S	695A	96020
N9941S	695A	96021
N9942S	**695A**	**96022**
N9943S	695A	96023
(N9944S)	695A	96024
N9945S	**695A**	**96025**
N9946S	695A	96026
N9947S	695A	96027
N9948S	**695A**	**96028**
(N9949S)	695A	96029
(N9950S)	695A	96030
N9951S	695A	96031
N9952S	695A	96032
(N9953S)	695A	96033
N9954S	695A	96034
(N9955S)	695A	96035
(N9956S)	695A	96036
N9957S	695A	96037
N9958S	695A	96038
N9959S	695A	96039
N9960S	695A	96040
N9961S	695A	96041
N9962S	695A	96042
N9963S	695A	96043
N9964S	695A	96044
N9965S	695A	96045
N9966S	**695A**	**96046**
N9967S	695A	96047
N9968S	**695A**	**96048**
N9969S	695A	96049
N9970S	695A	96050
N9971F	G1	17
N9971G	441	0006
N9971S	695A	96051
N9972S	695A	96052
N9973S	**695A**	**96053**
N9974S	695A	96054
N9975S	695A	96055
(N9976S)	695A	96056
(N9977S)	695A	96057
N9978S	695A	96058
(N9979S)	695A	96059
N9980S	695A	96060

N9981S	695A	96061
(N9982S)	695A	96062
(N9984S)	695A	96064
(N9985S)	695A	96065
(N9986S)	695A	96066
(N9987S)	695A	96067
N9988C	**200G**	**BY-67**
(N9988S)	695A	96068
(N9990S)	695A	96070
(N9991S)	695A	96071
(N9992S)	695A	96072
(N9993S)	695A	96073
N9998P	**C-12**	**BC-8**
N10024	300C	FM-9
N10053	MIII	T-314
N10057	MIII	T-319
N10058	MIII	T-315
N10058	PC6	522
N10061	MIII	T-345
N10063	MIII	T-341
N10074	MIII	T-330
N10118	MIII	T-387
N10119	MIII	T-388
N10120	90	LJ-561
N10121	90	LJ-325
N10126	MIII	T-400
N10127	90	LJ-222
N10127	MIII	TT-435
N10140	MIII	T-320
N10143	MIII	T-317
N10269	681B	6052
N10409	46T	97266
N10430	90	LJ-117
N10436	200	BB-1536
N10485	P68	171
N10563	46T	97276
N10655	**B100**	**BE-81**
N10656	46T	97273
N10691	350	FL-150
N10694	**46T**	**97297**
N10778	PC12	412
N10780	200	BB-1553
N10799	90	LJ-1340
N10803	46T	97282
N10817	350	FL-151
N10825	**200**	**BB-26**
N10827	200	BB-1519
N11176	350	FL-161
N11191	350	FL-191
N11216	BN2	759
N11232	31T	7520015
N11250	350	FL-193
N11278	350	FL-195
N11309	350	FL-176
N11310	350	FL-186
N11355	200	BB-1584
N11692	**90**	**LJ-772**
N11755	90	LJ-1092
(N12003)	C-12	BC-18
N12070	441	0312
(N12072)	441	0313
N12076	441	0314
N12093	441	0328
N12099	441	0329
N12109	200C	BL-68
N12114	441	0343
N12116	441	0344
N12125	441	0349
N12127	441	0350
(N12154)	200	BB-197
N12201	425	0187
N12214	425	0194
N12218	425	0195
N12235	PC6	556
N12238	425	0206
N12244	**425**	**0213**
(N12249)	425	0214
N12254	425	0220
N12256	425	0221
N12268	**425**	**0227**
N12270	425	0231
N12271	425	0232
N12321	**46D**	**96**
(N12383)	441	0362

N12450	PC6	514
N12827	441	0359
N12829	441	0360
N13200	PC6	581
N13201	PC6	582
N13202	PC6	583
N13303	100	B-3
N13309	90	LJ-9
N13392	P68	233
N13622	**690B**	**11469**
N13625	690B	11444
N14072	690D	15001
N14451	BN2	10
N14645	MU-2	320
N14886	**31T**	**7904036**
N15023	90	LJ-1192
N15098	200	BB-1491
N15116	90	LJ-1374
N15234	**90**	**LJ-1194**
N15509	200T	BT-35
N15527	90	LJ-1262
(N15527)	90	LJ-1369
N15542	90	LJ-1376
N15570	200	BB-1316
N15572	200	BB-1315
N15585	300	FA-178
N15587	200	BB-1325
N15588	200C	BL-133
N15591	300	FA-171
N15591	300	FA-187
N15599	200	BB-1353
N15599	90	LJ-1367
N15613	**300**	**FA-193**
N15615	90	LJ-1215
N15627	90	LJ-1222
N15628	90	LJ-1218
N15696	90	LJ-1242
N15710	200	BB-1343
N16776	G1	58
N17077	PC6	540
N17244	690	11031
N17508	B100	BE-17
N17510	90	LJ-713
N17530	200	BB-204
N17570	200	BB-234
N17573	**90**	**LJ-714**
N17580	B100	BE-20
N17582	G1	188
N17603	E90	LW-214
N17610	200	BB-335
N17619	E90	LW-220
N17620	E90	LW-222
N17640	200	BB-237
N17647	90	LJ-729
N17649	200	BB-239
N17690	680T	1577-31
N17723	200	BB-223
N17739	200	BB-292
N17743	200	BB-273
N17759	200	BB-277
N17776	90	LJ-7
N17792	**B100**	**BE-41**
N17799	200	BB-229
N17812	200	BB-236
N17821	B100	BE-21
N17822	B100	BE-22
N17844	E90	LW-241
N18080	90	LJ-972
N18112	200	BB-905
N18121	F90	LA-144
N18150	F90	LA-137
N18172	200	BB-914
N18182	90	LJ-1086
N18216	200	BB-922
N18237	350	FL-180
N18243	200	BB-274
N18243	E90	LW-218
N18251	200	BB-251
N18260	200	BB-900
N18261	200	BB-916
N18262	200	BB-927
N18264	90	LJ-1156
N18266	200	BB-266
N18267	90	LJ-988

N18269	200	BB-269
N18269	350	FL-185
N18297	350	FL-188
N18299	90	LJ-962
N18300	90	LJ-986
N18306	200	BB-279
N18317	B100	BE-36
N18335	200	BB-314
N18343	**E90**	**LW-243**
N18345	200	BB-303
N18347	200	BB-247
N18348	B100	BE-136
N18371	200	BB-913
N18379	200C	BL-44
N18383	90	LJ-733
N18409	200	BB-972
N18421	200	BB-304
N18426	B100	BE-26
N18429	B100	BE-29
N18430	B100	BE-30
N18436	B100	BE-32
N18436	F90	LA-189
N18450	200	BB-364
N18451	200C	BL-50
N18454	200	BB-311
N18460	90	LJ-1042
N18466	200	BB-1114
N18471	**F90**	**LA-161**
N18481	200	BB-955
N18481	**425**	**0105**
N18482	B100	BE-46
N18487	B100	BE-31
N18488	90	LJ-999
N18494	200	BB-294
N18495	B100	BE-50
N18500	200	BB-967
N18536	90	LJ-1000
N18544	200	BB-899
N18548	90	LJ-1001
N18571	F90	LA-165
N18750	E90	LW-250
N18753	E90	LW-253
N18754	E90	LW-286
N18758	200	BB-258
N18762	200	BB-262
N18991	90	LJ-369
N19112	F90	LA-106
N19500	46D	33
N19500	**46D**	**160**
N20004	200	BB-221
N20162	E90	LW-290
N20281	E90	LW-294
N20316	E90	LW-258
N20351	E90	LW-303
N20505	200	BB-268
N20505	200	BB-1569
N20506	90	LJ-814
N20509	E90	LW-312
N20564	E90	LW-314
N20620	200	BB-414
N20695	E90	LW-257
N20736	90	LJ-844
N20875	BN2	599
N20880	100	B-63
N20903	200	BB-319
N21428	FPC6	2037
N21429	FPC6	2038
N21438	FPC6	2063
N21441	FPC6	2047
N21441	FPC6	2064
N21442	FPC6	2046
N21442	FPC6	2065
N21443	FPC6	2045
N21443	FPC6	2066
(N21444)	FPC6	2067
N21722	MU-2	226
N21868	90	LJ-1498
N22071	200	BB-111
N22220	100	B-189
N22320	G1	323
N22453	E90	LW-245
N22522	MU-2	625
N22591	F406	0033
N22654	E90	LW-254

N22675	E90	LW-226	N23600	31T	7920059	N25655	E90	LW-72	N31008	46T	97191
N22844	E90	LW-228	N23600	E90	LW-236	N25674	90	LJ-574	N31010	46T	97315
N23086	350	FL-208	**N23605**	**100**	**B-236**	**N25677**	**MIII**	**T-254**	N31061	46T	97209
N23105	350	FL-210	N23617	31T	7920074	N25747	100	B-179	**N31062**	**46T**	**97208**
N23137	31T	7920029	N23627	31T	7920075	N26226	441	0109	N31064	46T	97211
N23138	31T	7920030	N23630	31T	7920077	(N26227)	441	0110	N31072	MIVC	AT-504
N23138	31T	7920031	N23634	B100	BE-33	(N26228)	441	0111	N31087	46T	97204
N23139	31T	7920032	**N23646**	**31T**	**7920078**	N26230	441	0118	**N31094**	**200**	**BB-1676**
N23140	31T	7920033	N23646	E90	LW-246	N26231	441	0119	N31098	46T	97205
N23140	31T	7920034	N23649	31T	7920079	(N26232)	441	0120	N31101	MIVC	AT-543
N23142	350	FL-217	N23658	31T	7904046	(N26233)	441	0121	N31105	46T	97229
N23152	31T	7920035	N23660	E90	LW-287	N26253	441	0133	N31108	MIVC	AT-546
N23159	31T	7920036	N23661	31T	7920080	(N26263)	441	0139	N31122	46T	97194
N23173	31T	7920037	N23665	31T	7920081	(N26264)	441	0140	N31134	MIVC	AT-569
N23185	31T	7920040	N23667	31T	7920082	N26267	441	0141	N31135	MIVC	AT-570
N23189	31T	7920041	N23669	90	LJ-769	(N26271)	441	0149	N31136	46T	97214
N23199	31T	7904011	N23675	90	LJ-757	N26296	441	0159	**N31136**	**46T**	**97309**
N23203	31T	7904012	N23676	31T	7920083	(N26308)	441	0160	N31136	MIVC	AT-577
N23215	31T	7904013	N23677	31T	7920084	N26540	90	LJ-270	N31141	46T	97239
N23216	31T	7904014	N23680	31T	7920085	N26732	200C	BL-35	N31141	46T	97249
N23216	350	FL-205	N23680	31T	7904047	N26803	90	LJ-939	**N31145**	**46T**	**97215**
N23217	31T	7920042	N23681	E90	LW-268	N26877	TRIS	1020	N31174	90	LJ-1167
N23217	31T	7920044	N23687	200	BB-307	N26902	E90	LW-166	N31187	90	LJ-1195
N23219	31T	7920045	N23687	31T	7920086	N26952	690B	11487	N31226	F406	0057
N23227	350	FL-206	N23687	31T	7904048	N27214	441	0165	N31240	46T	97236
N23235	31T	7904015	N23699	31T	7920073	(N27216)	441	0166	N31264	MIVA	AT-057
N23236	31T	7904016	N23700	90	LJ-700	N27219	441	0167	N31278	46T	97240
N23243	**31T**	**7904017**	N23707	200	BB-498	N27220	441	0174	N31279	90	LJ-1567
N23250	**31T**	**7904018**	N23707	E90	LW-237	(N27237)	441	0181	N31379	350	FL-266
N23250	E90	LW-232	N23718	31T	7920087	N27248	441	0187	N31398	90	LJ-1174
N23257	31T	7904019	N23721	90	LJ-721	N27252	441	0194	(N31418)	690A	11307
N23260	31T	7904020	N23726	E90	LW-267	N27353	300	FA-107	N31434	90	LJ-1186
N23263	31T	7904021	N23728	90	LJ-728	N27465	90	LJ-159	N31447	90	LJ-1187
N23268	200	BB-1732	N23731	90	LJ-731	N27563	MIII	T-311	N31480	MU-2	741SA
N23272	31T	7920046	N23735	B100	BE-35	N27856	300	FA-108	N31559	90	LJ-1207
N23272	31T	7904022	N23738	90	LJ-738	N27856	31T	7620041	N31780	90	LJ-1880
N23272	350	FL-222	N23743	200	BB-350	N28356	E90	LW-108	N31800	300	FA-165
N23285	31T	7904023	N23744	90	LJ-744	N28377	BN2	141	N31861	90	LJ-1861
N23310	31T	7920049	N23748	90	LJ-748	N28958	690A	11161	N31869	90	LJ-1869
N23313	200	BB-313	N23756	90	LJ-747	N29561	P68	266	N31872	90	LJ-1872
N23319	31T	7904023	N23756	B100	BE-28	N29773	690B	11403	N31882	90	LJ-1882
N23334	**31T**	**7904024**	N23761	200	BB-286	N29791	90	LJ-543	N31947	90	LJ-1847
N23338	31T	7904025	N23764	200	BB-260	N29825	31T	7920044	N31967	350	FL-567
N23340	31T	7920051	N23765	200	BB-297	**N29884**	**BN2**	**847**	N31973	350	FL-573
N23343	31T	7920052	N23779	h	BB-282	N29913	200	BB-617	N32017	200G	BY-17
N23352	200	BB-1639	N23780	90	LJ-778	N29929	TRIS	1013	N32029	200G	BY-29
N23352	31T	7920053	N23786	200	BB-320	N29978	300	FA-114	N32075	90	LJ-1875
N23355	200	BB-1641	N23794	200	BB-342	N29979	200	BB-1265	N32078	350	FL-578
N23356	200	BB-1643	N23796	90	LJ-737	N29985	300	FA-117	N32087	90	LJ-1887
N23358	31T	7904022	N23798	E90	LW-271	**N29997**	**200**	**BB-1268**	N32148	350	FL-568
N23363	31T	7904027	N23800	E90	LW-238	N30025	90	LJ-1725	N32154	350	FL-609
N23371	31T	7904028	N23802	E90	LW-269	N30042	MIII	T-357	N32166	200G	BY-16
N23373	31T	7904029	N23804	90	LJ-766	N30042	MIII	TT-441	N32211	90	LJ-1581
N23376	31T	7904030	N23807	200	BB-332	N30059	695B	96204	N32217	90	LJ-1717
N23381	31T	7904031	N23856	90	LJ-706	N30234	200	BB-1274	N32217	90	LJ-1914
N23384	31T	7904032	N23868	100	B-228	N30246	90	LJ-1746	**N32229**	**90**	**LJ-49**
N23404	**100**	**B-234**	N23875	90	LJ-711	N30296	300	FA-134	**N32238**	**90**	**LJ-1580**
N23406	31T	7920054	N23879	200	BB-222	N30296	MIII	TT-462A	N32268	200	BB-1684
N23407	31T	7920055	N23903	90	LJ-722	N30364	MIVC	AT-464	N32268	200T	BT-39
N23408	31T	7920057	N23915	200	BB-241	N30365	200	BB-1622	N32287	200	BB-1698
N23411	31T	7920058	N23917	90	LJ-719	N30391	200	BB-1270	N32323	300	FA-2
N23412	31T	7920060	N23929	90	LJ-720	**N30397**	**46T**	**97167**	N32434	200	BB-1651
N23414	31T	7920061	N23930	200	BB-245	N30417	300	FA-124	**N32643**	**200G**	**BY-43**
N23415	31T	7920062	N23947	90	LJ-726	N30469	46T	97173	N32745	31T	7920039
N23416	31T	7920063	N23959	90	LJ-730	N30486	200	BB-1273	N32868	100	B-228
N23418	31T	7904033	N24096	200	BB-336	N30573	90	LJ-1140	N32928	200G	BY-28
N23424	31T	7904034	N24099	680W	1777-15	N30614	46T	97174	N32974	90	LJ-1874
N23426	**31T**	**7904035**	N24110	200	BB-347	N30625	200	BB-1278	N33122	200G	BY-22
N23447	31T	7904026	N24138	200C	BL-1	N30663	46T	97180	N33226	90	LJ-1866
N23449	31T	7920065	N24144	PC6	729	N30721	200	BB-1281	N33511	680T	1709-84
N23457	31T	7920066	N24153	200	BB-278	N30757	300	FA-138	N33703	350	FL-563
N23466	31T	7920067	N24164	200	BB-264	N30832	441	0342	N33885	200G	BY-15
N23466	46D	89	**N24169**	**B100**	**BE-38**	N30833	90	LJ-1172	N33984	350	FL-584
N23475	31T	7920068	N24172	90	LJ-765	N30844	90	LJ-1169	N34003	90	LJ-1853
N23477	31T	7920064	N24176	90	LJ-762	N30850	200	BB-1288	N34004	200G	BY-14
N23493	31T	7904038	N24201	200	BB-242	**N30854**	**690A**	**11229**	N34008	200G	BY-8
N23497	31T	7904039	**N24203**	**B100**	**BE-40**	N30898	46T	97196	N34010	350	FL-580
N23509	E90	LW-259	N24346	31T	7904036	**N30898**	**46T**	**97202**	N34177	200G	BY-64
N23517	100	B-235	N25219	300	FA-94	N30908	46D	200	**N34269**	**P68**	**241**
N23521	31T	7904041	N25616	100	B-153	N30912	46T	97183	N34651	200G	BY-21
N23555	31T	7904042	N25620	90	LJ-573	N30912	46T	97210	N34687	350	FL-587
N23569	31T	7904044	N25623	100	B-209	N30953	46T	97304	N34712	200G	BY-12
N23591	31T	7920071	N25628	100	B-154	**N30983**	**46T**	**97189**	N34857	200G	BY-57
N23593	31T	7920072	N25652	100	B-152	N30993	46T	97190	N34923	200G	BY-23

N34975	90	LJ-1865
N35017	350	FL-136
N35436	90	LJ-1736
N36030	90	LJ-240
N36561	350	FL-461
N36566	200	BB-1936
N36579	200	BB-1879
N36585	200	BB-1885
N36620	350	FL-420
N36634	90	LJ-1734
N36635	350	FL-435
N36640	90	LJ-1740
N36644	200	BB-1904
N36648	90	LJ-1748
N36659	350	FL-459
N36667	90	LJ-1747
N36688	90	LJ-1772
N36705	200	BB-1905
N36715	**350**	**FL-415**
N36719	90	LJ-1719
N36720	90	LJ-1730
N36735	90	LJ-1735
N36739	200	BB-1889
N36741	200	BB-713
N36741	90	LJ-1741
N36742	90	LJ-1742
N36744	350	FL-444
N36745	90	LJ-1745
N36767	350	FL-467
N36782	200	BB-1932
N36784	200	BB-909
N36788	200	BB-1938
N36799	90	LJ-1769
N36801	200	BB-941
N36801	200	BB-1881
N36803	90	LJ-1036
N36805	90	LJ-1157
N36809	200	BB-1285
N36811	350	FL-411
N36813	350	FL-413
N36814	350	FL-414
N36839	90	LJ-1739
N36850	90	LJ-1750
N36851	350	FL-451
N36860	350	FL-460
N36871	200	BB-1911
N36880	90	LJ-914
N36883	90	LJ-1743
N36886	350	FL-486
N36888	90	LJ-1788
N36891	90	LJ-1751
N36893	200	BB-1893
N36898	200	BB-1948
N36916	200	BB-1916
N36919	350	FL-419
N36929	441	0009
N36929	**90**	**LJ-1729**
N36930	441	0010
N36931	441	0011
N36932	350	FL-452
N36932	441	0012
N36933	350	FL-463
(N36933)	441	0013
(N36934)	441	0014
N36936	441	0015
N36937	90	LJ-1737
N36938	441	0016
N36939	441	0017
N36941	350	FL-441
N36941	441	0018
N36942	441	0019
(N36943)	441	0020
(N36944)	441	0021
N36946	350	FL-471
(N36946)	441	0022
(N36947)	441	0023
N36948	200C	BL-148
(N36948)	441	0024
N36949	200C	BL-149
N36949	441	0025
N36951	441	0026
(N36952)	441	0027
N36953	350	FL-453
N36955	441	0028

N36956	200	BB-721
N36956	441	0029
N36957	350	FL-457
(N36957)	441	0030
N36958	441	0031
(N36961)	441	0032
N36962	350	FL-462
N36962	441	0033
(N36964)	441	0034
N36968	441	0036
(N36970)	441	0037
N36971	441	0038
N36972	200	BB-1902
N36972	441	0039
(N36974)	441	0040
N36975	350	FL-475
(N36975)	441	0041
N36984	350	FL-484
N36984	441	0042
(N36985)	441	0043
N36987	200	BB-1887
N36987	441	0044
N36988	**350**	**FL-488**
(N36988)	441	0045
(N36989)	441	0046
(N36990)	441	0047
N36992	441	0048
(N36993)	441	0049
(N36994)	441	0050
N36995	200	BB-1895
N36995	441	0051
(N36997)	441	0052
N36998	350	FL-498
N36999	350	FL-483
N37025	350	FL-425
N37026	350	FL-503
N37040	350	FL-504
N37046	200	BB-1946
N37058	200	BB-1958
N37064	90	LJ-1833
N37065	350	FL-465
N37066	200	BB-1966
N37069	350	FL-469
N37082	200	BB-1882
N37084	**350**	**FL-482**
N37085	350	FL-505
N37090	350	FL-490
N37093	90	LJ-1773
N37094	350	FL-494
N37097	200	BB-1917
N37101	**200**	**BB-1931**
N37123	90	LJ-1753
N37124	90	LJ-1784
N37132	90	LJ-932
N37134	200	BB-1934
N37149	90	LJ-1749
N37155	200	BB-1915
N37156	200	BB-1956
N37164	350	FL-464
N37172	350	FL-472
N37173	350	FL-473
N37174	350	FL-474
N37183	350	FL-443
N37198	90	LJ-1798
N37200	**90**	**LJ-1800**
N37222	**90**	**LJ-1722**
N37225	200	BB-762
N37244	200	BB-1944
N37246	350	FL-446
N37247	350	FL-447
N37307	200	BB-1907
N37308	200	BB-1908
N37312	200	BB-670
N37318	350	FL-481
N37324	90	LJ-1794
N37336	350	FL-436
N37390	**350**	**FL-11**
N37390	F90	LA-96
N37392	200	BB-768
N37546	690	11004
N37990	**F90**	**LA-101**
N38005	B100	BE-108
N38051	F90	LA-107
N38052	B100	BE-111

N38164	F90	LA-118
N38221	200	BB-769
N38246	F90	LA-123
N38280	**90**	**LJ-953**
N38295	200	BB-785
N38301	200	BB-837
N38314	200C	BL-34
N38340	200	BB-885
N38342	200	BB-928
N38353	90	LJ-959
N38381	200	BB-934
N38454	200	BB-824
N38473	200	BB-842
N38535	200	BB-845
(N38535)	TRIS	372
N38561	E90	LW-345
N38589	90	LJ-963
N38595	90	LJ-964
N38649	F90	LA-132
N38653	200	BB-865
N38789	31T	8120010
N38920	MU-2	031
N39130	B100	BE-5
N39272	P68	283
N39273	P68	285
N39274	P68	287
N39278	P68	293
N39289	G1	43
N39480	680W	1842-41
N39518	31T	7620054
N40191	**PC12**	**248**
N40480	200	BB-1695
N40481	200	BB-1696
N40483	200	BB-1697
N40490	90	LJ-1592
N40593	350	FL-162
N40764	PA42	8001030
N40833	PA42	5501007
N40833	PA42	5501013
N40837	PA42	8001039
N40844	PA42	8001057
N40880	PA42	8001033
N40886	PA42	8001042
N40889	PA42	8001040
N40946	PA42	8001051
N40980	PA42	8001063
N40981	PA42	8001064
N41054	425	0172
(N41090)	PA42	8001087
N41117	PA42	5501008
N41125	PA42	5527021
N41126	PA42	5527024
N41139	PA42	8001101
N41158	PA42	5501004
N41182	PA42	5501024
N41182	PA42	5501040
N41187	PA42	5527022
N41191	PA42	5527029
N41198	PA42	5527030
N41199	46D	10
N41199	PA42	5527031
(N41202)	31T	8275023
N41202	31T	5575001
N41212	46D	184
N41222	46D	175
N41244	46D	204
N41257	46D	32
N41270	46D	63
N41270	46D	78
N41346	46D	123
N41462	690C	11672
N41469	46D	162
N41647	46D	237
N41653	46D	94
N41653	46D	203
N41758	90	LJ-270
N41760	46D	171
N41842	46T	97008
N41848	46T	97011
N41851	46T	97010
N41865	46D	158
N41874	**46D**	**73**
N42091	200	BB-75
N42319	100	B-66

N42319	200	BB-9
N42327	200	BB-1727
N42327	200T	BT-43
N42495	BN2	384
N42540	BN2	3006
N42636	F90	LA-81
N42821	P68	357
N43046	90	LJ-1596
N43676	200	BB-809
N43866	**MU-2**	**757SA**
N43870	350	FL-287
N44264	MIII	T-230
N44287	MIII	TT-515A
N44319	31T	7920062
N44344	200C	BL-40
N44406	90	LJ-1610
N44454	90	LJ-499
N44486	90	LJ-874
N44640	200	BB-86
N44693	90	LJ-1593
N44717	200	BB-1717
N44717	200T	BT-40
N44721	200	BB-1721
N44721	200T	BT-41
N44724	200	BB-1724
N44724	200T	BT-42
N44776	**441**	**0121**
N44857	200	BB-1787
N44866	350	FL-304
N44869	200T	BT-45
N44882	F90	LA-102
N44917	90	LJ-801
N44919	200	BB-863
N44951	P68	322
N44955	P68	314
N44956	**P68**	**318**
N44959	**P68**	**319**
N44967	P68	295
N45591	MU-2	524
N45818	**MIII**	**T-235**
N45845	F90	LA-185
N45858	BN2	2014
N46663	690A	11153
N46802	690B	11427
N46809	P68	332
N46810	**P68**	**334**
N46866	690A	11108
N46906	690A	11338
N46958	BN2	584
N47074	MIII	T-206
N47150	690A	11150
N48213	681B	6052
N49401	G1	64
N49579	P68	259
N49855	200	BB-394
N49984	C-12	BD-3
N50130	200	BB-1830
N50152	200	BB-1842
N50344	90	LJ-1634
N50478	200	BB-1861
N50515	**C-12**	**BP-26**
N50525	**90**	**LJ-159**
N50655	**680T**	**1714-88**
N50693	**BN2**	**828**
N50758	46T	97058
N50778	90	LJ-1638
N50785	90	LJ-1636
N50807	200	BB-1827
N50847	90	LJ-1697
N50848	200	BB-1748
N50902	31T	7820033
N50969	200C	BN-9
N51139	90	LJ-1639
N51148	90	LJ-1738
N51151	46T	97064
N51151	46T	97078
N51161	200	BB-1811
N51214	200T	BT-44
N51228	695A	96047
N51283	200	BB-1833
N51342	200	BB-336
N51418	200	BB-1924
N51488	200C	BN-8
(N51798)	690B	11518

N51881	200	BB-1000
N52457	E90	LW-130
N53199	46T	97148
N53215	46T	97071
N53235	46T	97083
N53238	46T	97086
N53258	46T	97088
N53263	46T	97054
N53270	46T	97093
N53272	46T	97094
N53283	46T	97055
N53308	46T	97050
N53322	46T	97070
N53328	46T	97098
N53353	46T	97117B
N53353	46T	97118A
N53362	46T	97092
N53362	46T	97109
N53369	46T	97088
N53401	46T	97142A
N53401	46T	97143B
N53415	46T	97112
N53416	46T	97116
N53450	46T	97122B
N53453	46T	97117A
N53453	46T	97125B
N53474	F406	0023
N53487	46T	97150
N53511	46T	97128
N53516	46T	97132
N53554	46T	97143A
N53554	46T	97146B
N53599	46T	97155
N53599	46T	97168
N53599	46T	97172
N53667	46T	97158
N53677	46T	97155
N53689	46T	97163
N53695	P68	126
N53705	46T	97164
N53705	46T	97181
N54117	680T	1687-67
N54163	680W	1774-12
N54199	46T	97164
N54553	680T	1573-28
N54568	PA42	8001042
N54574	MIII	T-251
N54656	MU-2	253
N54959	31T	7520030
N54961	31T	7520018
N54964	31T	7520033
N54966	31T	7520034
N54967	31T	7520035
N54968	31T	7520036
N54969	31T	7520037
N54970	31T	7520038
N54971	31T	7520040
N54972	31T	7520041
N54973	31T	7520042
N54974	31T	7520043
N54975	31T	7520028
N54976	31T	7520044
N54976	31T	7620001
N54977	31T	7520045
N54977	31T	7620002
N54978	31T	7520047
N54978	31T	7620004
N54979	31T	7620005
N54980	31T	7620006
N54985	31T	7620007
N54986	31T	7620008
N54987	31T	7620009
N54988	31T	7620011
N54989	31T	7620012
N54990	31T	7520039
N54992	31T	7620013
N54993	31T	7620014
N54994	31T	7620015
N55008	90	LJ-1252
N55486	90	LJ-1254
N55495	90	LJ-1255
N55684	300C	FM-8
N55796	100	B-9
N55947	300C	FM-3
N56016	300C	FM-5
N56361	200T	BT-34
N56379	200	BB-1443
N56385	200	BB-1441
N56449	300	FA-224
N56456	350	FL-71
N56531	90	LJ-1258
N56534	90	LJ-1286
N56562	200	BB-1365
N56616	200	BB-1371
N56633	90	LJ-1248
N56638	90	LJ-1249
N56641	200C	BL-136
N56787	90	LJ-1261
N56800	350	FL-30
N56862	350	FL-13
N56872	350	FL-17
N56881	200	BB-1377
N57030	690A	11249
N57032	690A	11248
(N57035)	690A	11251
N57035	690A	11267
N57037	690A	11126
N57042	690A	11252
N57043	690A	11253
N57053	690A	11140
N57054	690A	11132
N57056	690A	11254
N57059	690A	11139
N57063	690A	11255
N57074	690A	11153
N57077	690A	11156
N57086	690A	11157
N57090	690A	11259
(N57091)	690A	11159
N57091	690A	11165
N57092	690A	11160
N57093	690A	11161
N57096	690A	11120
(N57097)	690A	11107
N57097	690A	11260
(N57098)	690A	11128
(N57098)	690A	11261
N57098	690A	11296
N57099	690A	11131
N57101	690A	11101
N57102	690A	11102
N57104	690A	11262
N57105	690A	11105
N57106	690A	11106
N57108	690A	11108
N57109	690A	11109
N57110	690A	11110
N57111	690A	11111
N57112	690A	11263
N57113	690A	11113
N57114	690A	11114
(N57115)	690A	11115
N57115	690A	11245
(N57115)	690A	11264
(N57116)	690A	11116
N57116	690A	11230
(N57117)	690A	11258
(N57118)	690A	11118
(N57118)	690A	11119
(N57118)	690A	11265
N57118	690A	11311
N57119	690A	11119
(N57121)	690A	11121
(N57121)	690A	11266
N57121	690A	11310
(N57122)	690A	11122
N57122	690A	11122
N57123	690A	11123
N57123	690A	11213
N57124	690A	11124
N57125	690A	11125
N57127	690A	11127
N57129	690A	11129
(N57130)	690A	11130
(N57130)	690A	11268
N57133	690A	11133
(N57134)	690A	11200
N57135	690A	11135
N57136	690A	11205
N57137	690A	11137
(N57138)	690A	11138
N57138	690A	11271
(N57141)	690A	11141
N57141	690A	11272
(N57142)	690A	11142
N57142	690A	11273
N57143	690A	11143
(N57143)	690A	11173
N57144	690A	11144
N57145	690A	11145
(N57146)	690A	11146
N57146	690A	11269
(N57147)	690A	11147
N57147	690A	11178
N57148	690A	11148
N57149	690A	11149
(N57150)	690A	11150
N57151	690A	11151
(N57152)	690A	11152
N57152	690A	11164
N57154	690A	11154
N57155	690A	11155
N57158	690A	11158
(N57162)	690A	11206
(N57163)	690A	11163
(N57163)	690A	11317
N57166	690A	11166
(N57167)	690A	11167
(N57167)	690A	11184
N57168	690A	11168
N57169	690A	11203
N57170	690A	11275
(N57170)	690A	11276
(N57170)	690A	11318
N57171	690A	11171
(N57172)	690A	11172
N57172	690A	11276
(N57172)	690A	11315
N57174	690A	11174
N57175	690	11004
(N57175)	690A	11175
N57175	690A	11277
N57176	690A	11278
N57177	690A	11177
N57179	690A	11179
(N57179)	690A	11279
(N57180)	690A	11180
(N57180)	690A	11184
N57180	690A	11279
N57181	690A	11185
N57183	690A	11281
N57186	690A	11186
N57187	690A	11187
N57189	690A	11189
N57190	690A	11190
N57191	690A	11191
N57192	690A	11192
N57193	690A	11282
N57194	690A	11194
(N57195)	690A	11195
N57195	690A	11274
(N57196)	690A	11196
(N57196)	690A	11207
(N57196)	690A	11317
N57196	690A	11333
(N57198)	690A	11198
(N57198)	690A	11318
N57198	690B	11518
N57208	690A	11209
(N57209)	690A	11204
N57210	690A	11210
N57212	690A	11219
N57214	690A	11214
N57215	690A	11215
N57216	690A	11216
(N57216)	690A	11234
(N57216)	690A	11238
N57217	690A	11239
N57218	690A	11227
(N57220)	690A	11220
(N57220)	690A	11224
N57220	690A	11229
N57221	690A	11221
(N57222)	690A	11222
N57223	690A	11223
(N57225)	690A	11225
N57227	690A	11226
N57228	690A	11283
N57229	690A	11242
N57230	690A	11243
N57231	690A	11245
N57232	690A	11246
N57233	690A	11247
N57235	690A	11235
(N57236)	690A	11248
N57236	690A	11289
N57237	690A	11237
N57252	690A	11314
N57263	690A	11244
(N57267)	690A	11330
N57267	690B	11519
N57268	690A	11248
(N57271)	690A	11239
N57273	690A	11284
N57275	690A	11285
N57280	690A	11286
(N57280)	690A	11330
N57286	690A	11287
N57287	690A	11288
N57292	690A	11270
N57294	690A	11290
(N57524)	31T	7620016
N57524	31T	7620016
N57526	31T	7620017
N57528	31T	7620018
N57656	31T	8120005
N57907	MU-2	027
N58009	200C	BL-83
N58018	MIII	T-254
N58022	200C	BL-88
N58237	MIII	TT-462A
N58244	200	BB-533
N58280	200	BB-61
N58309	100	B-198
N59360	BN2	2017
N60041	350	FL-631
N60049	31T	7520036
N60064	350	FL-644
N60102	200	BB-2002
N60125	350	FL-645
N60159	C-12	BD-16
N60162	350	FL-662
N60182	46T	97320
N60253	E90	LW-321
N60275	200	BB-1835
N60312	200	BB-2012
N60318	350	FL-638
N60322	200G	BY-72
(N60352)	441	0065
N60383	200	BB-1504
N60419	46T	97325
N60454	350	FL-354
N60476	200	BB-1836
N60533	90	LJ-845
N60575	B100	BE-26
N60575	E90	LW-325
N60576	200T	BT-11
N60581	200T	BT-12
N60587	200T	BT-13
N60603	200T	BT-16
N60616	BN2	399
N60659	90	LJ-880
N60690	46T	97329
N60724	90	LJ-1744
N60819	350	FL-619
N60887	46T	97338
N60897	46T	97344
N60910	46T	97341
N60914	200	BB-1814
N60925	46T	97366
N60935	46T	97349
N60951	46T	97355
N60954	350	FL-654
N60964	46T	97378
N61006	46T	97381
N61027	46T	97389

N61037	200	BB-1837
N61185	350	FL-395
N61188	90	LJ-1006
N61227	**350**	**FL-647**
N61228	**F90**	**LA-169**
N61254	90	LJ-1007
N61346	200T	BT-46
N61353	**350**	**FL-653**
N61369	200	BB-990
N61369	200	BB-1809
N61383	**90**	**LJ-1009**
N61408	200	BB-925
N61415	200	BB-949
N61425	200	BB-917
N61429	F90	LA-171
N61474	200	BB-998
N61508	695A	96063
N61592	200	BB-1859
N61638	350	FL-438
N61669	90	LJ-1690
N61675	200G	BY-75
N61678	**90**	**LJ-1958**
N61679	350	FL-379
N61698	**90**	**LJ-1698**
N61716	90	LJ-1716
N61726	200	BB-1926
N61726	**350**	**FL-626**
N61740	350	FL-410
N61767	200	BB-1877
N61775	MIIB	T26-178
N61776	90	LJ-983
N61788	**350**	**FL-648**
N61788	90	LJ-1763
N61797	90	LJ-1012
N61806	200	BB-1906
N61806	200	BB-2006
N61808	200	BB-1828
N61831	200	BB-1831
N61847	200	BB-1847
N61906	90	LJ-1696
N61907	350	FL-357
N61913	200	BB-1813
N61942	350	FL-382
N61956	200	BB-1856
N62012	200	BB-1812
N62148	PC6	631
N62149	PC6	672
N62150	PC6	517
N62153	PC6	632
N62154	PC6	620
N62156	PC6	667
N62157	FPC6	2011
N62158	PC6	523
N62160	PC6	704
N62161	PC6	669
N62162	PC6	705
N62183	BN2	592
N62286	31T	7820061
N62300	**90**	**LJ-989**
N62358	90	LJ-1020
N62360	200	BB-240
N62366	690A	11141
N62403	PC6	558
N62509	200	BB-2009
N62524	FPC6	2021
N62525	**90**	**LJ-691**
N62526	100	B-161
N62541	90	LJ-1941
N62546	200	BB-1023
N62569	200	BB-1028
N62760	F90	LA-184
N62780	200	BB-1035
N62825	31T	7720016
N62828	200	BB-1039
N62881	200	BB-1043
N62895	200	BB-1044
N63007	200	BB-2007
N63123	350	FL-643
N63255	**350**	**FL-655**
N63286	200	BB-1067
N63435	200	BB-1071
N63459	90	LJ-1041
N63494	**350**	**FL-674**
N63540	90	LJ-1940

N63560	**350**	**FL-656**
N63561	**350**	**FL-661**
N63563	**350**	**FL-663**
N63578	200	BB-2008
N63593	**200**	**BB-552**
N63669	**350**	**FL-639**
N63686	200	BB-1085
N63686	**200G**	**BY-86**
N63688	200	BB-1080
N63699	**350**	**FL-629**
N63740	**350**	**FL-640**
N63769	**350**	**FL-659**
N63791	200	BB-1100
N63799	**200G**	**BY-79**
N63802	200	BB-1101
N63815	**350**	**FL-665**
N63827	200	BB-1099
N63881	200G	BY-81
N63882	200	BB-1106
N63908	90	LJ-1054
N63924	200	BB-2004
N63937	**90**	**LJ-1937**
N63980	**200G**	**BY-80**
N63989	**200G**	**BY-89**
N63997	**350**	**FL-667**
N64255	**350**	**FL-635**
N64276	200G	BY-76
N64347	90	LJ-1947
N64386	**350**	**FL-646**
N64392	**90**	**LJ-1972**
N64406	90	LJ-392
N64478	200	BB-1108
N64576	**90**	**LJ-1957**
(N64783)	200	BB-328
N64795	E90	LW-101
N65103	MIIB	T26-140E
N65150	MIIB	T26-158E
N65169	690A	11119
N65171	200	BB-160
N65187	B100	BE-137
N65190	90	LJ-138
N65198	MU-2	549
N65323	BN2	667
N65558	300	FA-73
N65664	695	95044
N65912	F406	0055
N66000	**C-12**	**BC-66**
N66104	200	BB-1119
N66171	200	BB-364
N66177	BN2	626
N66218	425	0163
N66404	200	BB-1129
N66447	F90	LA-7
N66460	200	BB-1134
N66480	200	BB-1132
N66480	B100	BE-71
N66489	F90	LA-4
N66534	G1	85
N66549	200	BB-1141
N66549	F90	LA-9
N66585	200	BB-507
N66710	200	BB-572
N66712	90	LJ-876
N66775	90	LJ-1063
N66804	**B100**	**BE-82**
N66810	90	LJ-881
N66820	**B100**	**BE-68**
N66825	200	BB-1156
N66826	200	BB-1160
N66828	90	LJ-882
N66834	31T	7400005
N66835	31T	7400006
N66836	31T	7400007
N66837	31T	7400008
N66838	31T	7400009
N66839	31T	7400010
N66839	31T	7520001
N66840	31T	7400011
N66840	31T	7520002
N66841	31T	7400012
N66841	31T	7520003
N66843	31T	7520010
N66844	31T	7520011
N66845	31T	7520014

N66846	31T	7520017
N66847	**31T**	**7520019**
N66848	31T	7520020
N66849	31T	7520021
N66850	31T	7520022
N66851	31T	7520023
N66852	31T	7520024
N66853	90	LJ-853
N66854	31T	7520029
N66864	90	LJ-887
N66877	90	LJ-877
N66911	200	BB-1054
N66912	F90	LA-12
N67146	F90	LA-211
N67148	200	BB-1174
N67219	200	BB-1172
N67222	200	BB-630
N67224	200	BB-653
N67233	90	LJ-916
N67242	F90	LA-44
N67259	B100	BE-87
N67262	200	BB-1182
N67262	90	LJ-337
N67262	E90	LW-331
N67265	200	BB-1183
N67265	FPC6	2029
N67353	200	BB-654
N67460	B100	BE-90
N67470	200	BB-673
N67511	**90**	**LJ-888**
N67516	90	LJ-1069
N67554	90	LJ-1070
N67569	90	LJ-1071
N67599	90	LJ-898
N67683	300	FA-3
N67704	425	0015
N67720	425	0027
N67724	425	0028
N67725	425	0029
N67726	425	0030
N67735	425	0042
(N67741)	425	0049
N67743	425	0050
N67761	425	0057
N68395	90	LJ-245
N68436	425	0060
(N68439)	425	0061
N68439	441	0300
N68446	425	0068
(N68449)	425	0069
(N68451)	425	0075
N68455	425	0076
N68456	425	0077
N68474	90	LJ-1075
(N68476)	425	0090
N68478	425	0091
N68481	425	0095
N68489	425	0096
(N68493)	425	0102
N68496	425	0103
N68498	425	0104
(N68539)	441	0222
N68548	441	0229
N68559	441	0238
N68577	441	0249
N68586	441	0254
N68587	441	0255
N68594	441	0259
N68597	441	0260
(N68598)	441	0261
N68599	441	0302
N68721	425	0170
N68731	425	0180
N68732	425	0181
N68734	**425**	**0182**
(N68746)	425	0188
N68803	425	0114
N68807	425	0115
N68817	425	0120
N68822	425	0129
N68823	425	0130
N68844	425	0141
(N68854)	425	0150
N68859	425	0151

N68859	PC6	907
(N68860)	425	0157
N68863	425	0158
(N68864)	425	0159
N68865	425	0160
N68867	425	0161
(N68869)	425	0162
N68943	200	BB-1135
N69010	690A	11107
N69084	**F90**	**LA-157**
N69131	200	BB-1127
N69237	90	LJ-1084
N69261	90	LJ-1097
N69264	300	FA-105
N69275	90	LJ-1076
N69282	200	BB-1196
N69283	F90	LA-222
N69297	90	LJ-1077
N69301	**90**	**LJ-1079**
N70068	200	BB-1968
N70088	**U-21**	**LM-6**
N70118	200	BB-1978
N70132	F90	LA-195
N70135	U-21	LM-9
N70143	200	BB-1943
N70150	200	BB-1950
N70155	350	FL-515
N70161	BN2	905
N70189	90	LJ-1799
N70224	U-21	LM-14
N70264	U-21	LM-17
N70292	**U-21**	**LM-18**
N70315	MIVA	AT-036
N70318	695	95083
N70356	**U-21**	**LM-25**
N70491	90	LJ-1153
N70503	**U-21**	**LM-43**
N70505	695	95016
N70637	F90	LA-38
N70648	**U-21**	**LM-53**
N70689	90	LJ-1819
(N70733)	BN2	51
N70766	U-21	LM-64
N70783	200	BB-1983
N70841	U-21	LM-73
N70876	**U-21**	**LM-75**
N70879	**U-21**	**LM-76**
N70890	U-21	LM-78
N70904	U-21	LM-79
N70926	**U-21**	**LM-84**
N70944	90	LJ-1814
N70950	**U-21**	**LM-86**
N71089	200	BB-1979
N71296	90	LJ-1796
N71347	**U-21**	**LM-96**
N71351	**U-21**	**LM-97**
N71562	**46T**	**97081**
N71581	**U-21**	**LM-116**
N71588	31T	7620018
N71597	**U-21**	**LM-118**
N71612	F90	LA-221
N71650	90	LJ-1810
N71674	MU-2	125
N71764	U-21	LM-130
N71795	350	FL-495
N71797	**U-21**	**LM-131**
N71834	350	FL-534
N71837	350	FL-477
N71839	90	LJ-1829
N71850	200	BB-1985
N71873	90	LJ-1803
N71878	**90**	**LJ-1778**
N71885	**350**	**FL-485**
N71909	90	LJ-1809
N71957	90	LJ-1787
N71959	MU-2	277
N71966	**350**	**FL-533**
N71970	350	FL-537
N71982	U-21	LU-3
N71984	U-21	LU-4
N71992	U-21	LU-12
N71996	U-21	LU-13
N71998	U-21	LU-15
N72014	U-21	LM-124

N72055	90	LJ-1085
N72069	300	FA-22
N72073	90	LJ-1088
N72146	300	FA-29
N72149	90	LJ-1130
N72154	**90**	**LJ-619**
N72180	300	FA-41
N72188	300	FA-40
N72206	90	LJ-1101
N72223	90	LJ-1102
N72224	F90	LA-233
N72226	90	LJ-1103
N72231	300	FA-54
N72233	90	LJ-1105
N72260	90	LJ-1107
N72265	300	FA-82
(N72272)	200	BB-1216
N72294	200	BB-1220
N72302	300	FA-71
N72303	200	BB-1222
N72323	300	FA-58
N72345	300	FA-62
N72353	300	FA-89
N72357	200	BB-1244
N72369	90	LJ-1119
N72381	200C	BL-125
N72385	200C	BL-126
N72392	200T	BT-31
N72400	90	LJ-1146
N72401	200C	BL-129
N72405	300	FA-121
N72410	200	BB-1284
N72413	300	FA-139
N72448	300	FA-74
N72451	300	FA-70
N72470	**C-12**	**BC-4**
N72472	300	FA-77
N72472	**C-12**	**BC-11**
N72473	200	BB-1236
N72476	**C-12**	**BC-26**
N72479	300	FA-78
N72503	200	BB-1238
N72508	90	LJ-1131
N72524	200	BB-1242
N72583	300	FA-91
N72589	E90	LW-52
N72709	90	LJ-1839
N73220	90	LJ-1822
N73380	**350**	**FL-480**
N73413	BN2T	880
N73415	**90**	**LJ-1785**
N73542	MIII	T-241
N73555	200C	BL-65
N73712	90	LJ-1812
N73817	200	BB-1947
N73920	90	LJ-1840
N73991	90	LJ-1801
N74061	200	BB-1961
N74171	E90	LW-52
N74226	**350**	**FL-522**
N74753	200	BB-1973
N75368	**90**	**LJ-75**
N75465	31T	7720019
N77400	46T	97199
N77400	**46T**	**97206**
N77577	90	LJ-207
N77711	100	B-71
N77711	100	B-227
(N77711)	200	BB-1054
N77715	100	B-227
(N77773)	31T	8004004
N78011	200	BB-831
N80024	200T	BT-36
N80027	200T	BT-37
N80048	200T	BT-38
N80383	**P68**	**370**
N80398	MU-2	712SA
N80513	90	LJ-1303
N80605	300C	FM-6
N80663	350	FL-108
N80679	300	FA-230
N80775	300	FA-223
N80806	300	FA-228
N80904	90	LJ-1271
N80907	300	FA-226
N80927	90	LJ-1358
N80938	425	0233
N81148	200	BB-1434
(N81389)	690A	11292
N81389	690A	11313
(N81391)	690A	11267
N81392	690A	11305
(N81394)	690A	11280
(N81394)	690B	11579
(N81397)	690A	11291
N81398	690A	11297
N81399	690A	11299
(N81400)	690A	11301
N81400	690C	11600
N81405	695	95080
N81406	690A	11302
N81409	690A	11303
N81410	690A	11304
N81413	690A	11224
N81416	690A	11306
N81418	300	FA-227
N81418	690A	11307
N81419	690A	11308
N81427	690A	11295
(N81430)	690A	11316
N81430	690A	11321
(N81432)	690A	11315
N81432	695B	96207
N81434	690A	11319
N81436	690A	11320
N81437	690A	11322
N81438	690A	11323
N81441	690A	11324
N81442	690A	11325
N81444	690A	11326
N81448	**690A**	**11327**
N81449	690A	11328
(N81460)	690A	11329
N81460	690A	11329
(N81463)	690A	11331
N81464	690A	11332
(N81465)	690B	11408
N81467	690A	11334
(N81467)	690B	11410
N81470	690A	11335
N81473	690A	11336
N81476	690A	11337
(N81477)	690A	11338
N81483	690A	11339
N81491	690A	11340
N81493	690A	11341
N81497	690A	11342
(N81499)	690A	11343
N81500	690A	11344
N81502	31T	8166022
N81502	695A	96000
N81516	690B	11350
N81521	690B	11351
(N81523)	690B	11352
N81523	690B	11566
N81525	690B	11353
(N81526)	690B	11354
(N81526)	690B	11565
N81527	690B	11355
N81528	690B	11356
N81529	690B	11357
N81531	690B	11358
N81533	690B	11359
N81535	200	BB-1401
(N81535)	690B	11360
N81535	690B	11564
N81536	200	BB-1406
(N81536)	690B	11361
N81536	690B	11563
N81537	690B	11362
N81538	690B	11562
N81538	90	LJ-1281
N81540	690A	11265
N81541	690B	11363
(N81543)	690B	11364
(N81543)	690B	11561
(N81544)	690B	11365
N81544	690B	11560
N81546	690B	11366
N81547	690B	11367
N81548	690B	11368
N81550	690B	11369
(N81552)	690B	11559
(N81553)	690B	11370
(N81553)	690B	11558
N81556	690B	11371
N81557	690B	11372
N81558	690B	11373
N81562	690B	11374
N81563	690B	11375
N81567	690B	11376
N81567	BN2	470
(N81568)	690B	11377
(N81568)	690B	11557
(N81569)	690B	11378
(N81569)	690B	11556
(N81575)	690B	11379
N81575	695	95000
(N81579)	690B	11380
N81579	690B	11555
(N81582)	690B	11554
N81591	690B	11553
(N81592)	690B	11552
N81593	690B	11381
N81599	690B	11382
N81601	690B	11383
N81601	MU-2	577
N81602	690B	11384
N81603	690B	11385
N81604	350	FL-37
(N81604)	690B	11386
(N81604)	690B	11551
N81604	MU-2	783SA
N81609	690B	11387
N81610	690B	11388
N81615	690B	11389
(N81619)	690B	11390
N81621	690B	11391
(N81622)	690B	11392
N81622	690B	11549
N81623	350	FL-46
N81623	690B	11393
(N81625)	690B	11394
N81625	690B	11548
N81626	690B	11395
N81628	690B	11396
(N81631)	690B	11397
N81631	690B	11547
(N81632)	690B	11398
N81632	690B	11546
N81633	690B	11399
N81634	690B	11400
(N81636)	690B	11401
(N81636)	690B	11545
N81638	690B	11402
N81639	690B	11403
N81640	690B	11404
N81641	690B	11405
N81642	690B	11406
N81643	690B	11407
N81645	690B	11408
N81646	690B	11409
N81647	690B	11410
N81648	690B	11411
N81648	90	LJ-363
N81653	690B	11412
N81654	690B	11414
N81655	690B	11544
N81658	690B	11416
N81662	690B	11417
N81664	350	FL-52
N81664	690B	11418
N81668	690B	11419
N81671	690B	11420
N81672	690B	11421
N81673	690B	11422
N81674	690B	11423
N81677	690B	11424
N81680	690B	11425
N81682	690B	11426
N81683	690B	11427
(N81684)	690B	11428
(N81684)	690B	11543
(N81687)	690B	11429
N81687	690B	11542
(N81689)	690B	11430
N81689	690B	11541
(N81689)	690B	11550
N81692	690B	11431
N81694	690B	11432
N81695	690B	11433
(N81697)	690B	11434
N81697	690B	11540
N81698	690B	11435
(N81699)	690B	11436
N81699	690B	11539
(N81701)	690B	11437
(N81701)	690B	11442
N81701	690B	11538
(N81702)	690B	11442
N81702	690B	11537
N81703	**690B**	**11438**
N81706	690B	11439
(N81707)	690B	11440
N81707	690B	11536
N81708	690B	11441
(N81709)	690B	11443
N81709	690B	11535
(N81710)	690B	11444
(N81710)	690B	11534
N81717	690B	11445
(N81721)	690B	11446
N81721	690B	11533
(N81723)	690B	11447
(N81723)	690B	11532
N81726	690B	11448
(N81728)	690B	11449
(N81728)	690B	11531
N81729	690B	11450
N81733	690B	11451
(N81734)	690B	11452
N81734	690B	11530
N81736	690B	11453
N81737	690B	11454
N81746	690B	11521
N81748	690B	11455
(N81750)	690B	11456
N81750	690B	11529
N81752	690B	11457
N81754	690B	11458
N81756	690B	11459
N81762	690B	11460
(N81763)	690B	11461
N81763	690B	11528
N81763	90	LJ-1290
N81764	690B	11462
(N81765)	690B	11463
(N81765)	690B	11475
N81765	690B	11527
N81766	690B	11464
N81767	690B	11465
(N81769)	690B	11466
N81769	690B	11526
N81771	690B	11467
(N81772)	690B	11468
(N81773)	690B	11469
N81773	690B	11524
N81774	690B	11470
(N81775)	690B	11472
N81775	690B	11523
(N81776)	690B	11473
N81776	690B	11522
(N81783)	690B	11474
N81783	690B	11521
(N81785)	690B	11475
N81785	690B	11520
(N81795)	690B	11476
N81795	690B	11511
N81797	690B	11478
N81798	425	0151
(N81798)	690B	11479
N81799	690B	11480
(N81805)	690B	11482
(N81806)	690B	11483
N81809	690B	11485
N81811	690B	11487

(N81812)	690B	11488	N82102	31T	7720018	N82281	31T	7804003	N88879	100	B-59
(N81818)	690B	11489	N82105	31T	7720019	N82282	31T	7820055	N89315	200	BB-315
(N81819)	690B	11490	N82109	31T	7720020	N82285	31T	7820056	(N89809)	MU-2	726SA
N81820	690B	11491	N82112	31T	7720021	N82288	31T	7820045	N89991	90	LJ-145
N81822	690B	11492	N82112	350	FL-112	N82290	31T	7820058	N90090	MIVA	AT-035
N81826	690B	11494	N82115	31T	7720023	N82291	31T	7820059	N90165	MU-2	140
N81826	90	LJ-1292	N82116	31T	7720024	N82293	31T	7820060	(N90208)	100	B-116
N81827	350	FL-32	N82118	31T	7720026	N82294	31T	7820061	(N90233)	90	LJ-88
(N81827)	690B	11495	N82120	31T	7720027	N82295	31T	7820062	(N90255)	BN2	530
(N81830)	690B	11496	N82121	31T	7720028	N82298	31T	7820063	N90420	690A	11208
N81831	690B	11497	N82122	31T	7720029	N82307	90	LJ-519	N90466	200C	BL-45
N81832	690B	11499	**N82123**	**31T**	**7720030**	N82311	350	FL-101	"N90492"	690A	11208
N81833	690B	11500	N82125	31T	7720063	N82323	90	LJ-1335	N90541	TRIS	299
N81835	690B	11501	N82126	31T	7720032	N82324	300C	FM-7	N90589	31T	7520002
(N81842)	690B	11502	N82130	31T	7720034	N82326	90	LJ-1336	N90806	200	BB-33
N81843	690B	11503	N82136	31T	7720038	N82345	300	FA-216	N90874	MIIB	T26-154E
(N81845)	690B	11504	**N82139**	**31T**	**7720040**	N82349	90	LJ-1337	N91074	90	LJ-507
N81846	690B	11505	N82144	31T	7720031	N82366	90	LJ-1338	N91201	31T	1104016
(N81849)	690B	11506	N82144	31T	7720041	N82376	90	LJ-1339	N91204	31T	1104017
N81850	690B	11507	N82148	31T	7720042	N82378	200	BB-1469	N91296	31T	1166005
N81861	690B	11508	N82152	31T	7720033	N82396	300	FA-225	N91384	690A	11118
(N81863)	690B	11509	N82152	31T	7720043	N82410	200C	BL-140	N91575	695B	96205
N81865	690B	11510	N82155	31T	7720044	N82425	200	BB-1462	N91716	46D	23
(N81871)	690B	11516	**N82156**	**31T**	**7720045**	N82428	STAR	NC-28	N91782	46D	67
N81872	690B	11512	N82161	31T	7720049	N82430	90	LJ-1324	N91859	46D	140
N81873	690B	11513	N82163	31T	7720048	N82431	200C	BL-139	N91940	PA42	5527044
N81876	690B	11514	N82164	31T	7720051	N82446	300	FA-229	N91991	46D	28
N81877	690B	11484	N82165	31T	7720052	N82678	350	FL-93	N92091	46D	167
N81879	690B	11515	N82166	31T	7720053	N82682	350	FL-62	**N92156**	**46D**	**223**
N81918	31T	7920036	N82167	31T	7720054	N82687	300	FA-221	N92263	46D	44
N82000	31T	7620019	N82168	31T	7720055	N82696	200	BB-1431	N92263	46D	172
N82000	31T	7620030	N82169	31T	7720056	N82793	MU-2	136	N92264	PA42	5501048
N82000	31T	7620037	N82172	31T	7720057	N82982	100	B-119	N92266	PA42	5501049
N82002	31T	7620021	N82175	31T	7720046	N83908	G1	164	N92275	PA42	5501050
N82005	31T	7620022	N82176	31T	7720058	**N86000**	**46D**	**30**	N92402	PA42	5501052
N82006	31T	7620023	N82177	31T	7720059	N86345	690A	11145	N92409	PA42	5501054
N82009	31T	7620024	N82177	31T	7720061	N87494	441	0308	N92427	MIII	T-297
N82010	200	BB-1474	N82178	31T	7720060	**N87699**	**200**	**BB-887**	N92468	46D	47
N82010	31T	7620025	N82182	31T	7720062	N87720	90	LJ-499	N92474	46D	108
N82013	31T	7620027	N82186	31T	7720067	N87877	BN2	91	N92502	46D	202
N82016	31T	7620028	N82188	31T	7720065	N88598	441	0060	N92537	46D	70
N82017	31T	7620029	N82189	31T	7720066	**N88598**	**441**	**0242**	N92537	46D	220
N82019	31T	7620031	N82190	31T	7720068	N88638	441	0289	N92552	46D	99
N82021	31T	7620033	N82194	31T	7720003	**N88692**	**441**	**0290**	N92552	46D	193
N82022	31T	7620034	N82196	31T	7820003	N88707	441	0291	N92575	46D	122
N82023	31T	7620035	N82197	31T	7820004	N88716	441	0292	N92660	46D	120
N82025	200	BB-1423	N82204	31T	7820005	N88723	441	0293	N92660	46D	181
N82025	31T	7620036	N82207	31T	7820007	(N88724)	441	0294	N92671	46D	79
N82025	90	LJ-1294	N82209	31T	7820008	(N88726)	441	0067	N92735	46D	95
N82026	31T	7620043	N82210	31T	7820024	**N88727**	**441**	**0267**	N92735	46D	126
N82028	31T	7620038	N82211	31T	7820010	N88731	441	0262	**N92765**	**46D**	**69**
N82031	31T	7620039	N82212	31T	7820011	(N88791)	441	0054	N92771	46D	34
N82033	31T	7620041	N82216	31T	7820014	(N88791)	441	0263	N92819	46D	62
N82033	31T	7620044	N82217	31T	7820015	N88792	441	0055	**N92819**	**46D**	**147**
N82037	31T	7620046	N82218	31T	7820016	(N88795)	441	0056	N92832	46D	80
N82039	300	FA-219	N82222	31T	7820017	N88795	441	0264	N92849	46D	152
N82039	31T	7620047	N82223	31T	7820018	N88796	441	0057	N92880	46D	60
N82044	31T	7620048	N82225	31T	7820021	(N88797)	441	0058	N92880	46D	190
N82045	31T	7620049	N82226	31T	7820022	(N88798)	441	0059	**N92884**	**46D**	**125**
N82047	31T	7620050	N82228	31T	7820025	N88798	441	0265	N92929	46D	26
N82048	31T	7620051	N82229	31T	7820026	N88799	441	0060	N92996	90	LJ-575
N82053	31T	7620045	N82231	31T	7820027	N88800	441	0061	N93227	90	LJ-44
N82054	31T	7620052	N82232	31T	7820028	(N88822)	441	0063	N94490	680W	1828-36
N82055	31T	7620053	N82233	31T	7820029	N88823	441	0064	**N95590**	**690B**	**11482**
N82057	31T	7620054	N82236	31T	7820030	(N88824)	441	0065	(N96002)	695A	96002
N82058	31T	7620055	N82238	31T	7820031	(N88825)	441	0066	**N96954**	**MIII**	**T-311**
N82063	31T	7620056	N82242	31T	7820032	N88827	441	0068	N97011	680W	1763-9
N82064	31T	7720001	N82246	31T	7820035	(N88830)	441	0069	N97315	695B	96206
N82065	31T	7720002	N82249	31T	7820034	N88830	441	0268	N97696	690C	11697
N82071	31T	7720003	N82250	31T	7820019	N88831	441	0070	N98418	441	0271
N82073	31T	7720004	N82251	31T	7820036	N88832	441	0071	N98432	441	0272
N82075	31T	7720005	N82253	31T	7820037	N88833	441	0072	N98436	441	0273
N82076	31T	7720006	N82255	31T	7820038	N88834	441	0073	N98468	441	0274
N82077	31T	7720007	N82256	31T	7820039	**N88834**	**441**	**0269**	N98563	441	0275
N82081	31T	7720008	N82259	31T	7820040	N88836	441	0074	N98599	441	0276
N82084	31T	7720009	N82266	31T	7820042	(N88837)	441	0075	N98630	441	0126
N82085	31T	7720010	N82267	31T	7820043	(N88838)	441	0076	N98630	MU-2	607
N82086	31T	7720011	N82271	31T	7820044	(N88840)	441	0077	(N98682)	441	0277
N82091	31T	7720012	N82273	31T	7820046	(N88842)	441	0078	N98718	441	0278
N82092	31T	7720013	N82274	31T	7820047	(N88845)	441	0079	N98751	425	0003
N82094	**31T**	**7720014**	N82275	31T	7820048	N88846	441	0080	(N98784)	441	0279
N82096	31T	7720015	N82276	31T	7820049	**N88846**	**46D**	**92**	N98817	425	0004
N82097	31T	7720016	N82277	31T	7820050	(N88848)	441	0081	N98820	425	0005
N82100	31T	7720017	N82277	350	FL-77	N88849	441	0082	N98830	425	0006

N98858	425	0007
N98876	425	0008
(N98896)	425	0009
N98949	90	LJ-407
N99342	E90	LW-215
(N99358)	BN2	780
N99447	E90	LW-39
(N99517)	680T	1558-16
N99855	E90	LW-83
N535457	46D	205

Peru

OB-932	90	LJ-465
OB-1035	BN2	682
OB-1146	MIVA	AT-064E
OB-1163	PC6	756
OB-1164	PC6	760
OB-1165	PC6	720
OB-1166	PC6	722
OB-1168	PC6	737
OB-1169	PC6	738
OB-1170	PC6	739
OB-1176	31T	8020010
OB-1193	31T	8020069
OB-1207	BN2	859
OB-1212	690A	11222
OB-1219	MU-2	730SA
OB-1228	31T	8120048
OB-1234	PA42	8001019
OB-1272	BN2	105
OB-1284	MU-2	282
OB-1297	90	LJ-326
OB-1305	90	LJ-302
OB-1308	31T	7920075
OB-1330	300	FA-145
OB-1337	441	0341
OB-1361	90	LJ-451
OB-1362	90	LJ-448
OB-1364	90	LJ-330
OB-1365	PA42	8001018
OB-1403	31T	7720022
OB-1420	E90	LW-106
OB-1457	90	LJ-180
OB-1466	E90	LW-39
OB-1468	200	BB-193
OB-1495	90	LJ-333
OB-1497	31T	7820049
OB-1509	200	BB-20
OB-1558	90	LJ-405
OB-1567	90	LJ-228
OB-1593	90	LJ-477
OB-1594	90	LJ-322
OB-1595	90	LJ-400
OB-1598	E90	LW-36
OB-1600	PC6	789
OB-1602	E90	LW-22
OB-1629	PA42	8001067
OB-1630	PA42	8001022
(OB-1631)	PA42	8001009
OB-1633	PA42	7801003
OB-1649	PA42	8001009
OB-1687	PA42	8001016
OB-1700	200	BB-214
OB-1714	PA42	8001013
OB-1803	PA42	7800002
OB-1593-P	90	LJ-477
OB-1633-P	PA42	7801003
OB-1803-P	PA42	7800002
OB-1819-P	PA42	8001012
OB-1819-T	PA42	8001012
OB-1881-P	350	FL-470
OB-M-932	90	LJ-465
OB-M-1003	31T	7820057
OB-M-1031	690	11008
OB-M-1176	31T	8020010
OB-M-1193	31T	8020069
OB-M-1212	690A	11222
OB-M-1219	MU-2	730SA
OB-M-1228	31T	8120048
OB-M-1234	PA42	8001019
OB-M-1235	G1	152
OB-M-1330	300	FA-145
OB-R-1167	PC6	723
OB-R-1271	BN2	604
OB-R-1272	BN2	105
OB-S-932	90	LJ-465
OB-S-1176	31T	8020010
OB-S-1193	31T	8020069
OB-S-1228	31T	8120048
OB-S-1234	PA42	8001019
OB-S-1284	MU-2	282
OB-S-1308	31T	7920075
OB-T-924	680T	1565-21
OB-T-932	90	LJ-465
OB-T-1035	BN2	682
(OB-T-1196)	BN2	750
OB-T-1207	BN2	859
OB-T-1272	BN2	105
(OB-T-1282)	BN2T	2102
OB-T-1297	90	LJ-326

Austria

(OE-)	695	95036
OE-BAZ	G1	23
OE-BBB	200	BB-526
OE-BBL	PC6	664
OE-BIA	PC6	664
OE-DEM	PC6	513
OE-DMG	46T	97345
OE-ECS	PC6	848
OE-EDB	TBM7	7
OE-EDU	TBM7	73
OE-EEE	TBM8	464
OE-EHG	TBM7	28
OE-EKD	PC12	142
OE-EMC	PC12	663
OE-EMD	PC6	928
OE-EMS	TBM7	315
OE-EPC	PC12	536
OE-ESK	TBM7	279
OE-ESM	TBM7	1
OE-FAA	PA42	5501057
(OE-FAB)	PA42	5501059
OE-FAK	90	LJ-1125
OE-FAM	425	0131
OE-FAW	425	0074
OE-FAY	200	BB-224
OE-FBD	441	0102
OE-FBH	425	0035
OE-FBO	31T	7820051
OE-FCB	680T	1620-51
OE-FCC	441	0027
OE-FCL	441	0242
OE-FCO	425	0111
OE-FCP	441	0181
OE-FCS	690D	15036
OE-FCW	100	B-89
OE-FCY	441	0288
OE-FDH	31T	8020052
OE-FDS	31T	7720056
OE-FDU	90	LJ-434
OE-FDY	90	LJ-1908
OE-FED	425	0080
OE-FEM	100	B-7
OE-FEM	300	FA-210
OE-FFF	P68	221
OE-FFH	31T	7720018
OE-FGE	425	0063
OE-FGK	31T	8020052
OE-FGS	690D	15035
OE-FGW	P68	122
OE-FHF	PA42	8001011
OE-FHG	90	LJ-900
OE-FHL	90	LJ-1115
OE-FHM	90	LJ-1284
OE-FIB	425	0131
OE-FIJ	200	BB-1902
OE-FIL	P68	226
OE-FIM	200	BB-110
OE-FIT	690C	11672
OE-FIT	PA42	8001048
OE-FIX	690A	11163
OE-FJB	200	BB-1231
OE-FKG	31T	8020036
OE-FKH	31T	8104029
OE-FKW	200	BB-1005
OE-FLO	31T	8166044
OE-FLU	MIII	TT-536
OE-FMC	200	BB-93
OE-FME	300	FA-228
OE-FMG	90	LJ-1236
OE-FMI	200	BB-739
OE-FML	F90	LA-106
OE-FMM	PA42	5501030
OE-FMO	31T	8120058
OE-FMR	31T	7920086
OE-FMW	200	BB-263
OE-FOP	31T	7820048
OE-FOS	200	BB-1741
OE-FOW	MIII	T-318
OE-FPS	425	0024
OE-FRF	200	BB-933
OE-FRS	90	LJ-1124
OE-FRZ	441	0193
OE-FSO	300	FA-215
OE-FSY	31T	8120068
OE-FTA	MIVA	AT-042
OE-FUN	441	0150
OE-FYA	31T	8120035
OE-GSN	G1	146
OE-HAZ	G1	23
OE-HSN	G1	146
OE-KAB	46D	123
OE-KDM	46T	97111
OE-KFD	46D	82
OE-KGB	46T	97035
OE-LEA	200	BB-468

Finland

OH-ABE	200	BB-1038
OH-ACE	681	6032
OH-ACH	690	11072
OH-ACN	690A	11301
OH-ADA	MIII	T-248
OH-ALK	690A	11161
OH-ALU	F406	0044
OH-ALY	F406	0040
OH-BAX	90	LJ-984
OH-BCX	90	LJ-770
OH-BEX	90	LJ-978
OH-BIF	200	BB-847
OH-BKA	100	B-39
OH-BKB	100	B-20
OH-BKC	100	B-119
OH-BKI	90	LJ-898
OH-BKO	90	LJ-1041
OH-BNA	BN2	181
OH-BNB	BN2	218
OH-BNC	BN2	269
OH-BND	BN2	2171
OH-BSA	300	FA-205
OH-BSB	300	FA-206
OH-CIE	441	0257
OH-CIK	425	0142
OH-FCU	MIVC	AT-502
OH-KJJ	TBM7	258
OH-MIB	MU-2	532
OH-MIC	MU-2	557
OH-MIS	MU-2	673
OH-OTL	F406	0015
OH-PAY	PA42	5527040
OH-PHA	31T	7620001
OH-PNS	31T	7400002
OH-PNT	31T	7520007
OH-POA	PC6	341
OH-POB	PC6	651
OH-PVA	P68	10
OH-PVB	P68	13
OH-PVC	P68	44
OH-PYE	31T	7920094
OH-SHG	46T	97138
OH-STA	MU-2	1515SA
OH-TJJ	TBM7	166
OH-UTI	690A	11204
OH-WBA	MU-2	718SA
OH-WIB	200	BB-1355
OH-WWR	200	BB-483

Czech Republic

(OK-AAA)	PC12	837
OK-ALE	I270	008
OK-ATX	MU-2	239
OK-BKS	90	LJ-1430
OK-CTR	46T	97320
OK-DAG	46T	97349
OK-DKH	E90	LW-48
OK-DSH	90	LJ-837
OK-EMA	I270	001
OK-EVA	I270	007
OK-FLT	46T	97378
OK-GTJ	300	FA-223
OK-HLB	350	FL-557
OK-HLB	MU-2	718SA
OK-INA	I270	006
OK-JKB	200	BB-501
OK-LFB	200C	BL-49
OK-LFD	350	FL-322
OK-LIB	I270	005
OK-MAG	200	BB-221
OK-MPM	PA42	5501005
OK-NEA	G1	25
OK-NET	46T	97315
OK-NHR	90	LJ-1839
OK-NTG	46T	97407
OK-OKL	PA42	8001060
OK-PPP	PC12	1142
OK-PTP	PC6	947
OK-SAR	I270	003
OK-SKW	P750	128
(OK-TIP)	46T	97355
OK-TIP	46T	97355
(OK-TOP)	46T	97344
OK-TOP	46T	97344
OK-TOS	200	BB-1825
OK-UNO	200	BB-1905
(OK-VIP)	46T	97273
OK-VIP	46T	97273
OK-VKE	90	LJ-1222
OK-XKN	90	LJ-418
OK-YES	350	FL-221

Slovakia

OM-ALE	200	BB-1975
OM-FLY	200	BB-1565
OM-FUN	200G	BY-22
OM-M-1146	MIVA	AT-064E
OM-VIP	31T	7920002
OM-VKE	90	LJ-1222
OM-VPR	200G	BY-33

Belgium

OO-AER	PC6	645
OO-ARI	BN2	8
(OO-ARI)	BN2	9
OO-ARI	BN2	150
OO-ASL	200C	BL-49
OO-AST	BN2	8
OO-BOS	425	0197
OO-CTE	200	BB-399
OO-CTF	200	BB-431
OO-CVL	MU-2	1528SA
OO-DGS	31T	7820033
OO-EEC	P68	218
OO-ENG	MU-2	586
OO-FKT	P68	26
OO-FWJ	PC6	710
(OO-GMJ)	350	FL-460
OO-GMJ	350	FL-460
OO-GPL	690	11038
OO-GVS	BN2	236
OO-HJA	P68	210
OO-HJB	P68	241
OO-HJC	P68	216

OO-HJD	P68	245
(OO-HJE)	P68	255
OO-HSA	MIII	T-322
OO-HSC	MIII	T-345
OO-IAL	F90	LA-100
(OO-IBG)	G1	166
OO-INN	200	BB-1500
OO-JDV	PC6	911
OO-JMR	31T	8004044
OO-JPA	MIVA	AT-041
OO-JPN	MIV	AT-002
OO-JPN	MIVA	AT-038
OO-KNM	441	0344
OO-LAC	200C	BL-16
OO-LET	200	BB-1473
(OO-LFC)	425	0071
OO-LFJ	441	0021
OO-LFL	441	0184
OO-LMO	F406	0034
OO-LSA	P68	279
(OO-MLC)	90	LJ-649
OO-MMM	BN2	468
OO-MPC	BN2	461
OO-MRT	690B	11357
OO-MRU	690B	11374
OO-NAC	PC6	710
OO-NAN	441	0182
OO-NAP	PC6	914
OO-NMU	46D	194
(OO-PCM)	BN2	461
OO-PCV	PC6	882
OO-PJM	46D	159
OO-PKZ	PC6	909
OO-POF	PC6	524
OO-PSM	MIVA	AT-057
OO-PXL	P68	245
OO-RDW	31T	7720043
OO-ROB	690B	11409
OO-RVT	P68	156
OO-SAD	U-21	LM-126
(OO-SAL)	F90	LA-100
OO-SDU	350	FL-368
OO-SKF	680T	1720-91
OO-SKL	200	BB-1348
OO-SKM	200	BB-1407
(OO-SKN)	200C	BL-16
OO-SNA	100	B-217
OO-SXA	E121	121038
OO-SXB	E121	121040
OO-SXC	E121	121042
OO-SXD	E121	121043
OO-SXE	E121	121045
OO-TBM	TBM7	3
OO-TBW	MU-2	526
OO-TCA	690A	11208
(OO-TIA)	F406	0007
OO-TIK	F406	0003
OO-TIR	F406	0007
OO-TIS	F406	0002
OO-TIV	F406	0001
OO-TIW	F406	0018
OO-TIY	F406	0013
OO-TIZ	F406	0012
OO-TJG	P68	253
OO-TJH	P68	252
OO-TJI	P68	277
OO-TJJ	P68	284
OO-TJK	P68	372
OO-TLS	100	B-188
OO-TNY	P68	202
OO-TOF	P68	30
OO-TOP	BN2	424
OO-TPN	P68	88
OO-TPT	P68	197
OO-TZT	P68	238
OO-VGC	MIVA	AT-066
OO-VGD	MIVA	AT-062-2
OO-VHV	E90	LW-316
OO-WAT	690A	11125
OO-WIK	P68	152
OO-XJE	P68	255
OO-XJF	P68	244
(OO-XJG)	P68	253
(OO-XJI)	P68	277
OO-XSC	MIII	T-388

Denmark

OY-	PA42	7801004
OY-AJH	P68	113
OY-ANP	90	LJ-98
OY-ARV	MU-2	635
OY-ASF	100	B-138
OY-ASH	90	LJ-306
OY-ASI	90	LJ-723
OY-ASN	200	BB-928
(OY-ASO)	100	B-62
OY-ASS	200	BB-683
OY-AST	MIVA	AT-058
OY-ASU	E90	LW-244
OY-ATA	100	B-122
OY-ATS	100	B-185
OY-ATW	MIII	T-261
OY-ATZ	MU-2	626
OY-AUD	MIV	AT-014
OY-AUF	100	B-62
OY-AUI	MIV	AT-015
OY-AUJ	200	BB-119
OY-AUK	200	BB-199
OY-AUL	F90	LA-72
OY-AUM	200	BB-626
OY-AUV	90	LJ-890
(OY-AUY)	200	BB-703
OY-AUZ	200	BB-216
OY-AZA	90	LJ-593
OY-AZG	E90	LW-297
OY-AZV	90	LJ-799
OY-BAL	90	LJ-52
OY-BEB	90	LJ-971
OY-BEE	31T	8120010
OY-BEG	G1	177
OY-BEH	200	BB-773
OY-BEJ	690B	11367
OY-BEK	90	LJ-937
OY-BEL	F90	LA-129
OY-BEM	200	BB-861
OY-BEO	690A	11259
OY-BEP	200C	BL-43
OY-BER	200C	BL-41
OY-BET	200	BB-910
OY-BEY	200	BB-816
OY-BHA	100	B-245
OY-BHG	690C	11624
OY-BHM	441	0058
OY-BHO	690B	11357
OY-BHU	31T	7904004
OY-BHY	MU-2	1537SA
OY-BIS	MU-2	630
OY-BJH	P68	194
OY-BJY	MIII	T-403
OY-BNT	BN2	2209
OY-BPA	695A	96003
OY-BPE	MU-2	1562SA
OY-BPF	695A	96064
OY-BPG	200	BB-477
OY-BPK	MIII	TT-459A
OY-BPM	MIII	T-410
OY-BRL	31T	7820051
OY-BRV	31T	7820088
OY-BSB	31T	7620001
OY-BSE	P68	174
OY-BSG	690B	11415
OY-BTR	200	BB-211
OY-BVA	90	LJ-68
OY-BVB	200	BB-419
OY-BVC	200	BB-459
OY-BVD	F90	LA-4
OY-BVE	200C	BL-2
OY-BVL	200	BB-1070
OY-BVS	90	LJ-418
OY-BVW	200	BB-705
OY-BYS	P68	278
OY-CAA	P68	48
OY-CAB	P68	72
OY-CAC	P68	179
OY-CAD	P68	217
OY-CAE	P68	199
OY-CAF	P68	196
OY-CAG	P68	243
OY-CAT	BN2	2224
OY-CBK	200	BB-160
OY-CBL	200	BB-521
OY-CBP	200	BB-235
OY-CBV	200	BB-192
OY-CBW	MIII	T-283
OY-CBY	200	BB-545
OY-CCA	100	B-215
OY-CCC	F90	LA-184
OY-CCD	MIV	AT-018
OY-CCE	200	BB-932
OY-CCP	100	B-55
OY-CCS	100	B-160
(OY-CCW)	MIVA	AT-051
OY-CCZ	300	FA-200
OY-CDC	P68	211
OY-CDG	P68	363
OY-CDI	P68	392
OY-CEF	MU-2	683
OY-CEG	BN2	3009
OY-CEL	46D	219
OY-CEP	P68	44
OY-CEW	P68	30
OY-CEY	P68	62
OY-CFO	E90	LW-95
OY-CFT	P68	213
OY-CFV	BN2	2174
OY-CGH	PA42	8001046
OY-CGM	441	0229
OY-CGN	MU-2	755SA
OY-CGW	MU-2	459SA
OY-CHA	MIVA	AT-074
OY-CHB	MIVC	AT-461
OY-CHC	MIVC	AT-493
OY-CHE	200C	BL-25
OY-CHH	MIVC	AT-502
(OY-CKF)	MU-2	714SA
OY-CKP	200	BB-951
OY-CKS	BN2	553
OY-CRM	690C	11669
OY-CRU	MIII	TT-465
OY-CTJ	200	BB-619
OY-CTM	441	0235
OY-CUG	MU-2	557
OY-CVB	300	FA-175
OY-CVC	F90	LA-203
OY-CVL	350	FL-83
OY-DHS	BN2	188
OY-DJV	P68	22
OY-DLM	MU-2	187
OY-DSJ	MIV	AT-002
OY-DVJ	BN2	154
OY-DZR	P68	14
OY-DZV	BN2	702
OY-EEF	200	BB-1548
(OY-FCT)	200	BB-389
OY-FFD	MIVA	AT-062-2
OY-FFE	MIVA	AT-066
(OY-FTC)	200	BB-309
OY-GAP	100	B-33
OY-GCM	P68	367
OY-GEA	STAR	NC-8
OY-GEB	200C	BL-40
OY-GEF	90	LJ-1284
OY-GEH	200	BB-155
OY-GEL	300	FA-199
OY-GER	200	BB-1343
OY-GES	200	BB-1305
OY-GEU	200	BB-1341
OY-GEW	200	BB-1342
"OY-GEY"	200	BB-1343
OY-GIG	350	FL-167
OY-GMA	200	BB-1340
OY-GPT	46T	97019
OY-GRB	200	BB-845
OY-GSA	PC12	421
OY-IFH	90	LJ-1422
OY-JAB	90	LJ-1223
OY-JAJ	90	LJ-1097
OY-JAO	200	BB-401
OY-JAP	90	LJ-874
OY-JAR	200C	BL-13
(OY-JEL)	46D	142
"OY-JRB"	200	BB-364
OY-JRN	200	BB-364
OY-JRO	90	LJ-327
OY-JVL	350	FL-273
(OY-LAW)	46T	97122B
OY-LAW	46T	97138
OY-LDA	46T	97147
OY-LEL	350	FL-161
OY-LKH	200	BB-1325
OY-LKI	P68	366
OY-LKT	300	FA-108
OY-LLL	200	BB-1861
(OY-LMM)	46T	97108
OY-LMM	46T	97108
OY-LSA	90	LJ-1610
OY-MBA	90	LJ-846
OY-MBB	90	LJ-848
OY-MEN	350	FL-229
OY-MID	PC12	659
(OY-NEW)	46T	97014
(OY-NEW)	46T	97019
OY-NIR	MU-2	714SA
OY-NUK	200	BB-634
OY-NUS	PC12	1038
OY-NUT	PC12	677
OY-OCM	P68	180
OY-PAB	F406	0034
OY-PAL	200	BB-575
OY-PAM	200	BB-557
OY-PBA	PC6	678
OY-PBG	F406	0015
OY-PCL	200	BB-1675
OY-PCM	90	LJ-1889
OY-PEB	200	BB-309
OY-PED	F406	0046
OY-PEH	200	BB-643
OY-PEU	F406	0045
OY-PEZ	F406	0048
(OY-PHD)	46T	97178
OY-PHD	46T	97193
OY-PHO	46T	97240
*OY-PHS	BN2	2291
OY-PHY	BN2	2240
OY-PHZ	46T	97283
OY-PKB	46T	97309
OY-PKC	46T	97317
OY-PKE	46T	97350
OY-PLA	PC12	652
OY-PLB	PC12	803
OY-PLC	PC6	952
OY-PMM	46T	97387
*OY-PNG	PC12	1101
OY-PPP	BN2	2037
OY-PPP	PC12	697
OY-PRW	P68	79
OY-PRY	P68	102
OY-RPZ	BN2	433
OY-SBU	90	LJ-768
OY-SCI	PC12	496
OY-SFH	PC6	778
*OY-SKI	PC12	1074
OY-SUF	MU-2	719SA
OY-SUH	MU-2	762SA
OY-SUR	P68	246
OY-SUU	690B	11488
OY-SVE	46D	131
OY-SVG	690C	11662
OY-SVN	MU-2	792SA
OY-TLC	P68	147
OY-TLP	P180	1060
OY-TUS	PC12	230
OY-TWO	PC12	863
OY-VIN	PC12	872
OY-YES	PA42	8001043

Netherlands

PH-ACE	300	FA-80
PH-ACZ	200	BB-1215
PH-AJS	TBM7	24
PH-ALA	31T	8020088
PH-ALE	F406	0012

PH-ALK	F406	0003
PH-ALN	F406	0018
(PH-ALN)	F406	0047
PH-ALO	F406	0001
PH-ALP	F406	0046
(PH-ALR)	F406	0048
PH-ALU	F406	0044
PH-ALV	F406	0045
PH-ALX	F406	0038
PH-ALY	F406	0040
PH-ALZ	F406	0041
(PH-AMW)	200	BB-531
PH-ATM	200	BB-123
PH-AXS	E90	LW-297
(PH-BAM)	31T	7920078
PH-BDV	PA42	8001016
PH-BGY	200	BB-558
PH-BMP	441	0357
PH-BOA	MU-2	1507SA
PH-BRN	350	FL-80
PH-CAM	31T	7920059
(PH-CAV)	90	LJ-890
(PH-CCA)	90	LJ-890
PH-CLE	F406	0032
PH-CLZ	TBM7	299
(PH-CRT)	200	BB-988
(PH-CVA)	PC12	247
PH-DDB	200	BB-221
PH-DIX	PC12	309
PH-DKI	P68	297
(PH-DLN)	P180	1171
PH-DLN	P180	1175
PH-DMJ	90	LJ-848
PH-DRX	MU-2	1555SA
PH-DUS	200	BB-1296
PH-DYB	MIII	T-294
PH-ECC	PC12	107
PH-ECF	200	BB-956
PH-EEO	P68	62
PH-EMC	P68	253
(PH-EPB)	P68	75
(PH-EPS)	46T	97054
(PH-FHB)	46T	97282
PH-FHB	46T	97282
PH-FSB	TBM8	358
PH-FSS	90	LJ-32
PH-FWB	F406	0009
PH-FWC	F406	0007
PH-FWD	F406	0014
PH-FWE	F406	0015
PH-FWF	F406	0020
PH-FWG	F406	0021
PH-FWH	F406	0027
PH-FWI	F406	0029
PH-FWJ	F406	0030
PH-FWM	MU-2	1548SA
PH-GPX	F406	0058
(PH-GRO)	P68	278
PH-GRO	P68	278
PH-GUG	F406	0060
PH-GUI	F406	0063
PH-HRK	P180	1120
PH-HUB	TBM7	127
PH-ILG	200C	BL-13
PH-ILH	200	BB-737
PH-ILK	90	LJ-4
PH-IND	90	LJ-285
(PH-IPC)	200	BB-988
(PH-ISM)	690B	11409
PH-JAX	90	LJ-1913
PH-JDV	PA42	8001055
PH-JFD	PC6	909
PH-JFL	PC6	947
PH-JFS	PC12	477
(PH-JKS)	PC12	477
PH-JOE	425	0168
PH-KBB	90	LJ-1718
(PH-KJF)	BN2	111
PH-LAS	F406	0016
PH-LLL	PC6	954
PH-LMC	200	BB-988
PH-LTW	425	0148
PH-LUX	46D	36
PH-MEN	PC6	707
PH-MJM	F406	0037
PH-MNS	F406	0002
PH-NVA	BN2	111
*PH-OLS	PC12	1104
PH-OTB	PC6	518
PH-OTE	PC6	685
(PH-PAG)	P68	55
PH-PAR	BN2	206
PH-PEL	F406	0024
PH-PFS	BN2	788
PH-PHO	F406	0034
PH-PIX	MIII	T-267
PH-PNA	P68	38
PH-PNG	PC12	1121
PH-RAX	MIVC	AT-493
PH-RPM	BN2T	2190
PH-RPN	BN2T	2191
PH-RUL	PC12	1130
PH-RVR	P68	75
PH-RVS	P68	98
PH-RVT	P68	156
PH-RVU	P68	187
PH-SAT	200	BB-197
PH-SBK	200	BB-180
PH-SKP	200C	BL-11
(PH-SKS)	200	BB-531
PH-SLG	200	BB-397
(PH-SLK)	PA42	5527033
PH-SOK	P68	218
PH-SPB	P68	180
PH-SVX	31T	1166004
PH-SVY	31T	8020041
PH-TAX	31T	8020055
PH-TBD	TBM7	85
PH-TBM	TBM7	172
(PH-TCN)	P180	1020
PH-TCN	P180	1089
PH-TJA	TBM8	428
PH-UKK	TBM8	372
PH-VDO	P68	354
PH-VMC	425	0169
PH-VMP	200	BB-1538
PH-WMC	PC12	378
PH-XII	PC12	550

Philippines

See also RP-

PI-C202	90	LJ-356
PI-C282	100	B-78
PI-C710	100	B-15
PI-C797	680T	1573-28
PI-C990	90	LJ-247
PI-C1977	681	6036
PI-C1978	100	B-77

Netherlands Antilles

PJ-	690C	11606
PJ-	695A	96030
PJ-	695A	96065
PJ-AIW	BN2	2038
PJ-BIW	BN2	82
PJ-BRW	695	95010
PJ-CEB	690A	11292
PJ-CIW	BN2	876
PJ-EZR	BN2	592
PJ-NAF	695A	96008
PJ-SEA	BN2	311
PJ-SKY	BN2	885
PJ-SUN	BN2	377
PJ-TES	300	FA-26
PJ-WEA	BN2	659
PJ-WEB	BN2	2208
PJ-WIC	BN2	229
PJ-WIG	31T	8375005

Indonesia

PK-	PC12	842
PK-AFE	PC6	799
PK-AHA	TBM7	119
PK-AHC	TBM7	120
PK-BIG	BN2	837
PK-BTW	100	B-76
PK-CAE	100	B-222
PK-CAF	100	B-223
PK-CAK	200C	BL-140
PK-CAL	TBM7	114
PK-CAM	TBM7	121
PK-CDM	G1	177
PK-CTE	G1	177
PK-DYR	31T	7820054
PK-DYS	31T	7520028
PK-ENS	695B	96202
PK-ESS	BN2	697
PK-FKL	441	0179
PK-HNF	BN2	2250
PK-HNG	BN2	2249
PK-HPH	200	BB-1281
PK-HSN	200C	BL-134
PK-HTI	200	BB-1255
(PK-JAB)	PC6	943
PK-JBK	350	FL-619
PK-JCA	200C	BL-138
PK-KNA	BN2	308
PK-KNC	BN2	663
PK-KND	BN2	692
PK-KNE	BN2	675
PK-KNF	BN2	745
PK-KNG	BN2	749
(PK-KNH)	BN2	781
(PK-KNI)	BN2	782
PK-KTA	TRIS	1006
PK-KTC	TRIS	1017
PK-KTD	TRIS	1018
PK-KTH	TRIS	1022
PK-KTI	TRIS	1021
PK-KTJ	TRIS	1033
PK-LAV	BN2	697
PK-LTJ	PC6	959
PK-NPO	PC6	623
PK-NPP	PC6	622
PK-NPQ	PC6	621
PK-NPR	PC6	590
PK-NPS	PC6	589
PK-NPT	PC6	588
PK-NPU	PC6	577
PK-NPV	PC6	578
PK-NPW	PC6	579
PK-NPX	PC6	542
PK-NPY	PC6	538
PK-NPZ	PC6	560
PK-NSI	350	FL-30
PK-OAB	BN2	291
PK-OAN	BN2	235
PK-OAV	BN2	639
PK-OBB	680T	1573-28
PK-OBE	BN2	429
PK-ODR	695	95019
PK-PJH	31T	7620015
PK-PTI	31T	7920084
PK-RCD	P750	149
PK-RCQ	PC6	911
PK-RCS	PC6	948
PK-RCX	PC6	922
PK-RCY	PC6	923
PK-RCZ	PC6	903
PK-RGI	200	BB-1732
PK-RGP	BN2	2249
PK-RJA	G1	191
PK-RJR	350	FL-30
PK-SDI	PC6	760
PK-SYS	31T	7520028
PK-TAR	BN2	860
PK-TDR	350	FL-30
PK-TRA	200	BB-113
PK-TRB	200	BB-116
PK-TRC	BN2	545
PK-TRL	G1	60
PK-TRM	G1	57
PK-TRN	G1	193
PK-TRO	G1	130
PK-UCE	PC6	943
PK-UCF	PC6	945
PK-UCG	PC12	795
PK-UCI	PC6	927
PK-VIA	BN2	2250
PK-VIB	BN2	545
PK-VIM	BN2	634
PK-VIN	BN2	351
PK-VIO	BN2	693
PK-VIP	BN2	752
PK-VIQ	BN2	754
PK-VIR	BN2	392
PK-VIS	BN2	485
PK-VIT	BN2	595
PK-VIU	BN2	781
PK-VIV	BN2	852
PK-VIW	BN2	2026
PK-VIX	BN2	2027
PK-VIY	BN2	2133
PK-VIZ	BN2	697
PK-VKA	200	BB-732
PK-VKB	200	BB-794
PK-VKI	200C	BL-138
PK-VKY	90	LJ-197
PK-VKZ	90	LJ-189
PK-VVK	PC6	958
PK-VVP	PC6	957
*PK-VVQ	PC6	965
PK-VVX	P180	1192
PK-WBA	BN2	727
PK-WWG	G1	19
PK-YPC	PC6	726
PK-YPR	200C	BL-134
PK-YPS	200	BB-920
PK-YPW	200C	BL-136
PK-ZAA	BN2	730
PK-ZAD	BN2	732
PK-ZAE	BN2	565
PK-ZAL	BN2	780
PK-ZAM	BN2	782
PK-ZGZ	PA42	5527015
PK-ZNS	695B	96202

Brazil

PP-ACM	E121	121021
*PP-AGM	90	LJ-1955
PP-AGR	90	LJ-1896
PP-AMC	90	LJ-1727
PP-AMJ	90	LJ-1772
PP-ASD	90	LJ-1603
PP-BAF	90	LJ-1646
PP-BER	PC12	655
PP-CBD	200	BB-1062
PP-CHE	31T	8120008
PP-CIJ	90	LJ-105
(PP-CMA)	90	LJ-1906
PP-CMM	F90	LA-202
PP-COP	90	LJ-1618
PP-CSE	F90	LA-228
PP-DPS	F90	LA-163
PP-EEF	MU-2	136
PP-EFC	E90	LW-15
PP-EFI	BN2	314
PP-EFJ	BN2	327
PP-EFL	100	B-161
(PP-EGA)	E121	121039
PP-EGK	100	B-121
PP-EGT	E121	121016
PP-EGW	E121	121015
PP-EHE	90	LJ-638
PP-EHJ	E121	121027
PP-EIC	E121	121039
PP-EIJ	E121	121094
PP-EIL	E121	121028
PP-EJG	200	BB-1410
PP-EJO	300	FA-31
PP-EMN	E121	121035
PP-ENF	90	LJ-105
PP-EOC	90	LJ-346
PP-EOM	E121	121012
PP-EOP	200	BB-137
PP-EPB	PA42	8001035
PP-EPD	300	FA-92
PP-EPE	E121	121059
PP-EPS	90	LJ-1442

PP-ERG	200	BB-1603	PR-AGM	PC12	667	PR-JQM	90	LJ-1684	PT-DTL	MU-2	196
PP-ETR	90	LJ-1578	PR-AGR	PC12	652	PR-JSP	200	BB-304	PT-DUX	MIII	T-215
PP-EUE	90	LJ-409	PR-AGV	90	LJ-1725	PR-JUB	200G	BY-9	PT-DVE	BN2	258
PP-EUW	E121	121011	*PR-AJK	200	BB-1158	*PR-KRC	TBM8	484	PT-DVN	BN2	259
PP-FBT	100	B-121	PR-AJT	200	BB-1771	PR-LIA	200	BB-1798	PT-DYL	BN2	205
PP-FBU	BN2	650	PR-APJ	200	BB-1755	PR-LJA	350	FL-290	"PT-EFI"	BN2	314
PP-FBV	BN2	652	PR-ARC	90	LJ-1739	PR-LJR	PC12	738	PT-EFJ	BN2	327
PP-FBW	90	LJ-567	PR-ARN	200G	BY-21	*PR-LLL	90	LJ-1937	PT-FAN	E121	121012
"PP-FBY"	BN2	652	PR-ART	200	BB-806	PR-LMT	90	LJ-1853	PT-FAX	E121	121049
PP-FHE	E121	121051	PR-ATC	200	BB-1779	*PR-LMT	90	LJ-1876	PT-FAY	E121	121051
PP-FHG	90	LJ-346	PR-AVG	90	LJ-1891	*PR-LOL	90	LJ-1914	PT-FBU	BN2	650
PP-FNK	680W	1833-38	PR-AVT	90	LJ-1279	(PR-LOV)	90	LJ-1823	PT-FBV	BN2	652
PP-FNZ	90	LJ-346	PR-BHB	200G	BY-45	PR-LPM	200	BB-1981	PT-FBW	90	LJ-567
PP-FOY	100	B-142	PR-BIO	90	LJ-1803	PR-LYG	90	LJ-1886	PT-FCM	90	LJ-1471
PP-FPP	E90	LW-56	PR-BLP	200	BB-1199	PR-MCE	200	BB-1890	PT-FEG	E121	121057
PP-FRC	690	11036	PR-BOM	90	LJ-1763	(PR-MDA)	90	LJ-1940	PT-FFN	300	FA-174
PP-FRD	690	11037	PR-BTN	200	BB-1968	PR-MFG	90	LJ-1742	PT-FFS	200	BB-1578
PP-IAF	90	LJ-567	PR-BTS	90	LJ-1827	(PR-MJB)	90	LJ-1904	PT-FGA	E90	LW-56
PP-IAG	90	LJ-466	PR-BZE	PC12	580	PR-MLF	TBM8	457	PT-FGB	350	FL-42
PP-IKN	200	BB-137	PR-BZZ	PA42	8001106	PR-MLG	200	BB-1863	*PT-FLA	690B	11564
PP-JCA	F90	LA-107	PR-CAR	90	LJ-1826	PR-MLZ	90	LJ-1644	PT-FNK	680W	1833-38
PP-JJM	P68	451	PR-CCB	350	FL-541	*PR-MOG	200	BB-696	PT-FNZ	90	LJ-346
PP-JLM	200	BB-1591	PR-CCF	90	LJ-1608	PR-MOZ	350	FL-237	PT-FOA	90	LJ-353
PP-JSC	350	FL-289	PR-CEB	90	LJ-1807	PR-MPD	690B	11513	PT-FOB	100	B-200
PP-KIA	350	FL-608	(PR-CFA)	200G	BY-68	PR-MRF	350	FL-345	PT-FRC	690	11036
PP-KKG	350	FL-288	*PR-CGN	90	LJ-671	PR-MRN	695A	96023	PT-FRD	690	11037
(PP-KKK)	350	FL-288	PR-CMB	90	LJ-1780	(PR-MSM)	690B	11350	PT-FRG	E121	121044
PP-LCB	C-12	BC-65	PR-CMG	90	LJ-1940	PR-MSM	690B	11350	PT-FSA	350	FL-221
PP-LCQ	31T	7820046	PR-CMI	90	LJ-1715	PR-MSP	31T	8166052	PT-GAR	90	LJ-1813
PP-LOG	350	FL-434	PR-CMM	90	LJ-1769	PR-MZP	90	LJ-1311	PT-GAV	PC12	741
PP-LOV	200	BB-1992	PR-CVI	350	FL-550	*PR-NKA	200	BB-147	PT-IAS	BN2	216
*PP-MSE	90	LJ-1949	PR-DAH	350	FL-481	*PR-ORB	690B	11538	PT-IBE	90	LJ-531
PP-MVT	PC12	1066	PR-DBR	695	95069	PR-OTE	90	LJ-1862	PT-ICD	MU-2	215
*PP-NTX	200G	BY-84	PR-DCT	350	FL-579	PR-PDG	90	LJ-1799	PT-ICP	90	LJ-558
*PP-OPV	TBM8	429	PR-DGO	31T	8120035	PR-PIB	90	LJ-1784	PT-IEC	681B	6069
PP-OTK	90	LJ-221	(PR-DHA)	90	LJ-1825	PR-PJC	90	LJ-181	PT-IED	681B	6070
PP-PIV	TBM8	361	PR-DHD	90	LJ-1825	PR-RFB	90	LJ-1546	PT-IEE	681B	6071
PP-PPC	200G	BY-31	PR-DIN	90	LJ-1796	PR-RHH	90	LJ-1717	PT-IGD	E90	LW-9
(PP-RCA)	90	LJ-1861	PR-DOC	200G	BY-51	(PR-RIP)	90	LJ-1670	PT-IJE	BN2	304
PP-SAM	PC12	785	PR-DOG	PC12	814	PR-RMA	90	LJ-1693	PT-IJF	BN2	301
PP-UMU	90	LJ-1858	PR-DPR	TBM8	492	*PR-RPN	90	LJ-1939	PT-IKA	BN2	668
PP-UNI	90	LJ-1682	PR-DPS	200	BB-1501	PR-SDA	90	LJ-1770	PT-ILB	BN2	669
PP-WCA	90	LJ-1676	PR-EAO	200	BB-1912	PR-SGB	90	LJ-1794	PT-ILC	BN2	671
PP-ZCT	E121	121001	PR-ECT	PC12	359	PR-SIA	90	LJ-1272	PT-IMI	BN2	670
PP-ZDD	BN2	669	PR-EDF	350	FL-335	PR-SJE	90	LJ-1926	PT-JGA	MU-2	268
PP-ZDK	E121	121009	PR-EDP	90	LJ-1672	PR-SOF	90	LJ-1790	PT-JJI	BN2	642
PP-ZXA	E121	121054	PR-EDW	200	BB-623	PR-SRA	90	LJ-1861	PT-JNT	BN2	690
PP-ZXB	E121	121055	PR-EFN	200	BB-1932	PR-SYS	200	BB-1634	PT-JQF	BN2	645
PP-ZXD	E121	121065	PR-ENO	PC12	866	PR-TCA	90	LJ-1441	PT-JSC	BN2	695
PP-ZXF	E121	121069	PR-EPS	200	BB-1798	PR-TIN	90	LJ-1628	PT-JUB	200	BB-1455
PP-ZXG	E121	121070	*PR-EQM	90	LJ-1730	PR-TLL	90	LJ-713	PT-JYC	BN2	385
PP-ZXH	E121	121071	PR-ERM	90	LJ-1906	PR-TRD	200G	BY-15	(PT-JZJ)	BN2	390
PP-ZXI	E121	121001	PR-ESP	200G	BY-71	PR-UMU	90	LJ-1783	PT-JZJ	BN2	645
PP-ZXJ	E121	121072	PR-FAG	F406	0037	*PR-UNI	200G	BY-79	PT-JZN	BN2	370
PP-ZXL	E121	121073	PR-FAZ	90	LJ-1674	PR-USA	90	LJ-1679	PT-KAB	BN2	689
PP-ZXM	E121	121074	PR-FBI	MU-2	772SA	(PR-UTH)	MU-2	727SA	PT-KAB-X	BN2	689
PP-ZXN	E121	121075	PR-FCI	90	LJ-1904	PR-UTI	MU-2	727SA	PT-KAC	BN2	644
PP-ZXO	E121	121076	PR-FIC	TBM7	297	PR-VDQ	200	BB-1965	PT-KAC-X	BN2	644
PP-ZXP	E121	121077	PR-FKY	90	LJ-1701	PR-VIP	200	BB-384	PT-KCF	BN2	698
PP-ZXQ	E121	121078	PR-FRB	200	BB-1871	PR-VIT	90	LJ-1706	PT-KCF-X	BN2	698
PP-ZXR	E121	121079	PR-FVP	200	BB-1969	PR-VOT	90	LJ-1076	PT-KFV	90	LJ-638
PP-ZXS	E121	121080	PR-GAB	TBM8	418	PR-VZE	PC12	1088	PT-KGV	90	LJ-221
PP-ZXT	E121	121081	PR-GBI	200	BB-323	*PR-WFM	90	LJ-1301	PT-KHK	BN2	208
PP-ZXU	E121	121068	PR-GBS	90	LJ-1332	PR-WIT	200G	BY-13	PT-KME	31T	7520012
PP-ZXV	E121	121083	PR-GFB	90	LJ-1821	PR-WNF	90	LJ-1670	PT-KNE	BN2	696
PP-ZXW	E121	121084	PR-GPO	90	LJ-1658	PR-XAA	350	FL-408	PT-KNM	BN2	669
PP-ZXX	E121	121082	PR-GRB	PC12	856	PR-XGT	90	LJ-1846	PT-KQS	BN2	434
PP-ZXZ	E121	121085	PR-GSW	90	LJ-1712	PR-XIB	90	LJ-1639	PT-KRO	BN2	742
PP-ZYA	E121	121086	PR-HLT	TBM8	454	PR-XKY	90	LJ-586	PT-KRP	BN2	743
PP-ZYB	E121	121087	PR-HRM	31T	7620053	PT-	680T	1703-79	(PT-KSJ)	BN2	447
PP-ZYC	E121	121089	*PR-ILF	MU-2	1507SA	(PT-)	690B	11391	PT-KSJ	BN2	488
PP-ZYD	E121	121090	PR-IPI	90	LJ-1912	PT-	695	95038	PT-KSP	BN2	407
PP-ZYE	E121	121091	PR-IRB	90	LJ-1743	PT-	90	LJ-16	PT-KTP	BN2	491
PP-ZYF	E121	121092	PR-JAG	90	LJ-1771	PT-ASN	F90	LA-232	PT-KTQ	BN2	493
PP-ZYG	E121	121095	PR-JAV	90	LJ-1885	PT-BOY	MU-2	145	PT-KTR	BN2	495
PP-ZYH	E121	121096	*PR-JBT	200C	BL-133	PT-BPY	MU-2	158	PT-KTS	BN2	499
PP-ZYI	E121	121098	PR-JCA	90	LJ-1844	PT-BZW	MU-2	175	PT-KUO	BN2	512
PP-ZYJ	E121	121099	PR-JCC	350	FL-657	PT-BZY	MU-2	188	PT-KYA	BN2	301
PP-ZYK	E121	121100	PR-JCF	90	LJ-1938	PT-CGK	90	LJ-466	PT-KYF	G1	75
PR-	200	BB-25	PR-JDB	350	FL-435	PT-DEU	90	LJ-355	PT-KYY	680W	1833-38
PR-AAX	200	BB-736	PR-JFC	350	FL-381	PT-DIQ	90	LJ-398	PT-LBZ	90	LJ-181
PR-ACT	200	BB-1626	PR-JJM	90	LJ-1882	PT-DKV	100	B-43	PT-LCE	E90	LW-347
PR-ADM	350	FL-398	PR-JME	90	LJ-1841	PT-DNP	100	B-56	PT-LDA	690	11036
PR-AEF	350	FL-377	*PR-JPG	200	BB-306	PT-DQX	681	6018	PT-LDL	690	11037

PT-LER	F90	LA-148	PT-MAQ	E121	121024	PT-OEH	90	LJ-914	PT-OTG	90	LJ-1096
PT-LEW	MU-2	244	PT-MAR	E121	121025	PT-OEP	90	LJ-1019	PT-OTI	90	LJ-1237
PT-LFX	MU-2	650	PT-MAS	E121	121026	PT-OFB	F90	LA-200	PT-OTO	200	BB-694
PT-LHH	MU-2	1508SA	PT-MAT	E121	121027	PT-OFC	90	LJ-534	PT-OTV	31T	8104017
PT-LHJ	90	LJ-1010	(PT-MAU)	E121	121028	PT-OFD	F90	LA-118	PT-OUF	E90	LW-343
PT-LHM	90	LJ-105	PT-MAV	E121	121029	PT-OFF	90	LJ-1264	PT-OUH	E121	121012
PT-LHV	690B	11376	PT-MAW	E121	121030	PT-OFG	690A	11274	PT-OUJ	F90	LA-155
PT-LHZ	E90	LW-133	PT-MAX	E121	121031	PT-OFH	31T	7920034	PT-OUL	90	LJ-125
PT-LIF	F90	LA-223	PT-MAY	E121	121032	PT-OFS	F90	LA-225	PT-OUO	90	LJ-499
PT-LIK	MU-2	1546SA	PT-MAZ	E121	121033	PT-OFV	MU-2	298	PT-OUX	90	LJ-937
PT-LIR	MU-2	428SA	PT-MBA	E121	121028	PT-OFY	90	LJ-1094	PT-OVB	31T	8104051
PT-LIS	MU-2	749SA	PT-MBB	E121	121034	PT-OFZ	100	B-243	PT-OVD	PA42	5527005
PT-LJM	100	B-161	(PT-MBC)	E121	121035	PT-OHH	90	LJ-975	PT-OVE	31T	8004014
PT-LJN	100	B-121	PT-MBD	E121	121036	PT-OHK	MU-2	774SA	PT-OVN	90	LJ-1041
PT-LJR	F90	LA-93	PT-MBE	E121	121037	PT-OHR	F90	LA-177	PT-OVP	90	LJ-152
PT-LJS	MU-2	1568SA	PT-MBF	90	LJ-1823	PT-OHS	31T	8020041	PT-OVQ	100	B-137
PT-LLG	31T	8020054	PT-MBF	E121	121038	PT-OHX	F90	LA-211	PT-OVW	MU-2	350SA
PT-LLO	90	LJ-1225	PT-MBG	E121	121039	PT-OHZ	F90	LA-173	PT-OVY	90	LJ-835
PT-LLP	F90	LA-7	PT-MBH	E121	121040	PT-OIF	F90	LA-49	PT-OXG	200	BB-1473
PT-LLR	90	LJ-946	PT-MBI	E121	121041	PT-OIP	MU-2	354SA	PT-OXH	90	LJ-1127
PT-LLV	90	LJ-897	PT-MBJ	E121	121042	PT-OIU	90	LJ-515	PT-OXU	90	LJ-535
PT-LMC	F90	LA-171	PT-MBK	E121	121043	PT-OIV	F90	LA-163	PT-OXY	90	LJ-1092
PT-LMD	MU-2	026	PT-MBL	E121	121044	PT-OIY	MU-2	453SA	PT-OYD	90	LJ-455
PT-LMI	90	LJ-913	PT-MBM	E121	121045	PT-OIZ	90	LJ-1174	PT-OYN	90	LJ-1081
PT-LMJ	90	LJ-927	PT-MBN	E121	121014	PT-OJA	90	LJ-952	PT-OYR	200	BB-487
PT-LNG	31T	8120061	PT-MBO	E121	121046	PT-OJE	31T	8120031	PT-OZE	F90	LA-236
PT-LNJ	300	FA-31	PT-MBP	E121	121047	PT-OJI	90	LJ-812	PT-OZJ	90	LJ-951
PT-LOH	MU-2	126	PT-MBQ	E121	121048	PT-OJM	31T	8120070	PT-OZK	200	BB-45
PT-LPB	MU-2	1567SA	PT-MBR	E121	121049	PT-OJQ	300	FA-154	PT-OZL	90	LJ-1341
PT-LPD	90	LJ-1173	PT-MBS	E121	121050	PT-OJU	90	LJ-900	PT-OZN	31T	8020061
PT-LPG	200	BB-1271	PT-MBT	E121	121051	PT-OJZ	90	LJ-1193	PT-OZP	F90	LA-175
PT-LPJ	90	LJ-1026	PT-MBU	E121	121052	PT-OKL	PA42	8001103	PT-OZR	90	LJ-1059
PT-LPL	F90	LA-28	PT-MBV	E121	121053	PT-OKQ	90	LJ-1195	PT-OZS	E121	121015
PT-LPS	90	LJ-817	PT-MBW	E121	121054	PT-OKS	31T	8120020	PT-OZY	31T	7820030
PT-LQC	F90	LA-132	PT-MBX	E121	121055	PT-OKT	31T	8104041	PT-PAC	90	LJ-1555
PT-LQD	90	LJ-844	PT-MBY	E121	121056	PT-OKW	90	LJ-1023	PT-SBM	200G	BY-72
PT-LQE	90	LJ-1056	PT-MBZ	E121	121057	PT-OLF	31T	8004039	PT-TPU	PC12	326
PT-LQS	90	LJ-966	PT-MCA	E121	121058	PT-OLI	300	FA-26	PT-VXJ	PC12	1044
PT-LRQ	690C	11719	PT-MCB	E121	121059	PT-OLM	F90	LA-86	PT-WAC	350	FL-177
PT-LRT	31T	8120040	PT-MCC	E121	121061	PT-OLP	F90	LA-220	PT-WAE	90	LJ-191
PT-LSE	90	LJ-1063	PT-MCD	E121	121016	PT-OLQ	90	LJ-884	PT-WAG	E90	LW-138
PT-LSH	F90	LA-94	PT-MCE	E121	121094	PT-OLT	PA42	5501011	PT-WAH	90	LJ-1245
PT-LSO	90	LJ-794	PT-MCF	E121	121093	PT-OLW	90	LJ-985	PT-WBQ	90	LJ-460
PT-LSP	F90	LA-197	PT-MCG	E121	121088	PT-OLX	90	LJ-963	PT-WCB	200	BB-1419
PT-LSQ	MU-2	1530SA	PT-MCI	E121	121097	PT-OLZ	31T	8120005	PT-WCS	90	LJ-1377
PT-LTC	MU-2	314	PT-MCJ	E121	121100	PT-OMO	90	LJ-1294	PT-WDU	90	LJ-791
PT-LTF	90	LJ-543	PT-MCK	E121	121104	PT-OMZ	90	LJ-1220	PT-WEF	31T	8104034
PT-LTO	F90	LA-156	PT-MCM	300	FA-52	PT-ONE	F90	LA-144	PT-WEG	200	BB-875
PT-LTT	F90	LA-103	PT-MFL	PA42	8001080	PT-ONJ	90	LJ-1078	PT-WET	F90	LA-78
PT-LUF	90	LJ-651	PT-MFW	31T	8166067	PT-ONO	F90	LA-92	PT-WFB	31T	8020048
PT-LUJ	31T	7720039	PT-MGX	BN2	596	PT-ONQ	90	LJ-1018	PT-WFN	90	LJ-1346
PT-LUT	F90	LA-215	PT-MGZ	31T	8020058	PT-ONU	F90	LA-128	PT-WFQ	31T	7820049
PT-LVI	90	LJ-834	PT-MJD	200	BB-1589	PT-OOD	90	LJ-1000	PT-WGH	MIV	AT-011
PT-LVK	90	LJ-1201	PT-MJQ	90	LJ-1564	PT-OOG	90	LJ-1048	PT-WGJ	31T	8120101
PT-LXI	F90	LA-11	PT-MMB	200	BB-971	PT-OOS	MU-2	388SA	PT-WGS	200	BB-1446
PT-LXY	F90	LA-195	PT-MMC	300	FA-113	PT-OOT	90	LJ-995	PT-WGU	90	LJ-1363
PT-LYI	MU-2	213	PT-MMF	200	BB-1915	PT-OOX	F90	LA-162	PT-WHA	90	LJ-1253
PT-LYK	90	LJ-1188	PT-MPC	90	LJ-683	PT-OOY	90	LJ-882	PT-WHI	31T	7920077
PT-LYM	F90	LA-185	PT-MPN	690B	11465	PT-OOZ	F90	LA-203	PT-WHN	31T	8104073
PT-LYP	F90	LA-126	PT-MPR	200	BB-840	PT-OPC	31T	8120010	PT-WHP	90	LJ-1212
PT-LYT	90	LJ-1037	PT-MSA	E121	121011	PT-OPD	90	LJ-920	PT-WIC	690C	11625
PT-LYW	90	LJ-584	PT-MSC	350	FL-212	PT-OPE	90	LJ-940	PT-WIH	90	LJ-1396
PT-LYZ	F90	LA-109	PT-MTD	90	LJ-1219	PT-OPF	31T	8004038	PT-WIT	90	LJ-1394
PT-LZA	100	B-200	PT-MVJ	90	LJ-1498	PT-OPH	31T	7620044	PT-WIX	MU-2	232
PT-LZB	31T	7920063	PT-OAB	90	LJ-1022	PT-OPQ	31T	8004007	PT-WJD	90	LJ-1427
PT-LZD	PA42	8001038	PT-OAJ	31T	8004005	PT-OPR	90	LJ-870	PT-WJF	90	LJ-1386
PT-LZH	90	LJ-808	PT-OAM	31T	8020028	PT-OQH	690	11011	PT-WKF	PC12	141
PT-LZR	31T	7920083	PT-OAU	E121	121028	PT-OQP	100	B-7	PT-WKX	90	LJ-1494
PT-LZT	F90	LA-216	PT-OBF	90	LJ-1224	PT-OQQ	681	6021	PT-WLD	690D	15027
PT-MAA	E121	121001	PT-OBW	90	LJ-353	PT-OQS	90	LJ-1005	PT-WLF	200	BB-1528
PT-MAB	E121	121007	PT-OCC	90	LJ-960	PT-OQY	690D	15038	PT-WLJ	31T	8120011
PT-MAC	E121	121009	PT-OCE	F90	LA-217	PT-ORB	200	BB-1435	PT-WLK	200	BB-1543
PT-MAD	E121	121010	PT-OCI	90	LJ-998	PT-ORG	90	LJ-1308	PT-WLT	200	BB-1275
PT-MAE	E121	121011	PT-OCL	31T	8020033	PT-ORW	90	LJ-1004	PT-WLV	E121	121059
PT-MAG	E121	121013	PT-OCT	90	LJ-567	PT-ORY	F90	LA-153	PT-WME	31T	8020058
PT-MAH	E121	121015	PT-OCY	90	LJ-847	PT-ORZ	90	LJ-1233	PT-WMT	90	LJ-956
(PT-MAI)	E121	121016	PT-ODA	90	LJ-466	PT-OSI	90	LJ-936	PT-WMU	31T	8004043
PT-MAJ	E121	121017	PT-ODE	90	LJ-1159	PT-OSN	90	LJ-1260	PT-WMX	31T	8104062
PT-MAK	E121	121018	PT-ODH	90	LJ-1128	PT-OSO	90	LJ-927	PT-WMY	BN2	314
PT-MAL	E121	121019	PT-ODM	31T	8120042	PT-OSR	200	BB-784	PT-WNC	31T	8120020
PT-MAM	E121	121020	PT-ODN	F90	LA-85	PT-OSX	PA42	8001035	PT-WND	350	FL-141
PT-MAN	E121	121021	PT-ODO	F90	LA-213	PT-OSZ	300	FA-92	PT-WNG	31T	8166049
PT-MAO	E121	121022	PT-ODR	31T	8020079	PT-OTA	F90	LA-187	PT-WNI	90	LJ-1442
PT-MAP	E121	121023	PT-OED	31T	8020029	PT-OTF	31T	7920044	PT-WNL	350	FL-159

PT-WNN 200 BB-1558
PT-WNQ 200 BB-1584
PT-WNS MU-2 1501SA
PT-WNW 90 LJ-1092
PT-WNZ 31T 8004046
PT-WOF 200 BB-986
PT-WOR 31T 8120030
PT-WOU BN2 327
PT-WOZ 90 LJ-1498
PT-WPN 90 LJ-1294
PT-WPV B100 BE-45
PT-WQA PA42 5501053
PT-WQW 90 LJ-1577
PT-WRA 90 LJ-1385
PT-WRN 200 BB-1603
PT-WSI 350 FL-169
PT-WSJ 350 FL-152
PT-WST MU-2 711SA
PT-WSW 200 BB-1603
PT-WSX 200 BB-1266
PT-WTN 90 LJ-346
PT-WTU 90 LJ-1491
PT-WTW 350 FL-205
PT-WUA 350 FL-179
PT-WUG 90 LJ-1511
PT-WUT 350 FL-240
(PT-WVA) 350 FL-179
PT-WVI 90 LJ-1331
PT-WXH 90 LJ-1590
PT-WYO 350 FL-40
PT-WYT MU-2 722SA
PT-WYY 200 BB-1302
(PT-WZC) 350 FL-205
PT-WZC 90 LJ-1538
PT-WZE PC12 165
PT-XEG 200 BB-1190
PT-XHP 90 LJ-1473
PT-XOC 31T 8104064
PT-XOU 90 LJ-1501
PT-XOV 90 LJ-1569
PT-XTG PC12 214
PT-ZVB E123 123802
PT-ZVE E123 123801

Suriname

PZ- P68 142
PZ-TBL BN2 2153
PZ-TGT BN2 2116
PZ-TGU BN2 2108

Papua New Guinea

P2- BN2 81
P2-ALC BN2 36
P2-ALD BN2 76
P2-ALE BN2 100
P2-ALF BN2 395
P2-ALH BN2 761
P2-ALI BN2 73
P2-ALL BN2 448
P2-ALM BN2 124
P2-AND BN2 133
P2-APD BN2 133
P2-ATI BN2 28
P2-ATS BN2 36
P2-ATU BN2 119
P2-ATV BN2 100
P2-ATW BN2 67
P2-ATX BN2 126
P2-ATY BN2 94
P2-ATZ BN2 132
P2-BAB BN2 846
P2-BAC BN2 716
P2-BAY BN2 620
P2-BBC BN2 36
P2-BCL MIII T-226
P2-BPV BN2 134
P2-BWC P750 136
P2-CAA 200 BB-415
P2-CAI MIIB T26-103
P2-CBA BN2 753
P2-CBB BN2 140
P2-CBE BN2 438
P2-CBT BN2 393
P2-CCB 200C BL-38
P2-COB BN2 768
P2-COD BN2 813
P2-COG BN2 843
P2-DCA 90 LJ-552
P2-DNA P68 29
P2-DNB BN2 76
P2-DNC P68 37
P2-DNI BN2 28
P2-DNJ BN2 857
P2-DNK P68 33
P2-DNN TRIS 245
P2-DNP TRIS 372
P2-DNV BN2 100
P2-DNW BN2 67
P2-DNX TRIS 322
P2-DNY BN2 94
P2-DRS 90 LJ-1227
P2-DWA BN2 113
P2-EDI BN2 227
P2-EER BN2 832
(P2-FHC) BN2 356
P2-FHO BN2 336
P2-FHP BN2 168
P2-FHQ BN2 395
P2-FHR BN2 421
P2-GTZ P68 29
P2-HAC BN2 762
P2-HBE BN2 815
P2-HCN 200C BL-22
P2-IAC BN2 425
P2-IAD BN2 768
P2-IAG 200 BB-344
P2-IAH 200 BB-297
P2-ISA BN2 703
P2-ISA BN2 758
P2-ISB BN2 709
P2-ISC BN2 207
P2-ISC BN2 394
(P2-ISD) BN2 227
P2-ISD BN2 582
P2-ISE BN2 753
P2-ISF BN2 281
P2-ISG BN2 756
P2-ISH BN2 757
P2-ISI BN2 73
P2-ISJ BN2 89
P2-ISK BN2 805
P2-ISL BN2 806
P2-ISM BN2 81
P2-ISM BN2 227
P2-ISN BN2 194
P2-ISO BN2 761
P2-ISP BN2 763
P2-ISQ BN2 134
P2-ISR BN2 15
P2-ISS BN2 81
P2-IST BN2 180
P2-ISU BN2 605
(P2-ISW) BN2 172
P2-KAD BN2 800
P2-KAE BN2 489
P2-KAF BN2 425
P2-KAG BN2 503
P2-KCA 200 BB-579
P2-KSA 200 BB-1527
P2-KSN 200C BL-22
P2-KST BN2 2014
P2-MBD BN2 158
P2-MBE BN2 194
P2-MBF BN2 646
P2-MBH 200 BB-1423
P2-MBM 200 BB-550
P2-MBZ 200 BB-1420
P2-MCA BN2 2131
P2-MFI BN2 188
P2-MFT BN2 421
P2-MFW BN2 521
P2-MFZ BN2 759
P2-MIB BN2 217
P2-MKN BN2 73
P2-MKV BN2 703
P2-MKW BN2 709
P2-MKX BN2 394
P2-MML 200 BB-579
P2-NAA BN2 124
P2-NAJ BN2 100
P2-NAM BN2 76
P2-NAM BN2 207
P2-NAS BN2 36
P2-NAT 200 BB-463
P2-NCA P750 134
P2-NCE BN2 768
P2-NTJ 90 LJ-1024
P2-NTR 90 LJ-1021
P2-PAA BN2 81
(P2-PAB) BN2 194
P2-PAC BN2 761
P2-PAD BN2 763
P2-PJV 200C BL-22
P2-PNB 90 LJ-552
P2-PNG 200 BB-415
P2-PNG 350 FL-79
P2-PNG PC6 584
P2-PNH 200 BB-415
P2-PNO PC6 584
P2-ROV BN2 81
P2-RTK BN2 194
P2-SAA BN2 134
P2-SAB BN2 100
P2-SAC BN2 94
P2-SDB P750 124
P2-SEA PC6 584
P2-SEZ PC6 660
P2-SIA 200C BL-39
P2-SIV BN2T 2138
P2-SMB 200 BB-355
P2-SML 200 BB-365
P2-SWA BN2 805
P2-SWB BN2 758
P2-SWC BN2 835
P2-SWD BN2 660
P2-TCP BN2 721
P2-TFI BN2 432
P2-TND BN2 813
P2-TNT BN2 393
P2-TNT P750 143
P2-UIC PC6 660
P2-VAB BN2 759
P2-VIC 200 BB-990
P2-WGQ BN2 76
P2-WGT BN2 646

Aruba

P4-JML G1 76
P4-PHC 690A 11125
P4-SSI 90 LJ-1476

Russia

RA-01500 PC12 803
RA-01501 PC12 841
RA-01502 PC12 862
RA-01503 PC12 882
RA-01504 PC12 1026
RA-01505 PC12 1029
RA-01506 PC12 1061
RA-01507 PC12 1064
RA-01509 PC12 745
RA-01510 PC12 723
RA-0216G 46D 128
RA-15001 M101 1500001
(RA-15002) M101 1500002
RA-15003 M101 1500003
RA-15004 M101 1500004
RA-15100 M101 1501013
RA-15101 M101 1501001
RA-15102 M101 1501002
RA-15103 M101 1501003
RA-15104 M101 1501004
RA-15105 M101 1501005
RA-15106 M101 1501006
RA-15107 M101 1501007
RA-15108 M101 1501008
RA-15109 M101 1501009
RA-15110 M101 1501010
RA-15111 M101 1501011
RA-15112 M101 1501012
RA-15114 M101 1501014
RA-15122 M101 1501022
RA-15123 M101 1501023
RA-15124 M101 1501024
RA-15125 M101 1501025
RA-15126 M101 1501026
RF-14004 MIIB T26-129
RF-14424 MIIB T26-152

Philippines

See also PI-

RP-223 200 BB-66
RP-251 BN2 3002
RP-462 BN2 462
RP-463 BN2 463
RP-766 BN2T 3007
RP-2131 BN2 421
RP-2133 BN2 430
RP-2137 BN2 443
RP-2151 BN2 560
RP-2157 BN2 505
RP-2164 BN2 462
RP-2169 BN2 463
RP-4177 BN2 462
RP-1801 BN2 739
RP-C TRIS 1025
RP-C TRIS 361
RP-C22 200 BB-162
RP-C28 BN2 409
RP-C200 200 BB-47
RP-C201 E90 LW-126
RP-C202 90 LJ-356
RP-C203 MIII T-244
RP-C204 MIV AT-018
RP-C223 200 BB-66
RP-C243 200 BB-491
RP-C251 BN2 3002
RP-C258 BN2 3001
RP-C264 200 BB-692
RP-C267 200 BB-848
RP-C282 100 B-78
RP-C289 E90 LW-12
RP-C290 90 LJ-857
RP-C291 E90 LW-325
RP-C292 E90 LW-277
RP-C298 E90 LW-302
RP-C304 200 BB-503
RP-C319 E90 LW-331
RP-C323 MIII T-313
RP-C340 BN2 3005
RP-C346 441 0095
RP-C367 200 BB-963
RP-C410 F90 LA-136
RP-C415 E90 LW-190
RP-C471 BN2 473
RP-C530 BN2 3003
RP-C549 441 0115
RP-C552 BN2 3006
RP-C553 BN2 3008
RP-C574 425 0008
RP-C575 MU-2 310
RP-C578 BN2 3013
RP-C582 200 BB-785
RP-C585 MU-2 1536SA
RP-C604 BN2 3012
RP-C662 BN2 3004
RP-C664 BN2 3014
RP-C665 BN2 3015
RP-C684 BN2 723
RP-C685 441 0039
RP-C688 BN2 2042
RP-C693 BN2 2043
RP-C704 200 BB-615
RP-C710 100 B-15
RP-C711 200 BB-83
RP-C755 200 BB-975
RP-C764 BN2 318

RP-C766	BN2T	3007
RP-C775	681B	6066
RP-C788	BN2T	3010
RP-C797	680T	1573-28
RP-C809	BN2	755
RP-C850	BN2	469
RP-C868	BN2	725
RP-C879	E90	LW-145
RP-C898	90	LJ-1403
RP-C969	200	BB-951
RP-C990	90	LJ-247
RP-C1047	BN2	654
RP-C1048	BN2	500
RP-C1260	200	BB-595
RP-C1261	MIII	T-245
RP-C1262	BN2	408
RP-C1298	S600	008
RP-C1320	BN2	569
RP-C1321	BN2	547
RP-C1323	BN2	502
RP-C1324	BN2	539
RP-C1325	BN2	593
RP-C1502	200	BB-1500
RP-C1515	200	BB-1004
RP-C1577	200	BB-945
RP-C1587	350	FL-20
RP-C1728	350	FL-118
RP-C1801	BN2	739
RP-C1807	350	FL-153
RP-C1807	90	LJ-1181
RP-C1849	BN2	3009
RP-C1850	BN2	3011
RP-C1887	200	BB-1062
RP-C1890	300	FA-64
RP-C1956	690	11072
RP-C1966	BN2	725
RP-C1977	681	6036
RP-C1978	100	B-77
RP-C1979	200	BB-108
RP-C1990	E90	LW-341
RP-C1995	200	BB-1429
RP-C2100	200	BB-1405
RP-C2103	BN2	741
RP-C2130	BN2	721
RP-C2131	BN2	421
RP-C2132	BN2	422
RP-C2134	BN2	438
RP-C2135	BN2	439
RP-C2136	BN2	440
RP-C2137	BN2	443
RP-C2138	BN2	445
RP-C2139	BN2	448
RP-C2140	BN2	450
RP-C2141	BN2	452
RP-C2142	BN2	455
(RP-C2143)	BN2	456
RP-C2143	BN2	547
RP-C2144	BN2	458
RP-C2145	BN2	459
RP-C2146	BN2	462
RP-C2146	BN2	548
RP-C2147	BN2	460
RP-C2147	BN2	551
RP-C2148	BN2	453
RP-C2148	BN2	552
RP-C2149	BN2	471
(RP-C2150)	BN2	473
RP-C2150	BN2	559
RP-C2151	BN2	485
RP-C2151	BN2	560
RP-C2152	BN2	487
RP-C2153	BN2	494
RP-C2153	BN2	561
RP-C2154	BN2	500
RP-C2155	BN2	502
RP-C2156	BN2	503
RP-C2156	BN2	567
RP-C2157	BN2	505
RP-C2158	BN2	508
RP-C2159	BN2	509
RP-C2159	BN2	594
RP-C2160	BN2	527
RP-C2161	BN2	528
RP-C2162	BN2	538
RP-C2163	BN2	539
RP-C2165	BN2	568
RP-C2166	BN2	569
RP-C2167	BN2	509
RP-C2168	BN2	593
RP-C2169	BN2	463
RP-C2207	BN2	718
RP-C2208	90	LJ-365
RP-C2226	350	FL-563
RP-C2296	350	FL-196
RP-C2340	90	LJ-57
RP-C2446	90	LJ-1102
RP-C2528	350	FL-567
RP-C2638	350	FL-137
RP-C2750	BN2	692
RP-C2850	350	FL-145
RP-C3318	90	LJ-281
RP-C3500	350	FL-148
RP-C3650	90	LJ-662
RP-C3885	200	BB-1532
RP-C4188	200	BB-1359
RP-C4567	300	FA-64
RP-C4650	200	BB-762
RP-C5129	200	BB-358
RP-C5139	200	BB-692
RP-C5555	200	BB-1157
RP-C7000	350	FL-175
RP-C7188	200	BB-1077
RP-C8300	350	FL-83
RP-C8300	350	FL-505
RP-C8853	200	BB-1529

Sweden

SE-EDM	MU-2	011
SE-EDN	P166	413
SE-FGE	681	6033
SE-FGF	690	11004
~~SE-FGG~~	~~MU-2~~	~~526~~
SE-FGO	MU-2	102
SE-FGP	MU-2	028
SE-FLN	690A	11118
SE-FNU	90	LJ-150
SE-FTA	BN2	206
SE-FTB	BN2	208
SE-FTF	MU-2	630
SE-FTM	P68	24
SE-FTS	MU-2	277
SE-FUK	P68	39
(SE-GER)	690A	11118
SE-GEU	P68	174
SE-GFN	P68	56
SE-GHA	MU-2	283
SE-GHB	MU-2	287
SE-GHC	MU-2	289
SE-GHD	MU-2	293
SE-GHE	MU-2	294
SE-GHF	MU-2	299
SE-GHG	MU-2	191
SE-GHH	MU-2	222
SE-GHK	200	BB-501
~~SE-GHS~~	~~200~~	~~BB-155~~
SE-GHT	MU-2	621
SE-GHU	MU-2	308
SE-GHX	MU-2	250
SE-GHY	MU-2	626
SE-GLA	31T	7520031
SE-GLB	31T	7400002
SE-GNB	31T	7620057
SE-GRP	200	BB-192
SE-GRR	200	BB-208
SE-GSB	690A	11152
SE-GSL	690A	11161
SE-GSR	690A	11204
SE-GSS	690C	11613
SE-GSU	200	BB-133
SE-GTV	BN2	651
SE-GUI	P68	109
SE-GUU	90	LJ-470
SE-GXD	90	LJ-616
SE-GXK	90	LJ-868
SE-GXL	P68	194
SE-GXM	200	BB-521
SE-GXV	MIII	T-283
SE-GYC	441	0035
SE-IAB	31T	7820088
(SE-IBI)	441	0002
SE-IBM	441	0210
(SE-IBS)	441	0223
SE-ICS	31T	7920094
SE-IDM	31T	8020059
SE-IEH	200	BB-683
SE-IES	E90	LW-339
SE-IEZ	200	BB-754
SE-IFM	425	0059
(SE-IFU)	441	0206
SE-IGS	90	LJ-939
SE-IGV	200	BB-844
(SE-IHE)	441	0232
(SE-IHH)	441	0248
SE-IHM	425	0134
SE-IHX	441	0291
SE-IIA	BN2	48
SE-IIB	90	LJ-723
SE-IIE	100	B-62
SE-IIM	MIII	T-403
(SE-IIS)	200	BB-892
SE-IIU	E90	LW-106
SE-IKD	E90	LW-297
SE-IKM	E90	LW-283
SE-ILR	46T	97047
SE-ING	100	B-163
SE-INI	200	BB-687
SE-INM	BN2	84
SE-ION	46D	19
SE-IOU	MU-2	304
SE-IOV	MU-2	337
SE-IOX	MU-2	331
SE-IOY	MU-2	265
SE-IOZ	MU-2	320
SE-IPB	441	0254
(SE-IPH)	F406	0005
SE-IRH	100	B-122
SE-IRM	MIVC	AT-495B
SE-IRP	200	BB-288
SE-IRR	PC6	667
SE-IUA	MU-2	345
~~SE-IUB~~	~~MU-2~~	~~616~~
SE-IUG	31T	8104024
SE-IUN	200	BB-616
SE-IUP	200	BB-847
SE-IUV	690C	11681
SE-IUX	200	BB-675
SE-IUZ	200	BB-196
SE-IVA	MU-2	666
SE-IVI	200	BB-480
SE-IVZ	200	BB-1007
SE-IXA	200	BB-1175
~~SE-IXC~~	~~200~~	~~BB-1210~~
SE-IXL	46D	37
SE-IYB	31T	7920038
SE-IYU	200	BB-712
SE-IYX	690A	11259
SE-IZB	200	BB-521
SE-KBX	MU-2	247
SE-KBY	PA42	5501010
SE-KDG	31T	8020088
SE-KDK	200	BB-909
SE-KFP	200C	BL-132
SE-KGK	200	BB-1310
SE-KGO	MU-2	755SA
SE-KHM	31T	8166064
SE-KIP	46D	131
SE-KKM	200	BB-932
SE-KLC	200	BB-1333
SE-KND	200	BB-1070
(SE-KNX)	TBM7	60
SE-KOL	300	FA-189
SE-KOM	441	0257
SE-KON	200C	BL-4
SE-KVL	200	BB-829
SE-KXL	300	FA-204
SE-KXM	200	BB-459
SE-KXN	200	BB-619
SE-KYL	200	BB-221
SE-KYY	690A	11259
SE-LAX	BN2	431
SE-LBZ	P68	221
SE-LCB	200C	BL-139
SE-LCE	200	BB-1355
SE-LCT	300	FA-25
SE-LDL	100	B-213
SE-LDM	200	BB-531
SE-LDV	G1	82
SE-LEN	90	LJ-418
SE-LFV	G1	82
SE-LGN	BN2	377
SE-LKI	P68	366
SE-LKY	200C	BL-127
SE-LLU	350	FL-175
SE-LMM	200	BB-920
SE-LMN	200	BB-1255
SE-LMO	200	BB-1281
SE-LMP	200C	BL-134
SE-LTL	200	BB-582
SE-LTM	46T	97090
SE-LUB	31T	7820051
SE-LVU	200	BB-1692
SE-LVV	200	BB-1537
SE-LYG	P68	279
SE-LYL	46D	124
SE-LYY	PA42	5527010
SE-LYZ	P750	113
SE-LZU	690A	11121
SE-LZX	690B	11367
SE-MAZ	200	BB-1522
SE-MBE	P68	441

Slovenia

See also S5-

SL-CAE	441	0150

Poland

SP-DSA	200G	BY-3
(SP-FNH)	300	FA-227
SP-FNS	350	FL-134
SP-IKY	200	BB-1995
(SP-KEZ)	PC12	488
SP-KGW	200	BB-716
SP-KKH	31T	8120041
SP-KWA	P68	239
SP-KWB	P68	124
SP-MXH	P180	1079
SP-MXI	P180	1124
SP-NEB	90	LJ-1285
(SP-NLL)	46T	97338
SP-NLL	46T	97338

Sudan

ST-ADE	PC6	645
ST-ADF	PC6	650
ST-ADG	PC6	651
ST-ADH	PC6	655
ST-ADJ	BN2	116
ST-AEU	PC6	616
ST-AEV	PC6	666
ST-AEW	PC6	732
ST-AFO	90	LJ-669
ST-AFR	PC6	340
ST-AFU	BN2	750
ST-AGR	PC6	557
ST-AGW	PC6	599
ST-AGX	PC6	521
ST-AGY	PC6	600
ST-AGZ	90	LJ-726
ST-AHD	PC6	514
ST-AHE	PC6	565
ST-AIR	90	LJ-619
ST-AIY	BN2	144
ST-ANH	90	LJ-823
ST-APW	200C	BL-38
ST-BBA	200	BB-341
ST-DAL	300	FA-204
ST-HAL	200	BB-1695
ST-SFS	200	BB-539

Egypt

SU-AYB	BN2	728
SU-AYD	200	BB-353
SU-BAX	200	BB-353
SU-BMW	350	FL-173
SU-BNJ	200	BB-1664
SU-MMN	350	FL-476
SU-PAA	200	BB-1024
SU-PAC	90	LJ-1031
SU-UAA	90	LJ-1418
SU-ZAA	90	LJ-1353
SU-ZBA	200	BB-1518

Greece

SX-ABT	31T	7620023
SX-ABU	31T	7920071
SX-ABV	31T	7720062
SX-AFB	PC6	694
SX-AFC	PC6	691
SX-AGQ	MU-2	665
SX-APJ	200	BB-401
SX-AVA	31T	8020026
SX-AVB	31T	8020027
SX-AVC	31T	8020038
SX-AVE	31T	7620018
SX-BBS	BN2	621
SX-BBV	BN2	622
SX-BBX	BN2	334
SX-BBY	BN2	616
SX-BBZ	BN2	435
SX-BFA	BN2	399
SX-BFB	BN2	403
SX-BFC	BN2	316
SX-BFD	BN2	399
SX-BFE	BN2	435
SX-BFF	BN2	399
SX-BFG	BN2	316
SX-BFH	BN2	461
SX-BFQ	31T	7820039
SX-BFR	31T	7620018
SX-BGO	90	LJ-874
SX-BGT	MIVA	AT-038
SX-BKY	90	LJ-1334
SX-BNC	P180	1036
SX-BND	P180	1038
SX-CBN	TRIS	319
SX-CPG	TRIS	1055
SX-CVM	TRIS	1054
SX-DKA	BN2	2114
SX-DKB	BN2	2004
SX-ECG	200	BB-372
SX-FDC	31T	7720063

Bangladesh

S2-ACD	PC6	670
S2-AED	PC12	538
S2-AEV	P180	1193

Slovenia

See also SL-

S5-CAE	441	0150
S5-CAI	690A	11121
S5-CAM	S600	006
S5-CEC	200	BB-1662
S5-CEJ	31T	1104015
S5-CER	P68	231
S5-CGS	46D	22
S5-CMA	PC6	791
S5-CMO	90	LJ-1360
S5-DGN	46D	225
S5-DJC	46T	97366

Seychelles

See also VQ-S

S7-AAA	BN2	540
S7-AAC	BN2	814
S7-AAD	BN2	589
S7-AAE	BN2	603
S7-AAG	TRIS	1052
S7-AAH	BN2	384
S7-AAI	F406	0051
S7-AAJ	BN2	289
S7-AAK	BN2	748
S7-AAM	F406	0035
S7-AAN	TRIS	1026
S7-AAO	MIII	T-417
S7-AAU	BN2	589
S7-IDC	F406	0035
S7-IDO	F406	0035
S7-SMB	200	BB-1316

Sao Tome

S9-	G1	167
S9-BAA	350	FL-220
S9-CAM	350	FL-163
S9-CAN	350	FL-294
S9-IHD	F406	0048
S9-NAA	90	LJ-50
S9-NAO	200	BB-1348
S9-NAP	200C	BL-135
S9-NAQ	200	BB-836
S9-NAU	G1	6
S9-NAV	G1	323
S9-NAY	350	FL-59
S9-TAM	BN2	53
S9-TAP	350	FL-102

Turkey

TC-ACN	200	BB-791
TC-AEM	90	LJ-1275
TC-AUT	90	LJ-622
TC-AUV	90	LJ-587
TC-AUY	200	BB-333
TC-AYK	200	BB-1938
TC-BPS	MIVA	AT-044
TC-CHS	200	BB-1203
TC-CSA	90	LJ-801
TC-DBY	200	BB-791
TC-DBY	200	BB-821
TC-DBZ	90	LJ-703
TC-DHA	350	FL-37
(TC-DHC)	350	FL-63
TC-EEE	PA42	5527036
TC-FAG	PA42	5501031
TC-FAH	PA42	5501033
TC-FBI	BN2	3014
TC-FBK	BN2	2192
TC-FBL	BN2	2040
TC-FBZ	200	BB-110
TC-FIR	200	BB-1082
TC-FRT	90	LJ-910
(TC-HCY)	200	BB-883
TC-IHC	90	LJ-771
TC-KOC	200	BB-1312
TC-KUN	BN2	272
TC-KUR	BN2	290
TC-LMK	90	LJ-1080
TC-MAZ	90	LJ-1412
TC-MCK	90	LJ-962
TC-MDE	200	BB-1539
TC-MGB	200	BB-1375
TC-MNK	350	FL-63
TC-MSS	90	LJ-1276
TC-NAZ	90	LJ-787
TC-NML	F90	LA-104
TC-OPM	200	BB-1701
TC-OPN	425	0177
TC-OZD	200	BB-1496
TC-OZY	200	BB-1545
TC-RZL	690A	11265
TC-SAB	350	FL-63
TC-SAY	200	BB-1149
TC-SCM	PA42	5527036
TC-SDR	200	BB-1086
TC-SKO	200	BB-1334
TC-SMA	G1	172
TC-TAA	200	BB-122
TC-TAB	200	BB-131
TC-TAT	200	BB-1568
TC-THK	PA42	5501031
TC-TKG	BN2T	2231
TC-UPS	MIVA	AT-044
TC-YPI	200	BB-883
TC-YSM	200	BB-1086

Iceland

TF-ARA	BN2	2040
TF-ARB	BN2	2192
TF-ARG	BN2	3014
TF-BMW	P68	389
TF-DCA	E90	LW-84
TF-ELI	200	BB-468
TF-ELT	200	BB-276
TF-ELT	200	BB-468
TF-ELT	425	0163
TF-ELT	E90	LW-116
TF-ERR	690A	11172
TF-ETP	P68	219
TF-FHL	MU-2	660
TF-FHM	MU-2	1543SA
TF-FMS	200	BB-1221
TF-GTM	P68	79
TF-ISA	P68	79
TF-JMC	MU-2	669
TF-JVI	P68	79
TF-MYX	200	BB-1136
TF-ORD	F406	0047
TF-ORF	441	0057
TF-ORN	BN2	789
TF-RED	BN2	383
TF-REH	BN2	19
(TF-REJ)	BN2	8
TF-REJ	BN2	179
TF-RTO	BN2	142
"TF-UUU"	200	BB-1221
TF-VEB	P68	79
TF-VEG	BN2	2240
TF-VEJ	BN2	2209
TF-VEJ	P68	290
TF-VEL	P68	219
TF-VEN	P68	284
TF-VEY	P68	109
TF-VLH	31T	7720011

Guatemala

TG-	681	6036
TG-	690A	11162
TG-	200	BB-267
(TG-)	695	95047
TG-	F90	LA-54
TG-	MIII	T-240
TG-AKE	PC6	816
TG-AMI	681	6032
TG-ASC	PC12	767
TG-ASE	MU-2	407SA
TG-ATP	690A	11175
TG-AVE	31T	7820033
TG-BAC	90	LJ-1399
TG-BAD	690	11005
TG-BAQ	90	LJ-1399
TG-BET	E90	LW-251
TG-BOC	PC6	794
TG-CBI	200	BB-1959
TG-CCA	90	LJ-1364
TG-CFA	F90	LA-181
TG-COB	31T	8120003
TG-CPG	300	FA-47
TG-CYC	31T	8020003
TG-DAM	680W	1821-35
TG-EAB	31T	8020045
TG-EME	90	LJ-1364
TG-FRD	MU-2	253
TG-FYL	200	BB-1808
TG-GAP	31T	7820058
TG-GMI	681	6032
TG-GOL	31T	8020003
TG-HCR	31T	8020032
TG-HYD	200	BB-1479
TG-JAC	690	11005
(TG-JAC)	690	11030
TG-KAD	200	BB-481
TG-LAR	31T	7820084
TG-LEF	690C	11699
TG-LEM	695A	96002
TG-LIA	31T	7920024
TG-LIA	31T	8120043
TG-MDN	300	FA-105
TG-MDN-P	300	FA-105
TG-MEE	690B	11472
TG-OIL	200	BB-1794
TG-OIL	31T	8020003
TG-PAF	441	0111
TG-PAF	P68	357
TG-POL	90	LJ-859
TG-PYD	680T	1593-41
TG-RBL	90	LJ-698
TG-REB	BN2	101
TG-RWC	90	LJ-1373
TG-RWC	90	LJ-1822
TG-SAQ	90	LJ-1373
TG-SIK	31T	1166007
TG-SUS	425	0118
TG-SYV-PA	690C	11641
TG-TEG	FPC6	2026
TG-TJB	G1	33
TG-TUC	PC6	858
TG-UGA	200	BB-125
(TG-UGA)	200	BB-751
TG-UME	441	0024
TG-VAL	31T	8120045
TG-VAS	90	LJ-782
TG-VDG	31T	7920029
TG-WIZ	681	6022
TG-ZAZ	31T	7820033
TG-ZUM	90	LJ-270

Costa Rica

TI-	680T	1709-84
TI-1063C	BN2	14
TI-AIW	BN2	154
TI-AKC	BN2	766
TI-AKD	BN2	770
TI-AKI	BN2	464
TI-ALU	BN2	592
TI-AQM	690C	11719
TI-ART	BN2	497
TI-AWM	F90	LA-76
TI-AWN	31T	7520043
TI-AXM	690A	11168
TI-AXU	690A	11139
TI-AYA	BN2	626
TI-AYN	100	B-84
TI-AYU	BN2	198
TI-AZI	90	LJ-1468
TI-AZO	E90	LW-240
TI-BBN	E90	LW-250
TI-GEV	E90	LW-268
TI-MEL	690	11022
TI-MEL	695	95056
TI-SFC	E90	LW-141
TI-TCT	200	BB-87

Cameroon

TJ-AFJ	P68	89
TJ-AGR	31T	8275025
TJ-AGS	31T	7920069
TJ-AHZ	441	0001
TJ-AIM	31T	8166061
TJ-AIQ	31T	8275025
TJ-MJP	E90	LW-321
TJ-ROF	200	BB-531
TJ-TAC	31T	7620057
TJ-WIN	G1	20

Central African Republic

TL- E90 LW-97
TL-AAQ BN2 647
TL-ABL P68 373
TL-ABU BN2 2256
TL-ADN G1 42
TL-CUC BN2 346
TL-KAA BN2 346
TL-KAF BN2 2256

Congo

TN-ACO BN2 708
TN-ADD P68 81
TN-ADH P68 94
TN-ADN BN2 647
TN-ADO MIII T-211
TN-ADP MIVA AT-025
TN-ADS BN2 127
TN-ADY BN2 764
TN-AEQ BN2T 2147
TN-AFG E90 LW-326
TN-ATR 200 BB-603

Gabon

TR-AEM 350 FL-486
TR-LAE 100 B-137
TR-LAJ F90 LA-191
TR-LAT P68 89
TR-LBB 90 LJ-4
TR-LBE 441 0320
TR-LBG PA42 8001054
TR-LBJ BN2 2127
TR-LBP 200C BL-67
TR-LCM BN2 771
TR-LCN BN2 744
TR-LCP 200 BB-780
TR-LCS 90 LJ-848
TR-LDM 200 BB-1220
TR-LDU 200 BB-1110
TR-LDX 200 BB-121
TR-LEG 200 BB-620
TR-LEQ F406 0007
TR-LNF BN2 16
TR-LNG BN2 13
TR-LOC BN2 83
TR-LOD BN2 102
TR-LOL PC6 909
TR-LQL TRIS 245
TR-LRP BN2 332
TR-LRX E90 LW-97
(TR-LRY) BN2 700
TR-LSF BN2 387
TR-LTT E90 LW-136
TR-LUR BN2 740
TR-LVH E90 LW-151
TR-LVJ E90 LW-157
(TR-LWC) 200 BB-108
TR-LWI BN2 771
TR-LWL BN2 764
TR-LWO BN2 773
TR-LWZ 200 BB-106
TR-LXW BN2 151
TR-LXX BN2 829
TR-LXY 690A 11104
TR-LYA E90 LW-247
TR-LYU BN2 744
TR-LYW BN2 838
TR-LYZ P68 201
TR-LZD P68 163
TR-LZH 200C BL-12
TR-LZK BN2 869
TR-LZS MIV AT-008
TR-LZY BN2 2101

Tunisia

TS-LAZ 31T 7720041
TS-LMB 200 BB-1049
TS-POB P68 381

Tchad

TT-AAF PC12 128
TT-BAS 441 0197
TT-BAV PC6 763
TT-KAA PC6 762
TT-KAC PC6 763

Ivory Coast

TU- 200 BB-1623
TU-TDM G1 20
TU-TFW BN2 196
TU-TJE 200 BB-163
TU-TJL 31T 7720033
TU-TJQ MIII T-288
TU-TLC BN2 292
TU-TLQ P68 142
TU-TLW 31T 8120010
TU-TOG MIVA AT-051
TU-TXQ P68 142
TU-TXW MU-2 774SA
TU-VAC G1 133
TU-VBB 200 BB-295

Mali

TZ-ACF BN2 330
TZ-ACS BN2 910
TZ-ADN BN2 2161
TZ-APV BN2 2182
TZ-ASC BN2 397
TZ-ASM BN2 700
TZ-DDG 200 BB-589
TZ-ZBC 200 BB-86
TZ-ZBE U-21 LM-64

Kiribati

T3-ATD TRIS 391
T3-ATE TRIS 1004
T3-ATG BN2 611
T3-ATH BN2 52
T3-JMR BN2 494
T3-VIN BN2 2154

San Marino

T7-BMM P68T 9002
T7-PAC P750 135
T7-SFH PC6 778
T7-SMI 200 BB-1124

Micronesia

T8-A103 BN2 2042

Kazakhstan

UN-K9001 90 LJ-1236
UN-P3101 31T 1104010
UP- PA42 8001105
UP-K3501 350 FL-76
UP-K9001 90 LJ-1236

Ukraine

UR-CCZV 46T 97147
UR-CRV 90 LJ-1348
UR-CWA 350 FL-64
UR-CWB 350 FL-46
UR-HBD 350 FL-469

Australia

VH- MU-2 516
(VH-AAB) BN2 73
VH-AAD PC12 1068
VH-AAG 690A 11101
VH-AAV 200 BB-245
VH-AAZ 200 BB-241
VH-ABX P68 99
VH-ACV P166 354
VH-AEC BN2 2164
VH-AEU BN2 2130
VH-AGB 200 BB-951
VH-AGI BN2 835
VH-AIA BN2 15
VH-AIH 200 BB-365
VH-AJM 200C BL-138
VH-AJX P68 228
VH-AJZ 350 FL-125
VH-AKT 200 BB-579
VH-AKT 200 BB-595
VH-AKV 200C BL-10
VH-AMB 200C BL-131
VH-AMH 90 LJ-552
VH-AMM 200C BL-125
VH-AMQ 200 BB-1813
VH-AMR 200 BB-1812
VH-AMR 200C BL-126
VH-AMS 200 BB-1814
VH-AMS 200C BL-133
VH-ANH 200 BB-780
VH-ANJ 441 0132
VH-APA 200 BB-259
VH-APD BN2 133
VH-APH P68 351
VH-ARZ 200 BB-1019
VH-ASA P166 409
VH-ASJ G1 52
VH-ATF 690A 11158
VH-ATI BN2 28
VH-ATK BN2 29
VH-ATS BN2 36
VH-ATU BN2 119
VH-ATV BN2 100
VH-ATW BN2 67
VH-ATY BN2 94
VH-ATZ BN2 132
VH-AUI MU-2 516
VH-AUN BN2 660
VH-AUP 200C BL-126
VH-AWU MIII T-298
VH-AYC 200 BB-1575
VH-AZB 441 0182
VH-AZW 441 0026
VH-AZY 441 0091
VH-BAY BN2 620
VH-BBA MU-2 782SA
VH-BBG P166 403
VH-BCL MIII T-226
VH-BGK 46D 89
VH-BGS TRIS 322
VH-BHK P166 370
VH-BIB 90 LJ-227
VH-BLH 690 11062
(VH-BML) TRIS 360
VH-BNX BN2 2177
VH-BPB TRIS 1025
VH-BPH F406 0078
VH-BPH TRIS 1003
VH-BPV BN2 134
VH-BQR 200C BL-131
(VH-BRC) BN2 409
VH-BRF 200C BL-125
VH-BRQ 200C BL-133
VH-BRQ BN2 614
VH-BSG TRIS 279
VH-BSL BN2 302
VH-BSN BN2 3005
VH-BSO 690C 11640
VH-BSO BN2 2129
VH-BSP TRIS 372
VH-BSS 690 11044
VH-BTL 350 FL-122
VH-BUR PA42 5527019
VH-BUW PA42 8001047
VH-BWO BN2 2042
VH-CAC P166 375
VH-CAH MIIB T26-111
VH-CAI MIIB T26-103
VH-CAJ MIIB T26-119
VH-CAK MIIB T26-172E
VH-CAL MIII T-213
VH-CAM MIII T-210
VH-CBZ 200C BL-38
VH-CCR P68 50
VH-CCW 31T 7720046
VH-CCY 441 0178
VH-CFD 441 0141
VH-CFO MIVA AT-033
VH-CFT P68 414
VH-CFZ BN2 3015
VH-CGL 100 B-154
VH-CJJ P68 445
VH-CJP MU-2 505
VH-CLT 690A 11152
VH-CMT 90 LJ-114
VH-CPG BN2 236
VH-CPN BN2 180
VH-CRA G1 171
VH-CRG 90 LJ-564
VH-CRM F90 LA-86
VH-CSS BN2 2294
VH-CSU BN2 81
VH-CWE 200 BB-470
VH-CWG BN2 188
VH-CWO 200C BL-72
(VH-CYC) TRIS 322
VH-CZM TBM7 344
VH-DAX 200 BB-1037
VH-DBF P68 37
VH-DDG E90 LW-122
VH-DHP 350 FL-339
(VH-DHW) F90 LA-153
VH-DLK 690A 11321
VH-DNA P68 29
VH-DNK P68 33
VH-DQV PC12 827
VH-DRV 31T 7820079
VH-DTV MU-2 132
VH-DXD 31T 7520037
VH-DXI 31T 8020005
VH-DXQ P750 129
VH-DYN 200 BB-690
VH-DYN 90 LJ-281
VH-EAJ P750 132
VH-EAK P750 110
VH-ECO P68 99
VH-EDI BN2 227
VH-EEN MIVC AT-563
VH-EEO MIVC AT-564
VH-EEP MIVC AT-567
VH-EER BN2 832
VH-EGC MIII T-204
VH-EGE BN2 3015
VH-EGQ 425 0202
VH-EGR 425 0195
VH-EGS 425 0183
VH-EGT 425 0216
VH-EGU TRIS 1030
VH-EMJ 90 LJ-1374
VH-EMO MIII T-208
VH-ENH MU-2 718SA
VH-EQE BN2 113
VH-EQK BN2 146
VH-EQT BN2 124
VH-EQV BN2 172
VH-EQW BN2 173
VH-EQX BN2 164
VH-EQY BN2 168
VH-EQZ BN2 605
VH-EVP 441 0088
VH-EWQ 350 FL-122
VH-EXT 690B 11385
VH-FAB P68 42
VH-FAM PC12 161
VH-FAO P68 41
VH-FAP P68 45
VH-FAX P68 46

VH-FAZ	P68	53
(VH-FBK)	90	LJ-114
VH-FCJ	BN2	448
VH-FCO	BN2	845
VH-FCP	BN2	755
VH-FDA	200	BB-1986
VH-FDA	200C	BL-55
VH-FDB	200	BB-1977
VH-FDB	200C	BL-26
VH-FDC	PC12	426
VH-FDD	200	BB-1697
VH-FDE	PC12	332
VH-FDF	200	BB-1696
VH-FDG	200	BB-1172
VH-FDG	200	BB-2012
VH-FDI	200	BB-1037
VH-FDJ	PC12	861
VH-FDK	PC12	466
VH-FDM	90	LJ-1024
VH-FDM	PC12	428
VH-FDO	200	BB-1056
VH-FDP	90	LJ-968
VH-FDP	PC12	434
VH-FDR	200	BB-1881
VH-FDR	200C	BL-39
VH-FDS	200C	BL-68
VH-FDT	200	BB-1990
VH-FDT	90	LJ-842
VH-FDW	200	BB-1880
VH-FDW	90	LJ-1011
VH-FDZ	200	BB-1882
VH-FDZ	90	LJ-1021
VH-FGR	PC12	438
VH-FGS	PC12	440
VH-FGT	PC12	442
(VH-FHH)	P68	54
VH-FII	200	BB-653
VH-FIL	200	BB-617
(VH-FIS)	TBM7	52
VH-FIX	350	FL-90
VH-FLD	BN2	158
VH-FLE	BN2	89
(VH-FLF)	BN2	116
(VH-FLF)	BN2	124
VH-FLF	BN2	141
VH-FLO	G1	100
VH-FMC	PC12	109
VH-FMF	PC12	110
VH-FMN	200C	BL-47
VH-FMP	PC12	122
VH-FMQ	441	0109
VH-FMW	PC12	123
VH-FMZ	PC12	138
VH-FOM	90	LJ-1024
VH-FOP	90	LJ-968
VH-FOZ	690B	11380
VH-FSA	P166	360
VH-FSB	PC6	628
VH-FSC	P166	414
VH-FSE	MU-2	101
VH-FSH	P68	18
VH-FSI	P68	80
VH-FWA	441	0026
VH-FZB	PC6	634
VH-GAB	695A	96032
VH-GOA	P166	378
VH-GOB	P166	400
VH-GOC	P166	403
VH-GOE	P166	373
VH-GTI	90	LJ-1874
VH-HBM	425	0151
VH-HEO	200C	BL-41
VH-HIA	BN2	415
VH-HIG	PC12	772
VH-HLJ	200	BB-945
VH-HMA	31T	7520028
VH-HMZ	441	0017
VH-HPA	200	BB-1155
VH-HPJ	350	FL-166
VH-HPL	BN2	3004
VH-HPP	200C	BL-137
VH-HPT	350	FL-83
VH-HPW	200	BB-1504
VH-HPX	200	BB-1505

VH-HPZ	200C	BL-138
VH-HTU	200	BB-964
VH-HUU	P68	351
VH-HWD	441	0038
VH-HWO	200	BB-1641
VH-HXL	31T	8166055
VH-HXM	441	0106
VH-IAE	BN2T	2112
VH-IAM	MU-2	517
VH-IBC	200	BB-74
VH-IBD	200	BB-297
VH-IBE	200	BB-518
VH-IBF	200	BB-813
VH-IBS	BN2	761
VH-IBZ	BN2	785
VH-ICA	TBM7	205
VH-ICM	P68	356
VH-ICO	425	0202
VH-ICO	TBM7	69
VH-ICV	E90	LW-63
VH-IFA	BN2	856
VH-IGT	BN2	503
VH-IHJ	MIII	TT-459A
VH-IHK	31T	8120002
VH-IJQ	441	0174
VH-ILB	90	LJ-1375
VH-ILM	P68	356
VH-IMP	200	BB-1366
VH-INB	BN2	2177
VH-INO	BN2	2221
VH-IOA	BN2	842
VH-ISA	BN2	159
VH-ISB	BN2	195
VH-ISC	BN2	207
VH-ISD	BN2	145
VH-ISE	BN2	278
VH-ISF	BN2	281
VH-ISG	BN2	18
(VH-ISH)	BN2	325
VH-ISI	BN2	329
VH-ISL	BN2	432
VH-ISL	BN2	2131
VH-ISW	PA42	8001047
VH-ITA	200	BB-1244
VH-ITA	200T	BT-6
VH-ITH	200	BB-344
(VH-ITH)	200	BB-463
VH-ITM	200	BB-1512
VH-IWO	200	BB-1639
VH-IWT	31T	8166044
VH-IXB	P68	154
VH-IXC	P68	164
VH-IXD	P68	168
VH-IXE	P68	178
VH-IXH	P68	186
VH-IYA	P68	114
VH-IYB	P68	118
VH-IYC	P68	119
VH-IYD	P68	123
VH-IYE	P68	124
VH-IYF	P68	128
VH-IYG	P68	132
VH-IYH	P68	134
VH-IYI	P68	136
VH-IYJ	P68	112
VH-IYK	P68	138
VH-IYL	P68	140
VH-IYM	P68	143
VH-IYN	P68	146
VH-IYO	P68	148
VH-JCB	MIII	TT-468A
VH-JEB	441	0095
VH-JEC	425	0183
VH-JEJ	MU-2	612
VH-JER	425	0184
VH-JER	MU-2	521
VH-JES	MU-2	516
VH-JET	90	LJ-1464
VH-JFD	441	0095
VH-JHP	350	FL-343
VH-JJR	200	BB-1019
VH-JLK	PC12	126
VH-JLT	441	0138
VH-JMU	MU-2	549

VH-JMU	PC12	445
VH-JMZ	MU-2	561
VH-JPJ	G1	191
VH-JQM	P68	154
VH-JSO	TBM7	173
VH-JUU	BN2	632
VH-JVB	441	0231
VH-JVL	441	0352
VH-JVN	F406	0033
VH-JWO	681	6039
VH-JWO	MU-2	037
VH-KBH	200	BB-1189
VH-KBO	P68	448
VH-KCH	200	BB-1125
VH-KDJ	441	0070
VH-KDK	200	BB-908
VH-KDN	441	0130
VH-KDT	350	FL-443
VH-KDV	300	FA-165
VH-KDX	350	FL-361
VH-KFE	200	BB-1172
VH-KFG	90	LJ-777
VH-KFN	200C	BL-31
VH-KFT	TBM7	92
VH-KGT	200G	BY-8
VH-KGW	PA42	7800002
VH-KJD	350	FL-125
VH-KJD	350	FL-194
VH-KJD	350	FL-443
VH-KMS	200	BB-1667
VH-KNA	200	BB-813
VH-KNR	200	BB-813
VH-KOF	MU-2	544
VH-KOH	MU-2	521
VH-KQB	90	LJ-1350
VH-KRG	MIIB	T26-143
VH-KRX	680W	1751-4
VH-KTE	200	BB-320
VH-KUZ	441	0138
VH-KWO	PC12	363
VH-KZL	200C	BL-9
VH-LAB	200T	BT-23
VH-LBA	441	0042
VH-LBC	441	0164
VH-LBC	441	0236
VH-LBD	441	0296
VH-LBX	441	0091
VH-LBY	441	0023
VH-LBZ	441	0038
VH-LCA	P68	298
VH-LCI	BN2	857
VH-LEM	441	0081
VH-LFD	441	0164
VH-LFH	E90	LW-255
VH-LHA	BN2	856
VH-LHK	200	BB-344
VH-LJG	90	LJ-1020
VH-LJK	31T	7920026
VH-LJR	P68	41
VH-LKB	200	BB-259
VH-LKF	200	BB-660
VH-LLS	90	LJ-538
VH-LMC	690D	15026
VH-LMU	MU-2	689
VH-LNJ	200C	BL-41
VH-LOA	200	BB-1463
VH-LQH	90	LJ-644
VH-LRJ	46D	56
VH-LRX	BN2	504
VH-LTI	695A	96063
VH-LTJ	695A	96069
VH-LTK	695A	96075
VH-LTM	695B	96208
VH-LTN	695A	96078
VH-LTO	695A	96085
VH-LVG	690B	11551
VH-LWO	200	BB-1643
VH-LYG	90	LJ-1020
VH-MBF	BN2	646
VH-MBK	BN2	158
VH-MET	BN2	758
VH-MIB	BN2	217
VH-MIT	MU-2	720SA
VH-MIU	MU-2	798SA

VH-MKA	350	FL-110
VH-MKN	BN2	73
VH-MKR	200	BB-518
VH-MKT	PC6	689
VH-MLG	350	FL-389
VH-MLU	MU-2	1527SA
VH-MMP	P166	365
VH-MNG	350	FL-162
VH-MNU	MU-2	527
VH-MQZ	200	BB-1961
VH-MRJ	TBM8	389
VH-MRJ	TRIS	322
VH-MSB	200	BB-1812
VH-MSH	200	BB-1416
VH-MSH	200	BB-1787
VH-MSM	200	BB-1430
VH-MSM	200	BB-1464
VH-MSU	200C	BL-48
VH-MSU	MU-2	439SA
VH-MSZ	200	BB-866
VH-MTG	E90	LW-222
VH-MUA	MU-2	746SA
VH-MUG	MU-2	612
VH-MUK	MU-2	310
VH-MUO	MU-2	270
VH-MUT	MU-2	612
VH-MVJ	200	BB-1842
VH-MVL	200	BB-1333
VH-MVS	200	BB-1813
VH-MVU	MU-2	1502SA
VH-MVW	200	BB-1814
VH-MVW	200	BB-1980
VH-MVX	200C	BL-153
VH-MVY	200	BB-1324
VH-MWH	200	BB-2003
VH-MWK	200C	BL-152
VH-MWO	PC12	379
VH-MWQ	200	BB-1416
VH-MWT	31T	7820054
VH-MWU	200	BB-1418
VH-MWX	200	BB-1424
VH-MWZ	200	BB-1430
VH-MWZ	MU-2	290
VH-MXK	200	BB-653
VH-MYO	200	BB-605
VH-MYO	200	BB-1472
VH-MYU	200	BB-605
VH-MZV	200	BB-859
VH-NAI	P68	286
VH-NAV	P68	275
VH-NAX	441	0106
VH-NBT	681B	6047
VH-NCM	690C	11629
VH-NEY	690	11062
VH-NFD	441	0159
VH-NGC	PC12	102
VH-NIA	200	BB-470
VH-NIB	200	BB-259
VH-NIC	200	BB-487
VH-NIE	441	0043
VH-NIF	441	0232
VH-NIH	200	BB-12
VH-NKI	P68	100
VH-NKW	TRIS	381
VH-NMA	PA42	8001066
VH-NMT	690A	11152
VH-NMU	MU-2	707SA
VH-NPT	690B	11475
VH-NQH	90	LJ-655
VH-NSD	200C	BL-55
VH-NSE	200C	BL-10
VH-NSF	200C	BL-50
VH-NSG	200C	BL-9
VH-NSN	200	BB-1552
VH-NSR	200C	BL-40
VH-NSS	200	BB-12
VH-NTC	BN2	425
VH-NTE	200	BB-529
VH-NTG	200C	BL-9
VH-NTH	200C	BL-12
VH-NTS	200C	BL-30
VH-NWO	PC12	396
VH-NYA	690A	11152
VH-NYB	690	11039

VH-NYC	690	11026
VH-NYD	681	6034
VH-NYE	681B	6047
VH-NYF	681	6026
VH-NYG	681	6004
VH-NYH	681	6016
VH-NYM	MU-2	037
VH-NZA	F90	LA-153
VH-NZJ	P750	122
VH-OAA	441	0102
VH-OAP	P68	132
VH-OBJ	BN2	458
VH-OBL	BN2	2035
VH-OBS	P68	326
VH-OCH	BN2	660
VH-OCS	441	0030
VH-OIA	BN2	402
VH-OLV	P68	443
VH-OOI	PC12	827
VH-OOU	PC12	827
VH-OPM	441	0088
VH-ORE	MU-2	1513SA
VH-OTH	200C	BL-40
VH-OVC	MIII	T-318
VH-OWA	PC12	1115
VH-OWB	PC6	652
VH-OWN	200	BB-936
VH-OWP	PC12	1032
VH-OWQ	PC12	1052
VH-OWR	PC12	1082
VH-OXA	200	BB-1420
VH-OXE	350	FL-122
VH-OXF	350	FL-122
VH-OXF	350	FL-361
VH-OXL	200	BB-1423
(VH-OXR)	200C	BL-138
VH-OYA	200	BB-365
VH-OYC	200	BB-951
VH-OYD	200	BB-1041
VH-OYE	200	BB-355
VH-OYH	200	BB-148
VH-OYK	200C	BL-41
VH-OYT	200T	BT-6
VH-PAP	P166	357
VH-PAR	P166	401
VH-PAU	P166	366
VH-PCD	690B	11414
VH-PCE	PC12	551
VH-PCV	690A	11283
VH-PCX	P68	235
VH-PFJ	90	LJ-1586
VH-PFK	90	LJ-1586
VH-PFK	90	LJ-1915
VH-PFN	P68	78
VH-PFO	P68	90
VH-PFP	P68	91
VH-PFQ	P68	95
VH-PFR	P68	96
VH-PFS	P68	99
VH-PFU	P68	100
VH-PGA	P166	374
VH-PGN	P68	249
VH-PHP	350	FL-372
VH-PID	PC12	231
VH-PIL	200	BB-487
VH-PIL	PC12	231
VH-PIL	PC12	1007
VH-PIU	PC12	231
VH-PJC	690B	11475
VH-PJC	695B	96208
VH-PNC	P166	357
VH-PNC	P68	37
VH-PND	P166	401
VH-PNF	PC6	580
VH-PNG	PC6	584
VH-PNH	PC6	615
VH-PNJ	BN2	354
VH-PNN	P68	50
VH-PNP	P68	51
VH-PNQ	P68	63
VH-PNR	P68	64
VH-PNS	P68	71
VH-PNT	P68	73
VH-PNU	P68	84
VH-PNV	P68	85
VH-PNW	P68	65
VH-PNX	P68	66
VH-PNY	P68	70
VH-PNZ	P68	77
VH-PPJ	200T	BT-6
"VH-PQA"	P166	370
VH-PQA	P166	410
VH-PSK	350	FL-29
VH-PTG	PA42	5527034
VH-PTG	TBM7	52
VH-PTH	425	0044
(VH-PUE)	P68	270
(VH-PUG)	P68	271
VH-PUZ	P68	268
VH-PWK	200	BB-1019
VH-PYN	350	FL-525
VH-RCA	F406	0050
VH-RCB	F406	0033
VH-RCI	MIII	TT-474
VH-REL	PC6	693
VH-RFX	200	BB-1056
VH-ROV	BN2	81
VH-RQW	BN2	73
VH-RSW	31T	8166001
VH-RTK	BN2	194
VH-RTP	BN2	79
VH-RTV	BN2	152
VH-RUT	BN2	165
VH-SAM	90	LJ-655
VH-SBD	BN2	500
VH-SBH	BN2	406
VH-SBM	200	BB-964
VH-SCQ	350	FL-150
VH-SFV	690B	11475
VH-SGQ	350	FL-150
VH-SGQ	350	FL-461
VH-SGT	200	BB-73
VH-SGV	200	BB-718
VH-SJJ	31T	8304003
VH-SKC	200	BB-47
VH-SKG	BN2	609
VH-SKN	200	BB-690
VH-SKU	200	BB-165
VH-SLM	BN2	112
VH-SLS	P68	351
VH-SMA	PC6	656
VH-SMB	200	BB-355
VH-SMB	PC6	657
(VH-SMF)	P166	354
VH-SMF	P166	355
VH-SMO	441	0132
VH-SMT	200	BB-162
VH-SMZ	200	BB-1155
VH-SMZ	200	BB-1490
VH-SMZ	MU-2	741SA
VH-SMZ	TBM8	366
VH-SPQ	200	BB-355
VH-SQH	90	LJ-730
VH-SQS	BN2	494
VH-SSD	MIII	T-213
VH-SSL	MIII	T-210
VH-SSL	MU-2	712SA
VH-SSM	MIII	T-204
VH-SVQ	690B	11380
VH-SWC	200	BB-1329
VH-SWK	MIII	T-296
VH-SWO	200C	BL-12
VH-SWP	200	BB-529
VH-SWP	MIVA	AT-033
VH-SYU	BN2	769
VH-TAM	90	LJ-919
VH-TAZ	441	0005
VH-TBO	TBM7	220
VH-TCU	P68	239
VH-TFB	441	0260
VH-TFG	441	0236
VH-TFW	441	0023
VH-THS	200	BB-12
VH-TLD	441	0179
VH-TLQ	P68	33
VH-TLX	200	BB-550
VH-TNP	31T	7920026
VH-TNQ	200C	BL-30
VH-TNZ	31T	7920064
(VH-TPM)	46T	97089
VH-TPM	46T	97089
VH-TRS	200C	BL-2
VH-TRW	BN2	815
VH-TSS	690B	11463
VH-TTD	31T	8020005
VH-TWI	BN2	800
VH-TXC	BN2	761
VH-TXF	BN2	763
VH-TXG	BN2	768
VH-TXH	BN2	753
VH-TXL	BN2	756
(VH-TXL)	BN2	757
VH-TZH	BN2	75
VH-UBB	MIII	T-331
VH-UBD	BN2	140
VH-UBN	BN2	421
VH-UCR	MIII	TT-426A
VH-UHP	350	FL-346
VH-UIC	PC6	660
VH-UJG	690	11062
(VH-UJN)	681B	6047
VH-ULX	425	0124
VH-UQN	BN2	145
VH-URJ	BN2	402
VH-URU	200	BB-1150
VH-USD	200	BB-881
VH-USD	BN2	450
VH-UUA	MIVC	AT-502
VH-UUG	P68	227
VH-UUJ	MU-2	612
VH-UUP	P68	220
VH-UVT	690C	11619
VH-UWV	BN2	654
VH-UZA	MIII	TT-444A
VH-UZA	MIVC	AT-502
VH-UZB	MU-2	528
VH-UZC	MU-2	519
VH-UZD	MU-2	513
VH-UZI	MIVC	AT-570
VH-UZN	MU-2	527
VH-VAT	PC12	203
VH-VCB	200	BB-579
VH-VED	441	0272
VH-VEH	441	0238
VH-VEJ	441	0249
VH-VEM	441	0174
VH-VEW	441	0264
VH-VEY	441	0295
VH-VEZ	441	0182
VH-VHP	350	FL-348
VH-VME	P68	417
VH-VMV	P68	435
VH-VPC	BN2	521
VH-VRI	P68	430
VH-VTF	PC12	1045
VH-VWO	PC12	400
VH-WBI	PC12	617
VH-WCE	PA42	8001033
VH-WGQ	BN2	76
VH-WGT	BN2	646
VH-WHP	350	FL-349
VH-WHP	350	FL-389
VH-WJT	F90	LA-117
VH-WJY	200	BB-1875
VH-WLH	200C	BL-26
VH-WLO	690	11030
VH-WLS	690	11030
VH-WMU	MU-2	512
VH-WMW	MU-2	544
VH-WMY	46T	97165
VH-WNH	200	BB-148
VH-WNI	200	BB-185
VH-WNT	90	LJ-552
VH-WPA	G1	114
VH-WPE	PC12	704
VH-WPT	BN2	835
VH-WPY	PC12	720
VH-WRF	BN2	3004
VH-WRM	BN2	3015
VH-WRR	BN2	882
VH-WWA	90	LJ-504
VH-WYY	MU-2	521
VH-WZD	BN2	450
VH-WZE	BN2	354
VH-WZF	BN2	537
VH-WZG	P68	63
VH-WZK	BN2	421
VH-WZN	200	BB-963
VH-WZP	BN2	2284
VH-WZP	P68	228
VH-WZQ	P68	100
VH-XBC	441	0297
VH-XCB	200	BB-1472
VH-XDB	200	BB-533
VH-XDV	200	BB-1100
VH-XDW	200	BB-1258
VH-XFB	200	BB-531
VH-XFF	BN2	763
VH-XFI	BN2	605
VH-XHP	350	FL-350
VH-XHP	350	FL-426
VH-XLC	P750	120
VH-XLI	P68	228
VH-XLS	P750	105
VH-XMD	441	0025
VH-XMG	441	0130
VH-XMJ	441	0113
VH-XMZ	MU-2	371SA
VH-XRF	200	BB-165
VH-XRP	200	BB-327
VH-XTB	TBM7	166
VH-YBP	200G	BY-60
VH-YDH	200	BB-1401
VH-YDN	PC12	301
VH-YDO	PC12	102
VH-YEH	200	BB-1463
VH-YFD	441	0157
VH-YHP	350	FL-351
VH-YHP	350	FL-437
VH-YIE	BN2	2154
VH-YIF	P750	153
VH-YJG	690A	11308
VH-YJP	690A	11173
VH-YNE	200	BB-605
VH-YOJ	PC12	1122
VH-YOL	441	0106
VH-YVH	BN2T	2145
VH-YVH	BN2T	4009
VH-YWO	PC12	725
VH-YZE	F406	0076
VH-YZF	F406	0078
VH-YZG	F406	0079
VH-ZBD	PC12	837
VH-ZCZ	PC6	731
VH-ZEK	200	BB-1083
VH-ZGQ	90	LJ-1345
VH-ZGS	350	FL-484
VH-ZHP	350	FL-439
VH-ZHP	350	FL-651
VH-ZKA	350	FL-341
VH-ZKM	PC12	795
VH-ZKM	PC12	842
VH-ZMM	PC12	638
VH-ZMO	200	BB-470
VH-ZMP	200	BB-259
VH-ZOR	200	BB-762
VH-ZOS	200	BB-145
VH-ZVM	P750	126
VH-ZWJ	P68	112
VH-ZWO	PC12	467
VH-ZZE	F406	0076
VH-ZZF	F406	0078
VH-ZZG	F406	0079
VH-ZZT	BN2	2279
VH-ZZU	BN2	2280
VH-ZZV	BN2	2281
VH-ZZW	BN2	2282
VH-ZZX	BN2	2283
VH-ZZY	BN2	2284

Vietnam

VN-B444	350	FL-417
VN-B594	200	BB-1329

Anguilla

VP-AAA BN2 382
VP-AAB BN2 3008
VP-AAC BN2 919
VP-AAE BN2 905
VP-AAF BN2 2024
VP-AAG BN2 88
VP-AAS BN2 206

Bermuda
See also VR-B
VP-BBB PC12 407
VP-BBB PC12 422
VP-BBG P180 1037
VP-BBK 200 BB-1519
VP-BCT 695B 96208
VP-BDR 425 0199
VP-BJT 425 0027
VP-BKD PC12 369
VP-BKW 90 LJ-805
VP-BLK 690C 11672
VP-BLS PC12 176
VP-BMK 300 FA-202
VP-BMZ 690D 15033
VP-BNM 425 0027
VP-BRR 690A 11259
VP-BYR 200 BB-1202

Cayman Islands
See also VR-C
VP-CCT 90 LJ-1028
VP-CHE 200 BB-1569
VP-CII BN2 883
VP-CLA F90 LA-231
VP-CMA 200 BB-1564
VP-CRI 350 FL-66
VP-CRS P180 1011
VP-CYA P180 1166
VP-CYC P180 1185

Falkland Islands

VP-FAY BN2 872
VP-FBD BN2 2160
VP-FBF BN2 2125
VP-FBG BN2 2126
VP-FBI BN2 2188
VP-FBM BN2 2200
VP-FBN BN2 2216
VP-FBO BN2 2218
VP-FBR BN2 2252

Belize
See also V3-
VP-HBI BN2 177
VP-HBX BN2 627
VP-HCD BN2 374
VP-HCT BN2 571
VP-HCU BN2 610
VP-HDV BN2 908

Leeward & Windward Islands

VP-LAC BN2 80
VP-LAD BN2 153
VP-LAE BN2 160
VP-LAF BN2 161
VP-LAG BN2 163
VP-LCF BN2 557

Montserrat

VP-LMB TRIS 1041
VP-LMF BN2T 2102
VP-LMG BN2 70
VP-LMG BN2 2152
VP-LMH BN2 147

British Virgin Islands

VP-LV 100 B-166
VP-LVA BN2 635
VP-LVB BN2 193
VP-LVD BN2 170
"VP-LVE" BN2 170
VP-LVG BN2 389
VP-LVP BN2 2155

Solomon Islands

VP-PAM BN2 613
VP-PAO TRIS 349
VP-PAS BN2 173
VP-PAT BN2 172
VP-PAU BN2 605

St Vincent
See also J8-
VP-VAG TRIS 1037
VP-VAH BN2 2018

Rhodesia
See also Z-
VP-WEX BN2 619
VP-WHX BN2 192
VP-WLE P68 149
VP-WLL P68 245
VP-WMT P68 106

Fiji
See also DQ-
VQ-FBO BN2 195
VQ-FBP BN2 614

Grenada
See also J3-
VQ-GAB BN2 59

St Lucia
See also J6-
VQ-LAQ BN2 197
VQ-LAS BN2 612
VQ-LAT BN2 610

Seychelles
See also S7-
VQ-SAC BN2 287
VQ-SAH BN2 384
VQ-SAJ BN2 289
VQ-SAK BN2 748
VQ-SAN TRIS 1026

Turks & Caicos Islands

VQ-TAA BN2 2016
VQ-TAB BN2 2019
VQ-TAD TRIS 1029
VQ-TAG BN2 635
VQ-TAH BN2 154
VQ-TAJ TRIS 1009
VQ-TDA BN2 504
VQ-THL BN2 858
VQ-TIU 200C BL-131
VQ-TRS 200C BL-133

Swaziland
See also 3D-
VQ-ZIP G1 38
VQ-ZIZ MIIB T26-171E

Bermuda
See also VP-B
VR-BBI BN2 137
VR-BBK 200 BB-1519
VR-BBY G1 48
VR-BDM 200 BB-206
VR-BDM 200 BB-292
VR-BDR 425 0199
VR-BGN 200 BB-338
VR-BHQ MIII T-212
VR-BHT 90 LJ-352
VR-BKF 31T 8104070
VR-BKW 90 LJ-805
VR-BKX 200 BB-1321
VR-BLK 690C 11672
VR-BMZ 690D 15033
VR-BNM 425 0027
VR-BNN 200 BB-1180
VR-BPH 441 0268
VR-BTI G1 71

Cayman Islands
See also VP-C
VR-CAA TRIS 1008
VR-CAE G1 55
VR-CBP 695 95069
VR-CCI 200 BB-416
VR-CCT 90 LJ-1028
VR-CGK E90 LW-59
VR-CII BN2 883
VR-CRI 350 FL-66
VR-CSH 350 FL-9
VR-CTN G1 20

Hong Kong
See also B-H
VR-HZM 200C BL-128
VR-HZN 200C BL-130
(VR-HZO) BN2 615

British Cameroons

VR-NDO P166 377

Brunei

VR-UDV 90 LJ-338

India

VT- MIIB T26-101
VT-ACD 350 FL-465
VT-ACG PC12 562
VT-AEL 200 BB-1788
VT-AJV 90 LJ-1159
VT-ASB F406 0031
VT-ATX BN2 126
VT-AVB B100 BE-121
VT-BAF 200 BB-1939
VT-BAL 200 BB-1563
VT-BHL 350 FL-105
VT-BSA 200 BB-1485
VT-CIL 200 BB-1469
VT-CSK 200 BB-1567
VT-CTG 200 BB-1947
VT-DAF 200 BB-1563
VT-DAR PC12 251
VT-DAV PC12 252
VT-DDS 200 BB-1896
VT-DEJ 90 LJ-1404
VT-DXU 90 LJ-308
VT-DYZ BN2 606
VT-EAN BN2 608
VT-EBB 200 BB-1486
VT-EBG 90 LJ-1752
VT-ECA 90 LJ-537
VT-EFB 90 LJ-706
VT-EFE 90 LJ-711
VT-EFF 90 LJ-705
VT-EFG 90 LJ-719
VT-EFP 90 LJ-720
VT-EFZ 90 LJ-790
VT-EGQ B100 BE-121
VT-EGR 90 LJ-967
VT-EHB 200 BB-972
VT-EHK 200 BB-985
VT-EHY 90 LJ-1008
VT-EID 200C BL-56
VT-EIE 200C BL-63
VT-EJZ 90 LJ-1100
VT-ELZ F90 LA-233
VT-EMI 90 LJ-1135
VT-EMJ 90 LJ-1137
VT-ENL 200 BB-1248
VT-ENM 200 BB-1236
VT-EOA 200C BL-129
VT-EPA 200 BB-1254
VT-EPY 200 BB-1277
VT-EQD 200 BB-1272
VT-EQK 200 BB-1288
VT-EQM 300 FA-128
VT-EQN 90 LJ-1167
VT-EQO 90 LJ-1153
VT-ESR 200 BB-739
VT-ETI 90 LJ-1160
VT-EUJ 200 BB-1456
VT-FAE 200 BB-1918
VT-FIU 350 FL-478
VT-GUJ 200 BB-1687
VT-HIS 200 BB-1982
VT-HRA 200 BB-1906
VT-HYA 90 LJ-1376
VT-IOO PC12 568
VT-IRC 350 FL-112
VT-JIL 90 LJ-1573
VT-JKC 200 BB-1198
VT-JKK 350 FL-552
VT-JNK 350 FL-160
VT-JOY P68 436
VT-JPK 90 LJ-1278
VT-JRD 90 LJ-1485
VT-JSL PC12 782
VT-JVL 200 BB-1815
VT-KPC 90 LJ-1696
VT-LJS 350 FL-526
VT-LKK 200 BB-1895
VT-LMW 200 BB-1998
VT-LNT 200 BB-1468
VT-MEG PC12 135
VT-MGJ 350 FL-192
VT-MNM 350 FL-105
VT-MPG 200 BB-1445
VT-MPT 200 BB-1775
VT-NEF 90 LJ-890
VT-NEI 90 LJ-1116
VT-NKF 90 LJ-1402
VT-PPC 90 LJ-1371
VT-RAM 90 LJ-790
VT-REL 90 LJ-1604
VT-REM 200 BB-1700
VT-RJA 200 BB-1943
VT-RLK 90 LJ-1278
VT-RLL 90 LJ-1369
VT-RNB P180 1161
VT-RSB 200 BB-1317
VT-RSL 90 LJ-1560
VT-RSM 200 BB-1758
VT-RSN 200 BB-1631
VT-SAA F406 0050
VT-SAB 200 BB-1305
VT-SAC F406 0033
VT-SAD 200 BB-1341
VT-SAE 200 BB-1342
VT-SAF 200 BB-1343
VT-SAZ 200 BB-1831
VT-SDJ 200 BB-1567
VT-SFL 90 LJ-1496
VT-SKI BN2T 2264
VT-SKM 90 LJ-1810
VT-SLK 90 LJ-1270
VT-SLS 200 BB-575
VT-SRC 200C BL-139
VT-SSL 90 LJ-1751

VT-SUN	BN2T	2287
VT-TAA	PT68	001
VT-TAB	PT68	002
VT-TAC	PT68	003
VT-TAD	PT68	004
VT-TAE	PT68	005
VT-TAH	PT68	C-3006
VT-TAI	PT68	C-3007
VT-TAS	PC12	472
VT-TET	P180	1183
VT-TIS	90	LJ-1393
VT-TLA	PT68	C-3008
VT-TLB	PT68	C-3009
VT-TLC	PT68	C-3010
VT-TLD	PT68	C-3011
VT-TLE	PT68	C-3012
VT-TLF	PT68	C-3013
VT-TLH	PT68	C-3014
VT-TSA	PC12	445
VT-TVS	200	BB-1572
VT-UAB	200	BB-1914
VT-UBA	90	LJ-711
VT-UPA	300	FA-230
VT-UPR	200	BB-1818
VT-UPZ	90	LJ-1400
VT-VHL	200	BB-1267
VT-VIL	90	LJ-1374
VT-VSM	200	BB-1723
VT-XRM	NALS	SP02
VT-XSD	NALS	SP01
VT-YUD	200	BB-1764

Antigua

V2-	BN2	97
V2-LAC	BN2	80
V2-LAD	BN2	153
V2-LAE	BN2	160
V2-LAF	BN2	161
V2-LAG	BN2	163
V2-LCF	BN2	557
V2-LCI	TRIS	1037
V2-LCL	BN2	2006
V2-LCM	P68	280
V2-LDC	P68	365
V2-LDE	BN2	2152
V2-LDF	BN2T	2102
V2-LDI	BN2	919
V2-LDL	BN2	532
V2-LDM	BN2	2180
V2-LDR	P68	262
V2-LDV	BN2	741
V2-LEG	P68	302
V2-LFE	BN2	2251
V2-LFP	BN2	2211
V2-LMB	TRIS	1041

Belize
See also VP-H

V3-HBI	BN2	177
V3-HCT	BN2	571
V3-HCU	BN2	610
V3-HDV	BN2	908
V3-HEP	BN2	572
V3-HEZ	BN2	3008
V3-HFA	BN2	839
V3-HFB	BN2	907
V3-HFB	BN2	2023
V3-HFO	BN2	465
V3-HGE	BN2	911
V3-HGK	BN2	853
V3-HIA	BN2	2015
V3-HRT	BN2	876

St. Kitts & Nevis

V4-AAA	BN2	532

Namibia

V5-AAL	200C	BL-4
V5-AIR	441	0095
V5-BDL	200	BB-1325
V5-CCH	31T	7820085
V5-CIC	200	BB-85
V5-CSB	90	LJ-675
V5-DAC	690C	11732
V5-DHL	F406	0062
V5-EEZ	F406	0004
V5-FMR	F406	0093
V5-INN	90	LJ-523
V5-JKB	200	BB-72
V5-KLH	200	BB-630
V5-KLT	F90	LA-44
V5-LCA	PA42	8001030
V5-LIL	200	BB-1047
V5-LSY	31T	8166031
V5-LYZ	425	0021
V5-MAC	690B	11557
V5-MAD	F406	0013
V5-MDA	F406	0058
V5-MED	E90	LW-87
V5-MFN	690B	11422
V5-MGF	690B	11432
V5-MJW	425	0077
V5-MNF	200	BB-15
V5-MSK	200	BB-597
V5-ODH	PC6	874
V5-RTZ	300C	FM-1
V5-TSO	PC12	247
V5-WAK	F406	0048
V5-ZEN	PC12	125

Micronesia

V6-01FM	BN2	2014
V6-03FM	BN2	660
V6-SFM	BN2	2014

Marshall Islands

V7-0009	BN2	65

Mexico

XA-	425	0108
XA-	425	0216
XA-	441	0198
XA-	690B	11423
XA-	690B	11549
XA-	695A	96075
XA-	P68	315
XA-	100	B-158
XA-	200	BB-49
XA-	200	BB-79
XA-	200	BB-122
XA-	200	BB-240
XA-	200	BB-572
XA-	200	BB-610
XA-	200	BB-611
XA-	200	BB-618
XA-	200	BB-708
XA-	200	BB-833
XA-	200	BB-881
XA-	200	BB-915
XA-	200G	BY-6
XA-	31T	7620046
XA-	31T	7620049
XA-	31T	7720049
XA-	31T	7820060
XA-	31T	7820077
XA-	31T	7920062
XA-	31T	8020082
XA-	31T	8166025
XA-	90	LJ-200
XA-	90	LJ-287
XA-	90	LJ-399
XA-	90	LJ-536
XA-	90	LJ-1753
XA-	90	LJ-1773
XA-	90	LJ-1788
XA-	90	LJ-1840
XA-	90	LJ-1843
XA-	90	LJ-1872
XA-	90	LJ-1905
XA-	C-12	BC-23
XA-	E90	LW-14
XA-	E90	LW-238
XA-	E90	LW-263
XA-	F90	LA-168
XA-	MIIB	T26-149E
XA-	MIIB	T26-158
XA-	MIII	T-229
XA-	MIII	T-252
XA-	MIII	T-282
XA-	MIV	AT-009
XA-	PA42	5527007
XA-	PC12	456
XA-	PC12	674
XA-	PC12	1042
XA-ABB	MIII	T-251
XA-ABH	690B	11454
XA-ACG	90	LJ-548
XA-AFI	690B	11410
XA-AGG	F90	LA-193
XA-ALK	G1	138
XA-ALT	300	FA-176
XA-ANS	P180	1088
XA-ASR	200	BB-395
XA-AVJ	300	FA-95
XA-BLU	PC12	481
XA-BOG	690A	11218
XA-BUB	MU-2	104
XA-BWA	PC12	775
XA-CAB	350	FL-341
XA-CAG	681	6023
XA-CAH	200	BB-60
XA-CAK	90	LJ-92
XA-CAZ	BN2	427
XA-CGT	90	LJ-1829
XA-CHA	200	BB-516
XA-CHM	690D	15040
XA-CIC	90	LJ-342
XA-CIQ	BN2	300
XA-CLE	690A	11144
XA-COJ	31T	7520038
XA-COQ	90	LJ-469
XA-COS	690	11031
XA-CPR	90	LJ-1758
(XA-CUC)	TRIS	1060
XA-CUJ	BN2	324
XA-CUL	BN2	24
XA-CYR	PA42	5527032
XA-DAV	BN2	331
XA-DEA	100	B-68
XA-DER	690	11060
XA-DEU	BN2	326
XA-DEW	BN2	356
XA-DID	MU-2	635
XA-DID	MU-2	641
XA-DIF	690	11074
XA-DII	680W	1788-18
XA-DIM	BN2	681
XA-DIS	MU-2	608
XA-DOG	690A	11128
XA-EAM	90	LJ-1738
XA-EAM	90	LJ-1842
XA-EGE	90	LJ-1624
XA-EJS	PA42	5501008
XA-EMO	690D	15030
XA-EOC	690A	11225
XA-ESM	90	LJ-1138
XA-FCV	350	FL-251
XA-FEG	690A	11170
XA-FEQ	BN2	358
XA-FEX	E90	LW-113
XA-FFG	PC12	868
XA-FIC	BN2	390
XA-FIZ	690A	11188
XA-FUA	BN2	388
XA-FUB	200	BB-27
(XA-GAC)	690	11060
XA-GAS	PC12	832
XA-GAY	200	BB-48
XA-GAZ	BN2	486
XA-GEL	BN2	467
XA-GEM	690A	11267
XA-GFM	200	BB-1892
XA-GOL	MU-2	197
XA-GSA	90	LJ-1551
XA-GSM	90	LJ-1132
XA-GUT	BN2	490
XA-HAY	31T	7720008
XA-HER	31T	7400009
XA-HIT	BN2	819
XA-HNG	31T	7920041
(XA-HOI)	TRIS	1048
XA-HPS	200	BB-1838
XA-IEQ	31T	7720055
XA-IEX	BN2	2013
XA-IIM	BN2	598
XA-IIW	690	11050
XA-IIY	200	BB-395
XA-ILV	G1	93
XA-IOE	200	BB-37
XA-IOH	BN2	592
XA-ISL	90	LJ-961
XA-IUC	MU-2	397SA
XA-IUJ	MU-2	740SA
XA-JAG	90	LJ-1623
XA-JEA	MU-2	754SA
XA-JEK	BN2	855
XA-JET	MU-2	414SA
XA-JGS	31T	7820089
XA-JIM	200	BB-592
XA-JOF	31T	7520010
XA-JOS	PC12	504
XA-JPA	690C	11650
XA-JPE	TRIS	1051
XA-JPV	690B	11455
XA-JSC	MIII	T-294
XA-JUB	200	BB-346
XA-JUC	MU-2	512
XA-JUY	690A	11170
XA-JUY	690C	11621
XA-JYM	690C	11680
XA-KAB	690B	11468
XA-KEY	441	0108
XA-KGH	200	BB-1322
XA-KIB	MU-2	777SA
XA-KOM	90	LJ-910
XA-KOO	690C	11631
XA-KOP	TRIS	1046
XA-KOQ	TRIS	1045
XA-KUE	90	LJ-923
XA-KUR	F90	LA-79
XA-KUU	690	11042
(XA-LEI)	695	95044
XA-LEJ	695	95046
XA-LEK	695	95042
(XA-LEO)	441	0030
XA-LER	MU-2	689
XA-LEY	690A	11168
XA-LGT	F90	LA-45
XA-LIG	200	BB-802
XA-LIY	690B	11427
XA-LIZ	TRIS	1043
XA-LOJ	31T	8120030
XA-LOO	F90	LA-147
(XA-LOP)	90	LJ-961
XA-LOS	425	0051
(XA-LOT)	200C	BL-27
XA-LOW	200	BB-841
XA-LOZ	B100	BE-122
XA-LUL	425	0075
XA-LUU	695A	96004
XA-LUZ	200	BB-869
XA-MAO	BN2	2104
XA-MAP	BN2	2105
XA-MAS	G1	42
XA-MAW	200	BB-27
XA-MAY	200	BB-948
XA-MCB	200	BB-1151
XA-MCB	31T	8166034
XA-MHA	441	0108
XA-MHT	BN2	451
XA-MIA	200	BB-869

XA-MIC	PC12	884
XA-MII	200	BB-958
XA-MIM	90	LJ-342
XA-MIN	200C	BL-46
XA-MIX	300	FA-93
XA-MSC	90	LJ-1653
XA-MUR	90	LJ-63
XA-MUS	100	B-132
XA-MYR	G1	71
XA-NAZ	300	FA-47
XA-NTC	690B	11370
XA-OAC	441	0311
XA-OAC	MU-2	1544SA
XA-OCI	B100	BE-72
XA-PAC	690A	11320
XA-PAH	441	0108
XA-PAK	100	B-47
XA-PAU	200	BB-37
XA-PCA	PC12	680
XA-PCM	PC12	405
XA-PEE	300	FA-93
XA-PEH	441	0337
XA-PEL	441	0083
XA-PEM	F90	LA-204
XA-PES	300	FA-83
XA-PEU	200	BB-48
XA-PEW	690C	11699
XA-PEX	200	BB-60
XA-PEZ	441	0176
XA-PGT	31T	7620034
XA-PIE	300	FA-114
XA-PIF	300	FA-108
XA-PIQ	BN2	892
XA-PIR	690A	11302
XA-PJA	BN2	228
XA-PMX	200	BB-114
XA-PMX	200	BB-478
XA-POK	90	LJ-1138
XA-POW	690A	11178
XA-POX	BN2	907
XA-POY	300	FA-14
XA-PQZ	441	0142
XA-PSG	PA42	5501019
XA-PUA	G1	35
XA-PUD	300	FA-169
XA-PUM	690C	11632
XA-PUY	690	11018
XA-RAO	690A	11144
XA-RAS	690A	11155
XA-RCG	350	FL-277
XA-RDJ	200	BB-1907
XA-RDM	441	0083
XA-REB	690B	11382
XA-REC	690C	11721
XA-REF	441	0015
XA-REH	90	LJ-923
XA-RFG	690B	11400
XA-RFH	90	LJ-1741
XA-RFN	90	LJ-1246
XA-RGL	90	LJ-1232
XA-RIV	G1	199
XA-RJB	G1	159
XA-RJV	200	BB-559
XA-RKO	690C	11621
XA-RLB	31T	8104068
XA-RLK	G1	138
XA-RLN	425	0051
XA-RLW	PA42	7801004
XA-RLZ	MU-2	326
XA-RMG	690B	11371
XA-RMH	90	LJ-74
XA-RML	BN2	864
XA-RMR	B100	BE-122
XA-RMT	31T	7820060
XA-RMX	200	BB-814
XA-RMZ	690A	11254
XA-RNF	E90	LW-79
XA-RNL	MU-2	777SA
XA-ROE	F90	LA-147
XA-RPD	690A	11342
XA-RPY	690B	11551
XA-RQD	F90	LA-236
XA-RQM	90	LJ-1226
XA-RQQ	200	BB-588
XA-RRE	MU-2	757SA
XA-RRM	BN2	390
XA-RRV	441	0104
XA-RSC	200	BB-565
XA-RTQ	690A	11119
XA-RUI	90	LJ-519
XA-RVH	200	BB-1365
XA-RVJ	200	BB-995
XA-RWA	690C	11687
XA-RWJ	MIIB	T26-175
XA-RWP	MU-2	740SA
XA-RWR	31T	7920047
XA-RXE	90	LJ-1279
XA-RXT	90	LJ-1280
XA-RYF	690	11010
XA-RZH	200	BB-833
XA-RZS	690A	11161
XA-RZV	BN2	525
XA-SAW	F90	LA-95
XA-SBG	200	BB-60
XA-SBU	PA42	8001071
XA-SBW	31T	7720068
XA-SCG	90	LJ-1003
XA-SCJ	690B	11526
XA-SEK	PA42	8001017
XA-SEQ	690A	11252
XA-SFD	690B	11534
XA-SFY	200	BB-850
XA-SGQ	90	LJ-630
XA-SHP	681B	6063
XA-SKG	BN2	819
XA-SKJ	441	0021
(XA-SLL)	690B	11521
XA-SOE	690C	11731
XA-SPW	690A	11175
XA-STD	441	0015
XA-SUL	200	BB-1859
XA-SWE	100	B-34
XA-SXW	PC6	870
XA-SYV	690C	11641
XA-TAY	31T	7620034
XA-TAY	F90	LA-43
XA-TBM	441	0083
XA-TBT	G1	12
XA-TBT	G1	136
XA-TCK	690D	15001
XA-TCS	MU-2	375SA
XA-TDJ	G1	127
XA-TDW	90	LJ-1375
XA-TEH	TRIS	1056
XA-TFE	200	BB-1483
XA-TFQ	690A	11332
XA-THE	690B	11400
XA-TIL	PA42	8001071
XA-TJD	U-21	LM-16
XA-TJH	PA42	8001039
XA-TJN	200	BB-1681
XA-TLD	FPC6	2026
XA-TLW	441	0237
XA-TMP	F90	LA-44
XA-TNR	STAR	NC-36
XA-TOR	690C	11661
XA-TQD	690A	11185
XA-TQF	STAR	NC-49
XA-TTR	90	LJ-1524
XA-TTU	G1	58
XA-TVO	200	BB-1752
XA-TWB	F90	LA-147
XA-TWZ	PC12	461
XA-TXE	90	LJ-1645
XA-TXK	90	LJ-584
XA-TYU	TRIS	1040
XA-UAO	PC12	333
XA-UBA	PC12	512
XA-UBD	TRIS	1044
XA-UES	PC12	585
XA-UET	350	FL-455
XA-UFN	PC12	701
XA-UFZ	690C	11635
XA-ULE	90	LJ-1924
XA-ULF	90	LJ-1925
XA-VID	300	FA-14
XA-VIP	PA42	5501058
XA-XAL	200	BB-1661
XA-YAS	90	LJ-1479
XA-ZEC	200	BB-1803
(XB-)	690A	11111
XB-ACA	441	0232
XB-ACM	200	BB-48
XB-ACO	695	95051
XB-AEA	690A	11199
XB-AEB	690A	11202
XB-AEL	690	11074
XB-AEU	E90	LW-75
XB-AHK	90	LJ-1593
XB-AIN	PA42	5501048
XB-ALD	BN2	525
XB-AOC	695	95040
XB-AQQ	MU-2	632
XB-ARE	MU-2	605
XB-ARF	MU-2	687
XB-ATC	695A	96091
XB-ATO	441	0319
XB-AUR	681	6040
XB-AUV	MIII	T-251
XB-BED	690A	11188
XB-BGH	690B	11534
XB-BHP	MU-2	743SA
XB-BLU	MU-2	757SA
XB-BNB	690B	11519
XB-BOF	90	LJ-168
XB-BON	441	0155
XB-BRB	200	BB-395
XB-BRR	31T	8020042
XB-BXU	200	BB-654
XB-BZQ	90	LJ-316
XB-CDI	690B	11548
XB-CED	680T	1714-88
XB-CGP	F90	LA-95
XB-CIJ	G1	10
XB-CIO	90	LJ-387
XB-CIP	100	B-47
XB-CMY	31T	7820033
XB-CSB	441	0314
XB-CUF	681	6023
XB-CZX	690	11065
XB-DCT	200	BB-1068
XB-DIP	MIII	T-328
XB-DIV	695	95046
XB-DJN	681	6023
XB-DJX	MU-2	777SA
XB-DJZ	90	LJ-923
XB-DKJ	90	LJ-74
XB-DKQ	690B	11503
XB-DLS	E90	LW-238
XB-DMT	690B	11360
XB-DQP	F90	LA-79
XB-DSA	695	95046
XB-DSF	695A	96015
XB-DSH	690C	11631
XB-DTD	680W	1788-18
XB-DTO	695	95042
XB-DTW	690C	11650
XB-DVG	G1	35
XB-DVH	BN2	390
XB-DVV	MU-2	414SA
XB-DWX	690C	11621
XB-DXX	695	95042
XB-DYZ	690C	11699
XB-DZP	690B	11410
XB-DZV	PA42	7801004
XB-EBD	690A	11277
XB-EBZ	BN2	24
XB-ECL	90	LJ-1132
XB-ECT	695A	96004
XB-ECX	690A	11331
XB-EDZ	200	BB-48
XB-EFN	MU-2	034
XB-EFU	MU-2	740SA
XB-EFZ	MIII	T-328
XB-EGT	690B	11371
XB-EGZ	31T	7720055
XB-EHC	200	BB-1267
XB-EIH	690A	11214
XB-EJW	690A	11290
XB-ELW	31T	7720032
XB-EMA	BN2	901
XB-EQT	441	0044
XB-ESO	G1	15
XB-ETM	690B	11529
XB-EVU	PA42	8001081
XB-EWO	441	0235
XB-EXC	690A	11225
XB-EYL	46D	38
XB-EYZ	PA42	5527009
XB-EZL	PA42	8001057
XB-FBY	MU-2	754SA
XB-FCD	441	0142
XB-FDE	31T	8004033
XB-FJF	90	LJ-296
XB-FJM	90	LJ-315
XB-FKC	690B	11406
XB-FLF	690A	11169
XB-FLL	G1	58
XB-FMJ	90	LJ-1132
XB-FMS	425	0051
XB-FMV	MU-2	034
XB-FND	441	0155
XB-FNS	BN2	252
XB-FNU	BN2	901
XB-FOT	90	LJ-168
XB-FQC	690A	11144
XB-FQM	MU-2	458SA
XB-FRW	90	LJ-550
XB-FSG	31T	8166047
XB-FUB	G1	27
XB-FVK	441	0148
XB-FXK	425	0091
XB-FXS	690A	11107
XB-FXU	31T	7904053
XB-FYD	690	11065
XB-FYK	690A	11162
XB-GAL	31T	1104009
XB-GAS	90	LJ-519
XB-GAW	G1	136
XB-GBN	441	0021
XB-GBR	690C	11641
XB-GCU	690B	11460
XB-GCV	690C	11677
XB-GDS	690B	11371
XB-GDY	P68	214
XB-GEC	200	BB-1086
XB-GGZ	31T	7720068
XB-GIW	90	LJ-342
XB-GJL	690	11074
XB-GJQ	690B	11503
XB-GMT	690C	11677
XB-GMY	90	LJ-270
XB-GQI	31T	8004056
XB-GQU	690A	11277
XB-GRY	FPC6	2026
XB-GTP	90	LJ-63
XB-GUG	BN2	10
XB-GVI	31T	8020008
XB-HCL	90	LJ-388
XB-HDY	200	BB-423
XB-HGG	690A	11257
XB-HGY	31T	7720027
XB-HHA	300	FA-14
XB-HMI	90	LJ-1549
XB-HNA	31T	7920012
XB-HOV	MU-2	156
XB-HPC	F90	LA-17
XB-HQW	90	LJ-1280
XB-HSE	690A	11225
XB-HUL	681B	6063
XB-HVO	31T	7820012
XB-HYM	46D	232
XB-HYP	31T	8120030
XB-IEI	E90	LW-55
XB-IGG	690B	11503
XB-IHK	200	BB-423
XB-IHX	PC12	166
XB-IKO	PC12	493
XB-ILT	31T	7820032
XB-ILU	PC12	143
XB-IMT	200	BB-8
XB-ING	100	B-34
XB-IRY	690B	11503
XB-ISC	690A	11145
XB-IVQ	200	BB-6
XB-JCT	E90	LW-170

XB-JDK PC12 348
XB-JGR G1 161
XB-JIC 31T 7720060
XB-JII MU-2 170
XB-JIO 690C 11695
XB-JLA E90 LW-333
XB-JMC F90 LA-186
XB-JNA 690B 11503
XB-JNC PA42 8001104
XB-JNN 90 LJ-1199
XB-JQC MIII T-220
XB-JRF F90 LA-186
XB-JTA BN2 323
XB-JTE STAR NC-33
XB-JTJ 441 0153
XB-JVV 100 B-170
XB-JYE 200 BB-873
XB-JYM 690B 11521
XB-JYN 46D 182
XB-JZO 200 BB-65
XB-JZP 200 BB-225
XB-KBC 200 BB-1932
XB-KBI 441 0139
XB-KBX 441 0319
XB-KCQ 200 BB-160
XB-KCY 690B 11537
XB-KFC 441 0232
XB-KFD 695 95052
XB-KLY 690B 11563
XB-KSB MIII T-249
XB-KSW P180 1157
XB-KUE 690 11065
XB-KWX 690B 11375
XB-LGR 690B 11481
XB-LIJ MU-2 259
XB-LIJ MU-2 341
XB-LVE MU-2 641
XB-MAZ 90 LJ-410
XB-MCB 200 BB-1151
XB-MMR 31T 7720055
XB-MSF 90 LJ-1499
XB-MVG 350 FL-271
XB-NBI 690A 11144
XB-NEB MU-2 583
XB-NOE 100 B-34
XB-NUG MU-2 619
XB-NUV 100 B-128
XB-OCI 690B 11359
XB-ORA 200 BB-225
XB-ORA 695 95066
XB-PAO 681 6010
XB-PEZ 90 LJ-342
XB-PRO MU-2 743SA
XB-PSA 690B 11537
XB-PUF E90 LW-79
XB-QIY E90 LW-113
(XB-RAB) 690A 11188
XB-REA 100 B-68
XB-RHO 200 BB-395
XB-RLM 31T 7920023
XB-RRG MU-2 777SA
XB-RTG 31T 7920012
XB-RUE MU-2 637
XB-RYA 90 LJ-1533
XB-RZH 300 FA-203
XB-SAH 690B 11406
XB-SCH 31T 7904031
XB-SFS 90 LJ-173
XB-SHP 681B 6063
(XB-SIR) 90 LJ-498
XB-SLG 100 B-132
XB-SSL 90 LJ-1815
XB-SUR MU-2 197
XB-SYV 690C 11641
XB-TFS 200 BB-8
XB-TIM MU-2 103
XB-TON MU-2 525
XB-TWL 690B 11382
XB-TYS PA42 5501048
XB-UBA 90 LJ-1728
XB-VAD G1 27
XB-VIW G1 27
XB-VUW 90 LJ-92
XB-WAG BN2 24
XB-WID 681B 6052
XB-WOS 100 B-47
XB-WUI 100 B-4
XB-WWG PA42 5527006
XB-XOI MU-2 189
XB-XUC 690A 11115
XB-YAZ 90 LJ-44
XB-YET 681B 6061
XB-ZAA 90 LJ-63
XB-ZAO MIIB T26-149E
XB-ZAO MIII T-286
XB-ZIP MU-2 273
XC-AA10 441 0319
XC-AA11 441 0142
XC-AA12 441 0232
XC-AA15 695 95061
XC-AA16 695A 96084
XC-AA19 695A 96056
XC-AA20 300 FA-115
XC-AA20 695A 96091
XC-AA23 695A 96001
XC-AA27 690C 11652
XC-AA29 690C 11606
XC-AA33 695A 96024
XC-AA36 690C 11678
XC-AA37 441 0275
XC-AA38 200 BB-48
XC-AA38 695 95020
XC-AA39 690D 15009
XC-AA46 300 FA-95
XC-AA48 200 BB-369
XC-AA49 300 FA-83
XC-AA50 200 BB-1108
XC-AA53 G1 179
XC-AA54 300 FA-158
XC-AA56 690C 11695
XC-AA57 G1 103
XC-AA61 G1 42
XC-AA62 695 95068
XC-AA67 695 95000
XC-AA71 441 0189
XC-AA72 300 FA-87
XC-AA74 441 0019
XC-AA79 200 BB-156
XC-AA80 300 FA-74
XC-AA81 200 BB-928
XC-AA82 441 0155
XC-AA84 695 95052
XC-AA85 690B 11382
XC-AA98 695 95045
XC-ADP 200 BB-156
XC-AGS 90 LJ-1132
XC-ALB 695 95052
XC-ALI 690B 11503
XC-ALO 690C 11606
XC-BAD 690C 11659
XC-BAP 690A 11257
XC-BAU G1 85
XC-BCN 200 BB-435
XC-BCN 200 BB-874
XC-BDR 690D 15009
XC-BIB FPC6 2069
XC-BIC FPC6 2021
XC-BIO G1 21
XC-CAU 690A 11170
XC-CDA 690A 11280
XC-CEN 690C 11631
XC-CHI 350 FL-166
XC-CII BN2 819
XC-CIR 690A 11331
XC-CLQ 200 BB-1958
XC-COJ BN2 323
XC-COL 690B 11448
XC-CRM BN2 470
XC-CTL 200 BB-1661
XC-CUA 31T 7904026
XC-CUL 695A 96010
XC-DAB BN2 313
(XC-DAC) 695 95045
XC-DEY 90 LJ-92
XC-DIB BN2 864
XC-DIJ 200 BB-100
XC-DIK 200 BB-364
(XC-DIR) B100 BE-93
XC-DIS BN2 250
XC-DUI BN2 881
XC-DUJ BN2 892
XC-DUK BN2 883
XC-DUL BN2 882
XC-DUM BN2 893
XC-DUN BN2 884
XC-DUO BN2 885
XC-DUP BN2 894
XC-DUR BN2 891
XC-DUS BN2 895
XC-DUT BN2 900
XC-DUU BN2 897
XC-DUV BN2 906
XC-DUW BN2 901
XC-DUY BN2 907
XC-DUZ 690C 11641
XC-ENL 695 95052
XC-EZS MU-2 512
XC-FAJ MU-2 173
XC-FEE BN2 2022
(XC-FEL) 690 11042
XC-FEL MU-2 103
XC-FER 90 LJ-74
XC-FIK BN2 255
XC-FIK BN2 420
XC-FIS 100 B-101
XC-FIW 100 B-110
XC-FIX 100 B-114
XC-FIY BN2 294
XC-FNV BN2 895
XC-FOC 90 LJ-553
XC-FOE BN2 2031
XC-FOJ BN2 293
XC-FUC 100 B-132
XC-FUG MIV AT-006
XC-FUJ 690 11042
XC-FUR 90 LJ-92
XC-FUS 200 BB-825
XC-FUS 90 LJ-270
XC-FUT 695 95044
XC-FUV 690 11050
XC-FUY E90 LW-33
XC-GAS 690B 11556
XC-GAU BN2 307
XC-GEC BN2 2024
XC-GEI G1 66
XC-GFM 90 LJ-74
XC-GIG 690A 11128
XC-GIM 690A 11169
XC-GIR 690C 11621
XC-GOA BN2 378
XC-GOL 200 BB-435
XC-GON 441 0224
XC-GOO 441 0208
XC-GOQ BN2 286
XC-GRO BN2 911
XC-HAA 690C 11677
XC-HAB 690C 11688
XC-HAC 695A 96015
XC-HFA MIII T-238
XC-HFN 695A 96043
XC-HFV 695A 96056
XC-HFX 695 95020
XC-HFZ 695A 96035
XC-HGG 695 95051
XC-HGH 695 95072
XC-HGI 300 FA-114
XC-HGJ 690C 11652
XC-HGL 695 95061
XC-HGV 300 FA-83
XC-HGW 695A 96084
XC-HGX 695A 96091
XC-HHH 690C 11649
XC-HHI 695 95040
XC-HHM 695 95072
XC-HHS 690B 11450
XC-HHU 441 0275
XC-HHY 690C 11678
XC-HHZ 695A 96013
XC-HMO 690B 11560
XC-HUA 695A 96091
XC-HYC G1 51
XC-ICP 90 LJ-176
XC-IFA 690C 11609
XC-IMC B100 BE-93
XC-IMS G1 35
XC-JAI 200 BB-1108
XC-JAL 690B 11417
XC-JBP 690B 11382
XC-JCT 690A 11331
XC-JDB 690D 15009
XC-JDK BN2 774
XC-JDN BN2 820
XC-JEH 690C 11678
XC-KAG 690C 11621
XC-KAY 200 BB-369
XC-LAP 441 0245
XC-LGC 695A 96024
XC-LGE 441 0275
XC-LHD 695A 96056
XC-LIE G1 148
XC-LIM 690C 11606
XC-LJQ 690C 11662
XC-MLM 690A 11277
XC-MLM 690D 15028
XC-NAY 690A 11115
"XC-NCL" 695A 96086
XC-OAX 690C 11656
(XC-ONA) 100 B-101
XC-ONA 90 LJ-293
XC-PFB 695 95018
XC-PGB 690C 11652
XC-PGR 200 BB-317
XC-PPF 695 95061
XC-PPM 690A 11271
XC-QET 31T 8020019
XC-RAM 690 11021
XC-ROX 690A 11202
XC-ROX 690B 11471
XC-SAH 690B 11516
XC-SIB BN2 353
XC-SIC MIII T-235
XC-SLP 200 BB-725
XC-SPI 690B 11406
XC-SPP 690B 11410
XC-STA 690B 11447
XC-TAB 690A 11128
XC-TAB 690B 11504
XC-TAG 690B 11382
XC-TJN 200 BB-1681
XC-TXA 690C 11631
XC-TXA 695 95045
XC-UAT 200 BB-1674
XC-UAT 31T 7620046
XC-UJW 695 95000
XC-UJX 441 0019
XC-UPJ BN2 267
XC-UPJ BN2 307
XC-UPK BN2 286
XC-UPL BN2 323
XC-UPZ PA42 7801004
XC-UTA 695A 96001
XC-UTE MIII T-235
XC-UTF MIV AT-006
XC-UTG 90 LJ-270
XC-VER 690A 11280
XC-VES 690B 11481
XC-VNC G1 58
XC-ZCL 695A 96084

Burkina Faso

XT-IGB 200 BB-1487
XT-MAX 200 BB-742
XT-MBA 200 BB-698
XT-MBD 200 BB-1311

Kamphuchea

XU-008 200 BB-881
XU-999 90 LJ-281
XU-BAE BN2 190
XU-HBB 90 LJ-510
XU-MLA BN2 401
XU-MLB BN2 414

XU-MLC	BN2	400
XU-MTA	BN2	401
XU-MTB	BN2	414
XU-MTC	BN2	400

Laos

XW-PBI	PC6	553
XW-PBL	PC6	556
XW-PBQ	PC6	554
XW-PCB	PC6	567
XW-PCC	PC6	568
XW-PCE	PC6	571
XW-PCH	PC6	576
XW-PCI	PC6	523
XW-PCK	PC6	591
XW-PCL	PC6	583
XW-PCN	PC6	594
XW-PCO	PC6	595
XW-PCQ	PC6	602
XW-PCR	PC6	603
XW-PDC	PC6	547
XW-PDG	PC6	517
XW-PDI	PC6	620
XW-PDJ	PC6	626
(XW-PDK)	PC6	631
XW-PEF	PC6	672
XW-PEK	PC6	695
XW-PEO	PC6	704
XW-PFB	PC6	581
XW-PFC	PC6	631
XW-PFD	PC6	632
XW-PFQ	PC6	667
XW-PFR	PC6	668
XW-PFW	PC6	669
XW-PGN	PC6	705
XW-PHG	PC6	711
XW-PKI	FPC6	2011

Iraq

YI-AFZ	**BN2**	**298**
YI-AHE	**BN2**	**737**
YI-AHF	**BN2**	**735**
YI-AHG	**BN2**	**738**
YI-AHZ	**P166**	**463**
YI-AIA	**P166**	**464**

Vanuatu

YJ-0019	**TRIS**	**1055**
*YJ-007	BN2	2177
YJ-008	**BN2**	**2172**
YJ-AV3	**BN2**	**483**
YJ-009	**BN2**	**65**
YJ-RV16	**BN2**	**104**
YJ-RV19	BN2	152
YJ-RV2	BN2	145
YJ-RV2	**BN2**	**172**
YJ-RV20	BN2	585
YJ-RV3	TRIS	349
YJ-RV4	BN2	220
YJ-RV5	**BN2**	**173**
YJ-RV6	BN2	81
YJ-RV6	BN2	605

Latvia

YL-CCQ	**PC6**	**950**
YL-CHD	**46T**	**97283**
YL-FBI	**P68**	**433**

Romania

YR-	**PC12**	**1099**
YR-ANF	**PA42**	**8001041**
YR-BNA	BN2	93
YR-BNB	BN2	97
YR-BNC	BN2	122
YR-BND	BN2	130
(YR-BNE)	BN2	138
YR-BNE	BN2	779
YR-BNF	BN2	138
YR-BNG	BN2	641
YR-BNH	**BN2**	**775**
YR-BNI	BN2	776
YR-BNJ	BN2	777
YR-BNK	**BN2**	**778**
YR-BNL	**BN2**	**790**
YR-BNM	**BN2**	**808**
YR-BNN	**BN2**	**804**
YR-BNO	BN2	821
YR-BNP	**BN2**	**822**
YR-BNR	**BN2**	**824**
YR-BNS	BN2	812
YR-BNT	BN2	816
YR-BNU	**BN2**	**817**
YR-BNV	**BN2**	**840**
YR-BNW	BN2	853
YR-BNX	BN2	829
YR-BNX	BN2	841
YR-BNX	BN2	898
YR-BNY	BN2	56
YR-BNY	BN2	830
YR-BNY	BN2	843
YR-BNZ	BN2	831
YR-BPA	BN2	526
YR-BPB	BN2	562
YR-BPC	BN2	543
YR-BPD	BN2	797
YR-BPE	BN2	798
YR-BPF	BN2	801
YR-BPG	BN2	579
YR-BPG	BN2	802
YR-BPH	BN2	580
YR-BPH	BN2	803
YR-BPI	BN2	825
YR-BPJ	BN2	826
YR-BPK	BN2	827
YR-CAA	**350**	**FL-73**
YR-NBU	BN2	902
YR-NBV	BN2	903
YR-NBW	BN2	899
YR-NBY	BN2	896
YR-NBZ	BN2	890
YR-RAB	**BN2**	**816**
YR-RAD	**200**	**BB-1348**

El Salvador

YS-111-N	**200**	**BB-1707**
YS-111N	441	0024
YS-15C	F406	0062
YS-210P	**E90**	**LW-268**
YS-23C	BN2	627
YS-24C	BN2	627
YS-25C	BN2	101
YS-51C	BN2	610

Serbia

"YU-1100"	31T	8020021
YU-ALF	MIVA	AT-062-2
YU-ALG	MIVA	AT-066
YU-BKT	31T	7720042
YU-BLK	**31T**	**8020006**
YU-BLU	31T	7820090
YU-BLV	441	0097
YU-BLW	200	BB-490
YU-BMF	200	BB-652
YU-BMG	441	0150
YU-BMM	**31T**	**8020021**
YU-BPF	31T	8020006
YU-BPG	**31T**	**8020012**
YU-BPH	**31T**	**8020063**
*YU-BTC	350	FL-643

Venezuela

YV-01P	690A	11264
YV-02CP	F90	LA-127
YV-02P	690A	11244
YV-02P	90	LJ-659
YV-03CP	680T	1689-69
YV-04CP	100	B-73
(YV-04CP)	100	B-87
YV-04CP	31T	8120013
YV-04CP	MU-2	573
YV-04P	100	B-83
YV-05CP	MU-2	253
YV-06CP	681	6008
YV-06CP	90	LJ-306
YV-07CP	690A	11325
YV-07P	MU-2	126
YV-08CP	31T	7520027
YV-08CP	G1	117
YV-09CP	G1	24
YV-11CP	MU-2	418SA
YV-11CP	MU-2	645
YV-19P	MU-2	126
YV-25CP	441	0111
YV-26CP	F406	0022
YV-27P	E90	LW-231
YV-28CP	G1	119
YV-29CP	690A	11323
YV-30CP	MU-2	669
YV-31CP	690A	11253
YV-32P	**90**	**LJ-1191**
YV-33CP	690B	11380
YV-34CP	441	0304
YV-34CP	MU-2	632
YV-36CP	200	BB-52
YV-36CP	B100	BE-9
YV-38CP	31T	7820091
YV-39CP	690C	11618
YV-39CP	90	LJ-629
YV-40CP	90	LJ-370
YV-42CP	200	BB-201
YV-42CP	350	FL-32
YV-45CP	690A	11220
YV-45CP	690C	11723
(YV-46CP)	31T	7720003
YV-46CP	G1	56
YV-46CP	MU-2	663
(YV-52CP)	90	LJ-190
YV-53CP	**695A**	**96067**
YV-56CP	695	95017
YV-61CP	MU-2	543
YV-62CP	31T	7920072
YV-63CP	690B	11390
YV-66CP	E90	LW-144
YV-69CP	690A	11245
YV-69CP	690A	11250
YV-70CP	90	LJ-306
YV-70CP	MU-2	399SA
YV-71P	E90	LW-146
YV-72CP	E90	LW-14
YV-74CP	200	BB-323
YV-76CP	G1	192
YV-77CP	690B	11390
YV-78CP	200	BB-301
YV-79CP	90	LJ-316
YV-80CP	690A	11285
YV-81CP	690A	11285
YV-82CP	200	BB-344
YV-82CP	G1	26
YV-83CP	695	95016
YV-83CP	G1	199
YV-83P	690C	11636
YV-85CP	G1	97
YV-86CP	690A	11329
YV-87CP	**690C**	**11654**
YV-91CP	B100	BE-5
YV-92CP	200	BB-195
YV-93CP	200	BB-677
YV-94CP	MU-2	347
YV-94P	90	LJ-390
YV-95CP	**B100**	**BE-19**
YV-97CP	31T	7620050
YV-98CP	300	FA-10
YV-98CP	31T	7620054
YV-99CP	690B	11354
YV-101CP	100	B-94
YV-102CP	690B	11443
YV-102CP	MU-2	683
(YV-104CP)	690B	11466
YV-104CP	90	LJ-817
YV-105CP	200	BB-226
YV-105CP	690C	11685
YV-106CP	200	BB-238
YV-108CP	MU-2	615
YV-108CP	MU-2	1514SA
YV-109CP	690A	11244
YV-112CP	200	BB-232
YV-112CP	350	FL-55
YV-114CP	200	BB-259
YV-116CP	690B	11377
YV-117CP	B100	BE-24
YV-118CP	E90	LW-234
YV-119CP	695	95020
YV-121CP	**200**	**BB-1398**
YV-121CP	G1	150
YV-122CP	200	BB-394
YV-122CP	E90	LW-231
YV-122CP	MU-2	629
YV-123CP	31T	7720036
YV-124CP	31T	7720047
YV-125CP	B100	BE-28
(YV-126CP)	B100	BE-28
YV-127CP	B100	BE-28
YV-127P	90	LJ-651
YV-128CP	441	0007
YV-129CP	B100	BE-39
YV-129P	695	95012
YV-129P	FPC6	2048
YV-131CP	h	BB-282
YV-132CP	31T	7720043
YV-133CP	31T	7820076
YV-134CP	200	BB-812
YV-134CP	PA42	8001010
YV-136CP	441	0022
YV-141CP	**200**	**BB-265**
YV-142CP	BN2	573
YV-143CP	200	BB-421
YV-143CP	690B	11378
YV-144CP	**MU-2**	**702SA**
YV-145CP	690B	11403
YV-145P	BN2	711
YV-146CP	31T	7400006
YV-149CP	690B	11383
YV-150CP	MU-2	212
YV-152CP	90	LJ-739
YV-158CP	**90**	**LJ-742**
YV-161CP	200	BB-290
YV-167CP	**90**	**LJ-751**
YV-168CP	200	BB-316
(YV-168P)	MU-2	539
YV-170CP	690C	11603
YV-170P	690C	11726
(YV-171CP)	E90	LW-260
YV-171P	31T	7904013
YV-172CP	90	LJ-756
YV-174CP	MU-2	695
YV-176CP	441	0063
YV-176P	MU-2	615
YV-177CP	690B	11376
YV-178CP	90	LJ-952
YV-179CP	MIII	T-273
YV-180CP	MIII	T-287
YV-181CP	690B	11402
YV-181P	90	LJ-801
YV-182CP	690B	11454
YV-187CP	31T	7920054
YV-188CP	**690B**	**11461**
YV-192CP	690A	11288
YV-193CP	31T	7720050
YV-193CP	90	LJ-766
YV-194CP	31T	7820052
YV-195CP	E90	LW-278
YV-202CP	90	LJ-786
YV-204CP	690B	11466
YV-207CP	E90	LW-296
YV-209CP	690B	11490
YV-212CP	690B	11482
YV-212P	690C	11735

YV-215CP	31T	7820071	YV-355CP	90	LJ-895	YV-477CP	90	LJ-1647	YV-726CP	E90	LW-182
YV-216CP	90	LJ-797	(YV-360CP)	690B	11568	YV-483CP	690C	11678	YV-731CP	90	LJ-1659
YV-217CP	90	LJ-801	YV-363CP	31T	8020029	YV-484CP	695A	96024	YV-732P	200	BB-35
YV-218CP	690B	11483	**YV-364C**	**695A**	**96018**	YV-485CP	690C	11698	YV-733P	690A	11207
YV-220CP	690B	11490	YV-364CP	BN2	863	YV-486C	TRIS	1047	YV-734CP	200	BB-35
YV-223CP	**90**	**LJ-789**	YV-365CP	BN2	2014	YV-486CP	F90	LA-179	YV-735P	E90	LW-176
YV-225CP	441	0067	YV-366CP	695	95006	YV-487C	TRIS	1044	YV-740CP	MIII	TT-456A
YV-227CP	690B	11464	YV-368CP	441	0273	(YV-487CP)	200C	BL-51	YV-741CP	90	LJ-898
YV-229CP	690B	11502	(YV-371CP)	F90	LA-54	YV-488C	TRIS	1012	YV-744CP	680T	1685-66
YV-229P	**690B**	**11502**	YV-371CP	F90	LA-97	YV-488CP	200	BB-1020	YV-757P	690A	11288
YV-230C	BN2	19	(YV-372CP)	F90	LA-79	YV-490CP	F90	LA-193	YV-762CP	31T	7820024
YV-236P	690A	11220	(YV-373CP)	F90	LA-66	**YV-492CP**	**690D**	**15006**	**YV-770CP**	**MIII**	**T-384**
YV-238CP	200	BB-440	(YV-377CP)	BN2	874	YV-493CP	200	BB-1090	YV-773CP	690C	11666
YV-239CP	31T	7904040	(YV-381CP)	200	BB-731	YV-494CP	200	BB-1706	YV-775CP	690B	11366
YV-242CP	**MIII**	**T-357**	YV-381CP	90	LJ-948	YV-494CP	F90	LA-197	YV-777CP	690D	15032
YV-243CP	690B	11488	(YV-384CP)	200	BB-719	YV-500CP	MIII	T-252	YV-779CP	690C	11673
YV-246CP	690A	11278	YV-385CP	200	BB-740	YV-505CP	690C	11726	YV-783CP	350	FL-313
YV-247CP	200	BB-472	(YV-386CP)	200	BB-731	(YV-506CP)	695A	96058	YV-783P	200	BB-656
YV-248CP	B100	BE-64	(YV-386CP)	200	BB-770	YV-507CP	MIII	TT-515A	YV-787CP	695	95084
YV-249CP	90	LJ-841	YV-386CP	690A	11274	YV-508C	BN2	30	YV-788CP	MIII	T-330
YV-250CP	90	LJ-852	YV-390CP	31T	8020062	YV-509C	BN2	369	YV-791CP	200	BB-261
YV-251CP	**31T**	**7920022**	YV-391P	P68	334	**YV-516CP**	**E90**	**LW-322**	YV-792CP	690C	11725
YV-252CP	690B	11512	**YV-394CP**	**690C**	**11637**	YV-521CP	690D	15022	YV-795P	BN2	345
YV-254CP	90	LJ-784	YV-395CP	MIII	T-354	**YV-522C**	**BN2**	**310**	YV-797CP	690B	11468
YV-256CP	200	BB-511	YV-397CP	200	BB-782	YV-525C	F406	0022	YV-801CP	100	B-16
YV-257CP	**200**	**BB-517**	YV-399CP	F90	LA-102	YV-527P	BN2	712	YV-804CP	P68	302
YV-258CP	31T	7920038	YV-400CP	F90	LA-108	YV-532CP	690B	11547	YV-806CP	200	BB-352
YV-258CP	**90**	**LJ-488**	**YV-401CP**	**200**	**BB-796**	**YV-533P**	**441**	**0227**	**YV-808CP**	**MIII**	**TT-435**
YV-260CP	200	BB-500	(YV-402CP)	200	BB-802	YV-533P	680W	1813-30	YV-818P	690A	11285
YV-260CP	690C	11725	(YV-402CP)	200	BB-812	YV-535CP	690C	11725	YV-818P	90	LJ-556
(YV-261CP)	200	BB-522	YV-402CP	200	BB-836	**YV-536P**	**680W**	**1813-30**	**YV-820CP**	**680W**	**1775-13**
YV-262CP	200	BB-533	YV-402CP	690A	11318	YV-539CP	MIII	TT-507	YV-822CP	690D	15030
YV-262CP	**MIII**	**TT-521**	**YV-403CP**	**200C**	**BL-23**	(YV-546CP)	695A	96031	YV-834CP	690A	11114
YV-263CP	90	LJ-865	YV-406CP	690C	11655	YV-547CP	425	0162	YV-834P	680T	1689-69
YV-266CP	425	0155	**YV-407CP**	**695**	**95067**	YV-548CP	425	0189	YV-839CP	90	LJ-1329
(YV-268CP)	690B	11534	YV-409P	MU-2	663	YV-554CP	200	BB-1026	YV-842C	690B	11547
(YV-268CP)	690B	11564	YV-410CP	90	LJ-659	(YV-554CP)	200	BB-1109	YV-849CP	690C	11610
YV-269C	BN2	345	YV-410CP	F90	LA-127	(YV-555CP)	200	BB-1092	YV-852CP	MIII	TT-447
YV-269C	BN2	2003	YV-414CP	425	0102	YV-555CP	200	BB-1092	YV-853CP	690	11061
YV-270C	**BN2**	**573**	YV-415CP	690C	11680	(YV-555CP)	200	BB-1132	YV-854CP	690	11061
YV-272P	P166	367	YV-416CP	690B	11546	YV-555CP	90	LJ-370	YV-870P	P68	54
YV-273P	90	LJ-499	YV-416CP	695A	96018	YV-581CP	695	95007	YV-872C	TRIS	1034
YV-277CP	MIII	TT-441	YV-416P	E90	LW-81	YV-597CP	200	BB-394	YV-877CP	300C	FM-8
YV-279CP	31T	7720063	YV-417C	BN2	19	YV-601P	690C	11698	YV-880CP	690D	15017
(YV-280CP)	690B	11546	YV-417CP	690C	11668	YV-606CP	F90	LA-174	YV-880P	MU-2	331
YV-281CP	690B	11532	YV-419CP	200	BB-863	YV-609CP	690C	11610	YV-886CP	F90	LA-179
YV-288CP	F90	LA-8	YV-420CP	690B	11408	YV-612CP	MIII	TT-468A	YV-893CP	695	95058
YV-289CP	F90	LA-16	YV-422CP	200	BB-887	YV-620CP	G1	170	YV-898CP	90	LJ-370
YV-290CP	F90	LA-35	YV-423CP	200	BB-857	YV-621CP	G1	171	YV-900P	690A	11180
YV-291C	**BN2**	**586**	(YV-424CP)	90	LJ-965	**YV-622CP**	**F90**	**LA-207**	YV-902P	690A	11318
YV-291CP	BN2	586	YV-426P	200	BB-142	YV-626CP	690C	11666	**YV-903CP**	**G1**	**173**
YV-292CP	MIII	TT-459A	YV-428CP	F90	LA-140	**YV-627C**	**G1**	**170**	**YV-903P**	**690D**	**15012**
YV-295CP	31T	8166020	(YV-429CP)	200	BB-872	YV-627CP	G1	170	YV-907CP	690A	11180
YV-296CP	200	BB-565	YV-435CP	690C	11666	YV-628C	G1	171	**YV-910CP**	**350**	**FL-206**
YV-299P	90	LJ-72	YV-436CP	90	LJ-973	YV-628CP	G1	171	YV-914CP	690C	11640
YV-307CP	31T	7920062	YV-437CP	200	BB-906	YV-630CP	690C	11640	YV-918CP	690B	11490
YV-309CP	B100	BE-61	YV-438CP	MU-2	1505SA	YV-631CP	100	B-83	YV-920C	BN2	56
YV-310CP	690C	11645	YV-439CP	690C	11671	YV-639CP	200	BB-1712	YV-920P	P68	198
YV-312P	200	BB-86	YV-441CP	695A	96020	YV-640P	MIII	T-252	YV-921C	BN2	149
YV-313CP	MU-2	409SA	(YV-442CP)	90	LJ-989	YV-649P	690B	11390	YV-928P	P68	203
YV-314CP	31T	8020005	(YV-442CP)	90	LJ-991	**YV-652CP**	**MIII**	**TT-515A**	YV-931CP	90	LJ-1659
YV-316P	690A	11274	YV-443CP	200	BB-930	YV-655CP	31T	7920018	YV-940P	E90	LW-183
(YV-317CP)	690B	11572	YV-444C	BN2	863	YV-660CP	90	LJ-1401	YV-941CP	MIIB	T26-175
(YV-318CP)	690B	11576	YV-445CP	F90	LA-151	YV-663CP	690B	11358	YV-943CP	TRIS	1040
(YV-319CP)	690B	11578	YV-450CP	425	0028	YV-665CP	200	BB-160	YV-946CP	200	BB-540
YV-321CP	B100	BE-72	YV-453CP	G1	175	YV-670CP	690B	11547	YV-949CP	200	BB-1671
(YV-322CP)	90	LJ-910	YV-453CP	MIII	TT-462A	**YV-689C**	**BN2**	**863**	YV-950CP	690A	11329
(YV-322CP)	B100	BE-76	YV-454CP	690B	11405	YV-690P	690B	11532	(YV-971P)	690A	11285
YV-325P	300	FA-158	YV-454CP	90	LJ-927	YV-693CP	MIII	T-287	YV-972CP	90	LJ-786
YV-326P	E90	LW-172	YV-459CP	31T	8120049	YV-695CP	31T	7820008	YV-977CP	441	0111
YV-333CP	90	LJ-1153	(YV-461CP)	695A	96017	YV-695CP	MIII	TT-465	YV-979CP	100	B-155
YV-335CP	200	BB-598	YV-461CP	695A	96036	YV-696P	P68T	8005	**YV-980CP**	**695**	**95028**
YV-337CP	BN2	2003	YV-464CP	90	LJ-1005	YV-702CP	F90	LA-174	YV-980CP	695	95074
YV-340CP	680T	1718-89	(YV-465CP)	200C	BL-45	YV-703CP	31T	7820008	YV-980P	690A	11318
YV-342CP	F90	LA-39	YV-465CP	90	LJ-556	**YV-706P**	**E90**	**LW-208**	(YV-980P)	90	LJ-83
YV-344P	680T	1718-89	(YV-466CP)	200	BB-976	YV-710CP	MIII	T-301	YV-986CP	200	BB-1671
YV-349P	MU-2	302	YV-466CP	200	BB-980	YV-711P	690A	11323	YV-988C	G1	173
YV-350CP	200	BB-619	**YV-467CP**	**E90**	**LW-94**	YV-714CP	680T	1689-69	YV-988CP	200	BB-1194
(YV-350CP)	350	FL-32	**YV-472CP**	**MIII**	**TT-471**	YV-717P	690C	11666	YV-989C	G1	194
(YV-351CP)	690C	11621	YV-473C	BN2	116	YV-717P	MU-2	727SA	YV-990CP	F406	0022
(YV-352CP)	200	BB-656	YV-474C	BN2	2023	YV-718CP	MIII	TT-447	YV-991CP	PA42	5527009
YV-352CP	200	BB-708	YV-475C	BN2	905	YV-722P	90	LJ-306	YV-991P	690B	11390
YV-353CP	200	BB-701	YV-476CP	200	BB-961	YV-723P	31T	7920021	YV-993CP	690C	11640
YV-354CP	90	LJ-889	(YV-477CP)	695A	96016	(YV-723P)	680W	1843-42	YV-994P	90	LJ-693

YV-998C 690B 11546
YV-1000CP 90 LJ-1273
YV-1001P 200 BB-930
YV-1006CP 200 BB-880
YV-1013P F90 LA-16
(YV-1020P) 690A 11325
YV-1030CP 350 FL-143
YV-1031CP 200 BB-1556
YV-1037CP 90 LJ-659
YV-1049P MU-2 543
YV-1050P 690B 11443
(YV-1050P) MU-2 347
YV-1051P 200 BB-656
YV-1062CP 441 0356
YV-1066CP 90 LJ-1586
YV-1067P MU-2 165
YV-1069CP 90 LJ-1329
YV-1073P BN2 520
YV-1074CP 90 LJ-1605
YV-1076CP G1 194
YV-1077CP 300 FA-157
YV-1082P 31T 7920053
YV-1102CP 690C 11698
YV-1104CP 100 B-237
YV-1115C BN2 296
YV-1116C BN2 242
YV-1116P BN2 679
YV-1117C TRIS 1007
YV-1131C BN2 679
YV-1132C BN2 369
YV-1148CP 100 B-231
YV-1151CP 680T 1538-5
YV-1170P P68 76
YV-1276P B100 BE-28
YV-1300P h BB-282
YV-1341P 200 BB-812
YV-1391P 90 LJ-190
YV-1402P 31T 7820008
YV-1402P 31T 7820067
YV-1405P 680T 1719-90
YV-1444P 690B 11493
YV-1471P P68 157
YV-1477P P68 130
YV-1478P P68 126
YV-1500P E90 LW-270
YV-1538P P68 160
YV-1700P 90 LJ-205
YV-1765P E90 LW-28
(YV-1834P) P68 175
YV-1835P P68 185
YV-1860P MU-2 573
YV-1873P 200 BB-632
YV-1894P E90 LW-69
YV-1930P 90 LJ-766
YV-1947P 90 LJ-370
YV-1978P MU-2 212
YV-1990P 31T 7520027
YV-1995P 31T 8120013
YV-2034P 90 LJ-659
YV-2083P P68 263
YV-2084P P68 250
YV-2085P P68 242
YV-2096P 690B 11490
(YV-2173P) BN2T 880
(YV-2174P) BN2 2107
YV-2175P 680W 1777-15
YV-2200P 31T 7400006
YV-2222P 200 BB-887
YV-2222P P68 364
YV-2229P 90 LJ-488
YV-2235P BN2 863
YV-2244P BN2 19
YV-2246P 425 0102
(YV-2248P) 200 BB-1020
(YV-2250P) 200 BB-1092
YV-2251P 200 BB-1026
(YV-2253P) F90 LA-193
(YV-2254P) 200 BB-1090
YV-2260P 90 LJ-1005
YV-2263P 425 0162
YV-2274P P68 306
YV-2280P 680W 1804-26
YV-2282P 90 LJ-1273
YV-2289P F90 LA-16
(YV-2301P) 90 LJ-770
YV-2302P 690B 11494
YV-2310P P68 355
YV-2317P 690A 11239
YV-2318P P68 288
YV-2323P 200C BL-66
YV-2323P P68 368
YV-2331P 31T 7820070
YV-2344P P68 353
YV-2346P 690C 11671
YV-2350P 200 BB-906
YV-2352P 200 BB-1092
YV-2354P 200 BB-656
YV-2357P P68 233
YV-2359P 200 BB-226
YV-2362C P68 299
YV-2365P 31T 7820037
YV-2370P P68 311
YV-2373P P68T 8009
YV-2380P P68 285
YV-2383P 681 6005
YV-2384P BN2 405
YV-2390P 441 0063
YV-2395P MIII T-384
YV-2401P 300 FA-158
YV-2404P 681 6029
YV-2413P 690C 11668
YV-2418P P68 291
YV-2422P 690B 11515
YV-2423P 100 B-90
YV-2424P P68 265
YV-2425P BN2 2023
YV-2435P 680T 1685-66
YV-2436P 680W 1814-31
YV-2437P 690A 11323
YV-2451P 31T 7720050
YV-2466P 90 LJ-591
YV-2475P 681B 6052
YV-2478P BN2 369
YV-2484P 200 BB-160
YV-2488P 690A 11190
YV-2501P 681 6024
YV-2503P E90 LW-144
YV-2505P 690C 11726
YV-2510P P68T 8002
YV-2521P TRIS 1012
YV-2523P TRIS 1044
YV-2566P 695 95009
YV-2576P 200 BB-656
YV-2584P 200 BB-316
YV-2588P 690B 11468
YV-2593P 690A 11253
YV-2604P MU-2 348SA
YV-2615P 100 B-161
YV-2616P 441 0097
YV-2620P 90 LJ-786
YV-2631P 690B 11466
YV-2663P 350 FL-313
YV-2683P 90 LJ-306
YV-2694P 690B 11472
YV-2697P 681 6044
YV-2703P 200 BB-167
YV-2710P 200 BB-632
YV-2737P 690B 11546
YV-2740P 680T 1685-66
YV-2745P 200 BB-656
YV-2767P 425 0189
YV-2772P 690B 11547
YV-2800P 31T 8120013
YV-2812P 690A 11228
YV-2816P 90 LJ-378
YV-2822P 31T 7920076
YV-2834P 200 BB-346
YV-2835P 90 LJ-784
YV-C-AJG BN2 711
YV-C-AKL BN2 405
YV-C-MTM BN2 712
YV-E-APM 90 LJ-629
YV-E-DPK 690A 11207
YV-O-MC-5 690A 11281
YV-O-BDA-3 MU-2 685
YV-O-BIV-1 200 BB-731
YV-O-BIV-2 E90 LW-182
YV-O-BND-1 200 BB-701
YV-O-CBL-5 90 LJ-889
YV-O-CDA-2 MU-2 629
YV-O-CDM-1 MU-2 525
YV-O-CPI-1 200 BB-770
YV-O-CPI-2 B100 BE-15
YV-O-CVF-1 200 BB-644
YV-O-CVG-2 680T 1719-90
YV-O-CVG-4 100 B-176
YV-O-CVG-5 200 BB-223
YV-O-CVG-8 200 BB-273
(YV-O-DAC-2) 690B 11383
YV-O-DAC-2 690B 11430
YV-O-FDN-1 BN2 520
YV-O-FDU-1 690B 11500
YV-O-FMO-5 200 BB-223
YV-O-FMO-8 200 BB-273
YV-O-GPA-1 690A 11198
YV-O-GSF-6 BN2 520
YV-O-ICA-1 PA42 8001010
YV-O-IGV-1 MIII T-287
YV-O-INAV-3 E90 LW-189
YV-O-INH-2 200 BB-701
YV-O-INOS-3 680W 1804-26
YV-O-INV-3 E90 LW-189
YV-O-KWH-1 90 LJ-488
YV-O-KWH-3 690C 11657
YV-O-MAC-1 200 BB-701
YV-O-MAC-1 PA42 8001010
YV-O-MAC-2 31T 7904040
YV-O-MAC-6 E90 LW-82
YV-O-MAR-10 690A 11323
YV-O-MAR-2 680T 1683-64
YV-O-MAR-6 BN2 203
YV-O-MH-01 E90 LW-82
YV-O-MIF-1 695A 96016
YV-O-MIF-2 690B 11430
YV-O-MMH-2 90 LJ-190
YV-O-MMH-9 200 BB-261
YV-O-MOP-12 BN2 203
YV-O-MOP-8 680T 1683-64
YV-O-MRI-2 MU-2 629
YV-O-MTC-1 695A 96016
YV-O-MTC-12 690B 11430
YV-O-MTC-2 690B 11430
YV-O-MTC-5 690A 11281
YV-O-NCE-2 E90 LW-201
YV-O-PTJ-2 200 BB-1092
YV-O-SAS-3 E90 LW-82
YV-O-SAS-3 E90 LW-203
YV-O-SATA-1 200 BB-223
YV-O-SATA-2 200 BB-261
YV-O-SATA-3 200 BB-273
YV-O-SATA-4 200 BB-701
YV-O-SATA-5 200 BB-731
YV-O-SATA-6 200 BB-5
YV-O-SATA-6 200 BB-770
YV-O-SATA-7 E90 LW-189
YV-O-SATA-8 PA42 8001010
YV-O-SID-2 100 B-155
YV-P-AEA G1 24
YV-P-DPN 90 LJ-370
YV-P-EPC G1 119
YV-P-HPN 90 LJ-488
YV-T-ABH MU-2 615
YV-T-ADD MU-2 573
YV-T-ADF 90 LJ-556
YV-T-AEW BN2 345
YV-T-AFD MU-2 253
YV-T-AJG BN2 711
YV-T-AJP E90 LW-81
YV-T-AKL BN2 405
YV-T-ANH MU-2 632
YV-T-ANI MU-2 126
(YV-T-AOL) E90 LW-146
YV-T-AOU 200 BB-52
YV-T-AOV 90 LJ-659
YV-T-APD E90 LW-144
YV-T-ART MIII T-252
YV-T-ASS 90 LJ-651
YV-T-ETM 100 B-83
YV-T-GTX 90 LJ-190
YV-T-HTZ E90 LW-146
YV-T-MTI 200 BB-35
YV-T-MTM BN2 7
YV-T-MTM BN2 712
YV-T-NDD MU-2 645
YV-T-OTZ 680T 1689-69
YV-T-QTO MU-2 543
YV-T-VTY 680W 1813-30
YV-T-WTI MU-2 115
YV-T-ZTA 680T 1689-69
YV-T-ZTA 690A 11180
YV-T-ZTZ 680T 1689-69
YV-TADJ E90 LW-53
YV-TAKP 680T 1689-69
YV-TAPP 690A 11207
YV-TARW 690A 11250
YV-TASK 90 LJ-499
YV-TAYA 31T 7520027
YV-TAYT 690A 11220
YV-TOCO 690A 11244
YV-TSJM 690A 11253
YV0100 695A 96016
YV0101 200 BB-223
YV0102 200 BB-261
YV0103 200 BB-273
YV0104 200 BB-701
YV0105 200 BB-731
YV0106 200 BB-5
YV0107 E90 LW-189
YV0108 PA42 8001010
YV0112 690B 11430
YV0115 690B 11500
YV0132 MIII T-287
YV0136 90 LJ-889
YV0138 350 FL-55
YV0145 690A 11198
YV0149 690C 11657
YV0154 695 95010
YV 100 B-34
YV 100 B-168
YV 100 B-240
YV 200 BB-8
YV 200 BB-17
YV 200 BB-31
YV 200 BB-67
YV 200 BB-78
YV 200 BB-107
YV 200 BB-133
YV 200 BB-176
YV 200 BB-279
YV 200 BB-391
YV 200 BB-427
YV 200 BB-472
YV 200 BB-506
YV 200 BB-507
YV 200 BB-562
YV 200 BB-613
YV 200 BB-779
YV 200 BB-976
YV 200 BB-1479
YV 200C BL-55
YV 300 FA-9
YV 300 FA-40
YV 300 FA-137
YV 31T 8020086
YV 350 FL-513
YV 350 FL-514
YV 441 0001
YV 441 0022
YV 441 0040
YV 441 0195
YV 441 0250
YV 441 0259
YV 681 6014
YV 690 11012
YV 690 11030
YV 690A 11160
YV 690A 11177
YV 690A 11191
YV 690A 11276
YV 690B 11363
YV 690B 11410
YV 690B 11428
YV 690B 11431
YV 690B 11510
YV 690B 11524
YV 690B 11550

YV 690B 11561
YV 690C 11632
YV 690C 11694
YV 690D 15034
YV 695 95000
YV 695 95043
YV 90 LJ-53
YV 90 LJ-124
YV 90 LJ-130
YV 90 LJ-146
YV 90 LJ-147
YV 90 LJ-151
YV 90 LJ-167
YV 90 LJ-195
YV 90 LJ-202
YV 90 LJ-210
YV 90 LJ-222
YV 90 LJ-224
YV 90 LJ-240
YV 90 LJ-266
YV 90 LJ-341
YV 90 LJ-357
YV 90 LJ-358
YV 90 LJ-383
YV 90 LJ-396
YV 90 LJ-452
YV 90 LJ-464
YV 90 LJ-495
YV 90 LJ-649
YV 90 LJ-1041
YV 90 LJ-1834
YV 90 LJ-1941
YV B100 BE-18
YV B100 BE-114
YV BN2 171
YV BN2 228
YV BN2 533
YV E90 LW-25
YV E90 LW-262
YV E90 LW-309
YV F90 LA-209
YV G1 92
YV G1 129
YV MIIB T26-142
YV MIV AT-002
YV123T MIIB T26-175
YV128T MIII TT-507
YV144T 90 LJ-511
YV175T 31T 7920053
YV177T MIII T-268
YV178T BN2 242
YV189T 690B 11359
YV196T 200 BB-540
YV197T 90 LJ-1605
YV217T 31T 7920021
YV218T 90 LJ-1659
YV223T 690B 11472
YV224T 695 95009
YV228T 441 0100
YV246T 690B 11539
YV258T BN2 323
YV261T MIII T-292
YV303T 690A 11171
YV306T 690B 11517
YV313T MIII T-407
YV319T 690B 11471
YV334T MIII T-290
YV352T 200G BY-29
(YV1019) 690B 11359
YV1020 G1 106
YV1031 31T 7820032
YV1035 680T 1538-5
YV1044 680W 1762-8
YV1054 90 LJ-786
YV1066 681B 6061
YV1081 31T 7920018
YV1082 690B 11466
YV1085 690B 11390
YV1104 100 B-231
YV1137 31T 7820052
YV1146 90 LJ-1388
YV1153 31T 7920076
YV1159 B100 BE-61
YV1165 31T 7820067
YV1167 E90 LW-172
YV1173 690D 15022
YV1177 690A 11245
YV1187 F406 0022
YV1191 B100 BE-128
YV1197 BN2 712
YV1204 BN2 56
(YV1217) 680T 1718-89
YV1226 31T 7720047
YV1239 100 B-214
YV1240 200 BB-790
YV1241 BN2 149
YV1245 90 LJ-756
YV1250 90 LJ-511
(YV1254) 681 6044
YV1257 100 B-161
YV1271 690B 11464
YV1300 100 B-73
YV1303 P68 353
YV1304 200 BB-656
YV1306 100 B-237
YV1315 690C 11618
YV1323 P68 185
YV1325 690C 11698
YV1342 90 LJ-405
YV1348 690A 11131
YV1349 90 LJ-784
YV1375 P68 265
YV1385 690C 11666
YV1387 200 BB-602
YV1391 PA42 5527009
YV1397 31T 8120013
YV1412 MIII TT-465
YV1416 TRIS 1034
YV1443 31T 7904013
YV1456 690B 11490
YV1459 690A 11207
YV1465 E90 LW-234
YV1482 441 0276
YV1486 100 B-16
YV1497 350 FL-32
YV1498 300C FM-8
YV1504 441 0319
YV1507 100 B-155
YV1532 695 95034
YV1537 F90 LA-35
YV1540 690B 11546
(YV1551) 680T 1689-69
(YV1566) 690A 11216
YV1568 90 LJ-374
YV1591 200 BB-556
YV1595 90 LJ-659
YV1599 90 LJ-370
YV1601 F90 LA-179
YV1603 200 BB-1712
YV1607 90 LJ-973
YV1617 690D 15017
YV1632 690B 11377
YV1641 BN2 711
YV1647 441 0072
YV1649 90 LJ-1329
YV1651 31T 7820008
YV1657 MIII TT-456A
YV1675 300 FA-51
YV1676 P180 1086
YV1690 441 0060
YV1693 F90 LA-174
YV1694 200 BB-1671
YV1695 90 LJ-865
YV1699 PA42 5527009
YV1705 441 0063
YV1706 P68 242
YV1726 90 LJ-1273
YV1730 200 BB-440
YV1731 200 BB-598
YV1733 200 BB-1020
YV1740 200 BB-1706
YV1750 425 0189
YV1753 441 0067
YV1758 690A 11244
YV1762 P68 130
YV1775 681 6005
YV1777 690D 15032
YV1787 690A 11264
YV1796 690A 11329
YV1832 P68T 8002
YV1835 690C 11725
YV1838 100 B-136
YV1839 300 FA-158
YV1841 690A 11239
YV1846 690A 11288
YV1849 300 FA-169
YV1851 690C 11735
YV1855 441 0140
YV1857 441 0356
YV1871 200 BB-632
YV1892 690C 11726
YV1898 P68 157
YV1906 441 0097
YV1909 200 BB-195
YV1912 FPC6 2048
YV1923 MIII TT-447
YV1932 690B 11515
YV1957 425 0162
YV1959 690A 11253
YV1973 90 LJ-810
YV1980 P68 368
YV1987 BN2 2023
YV1994 690B 11547
YV1996 BN2 242
YV1998 690B 11483
YV1999 P68 263
YV2001 690B 11532
YV2005 P68 299
YV2006 31T 7820052
YV2009 690B 11499
YV2010 100 B-80
YV2020 695 95084
YV2037 690A 11325
YV2045 MIII TT-459A
YV2047 P68 364
YV2048 690B 11448
YV2054 G1 171
YV2056 690B 11443
YV2078 200 BB-1157
YV2090 695 95017
YV2094 690B 11366
YV2096 690B 11358
YV2099 690C 11603
YV2122 690B 11378
YV2129 100 B-83
YV2135 MIII T-301
(YV2143) 690A 11278
YV2152 90 LJ-1787
YV2160 690B 11405
YV2175 695 95058
YV2176 690B 11488
YV2178 681B 6052
YV2182 690B 11359
YV2184 690A 11285
YV2186 441 0153
YV2188 MU-2 348SA
YV2199 P68T 8005
YV2222 690B 11468
YV2224 680T 1718-89
YV2226 B100 BE-28
YV2229 690A 11180
YV2247 690A 11114
YV2249 690D 15030
YV2252 690 11061
YV2256 690A 11228
YV2278 P68 233
YV2299 P68T 8009
YV2310 MIII TT-468A
YV2327 90 LJ-499
YV2341 690B 11413
YV2343 F90 LA-60
YV2350 90 LJ-1401
YV2352 E90 LW-189
YV2392 200 BB-1966
YV2406 690B 11388
YV2410 90 LJ-554
YV2418 690A 11190
YV2419 90 LJ-1828
YV2424 100 B-209
YV2428 690A 11161
YV2458 100 B-230
YV2490 690A 11257
YV2499 31T 8104057
YV2525 350 FL-573
YV2538 690A 11171
YV2576 690B 11392

Zimbabwe

See also VP-W

Z-AHL E90 LW-205
Z-AIR TRIS 1054
Z-APG 200 BB-1046
Z-CAA BN2 2254
Z-DDD F406 0069
Z-DDE F406 0068
Z-DDF F406 0071
Z-DDG F406 0067
Z-DJF E90 LW-205
Z-KEN PC12 126
Z-LCS 90 LJ-848
Z-MKI 200 BB-1476
Z-MKI 90 LJ-1099
Z-MRS 200 BB-286
Z-TAB 200 BB-315
Z-TAB 90 LJ-609
Z-TAM 200C BL-49
Z-UAS BN2 155
Z-UTD TRIS 1055
Z-WEX BN2 619
Z-WHX BN2 192
Z-WLE P68 149
Z-WLL P68 245
Z-WMT P68 106
Z-WNB 90 LJ-485
Z-WPR BN2 396
Z-WRD 90 LJ-687
Z-WSG 200 BB-748
Z-WSG 90 LJ-609
Z-ZLT 200 BB-1196

New Zealand

ZK- BN2 550
ZK-CGS 200 BB-301
ZK-CII F406 0012
(ZK-CJS) TRIS 1042
(ZK-CMO) 200 BB-259
ZK-CRA BN2 609
ZK-DAI P166 410
ZK-DBV BN2 164
ZK-DBW BN2 168
ZK-DFJ PC6 628
ZK-DKN BN2 278
ZK-DLA BN2 2131
ZK-DMA P68 68
ZK-ECR MU-2 371SA
ZK-EKZ MU-2 519
ZK-EON MU-2 513
ZK-ERA P68 123
ZK-ESM MU-2 528
ZK-EVK BN2 583
ZK-EVO BN2 785
ZK-EVT BN2 152
(ZK-FCS) P68 228
ZK-FFL BN2 614
ZK-FGR BN2 741
ZK-FIF BN2 417
ZK-FLU BN2 104
ZK-FMS BN2 42
ZK-FNZ P750 102
ZK-FPL 31T 8475001
ZK-FRC 695A 96036
ZK-FUZ P68 327
ZK-FVD BN2 316
ZK-FWH BN2 43
ZK-FWZ BN2 52
ZK-FXE BN2 110
ZK-FXY BN2 611
ZK-FZB PC6 634
ZK-IAS BN2 182
ZK-JAD P750 122
ZK-JAY P750 120
ZK-JBC P750 119
ZK-JBD P750 121

ZK-JDQ	P750	139
ZK-JFM	P750	141
ZK-JGI	P750	113
ZK-JGJ	P750	115
ZK-JHA	P750	147
ZK-JHM	P750	152
ZK-JIF	P750	153
ZK-JJH	P750	154
ZK-JML	PC6	653
ZK-JMP	PC6	693
ZK-JNA	P750	133
ZK-JNF	P750	135
ZK-JNG	P750	143
ZK-JNH	P750	131
ZK-JNV	P750	114
ZK-JNV	P750	130
ZK-JOA	P750	124
ZK-JPH	P750	108
ZK-JPP	P750	106
ZK-JPQ	P750	112
ZK-JPU	P750	117
ZK-JPV	P750	105
ZK-JQA	P750	109
ZK-JQB	BN2	2217
ZK-JQC	BN2	2220
ZK-JQE	P750	110
ZK-JQF	P750	111
ZK-JQK	P750	118
ZK-JQO	P750	123
ZK-JQO	P750	134
ZK-JQP	P750	116
ZK-JQQ	P750	128
ZK-JQQ	P750	136
ZK-JQR	P750	126
ZK-JQV	P750	127
ZK-JRB	P750	129
ZK-JRQ	P750	132
ZK-JRR	P750	137
ZK-JRS	P750	138
ZK-JSB	BN2	458
ZK-JSE	P750	144
ZK-JSQ	P750	142
ZK-JSU	P750	148
ZK-JZI	P750	155
ZK-JZL	P750	156
ZK-KAB	200	BB-1054
ZK-KAC	200	BB-1008
ZK-KAD	200	BB-1087
ZK-KAF	200	BB-1178
ZK-KAG	200	BB-968
ZK-KAH	P750	149
ZK-KAJ	P750	150
ZK-KAK	P750	157
ZK-KAP	P68	327
ZK-KAV	P750	158
ZK-KAX	P750	159
ZK-KAY	P750	107
ZK-KDF	P750	146
ZK-KHA	BN2	661
(ZK-KHB)	BN2	447
ZK-KHB	BN2	511
ZK-KOH	MU-2	521
ZK-KPH	31T	8004036
ZK-KSL	300	FA-105
ZK-KTR	BN2	759
ZK-LAL	P68	70
ZK-LAQ	P750	125
ZK-LGC	TRIS	381
ZK-LGC	TRIS	1042
ZK-LGO	P68	25
ZK-LGR	TRIS	372
ZK-LHL	425	0171
ZK-LOU	TRIS	322
ZK-LYP	BN2	821
(ZK-MAA)	MIVA	AT-033
(ZK-MAB)	300	FA-105
ZK-MAN	200	BB-1366
ZK-MCB	BN2	336
ZK-MCC	BN2	395
ZK-MCD	BN2	719
ZK-MCE	BN2	724
ZK-MCK	PC6	809
ZK-MCN	PC6	824
ZK-MCT	PC6	841
ZK-MFN	BN2	2168
ZK-MGP	300	FA-63
ZK-MIR	P68	227
ZK-MKG	90	LJ-1367
ZK-MOH	690	11006
ZK-MPI	31T	7720009
ZK-MSF	BN2	2037
ZK-MYF	P68	123
ZK-MYO	P68	417
ZK-NFD	441	0141
ZK-NMK	P68	114
ZK-NNE	BN2	661
ZK-OBL	BN2	2035
ZK-PBG	200	BB-866
ZK-PCI	PC6	523
ZK-PDC	31T	7520028
ZK-PFT	P68	42
ZK-PIP	690B	11380
ZK-PIY	BN2	344
ZK-PIZ	BN2	2012
ZK-PLA	P68	86
ZK-PLK	200C	BL-64
ZK-POD	31T	7720009
ZK-PTP	PC6	656
ZK-PVA	690B	11476
ZK-PVB	690A	11321
ZK-REA	BN2	43
ZK-RGA	200	BB-961
ZK-RIL	E90	LW-318
ZK-ROM	31T	7620055
ZK-RUR	PA42	5527015
ZK-SDF	P750	145
ZK-SFE	BN2	406
ZK-SFF	TRIS	1025
ZK-SFG	TRIS	1039
ZK-SFK	BN2	236
ZK-SMB	P68	308
ZK-SWA	P750	130
ZK-SWB	MIVA	AT-033
ZK-TCP	P68	371
ZK-TSS	BN2	2043
ZK-TTL	P750	104
ZK-TZY	P68	414
ZK-TZZ	P68	376
ZK-UAC	P750	103
(ZK-UPA)	200	BB-617
ZK-UPA	90	LJ-525
ZK-VAA	F406	0012
ZK-VAF	F406	0057
ZK-WAL	MU-2	037
ZK-WIL	200	BB-1015
ZK-WLH	690B	11475
ZK-WNL	200	BB-690
ZK-WNZ	BN2	278
ZK-XLA	P750	101
ZK-XLB	P750	140
ZK-XLC	F406	0012
ZK-XLE	P750	151
ZK-XLF	F406	0057
ZK-XLG	P750	122
ZK-YCL	MIII	T-360
ZK-ZQN	BN2	2197
ZK-ZSP	P68	129

Paraguay

ZP-	425	0223
(ZP-)	690	11052
ZP-	690C	11606
ZP-	690D	15021
ZP-	695	95035
ZP-	695A	96093
ZP-	MIII	TT-462A
ZP-ASH	690C	11625
ZP-CCQ	MU-2	028
ZP-GAR	690B	11425
ZP-PMX	E90	LW-259
ZP-PRY	690A	11222
(ZP-PSP)	B100	BE-87
ZP-PTC	200	BB-209
ZP-PTU	695	95021
ZP-PVO	690A	11110
ZP-TFV	695	95053
ZP-THN	690A	11274
ZP-TIW	690B	11394
ZP-TJW	E90	LW-284
ZP-TKN	200	BB-137
ZP-TMA	E90	LW-284
ZP-TTC	200	BB-209
ZP-TTU	695	95021
ZP-TVO	690A	11110
ZP-TWN	200	BB-1008
ZP-TWT	E90	LW-69
ZP-TWV	690B	11425
ZP-TWY	695A	96095
ZP-TWZ	690D	15005
ZP-TXE	90	LJ-799
ZP-TXF	695A	96079
ZP-TXG	695B	96203
ZP-TXP	90	LJ-195
ZP-TXR	200	BB-1008
ZP-TYE	680T	1620-51
ZP-TYF	90	LJ-132
ZP-TYI	31T	8020066
ZP-TYZ	PA42	8001044
ZP-TZF	F90	LA-46
ZP-TZW	E90	LW-261

South Africa

ZS-	200	BB-1291
ZS-	46T	97031
ZS-AAA	200	BB-33
ZS-AAC	G1	38
ZS-AAU	90	LJ-485
ZS-ACS	200	BB-961
ZS-AFE	PC6	678
ZS-AGI	PC12	471
ZS-AIL	P750	131
ZS-ALD	F90	LA-160
ZS-ALE	200	BB-643
ZS-ALX	G1	86
ZS-AMC	425	0169
ZS-AMR	E90	LW-130
ZS-AMS	PC12	203
ZS-AMS	PC12	845
ZS-APG	200	BB-1046
ZS-APS	PC12	771
ZS-ARL	200	BB-1537
ZS-ASB	200	BB-903
ZS-ASM	441	698
ZS-AVH	PC12	713
(ZS-BBO)	PC12	108
ZS-BCI	TBM8	397
ZS-BDZ	P750	133
ZS-BEB	PC12	180
ZS-BEL	PC12	143
ZS-BEN	90	LJ-397
ZS-BHK	200	BB-387
ZS-BLU	P750	123
ZS-BLV	BN2	683
ZS-CBL	200	BB-1742
ZS-CCK	200	BB-1987
ZS-COH	PC12	436
ZS-COP	90	LJ-1204
ZS-CPD	PC12	1037
ZS-CPM	200	BB-1911
ZS-CPM	90	LJ-1034
ZS-CPX	425	0071
ZS-CSC	90	LJ-1034
*ZS-CSI	F90	LA-47
ZS-CTR	PC12	1135
ZS-CVH	200C	BL-32
ZS-CWM	PC12	739
ZS-DAT	PC12	242
(ZS-DCG)	46T	97055
ZS-DCG	46T	97055
ZS-DER	PC12	554
ZS-DET	PC12	245
ZS-DEV	200	BB-1885
"ZS-DGC"	90	LJ-1875
ZS-DJA	200	BB-1607
ZS-DLB	PC12	791
ZS-DMM	PC12	198
ZS-DSL	200	BB-531
(ZS-DSL)	200	BB-1152
ZS-EFC	90	LJ-161
ZS-EPV	P750	144
(ZS-EUI)	680T	1532-2
ZS-EXC	PC12	220
ZS-FDR	200	BB-1234
(ZS-FDS)	PC12	147
ZS-FEM	PC6	638
(ZS-FEP)	TBM7	306
ZS-FIN	P166	444
ZS-FML	350	FL-534
ZS-FON	90	LJ-1735
ZS-FTG	PC12	615
ZS-GAA	PC12	858
(ZS-GCC)	690A	11122
ZS-GCO	P750	146
ZS-GDC	90	LJ-1875
ZS-GJV	200	BB-1167
ZS-GKR	690A	11122
ZS-GMC	PC12	797
ZS-HSA	680T	1709-84
ZS-IAN	E90	LW-169
ZS-IBE	90	LJ-402
ZS-IHB	PC6	713
ZS-IHZ	90	LJ-497
ZS-IJA	BN2	182
ZS-IJB	BN2	192
ZS-IJC	BN2	253
ZS-IJD	BN2	288
ZS-ILA	MIIB	T26-180E
ZS-INN	90	LJ-523
ZS-INY	100	B-105
ZS-INY	90	LJ-397
ZS-IRC	BN2	271
ZS-IRJ	90	LJ-161
ZS-ITH	90	LJ-551
ZS-IZZ	BN2	317
ZS-JDD	PC12	805
(ZS-JEM)	PC12	202
ZS-JFW	E90	LW-141
ZS-JIS	G1	193
ZS-JJC	TRIS	360
ZS-JJK	MU-2	659
ZS-JKB	200	BB-72
ZS-JLR	31T	7520029
ZS-JLZ	MIVA	AT-040
ZS-JMA	441	0095
ZS-JMA	MIVA	AT-037
ZS-JMF	681B	6048
ZS-JPD	200	BB-95
ZS-JRA	690A	11284
ZS-JRB	690A	11248
ZS-JRC	690B	11432
ZS-JRD	690B	11371
ZS-JRE	690A	11344
ZS-JRF	690B	11491
ZS-JRH	690B	11421
ZS-JRL	690A	11339
ZS-JRZ	690A	11249
ZS-JSC	200	BB-1985
ZS-JTP	31T	7620012
ZS-JWA	P68	28
ZS-JWS	690A	11151
ZS-JXT	BN2	774
ZS-JYF	TRIS	1031
ZS-JZO	BN2	678
ZS-KAA	200	BB-222
ZS-KAB	200	BB-245
ZS-KAG	BN2	556
ZS-KAL	PC12	508
ZS-KAL	PC12	1023
ZS-KAM	90	LJ-730
ZS-KAO	200	BB-286
ZS-KCB	200	BB-347
ZS-KCE	E90	LW-170
ZS-KDP	441	0055
(ZS-KEC)	E90	LW-170
ZS-KEF	690B	11458
ZS-KGO	90	LJ-805
ZS-KGS	200	BB-470
ZS-KGW	200	BB-381
ZS-KHB	90	LJ-844
ZS-KHK	200	BB-564
ZS-KJP	200	BB-593
ZS-KLC	90	LJ-880

ZS-KLH	200	BB-630
ZS-KLK	BN2	862
ZS-KLM	200	BB-682
ZS-KLO	200	BB-704
ZS-KLT	F90	LA-44
ZS-KLW	90	LJ-484
ZS-KLZ	F90	LA-69
ZS-KMA	90	LJ-930
ZS-KMD	BN2	854
ZS-KME	TRIS	1044
ZS-KMF	TRIS	1058
ZS-KMG	BN2	857
ZS-KMH	TRIS	362
ZS-KMT	200	BB-767
ZS-KOF	690C	11617
ZS-KOG	690B	11441
ZS-KPB	441	0215
ZS-KRS	690C	11644
ZS-KST	425	0016
ZS-KSU	425	0115
ZS-KTG	31T	8120010
ZS-KUS	690B	11545
ZS-KVB	695	95005
ZS-KVX	425	0033
ZS-KXB	425	0130
ZS-KXL	425	0126
ZS-KXU	425	0047
ZS-KYH	E90	LW-307
ZS-KYU	690C	11659
ZS-KZI	90	LJ-959
ZS-KZM	690C	11709
ZS-KZN	695	95063
ZS-KZO	690C	11681
ZS-KZP	690C	11670
ZS-KZR	695	95068
ZS-KZS	695A	96034
ZS-KZT	690D	15008
ZS-KZU	200	BB-416
ZS-KZV	695A	96023
ZS-KZW	695	95009
ZS-KZX	695A	96050
ZS-KZY	695A	96051
ZS-KZZ	695A	96052
ZS-LAD	350	FL-75
ZS-LAJ	P68	210
ZS-LAK	P68	241
ZS-LAW	200	BB-889
ZS-LAY	200C	BL-34
ZS-LBC	F90	LA-122
ZS-LBD	200	BB-837
ZS-LBE	200	BB-903
ZS-LBF	90	LJ-978
ZS-LCA	PA42	8001030
ZS-LDR	425	0176
ZS-LEE	90	LJ-1565
(ZS-LES)	C-12	BC-28
ZS-LFF	F90	LA-158
ZS-LFL	90	LJ-1033
ZS-LFM	200	BB-954
ZS-LFN	90	LJ-1031
ZS-LFP	F90	LA-189
ZS-LFT	200	BB-915
ZS-LFU	200	BB-1018
ZS-LFW	200	BB-999
ZS-LID	MIVA	AT-043
ZS-LIL	200	BB-1047
ZS-LIM	BN2	849
ZS-LIN	90	LJ-1053
ZS-LIZ	200	BB-1135
ZS-LJA	200	BB-910
ZS-LJB	PC12	1135
ZS-LJF	E90	LW-76
ZS-LJR	MIVA	AT-035
ZS-LJY	PC6	677
ZS-LKA	200	BB-614
ZS-LKE	BN2	271
ZS-LKF	BN2	729
ZS-LKL	PA42	8001075
ZS-LLL	695A	96003
ZS-LMJ	P68	80
ZS-LNR	200	BB-1222
ZS-LNT	200C	BL-70
ZS-LNV	200C	BL-71
ZS-LOF	200C	BL-50

ZS-LOI	300	FA-71
ZS-LOK	90	LJ-1071
ZS-LOL	90	LJ-890
ZS-LRE	200	BB-1195
ZS-LRG	300	FA-7
ZS-LRM	690A	11105
ZS-LRS	200C	BL-20
ZS-LSE	BN2	834
ZS-LST	200	BB-51
ZS-LSU	300	FA-104
ZS-LSX	P68	323
ZS-LSY	31T	8166031
ZS-LTD	F90	LA-63
ZS-LTE	200	BB-607
ZS-LTF	90	LJ-613
ZS-LTG	200	BB-1251
ZS-LTZ	90	LJ-919
ZS-LUC	31T	7820092
ZS-LUU	90	LJ-988
ZS-LVK	200	BB-1111
ZS-LVL	100	B-228
ZS-LWD	200	BB-756
ZS-LWE	200	BB-1284
ZS-LWM	200	BB-341
ZS-LWZ	90	LJ-338
ZS-LXF	200	BB-1143
ZS-LXL	90	LJ-660
ZS-LXS	200C	BL-45
ZS-LXW	200	BB-1015
ZS-LYA	200	BB-26
ZS-LYZ	425	0021
ZS-LZP	90	LJ-987
ZS-LZR	90	LJ-1118
ZS-LZU	200	BB-444
ZS-MAD	F406	0013
ZS-MAN	90	LJ-161
ZS-MBN	200	BB-1046
ZS-MBZ	90	LJ-795
ZS-MCA	90	LJ-551
ZS-MCC	200	BB-1195
ZS-MCO	350	FL-543
ZS-MES	200	BB-1038
ZS-MFA	90	LJ-839
ZS-MFB	200	BB-1316
ZS-MFC	200	BB-525
ZS-MFW	300	FA-72
ZS-MGF	MU-2	622
ZS-MGG	200	BB-586
ZS-MGI	P68T	9004
ZS-MGR	200	BB-19
ZS-MGV	MU-2	622
ZS-MHK	300	FA-118
ZS-MHM	F90	LA-47
ZS-MIG	425	0064
ZS-MIL	90	LJ-1164
ZS-MIM	200	BB-846
ZS-MIN	200	BB-941
ZS-MIP	300	FA-173
ZS-MIZ	P750	127
ZS-MJH	200	BB-480
ZS-MJW	425	0077
ZS-MJX	P68	277
ZS-MJZ	P68	241
ZS-MKI	90	LJ-1099
ZS-MLL	300	FA-139
ZS-MLO	90	LJ-526
ZS-MMB	350	FL-86
ZS-MMI	P166	462
ZS-MMO	200	BB-1124
ZS-MMV	200	BB-1318
ZS-MNC	90	LJ-671
ZS-MNE	200	BB-812
ZS-MNF	200	BB-15
ZS-MNG	300	FA-178
ZS-MNT	90	LJ-528
(ZS-MRI)	200	BB-256
ZS-MRJ	MU-2	1539SA
ZS-MRZ	90	LJ-748
ZS-MSD	46T	97384
ZS-MSD	90	LJ-956
ZS-MSF	PC12	506
ZS-MSG	B100	BE-75
ZS-MSG	PC12	1030
ZS-MSK	200	BB-597

ZS-MSL	200	BB-815
ZS-MSZ	PC6	866
ZS-MTP	PC6	840
ZS-MTW	200	BB-1076
ZS-MUK	MU-2	308
ZS-MUM	90	LJ-408
ZS-MUZ	MU-2	588
ZS-MUZ	MU-2	621
ZS-MVK	MU-2	627
ZS-MVW	425	0041
ZS-MWA	200	BB-1317
ZS-MWB	200	BB-1359
ZS-MXE	690A	11105
ZS-MXH	200	BB-914
ZS-MYA	200	BB-101
ZS-MYE	300	FA-211
ZS-MZG	90	LJ-810
ZS-MZS	B100	BE-72
ZS-NAG	90	LJ-1298
ZS-NAT	BN2T	2158
ZS-NAV	350	FL-29
ZS-NAW	200	BB-1027
ZS-NAX	200C	BL-8
ZS-NBA	200	BB-1186
ZS-NBJ	200	BB-1070
ZS-NBO	200	BB-706
ZS-NCH	200	BB-918
(ZS-NDH)	90	LJ-619
ZS-NDH	90	LJ-619
ZS-NDM	MU-2	629
ZS-NDR	E90	LW-205
ZS-NED	90	LJ-80
ZS-NEP	200	BB-838
ZS-NES	425	0046
ZS-NFE	200	BB-1418
ZS-NFO	F90	LA-51
ZS-NGC	200	BB-215
ZS-NGI	350	FL-22
ZS-NHG	690	11007
ZS-NHR	P166	461
ZS-NHW	G1	141
ZS-NHX	200	BB-386
ZS-NIP	200	BB-547
ZS-NIR	PC6	885
ZS-NIS	PC6	886
ZS-NIT	PC6	896
ZS-NIU	PC6	897
ZS-NIV	PC6	898
ZS-NIW	PC6	899
ZS-NIX	PC6	900
ZS-NIY	MU-2	380SA
ZS-NJI	300	FA-156
ZS-NJM	200	BB-1152
ZS-NJP	P166	457
ZS-NJR	P166	455
ZS-NJS	P166	454
ZS-NJT	P166	453
ZS-NJU	P166	452
ZS-NJV	P166	450
ZS-NJV	P68	277
ZS-NJW	P166	448
ZS-NJX	P166	446
ZS-NJY	P166	445
ZS-NJZ	P166	460
ZS-NKC	200	BB-1474
ZS-NKE	200	BB-1475
ZS-NKN	P166	459
ZS-NKT	G1	124
ZS-NNA	F406	0005
ZS-NNS	200	BB-266
ZS-NOC	200	BB-715
ZS-NOH	200	BB-1083
ZS-NOK	90	LJ-337
ZS-NOW	200	BB-1427
ZS-NPL	300	FA-110
ZS-NPO	200	BB-367
ZS-NPY	200	BB-769
ZS-NRR	200	BB-288
ZS-NRT	200	BB-334
ZS-NRW	200	BB-201
ZS-NSC	F90	LA-15
ZS-NSD	200C	BL-137
ZS-NTH	46D	64
ZS-NTL	200	BB-85

ZS-NTM	200	BB-256
ZS-NTT	200	BB-350
ZS-NUC	200	BB-407
ZS-NUE	90	LJ-1441
ZS-NUF	200C	BL-4
ZS-NVG	G1	1
ZS-NVP	200	BB-1325
ZS-NWC	90	LJ-625
ZS-NWK	200	BB-52
ZS-NWT	200	BB-1144
ZS-NWZ	PC12	103
ZS-NXH	200	BB-37
ZS-NXI	E90	LW-224
ZS-NXK	690A	11286
ZS-NXT	200	BB-1502
ZS-NXY	90	LJ-1058
ZS-NYE	E90	LW-222
ZS-NYI	F406	0030
ZS-NYM	PC12	147
ZS-NZH	200	BB-206
ZS-NZI	200	BB-593
ZS-NZJ	200	BB-630
ZS-NZK	200	BB-1553
ZS-NZN	200	BB-1552
ZS-NZZ	200	BB-1323
ZS-OAE	E90	LW-151
ZS-OAK	200	BB-197
ZS-OBB	200	BB-1522
ZS-OCA	G1	42
ZS-OCI	200	BB-121
ZS-ODI	200	BB-1542
ZS-ODU	200	BB-1476
ZS-ODV	90	LJ-675
ZS-OEB	200T	BT-7
ZS-OED	200	BB-1149
ZS-OEE	F406	0023
ZS-OEV	PC12	207
ZS-OEW	PC12	211
ZS-OFB	PC12	205
ZS-OFC	PC12	206
ZS-OFD	PC12	208
ZS-OFN	PC12	190
(ZS-OGB)	200	BB-1077
ZS-OGT	E90	LW-87
ZS-OGV	200	BB-620
ZS-OGY	F406	0035
ZS-OHB	90	LJ-431
(ZS-OHJ)	46D	167
ZS-OHJ	46D	167
ZS-OHR	90	LJ-669
ZS-OIG	F406	0041
ZS-OLM	200	BB-1654
ZS-OLO	PC6	871
ZS-OMK	46D	56
ZS-ONB	MU-2	674
(ZS-ONC)	MU-2	672
ZS-ONC	MU-2	727SA
ZS-ONO	G1	134
ZS-ONR	PC12	108
ZS-ONZ	425	0075
ZS-OOE	G1	5
ZS-OPR	200T	BT-8
ZS-ORD	BN2	412
(ZS-ORM)	46T	97034
ZS-OSB	200	BB-327
ZS-OSD	BN2	461
ZS-OSH	200	BB-1296
ZS-OTK	90	LJ-1193
ZS-OTL	31T	8275011
ZS-OTP	200	BB-683
ZS-OTS	200	BB-1113
ZS-OTT	F406	0040
ZS-OUI	200	BB-688
ZS-OUO	46T	97116
ZS-OUP	31T	8275002
ZS-OUS	100	B-57
ZS-OUT	200	BB-764
ZS-OVX	200	BB-1253
ZS-OWH	200	BB-643
ZS-OWL	P68	106
ZS-OXE	F406	0058
ZS-OXT	P68	240
(ZS-OYN)	90	LJ-397
ZS-OYN	PT68	002

ZS-OYP 200 BB-594
ZS-OYS 90 LJ-397
ZS-PAM 200 BB-813
ZS-PAN 200 BB-1344
ZS-PAO BN2 2203
ZS-PAY PC12 204
ZS-PAZ 300 FA-25
ZS-PBB 200 BB-126
ZS-PBH 100 B-9
ZS-PBL 200 BB-468
ZS-PBP P68 307
ZS-PBR P68 359
ZS-PBS 31T 8120054
ZS-PBT 31T 1166004
ZS-PCH 200 BB-1856
ZS-PCJ BN2 869
ZS-PCT P68 287
ZS-PCU P68 223
ZS-PDJ BN2 773
ZS-PDZ PC12 525
ZS-PEA 200C BL-29
ZS-PEF BN2 2002
ZS-PEI 200 BB-1789
ZS-PES 425 0028
ZS-PES 441 0007
ZS-PEZ 200 BB-1528
ZS-PFA 90 LJ-395
ZS-PFD 690B 11422
ZS-PGB 200 BB-1764
ZS-PGN PC12 1089
ZS-PGW F90 LA-120
ZS-PGX PC12 560
ZS-PHG P750 137
ZS-PHI G1 164
ZS-PHJ G1 134
ZS-PHK G1 25
ZS-PHO PA42 5527003
ZS-PJR 300 FA-89
ZS-PKJ BN2T 2151
ZS-PKK BN2T 2141
ZS-PKM 200 BB-382
(ZS-PLG) 46T 97199
ZS-PLG 46T 97199
ZS-PLJ 200 BB-1401
ZS-PLK 200 BB-1463
ZS-PLL 200 BB-1189
ZS-PLY 200 BB-687
(ZS-PMA) 441 0159
ZS-PMC 441 0162
ZS-PMM 200 BB-1654
ZS-PNP 425 0075
ZS-PNR 200 BB-1344
ZS-PNZ 200C BL-8
ZS-POZ P750 125
ZS-PPG 200 BB-1562
ZS-PPU F406 0037
ZS-PPZ 200 BB-419
ZS-PRA 200 BB-1340
ZS-PRB 200C BL-40
ZS-PRC 200 BB-1341
ZS-PRK PC12 690
ZS-PRT 90 LJ-485
ZS-PRX PC12 634
ZS-PSP 200 BB-650
ZS-PTX PC12 695
*ZS-PUB 200 BB-197
ZS-PUF 200 BB-867
ZS-PVT PC12 121
ZS-PWS PC6 952
ZS-PXB 31T 7920056
ZS-PXF 350 FL-532
ZS-PXR 690A 11259
ZS-PYD 425 0067
ZS-PZB PC12 479
ZS-PZU 200 BB-315
ZS-RAF 200 BB-1673
ZS-RGS 441 0353
ZS-RSM 680W 1763-9
ZS-RTZ MIIB T26-179
ZS-RVL PC12 1043
ZS-SBI 200C BL-21
ZS-SBW P750 138
ZS-SDO PC12 282
ZS-SDP PC12 286
ZS-SDS 200 BB-803
ZS-SFB 200C BL-37
ZS-SFS PC12 525
ZS-SGJ PC12 1113
ZS-SGO 90 LJ-954
ZS-SGP 200 BB-407
ZS-SHJ P750 148
ZS-SHY 350 FL-543
ZS-SLI 690A 11211
ZS-SLL 690C 11679
(ZS-SMA) 441 0157
ZS-SMA 441 0164
ZS-SMC 200 BB-1489
ZS-SMY PC12 113
ZS-SOL 200 BB-1138
ZS-SON 200C BL-136
(ZS-SPD) 46T 97266
ZS-SPD 46T 97266
ZS-SRH PC12 313
(ZS-SRI) PC12 325
(ZS-SRI) PC12 352
(ZS-SRJ) PC12 329
(ZS-SRJ) PC12 342
ZS-SRK PC12 202
ZS-SRL PC12 251
ZS-SRM PC12 252
(ZS-SRO) PC12 316
(ZS-SRO) PC12 349
ZS-SRP PC12 317
ZS-SRR PC12 319
ZS-SSC F406 0032
ZS-SSD F406 0027
ZS-SSE F406 0043
(ZS-SWV) PC12 203
ZS-TAB 200 BB-315
ZS-TAY 46T 97304
ZS-TBM TBM7 164
ZS-TBM TBM7 245
ZS-TBS 100 B-105
ZS-TBS 441 0192
ZS-TBS 90 LJ-397
ZS-TCL MU-2 588
ZS-TGM 200 BB-1938
ZS-TGM 90 LJ-1802
ZS-TIP 200 BB-1805
ZS-TKB 90 LJ-1492
(ZS-TLA) PC12 352
ZS-TLA PC12 383
ZS-TMA 441 0159
(ZS-TMA) 441 0164
ZS-TNY 200 BB-914
ZS-TOB 200 BB-1515
ZS-TON 200 BB-1060
ZS-TSW PC12 750
ZS-TWP 200G BY-46
ZS-TWP 90 LJ-1802
ZS-TWZ 46D 186
ZS-VIS BN2 660
ZS-XAC 90 LJ-551
ZS-XAT 31T 7620012
ZS-XGB 100 B-228
ZS-XGC BN2 774
ZS-XGD 200 BB-286
ZS-XGF BN2 736
ZS-YEA PC12 621
ZS-ZAZ 350 FL-459
ZS-ZBR PC12 1069
ZS-ZEN PC12 125
ZS-ZOB MIVA AT-051
ZS-ZXX 200 BB-1077
ZS-ZZZ 300 FA-156
ZU-ABL P166 461
ZU-ABM P166 451
ZU-ABN P166 462
ZU-ABO P166 460
ZU-ABU P166 444
ZU-ABU P166 450
ZU-ABV P166 449
ZU-ACI P166 447
ZU-ADD P166 454
ZU-ADO P166 445
ZU-AGM P166 459
ZU-DFI P166 417

Macedonia

Z3-BAB 200 BB-652

Monaco

3A-MBA 31T 7720018
3A-MBD 200 BB-722
3A-MBT 31T 7920039
3A-MCR 441 0058
3A-MIE 90 LJ-628
3A-MIO 31T 7920001
3A-MKB 90 LJ-867
3A-MOI P68 19
3A-MON 90 LJ-710
3A-MON F90 LA-129
3A-MRL 90 LJ-1391
3A-MSB 31T 7820010
3A-MSI 31T 7904026
3A-MTD 31T 7920039

Mauritius

3B-SKY 200 BB-1363

Equatorial Guinea

3C- G1 82
3C-JJP 31T 8275025
3C-PBH 100 B-9

Swaziland
See also VQ-Z
3D-AAC G1 38
3D-AAG MIIB T26-171E
3D-ABH 695 95009
3D-ABY 200 BB-72
3D-ACO 90 LJ-730
3D-ADF MU-2 588
3D-ADM 690A 11286
3D-ADO BN2 396
3D-ADS 200 BB-347
3D-AFH MU-2 622
3D-AFO 200 BB-812
3D-ARF G1 134
3D-BYZ 690A 11151
3D-DLN G1 25
3D-DOM G1 42
3D-DUE G1 134
3D-IAN 425 0067
3D-LKK 200 BB-1018
3D-TRE G1 42
3D-TRN G1 193

Guinea

3X-GEF BN2 466
3X-GER G1 1

Sri Lanka

4R- 200 BB-1900
4R-HVE 200T BT-30

Israel

4X-AIY PC6 729
4X-ARD 200 BB-279
4X-ARF G1 134
4X-ARG G1 166
4X-ARH G1 25
4X-ARV G1 101
4X-AYA BN2 171
4X-AYB BN2 214
4X-AYC BN2 166
4X-AYE BN2 717
4X-AYF BN2 101
4X-AYG BN2 403
4X-AYH BN2 446
4X-AYI BN2 435
4X-AYK BN2 285
4X-AYL BN2 316
4X-AYN BN2 616
4X-AYO BN2 283
4X-AYP BN2 399
4X-AYR BN2 334
4X-AYS BN2 376
4X-AYT BN2 96
4X-AYV BN2 86
4X-AYW BN2 107
4X-CAH BN2 150
4X-CAY BN2 640
4X-CBF PA42 8001064
4X-CBL 31T 8020080
4X-CBS 31T 7904041
(4X-CCI) TRIS 1024
4X-CCK TRIS 366
4X-CCL TRIS 1042
4X-CCO BN2 139
4X-CCV P68 09
4X-CIC PA42 8001073
4X-CIE 31T 7920030
4X-CIM PA42 8001101
4X-CIN 31T 7820042
4X-CIZ MIII T-271
4X-COD ST50 001
4X-CST G1 194
4X-DZK 200 BB-306
4X-DZT 90 LJ-513
4X-FEA 200 BB-1385
4X-FEB 200 BB-1386
4X-FEC 200 BB-1387
4X-FED 200 BB-1388
4X-FN BN2 107
4X-FNP BN2 285
4X-FSA C-12 BP-7
4X-FSB C-12 BP-8
4X-FSC C-12 BP-9
4X-FSD C-12 BP-10
4X-FSE C-12 BP-11
4X-FSF RC12 FG-1
4X-FSG RC12 FG-2
4X-IPA P68 09
4X-JUD G1 146
4X-SVV PC6 529

Libya

5A-BBA BN2 55
5A-DDT 200C BL-1
5A-DDY 200C BL-6
5A-DEA BN2 55
5A-DHU BN2 865
5A-DHZ MIII T-345
5A-DJB MIII T-388
5A-DKW F406 0092
5A-DSD P68T 8008
5A-DSE P68 397
5A-DSF P68 396
5A-DUA 200 BB-1729

Cyprus

(5B-CFP) BN2 2106
5B-CGM 100 B-27
5B-CHD BN2 166
5B-CHG BN2 870
5B-CHV BN2 878
5B-CIL 31T 7920071
5B-CIM 31T 7620023
5B-CIP 31T 7720062
5B-CJC 31T 7820039
5B-CJD 31T 7620018
5B-CJL 90 LJ-979
5B-CJM 200 BB-1406
(5B-CJM) 200C BL-11
5B-CKJ 200 BB-1729
(5B-CKS) PC6 946
5B-CPA BN2T 2207

5B-ICV BN2 2106

Tanzania

5H-ABN 200C BL-17
5H-ANS F406 0030
5H-ASP 690B 11474
5H-AWK F406 0030
5H-AZD TRIS 1042
5H-AZP TRIS 1041
5H-AZY P68 149
5H-CAM BN2 619
5H-EXC PC12 220
5H-KLA BN2 2002
5H-MCW 100 B-198
(5H-MPD) 100 B-198
(5H-MPE) 100 B-202
5H-MTX 31T 8275011
5H-MTY 690B 11474
5H-MUN 200 BB-467
5H-MVE BN2 2203
5H-PAY F406 0035
5H-RAS F406 0005
5H-SCB 425 0183
5H-SRP PC12 317
5H-SUZ PC12 557
5H-SXB F406 0040
5H-TAA 690B 11473
5H-TRA 100 B-202
5H-TWD F406 0028
5H-TZC F406 0028
5H-TZD F406 0029
5H-TZE F406 0046
5H-TZO P68 120
5H-TZW 200C BL-17
5H-TZX 200 BB-1196
5H-TZY P68 149
5H-UNT BN2 773
5H-WOW F406 0060
5H-ZAA P68 120

Nigeria

5N-AAI G1 58
5N-ABE P166 377
5N-ADG PC6 527
5N-ADP P166 406
5N-ADQ P166 364
5N-AIJ BN2 121
5N-AIK BN2 135
5N-AIL BN2 137
5N-AIQ BN2 156
5N-AKL BN2 330
5N-AKR 200 BB-180
5N-AKS 690A 11221
5N-ALA 690B 11374
5N-ALF 200 BB-397
5N-ALP MU-2 415SA
5N-ALW 200 BB-387
5N-AMT 200 BB-663
5N-AMU 200 BB-809
5N-AMW 425 0067
5N-AMZ 90 LJ-755
5N-AOI BN2 726
5N-APZ 441 0118
5N-ARG E121 121048
5N-ASI BN2 794
5N-ATE P68 244
5N-ATR 441 0353
5N-ATU 90 LJ-136
5N-AUT 31T 7520016
5N-AVH 200 BB-538
5N-AVI BN2 904
5N-AYC P68 252
5N-BHL 200 BB-387
5N-BLF 200 BB-1213
5N-DOV 441 0118
5N-FLS 350 FL-246
5N-FLY 350 FL-279
5N-IHS 200 BB-663
5N-JBN 441 698
5N-MAG 350 FL-153
5N-MPB 350 FL-238
5N-WNL 90 LJ-765

Madagascar

5R- 425 0061
5R- 31T 7720036
5R- E90 LW-47
(5R-M) 90 LJ-528
5R-MGH 200 BB-688
5R-MGV 425 0032
5R-MHC 100 B-122
5R-MIM 31T 7720059
5R-MKA P68 282
5R-MKC P68T 9002
5R-MKI P750 138
5R-MLG BN2 651
5R-MSA BN2 382
5R-MSK F406 0005
5R-MVF BN2 651

Mauritania

5T-BSA BN2T 2144
5T-MAA BN2 577
5T-MAB 31T 8120024
5T-MAC 31T 8120026
5T-MAQ BN2 786
5T-MAR BN2 787
5T-MAS BN2 747
5T-MAT BN2 765
5T-MAU BN2 793
5T-MAV BN2 587
5T-MAY BN2 574
5T-MAZ BN2 576
5T-TJV BN2 377
5T-TJY 31T 7920056

Niger

5U-AAN BN2 674
5U-AAS BN2 744
5U-ABJ BN2 771
5U-ABV E90 LW-291
5U-ABX 200 BB-531
5U-ABY 200 BB-431
5U-ABZ BN2 702
5U-ACC 31T 7920056

Togo

5V- 31T 7820013
5V- F406 0023
5V-MCG 200 BB-857
5V-MCH 200 BB-858
5V-TPH 300 FA-173
5V-TTB BN2 717
5V-TTD 90 LJ-453

Western Samoa

5W-FAF BN2 109
5W-FAQ BN2 785
5W-FAV BN2 42

Uganda

5X-BEE BN2 143
5X-EMM BN2 861
5X-INS 200 BB-914
5X-INS 200 BB-1650
5X-MHB BN2 2002
5X-UAF P68 416
5X-UAS TRIS 373
5X-UDC TRIS 1001
5X-UWS 100 B-188
5X-UWT 100 B-197

Kenya

(5Y-) 690 11069
5Y-AHR PC6 629
5Y-AHY PC6 627
5Y-AMG BN2 601
5Y-AMU BN2 251
5Y-ANU BN2 287
5Y-ANV BN2 284
5Y-AOY TRIS 320
5Y-ARZ BN2 330
(5Y-ARZ) BN2 673
5Y-AUA BN2 275
5Y-AYE BN2 736
5Y-BAO P68 74
5Y-BAV P68 80
5Y-BBA P68 93
5Y-BBB BN2 809
5Y-BBC BN2 810
5Y-BBE P68 106
5Y-BBF P68 107
5Y-BBT P68 125
5Y-BBY P68 131
5Y-BCB P68 139
5Y-BCG P68 145
5Y-BCH P68 149
5Y-BCI P68 153
5Y-BCR BN2 820
5Y-BCS BN2 818
5Y-BCT P68 162
5Y-BDC P68 192
5Y-BDK P68 167
5Y-BFR P68 363
5Y-BHZ BN2 814
5Y-BIG 31T 8275011
(5Y-BIQ) 200 BB-51
5Y-BIR 200 BB-51
5Y-BIS F406 0037
5Y-BIW 200 BB-782
5Y-BIX F406 0055
5Y-BIZ MU-2 1528SA
5Y-BJC 200 BB-597
5Y-BJM 200 BB-1152
5Y-BJX MU-2 627
5Y-BKA 200 BB-846
5Y-BKM 200 BB-86
5Y-BKN F406 0021
5Y-BKS 200 BB-201
5Y-BKT 200 BB-256
5Y-BLA 200C BL-10
5Y-BLF G1 131
5Y-BLR G1 34
5Y-BMA 200 BB-155
5Y-BMC 200 BB-211
5Y-BMR G1 81
5Y-BMS G1 194
"5Y-BMT" G1 81
5Y-BMT G1 173
5Y-BMY 690B 11474
5Y-BPJ 200 BB-327
5Y-BRZ 441 0164
5Y-BSR MU-2 727SA
5Y-BSU 200 BB-222
5Y-BTL 690A 11103
5Y-BTO 200 BB-407
5Y-BTV 200 BB-1342
5Y-BVU 200 BB-286
5Y-BWD 200 BB-756
5Y-BYX F406 0010
5Y-CDO 200 BB-610
5Y-CMC TRIS 1032
5Y-DDE 200 BB-379
5Y-DLC BN2 155
5Y-ECO 200 BB-1343
5Y-EKO 200C BL-2
5Y-EMJ G1 158
5Y-EMK G1 1
5Y-EOB 200 BB-1305
5Y-FDK 200 BB-531
5Y-GJW P68 394
5Y-GRD 200 BB-552
5Y-HHA 200 BB-988
5Y-HHD 200 BB-643
5Y-HHE 200 BB-547
5Y-HHG 200 BB-288
(5Y-HHJ) F406 0040
5Y-HHK 200 BB-696
5Y-HHM 200 BB-1152
5Y-ING F406 0024
5Y-JAI 200 BB-557
5Y-JAK BN2 2002
5Y-JET G1 44
5Y-JJA F406 0013
5Y-JJB 31T 8375001
5Y-JJC F406 0040
5Y-JJG F406 0003
5Y-JJZ 200 BB-1127
5Y-JKB 200 BB-72
5Y-JMR 200C BL-17
5Y-KXU 425 0047
5Y-LAN F406 0045
5Y-LRS 200C BL-20
5Y-MAF PC12 243
5Y-MAL 90 LJ-619
5Y-MAX BN2 748
"5Y-MEL" 90 LJ-619
5Y-MIA G1 158
5Y-MKM F406 0044
5Y-MMJ F406 0030
5Y-NAL F406 0038
5Y-NAX 200C BL-8
5Y-NBB 90 LJ-528
5Y-NCA 441 0072
5Y-NJS 200 BB-837
5Y-NKI 200 BB-525
5Y-NPO 200 BB-367
(5Y-NRW) 200 BB-201
(5Y-NTM) 200 BB-256
5Y-NUN 200 BB-643
5Y-NUR 200 BB-309
5Y-PLM 200 BB-812
5Y-RAJ BN2 537
5Y-RJA 200 BB-619
5Y-SEL 200 BB-99
5Y-SJB 200 BB-467
5Y-SMB 200 BB-379
5Y-SPR MU-2 1566SA
5Y-SRS P68 392
5Y-TAL F406 0009
5Y-THS 200 BB-643
5Y-TNT MIII T-211
5Y-TWA 200 BB-803
5Y-TWB 200 BB-696
5Y-TWC 200C BL-37
5Y-UAC 31T 8375002
5Y-UAL 31T 8275002
5Y-WAW F406 0012
5Y-XXC 200 BB-531
5Y-XXX G1 1
5Y-ZBK 200 BB-1714

Somalia

6O-SBB P68 139
6O-SBI P166 467
6O-SBJ P166 468
6O-SBK P166 469
6O-SBL P166 470
6O-SBQ 690A 11151
6O-SBV MIII TT-477A

Senegal

6V- 100 B-91
6V- 100 B-150
6V-ADJ BN2 700
6V-AES BN2 700
6V-AGO 31T 7620057
6V-AGS 200 BB-28
6V-AHW BN2T 2146

Jamaica

6Y-JAP BN2 621
6Y-JDB MU-2 353SA

6Y-JFL	BN2	54
6Y-JHU	BN2	257
6Y-JJA	BN2	368
6Y-JJH	TRIS	1009
6Y-JJI	TRIS	1012
6Y-JKJ	BN2	2103
6Y-JLA	BN2	341
6Y-JLB	BN2	78
6Y-JLG	BN2	2170
6Y-JLU	BN2	2170
6Y-JNS	BN2	2289
6Y-JQA	BN2	368
6Y-JQE	TRIS	1056
6Y-JQF	TRIS	1058
6Y-JQJ	BN2	2103
6Y-JQK	TRIS	1059
6Y-JRC	BN2	339
(6Y-JRD)	BN2	340
6Y-JSM	BN2	116
6Y-JSX	BN2	78

Lesotho

7P-AAA	300	FA-72
7P-FDG	PC6	682
7P-IRC	BN2	271
7P-LAC	BN2	729
7P-LAD	BN2	271
7P-LAE	BN2	556

Malawi

7Q-NXB	200	BB-286
7Q-ULC	350	FL-595
7Q-YAU	BN2T	2151
7Q-YAV	BN2T	2158
7Q-YAW	BN2T	2141
7Q-YAX	BN2	792
7Q-YAZ	BN2	492
7Q-YFZ	P68	277
7Q-YKC	BN2	105
7Q-YKD	BN2	604
7Q-YLL	690B	11384
7Q-YLT	PC12	525
7Q-YMM	90	LJ-880
7Q-YMP	200	BB-903
7Q-YSC	690A	11286
7Q-YST	300	FA-139
7Q-YTC	200	BB-215

Algeria

7T-VBE	200	BB-1453
7T-VBV	PC6	541
7T-VCG	PC6	917
7T-VCH	PC6	929
7T-VCI	PC6	930
7T-VCJ	PC6	933
7T-VCK	PC6	934
7T-VCV	100	B-93
7T-VNA	PC6	817
7T-VRF	100	B-147
7T-VRG	200	BB-184
7T-VRH	200	BB-175
7T-VRI	200	BB-171
7T-VRO	200	BB-807
7T-VRS	200	BB-759
7T-VRT	200	BB-775
7T-VRY	200T	BT-20
7T-VRZ	200T	BT-21
7T-VSH	90	LJ-423
7T-VSV	PC6	541
7T-WCF	90	LJ-1359
7T-WCG	90	LJ-1379
7T-WCH	90	LJ-1380
7T-WLA	PC6	919
7T-WLD	PC6	937
7T-WLE	PC6	920
7T-WRG	200	BB-184
7T-WRH	200	BB-175
7T-WRI	200	BB-171
7T-WRO	200	BB-807
7T-WRS	200	BB-759
7T-WRT	200	BB-775
7T-WRY	200T	BT-20
7T-WRZ	200T	BT-21

Barbados

8P-ASC	BN2	610
8P-ASC	TRIS	1027
8P-ASD	BN2	33
8P-ASE	BN2	532
8P-ASF	BN2	2128
8P-ASF	TRIS	1035
8P-ASL	BN2	2152
8P-BAR	200	BB-1313
8P-BAR	90	LJ-499
8P-BAR	E90	LW-140
8P-DIS	BN2	54
(8P-DON)	BN2	388
8P-HEC	BN2	54
8P-PAT	BN2	694
8P-RAD	BN2	2018
(8P-SCA)	BN2	2208
8P-TAC	BN2	2128
8P-TAD	BN2	2152
(8P-TAF)	BN2	2203
8P-TAG	BN2	2208
(8P-TAH)	BN2	2204
8P-TAI	BN2	2211
8P-TAJ	BN2	2210

Guyana

8R-	BN2	431
8R-GAC	BN2	694
8R-GAR	BN2	306
8R-GDJ	BN2	148
8R-GDN	BN2	118
8R-GDN	BN2	230
(8R-GDQ)	BN2	125
8R-GDQ	BN2	231
8R-GDS	BN2	610
8R-GDT	BN2	612
8R-GEE	BN2	720
8R-GEH	BN2	348
8R-GER	BN2	478
8R-GES	BN2	482
8R-GET	BN2	484
8R-GFB	200	BB-82
8R-GFI	BN2	677
8R-GFL	BN2	384
8R-GFN	BN2	289
8R-GFQ	BN2	33
8R-GGL	BN2	54
8R-GGN	BN2	694
8R-GGR	BN2	230
8R-GGT	BN2	635
8R-GGU	BN2	251
8R-GGY	BN2	470
8R-GHB	BN2	269
8R-GHC	BN2	306
8R-GHD	BN2	622
8R-GHE	BN2	269
8R-GHG	BN2	116
8R-GHM	BN2	216
8R-GMM	BN2	2021
8R-GRA	BN2	3006
8R-GRC	BN2	2114

Croatia

9A-BIH	31T	1104016
9A-BKB	200	BB-1983
9A-BOR	31T	8004011
9A-BZG	31T	8104032
9A-CZG	31T	8104046
9A-DAC	90	LJ-1263

Ghana

9G-AGC	200C	BL-137
9G-SAM	90	LJ-839

Malta

9H-AAB	BN2	73
9H-ACI	F406	0041
9H-ACU	BN2	2159
9H-ADD	PA42	8001101
9H-ADF	BN2	2156
9H-ADV	350	FL-279
9H-AFF	P68	397
9H-AFO	P68T	8008

Zambia

9J-AAT	90	LJ-484
9J-AAU	90	LJ-485
9J-AAV	90	LJ-486
9J-ACB	BN2	246
9J-ACC	BN2	254
9J-ACE	BN2	260
9J-ACF	BN2	261
9J-ACG	BN2	270
"9J-ACH"	BN2	275
9J-ACL	BN2	275
9J-ACM	BN2	280
9J-AEO	BN2	849
9J-AEV	200	BB-715
9J-AFI	300	FA-166
9J-AFK	BN2	155
9J-DCF	90	LJ-575
9J-GCF	90	LJ-590
9J-MAC	BN2	619
9J-MED	200	BB-1046
9J-OGT	E90	LW-87
9J-PLJ	BN2	799
9J-RGD	680T	1709-84
9J-SKY	BN2	270
9J-STA	E90	LW-116
9J-TAF	90	LJ-485
9J-UAS	BN2	155
9J-WHX	BN2	192
9J-YVZ	90	LJ-338

Kuwait

9K-ACP	690A	11141
9K-ACW	MIIB	T26-171E
(9K-ANP)	690A	11141

Sierra Leone

9L-LAF	P166	406
9L-LAQ	TRIS	363
9L-LAR	TRIS	366
(9L-LAR)	TRIS	373
9L-LAU	TRIS	1028
9L-LAV	BN2	767
9L-LBC	P68T	9003
9L-LDA	90	LJ-281

Malaysia

9M-	350	FL-598
9M-APD	BN2	41
9M-APE	BN2	63
(9M-API)	PC6	650
9M-APJ	PC6	655
9M-APK	BN2	602
9M-APQ	PC6	627
9M-ARM	BN2	42
9M-ARQ	BN2	632
9M-ASH	200	BB-881
9M-ASL	BN2	684
9M-ATM	BN2	693
9M-ATN	BN2	701
9M-ATS	BN2	379
9M-AUD	BN2	392
9M-AUQ	BN2	741
9M-AXL	441	0039
9M-AXU	BN2	584
9M-AXZ	425	0063
9M-AYJ	BN2	42
9M-AZM	690B	11414
9M-AZV	BN2	2177
9M-BSM	BN2	3005
9M-BSS	BN2T	2112
9M-CAA	100	B-27
9M-CAM	200T	BT-10
9M-DSL	350	FL-122
9M-DSR	TBM7	69
9M-JPA	100	B-27
9M-JPA	200T	BT-10
9M-JPC	BN2	379
9M-JPD	200T	BT-24
(9M-JPE)	200T	BT-24
9M-JPL	90	LJ-1809
9M-KNS	200	BB-294
9M-LYG	BN2T	2138
9M-MDA	BN2	41
9M-MDB	BN2	42
9M-MDC	BN2	602
9M-MDD	BN2	684
9M-PMS	F406	0049
9M-PSE	PC6	849
9M-PSF	PC6	850
9M-PSG	PC6	851
9M-PSH	PC6	852
9M-PSI	PC6	853
9M-PSJ	PC6	854
9M-PSK	PC6	855
9M-PTA	350	FL-587
9M-PTB	350	FL-593
9M-TAC	BN2	2251
9M-TAD	BN2	2159
9M-TAM	BN2	2234
9M-TBM	TBM7	166
9M-TDM	PA42	5527032
9M-TIR	BN2T	2138
(9M-TPD)	BN2T	4011
9M-TPS	BN2T	4009
9M-UMW	200	BB-590
9M-WKC	BN2	2038
9M-WSK	200G	BY-8
9M-ZAA	200	BB-452

Nepal

9N-AAF	PC6	346
9N-AAG	PC6	347
9N-AAW	PC6	716
9N-AAZ	PC6	727
9N-ABC	PC6	728
9N-ABJ	PC6	746
9N-ABK	PC6	755
9N-AIU	PC6	962
9N-AIV	PC6	963
9N-AIZ	P750	154

DR Congo

9Q-	G1	193
9Q-	P68	216
9Q-CAA	MU-2	618
9Q-CAD	P68	131
9Q-CAE	BN2	630
9Q-CAJ	C-12	BD-5
9Q-CAK	P68	205
9Q-CAZ	MU-2	586
9Q-CBC	P68	116
9Q-CBD	G1	35
9Q-CBL	P68	131
9Q-CBU	681B	6045
9Q-CBY	G1	33
9Q-CCB	690A	11151
9Q-CCE	200	BB-934
9Q-CCG	E90	LW-110
9Q-CDB	P68	127

9Q-CDV	**P68**	**207**
9Q-CEM	**100**	**B-105**
9Q-CEW	P68	120
9Q-CEZ	**P68**	**163**
9Q-CEZ	P68	197
9Q-CFE	200	BB-722
9Q-CFK	G1	77
9Q-CFK	MIVC	AT-423
9Q-CFZ	**P68**	**202**
9Q-CGE	681B	6060
9Q-CGL	681	6030
9Q-CHE	90	LJ-969
9Q-CHV	P68	208
9Q-CIH	690	11039
9Q-CIN	**BN2**	**746**
9Q-CJA	**BN2**	**898**
9Q-CJB	**G1**	**155**
9Q-CJT	200C	BL-53
9Q-CKM	**90**	**LJ-402**
(9Q-CKR)	BN2	2127
9Q-CKS	300	FA-110
9Q-CKT	P68	255
9Q-CKV	**P68**	**26**
9Q-CKW	**P68**	**289**
9Q-CKZ	90	LJ-494
9Q-CLW	BN2T	2030
9Q-CMJ	BN2	591
9Q-CMM	**BN2**	**814**
9Q-CMQ	P68	38
9Q-CNV	**P68**	**171**
9Q-COE	**G1**	**156**
9Q-COI	MIII	T-302
9Q-CPT	BN2	461
9Q-CPV	200	BB-999
9Q-CQP	MIII	T-342
9Q-CRF	**100**	**B-33**
9Q-CRF	BN2	157
9Q-CRP	**BN2**	**631**
9Q-CTE	200	BB-399
9Q-CTF	200	BB-431
9Q-CTG	**200**	**BB-629**
9Q-CTH	PC6	817
9Q-CTK	200	BB-160
9Q-CTL	**P68**	**145**
9Q-CTN	**P68**	**238**
9Q-CTO	**P68**	**162**
9Q-CTQ	E90	LW-88
9Q-CTS	BN2	607
9Q-CTS	P68	116
(9Q-CTZ)	200T	BT-14
9Q-CVB	**P68**	**177**
9Q-CVT	90	LJ-431
9Q-CYA	**BN2**	**617**
9Q-CYB	BN2	633
9Q-CYC	**BN2**	**638**
9Q-CYK	P68	240
9Q-CYS	200	BB-999
9Q-CYS	300	FA-156
9Q-CYZ	300	FA-173
9Q-CZD	E90	LW-76
9Q-CZG	PC6	916
9Q-CZV	**P68**	**209**
"9Q-XJF"	P68	255

Burundi

9U-BRV	BN2	814

Singapore

9V-BBS	BN2	42
9V-BDH	BN2	632
9V-BDT	BN2	235
(9V-BDW)	BN2	615
9V-BEB	BN2	634
9V-BEC	BN2	639
9V-BGA	BN2	380
(9V-BGD)	BN2	426
9V-BGJ	BN2	392
9V-BGT	BN2	752
9V-BGV	BN2	754
9V-BHF	31T	7620015
9V-BHX	BN2	780
9V-BJF	BN2	782
9V-BJG	BN2	785
9V-BJN	BN2	595
9V-BJO	BN2	781
9V-BKQ	BN2	831
9V-BLM	BN2	584
9V-BMA	31T	8004036

Rwanda

9XR-GV	BN2	751
9XR-GW	**BN2**	**811**
9XR-KA	BN2	662
9XR-KG	BN2	664
9XR-WR	G1	106

Trinidad & Tobago

9Y-TGR	200	BB-676
9Y-TGY	200	BB-1048
9Y-THI	P68T	8007
9Y-TJA	100	B-208

MILITARY INDEX

Angola

1723	PC6	715
2451	BN2	526
2452	BN2	562
2453	BN2	543
2454	BN2	797
2455	BN2	801
2456	BN2	798
2457	BN2	802
2458	BN2	803
I-301	BN2	898
I-302	BN2	896
I-303	BN2	890
I-304	BN2	899
I-305	BN2	902
I-306	BN2	903
R-201	BN2	526
R-202	BN2	562
R-203	BN2	543
R-205	BN2	801
R-206	BN2	798
R-207	BN2	802
R-208	BN2	803
R-209	BN2	898
R-210	BN2	896
R-211	BN2	890

Argentina

0674	FPC6	2034
0684	FPC6	2045
0684	FPC6	2046
0685	FPC6	2046
0686	FPC6	2047
0697	200	BB-54
0698	200	BB-71
0745	200	BB-460
0746	200	BB-471
0746	200	BB-543
0747	200	BB-488
0748	200	BB-546
0749	200	BB-549
1-G-31	200	BB-54
4-G-1	FPC6	2046
4-G-2	FPC6	2045
4-G-3	FPC6	2046
4-G-4	FPC6	2047
4-F-42	200	BB-71
4-F-43	200	BB-460
4-G-42	200	BB-71
4-G-43	200	BB-460
4-G-44	200	BB-471
4-G-45	200	BB-488
4-G-46	200	BB-543
4-G-47	200	BB-546
4-G-48	200	BB-549
5-T-31	200	BB-54
5-T-32	200	BB-71
5-T-33	200	BB-460
6-G-1	FPC6	2034
6-G-41	200	BB-54
6-P-44	200	BB-471
6-P-45	200	BB-488
6-P-47	200	BB-546
6-P-48	200	BB-549
AE100	100	B-82
AE104	680T	1681-63
AE128	680T	1681-63
AE129	680T	1681-63
AE176	MIII	T-275
AE177	MIII	T-277
AE178	MIII	T-280
AE179	MIII	T-281
AE180	MIVA	AT-071E
AE181	MIVA	AT-063
AE182	MIVA	AT-064
GN-705	31T	8020092
GN-804	PC6	786
GN-805	PC6	787
GN-806	PC6	788
GN-807	PC6	805
GN-808	PC6	806
GN-809	PC6	807
GN-810	PC12	294
GN-853	PC6	953
TS-01	MIVA	AT-063
TS-02	MIVA	AT-064

Australia

A14-652	PC6	652
A14-653	PC6	653
A14-661	PC6	661
A14-662	PC6	662
A14-680	PC6	680
A14-681	PC6	681
A14-683	PC6	683
A14-684	PC6	684
A14-686	PC6	686
A14-687	PC6	687
A14-689	PC6	689
A14-690	PC6	690
A14-692	PC6	692
A14-693	PC6	693
A14-701	PC6	701
A14-702	PC6	725
A14-703	PC6	729
A14-704	PC6	730
A14-705	PC6	731
A14-725	PC6	725
(A14-729)	PC6	729
(A14-730)	PC6	730
(A14-731)	PC6	731
A32-001	200	BB-1189
A32-002	200	BB-1125
A32-003	200	BB-1401
A32-004	200	BB-1463
A32-339	350	FL-339
A32-343	350	FL-343
A32-346	350	FL-346
A32-348	350	FL-348
A32-349	350	FL-349
A32-350	350	FL-350
A32-351	350	FL-351
A32-372	350	FL-372
A32-426	350	FL-426
A32-437	350	FL-437
A32-439	350	FL-439
*A32-651	350	FL-651

Austria

3G-EA	PC6	752
3G-EB	PC6	758
3G-EC	PC6	764
3G-ED	PC6	765
3G-EE	PC6	766
3G-EF	PC6	769
3G-EG	PC6	770
3G-EH	PC6	771
3G-EI	PC6	774
3G-EJ	PC6	775
3G-EK	PC6	776
3G-EL	PC6	777
3G-EM	PC6	856
3G-EN	PC6	664

Bahamas

DF-103	350	FL-95

Bangladesh

S3-BHN	31T	1104007

Belgium

B-01	BN2	466
B-02	BN2	468
B-03	BN2	476
B-04	BN2	498
B-05	BN2	501
B-06	BN2	510
B-07	BN2	523
B-08	BN2	531
B-09	BN2	533
B-10	BN2	541
B-11	BN2	549
B-12	BN2	553
CF-01	MIII	T-259
CF-02	MIII	T-260
CF-03	MIII	T-262
CF-04	MIII	T-264
CF-05	MIII	T-265
CF-06	MIII	T-267
G-05	BN2T	2146
OT-ALC	BN2	476
OT-ALD	BN2	498
OT-ALE	BN2	501
OT-ALF	BN2	510
OT-ALG	BN2	523
OT-ALH	BN2	531
OT-ALI	BN2	533
OT-ALJ	BN2	541
OT-ALK	BN2	549
OT-ALL	BN2	553
OT-GLA	BN2T	2146

Belize

BDF-01	BN2	2137
BDF-02	BN2	2136
BDF-05	BN2	277
BDF-06	90	LJ-270

Bolivia

EB-001	200	BB-209
EB-002	200C	BL-33
EB-003	90	LJ-905
EB-004	31T	8120017
FAB-001	200	BB-11
FAB-001	90	LJ-413
FAB-002	200	BB-11
FAB-002	200C	BL-33
FAB-005	FPC6	2072
FAB-006	90	LJ-413
FAB-009	FPC6	2070
FAB-018	200C	BL-28
FAB-019	695	95049
FAB-023	690B	11562
FAB-026	E90	LW-28
FAB-028	690	11067

Botswana

OA1	BN2	791
OA2	BN2	783
OA2	BN2	795
OA3	BN2	799
OA4	BN2	772
OA5	BN2	836
OA6	BN2	918
OA7	BN2	2226
OA8	BN2	2227
OA9	BN2	2257
OA10	BN2	2258
OA11	BN2	2265
OA12	BN2	2295
OB1	200	BB-1352
OB2	200	BB-1352
OE1	TRIS	1054
OE2	TRIS	1055

Brazil

2650	E121	121002
2651	E121	121003
2652	E121	121004
2653	E121	121005
2654	E121	121006
2655	E121	121008
2656	E121	121060
2657	E121	121037

Bulgaria

020	PC12	518

Canada

145201	200	BB-77
145201	200	BB-92
145202	200	BB-170

Chile

209	90	LJ-441
331	100	B-219
336	200	BB-1530
C-51	31T	8020090
C-52	200G	BY-19
FAC498	E90	LW-153
FAC499	200C	BN-1

Colombia

ARC601	690	11055
EJC-010	90	LJ-739
EJC-021	690D	15024
EJC-022	695	95066
EJC-103	690D	15024
EJC-111	690D	15024
EJC-112	695A	96076
EJC-114	695A	96083
EJC-115	695	95066
EJC-116	90	LJ-739
EJC-117	200	BB-694
EJC-118	200	BB-1452
EJC-119	200	BB-1615
EJC-124	200	BB-6
FAC	690C	11685
FAC	690C	11723
FAC160	PC6	349
FAC542	680T	1563-19
FAC551	680T	1519-95
FAC570	90	LJ-752
FAC1110	PC6	818
FAC1111	PC6	819
FAC1112	PC6	821
FAC1113	PC6	822
FAC1114	PC6	823
FAC1115	PC6	820
FAC5194	31T	7520014
FAC5198	695A	96030
FAC5454	690D	15010
FAC5553	695	95055
FAC5570	90	LJ-752
FAC5600	695A	96044
FAC5625	300	FA-22
FAC5730	90	LJ-503
FAC5739	31T	7520014

FAC5743	PA42	5501039
FAC5744	PA42	8001062
FAC5746	350	FL-282
FAC5747	350	FL-454
FAC5750	300	FA-22
PNC-204	441	0031
PNC-0208	300	FA-159
PNC-209	200	BB-212
PNC-221	200	BB-833
PNC-0225	200	BB-1644
PNC-0236	200	BB-512

Cyprus

12106	BN2	2106
CP-1	BN2T	2207

DR Congo

9T-BHB	BN2	630
9T-MBA	MU-2	618
9T-MBD	MU-2	620

Dominican Republic

1521	MU-2	548

Ecuador

723	200	BB-723
AEE-001	200	BB-811
AEE-101	200	BB-811
AN-231	200	BB-771
AN-232	300	FA-75
AN-233	200	BB-458
AN-234	200	BB-580
AN-235	350	FL-85
AN-236	200	BB-703
E-180	PC6	750
E-185	PC6	859
E-190	PC6	743
E-195	PC6	903
IGM-240	100	B-242
SAE-T-1540	FPC6	2037
SAE-T-1545	FPC6	2038
T-180	PC6	750
T-185	PC6	743
T-185	PC6	859

Falkland Islands

619	PC6	619

Finland

BN-1	BN2	269

France

0006	F406	0006
0008	F406	0008
0010	F406	0010
0025	F406	0025
27	E121	121027
30	E121	121030
33	TBM7	33
35	TBM7	35
0039	F406	0039
47	E121	121047
054	E121	121054
055	E121	121055
55	E121	121055
56	E121	121056
0064	31T	8120064
064	E121	121064
65	E121	121065
066	E121	121066
67	E121	121067
68	E121	121068
069	E121	121069
69	E121	121069
070	E121	121070
70	TBM7	70
71	E121	121071
072	E121	121072
073	E121	121073
74	E121	121074
075	E121	121075
076	E121	121076
77	E121	121077
077	E121	121077
77	TBM7	77
078	E121	121078
78	TBM7	78
79	E121	121079
080	E121	121080
80	TBM7	80
81	E121	121081
082	E121	121082
083	E121	121083
83	E121	121083
084	E121	121084
85	E121	121085
086	E121	121086
87	E121	121087
089	E121	121089
090	E121	121090
90	E121	121090
091	E121	121091
092	E121	121092
93	TBM7	93
94	TBM7	94
095	E121	121095
95	TBM7	95
096	E121	121096
098	E121	121098
099	E121	121099
99	TBM7	99
100	TBM7	100
101	E121	121101
102	E121	121102
103	E121	121103
103	TBM7	103
104	TBM7	104
105	E121	121105
105	TBM7	105
106	TBM7	106
107	E121	121107
108	E121	121108
110	TBM7	110
111	E121	121111
111	TBM7	111
115	TBM7	115
117	TBM7	117
125	TBM7	125
131	TBM7	131
136	TBM7	136
139	TBM7	139
146	TBM7	146
147	TBM7	147
156	TBM7	156
159	TBM7	159
160	TBM7	160
518	90	LJ-518
887	PC6	887
888	PC6	888
889	PC6	889
890	PC6	890
891	PC6	891
330-IC	TBM7	93
330-ID	TBM7	33
40-XD	TBM7	77
40-XF	TBM7	80
40-XP	TBM7	110
41-XF	TBM7	80
41-XI	TBM7	103
41-XJ	TBM7	104
41-XP	TBM7	110
43-VX	TBM7	70
43-XA	TBM7	33
43-XB	TBM7	35
43-XC	TBM7	70
43-XL	TBM7	93
44-XE	TBM7	78
44-XG	TBM7	94
44-XN	TBM7	117
65-XA	TBM7	33
65-XB	TBM7	35
65-XD	TBM7	77
65-XE	TBM7	78
65-XF	TBM7	80
65-XG	TBM7	94
65-XH	TBM7	95
65-XI	TBM7	103
65-XJ	TBM7	104
65-XK	TBM7	105
65-XL	TBM7	110
65-XM	TBM7	111
65-XN	TBM7	117
65-XO	TBM7	125
65-XQ	TBM7	131
65-XR	TBM7	146
65-XS	TBM7	147
70-XG	TBM7	94
70-XJ	TBM7	104
ABO	TBM7	99
ABP	TBM7	100
ABQ	TBM7	115
ABR	TBM7	136
ABS	TBM7	139
ABT	TBM7	156
ABU	TBM7	159
ABV	TBM7	160
ABW	TBM7	35
ABX	TBM7	70
ABY	TBM7	80
ABZ	TBM7	94

Ghana

G350	BN2	333
G351	BN2	337
G352	BN2	338
G353	BN2	339
G354	BN2	340
G355	BN2	341
G356	BN2	342
G357	BN2	343
G360	BN2T	2225
G361	BN2T	2222
G362	BN2T	2223
G363	BN2T	2229

Greece

401	C-12	BC-34
402	200	BB-1733
403	200	BB-1744
AC-21	F406	0087
AC-22	F406	0088
AC-23	F406	0089
P-9	G1	120

Guatemala

070	695A	96006
458	90	LJ-458
633	690	11005
700	F90	LA-181
FAG001	200	BB-125
R701	90	LJ-296
R704	200	BB-310

Haiti

1270	BN2	410

Honduras

FAH006	695A	96060
FAH012	PA42	8001056

Hong Kong

HKG-7	BN2	615
HKG-8	200C	BL-128
HKG-9	200C	BL-130

India

IN126	BN2T	477
IN127	BN2T	480
IN128	BN2T	481
IN129	BN2T	506
IN130	BN2T	507
IN131	BN2	873
IN132	BN2	875
IN133	BN2T	886
IN134	BN2	887
IN135	BN2T	888
IN136	BN2	889
IN137	BN2	2123
IN138	BN2	2134
IN139	BN2	2135
IN140	BN2	2148
IN141	BN2	2149
IN142	BN2	2150

Indonesia

A-10021	BN2	713
AG-601	PC6	785
AG-602	PC6	792
AG-603	PC6	798
AG-604	PC6	799
AG-605	PC6	801
ST-0601	PC6	785
ST-0602	PC6	792
ST-0603	PC6	798
ST-0604	PC6	799
ST-0605	PC6	801

Iran

501	690	11049
501	690	11076
1401	690A	11181
1402	690A	11293
1403	690	11049
1405	690	11075
1406	690	11045
4-901	690	11077
4-902	690	11078
4-903	690	11079
4-9801	PC6	825
4-9802	PC6	826
4-9803	PC6	827
4-9804	PC6	828
4-9805	PC6	829
4-9806	PC6	830
4-9807	PC6	831
4-9808	PC6	832
4-9809	PC6	833
4-9810	PC6	834
4-9811	PC6	835
4-9812	PC6	836
4-9813	PC6	837
4-9814	PC6	838
4-9815	PC6	839
5-59	681	6009
5-280	681B	6062
5-281	681B	6068
5-282	681B	6072
5-2501	690	11076
5-2505	690A	11183
5-4035	690A	11294
5-4036	690A	11295

5-4037	690A	11333
5-4038	690A	11334
5-4081	681	6009
5-8901	681B	6062
5-8902	681B	6068
5-8903	681B	6072
5-8997	690	11049
6-3201	690A	11181
6-3202	690A	11293
G-3201	690A	11181
G-3202	690A	11293

Iraq

5821	PC6	846
5822	PC6	847
YI-321	350	FL-521

Ireland

232	200	BB-208
234	200	BB-376
240	200	BB-672
254	BN2T	4008

Israel

00.	BN2	96
001	G1	146
02	PC6	529
004	BN2	285
006	200	BB-1388
006	BN2	107
06	PC6	646
007	200	BB-1387
008	200	BB-1386
009	200	BB-1385
501	200	BB-1385
504	200	BB-1386
507	200	BB-1387
510	200	BB-1388
622	200T	BT-39
625	200T	BT-40
629	200T	BT-41
633	200T	BT-42
636	200T	BT-43
703	200C	BN-5
709	200C	BN-6
711	200C	BN-7
714	200C	BN-8
719	200C	BN-9
721	200T	BT-44
730	200T	BT-45
735	200T	BT-46
842	200	BB-1806
844	200	BB-1809
848	200	BB-1811
856	200	BB-1804
859	200	BB-1819
974	C-12	BP-7
977	C-12	BP-8
980	C-12	BP-9
982	C-12	BP-10
985	C-12	BP-11
987	RC12	FG-1
990	RC12	FG-2

Italy

303-10	P166	434
303-20	P166	472
303-21	P166	473
303-22	P166	474
303-23	P166	475
303-24	P166	476
303-25	P166	477
303-28	P166	383
303-28	P166	421
303-31	P166	397
303-31	P166	407
303-32	P166	384
303-33	P166	393
303-33	P166	430
303-36	P166	404
303-37	P166	425
303-39	P166	438
36-65	P166	435
36-66	P166	433
36-66	P166	442
36-74	P166	379
36-75	P166	387
36-75	P166	395
36-76	P166	391
4-4	P166	422
53-34	P166	437
53-34	P166	443
53-35	P166	432
53-35	P166	440
53-72	P166	418
53-73	P166	420
53-76	P166	394
8-01	P166	478
8-02	P166	479
8-03	P166	480
8-04	P166	481
8-05	P166	482
8-06	P166	483
8-07	P166	484
8-08	P166	485
8-09	P166	486
8-10	P166	487
8-11	P166	488
8-12	P166	489
9-01	P180	1076
9-02	P180	1085
9-03	P180	1090
CC-112	P180	1114
CFS-181	P180	1094
CSX5172	P166	466
CSX62164	P180	1030
CSX62211	P180	1085
CSX62213	P180	1090
CSX62246	P180	1114
CSX62247	P180	1113
CSX62249	P180	1126
GF-01	P166	465
GF-02	P166	466
GF-03	P166	490
GF-04	P166	491
GF-05	P166	492
GF-06	P166	493
GF-07	P166	494
GF-08	P166	495
GF-09	P166	496
GF-10	P166	601
GF-11	P166	602
GF-12	P166	603
GF-18	P180	1118
GF-19	P180	1126
MM25153	P166	472
MM25154	P166	473
MM25155	P166	474
MM25156	P166	475
MM25157	P166	476
MM25158	P166	477
MM25159	P166	478
MM25160	P166	479
MM25161	P166	480
MM25162	P166	481
MM25163	P166	482
MM25164	P166	483
MM25165	P166	484
MM25166	P166	485
MM25167	P166	486
MM25168	P166	487
MM25169	P166	488
MM25170	P166	489
MM25171	P166	465
MM25172	P166	466
MM25173	P166	490
MM25174	P166	491
MM25175	P166	492
MM25176	P166	493
MM25177	P166	494
MM25178	P166	495
MM25179	P166	496
MM25180	P166	601
MM25181	P166	602
MM25182	P166	603
MM61871	P166	379
MM61872	P166	380
MM61873	P166	381
MM61874	P166	382
MM61875	P166	383
MM61876	P166	384
MM61877	P166	385
MM61878	P166	386
MM61879	P166	387
MM61880	P166	388
MM61881	P166	389
MM61882	P166	390
MM61883	P166	391
MM61884	P166	392
MM61885	P166	393
MM61886	P166	394
MM61887	P166	395
MM61888	P166	396
MM61889	P166	397
MM61890	P166	398
MM61891	P166	399
MM61902	P166	404
MM61903	P166	405
MM61904	P166	407
MM61905	P166	408
MM61906	P166	418
MM61907	P166	419
MM61908	P166	420
MM61909	P166	421
MM61910	P166	422
MM61911	P166	423
MM61912	P166	424
MM61913	P166	425
MM61914	P166	426
MM61915	P166	427
MM61916	P166	428
MM61917	P166	429
MM61918	P166	430
MM61919	P166	431
MM61920	P166	432
MM61921	P166	433
MM61924	P166	434
MM61925	P166	435
MM61926	P166	436
MM61927	P166	437
MM61928	P166	438
MM61929	P166	439
MM61930	P166	440
MM61931	P166	441
MM61932	P166	442
MM61933	P166	443
MM62159	P180	1023
MM62160	P180	1024
MM62161	P180	1025
MM62162	P180	1028
MM62163	P180	1029
MM62164	P180	1030
MM62167	P180	1026
MM62168	P180	1027
MM62169	P180	1031
MM62199	P180	1041
MM62200	P180	1047
MM62201	P180	1053
MM62202	P180	1058
MM62203	P180	1071
MM62204	P180	1082
MM62205	P180	1075
MM62206	P180	1087
MM62207	P180	1096
MM62211	P180	1085
MM62212	P180	1076
MM62213	P180	1090
MM62246	P180	1114
MM62247	P180	1113
MM62248	P180	1118
MM62249	P180	1126
PS-A94	P68	333
PS-A95	P68	336
PS-A96	P68	337
PS-A97	P68	338
PS-A98	P68	339
PS-A99	P68	378
PS-B02	P68	382
PS-B03	P68	383
PS-B04	P68	385
PS-B05	P68	386
PS-B06	P68	388
PS-B07	P68	401
PS-B08	P68	403
PS-B09	P68	404
PS-B10	P68	405
PS-B11	P68	406
PS-B12	P68	408
PS-B13	P68	409
PS-B14	P68	410
PS-B15	P180	1113
RM-79	P166	382
RM-80	P166	396
RR-05	P166	441
SP-30	P166	381
SP-33	P166	405
SP-34	P166	389
SP-35	P166	386
SP-36	P166	423
SP-37	P166	385
SP-37	P166	429
SP-38	P166	388
SP-40	P166	431
SP-81	P166	380
VF-181	P180	1078
VF-182	P180	1142
VV-12	P166	424
VV-14	P166	426
VV-26	P166	436
VV-33	P166	439

Jamaica

T-2	BN2	699
T-3	100	B-216
T-5	BN2	796
T-8	695A	96077

Japan

6801	90	LJ-597
6802	90	LJ-598
6803	90	LJ-599
6804	90	LJ-642
6805	90	LJ-670
6806	90	LJ-778
6807	90	LJ-855
6808	90	LJ-916
6809	90	LJ-917
6810	90	LJ-976
6811	90	LJ-980
6812	90	LJ-1042
6813	90	LJ-1043
6814	90	LJ-1044
6815	90	LJ-1047
6816	90	LJ-1060
6817	90	LJ-1061
6818	90	LJ-1062
6819	90	LJ-1083
6820	90	LJ-1084
6821	90	LJ-1110
6822	90	LJ-1146
6823	90	LJ-1335
6824	90	LJ-1336
6825	90	LJ-1337
6826	90	LJ-1338
6827	90	LJ-1339
6828	90	LJ-1584
6829	90	LJ-1592
6830	90	LJ-1596
6831	90	LJ-1634
6832	90	LJ-1636
6833	90	LJ-1638
6834	90	LJ-1690
6835	90	LJ-1851
6836	90	LJ-1852

9102	90	LJ-1038
9301	90	LJ-1182
9302	90	LJ-1248
9303	90	LJ-1249
9304	90	LJ-1281
9305	90	LJ-1282
9306	90	LJ-1335
9307	90	LJ-1336
9308	90	LJ-1337
9309	90	LJ-1338
9310	90	LJ-1339
03-3207	MU-2	907
03-3208	MU-2	908
13-3209	MU-2	909
13-3210	MU-2	910
13-3211	MU-2	911
13-3212	MU-2	912
22-001	MU-2	801
22-002	MU-2	802
22-003	MU-2	803
22-004	MU-2	804
22-005	MU-2	805
22-006	MU-2	806
22-007	MU-2	807
22-008	MU-2	808
22-009	MU-2	809
22-010	MU-2	810
22-011	MU-2	811
22-012	MU-2	812
22-013	MU-2	813
22-014	MU-2	814
22-015	MU-2	815
22-016	MU-2	816
22-017	MU-2	817
22-018	MU-2	818
22-019	MU-2	819
22-020	MU-2	820
23-050	350	FL-15
23-051	350	FL-176
23-052	350	FL-186
23-053	350	FL-266
23-054	350	FL-307
23-055	350	FL-331
23-056	350	FL-382
23-3213	MU-2	913
23-3214	MU-2	914
23-3226	MU-2	926
33-3215	MU-2	915
33-3216	MU-2	916
33-3217	MU-2	917
33-3227	MU-2	927
43-3218	MU-2	918
53-3219	MU-2	919
53-3271	MU-2	951
63-3220	MU-2	920
63-3221	MU-2	921
63-3228	MU-2	928
73-3201	MU-2	901
73-3202	MU-2	902
73-3222	MU-2	922
73-3229	MU-2	929
73-3272	MU-2	952
83-3203	MU-2	903
83-3204	MU-2	904
83-3223	MU-2	923
83-3224	MU-2	924
83-3273	MU-2	953
93-3205	MU-2	905
93-3206	MU-2	906
93-3225	MU-2	925
93-3274	MU-2	954

Jordan

330	BN2	861

Kamphuchea

ML501	BN2	400

Lebanon

L-701	690A	11157

Madagascar

382	BN2	382

Malaysia

M41-01	200T	BT-35
M41-02	200T	BT-36
M41-03	200T	BT-37
M41-04	200T	BT-38

Malta

AS9516	BN2	2159
AS9819	BN2	2156

Mauritius

MP-CG-02	BN2T	2238

Mexico

2201	90	LJ-1166
2202	90	LJ-1176
2203	90	LJ-1168
2204	90	LJ-1175
2205	90	LJ-1171
3301	PC6	880
3302	PC6	881
3303	PC6	883
3304	PC6	884
3918	695A	96041
3932	690A	11296
3958	695A	96056
3960	695A	96061
3963	695A	96010
3971	300	FA-95
5201	90	LJ-1166
5202	90	LJ-1176
5203	90	LJ-1168
5204	90	LJ-1175
5205	90	LJ-1171
AMP-130	695	95046
AMP-131	695	95051
AMP-132	695A	96040
AMP-133	695	95082
ETE-1318	695A	96041
ETE-1328	MIII	T-328
ETE-1332	690B	11494
ETE-1349	695A	96020
ETE-1358	695A	96056
ETE-1361	690C	11660
ETE-1363	695A	96010
MT-213	90	LJ-270
MT-214	695A	96040
MT-217	695A	96026
MT-218	695A	96013
MT-219	695	95040
MT-221	695	95046
MT-222	695	95082
MT-223	MU-2	122
MT-224	441	0101
MT-224	695	95051
MU-1550	MU-2	566
PF-209	BN2	255
TP-206	MIII	T-235
TP-0207	BN2	250
TP-207	BN2	250
TP-0207	MIV	AT-006
TP-0208	BN2	252
TP-208	BN2	252
TP-209	200	BB-725
TP-0209	BN2	255
TP-0209	BN2	420
TP-0210	BN2	294
TP-210	BN2	294
TP-211	BN2	293
TP-0211	BN2	293
TP-0212	BN2	286
TP-212	BN2	286
TP-213	90	LJ-270
TP-216	695A	96001
TP-310	BN2	267
TR-301	PC6	883
TR-302	PC6	884
TR-303	PC6	880
TR-304	PC6	881

Morocco

CNA-NA	100	B-180
CNA-NB	100	B-181
CNA-NC	100	B-182
CNA-ND	100	B-183
CNA-NE	100	B-186
CNA-NF	100	B-187
CNA-NG	200	BB-1072
CNA-NH	200	BB-1073
CNA-NI	200C	BL-57
CNA-NX	300	FA-207
CNA-NY	300	FA-208

Myanmar

4001	PC6	772
4002	PC6	773
4003	PC6	780
4004	PC6	781
4005	PC6	795
4006	PC6	796
4007	PC6	797

Nepal

RAN-49	BN2T	2191
RAN-50	BN2T	2190

New Zealand

NZ1881	200	BB-1054
NZ1882	200	BB-1008
NZ1883	200	BB-1087
NZ1884	200	BB-1178
NZ1885	200	BB-968

Nicaragua

FAN002	C-12	BC-37

Oman

301	BN2	400
302	BN2	401
303	BN2	402
304	BN2	413
305	BN2	414
306	BN2	415
307	BN2	417
308	BN2	418

Pakistan

08	BN2	2308
42	BN2T	2242
46	BN2T	2246
419	350	FL-419
444	350	FL-444
927	200	BB-927
11667	690C	11667
11733	690C	11733
AR-NYB	BN2T	2242
AR-NYC	BN2T	2246
AR-NYD	BN2	2308

Panama

018	695A	96006
FAP-200	31T	7620046
FAP-207	BN2	722
FAP-208	BN2	256
SAN-207	BN2	722
SAN-208	BN2	256
SAN-209	BN2	44

Paraguay

FAP-01	350	FL-45

Peru

708	690B	11391
AE571	200C	BN-2
AE572	200C	BN-3
AE573	200C	BN-4
AE574	200T	BT-25
AE575	200T	BT-26
(AE576)	200T	BT-27
EP-825	350	FL-21
FAP-18	300	FA-41
FAP-314	PC6	717
FAP-314	PC6	756
FAP-316	PC6	718
FAP-316	PC6	760
FAP-319	PC6	719
FAP-320	PC6	720
FAP-331	PC6	722
FAP-332	PC6	723
FAP-334	PC6	737
FAP-336	PC6	738
FAP-337	PC6	723
FAP-338	PC6	739
(FAP-339)	PC6	744
FAP-340	PC6	744
FAP-341	PC6	745
FP-006	BN2	2113
FP-15	BN2	2176
GC-006	BN2	2113
PNP-215	BN2	2176
PNP-218	695	95080
PNP-230	E90	LW-36
UAP-6	BN2	2113

Philippines

301	BN2	428
302	BN2	453
303	BN2	460
304	BN2	456
310	BN2	430
311	BN2	538
312	BN2	567
314	BN2	568
320	BN2	552
426	BN2	426
428	BN2	428
430	BN2	430
453	BN2	453
455	BN2	455
456	BN2	456
459	BN2	459
460	BN2	460
462	BN2	462
463	BN2	463
471	BN2	471
502	BN2	502
508	BN2	508
509	BN2	509
527	BN2	527
528	BN2	528
538	BN2	538
539	BN2	539
547	BN2	547

548 BN2 548
551 BN2 551
552 BN2 552
559 BN2 559
560 BN2 560
561 BN2 561
567 BN2 567
568 BN2 568
569 BN2 569
593 BN2 593
594 BN2 594
3001 BN2 3001
3003 BN2 3003
11250 690A 11250
PCG-251 BN2 3002
PCG-684 BN2 723

Rhodesia

3718 BN2 705
7136 BN2 707
7213 BN2 412
7317 BN2 658
7319 BN2 656
7323 BN2 678

Romania

93 BN2 93
97 BN2 97
122 BN2 122
130 BN2 130
816 BN2 816

Saudi Arabia

25 200 BB-76

Seychelles

A2-01M BN2 589
SY-005 MIII T-417
SY-006 F406 0035

Slovenia

L6-02 PC6 925
L6-03 PC6 926

Somalia

AM-75 PC6 642
MM60210 P166 467
MM60211 P166 468
MM60212 P166 469
MM60213 P166 470
MM60222 BN2 34
MM60223 BN2 47
MM60224 BN2 117
MM60225 BN2 648

South Africa

9 MIVA AT-037
10 MIVA AT-035
11 MIVA AT-036
12 MIVA AT-038
14 MIVA AT-041
15 MIVA AT-043
16 BN2 862
16 MIVA AT-040
17 BN2 834
650 200C BL-70
651 200C BL-45
652 200C BL-34
653 300 FA-118
654 200C BL-70

881 P166 417
882 P166 444
883 P166 445
884 P166 446
885 P166 447
886 P166 448
887 P166 449
888 P166 450
889 P166 451
890 P166 452
891 P166 453
892 P166 454
893 P166 455
894 P166 456
895 P166 457
896 P166 458
897 P166 459
898 P166 460
899 P166 461
900 P166 462
2070 PC6 871
8030 PC12 145
T180 P68 277
T190 P68 241
T320 PC6 871

South Korea

67-18086 U-21 LM-85
98-1001 F406 0081
98-1002 F406 0082
98-1003 F406 0083
99-1005 F406 0084
99-1006 F406 0085

Spain

409-30 90 LJ-666
409-31 90 LJ-621
409-33 90 LJ-603
409-34 90 LJ-605
42-30 90 LJ-666
42-31 90 LJ-621
42-32 90 LJ-624
42-33 90 LJ-603
42-34 90 LJ-605
E.22-1 90 LJ-603
E.22-01 90 LJ-666
E.22-2 90 LJ-605
E.22-02 90 LJ-621
E.22-3 90 LJ-608
E.22-03 90 LJ-624
E.22-04 90 LJ-603
E.22-4 90 LJ-621
E.22-05 90 LJ-605
E.22-5 90 LJ-623
E.22-6 90 LJ-624
E.22-7 90 LJ-663
E.22-8 90 LJ-664
E.22-9 90 LJ-665
E.22-10 90 LJ-666
E.23-1 100 B-193
E.23-2 100 B-195

Sri Lanka

CR841 200T BT-30
CR842 200T BT-30
CR843 200 BB-1314

Suriname

SAF-001 BN2 916
SAF-002 BN2 2108
SAF-003 BN2 2116
SAF-004 BN2 2117

Sweden

90 PC6 570
88002 MIVC AT-495B
101001 200C BL-25
~~101002 200 BB-459~~
101003 200 BB-619
101004 200 BB-932

Switzerland

T-721 350C FN-1
V-611 PC6 530
V-612 PC6 624
V-613 PC6 630
V-614 PC6 633
V-615 PC6 635
V-616 PC6 639
V-617 PC6 640
V-618 PC6 641
V-619 PC6 643
V-620 PC6 644
V-621 PC6 647
V-622 PC6 648
V-623 PC6 649
V-630 PC6 747
V-631 PC6 749
V-632 PC6 751
V-633 PC6 757
V-634 PC6 759
V-635 PC6 761

Taiwan

NA-301 200 BB-449
NA-302 350 FL-108

Tanzania

JW9027 100 B-197

Thailand

342 200 BB-342
348 MIII T-348
501 BN2 26
0517 PC6 517
0523 PC6 523
0631 PC6 631
0632 PC6 632
0669 PC6 669
0704 PC6 704
0705 PC6 705
794 200 BB-342
00-923 E90 LW-26
1165 200 BB-1165
1311 PC6 753
1312 PC6 754
1313 PC6 767
1314 PC6 768
1315 PC6 782
1316 PC6 783
1317 PC6 784
1601 FPC6 2030
1602 FPC6 2031
1603 FPC6 2032
1604 FPC6 2043
1605 FPC6 2063
1606 FPC6 2064
1607 FPC6 2065
1608 FPC6 2066
1609 FPC6 2067
1609 PC6 733
1769 E90 LW-26
2011 350 FL-146
2011 FPC6 2011
2012 350 FL-147
11340 690A 11340
56379 200 BB-1443
56385 200 BB-1441
60301 MIVA AT-071
60302 MIVA AT-072
60303 MIVA AT-073
60501 MIVA AT-071
60502 MIVA AT-072
60503 MIVA AT-073
81491 690A 11340
93303 200 BB-1436
93304 200 BB-1441
93305 200 BB-1443
21-111 MIVA AT-062E
29-999 MIVA AT-065
72-1304 FPC6 2050
72-1305 FPC6 2051
72-1306 FPC6 2052
72-1307 FPC6 2053
72-1308 FPC6 2054
72-1310 FPC6 2056
72-1311 FPC6 2057
72-1312 FPC6 2058
72-1313 FPC6 2059
72-1314 FPC6 2060
72-1315 FPC6 2061
72-1316 FPC6 2062
72-1317 FPC6 2039
72-1318 FPC6 2020
74-2073 FPC6 2073
74-2074 FPC6 2074
74-2075 FPC6 2075
74-2076 FPC6 2076
74-2077 FPC6 2077
74-2078 FPC6 2078
74-2079 FPC6 2079
74-2080 FPC6 2080
74-2081 FPC6 2081
74-2082 FPC6 2082
74-2083 FPC6 2083
74-2084 FPC6 2084
74-2085 FPC6 2085
74-2086 FPC6 2086
74-2087 FPC6 2087
74-2088 FPC6 2088
74-2089 FPC6 2089
74-2090 FPC6 2090
74-2091 FPC6 2091
74-2092 FPC6 2092
B.JTh2-1\15 FPC6 2050
B.JTh2-2\15 FPC6 2051
B.JTh2-3\15 FPC6 2052
B.JTh2-4\15 FPC6 2054
B.JTh2-5\15 FPC6 2056
B.JTh2-6\15 FPC6 2057
B.JTh2-7\15 FPC6 2058
B.JTh2-8\15 FPC6 2059
B.JTh2-9\15 FPC6 2060
B.JTh2-10\15 FPC6 2061
B.JTh2-11\15 FPC6 2062
B.JTh2-12\15 FPC6 2039
B.JTh2-13\15 FPC6 2020
B.JTh2-14\19 FPC6 2073
B.JTh2-15\19 FPC6 2074
B.JTh2-16\19 FPC6 2075
B.JTh2-17\19 FPC6 2076
B.JTh2-18\19 FPC6 2077
B.JTh2-19\19 FPC6 2078
B.JTh2-20\19 FPC6 2079
B.JTh2-21\19 FPC6 2080
B.JTh2-22\19 FPC6 2081
B.JTh2-23\19 FPC6 2082
B.JTh2-24\19 FPC6 2083
B.JTh2-25\19 FPC6 2084
B.JTh2-26\19 FPC6 2085
B.JTh2-27\19 FPC6 2086
B.JTh2-28\19 FPC6 2087
B.JTh2-29\19 FPC6 2088
B.JTh2-30\19 FPC6 2089
B.JTh2-31\19 FPC6 2090
B.JTh2-32\19 FPC6 2091
B.JTh2-33\19 FPC6 2092
B.JTh2-34\20 FPC6 2053

Turkey

4005	200	BB-1434
4006	200	BB-1375
10010	200	BB-1409
10011	200	BB-1411
10012	200	BB-1413
10013	200	BB-1414
10014	200	BB-1415
J-11265	690A	11265
M-1375	200	BB-1375

United Arab Emirates

201	BN2	34
202	BN2	47
203	BN2	117
204	BN2	648
318	BN2T	2118
321	PC6	863
322	PC6	864
411	BN2T	2118
801	350	FL-131
801	BN2	34
802	350	FL-132
802	BN2	47
803	BN2	117
804	BN2	648
825	350	FL-132
2215	PC6	863
2216	PC6	864

United Kingdom

(ZB503)	BN2	2011
ZF573	BN2T	2034
ZG844	BN2	2184
ZG845	BN2	2194
ZG846	BN2	2195
ZG847	BN2	2196
ZG848	BN2	2199
ZG989	BN2T	2140
ZG993	BN2	2202
ZG994	BN2	2206
ZG995	BN2T	4005
ZG996	BN2T	4010
ZG997	BN2T	4012
(ZG998)	BN2T	2118
ZG998	BN2T	4014
ZH001	BN2T	4015
ZH002	BN2T	4016
*ZH003	BN2T	4017
ZH004	BN2T	4009
ZH536	BN2T	2235
ZH537	BN2T	2118
ZK450	200	BB-1829
ZK451	200	BB-1830
ZK452	200	BB-1832
ZK453	200	BB-1833
ZK454	200	BB-1835
*ZK455	200	BB-1836
*ZK456	200	BB-1837
ZK457	200	BB-684
*ZK458	200G	BY-32
*ZK459	200G	BY-36
ZZ416	300C	FM-14
ZZ417	300C	FM-16
*ZZ418	300C	FM-17
*ZZ419	300C	FM-18
*ZZ500	350	FL-597
*ZZ501	350	FL-618
*ZZ502	350	FL-629
*ZZ503	350	FL-633

United Nations

UN-1	BN2	810
UN-1	PC6	350
UN77	690A	11265
UN454	200	BB-419

United States of America

02	G1	91
02	G1	92
03	G1	91
1380	G1	91
155722	G1	176
155723	G1	178
155724	G1	180
155725	G1	182
155726	G1	183
155727	G1	184
155728	G1	185
155729	G1	186
155730	G1	187
160839	T-44	LL-1
160840	T-44	LL-2
160841	T-44	LL-3
160842	T-44	LL-4
160843	T-44	LL-5
160844	T-44	LL-6
160845	T-44	LL-7
160846	T-44	LL-8
160847	T-44	LL-9
160848	T-44	LL-10
160849	T-44	LL-11
160850	T-44	LL-12
160851	T-44	LL-13
160852	T-44	LL-14
160853	T-44	LL-15
160854	T-44	LL-16
160855	T-44	LL-17
160856	T-44	LL-18
160967	T-44	LL-19
160968	T-44	LL-20
160969	T-44	LL-21
160970	T-44	LL-22
160971	T-44	LL-23
160972	T-44	LL-24
160973	T-44	LL-25
160974	T-44	LL-26
160975	T-44	LL-27
160976	T-44	LL-28
160977	T-44	LL-29
160978	T-44	LL-30
160979	T-44	LL-31
160980	T-44	LL-32
160981	T-44	LL-33
160982	T-44	LL-34
160983	T-44	LL-35
160984	T-44	LL-36
160985	T-44	LL-37
160986	T-44	LL-38
161057	T-44	LL-39
161058	T-44	LL-40
161059	T-44	LL-41
161060	T-44	LL-42
161061	T-44	LL-43
161062	T-44	LL-44
161063	T-44	LL-45
161064	T-44	LL-46
161065	T-44	LL-47
161066	T-44	LL-48
161067	T-44	LL-49
161068	T-44	LL-50
161069	T-44	LL-51
161070	T-44	LL-52
161071	T-44	LL-53
161072	T-44	LL-54
161073	T-44	LL-55
161074	T-44	LL-56
161075	T-44	LL-57
161076	T-44	LL-58
161077	T-44	LL-59
161078	T-44	LL-60
161079	T-44	LL-61
161185	C-12	BJ-1
161186	C-12	BJ-2
161187	C-12	BJ-3
161188	C-12	BJ-4
161189	C-12	BJ-5
161190	C-12	BJ-6
161191	C-12	BJ-7
161192	C-12	BJ-8
161193	C-12	BJ-9
161194	C-12	BJ-10
161195	C-12	BJ-11
161196	C-12	BJ-12
161197	C-12	BJ-13
161198	C-12	BJ-14
161199	C-12	BJ-15
161200	C-12	BJ-16
161201	C-12	BJ-17
161202	C-12	BJ-18
161203	C-12	BJ-19
161204	C-12	BJ-20
161205	C-12	BJ-21
161206	C-12	BJ-22
161306	C-12	BJ-23
161307	C-12	BJ-24
161308	C-12	BJ-25
161309	C-12	BJ-26
161310	C-12	BJ-27
161311	C-12	BJ-28
161312	C-12	BJ-29
161313	C-12	BJ-30
161314	C-12	BJ-31
161315	C-12	BJ-32
161316	C-12	BJ-33
161317	C-12	BJ-34
161318	C-12	BJ-35
161319	C-12	BJ-36
161320	C-12	BJ-37
161321	C-12	BJ-38
161322	C-12	BJ-39
161323	C-12	BJ-40
161324	C-12	BJ-41
161325	C-12	BJ-42
161326	C-12	BJ-43
161327	C-12	BJ-44
161497	C-12	BJ-45
161498	C-12	BJ-46
161499	C-12	BJ-47
161500	C-12	BJ-48
161501	C-12	BJ-49
161502	C-12	BJ-50
161503	C-12	BJ-51
161504	C-12	BJ-52
161505	C-12	BJ-53
161506	C-12	BJ-54
161507	C-12	BJ-55
161508	C-12	BJ-56
161509	C-12	BJ-57
161510	C-12	BJ-58
161511	C-12	BJ-59
161512	C-12	BJ-60
161513	C-12	BJ-61
161514	C-12	BJ-62
161515	C-12	BJ-63
161516	C-12	BJ-64
161517	C-12	BJ-65
161518	C-12	BJ-66
163553	UC12	BU-1
163554	UC12	BU-2
163555	UC12	BU-3
163556	UC12	BU-4
163557	UC12	BU-5
163558	UC12	BU-6
163559	UC12	BU-7
163560	UC12	BU-8
163561	UC12	BU-9
163562	UC12	BU-10
163563	UC12	BU-11
163564	UC12	BU-12
163836	UC12	BV-1
163837	UC12	BV-2
163838	UC12	BV-3
163839	UC12	BV-4
163840	UC12	BV-5
163841	UC12	BV-6
163842	UC12	BV-7
163843	UC12	BV-8
163844	UC12	BV-9
163845	UC12	BV-10
163846	UC12	BV-11
163847	UC12	BV-12
(164579)	T-44	LL-62
(164580)	T-44	LL-63
(164581)	T-44	LL-64
(164582)	T-44	LL-65
(164583)	T-44	LL-66
760172	C-12	BD-29
823132	C-12	BC-68
823133	C-12	BC-69
04-0602	PC12	602
05-0409	PC12	409
05-0419	PC12	419
05-0424	PC12	424
05-0447	PC12	447
05-0482	PC12	482
05-0573	PC12	573
05-0646	PC12	646
05-52305	200	BB-924
07-0736	PC12	736
07-0821	PC12	821
07-0838	PC12	838
07-0840	PC12	840
07-21907	200	BB-1114
08-0293	350	FL-293
08-0309	350	FL-309
08-0329	350	FL-329
08-0336	350	FL-336
08-0353	350	FL-353
08-0376	350	FL-376
08-0462	350	FL-462
08-0546	350	FL-546
66-7943	90	LJ-320
66-15361	90	LJ-153
66-18000	U-21	LM-1
66-18001	U-21	LM-2
66-18002	U-21	LM-3
66-18003	U-21	LM-4
66-18004	U-21	LM-5
66-18005	U-21	LM-6
66-18006	U-21	LM-7
66-18007	U-21	LM-8
66-18008	U-21	LM-9
66-18009	U-21	LM-10
66-18010	U-21	LM-11
66-18011	U-21	LM-12
66-18012	U-21	LM-13
66-18013	U-21	LM-14
66-18014	U-21	LM-15
66-18015	U-21	LM-16
66-18016	U-21	LM-17
66-18017	U-21	LM-18
66-18018	U-21	LM-19
66-18019	U-21	LM-20
66-18020	U-21	LM-21
66-18021	U-21	LM-22
66-18022	U-21	LM-23
66-18023	U-21	LM-24
66-18024	U-21	LM-25
66-18025	U-21	LM-26
66-18026	U-21	LM-27
66-18027	U-21	LM-28
66-18028	U-21	LM-29
66-18029	U-21	LM-30
66-18030	U-21	LM-31
66-18031	U-21	LM-32
66-18032	U-21	LM-33
66-18033	U-21	LM-34
66-18034	U-21	LM-35
66-18035	U-21	LM-36
66-18036	U-21	LM-37
66-18037	U-21	LM-38
66-18038	U-21	LM-39
66-18039	U-21	LM-40
66-18040	U-21	LM-41
66-18041	U-21	LM-42
66-18042	U-21	LM-43
66-18043	U-21	LM-44
66-18044	U-21	LM-45
66-18045	U-21	LM-46
66-18046	U-21	LM-47
66-18047	U-21	LM-48
67-18048	U-21	LM-49
67-18049	U-21	LM-50
67-18050	U-21	LM-51
67-18051	U-21	LM-52
67-18052	U-21	LM-53
67-18053	U-21	LM-54

67-18054	U-21	LM-55	70-15884	U-21	LU-10	76-0161	C-12	BD-18	80-23379	RC12	FC-1
67-18055	U-21	LM-56	70-15885	U-21	LU-11	76-0162	C-12	BD-19	80-23380	RC12	FC-2
67-18056	U-21	LM-57	70-15886	U-21	LU-12	76-0163	C-12	BD-20	81-23541	C-12	BP-22
67-18057	U-21	LM-58	70-15887	U-21	LU-13	76-0164	C-12	BD-21	81-23542	RC12	GR-1
67-18058	U-21	LM-59	70-15888	U-21	LU-14	76-0165	C-12	BD-22	81-23543	C-12	BP-24
67-18059	U-21	LM-60	70-15889	U-21	LU-15	76-0166	C-12	BD-23	81-23544	C-12	BP-25
67-18060	U-21	LM-61	70-15890	U-21	LU-16	76-0167	C-12	BD-24	81-23545	C-12	BP-26
67-18061	U-21	LM-62	70-15891	U-21	LM-125	76-0168	C-12	BD-25	81-23546	C-12	BP-27
67-18062	U-21	LM-63	70-15892	U-21	LM-126	76-0169	C-12	BD-26	81-23638	C-12	BP-7
67-18063	U-21	LM-64	70-15893	U-21	LM-127	76-0170	C-12	BD-27	81-23639	C-12	BP-8
67-18064	U-21	LM-65	70-15894	U-21	LM-128	76-0171	C-12	BD-28	81-23640	C-12	BP-9
67-18065	U-21	LM-66	70-15895	U-21	LM-129	76-0172	C-12	BD-29	81-23641	C-12	BP-10
67-18066	U-21	LM-67	70-15896	U-21	LM-130	76-0173	C-12	BD-30	81-23642	C-12	BP-11
67-18067	U-21	LM-68	70-15897	U-21	LM-131	76-3239	C-12	BD-24	82-23780	C-12	BP-28
67-18068	U-21	LM-69	70-15898	U-21	LM-132	76-22545	C-12	BC-21	82-23781	C-12	BP-29
67-18069	U-21	LM-70	70-15899	U-21	LM-133	76-22546	C-12	BC-22	82-23782	C-12	BP-30
67-18070	U-21	LM-71	70-15900	U-21	LM-134	76-22547	C-12	BC-23	82-23783	C-12	BP-31
67-18071	U-21	LM-72	70-15901	U-21	LM-135	76-22548	C-12	BC-24	82-23784	C-12	BP-32
67-18072	U-21	LM-73	70-15902	U-21	LM-136	76-22549	C-12	BC-25	82-23785	C-12	BP-33
67-18073	U-21	LM-74	70-15903	U-21	LM-137	76-22550	C-12	BC-26	83-0494	C-12	BP-40
67-18074	U-21	LM-75	70-15904	U-21	LM-138	76-22551	C-12	BC-27	83-0495	C-12	BP-41
67-18075	U-21	LM-76	70-15905	U-21	LM-139	76-22552	C-12	BC-28	83-0496	C-12	BP-42
67-18076	U-21	LM-77	70-15906	U-21	LM-140	76-22553	C-12	BC-29	83-0497	C-12	BP-43
67-18077	U-21	LS-1	70-15907	U-21	LM-141	76-22554	C-12	BC-30	83-0498	C-12	BP-44
67-18078	U-21	LM-78	70-15908	100	B-95	76-22555	C-12	BC-31	83-0499	C-12	BP-45
67-18079	U-21	LM-79	70-15909	100	B-96	76-22556	C-12	BC-32	83-24126	680W	1772-10
67-18080	U-21	LM-80	70-15910	100	B-97	76-22557	C-12	BC-33	83-24145	C-12	BP-34
67-18081	U-21	LM-81	70-15911	100	B-98	76-22558	C-12	BC-35	83-24146	C-12	BP-35
67-18082	U-21	LM-82	70-15912	100	B-99	76-22559	C-12	BC-36	83-24147	C-12	BP-36
67-18083	U-21	LM-83	72-1304	FPC6	2050	76-22560	C-12	BC-37	83-24148	C-12	BP-37
67-18084	U-21	LM-84	72-1305	FPC6	2051	76-22561	C-12	BC-38	83-24149	C-12	BP-38
67-18085	U-21	LT-1	72-1306	FPC6	2052	76-22562	C-12	BC-39	83-24150	C-12	BP-39
67-18086	U-21	LM-85	72-1307	FPC6	2053	76-22563	C-12	BC-40	83-24313	RC12	GR-14
67-18087	U-21	LS-2	72-1308	FPC6	2054	76-22564	C-12	BC-41	83-24314	RC12	GR-15
67-18088	U-21	LM-86	72-1309	FPC6	2055	77-22931	C-12	BC-42	83-24315	RC12	GR-16
67-18089	U-21	LT-2	72-1310	FPC6	2056	77-22932	C-12	BC-43	83-24316	RC12	GR-17
67-18090	U-21	LM-87	72-1311	FPC6	2057	77-22933	C-12	BC-44	83-24317	RC12	GR-18
67-18091	U-21	LM-88	72-1312	FPC6	2058	77-22934	C-12	BC-45	83-24318	RC12	GR-19
67-18092	U-21	LM-89	72-1313	FPC6	2059	77-22935	C-12	BC-46	84-0143	200C	BL-73
67-18093	U-21	LS-3	72-1314	FPC6	2060	77-22936	C-12	BC-47	84-0144	200C	BL-74
67-18094	U-21	LM-90	72-1315	FPC6	2061	77-22937	C-12	BC-48	84-0145	200C	BL-75
67-18095	U-21	LM-91	72-1316	FPC6	2062	77-22938	C-12	BC-49	84-0146	200C	BL-76
67-18096	U-21	LM-92	72-1317	FPC6	2039	77-22939	C-12	BC-50	84-0147	200C	BL-77
67-18097	U-21	LM-93	72-1318	FPC6	2020	77-22940	C-12	BC-51	84-0148	200C	BL-78
67-18098	U-21	LM-94	72-21058	200	BB-3	77-22941	C-12	BC-52	84-0149	200C	BL-79
67-18099	U-21	LM-95	72-21059	200	BB-4	77-22942	C-12	BC-53	84-0150	200C	BL-80
67-18100	U-21	LM-96	72-21060	200	BB-5	77-22943	C-12	BC-54	84-0151	200C	BL-81
67-18101	U-21	LM-97	73-1205	C-12	BD-1	77-22944	C-12	BC-55	84-0152	200C	BL-82
67-18102	U-21	LM-98	73-1206	C-12	BD-2	77-22945	C-12	BC-56	84-0153	200C	BL-83
67-18103	U-21	LM-99	73-1207	C-12	BD-3	77-22946	C-12	BC-57	84-0154	200C	BL-84
67-18104	U-21	LM-100	73-1208	C-12	BD-4	77-22947	C-12	BC-58	84-0155	200C	BL-85
67-18105	U-21	LM-101	73-1209	C-12	BD-5	77-22948	C-12	BC-59	84-0156	200C	BL-86
67-18106	U-21	LM-102	73-1210	C-12	BD-6	77-22949	C-12	BC-60	84-0157	200C	BL-87
67-18107	U-21	LM-103	73-1211	C-12	BD-7	77-22950	C-12	BC-61	84-0158	200C	BL-88
67-18108	U-21	LM-104	73-1212	C-12	BD-8	78-23126	C-12	BC-62	84-0159	200C	BL-89
67-18109	U-21	LM-105	73-1213	C-12	BD-9	78-23127	C-12	BC-63	84-0160	200C	BL-90
67-18110	U-21	LM-106	73-1214	C-12	BD-10	78-23128	C-12	BC-64	84-0161	200C	BL-91
67-18111	U-21	LM-107	73-1215	C-12	BD-11	78-23129	C-12	BC-65	84-0162	200C	BL-92
67-18112	U-21	LM-108	73-1216	C-12	BD-12	78-23130	C-12	BC-66	84-0163	200C	BL-93
67-18113	U-21	LM-109	73-1217	C-12	BD-13	78-23131	C-12	BC-67	84-0164	200C	BL-94
67-18114	U-21	LM-110	73-1218	C-12	BD-14	78-23132	C-12	BC-68	84-0165	200C	BL-95
67-18115	U-21	LM-111	73-22250	C-12	BC-1	78-23133	C-12	BC-69	84-0166	200C	BL-96
67-18116	U-21	LM-112	73-22251	C-12	BC-2	78-23134	C-12	BC-70	84-0167	200C	BL-97
67-18117	U-21	LM-113	73-22252	C-12	BC-3	78-23135	C-12	BC-71	84-0168	200C	BL-98
67-18118	U-21	LM-114	73-22253	C-12	BC-4	78-23136	C-12	BC-72	84-0169	200C	BL-99
67-18119	U-21	LM-115	73-22254	C-12	BC-5	78-23137	C-12	BC-73	84-0170	200C	BL-100
67-18120	U-21	LM-116	73-22255	C-12	BC-6	78-23138	C-12	BC-74	84-0171	200C	BL-101
67-18121	U-21	LM-117	73-22256	C-12	BC-7	78-23139	C-12	BC-75	84-0172	200C	BL-102
67-18122	U-21	LM-118	73-22257	C-12	BC-8	78-23140	C-12	BP-1	84-0173	200C	BL-103
67-18123	U-21	LM-119	73-22258	C-12	BC-14	78-23141	RC12	GR-6	84-0174	200C	BL-104
67-18124	U-21	LM-120	73-22259	C-12	BC-15	78-23142	RC12	GR-7	84-0175	200C	BL-105
67-18125	U-21	LM-121	73-22260	C-12	BC-16	78-23143	RC12	GR-8	84-0176	200C	BL-106
67-18126	U-21	LM-122	73-22261	C-12	BC-9	78-23144	RC12	GR-9	84-0177	200C	BL-107
67-18127	U-21	LM-123	73-22262	C-12	BC-10	78-23145	RC12	GR-10	84-0178	200C	BL-108
67-18128	U-21	LM-124	73-22263	C-12	BC-11	79-23253	PC6	802	84-0179	200C	BL-109
70-15875	U-21	LU-1	73-22264	C-12	BC-12	79-23254	PC6	803	84-0180	200C	BL-110
70-15876	U-21	LU-2	73-22265	C-12	BC-13	80-23371	RC12	GR-2	84-0181	200C	BL-111
70-15877	U-21	LU-3	73-22266	C-12	BC-17	80-23372	RC12	FC-3	84-0182	200C	BL-112
70-15878	U-21	LU-4	73-22267	C-12	BC-18	80-23373	RC12	GR-4	84-0484	200C	BL-118
70-15879	U-21	LU-5	73-22268	C-12	BC-19	80-23374	RC12	GR-12	84-0485	200C	BL-119
70-15880	U-21	LU-6	73-22269	C-12	BC-20	80-23375	RC12	GR-5	84-0486	200C	BL-120
70-15881	U-21	LU-7	76-0158	C-12	BD-15	80-23376	RC12	GR-11	84-0487	200C	BL-121
70-15882	U-21	LU-8	76-0159	C-12	BD-16	80-23377	RC12	GR-3	84-0488	200C	BL-122
70-15883	U-21	LU-9	76-0160	C-12	BD-17	80-23378	RC12	GR-13	84-0489	200C	BL-123

84-24375	C-12	BP-46
84-24376	C-12	BP-47
84-24377	C-12	BP-48
84-24378	C-12	BP-49
84-24379	C-12	BP-50
84-24380	C-12	BP-51
85-0147	RC12	FE-1
85-0148	RC12	FE-2
85-0149	RC12	FE-3
85-0150	RC12	FE-4
85-0151	RC12	FE-5
85-0152	RC12	FE-6
85-0153	RC12	FE-7
85-0154	RC12	FE-8
85-0155	RC12	FE-9
85-1261	C-12	BP-52
85-1262	C-12	BP-53
85-1263	C-12	BP-54
85-1264	C-12	BP-55
85-1265	C-12	BP-56
85-1266	C-12	BP-57
85-1267	C-12	BP-58
85-1268	C-12	BP-59
85-1269	C-12	BP-60
85-1270	C-12	BP-61
85-1271	C-12	BP-62
85-1272	C-12	BP-63
85-1609	31T	7720051
86-0084	C-12	BP-64
86-0085	C-12	BP-65
86-0086	C-12	BP-66
86-0087	C-12	BP-67
86-0088	C-12	BP-68
86-0089	C-12	BP-69
86-0092	90	LJ-159
86-0402	G1	2
86-1683	90	LJ-129
87-0160	C-12	BP-70
87-0161	C-12	BP-71
88-0196	BN2T	880
88-0325	RC12	FE-10
88-0326	RC12	FE-11
88-0327	RC12	FE-12
89-0267	RC12	FE-13
89-0268	RC12	FE-14
89-0269	RC12	FE-15
89-0270	RC12	FE-16
89-0271	RC12	FE-17
89-0272	RC12	FE-18
89-0273	RC12	FE-19
89-0274	RC12	FE-20
89-0275	RC12	FE-21
89-0276	RC12	FE-22
89-1471	MIVC	AT-549B
90-0060	B100	BE-67
91-0516	RC12	FE-23
91-0517	RC12	FE-24
91-0518	RC12	FE-25
92-3327	UC12	BW-1
92-3328	UC12	BW-2
92-3329	UC12	BW-3
92-13120	RC12	FE-26
92-13121	RC12	FE-27
92-13122	RC12	FE-28
92-13123	RC12	FE-29
92-13124	RC12	FE-30
92-13125	RC12	FE-31
93-0697	RC12	FE-32
93-0698	RC12	FE-33
93-0699	RC12	FE-34
93-0700	RC12	FE-35
93-0701	RC12	FE-36
94-0315	UC12	BW-4
94-0316	UC12	BW-5
94-0317	UC12	BW-6
94-0318	UC12	BW-7
94-0319	UC12	BW-8
94-0320	UC12	BW-9
94-0321	UC12	BW-10
94-0322	UC12	BW-11
94-0323	UC12	BW-12
94-0324	UC12	BW-13
94-0325	UC12	BW-14
94-0326	UC12	BW-15
95-0088	UC12	BW-16
95-0089	UC12	BW-17
95-0090	UC12	BW-18
95-0091	UC12	BW-19
95-0092	UC12	BW-20
95-0093	UC12	BW-21
95-0094	UC12	BW-22
95-0095	UC12	BW-23
95-0096	UC12	BW-24
95-0097	UC12	BW-25
95-0098	UC12	BW-26
95-0099	UC12	BW-27
95-0100	UC12	BW-28
95-0101	UC12	BW-29
95-6039	PC6	907
NASA1	G1	96
NASA2	G1	98
NASA3	G1	92
NASA4	G1	151

__Uruguay__

871	200T	BT-4

__Venezuela__

2840	200	BB-520
3150	200	BB-522
3240	200C	BL-19
3250	200	BB-92
3280	200C	BL-18
ARBV-0201	E90	LW-264
ARV-0201	E90	LW-264
ARV-0211	695	95007
ARV-0212	200	BB-906
EV-7702	E90	LW-229
EV-7910	200	BB-495
EV-7911	BN2	851
GN-7432	BN2	405
GN-7593	E90	LW-154
GN-7839	E90	LW-260
GN-8270	200C	BL-51
GN-8274	200	BB-980
TR-0201	E90	LW-264

__Zimbabwe__

14	F406	0067
15	F406	0068
16	F406	0071
17	F406	0069
3718	BN2	705
7136	BN2	707
7213	BN2	412
7317	BN2	658
7319	BN2	656
7323	BN2	678

AIR-BRITAIN SALES

Companion volumes to this publication are also available by post-free mail order from

Air-Britain Sales Department (Dept BTI09)
41 Penshurst Road, Leigh,
Tonbridge, Kent TN11 8HL

For a full list of current titles and details of how to order, visit our secure e-commerce site at www.air-britain.co.uk
Visa / Mastercard / Solo / Maestro accepted - please give full details of card number and expiry date.

ANNUAL PUBLICATIONS - 2009 - NOW AVAILABLE

UK and IRELAND QUICK REFERENCE 2009 £6.95 (Members) £7.95 (Non-members)
Basic easy-to-carry current registration and type listing, foreign aircraft based in UK, IoM and Ireland, current military serials UK and Ireland, aircraft museums and expanded base index. A5 size, 176 pages.

BUSINESS JETS & TURBOPROPS QUICK REFERENCE 2009 £6.95 (Members) £7.95 (Non-members)
Now expanded to include all purpose-built business jets and business turboprops, in both civil and military use, in registration or serial order by country. Easy-to-carry A5 size, 160 pages.

AIRLINE FLEETS QUICK REFERENCE 2009 £6.95 (Members) £7.95 (Non-members)
Pocket guide now includes airliners of over 19 seats of 1700 major operators likely to be seen worldwide; regn, type, c/n, fleet numbers. Listed by country and airline. A5 size, 240 pages.

UK/IRELAND/IoM CIVIL REGISTERS 2009 £19.95 (Members) £26.00 (Non-members)
The 45th annual edition of our longest-running title lists all current G-, M- and EI- allocations, plus overseas-registered aircraft based in the British Isles , alphabetical index by type, military/civil marks decode, full BGA and microlight details, museum aircraft, etc. At 672 pages this is the UK civil aircraft register standard reference.

BUSINESS JETS INTERNATIONAL 2009 £18.00 (Members) £23.00 (Non-members)
Full production listing for business jets in c/n order with complete registration/serial details, model details and fates of over 19,400 aircraft. Comprehensive index of nearly 74,000 business jet registrations past and present, cross-referenced by type and c/n with all current marks highlighted - the perfect companion to this book. Now 576 pages hardback.

AIRLINE FLEETS 2009 £19.95 (Members) £25.00 (Non-members)
Listing over 2,800 operators'fleets by country with registrations, c/ns, line numbers, fleet numbers and names, plus numerous appendices including airliners in non-airline service, IATA and ICAO airline and base codes, operator index, etc. Now 720 pages A5 size hardback.

EUROPEAN REGISTERS HANDBOOK 2009 £17.50 (Members) £26.25 (Non-members)
Current civil registers of 44 European countries between the Atlantic and Russia, all powered aircraft, balloons, gliders, microlights. Now in new dual format A5 softback easy-carry book in QR format combined with CD containing all the usual data with c/ns, full previous identities and many extra permit and reservation details.

JET AIRLINERS OF THE WORLD 1949-2007 £26.50 (Members) £37.50 (Non-members)
This two-volume set contains details of over 33,000 aircraft in past or current production. The first volume of 656 pages covers production lists of all jet airliners including Soviet types and military transports. In the second volume there are line number cross references and a master index of nearly 75,000 registrations and military serials.

For details of other Air-Britain civil aviation titles including type histories, airline histories and complete civil registers, please check our sales website for current availability. Air-Britain also publishes a comprehensive range of military titles, please check for latest details of RAF Serial Registers, detailed RAF aircraft type "Files", Squadron Histories and Royal Navy Aircraft Histories.

IMPORTANT NOTE – Members receive substantial discounts on prices of all the above Air-Britain publications.
Membership subscription rates start from as little as £20 per annum (2009), and this amount provides a copy of 'Air-Britain Aviation World' quarterly as well as many other benefits. Subscriptions to include any or all of our other three magazines vary between £25 and £62 per annum (slightly higher to overseas).

For full details of membership, magazines and current books visit our website at http://www.air-britain.co.uk where you can also join on-line.

Alternatively write to 'Air-Britain' at 1 Rose Cottages, 179 Penn Road, Hazlemere, High Wycombe, Bucks HP15 7NE, UK. Or telephone 01394 450767 (+44 1394 450767 from outside UK) or e-mail: membenquiry@air-britain.co.uk and ask for a membership pack containing the full details of subscription rates, samples of our magazines and a book list.